Psychology
of
Exceptional Children
and Youth

PSYCHOLOGY OF EXCEPTIONAL CHILDREN AND YOUTH

Third Edition

Edited by

WILLIAM M. CRUICKSHANK, PH.D., SC.D.

The University of Michigan

Prentice-Hall, Inc.

Englewood Cliffs, N.J.

PRENTICE-HALL PSYCHOLOGY SERIES

Arthur T. Jersild, Editor

13-733931-3

Library of Congress Catalog Card No. 71-142162

Current printing (last digit)
10 9 8 7 6 5 4 3 2 1

PRINTED IN THE UNITED STATES OF AMERICA

Prentice-Hall International, Inc., London
Prentice-Hall of Australia, Pty. Ltd., Sydney
Prentice-Hall of Canada, Ltd., Toronto
Prentice-Hall of India Private Limited, New Delhi
Prentice-Hall of Japan, Inc., Tokyo

CONTENTS

PREFACE

Since 1920, the combined effect of several important influences has brought the exceptional child and youth to the attention of professional people in a very dramatic way. World Wars I and II, with their universal military conscription, subjected almost the entire male population of the United States to complete physical, psychological, and psychiatric examinations, and directed public attention to the large percentage of men who, due to physical disability, mental retardation, illiteracy, or psychiatric disorders, were rejected as unfit to assume this major responsibility of citizenship. Similarly, the results of the two wars, together with the conflicts of Korea and Vietnam, have created widespread interest in and concern about the general problems of rehabilitation.

Medicine and allied sciences have progressed markedly since the twenties. Psychological inquiries and research have added much to our understanding of the role of handicaps in the lives of children, their parents, and society in general. Medical inquiries have contributed greatly to the control of epilepsy, to an understanding of cardiac disturbances, and to the basic information regarding congenital disorders. True congenital deformities, retrolental fibroplasia, cerebral injuries, and many other problems still pose unanswered questions to the professions. Nevertheless, many advances have been observed in psychological and medical knowledge.

Since 1955, much has happened in the United States and elsewhere in the interest of exceptional children, youth, and adults. The Congress of the United States has provided grants for research and study which have stimulated the total growth of the field. Leadership personnel have been trained in major universities and colleges through such funds, and these people are beginning to take their places in positions of responsibility throughout the country. The U.S. Department of Health, Education and Welfare, through many of its agencies, has brought new life and direction to its program in the several states through direct grants for research, service, and study. The National Institutes of Health have provided leadership for research, training, and the pursuit of knowledge in many related fields, thus bringing new insights to this area of human development. Private foundations have invested their funds generously in major studies and in direct services for all types of children and youth with disabilities. The Panel on Mental Retardation initiated by executive order of President John F. Kennedy and the continuing significant contribution of the President's Committees on the Employment of the Handicapped and on Mental Retardation express a national concern with these significant problems. Many colleges and universities have responded to this stimulation with stronger programs of teacher and leadership preparation in special education and rehabilitation. Some of these institutions of higher education, utilizing the generous funds of government and private foundations as well as their own resources, have initiated important programs of research, the results of which are turning conjecture and hypothesis into concrete fact and basic knowledge.

Although much remains to be investigated concerning the psychological growth and development of exceptional children and youth, psychological understanding has grown sufficiently exact to warrant a single publication dealing with this problem. This symposium, prepared by psychologists, is devoted solely to the psychological considerations of the influence of physical deviation upon the normative growth and development of children and young people. The term "exceptional child" means one who, by reason of a physical or intellectual deviation, is considered unique among children. Thus, chapters that deal with the psychology of the intellectually superior child, as well as with the intellectually inferior child, are included in the book. Chapters that deal with all the major groups of physically disabled children are also included.

Since the publication of the first editon of this book in 1955, a companion volume, the *Education of Exceptional Children and Youth,* has been published by Prentice-Hall, Inc. Together these two volumes provide a remarkable background for the total field of the psychology and education of exceptional children and youth.

As has been stated elsewhere, the editor of this volume and the contributing authors are of the opinon that the field of the psychology of exceptional children is too complicated and diverse to be treated adequately by a single author. No one individual can be so uniformly authoritative on all facets of this broad field as to be able to treat each with experience, personal investigation, and deep understanding. The strength of this book and of its companion in the field of education lies in part in the fact that each chapter has been prepared by an authority in a given field.

In the revision of this work, attempts have been made to strengthen the book even more. Certain chapters have been completely rewritten. Dr. Berthold Lowenfeld has prepared what is undoubtedly the definitive chapter on the psychology of the visually impaired. The psychology of the deaf has been given a different perspective by Dr. John Wiley, and Dr. E. Paul Torrance has prepared a new chapter on the psychology of the gifted. Dr. Peter Knoblock has added a new dimension to the book in his chapter dealing with basic psychological issues regarding the emotionally disturbed child. Other new authors in this edition include Drs. Frances Connor, Herbert Rusalem, and James L. Paul, who in cooperation with the editor, have provided a new focus and new material on the orthopedically and neurologically handicapped child. Of great significance is a new aspect of the book, namely, the treatment of handicapping conditions as a social phenomenon which has been written by Drs. Nettie Bartel and Samuel L. Guskin.

Chapter I has only been revised modestly. This theoretical chapter is relatively timeless, and stands as well today as it did at the time of the first printing of the first edition of this book. It contains concepts which are basic and essential to the total field of disability. The reader will find a significant amount of material incorporated into Chapter I which was taken from the writings of Dr. Meyerson and which appeared in the first two editions of this book. This material is of such importance to the profession and is so germane to the contents of the chapter that in the opinion of the editor and author it should not be lost to the reader of this edition.

The remaining chapters have been revised significantly. Individual authors have preferred to permit their chapters to stand as in the original edition, but to integrate new research, ideas, and concepts which have developed in the intervening period. However, the editor and each author have seriously considered each chapter to determine whether or not it still provides for the student a continuing base for understanding and appreciation of the essential concepts regarding disability and exceptionality.

While almost every new insight derived from research brings to light two others which need study, the period since the publication of the first edition of this book has been marked essentially by critical investigation. Techniques and research methods, as Drs. Meyerson and Newland so well emphasize in their chapters, need yet to be refined for the investigation of many problems of human life. Suffice it to say, however, that there is a current critical attitude toward this professional field which can only result in a significant understanding in the future. The contributing authors of this edition commend their chapters to the serious student of psychology and education in the expectancy that many will be motivated to further study, research, and contribution to the understanding of exceptional children and youth.

PART I

Foundation Concepts

ONE

Somatopsychology of Physical Disability

LEE MEYERSON

Lee Meyerson is Professor of Psychology at Arizona State University. He is a Fellow of the American Psychological Association and holds memberships in the American Public Health Association and the Society for Research in Child Development.

At one time many people believed that continuing progress in the medical sciences would lead eventually to the prevention or cure of all the disorders we classify as physical disabilities. Today it is clear that we have made great strides in preventing some disabilities and in reducing the severity of others. Blindness as a consequence of untreated syphilis in the mother is practically nonexistent in the United States. Severe crippling following poliomyelitis, which was once common, is now rare. The deformities resulting from osteomyelitis are now prevented by the miracle of antibiotic drugs.

The other side of the picture, however, is not as hopeful. It is becoming increasingly evident that modern medicine is saving lives at the cost of permanent physical disabilities. Premature infants, children, and adults ill with acute infections or the injuries of accidents, and the enfeebled aged, all of whom once would have died, now live; but they live with gross alterations in physique and with severe impairments in physiological functioning.

There is presently little hope that illness and disability will disappear. Instead the number, and perhaps the rate, of physically disabled persons is increasing so that today there are more people with physical disabilities in the world than ever before.

Are these millions of people with physical disabilities different kinds of people from others? Are they treated in ways that are unique to those with imperfect bodies? Have they been exposed to life situations that exert a unique effect on behavior? Do we require a special psychology or unique psychological laws to understand them?

Large numbers of professional men all over the world are devoting their lives to the practice of rehabilitation. They make great efforts to assist the disabled person to return to normal society and normal living. Sometimes their efforts result in great success. More often success is limited by variables that are as yet imperfectly understood.

It is clearly important to study the problems that arise from the possession of an atypical physique and to attempt to find answers. A direct attack upon problems that are not well understood, however, is not always the most fruitful. Here we shall begin indirectly by considering the significance that may be assigned to physique generally, without special reference to the physical variations we call physical disability.

Somatopsychology (*soma:* body; *psyche:* mind, soul) is the study of some of the relationships that bind physique and behavior. All of us in everyday life tend to make judgments of people in terms of their physiques and also to evaluate physique in terms of behavior. We may say, "She's a redhead; I'll bet she has a temper," or "He might be a handsome fellow if he didn't scowl all the time." On a more sophisticated level we may say, "She's shy and withdrawn because she's ashamed of being so fat," or "She's fat because she's shy and withdrawn, and eating is her only pleasure."

It is not easy to disentangle the threads of cause-effect, and moreover, there always seem to be many exceptions. Some fat people are jolly, and some perfectly proportioned people are shy and withdrawn. It is a matter of common observation that the same kinds of behavior may be shown by people who have widely differing physiques, and that among individuals who have the same kind of physique can be found widely differing behavior.

It is the function of somatopsychology as a science to try to make sense out of this confusing array of data. Are there any invariable relationships between physique and behavior so that a science of somatopsychology can be developed, or must we say that each person is a law unto himself?

There are several ways of attacking this problem, and for each way there is some confirming evidence.

1. There is no relationship between physique and behavior. It is evident that normal variations in specific aspects of physique such as the length of fingers, toes, lips, or tongue are not critical factors in behavior. Similarly, it is obvious from impressionistic evaluation of the whole physique that individuals who engage in similar behavior may come in all shapes and sizes. Groups of writers or lawyers or psychologists or realtors are not noted for their physical similarity.

It is equally evident, however, that girls with generous chest measurements seem to behave in ways that are different from girls who are less well endowed. Boys with well-developed muscles engage in activities that are rare for weaker youths. Athletes as a group do not look like bankers or bookkeepers. Men, as identified by physique, behave differently than women.

In addition to common observation, we must also note that there is a large and increasing research literature whose findings lead in a consistent direction. Most of the studies that have been made show a positive correlation between certain aspects of physique and certain kinds of behavior. For example, children who are physically larger in height and weight tend to show leadership, popularity, social success, and good adjustment more frequently than smaller children (Barker *et al.,* 1953). The correlations obtained are usually low, but they are positive in relating "good" physique to "good'" behavior; and some of the correlations are statistically significant.

How can such data be explained? It must be emphasized that correlation is not explanation. We can be certain only that there are some relationships between physique and some aspects of behavior, but we are still faced with the problem of determining whether these relationships are meaningful. In terms of what concepts can the obtained relationships be explained?

Some of the research findings seem easy to understand. No one in our culture is likely to be surprised that most men tend to marry women who are slighly shorter than they are. This may be a matter of social expectancy. In our culture men are supposed to be taller than their wives. There is no necessary relationship, however. Many men are shorter than their wives. It is also unsurprising that behavioral skill in games is associated with physical strength. To the degree that strength is required for skill, this would appear to be a comprehensible, direct relationship.

It is more difficult, however, to understand Gowin's finding that railroad presidents were significantly taller than railroad station agents, university presidents were taller than small-college presidents, and bishops were taller than small-town preachers (Gowin, 1927). Why do the two characteristics seem to go together with greater than chance expectancy? Similarly, it is not clear why Blair (1940), in a survey of 270,000 men who owned life insurance, found an almost perfect relationship between a person's height and the amount of his insurance policy. The average amount per policy for men who were 6 feet 4 inches tall was $6,180, and the amount consistently decreased with each decrease of 1 inch in height until the average amount per policy for men who were 5 feet tall was only $2,979. Should we say that tall men are more able and therefore earn more money than shorter men? That there are special social reasons why tall men need more insurance than others? Or that tallness and the increased ability to buy insurance are both functions of a superior nutritional and social environment?

2. Physique determines behavior. One of the oldest ideas in the history of psychology is based on the observation that some individuals are relatively taller than they are wide; some are relatively wider than they are tall; some are relatively well proportioned in both directions; and many cannot be exactly classified.

Since the time of Hippocrates, 2,500 years ago, thoughtful and observant men have believed that there is a systematic and intrinsic connection between physique, or body type, and personality. The connection has been variously conceived to be genetic or biochemical or physiological so that once the body type or body was established, predictable behavior necessarily followed.

It is conceivable that the same genes or biochemical conditions that influence the development of body type also directly influence personality and behavior, but the evidence lends little support to this idea. Correlations, obtained from normal populations, between physical type and psychological type almost invariably have been so low as to be useless for prediction (Burt, 1944; Cabot, 1938; Eysenck, 1947; Fiske, 1944; Klineberg, Asch, and Block, 1934; Paterson, 1930; Sanford *et al.*, 1943).

Sheldon and associates have developed the most promising modern constitutional typology (Sheldon, 1944; Sheldon, Hartl, and McDermott, 1949; Sheldon and Stevens, 1942; Sheldon, Stevens, and Tucker, 1940). They have described three components of structural variation, which they claim are independent of nutrition and weight, and three basic components of temperament. In this scheme, a subject is rated on a scale from 1 to 7 for each component of physique and of temperament. Thus, the extreme endomorph (fat and flabby physique) would have a somatotype of 7–1–1; an extreme mesomorph (strong and muscular physique) would have a somatotype of 1–7–1; and an extreme ectomorph (frail and delicate physique) would have a somatotype of 1–1–7. A person who had an average degree of each component would be rated 4–4–4. Similar ratings are made for each of the three primary components of temperament; namely, viscerotonia (general relaxation, love of comfort, food, and people), somatotonia (muscular activity and bodily assertiveness), and cerebrotonia (restraint and inhibition). The creators of this classification reported correlations of the order of + .8 between endomorphic physique and viscerotonic temperament; mesomorphic physique and somatotonic temperament; and ectomorphic physique and cerebrotonic temperament (Sheldon, 1944).

These findings, however, have been criticized on the ground that the criteria for the temperament ratings were often expressed in physical terms. For example, the trait of physical courage for combat was defined as a "confident dependence upon the sturdiness, skill, and muscular strength of the body." The temperamental characteristic of restraint in posture and movement was defined as meaning that the body as a whole is carried stiffly. If temperament ratings are contaminated by body characteristics from the very beginning, it is not surprising that high correlations between physique and temperament were found.

Nevertheless, this theory is a great improvement over earlier typologies, for it recognizes that pure or extreme types of physique or temperament rarely exist and makes provision for the classification of the great mass of men whose physiques and temperaments do not fit exactly into just one of three classifications.

The theory of somatotypes may eventually add to our knowledge of intrinsic relationships between physique and temperament. A somatotyping study of congenitally handicapped persons would be of great interest. At present, however, the theory offers no aid in understanding the behavior of the physically handicapped.

Physique may also determine behavior in ways that do not require assumptions about body type. Men are biological organisms, and as such they are amenable to biological forces, especially deprivations and disease. Lack of necessary endocrine products, for example, may affect both physical and psychological development, although there is little evidence that normal variation in endocrine secretion is related to personality (Haskins, 1941).

Sexual maturity and interest in the opposite sex ordinarily develop together. A person may be sexually mature, however, without being interested in the opposite sex, and a sexually immature child may be highly interested in sexual contact with adults (Bender and Blau, 1937). The presence of the appropriate physique may not necessarily require a particular kind of behavior, and the absence of appropriate physique may not prohibit behavior.

It is predictable that a totally blind child will not respond to visual stimuli nor a totally deaf child to auditory stimuli. It must be remembered, however, that these highly specific limitations on behavior may be resolved in countless ways. Children with the same physical limitation may present markedly diverse personality pictures. It is not possible to predict with accuracy the molar psychological behavior of a child solely from knowledge of the nature and degree of his disability.

Men are also social organisms. In our culture it is predictable that children with male physiques will play with mechanical toys, whereas children with female physiques will play with dolls. Adults with male physiques will usually be the breadwinners who work outside the home while adults with female physiques will concern themselves primarily with pursuits inside the home. Again, however, it must be noted that exceptions exist. There is no necessary relationship between the physique and the behavior. In some cultures, in fact, women do the sort of work we consider appropriate for men, and men do the work we consider appropriate for women (Benedict, 1934).

3. Behavior determines physique. White individuals who uncover their bodies to the sun develop red or brown skins. Individuals who practice the sport of weight lifting develop large biceps. The academic class of a coed at Cornell University in Ithaca, New York, where hills are frequent and steep, can be predicted with considerable accuracy from the relative development of the muscles of the calf.

In recent years great emphasis has been placed upon functional or psychosomatic disabilities. It is now well known that how a person thinks and feels may affect his physique. A soldier who runs away from the cries of his wounded buddies may develop "psychogenic" deafness. Highpowered executives who function under great pressure for long periods of time are more likely to develop peptic ulcers than individuals who lead calmer lives. Negroes in Africa and Chinese in China rarely develop the heart condition known as essential hypertension, but Negroes and Chi-

nese who live and behave like Americans are as susceptible as other Americans. Similarly, American-born Japanese grow taller and develop a different type of chest structure than their countrymen who grew up in Japan, although there is no reason to believe that the genetic structures of the two groups are different.

A similar process is not unknown among Americans. Theodore Roosevelt was frail and delicate as a youngster. The change in his physique with exercise was not paralleled by similar changes in other frail youngsters who were unable to live in the open and did not develop his interest in "roughing it."

It is evident that all human functions are psychosomatic. Nothing is ever determined simply by heredity or simply by environment.

4. Behavior and physique may be simultaneously determined by a third variable.

The untreated congenital hypothyroid child simultaneously develops cretin physique and behavioral sluggishness. Both deafness and mental deficiency in a child may be residuals of an attack of meningitis. Development of secondary sexual characteristics and becoming interested in the opposite sex may result from the injection of sex hormones. Some of these relationships have a *must* characteristic so that direct and accurate prediction from physique to behavior is possible; for example, no cases have been reported of untreated congenital hypothyroid children who did not simultaneously manifest cretin physique and behavioral sluggishness. Other relationships, however, like those in the previous classifications refer to statistical probabilities. Meningitis may or may not cause deafness, mental deficiency, or both.

5. Behavior is a function of a person interacting with his environment, B = f(PE)

(Lewin, 1936). It is now obvious that this is the only formulation that will adequately account for all of the evidence. Behavior is never the result of the person or the environment alone. It is not certain, however, that knowledge of this formula greatly increases our understanding or our ability to predict and control behavior in the individual case. To study all aspects of a person, all aspects of the environment, and all aspects of the interaction between the two is clearly an impossible task. We may limit the field to more manageable dimensions by concentrating not on an understanding of all behavior but rather the more modest aim of understanding what behavior occurs because a person has a particular physique. Even more specifically, we wish to find some way of ordering and understanding the behavior of individuals whose physique is "exceptional" in a negative way—that is, the behavior of individuals whom we call physically disabled.

In the past, one unfortunate effect of formulating a psychological problem in terms of physical characteristics has been to imply that a disability per se is directly responsible for behavior. It is not uncommon to read that the deaf are suspicious, the blind are withdrawn, and the crippled are maladjusted. It is known, however, that some of our deaf, blind, and crippled children are very well-adjusted individuals whose mental health is superior to that achieved by the average physically normal child. For such cases the tendency has been to fall back on the bromide that "it all depends upon the person." Since all degrees and kinds of adjustment may be found in the physically disabled, it has been claimed that adjustment depends upon the individual. It is the individual child who with "help" must "accept" or "compensate" or "make up for" so that he

may "act as normal as possible" and "be treated as normal," "in spite of" his disability. These formulations place an impossible task and needless strains upon disabled children. As we shall see, except for certain specific behavioral limitations that are directly tied to physique, placing the source of behavior either in the disability itself or in the person is neither helpful nor true.

UNDERSTANDING THE BEHAVIOR OF THE PHYSICALLY DISABLED: THE CULTURAL RELATIVITY OF DISABILITY

The history of science shows that progress in understanding phenomena has often been impeded by the acceptance of "obvious" assumptions that are not true. It may be of value, therefore, to examine certain assumptions in somatopsychology that appear to be self-evident. For example, what is a physical disability? What is a physical handicap? For many years, the two terms were frequently used interchangeably, for it seemed clear that if a person had a disability, he was handicapped for that ability and the handicap would spread to other behavior also. Undoubtedly there is some truth in this view. A crippled child is limited not only in physical ability. He *may* also be limited in the kinds of play experiences that are open to him. His parents, other adults, and children *may* treat him differently than if he were not crippled, and he himself *may* come to feel that he is not only different, but also a less worthy person than others. It will be observed that different verbs have been used in this description. The child is physically limited, but the effects of the limitation are restricted to a conditional *may*. Handicaps may or may not follow from a disability. In recent years it has become common to make this sort of distinction between the two terms. A disability is seen as an impairment having an objective or medical aspect (Hamilton, 1950), whereas a handicap is seen as an impairment in a particular kind of social and psychological behavior. Although behavioral data may be equally as objective as physique, this is a useful distinction. It makes explicit the common observation that children with identical physical impairments may behave in radically different ways and children who behave is essentially similar ways may have widely differing physiques. It is not certain, however, that such a distinction is of maximum utility in understanding the behavior of the people we call disabled. It may be of greater value to postulate that neither disability nor handicap is objective in the sense of being simply descriptive. Both are *judgments* that tend to conceal the implicit values upon which they are based. In strictly objective terms it can be said only that variations in physique exist. Which variations will be considered disabilities, impairments, or handicaps is strictly relative to the expectations of the culture in which the person lives, the tasks that are required of him, and the meaning the person himself and others may assign to the variation.

Variations in Physique Leading to Limitation in Ability

Consider a female adolescent whose feet from heel to toe measure just four inches and appear to be deformed. On observation it is noted that the girl walks mostly on her toes with a shuffling movement, that she cannot walk with the free stride of the typical American girl, and that she cannot run. Does this person have a disability? If she were an American girl living in the United States, obviously it would be difficult or impossible for her to engage in many of the activities that we consider appropriate and desirable for teen-age girls. Suppose, however, that this adolescent lived in China a hundred years ago when it was customary to bind the feet of females. In terms of the culture in which she lived, was she disabled? Who should be the judge? There is no question about the variation in physique. The feet of this adolescent and the feet of an American contemporary would differ. An American might say, "She's crippled. Why, she could never play softball like a real American girl." A Chinese might reply, "Barbarians! It is not appropriate for a woman to play softball. This girl has delightfully small feet that her husband will cherish, and she walks with the light and mincing step that is appropriate for a woman. Your American girls with their big gross feet walk like men. We would not allow it in China."

Obviously, it cannot be said that the Chinese girl in the Chinese culture of that time had a disability; on the contrary, the variation in the structure of her foot gave her a positive ability—the ability to walk in the way a woman "ought" to walk. An American girl in China would lack this ability. She would be "different." It would be seen by all that her feet were large and repulsive. She would be handicapped in behaving like a woman, and if social disapproval were great enough, she might very well develop the maladjusted behavior we commonly refer to as psychological handicap.

Another example from Chinese culture is instructive. It is said that when a powerful man approached the peak of his power, he closed his hands into fists and allowed his fingernails to grow through the palms to the other side. Physically, such a person was in a position similar to that of a bilateral hand amputee, but we cannot say that he was handicapped or disabled. He was in a highly desirable and envied position. He had the ability to live without caring for himself or lowering himself to any kind of labor. In effect such a person was saying to the world, "You see how wealthy and powerful I am? See how fearless I am of the future? See what a wonderful and privileged life I lead? There is nothing I have to do for myself. In all things I have servants at my beck and call."

In our culture, where we value purposeful activity, such a "deformity" would be a horrible disability. Among the elite of China, who value the contemplative life, it was not horrible. It was the height of social distinction. No doubt such behavior sounds very queer and abnormal to us but only because we are accustomed to different forms of social honor. The Chinese might very well point to the "deformities" we imposed upon physique when the whalebone-corseted wasp waist and the hourglass figure were considered appropriate for women. The fainting spells and many of the varied "female troubles" common in Queen Victoria's day undoubtedly were traceable to these imposed variations in physique. Similarly, binding of the breasts, required for the boyish figure of the 1920 flapper, which led to the breakdown of breast tissue and disturbances in lactating ability, probably was not unrelated to the increasing popularity of infant bottle-feeding during the same period. The Chinese might also point to the frequency with which our men, in their unceasing struggle for wealth, success, and power, drive themselves into physical disability and early death from heart disease. Our "jokes" about one-ulcer or two-ulcer executives in the advertising business, as indicators of productivity and merit, would not seem funny to the Chinese.

Other examples of the cultural relativity of disability are easy to find. In our culture, women who have epileptic seizures are considered to have a disability. Among the Shasta Indians of California, however, similar seizures are a rare and valued ability which lead a person to positions of importance, power, and honor. The Ubangi, whom many of us have seen in the circus side show, place wooden plugs in their lips to stretch them, so that at adulthood the lips extend five or six inches in front of the face. It is obvious that functions such as eating, speaking, and (for them) the uncommon emotional expression we call kissing must be affected.

Are these people "normal"? Are they "disabled"? One must remember that the Ubangi do not kiss; their lips are not an impediment to their own speech or to their nutrition. They may be considered to have a disability only if kissing were as valued in Africa as it is in the United States, only if they were required to speak English, and only if it were necessary for them to eat American foods. Obviously, however, an American among the Ubangi would have a disability by reason of his shallow lips.

Physical variation among the people of the earth seems to be the rule rather than the exception. There are people who "complete" the body by elongating the neck or molding the skull, by knocking out front teeth, blackening them, or filing them to points. Among some primitive people, it is customary to stretch the labia of the female genitals until they reach the knees. Other groups insert objects into the prepuce of the male genitals. All are examples of variation in physique that, in our culture, would lead us to the judgment of "disability," although they do not do so in the cultures in which they are found.

In addition to imposed variations in physique, it is easy to see that normal variations in height or in musculature may also lead directly to limitations in ability and indirectly to a judgment of "disability." The Pigmy lacks the ability to function efficiently in a society built for tall people. The normal white man is relatively lacking in a similar way if he is required to hunt animals by crawling through low grass without being seen. The clothes model of our culture, the highly valued, frail female with the pipestem shape, would be devalued and handicapped in Okinawa where it is customary for women to be able to row a boat, hoe a plot of ground, and haul in large fishing nets. Where big husky women are required and valued, our beautiful model, by reason of her physique, would lack important physical abilities.

In other words, it cannot be said that a person has a disability without specifying the situation in which he is expected to behave. Disability is not an objective *thing in a person,* but a social value judgment. A society makes a disability by creating a culture in which certain tools are required for behavior. Variations in physique by themselves have little psychological meaning outside of the frame of reference in which they are evaluated.

These examples may seem somewhat unreal analogies since there is little communication between primitive cultures and our own and we are convinced of our own superiority. Nevertheless, they may help to clarify and make explicit the relativity character of normal physique and the judgmental character of the term "disability." Moreover, it can be shown that such

analogies are not simply speculations but are similar to culture contacts that have occurred on a large scale. For example, in comparison with the American Indian, who was able to hear the faintest sound of animals in the wilderness and to see the buffalo herds when they were no more than a tiny speck on the plains, the average American pioneer was half deaf and half blind. It is probable that much of the Indians' superiority was a function of training, but it is possible also that they had real physiological superiorities in auditory and visual capacities. It is certain that some early pioneers who did not have or did not differentiate the important abilities of hearing and seeing at a distance sometimes paid for their disabilities with their lives.

The frequency with which intercultural comparisons have been made does not mean that the effects of culture on the judgment of disability can be found only by comparing primitive and civilized groups. Intracultural comparisons can be made also. Consider the German male who received a sabre cut on the face in a duel. Such wounds sometimes resulted in muscular and neurological injuries which, like the lips of the Ubangi, affected the person's ability to eat, speak, and kiss. In the United States such an injury might lead to prompt and vigorous application of rehabilitative measures to restore or improve the affected functions. There is no evidence, however, that such "marks of honor" were perceived in pre-World War I Germany as disabilities or as defects that required remedial treatment. They were visible proof of the positive abilities "to be brave" and "to defend one's honor."

Similarly, it is instructive to consider physical abilities (such as acuity for sounds) which have little practical importance in our culture. Some Americans are able to perceive sounds having a frequency of 20,000 cycles per second, but many persons are either lacking or severely impaired in this ability. The perception of such high-frequency sounds is presently of no practical importance in our culture and is hardly differentiated from other hearing abilities except by a few psychophysicists. Impairment in this ability can be precisely measured and rigorously demonstrated. Yet, when it is found, there is no suggestion that it is of any importance, that it has physical, psychological, or social effects upon the person, that he should seek remedial measures, or that he should compensate in some way for his lack. The variation in physique leading to limitation in ability is evident; but the judgment of "disability" is withheld. Suppose that sometime in the future the ability to hear frequencies of 20,000 cycles per second should become important. The sequence of social and psychological effects that would follow is clearly predictable.

This type of analysis of the meaning of physique suggests that it may be fruitful to think of physique, and the abilities that are associated with particular variations in physique, simply as tools for behavior. We can then make the following generalization: a disability exists only when a person lacks an adequate physical tool for behavior and when this lack is perceived by the culture in which the person lives as making him less able than his fellows. If a particular tool is not differentiated or required by a culture, its lack or impairment in a person cannot be a disability. If the tool is differentiated and valued by a culture but conflicts with a "higher" physical, social, and psychological ability, the lack or impairment will not be perceived as a disability.

Variations in Physique Leading to Socially Imposed Handicaps

There are some variations in physique that are socially handicapping only. These variations do not directly impose limitations on the abilities that are required by the culture in which the person lives, but they are perceived by the majority as being undesirable.

For example, in some cultures all redheaded infants are considered evil and killed immediately. In our own culture, a black skin, regardless of the brain power that may be under the skin, disqualifies a person from attending some universities. A female physique is a disqualification for many jobs that are well within the capacities of women. Women in the United States do not become barbers to men, although this is a common occupation for women in other countries. Surgeons are rarely female, although the skilled cutting and sewing of small objects that surgery requires is often considered a task at which women excel.

The social discrimination and prejudice against women (and Negroes and members of other minority groups who can be distinguished by their physiques) are commonly known and do not require additional emphasis here. It is evident that some limitations on behavior are not disabilities but socially imposed handicaps. Moreover, it is clear that the handicap is not *in* the body nor *in* the person but is a function of the society in which the person lives. This is true also of handicaps that arise from physical standards. These standards often seem as arbitrary and nonsensical as the killing of redheaded infants. Although they are readily seen to be "funny" rules, and they do not circumscribe behavior as completely as prejudice, they may have as drastic psychological effects in situations where they are imposed. Carious teeth, for example, may prevent a person from securing a teaching credential in the state of California. An airline hostess must be between 5 feet 3 and 5 feet 7 inches tall. Individuals who are "too tall" or "too short" relative to an arbitrary standard may not serve in certain police departments or in the armed forces. The newspapers recently reported the case of twins from Worcester, Massachusetts, who wished to enlist in the Naval Reserve. One was accepted, but his twin, who was a quarter-inch shorter, did not meet the height requirement and therefore was rejected!

We cannot discuss here the origin of social stereotypes, the reasonableness of arbitrary standards for physique, or the social expectation that certain behavior necessarily follows directly from physique. It may be sufficient to note only that physique is one of the criteria for social classification. It often determines how a person is expected to behave and what he will be permitted to do.

The social criteria are neither universal nor permanent. They may be different for different cultures, and even in the same culture they may change over a period of time.

The criteria for beauty offer an example. The concept of beauty is a relatively simple one. By the time the average child is four and a half years old, according to the norms of the Revised Stanford Binet Tests, Form L, he is able to perceive and understand that curly hair is more beautiful than straight hair; a Grecian nose is prettier than a broad, flat, or curved nose; relatively thin lips, and ears that lie close to the skull are nicer than their opposites. Like their elders, children do not see physical characteristics in isolation. Beauty, goodness, prestige, high moral qualities, and social acceptance can rarely be disentangled (Spiegel, 1950).

In the light of the evidence cited in the previous section, the cultural relativity of the physical characteristics considered beautiful need not be labored. The cross-cultural evidence makes it clear that, as the philosopher says, beauty is in the eye of the beholder.

There are few, if any, universal standards of attractiveness. In the female, for example, thinness and fatness, powerful muscular physiques and fragile delicate physiques, large, long, pendulous breasts and small upright breasts, flat and narrow buttocks and buttocks protruding to the point of steatopygia are all valued and considered beautiful in some cultures.

Among the Kwoma "the big strapping women, who could carry large loads of produce or firewood up the mountainside ... were the females that caused Kwoma men to smack their lips and make lewd comments" (Whiting, 1941). How would these women behave if they lived in Japan and were required to learn the routine of the delicate, graceful tea ceremony?

Within our own culture, standards for beauty have changed radically in less than two generations. It was not long ago that women who had "skinny" hips emulated Lillian Russell, the glamour girl of the 1890s, by tying pillows over their buttocks and eating without stint to fatten the neck, the shoulders, and the arms. It was only yesterday that the skinny, breastless, hipless flapper was the beauty ideal. Today, a casual leafing of any magazine will reveal the social necessity of large breasts on a slender figure.

Assume that three women, each having one of the valued physiques, but entirely unchanged in other respects, were systematically placed in each of the three periods from 1890 to 1970. Would they be likely to change in behavior? Would they become different kinds of people? What would be the critical variable, their physiques or the differing life situations with which they had to cope?

It is evident that social expectations which have the force of standards will influence behavior. A person who has a socially approved physique will be treated differently and will be expected to behave differently from persons whose physiques deviate from the social ideal. Obviously, therefore, the self-image of the person will also be affected. It is difficult to escape becoming the person that others believe one to be. In large measure the self is created by social interaction with others. No person can develop a wholesome personality if he encounters only derogatory attitudes.

It cannot be claimed that the physically disabled are exceptions to these generalizations. It is not correct to state that the physical limitations we have called *disabilities* invariably call forth universal social expectations. The roles assigned to the disabled and the behavior expected from them are not fixed. In Turkey blind men are preferred as readers of the Koran, for their prayers are believed to be more welcome to God than the prayers of others. A blind Catholic, however, cannot become a priest. If the person with a disability has sufficient prestige and status, the desirability of his role may be so great that his disability will be imitated. Princess Alexandra, who became the wife of Edward VII, walked with a limp. At the time she married, a fad spread among thousands of women on the European continent so that they walked with the special, prestigeful, limping gait known as the Princess Alexandra Walk!

Hanks and Hanks, Jr., (1948) have shown that individuals with physical variations that are perceived as disabilities are assigned different roles in different cultures. They may be treated as pariahs or as economic liabilities; they may be tolerantly utilized, granted limited social participation, or just left alone. These variations in assigned role, social treatment, and behavioral expectations are not functions of the disability. Instead, the Hankses hypothesize, the adverse treatment of the disabled is a function of low productivity or unequal distribution of goods in proportion to the size of the population, the maximizing of competitive factors in achievement, and the evaluation of criteria for achievement in absolute ways rather than relative ways.

These are promising hypotheses that appear to agree with the available evidence. Whether or not they are true, or whether other hypotheses are equally tenable, are problems for further investigation. It would be of great help to know why and how variations in physique lead to the imposing of social limitations or handicaps. The origin of social behavior is a problem that cannot be discussed here, however. It is sufficient for our present purpose simply to note that variations in physique, with or without ability limitations, may lead to social emulation, social approval, or social limitation.

It is society, far more than the condition of the body, which determines what a person will be permitted to do and how he will behave. All cultures place values upon certain aspects of physique, although different aspects of physique may be differentiated as important in different cultures, and different values may be assigned to the same variations. Nevertheless, certain generalizations may be made:

1. Physique is a social stimulus.
2. It arouses expectations for behavior.

3. It is one of the criteria for assigning a person to a social role.
4. It influences the person's perception of himself both directly through comparison with others and indirectly through others' expectations of him.
5. Comprehension of the kind, extent, and degree of socially imposed handicaps on persons with atypical physiques is basic to an understanding of the somatopsychology of physical disability.

Variations in Physique Leading to Emotional Handicaps

Some variations in physique do not produce ability limitations, nor do they instigate social handicaps. They may be seized upon, however, and utilized by the person as a defense against facing other problems. For example, a girl may fixate on a small facial mole and moan that it is ruining her life. If only she didn't have the mole— boys would like her better, she'd be less irritable, she'd get along better with her parents, and she'd be able to study better because she wouldn't need to worry about whether other children were looking at her, laughing at her, and criticizing her. There is clearly no ability limitation. In addition, her friends may honestly say that the mole is so small few people even notice it, or if they do, more frequently than not it is considered an attractive beauty mark. Nonetheless, the girl refuses to be comforted. If she seems unfriendly, irritable, and inconsiderate of others, it is because the mole on her face makes her so. A similar situation may be encountered in individuals who have normal variations in physique that are socially undifferentiated or not assigned social meaning.

Macgregor and Schaffner (1950) have reported that such indiviuals sometimes seek plastic surgery on the assumption that the change in physique will automatically lead to great social and emotional improvements. They show clearly, however, that the basic problems are psychiatric and not somatopsychologic. If one "blemish" is removed, the individual is either dissatisfied with the result or he readily finds another physical characteristic upon which to project his feelings of insecurity. Physique for such individuals has unique personal meanings that are entirely unrelated to ability limitations or to social handicaps. Moreover, it is questionable whether there is any direct relationship between the variation in physique and the emotional handicap. The body in these cases is simply the excuse for, not the cause of, psychological maladjustment.

These psychiatric cases present separate and complex problems that cannot be considered within the framework of somatopsychology. They are mentioned here primarily because their surface similarity to somatopsychologic problems may confuse the unwary investigator and obscure the essential, underlying relationships between physique and behavior.

It is unquestionable that normal variations in physique and physical disabilities are sources of psychological disturbance for some children. It is equally unquestionable that similar variations and disabilities in other children are not sources of psychological disturbance (Barker, Wright, and Meyerson, 1953; Stolz and Stolz, 1944). Workers in somatopsychology may differ as to the reasons why the same physical variation leads to emotional disturbance in one child and not in another, but there is universal agreement that variations in physique need not necessarily lead to emotional handicaps.

Except for the psychiatric cases, the following generalizations seem reasonable:

1. No variation in physique requires psychological maladjustment.
2. If an emotional handicap exists in a person who has a physical disability, it does not stem directly from the disability but has been mediated by social variables.
3. The mediation between physical status and psychological behavior occurs in the following way:
   (a) The person lacks a tool that is required for behavior in the culture in which he lives, and he knows that he lacks it.
   (b) Other individuals perceive that he lacks an important tool and devaluate him for his lack.
   (c) The person accepts the judgment of others that he is less worthy (or, to the degree that he is a product of his own culture, he judges himself as less worthy) and devaluates himself.

The (a) (b) (c) sequence is a unit. If (a) or (b) do not occur, (c) does not occur. If (c) does not occur, there is no emotional handicap.

Variations in Physique Leading to a Combination of Disability and Handicaps

Disability, social handicap, and emotional handicap have been isolated in order to show that they are separate and independent phenomena. Of course, we must now say at once that various combinations are the rule rather than the exception.

The analysis in itself, however, helps to account for the great variation in behavior that may be observed in people who vary in physique. Knowing the components of a combination and their interrelationships, especially in the light of cross-cultural contexts, enables us to begin to understand diverse phenomena that previously were obscure and incomprehensible.

We can begin to understand not only the major question of how it is that two similar individuals with similar disabilities can behave in different ways, but also such apparently diverse phenomena as why the behavior of a child who is blind may change when he understands for the first time that he is blind, and why the task of telling the child is so traumatic for parents.

Moreover, the analysis points to some of the critical variables that affect the behavior of those who have been judged to be disabled. If we are faced with behavior that is undesirable, it is possible to see what has to be changed. We need no longer conceal our ignorance under the guise of respecting individuality. It may be true that "each person is different," but it is neither true nor helpful to "explain" all reactions to disability in terms of characteristic and unchangeable functions of the disability itself or the person.

In actual practice, within a culture that has established standards for physique which seem right and natural, it is difficult for the somatopsychologist to step outside of his own ethnocentrism. An example from within the culture may help to clarify the issue.

Ever since he was a small boy, Edward G. knew that he wanted to be a policeman. When he was twenty-one years old, he took the Civil Service Examination for patrolmen, and he passed the mental and physical tests with flying colors—except for one item. He was 5 feet 3½ inches tall, and the regulations said that a policeman had to be 5 feet 4 inches tall.

Edward was desolate. Although he knew that it was not true, he claimed that a mistake had been made in measuring him, and he demanded a remeasurement of his height.

For three days Edward remained in bed and had his friends pull on his legs and his head so that he was stretched out to the fullest possible inch. Then, thirty minutes before he was due to be measured, Edward persuaded a friend to hit him a sharp blow on the top of the head with a piece of wood. The blow raised a lump of considerable size.

Edward immediately raced to the examination and had himself measured. The stretching of the previous few days together with the bump on his head was more than enough to raise his stature to the required 5 feet 4 inches, and he was sworn in as a policeman.

Edward was a good policeman. In three years' service he received several commendations and one award for bravery in capturing an armed robber. One day, however, he was called out to march in a parade and lined up with other policemen who also were supposed to be of minimum height. By comparison, it could be seen immediately that Edward was perceptibly shorter than the others. A "spit and polish" officer measured him on the spot and found he was only 5 feet 3 inches tall. Two weeks later, Edward was no longer a policeman.

Dismissal from the police force was a great shock. Some of the people Edward had dealt with in the line of duty now taunted him; others laughed. Edward became more and more convinced that he was no good, not useful for anything. If anyone called him "shorty" he flew into a rage. If he couldn't reach something on a high shelf, he was morose for days. "If only I were taller," he said again and again.

At last report Edward was in a "nursing home." He was not psychotic, but neither was he mentally well. Severely maladjusted is probably the term that best describes him.

Now how can we explain this case? Did his shortness *cause* his behavior? Obvi-ously, just to ask the question is to realize its absurdity. Did his shortness prevent him from being a good policeman? Well, yes and no. When he was a policeman, he was a good one, but according to the standards, he had a disability for being a policeman and therefore he couldn't be one. Should we say that if Edward had been a different kind of person, if he had courage and social interest, he would not have broken down? Again, all we can answer is yes and no. Every person has his breaking point, and Edward reached his. On the other hand, while he was a policeman, he was a good policeman and a worthy citizen. He did not become maladjusted until he accepted the evaluations of the important others and agreed he was "no good."

Although this case has many important aspects, it is relatively simple in structure and uncluttered with the emotionality that often surrounds the discusion of "real" disabilities. The tool loss leading to social handicap and emotional handicap can readily be seen. It is a good case to remember when platitudes about deafness, blindness, and crippling are offered as explanations for behavior. *"Because* the deaf, blind, or crippled are . . . " or *"because* that's the kind of person he is" are rarely true or useful answers.

In somatopsychology we deal primarily with processes and interrelationships and not with static phenomena. Our further understanding depends upon the development of a human psychological ecology that will permit us to describe in concrete detail the relationships between human beings and their psychological environments in ecological rather than valuative or judgmental terms. A beginning has been made in this section with describing when and how a variation in physique may become a disability and a handicap.

UNDERSTANDING THE BEHAVIOR OF THE PHYSICALLY HANDICAPPED: SCIENCE AND THEORY IN SOMATOPSYCHOLOGY

It is not enough to have some background knowledge of how disabilities and handicaps are created, in general. Our culture has a well-developed value system relating to variations in physique. To change the negative attitudes of the culture toward those who are judged to be disabled may require hundreds of years of systematic labor. In the meantime we are confronted with the practical problem of helping the handicapped to live with some measure of usefulness and happiness.

The evidence on one point is clear. Children who have disabilities, as a group, tend to have more frequent and more severe psychological problems than others. Why does this occur, and what can be done about it?

It is evident from our earlier analysis that it is not sufficient to say, for example, "John is blind; therefore he has severe problems of adjustment." It is necessary to say, "John is blind. In the culture in which he lives people pity those who cannot see. The blind are perceived as dependent individuals who must be taken care of and who cannot compete for many of the most desirable goals in life. John, as a member of his own culture, tends to see himself in this way also. He perceives clearly the low esteem in which he, as a blind person, is held, the prejudice and discrimination that are raised against him, and his lack of status in society. He agrees that he is a less worthy person than those who can see. Therefore, John feels inferior and has severe problems of adjustment."

Expressed in this way, it is clear that not blindness but the social problem is the critical variable. This is true not only of blindness but of other variations in physique also. Some individuals who shrink from the physically deformed are aware that a person is not responsible for how he looks and that avoidance is ethically unjustified. It is contended, therefore, that the repugnance is instinctive, natural, and really can't be helped. There is no reason to believe that this is true. There is every reason to believe that attitudes toward variations in physique are learned. First, the variations that are perceived with horror in one culture are accepted without emotion in another culture. Second, within a culture there are many individuals who do not feel the culturally sanctioned emotions. Not everyone in the United States is emotionally disturbed by the sight of a cerebral-palsied child or a congenital amputee. Third, many who do experience emotional distress on first exposure to a particular disability also experience rapid adaptation. The horrified student who sees only disabled bodies at a school for the handicapped changes quickly to the experienced therapist who is only faintly aware of differences in physique but keenly aware of differences in personality.

Disability appears to be as much a problem of the nondisabled majority as it is of the disabled minority. Maladjustment in normal individuals with respect to physical disability is widespread. However, we cannot change our society overnight, and social attitudes often present problems that can be dealt with only indirectly.

It appears that a dead end has been reached. If disability is relatively fixed and society is relatively inflexible, that leaves only the person. Inasmuch as the source of behavior is not *in* the person in any psychological meaningful sense, what can be done?

Suppose you are approached by a

mother who has a deaf child. "I understand that deaf children tend to become maladjusted," she says. "What can I do to prevent this?"

"Well," you say, "how old is your child? Is it a boy or a girl? How much hearing does he have? Are there any other children in the family? Do they hear well? How old were you when the child was born? Were you ill during pregrancy? Was birth normal? How old is your husband? Is anyone else in your family deaf or hard of hearing? Does the child show signs of maladjustment now?"

The questions, of course, can be endless. A curious thing about them is that there are only common sense reasons, or often no reasons, for believing the answers have any direct relationship to the child's behavior. After the answers are received you may say, "Treat him as if he were normal, but *don't* expect as much of him as if he were normal. Don't spoil him, but on the other hand *do* make allowances for his disability. A special nursery school for deaf children would be a good thing, but then he has to live in a world with normally hearing people, so a regular nursery school would be a good thing too. It all depends on what kind of child he is." In other words, we don't know. We don't know in general, and we don't know what it depends on. The responsibility is passed back to the parent with directions that are contradictory and impossible to fulfill.

Similarly, suppose a parent brings a six-year-old cerebral palsied child and raises the specific question: "Can my child get along in school?" Often we don't know. After asking innumerable questions all that can be said is, "Let's try him out and see." If he gets along, then he gets along, and that's fine. Of course, the waste, frustration, anxiety, and psychological damage to the child if he doesn't get along are unfortunate but inevitable. Clearly this is an unsatisfactory state of affairs.

It is true that in some instances an individual child can be studied. To some degree it can be determined what "kind" of child he is and how he interacts with his environment. The function of science, however, is to solve problems by means of general laws that can be applied to the individual case. Generalization and certainty of prediction are at the heart of science. Progress in other sciences has occurred only to the degree that the theories were constructed which led to general laws that held without exception. If each case must be studied individually and nothing can be said about the psychological effects of disability in general, there can be no science of somatopsychology.

The problem of individual differences and the search for generalizations that can be applied to every individual case are not unique to psychology. They are common to all science.

Consider the following example from the field of mathematics. What is the area of a circle? In one sense this is a stupid and unanswerable question. It is possible to complain that there are infinite numbers of circles, from a pin point to the circle of the universe, all differing in area. What circle is meant? Where is it? How is it possible to say anything about circles in the abstract? It is indisputably true that the answer to the question depends upon what kind of circle it is. If little is known about circles in general, it may be reasonable to ask the following questions: Where is this circle? Is it here on earth, up in the air, or underground? How did it get there? Are there any other circles nearby? Is it hollow or solid? What color is it? Is it made of steel, wood, soap, or is it just a line on paper? How was it formed? When did it get there? Does it surround anything?

Every person who knows the general law, Area $= \pi r^2$, however, knows that these questions are irrelevant and meaningless. The general and invariable relationship between circles and their areas makes only one measurement of importance in determining the area of a particular circle. If this relevant context is known, it is possible to understand and predict the area of any circle by asking just one question: What is the radius? It is then possible to forget the thousand-and-one ways in which circles may differ. These other variables may be important in other relevant contexts, but they are of no value in predicting or controlling area.

If the relevant context is not known, two procedures are possible: (1) An attempt can be made to cover ignorance by asking many irrelevant questions, as is often done in somatopsychology. This procedure will yield meaningless answers that leave us little wiser than before (2) If, by some fortuitous circumstance, we lived in a world where red circles tended to be larger than black ones, it would be possible to compute a correlation and reach the empirical generalization that red circles tend to be larger in area than black ones. In such a case predictions might be made with better than chance success, but there would still be much uncertainty. Some black circles would have a greater area than some red ones. We could speak only of "tendency" and not of "certainty." Proceeding on the basis of correlational evidence and empirical generalization, as is now often done in somatopsychology, it might be contended that every circle is really different and therefore must be treated individually. The only way to be sure would be to produce a specific circle about which information was desired and measure it. Obviously, this procedure is possible, but it is much more useful to have a general formula that can be applied

to any circle. General laws in somatopsychology would be equally useful.

Our goal is to be able to make psychological predictions. The mathematician requires mathematical data in order to make mathematical predictions. Physical characteristics such as color, material, or position in space are not helpful to him. The geneticist requires genetic data in order to make genetic predictions. Physical data such as weight, psychological data such as temperament, or social data such as the number of animals in a cage are useless for genetic prediction.

Is it reasonable to suppose that somatopsychological predictions can be made from the physical data classified as disabilities? Physical characteristics must be the starting point, but they are just as phenotypic or superficial for somatopsychology as they are for genetics. Progress in somatopsychology will come only when a somatopsychological theory is developed which permits the transformation of physical data into psychological data.

A WAY OF THINKING IN SOMATOPSYCHOLOGY

A commonplace remark is that we need more research on disabled persons. Undoubtedly that is true, but it is well to understand the kind of research that is required.

There is a myth in our culture about the open-minded scientist who approaches a problem without preconceptions and reports only the "facts." As we have seen, however, the number of questions that can be asked about any phenomenon is limited only by our ingenuity. Not all questions are equally good questions, and not all facts are equally useful in the sense that they lead to further understanding.

LEE MEYERSON

For example, we may adopt the role of the open-minded scientist who wishes to study the psychology of the exceptional. What shall be investigated? It is perfectly possible to measure the big toes or the length of the eyelashes of children who are blind and compare the findings with similar data from children who see. No one has done such a study, however, and no one is likely to. Why? Because there is no reason for believing that such measurements will contribute anything to our knowledge of behavior. Even if the two groups were completely different in these characteristics, the result would have no meaning unless there was some way of explaining it. Similarly, it is possible to study the psychology of people who wear size 9 shoes—or even the behavior of people with size 10 feet who wear size 9 shoes—but no one does this. In other words, open-minded is not synonymous with empty-headed. A scientist does not study a problem unless he has some reason for believing it to be important. If he believes that a particular investigation is important, obviously he must have some hunch, reason, or theory for believing so. Before he begins, his preconceptions have already been expressed by the problem he has selected for study and the methods of collecting data that he plans to use. In other words, he has a theory. The random collection of facts is not science. Research undirected by a theory of probable relationships is blind and rarely productive. The investigator, before he begins, must have a clear idea of what he is going to look for and how he is going to look. The questions that he asks, in great measure, determine what he will find. If his hunch, hypothesis, or theory is approximately correct to begin with, it is likely that his work will be fruitful.

In somatopsychology it is evident that despite considerable research effort, only limited progress has been made in answering the basic question of how physique may be related to behavior. Examination of the literature shows that considerable progress has been made in other fields, such as medicine, in coping with the problems of disability. In somatopsychology there is still much discussion of the same problems that were seen to be critical one hundred years ago. Answers to these problems are scarce or contradictory and exceptions to the rule are frequent.

Whenever a question is posed that does not yield generalizations that can be applied without exception to the individual case, it is time to ask whether the questions are meaningful and whether they are answerable.

What Is an Answer or Explanation?

All scientific explanations are essentially descriptions, but there are different levels of adequacy. The least adequate explanation is simply to recognize and affirm that something is and perhaps give it a name. The best explanation describes the greatest amount of data in the fewest terms. A few examples may make these statements more meaningful.

Naming Explanations

It has been observed that salmon are spawned far up in the headwaters of streams. In their second year, they travel downstream to the ocean, which is warmer and saltier and contains less oxygen than do mountain streams. Why do they do this?

In the past it has been customary to label behavior of this kind as instinctive. There is an instinct *in* the fish to behave as it does. This naming of a behavior often yields a satisfying feeling that the behavior has been explained. Actually nothing has been explained. A word has been substituted for an observation of behavior, but we are no wiser than before. The salmon does what it does. First, it is observed that the salmon swims to the ocean. Second, the behavior is labeled an instinct. Third, the behavior is "explained" by saying there is an unknown "something" in the fish that makes it behave this way. It is precisely this unknown that must be investigated. Why do salmon behave this way? Naming the unknown an instinct does not contribute to understanding, and to the extent that it tends to choke off further research, naming is not helpful.

Not long ago it was discovered that the essential factor was the relationship between light and photosensitive receptors in the skin of the salmon. The receptors are covered by pigment which is gradually lost. As the photoreceptors are stimulated by light the fish seeks deeper and deeper streams until eventually it reaches the ocean. This is an explanation. It explains both "instinct" and the lack of it. Prediction and control are possible. If a fish doesn't migrate, the investigator now knows where to look—at the photoreceptors. If it is desirable to prevent fish from migrating, the investigator knows what to control—light.

Young children and primitive people employ many naming explanations. Things are because they are. They act as they do because that is their nature. Heavy objects have the essential nature of heaviness; that's why they fall to earth. A sailboat moves because it *is* a sailboat, and that is its nature.

Of course, older people and civilized people see immediately that an object falls because of its relationship to the earth; a boat moves not because that is its nature but because of the relationship between the area of its sails and the strength of the wind. Expressed in this way, it is clear that prediction is possible because the relevant context is understood. Nothing *is* in itself. Everything occurs in a relevant context.

But how quickly we forget once we move out of the area where the essential relationships are known.

It is observed that a child appears to be wary of adults and clings closely to his mother. He does not mix easily with other children. He is often seen watching other children as if he'd like to join them. Why does the child behave in this way? "Because," we say, "he *is* shy"; that is, the shyness is something *in* the child. It is a "thing" that he carries around with him. This is essentially the same kind of "explanation" that was considered unsatisfactory for the salmon. First the behavior is described, then a name is assigned to the behavior, and finally the behavior is "explained" by the name. The question, "Why does the child behave in this way?" has now been changed to, "Why is the child shy?" But an answer in terms of the relevant relationships has not been given.

The same naming phenomena occur in somatopsychology on a more sophisticated level. It may be observed that a certain person is deaf. He also engages in the behavior that may be classified or described as being suspicious of others. Why does he behave this way?

"Well, this person is deaf. Now it is a finding of psychology that deaf people tend to be suspicious. If this person were blind and suspicious, that would be unusual, but he is deaf and it is not unusual for deaf people to be suspicious. He is deaf. That's why he's suspicious. It is in the nature of deafness or deaf people to be suspicious."

It should be clear at this point that another circular explanation has been given that is no more adequate than the concept of instinct. It doesn't help to add that deaf people are suspicious because they believe that other people are talking about them. Not every deaf person is suspicious. Some do not believe others talk about them. Other deaf people may believe it but don't care. Neither the behavior of the suspicious deaf person nor the behavior of the unsuspicious deaf person has been explained.

Naming is not explanation.

Historical and Contemporaneous Explanations

Assume that your class meets in a room without windows. The sun is shining outside, but it is not shining on you. Why isn't the sun shining on you?

Two kinds of explanations are possible. One is based on the history of the objects and might go something like this:

The sun isn't shining on me because I'm sitting in this room.
Why are you sitting in this room?
Well, because I'm going to the university.
Why are you going to the university?
There are two reasons, First, because the university is here to go to. Back in 1860 a leading citizen decided to build a university. He made a lot of money in the slave trade and didn't know what else to do with it, so he thought a university would be a good idea. Of course, he made all of this money in the first place because his family had disowned him, and he wanted to prove himself. So, in one sense the sun isn't shining on me or any of the others in the class because the university benefactor wanted to prove himself. The second reason is purely personal and applies only to me. You see, back in 1800 my paternal great-grandfather took his four boys and headed west for Kansas . . .

It is evident that a complete historical explanation is an infinite regress that leads back to the origins of the universe and to the detailed history of every individual involved. Various shortcuts, of course, can be taken, but the final answer to the question posted must be different for every person in the class. The sun isn't shining on Joe because he is studying to be a doctor. The sun isn't shining on Jim because his parents made him come to college. The sun isn't shining on Mary because she is looking for a husband. Every case is different. These answers sound queer and unbelievable, not because they are false, but because they do not "explain" the relevant context that most of us already know.

In a contemporaneous explanation, no attention would be paid to particular objects. Instead, since this is a physical question, attention would be directed to the physical field forces that are operating: The sun does not penetrate opaque objects. The psychological or social motivations of the individual are irrelevant. A statement may now be made in if-then terms which is always true: If a person is sitting in a room made entirely of opaque substances, then the sun will not shine on him. There are no exceptions. In every case, regardless of whether the room is built of brick or stone or building paper, and regardless of whether the person is Joe or Jim or Mary, an immediate correct prediction for individual cases can be made. Moreover, since the phenomenon is now understood, it is possible to make the prediction before a room is built and to control the shining of-the-sun-on-persons-or-objects as we wish. It will be observed that this kind of explanation accounts for both sun-shining-on-objects and sun-not-shining-on-objects. It is independent of any particular objects, and it is independent of the past.

Consider a similar situation in medicine. A child is limping down the street. Why does he limp? Because he had polio when he was five years old. It should be evident immediately that this is a historical explanation which does not explain. The child does not limp because he had polio when he was five years old any more than the sun does not shine on Mary because she is looking for a husband. There are many children who had polio when they were five years old who do not limp. It can be said, of course, that each case is different. Some children who have polio become crippled, and some do not. It all depends on the child. But *what* does it depend on? What should be investigated? If the case histories show that bright children contract crippling polio more frequently than less bright children, as is sometimes claimed, should physicians investigate intelligence?

Fortunately the physician has a contemporaneous explanation that he can apply to individual cases. He may say that if nerves *x, y,* or *z* are destroyed the muscles in the legs that are innervated by these nerves will atrophy, and the child will limp. It will be observed that this explanation is independent of any particular child and of any particular disease. It holds without exception in every case. Any injury that destroyed nerves *x, y,* or *z* will produce the same behavior. The physician is thereby able to understand why two similar children who had the same disease at the same age may walk differently, while two children who had different diseases may walk in the same way. By testing the nervous function of a particular case he is able to predict before the child takes his first step whether or not limping will occur. The prediction can be made even if the physician has never seen the child before and knows nothing else about

him. Control of this behavior is not yet possible, but knowledge of the relevant context between nerves and muscles and limping guides future investigation. It tells the researcher where to look and what to study. The thousand-and-one other ways in which children differ in health and in illness are irrelevant at this point.

Of course, contemporaneous explanation also leads to an infinite regress. How and why are nerves destroyed by disease? The answer to this question will, in turn, permit further questions to be seen. The questions, however, are meaningful, and they are answerable. Historical explanations, except perhaps for certain problems in public health, are dead ends. The implications of this statement deserve to be spelled out.

If a child limps because he had polio, and polio causes crippling, and the polio attack occurred last year, what can be done now? The polio is a past event. It is not possible to influence past events but only the factors that are operating in the present. Historical and contemporaneous explanations lead in two radically different directions, and the influence of direction cannot be overestimated. Historical explanations lead from the present to the past: "It is too bad that the child is crippled because he had polio last year, but that's the way the ball bounces." Contemporaneous explanation leads from the present to the future: "The child is crippled because nerves *x, y,* or *z* are destroyed. Is there some way of regenerating these nerves? Is it possible that other intact nerves may be attached to the affected muscles?" Historical explanations lead to excuses. Contemporaneous explanations lead to continuous investigation.

Rehabilitation of the disabled is presently plagued with this problem. Few researchers in somatopsychology are as yet thinking in terms of contemporaneous, field-contextual descriptions. Almost all explanations are in terms of naming, assigning qualities to the individual, or tracing history. For example, a child doesn't talk. Why? Because he lost his hearing when he was two years old, that's why he doesn't talk. An adolescent is very dependent. Why? Because he's been blind since birth. It is too bad, but that is the way deaf children and blind children are.

It is necessary only to see a deaf child who talks and a blind child who is not dependent to realize that historical explanations do not explain. From the standpoint of contemporaneous explanation children who have physical disabilities may tend to show certain kinds of psychological behavior, not because of their histories but because of the psychological forces that are presently acting. If these forces can be understood, behavior will be amenable to change.

Empirical or Correlational Explanations

One way of attempting to solve a problem is to investigate the frequency with which two variables occur together. This is a form of historical explanation projected to the future. It contains certain pitfalls, however, that deserve special mention.

Empirical *method* is basic to science. There are two ways of employing the method, however. One way is to make observations or conduct experiments to test a working hypothesis or a theory. A second way is to try to build up an explanatory theory from the observations. The first way is in general and productive use. The second way has sometimes been characterized as a determined attempt to obtain knowledge from ignorance. The difficulty with the second way is the ease with

which human reason may be misled when the relevant context is not known.

For example, there is a statistically significant relationship between sight and intelligence. Blind children, as a group, earn lower IQs than children who see. There is nothing wrong with such a statement as a description, but it is misleading if it used as a cause-effect explanation or as a means of prediction for the individual case. It cannot be said that blind children obtain lower IQs *because* they are blind. There are some blind children who test at the genius level. If the IQ of a particular blind child is explained in terms of his blindness, there is no way of explaining the high IQs of other equally blind children. An example from a field where the true context is known may clarify the matter.

In everyday life there appears to be a close correlation between the lightness of objects and their ability to float in water. Suppose a cild shows you a 10-pound iron boat and asks you whether it will float. Depending on your own observations, you reply that it will not because it is "too heavy." Only "light" things will float and not heavy ones. If the boat were made of wood, then it would float, but since it is made of iron it won't. If the child now tells you about a visit to the seashore in which he saw big iron boats floating that weighed ten thousand tons, what can you say? It is apparent that you do not have the correct explanation.

Similarly, consider these empirical observations: An almost perfect correlation has been found between the number of births that occur yearly in the city of Stockholm and the number of storks' nests that are built yearly in Stockholm chimneys. What conclusion can be drawn? Would you draw it even if the correlation over a period of fifty years were perfect? There is a very close correlation between the number of fire engines that go to a fire and the amount of damage that occurs. Assume that you wish to reduce the amount of damage that occurs at fires, would you suggest that the number of fire engines be reduced?

These are not simply academic examples. They are essentially similar to empirical observations which have misled investigators in the past and continue to mislead in the present. A hundred years ago in the lowlands of Italy it was observed that individuals who left their windows open at night became ill, while those who closed their houses tightly remained well. The disease was malaria, for obviously it came from the bad night air. The man who had a theory that not bad air but the mosquitoes that fly at night were responsible for the disease was obviously a crackpot. In France a hundred years ago it was observed that children who were fed cow's milk sickened and died, whereas those who were fed wine remained well. In the absence of a correct theory to explain the observation the French were quite right in praising alcohol and condemning milk as food for infants.

It is easy to see the "foolish" errors of others when the true relationships are known. The dangers of empirical explanation are less evident when the relevant contexts are not known.

Suppose a child plays hookey from school. Why is he a truant? An empirical investigation might determine that the school was directly northwest of the child's house. Further, if he left his house and continued in a northwest direction—regardless of whether he walked, roller-skated, or rode his bike—he went to school. On the other hand, if he didn't start out in a northwest direction or didn't continue long enough, he didn't go to

school. These are the facts. What should be done? Clearly, it is necessary to give the child training in walking, roller-skating, and riding his bike in a northwest direction! That will correct his truancy.

No doubt this sounds very funny, but consider these situations. A child says the *w* sound for *r*. It has been found that if a child moves his speech organs in a particular way he will say *r* and not *w*. Therefore, if a child has such a defect, give him training in saying the *r* sound. A child doesn't read. It has been found that in order to read, a child must recognize words. This child doesn't recognize words. Therefore, give him special remedial work in recognizing words. These do not sound so funny, but they are based on the same principle as the earlier examples and they are just as likely to be wrong. Recent research on the successful treatment of reading disabilities by counseling, without remedial work, is highly suggestive.

The world is presently disturbed by the fact that there appears to be a correlation between the number of cigarettes smoked daily and the incidence of lung cancer. On a purely empirical basis, it can also be demonstrated that there is a close relationship between the increased incidence of lung cancer and increase in the following:

1. Consumption of margarine
2. Membership in the Democratic party
3. Output of comic books
4. Number of aged in the population
5. Social freedom for women
6. Civil liberties for Negroes and other minority groups
7. Number of people who work for a living
8. Cost of living

LEE MEYERSON

It is immediately evident that some of these relationships are meaningless or chance relationships that result from the simultaneous operation of independent forces. Some may reflect the influence of a third variable which is not listed here; for example, "tense" individuals may smoke more than others and also be predisposed toward lung cancer. None of the variables will permit precise prediction. Many career women who smoke a lot, eat margarine, belong to the Democratic party, and read comic books do not get lung cancer.

Correlation is not explanation. An obtained correlation or empirical relationship is meaningless aside from the theory that is used to explain it. The most adequate theory will account for the negative cases in terms of the same concepts that are used to explain the positive cases. The collection of data is not the essence of science. A scientific investigation may be considered successful to the degree that it contributes to the reduction of empirical and quantitative statements and increases the number of qualitative statements that can be made about phenomena.

Inasmuch as many of the conclusions in somatopsychology are based on empirical evidence, these cautions may be worth heeding.

Summary

The task of all science is to order or transform observational data to theoretical constructs in such a way that understanding, prediction, and control of phenomena are possible. The observational data provide a test of the "truth" of a theory, but the theoretical constructs are not directly derived from the data.

If a theory leads to increased understanding, it is considered an explanation.

Complete explanation, however, is impossible. Science is truly an "endless frontier" in which a correct answer leads inevitably to further questions.

Adequate explanations appear to have several characteristics in common:

1. They are generalizations that permit application to the individual case.
2. They describe the greatest amount of data in the fewest terms.
3. They reflect a necessary and invariable relationship between certain events that occur in a specified context. The relationship is important rather than the qualities in an object.
4. They lead to understanding of what has to be changed in a relationship in order to bring about change in behavior.
5. They are expressed in dynamic, genotypic, contemporaneous terms and not in empirical, phenotypic, historical terms.
6. They point to further relevant research.

Progress in somatopsychology depends upon discovering adequate theoretical concepts to which data can be ordered. It has been pointed out that revolutionary advances in science have come not from empiricism but from new theories (Conant, 1953).

UNDERSTANDING THE BEHAVIOR OF THE PHYSICALLY HANDICAPPED: SOME CONCEPTS FOR SOMATOPSYCHOLOGY

Physical disabilities are physical. How is it possible to make psychological sense out of data that are not psychological? It is evident from earlier discussion that physique must be phenotypic for psychology. Psychological investigations based directly upon physique can lead only to naming or to empirical generalizations. Such generalizations can be expressed only in terms of tendency, correlation, or group differences that are significantly different from chance expectancy. If-then-always statements will not be made. There will always be many exceptions, and precise prediction will be impossible.

Examination of the research findings on physical disability indicates that this is an accurate reflection of the current state of affairs.

In this section an attempt will be made to develop a new way of thinking about somatopsychology in dynamic, genotypic, contemporaneous terms. Discussion will be restricted to social psychological adjustment problems. The problems of individual differences, educational method, and physical rehabilitation require extended discussion which cannot be given here.

As psychologists, we are not concerned with physical disability per se, but with the *behavior* that is associated with or appears to result from physical disability. The emphasis is on behavior. Psychological concepts, therefore, are required. Two such psychological concepts which permit the ordering of social-emotional behavior will be described. These are the concepts of *new psychological situations* and *overlapping psychological roles*. These ideas are not original with the present author. They were formulated by the late Kurt Lewin. Their elaboration and application to the physically handicapped were accomplishments of Roger G. Barker and associates. The following discussion draws heavily on their work (Barker, Wright, and Meyerson, 1953).

NEW PSYCHOLOGICAL SITUATIONS

Figure 1–1 represents a momentary point in time in the life space of a person.* It shows a schematic representation of an old or familiar psychological situation and a new psychological situation.

It will be seen that there are many known subregions in the old psychological situation. Some of the subregions have been labeled "plus" to indicate that they are desired by the person, and some have been labeled "minus" to indicate that they are not desired. Some paths to particular subregions have been indicated. Path A, for example, may represent going to the movies with a friend. The lines between subregions represent barriers that must be overcome. In this case, the barrier in subregion A_1 may represent getting permission from mother to go, A_2 may represent finding a friend to go with, and A_3 may represent having the money to get into the movies. Path B may represent "getting praise from mother;" the subregions to be passed through include making the bed in one's room, picking up toys, and washing one's hands and face before dinner. Path C may represent getting punishment from father, and single subregions may represent "being impudent."

*This figure and the following ones may have practical as well as didactic value. It is suggested that the student attempt to diagram the psychological situations of individuals whose behavior he wishes to study. The diagraming process will help to indicate the information that must be be obtained to understand the existing situation and the actions that are necessary to bring about a change in behavior. B. Wright in *Physical Disability—A Psychological Approach* (New York: Harper & Row, 1960) provides a rich source of case material on which to practice. N. Cohn in "Understanding the Process of Adjustment to Disability" (*Journal of Rehabilitation,* November–December, 1961) illustrates some simpler diagrams and shows their utility.

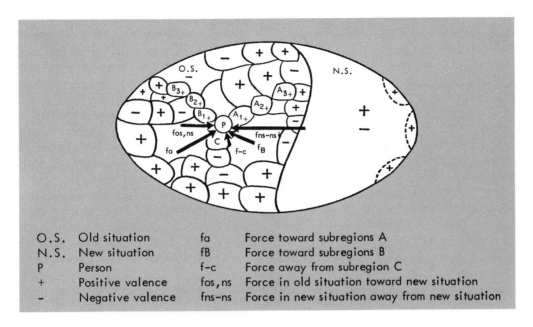

O.S.	Old situation	fa	Force toward subregions A
N.S.	New situation	fB	Force toward subregions B
P	Person	f-c	Force away from subregion C
+	Positive valence	fos, ns	Force in old situation toward new situation
−	Negative valence	fns-ns	Force in new situation away from new situation

Fig. 1–1. Old and new psychological situations.

In general, the behavioral possibilities are well structured in an old situation. The person knows where different positive or negative goals are and what paths lead to them. This is true for everyone, handicapped and nonhandicapped, adults and children.

In a new psychological situation the entire region is understructured except for a belief that a positive goal lies out there. In order to reach that goal it is necessary for the person to move out into this unknown region. Because the goal is positive and attractive, but its unfamiliarity is repelling, the region is labeled both plus and minus. An example of a new psychological situation might be leaving home and mother for the first time in order to go to school when all that is known about school is that mother says, "you will have lots of fun there."

From the structure of new psychological situations, the following statements can be made immediately:

1. The location of the goal and the path by which it can be reached are not known.
2. Entering the region in which the goal is located both attracts and repels.
3. The person's perception of the region in which the goal is located will not be stable. The region and the position of the goal will appear to change as the person's psychological position changes.

From these statements the following behavioral predictions can be derived:

1. A person in a new psychological situation will engage in wandering, vacillating, unstable trial-and-error behavior. Since the location of the goal and the paths by which it may be reached are unknown, behavior cannot be parsimonious. It must be tentative and cautious. The person will be alert to small cues. He will be easily influenced by peripheral stimuli.

Behavior will change as the person's perception of the situation changes. If it appears that he is getting closer to the goal, he will do more of what he has been doing. If it appears that he is moving away from the goal, he will change behavior. Early behavior will be cautious, but if it is unsuccessful, it will be followed by more extreme behavior.

2. The frustration that accompanies repeated trial-and-error behavior will occur. The person will show the emotionality and the disruption of behavior that result from frustration.

3. The person will be in conflict. He will attempt simultaneously to reach the goal in the new situation and to withdraw to the safety of the old situation. The conflict will be intensified if the goal is highly attractive and the old situation relatively unattractive. Conflict will be intensified further if induced forces, external to the person, block the return to the old situation or add strength to the vectors toward the new situation.

It is now possible to make some if-then-always statements: A person will enter a new psychological situation if the psychological forces acting upon him toward the new psychological situation are greater than the forces away from it. (The impelling and restraining forces are amenable to more detailed description, but this will not be attempted here.) If a person enters a new psychological situation, frustration and conflict, and the emotionality and behavior disruption that accompany frustration and conflict, will occur. There are no exceptions. It is true for adults as well as for children. It is true for the physically normal as well as for the physically handicapped.

If this is true, the concept of new psychological situations provides a powerful tool for the understanding, prediction, and control of behavior. The multitudinous, but irrelevant, questions about the past need no longer be asked. The innumerable ways in which individuals differ may be ignored. For this aspect of behavior only one question is relevant: Is the person in a new psychological situation? If the answer is affirmative, the predicted behavior will occur.

We are now in a position to understand why the physically disabled, as a group, tend to have more frequent and more severe problems of adjustment: They are more frequently placed in new psychological situations which place severe, traumatic demands upon them. When a person is placed in a new psychological situation, he *must* behave according to the demands of the situation. People who incur physical disabilities do not become different kinds of people as a direct physical or physiological function of the disability. They remain the same kinds of people, but now, by reason of their disability, they may be placed in different life situations. Especially, they may be placed much more frequently in new psychological situations. Their behavior will change according to the frequency and the degree of "newness" in the situations they encounter.

The behavior of individual, physically disabled persons who are not maladjusted may be understood in the same terms and placed on the same continuum. These individuals, for reasons which remain to be more fully described, are not in new psychological situations.

It may be speculated that some disabled persons may be in positions of special status or power. For example, the situation of a blind college instructor who is in a position of power where he can demand the attention of his class is markedly different from the situation of a blind college student. If only because of his greater knowledge of the material that students must learn and his power to give or to withhold grades, the blind instructor is on familiar ground. In high degree he can arrange the class to suit himself, taking full advantage of his skill with words and avoiding his limitations in writing or drawing on the blackboard. In many fields vocal dramatics and the ability to paint compelling verbal pictures are by no means less desired by listeners or inferior to diagrams.

In this instance the blind instructor is not in a new psychological situation and cannot be expected to show the behavior that results from new psychological situations. If he is equally powerful or skillful in other life situations, he will be a blind man who is not maladjusted, and we can readily understand why he is not emotionally disturbed. He would not be an unexplainable exception.

The personal characteristics and the past history of different disabled individuals, of course, may lead to behavior in new situations that is superficially different. Some individuals may be self-conscious, some may withdraw, some may seem to be aggressive. These behaviors, however, are only phenotypically different. Genotypically, they may all be ordered to the "cautiousness" that is required by the new psychological situation. A person can be cautious in different ways. The loud, boisterous person will often agree that he was only putting on a bold front while actually he was quaking in his boots.

One great value of this formulation, like useful concepts in other disciplines, is that it leads immediately to methods of control. If it is undesirable for the physically disabled to be maladjusted, one remedy is clear: *Reduce the "newness" of their life situations.*

It will be observed that a basic requirement for fruitful scientific thinking has been met. Physical data have been transformed to psychological data. The critical variable is no longer the physical disability, with which psychologists can't deal, but the psychological situation of newness. Disabilities have psychological effects not because it is in the nature of disabilities to require certain behavior but because they force the person more frequently into new psychological situations. It is evident that from psychological data, psychological predictions can be made.

Some Dynamics of New Psychological Situations

The situation of a blind student may be taken as an example. In contrast to the well-ordered structure that may be created by a blind professor, the situation of a blind student may become new whenever an instructor writes on the blackboard. The psychological effects of this situation depend upon whether the student is required to enter it.

Figure 1–2a illustrates the critical forces in the situation if the instructor says, "These two words, phenotypic and genotypic, which I have written on the board are important. You must remember them." The situation is not new for the blind student. He can remember the concepts without seeing them written. The goal of remembering is within an old and familiar situation. His blindness will cause no emotionality, no frustration.

Figure 1–2b shows how the situation may change if the instructor draws a diagram but then says, "The diagram shows only what I have just told you. You need not remember it." The situation may be new, but the blind student is not required to enter it. The vectors away from the new situation are greater than the vectors toward it.

Figure 1–2c illustrates the situation if the instructor says, "This diagram is basic. You must be able to reproduce it. I will ask for it on the next examination." If the student does not know how to reach the goal of learning to reproduce the diagram, the situation is new and the student must enter it. The strength of the forces acting

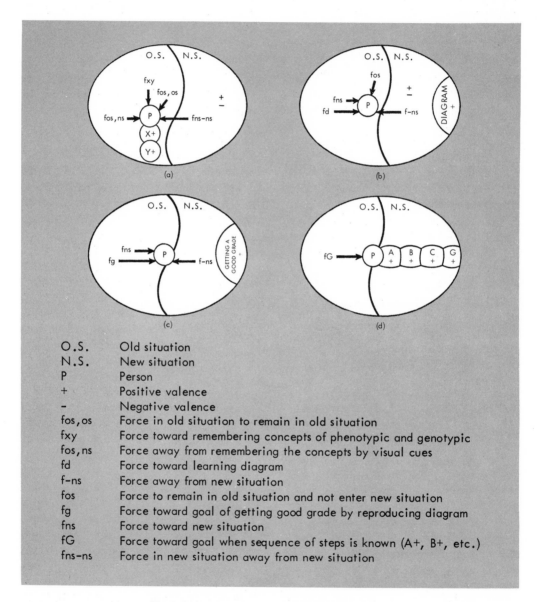

O.S.	Old situation
N.S.	New situation
P	Person
+	Positive valence
–	Negative valence
fos,os	Force in old situation to remain in old situation
fxy	Force toward remembering concepts of phenotypic and genotypic
fos,ns	Force away from remembering the concepts by visual cues
fd	Force toward learning diagram
f-ns	Force away from new situation
fos	Force to remain in old situation and not enter new situation
fg	Force toward goal of getting good grade by reproducing diagram
fns	Force toward new situation
fG	Force toward goal when sequence of steps is known (A+, B+, etc.)
fns-ns	Force in new situation away from new situation

Fig. 1–2. Varieties of new psychological situations.

on the student in the direction of the new situation is directly proportional to the attractiveness of the goal, that is, the student's aspiration to attain it. The greater the aspiration, either directly for knowledge or indirectly for the ability to give a correct answer on the examination sheet and thereby obtain a high grade, the greater the emotionality and behavioral disruption that will occur.

Obviously, the same analysis is possible for other kinds of physical situations and other kinds of physical disabilities.

Individual Differences

In these terms, it is now possible to discuss individual differences in a meaningful way. Not all blind individuals react emotionally when another person draws on the blackboard. Some blind people don't go to college in the first place and thereby avoid the many traumatic, new psychological situations in which blind students may be placed. Among those who do go to college, some, by reason of greater intelligence or better guidance, may prepare themselves in advance so as to reduce the newness of the situations that may be encountered. The blind student who has arranged for a classmate to trace every diagram into his hand, to reproduce it later in three dimensions, and to check the correctness of his practice drawings has made great progress toward his goal. His situation is shown in Figure 1–2d. It will be seen that the situation is not new; it is well structured. The sequence of steps that will lead him toward both momentary and long-range goals is known. The behavior predicted for new psychological situations, therefore, will not appear.

Another kind of blind student—perhaps one who is less intelligent, less well guided, or too proud to seek or accept the help he needs, who does not know the sequence of steps that will lead to attainment of the goal—will be in a new psychological situation and will show the predicted behavior. It is evident, however, that this will occur only indirectly because of the kind of person he is. The behavior is amenable to change with change in the structuring of the new situation.

New Psychological Situations in Physical Disability

There are three kinds of new psychological situations that may be encountered by the physically disabled person.

1. There are situations that are new because the person has never experienced them. It is common knowledge that the child with a disability is frequently overprotected or rejected by his parents and others. He may be deprived of common cultural experiences that are open to the nondisabled. The cerebral-palsied child or the blind child may infrequently or never have been exposed to the learning experiences of "going downtown with mother," "playing outside with the neighbors' children," "going to look at the fire engines with father," or "selecting and buying a toy from his own allowance." Experiential backgrounds in such cases are obviously limited. The capacity to cope successfully with a wide variety of life situations has not been permitted to develop. In technical terms, the psychological worlds of disabled children may be smaller and less well differentiated than the life spaces of physically normal children.

The practice of institutionalizing disabled children imposes some further restrictions upon the development of their ability to cope with the culture in which they live. Family living experiences, in all their warmth and all their opportunities for learning vicariously, may be drastically reduced. Practice in making decisions, even about such simple things as the time of arising or going to sleep, or when, where, and with whom to play, may be sacrificed to the need for running an institution efficiently. It is not surprising, therefore, that disabled children may reach adulthood without knowledge of the sequence of actions that will lead to the attainment of desired goals. To the degree that they do encounter such new, unstructured situations, they will behave as the situation demands. A schematic representation of the life space of disabled children and the life space of more favored children is shown in Figure 1–3.

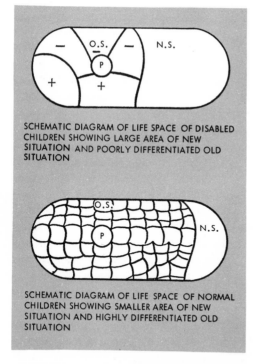

SCHEMATIC DIAGRAM OF LIFE SPACE OF DISABLED CHILDREN SHOWING LARGE AREA OF NEW SITUATION AND POORLY DIFFERENTIATED OLD SITUATION

SCHEMATIC DIAGRAM OF LIFE SPACE OF NORMAL CHILDREN SHOWING SMALLER AREA OF NEW SITUATION AND HIGHLY DIFFERENTIATED OLD SITUATION

Fig. 1–3. Life space for disabled and physically normal children (see Fig. 1–1 for key).

It is evident that many situations that are new because they have not been experienced are unrelated to disability. Activities which lead to increasing the scope of behavioral possibilities, and to the structuring of these regions, therefore, will reduce the maladjusted behavior that is a function of newness.

2. Some situations are new because the person lacks a culturally required tool for behavior. He is partially or totally unable to structure the new situations.

It must be emphasized that psychological newness is not equivalent to geographical or physical newness. A motorist may never have driven to Alaska, but if he is able to read maps and follow route markers, such a trip would not be psychologically new. The field is well structured. Similarly, if a person is confident of the technique for acknowledging introductions and the etiquette of behavior at a party, he may meet many new people in new surroundings, but since the sequence of steps to "making a good impression on others" is known, the situation is not psychologically new.

On the other hand, a disabled person may enter the same physical situation repeatedly, and it may be new each time. The blind child, for example, may be in a new psychological situation every time he leaves his home to walk around the block. Ditches may have been dug, barriers erected, or there may be obstacles on the sidewalk in places that cannot be anticipated in advance. Each walk, each street to be crossed, may be a new adventure that requires great cautiousness. Similarly, the congenitally deaf child rarely knows in advance if he is going to be able to read the lips of the people who speak to him or if others will understand his laboriously acquired, but imperfect, speech.

Each time he tries to speak or to lip-read, the situation is new if it cannot be structured. Knowledge from past experience that communication will be easy, of course, will reduce newness, but knowledge that communication will be difficult leaves the field unstructured.

Behavior in new situations, it will be recalled, is oriented to a goal. The forces toward the goal may arise from the motives of the child, from induced forces from without, or from a combination of both. The deaf child may wish to attend a regular school for normally hearing children or his mother may insist on this. In order to stay it is vital that he "make a good impression" on the teacher. One means to this goal is to have speech that can be understood and to be able to read the lips of others. If, however, the teacher and the other children only sometimes understand the deaf child and only sometimes does the deaf child understand others, each act of communication is psychologically new. The child can't plan consistently. He can never be sure of what to expect. New situations, therefore, are encountered with a frequency that is rarely, if ever, experienced by normally hearing persons. This is true for individuals with other kinds of disabilities, also.

This is inescapable: Every disabled person in our culture is going to be frustrated by those new psychological situations that arise because he lacks an appropriate tool for behavior. The deaf person does not live in an Indian culture, where signs are generally understood and sometimes preferred for communication. The crippled person does not live in an environment where there are no steps to be climbed. He lives in a culture where vocal communication and good locomotor ability are required. To some degree a disabled person is going to be able to function in our culture as well as he would if he were not disabled. But he is going to be exposed more frequently to new psychological situations that are directly related to the disability.

There are no magic solutions here, but the concept of new psychological situations points clearly to the relevant contexts that must be investigated:

(a) Many new situations can be avoided. The deaf person can associate only with individuals who know the language of signs. The blind person can sit at home and listen to the radio or the talking book, What are the positive and negative consequences of such behavior?

(b) Specific skills to reduce newness can be taught. What should a deaf child do if another person cannot understand his speech? What should a crippled child do if he wishes to enter a building but cannot open the door?

(c) It is probable that tolerance for frustration can be learned. Under what conditions is this feasible and desirable?

(d) The potency of some goals can be reduced. For which goals and under what conditions should the disabled person not strive?

3. Some situations are new because of the social stimulus value of the disabled person. Disability has many meanings to others. The disabled person often does not know when he enters a social situation whether he will be an object of curiosity, pitied, sympathized with, "helped," patronized, exhibited, praised for his spunk, avoided, or actively rejected. Only rarely will he be seen as a person who has psy-

chological properties beyond the disability. More frequently he will be identified with the disability and be reacted to in terms of whatever the disability means to the other person. These meanings are often extreme. They are rarely neutral.

Reduction of newness in this situation has two aspects:

(a) The education of the public as to the nonidentity of physical characteristics and psychological characteristics.

This requires a change in well-developed stereotypes, and it may be difficult to accomplish. It may be difficult not only because able-bodied persons may have a need to perceive the physically disabled as inferior persons but also because disability is not infrequently phenotypically related to other undesirable characteristics. For example, if large numbers of cerebral-palsied persons, through no fault of their own, are poorly educated, or if an appreciable proportion of the cerebral-palsied are also cortically brain-damaged, a drastic change in customary modes of thinking is required to reserve judgment about a particular, unknown individual who is seen to have cerebral palsy. This is a part of the general problem of prejudice that is experienced by other minority groups also. Enough progress has been made toward the solution of this problem to indicate that reduction of prejudice in the public is possible (Allport, 1954). Change will not be easy, however, and it will not be accomplished quickly.

(b) The education of the disabled person in specific social skills which will facilitate his acceptance as a person.

The physically normal person is often well-meaning, but he does not know how to behave toward another whom he perceives to be different. What sorts of behavior will reduce the newness of the situation both for the disabled and for the nondisabled person?

This analysis indicates that the disabled person lives in a world that is frequently ambiguous both for himself and for others. He may frequently be placed in a strange and terrifying world in which he is expected to cope with new situations to which he has not previously been exposed; new situations in which his lack of a tool hampers adequate structuring; and new situations in which his social role is not clear.

If new psychological situations have the properties that we have derived, and if disabled persons are more frequently placed in new psychological situations, it is not surprising that, on the average, the disabled have been found to be less well adjusted than others. If the theory is true, however, the sequence of steps that will lead to good adjustment is equally clear.

OVERLAPPING PSYCHOLOGICAL ROLES

The disabled person lives in two psychological worlds. Like everyone else, he lives in the world of the nondisabled majority. He also lives in the special psychological world that his disability creates for him. These worlds overlap, as shown in Figure 1–4.

Many activities are common to both worlds, but some activities are engaged in primarily by disabled persons, whereas other activities are open only to the physically normal. The world of the physically normal is larger in the sense that it contains relatively more behavior possibilities and is amenable to greater differentiation. This dichotomy is not unique to disability, how-

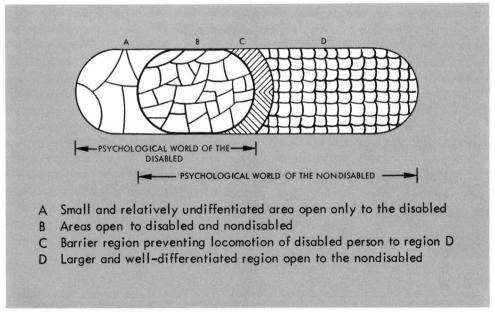

A Small and relatively undiffentiated area open only to the disabled
B Areas open to disabled and nondisabled
C Barrier region preventing locomotion of disabled person to region D
D Larger and well–differentiated region open to the nondisabled

Fig. 1–4. Overlapping psychological role situation.

ever. It can also be applied to any of the ways in which individuals differ. There is a psychological world of women and a psychological world of men; a world of Negroes and a world of whites; a world of Catholics and a world of those who have other beliefs; a world of the stupid and a world of those with greater intelligence; a world of the poor and a world of the rich. Inasmuch as every person holds membership in many different groups, he must play multiple overlaping roles. This in itself is not a source of difficulty. For example, a young man can be simultaneously a son, a brother, a nephew, a fiancé, a college student, a major in English, a fraternity pledge, a Protestant, a football player, and a musician. Each of these roles, in some degree, requires different behavior than the others; but in general they are compatible with each other. The person is able to play the role that is required by the different constellations of psychological and social forces that act upon him.

Interfering Overlapping Roles

At particular times, however, the different roles may be interfering. A man can play football in the afternoon and be a dance band leader in the evening; but he cannot play on the university football team and play in the band simultaneously. The latter situation will create conflict in the degree that the two roles are considered equally desirable and are not seen as different, but equally good avenues of recreation.

The conflict will be resolved as the interplay of psychological forces acting upon the person impels him in the direction of one goal or the other. These psychological forces may arise from the greater, intrinsic desirability of one goal, differences in social prestige attached to the different behaviors, the relative ability of the person to do one or the other well (for example, first trumpet player versus third-string tackle), the amount of time that is required for practice relative to the amount of time needed for study or the wish to have an active social life, the relative scholarships given to football players and trumpet players, plans for the future, and other factors. The important point here is that the person is amenable to the forces that arise from each situation. Both roles are open to him. He can play either or, within limits, change from one to the other.

Antagonistic Overlapping Roles

Conflict will be intensified if the overlapping roles are antagonistic so that responding to one set of role-determiners automatically rules out the other. If a college student brings his fiancée home for a visit, his fiancée-oriented role as a mature person who plans soon to marry, have his own home, and raise a family may interfere with his mother-oriented role as a dutiful son. Suppose one evening his doting mother, who still sees him as a child, says, "Junior, dear. It is raining outside. Be sure to put on your rubbers before you go out." How can the student respond to this childish role to which he has been assigned? If he behaves as a dutiful, docile son he loses status as a mature, capable person in the eyes of his fiancée and of himself. If he rejects his mother's well-meaning meddling in word or action, he loses his role as a dutiful son. He cannot behave both as a mature person and as an immature person; whatever he does, someone will be hurt. The situation will be resolved as before in terms of the relative attractiveness of the two roles and the potency of the psychological forces acting. College students understand why the mother's perception of her son as "my little baby" is unacceptable to him, and why it causes conflict. There are more, and

more attractive, behavioral possibilities in the mature role. It is true that college students often are dependent upon their parents in some ways. However, they see no reason why financial dependency, for example, should "spread" to an assumed general immaturity of such degree that they do not know when to come in out of the rain. This sort of role pervasiveness is considered unnecessary and unacceptable. We shall see that this is a serious problem in disability also.

Overlapping Excluding Roles

The greatest conflict occurs when the person rejects the roles that are open to him and strives for a role that he cannot attain or at least that is relatively inaccessible to him. We shall call these "overlapping excluding roles." It does not matter greatly at the momentary point of conflict whether the barrier between the person and a desired role is an ability barrier or a social barrier.

The psychological world of the homely girl, for example, in contrast to the world of the beautiful girl, can be ordered to Figure 1-4. For this variable of beauty, it is evident to any observer that a beautiful girl may behave in ways that are impossible for others. Other things being equal, the beautiful girl will be sought out more frequently. She can be highly selective in whom she will date and where she will go. Even in the classroom, as the author knows from experience, beauty is not unrelated to academic grading. Prestige, status, and privileged behavioral possibilities, not open to homely girls, are open to college "queens." The gains are not only immediate but extend far into the future. Favorable marriages and social mobility as a function of beauty are not unknown.

These are no trivial or insignificant

goals for many college women. It is not surprising that many college girls, when they perceive the great value placed on beauty and the attractive behavioral possibilities it creates, desire this role for themselves. It is possible, within limits, for a homely girl to make the most of what she's got by reducing weight, by adopting culturally approved forms of dress, and by using cosmetics; but only rarely is it possible for a homely girl to become beautiful or to play the role of a beauty.

Many girls who are not endowed with great beauty handle this problem very well. They do not place a high value on the role from which they are excluded. If the beauty behaves as if "beauty is as beauty does," they reply, "Beauty is only skin deep. Other things are more important than how you look."

Some homely girls, however, because of the psychological forces acting upon them, are unable to relinquish the goal of beauty. Perhaps beauty is important to family and friends, and the girl is never permitted to forget that she is not beautiful. She may be referred to as ugly and treated with the rejection and disdain that are reserved for those who lack important attributes. Inasmuch as everyone tends to accept the judgments of important "others," it is extremely difficult to avoid internalizing feelings of inferiority and unworthiness.

For some individuals, beauty is not an end in itself but a means to a goal, so that the psychological forces arise, in part, from within. A girl who wishes to be a movie heroine may perceive that she lacks the necessary pulchritude for this role but be unable to give it up. She may try all sorts of tricks to attain beauty, but she may also make herself perfectly miserable by sitting in front of a mirror and examining herself: "If only my nose weren't quite so long; if my ears were smaller; if my hair

weren't so dry and stringy; if my eyelashes were longer—then the satisfactions that are open to beautiful women would be open to me too. I could be a movie star. I could meet and maybe marry a wealthy and attractive man. I could have fame and other good things."

No doubt, in some degree, this kind of behavior occurs in all psychologically adolescent women in our culture, for there are undoubtedly real advantages in being able to play the role of beauty. If the goal is inaccessible or unattainable, however, it does no good to continue to place a high value on it simply because one feels beautiful inside. Most mature individuals, both male and female, appear to place less value on physical beauty than adolescents do. It is nice to have, but its absence or relative lack does not make a person less worthy nor is it decisive for the judgment of the person.

Similarly, a goal may be unattainable because the path to the goal is blocked by a social barrier. A college girl's highest aspiration may be to pledge Alpha Alpha Alpha sorority. Perhaps, however, she once wore bobby socks on campus or committed the unpardonable faux pas of wearing a slip under an evening gown. Perhaps her family is of the "wrong" race, religion, or economic status. Otherwise she may be beautiful, talented, and a BWOC, but she is blackballed from the sorority. She is now just as effectively prevented from playing the role of "member of Alpha Alpha Alpha" with all its advantages as she would be if she lacked an intrinsic ability. It doesn't matter from the standpoint of behavioral consequences whether the social prejudice is unjust. If the social barrier is strong, only rarely is it possible for the determined person to break through it. Prejudice is usually not amenable to reason nor will it be decreased by "good" behavior on the part of the person. If the person is unable to relinquish a strong emotional attachment to an unattainable goal, the resulting behavior is clearly predictable.

An implicit understanding of this principle is perhaps one reason why it is a normal human tendency to stop comparing oneself with others who are different. The average college student compares his test papers not with Phi Beta Kappas but with others on his own level. The athlete who plays both football and basketball but is able to make only the football team not only plays football and less basketball, but he comes to consider football a "better" game. The path to mental health is traveled when a person places his highest values on what he has got or can attain and places lower, neutral values or noncomparative values on what he hasn't got or cannot attain.

We are now in a position to make an additional if-then-always statement: If a person, because of his own forces or induced forces, is impelled to strive for a goal that is unattainable because of ability or social barriers, the constellation of behavior commonly referred to as psychological maladjustment will occur. The greater the vectors toward the goal and the stronger the barriers that surround the goal, the greater will be the behavioral disruption.

Application to the Physically Disabled

Individuals who have physical disabilities also have other roles. Like others, they encounter their fair share of overlapping compatible, overlapping interfering, and overlapping antagonistic roles. They are almost unique, however, in being exposed more frequently, sometimes for a lifetime, to overlapping excluding roles. If

this is true, it is not surprising that according to available evidence, disabled persons tend to be maladjusted more frequently than others.

The excluding overlap occurs between the role of the disabled person and the role of the physically normal person. They dynamics of the situation are shown in Figure 1–5. It will be seen that the psychological forces acting upon the person in the direction of the world of the physically normal are greater than the vectors toward the world of the physically handicapped. In popular language, it is "better" to be physically normal than to be physically disabled. The reasons are easy to understand. The world of the physically normal is larger and better structured with desirable behavioral possibilities. The world of the physically handicapped is relatively underprivileged.

The slogans prevalent in rehabilitation, that the goal of the handicapped is to "be normal, achieve normality, become as normal as possible, be treated like normal children, do the same thing as normal children and in the same way" are not simply figures of speech. They reflect the reality of underlying psychological and social forces. However, the role of the disabled person excludes the role of the nondisabled person in every situation where the disability makes a difference. The disabled person is separated from some desirable normal goals by a strong barrier. This barrier is constructed of ability limitations and social limitations, and both are relatively impermeable. It is dynamically clear, therefore, that disabled persons are often placed in a position where they are impelled to strive for relatively inaccessible or unattainable goals. When the barrier is impermeable and the goal unattainable, the behavior predicted for overlapping excluding roles will occur. Living on the bar-

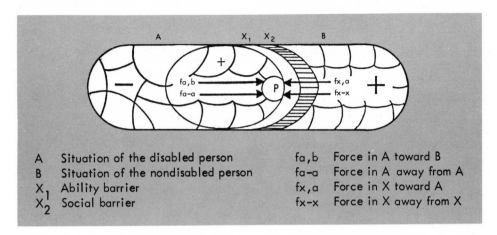

A	Situation of the disabled person	fa,b	Force in A toward B
B	Situation of the nondisabled person	fa-a	Force in A away from A
X_1	Ability barrier	fx,a	Force in X toward A
X_2	Social barrier	fx-x	Force in X away from X

Fig. 1–5. Overlapping role situation in disability.

rier between overlapping excluding roles may be considered a form of psychological suicide.

If it is undesirable for disabled persons to be maladjusted, another solution has become clear: Reduce the frequency of overlapping excluding role situations. A few examples of specific situations may clarify this abstract formulation.

Assume that a person who is blind wishes to be treated like a regular person, just like anyone else. His hostess at a party takes him at his word and asks him to pour the cocktails. How should he behave? Theoretically he has a choice. He can pour like a blind man or he can try to pour like a seeing person. If he pours like a blind man, he will hook a finger over the lip of the glass. When the liquid reaches his fingertip, it is full. Many people, however, are somewhat squeamish about having other people's fingers in their drinks. If he poured in this fashion he would call down upon himself the intense hostility of the assembled group. Perhaps he would hear derogatory comments about blind people being invited to parties. However, he has already rejected the role of the blind person and decided to try to play the role of a normally seeing person. He must, therefore, accept the assignment and attempt to pour drinks like a normally seeing person. He cannot bring out his blindness as an "excuse." He is not a seeing person, however. He is blind. In this situation he cannot behave like a normally seeing person, for he does not have the necessary visual tool. The best he can do is to depend on change in weight or change in sound to estimate when a glass is full. This is both a more difficult and a less effective procedure than visual inspection. Some glasses may be correctly filled, but it would not be surprising if some glasses were filled to overflowing and some were left only partially full. He may go through the motions of behaving like a seeing person, but he cannot actually play the role. He knows, and all who see him will know, that he is blind.

The significance of this example is that similar situations occur with great frequency in the life of every disabled person who rejects the behavioral possibilities that are open to him as a disabled person and strives instead to live a role that is not possible. To the degree that the person's life situation requires normal behavior, and to the degree that the person places a high value on entering regions that are partially or totally closed to him, he will be maladjusted. Moreover, the denial of the disabled role will not protect him from the social discrimination of those who perceive that he is disabled. He will be denied acceptance and entrance into privileged situations by those who respond to his disability no less frequently than disabled persons who accept the disabled role when the disabled role is appropriate.

It is easy to contend that the disabled person must accept his disability, but this is only a meaningless and contradictory platitude if the underlying situation of disability is not understood. If acceptance means that the person must be content with an inferior position that requires him to acknowledge his inferiority as a person and permits him to strive only for intrinsically less satisfying goals, acceptance is difficult. If there is no assurance that society will accept the disability also and not penalize the person for it, it is unrealistic to endow acceptance with the qualities of a panacea.

The Problem of Acceptance

In almost every other overlapping excluding role situation, there are some who will contend sincerely, and not as a sour-grapes mechanism, that the possible role is just as good or better than the excluded role. It is just as good to be a woman as a man; it is just as good to be a Negro as to be white; it is just as good to be Catholic as to hold other faiths; it is just as good to be an independent as it is to be a fraternity man. Many more people believe that it is not good to be too smart, too rich, too beautiful, or too successful. Disability is unique in that almost no one believes it is just as good or better, in any sense, to be

disabled than to be nondisabled. No one believes that it is not good to be too healthy. This means that some of the strongest forces in our society act upon disabled people to deny their disabilities and impel them to strive to be nondisabled. We do not wish the disabled to accept their disability. On the contrary, we insist that they deny it.

Consider the case of a Negro who feels that many of the most valued goals in our culture are reserved for whites. He aspires, therefore, to the role and position of a white man. How would we evaluate such a person if he exposed himself to X-rays and bought quantities of drugs to lighten his skin, pomades to straighten his hair, and sought plastic surgery to reduce the width of his nose? Every psychologist would say that such a person is seriously maladjusted. His wish to be white in a culture that rewards white skin and penalizes black skin is understandable, but mental health lies only in the direction of accepting himself as a Negro and taking pride in the group to which he belongs.

Consider also the case of a Jew named Goldstein who believes that, like members of numerous other minority groups, he is excluded from highly desirable goals. He suddenly changes his name to Brown and joins the Episcopal Church. Most would agree that he cannot deny himself. Like the blind man pouring drinks, he is only going through the motions. He cannot really be Brown, the Episcopalian. To himself and to his friends he is still Goldstein underneath. To attempt to change in this way is prima-facie evidence of emotional disturbance. It would be better to accept himself and take pride in the group to which he belongs.

Consider now the treatment and evaluation of the disabled. A child is deaf. On the one hand we say he must accept the

LEE MEYERSON

deafness. On the other hand, however, we give him a hearing aid, and compel him to spend most of his waking hours in listening to sounds that he perceives so faintly and distortedly that he cannot interpret them; we urge him to attempt to say sounds that he himself cannot hear or monitor for himself; and we drill him in assigning meaning to the fleeting movements of the lips that are only by-products of the vocal noises of others. In some cases this process is crowned with striking success. Some degree of adaptation occurs in many. For all deaf children, however, we make it clear that the child is not to accept his deafness. On the contrary, he is to exert himself to the utmost to be not deaf. He is not to use the signs which are easier for him. He is to speak, even though his speech will never be as good or as normal as the speech of a normally hearing person. He must continue to strive with all his energy for goals that, at best, are only partially attainable. In addition, his adjustment is evaluated, in part, according to the degree to which he associates with normally hearing people and avoids other deaf persons. The inferiority of the deaf is made clear to him, for he is encouraged to assert his membership in every other group to which he belongs, but he is not to take pride or seek satisfactions in the psychological world of the deaf.

Deaf children learn quickly that it is better to be a hearing person than a deaf person. In the most progressive schools where deaf teachers of the deaf are never employed "because they can't teach speech," the children see that the important people, the teachers, the supervisors, and the technicians are hearing people; the janitors, the junior cooks, and the servants are deaf people. Little children who wear individual hearing aids point to them pridefully and indicate, "I hear." Others point to their own empty ears and shrug their dismay.

Similarly, a child has cerebral palsy and doesn't walk. Of course, it is necessary to accept the disability; but, of course, it is equally necessary for the child to struggle with all sorts of therapies to try to overcome at least some aspects of the disability.

This is not an argument for or against particular methods of education but an attempt to attain clarity. It may be socially desirable that deaf, blind, and crippled children behave, as far as possible, as not deaf, not blind, and not crippled. It may be necessary for them to live on the barrier between overlapping excluding roles. If this is so, however, it is a great advantage to understand clearly the structure of the situation. We cannot justly create situations which lead to maladjustment on one hand and belabor the disabled for their maladjustment on the other.

It is conceivable that there are advantages and values in maladjustment. George Matthew Adams (1954), a newspaper columnist who often reflects popular feeling, advised his readers, "Be anxious." Everything worthwhile has been accomplished by people who were anxious to "get ahead."

In a society that worships achievement and success, perhaps anxiety and insecurity are a small price for progress. It is certain that among the disabled, the highest accolades have gone to those who did not accept but denied and achieved "in spite of." It is equally certain, however, that they paid for this recognition and praise with anxiety, conflict, and frustration. The former undoubtedly are valuable, but the latter are not the fruits of adjustment. There is nothing to be gained by confusing accomplishment with adjustment. Fortunately, we need not be caught on either horn of the dilemma. If the theory of disability presented in this chapter is true, solutions for some of the critical problems of disability are implicit within it.

The Problem of Adjustment

Some crucial psychological situations, frequently encountered by the person with a disability, have been ordered to the diagrams shown in Figures 1–6 through 1–11.

We have noted that one effect of the lack of a tool for behavior, such as is created by an impairment in physique, is that it places the person more frequently in new psychological situations and antagonistic, overlapping role situations. These situations have inevitable, psychologically maladjusting consequences. For adjustment to occur, psychological newness and antagonsitic overlapping must be reduced. There are three major ways in which this reduction in exposure to conflict-inducing situations may be accomplished.

A most effective, but nonpsychological, way of reducing the somatopsychological problems arising from situational determiners is to remove, limit, or replace with a functionally adequate substitute tool, the physical impairment that acts as a barrier to the structuring of new regions. Medical and surgical procedures now commonly remove or reduce many potential or existing disabilities. They thereby simultaneously eliminate or reduce the new psychological situations to which a person may be exposed if he lacks a culturally required tool for behavior. For example, if stapes mobilization surgery results in restoration of hearing or a laser beam procedure restores vision by welding a detached retina back into place, the individuals served will not be placed in new psychological situations or antagonistic, overlapping situations by reason of their deafness or blindness: they are no longer either deaf or blind. Prosthetic aids also—eyeglasses, hearing aids, electronic larynxes, cardiac pacemakers, and, in lesser degree, wheelchairs—often serve with great success in removing or reducing physical barriers that impede coping behaviors.

Further advances are clearly on the horizon. In the distant future, we may anticipate confidently the invention of packaged transducers and analyzers that will plug into the human brain and serve as mechanical substitutes for those with peripheral impairments of sight or hearing.

A second way of reducing newness is to teach the client the specific behaviors and general skills that facilitate the structuring of new situations and permit desired goals to be reached. If a nonambulant child learns to walk or a speech-impaired child learns to speak correctly, the physical forces limiting the structuring of new regions have been removed as completely as if a surgical procedure had been used.

Even now, specific educational treatment—mobility training for the blind, lip reading and auditory training for the hearing-impaired, activities of daily living training for the crippled—often is highly effective in enlarging the life space and in reducing areas of newness. Therapists may not always appreciate how many situations are new to disabled children because the situations have never been entered, and there are no available models to facilitate vicarious learning. Therapists, also may underestimate how much may be achieved not only by the direct teaching of a skill but also by teaching problem-solving procedures and fostering the systematic consideration of the alternative routes by which positive goals can be reached or negative regions avoided. For

LEE MEYERSON

example, how many special schools or rehabilitation centers teach their clients how to ask for help or how to refuse it? How many schools teach how to respond to well-meaning but impertinent questions or aversive social behavior? How can advance information be obtained that may reduce newness (such as lighting conditions for the deaf, architectural barriers or their absence for the orthopedically handicapped, lavatory accessibility for wheelchair users)?

Education of the public in the direction of altering the social-stimulus value of physical disability is also an effective way of reducing newness and antagonistic overlap. This important task for the psychologist shows signs of increasing effectiveness. Legislation in many states to eliminate architectural barriers have literally paved the way for people with orthopedic disabilities to become mobile. Their greater mobility on the streets, on university campuses, and in restaurants, hotels, airlines, and public buildings has, in turn, made crutches and wheelchairs a much more common and familiar occurrence in the lives of innumerable people who, otherwise, might not be exposed to well-functioning disabled persons. The exposure alone may permit desensitization of "visual allergies" in the able-bodied, and it may tend to extinguish some irrational social behaviors.

A third way of reducing newness, open to those who are prepared to occupy fully the professional role for which their educational and professional experience may qualify them, is to strengthen clients who choose not to strive for inaccessible or inappropriate goals, that is, who choose not to enter certain new or overlapping situations. The role requires great wisdom, for psychologically more powerful people are tempted to impose their needs and values upon less powerful people. Yet, every psychologist is familiar with individuals who are subject to psychological forces that result in persistent self-defeating behavior, and he is ethically required to help such persons modify that behavior if he can. Striving for an unattainable goal inevitably must result in failure, but it is not easy to distinguish which situations are new but structurable from situations that should be avoided because the possibility of successful structuring is slight.

Wright (1960), in a unique and valuable book, offers a wealth of specific procedures for reducing newness and enhancing coping behavior. Kerr (1961) has described in field-theoretical terms, with uncluttered schematic diagrams, the process of adjustment to acquired disability.

We shall illustrate and discuss here, in the light of the forgoing considerations, three kinds of adjustment patterns to disability and the advantages and consequences that result from each. In the interest of unity and coherence, the exposition focuses on the adjustment of the person with impaired hearing. The same kind of analysis is possible for other disabilities, and the student may gain much by attempting it.

Adjustment Pattern 1

Figure 1–6a shows a type of adjustment pattern that is selected by many persons who have impaired hearing. These individuals withdraw to the relatively small, restricted, but safe, life spaces provided by clubs of the deaf and societies for the hard of hearing. They reject and are rejected by the world of the normally hearing. Their major goals and aspirations are confined to situations in which they can function at equal advantage with the hearing. The amount of overlap or commonality with

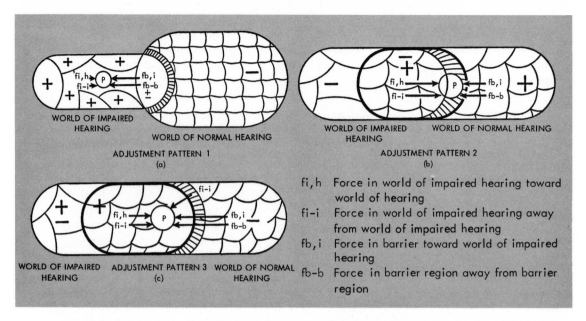

fi,h   Force in world of impaired hearing toward world of hearing

fi-i   Force in world of impaired hearing away from world of impaired hearing

fb,i   Force in barrier toward world of impaired hearing

fb-b   Force in barrier region away from barrier region

Fig. 1–6. Varieties of adjustment patterns.

the life space of the normally hearing is slight. The valence of the overlap is simultaneously positive and negative. It is positive because some areas, like earning a living, cannot often be restricted to the psychological world of impaired hearing. It is negative because a situation open equally to hearers and impaired hearers often requires the impaired hearers to function at a disadvantage. For example, the deaf individual in applying for a job is not certain whether he will be evaluated negatively as a deaf person or positively as a person who has the necessary skills for the position. Because of the communication barrier he is often less able to present his qualifications in a favorable light.

Similarly, a person with impaired hearing may enjoy driving his car—a region that is open to both groups—but if he has an accident, his case may be prejudged because of unwarranted assumptions about the influence of hearing on driving skills. It is not surprising that many deaf in-

dividuals perceive safety in a small and restricted but well-organized world.

Adjustment Pattern 2

Figure 1–6b shows the life space of a person who rejects the world of impaired hearing and aspires to the world of the normally hearing. He desires to do exactly the same things as the normally hearing and in exactly the same way. As in 1–6a, however, the ability and social barriers to participation in the world of the normally hearing are strong. Individuals who select this adjustment pattern live on the barrier between two ways of life—a world whose goals are relatively inaccessible to them and a world whose goals they reject. Sometimes the efforts of an extremely able person are strikingly successful. He is admitted to some limited areas of the normal world where others who have similar disabilities are not accepted. It is not always certain that the gains achieved are in proportion to the amount of effort that has been required to attain them. For others who are less able or in less favorable social situations the barriers are never breached, even after a lifetime of intensive effort and years of insecurity and anxiety.

Adjustment Pattern 3

Figure 1–6c is a schematic representation of the life space of a person who eagerly enters and values the large area of commonality that exists between those who have impaired hearing and those who have normal hearing. Such a person perceives himself as one who shares many behavioral areas with others. Impaired hearing is correctly perceived to be only one of his characteristics: he has many others. For example, he may be a bowler, an amateur photographer, a professional printer, a parent, and a worker for the Community Chest. Hearing does not necessarily have a central position in these activities. The person may feel as able to participate in them as normally hearing individuals.

Other activities which require hearing can be entered by different methods. A lecture can be listened to, translated into signs, or written down. The same goal can be reached by a variety of methods.

The special activities in the psychological world of impaired hearing are accepted also as additional regions for rich and fruitful living. For example, a hard-of-hearing man may attend a special class in lip reading—an activity not usually entered by those with normal hearing, but of interest and value to him. A deaf person may attend an alumni meeting of his state school and communicate with some of his friends by means of signs and finger spelling.

These special activities may have negative as well as positive valence for some.

The negative valence may arise because the person perceives the negative values that are attached to impaired hearing in our culture. If deaf people are considered inferior, and if it is true that a person is judged by the company he keeps, participation in the special activities of the deaf may have clear negative components.

There is no uncertainty, however, about the special areas that require hearing for participation. The person whose life space is represented in Figure 1–6c rejects them. He does not attend musical concerts simply to show that he behaves like normal people. He has no desire to play the piano like a typewriter. He does not aspire to jobs such as telephone operator, radio announcer, or opera singer. He perceives clearly that specific ways of behaving may be different without being better or worse.

There are numerous other arrangements of commonality, barriers, and valences. The three that have been outlined, however, may be considered examples of the major types.

Which adjustment pattern is best? This is a question that cannot be answered by a scientific psychology. The solution must be approached through a philosophy of counseling.

THE PROBLEM OF COUNSELING

It is not usually the function of the counselor to advise that one pattern of adjustment is better than another. This is a problem that every person should be free to decide for himself. It is the function of the counselor, like the scientific advisor in any field, to understand the field forces that affect behavior and to help apply them to the individual case.

The patterns of adjustment that have been outlined are all useful, but for different purposes. Their suitability depends in large part upon the cognitive, perceptual, and motor capacities of the behaving person; upon his needs, tensions, strengths, and skills; and upon the host of variables that may be specific to his situation.

Undoubtedly there are some individuals who are exceptionally able in using cues other than hearing to structure new psychological situations quickly. Others may have greater tolerance for the ambiguity of overlapping psychological roles. The good counselor helps the client to discover his own needs and abilities and to match them to the best fitting adjustment pattern. The type of adjustment that may be satisfying and self-actualizing for a congenitally deaf child of average ability may be highly inappropriate and unrewarding for a recently deafened war veteran. There is no one best pattern.

Adjustment Pattern 1

Adjustment Pattern 1 is often called "withdrawal" and condemned as undesirable by practically all except those who practice it. It is a threat to many normally hearing people because it amounts to challenging the values of the normally hearing world as the only values or the best values. It is a claim that one can live a full and happy life without speech, without lip reading, and with limited language that is communicated by finger spelling, signs, and writing.

Is it better to be a big frog in a small and quiet puddle or a small frog in a big and dangerous pond? The answer depends more on the values and philosophy of the person who judges than upon the objective situation. Psychology can only point out the consequences of each role.

It is evident that the psychological world of impaired hearing is smaller and less well differentiated than the world of hearing. There is safety in it, however. The demands upon the person are fewer, more readily anticipated, and more easily met.

Withdrawal is not necessarily an undesirable or maladjusted reaction. In many cases it is appropriate and realistic. In some degree it decreases the opportunities for varied satisfactions and gratifications. However, it also solves the problem of antagonistic overlapping role situations.

Advantages and Consequences of Adjustment Pattern 1

The deaf individual who chooses Adjustment Pattern 1 knows clearly the group to which he belongs and the role that he will play. In great measure he is protected from conflict, insecurity, frustration, and the anxiety and humiliations that are a consequence of trying to compete on equal terms with unequal tools. He does not devaluate himself as an inferior person because he cannot meet normal standards for speech and hearing, nor does he pursue the ghost of a different, but not necessarily better, ideal—the life of a normally hearing person. Within his world he may find understanding, friendship, love, status, success, and other gratifications that might never fall to his lot as a marginal person.

He does not carry the burden of trying to behave as if he had normal hearing. The boundaries of his world are clear. He is able to accept help when it is needed without feeling inferior. He refuses to judge himself as a person, or to allow himself to be judged, only on tasks where he is inferior because he lacks the appropriate tools. He insists that other qualities and abilities, for which he has adequate tools, are equally important. From a psychological standpoint such an adjustment is based upon reality. It may not be optimal but it is not unhealthy unless the scope for behavior is unduly restricted.

It is significant that many of the adult deaf, including some who have been educated in oral schools, seem eventually to fall into this pattern. They maintain stoutly that as persons they are just as good as hearing people, that signs and finger spelling are just as good as speech, and that pad and pencil are just as good, or better, for effective communication as lip reading. They appear to have a strong group "we feeling," and are active in defending what they consider their inalienable rights.

The relative narrowness of the deaf world, and the tendency toward egocentricity and provinciality that it induces in its inhabitants, should not be overlooked. Neither, however, should it be unduly exaggerated. The deaf are often pictured as miserable, maladjusted, isolated individuals who are burdens to themselves, their parents, and their community. Nothing could be farther from fact. Within the psychological world of the deaf, once it and its values are accepted, there are numerous opportunities for self-fulfillment. Because they are not widely publicized, normally hearing people are often unaware that these opportunities exist.

The deaf hold numerous social events and have many clubs and organizations for varied interests. For example, in New York City the Union League of the Deaf is so large that it occupies a building which rents for $6,000 a year. The deaf publish their own magazines and newspapers. They own their own insurance company. They sponsor a periodic World Conference of the Deaf and a World Deaf Olympics in addition to regular nationwide and regional conventions in the

United States. They have their own churches and spiritual advisors. They love, work, and play in ways which do not appear dynamically different from the way others do these things. Their family life does not appear to be less stable. Their children—both deaf and hearing—are often outstandingly successful by any standards. As a group they are employed, law-abiding, home-owning, respectable members of their communities.

Unlike some other disabled groups they have always taken care of their own social service work. It is not a grammatical error that leads them to call their organizations Clubs *of* the Deaf. It is their way of emphasizing that they are not the recipients of other people's charity. They have organized and supported these clubs themselves, with relatively little help from the normally hearing. Their disability is deafness, not incompetence. They are vigilant in combating the small group of deaf peddlers or beggars who try to trade upon their deafness and thereby infringe upon the good name and self-respect of other deaf people.

Their independence is shown in other ways also. In recent years, when Senator Langer of North Dakota proposed that the deaf be permitted an additional $600 income tax exemption, similar to what is now allowed the blind, the organizations for the deaf were unanimous in opposition. They successfully killed the bill with their statement that they wished no favors. There are practically no legal benefits for the deaf, in contrast to many special privileges for the blind, for example.

This description, of course, has meaning largely for deaf children who grow up to identify themselves with the deaf. It is not an easy process. An analogy is sometimes made between the disabled and other types of social and cultural minority groups. This is only an analogy, however, and must not be pushed too far. Most deaf chilren are born to normally hearing parents, and not infrequently they have normally hearing siblings. The deaf child, especially outside of the larger cities, may not be a member of a minority group. He may be simply an isolated and rejected individual without group support. For years he may not know that there are others like him in the world. He may be the recipient of ambivalent and hostile attitudes. His parents may feel guilty over having brought a defective child into the world. Their oversolicitude or rejection may fail to meet his needs for social and emotional approval until the child stigmatizes himself as inferior, unworthy, or evil. Unlike members of religious or racial minority groups, which have a high degree of continuity and tend to encourage group pride and group belongingness, he actually has no group with which he can identify. He has no group support to sustain his courage and reinforce his claim of equal worthiness. He is a maverick, subject to all the psychological forces that act upon mavericks and ugly ducklings. His parents and sibs are likely to be normally hearing and to maintain the standards of the normally hearing.

Even schooling may not change this situation. In many schools for the deaf he and his classmates are evaluated in terms of the degree to which they meet hearing standards. There may be no deaf teachers to serve as models for an ego ideal. If there is a conflict between adjusting to self and adjusting to a normally hearing society, the former must yield.

For many children it is not until after they leave school that they have an opportunity to choose their own adjustment pattern. Then, however, they encounter additional problems. Unlike the Negro, who is often discriminated against from childhood and may learn to cope with it (Goodwin, 1953), the disabled child frequently lives in an outwardly protective and sentimental environment. Many of us have different attitudes toward sweet and "helpless" handicapped children than toward the grosser disabled adult. Benedict (1938) has ably described, in another context, the devastating psychological effects of such cultural discontinuities. It is not until postschool experience that the deaf child encounters the full force of the hostility and discrimination that is directed against his group. From the standpoint of mental hygiene, fewer problems might arise if deaf and other kinds of physically disabled children were actually members of a psychological minority group from birth.

A second problem the child faces is that the world of the deaf does overlap with the world of the hearing. The deaf person must live and work in a world that is composed largely of nondeaf individuals. If he does not wish to cut himself off from family and from sources of livelihood, he must make an effort to meet some of the standards of others. Apparently this can usually be done. The individuals who employ Adjustment Pattern 1, like normally hearing people in similar psychological situations, can comply with foreign standards without placing a high value on them or considering them better than their own.

Although the *deaf* child has been used in this discussion as a basic frame of reference, it must not be thought that Adjustment Pattern 1 is limited to the deaf. There is in much lesser degree a psychological world of the hard of hearing also. There are some individuals whose entire lives seem to revolve about the activities of the local Society for the Hard of Hearing.

It must be noted, also, that the suitability of Adjustment Pattern 1 is not necessarily dependent upon the degree of hearing loss. A child may have a great amount of residual hearing, passable speech, and fair lip-reading ability, but he may lack other qualifications for living in a normally hearing world. If he has lived a marginal and frustrating life of failure and humiliation during his school years, he may wish to enter the world of the deaf where greater satisfactions may be open to him. He may live thereafter as a deaf person who has some hearing rather than as a psychologically hearing person whose auding is impaired. In some cases that the author has counseled, this kind of adjustment has seemed to be the most realistic and appropriate.

Adjustment Pattern 2

In Adjustment Pattern 2, there are also positive and negative aspects. On the one hand, the psychological world may be larger and better differentiated. On the other hand, the person may be uncertain about the boundaries of his world, about the group to which he belongs, and about his status in the world of the normally hearing. This pattern is often considered best by the normally hearing. It is an affirmation that the role of the normally hearing person is preferable. It does not challenge the values of the dominant majority. The person who employs this pattern is frequently perceived to have spunk and courage. He does not withdraw from the activities of the dominant world. He fights and compensates. Because of his impaired hearing, or to make up for it, he tries to be better than others. By identifying himself with values of the majority and rejecting the values of the deaf minority, he hopes to escape the imputation of inferiority and the underprivileged status that is the fate of other individuals with impaired hearing.

The counselor must remember that the social and ability barriers are not completely impermeable. They can be breached. Sometimes because of exceptional skills, exceptional wealth, or exceptional social connections, the barriers are successfully penetrated. For example, one would not ordinarily expect a deaf man to be a psychiatrist (Farber, 1953), a dentist, a heart specialist, a professor, or a world famous advertising executive (Calkins, 1946). Yet there are adventitiously deafened men who are successfully functioning in these roles. Congenitally deaf men, known to the author, are successfully functioning among the normally hearing as insurance salesmen, engineers, medical illustrators, editors, bacteriologists, librarians, cartographers, and chemists. This is not to say that the adjustment pattern can be predicted from knowledge of occupations. It is necessary to know the values of deaf individuals.

For some in professional occupations, impaired hearing may be simply one of their acknowledged characteristics. It is neither more nor less important than any other characteristic. It would be a good thing to have better hearing just as it would be a good thing to be more intelligent, own a better home, look handsomer, or earn more money. The possession of good things is an asset, but lack of them does not make the *person* inferior or less valuable. Individuals who have a value system of this kind are not in an antagonistic overlapping role situation, and they will not behave as that situation requires. They see themselves as people who are entirely worthy of full acceptance by society. They do not devalue themselves or feel inferior to people who have good hearing. Other possessions of the person are of equal or greater importance.

For others, impaired hearing may become the center of existence with great effort being devoted to reduce it, disguise it, or compensate for it. Some acoustically handicapped individuals, for example, avoid like the plague all others who have a similar impairment. They live among the normally hearing and share their values. They devalue the nonspeaking, non-lipreading deaf, or those who are members of a society for the hard-of-hearing more strongly than their hearing counterparts do. They are sure that it is better to associate with hearing people than with acoustically handicapped people. Hearing people as *people* are better, more valuable, more likable, than those who have impaired hearing. These individuals suffer from the fact that fate has short-changed them and dealt them a bitter blow. Nevertheless, if they themselves are the objects of impatience, discrimination, and hostility, it is only right and natural because people with impaired hearing *are* inferior and less worthy. The most one can do about it is to double and redouble one's efforts to make up for it. Such persons are in an antagonistic overlapping role situation and they will behave with the guilt and conflict that the situation requires. They share the stigmatizing attitudes of the majority, and they do devalue themselves. They refuse to be comforted by the assurances of friends with more insight that "your deafness is not you" (Murphy, 1954). Regardless of their ability, if they are ashamed of their disability, if they try to deny it, or to behave as if it did not exist, they divorce themselves from reality without gaining the general social acceptance they crave. There is no assurance that penetrating a particular ability barrier

will automatically lead to a relaxation of social barriers. The ability barrier may be breached in the occupational region while the social barriers remain as strong as before. This is shown in Figure 1–7. The deaf psychiatrist, for example, is more likely to be perceived as a deaf person than as a psychiatrist, and he may have great difficulty in building a practice.

It is probable that both the person who is ashamed of his impaired hearing and the person who is not will be pitied and devalued by others who place a high value on hearing. They will both be discriminated against, avoided, and denied entrance to desirable behavioral regions.

There is an important difference between the two attitudes, however. As Dembo, Ladieu, and Wright (1948) have pointed out, the person who is ashamed will feel that his nonacceptance is logical, reasonable, and justifiable. The person who is not ashamed will see clearly that it is the maladjustment of the normally hearing individuals which leads them to devaluate and reject him. He will see that the difficulty is not in the disabled person who has adjusted and coped adequately with his loss of a tool. It is the nondisabled persons who show maladjustment and lack of respect for reality by their inability to understand that hearing is only a tool.

A considerable part of the suffering due to nonacceptance by others is thereby removed; because the negative evaluations of others are seen as unwarranted, because the injured person does not blame himself, they hurt less. Instead, the person who holds them may in turn be devaluated and seen as ignorant and prejudiced.

Whereas the maladjusted injured person wishes to be accepted by the non-injured though he feels he ought not to be accepted, the adjusted person will care less to associate with those whose values he does not share or respect. The adjusted injured person gains a considerable

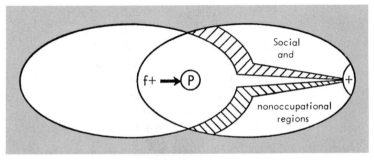

Fig. 1–7. Schematic life space of hearing-impaired individual showing penetration of occupational barrier and achievement of occupational goals while social and other barriers remain strong toward goal (ft = force toward goal; + = occupational goal).

degree of emotional independence and freedom from the non-injured (Dembo, Ladieu, and Wright, n.d.).

The kinds of suffering that result from attempting to meet artificial and inappropriate standards can be easily perceived in several autobiographies (Murphy, 1954).

To apply this reasoning to children, it is necessary to begin with parents. Although a child often shows a healthy respect for what he can do and a noncommittal or neutral attitude toward what he can't do, he sees parents as all-powerful beings. From them he tends to derive standards, values, and self-image. A harsh, uncertain, or overprotective parent with extreme ideas about normality may easily lead to the child's perception of himself as one who is inferior and unable to deal with his environment. He will then behave as if he were inadequate even though he has the necessary capacities. If parents are able to understand that hearing is only a tool, one characteristic, one value, and that a child has many others, they will not feel ashamed. They will not consider their child inferior or less valuable than other children, and the child will not blame himself.

This is rarely a problem for deaf parents. Normally hearing parents not unrea-

sonably wish to build the child in their own image. For some it is unquestionable that every person, to be a complete human being, *ought* to be able to hear well. They are unable to adjust themselves to the fact that an individual can be a very fine person and yet not hear or not see or not walk. For others, the *ought*, as an imperative, applies to speaking, understanding the speech of others, appreciation of music, or whatever the particular function that the physical impairment interferes with. They may say, "I want my deaf child to learn to speak and to become as normal as possible." They advise each other that the best way to evaluate a school is to talk with some of the older pupils and see how good their speech is—"and beware of schools that permit signing or finger spelling or have deaf teachers. Deaf teachers can't teach speech and they have queer ideas" (that is, different values). Why this harping on the very areas in which the child is handicapped?

Everyone will agree that speech and lip reading are useful tools for the deaf child. In their finest development they enlarge the life space of the child tremendously, permit increasingly finer differentations or growth, and reduce the communication barriers between the child, his family, and the world. For reasons that are presently unknown, however, not every deaf child learns to speak and lip read. For reasons we can only conjecture, many who do learn, after twelve to fifteen years of continuous drill, later do not use their hard-won skills. Perhaps they discover the deceit of the implicit promises held out to them that "if only you learn these skills and behave like other people, society will accept you." Perhaps many discover that their speech and lip reading are good only in limited circle of family and friends. Outside of it they may experience great difficulty in understanding or being understood. They may discover that others are amused or annoyed at their voices.

Is a child necessarily a less valuable child if he uses other modalities and communicates by finger spelling or pad and pencil? Is nothing else so important as speech and lip reading? It is true that in some schools there is a tendency to establish a status hierarchy of good oral pupils and poorer manual pupils, but there is no psychological justification for this. Perhaps parents should evaluate a school by determining whether its students have anything worthwhile to communicate beyond being able to say "a top, a ball, a fish." Perhaps they should ask if the children have learned to solve problems by themselves, whether they have learned to take turns and respect the rights of others, and whether they have good adult power figures with whom they can easily identify.

This discussion should not be misconstrued. Speech and lip reading or any communication skill, are valuable and worthy of great effort to acquire. When they are effective, they may produce near-miraculous changes and open vast behavioral possibilities. Parents perceive this. They would be less than human if they did

desire these fruits for their own. Speech and lip reading may be a way of salvation after what seems to be catastrophic misfortune. It is not surprising that they apply great pressure on the child to learn these difficult things. Deaf children, however, like other children, respond to parental and educational pressure with tension, frustration, anxiety, guilt, and shame. How can they help but feel inferior when they cannot satisfy the expectations of those upon whom they are most dependent (Barker, Dembo, and Lewin, 1941)?

Most parents undoubtedly wish their children to be happy. They are not to blame if they follow their own values and the best advice they can find. They may not anticipate the pathological reactions that may occur when a person is faced with a task that is impossible to cope with and yet must be coped with. They may not know the hazards of creating emotional attachments to unattainable goals. If they do know, they may still hope that their child may be one of those who has exceptional aptitude for language. Language aptitude is sufficiently well distributed that the hope is perhaps not unrealistic.

It is fortunate that deaf children who are not talented in this respect are sufficiently flexible to resolve as well as they do the great tensions that beset them. It is puzzling that the sensory, educational, and social deprivations presently associated with impaired hearing can be resolved with so relatively little overt psychological disturbance. By any standards the postschool adjustment of the deaf must be considered a tribute to the deaf themselves, their parents, their teachers, and others who have had a part in their rearing. Nevertheless, there is much to be said, from the standpoint of mental hygiene, for educational practices based on normal growth motivation rather than on deficiency motivation.

The Adequacy of Pattern 2

In considering the suitability of Adjustment Pattern 2 for the deaf child, or the adult he will become, it is necessary to remember two things:

1. There is no evidence and no reason to believe that deafness carries with it any kind of superiority. Exceptionally able children will be found among the deaf no more frequently than in other groups. The number of deaf individuals who will be able to penetrate even the ability barrier will be small.

2. The deaf person to survive in this antagonistic overlapping role situation must have not only exceptional ability but also highly developed tolerance for frustration. Entrance to the privileged situations of the normally hearing requires the very tools that the deaf person lacks. His voice and speech may not meet the standards of the normally hearing in pleasantness, modulation, rhythm, speed, accent, or pronunciation. Lip reading is more fatiguing, less easy, less flexible, and less certain than communications by hearing. There will be times when neither his speech nor his lip reading will be adequate to the demands of the situation. He will frequently be placed in new psychological situations in which his tool loss will hinder him from structuring the unknown regions. He will frequently have to deny his own perceptions in favor of the perceptions of others who have better tools. No matter whether he behaves then as if he were normally hearing or with behavior appropriate for the deaf, he will be seen as inferior and devalued. He will meet with ambiguous and hostile attitudes, and he will not have the emotional support of others whose perceptions are like his own. Frustration, tension, and conflict in high degree are inevitable. In brief, while he may make a more or less effective adjustment to normally hearing society, he will be more or less disorganized and maladjusted as a person.

The second point should not be misinterpreted. Maladjustment is a description whose meanings have been specified. The values of maladjustment to self must be weighed against the values of maladjustment to society with the person himself as the judge.

Although little attention has been devoted to the hard of hearing in the discussion of Adjustment Pattern 2, the dynamics are the same as for the deaf. The tool loss in moderately impaired hearing is smaller and creates a less rigid ability barrier than deafness. It is easier for the hard of hearing to pass through. At the same time, however, to the degree that the lacking tool is necessary for achievement, and uncertainty exists about meeting normal communication standards, the hard-of-hearing person will be subject to the same forces and show the same psychological reactions as the deaf person.

Adjustment Pattern 3

In the light of these considerations, Adjustment Pattern 3, or some variation of it, would appear to encompass great advantages. On the one hand it avoids the provinciality and egocentrism inherent in small, restricted, and poorly differentiated psychological worlds. On the other hand it also avoids the heart-searing conflicts, the disorganization, and the growth-inhibiting threats that inevitably arise from strong emotional attachments to unattainable, or only partially attainable, goals. Simultaneously, it offers a sufficiently large scope for a full and rich life. The increase in commonality between the world of those with impaired hearing and the world of the normally hearing can be increased gradually as the ability of the person increases and the resistance of social barriers decreases. Moreover, the enlargement of the life space can be accomplished without emotional disturbance because the person sees each increase as a positive gain. He may perceive that some have skills and privileges that he does not have and others do not have some of the skills and privileges that he has. However, he does not feel the necessity for making value comparisons and does not overvalue the former or devalue the latter. He places his highest values on what he can do and what he has reasonable expectations of achieving. Other abilities may be a good thing, but they do not make the person who has them better nor the person who does not have them worse. They are neutral.

To many the face value of this type of adjustment appears compelling. Why don't individuals with impaired hearing just accept it when it is so reasonable to do so? It is not a simple task, but difficult and complex. Some reasons for the difficulty have already been discussed.

It should not be necessary to point out that the problem is not unique to the acoustically handicapped. Ordinary psychotherapy for the physically normal is basically a process of leading a client to explore his limitations and disabilities and accept them as *part* of himself without devaluing himself as a person. The dynamics of adjustment that have been outlined have great generality. They are equally applicable to everyone. An example from everyday life may illuminate the issue.

Jim Smith is the son, grandson, and great-grandson of physicians. He, too, aspires to be a physician. Unfortunately, however, he lacks a tool for adequate behavior as a physician: he is not bright. His IQ is of the order of 100, and his academic record is poor. Despite rigorous application to his studies, he just isn't smart enough to gain the necessary knowledge that will enable him to be a good physician. What are the alternatives in this situation? He can say, "I'm stupid," or "I do not have the aptitudes for medicine." He can say, "It's a good thing to be a physician, but many occupations are just as good. Medicine is not for me. I'm pretty good at athletics, though. Maybe I'll become a football coach."

Jim, however, cannot say this. In part he is under great pressure from his family to carry on the tradition, and has accepted their values. In part, he has seen for himself the desirable and privileged life that physicians lead. In addition to their rewards of "serving humanity" and receiving the gratitude of patients who have been helped, there are better pay, high social status, and many other desirable goals in the life space of a physician. For these reasons also, Jim is unable to accept the suggestion that he become a medical technician. This would bring him closer to the desirable areas, but he would still be outside of the highly privileged regions.

Jim, therefore, continued to strive persistently. Because of this persistence, family influence, and other factors, Jim managed to squeak through college and medical school, although it took him ten years instead of eight. His family and others applauded his spunk. He now had an M.D. Is he really a physician, however? Is he really in the privileged area of medicine if he practices?

The life situation of a capable physician is markedly different from the life space of one who is not confident of his skills. The able M.D. feels secure in his ability to meet new situations as they arise. His training has already partially structured them. He knows in a general way the sequence of steps that will lead to help for the patient. This was not the situation for Jim. Jim, despite his degree, was simultaneously in the situation of a person lacking medical ability and important knowledge, and in the situation of a person who was expected and required to behave as a competent physi-

LEE MEYERSON

cian. He was attempting to play an antagonistic overlapping role. Like the blind person pouring cocktails, he could go through the motions but he could not simultaneously play both roles.

From this information alone it is predictable that Jim will have attacks of acute anxiety whenever he is called to a case. He can't know in advance whether he will be able to handle it. He will not behave adequately in emergencies, but will try to cover up as best he can. He will be afraid and ashamed to talk with other physicians and will have few friends among them. Since he is behaving only as if he were a physician, he can't have close friends for fear that someone will find him out. It is like living a lie—one can neither advance nor withdraw. He must continue to strive to be something he is not. As a consequence of striving for goals that he can never reach, Jim will be a frustrated, anxious, and unhappy person despite the prerogatives of his degree. The unhappiness will not be localized to medicine but will spread to other regions and relationships also. This, in fact, is what happened.

Most people, upon reading the case history, seem to agree that Jim would have been "better off" if he had been able to accept his limitations and to value the other good behavioral possibilities that were open to him.

The situation is not different for the disabled person who tries to behave "as if" he were not disabled. The anticipated advantages of the large life space, in reality, may be greatly circumscribed. It is not a larger life space if one is unable to move about freely within it. It is not greater freedom to live a fuller life if one must constantly compare himself unfavorably with others on abilities that the objective situation demands. There may be more real freedom in a life space that has fewer "objective" advantages but also fewer barriers. Freedom exists when one can cope adequately with the environment and feel successful. Adjustment exists when a person's values are consistent with his needs and abilities.

The development of values and the process of value change are not well understood. That is one reason why psychotherapy is such a long, expensive, and painful process. It seems certain, however, that children, as more helpless and dependent persons, have less freedom in selecting values than adults. The responsibility of their parents and teachers, therefore, is great.

In fulfilling this responsibility some other advantages of Adjustment Pattern 3 may be considered.

Advantages of Pattern 3

1. It allows and encourages the child to believe in his own perceptions. We have noted that some of the skills and much of the behavior that children with impaired hearing may be socially required to learn are based on the needs and the perceptions of others. In speech and lip reading, for example, the child may be unable to monitor his own productions. He must constantly look to a helper to tell him when he is right and when he is wrong, for he frequently cannot perceive the stimuli that would enable him to know for himself. It is something like learning to shoot a rifle at a target that cannot be seen, with a helper to punish poor shots and reward good ones; or learning to drive a car when blindfolded. It is possible, and some may develop great skill, but it is nerve-racking. One soon learns to respond to the promptings of others rather than to the goal.

This situation, in itself, may account for a large part of the rigid, drilled, anxious, submissive, and insecure behavior of the deaf that has been reported by many observers. Could it also be one reason it is so difficult to make speech and lip reading training stick? Have deaf children learned to please their teachers rather than to structure paths to goals?

There have been no investigations of this problem among the deaf. Asch (1952), however, in a brilliant investigation, has described some of the psychological effects of social pressures upon a person to deny his own perceptions. He presented a group of subjects the task of selecting one of three lines that most nearly matched the length of a standard line. Two of the comparison lines were always perceptibly different from the standard line, as in Figure 1–8.

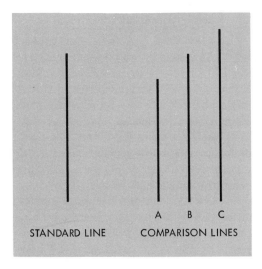

STANDARD LINE   COMPARISON LINES

Fig. 1–8. Lines used in Asch's (1952) experiments [from Solomon E. Asch, *Social Psychology* (Englewood Cliffs, N. J.: Prentice-Hall, Inc., 1952), reproduced with permission].

When the subject did the task alone he was able to make the correct matches.

Asch then formed groups of seven subjects in which each person was required to announce publicly his decisions about the correct matching lines. However, six of the seven subjects in the group were collaborators of the experimenter. They had been instructed to give a certain number of false reports. In Figure 1–8, for example, they would respond that Line C best matched the standard line. The seventh subject—a minority of one—was the critical person. The task was exquisitely simple. The evidence was right in front of him. From a purely perceptual standpoint the experimental subject could always answer correctly and be sure that he was right.

What actually happened when the experimental subjects found that their perceptions were different from the majority? As a group, they yielded! No subject disregarded the judgments of the group. Most of them saw the difficulty as being not in the false reports of the majority but in themselves. They assumed the blame for lack of agreement and disruption of the experiment. They doubted and condemned themselves. They felt shame, guilt, and inferiority. They assumed from the outset that they were wrong and the majority was right. By doing so they became less free to look at the evidence in front of their eyes. Being correct and not exposing oneself as different was of greater concern than mastering the task. Because they had a great need not to be excluded from the group, they tried hard to see the lines in the same way as the majority. Sometimes they suceeded in inducing this confusion in themselves. If they could not succeed, they knowingly falsified their reports. Few were able to remain independent and report their own true perceptions without anxiety, tension, and conflict. Most would not say or imply that the group might be in error. Like disabled persons who employ Adjustment Pattern 2, when they have a similar need not to appear different although they perceive differently, Asch's subjects transferred an external conflict in percepts to a conflict within themselves.

Asch's eloquent discussion of the meaning of this experiment offers strong support for the theory that has been described in this chapter. Sharing foreign or inappropriate values by suppressing one's own experiences is not beneficial to society or to the person. It is a malignant process. To deny the worth of one's own experience, to permit oneself to become confused about it, or to suppress experiences that cannot be assimilated by the larger group is to renounce an essential condition upon which one's capacity to function depends. To live up to the demands of others when they are inappropriate may require that the person blunt his experiences, restrict his awareness of reality, and develop a self that is shadowy and superficial. Such conditions chronically overtax the capacity for orientation, for reality appears always to be shifting. There is no common ground with others, but only yielding to others. These conditions put a stop to the testing of reality so that the person tries not to observe, not to understand, and not to feel. Contact with reality is impossible when one must behave in a contradictory and threatening world as if it were a consistent and understandable world.

Human beings faced with demands beyond their capacities for orientation and lacking the perceptions for independent action do more than distort and exclude the content of unmanageble situations. In the effort to achieve a new but now artificial stability they are forced to modify their mode of orientation in the direction of *not* responding adequately to objective requirements, including their own needs. The consequences are that ultimately they become estranged from both their culture and themselves.

It is not a contrary argument that some with impaired hearing or other disabilities embrace the injustice from which they suffer. This is a common effect of extreme social pressures. Men cannot endure being only losers and victims; they cannot face indefinitely the consequences of resignation and defeat.

Asch (1952) continued his experiments by introducing *two* naïve subjects into a group of five collaborators. The results now were strikingly different. The two naïve subjects might not show any evidence of being aware of each other, but their emotional disturbance was much less. "The presence of a single voice pointing to the true state of affairs had an unmistakable liberating effect. With one person at their side most subjects were able to face the majority with independence and the weakest were spared the extremes of yielding."

These experiments suggest a basic function of the counselor: he must supply at least one single voice that encourages the disabled child to believe in the worth and validity of his own perceptions. The perceptions of children with impaired hearing may be different, but they are just as true as the perceptions of the hearing. It is vital to the mental health and adjustment of the acoustically handicapped that the counselor does not try to force them into a psychological "iron maiden." He must be able to say that the majority—society—is wrong. You do not have to submit by denying yourself.

There is no direct evidence on this problem for the acoustically handicapped, although it is one of the most potentially rewarding areas for future investigation. Cutsforth (1932) offers some evidence concerning the blind which is in general agreement with Asch's later work. He asked blind children what they would say about certain stimulus words. These words had been selected because they could be responded to in terms of several modalities. For example, a rose may be red, sweet-smelling, soft, velvety, and bitter-tasting. Cutsforth found that the great majority of responses were of visual qualities, especially color. When there was a double response, the children tended to feel that the visual attribute was the more valid. In responding to blood, a child said, "Sticky-red. It's sticky, but it's *really* red." What is the experiential significance of color for the blind?

Cutsforth raised the important question of whether we are justified in leading the blind child into the realm of visual unreality and away from his own world of valid experience. Why should the blind child employ visual concepts when other sensory concepts are equally available and much more meaningful in experience. Why should they overvalue the experiences of others and undervalue their own. We may well raise similar questions for the deaf. Do we wish to live by words rather than in reality, and what are the implications of the former behavior on personality and social adjustment?

Adjustment Pattern 3 does not require the child to deny his own perceptions or encourage him to place a high value on the perceptions of others.

2. A related characteristic of Adjustment Pattern 3 is that it facilitates cognitive clarity. The boundaries of the situation are clear so that at a given point in time the child is not uncertain about what behavior is possible and what is not. Of course, as the child grows, the life space may be greatly enlarged and the boundaries pushed back. His behavior, however, is cognitively guided. He is not at the mercy of the perceptions and values of others nor is he impelled to react automatically to stimuli that are inappropriate for him. With respect to his hearing characteristics, he is able to answer the question: Who am I? In what psychological world do I live?

Everyone, it will be recalled, lives in multiple overlapping role situations. The hearing-impaired: hearing dichotomy has been singled out for analysis here, but it should not be forgotten that there are many additional multiple overlaps—all of which sometimes operate simultaneously. For example, the person with impaired hearing may also play the roles of the white, middle-class, Jewish adolescent. All of these, in some degree, require different behavior than is appropriate for a Negro, upperclass, Christian child. Cognitive clarity for these other group membership roles is also desirable. A large and well-balanced variety of group memberships does not cause disturbance. It is uncertainty about one's belongingness that creates psychological conflict. Where fate has made a child a member of one minority group, it is essential that he should recognize and accept it and take pride in his membership. This is a necessary basis for developing strong and secure loyalties to other groups (Lewin, 1948). Shame and attempts to escape identification with an undervalued minority make the child uncertain about where he belongs. Pride in group membership, identification with group goals, and achievements and concern for favorable changes in the social status of the group are adjustive behaviors.

No part of the devaluation and discrimination against the deaf is necessarily directed to them as persons. Rather, it may be prejudice against the group to which they belong.

The counselor who insists on the following is not helpful: (a) The person with impaired hearing is only an individual and not a member of a group; (b) he is not different from others who hear; and (c) behavior which appears normal or most closely approaches normality is the most highly desirable goal. All of these values impose great and unnecessary burdens

LEE MEYERSON

upon the person. They demand behavior which may be considered undesirable for mental health if it is achieved. In effect they demand that the person with impaired hearing place himself on the barrier between the life spaces of hearing roles and impaired-hearing roles and submit to the buffeting forces that inevitably act upon persons in antagonistic role situations.

The person with impaired hearing who has no pride in the group to which fate has assigned him and tries to escape does not thereby free himself from the treatment that is directed toward other members of the group. He simply loses the valuable support of others who are attempting to cope with a similar situation. The independence, respectability, and courage of the deaf provide an excellent base for the feeling of group belongingness.

Consequences of Pattern 3

Some consequences of Adjustment Pattern 3, therefore, are the following:

The person is easily able to say, "I have impaired hearing." He does not devalue himself or his group. Differences can be neutral. He sees the value of hearing behavior as an asset, but impaired-hearing behavior does not affect the worth of the person. If he is placed at a disadvantage in a normally hearing world, it is because of the difficulty of the task and not the incompetence of the person. He, therefore, does not blame himself or feel guilt and shame. Because he is cognitively clear about this, his behavior is flexible and not bound by anxiety. He can cognitively guide his behavior in a conscious, goal directed, and voluntary way and describe what he is doing to others. At one stroke he frees himself from ambiguous group memberships and their conflicting group demands.

COUNSELING ADVENTITIOUSLY IMPAIRED PERSONS

The same principles that apply to individuals with congenital impairments apply also to those who have incurred impairments. The latter are more likely to be attracted to Adjustment Pattern 2 and to reject Adjustment Pattern 1, but this does not invariably occur.

A major difference between the two groups is that the life space of the congenitally impaired is gradually built up and differentiated. The adventitiously impaired, however, may already have a well-organized life space which must now be restructured. The counselor must not be too cheerful too soon. Hearing is a valuable asset. It is necessary and desirable for the person to mourn his loss before he is able to assimilate his present situation and reassess his goals. Unlike the congenitally impaired, who can easily see new enlargement and differentiation of the life space as a gain, the adventitiously impaired person must set up a new base line from which to evaluate himself. If he previously shared the stigmatizing attitudes of the majority toward the group to which he now belongs, he will apply these judgments to himself. He will devalue himself as an imperfect normal person and be unable to see himself as a whole and good person whose impaired hearing is just one attribute. In this situation no matter how often he does as well or better than normally hearing persons, he will still feel inferior. If it were not for his defective hearing, he might have done even better.

The function of the counselor is to help set up a new base line which is rooted in the present and does not require any comparisons with the previous state of the person. From this new base line the adventitiously impaired, also, will be able to perceive each positive gain as a gain. If an individual was not able to lip read and can now lip read a little, that is an objective gain. There is no need to devalue it because hearing was easier.

The basic principles have already been stated. Figures 1–9, 1–10, and 1–11 show some additional ways in which the counselor can assist in the restructuring process.

The client often comes with the feeling that he is imprisoned by impaired hearing. The barrier, however, in reality need not surround the person, but only certain areas of the life space. Many activities do not require hearing. It is possible to show also, as in Figure 1–10, that desirable activities which appear to require hearing do not so. Effective communication, for example, may be mediated by vision, as in lip reading or finger spelling; by motor activities, as in writing; and by emotions, as in scowling or kissing. In addition, the counselor can show, as in Figure 1–11, the relatively small portion of human capacities that are effectively utilized by the average person. There are persons with excellent hearing who engage in conversation no more stimulating than "He said, and then I said." They may never attend a lecture or a concert or use their auditory capacities for enriching their lives. The same is true of other modalities. The child with impaired hearing has a greater potential for psychological growth than he will ever develop to the full.

DOING SOMETHING FOR THE DISABLED: A TECHNOLOGY FOR PSYCHOLOGISTS

One reasonably systematic, social psychological approach to the specification of the conditions under which some kinds of psychological maladjustment may occur has been presented. The occasional application of the model to nonphysically disabled persons as well as to disabled persons, and the use of the same concepts in accounting for both adjustment and maladjustment, enhance our confidence in the generality and probable correctness of the propositions.

Additional support for the belief that the relationships between physical disability and behavior must be mediated by intervening variables such as the psychological situations described is given by Shontz (1970). His review of the recent experimental literature attempting to relate physical disability and personality led him to reaffirm earlier conclusions (Barker, *et al.,* 1953) that, despite persistent search for it, there is no evidence of systematic association of type or degree of disability with type or degree of personality adjustment.

This kind of analysis, leading to increased understanding of some relevant variables in somatopsychology, may not be fully satisfying to those who are charged to "do something" for disabled persons. Rehabilitation workers may understand better the conditions under which a physical impairment becomes a psychological handicap and coerces the behaviors that are categorized as maladjusted. Simultaneously, however, there is a strong demand for behavioral engineering support: a detailed technology for the prevention of psychological disturbance and for immediate utilization in day-to-day therapy.

Considering the purpose of this chapter, the demand for a detailed technology for psychologists cannot be fulfilled here. One would not expect to find a book on the servicing and repair of home appliances in a textbook on physics. On the other hand,

Fig. 1–9. Perception of life situation.

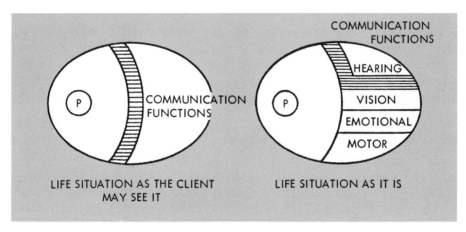

Fig. 1–10. Perception of life situation.

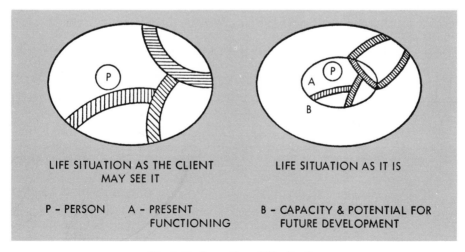

Fig. 1–11. Perception of life situation.

a book on effective therapeutic procedures in rehabilitation is urgently needed. Psychology is in great part an applied science, and it is not unreasonable that rehabilitation workers should expect psychological knowledge to help solve practical problems. Accordingly, some sources of ineffectiveness of present applied research in disability will be mentioned, and some examples of one promising, developing technology will be presented.

Some Limitations of Present Research

A science develops, after an initial description and classification of phenomena, by manipulation or observation of an independent variable that produces some change in a dependent variable. Through this manipulation or observation, knowledge is obtained about the functional relationships that exist between one variable and another.

In much current research on disability, however, variables are not manipulated in any experimental way. Instead, relatively unmanipulable characteristics or conditions such as age, sex, intelligence, kind or degree of disability, personality, and other global descriptions are simply counted, measured, correlated, or compared. This kind of research results in the continued piling up of static information that is no longer sufficient, particularly needed, or helpful. One recently published curiosity, for example, plotted children's improvement in speech as a function of the occupations of their fathers!

In addition, there is no dearth of phenomenological studies describing how persons who are disabled perceive their situations and themselves (Levine, 1962; Zunich and Ledwith, 1965; Kemph, 1967; Kleck, 1968; Klein and Parson, 1968; Caffrey, 1968; Abram, 1969) or of social-psychological studies describing how disabled persons are perceived by others (Yuker, Block and Young, 1966; Siller *et al.,* 1967; McDonald and Hall, 1969).

We know a great deal now about the verbally reported attitudes of disabled and nondisabled persons. Some basic data, too, are now available on how the body is perceived (Shontz, 1969).

Psychological contributions focusing on behavior and behavioral improvement in disability, however, are meager. Entire books are in print whose conclusions seem to be that nothing of psychological importance can be done for persons with disabilities except to diagnose and measure their psychological characteristics and try to separate the rehabilitatable sheep, who already possess the good or strong qualities that are believed to be associated with successful rehabilitation, from the unrehabilitatable goats (Meyerson, 1963). Only rarely does one encounter a treatment such as Wright's (1960) in which implications for therapy, improvement, and change are frequently derived from explicitly stated psychological principles.

Part of the restiveness among students and professionals alike stems from disenchantment with "diagnostic" psychological procedures in which a new name, placed on observational data, passes for explanation. For example, a teacher or parent may observe that a child does not stick to one task very long but flits rapidly from object to object and activity to activity. After the psychologist tests the child, he may observe profoundly that the child has a low attention span. Similarly, it may be observed by a layman that a child has difficulty in picking up or precisely depositing an object. The psychologist will confirm that hand-eye coordination is poorly developed or retarded. The terminology that the psychologist may offer does not say anything more than the first description. He is simply placing a different and more impressive name on the same behavior. Other kinds of diagnostic effort, if they lead to no more than categorizing the client or his behavior, are equally unhelpful. It is not unreasonable for a therapist to ask, "Well, what can I *do* about that?" and to feel unsatisfied if a reasonable technology for behavior change is not forthcoming.

Another part of the problem is that somatopsychological theorists have been concerned with understanding and elaborating the ways in which the interactions of a person with his environment determine behavior. They search for general principles upon which a technology may be based, but they have not devoted equal effort to building that technology. Practitioners are concerned with, and in need of, much more concrete and specific procedures for coping with day-to-day, overt behaviors.

Some Practice Conclusions Concerning Therapy

The therapist's observations often can be reduced to the following:

1. The client is not engaging in some overt behavior that, in the opinion of some wise, authoritative, or responsible expert or agency, he should engage in.
2. The client is engaging in some behavior that he should not engage in.
3. The client does some things that he should do, but he does not do them often enough or strongly enough, or they are interspersed with undesired behaviors which interfere with his education or rehabilitation.

The ethical questions so frequently discussed in connection with psychotherapy as to when, in what degree, and by what procedures it is permissible to influence the behavior of another rarely arise in physical-rehabilitation or special-education settings. The basic decisions, not unlike other socially imposed standards, have already been made for all persons who enter. These decisions are that it is better to be as much like a physically normal person as possible, better to walk than not to walk, better to be mobile or partially mobile than immobile, better to speak correctly than with a speech impairment, and better to learn a task or skill than not to learn it.

The teacher or therapist may ask, "How can I motivate the client?" but what he may mean is "How can I change his behavior?" He is convinced that what he does and what he wishes the client to do are correct and valuable. He knows that the requirements placed on the client "to do" or "not to do" may be unpleasant, difficult, effortful, or painful, and these efforts may not be crowned with success. He believes, nevertheless, that the possible advantages outweigh the disadvantages and the task should be attempted. What he is asking for are better methods for generating desirable new behavior, maintaining a good behavior, and altering bad behavior; he has no difficulty in distinguishing what is good and desirable behavior from bad behavior. Dembo (1969) contended that this kind of formulation of the therapeutic endeavor is insufficient, incorrect, and inappropriate. Like Wright (1960), who urges that the client be the comanager in his rehabilitation, Dembo believes that the client's viewpoint is important and must be taken into account. An excellent and powerful technology has developed, however, which serves the demands of the pragmatic therapist and places little emphasis upon the client's perceptions. This rehabilitation approach is called *behavior modification.*

Behavior Modification

The behavior modification approach to learning and rehabilitation is different from the field-theoretical approach in some important respects. It is simpler and more elegant than field theory. In its conceptualizations of relevant variables, the overwhelming emphasis is upon the consequences of behavior. Intervening variables, hypothetical constructs, and other "mentalistic explanatory fictions" are rejected as unnecessary and misleading. What is important is the direct, empirical study of *how* the environment acts upon the behavior that is emitted by an organism and thereby controls the shape and frequency of future acts. The crucial variable to understanding behavior or changing it is to observe and manipulate its consequences.

As an operational, molecular technology, behavior modification is not incompatible with field theory or other learning approaches to behavior, although the behavior modification approach may assign different reasons for results obtained. Behavior theory does not take into account, or omits unneeded, certain complexities of the person and environment that other approaches consider of great importance. However, there is increasing agreement, among psychologists of diverse theoretical orientations, that behavior modification works as far as it goes. There is disagreement as to whether a positivistic, mechanistic system is sufficient to account for behaviors that some consider uniquely human. But on a practical level, the behavior modification approach does have the advantages of system, clarity, precision, and control, and the approach is exerting great influence on applied practice in many fields. This influence is possible because an effective technology is not "owned" by the group that develops it. Anyone can use the technology for his own purposes without necessarily accepting the theoretical structure from which it stems, and the therapist is free to place his own interpretations on why the technology is effective (Michael and Meyerson, 1962).

Only a grossly oversimplified and schematic account of the approach can be given here. The basic reference is Skinner's book *Science and Human Behavior* (1953). For later and more technical expositions, the interested reader should see Ferster and Perrott (1968), Bandura (1969), Skinner (1968), and Reynolds (1968). Patterson and Gullion (1968) have prepared an elementary, programmed introduction for parents and teachers. Ullmann and Krasner (1965) and Ulrich, Stachnik, and Mabry (1966) present some illustrative case studies. Michael (1970) discusses applications to rehabilitation.

Essentially, the behavior modification approach is based upon several observations:

1. Behavior has consequences.
2. The consequences of a particular action influence the probability that the same act will occur in the future when the environmental conditions are similar.
   a. If good consequences (reinforcers) follow an action—particularly if they follow immediately or very quickly—that act (behavior) tends to occur more frequently under similar conditions.
   b. If bad consequences (punishments) follow an action—particu-

larly if they follow immediately or very quickly—that act (behavior) tends to occur less frequently in the future.

3. One can encourage and strengthen or discourage and weaken a behavior by arranging the environment so that good things, from the learner's viewpoint, quickly follow the behavior that should be strengthened (reinforcement) and bad things or no consequences follow the behavior that one wishes to weaken (punishment, extinction). "Good things" means the presentation of satisfying conditions or the withdrawal of aversive conditions. "Bad things" means the presentation of aversive conditions or the withdrawal of satisfying conditions.

  a. A particularly effective influence on behavior results if a teacher or therapist has a monopoly or a high degree of control over certain good things which he dispenses to a learner only after certain desired responses have been made. (Reinforcement contingent upon a behavior.)

  b. Many complex behaviors are learned most readily if important subordinate behaviors are discriminated by the therapist; and the correct responding by the learner, in stepwise, sequential fashion, is reinforced quickly and frequently at each step before going on to the next step. (Shaping successive approximations, teaching).

Researchers in the experimental analysis of behavior emphasize that observations are not theoretical statements. The observations are presented as an empirical description of what has occurred in thousands of experiments and what appears to occur naturally when behavior changes in the special way that is called learning.

The observations are not new. They have deep roots in the wisdom of the past. Grandmother, and her grandmother, quoted the proverbs: "You can catch more flies with honey than with vinegar" (reinforcement) and "the burned child dreads the fire" (punishment). Similarly, the teaching procedures that can be derived from the observations were probably known intuitevely by every good teacher who ever lived; and they are implicit in the modern dictum: "Begin where the client is, and lead him very gradually with a maximum of success experiences." As grandmother would say it, "Nothing succeeds like success."

What is new is that gross observations, proverbs, folk wisdom, and teaching maxims are yielding to the detailed experimental study of the necessary and sufficient conditions for behavior change. Some basic principles have been identified, verified, systematized, and pinned down to a teachable format that is easily learned.

The natural or manipulated consequences of actions are not the only determiners of behavior, but they are important ones. The appropriate and systematic management of consequences, with particular emphasis on reinforcing consequences, may be sufficient in itself to improve greatly the effectiveness of every teacher and therapist.

Examples of Behavior Modification

Meyerson, Kerr, and Lazar (1969 a, 1969 b) produced a motion picture showing some behavior modification procedures and outcomes in teaching Terry, an eight-year-old, profoundly retarded, nonambulant child, to walk; correcting Johnny's speech defect—a frontal lisp; and teaching Jenny, an immature, preschool child, to tie her shoe. These are all very practical behaviors that are of immediate concern to rehabilitation workers.

For each case, the authors proposed the same framework of four basic steps:

1. Specify the specific, concrete, overt behavior that you wish the child to engage in.
2. Specify the successive approximations. What are the smaller behaviors, the steps-along-the-way, that will lead the child from what he does now to the desired terminal, molar behavior?
3. Find a reinforcer. What will the child work for? It is not a reinforcer if it does not strengthen a specific behavior when dispensed in a contingency relationship.
4. Give the reinforcer to the child, immediately and frequently, contingent upon his successful performance of the successive approximations. If the child does not earn reinforcers frequently, you may be raising the requirement for reinforcement too rapidly, the size of the steps in your successive approximations may be too large, or you may not have an adequate reinforcer.

The motion pictures of Terry learning to walk show a child who appears to be profoundly retarded. Her complex diagnosis made reference to defective central processes and immaturity or impairment of her neuromuscular apparatus, which can be summarized in colloquial language as follows: There is nothing wrong with her legs. She is just too stupid to maintain balance while simultaneously putting one foot ahead of another.

Attempts had been made for a year to teach her to walk using regular physical therapy procedures, but having neither speech nor ability to understand speech, she did not understand what was required. Moreover, she "didn't want to walk." She screamed, fussed, and balked when she was coaxed or coerced in exercises leading to walking, and it was concluded that she was incapable of learning this behavior.

The film shows the establishment and maintenance of walking behavior after less than ten hours of teaching time. Frequent, positive reinforcement of successive approximations to walking, administered in short training sessions over many days, led to the rapid, easy, and painless acquisition of a basic behavior. Meyerson, Kerr, and Michael (1967) present data on a similar case.

The behavior modification procedures carried out in the film are presented in the following cases.

CASE I

Terry—Walking

I. *Define the Behavior.*
   A. Terminal behavior.
     Walking independently in everyday life.
   B. Beginning behavior
     She would stand for considerable periods of time holding on to a chair with one or both hands, but she refused to let go, to move to another firm support, or to take a step on her own.

II. *Decide on Successive Approximations.*
   A. With Terry, the following approximations were used:
     1. Standing holding onto the chair.
     2. Switching from one chair to another without letting go.
     3. Moving the chairs apart so that the

switch required letting go of one chair momentarily.

4. Taking a step of sorts while switching from one chair to another.

5. With support from taut rope suspended from ceiling of therapy room, taking, first, one step and then gradually increasing numbers of steps.

6. Walking farther and farther with rope slackened.

7. Walking across room with long piece of rope in one hand.

8. Walking across room with smaller and smaller piece of rope on each trip.

9. Walking with only a wad of string clenched in fist.

10. Walking in room without any string in fist.

11. Walking on other surfaces (grass, gravel, etc.).

12. Walking independently in everyday life.

B. It is wise to make some plan in advance about what approximations will lead the child from the beginning behavior to the terminal behavior. However, it is not always possible to have a predetermined program as was set up for shoelace tying.

C. At times, the next approximation has to be determined by what the child is doing. For example, some children, once they have reached Step 4, will quite readily take an independent step toward the outstretched arms of a therapist, with seeming confidence that no one will let him fall. Soon such a child takes more steps between two people. Other children who, like Terry, insist on something to hang onto, immediately drop to the floor when the rope is cut. With such a child, it is possible for the therapist to give support by holding onto one end of a stick and walking with the child holding on to the other end. By gradually reducing the amount of support actually given, the child eventually walks independently.

III. *Find a Reinforcer.*

A. The initial reinforcers for Terry were bites of ice cream, or sips of fruit juice. Later, of course, when she could walk well, the natural reinforcers in the environment were sufficient to keep her walking.

B. Terry is severely retarded. It was impossible to "explain" anything to her, and she was totally unresponsive to verbal approval from an adult. With considerable training, it probably would have been possible to teach her to work for tokens that could be cashed in later for ice cream. However, teaching her the significance of a token was not a necessary step in learning to walk and in practice it was easier to show her a spoonful of ice cream.

IV. *Give the Reinforcer Immediately and Frequently.*

A. At the point in Terry's development shown in the film, the only way she learned anything was by experiencing the consequences that followed her behavior. In this case, and perhaps more generally, cognitive "goals" are not necessary if consequences are satisfying.

B. Terry would not understand if someone said, "Now turn and grab the other chair." Nor would she understand if an hour after she had turned from one chair to another someone came along and said, "Here's some ice cream. I'm giving it to you because you turned from one chair to another." In her case, immediate and frequent reinforcement was not only desirable but absolutely essential if learning was to occur. However, as in other cases, it was possible at later stages to reduce the frequency of reinforcement and gradually withdraw artificial reinforcers altogether (Meyerson, Kerr, and Lazar, 1969 b).

CASE II

Johnny had a frontal lisp. In pronouncing the /s/ sound, his tongue protruded through his teeth, and the resulting sound came out /th/ as in "thoap," "thuit," "thun." Correction of this impairment, which is not considered a particularly severe or difficult speech problem although it occurs frequently, may require six to twelve months of traditional therapeutic effort. The film shows the correction of the frontal lisp in this child in two 15-minute, behavior modification sessions. Mowrer, Baker, and Schutz (1968) present data on similar cases.

Johnny—Speech Correction

The desired behavior for this child was the use of the /s/ sound correctly in conversational speech. The successive approximations began with the crucial one, namely, closing the teeth and saying /s/. This procedure relied completely on the shaping of an incompatible response. Closing the teeth to say /s/ is incompatible with sticking out the tongue. The therapist, in fact, never once told the child, "Don't stick your tongue out." Instead, she emphasized the positive instruction, "Keep your teeth closed."

Every correct response was immediately followed by a click and the illumination of one light on a multiple-light reinforcer box. Every incorrect response was immediately followed by a buzzer noise. Periodically, as the child completed a run of correct responses, he was allowed to select a small piece of candy to take home with him. This reinforcement procedure allowed hundreds of correct responses to be made in a brief period of time. Once the first approximation to the correct /s/ sound was mastered and consolidated, the outcome was never in doubt. Acquisition

of the correct speech behavior was completed in thirty minutes. The new behavior was maintained thereafter by natural social reinforcement provided by the school environment.

CASE III

Responsibility for failure or lack of progress in teaching or therapy often is assigned to some impeding characteristic in the client about which the therapist, seemingly, can do little or nothing. It is the client's immaturity, his developmental or experiential unreadiness, his lack of motivation, his fearfulness, his neuromuscular impairment, his sensory deficit, or some other inadequacy that is responsible for his undesirable behavior. The author has observed with interest that users of operant conditioning procedures almost invariably remove the label of inadequacy from the backs of their clients and place the burden on their own shoulders. There is general agreement among behavior modifiers that if a client does not learn a specified behavior, the fault is more likely to rest on some inadequacy of the program of successive approximations or on the reinforcement contingencies than upon some irremediable inadequacy of the client. Behavior modifiers do not always succeed, but they do not "cop out" with the easy, conventional explanations.

Jenny's inability to tie her shoe was not surprising. Children are usually six or seven years old before they learn this complex behavior, and Jenny was less than four. It could be said that in time, as she matured and gained more experience, she would become ready to learn to tie her shoe and learn this behavior at the natural time—that is, at the age when even poor teaching usually results in learning. Perhaps, as some say, one must wait for the maturation of eye-hand coordination, although Jenny's present, fine-motor coordination allowed her to perform more delicate tasks than shoe tying.

Etzel (1968) described the shoe-tying program that Jenny learned. Ordinarily, preschool children work with the program for only five to fifteen minutes in many sessions spread over several weeks. For the film production, however, Jenny was allowed to take several sessions of shoe tying in the same day. She learned to tie her shoes before the day was out.

What kind of phenomenon is "maturation of eye-hand coordination" if the maturation can occur so rapidly in children who receive the reinforced, programmed instruction, whereas children who do not work with the program remain "immature and unready"? There is reason to believe that many behavioral deficiencies, including those that often seem to be lessened by additional time, trial-and-error experience, and increased maturity, are functions of exposure to a meager, unsystematic, or unrewarding environment. Such deficits may be overcome, and overcome quickly, if the therapist will skillfully reinforce the client's responding to successive approximations in a well-designed program.

The behavior-modification procedures for Jenny, were as follows:

Jenny—Shoe Tying

I. *Define the Behavior.*
  A. Terminal behavior.
     We want the child to tie her shoelaces in a tight bow without assistance.
  B. Beginning behavior.
     When asked to tie her shoes, she fiddles with the laces and attempts unsuccessfully to tie them. She demonstrates that she knows what shoelaces

are and that she is supposed to do something with them—but clearly she doesn't know *what* to do.

II. *Decide on Successive Approximations.*
  A. The following things were done initially to make the whole task an easier one.
     1. The child worked at a table instead of leaning over to reach her foot
     2. The shoe was nailed to a board so that it would be stable.
     3. One lace was white and the other red.
     4. The place on the board where each lace should go was marked with a small piece of appropriately colored tape.
     5. In the beginning, extra long laces were used.
     6. The laces were marked to show the child where to make the loops and where to place them together.
     7. The verbal instructions were simple enough to be easily understood by a young child, and the demonstrations could be comprehended without language.
  B. The actual tying of the bow was broken into 12 distinct steps. The steps, along with the verbal directions given by the teacher, were as follows:
     1. This is a white lace. Pick up the white lace.
     2. This is the red lace. Pick up the red lace.
     3. Make the white lace fly (to marker on opposite side)
     4. Make the red lace fly (to marker on opposite side)
     5. Here is a white tunnel. You make a white tunnel like this. You make a white tunnel.
     6. This red road goes under the tunnel like this. You make the red road go under the tunnel.
     7. Now pull both laces to make a knot.
     8. Put the two marks together to make a white rabbit ear. You make a white ear.

9. The red lace is an ear like this. Put the two marks together to make a red ear.
10. Place the red ear across the white ear like this (across a yellow mark on the white ear holding both ears in one hand).
11. See the big hole? Point to the big hole. Put the red lace under and up through the hole.
12. Now pull the red ear and the white ear. You tied the shoe! . . . and you get a token.

III. *Find a Reinforcer.*
A. In searching for an effective reinforcer it is necessary to keep several things in mind.
   1. A reinforcer provides feedback that tells a child *what* he has done correctly. For this reason, it should be something that can be given just as soon as a correct approximation has been made. In Jenny's case a chip dropped in her cup every time she did one step correctly, and her teacher's approval, gave her such feedback.
   2. A reinforcer should also serve to motivate the child to practice until his skill is developed to the point that the behavior carries its own reward. For example, the conveniece of being able to tie shoes is obvious, once it can be done with little effort. However, the extrinsic reinforcer gives the child a good reason for sticking at the task of learning the skill. It is unlikely that Jenny would be very enthusiastic about merely acquiring tokens. However, her tokens can be exchanged for a ride on the hobby horse. The things that tokens or points can be traded for are called "back-up reinforcers." The tokens themselves are conditioned reinforcers.
   3. A reinforcer must be something that is meaningful to the child—something that he will work for. There are several ways to find out what may be effective for a particular child.
      a. Observe his play activities and see what he chooses to do. In Jenny's case, she was very attracted to the hobby horse.
      b. Give a child a choice of a number of trinkets or kinds of candy and ask him which one he would buy if he had the money.
      c. Simply ask children (or the parents of young or non-verbal children) what things they like most to have or do.
      d. Test out possible reinforcers by seeing whether the child will work to obtain them.

IV. *Give the Reinforcer Immediately and Frequently.*
A. The importance of giving reinforcers immediately and frequently, especially in the beginning stages of learning, cannot be overemphasized. Any place where it is possible to make a mistake, is a place where a correct response should be reinforced. Jenny earned many tokens in the process of learning to tie her shoe. She got tokens for each correct step even when, as was always the case, she started at the beginning and practiced steps that she had done correctly previously (Meyerson, Kerr, and Lazar, 1969 b).

These examples emphasize only two of the principles of operant conditioning—positive reinforcement and shaping. There are other principles also, and many ingenious ways of applying them to specific problems have been reported.

Osborne and Wageman (1969) discussed the use of operant techniques in schools for the deaf, and Osborne (1970) described an experimental example. Whelan (1966) reviewed behavior modification procedures for emotionally disturbed children, whereas Gardner and Watson

(1969) compiled an annotated bibliography of studies with the retarded. Applications to remedial speech and language are presented in a book edited by Sloane and MacAulay (1968). A special behavioral counseling issue of the journal *The Counseling Psychologist* (1969) and a book edited by Krumboltz and Thoresen (1969) may be of considerable interest to rehabilitation counselors, whereas rehabilitation psychologists may be stimulated by Ullmann and Krasner's (1969) text on abnormal behavior and McGinnies and Ferster's (1970) readings on the reinforcement of social behavior.

The rapidly increasing and widespread current literature is indexed conveniently in *Psychological Abstracts*. Specialized journals such as the *Journal of Applied Behavior Analysis* and the *Journal of Experimental Child Psychology* are frequent outlets for studies using the behavior-modification paradigm.

EPILOGUE

This chapter is long and detailed, but the major topics are few. The reader has covered the material if he can discuss, with appropriate evidence and examples, the following questions:

1. What are some of the relationships that may exist between physique and behavior?
2. Under what conditons is a variation in physique categorized as a disability?
3. Under what conditions does a disability become a handicap?
4. Identify three kinds of explanations and characterize an adequate explanation.
5. What are new and overlapping situations, and what relevance do they have for an understanding of behavior in human disability?
6. Elaborate on the kinds and values of the psychological adjustment patterns that may be observed in disabled and nondisabled persons.
7. Compare and contrast the behavior modification approach to human problems with other approaches that are known to you. Can the concepts of each be translated into the terminology and language of the others?

References

Abram, H. S. The psychiatrist, the treatment of chronic renal failure, and the prolongation of life. II. *American Journal of Psychiatry,* 1969, *126,* 157–167.

Adams, G. M. Be anxious. *Easton Express,* April 29, 1954, p. 6.

Allport, G. W. *The nature of prejudice.* Reading, Mass.: Addison-Wesley Publishing Company, Inc., 1954.

Asch, S. A. *Social psychology.* Englewood Cliffs, N.J.: Prentice-Hall, Inc., 1952.

Bandura, A. *Principles of behavior modification.* New York: Holt, Rinehart & Winston, Inc., 1969.

Barker, R. G. *et al. Adjustment to physical handicap and illness: A survey of the social psychology of physique and disability.* New York: Social Science Research Council, 1953.

Bender, L., & Blau, A. The reaction of children in sexual relations with adults. *American Journal of Orthopsychiatry,* 1937, *7,* 500–518.

————. Continuities and discontinuities in cultural conditioning, *Psychiatry,* 1938, 161–167.

Benedict, R. *Patterns of culture.* Boston: Houghton Mifflin Company, 1934.

Blair, F. B. Relations between the average amount of insurance per policy and the height and the weight of the insured. *The Record* (American Institute of Actuaries), 1940, *29,* 211–223.

Burt, C. The factorial study of physical types. *Man,* 1944, *72,* 82–86.

Cabot, P. S. de Q. The relationship between characteristics of personality and physique in adolescents. *Genetic Psychology Monographs,* 1938, p. 20.

Caffrey, B. Reliability and validity of personality and behavioral measures in a study of coronary heart disease. *Journal of Chronic Diseases,* 1968, *21,* 191–204.

Calkins, E. E. *And hearing not—.* New York: Charles Scribner's Sons, 1946.

Conant, J. B. *Modern science and modern man.* Garden City, N. Y.: Doubleday & Company, Inc., 1953.

The Counseling Psychologist, 1969, *1* (4).

Cutsforth, T. D. The unreality of words to the blind. *Teachers Forum,* 1932, *4,* 86–89.

Dembo, T. Rehabilitation psychology and its immediate future. *Psychological Aspects of Disability,* 1969, *16,* 63–72.

Dembo, T., Ladieu, G., & Wright, B. A. Acceptance of loss-amputations. *Psychological Aspects of Physical Disability.* Washington, D. C.: Rehabilitation Service Series No. 210. Superintendent of Documents, *n.d.*

———. *Adjustment to misfortune, a study of the social-emotional relationships between injured and non-injured people.* Washington, D.C.: Army Medical Research and Development Board, Office of the Surgeon General, War Department, April, 1948.

Etzel, B. C. *Programming preacademic skills for preschool children.* Mimeograph. Lawrence, Kan.:University of Kansas Child Development Preschool Laboratories, 1968.

Eysenck, H. J. *Dimensions of personality.* London: Routledge & Kegan Paul, Ltd., 1947.

Farber, D. J. Written Communication in psychotherapy. *Psychiatry,* 1963 *16,* 365–374.

Ferster, C. B., & Perrott, M. C. *Behavior principles.* New York: Appleton-Century-Crofts, 1968.

Fiske, D. W. A study of relationships to somatotype. *Journal of Applied Psychology,* 1944, *28,* 504–519.

Gardner, J. M. & Watson, L. S., Jr. Behavior modification of the mentally retarded: An annotated bibliography. *Mental Retardation Abstracts,* 1969, *6,* 181–193.

Goodwin, R. B. *It's good to be black.* Garden City, N.Y.: Doubleday & Company, 1953.

Gowin, E. B. *The executive and his control of men.* New York: The Macmillan Company, 1927.

Hamilton, K. W. *Counseling the handicapped in the rehabilitation process.* New York: The Ronald Press Company, 1950.

Hanks, J. R., & Hanks, L. M., Jr. The physically handicapped in certain nonoccidental societies. *Journal of Social Issues,* 1948, *4,* 11–20.

Haskins, R. G. *Endocrinology.* New York: W. W. Norton & Company, Inc., 1941.

Kemph, J. P. Psychotherapy with patients receiving kidney transplants. *American Journal of Psychiatry,* 1967, *124,* 623–629.

Kerr, N. C. The process of adjustment to disability. *Journal of Rehabilitation,* 1961, *27.*

Kleck, R. Self-disclosure patterns of the nonobviously disabled. *Psychological Reports,* 1968, *23,* 1239–1248.

Klein, H. P. & Parson, O. A. Self-descriptions of patients with coronary disease. *Perceptual and Motor Skills,* 1968, *26,* 1099.

Klineberg, O., Asch, S. E., & Block, H. An experimental study of constitutional types. *Genetic Psychology Monographs,* 1934, *16,* 145–221.

Krumboltz, J. D., & Thoresen C. E. (Eds.). *Behavioral counseling: Cases and techniques.* New York: Holt, Rinehart & Winston, Inc., 1969.

Levine, E. Auditory disability. In J. F. Garrett and Edna S. Levine (Eds.), *Psychological practices with the physically disabled.* New York: Columbia University Press, 1962.

Lewin, K. *Principles of topological psychology.* New York: McGraw-Hill Book Co., 1936.

———. *Resolving social conflicts.* New York: Harper & Row, Publishers, 1948.

Macgregor, F. C., & Schaffner, B. Screening patients for nasal plastic operations. *Psychosomatic Medicine,* 1950, *12,* 227–291.

McDonald, A. P., & Hall, J. Perception of disability by the non-disabled. *Journal of Consulting and Clinical Psychology,* 1969, *33,* 654–660.

McGinnies, E. & Ferster, C. B. *The reinforcement of social behavior: Selected readings.* New York: Houghton Mifflin Company, 1970.

Meyerson, L. The life and times of Division

22. *Psychological Aspects of Disability,* 1963, *10,* 40–46.

Meyerson, L., Kerr, C., & Lazar, I. *Rewards and reinforcements in learning.* 16mm motion picture, black and white, sound. Scottsdale, Ariz.: Behavior Modification Productions, 1969. (*a*)

_____. *Study guide for film: Rewards and reinforcements in learning.* Cincinnati: Board of Education, 1969. (*b*)

Meyerson, L., Kerr, C., & Michael, J. L. Behavior modification in rehabilitation. In S. B. Bijou and D. M. Baer (Eds.), *Child development: Readings in experimental analysis.* New York: Appleton-Century-Crofts, 1967.

Michael, J. L. Rehabilitation. In C. Neuringer and J. Michael (Eds.), *Behavior modification in clinical psychology.* New York: Appleton-Century-Crofts, 1970.

Michael, J., & Meyerson, L. A behavioral approach to counseling and guidance. *Harvard Educational Review,* 1962, *32,* 382–402.

Mowrer, D. E., Baker, R. L., & Schutz, R. E. Operant procedures in the control of speech articulation. In H. N. Sloane, Jr., and B.D. MacAulay (Eds.), *Operant procedures in remedial speech and language training.* New York: Houghton Mifflin Company, 1968.

Murphy, G. E. *Your deafness is not you.* New York: Harper & Row, Publishers, 1954.

Osborne, J. G. Behavior modification with a deaf student: A case study. *Psychological Aspects of Disability,* 1970, *17.*

Osborne, J. G. & Wageman, R. M. Some operant conditioning techniques and their use in schools for the deaf. *American Annals of the Deaf,* 1969, *114,* 741–743.

Paterson, D. G. *Physique and intellect.* New York: Appleton-Century-Crofts, 1930.

Patterson, G. R., & Gullion, M. E. *Living with children: new methods for parents and teachers.* Champaign, Ill.: Research Press, 1968.

Reynolds, G. S. *A primer of operant conditioning.* Glenwood, Ill.: Scott Foresman & Company, 1968.

Sanford, R. N. *et al.* Physique, personality and scholarship. *Monographs of the Society for Research in Child Development,* 1943, *8,* (1).

Sheldon, W. H. Constitutional factors in personality. In J. M. Hunt (Ed.), *Personality and the behavior disorder.* New York: The Ronald Press Company, 1944, Chap. 17.

Sheldon, W. H., Hartl, E. M., & McDermott, E. *Varities of delinquent youth.* New York: Harper & Row, Publishers, 1949.

Sheldon, W. H., & Stevens, S. S. *The varieties of temperament.* New York: Harper & Row, Publishers, 1942.

Sheldon, W. H., Stevens, S. S., & Tucker, W. B. *The varieties of human physique.* New York: Harper & Row, Publishers, 1940.

Shontz, F. C. *Perceptual and cognitive aspects of body experience.* New York: Academic Press, Inc., 1969.

_____. Physical disability and personality: Theory and research. *Psychological Aspects of Disability,* 1970, *17.*

Siller, J. *et al.* Attitudes of the non-disabled toward the physically disabled. New York: New York University School of Education, 1967.

Skinner, B. F. *Science and human behavior.* New York: The Macmillan Company, 1953.

_____. *The technology of teaching.* New York: Appleton-Century-Crofts, 1968.

Sloane, H. N., Jr., & MacAulay, B. D. (Eds.). *Operant procedures in remedial speech and language training.* New York: Houghton Mifflin Company, 1968.

Spiegel, L. A. The child's concept of beauty. *Journal of Genetic Psychology,* 1950, *77,* 11–23.

Stolz, H. R., & Stolz, L. M. Adolescent problems related to somatic variations. *National Society for the Study of Education, Forty-Third Yearbook,* Part 1. Chicago: University of Chicago Press, 1944.

Ullmann, L. P., & Krasner, L. (Eds.). *Case studies in behavior modification.* New York: Holt, Rinehart & Winston, Inc., 1965.

_____. *A psychological approach to abnormal behavior.* Englewood Cliffs, N. J.: Prentice-Hall, Inc., 1965.

Ulrich, R., Stachnik, T., & Mabry, J. (Eds.). *Control of human behavior.* Glenwood, Ill.: Scott Foresman & Company, 1966.

Whelan, J. R. The relevance of behavior modification procedures for teachers of emotionally disturbed children. In P. Knoblock (Ed.), *Intervention approaches in edu-*

cating emotionally disturbed children. Syracuse, N.Y.: Syracuse University Press, 1966.

Whiting, J. W. M. *Becoming a Kwoma.* New Haven, Conn: Yale University Press, 1941.

Wright, B. A. *Physical disability—a psychological approach.* New York: Harper & Row, Publishers, 1960.

Yuker, H. E., Block, J. R., & Young, J. H. *The measurement of attitudes toward disabled persons.* Albertson, N .Y.: Human Resources Foundation, 1966.

Zunich, M., & Ledwith, B. E. Self-concepts of visually handicapped and sighted children. *Perceptual and Motor Skills,* 1965, *21,* 771–774.

TWO

A Handicap as a Social Phenomenon

NETTIE R. BARTEL and
SAMUEL L. GUSKIN

Nettie R. Bartel, who is an Assistant Professor of Special Education at Temple University, was formerly with the Department of Special Education, Indiana University. Samuel L. Guskin is currently Professor of Education, Department of Special Education, Indiana University.

INTRODUCTION: SOCIAL VERSUS MEDICAL DEFINITIONS OF HANDICAP

In the fields of special education and rehabilitation it is generally assumed that one is dealing with disabled or handicapped individuals, that is, persons who have certain intrinsically unhealthy or undesirable characteristics which have been or may be diagnosed by a physician or psychologist and which require a distinctive treatment procedure. In this chapter we take the position that what is distinctive about and common to all handicapped individuals is not so much their own characteristics as the characteristic response of others to them. A handicapped person is someone whom others think is incompetent or unattractive, someone whom others want to help or protect or avoid. Physicians, psychologists, educators, and rehabilitation experts merely rationalize and institutionalize the layman's pity and antipathy. That is, professionals create terminology, organizations, and treatment patterns which foster and stabilize the distinctive status relationship between handicapped persons and others.

The fields of special education and rehabilitation exist not because many children have certain distinctive physical and behavioral characteristics but because our society chooses to treat such children differentially, because other people define them as creating a problem, because social agencies, particularly the schools, choose to create special arrangements for dealing with them. In this chapter we shall draw out the implications of this definition of the exceptional child and adult in terms of social response rather than individual characteristics. In doing so we shall find that the traditional categories of exceptionality vary considerably in their appropriateness and that further categories such as racial or ethnic minorities fit these social definitions as well as do conventional categories such as mental retardation and orthopedic disability.

We are not the first to take this approach, and we shall draw heavily on other sociological and social-psychological writings in the area, especially Barker and Wright (1952), Freidson (1965), Goffman (1963), Guskin (1963), and Kelley *et al.* (1960). Probably Freidson's social definition of handicap is closest to our own. He states (p. 72): "What is a handicap in social terms? It is an imputation of difference from others; more particularly, imputation of an *undesirable* difference. By definition, then, a person said to be handicapped is so defined because he deviates from what he himself or others believe to be normal or appropriate."

It has probably always been recognized that disabilities have social consequences. Among the points mentioned in popular and professional lore are that nondisabled persons behave differently toward the disabled, that the disabled feel uncomfortable in normal social situations, that frustration and feelings of inadequacy stemming from limited competence lead to inappropriate social behavior, that the sensory, motor, or intellectua· limitations themselves make ·normal social interchange difficult. Educational and rehabilitation agencies have usually included the reduction of social inadequacies and social problems as major goals of their activities. Perhaps the major weakness in our understanding has been the nature and consequences of our own professional activities. We have largely operated or been trained in medical settings with the result that we see our role as diagnosing and treating the illness of the individual. We tend to see social adjustment problems as a function of problems within the individual and we are so enamoured with our diagnostic skills that we see the client's acceptance of our diagnosis as the major prerequisite for his "recovery" or adjustment.

This approach is analogous to that of a physician diagnosing the symptoms of a patient in an attempt to discover his "real" condition—is the patient suffering from an iron deficiency or a malfunctioning thyroid? Similarly, the psychologist pores over responses to the Rorschach or the Stanford-Binet in attempts to decide whether the subject is, or is not, a sociopathic personality with or without schizoid features; whether the individual is a low educable retardate or really a high trainable; whether his IQ is 51 or 48. In each case a social consequence follows the diagnosis. Thus, depending on the diagnosis of the physician or psychologist, the subject may be placed in a community hospital, a convalescent home, a mental health clinic, an institution for the mentally ill or mentally retarded, or a school or class for the educable or trainable retarded—in each case, with others of his kind. The assumption is that some individuals *are* mentally ill, mentally retarded, physically disabled, or delinquent and that a society is simply acknowledging the presence of preexisting, objective characteristics when it labels them as such and groups them according to their own kind.

In contrast to the preceding approach, which emphasizes individual traits or individual behaviors, a social systemic analysis is concerned with a broad spectrum of questions concerning social relationships and interrelationships. In what social circumstances are individuals likely to be designated as different, disabled, or deviant? What are the processes through which deviant social identities are acquired? How will the subject and his audi-

NETTIE R. BARTEL AND SAMUEL L. GUSKIN

ence react to the social redefinition? What changes in group membership and group interactions are likely to ensue?

The purpose of this chapter is to reorient thinking about disabled persons, to shift from a focus on the problems of the disabled individual to a focus on the disabling reactions of other persons and society as a whole. The thesis of this chapter is basically that society creates and exacerbates a handicap by identifying and labeling a "condition" and by responding or treating differentially persons so labeled. The hope of this argument is that by identifying society and social response as the source of handicapped behavior we can develop some effective methods of reducing the degree of handicap.

SOCIETY AS A CREATOR OF HANDICAP

Let us assume that you now have no diagnosed disability. Is it possible that without changing your personal, physical, or social characteristics directly you can become a handicapped person? What would be required for society to define you as handicapped? Some attribute of yours would have to be reacted to as seriously unattractive or incompetent to the extent that others would want to avoid you or protect you. Consider the following possibility: You're white and you take a summer job in a camp for poor children, having answered an advertisement and applied by mail. You know a substantial proportion of the children will be black. When you arrive at the orientation session for counselors and children, you find that all the children and all the remaining counselors are black. They are surprised to find a white member on their staff. The counselors are not only black but are

highly involved in asserting the value of blackness, "soul," and so forth. You have eight weeks ahead of you in this environment. Isn't your "whiteness" going to be a physical disfigurement or disability in this setting? Given the norms of this black group, everyone is courteous but careful not to be seen as your friend or your date. You are faced with a difficult adjustment problem—you can't pass. Perhaps you can minimize your white social characteristics and be sure not to be seen as attempting to assert the appropriateness of your own standards or appearance. But regardless of your strategy, it is impossible for you to have normal social relationships in this setting. You must do the best you can, recognizing that all will see you as different and as less adequate in a critical characteristic. The essence of being handicapped is present. A social group defines standards that an individual cannot meet and then treats him as unacceptable or of lower status for failing to meet these standards.

This exercise must surely convince you that you can be handicapped without changing your own characteristics, merely by a change in society's reaction to you. Furthermore, what initially starts out as an evaluation by *others* that you have lesser status, attractiveness, or competence quickly presents *you* with problems of self-esteem, social adjustment, and emotional tension which may, in fact, lead to less competent behavior on your part than would otherwise be the case. By reversing the racial properties in the illustration you can also see that being black must surely be a handicap in a white society, which may help explain why blacks are moving away from the strain of integration to the comfort of homogeneous black subgroups. This influence of others' expectations about one's self upon one's own self-evaluation and behavior will be discussed at some length later.

In a more formal way, society creates deviants by selecting certain attributes or norms and calling them desirable—individuals who fail to measure up on these attributes or norms are then considered deviant and treated accordingly. The processes underlying this phenomenon are considered in the following section.

SOCIAL CATEGORIZATION

Although human beings are presumed to differ on a great number of traits, attributes, behaviors, and beliefs, classifications are ordinarily made according to only a few of these. Thus, individuals are commonly thought of as belonging to similar groups according to skin color but not according to the color of eyes or hair. Similarly, individuals are sorted (in schools) according to intellectual ability but not according to perceptual or motor ability.

In some instances school children have been (and still are) grouped on the basis of attributes which are completely irrelevant to school achievement or grouped in ways that clearly attenuate their academic performance. The most conspicuous example of this occurrence is in the grouping of school children on the basis of skin color (Coleman, *et al.,* 1966). Again, orthopedically handicapped children are frequently excluded from school but not necessarily because they are unable to benefit from classroom instruction.

In other areas of life classification patterns of various public and private institutions of the society reveal inconsistencies. To cite an example from a professional field, Peterson (1965) notes that psychiatric classification schemes have little to do with observable behavior in real life situations and typically carry no implications for the treatment that the client should undergo. The classification of individuals as delinquent varies greatly from state to state and within the same state as to what behaviors shall determine such a status. An informal type of classification operates in a belief of many employers that high school dropouts are necessarily incompetent workers. Actually, these employers' refusals to hire dropouts probably are more the result of custom than of any rational belief that skills learned in the later years of high school make the individual a more competent waitress, truck driver, gasoline station attendant, or whatever. Perhaps the best-known inconsistency in classification practices in this country is the fact that an individual eighteen to twenty-one years old is considered a juvenile as far as voting (in most states) is concerned but is considered an adult as far as the draft is concerned.

These examples are meant to illustrate that much of the everyday categorizing and classifying of people is not highly rational, consistent, relevant, or useful. Even if we are willing to posit some kind of innately given "urge to classify" (Menninger, Mayman, and Preger, 1963) that is characteristic of Homo sapiens, we are still left with the question of who gets classified and into what kind of group.

Dexter (1958, 1964) has been more specifically concerned with the antecedents of classification patterns in this country. In particular he has raised the question of why intellectual deviance rather than other forms of deviance (such as, for example, awkwardness) forms the basis upon which individuals are categorized. Dexter suggests that the practice of classifying persons as mildly retarded is an outgrowth of the ideology of (1) the "Protestant

NETTIE R. BARTEL AND SAMUEL L. GUSKIN

ethic" with its emphasis upon achievement as a justification of one's righteousness and of (2) the French Revolutionary notion of equality with its concern not only that the *opportunity* be equal but that the obligation to take advantage of the opportunity be equal. Dexter further contends that these twin ideologies led to compulsory education in America and, consequently, that a requirement for initiation into adult social status has become a "demonstration of formal skill in coordinating meaning"—that is, in reading, writing and arithmetic. He postulates that some retardates become social problems only because of this requirement and not because of any inherent biological attribute. If this is true, much of the cost and trouble of retardates in our society is due to the socially prescribed role of retardate rather than to any actual deficit in intelligence.

It may be that it is quite appropriate for the school to "discover" a child's intellectual deviance. Festinger (1954) suggests that a group is likely to be differentiated on the basis of some ability that is relevant and important to it. In the school intellectual ability is of great relevance and importance and, consequently, the school population is likely to be sorted according to intellectual criteria. We could hypothesize that when the school is made particularly aware of intellectual performance, or when its level of intellectual capability is made suspect, it would tend to redefine and sharpen the boundaries of where normalcy in intelligence ends and where deviance begins or, to quote Dentler and Erikson (1959), "to locate its position in social space by defining its symbolic boundaries" (p. 106).

Beatrice Wright (1960) has some suggestions as to why certain traits of individuals rather than others tend to be used by particular groups as the basis of differentiating the deviant from the nondeviant. She suggests that there are at least two aspects of a particular trait that help determine its importance: (1) *Self-connection gradient* refers to the degree to which traits are seen as more or less related to the central "core" of the individual himself. For example, the size of a person's feet is not seen as closely related to the "real" person, and we do not ordinarily categorize people on the size of their feet. On the other hand, such traits as skin color or ethnic origin are seen by many people as integral to what kind of a person an individual "really" is. Wright suggests that traits described by the verb "to be" are more closely connected to self than those described by the verb "to have." Thus we speak of an individual as *being* intelligent or retarded but as *having* brown or blond hair. (2) *Status value gradient* refers to the degree that certain attributes are more highly prized in our society than are other attributes. For example, the ability to achieve (intelligence) has high status value in our culture; therefore persons lacking in this ability will be perceived as deficient in a part of the "self." Athletic ability is also highly prized in this society (witness the size of the salaries paid to professional athletes). Consequently, individuals who exhibit physical disabilities that interfere with their motor functioning are likely to be classified unfavorably.

SIMILARITIES AND DIFFERENCES AMONG DEVIANT TYPES

If handicaps are created largely by social response and if we include within the notion of handicap such diverse phenomena as minority group membership and physical deformity, it is as if we are equating all social differences with one another and as if all distinctive characteristics may be thought of as handicapping and as resulting in quite comparable societal response. Guskin (1963a) made a study to determine the extent to which a variety of deviant types were seen as similar to one another. College students were asked to compare pairs of persons who were described briefly in a sentence such as "A child who has a heart condition and can't play vigorous games." The groups compared included a normal or typical child, an educationally inadequate child, an institutionalized "feeble-minded" child, a child grossly deficient in development, a delinquent child, a lower social class child, a physically handicapped child, an emotionally disturbed child, an autistic child (severely withdrawn), and an unpopular child. The students were asked to rate each pair on the degree of similarity between the two types of children.

Some of the more relevant results are shown in Table 2–1. Most of the groups are seen as very different from the normal child, but the lower social class child and the physically handicapped child are seen as only somewhat different from the normal. The seriously retarded are seen as not very different from other retarded and disturbed types but as extremly different from the physically handicapped. The physically handicapped child was seen as also very different from the delinquent child and lower social class child but not very different from the withdrawn and unpopular children.Since the relationships found might be limited to the specific description of the handicap, alternate specific descriptions were presented to another group. For example, the physically handicapped child was presented as "a child who wears braces as a result of hav-

ing had polio" rather than a child with a heart condition. Similar results were obtained.

Although there is some basis for grouping very diverse kinds of deviation with the traditional handicapping conditions, there are also substantial distinctions among deviant groups. However, distinctions exist among the traditional handicaps (for example, physical versus severe mental handicap) and not merely between the traditional handicaps and other kinds of deviance.

TABLE 2-1

PERCEIVED DIFFERENCES
AMONG DEVIANT GROUPS

	Mean Perceived Difference from:		
Comparison Child	Normal or Typical Child	Institutionalized "Feeble-minded"	Physically Handicapped
Normal or typical	–	3.7	1.9
Institutionalized feeble-minded	3.7	–	3.6
Grossly deficient developmentally	3.1	1.4	2.6
Educationally inadequate	3.3	1.7	3.0
Autistic	2.8	2.5	2.2
Emotionally disturbed	2.7	1.8	2.6
Unpopular	3.1	1.9	2.0
Delinquent	3.3	2.7	3.9
Lower social class	1.7	3.1	3.1
Physically handicapped	1.9	3.6	–

Approximate meaning of scale:
0.0–no difference at all   3.0–very different
1.0–slightly different   4.0–extremely different
2.0–fairly different

NETTIE R. BARTEL AND SAMUEL L. GUSKIN

What other criteria may be used for grouping together very different kinds of behavior under the common category of handicap? Consistent with our approach to examine closely the professional's response to handicapping conditions, it is important to note that what is common to many of the categories we call handicapped here is a common form of social treatment, either formal or informal; for example, segregation, institutionalization, or creation of special educational arrangements. Arrangements for the mentally ill, the mentally retarded, criminals, and the severely sensory disabled have much in common. These common treatment patterns will be discussed in greater depth later in this chapter.

Are there more general criteria we can use for recognizing a handicap? It seems that what is common to all those conditions we are here calling handicaps is that society or a social group or other individuals have raised some question about the competence of another individual or group or about the attractiveness of the individual or group. The questioning of competence can be seen in the protective behavior of others, a dependency relationship which society provides members of that particular type, for example, the mentally ill or mentally retarded. The failure to meet standards of attractiveness is noticeable in the avoidance behavior of others toward members of that category, as, for example, the facially disfigured.

The distinction between unattractiveness and incompetence is more observable is some instances than others. Although a prominent facial scar or disfigurement presents a clear case of unattractiveness with no implications for incompetence, and the "dumb blond" represents incompetence but not unattractiveness, there are individuals whose stimulus value involves

both dimensions. Thus the orthopedically handicapped may well be limited in actual ability as well as in attractiveness; similarly, the mentally ill may elicit in others feelings of both protectiveness and avoidance.

LABELING, DEFINING, AND RECOGNIZING HANDICAPS

We have suggested how society creates handicaps through defining standards that others cannot meet and through creating distinctive modes of treatment for those who fail to come up to the arbitrary standards of a group. Society and social groups have a much more efficient way of handicapping an individual or group. Without clearly evaluating the extent to which an individual or group meets their own standards, a person may be rapidly identified as distinctively incompetent or unattractive as a result of merely placing a label upon him, for example, the label "mentally retarded" or "mentally ill." There are few who feel that such a label is acceptable for themselves. As a matter of fact, a study by Edgerton (1967) shows that among forty-eight subjects leaving an institution for the mentally retarded, he was unable to find one who accepted the definition of himself as retarded. It is obvious why this is the case. The label "mentally retarded" or "mentally ill" immediately sets into operation a series of value judgments about the individual and perhaps a series of important consequences for social interactions and even legal intervention and a major change in life circumstances.

The application of the label "mentally ill" is so significant for the individual and his associates that there is often an extensive period of negotiation, in both "non-developed" as well as modern western societies, before such labels are accepted as legitimate. A study by Edgerton (1969) of the recognition of mental illness in certain East African groups illustrates how a large proportion of those labeled "mentally ill" are labeled as such because the label is functional for the individual or his clan or some other group. In one instance a clan was able to avoid retribution for a murderer who was labeled "psychotic." In another case an individual who was diagnosed as being mentally ill was rediagnosed as being only temporarily disturbed in response to pressure from the members of his family who had high personal involvement in the future professional success of the child. In our own society we see similar negotiations in the case of murderers whose attorneys are attempting to keep them from facing the death penalty or by spouses attempting to rid themselves of unhappy marriages. A more common situation involves placing the label "mentally retarded" on a child within the public schools, where teacher, psychologist, principal, and parents may become involved in the negotiations (which the parents usually lose). A study by Hersh (1969) suggests there may be at least an unconscious conspiracy between teacher and psychologist to define a child as "incompetent." In Hersh's investigation, examiners were given biased referrals from teachers indicating the teacher's estimate of the child's competence. Unknown to the testers, the referrals were assigned at random to children. Examiners obtained lower IQ scores on an individual intelligence test for those children with negative referrals than they did for comparable children on whom they had received favorable referrals. In a more typical public school situation, the psychologist may know that a teacher and principal desperately want to

remove a child from his regular class and the only place for him to go is a "special class for the mentally retarded" for which the child must obtain an IQ of 79 or less to qualify. It seems unlikely that under these conditions the psychologist will expend effort in motivating the child or give him the benefit of the doubt.

Why is labeling so prevalent? We have already suggested its efficiency. If a person has been provided with the label, he does not need to go through the full evaluation process with each individual he meets. The major advantage of this is to protect the observer from a serious error based on inadequate information. The problem with the control that labels have over our behavior is that most labels either are not based on valid information or lead to invalid treatment assumptions. The label "mentally retarded," for example, may be assigned to a child on the basis of his performance on an intelligence test given in a language that he is only beginning to learn. The label "emotionally disturbed" may be the result of the teacher's inability to cope with an overactive child. The treatment for the "retarded" child may be placement in a class where the teacher avoids teaching academic subject matter, thus further retarding his academic growth. For the "disturbed" child, treatment may consist of placing him with a group of aggressive children equally unacceptable to their teachers, and also termed "disturbed," who may teach him more unacceptable behavior. Notice how the treatment may only compound the problem and foster greater incompetence or unacceptable behavior in the child.

The potential advantage of the labeling process can be seen in those cases where the label prevents mistreatment of a person who would otherwise be assumed to be capable of more acceptable behavior.

Nettie R. Bartel and Samuel L. Guskin

Knowing a person is deaf prevents us from treating him as insulting when he doesn't respond to our requests. Being forewarned that a child is retarded will enable us to be wary of interpreting failure on a task as intentional uncooperativeness. Nevertheless, even an appropriate-seeming interpretation of a label can have unfortunate effects. As we have suggested above, children legitimately labeled retarded or disturbed are frequently placed in an environment with other children of similar diagnosis. This treatment appears self-defeating when one considers that their problem might in fact derive from having lived in an emotionally, socially, or intellectually inadequate environment. In fact an influential theory on the etiology of delinquent behaviors suggests that this undesirable behavior is the result of excess association with persons exhibiting the behavior (Sutherland and Cressey, 1960). If children learn from their peers—and most persons agree that they do—then placing deviant children with others of their own kind is disastrous, for they will simply learn more delinquent, disturbing, or retarded behavior. The normal classroom and community environment might be a much more positive place for them.

The greatest problem of labels is their tendency to become overgeneralized. Instead of thinking of a child who has intellectual limitations or emotional problems, we think of a "mentally retarded child" or an "emotionally disturbed child." Beatrice Wright (1960) has called this generalizing of the defect to the whole person a "spread effect." Persons expect that a child so labeled will differ from others in many respects aside from the specifically diagnosed disability. Some labels are particularly open to this misinterpretation. The label "mentally ill" is one of these. Although most persons seem to think that mentally ill persons differ from other people in almost all respects, some writers (for example, Braginsky, Braginsky, and Ring, 1969) have presented evidence that those considered to be chronically mentally ill show patterns of behavior very similar to those of other persons.

Stereotyping, or responding to labels, is most understandable when no other information is available about persons. It seems least justifiable when we know much from direct contact with an individual. One of the authors has investigated what happens when the label "mentally retarded" and other labels are presented alone and presented as a characteristic of an observed individual.It is clear that persons, whether they be college students or typical members of the community, have some conception of what a "mentally retarded" individual is like (Guskin, 1963b). Table 2–2 compares the judgments held by noncollege people of the characteristics of a "typical child, an average 18-year-old boy who has just finished high school" and an "18-year-old boy who has just returned home to live after being in a state training school for the feebleminded or mentally defective." On the basis of these differences, we can construct a stereotype of the retarded and then evaluate the extent to which specific persons' judgments of individuals resemble or differ from the stereotype. Such an index may be called "perceived subnormality," a high score representing the assignment of more of the retarded traits to an observed person. In the studies carried out thus far, the observed person has once been a written character sketch or case study, another time an actual mentally retarded child observed through a one-way mirror, and in a third investigation a film of a retarded child. In each study, the observed or stimulus person was presented with and

TABLE 2-2

TABLE 2-3

STEREOTYPE OF DEFECTIVES COMPARED WITH DESCRIPTION OF AVERAGE PERSON

MEAN PERCEIVED SUBNORMALITY SCORES

Stimulus Person	Label (n = 25)	Control (n = 25)
Bob	24.04	20.52
Alice	26.16	17.48

	Percent of 50 Non-college Persons Choosing Sub-normal Term in Describing an Individual Who Is:	
	Defective	Average
Quiet (talkative)	88	8
Timid (confident)	86	14
Unintelligent (bright)	74	6
Abnormal (normal)	68	4
Strange (ordinary)	84	22
Helpless (capable)	72	12
Clumsy (skillful)	80	24
Unpleasant (likeable)	40	2
Unfriendly (friendly)	38	0
Lazy (ambitious)	36	16
Irresponsible (reliable)	76	36
Sloppy (neat)	54	16
Careless (careful)	68	32
Nervous (calm)	80	40
Dissatisfied (happy)	48	22
Quick-tempered (self-controlled)	56	36
Inconsiderate (good)	30	28

without labels to different observers. Table 2–3 shows the mean perceived subnormality score obtained for two typewritten character sketches, each with and without the label (Guskin, 1963*b*). The specific stimulus persons are described below:

Bob Jackson is about 31 years old, is not married, and lives in a small town in a midwestern state. Since leaving (high school/a state training school for the feebleminded) at age 18, he has worked off and on at several jobs. He works most of the time, but rarely holds a job for more than a year. Two or three evenings a week he goes out for a beer and occasionally picks up a girl. Most of the other men his age in town are married and many of them have left town to look for jobs elsewhere. Bob doesn't appear to be bothered by this and seems fairly settled with his way of life (p. 571).

Alice Carter is a single girl of about 20 who lives with her parents in a fairly large southern city. She went to school until she was 16, (but was in a special class for mentally retarded or backward children/and was doing average school work before she left school). Her parents have had a good deal of trouble with her outside of school since she was about 13, and by the time she was 16 she had gotten a reputation for looseness among the young men of the neighborhood. Her parents have decided to do something about it, and so they are thinking of sending her to (a state training school for the feebleminded/live with some relatives in another city) (p. 572).

The labeled sketches were perceived as significantly more subnormal than the unlabeled sketch. Equally interesting is the greater impact of the label on the judgment of Alice than on the judgment of Bob. An examination of the personality sketches may suggest reasons for this difference. For example, Bob may be seen as "cured" by some because his label was applied in the past and not in the present, whereas Alice's present as well as past behavior has been labeled retarded. Other interpretations are, of course, possible. But the important point here is that labeling is not as simple a process as we might think. It is not indiscriminate in its impact.

Utilizing the personality sketch approach, Jaffe (1965) carried out a similar investigation with physical disability and found that the person with the label was responded to much more favorably than the label and even more favorably than the same person without the label. Some disability labels may then lead to more positive reactions to individuals.

In the second study mentioned earlier (Guskin, 1962b) four mentally retarded children (two boys, two girls; IQ 45 to 55; ages nine to fourteen; no dramatic physical symptoms) were observed twice, initially at play and then talking to a female teacher. Ratings were made of the child after each of the two brief (ten-minute) periods of observation. Observers of the same child were given different labeling information about the child prior to observation, either that the child was mentally retarded, the child's correct age, or the fact that the child had a speech defect. (In fact, all labels provided relatively accurate information.) Other observers in a control condition were given no such information. Findings on perceived subnormality are shown in Table 2–4.

TABLE 2-4

INFLUENCE OF LABELS ON
JUDGMENTS OF OBSERVED CHILDREN

| Label | Number of Observers | Mean Perceived Subnormality | |
		Judgment 1	Judgment 2
None	11	14.64	15.18
Speech defect	11	12.45	11.73
Correct age	11	15.45	17.73
Mentally retarded	12	14.67	16.00

Differences were greater after the second (verbal) period of observation. The lowest perceived subnormality occurred when the child was said to have a speech problem. It seems that one of the key cues to subnormality is inadequate language and the speech-problem label limits the degree to which an observer will generalize from such inadequate language. The most subnormality was perceived when the child's correct age was given. Apparently, observers tend to normalize others if they can. Less competent behavior can be attributed to younger age unless the child's age is known. The mental retardation label did not result in significant differences from the control condition.

Once again we have seen that labeling is more complex than one might assume. In this study one defect label (speech problem) had a somewhat positive effect, another neutral label (correct age) had a detrimental effect, and the most negative label (mental retardation) had no demonstrable effect. Negative labels can prevent negative evaluation by limiting an overresponse to observed inadequacies. ("This child only has a speech defect not a more general mental defect.") Neutral labels can induce negative evaluation by providing a frame of reference within which the observed behavior is seen as more inadequate. ("Is he really that old? If so, there must be something seriously wrong with him.") Finally, negative labels ("mental retardation") can be ineffective for some reason undetermined from this study.

The final study to be described here (Guskin, 1962a) attempted to see if the label "mental retardation" might be demonstrated to have an effect if we collected more observations on individual children. Short films of two of the children who had participated in the previous study were shown to forty-two observers. Each child was observed in two sequences, first without sound (the child shooting a dart gun at a target for about one minute) and then with sound (talking to a teacher or playing verbally with the teacher, for about two minutes). Half of the observers received instructions indicating both children were in special classes for mentally retarded children; the other half were informed only that the children were in public school classes.

The findings are shown in Table 2-5.

TABLE 2-5

INFLUENCE OF LABEL "RETARDED" ON JUDGMENTS OF TWO RETARDED CHILDREN OBSERVED IN TWO SHORT FILM SEQUENCES

	N	Mean Perceived Subnormality Scores	
		Girl	Boy
Control	21	16.07	16.19
Retarded	21	16.00	18.64
Judgment 1	42	14.85	17.85
Judgment 2	42	17.21	16.97

They seem quite clear. The label "mentally retarded" had absolutely no effect on judgments of the girl, but it resulted in the boy's being perceived as more subnormal. Equally clearly, having a second chance at observing (and more information on which to make judgments) had almost no effect or even a slight positive effect on judgment of the boy, but it resulted in the girl's being seen as substantially more subnormal. Another way of summarizing the findings is to say that these two children are perceived as similar in subnormality if no label is presented or if a more extensive period of observation is allowed. But if *either* the "retarded" label *is* presented or the children's language behavior is *not* presented, the girl is seen as more competent than the boy. Again, no simple labeling phenomenon can explain these findings. A better knowledge of the children's stimulus characteristics does help. The boy is awkward and holds his head tilted and his mouth open, whereas the girl is relatively normal in appearance and gross motor behavior. This explains why on initial observation the girl appeared more competent. Her language behavior, however, shows her to be no more verbally capable than a young preschooler, whereas the boy shows great motor difficulties in verbal expression, but, if anything, greater language sophistication than was implied by his initial gross motor difficulties. Thus, they are seen very similarly on the second observation.

The different effect of the label on the two children may possibly be attributed to the ambiguity of the boy as a stimulus. There does seem to be something wrong with him right from the beginning, but observers must have had difficulty determining what was special about him. The label "mentally retarded" seems to have been accepted as an explanation of this unusual behavior. In contrast the girl acted and looked quite normal initially, which might have led judges to interpret the label as very mild retardation, in effect, ignoring or underplaying the label. After being observed speaking, she appeared so inadequate that the label did not add information. To summarize, labeling seems to have no function and little use when clearcut observational evidence is available on which to make judgments. When there is little observational evidence or ambiguous evidence, judgments tend to be invalid, unstable, and open to strong influence from labels.

NETTIE R. BARTEL AND SAMUEL L. GUSKIN

SOCIAL ROLES AND EXPECTATIONS

We have seen how labels can have varied consequences for the way persons are perceived by others. However, the importance of these consequences is limited by the extent to which such perceptions lead to differences in behavior. Those labels that refer to specific positions in our society, such as occupations, not only lead to perceptions of likely personal characteristics but also to perceptions regarding likely and desired behaviors to be shown by members of this category (Hughes, 1945). Such perceptions are often called "role expectations," that is, expectations of behavior to be found in particular roles. Teachers are expected to do different things than secretaries; parents are expected to do different things than children; husbands to behave differently than wives. Are disabled persons expected to do things differently than nondisabled persons?

"Expectation" has two meanings—the belief that something is likely to happen and the desire or demand or obligation that a particular thing happen. Both meanings are relevant in the processes through which an individual comes to view another as deviant and in the viewer's subsequent attitudes toward the deviant. Goffman (1963) has pointed out that the anticipation in meeting a stranger has a component of expecting that he will possess certain attributes—a sound, whole body, functioning sensory abilities, normal intellectual ability, and so on. However, people do not merely anticipate that this will be the case—they transform their anticipations into "normative expectations, into righteously presented demands" (p. 2).

If people see a person with dark glasses and a white cane, they are more careful in how they walk near him and may offer him help in crossing a street. He may accept, despite a lack of need, because he has found that people respond more pleasantly when he lets them lead him than when he refuses their offer. His family and friends may assume that he will never be self-supporting and never marry and his attempts at courtship and independence may be rebuffed by others who can't see his competencies, only his disability. In such an instance, the social group has defined the role blind person as one similar to that of a child, and the result may be childlike role behavior, that is, withdrawal into a comfortable dependency on his parents and friends.

The existence and implications of the role of blind person have recently been studied by Scott (1969). Scott points out that many activities termed rehabilitative are in fact socialization procedures by which the person with impaired vision is inducted into the role of blind person. Thus Scott argues that there is nothing intrinsic to blindness that causes blind people to be docile, helpless, or dependent. "Blindness is a social role that people must learn to play. Blind men are made."

When the assumption of dependence leads to dependent behavior, we are observing an instance of what has been called a "self-fulfilling prophecy." Robert Rosenthal has written much and carried out many studies on this topic. In his earlier studies Rosenthal (1966) found that the results of psychological experiments were influenced by the experimenter's beliefs. For example, if the experimenter was told he was working with bright rats, the rats earned better learning scores than if the experimenter had been told he was studying dull rats. Rosenthal felt that the results of these studies had considerable applicability to educational problems, that teachers who believed that they had good students would get better work from the same students than if they expected poor performance.

In one well-publicized study, Rosenthal and Jacobson (1968) gave all the children in one elementary school a test that they indicated to teachers was a measure of children's readiness to show an intellectual growth spurt. The investigators later gave each teacher a list of those in her class who were supposed to show such spurts. Unknown to the teachers, the names had been drawn at random. That is, the experimenters chose about 20 percent of the children's names at random from a list of all the children in the class and arbitrarily designated these as the "potential bloomers."

Later in the school year, the investigators returned to give the children the same test again. The test was actually a group intelligence test with which the teachers were not familiar. The authors reported that the experimental children, that is, the predicted "bloomers," gained significantly more in intelligence than the control children. The prophecy, they claimed, was fulfilled. Unfortunately, the study has several weaknesses in experimental methodology and reporting. (See, for example, Thorndike, 1968.) Nevertheless, the interest it aroused has led to several other studies.

Rosenthal and Jacobson proposed that the effect they found might have resulted from unconscious cues about the child's competence which were conveyed from the teacher to the child through the teacher's facial expression, gesture, tone of voice, and so forth. The child's feelings of competence might then lead him to try harder and do better. An alternative interpretation is that teacher expectancy is most likely to influence pupil behavior when the expectation results in very overt changes in the pattern of teaching. Thus, a teacher may put a first-grade child into a higher or lower reading group, based on either tests or knowledge of the child's family, and how quickly the child learns to read may be determined by his reading group's rate of exposure to new reading material.

Beez (1968) carried out an investigation of this kind of phenomenon in a controlled teaching situation. Each of sixty summer school graduate students was asked to tutor a five-year-old Headstart child for half an hour. The first task consisted of teaching the child to recognize as many words or signs (for example, "stop," "men") as possible in ten minutes. Each tutor was shown a realistic looking but actually contrived psychological report on his child. Half of these reports indicated that the child had low potential for school learning, the other half that he had high. The reports were assigned at random to both tutors and pupils. The group of tutors who received the "low" reports were comparable in terms of teaching experience and educational background to those receiving the positively biased reports. Similarly, the group of pupils on whom the negatively biased reports were made were comparable in terms of age and vocabulary level to the group on whom "high" reports were made. Tutors who were given reports that indicated a high expectancy for their pupils presented more words for their pupils to learn; out of a possible twenty words they presented an average of about ten, whereas for tutors with reports indicating a low expectancy for their pupils the average was about five words presented. The learning achievement of the pupils reflected the tutors' expectancy with the high group averaging about six words learned to three for the low. Few low tutors and pupils performed as well as high tutors and pupils. In short, what the teacher believed as a consequence of the prior report influenced the number of words presented by teachers, which, in turn influenced the number of words learned by pupils. Pupil response thus supported the teacher's initial belief about the pupil, though in reality it was directly a result of teacher behavior and not pupil competence. Observations showed that the fewer words presented and learned when the teachers' expectancy of pupil ability was low came about because the teachers spent more time explaining and repeating words.

The possible effect of either actual pupil competence or teacher experience was also examined. Peabody Picture Vocabulary Test scores were available for all children with vocabulary quotients (roughly comparable to IQs) ranging from about 65 to 125. Yet no substantial relationship could be found between pupil vocabulary score and either teacher behavior or pupil word-learning. Likewise, no relationship was found between teacher behavior and amount of teaching experience, though experience ranged from zero to twenty years. Differences in learning could be accounted for by teacher expectancy but not by teacher experience or pupil competence. The study also found that tutors rated the two groups of children differently, and in accord with expectancies—on ratings of competence, task performance, future school success, and other measures.

The dramatic findings of this study—that critical differences in teaching pattern and resulting learning can be dependent upon the expectancies for pupils held by teachers—seem to have enormous implications for the education and treatment of the physically and mentally disabled. The handicapped may have less chance of becoming normal because they are felt to need special treatment, that is, teaching at a lower level of competence. What seems to be critical here is whether the assumption is made that the person has potential for intellectual or motor or social development or whether it is assumed that he can make little progress. A parallel belief is that of the teacher or rehabilitation worker that he can have an impact on the learning or adjustment of the pupil or client.

An investigation by Carter (1969) was concerned with this issue of whether the teacher's belief in his ability to control his environment has an influence on his teaching response to information about the child's potential. Tutors were selected who were either internal or external in locus of control (Rotter, 1966). Internally controlled persons are those who see events as a consequence of their own behavior; externally controlled persons see events as outside of their control and unrelated to their own behavior. As in Beez's study, the tutors were then given psychological reports and asked to teach sight vocabulary to preschool children. Carter anticipated that internal tutors would ignore the biasing information and respond equally effectively to children regardless of the psychological report, whereas the externals would rely heavily on the report and treat pupils in accord with expected differences. The results were quite in the opposite direction. Externally controlled tutors showed no expectancy effect, whereas internal tutors showed results similar to those found by Beez; they taught more words to the high expectancy children than to the low expectancy children.

What might explain these findings? Other research has shown that internal persons tend to be more effective utilizers of information. They seek out more task-relevant information, apparently because they think that what they do does make a difference, and they modify their behavior accordingly to cope with special problems. In this experimental situation their behavior was not more effective because (1) the information they were provided was incorrect and (2) the strategies they thought would improve learning (going more slowly and repeating more often for less able children) were not appropriate for the level of difficulty of this learning task.

The results of the Carter study force us to reexamine our assumptions regarding the nature of the expectancy effect and ways of coping with it. As with stereotypes the first assumption generally made about this type of response is that it is naive, inappropriate, and ineffective. Now we have found that those persons (internals) usually thought to be more effective are the same persons who are most responsive to this expectancy phenomenon. They explore and utilize whatever information is available and apparently relevant to their performance. It seems that the psychological report is assumed by most teachers and prospective teachers to be a valid and useful source of information. If responses by teachers to the implications or recommendations of a psychological report are inappropriate, it means either we are providing inaccurate information (which was the case in the Beez and Carter studies) or that we have not given teachers the training or task-relevant information necessary to carry out effective teaching. The solution to the problem is not then to select only those teachers who do not hold or utilize expectancies about pupil behavior or to train teachers to come without biases to the teaching situation. It seems that we must give teachers strategies for finding the most appropriate sources of information, provide more valid information, and provide techniques, training, and materials to implement the implied suggestions of the information. This approach would seem useful for the various professions that deal with disabled individuals.

The expectancy studies we have presented examined reactions to information *about* a person rather than cues from the person. One could build expectancies from interaction with the person, rather than seeking information about the person from other sources. The empathy or individual sensitivity orientation often found in the helping professions emphasizes the need for accurate perception of the characteristics and feelings of the individual with whom one is working. Much research has investigated the possibility that one could identify persons who are particularly accurate in perceiving others and that these persons would be particularly effective in dealing with others. Unfortunately, these hypotheses have not been supported. Accuracy in judging one person has little relationship to accuracy in judging other persons; accuracy in judging one kind of behavior is largely unrelated to accuracy in judging other kinds of behavior. Much of whatever accuracy does exist in judging others is the result of accurate stereotypes. That is, a judge can more accurately size up an individual if he has an accurate perception of what people in general are like; he can more accurately evaluate a specific eight-year-old if he knows what eight-year-olds in general are like. Very little accuracy is added by the degree to which the judge individualizes his evaluation (Cline, 1964). In other words, the understanding a perceiver has of persons in a particular position or place in society is his best

NETTIE R. BARTEL AND SAMUEL L. GUSKIN

clue to understanding individuals. This fits very well with the importance that role expectations have for behavior.

ROLE EXPECTATIONS, SELF-CONCEPT, AND BEHAVIOR

It has been shown that expectancies held by others may influence role performance. The general phenomenon is not difficult to understand. When speaking to a young child, an adult talks differently than when speaking to another adult. When an adult talks to an adolescent whom he thinks is childlike, he will speak differently than to an adolescent he thinks is adultlike. The result of talking at a lower level may be to arouse a lower level response. If you ask a simple question, you are likely to get a simple answer. This expectancy effect is then mediated by the behavioral changes in the person holding the expectations and may not require that the actor (the person for whom expectations are held) be aware of the expectations. The Beez and Carter studies illustrated this. The preschool children were probably not aware of what tutors' expectancies were. The children tried equally to learn the material they were presented, but tutors' expectancies led to different presentation rates.

In contrast to this behaviorally mediated effect is the kind of mediation proposed by Rosenthal and Jacobson (1968) in which the teacher unconsciously and subtly communicates a positive or negative evaluation of the child to him. This then leads the child to see himself as relatively adequate or inadequate. His own self-estimate then influences his behavior. If he thinks he can cope with something difficult he will attempt it. If he thinks he is incompetent he gives up.

There is considerable evidence that children who achieve more poorly in school see themselves as less academically competent than their peers (Brookover *et al.* 1965). However, it is difficult to demonstrate that the low self-evaluation leads to low performance. (It is more obvious that poor performance leads to recognition of relatively low ability.) The most dramatic way of demonstrating the influence of self-perception on performance is to try to influence self-perception and note its effects on behavior. Few studies have shown this effect. One interesting investigation by Brookover and his colleagues (1965) involved training parents to improve their children's self-evaluation regarding academic ability. The training program resulted in improved academic performance on the part of their children. However, this effect did not carry over to the next academic year. Furthermore, similar training programs with teachers and other personnel failed to modify children's achievement. It appears, then, that the most effective way to modify children's self-evaluation is to improve their performance, but the reverse effect, getting self-evaluation to influence performance, is more difficult to institute.

The self-evaluation referred to above is a direct estimate by the child of how well he does in school. Another kind of self-concept that might mediate between others' expectations and a child's behavior is locus of control, which was examined earlier as it influenced teachers' behavior. The child's feeling that what he does really makes a difference is related to how well he performs in school. Generally, as he gets older and more competent, he comes to feel more internally controlled (Bialer, 1961). The degree of internal control is related, however, to the child's ability and achievement in school; the lower the ability and achievement, the more external the control. Those groups that perform more poorly in school, (for example, lower socio-economic class and Negro children) are as a group more external (Battle and Rotter, 1963; Bartel, 1968; Coleman *et al.,* 1966). As a result of failure in school and/or poor opportunities outside of school to influence their environment, these children feel less potent. Again, the most likely way to increase a person's feeling of potency is probably to demonstrate that one can have some impact in obtaining rewards from the environment.

In a recent study, Lipp *et al.* (1968) attempted to measure the way in which internally controlled and externally controlled physically disabled subjects performed on a perceptual task measuring defensiveness about disability. Contrary to their hypothesis, Lipp and his associates found that externally controlled subjects were less denying of their disability than were internally controlled subjects. This finding is consistent with the logic expressed by Bialer (1961, p. 317) when he states that externally controlled subjects are not likely to have, or are incapable of having feelings of inferiority, because they do not see themselves as responsible for their failures. Thus, it is interesting to note the possibility that in the case of handicapped persons, the externally controlled individuals may manifest satisfactory adjustments, feeling that their condition is due to luck, fate, chance, or the will of God. The internally controlled handicapped person on the other hand, who by definition believes that his success or failure in the world is a result of his own doing, may feel guilt-ridden and blameworthy.

Though there is little evidence that disabled persons have lower general self-evaluation than others, it seems reasonable to expect that disabled persons have particular areas in which they feel impotent or incompetent. These may be based on realistic limitations. As Wright (1960) has indicated, the problem is to prevent the spread of this effect to the rest of the self-concept.

Two possible mediators for expectancy effects have been discussed: changes in the behavior of others and changes in self-evaluation. A third method is the societal institutionalization of expectancies, that is, the creation of formal procedures for handling persons for whom special expectancies exist. A child is placed in a special class for the physically or mentally handicapped; an adult is sent to a residential "school"; rehabilitation agencies are charged with responsibility for specific tasks. In these cases, the disabled person is treated differently from others as a result of formal rules, regulations, and laws and not merely because other individuals who interact with him hold special expectations for him. The effects of treatment arrangements for the disabled will be discussed later in this chapter.

PLAYING THE DISABLED ROLE

The discussion thus far has focused on the individual as a relatively passive receiver of others' expectations. An alternative view sees the individual as actively seeking a satisfying role by matching those expectations that fit the desired role and violating those expectations associated with distasteful roles. This way of viewing the disabled role may be seen in the work of Braginsky, Braginsky, and Ring (1969) in the area of mental illness.

Braginsky, Braginsky, and Ring (1969) claim that mentally ill persons are largely

NETTIE R. BARTEL AND SAMUEL L. GUSKIN

like other people and that their distinctive behavior results from the special situation in which they are placed. Thus they feel that chronically mentally ill persons in institutions are there because they want to be there and that they treat the residential hospital much as other people would treat a resort hotel, as a place of leisure which enables them to avoid the stresses of daily living. To demonstrate the self-motivated aspect of the behavior of such patients, these investigators noted what happened when they told one group of patients they were about to be interviewed to determine whether they should leave the hospital and told a comparable group that the purpose of the interview was to determine if they should be placed in a "locked ward." The first group acted much sicker in the interview, describing more serious symptoms to the interviewer and in general describing themselves less favorably than the patients in the second group. Thus, the long-term institutionalized mental patient can make himself look healthy to prevent being thrown into an unpleasant locked ward or he can appear disturbed to prevent being put back into the nonhospital community, where he does not have the skill with which to cope with the demands of living.

This analysis may be appropriate for other handicapped persons as well. Handicapped persons may make themselves appear more or less competent and attractive to maximize their personal satisfaction. An extreme, and obvious, case would be beggars as in Brecht's *Threepenny Opera*, who simulate or emphasize handicaps to arouse pity and collect money. In *The Threepenny Opera* Mr. Peachum is a businessman who provides the training and equipment to enable poor persons to simulate helpless, pitiful, handicapped persons. One can move from this extreme to the fund-raising campaigns of some agencies for the handicapped which have been criticized for portraying overly dependent persons (Wright, 1960). Another illustration might be a blind person who carries a cane, not for mobility reasons, but to be sure that others recognize his disability and make allowances for it. In contrast, another blind person who has serious difficulty getting around may avoid use of guide dogs or canes and put himself through an extremely difficult and dangerous training process to master simulation of normal mobility patterns.

The child who has been having school difficulty, who has been referred for testing for special class placement, and is about to be classified as mentally retarded by the schools may pass or fail the psychological (IQ) examination depending on his awareness of the purposes of the testing and his motivation to remain in the regular class. Similarly, a child who is retested by the schools after placement may modify his performance to match his desire to remain in or leave the special class. Thus, a child who has been in special classes for three years may perform well if he thinks there is some danger of being placed in a class for the more severely retarded children and perform poorly if he anticipates that he might be thrown back into a regular class. As a matter of fact, such performance discrepancies might be used as an objective criterion for child satisfaction with special classes.

In summary, it may be that much behavior that we think of as intrinsic characteristics of mentally ill, mentally retarded, or physically handicapped persons may be attributed to their desire to match role expectations associated with more satisfactory outcomes and to violate expectations associated with unsatisfactory outcomes.

PERSONAL MANAGEMENT OF STIGMA

The individual's problems in management of his life circumstances within a "treatment" setting are very different from those out in the "real world," where the disability may open the person to devaluation by others.

In a penetrating analysis, Goffman (1963) has examined the question of personal management of a stigma. Goffman sees the problem as one that is common to the human situation; at one time or another the most normal individual finds himself in a social situation in which some little failing or trait becomes salient, threatening relationships with shame or embarrassment. Thus, there are situations in which it is a disadvantage to be black or white, Jew or Gentile, rich or poor, intellectual or retardate. From Goffman's point of view, then, the visibly stigmatized form one end of a continuum—from those who frequently or constantly find themselves in situations where an attribute must be actively managed to "normals" who only occasionally need to manage unfavorable information about themselves.

The degree of visibility of a handicap affects the degree to which an individual needs to be concerned with stigma management. This factor is involved in the distinction that Goffman makes between the *discredited* and the *discreditable*. Individuals with highly visible blemishes, such as disfiguring scars or amputations, are discredited—they rarely, if ever, are able to pass successfully, because the stigma is immediately evident to normals. The major problem faced by this group of individuals is that of tension management—how to minimize the obtrusive and disruptive effects of the attribute.

Discreditable individuals, on the other hand, are those whose disabilities are less visible and more easily concealed: for example, the epileptic, homosexual, or mentally ill. The prime concern of this group is that of information control—when, where, and to whom to reveal what. Whereas the discredited concentrate on covering or minimizing the effects of their disability on others, the discreditable exert effort in the precarious task of passing—trying to conceal those bits of personal information that might identify them as different. Both represent attempts to approximate normalcy, probably because of the great social rewards that inhere in being considered normal.

Whether the possessor of a given attribute will expose his trait or try to cover or pass depends, of course, on the value assigned to the deviant trait by the society in which he finds himself and also on the values that the individual himself attributes to the trait.

Special situations arise when the values of the individual and the larger group in which he finds himself do not coincide. This situation may arise from a need of the group to feel that its value system is not being challenged. For example, if intellectual competence or physical prowess are valued by members of the group, it follows that individuals deficient in these areas are expected to feel inferior, guilty, and blameworthy. This kind of expectation is articulated by the friend of an individual recently blinded—"You're a blind man now, you'll be expected to act like one. . . . People will be firmly convinced that you consider yourself a tragedy. They'll be disconcerted and even shocked to discover that you don't" (Chevigny, 1946, p. 71 and 76, cited in Wright, 1960, p. 15). Similarly, whites are frequently taken aback by blacks who confidently assert that "Black is beautiful," when for

NETTIE R. BARTEL AND SAMUEL L. GUSKIN

years whites had tried to believe that "they (Negroes) were to be sub-human—quasi-humans who not only preferred slavery but felt it best for them" (Grier and Cobbs, 1968, p. 32). The "nice" black was the one who had made a virtue of identification with the aggressor (whites) and who had adopted an ingratiating and compliant manner, implying his own inferiority (Grier and Cobbs, 1968, p. 66).

One factor that all forms of physical and mental disability have in common is that their presence is disturbing to others with whom the individual possessing the characteristic interacts. Goffman (1963) describes this disturbance as arising out of a discrepancy between a virtual social identity and an actual social identity, between the expectation that an individual will be whole, normal, and unblemished and the observation that he is in fact deformed, defective, or blemished (Goffman, 1963, pp. 2–3). The expectation becomes a righteously presented demand that the individual should approximate an ideal of what is normal, conforming, or good. By definition, the individual who fails to do so is considered not quite human.

There is some experimental evidence bearing on others' reactions to the disabled. Kleck (1968) has carried out a series of experimental studies on reactions to a person with a simulated leg amputation. In one investigation, in which the "amputee" was an interviewer, it was found that there was greater physiological arousal (GSR) when interacting with the amputee than when interacting with a nondisabled interviewer; shorter answers were given to questions from the amputee than from the nondisabled; and the person interviewed expressed more frequent conformity to the interviewer's beliefs when the interviewer was an amputee. The results suggest greater anxiety or tension

and less naturalness when interacting with a disabled person.

In a second similar study Kleck filmed the behavior of the subject being interviewed and had him rate the interviewer. Kleck found more favorable impressions of the disabled interviewer than the nondisabled, less movement in the presence of the disabled, and less variation in focus of visual attention when being interviewed by the amputee. As in the earlier study, opinions were distorted in the direction of that of the amputee. These findings also imply less freedom or more tension when interacting with the disabled.

In a third study the nondisabled person was asked to train two other persons in origami (Oriental paper folding) after being trained himself. One of the persons he trained was an "amputee"; both were confederates of the experimenter. The training sessions were monitored by a hidden television camera. Kleck measured the distance between the trainer and his student and found that the average interaction distance was less when interacting with the "normal" than the "disabled" person. However, this effect occurred only in the first teaching session, not the second. Similarly, a difference in impressions occurred only after the first and not the second session. The difference favored the amputee. Finally, disabled learners in both sessions were rated as more interested and motivated in the learning task. As in the first two investigations, verbal statements by the nondisabled seemed to be biased in favor of the disabled, but nonverbal measures suggested less comfort with the disabled. The third study adds the suggestive finding that some of the differences wear off after a period of time.

A series of studies by Jones (1968) examined the influence of the presence of a simulated "blind" person on the performance of other persons on a learning task. Although there was no observable influence on the learning task, subjects *said* their performance was impaired as a result of interaction with the blind person. This effect seems likely to appear in desegregation situations, where white teachers and students may complain about the harm done to the teaching and learning process. Similarly, teachers may complain that the presence of a retarded child reduces teaching efficiency, though this has not yet been demonstrated. Persons do experience tension while in such situations; this may lead them to think their performance is impaired when in fact it is not.

Farina and his associates have conducted a related series of investigations. Farina and Ring (1965) examined the influence of interaction with a presumed mentally ill person on performance on a cooperative game. Both persons were naïve subjects, but none, one, or both were privately informed that the other was mentally ill. It was found that perceiving the coworker as mentally ill enhanced performance. However, when the coworker was perceived as mentally ill, subjects preferred to work alone; they also tended to blame the mentally ill partner for inadequacies in their joint performance. The results make clear that discomfort may accompany improved performance under certain conditions.

These investigations were carried out in laboratory settings, which enabled control and measurement but raise questions about how well we can generalize to more typical situations. Schoggin (1965) reported an investigation in which observations were obtained in natural settings. Patterns of reactions of parents and teachers to physically handicapped children and to the nondisabled were found to be very similar. The children in this study were, however, only mildly disabled and were attending regular classes.

PARENTAL RESPONSE TO DISABILITY

Probably the most widely discussed reactions to disability are the responses of family members to disability. The distinctive impact of a handicapped child on family relations probably begins at the point of the parents' definition or labeling of a child as handicapped (Farber, 1968, p. 153). In the case of children who exhibit obvious disabilities at the time of birth, a major revision is required in the general expectancy of the parents that the infant will be normal. Thus, many parents find an unfavorable diagnosis of their child unacceptable and spend time and resources seeking a physician or an agency which will yield a diagnosis that is more amenable to their beliefs (Wolfensberger, 1967). One would expect that in cases where the observable stimulus properties of the child were relatively discongruous, as in the case of a physically normal-looking child with greatly impaired motor or intellectual development, the parent might be even more reluctant to relinquish beliefs of normalcy as compared to cases where the stimulus properties of the child are congruous and unambiguous, as in the case of the variety of physical stigmata associated with Down's syndrome (Tallman, 1965).

Where prior beliefs regarding a child's essential normalcy are well entrenched (through verification over a period of years), as with an older child adventitiously brain-damaged or suffering from Wilson's disease, parents' belief systems would have to undergo drastic changes to accommodate the changed characteristics of the child. One would expect from stud-

NETTIE R. BARTEL AND SAMUEL L. GUSKIN

ies of selective perception and attitude change that rather convincing evidence would be needed to bring about belief changes (Bruner, 1951).

Once a member of a family is defined as "different," changes are made in the way the remaining members of the family interact with him, with each other, and with the community (Farber, 1968, pp. 152–176). Several investigations have examined the extent of change in family life due to the presence of a child who is defined as handicapped. Some of the effects of a handicapped child on the mother are common to different kinds of disabilities, whereas others are more specific. Klebanoff (1959) reported that mothers of brain-injured and retarded, and schizophrenic children were similar in child-rearing attitudes and that these attitudes were different from those of mothers of normal children. On the other hand, Cummings, Bayley, and Rie (1966) found differences in evidence of maternal stress in comparisons between the mothers of mentally retarded, chronically ill, and neurotic children. These results may suggest the existence of both a general change in attitude of mothers who learn there is something "wrong" or "different" about their child, plus additional effects that are dependent upon the unique nature of the child's disability and the management and personal adjustment problems it creates.

Although studies have been done on the extent to which college students and others make distinctions between various types of exceptionality (Guskin, 1963a), no studies have yet been reported on the extent to which parents of exceptional children distinguish their children from those with other forms of deviance. This question is an important one because the degree to which the parent believes his child is like or unlike another type of exceptionality may influence the way he interacts with his child and the behavior that he elicits from him. Thus the parent of a hyperactive brain-impaired child may reinforce infantile, incompetent behavior if he believes his child is similar to mentally retarded children; on the other hand, if he believes brain injury is akin to emotional disturbance he may tolerate outbursts of uncontrolled temper but not immature behavior. The degree to which parents identify their child with specific types of deviance is also likely to affect decisions regarding whether and where to institutionalize, prognosis for school and employment success, possibility of a "cure," and so on.

Parents' perception of the disability may or may not resemble that of professionals. There is a wide variation in the extent to which parents accept the diagnostic label that professionals deem appropriate for their child. From the researcher's point of view, this is an especially difficult question to work with, because those parents who reject the negative evaluation of their child (such as emotionally disturbed, mentally retarded, brain-injured) are generally not available for research purposes, because (1) they do not bring their child to the attention of professional agencies, or (2) if they do bring their child to a child-guidance clinic, psychologist, or the like and refuse to accept the proferred diagnosis, they are not likely to remain available for further study. Families (or teachers or employers) who are able to successfully cope with the different or unusual individual to the extent that he is able to pass as normal should be intensively studied—their coping strategies might provide clues to formal treatment and rehabilitation agencies on how to successfully integrate these individuals into the larger society. At present, most of the research information on the families of the exceptional has been gleaned from families that have not been successful in avoiding the formal classifying of their child as deviant—that is, most of the studies have been done with families who bring their children (or have them brought) to psychiatrists, family or child clinics, and courts, or with families that belong to such organizations as the National Association for Retarded Children. In one sense we have been studying only those families that have been unable to induct their children into normal roles, either as a result of the severity of the child's disability or the inadequacy of the family's coping strategies.

An interesting situation presents itself in cases in which children are professionally diagnosed and categorized as exceptional without the consent of the parents. Such a situation exists in most American public schools, where, due to compulsory education laws, a captive population is present. Routine administrations of intelligence tests effectively stratify children into normal and subnormal groups. This classification procedure has important implications for the child—changes are made in the type of curriculum to which he will be exposed, the kind of classmates he will have, the type of vocation he will be trained for, and the type of diploma he will receive when he graduates. How does the parent react to this? The question is an intriguing one, since most of the children classified as mildly retarded have no salient distinguishing characteristics, and most have been considered normal by their parents to that point (Meyerowitz, 1967).

What evidence is available (Meyerowitz, 1967; Olshansky and Schonfield, 1965) indicates that most parents in this situation do not accept the professional diagnosis which is imposed by the schools but persist in expressing their beliefs in the child's normalcy.

FORMAL MANAGEMENT OF DEVIANCE

All social systems, whether the family, peer group, school, or society at large, develop machinery for the detecting and processing of individuals who are considered different in characteristics important to the group. The identification and management of deviants occurs both formally and informally. Detection and processing of deviance may be as informal and uncomplicated as a parent discovering his child engaging in forbidden sexual activity, spanking him, and sending him to bed without supper, or a teacher having a child stand in the corner for hitting another child. However, of greater interest here are the formal agencies in a society that are established for the sole purpose of identifying and controlling individuals who are considered in need of such control. Depending on whether one is interested in behavioral, physical, or mental deviance, these agencies might include the police force, courts, and prisons, or rehabilitation workers and hospitals, or systematic procedures in the public schools for testing children's intelligence and placing them appropriately in special classes, schools, or institutions. Freidson (1965) in his elucidation of the functions of rehabilitation agencies notes that they carry on four major activities: (1) they specify what personal attributes shall be called handicaps, (2) they identify the population that meets the specifications, (3) they attempt to gain access to the target population, and (4) they attempt to modify the behavior of the target popula-

NETTIE R. BARTEL AND SAMUEL L. GUSKIN

tion to conform more closely to what the institutions believe are its potentialities.

The specification of one attribute rather than another as a manifestation of differentness is not frequently considered to be an aspect of social control. However, several interesting observations can be made if one takes seriously the possibility that the labeling of a particular characteristic as a handicap itself constitutes a first step in the management of deviance.

It has been documented that the incidence of a variety of deviant behaviors and characteristics varies with such factors as social class and ethnic background. Many possible interpretations may be suggested for this phenomenon. First, there may be systematic differences in the rate at which lower class, as compared with middle-class, individuals do in fact violate rules that are commonly accepted by both groups. A second alternative exists in the possibility that selective recording of deviation occurs—for example, individuals with high incomes are more likely to be able to afford a psychiatrist than are lower income individuals. Although psychiatrists may thus see more high-income patients, we cannot therefore argue that high-income individuals have a higher rate of mental illness than do low-income people. Similarly, the recording of criminal behavior is usually the function of police departments. If systematic biases in the attitude of the police toward certain groups, or systematic political pressure is brought to bear on police to clean up crime in certain neighborhoods, official records will show variations in crime rate that have very little to do with the actual rate of crime.

Another possibility is that the rules are made by groups of individuals that do not adequately represent the social norms of all social classes. Thus middle-class city councils may pass laws against hustling—laws that legitimately represent the interests of the middle-class residents but not those of the lower class residents (Reiss, 1961). In this kind of situation, the hustling rate of the middle-class group means something quite different from the rate of the lower class group. One group is violating a commonly held and supported norm; the other group may be violating a norm that is perceived as neither valid nor appropriate. A fourth possibility is that a rule is made by one group explicitly or implicitly for the purpose of controlling the behavior of another group. Thus stringent laws may be developed for the purpose of limiting vagrancy; when it is well known that this is a behavior that is engaged in by persons who are disproportionately of lower socioeconomic status. On the other hand, price fixing or tax evasion through loopholes in the laws (behavior typically more characteristic of the middle class) may be regulated only loosely and be enforced even more loosely. A fifth possible interpretation of varying indexes of incidence of deviance is that the regulations apply equally to all groups but that sanctions are brought to bear disproportionately against one group as opposed to another. An example of this practice is illustrated by the studies of Cohen and Short (1961) in which it was reported that middle-class boys do not get as far in the legal process when they are apprehended for delinquent acts as do boys from slum areas—that is, proportionately fewer middle-class boys get taken to the police station, get booked at the station, have a hearing before a judge, are convicted and finally sentenced. The dropout rate of middle-class boys along the route of legal processing is so high that sentencing and commitment to a corrective institution involves mostly lower class boys. Similarly, Garfinkel (1949) reported that the punishment rates of whites and Negroes who are believed to have committed homicide vary greatly. The point is that practically nothing can be said regarding the actual behavior of lower and middle-class groups, whites and Negroes, if only conviction rates are looked at.

Similar interpretations are tenable as explanations of higher or lower rates of exceptionality for one or another ethnic or social class group. Consider the following fact: a disproportionately large number of children in classes for the educable mentally retarded are lower class and/or black (Dunn, 1968, p. 6). How is this phenomenon to be explained? The following alternative explanations present themselves: (1) proportionately more blacks than whites are mentally retarded; (2) present tests are appropriate measures of the intelligence of white children but not of black children; (3) white legislators and school officials are aware of the fact that black children do more poorly than white children on conventional IQ tests; they have therefore decided that IQ testing presents a convenient, presumably valid, "scientific" procedure for separating middle-class children from certain blacks (and lower class whites); (4) equal proportions of black and white children are mentally retarded, but due to differential referrals by classroom teachers, and differential reactions to the testing situation by pupils, and differences in urgency for placement of blacks and whites on waiting lists, black children are more likely to end up in special classes for the mentally retarded.

The above interpretations of the identification and sorting processes engaged in by just one institution—the public schools—are not meant to be exhaustive but illustrative of the way institutions are created for and exist for the maintenance of a particular social system, in this instance, a social system that is interested in the maintenance of a stratification pattern that allocates most of its resources to the people at the top and very little to people at the bottom (Farber, 1968). It is not coincidental that the social system that is being maintained represents powerful factions of the social structure. Thus, Becker (1963) states:

Differences in the ability to make rules and apply them to other people are essentially power differentials (either legal or extralegal). Those groups whose social position gives them weapons and power are best able to enforce their rules. Distinctions of age, sex, ethnicity, and class are all related to differences in power, which accounts for differences in the degree to which groups so distinguished can make rules for others. . . . Enforcement is selective, and selective differentially among different kinds of people, at different times, and in different situations (pp. 17–18, 133).

Once a deviant is detected, what procedures are engaged in by others to rehabilitate or treat him? Societal notions about how certain deviants should be treated have varied from time to time and from place to place. Although there are cases where deviates are exalted and others where they are integrated into society, almost all forms of treatment have involved some variation of segregation (Freidson, 1965, p. 76). The degree of segregation may range from seeing a psychiatrist, parole officer, or itinerant speech therapist once a week to drastic, permanent separation–extermination. Historically, this latter procedure has been used to rid societies of individuals who represented differentness on a variety of criteria. Among the Wogeo, a New Guinea tribe, deformed infants are buried alive (cited in Wright, 1960, p. 254); during the Middle Ages among Europeans, countless individuals

NETTIE R. BARTEL AND SAMUEL L. GUSKIN

were burned at the stake because they were believed to be witches; in more recent times, and among presumably civilized people, millions of Jews were put to death within one decade. All of these actions, and many others, have been justified at one time or another as essential for protecting the tribe from evil spirits, keeping the society "pure," or providing a "solution" to a national "problem."

Extermination as a solution to social problems is also implicit in such practices as sterilization.* Although sterilization as a form of social control has been losing popularity in recent years, genetic and eugenic thinking have had a recent revival (Gottesman, 1968; Jensen, 1969; Reed and Reed, 1965). Certainly, birth control is being widely suggested as a solution to both national and international social problems.

At present our most common forms of segregation are our prisons for the behaviorally different, special schools and residence centers for those with impaired sight and hearing, mental institutions for the emotionally different, residential institutions and public school special classes for the intellectually different, rehabilitation centers and hospitals for the physically different, and ghettos for the ethnically and racially different. Most of these settings are typically justified because of some presumed habilitative or rehabilitative function that is supposed to be occurring. In fact, however, no defensible data has yet been published that indicates that these arrangements are effective in facili-

tating the inmates' return to and adjustment within the larger society (Braginsky, Braginsky, and Ring; 1969; Dentler, 1967; Edgerton, 1967; Goffman, 1961; Plaut and Kaplan, 1956; Roth and Eddy, 1967; Tappan, 1951).

The different types of segregation vary in the degree to which they are able to exert control over individuals. Thus, Goffman (1961) in his discussion of asylums states:

When we review the different institutions in our Western society, we find that some are encompassing to a degree discontinuously greater than the ones next in line. Their encompassing or total character is symbolized by the barrier to social intercourse with the outside and to departure that is often built right into the physical plant, such as locked doors, high walls, barbed wire, cliffs, water, forests or moors; these establishments I am calling total institutions (p.4).

Roth and Eddy (1967) from their study of a rehabilitation hospital conclude that total institutions serve social control functions by becoming the chief depositories for unwanted members of a society. The relevant characteristic that the inmates of the institution have in common then, is not some physical, mental, or behavioral trait—these only determine what *kind* of institutional placement they are technically eligible for—but the fact that all of them are unwanted members of society.

Our society has many homes for unwanted people. In addition to our custodial homes, . . . we have numerous mental hospitals, institutions for the retarded, nursing homes, old-age homes, training schools for delinquents and so on. The specific kind of institution a person "qualifies" for is often arbitrary. . . . Such institutions all perform much the same function, and we suspect that the choice of which institution the patient goes to is often an accident of the person or agency he happens to fall into the

*At the time of this writing, the Supreme Court of the United States has agreed to review the right of states to take such action. The litigation is sought on behalf of a Nebraska woman whose sterilization has been ordered as a prerequisite to her release from a mental institution. At present sixteen states have sterilization laws still in effect.

A Handicap as a Social Phenomenon

hands of. . . . To the patient who is stuck in such an institution, it often makes little difference which one he ends up in, except that the facilities and personnel at one may be somewhat more tolerable than those at another (Roth and Eddy, pp. 198–199).

Whatever the kind of total institution, society offers some organizational rationale for its existence. As Roth and Eddy put it (p. 199), "Although institutions for the unwanted all do much the same thing, they have differing 'excuses' for their existence, and these excuses make some difference in how they operate."

The handling of many human needs by the bureaucratic organization of blocks of people fits in closely with the function which the total institution serves—the effective disposition of the unwanted.

The official rationale for the existence of the institution varies with the real or imputed characteristics of the clients to be taken care of—in particular, whether or not the inmate's condition is seen as being caused by volitional acts of the individual. In cases where the responsibility for the condition is seen as residing within the individual, as in certain conceptions of criminality, management consists of some form of punishment; in cases where no motivation toward deviance is seen in the individual, as in the blind, treatment tends to be couched in "caretaker" or permissive terms (Freidson, 1965, p. 76). Nevertheless, the question of causality is not easily resolved, even within each form of exceptionality. This appears to be particularly so when competing conceptual models regarding the nature of the exceptionality are contrasted. Thus, if a disease or illness model is used to explain the occurrence of delinquency, quite different assumptions are made concerning the cau-

sality of the condition, as compared to the assumptions made when a nonmedical model is employed. The "sick" boy is not responsible for his condition—it is contracted from a contaminating environment; the "bad" boy is responsible for his condition—he is making the wrong decisions and thus messing up his life. In the former case, treatment will emphasize a therapeutic, "healthy" environment; in the latter, treatment will be rationalized in terms of getting the individual to change his mind about how he is going to behave, through punishment of the "bad" behavior and/or encouragement of "good" behavior.

Within the United States, the official rationale for the existence of institutions has undergone changes from time to time (Davies, 1959). These changes have been accompanied by concomitant variations in clientele being served. For example, the emphasis on institutional care for the retarded shifted from a rehabilitative thrust to a custodial orientation when the nature of the population considered to be in need of this particular form of control changed from the mildly retarded to the more severely retarded. It became necessary to reformulate the raison d'être, of the institution.

Institutionalization remains a popular social response to exceptionality in the United States, although there are systematic differences in the extent to which the various religious and ethnic groups use this form of social control with members of their own group. Saenger (1957) reports that Jewish families are more likely to institutionalize a severely retarded child than are Protestant and Catholic families; Catholics are most likely to care for the child in his home. Plaut and Kaplan (1956) in their study of Hutterite communities found that these groups rarely, if

Nettie R. Bartel and Samuel L. Guskin

ever, commit a member of their community to public or private institutions but prefer to care for their deviants in the communal setting. It is also noteworthy that the reported rate of mental illness among Hutterites is lower than that of the American population as a whole.

In spite of the fact that the impetus for the American system of institutions has its origins in Europe (Davies, 1959), this form of social control is by no means the only one used there today. In fact, dating from the fifteenth century to the present, the small town of Geel, Belgium, has developed and maintained a system of foster homes that provides a unique and successful treatment for both the mentally retarded and mentally ill.*

The Geel tradition of foster home placement provides a good illustration of the diversity of the antecedents of particular practices with the exceptional. This particular approach is the product of a centuries-old religious legend, which led to the establishment of Geel as a kind of Mecca for the mentally afflicted. The local peasants, in a canny combination of religious devotion and economic advantage, took in the pilgrims as boarders. Originally the Catholic Church was the overseer of the program; today Belgium's government reimburses families for their care of the impaired. What began five hundred years ago as a practical response to a unique situation arising from a revered superstition today is considered one of the more successful ways of coping with the severely mentally impaired (*Time*, March 14, 1969). The particular form of the

Time Magazine, March 14, 1969, p. 74 reports that although the service is designed particularly for chronic patients, about half of newly placed patients are able to go home in sixteen months or less. This rate compares very favorably with current "cure" rates reported in the United States.

treatment a society imposes on its deviants may be due as much to accidental occurrences as to logically justifiable treatment rationales.

Special class placement constitutes the most common method of treating the mildly mentally retarded in this society. On the basis of the presumed appropriateness of such placement, the numbers of such special classes have increased greatly in the past decades. These increases have been generally lauded as surely representing some kind of progress, and the disquieting findings of a whole sequence of efficacy studies have been either ignored or explained away.

What are the effects of special class placement for the mildly retarded? Do children undergoing such placement show evidence of superior personal, social, academic, and vocational skills development? What differences does it make as far as parents, siblings, peers, teachers, and employers are concerned?

Cluttered as the literature is with studies comparing the performance and adjustment of special-class and regular-class retardates, one could hope for definitive answers to these questions. Unfortunately, most of the studies are vulnerable to devastating criticisms of methodology, as pointed out by a number of reviewers (Gardner, 1966; Guskin and Spicker, 1968; Kirk, 1964; Spicker and Bartel, 1968). Most of the methodological criticisms directed at the earlier studies were circumvented by Goldstein, Moss and Jordan (1965). These investigators randomly assigned beginning first-grade children, IQs 50 to 85, to either regular classes or newly created special classes, thus avoiding biased sampling and the problem of the effects of previous academic failure on school performance. A special curriculum was implemented, the special class teachers were specially trained and supervised, and measures were developed to assess social and functional skills as well as academic achievement. Essentially, the results of this careful four-year study confirm the findings of the earlier studies: Educable mentally retarded children in special classes perform no better and no worse than EMRs in the regular grades.

Investigations comparing the social and emotional adjustment of regular and special-class children have to a large extent employed measures of undemonstrated validity or reliability; in addition many of the studies were subject to serious sampling bias. The best designed of the investigations—two substudies of the Goldstein, Moss, and Jordan (1965) study, were conducted by Meyerowitz (Goldstein, Moss, and Jordan, 1965; Meyerowitz, 1962). These two studies of personal and social adjustment found special-class retardates more likely to subscribe to self-derogatory statements and to interact less with neighborhood peers than children left in the regular grades. One can only conclude that the superiority of special-class retardates' personal and social adjustment remains to be demonstrated (Gardner, 1966; Guskin and Spicker, 1968; Spicker and Bartel, 1968).

Similarly, comparisons of the postschool adjustment of special class and regular class retardates (Carriker, 1957; Peck, 1964) fail to present convincing evidence that special class placement results in clearcut, overall long-term benefits in terms of social and vocational adjustment.

The major finding that can be gleaned from the assortment of inschool and postschool studies just referred to is that attaching the label of mental retardation to an individual and segregating him in a special class with other individuals of similar evaluation has yet to be shown to result in

unique social, educational, or vocational advantages for that individual. If singling out individuals as deviant (that is, placing them in special classes) is to be justified as of benefit to the individual, it must be justified in terms of positive, favorable evidence rather than on the basis of a lack of negative, unfavorable evidence. Society, of course, may be forced to recognize (or admit) that its goal is not individual benefit of the handicapped but comfort or protection of others.

It is noteworthy that most EMR children pass as normal throughout their lives except during the school years, during which the availability and presumed appropriateness of intelligence tests provides a convenient "scientific" basis for identifying intellectual deviants and subjecting them to special treatment. The high prevalence rate of identified retardates in the chronological age (CA) eight to fifteen range has been noted by Gruenberg (1964) and Farber (1968) in their reviews of epidemiological studies. Although Gruenberg cites the finding of increased prevalence during the school years and a decline thereafter as "the most important single finding of these surveys" and that "the phenomenon cries out for investigation," no such investigation has, to date, been reported. It is our opinion that this finding is more related to the schools' remarkable propensity for labeling children as retarded than to a propensity for children to become retarded during their school years and again unretarded after they drop out of school.

Related to this observation are the findings of two studies—Meyerowitz (1967) and Olshansky and Schonfield (1965). Both of these studies reported that most parents of mildly retarded children rated their child as normal or above in intelligence when asked to evaluate his

NETTIE R. BARTEL AND SAMUEL L. GUSKIN

mental status. One conclusion that may be drawn from these studies is that the criteria employed by the schools to relegate an individual to the status of EMR are irrelevant to or ignored by that group of most significant others—the individuals' families. According to Olshansky, Schonfield and Sternfeld (1962), "the majority of the (so-called) mentally retarded children are able to meet most of life's changing expectations except those of the schools as currently structured."

It is particularly important that the special class "solution" be questioned now, because similar treatment strategies are becoming popular for other deviant children under the rubrics of classes for the "emotionally disturbed" or for the "learning-disabled." Although some children may require extensive education or training of a very different kind from that found in the regular classroom, most of the children likely to be placed will probably be rather ordinary children who present problems in management or academic achievement and who are not being successfully coped with by teachers, either because of the teachers' poor training, lack of resources, or both.

CAREERS OF THE EXCEPTIONAL

The particular danger of any form of segregated treatment of a deviant or disabled individual is that it may lead to still more deviant behavior rather than a return to a normal life pattern. In examining the long-term consequences of any event, it is useful to think of the impact of the event on the career of the individual.

The concept of the career of an individual who is considered different by others has been usefully employed to facilitate an understanding of the sequence of self-other interactions of the mentally ill (Goffman, 1963) and the socially deviant (Cohen, 1966). Becker (1963) uses a similar orientation when he describes a sequential, as opposed to a simultaneous model of deviance (p. 22–25). This orientation is of special utility in attempts to understand deviance in that it draws attention to the fact that (1) a series, rather than a single episode of social interactions, rituals, and circumstances, leads to a stable deviant career, (2) decisions that are made at a given point in time effectively foreclose or attenuate the possibility of certain subsequent options, and (3) the impact of a given event on the development of a deviant career varies with the time of its occurrence, that is, an event may have a dramatic impact at one stage of a career but no discernable effect at another.

The sequential aspects underlying the notion of career appear to be of crucial pertinence in a consideration of individuals whose competence is in question. By its very nature competence or skill in a given behavior, be it reading, basket weaving, or performance on the Stanford-Binet, is dependent upon previous experience in the same or similar situations. Children who are considered to be too dull to benefit from instruction in simple arithmetic are not going to be given the opportunity to learn to perform well on quadratic equations; subjects living in an unstimulating institution are not likely to excel on vocabulary tests that question their knowledge of such words as "amanuensis." The point is that the general or specific competence of an individual at a given time cannot be accounted for without a consideration of previous experiences, opportunities, and circumstances.

Certain key decisions, made by the individual himself or by others in positions of power, effectively alter the possibility of his being considered handicapped or normal, or in some cases being labeled as possessing a particular kind of handicap, as opposed to some other handicap. Thus the decision of a young draftee returning from combat to seek or not to seek eligibility for veteran's compensation for some relatively minor physical impairment (such as reduced vision) resulting from engagement in action is likely to have a long-lasting impact on whether the individual sees himself as normal or as disabled in some way. Such a decision may initially be influenced by factors other than degree of impairment (such as probability of obtaining veteran's benefits); nevertheless, the decision is likely to become the basis for subsequent decisions, such as whether to seek employment or not. It is not difficult to see how a series of such decisions forecloses certain options and opens others—leading to the permanent adoption by the individual of the role of normal or of the partially sighted.

Freidson (1965) describes the career of the handicapped in the following way:

In this type of deviance (the handicapped), then, the career may be said to consist in large part in an attempt to *avoid* the role (rather than play the role and seek to avoid punishment for it). But characteristically, the career consists of a progressive narrowing of alternatives until none but the deviant role remains.... The most important point of the career of the prospective deviant lies in the events that establish his new role beyond any doubt—when he is trapped and cannot turn back ... one suddenly discovers that the cost of turning back is greater than that of continuing and that he is committed (Freidson, 1965, p. 89, 91, 92).

Several typical sequences, or careers, of the exceptional child may be contrasted with those of the normal child. (1) Shortly after birth, a severely handicapped child is permanently committed by the family to an institution. The parents consult with the family doctor and receiving personnel of the institution in arriving at their decision. All subsequent significant decisions concerning the individual are made by institutional personnel. (2) A severely handicapped child remains in the family until school age, is enrolled in a public school special day class from age seven to sixteen, then is given limited part-time employment in a sheltered workshop. His placements are governed by his parents' decisions and the availability and admission requirements of the day classes and sheltered workshop. (3) A lower class child spends his preschool years with his family. He enters school and achieves poorly, as do his school-age siblings. A psychological examination in the early grades indicates that the child is mildly retarded or otherwise handicapped in learning. The rest of his school years are spent in special day classes for children with similar learning impairments. After dropping out of school at age sixteen, he is alternatively unemployed or working at an unskilled job. (4) A middle-class child with a mild disability (for example, brain injury, sensory loss, physical disability) has his condition diagnosed at age two when his family first suspects there is something "wrong" with him. Rehabilitative and corrective steps are taken (for example, physical therapy, hearing aid, remedial reading), and the child proceeds through regular school with barely passing grades. After graduation he obtains, through a family connection, a white-collar job that makes minimal demands in the area of his disability. (5) A sixth-grade, lower class boy is caught setting fires in abandoned houses with a group of other boys, including his brother. A court-

NETTIE R. BARTEL AND SAMUEL L. GUSKIN

appointed psychologist obtains an IQ of 75 from the boy and an IQ of 83 from his brother. Subsequently, a judge decides that the appropriate placement for the boy is an institution for the retarded (since he scored in the retarded range); his brother is sent to a boys' farm (which accepts only juveniles of normal IQ). Until the age of eighteen years the brothers are in and out of their respective institutions several times.

LIFE CHANCES

How do individuals fall into one or another career pattern, and what factors affect the probability that a career will take one direction rather than another? One concept that is useful in considering these questions is that of life chances. This concept is also useful for understanding how individuals with handicaps fit into the overall stratification pattern of a social group. Gerth and Mills (1953, p. 313) develop the concept of life chances as

... everything from the chance to stay alive during the first year after birth to the chance to view fine arts, the chance to remain healthy and grow tall, and if sick to become well again quickly, the chance to avoid becoming a juvenile delinquent—and very crucially, the chance to complete an intermediary or higher educational grade.

It is immediately apparent that certain groups have restricted life-chances from almost any perspective. Thus black Americans (as opposed to whites) have a higher infant mortality rate, lower life expectancy, higher recorded rates of crime and delinquency, and lower educational level.

It appears that reciprocal relationships exist among the various facets of life chances. The individual who is physically handicapped frequently has low earning power. The resulting decrement in income may drastically affect the quality of the health care he can afford. Similarly, the intellectually limited individual is restricted in the degree of education he can attain; his educational level influences his expected income. [Miller (1965) estimates that expected lifetime earnings range from $143,000 for individuals with less than eight years of schooling to $425,000 for individuals with sixteen or more years of schooling]; income is related to such variables as mortality, suicide, and divorce rates (Tumin, 1967, p. 51). It is interesting to note that the relationship between the various aspects of life chances can be disrupted by the presence of a third factor. For example, the relationship between education and income is much stronger for whites than it is for blacks (Miller 1965, p. 164). Certain key variables seem to account for whole clusters of life chances; in this society two of these variables are race and social class.

Few persons would deny that handicapped individuals have reduced life chances. What factors enter into this limitation? It appears that the following elements are present in the life chances of the handicapped: (1) their actual competence, (2) the resources of their families and communities, (3) a number of unpredictable happenstances, and (4) the place of the individual in the social structure. These factors, in turn, depend on more specific variables. Competence is related to the type and severity of the disability and learning opportunities; family resources are determined by such factors as social class, religious beliefs, attitudes, family integration, and the decisions that these lead the family to make.

A great many of the decisions that influence the life chances of an individual are made by persons other than himself, often his family. This is likely to be especially true in cases where the individual's competence is in question. Individuals who are severely impaired in sensory, physical, or intellectual abilities typically do not make the significant decisions concerning their own welfare and future.

On the one hand, the opportunities available to these individuals are determined to a large extent by the objective facts of their physical limitations (such as extensive cerebral dysfunction, profound loss of visual or auditory acuity, gross motor disabilities or paralysis). In this sense, there are fewer decisions that need to be made for such an individual, his performance limitations foreclosing such options as college education or certain employment possibilities. On the other hand, because of his manifest disability, such decisions as remain to be made (such as to institutionalize or not to institutionalize) are made not by the individual himself, but by parents or guardians. This situation is in contrast to that of more competent individuals about whom more decisions must be made (more alternatives typically being available) and who are given progressively greater responsibility for making these decisions themselves as they progress from early childhood to maturity. This progression occurs very slowly and to a limited extent, or not at all, with severely disabled individuals, who, for the most part, must assume a rather permanent role of dependence and incompetence relative to others throughout life.

The acknowledgment of the role of unpredictable circumstances in the determination of life chances is shown in the following: The subject was feeling somewhat ill the day he was given the Stanford-Binet, thus he scored 79 (instead of say 80 or 81), which made him eligible for special class placement, which determined the nature of his schooling, which in turn affected his chances for employment after graduation. Or, to consider another possibility, a Negro child happens to be assigned to a teacher who is not free of racial prejudice. The ensuing year has two unhappy effects: the child fails to make progress in academic subjects, and he decides he hates school, "honkies, and the System." Similarly, the presence or absence of a policeman's patrol car at a particular street corner on a particular night sometimes determines whether a youngster's delinquent career terminates after one or more episodes of hub stealing or whether it blossoms into a full-blown criminal career.

Farber (1959, p. 9) notes that as a normal child proceeds in his career, the parents redefine and shift their conceptions and roles to adjust to the changing role of the child. In his discussion of "arrest in the family cycle," he points out that "regardless of his birth order in the family, the severely mentally retarded child eventually becomes the youngest child socially."

In the normal or average family, the sequence of family-child interactions proceeds somewhat as follows: In early infancy, most significant decisions concerning the child are made by the parents. As the child develops in ability, he is given increasing responsibility in the determination of his life chances until some time in the late teens or early twenties, when the family ceases to have the power or the responsibility to make decisions concerning his future. During the period that the family progressively relinquishes control over the child, a variety of other individuals, groups, and agencies—many of which

NETTIE R. BARTEL AND SAMUEL L. GUSKIN

are not particularly selected by or approved of by the family—come to exercise significant influences over the course of the individual's life. Examples of such personnel and institutions are teachers, counselors, school peers, neighborhood peers, church groups, law enforcement agencies and personnel, the draft, and college entrance policies and personnel. No one group can claim a monopoly of influence.

For the severely disabled, however, most decisions regarding his life chances are imposed primarily by the parents, sometimes with the assistance of a religious leader, family doctor, rehabilitation agency, or institution. Moreover, the nature of those who are permitted to influence the decisions made by the family are usually carefully selected by the family. From this point of view, as compared to the average individual, the impact of the family on the handicapped individual is indeed overwhelming.

The place of the handicapped individual in the overall social structure is an important element in what options are available. Farber (1968) has suggested that the life chances of most handicapped persons are reduced because they form part of the "surplus population" of the society. Reciprocally, they are part of the surplus population because their life chances are so limited. Farber assumes that the social structure establishes and rigidly controls the number of slots or offices in a social organization. Because the controlling groups will establish a division of labor that will maximize power, output of goods, knowledge, or other product, and because there is a limited number of available slots to be filled, there are always persons who don't fit in any niche of the structure. These individuals are the sur-

plus population, and the mentally retarded comprise one segment of this group (along with the physically or emotionally handicapped, the aged, certain minority groups, delinquents, and so forth). Thus, for Farber, the answer to the question of when individuals are likely to be designated disabled or deviant is that this occurs when individuals are incapable of filling slots in the social organization. From his point of view, the classification and grouping of individuals does not result from any conscious, deliberate act on the part of individuals; it is simply the outcome of a social order that gives rewards only to individuals who can fill needed roles in a stratification pattern based on a division of labor that is geared to efficiency as a top-priority goal. Farber views a surplus population as inevitable and even useful in a society, contributing to the stability of the social structure by (1) requiring, for its remediation and control, a series of institutions to meet the legal, welfare, health, and educational difficulties involved, and by (2) contributing to the efficiency of economic, political, family, and educational institutions by supplying a pool of personnel from which can be drawn appropriate matches for organizational slots, and by (3) contributing to the perpetuation of the social classes by comprising a group whose life chances are minimal.

Farber's formulation is useful in pointing out how the minimization of certain individuals' life chances can be institutionalized by a society and how the conjunction of clusters of undesirable characteristics (for example, low IQ, low social class, physical disability, membership in a minority group) in one individual contributes to his gravitation to the bottom of the stratification hierarchy.

SOCIETAL REDUCTION OF HANDICAPPING

If society can be held responsible for creating handicap, it should be possible for society to reverse the process and reduce handicap. One implication of much we have written here is that handicapping could be reduced by minimizing the segregation of disabled or otherwise different individuals. A second implied suggestion is elimination of diagnostic procedures that cannot be demonstrated to result in successful treatment attempts. A third implication is that reduction of handicapping might occur through totally avoiding treatment whenever the effectiveness of the treatment cannot be demonstrated. The suggested elimination of ineffective diagnostic and treatment procedures is based on our assumption that diagnosis and treatment may sharply reduce the likelihood of progression through a normal life career. A related implication is that if treatment is necessary and useful, the more invisible the service the more likely its reduction of the social condition known as "handicap."

Much else we have discussed has implied that labeling and "handicapping" serve important functions for society and thus that society will resist reduction of this process. Dentler and Erikson (1959) imply in their discussion of deviance that improving the status of the handicapped within a group may reduce the effectiveness with which the group can motivate others to meet norms. Thus it seems that it would be easier to convince social groups to keep deviant members in their midst than it will be to convince them not to differentially label and treat them within the group. Most importantly, it is necessary that in suggesting realistic change we consider the needs actually served by social treatment patterns rather than the humane rationale publicly presented.

SUMMARY

A handicap is a social condition, a condition created by society. A person's bodily or behavioral condition becomes a handicap only to the extent that society, other people, or the person himself define his condition as distinctive and undesirable. This definition consists of verbal labeling, distinctive interpersonal reactions, and/or special treatment techniques, all of which imply either unattractiveness or incompetence or both. The result of this social definition is to create distinctive environments and behaviors which sequentially remove the person further and further from normal life patterns and in time convince all concerned that the person truly is handicapped. Because most persons sense the serious social consequences of being different, they exert great effort to avoid being seen as different by those whom they value. When they are known to be different, they exert great effort to cover their differentness, that is, to remove it from the focus of negative attention. These attempts to pass and cover along with the substantial creations of society to cope with those who are different provide extensive evidence for the need to examine handicaps as social conditions. Finally, this approach suggests directions for prevention and treatment of handicap which are antithetical to the current approaches of our educational and rehabilitation agencies.

NETTIE R. BARTEL AND SAMUEL L. GUSKIN

References

Asch, S. E. Forming impressions of personality. *Journal of Abnormal and Social Psychology,* 1946, *41,* 258–290.

Barker, R. G., & Wright, B. A. The social psychology of adjustment to physical disability. In J. F. Garrett (Ed.), *Psychological aspects of physical disability.* Rehabilitation Service series No. 210. Washington, D. C.: Federal Security Agency, Office of Vocational Rehabilitation, 1952. Pp. 18–32.

Bartel, N. R. Locus of control and achievement in middle class and lower class children. Unpublished doctoral dissertation, Indiana University, 1968.

Battle, E. S., & Rotter, J. B. Children's feelings of personal control as related to social class and ethnic group. *Journal of Personality,* 1963, *31,* 482–490.

Becker, H. S. *Outsiders: Studies in the sociology of deviance.* New York: The Free Press, 1963.

Beez, W. V. Influence of biased psychological reports on teacher behavior and pupil performance. *Proceedings of the 75th APA Annual Convention.* Washington, D. C.: American Psychological Association, 1968. Pp. 605–606.

Bialer, I. Conceptualization of success and failure in mentally retarded and normal children. *Journal of Personality,* 1961, *29,* 303–320.

Braginsky, B. M., Braginsky, D. D., & Ring, K. *Methods of madness: The mental hospital as a last resort.* New York: Holt, Rinehart & Winston, Inc., 1969.

Brookover, W. *et al.* Self-concept of ability and school achievement II. U. S. Office of Education Cooperative Research Project, No. 1636, Lansing: Michigan State University, 1965. (ERIC ED003294).

Bruner, J. S. Personality dynamics and the process of perceiving. In R. P. Blake & G. V. Ramsey (Eds.), *Perception—an approach to personality.* New York: The Ronald Press Company, 1951. Pp. 121–147.

Carriker, W. J. A comparison of post-school adjustment of regular and special class retarded individuals served in Lincoln and Omaha. U. S. Office of Education Cooperative Research Project, No. 146. 1957.

Carter, R. Locus of control and teacher expectancy as related to achievement of young school children. Unpublished doctoral dissertation, Indiana University, 1969.

Clark, S. M., & Farber, B. The handicapped child in the family: A literature survey. In B. V. Sheets and B. Farber (Eds.), *The handicapped child in the family.* New York: United Cerebral Palsy Research & Educational Foundation, n. d.

Cline, W. B. Interpersonal perception. In B. A. Maher (Ed.), *Progress in experimental personality research.* Vol. I. New York: Academic Press, Inc., 1964. Pp. 221–284.

Cohen, A. K. *Deviance and control.* Englewood Cliffs, N. J.: Prentice-Hall, Inc., 1966.

―――, & Short, J. F. Juvenile delinquency. In R. K. Merton & R. A. Nisbet (Eds.), *Contemporary social problems.* New York: Harcourt, Brace & World, Inc., 1961. Pp. 77–126.

Coleman, J. S. *et al. Equality of educational opportunity.* Washington, D.C.: U. S. Department of Health, Education, and Welfare, 1966.

Cummings, S. T., Bayley, H. C., & Rie, H. E. Effects of the child's deficiency on the mother: A study of mothers of mentally retarded, chronically ill and neurotic children. *American Journal of Orthopsychiatry,* 1966, *36,* 595–609.

Davies, S. P. *The mentally retarded in society.* New York: Columbia University Press, 1959.

Dentler, R. A. *Major American social problems.* Chicago: Rand McNally & Co., 1967.

―――, & Erikson, K. T. The functions of deviance in groups. *Social Problems,* 1959, *7,* 98–107.

Dexter, L. A. A social theory of mental deficiency. *American Journal of Mental Deficiency,* 1958, *62,* 920–928.

―――. On the politics and sociology of stupidity in our society. In H. S. Becker (Ed.), *The other side: Perspectives on deviance.* New York: The Free Press, 1964. Pp. 37–49.

Dunn, L. M. Special education for the mildly retarded—Is much of it justifiable? *Exceptional Children,* 1968, *35,* 5–22.

Edgerton, R. B. *The cloak of competence: Stigma in the lives of the mentally retarded.*

Berkeley: University of California Press, 1967.

————. On the "recognition" of mental illness. In S. C. Plog & R. B. Edgerton (Eds.), *Changing perspectives in mental illness.* New York: Holt, Rinehart & Winston, Inc., 1969.

Farber, B. Effects of a severely mentally retarded child on family intergration. *Monographs of the Society for Research in Child Development*, serial No. 71, 1959, *24* (2).

————. *Mental retardation: Its social context and social consequences.* Boston: Houghton Mifflin Company, 1968.

————, Jenne, W. C., & Toigo, R. Family crisis and the decision to institutionalize the retarded child. *CEC Research Monograph*, series A., 1960 (1).

Farina, A., & Ring, K. The influence of perceived mental illness on inter-personal relations. *Journal of Abnormal Psychology*, 1965, *70*, 47–51.

Festinger, L. A theory of social comparison processes. *Human Relations*, 1954, *7*, 117–140.

Freidson, E. Disability as social deviance. In M. B. Sussman (Ed.), *Sociology and rehabilitation.* Washington, D.C.: American Sociological Association, 1965. Pp. 71–99.

Gardner, W. I. Social and emotional adjustment of mildly retarded children and adolescents: Critical review. *Exceptional Children*, 1966, *33*, 97–105.

Garfinkel, H. Research notes on inter- and intra- racial homicides. *Social Forces*, 1949, *27*, 369-381.

Gerth, H., & Mills, C. W. *Character and social structure.* New York: Harcourt, Brace & World, Inc., 1953.

Goffman, E. *Ayslums: Essays on the social situation of mental patients and other inmates.* Chicago: Aldine Publishing Company, 1961.

————. *Stigma: Notes on the management of spoiled identity.* Englewood Cliffs, N. J.: Prentice-Hall, Inc., 1963.

Goldstein, H., Moss, J.W., & Jordan, L. J. The efficacy of special class training on the development of mentally retarded children. U. S. Office of Education Cooperative Research Project, No. 619. Urbana: University of Illinois, 1965.

Gottesman, I. I. Biogenetics of race and class.

In M. Deutsch, I. Katz, & A. R. Jensen (Eds.), *Social class, race and psychological development.* New York: Holt, Rinehart & Winston, Inc., 1968. Pp. 11–51.

Grier, W. H., & Cobbs, P.M. *Black rage.* New York: Basic Books, Inc., Publishers, 1968.

Gruenberg, E. M. Epidemiology. In H. A. Stevens & R. Heber (Eds.), *Mental retardation: A review of research.* Chicago: University of Chicago Press, 1964. Pp. 259–306.

Guskin, S. L. The influence of labeling upon the perception of subnormality in mentally defective children. *American Journal of Mental Deficiency*, 1962, *67*, 402–406. (*a*)

————. The perception of subnormality in mentally defective children. *American Journal of Mental Deficiency*, 1962, *67*, 53–60. (b)

————. Dimensions of judged similarity among deviant types. *American Journal of Mental Deficiency*, 1963, *68*, 218–224. (*a*)

————. Measuring the strength of the stereotype of the mental defective. *American Journal of Mental Deficiency*, 1963, *67*, 569–575. (*b*)

————. Social psychologies of mental deficiency. In N. R. Ellis (Ed.), *Handbook of mental deficiency.* New York: McGraw-Hill, 1963. Pp. 325–352. (*c*)

————, & Spicker, H. H. Educational research in mental retardation. In N.R. Ellis (Ed.), *International review of research in mental retardation.* Vol. 3. New York: Academic Press, Inc., 1968. Pp. 217–278.

Hersh, J. B. Influence of biased referral reports in a clinical testing situation. Unpublished manuscript, Indiana University, 1969.

Hughes, E. C. Dilemmas and contradictions in status. *American Journal of Sociology*, 1945, *50*, 353–359.

Jaffe, J. Attitudes of adolescents toward persons with disabilities. Paper presented at the meeting of the American Psychological Association, New York, 1965.

Jensen, A. R. How much can we boost IQ and scholastic achievement? *Harvard Educational Review*, 1969, *39*, 1–123.

Jones, R. L. Cognitive functioning in the presence of the disabled. Paper presented at the meeting of the American Psychological Association, San Francisco, 1968.

Kelley, H. H. *et al.* Some implications of social psychological theory for research on the handicapped. In L. H. Lofquist (Ed.), *Psychological research and rehabilitation.* Washington, D. C.: American Psychological Association, 1960. Pp. 172–204.

Kirk, S. A. Research in education. In H. A. Stevens & R. Heber (Eds.), *Mental retardation: A review of research.* Chicago: University of Chicago Press, 1964. Pp. 57–99.

Klebanoff, L. Parental attitudes of mothers of schizophrenics, brain-injured and retarded, and normal children. *American Journal of Orthopsychiatry,* 1959, *29,* 445–454.

Kleck, R. E. Stigma conditions as elicitors of behavior in face-to-face inter-action. Paper presented at the meeting of the American Psychological Association, San Francisco, 1968.

Lipp, L. *et al.* Denial of disability and internal control of reinforcement: A study using a perceptual defense paradigm. *Journal of Consulting and Clinical Psychology,* 1968, *32,* 72–75.

Menninger, K., Mayman, M., & Preger, P. The urge to classify. In K. Menninger (Ed.), *The vital balance.* New York: The Viking Press, Inc., 1963. Pp. 9–34.

Meyerowitz, J. H. Self-derogations in young retardates and special class placement. *Child Development,* 1962, *33,* 443-451.

———. Parental awareness of retardation. *American Journal of Mental Deficiency,* 1967, *71,* 637–643.

Miller, H. *Rich man poor man.* Signet Book. The New American Library of World Literature, Inc., New York, 1965.

Olshansky, S., & Schonfield, J., Parental perceptions of the mental status of graduates of special classes. *Mental Retardation,* 1965, *3,* 16–20.

———, & Sternfeld, L. Mentally retarded or culturally different? *Training School Bulletin,* 1962, *59,* 18–21.

Peck, J. R. Success of young adult male retardates. U. S. Office of Education Cooperative Research Project, No. 1533. Austin: University of Texas, 1964.

Peterson, D. R. *The clinical study of social behavior.* New York: Appleton-Century-Crofts, 1968.

Plaut, T. F. A., & Kaplan, B. *Personality in a communal society: An analysis of the mental health of the Hutterites.* Law-

rence: University of Kansas, 1956, Pp. 50-55.

Reiss, A. J., Jr. The social integration of queers and peers. *Social Problems,* 1961, *9,* 102–120.

Reed, E. W., & Reed, S. C. *Mental retardation: A family study.* Philadelphia: W. B. Saunders Company, 1965.

Rosenthal, R. *Experimenter effects in behavioral research.* New York: Appleton-Century-Crofts, 1966.

———, & Jacobson, L. *Pygmalion in the classroom: Teacher expectation and pupils' intellectual development.* New York: Holt, Rinehart & Winston, Inc., 1968. (*a*)

———. Teacher expectations for the disadvantaged. *Scientific American,* 1968, *218*(4), 19–23. (*b*)

Roth, J. A., & Eddy, E. M. *Rehabilitation of the unwanted.* New York: Atherton Press, Inc., 1967.

Rotter, J. B. Generalized expectancies for internal versus external control of reinforcement. *Psychological Monographs,* 1966, *80* (1, whole No. 609).

Saenger, G. The adjustment of severely retarded adults in the community. A report to the New York State Interdepartmental Health Resources Board. Albany, New York, 1957.

Scheff, T. J. *Being mentally ill: A sociological theory.* Chicago: Aldine Publishing Company, 1966.

Schoggin, P. Observed behavior of mothers and teachers toward children with physical disabilities in natural situations. Paper presented at the meeting of the American Psychological Association, New York, 1965.

Scott, R. A. *The making of blind men.* New York: Russell Sage Foundation, 1969.

Spicker, H. H., & Bartel N. R. The mentally retarded. In G. O. Johnson & H. Blank (Eds.), *Exceptional children research review.* Washington, D. C.: Council for Exceptional Children, 1968. Pp. 39–109.

Sutherland, E. H., & Cressey, D. R. *Principles of criminology.* (6th ed.). Chicago: Lippincott, 1960.

Tallman, I. Spousal role differentiation and socialization of severely retarded children. *Journal of Marriage and the Family,* 1965, *27,* 37–42.

Tappan, P. W. Objectives and methods in correction. In P.W. Tappan (Ed.), *Contemporary correction.* New York: McGraw-Hill Book Company, 1951.

Time Magazine, 1969, March 14, p. 74.

Thorndike, R. L. "Pygmalion in the classroom" by Robert Rosenthal and Lenore Jacobson. *American Educational Research Journal,* 1968, *5,* 708–711.

Tumin, M. M. *Social stratification: the forms and functions of inequality.* Englewood Cliffs, N.J.: Prentice-Hall, Inc., 1967.

Wolfensberger, W. Counseling the parents of the retarded. In A. A. Baumeister (Ed.), *Mental retardation: Appraisal, education, and rehabilitation.* Chicago: Aldine Publishing Company, 1967.

Wright, B. A. *Physical disability: A psychological approach.* New York: Harper & Row, Publishers, 1960.

THREE

Psychological Assessment of Exceptional Children and Youth

T. ERNEST NEWLAND

T. Ernest Newland is Professor of Educational Psychology and Director of the School Psychology Program, College of Education, University of Illinois. He was formerly Chief of the Division of Special Education, Pennsylvania State Department of Public Instruction, and Professor of Psychology, University of Tennessee.

The purposes of this chapter are to review briefly the major assumptions that underlie psychological testing and to indicate major measurement problems regarding these assumptions with respect to exceptional children and youth. Results actually obtained in testing in the different areas of exceptionality will be presented only for the purpose of illustrating assessment problems in this field, since the major psychological findings are incorporated in the chapters on the several kinds of exceptionality. Only a few of the hundreds of devices and techniques will be mentioned—solely to illustrate the problems or attempts at solution of some of the problems which are indicated.

Our discussion of examination procedures and problems will be pointed toward the accomplishment of a maximally meaningful psychological assessment of exceptional children and youth. Yet, to attain this, we would need the contributions of a full and competent staff. Case studies, social studies, the reports of medical diagnostic and treatment specialists, and full educational histories would be required, and we should need to "staff" such children in the light of all such information before we could expect to have complete bases for sound and complete psychological assessments of the children. This is beyond the scope of this chapter. We shall limit our concern to problems involved in the obtaining and integrating of information within the framework of the psychological or psychoeducational clinic. Further, we shall confine ourselves to a consideration of the nature of the content of psychological reports rather than the reports themselves.

If this chapter identifies more problems than it settles, it is in part a result of the status of examination procedures in this field and in part a result of the author's desire to have this kind of educational impact upon the student.

The words "testing" and "assessing" mean definitely different activities. The term "testing" will be used to denote the exposure of a client to any given device, whether group or individual, essentially for the purpose of obtaining a quantitative characterization of one or more traits of that client. "Assessing," on the other hand, includes both this quantitative depiction of the client, and the qualitative and integrated characterization of the client as a dynamic, ongoing total organism functioning in a social setting. Without resorting to an illustrative full-length report of the assessment of a child, the following excerpted statements from a clinical case folder may suggest more clearly the contrast between qualitative and quantitative characterizations:

(a) He was 5 feet 4 inches tall [quantitative], but he didn't really stand up straight while he was being measured [qualitative].

(b) She earned an I.Q. of 67 on this test [quantitative], but she didn't seem to apply herself in the examination situation [qualitative].

(c) It is interesting to note that he consistently named differences but did not name similarities [qualitative], even though he did fail this part of the test [quantitative].

(d) Her constantly asking the examiner if her responses were correct and her frequent biting of her fingernails during the examination session suggested feelings of insecurity [qualitative]. This behavior, and some others like it, make me wonder if the I.Q. of 83 which she got on the Binet [quantitative] gives us a true picture of her rate of mental development.

There tends to be relatively less of the qualitative aspect in testing than there is of the quantitative aspect in assessing. Even though much of the following discussion will deal with the testing approach, the greater significance of the use of the assessment approach will, it is hoped, become apparent.

Even though this book is concerned with exceptional children and youth up to the chronological age of twenty-one, most of the discussion and the research cited will pertain to exceptional children from the high school level downward. The term "exceptional children," as used in this chapter, will signify either this more limited age range or a specific part of it.

It is particularly important in this chapter to bear in mind the fact that the terminology used to denote different kinds of exceptional children is confusing. In the first place, the term "physically handicapped" will be used here to refer to a group of exceptionalities—the orthopedic, the sensorily handicapped, the physically delicate, the brain-injured, the epileptic, and the like. The brain-injured will include both the cerebral-palsied and those who have, or are believed to have, higher-level neural impairment not reflected in motor dysfuntion. The deaf will be regarded as a part of the acoustically handicapped, just as the blind will be regarded as falling in the category of the visually handicapped. The term "mentally retarded" will be used, albeit illogically, to refer to those exceptional children whose intellectual retardation is not so severe as to warrant their falling in the range of mental deficiency nor so slight as to warrant their being regarded as "slow learners." The mentally retarded, then, will be thought of as having intelligence quotients roughly comparable to 1960 (L-M) Stanford-Binet IQs falling between approximately 50 and 75 or 80.*

*Hereafter, any unqualified reference to intelligence quotients or mental ages will be in terms of the 1960 Binet. If either has been ascertained by any

The mentally superior and gifted will be regarded as those with Stanford-Binet IQs of 125 and above.

In the second place, it certainly is not safe to assume that the different types of exceptionalities are "pure" types. A child with a speech impairment, for instance, also may have a hearing loss, or some higher central nervous system involvement, or he may be socially and emotionally maladjusted. A visually impaired child may be mentally superior or he may have a speech impairment, or he may also be brain-injured. However, our discussion will be restricted intentionally either to such "simple" types of exceptionality or to types of exceptionality in which the designated conditions are regarded as the *primary,* but not the sole, bases upon which the educational and social needs of such children are being met or are being studied. The psychological examination and assessment of children of any multiple-exception type involve a compounding of the problems peculiar to each of the involved areas of exceptionality, as in cases such as the mentally superior, severely involved athetoid; the deaf-blind; the blind cerebral-palsied; or the speech-impaired emotionally maladjusted.

ASSUMPTIONS UNDERLYING PSYCHOLOGICAL TESTING

In considering the following assumptions, it is quite likely that the student will think most often in terms of the measurement of the intelligence of a child. The assumptions, however, also underlie the processes of ascertaining such things as the nature of the child's emotionality,

---

other test, the name of that test will be used—as Otis IQ, or PMA mental age, or WISC verbal test age.

his educational achievement, his vocational aptitudes, his motor skills, his height, his weight, or even his temperature.

In this connection let us use the word "testing" to mean the process of using any device (test, inventory, scale, thermometer) in the examination of an individual. More explicitly, *testing is the controlled observation of the behavior of an individual to whom stimuli of known characteristics are applied in a known manner.* It would follow, then, that if the same stimulus (from the observer's point of view) were applied in the same manner (from the observer's point of view), the differences in the responses of the individuals so stimulated would be a function of differences within the individuals. The following assumptions inhere in this process:

1. It is assumed that *the observer is adequately trained* and skilled in the procedures of getting the subject to respond effectively (rapport), of applying the stimuli (test or test items), of recording the responses of the subject, and of evaluating (scoring) those responses according to the instructions for the standardized use of the device. In the majority of cases, the standardized procedures are adhered to rigidly. Later we shall consider certain studied departures from these procedures in connection with the examination of certain kinds of exceptional children.
2. It is assumed that *the sampling of behavior* in the test situation *is both adequate in amount and representative in area.* The safest way to judge a basket of strawberries would be to examine each strawberry and then base one's judgment on the total

sample. But people don't do that. Some look only at the top, and others tip up the basket and look at a few more. In the area of human behavior, we can't sample all of it, but by acceptable statistical methods we can determine how small a sample we can safely take. Similarly, we can't sample every different area of behavior, but we can and do sample those that, statistically, have been found to yield adequate reliability and validity.

3. It is assumed that *the subjects* being tested *have been exposed to comparable,* but not necessarily identical, *acculturation.* Even if the language problem is ignored, a personality test or inventory or a vocational aptitude test developed for use in the United States could well be of little or no value if used in Thailand or on the Zulus. Certain other tests are nearly as inappropriate when used on certain types of the physically handicapped whose worlds have been seriously circumscribed, as, for instance, Berko (1953) pointed out in connection with the cerebral palsied. Less often, but equally important, certain children may give evidence of having been "hothoused," given rather intensive cultural training consciously or unconsciously, by adults who, quite understandably, want their children to do well.

4. It is assumed that *error will be present* in the measurement of human behavior. Error is present in any measurement, whether it be in the distance to Jupiter, in the weight on the bathroom scales, in the length of a table, or in vocational aptitude, intelligence, or emotional adjustment. Statistical procedures enable us both to ascertain the magnitude of error in any given kind of measurement and to allow for that error in connection with any given measurement. We do not think of a child as having earned an absolute or infallible IQ on any given test but as having an IQ on that test falling between a point some 5, 10, or more points above the obtained one and another point some 5, 10, or more points below it.

5. It is assumed that only *present behavior is observed.* Behavior on any given test is as of that particular time on that particular test. It is a sample within a relatively long period of time. It must be remembered that a child is observed as reacting in this way (or these ways) to this stimulation (test) at the time and under the conditions of this test. But this condition does not make futile or meaningless the process of testing or examining because of the next assumption, plus certain kinds of statistical insurance that has been or can be taken out with respect to the validity of the behavior sampled.

6. It is assumed that *future behavior* of the child *is inferred.* The statement "Every diagnosis is a prognosis" illustrates the close association between the process of measuring present behavior and the act of using the results of that measurement in endeavoring to predict how the subject will act, regarding the particular areas of behavior observed, at some later time. The man is significantly overweight now; therefore he will be a less desirable insurance risk. The woman just passed her driver's examination; therefore, the state issues her a permit for future driving. The

child does very well on an intelligence test, and someone says he should be good college material. Another child does quite poorly in an examination situation and is therefore regarded as unlikely to respond effectively in future learning situations. Or, even, a child who actually has performed ineffectively in an examination situation is judged (inferred) to be actually capable of profiting from a treatment or training program, because certain conditions are believed to have impaired or distorted his present performance.

This two-step process of measuring and inferring is both reasonable and dangerous. On the one hand, it is the only thing we can do. A child performs normally in the first and second grades. That is to say, he is promoted to the next higher grade in the average amount of time. Therefore we make the guess that he will perform normally in the next higher grade, assuming no intervening distraction. Similarly, he answers correctly the same number of test items as did the average third grader, therefore, we *assume* that he is likely, in other related situations, to behave the way other third graders have behaved. On the other hand, such predictions have three important sources of potential error. Predictions may be faultily based either upon too limited a sample of behavior or upon a sample of behavior that bears no sound relationship to the predicted behavior. A fifteen-minute test involving the manipulation of some blocks can well provide a precarious basis upon which to predict that a child can acquire verbal symbols and use them meaningfully. Even a good sample of behavior which would serve satisfactorily for predicting behavior within the next year or so can lose much

of its value for the prediction of behavior five to ten years later. It must be remembered, too, that these predictions are not statements of certainty; they are actually probability statements, made in the sense of "the chances are . . . "

Measurement in the areas of intelligence and emotionality quite commonly involves an additional inferring process. In the case of intelligence, some kind of achievement often is measured, and then an inference is drawn concerning the capacity that made such achievement possible. In projective testing, for instance, we see inferences drawn with respect to basic personality structures from what often appear to the clinically untrained to be irrelevant behavior samples.

Thus we see that inferences are drawn from a present sample of behavior both with respect to what later behavior will be and with respect to what caused the behavior that was observed in the process of examination or measurement. It is particularly important to recognize that the results obtained in testing or assessing are used as the basis for inferences which have varying degrees of predictive strength. Especially is this realization necessary in dealing with exceptional children because they are, by the varying natures and complexities of their exceptionalities, the ones for whom many of our testing devices and procedures may be at least in part inappropriate.

VARIABILITY AMONG TESTS

Only very slowly are those who deal in the school setting with the results of tests of "intelligence" coming to recognize the necessity of differentiating among those devices. Perhaps even slower is their realization of the extreme importance of clearly denoting the specific measures obtained by means of these devices. Let us examine the importance of such precise communication with respect to "average" children and youth; the major implications of this with respect to the exceptional will become apparent repeatedly.

In order to simplify our consideration, we shall assume that normal, adequate, and otherwise satisfactory conditions existed in all the testings which are discussed. One further clarification is needed as regards the connotation of the term "IQ" as used in this portion of the chapter. Not infrequently—as in the question, Is the IQ constant?—one discovers that the person posing the question may use the IQ to denote, in some global fashion, the child's biologically determined potential for learning, a characteristic minimally reflecting the effects of any environmental influence upon it. Others may use the IQ to denote not only this basic capacity of the organism but also the extent to which it may have been modified by the child's rearing and culture, whether in a nurturant manner, in a nonnurturant manner, or in a detrimental way. In this second sense the IQ is used to denote what may well be regarded as the child's "effective intelligence." However, in addition to this ambiguity—as between just basic, native, biological potential, and potential-as-realized-and-operating—the IQ may denote simply some kind of score by which the child's performance on some test of "intelligence" is characterized. For our purpose in this section, we shall use IQ in this third sense—a score earned on some test of intelligence. As we shall see, this will improve our communication *somewhat,* but even this has come to contain disconcerting ambiguity.

In the 1920s, the early days of school group intelligence testing, when a group was said to have an average group test IQ of 121, or when any given child was referred to as having an IQ of 85 on some group test, the idea being conveyed was reasonably clear to those communicating. In most communities, a class so characterized would have been a fairly "bright" class; the child was possibly a "slow learner." *As of that time,* when teachers thus described or compared their classes or children, different teachers talked in terms of pretty much the same characteristic. This was due primarily to the fact that the group tests then in use were so similar in content. The behaviors sampled by the group tests of that time tended to be much the same from test to test. (The individual tests of those days, many of them the forerunners of most of our present "performance" tests sampled considerably more diverse forms of behavior.)

Subsequently, the predominantly verbal group tests came increasingly to be infused with or replaceable by tests that involved less reading and/or less use of verbal response by those taking them. Interspersed among items like "Boy is to girl as man is to (1) house (2) animal (3) woman (4) business," there were items such as "◁ is to ◁ as ▢○ is to (1) ◖ (2) ◫ (3) ▢ (4) ꝑ." The child reacting to both of these types of items was called upon to do the same *kind* of thing, but, in the first case, he employed words whose meanings he had learned, whereas, in the second, he did not need to use words to perform successfully. Then there developed complete tests, such as the Cattell Culture-Fair Tests, that employed no verbal content. Later came the kind of group test of intelligence which is more common now—that having one section of verbal items and another section of nonverbal, or "nonlanguage" items.

As a result, present group tests of intel-

T. ERNEST NEWLAND

ligence have become much more heterogeneous: some depending upon sampling only what has been learned by means of fundamental psychological processes; some involving a sampling not only of what has been learned but also of the processes which have been involved in that learning; and some which sample predominantly, or (hopefully) solely, processes which are essential to school learning. The scores (IQs) earned by means of these different kinds of behavior samplings therefore no longer are as likely to connote the relatively homogeneous sampling of earlier group tests. As a result it has become even more necessary to qualify the obtained score by the name of the test, such as Kuhlmann-Anderson IQ, Otis Gamma IQ, or Cattell Culture-Fair IQ. This kind of specificaton is additionally necessary by virtue of variations among tests in validity, adequacy of standardization, and other respects. For similar reasons it is necessary to identify clearly the individual test by means of which an IQ has been obtained.

If intelligence tests or, better, tests of learning aptitude are to be used to make a sampling of behavior on the basis of which to make some predictions as to likely ease of learning in school, and if the major kind of learning to be predicted is symbol acquisition, the devices used to measure that aptitude should yield reasonably consistent results. Disconcertingly often, educators find this not to be the case, as illustrated by five different average IQs obtained on 284 different twelfth-grade students tested within a single semester: 96.4, 103.7, 105.5, 114.2, and 118.2. One of the tests used was entirely nonverbal; another, a mixture of verbal and nonverbal; and a third, the heavily verbal Primary Mental Abilities Test. Equally extreme variations have been found on first-

grade children when they have been given even well-standardized group tests of "intelligence" or "mental maturity."

Chronologically paralleling this confusing state of affairs as regards group tests has been that of individual intelligence testing. Even as the Binet and early adaptations of it were coming into use, "performance" tests were being developed and used. The Seguin Form Board and its adaptations, the Witmer Cylinder, a myriad of form board tests from the Wallin Peg Boards to the more complicated Dearborn and Lincoln Hollow Square tests, picture and figure completion tests, the Kohs Color Cube Test, and maze tests first appeared as separate tests. They then were incorporated, as they were or in modified form, into batteries such as the Pintner-Patterson, the Grace Arthur, the Merrill-Palmer, and the Cattell scales. Because these were individual tests, they were used only clinically. It was out of such a background that the performance part of the Wechsler-Bellevue came into being and thus was included in the Wechsler Intelligence Scale for Children. That children's scores on such nonverbal tests contributed a much less adequate basis for predicting their verbal learning behavior than did their performance on verbal tests was early established, although that fact now appears to be largely overlooked.

The semirelevance of what has just been said about this group of performance tests to what was said earlier about nonverbal group-testing attempts must be considered most critically. There is the danger, as shown by uses to which the results of such testing have been put, particularly with respect to certain kinds of handicapped children, of assuming implicitly that because the item " ◁ is to ◁ as ... " is a nonverbal kind of item and because, say, a figure completion item such as the Feature Profile also is a nonverbal kind of item, they both sample the same kind of psychological process and, therefore, are likely to have the same or similar predictive value with respect to the child's primary chore in school—that of symbol acquisition. That such an assumption is not warranted is shown by the low correlations, long a matter of record, between the two kinds of performance and with educational achievement.

At least some of the confusion regarding results of widely differing tests—all purporting to measure intelligence—would seem to be capable of resolution by thinking about such tests in terms of factors that appear to be related to the extent to which scores earned on them increase with age. On the average, scores on the Raven Progressive Matrices, for instance, increase discriminatingly until the age of twelve or thirteen. At the other extreme, increases in scores on the Concept Mastery Test (CMT) can occur up to the age of fifty. "Maturity" on the Binet is reached from thirteen to fifteen years. Adult performance on the Wechsler increases until twenty to thirty years. Miller Analogies scores may "peak" somewhat after that, but significantly below the CMT (*See* Bayley, 1955; Bayley and Oden, 1955; Guertin, Frank, and Ladd, 1962). In part these differences well may be the result of the way in which these tests have been standardized, but, for our purposes here, another psychologically important variable, which may well be thought of as a continuum, seems to parallel the range from the Matrices to the CMT. If we examine the kinds of behavior sampled by the devices mentioned, we note that neither the administration of nor the responding to the matrices necessitates the use of verbal behavior. Given, for

instance, a box with three Xs and a blank space in it occupied by a ? to be replaced with one of the following: $\circ$, $\triangle$, $-$, X, $\bigcirc$, the subject quickly and easily can point to the X in the series as belonging in the box with the three other Xs. The product of nonverbal learning is needed in comprehending and solving the item. However, if we take an imaginary item to represent those in tests "peaking" later, we find a behavior sampling of this sort: "mortarboard : commencement :: bikini : —— (1) dancing (2) swimming (3) preaching (4) drawing." Here, the meaning of the pattern —:—::—:—long since has been learned, thus causing the difficulty of the item to inhere in the meanings of the words in order to satisfy the relationship called for in the proportion. It is suggested, then, that the continuum from Matrices-type tests to CMT-type tests can be paralleled by a continuum ranging from sampling learning potential in terms of *psychological processes fundamental to learning* to the sampling of learning potential essential in terms of the *products of learning.**

Graphically shown below is what is involved in a process-product perception of tested intelligence, in regard to at least educational achievement. Intelligence tests make behavior samplings that consist of varying mixtures of process and product. (Probably no sampling is purely process or purely product.) On the basis of the subject's performance on any pool of items, inferences are drawn regarding the subject's capacity to achieve in school

*Interestingly related to this conceptualization, which was arrived at clinically, is Cattell's positing, on the basis of results obtained by factor analysis, a fluid general ability, perhaps somewhat similar to the author's "process," and a crystallized general ability, quite similar to the author's "product." "Process" is relatable to Guilford's description (1967) of "operations;" "product," is relatable to his "products."

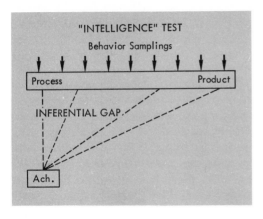

Fig. 3-1.

learning. The more the sampling is dominated by process, the shorter the inferential gap is; the more the sampling is dominated by product, the longer is the inferential gap.

The other tests mentioned, as well as still other intelligence tests not specifically referred to, can profitably be examined in terms of the extent to which they sample the psychological processes necessary to learning and in terms of the extent to which they sample behavior in terms of what has been learned. Two generalizations integrate the illustrative material that has been presented in this connection:

1. To the extent that the behavior sampled may be regarded as *product* (the result of learning), "maturity" tends to be attained later; whereas, to the extent that the behavior sampled constitutes *process*, "maturity" tends to be attained earlier. Or, intelligence test scores that reflect *process* tend to stop increasing at earlier ages than do scores of such tests that reflect *product*. It seems quite possible that at least certain essential psychological processes by which people learn may mature considerably

earlier than may have been assumed.

2. To the extent that the behavior sampled may be regarded as *product,* the impact of acculturation upon test performance tends to increase; whereas, to the extent that the behavior sampled constitutes *process,* the impact of acculturation on test performance tends to be reduced.

Such a consideration of the nature of behavior sampled by different kinds of intelligence tests should result in much less confusion regarding the varied scores that have been earned. As we shall see, this process-product concept has very definite implications regarding the assessment of the learning potential of exceptional children and youth.

THE MEANING OF NORMS

Individual test performances take on meaning when they are thrown into social perspective by means of norms. Measurements that are recorded have to be compared in order to give them meaning. For instance, we say Mary is 51 inches tall—a fact that, in and of itself, is meaningless. It takes on meaning when we are able to say that Mary is taller than her twin brother or is as tall as the average nine-year-old girl or is taller than 80 percent of her fellow seven-year-olds. Knowing how average seven-year-olds, average eight-year-olds, and average nine-year-olds learn, we have a somewhat fuller understanding of Jim's probable ease of learning when we know his mental age to be seven years six months. This was made possible by the fact that the person standardizing the test which was used on Jim had ascertained how a *typical* population at each age level in question had performed on that test. It is of particular importance here to note that a studiously typical population is sought for the standardization of the bulk of the measuring devices used. Mechanically using such devices on certain types of exceptional children, therefore, may be completely without justification. To make modifications of such devices by using only parts of the original standardized device, to modify slightly the material or procedure for even parts of the original standardized device, or to try to combine usable parts of differently standardized devices—each necessitates the carrying out of sound research to show that such tamperings do not invalidate the process of comparing the findings with the original norms.

Obviously, the significance attached to this varies with the kind of exceptional child being examined. If the child is exceptional *only* by virtue of some deviation in intelligence, devices standardized to measure this kind of behavior are applicable as standardized. On the other hand, tests involving speech to any significant extent would yield ambiguous results if used on children with serious motor involvements affecting speech. Certain manipulation tests, used in a standardized, timed manner on certain kinds of motor-handicapped children, would yield completely misleading results. When tests which include a considerable sample of acculturation are used on children who have not had a broadly "normal" exposure to that culture, it is inevitable that questions will be raised as to the validity of the results obtained.

Mainly in areas of exceptionality other than those of the intellectual deviant there is a very real question as to the extent to which the test performances of the severely orthopedically handicapped, or the sensorily handicapped, or of those with marked speech impairments, or even of those who are emotionally maladjusted should be depicted in terms of scores that have been obtained in the normal standardizations and uses of the device. If only devices standardized on a random sampling of a normal population are used on the exceptional, still excluding from our consideration the intellectual deviant, should the performances of the exceptional be stated in terms of the normal? If so, the exceptional stands to suffer by such a comparison because many of the conditions that constitute exceptionality are recognized clinically as conditions that tend to impair rather than to enhance an individual's performance. If, on the other hand, devices are standardized, for instance, on only the specific populations of the physically handicapped, there remains a problem of giving a meaningful social perspective to the performances of such persons on such devices. If, further, normally standardized devices are modified or "adapted" to the conditions of the exceptional, the meaning of the results so obtained, when compared with the norms for the original unmodified or unadapted device, becomes at best ambiguous.

In one sense the last three sentences in the above paragraph may be regarded as overstatements. Take, for instance, a bead-stringing task for which there are age norms. Assume that an athetotic ten-year-old takes the test and, in the prescribed amount of test time, is able to string only as many beads as the average five-year-old. It still may be socially worthwhile to know the level of the ten-year-old's functioning in this skill even though the test was not standardized on children with a motor involvement such as his. Whether the test was "fair" to this child depends upon the inferences that someone may draw with respect to his performance. In fact, logically, no test is "unfair"; only the user of a test can be "unfair," and his inferences may be unwarranted.

Assuming the appropriateness of norms for the different types of exceptionality, how should the performance of a given exceptional child on a particular device be characterized or interpreted? Should this child be described as being in the bottom 1 percent of the general population on a given trait, or should he be regarded as doing very well in view of the conditions operating in his case? On the one hand, his scholastic standing may be far below the grade level at which some persons might expect him to be working. On the other hand, he may be doing as well as he is capable of doing. The mental retardate, for instance, may be succeeding in school as well as can be expected on the basis of his mental capacity, but he still may be doing so poorly that he cannot be expected to succeed as a clerk in a small grocery where he would be required to make out slips, read invoices to check incoming goods, or even read names and addresses when making deliveries. The problem here is not an out-and-out either/or choice; it is, rather, one of deciding which to use when. For purposes of educational planning and motivation, we consider the child's performance in terms of *his* potential. For purposes of vocational planning, and for certain research purposes, however, his status must be conceived of in terms of his skills, or lack of them, in comparison with comparable skills in others. The assumption of a constant frame of reference, or a failure to distinguish clearly between different frames of reference, often causes considerable confusion in the assessment of exceptional children and youth.

We have seen, thus far (1) that when any client is tested or assessed, he is, in effect, being observed under conditions that are controlled as much as possible; (2) that certain concepts and assumptions are involved in any testing or assessing, whether the client be average or exceptional; (3) that special problems are encountered in testing or assessing the exceptional—whether it be attempted by the mechanical use on the exceptional of a device developed for and standardized upon the nonexceptional, or whether it be attempted by means of a device standardized upon a given kind of exceptional children, or whether one tries to take the shortcut of "adapting" conventional devices for use with the exceptional; and (4) that while these problems vary somewhat from one kind of exceptionality to another, the problems are common to various areas of measurement. Certainly, the more one is sensitive to the problems which have been indicated, the more one is hesitant to accept uncritically IQs reported on various kinds of the physically handicapped, especially when there lurk in the background implicit assumptions that IQs (or other quantifications) are comparable in a one-to-one relationship from one device to another, or from one handicapped group to another, or from one handicapped group to a nonhandicapped group.

As has been indicated, practically all of the devices that have been used in trying to ascertain the psychological picture of the physically handicapped have been developed on essentially normal populations. This is understandable in view of the fact that, in most cases, such devices were the only ones available and because it was desired to depict or describe the handicapped in terms of the nonhandicapped population with whom they had to live and compete. Take, for instance, the reporting of mental, or even achievement, test results on the deaf in terms of how they performed on devices that had been standardized on essentially nondeaf subjects. Consider, likewise, the dangers of this type of characterization of the performances of the severely orthopedically handicapped. However, no research evidence has been presented which demonstrates that the basic assumption regarding exposure to comparable acculturation has been satisfied.

TEST ADAPTATIONS

The point has been made that any test must be thought of as a controlled pattern of stimuli which is presented to a client in a uniform manner in order that the client's responses to those stimuli can be recorded and measured. Whether or not the original standardized pattern of items can be altered without lowering the validity of the total performance is an important question since, in examining children who are emotionally disturbed or even seriously ill at ease in the examination situation, some psychologists prefer to start their testing with performance or nonverbal items rather than with the verbal items with which the test was started when it was standardized. That such an approach tends more quickly to establish rapport with such subjects is generally accepted among clinicians. Fortunately, some research (Frandsen, McCullough, and Stone, 1950) on the effects of so altering the stimulus pattern of the 1937 Binet indicates that the validity of the total test response is not impaired by this particular type of modification of the test procedure.

It is a not infrequent practice among those making psychological examinations of the motor-handicapped to make other adaptations of tests to their clients by omitting certain items on which the examiner feels certain the client cannot perform. Certain vocabulary items are omitted if speech is severely impaired, and manipulation and drawing items are omitted if the client's hands are severely involved. This departure from the standardized stimulus concept of a test both involves a decrease in the sample of the client's behavior and, when "corrections" are made for the whole test on the basis of the parts of the test which were used, usually implies that each item in the test has equivalent measurement value.

Table 3-1 depicts the problem in a considerably oversimplified form. Let us assume that in the test in question ten kinds or "areas" of behavior are sampled, such as vocabulary, comprehension, maze tracing, picture identification, identification of similarities, and so on. Let us assume, also, that four nine-year-olds are examined by means of this device. Child 1 is examined in all ten areas and earns an IQ of 150, which becomes part of the basis upon which he may be characterized as mentally superior. Child 2, tested in the same ten areas, performs in a manner that suggests that he may be a candidate for a class for the mentally retarded. Child 3, who has a gross speech impairment, is examined in only eight of the ten areas, and he earns an IQ on that test of 65, numerically comparable to the one earned by Child 2. In like manner, Child 4, a manually impaired child, is examined by the same test, which has been adapted to his condition, and he is found to have an IQ numerically comparable to those of Child 2 and Child 3. We are justified in assuming psychological comparability among these total test performances only insofar as it has been shown by research that behavior samplings in each of the areas III, IV, VI, and VII are of equal psycho-

TABLE 3-1

HYPOTHETICAL TEST BEHAVIOR SAMPLING OF FOUR CHILDREN

	"Areas" of Behavior Sampled in the Total Test										
Child	I	II	III	IV	V	VI	VII	VIII	IX	X	I.Q.
1	x	x	x	x	x	x	x	x	x	x	150
2	x	x	x	x	x	x	x	x	x	x	65
3	x	x	x		x	x		x	x	x	65
4	x	x		x	x		x	x	x	x	65

logical value among themselves and also as related to the other areas of behavior sampled. In spite of the fact that it is yet to be shown by research that these conditions have been met, numerous studies have been published in the field of the exceptional, purporting to show comparisons among exceptionalities, between certain exceptionalities and the nonhandicapped, and within certain areas of exceptionality. Such studies have included test adaptations grossly lacking in psychological or statistical justification.

Although this problem is more clearly recognizable in connection with attempts to measure intelligence, it exists in a slightly modified form with respect to attempts to measure emotional adjustment, vocational aptitudes, and educational achievement. Whereas it is present in such attempts at measurement with the acoustically impaired and the speech-impaired, it is more commonly, and perhaps more dangerously, encountered with the cerebral-palsied.

Illustrative of ambiguous, if not misleading, data presented about the cerebral-palsied are the IQ data given in table 3-2. On the basis of these data, Bond (1953) stated that 40 percent of his 300 cases "must be classed as aments".

From a psychological point of view, one

TABLE 3-2

I.Q.	Per Cent	Age	Per Cent
Below 25	7	1-5 years	40
25-50	16	6-10	31
51-70	15	11-15	20
71-80	13	Over 15	9
81-90	17		
91-110	18	Speech	
111-130	4		
131-150	0.3	Poor	61
Undetermined	10	Fair	28
		Good	11

immediately asks questions such as these about such data: By means of what test or tests were these IQs obtained? Because the IQs were all thrown together in the same tabulation, is it not assumed that these IQs have both numerical and psychological comparability? Were the tests adapted to the subjects? If so, do the results from such adaptations have numerical and psychological comparability? In view of the fact that 40 percent of these cerebral-palsied clients were less than six years of age, how psychologically meaningful are such IQs? Because we know that the younger the child the greater the size of error in the psychological measurement of him, how much additional possible distortion resulted due to the crippled condition of these children? Since 61 percent were reported as having "poor" (presumably including "no") speech, to what extent are these data further clouded by that factor? What skill did this psychologist possess that enabled him to determine IQs in all but 10 percent of his 300 cerebral-palsied clients, 40 percent of whom were under six years of age and 61 percent of whom had poor speech? No small amount of curiosity would be evidenced as to the extent to which these intelligence quotient data would be affected by hearing impairments in these subjects. Questions such as these can well be raised with respect to a number of other reports on the intelligence quotients of the cerebral-palsied and certain other orthopedically handicapped children.

When one turns to the severely acoustically handicapped—particularly those born with this handicap or having it from an early age*—some of the same questions arise, and new ones occur due to the fact that the psychological conditions attending this latter group differ significantly from those attending, say, those cerebral-palsied who have normal hearing acuity. We shall confine our consideration here to problems attending the attempts at the measurement of general mental capacity but recognize that measurement of emotional adjustment, vocational aptitude, and educational achievement involves certain directly comparable problems. We have difficulty, for instance, in believing that our basic assumption concerning the general comparability of the acculturation of such handicapped subjects has been satisfied, particularly if devices developed for use with the nonhandicapped have been used on them and the results stated in terms of a normal population. For a

*For convenience, hereafter called the "deaf."

long time, devices standardized on a hearing population were administered to deaf children and youth and their performances characterized in terms of mental ages or IQs derived from data on children with normal hearing. That the deaf did significantly less well on these devices than the hearing was clearly evident. But did this fact indicate that the basic capacities of the deaf were as low as the test results suggested? Because at least most of the devices which were used sampled heavily in the verbal and conceptual areas, particularly regarding hearing subjects, one very properly can raise the question Was the acculturation of the deaf enough like that of the hearing (on whom the devices were standarized) to warrant the use of the same device on the two groups? Because even most mental measuring devices measure achievement (from which capacity to achieve is inferred), had the deaf the same opportunities to achieve (acquire percepts and form concepts) as did the nondeaf standardizing population?

This fact was early recognized and led to two lines of endeavor. Reasoning from the assumption that basic intelligence is likely to be "normally" distributed within a large population (such as the deaf) unless there are factors known to be operating to impair or distort it (as contrasted with affecting the *manifestation* of that intelligence), and that the average of that distribution should not be much, if at all, below the average of a comparable hearing population, ways were sought to obtain a "truer" picture of the basic mental capacities of the deaf. Because devices used were predominantly verbal, it seemed reasonable to get at the basic learning capacity of the deaf in a nonverbal manner. This seems like a wonderful idea, and it would be if we could be certain that the kinds of nonverbal behavior sampled provided as good a predictive basis (of subsequent school learning) as did the verbal behavior samplings. However, most measures of nonverbal behavior developed on a hearing population do not provide as good a basis for predicting success in school learning as do measures of verbal behavior. In the case of the deaf, the use of hearing-standardized nonverbal tests was found to be more effective in indicating school learning than was the use of hearing-standardized verbal tests. Steps were taken next to improve upon this admittedly makeshift situation by developing nonverbal tests that could be used with the deaf and standardizing these materials on the deaf. A roughly parallel developmental history has existed with respect to the areas of the cerebral-palsied and the blind. First, existing devices were employed, with little if any modification from their original form; certain parts of the devices were then omitted and/or substitutes made; then either wholly new devices were made or planned, or administration procedures and norms were developed for the particular exceptionality.*

*Regarding the initial basic assumption (concerning the normality of learning potential distribution) as equally plausible with respect to the deaf and the blind may seem, at first blush, defensible. However, the author questions its validity with respect to at least those who have been born deaf. He suspects that in persons born deaf the major psychological process underlyng all learning—the innate predisposition of the organism to generalize—does not receive as much reinforcement, both intentional and incidental, as is true in the case of individuals without such acoustic disability. As a result, it is believed, this process which originally may have had a potential of "normal" operation, well may come to function at something lower than its original potential due to lack of stimulation. This concept of reduced effective stimulation logically is part of a picture of deprived acculturation, a special case of faulty acculturation as that term is used in this chapter. The possible fruitfulness of this concept with respect to other kinds of exceptional children also should be explored. See, for instance, Newland (1960).

Making adaptations in the individual examination of exceptional children may consist, then, in those adaptations that are made in the testing procedures and in those that involve modifications of the device or devices used. Adapting testing procedures where the content of the device employed remains intact—although possibly presented in a modified order—is essentially a matter of employing psychological tactics in the testing situation. Here, the examiner may read the standardized test items to blind subjects, may allow a child to use a typewriter in giving his responses if he has a major speech or handwriting problem, may observe the eye movements of the subject as he identifies parts of a test item (where other children might write or point with their fingers in responding), might start with motor items rather than with verbal items in the case of a child whose problem involves the communication area, or might even rearrange some Binet items into WISC form if research warranted taking such liberties with the material. Here the primary objective is to obtain as psychologically meaningful responses as possible from the child to the total content of the test employed.

Adaptations that involve modifications of devices, either by the omission of a few of the kinds of behavior samplings or by selecting only certain parts of tests or scales, constitute something quite different. As was indicated earlier, this is done sometimes with no regard for the major psychological and statistical problems involved. Adaptations such as these are made for two reasons. Perhaps more commonly, the examiner employs only those parts of the device for which he can communicate the directions and to which he believes the child is capable of responding. The extreme of this is seen in the case of the use of "performance," nonverbal tests with the acoustically impaired. Attempts have been made to describe adaptations of a number of tests for use with the cerebral-palsied, as reported by Sièvers and Norman (1953) Allen and Collins (1955, 1958), and Katz (1956, 1958). In some instances, only some of the tests that make up a Wechsler or Binet may be utilized, because of insufficient time to administer the entire device or because the examiner believes, for one reason or another, that certain tests, or items, cannot be employed. Usually, arithmetically neat extrapolation procedures (sometimes of questionable psychological validity and limited in statistical justification) are specified for use in estimating what the "whole" behavior sample would have yielded. Generally, however, the communication problem is the major determinant of such adaptations, particularly in the cases of disabled subjects.

On the other hand, the psychologist may decide that he wants to study a child with respect to certain kinds of psychological functionings. He then employs only those parts of tests that he knows, or believes, involve the kind of behavior in which he is interested. He may, for instance, be particularly interested in the child's conceptualization behavior, or in the child's memory span, or in the child's fund of general information, or how he functions arithmetically, or how he learns in the clinic situation, and the like. Three conditions must be satisfied if the psychologist is going to use test materials in this manner. He must know the parts played by different kinds of behavior in the learning process. He must have evidence that the tests which he uses to obtain such behavior samples throw valid light upon such facets of learning. And he must have a normative background in terms of which he can interpret the results of his sampling. He must understand, for example, the difference in conceptualization behavior between a child who says that a bus and a railroad car are alike because they both have wheels and a child who says that they are alike because they are means of transportation. And he needs to know at what ages children are likely to respond in each of these two manners.

This type of clinical evaluation of children with cerebral defects is well described by Taylor (1959). By means of a variety of tests, for which she provides rationale, directions, and normative data, she samples behavior in terms of perception, reasoning, and learning—paying somewhat more attention to how the child functions than to the rate of development in these areas. Clinically, the procedures she describes have potential value beyond work with the cerebral-palsied.

The decisions as to whether and how test adaptations should be made must therefore be based, first, upon the assumptions initially made regarding the distribution of the trait being studied in the particular kind of exceptional subject. Is an essentially normal distribution of learning aptitude assumed as in the case of the visually impaired, the socioemotionally maladjusted, the orthopedically disabled, or of the total population in terms of which the mentally retarded and the mentally superior are described? Are test adaptations (or selections) made for the usually unstated purpose of causing the deviant to be perceived as less deviant than he really is (for school learning), as in the use of somewhat higher nonverbal performance scores in place of the predictively more meaningful verbal scores? The psychologist must make his basic assumptions explicit and is obligated to try to help the educator understand them and interpret test results in terms of them.

Other adaptations are necessary for certain of the exceptional. One kind of such adaptation involves the modification of methods of evoking the desired kinds of responses. These adaptations of the administration of the test are made only for the purpose of improving communication between the examiner and the examined, and every effort must be exerted to do nothing that will alter the psychological nature of the behavior being sampled. Imagine, for instance, a card that had printed on it, in randomly related positions, pictures of a cat, a tree, a bat (mammal), a tricycle, a flower, an elephant, and a house. Suppose that a speech-impaired child is shown a picture of a mouse and is asked, "show me all here (on the large card) like that (the mouse)." The child can, by pointing, give the examiner a psychologically meaningful indication as to whether he functions at a low conceptual level (selecting the cat because of the commonality of the whiskers), or go so far as to include the bat (as one kind of animal), indicating a high level of conceptualization. However, to use a picture of a person as a means of helping the deaf understand that they are to "draw a person" would help him to get the idea of what he is to do but would limit or invalidate the psychological intent of the test.

Another concept to be kept in mind in making test adaptations is one that was developed earlier to the effect that in certain instances, at least in the cases of the blind and in some of the orthopedically handicapped, learning potential may be more meaningfully sampled only, or primarily, in terms of process rather than in terms of product. The extent to which this kind of adaptation will have merit will necessarily depend upon the age level of the subject whose learning behavior is being predicted. It is quite likely that predicting school learning solely or primarily on the basis of samples of psychological process (classification, eduction of relationships and correlates, and the like) may be much more defensible in the case of young children than in the case, say, of high school level children. This is likely to be true due to the fact that learning at the higher level, or even at the later elementary school level, depends not only upon the pupil's being adequate in regard to the psychological processes essential to his learning but also to his having benefited from those processes by learning some things (products) that are needed in order to learn higher order things. At the kindergarten or preschool level, psychological processes are the primary means by which the child comes to learn that many different objects can be called "dog"; this concept must be acquired (product) before he later can differentiate between the labels "canine" and "feline"—it can be a contributive step to his learning what "animal life," or "transportation," or "shepherding" means.

The matter of adapting tests for use with the exceptional must be evaluated in terms of the whole range of points developed in this section. Particular areas of exceptionality present their unique demands, and the nature of the adaptations justifiably will need to vary also among the areas of psychological measurement—whether learning aptitude, academic achievement, socioemotional adjustment, or vocational aptitude.

MEASUREMENT APPROACHES AND PROBLEMS

We have considered at some length certain assumptions basic to and difficulties inherent in attempts to examine the exceptional. On the basis of these, the student should be able to determine for himself certain possible uses of specific devices and procedures.

The number of devices that have been well developed for the purpose of sampling different kinds of human behavior runs frustratingly into the hundreds. Other less well-standardized and validated devices that have been used, many of which might add significantly to our understanding of human behavior if they were provided with scientifically acceptable bases, increase the total amazingly. To consider each of the best and most promising of these, with respect to particular types of exceptionality, would lead us into a mass of detail that would be interesting but, in large part, highly transitory. It will better serve our purpose here to consider only illustrative attempts at measurement of certain types of behavior in certain of the areas of exceptionality. Some of these attempts have been made, others are being initiated, and some need to be undertaken.

Psychologically, we strive continuously to think in terms of the "whole individual" reacting in varying situations. However, measurement in this molar sense has not been accomplished. What we have to do is, consciously, artificially, to deal, one at a time, with certain facets of the individual, and then to reconstitute the individual into a dynamically meaningful whole. For our purpose, we shall concern ourselves with selected measurement approaches and problems in specific areas: limited aspects of physical condition, intellectual potential, socioemotional adjustment, educational achievement, and vocational aptitude.

As we consider these facets of different kinds of exceptional children and youth, we recognize that some evidences of some of these areas overlap to varying extents with certain evidences of others. A child needs a certain amount of intellectual capital and educational achievement in order to comprehend and react meaningfully to an inventory on social adjustment or to certain tests of vocational interest. Even if the items in such devices were read to him, he must be able to understand and remember what is read if his responses are to have even elementary validity. In spite of this, the areas can be regarded as partially and, if competent research has been done on the devices used, identifiably discrete. Bear in mind, too, that we shall refer to the exceptionalities as though they were single rather than multiple exceptionalities.

The Physical Area

During the early years of an individual's life, inferences concerning intellectual growth are based essentially upon evidences of physical growth and development. This is understandable because the nervous system must grow in order that muscles will function and, probably, for cognitive behavior to occur. When certain muscles are seen to function, this is taken as evidence that certain neural growth has occurred. When normal stimulation does not evoke a given motor response, it is inferred that neural growth has not occurred, due either to lack of time for such growth or to the presence of some pathological condition. If the nature of a variety of motor responses of an eighteen-month-old infant is comparable to the nature of those of only a nine-month-old, then one is usually highly suspicious of mental retardation or of some contributing pathology, or of both. (One does not generalize wisely on a single sample of behavior!) As a result, the physical developmental picture serves as a major basis on which inferences are drawn concerning mental development. Particularly useful in ascertaining and interpreting this physical developmental picture of infants and young children is Gesell and Amatruda's *Developmental Diagnosis*, although, in using the information in this book, one must constantly bear in mind the fact that the normative statements are in terms of averages and that perfectly normal individuals can fall somewhat above and below the averages which are presented.

Using the normative data of the Gesell Developmental Schedules, Blum and Fieldsteel have prepared development charts on which child growth may be plotted. The charts provide for the systematic recording of twenty-eight samples of motor behavior and of thirty-two samples of functional behavior. The systematic description of the motor performances (and functions) of children of whatever type of exceptionality has value, even when their behavior is compared with that of nonexceptional children, since in doing so, the *range* of any child's behaviors may be more suggestive than the fact of his having deviated from the "normal" in any of them. Assets thus tend more quickly to be capitalized upon and liabilities often may suggest remedial or corrective steps to be taken.

In interpreting behavior samples of this sort, one must remember that the manifestations of some mild neuropathological conditions may not appear until later. Illustrative of this is the case of a child who, at the age of eighteen months, was very thoroughly and apparently competently examined, both neurologically and psychologically, in a clinic of high repute. The official report of that clinic, undoubtedly justified at that time, contained not even a suspicion of any neurological involvement. When the writer saw the child, at the age of five, there were motor and sensory responses that suggested some neural involvement. Subsequent examination of the child by a competent medical authority confirmed the suspicion of mild athetoid involvement with an accompanying moderate hearing loss.

The problem of characterizing the motor levels of children handicapped by neuromuscular disorders has has been attacked by Johnson, Zuck, and Wingate (1951). Drawing upon Gesell's developmental data and preparing situations and devices which call for more complex behaviors, they have constructed an individual test by which they endeavor to ascribe motor ages to such handicapped children. Standardized originally on "normal" children, for which the original data unfortunately are not available, norms are established for functioning both with upper extremities and with lower extremities. The children can be examined both with and without braces, thus making possible a determination of the benefits of bracing and the effects of other corrective work.

Illustrative of a different basis for the study of the motor competencies of children, youth, and adults with neuromuscular involvements are the check lists prepared by Brown (1950a,b) and others. Her Daily Activity Record provides a means for checking 100 routine behaviors—including speech, dressing, undressing, eating, locomotion, rising, and sitting down—and for recording progress in learning such physical activities. The Brown-Bogert Pre-Vocational Motor Skill Inventory is intended for use with "any person of any age who has one or more extremities free for motor skills." One hundred activities are listed in this device, also, but they differ from the essentially self-care activities of the Daily Activity Record by including behaviors such as fixing a plug on an electric cord, extracting a nail, packing groceries in a carton, and putting a key in a padlock. Although the time allowances for both these devices and the age placements of the items in the latter inventory still may require more rigid statistical validation, the instruments and their underlying rationale have much to commend them. Distefano, Ellis, and Sloan (1958) have made some evaluations of over-all motor coordination especially with the mentally retarded, by means of the Oseretsky test.

If we disregard the psychogenic aspects of speech impairment and instead deal with it essentially as a motor function, then the problem of identifying the behaviors that constitute speech impairment is facilitated by the many check lists, sets of pictures, and other stimuli for evoking speech behavior which are described in the chapter on speech-handicapped children.

Although it is not within the proper domain of the psychologist to make diagnoses regarding the presence or absence of brain damage, he often can detect behavioral cues on the basis of which to invite consideration by the neurologist. Sometimes his suspicions are aroused by electroencephalographic tracings, by digit, letter, or figure reversals, or rotations on intelligence and on some projective tests, or by certain bizarre or stereotyped perceptual behavior (Piotrowski, 1940). Such hunches tend to be dangerous when they are expressed by the neophyte; they are not 100 percent certain with experts as voiced by Doll (1947) and Wittenborn (1949). Illustrative of psychologists' validated attempts to ascertain the presence of brain injury are the Graham-Kendall Memory-for-Designs Test, Benton's Visual Retention Test, and the work of Rei-

tan. No research has yet been done to ascertain whether these approaches can validly be used with the deaf or the blind.

The measurement of auditory and visual efficiency will not be discussed here, since those procedures and problems are discussed in the chapters on the acoustically and the visually handicapped. Suffice it to point out here that certain problems in these areas parallel those in the area of measuring intelligence. In all three areas, for instance, there is first the problem of gross and reasonably effective screening, as a result of which children so screened out undergo more intensive and extensive individual examination by more highly trained persons. Audiometric and vision screening procedures vary in validity just as group intelligence tests do. Further, just as a child of normal or above-average mental capacity may not do well on a group intelligence test because of emotionality or a number of other factors, just so, for instance, may a child "fail" in a group testing situation because of wax in his ears, a cold, or other causes.

Helpful to some extent in the total psychological assessment of exceptional children and youth are the evaluated measurements of their different gross structural features. Clinicians vary in the amount of attention they give to such aspects as body type, head girth, cephalic index, changes in chest size with inspiration and expiration, and stage of development of the wrist bones. Height and weight norms, interpreted in the light of the nature of the child's parental stock and health history, can be helpful in understanding and characterizing these aspects of the child. Widely used norms continue to be those of Baldwin and Wood (1932). Martin's (1955) much more recent and carefully obtained data on the heights and weights of children and youth, ages five through twenty, are now available, however. Developmental age-normative data, compiled by Olson, include additional information on permanent dentition and strength of grip, and extend the height-weight norms by sex down to the thirty-month level (Olson and Hughes, 1950). Recording and studying the physical developmental history of children, by teachers and parents in checking gross growth and by pediatricians in working correctively on growth problems, are facilitated by the Wetzel Grid technique (Wetzel, 1948). Based upon the fact that children tend to have their own physical growth rates, successive plottings of height-weight status can reveal departures from the children's channels which, in turn, are taken to be indicative of some disturbance of growth patterns due to physical or emotional factors.

The physical behavior pattern of a child may be distorted not only by neuromuscular and structural anomalies and physiological dysfunctions but also, with at least equal prevalence, by excessively solicitous and inhibiting parental care. Unless one is clinically highly perceptive of traces of cues in such cases, the degree of physical involvement is likely to be regarded as considerably greater than it actually is. In such instances, the orthopedist, the neurologist, or the pediatrician can give the psychologist some valuable cues and, often, the psychologist can find behavior potentialities of much value to the medical specialists.

The Area of Intelligence

The earlier discussion of assumptions and problems of measurement in general and the illustrations presented to show how easily the results of attempts at measurement of intelligence in particular can be contaminated are both of particular import with respect to the problem of ascertaining the learning capacity of all types of exceptional children.

General problems. As this discussion has progressed, the reader has probably become concerned about the seeming confusion of the measurement of "intelligence" as a total, all-inclusive something with the measurement of aptitude for school learning. It is hoped, also, that he has become concerned with allusions to "basic" learning capacity and illustrations of measured learning capacity. An understanding of these terms will contribute much to a comprehension of the significant measurement problems of the exceptional, to a sound basis for critical evaluation of the studies reported in this field, and to an adequate background in light of which to perceive the strengths and weaknesses of current and future attempts at measurement in this area.

Granted that it would be psychologically convenient to be able to measure an overall, all-inclusive intelligence either within a given area of exceptionality or among all areas, the bulk of the efforts have been, and probably will continue to be, directed toward the measurement of those aspects, or kinds, of intelligence which are most directly related to the learning of a certain kind of behavior that seems to play a major part both in just living with people and, more specifically, in learning in school situations. Because the provision of school learning situations constitutes the bulk of society's organized efforts in the interests of children, the measurement of the "intelligence," or "mental capacity," of these children becomes largely, if not essentially, the measurement of learning aptitude geared primarily to school situations but also to many nonschool situations. In the discussion here, it is assumed that the major learning activity is the acquisition of symbols.

Within this structure, then, the following definition of "intelligence" is employed: *Intelligence is the potential of the organism to acquire symbols, to retain those symbols, and to communicate meaningfully by means of those symbols.* This "educator's definition" includes much more than vocabulary acquisition. Symbols may be spoken or written. They may be verbalized or nonverbalized. Symbols represent both objects and relationships between objects. The child, for instance, may rub his stomach as a nonverbalized symbol to communicate the idea that he is hungry, that he likes something, or that he has a stomach ache. He may say, "John is taller than Sue," using the symbol "taller" for the relationship between two persons. He may cringe, in a completely unverbalized manner, at a frown because this facial "symbol" in another portends a threatening relationship between another and himself. Having acquired these symbols he uses them in "intelligence" tests, in personality inventories, in vocational aptitude tests (either verbal or nonverbal), in educational achievement tests, or in projective devices. In the light of this, then, the measurement of this aspect of intelligence becomes the measurement of the child's susceptibility to acquire symbols.

Lest this perception of intelligence be regarded as rejective of/or insensitive to Guilford's "Structure of Intellect," it should be observed that the orientation here is intentionally molar, in contrast to his highly differentiated (and integrated) conceptualization. In a sense the view presented here can be perceived as including all of his "operations" primarily with regard to his "semantic" category of "content." Symbols, as the term is used here,

would be involved in all of his "products."

"Creative" behavior, the educator's extrapolated implication of Guilford's psychological construct of "divergent thinking," has been the focus of a spate of educational literature. A failure to apply a social contribution criterion in differentiating between divergent thinking and creativity has underlain research seeking evidence of creativity in the mentally retarded, as illustrated in Tisdall's study. (If divergent thinking equals creativity, it would appear to follow logically that any error response is a creative response.) Creative production by different kinds of exceptional children and youth is yet to be validly researched and undoubtedly needs to be nurtured. Some of the testing efforts in this area could have relevance and promise. At least the bulk of this behavior will be symbolic in nature.

The second terminological problem here arises with respect to our belief, or evidence, as to how close we come to the measurement of this susceptibility to symbol acquisition. When test performance is minimally contaminated by such conditions as emotional overlay, sensory impairment, motor involvement, or abnormal acculturation ("hothousing" or gross deprivation), we regard such test behavior as very strongly indicative of basic capacity. To the extent that test performance is clouded by any of these conditions, we get results that do not accurately reflect that *basic* capacity. The term "basic capacity," or "basic intelligence," is used here to denote more nearly the biologically inherent learning-potential of an organism. We continually hope that the behavior which reflects it is as little culturally contaminated as possible but have the constantly lingering suspicion that it is at least a little so distorted.

The likelihood of test performances validly reflecting the basic capacities of children varies with the population of which those children are a part. If they were a group randomly selected out of a large heterogeneous public school population, basic capacities would be likely to be fairly accurately reflected in significantly more than half of those in such a group. If the children were among a random selection of those brought into a psychological clinic for examination, the basic capacities would be reasonably clearly reflected in only a small minority of them. Again, (and this is most important for us here) if the children were all exceptional, it would be highly unlikely that basic capacities would be reasonably clearly reflected in more than a very small percentage of the group. For reasons that have been suggested in this chapter and that have been presented in the other chapters of this book, the test performances of a very large percentage of exceptional children tend to be clouded by these conditions of emotional overlay, sensory impairment, motor involvement, and abnormal acculturation. Whereas such likely contaminations are recognized in the area of tested educational achievement and are suspected in the areas of emotionality and vocational aptitudes, they are particularly significant psychologically in the area of mental capacity measurement, both because of the higher frequency of attempts at measurement in this area and because of the cruciality of attempts at such measurement.

It appears desirable, then, to distinguish clearly between *basic* capacity and *manifest* capacity. We shall use the term "manifest capacity" to denote that performance level which is immediately and most easily apparent in the test situation, the interpretation of which is unaffected by any qualitative explanations. It is the test indication of what the client did—

how he scored according to standardized procedure of test administration. It involves no guessing by the examiner as to how much better or worse the client really is. It is the unmitigated performance at the time of testing. It is reasonably safe to assume that by far the major percentage of published reports of the intelligence of various types of exceptional children are reports of this manifest capacity. To the extent that readers of such reports assume that these manifest capacities are synonymous with the basic capacities of these children—to that extent may harm be done these children by means of distorted educational and social planning for them.

Because it is the manifest capacity which is indicated by the gross performance on the test, it should be noted that the basic capacity is inferred by the clinician. To the uninitiated, this inferring process may seem quite nebulous and the result of such inferring as only a wild guess. To the person who has worked clinically, rather than mechanically psychometrically, with children, this process is psychologically sound and real, and the results of it are supportable estimates. In some instances, basic capacity is taken to be indicated more by certain parts of certain tests (vocabulary versus memory span, for instance); in other instances, the clinician's inference as to basic capacity stems from the quality of performance rather than from the quantity of performance in the examining situation. This is admittedly a subjective process, but the subjectivity occurs within a trained clinician's frame of reference rather than within the frame of reference of a psychologically untrained person. The chances for and magnitude of error in such "measurement" of this basic capacity are clearly greater in such estimation by properly trained persons than is the case in the standardized use of psychological devices in ascertaining evidence of manifest capacity, but the clinician believes that a more meaningful psychological indication of the child's real potential is thereby obtained.

An illustration or two may help clarify the matter. An emotionally disturbed ten-year-old boy earned a Revised Binet Form L mental age of eight years and six months under competent examination (his manifest capacity). However, it was apparent to the examiner that the boy's basic capacity was greater than the one reflected in the examination situation. In fact, it was estimated that the boy's real potential would be nearer that of an average ten- or ten-and-a-half-year-old if the boy could be helped in his emotional adjustment. After the boy was put for a year in a therapeutic situation, which, in the judgment of the clinical staff, had been partially successful, he earned a Revised Binet IQ of 105. This was still believed to be somewhat below his "true" rate of intellectual development. A seven-year-old cerebral-palsied girl was examined by a psychometrist by means of parts of the Revised Binet and parts of several performance scales. The results were reported in terms of intelligence quotients, and the girl was recommended for exclusion from the public schools because her performance (manifest capacity) appeared to indicate that she was considerably lower than a Binet IQ of 50 would suggest. Yet, on reexamination by a psychologist, there were qualitative indications that she was functioning then, with allowances made for the motor handicap, at a five- or six-year level (her basic capacity). The results of a year's trial in a treatment center and special class for the cerebral-palsied supported the findings of the psychologist rather than those of the psychometrist.

It should not be assumed from the foregoing that only the basic capacity is psychologically and socially significant. Knowing the manifest capacity of a child, one is helped to know his "effective intelligence"—the level at which one can expect the child to function *at that time*. Having some idea of the basic capacity of that same child, if the two be different, one can know what to expect of that child, if and when the extenuating conditions or factors have been changed or if the child is helped to learn methods of compensating, in whole or in part, for them.

It should be emphasized that such disparities between manifest and basic capacities do not always exist. In a few cases, they are large; in some, little, if any, disparity exists. The likelihood of such disparities in the case of the exceptional is greater than in the case of the nonexceptional. As a rule, basic capacity tends to be greater than manifest capacity, although clinics are not without instances of children "testing beyond themselves." The frequency and size of error tend to be greater in the case of group devices than in the case of devices competently individually administered. Certain group devices have greater chances for error than others, even when they are competently administered and scored. The age of the child tested is also a factor to be considered. A comparable situation exists with respect to the various individual tests and scales. For reasons of this kind alone it will be seen why no small number of published studies presenting the IQs of handicapped children, or even of studies on reportedly nonhandicapped children, have been confusing and actually misleading to the uninformed. As has been suggested, the very fact that some children are exceptional should make us at once highly critical of the results obtained on such children by merely conventional approaches to the measurement of their mental capacities. This in no way vitiates devices used in conventional ways to ascertain the intelligence of not less than three-fourths of our school-age children, under the assumptions that have been stated; it suggests only that an intelligent caution by exercised with respect to the undertaking of this task in the cases of at least those 15 to 20 percent of our preschool and school-age children and youth who constitute the exceptional group. Healthy skepticism is rightly maintained at all times with respect to all test results; it is only more so with respect to the exceptional.

It is essential to emphasize, then, especially regarding group tests, that low test scores always are much more suspect than are high scores. The chances of error being present in an obtained low score are much greater than in high scores. A low score that is "untrue," or is not accurately indicative of the basic capacity of a child, still has psychological significance because it is of value to know that the child scored "artificially" low and to know that there are, or can be, times when he can or will stumble.

Good group intelligence tests have their major value (still short of perfection), as screening devices, for the initial indentification of the mentally superior; have decreased screening value (but still practical) with respect to the mentally retarded; and are of still less screening value in reflecting verbal learning capacity as we go from the socially and emotionally maladjusted to the speech-impaired, the sensorily handicapped, and the seriously involved orthopedically handicapped. In the case of the orthopedically handicapped, the tests have high practical screening value provided the children on whom they are used

have no interfering motor impairments and no major cultural impoverishment. With respect to some children with cerebral-palsied conditions and certain others who are known to be brain-damaged, the possible effect of conceptual dysfunctions needs also to be considered.

The need for more definitive depiction of the learning capacities of exceptional children and for reduction in the error of such measurement necessitates individual examination of them. In such an individual examination approach, greater adaptation of the procedure is possible in terms of the characteristics of the child. Rapport is established in the face-to-face situation, whereas indifference or fright may exist under group testing. The child who, for purely physical reasons, is enabled under individual examination procedures to take his time or to react only to situations that have been selected so as not to prejudice the sampling of his behavior, is not cut short by time limits or forced to enter into, or to avoid completely (fail), a variety of test situations that were found to have meaning with respect to the nonhandicapped. Less culturally contaminated behavior samplings can be made by means of certain individual procedures in the case of the child who presents a history of marked cultural deprivation as a result of sustained physical confinement, whereas most conventional group devices may involve a heavy sampling of behaviors that are completely irrelevant to such a child's psychological history.

The way in which an exceptional child's performances in test situations may be represented varies with the social and clinical factors attending those examinations. Most frequent characterizations of these performances have tended to be in terms of intelligence quotients. Less frequently, mental ages, test ages, centile, stanine, and standard score designations have been used. Still less frequently in the past, though increasingly now in most clinics, these performances have been characterized in broader, less definitive, terms. Intelligence quotients indicate only *rates* of mental development. The "deviation quotients" of the Wechsler scales and of the 1960 (L-M) Stanford-Binet can be taken roughly to indicate relative rates of development, but differ in certain respects from their forerunner, the computed intelligence quotient, which was obtained by dividing an obtained mental age by the chronological age and multiplying the result by 100. All such quotients, however, have primarily administrative value. Educationally, they have somewhat more value at the time a child normally enters school, have very limited value between that point and the high school level, and acquire more value from the high school age on up. Mental ages, however, have primarily educational value, because they indicate *levels* of mental development and thereby can be suggestive of the levels at which the child might be expected to work in school. Test ages, in the sense employed with respect to the WISC, and WPPSI, may have somewhat less educational value, depending upon the relationship known to exist between the behavior sampled by any particular test and the educational performances under consideration. Centile and standard score characterizations have less educational value below the high school level. Some rightly regard all such specific designations as unwarranted with respect to certain of the more physically handicapped and use such characterizations as "roughly the potential level of an average nine-year-old," or "educable," "trainable," and "subtrainable." The majority of our considerations

in this chapter are in terms of *level* characterizations.

We shall consider, mainly, representative examples of individual examination approaches that have been tried, adapted, and developed for certain of the exceptionalities. Some of these devices and approaches will be seen to be employable with more than one kind of exceptional child; some will be usable with only one kind.

The cerebral-palsied. * Children who have neuromuscular involvements present difficult assessment problems. The picture is considerably more complicated with respect to those handicapped by cerebral palsy. Although this section deals with problems pertaining only to the latter group, it will be apparent that many of these exist in the cases of children with orthopedic involvements.

The greatest liberties in endeavoring to adapt individual examinations have been taken with respect to the cerebral-palsied. The greater the physical involvement of such children, the greater has been the need either to make such adaptations or to develop examination procedures appropriate to the demands of this type of exceptionality. In fact, in the absence of individual devices suitable for use with the cerebral-palsied, a "cafeteria" approach generally has been used. Depending upon the condition of the particular child, certain items from one scale are used in connection with other items lifted from other scales on the assumption that all such items, taken together, psychologically rather than additively, would give at least a general idea of the mental level at which

*The term "cerebral palsy" is used in the sense of the definition. "Any abnormal alteration of movement or motor function arising from defect, injury, or disease of the nervous tissue within the cranial cavity."

the child was functioning, or could function. In the hands of the psychologically less well trained, this procedure can be dangerous, particularly if the assumption is implied that such items from different devices, and often sampling quite different kinds of behavior, are comparable on a one-to-one basis. However, when such items are selected with a view to the sampling of consciously presumed or known types of psychological functioning, and when the examiner has an adequate background of training and experience with normal children, reasonably meaningful qualitative and quantitative approximations of the intellectual potential of such a child can be obtained. Obviously, a definitive IQ characterization of the cerebral-palsied child by the former procedure is based upon assumptions that still need to be supported by research and hence may be misleading. Some rough ideas of the rates of mental development of these children by these procedures can be inferred, but by pinpointing by IQs is a psychometrist's and statistician's dream rather than a psychological reality.

The measurement of the learning capacities of the cerebral-palsied, early discussed by Bice (1948) and Haussermann (1952), presents problems that are considerably more challenging than is the case with respect to the other types of exceptionality. Test results obtained in the process of identifying the mentally superior and the mentally retarded are comparatively easy to verify in terms of social and educational criteria, even though the extent to which such test results are a function of nonhereditary organic pathology in the mentally handicapped is not yet clear. In the cases of children with other handicapping conditions, excepting *perhaps* those with aphasia and epilepsy, there is reason to assume that organic pathology

per se plays little or no part in the actual lowering of the basic learning capacities of such groups. When we come to the cerebral-palsied, however, our realization that the condition results from brain-centered nervous system pathology and our still relatively great ignorance of the extent to which basic learning capacity is thus impaired combine to provide us with extremely ambiguous criteria on which to evaluate results obtained from existing measuring devices or on which to standardize new devices suited to the unique perceptual and communication needs of this handicapped group. Some psychological research reveals a limited picture of their perceptualization processes, and these can contribute to, or even be a part of, faulty conceptualization. With our definition of basic learning capacity, such conceptualization impairment would appear to be grounds on which reasonably to suspect some basic retardation. The question is How much?

The need, therefore, for the development of devices and procedures that can be used with the cerebral-palsied is at once apparent. The problem here is not so much with those who are only mildly involved, since, with moderate caution, available approaches can be used. The major difficulties exist with respect to the examination of those of moderate and severe neuromuscular involvement. In such cases communication is a problem, both regarding the use of verbal responses by the subjects and, in some cases, regarding the sensory impairment of such cerebral-palsied children. In some instances, where these handicapped children are physically unable to speak, they also are unable to point. In such cases the examiner may have to rely upon the child's eye movements, and, if nystagmus renders this avenue of communication doubtful, even upon the facial expression of the child.* In addition to the problem of communication, there are those of the meaninglessness of rigid time limits, the highly varying and often grossly distorted cultural backgrounds, the possibility of the confusion of figure and ground in at least the visual field, the wide age range, the possible relatively higher fatigability as compared with the nonhandicapped, the possible interference of more and greater emotional factors such as excessive dependency on the parents, and conditioning against clinical settings. Add to all these problems the fact that the term "cerebral palsy" has come to include a variety of conditions that might materially complicate the psychological picture, and it will be seen how difficult the intellectual evaluation of these handicapped children actually is. The fact that this handicapped group is numerically smaller, for instance, than the blind group, even after correcting for Phelps' underestimation of prevalence, and regarding as blind those with a Snellen rating of 20/200 and worse in the better eye after maximal correction, also adds to the difficulty of soundly standardizing a test or a test battery on this population.

Because some of the difficulties attending the intellectual evaluation of the cerebral-palsied are in common with those encountered with other types of exceptional children, it is understandable that attempts would be made to develop devices that could be used with other kinds of children as well. Illustrative of one attempt of this sort is the Columbia Mental Maturity Scale (Blum, Burgemeister, and Lorge, 1951), which was developed for individual use with children in the mental age range from three to at least ten years. Somewhat sensitive to acculturation, especially in items at the upper end of the scale, this device may be administered either orally or by pantomime, although no data indicate whether the latter procedure affects the results.

From the time of the early Binets, young subjects have been asked to point out parts of a pictured doll, to give the verbal symbols for pictured objects, and to use words in describing pictures. That there would appear complete tests based upon vocabulary (symbol acquisition, in the terminology of this chapter) should be quite understandable, since measures of this kind of achievement would be highly predictive of further, similar achievement. Some of the group intelligence tests of the 1920s were entirely vocabulary tests, and vocabulary per se constituted a significant portion of the total behavior sampling of many others. Among individual intelligence tests the 1929 Van Alstyne Picture Vocabulary Test, revised in 1960, antedated the Ammons Full-Range Picture Vocabulary Test and the Peabody Picture Vocabulary Test. The Van Alstyne Test is limited to the mental age range of two through seven years, the Ammons Test has norms ranging from kindergarten through the twelfth grade, and the Peabody Test has normative data for levels from one year nine months to eighteen years. Each of these devices involves confronting the subject with cards, each bearing pictures about which the subject is asked questions and to which the subject can point in giving his responses. For exceptional children and youth who have gross difficulty in speaking, these tests help meet the communication problem; but it must be remembered that tests such as these sample recognition behavior rather than recall and verbal production,

---

*The author worked with one cerebral-palsied child who indicated "yes" by thumping his fist against his chest and "no" by hitting his leg.

T. ERNEST NEWLAND

as in the vocabulary test of the Binets and Wechslers. On any of these tests involving cards with pictures, differences among scores for preschool and for inschool children have quite different connotations, since they so fully sample *product,* in contrast with the Columbia Mental Maturity test which heavily samples *process.*

Less culturally contaminated are the Raven Progressive Matrices,* which consist of geometrical designs among which relationships must be ascertained in order that the subject can select, from a multiple choice situation, that design which will complete correctly the whole pattern, or matrix. Tracht and Taibl have used the 1938 matrices with the cerebral-palsied. The psychometric results obtained by means of this device (some suggesting less mental retardation among the cerebral-palsied than has been generally reported) do not concern us particularly here, since they, too, need to be evaluated in terms of the concepts developed thus far in the chapter. The theory underlying the construction of the items in this test gives it psychological appeal. Its adaptability, especially with respect to means of communication by the one using it and by the one taking it, makes it clinically desirable. However, some of its users, on both the handicapped and nonhandicapped, have felt some dissatisfaction with the adequacy of its standardization, even on British subjects. With well-established

*There are three series of these matrices. The 1938 series consists of five sets of twelve items each, the items arranged in a presumed order of difficulty and the sets increasing, overlappingly, in difficulty. The 1947 series, intended for children from five through eleven years of age, consists of the first two sets of the 1938 items plus an interposed set, with colors used in all three sets. The 1962 revision, the Advanced Progressive Matrices, Sets I and II, consists of twelve and thirty-six plates, respectively, and provides more "ceiling" than did the earlier series. The normative data are British.

American norms, and with research showing that the figure-ground idiosyncrasies of the cerebral-palsied are not clouding the picture, this device could well be found to have much value in psychometric work with this kind of exceptional child. Regardless of the extent to which Taibl's psychometric data may be found to be valid, the pains to which he went in ascertaining and establishing a pyschologically sound means of communication with the cerebral-palsied children can well serve as a goal for those who would examine such children.

Not completely unrewarding and unpromising, but as yet nondefinitive, exploratory attempts have been made to adapt other devices for use with the cerebral-palsied. These have consisted of taking extant test items and setting them up in a multiple-choice form in which the child can point to his answer to the question; of "blowing up" items, such as the Porteus Mazes, which the child may normally attempt or in which the child may direct the examiner how to proceed; or of the examiner's offering test item responses with respect to which the child indicates the correctness or incorrectness of the examiner's statements.

It is well to keep in mind the fact that the learning behavior of cerebral-palsied children, and other children with at least major orthopedic involvements, is, perhaps much more so than in the cases of other exceptional children, only partly a function of their basic capacities. Of at least equal importance are the nature and strength of his motivation. The cerebral-palsied child who communicated by hitting his chest or leg to indicate "yes" or "no," and the one who used a typewriter as a means of communication, and the one who turned pages by means of a rubber-tipped stick, and countless ingenious others, all give evidence of learning and, therefore, can be presumed to have significant capacities to learn. But of at least equal importance is the fact that they have a *drive* to do that learning.* The different combinations of drive and intelligence in such children present different kinds of challenges to the clinician. Consider, for example, the following kinds of children:

1. The child who has a strong drive and high intelligence presents the simplest clinical challenge because he is so highly responsive.
2. The child who has a strong drive and low intelligence presents less of a challenge to the clinician because there is a good basis for communication, although the parents of such a child often mistake effort or perseveration for achievement.
3. The child who has a weak drive and low intelligence usually is reasonably quickly and clearly identified as such, but the clinician needs, nevertheless, to make additional efforts to check the intellectual aspects very carefully lest he be misled by the behavior sampled.
4. The child who has a weak drive and high intelligence is most likely to be faultily diagnosed, since communication has badly broken down.

Teachers and therapists who work with such physically handicapped children ben-

*For our purpose here, a child is regarded as having a "strong drive" to the extent that he appears to be outgoing in his relationships with his environment (people, objects, and conditions), if he is inquisitive and curious, if he "bores in," if he is active. Aggressive behavior is regarded psychologically as more of an asset than a liability. The significance of a "strong drive" is tempered but not lost if it is compensatory in nature.

efit little from evaluations that throw light only upon learning capacity.

The brain-injured. The importance of the effectiveness of communication to and from the exceptional demands constant consideration in the assessment process. Is the input, the stimulus, properly controlled and delivered so that we have reasonable assurance that the subject "receives" it? Is the output, the subject's response, received by the examiner to such an extent that it can be scored or evaluated? On the basis of the responses evoked, inferences are drawn regarding the capacity of the individual to perform in certain ways, usually with respect to how he is likely to learn. It is necessary, now, to give a bit more consideration to what there is and what may happen between input and output. That which is, or occurs, between stimulus reception and response manifestation, aptly denoted by some as "the black box," is regarded here as the "mediational process."

The term "mediational process" is taken here to denote either or both the neural structure between sensory and motor structures or/and the way in which that intervening neural structure operates. In the case of the cerebral-palsied, the problem is relatively simplified by virtue of the fact that aberrations in their gross behavior are attributed to neuropathology in the motor area of the brain. Aberrations in their perceptual and cognitive behavior would suggest neuropathology in more than the motor area.

According to this definition, when there is known or validly inferred pathology in this intervening neural structure, we may more properly speak of brain damage. The neuronal deficiency of the familial mental retardate tends not to be regarded as a kind of brain damage, but when extragenetic conditions arrest or otherwise impair the normal growth and development of this intervening neural tissue, the term "brain damage" has been used to denote such sequelae. This structural aspect of the mediational process is not, per se, the proper concern of the educator, nor of most psychologists (excepting those concerned with neurophysiology).* However, when this intervening neural structure functions in certain ways, the learning of the individuals in school and social situations may be impaired. The psychologist observes behavior that appears unusual, and he then tries to find out if it is related to known or inferred difference in the intervening structure. He then infers that the different behavior he has observed is caused by the presumed or established difference in the neural structure. The results of his inferential procedure, about what there "is" between the stimulus and response, can be clouded by the fact that at least most of the different behaviors that have been reasonably validly attributed to some kind of brain damage also have been equally validly attributed to learning, usually accompanied by a large emotional component. The question as to whether there really is a brain syndrome has been raised by Pond (1960). The psychological assessment of the exceptional in terms of brain damage, a disturbingly oversimplified and a distressingly heterogeneous category, must be made with a full sensitivity to the numbers and kinds of facts and inferences that are involved, as well as with a proper regard for the law of probability (emotional factors more probable than neural factors) and the law of parsimony.

Ever since the 1930s when Werner and

*See, for instance, the provocative review of research on the effects of inadequate nutrition on neuronal development in animals and infants by Eichenwald and Frey (1969).

Strauss differentiated between the endogenous and the exogenous, the reports of psychologists and the literature of psychology and education have teemed with references to and reports of research on the "brain-injured." With the increasing sensitivity to and growing literature on this group, there has been an attending proliferation of relevant and semirelevant terminology, in fact to a point where now one authority in the field has noted that some forty different such terms have been used denoting or relating to such a condition. Understandably, certain learning problems were found to be related to, or even attributable to, brain injury. Out of this background, "learning disabilities" has become an area of increasing concern. Unfortunately, sufficiently definitive differential diagnostic information is not adequate to make at all clear the extent to which the two categories of children who are brain-injured and children who have learning disabilities overlap.

Generally, research on such differential diagnosis has been more frustrating than fruitful. Only very limited illustrative research is referred to here; the spectrum can be sampled in the works of Benton (1955), Reitan (1958), Rowley (1961), Hunt (1961), Lessing (1961), Scherer (1961), and Cruickshank (1966). Herbert, in reviewing the concept and testing of brain damage in children, observes: "If a child was found to be suffering from some learning disability or perceptual abnormality, such a finding would be more useful than the label 'brain damage'" (1964, p. 211). Kirk, McCarthy, and Kirk's 1968 revised Illinois Test of Psycholinguistic Abilities and Frostig's tests and training materials are illustrative of a number of attempts along the lines suggested by Herbert.

It should be borne constantly in mind

that only inferences are being drawn about what takes place (or exists) in the mediational process. It is hoped that some programmatic research on bona fide brain-injured children (somehow sharply defined as to kinds and extents of involvement) will be undertaken in terms of some systematic theory of intelligence, such as Guilford's operations in cognition, memory, divergent thinking (a rich field here!), convergent thinking, and evaluation.

One of the continuing questions that bothers the person who tries to make a psychological assessment of the brain-injured concerns the extent to which the aberrations which he finds in his behavior samplings can validly be attributed to the neural damage per se and to what extent they may be as plausibly, and more simply, attributed to some other condition. Nudd (1957), for instance, compared the free responses of brain-injured children and those of nonbrain-injured children to pictures depicting social interaction and found that nonbrain-injured children gave more of the kind of response usually expected of the brain-injured. Some of her evidence suggested that emotional rather than neurological factors might be playing the larger determining role.

The deaf. The psychological problems associated with attempts at the measurement of the intelligence of the deaf are of particular significance. Here the problems of cultural deprivation and emotional overlay continue to demand recognition. But more important and fundamental factors enter the picture. Whereas in the case of the cerebral-palsied a major problem is the means and clarity of communication by the child to the examiner, in the case of the deaf a major problem is the communication of the examiner to the child. Of at least equal psychological significance is the fact that the conceptuali-

zations, if not actually the conceptualization process, of the deaf may well be grossly impaired. The deaf child not only receives fewer stimuli on which to conceptualize but also runs a greater risk of perceiving those stimuli in manners other than those intended by the examiner. Whether or not this impairs the conceptualization process is not the concern of the chapter; the fact that conceptualizations are impaired is relevant, since normal or average acculturation consists of the acquisition of enough conceptualizations for ordinary communication. The significance of this is at once apparent with respect to the possibility of measuring the learning potential of the deaf. Such measurement aims at getting evidence of either the capacity of the individual to conceptualize on presumably novel stimuli, or the extent to which conceptualization has occurred (achievement), from which the capacity to do so is inferred. As the ease and adequacy of communication increase, both conceptually and auditorially, the unique measurement difficulties tend to disappear, and we approach only the normal problems of measuring basic learning capacity.

As is apparent in the chapter on the acoustically impaired, the deaf do not constitute a homogeneous group, whether defined in terms of hearing acuity or in terms of adequacy of communication, or some combination of both. Our line of reasoning concerning these is at once seen as more plausible with respect to those born with the hearing losses indicated in our definition, or acquiring them early as a result of conditions other than, say, scarlet fever, meningitis, and athetosis. In such cases the part played by neural pathology raises still further complicating questions.

Intentionally omitted from specific mention here are the numerous studies of the performances of the acoustically im-

T. Ernest Newland

paired on tests originally developed for use with the nonhandicapped, attempts at standardization on this group of such devices, and studies of the correlations between tests highly varied in purpose. These can be investigated more fruitfully by the interested student in the summaries in Pintner, Eisenson, and Stanton (1941) and in original form in the *Volta Review,* in the *American Annals of the Deaf,* and in *Exceptional Children.*

The Pintner Non-Language Mental Tests constituted the first and most extensive approach made to the group intelligence testing of the deaf by one who comprehended the complexities of the problem. The difficulties of communicating, even in the necessarily small group situations, and the highly varied structurings of the different psychological and physical characteristics of deaf children helped materially to shift interest to individual examination of the deaf. Illustrative of attempts to develop devices specifically for the individual examination of deaf children are the Ontario School Ability Examination, which appeared in 1936, and the Hiskey-Nebraska Test of Learning Aptitude, which became available in 1941 and was revised in 1966. Both of these devices were standardized on and for deaf subjects. The Ontario was standardized on an age range of five through twenty-two, whereas the norms for the Nebraska are for children between the ages of four and ten inclusive, although one-year extrapolations are provided at both extremes.

Without attempting to delineate the strong points and weaknesses of these tests, it is interesting to observe how they both illustrate a common step in adapting and developing measuring devices for the handicapped. On page 148 are listed the names of the items that constitute each test. No significance as to item placement in the test is indicated in the listing, although mental level increase is vaguely reflected in the Ontario from Examination I through Examination VI.

Here, again, we see the evidences of the cafeteria approach, which was mentioned with respect to examination procedures employed on the cerebral-palsied with, however, the manner of communication altered in view of the impaired hearing acuity. Here, though, the items selected in the cafeteria have been assembled and abetted by others statistically into what the authors believe to be effective devices for the indication of the learning potential. This is one step slightly in advance of the present status of testing the cerebral-palsied. This step, it will be noted, is predicated upon the assumption that the types of behavior sampled by the Binet and others from which the items were adapted or upon which they were modeled are psychologically crucial in the measurement, either directly or indirectly, of basic learning capacity. In fact, this kind of test construction dominantly characterizes the numerous "school readiness" tests, many of them individual, which first saw light during the 1960s. In large part, items were selected for tests because the test maker liked them and/or because they had been found to discriminate well and correlate well with school learning behavior. Evidence that some theory of intelligence supported the item selection process is seldom found.

The nonverbal parts of the Wechsler Adult Intelligence Scale and the Wechsler Intelligence Scale for Children are being tried on deaf children and youth. Undoubtedly parts of the Wechsler Preschool and Primary Scale of Intelligence will be found to be helpful with young deaf children. Opinions, yet to be supported systematically by meaningful data, are gener-

Ontario

Examination—Manipulation

Series A. Locomotion (standing and stepping alone)

Series B. Paper folding (similar to Gesell and Binet)

Series C. Block building (adapted from Gesell)

Series D. Form identification and construction (adapted from Stanford Revision IV, 2 and V, 5)

Series E. Knot tying (adapted from Stanford Revision VII, 4)

Series F. Healy-Fernald Puzzle (Stanford Revision, X, alt. 3)

Series G. Weight discrimination (adapted from Drever and Collins)

Examination II—Color patterns (adapted from Drever and Collins, Kohs)

Examination III—Knox blocks

Examination IV—Dominoes (adapted from Drever and Collins Visual number memory)

Examination V—Drawings

Series A. Imitative (adapted from Gesell)

Series B. Copying (adapted from Gesell and the Stanford Revision)

Series C. Design Pair (adapted from Stanford Revision X, 3)

Series D. Ring design

Examination VI—Tapping

Nebraska

Memory for colored sticks

Bead stringing (copying and memory)

Pictorial association

Block building (from pictures)

Memory for digits (subject reproduces one to five digits, presented visually and then hidden)

Completion of drawings

Pictorial identification

Paper folding

Visual attention span (one to six pictures briefly exposed to be selected from 15 possibilities)

Puzzle blocks (cubes, variously cut up to be reassembled)

Pictorial analogies (pictorial equivalents of the type: Man: House: Bird:——)

ally favorable to such partial uses of the Wechslers, just as they were with respect to the desirability of the earlier performance tests over verbal tests. Arthur Adaptation of the Leiter International Performance Scale, although not specifically developed for use with the deaf, has been used on them. Leiter results on deaf children have been reported by Birch and Birch (1951) with interesting and ambiguous disparities found between them and those obtained on the Arthur Performance Scale and on the early Nebraska. A few are trying the Progressive Matrices on the deaf and are entertaining the suspicion that this device will be found to be still more rewarding. On the basis of the responses of 1,400 hearing and 1,054 deaf subjects, all between the ages of three and sixteen, a revision of the Snjiders-Oomen Non-Verbal Intelligence Scale has been made. It involves a variety of behavior sampling—block design, picture completion, picture arrangement, visual memory, drawing and copying of designs, and sorting of objects and cards. The scale is structured in terms of "psychological viewpoints": form, combination, abstraction, and memory.

Considerable work in the area of individual intelligence testing of the deaf is still needed before the situation can be reasonably stabilized. Particularly germane with respect to testing in this area of exceptionality is the general question of what kind of behavior sample can provide the best basis for predicting the school learning of those so tested. The tendency has been for workers in this area to take those parts of tests which most easily can be communicated to the deaf and then to seek to identify that pattern of such tests which either discriminated between successive year levels or which yielded positive correlations with the amounts learned, or both. The size of such correla-

T. ERNEST NEWLAND

tions leaves much to be desired. This approach has tended to result in almost exclusive use of performance-type tests—long known to yield results that correlate poorly with the results of schooling, at least in the case of the hearing. The convenience in the use of such performance tests plus the chance of evoking higher scoring responses on such tests (this latter being a boon at times to many working with the mentally retarded as well) have tended to impede the development of a pattern of behavior sampling that might be significantly more predictive of the deaf's acquisition and use of symbols. Many of these tests appear to sample *process* more heavily than *product*. Here the problem would appear to lie, however, in the possibility that secondary psychological processes are being sampled rather than those processes more fundamental to the symbolic learning of the deaf. On the basis of the process-product concept developed earlier, one would assume that the kinds of behavior sampling involved in the Leiter and the Raven Matrices should be more fruitful, particularly with the young deaf.

It must be remembered that learning capacity tests are given for the purpose of getting indications of how well children will learn in school. The learning product of the public schools, with the nonhandicapped children, is still a great deal more clearcut and generally agreed upon than is the learning product of the deaf. Here the picture is tremendously clouded by a confusion of goals such as "learning speechreading, language, speech, and school subjects," "learning in a sign-dominated world," "learning in a speech-reading-dominated world," "learning to adjust," and the like. The ambiguity of any one of these and the use of different ones in different studies make for an elusive pre-

dictive target against which to validate any test of the learning aptitude of the deaf.

The blind. With the blind, as with the other kinds of physically handicapped, the a priori assumption has been made that their learning potential, whether basic or manifest, is made up of the same component parts which are present and operative to the same extent in the case of the nonhandicapped. This is probably a much more convenient point at which to start than if we were to assume the psychological naïveté of, say, Binet when he first undertook the task of identifying those kinds of behavior that served as indicators of learning capacity, or if we were to start back at the point where many performance tests were made in the hope that some of them would have predictive value for at least something. Our success in discovering those kinds of behavior that in combination are reasonably predictive of the learning behavior of children who are predominantly nonhandicapped, while helpfully suggestive in attacking this problem for the handicapped, must be regarded as potentially restrictive of our perception of all the psychological factors operating in the case of the handicapped. Because of perceptual or conceptual impairment or distortion and because of the unique communication problems of the various handicapped groups, certain behavior samples that are important with respect to the nonhandicapped may be of much less or of no significance with respect to the handicapped, and vice versa. For a thoroughly adequate approach to this area of measurement, we need a factor analysis, within each handicap area, of a wide variety of both old and new test approaches in order to ascertain for the different kinds of handicapped what the primary mental abilities are and the relative part each such ability plays. Until we know that the primary mental-ability pictures for all the kinds of handicapped are the same as those for the nonhandicapped, we must accept only provisionally the majority of our current testing approaches in this area.

This is not to imply that what has been done in the area of the total and severely visually impaired is without value. Research evidence that has been accumulated by Samuel P. Hayes, his early coworkers, and his students on the improvement of mental test scores with chronological age, on the relative stability of the intelligence quotients of blind children, and on the correlations between intelligence test performance and educational achievement indicates quite the contrary. The question remains whether or not the adaptations of the Binets and the Wechslers, significant as they have been, represent a psychologically adequate sampling of the behavior of the blind and severely visually impaired.

Viewing this area, as we did the cerebral-palsied and the deaf, we again see that unique problems arise with respect to communication, perception, and conceptualization. Communication is much more nearly normal than in the former areas; when it is impaired, it is essentially as a result of perceptual and conceptual distortions. "White as the driven snow," "blood red," and "sneeringly" mean something quite different to the blind than they mean to other physically handicapped who can see, since to the blind they may well mean "cold-wet-slippery," "warm-wet," and a particular voice quality or word sequence. Perceptual restrictions of this sort, with the attending conceptual impoverishment, have a direct bearing upon our assumptions of comparable acculturation. Test items that are known to involve this kind

of contamination are, fortunately, identifiable and replaceable. Whereas no small part of the blind child's communication with his world is through the senses of touch and kinesthesis, we have yet to ascertain, statistically, the part these as well as other senses play in his learning behavior. These avenues are only slightly tapped and little explored in present intelligence test procedures.

C. J. Davis, at Perkins, has under way the standardization of an adaptation of the 1960 Binet for the blind. The standardization of the Blind Learning Aptitude Test (BLAT) on 961 educationally blind residential and day-school children, aged six through sixteen, in twelve states was completed in 1969. Aimed at sampling behavior in terms of Spearman's "g" factor, the BLAT is an individual, nonverbal test, the items of which are solved by cutaneous-kinesthetic exploration involving no braille reading ability. Although the nature and the extent of its contribution to the assessment of the learning potential of blind children is yet to be ascertained by research, it is known to discriminate better in the six-to-twelve-year age range, and, because it so heavily taps *process,* it should have particular value in the cases of the younger children entering educational programs from highly divergent backgrounds of acculturation. Although Hecht (1965) found that BLAT scores in combination with Hayes-Binet and WISC Verbal scores yielded higher correlations with measured educational achievement than did any of them singly, this was not found to be the case in three schools in the South.

In the physical exploration of their total environment, the blind are markedly less mobile than the deaf. In the psychologically crucial years of infancy and early childhood, their physical dependency has tended to approach that of the severely orthopedically handicapped. This often contributes to the impairment of the communication process in the examination situation. The sampling of the behavior of any dependent child is always a real problem for the clinician; it is considerably more so in the case of the blind. It must constantly be kept in mind that, first, it is difficult to get certain behavior samples from such children and, second, there is the ever-present question of the extent to which the sample that is obtained has been psychologically contaminated by a long, impoverishing, constricting relationship with adults. A further problem, perhaps a psychological corollate of the above, that often affects communication between the psychological examiner and the blind is the occasional presence of "blindisms," those socially irrelevant, and often bizarre, motor behavior patterns (twisting, squirming, gesticulating, posturing) that are often misleading to the lay person and distracting to the clinician, especially if he has had limited experience with the blind.

With respect to this area, too, we need to raise questions on the validity and implications of this generalization: To the extent that blindness is independent of an inheritable defective syndrome, and to the extent that blindness is independent of neural pathology directly involving the higher mental processes—to such an extent we should expect a distribution of basic learning capacity similar to that of the total (normal) population. Note that this has been suggested with respect to only *basic* capacity and not to manifest capacity, since we already have considered some of the major factors that can contribute to considerable disparity between the two.

As has been indicated with respect to

the deaf, the accuracy of the measurement of learning capacity is reflected in the degree to which such measurements agree with the amounts learned. The learnings of the blind are quite different from those of the nonhandicapped, though probably less so than those of the deaf, and the presence of emotional problems often impairs the efficiency of the learning process, particularly in the cases of the adventitiously blind.

The disadvantaged. That this category should be included with those of the deaf and blind, as we consider the problems involved in assessing the learning potential of exceptional children and youth, may seem illogical. From the time that Witmer, at the beginning of this century, introduced the term "clinical psychology" to denote intensive work with individual children who were having trouble learning, clinicians have worked with one kind or another of disadvantaged children.

In large part, it was the group testers of intelligence who contributed to a limited sensitivity to the unique evaluation problem of the disadvantaged. Their reasonable commitment to the assumption of the commonality of acculturation, tenable to probably 80 percent of the population, may have carried with it an implicit assumption that some kind of clinical common sense would be exercised with respect to the other 20 percent of the population tested. But the growing social, educational, and psychological concern for the deviant minority, from roughly 1945 to 1965, resulted in a more critical consideration of the ways in which the acculturation of this minority differed from that of the majority.

Logically, the term "disadvantaged" is applicable to a wide range of the exceptional. Pintner, in the 1920s, made much of the fact that gifted children were the most retarded children in the schools, although he didn't use the term "disadvantaged" in this connection. A quite gifted child was a disadvantaged child because his gross inadequacy in the quantitative area was a function of his having been reared in a highly verbal, nonquantitative college professor's home; yet, with very little help and exposure to quantitative learning opportunities, he quickly acquired competence in the quantitative area. A fairly intensive examination of educational efforts exerted especially with the young deaf and blind will reveal the compensatory nature of this work, although these kinds of children are not currently perceived as disadvantaged. The same is true with regard to many of the "back room" orthopedically disabled and even the brain-damaged. Those factors, or conditions, to which many clinicians have long been sensitive, continue to be regarded as important in assessing and educating the exceptional. But the term "disadvantaged" has taken on a broader social and cultural dimension, as reflected, for instance, in the finding that Mexican children have particular difficulty with gerunds in the Peabody Picture Vocabulary Test because of an idiosyncrasy in their language. Further illustrative of this broadened sensitivity is the work of Klaus and Gray (1968) in their compensatory work with young disadvantaged rural children.

Although the fundamentals of good assessment of the learning potentials of the (current) disadvantaged are no different from what is described in this chapter, it should be recognized that two discernibly different (but often greatly overlapping) kinds of compensatory effort are being exerted in the interests of the disadvantaged. There is an effort to compensate for their *acculturation*, which largely is addressed to helping them acquire "experiences" that have been taken for granted among most children. This is essentially with respect to making it possible for disadvantaged children to learn things that the majority of children have learned while growing up in their more favorable environments. There is also a discernibly different effort that is *nurturant* in nature. Here, as illustrated at least in parts by the Klaus and Gray approach, the attempt is made to stimulate and facilitate the working of psychological operations that are fundamental to learning—that, in effect, make possible, or enhance, the learnings which are sought in the acculturation efforts. It is apparent that, in any assessment procedure with the disadvantaged, the effects of acculturation will be reflected in the *product* component of tested intelligence, whereas the effects of nurturance will be reflected in the *process* component. As a general rule, the younger the children and the more heterogeneous, or deviant, their acculturation backgrounds (these two have much in common), the more it becomes necessary to assess their learning potential in terms of process; the older they are, and the more their acculturations have in common, the more this can be done in terms of product, although process may still be contributive, as the author found in ascertaining the intellectual eligibility for rehabilitation of a group of adults from Appalachia. Although a full consideration of the role that process plays in the early learning by disadvantaged children is necessary, the contributive value of product must not be overlooked, as Anastasi (1967, p. 299) points out so well.

As we consider the whole area of intellectual measurement of the exceptional, we see that the problems related to it, particularly with respect to those who are seriously handicapped, are numerous and complicated. The professional and scientific literature on exceptional children teems with reports of results obtained by administering intelligence tests to these children. To the psychologically untrained, the reported results may well seem hopelessly confusing. Some data are taken to indicate improvement of basic intelligence; some, to indicate the uselessness of the tests by which the results were obtained; some, to indicate the relative brightness of different types of exceptional children. The differences between IQs obtained at successive times on the same populations, or between children with different kinds of problems, or between different kinds of tests on the same groups of children have caused some to jump almost blindly to conclusions on the nature of the social promise of some groups of children, or of some specific children; to enthuse hastily concerning the merits of given methods of treatment, education, or medication; or, even, to solve dilemmas by arbitrarily, and with no small amount of psychological blindness, taking the highest of a number of scores or performances as valid. It is no wonder that so many psychologically less well oriented educators have decided to avoid these apparent contradictions and confusions by avoiding the use of even well standardized intelligence tests, or that they have protected their teachers and children by salting away in their files such seemingly errant data.

If, hypothetically, only one person were to have used only one measuring device, variations or differences still would have existed for the reasons we have considered thus far. But different people used different devices intended to measure different aspects of the potential of different children at different times and under differing conditions. Even had the proper persons used the proper devices on the proper subjects, normal errors of measurement would have been disconcerting to the uninitiated. The presence of the highly varied and major psychological problems in the examination of different types of exceptional children, especially the physically handicapped, serves to complicate the picture to such an extent that one actually tends to be surprised at the relative consistency of such results as reported by Street (1942) for instance, rather than to be dismayed at seeming discrepancies. Two understanding and protective attitudes will help:

1. We need to entertain a persistent and healthy concern and to employ every legitimate checking procedure we know in the cases of all children who make test scores that suggest mental retardation.
2. So long as we recognize that our examination procedures, with their inherent assumptions, shed immediate, quantitative light on what the operating levels of the children are at the times of those procedures—their manifest capacities—and so long as we, or some others, draw careful inferences from those examination results as to what the basic capacities are, we shall be safeguarding the interests of those children, their parents, their teachers, their therapists, and society.

The Socioemotional Area

The designation of this area is intentionally broad because it is the bias here that, whatever the emotional picture of the individual may be, it is the impact of that emotionality upon interpersonal relationships that is of major importance. This is not to deny the value of studying the social development or status, or the emotional development or status, per se in order to obtain a psychologically sound picture of an individual; it is, rather, to emphasize the interrelatedness of these aspects of behavior in that individual. Whenever we consider these subareas separately, it will be with the constant realization that they have been only artificially isolated for the sake of descriptive convenience.

In fact, it is difficult, if not impossible, to consider the social behavior of a child without introducing factors or conditions that, in themselves, are not social but are really physical, intellectual, or emotional. Regarding the child socially, we can think of a child's ability to get around in his environment. (Does he play in different parts of the house, at times away from his adults? Does he play with children in the block? Does he go to the store for his mother? Does he participate in social group activity such as clubs, games, and so forth? Does he date?) Or we can think in terms of his physical growth and development (Can he crawl, walk or run?), or we can think in terms of his being able to communicate with those in his environment (speech, sensory adequacy, conceptual development). We can think in terms of his having sufficient mental maturity to enable him to go about the neighborhood with reasonable caution, or to enable him to remember what he went to the store for or how to go to and from the store, or to enable him to understand or count when he plays games, or we can think in terms of whether he is sufficiently emotionally independent of his parents to explore his house or his neighborhood, or of whether he is sufficiently outgoing to enjoy being with and to be accepted by his peers.

Take, for instance, the item, "Cares for self at table," which appears at the IX-X level of Doll's Vineland Social Maturity

Scale. The extent to which a child can do this adequately can be determined by a number of factors, singly or in combination, as in the case of any of the following nine-year-olds: a child, of average intelligence, having a highly overprotective or exacting mother, or a blind child, or a manually involved cerebral-palsied child. The scale is a highly useful device with which to quantify social competence, but its author and wary users of it are well aware that it reflects also "limitations imposed by intelligence level, emotional attitudes, social conditioning, disposition, and the like," and fully recognize that scores earned on it must "be interpreted with due regard for special limiting circumstances," which include physical handicapping conditions.* The difficulty of conceiving of social development and/or maturation as a completely discrete behavioral entity has resulted in the development of very few devices purporting to measure it, and helps account for the larger number forthrightly purporting to measure socioemotional development or adjustment.

The social frame of reference. The determination of overall social status, in terms of social distance from the group, or from members of the group, by means of a sociometric approach has been attempted with a number of the types of exceptional children, as illustrated by the studies by Force (1954) and Soldwedel (1951). This seemingly innocuous and

*This type of device has been used for goal-setting purposes by following this line of reasoning: Granting that the various behaviors which are to be checked on such a scale represent competency expectancies for the different age levels, to what extent can children not yet having the competencies normally expected at or near their age levels be helped or trained to do such things for themselves? The possibilities of this use of the Vineland, not unrecognized by workers with the handicapped, are, for instance, at once apparent with respect to the mentally handicapped, the blind, and the deaf.

plausible method of asking children to name those of their classmates whom they like as leaders, playmates, friends, neighbors, and the like (to mention only the positive nominations), recording frequency of nomination, and plotting the interrelationships indicated by the nominations has raised disturbing questions as to the validity (Is actual social status thus identified?), the permanence (How evanescent is the status identified?), and the generality (Is overall social status truly represented by high frequency of nomination as a seat neighbor, for instance?) of the data so obtained. The fact that this and other sociometric approaches, such as the "guess who" technique which was first used by Hartshorne and May (1929), must be used only on those children who either can read or can comprehend the statements that are presented to them tends to limit their valid use insofar as young children or mentally handicapped children are concerned.

The majority of attempts to ascertain "social adjustment," "socioemotional adjustment," or "emotional adjustment," whether so named or only implied, by means of rating scales, check lists, and inventories have been for the purpose of finding out whether or not the kind of exceptionality under study differs from the normal group, or whether or not a specific exceptional child is normal. Reports of the extent to which the sensorily handicapped, the orthopedically handicapped, and the intellectual deviants have problems, or are "maladjusted," have appeared with considerable frequency in the literature of this field. With respect to these the student may feel obliged to raise questions such as the following concerning the meaning of such findings. Generally, are the norms, on the basis of which any such comparative observations are made, psy-

chologically meaningful with respect to the kind of exceptional children on whom the device was used? Certain personality inventories and check lists may be used quite appropriately with mentally superior children of given ages, but how appropriate are they when used on mentally retarded children who cannot read effectively enough to respond meaningfully, or on some physically handicapped children whose backgrounds and experiences have been distorted in the sense of their not having had certain opportunities to respond in situations sampled by means of the devices? The reading of the items to children of either of these handicapped groups not only does not avoid these difficulties but also introduces at least two others—auditory memory span and auditory comprehension. Often overlooked in the uses of generally standardized devices involving the child's responding, either directly or indirectly, concerning himself are the nature and extent of conceptualization present in the child so responding. In one kind of examination setting it is definitely psychologically meaningful for a child to respond to the word "spells" either as a verb or as a noun, but to assume, as is the case in the normative uses of these devices, that all children will respond solely in terms of only one meaning can lead to at least ambiguous results. Consider the difference in the underlying meaning attached to the same answer "yes" to the question "Do you prefer a play to a dance?" when that reply is given by a youth with no orthopedic or other physical involvements and by a paraplegic. Both would receive the same score, but each would have different psychological meaning.

The use of rating scales, the results of which are evaluated in terms of norms, involves some of these same problems. In these the behaviors tend to be more objectively described in order to facilitate the use of such devices. However, the term "withdrawing" can have one meaning when checked for a physically handicapped child in a nonhandicapped group and quite another for a nonhandicapped child in the same group. Further, unless the behavior is quite specifically described, such a term can be interpreted variously by different raters. In fact, a very real question remains concerning the extent to which the one doing the rating of a child projects himself into the ratings, thus producing a picture that is a mixture of what some of the child's behavior may be and of how the rater feels about, or perceives, that behavior. The distortion of "true" pictures, obtained by such inventories, check lists, and rating scales, or by the subject's so describing himself, or by having another describe him is a factor that always has to be taken into consideration, but, with judicious use and cautious interpretation, such evaluations can be of some value.

A recent attempt to get around the verbal aspects of self-reporting on social adjustment is Jay's *A Book About Me* intended for use by kindergarten and first-grade children. With this device the child is confronted with a variety of pictured situations under headings such as "My Mother," "My Daddy," "My House," "Things We Have at Our House," "Things I Do at Home," "Things I Can Do All by Myself," "People I Know, See, and Like," and "Which I'd Rather Do"—all situations in which he is to identify himself. Pictured under "Things I Am Afraid Of," for instance, are a fire, a child being spanked, a storm, a snake, a policeman, a doctor, a father scolding a child, a larger boy shaking his fist at a smaller one, an oncoming car at a street intersection, a child going into a dark room, a bulldog, and bugs, flies, and a spider. Although this has been intended primarily for the average early school child, it itself, and other possible approaches patterned after it, should be of much value if used individually with a variety of exceptional children.

The individual frame of reference. The approaches illustrated thus far are intended primarily to throw light on the adjustment of individuals to groups or how individuals representing the groups react to other members in that group. The emphasis was on the social frame of reference within which the individual is operating. In addition to this necessary and useful conception of the problem of adjustment, it is very helpful to find out, if possible, the dynamic emotional structure with which the individual reacts to the members of his group and in terms of which his social peers react to him. The emphasis here is upon such aspects of the individual as his perceptions of himself, his needs, drives, and emotional tensions.

The responses of any person to any stimulus at any time are psychologically colored, often unconsciously, by the way he feels at the time and by his background of emotional and intellectual experiences. No small amount of research has been done to tease out and identify emotional manifestations involved in, or constituting parts of, performances on intellectual, achievement, and aptitude measuring instruments. Enthusiasms having varying amounts of validity have been expressed, for instance, with respect to intelligence test responses wherein a child consistently goes the longer way in the Binet child-to-school mazes, or wherein a child completely ignores (rejects) his immediate environment in the word-naming item, or wherein digit memory span is at variance with other test behavior. Starting at least with the early work of Binet and the users of free-association tests, many psychologists have endeavored to devise test stimuli which, without appearing to the subject to do so, would evoke responses that would throw greater light on the emotionality of subjects. The assumption here is that the nature of his responses to such stimuli will be more a function of the subject's emotionality than of the stimuli themselves. In current terminology the subject "projects" himself into the stimuli in terms of his own needs, tensions, and emotional outlook on life, and the devices are called projective tests. Only representative of a voluminous literature in this area are: Frank (1948), Goodenough (1948), Ames *et al.* (1952, 1959), Abt and Bellak (1959), Ledwith (1959), Rabin and Haworth (1960), and Mursten (1965).

The apparent plausibility and the seeming lack of threat to the subject being so examined have contributed heavily to the development of some 200 of these devices on the basis of varying kinds and qualities of research. A child may model an innocuous chunk of clay into a person, a chair, a cube, a ball, a snake, or some other object or animal. He may complete the sentence. "What I want is . . . " by adding "to go home," "to be an aviator," "to get even with Harry," or a number of other possibilities. He may draw lines more away from himself than toward himself. He may fill in solidly a geometric figure, or only a part of it, or he may attach drawings to it. He may draw a house with smoke coming out of the chimney, or with many or few openings, using a whole page for his drawing or using only a very small portion of it. In all these and other projective test stimuli situations, there is at least reduced likelihood of his feeling personally threatened by his being asked, or allowed, to do these things, and he is not likely to be aware that he is throwing some light on his emotional adjustment—a thing about which he may not feel able to talk and for which he may not have the verbalizations or concepts with which to talk.

With the blind, verbal and other ambiguous sound stimuli have been used, and they have been provided with objects and materials which they can manipulate in unstructured situations. Special sets of ambiguous pictures involving discernibly physically disabled individuals have been employed with the orthopedically disabled. Solomon and Starr have developed the School Apperception Method, using a series of ambiguously pictured school situations.

The potential clinical values of using such tests with the exceptional appear to be great even though most of the tests are regarded by many as not well validated in a predictive or normative sense. The importance of the emotional adjustment of the various kinds of exceptional children and youth, especially the handicapped, with respect to their education, their social adjustment and their vocational placement and adjustment, is only beginning to be recognized. That each area of exceptionality would be explored, at least in part, by this time by means of at least one kind of projective approach is understandable. Thus far, children who were mentally retarded, blind, and nonsensorily physically handicapped have been studied the most by projective approaches.

Our concern here is with the problems attending the use of projective approaches as a part of the total examination or psychological assessment process, rather than with the enumeration of the types used or with the study of the results reported. It is interesting to observe that, in general, the initial use of projective methods of getting at the nature of the emotionality, or of the emotional adjustment, of individuals has followed much the same basic pattern as characterized the initial use of tests of mental capacity. In both a very few were well standardized before they were generally used, but a large number of devices have sprung up mushroomlike. Just as certain responses to intelligence tests were regarded as throwing some light upon the emotionality of those taking them, just so have some responses to projective devices been interpreted as throwing light upon the mental capacity of the subjects. In both cases many inadequately trained persons made use of the devices, gaining a false sense of competency and dealing with their response data with an unwarranted sense of the definitiveness and implications of the behavior so elicited.

Attending the use of projective approaches are essentially the same assumptions and the same problems as in the use of mental capacity measures. Behavior is sampled. A general comparability of background, both experiential and developmental, is assumed. Responses are taken as *indicative* of emotional conditions rather than being taken as the condition they indicate, and thus these behavior samples are taken as the bases for inferences. There is error in such measurement due to sizes and natures of samplings and to the possible variability within the individual from time to time. The validation problem is, perhaps, greater in the projective area due to the difficulty in setting up acceptable criteria and to the greater possible impact of subjectivity on the scoring and analysis of the subject's responses.

To these disturbing but not necessarily invalidating difficulties or problems, which are present in the use of such approaches on the nonexceptional, we must add also those that are involved in working with the exceptional. Here, too, are the prob-

lems of communication and conceptualization. We can't present the ambiguous sound stimuli of one device to the deaf, but we can use it with certain other types of exceptionality. If for projective purposes we present bas-relief outlines of a horse to blind subjects, to what extent and in what ways can we safely compare their responses with those of sighted subjects? Deviant experiential backgrounds, perhaps even further impaired by mental retardation, may render useless pictorial or incomplete-sentence projective materials. The verbal responses to certain projective stimuli may be impaired or distorted due to limited conceptualization; such responses may well have a significance that renders them noncomparable with those of nonhandicapped subjects.

In spite of all these problems that figure importantly in the use of projective devices and procedures on the exceptional, important additional information can be obtained by this type of approach. This is true, however, only under these conditions, which are not unique to this area:

1. The devices must be used by persons who are competently trained in their uses and well oriented in the personality dynamics in the light of which inferences are drawn concerning emotionality, and in the assumptions underlying psychological measurement.
2. The devices must have validity that has been established with respect to the type or types of exceptionality on which they are used. Implied or expressed assumptions of such validity, however plausible they may seem, must be based on sound research.
3. The devices must be such as to permit clear communication *to* the ex-

ceptional child or youth, to permit unambiguous and adequate communication *from* the subject, and must not presume the use of concepts, verbalized or otherwise, which, for any physical, social, or intellectual reason are not reasonably likely to be in the repertoire of the subject.

Commonality of acculturation. We have emphasized, with respect to both the intelligence and socioemotional areas, the effect of the impact of grossly deviant backgrounds upon the responses of exceptional children and youth to devices in these areas. To understand the significance of this acculturation problem, two questions need to be answered: (1) How much can a child's background differ from those of other children and still be within the normal range? (2) When does a child's response become bizarre—completely at odds with the normality of the responses upon which the test is statistically or clinically standardized—and therefore have some special significance? To some, these questions are regarded as so unanswerable that they view the use of standardized examination procedures with thorough apprehension. This extremist position of throwing the baby out with the bath does not seem warranted, even though specific categorical answers may not be given to the questions. Rough limits within which the answers can be sought can, however, be indicated.

Environmental backgrounds can be thought of as ranging from psychologically impossible, absolutely identical environments of two or more persons through some that are quite similar, through some others that are roughly similar, to highly dissimilar, and on out on the continuum to the completely unique background for a single person. No test is standardized for

general use on an unattainable identity of backgrounds. Nor are any tests standardized on the logical impossibility of unique personal backgrounds. The use of "unselected" populations for standardization purposes, even on the basis of prior selections such as deaf children, blind children, cerebral-palsied children, or even mentally retarded or gifted children, carries with it the recognition of the presence of an admittedly wide variety of normally different yet roughly common backgrounds. Here, also, normality is a range and not a point on our continuum, but the range does not include the extremes of gross cultural deprivation we have mentioned. Put more specifically, our cerebral-palsied, for instance, come from homes that vary considerably in emotional atmosphere, cultural level and opportunity, presence and kind of siblings, amount and kind of orthopedic attention, educational facilities, and the like. But a few children, and these occur also in other areas of exceptionality, come from backgrounds that are even more different and will have had even more limited opportunity to come into contact with magazines, television, radios, and interpersonal and interobject contacts. Hence they will have lacked in both the stimulation value and in the experiential value that normally, though still in widely varied manners, would have been present in the lives of their more fortunate peers. In the cases of exceptional children, then it is not the response alone of the child who has been so deprived but rather the response-as-having-come-out-of-his-background. Again, once a device is selected by the clinician as appropriate to a child of a given type of exceptionality, it can be used rather forthrightly on a major percentage of his group (hence, such testing tends to have an overall value), but great care must constantly be exercised with certain other children of this type of exceptionality regarding the nature of their responses in the light of their backgrounds.

The Area of Educational Achievement

In considering the problems of measurement in this area, we concern ourselves more with the *what* of the individual than with the *why* and *how*. Here, the primary concern in examining the individual is to find out what he has learned, what he can do educationally. Regardless of his handicaps or his superiority, he reads at some part of a particular grade level, and that is the place at which the educator must work with him in reading. Such educational levels are the points from which the educators try to bring him up to those indicated by capacity tests and in the light of the facilitating or hampering effects of his emotionality and exceptionality. Measurements in the areas of learning capacity and socioemotional adjustment contribute to the total picture of the individual by helping us understand how he was able to achieve as much as he did or why he wasn't able to achieve any more than he did.

This contrast between the purpose and the nature of the results of measurement in this area and those of the areas considered earlier is of value primarily in showing the reasons why some of the assumptions made with respect to measurement of learning capacity and emotional adjustment do not apply here. We try to measure educational achievements in order to find out what they are; we do not draw inferences on the basis of them as to how well adjusted a child is socially or emotionally (although we may well want to find out if his emotional condition is or has been such as to impair the effectiveness of his learning). Regarding the results of measured educational achievement themselves, we do not have the manifest performance-basic capacity gap problem that we have with respect to measured learning capacity. Nor do we have in this area, quite as much as in the measured emotional adjustment, the tendency to generalize with respect to more global behavior. As in other measurement areas we accept, understand, and allow for, both statistically and clinically, the presence of our errors of measurement, both because we are working with a normally varying individual and because we have to use a sampling approach in our measurement. Similarly, we use the depictions of educational performance, whether they be in terms of educational grade status or stanines, as having meaning only in terms of the population on which the achievement tests were standardized.

Insofar as most of the types of exceptionality are concerned, we recognize the appropriateness of the use of such norms in understanding the particular child, but in some cases we purposely depart from certain stardardized test administration procedures and, at times, certain of the content. In the case of an emotionally disturbed child, or of a motor-involved child, we may give the test under normal, timed conditions, but have him mark how far he got at the designated time limits. We may then let him proceed with the tests as far as he can in the hope of getting fuller understanding of his total educational output. Spelling tests, usually administered orally, may have to be adapted into multiple choice, synonym, or some other method of presentation. Special consideration must be given to test items involving either sound words—the crowing of a rooster, the screeching of a car's brakes, and the like, or color and certain object depiction words in the cases of deaf or blind children who may encounter them in standardized tests or word lists. These alterations have to be kept in mind in trying to interpret the test performances of such children in the light of the norms which are provided. Some have endeavored to regard any such limited performances as percentages of what the total might have been and then have characterized the child's "true" educational performance in terms of this "corrected" total. So long as the results so obtained are regarded as even coarser approximations than are obtained in the normal use of such devices, this method can have some value.

The conceptualization-communication problem exists in this area, too, but with impacts that differ somewhat from the situation in the two previous areas of measurement. Achievement test approaches have been modified by the use of large-type achievement tests for children who are partially sighted, by the development of achievement tests in braille for those who are blind, by the motor handicappeds' use of the typewriter, by use of objective test items in the place of handwritten responses for children with certain motor handicaps, and by the reading of test items to children with other kinds of handicaps, thus facilitating communication both to and from these kinds of children. Regarding the conceptualization aspect of our examination problem, it takes on a different significance in this area of measurement since our interest here is in ascertaining whether or not the conceptualizations being tested have been acquired by the children as a means both of communication and of acquiring other concepts. Here the conceptualizations are the products being measured rather than the means by which one tries to get a picture of learning capacity or emotional adjustment.

Thus far no mention has been made of group averages. At times there may be merit in endeavoring to find out the average educational test performances of epileptic, cerebral-palsied, blind, or deaf children of different ages (ignoring the false implications as to any homogeneity of such age groups). From the standpoint of stimulating research on the learning processes of, especially, the sensorily handicapped, there may well be some value in knowing, for instance, that the educational achievements of the deaf tend with frustrating consistency to run below those of their chronological peers. This type of information by itself is of limited value; when it is thrown into relationship with their learning potentials, it takes on added and truly provocative meaning. But with exceptional children and youth in particular we are obligated to deal with and think in terms of *individual* performances. In the area of educational measurement, the key problem is the consideration of the amount of achievement in the light of the individual's capacity to achieve. In terms of their ages or grades, the mentally superior tend to do exceptionally well, in one sense, on such achievement tests, and the mentally retarded tend to do poorly. But these performances take on entirely different meanings when we view them in light of the learning potentials out of which they come. It is then that we see clearly that the mentally retarded tend to work up to their capacities and that the mentally superior are the more educationally retarded. Allowing for all of the errors which we know exist in our measurements of the exceptional, it is still beneficial and desirable to evaluate each individual's educational achievements in terms of his capacity to achieve. For the psychologist, teacher, and parent, the consideration of his performance in each of the different parts of an achievement test, with respect to his capacity to achieve, is of much more value than any "battery median" or average, although the latter, by itself, may have information value for a school administrator, as could "class medians" or averages.

The Area of Aptitude Measurement

In the preceding paragraphs we consider the outcomes of such educational measurement primarily as direct evidence on status. The child was found to read at third-grade level, could perform simple arithmetic operations at a fith-grade level, or had language-usage competence similar to that on an average fourth-grader. This contrasted with the purposes of measurement in the two preceding areas which, to varying degrees, were to ascertain *the basis for* further work with the exceptional child or youth—his susceptibility to learning in school and, perhaps, certain aspects of his promise under therapy. In a manner largely similar to the orientation in physical and educational status measurement, measurement of aptitudes is largely the ascertainment of the amounts of particular skills and interests that can function as they are, and partly measurement of susceptibilities to further training toward given job competencies.

The term "aptitude" is taken here to refer to certain of those habits (including attitudes) and muscular coordinations of an individual that are known to predispose him to acceptably efficient performance in a given type of activity. Unless specifically indicated, this activity is regarded as either vocational or prevocational in nature. This predisposition may be "embryonic" and relatively simple, as in the case of certain speed of movement tests; or it may be heavily structured and involved, as in the case of the use of pliers or other tools in

an object assembly test of considerable complexity. Intelligence has been dealt with in this chapter as learning aptitude or susceptibility to learning. Reading readiness tests are intended to measure a certain kind of aptitude for, or susceptibility to, learning to read. Emotional adjustment can affect general aptitude as in the case of an "unstable" person, or it can be a factor in determining whether an individual would do well in a given kind of work, as in the case of an "outgoing" person, or as in the case of a person who would feel more secure in the laboratory or among bookshelves. A "motor age" of an individual who is crippled may well have an important bearing on whether he can be expected to work at a drill press, or on a watch repair job, or as a keeper of a tool cage in a large plant. In like manner, whether a person can read or compute (educational achievement) can have particular significance with respect to a wide variety of occupations. All of these areas of potentiality and skills have a bearing upon, and can well be a large part of, the basis for vocational placement, as can sensory acuity, yet there remain certain other behavior samplings that research has shown to be relevant to success in certain occupations. It is in the sense of these areas of behavior that we shall consider the measurement of aptitude.

Behavior sampling in this area has been essentially of two kinds: attempts to ascertain the nature of the interests of the individual, insofar as they are known to be relevant to certain occupations, and attempts to ascertain the nature of muscular coordinations that are known to be or are regarded as playing important parts in the performance of given tasks. The inference gap, to which we have referred in other areas of measurement, is greater with respect to the measurement of interests than

T. Ernest Newland

in the case of measurement of motor skills. But the reasoning is straightforward and the limitations are reasonably apparent. If the interests and preferences of, say, successful architects can be found to be significantly different from those, say, of successful computing machine operators or real estate salesmen, then, depending to some extent on the age of the individual, if a person's interests and preferences most closely resemble those of architects, such a person has at least that much in his favor if he desires to become an architect. If a person just doesn't have fine motor coordinations and, perhaps, good visual memory, he might well have difficulty in succeeding at watch repairing.*

In each of the other areas, measurement in only one of them has little, if any, value. Just so does aptitude measurement alone have limited value. Interests have value in suggesting aptitudes but must be supported by certain amounts of intelligence, certain kinds of emotionality, mobility and other motor competencies, and educational skills. Similarly, errors are present in our behavior samplings, and we need research assurance that the behavior sampled has adequate predictive value with respect to given occupations or occu-

pational areas. Rapport and good motivation are needed in the examination, just as in any other area.

Because our primary concern here is with direct evidence of the compatibility of present interests and preferences with given established occupational areas and also with the present susceptibility of the individual to training to a competency level in a given occupation, or family of occupations, it is understandable that few tests need to be developed specially for the exceptional. As a result only a few aptitude measuring devices have been developed specifically for the exceptional, and the major effort has been in improving the means of communication with respect to existing devices. This has resulted in more work with the blind than with other exceptionalities. The relative instability of interests in the younger age groups and the attending delay in specific vocational guidance have understandably narrowed to the upper end of the age scale of our group the approaches to the measurement of their aptitudes. However, in the case of the mentally retarded, it is apparent that at least certain of the measurement approaches present unique problems in the area of concept adequacy on their part and the resulting communication efficacy of the devices which might be used. The most promising area of exploration with respect to this problem might well be the development and use of pictorial approaches involving the use of pictures to be checked in addition to the pictures of tools, machines, gear movements, and belt or rope routings over pulleys.

Some work along this line has been done by Weingarten (1958), and Geist (1959) developed a picture interest inventory for use with adults. Parnicky, Kahn, and Burnett (1968) have developed the Vocational Interest and Sophistication As-

---

*Intentionally omitted here is the consideration of the usual gamut of aptitude tests. Devices such as the Detroit Mechanical Aptitude Test are heavily loaded with samplings of knowledge about things mechanical—whether, for instance, the subject knows a pipe wrench from a claw hammer. In a sense, one who is better informed regarding an area of activity has a better aptitude for it. In the case of tests of musical aptitude, behavior is sampled in terms of aspects such as tonal discrimination, tempo discrimination, memory for each, and the like. Graphic artistic aptitude tends to be tested in terms of appreciation. Certain recently publicized tests of "creative writing ability" depend so heavily upon verbal factors already identified in most intelligence testing that their unique contribution as tests of creative writing aptitude is by no means clearly established.

sessment sets of pictures on the basis of the interests expressed by 3,000 male and female retarded youths and adults. The San Francisco Vocational Competency Scale (1968), usable with retardates, has become available. The Minnesota Vocational Interest Inventory (1968), for use with ninth-graders and up, limits its verbal sampling to skilled and semiskilled levels.

It is well to keep in mind that in this area, too, we are dealing in terms of probabilities. We are still in the realm of "the chances are . . . " Further, we are safer in our guesses or estimates when we recognize the fact that we use the results of some of our measures of vocational interest more to suggest the undesirability of a given occupation or group of occupations than to indicate clearly the desirability of a given occupation or group of occupations. Given the results of one or more vocational interest inventories on a youth, our statement to him might well run in this fashion: "More than your responses or scores on these devices is needed to help you make a decision about what you might consider as a kind of life work. However, as far as the results of these devices alone are concerned, the chances are about seven out of ten that——might be a good type of work for you to consider favorably, but the chances are eight or so out of ten that——would be a good area to avoid."

THE ASSESSMENT PROCESS

Analysis

Regardless of the kind of exceptionality the individual possesses and regardless of the age of the exceptional individual, the sampling of various areas of behavior must be carried out for the purpose of throwing light upon specifiable and psychologically significant aspects of the individual. In contrast to a testing approach that results from giving *a* test to get *a* score, there is the more important need to study the individual in terms of certain psychological constructs, or from certain psychological frames of reference that bear clearly upon the situation with respect to which the individual is being studied. A very significant approach of this sort is the one described by Taylor, as mentioned on page 130. A somewhat different structuring of the clinician's task is presented in the next few paragraphs. The assessment process will be considered in terms of obtaining behavior samples that will enlighten the clinician regarding the subject's conceptualization behavior, his interpersonal relationships, his communication, his energy level, and the validity of information obtained about the subject from others. This will be done by stating only a few questions that illustrate what the clinician must be asking himself about the client as he works with him.

Conceptualization. What is his present level and quality of conceptualization? In view of the subject's history, what reasonable implications can be drawn regarding the client's subsequent conceptualization—his rate and ultimate level of growth in this area? What has been the nature of the subject's acculturation? Has he had a normal exposure? Or has he been reared in an impoverished or culturally sterile environment? Or has he been hothoused? If the child shows the effects of such hothousing, what are the implications of the results of such activity with respect to the child's capacity to benefit from it? How does he learn in the clinic situation?

Interpersonal relationships. How does the subject relate to the clinician? How has he related to others in his environment? Is he "outgoing"? If so, is this behavior of good quality? Does it have a compensatory basis? Is it soundly compensatory, or is it overcompensatory? Is he "withdrawing"? Is this behavior really a manifestation of good quality self-sufficiency? Or is it the result of his having learned to retire to situations that must be, for him, less threatening? Is he quite distractible? Is this a function of his basic insecurity or other emotional tension? Or is it better attributable to low mentality? Or to hearing loss? How does he respond to motivation in the clinic situation? Does he become interested in the test situation, or is he concerned primarily with pleasing you? Is he excessively concerned with meeting time limits, or does he excessively seek approbation? Is he aggressive in the clinic situation? If so, is he justified in being so? Have the significant adults in his world taken him so often to clinics for examination and treatment that he resents being with you in another one? Or has he become resigned to it? How much residual psychological integrity has he?

Communication. How well is he receiving? Does he, possibly due to a hearing loss, give evidence of misinterpretation of words he hears? Is his asking for repetition of directions due to hearing loss, emotional need, or short attention span? Are any of his posturings or the closeness with which he watches you suggestive of any possible hearing loss? Is inattentiveness due to hearing loss, legitimate fatigue, or some other condition? Does he see well what is shown him? Are there any posturings or other physical adjustments that may be compensatory for poor vision? Are there any cutaneous-kinesthetic anomalies affecting his reception of stimuli? Are there any anomalies in the motor area? May they be due to inadequate maturation? To neural impairment? To emotional tension? Is motor anomaly limited to eye movement, speech, locomotion, manipulation, breathing, or common to two or more? (Questions regarding the mediation aspect of the communication process—what happens after the stimulus is received and before the response is made—will not be raised here specifically, since much that has been said [and asked] in regard to conceptualization and in regard to Taylor's procedures applies here.)

Energy level. Is the vigor of his response appropriate to the demands of the situation? Does he overreact? If so, is this a healthy, animal energy? Does it have a plausible emotional basis, as in certain overcompensatory behavior? If below the demands of the situation, may it have resulted from repressive treatment? From a debilitated physical condition? From understandable fatigue? From medication? From his rejection of the clinical situation?

Nature of information. To what extent is your clinical evaluation of the subject based primarily upon what you have actually observed? To what extent are you dealing with your own inferences as though they were observed behavior? To what extent is the developmental and social background information that you obtained from someone else a careful report of specific behavior, or to what extent does it consist of ambiguous, inferred generalities, such as "nervous," "stubborn," "withdrawn," and the like? Has your information about the subject come from a hyper-critical or excitable or basically insecure person? To what extent has your background information on the child come from an adult who is excessively ambitious for (or rejecting of) the child? Or has it come from a person of low psychological perceptive acuity?

These are only some of the many questions the psychologist always asks himself as he seeks to acquire an understanding of any individual—exceptional or otherwise—in order to try to make a psychologically sound assessment of him. It is apparent that, to do so, he cannot be "test-bound." But, in doing so, he needs four things:

1. To have a normative background in terms of which he can decide that a given child's conceptualization is that of an average ten-year-old, or decide that the child is insecure, or that he has good psychological integrity. To be able to do this, he needs to have acquired much experience in terms of which he has valid expectancies for average nine-month-old infants, seven-year-olds, ten- and fifteen-year-olds. He needs to know the various ways in which children handle their feelings of insecurity. He must be able to differentiate between psychological integrity, or ego strength, and psychological facade.

2. To have a knowledge of what behaviors may *not* suggest as well as of what they may suggest. The child hastily diagnosed as a "mirror writer" may after all be only a youngster, like one with whom the writer worked, who "saw her sister write this way and get a lot of attention" and similarly wanted attention. Or perhaps the child reported as "shifty eyed" and untrustworthy is actually nystagmic. Or, the child reported as "clumsy" may be a developmental problem; or he may be fearful of running and going up and down stairs because his crossed eyes render him deficient in depth perception; or he may be "clumsy" be-

cause he is muscularly tense as an integral part of an emotional problem; or, least likely, he may have some central nervous system impairment. Or, the situation may be something like the case of the child who had shown "uncontrollable behavior" at various times over a period of three years and who was found to have an infection of the ear that became severe and "drove the child wild."

3. To have a sound understanding of and a deep feeling for the legitimacy of differentness. While the clinician must have an understanding of the normal, in terms of which he can understand deviants, he, perhaps more fully than most parents and teachers, is constantly aware that in the psychological sense a norm is only a statistical statement, an average, for some defined group. To him such a norm need not be something to be attained by a given youngster, because it may be unreasonably high for one child or restrictingly low for another. The exceptional child has a "right to be different" and to expect the school and society both to understand his difference and to capitalize upon it.

4. To be sensitive constantly to the importance of the interaction of the many facets of behavior that he necessarily explores in isolation.

Synthesis

Let us imagine a piece of cloth that has been woven out of a variety of colored threads. An intricate design is woven into this piece of cloth. Due to the nature of some of the dyes, parts of some of the exposed threads have faded and other

T. ERNEST NEWLAND

parts have been soiled, so that the color you see in them is quite different from that you would find if you turned the cloth over or if you pulled those threads out of their sheltered positions within that pattern. Some of the cloth is well worn, meaning that some of these threads are thinner, even a bit shaggy, in spots. Perhaps, by some fluke in the patterning and weaving process, some particularly strong or well-dyed thread figures only to a very minor extent in what one sees on looking at the whole piece of cloth. One could look at the whole piece of cloth and make certain meaningful observations to the effect that it is soiled, faded, thin, worn, in need of replacing, usable for certain things, and so on. These are socially appropriate evaluations of this piece of cloth, given the implied frames of reference for them.

Certain persons, because of their particular functions in society—such as the weaver, the dyer and the patternmaker—may well decide to describe (an elementary kind of evaluation) the pattern in terms of the number of threads per inch, the percentage of color to a square inch, the use of straight-line or curved-line elements in the pattern, the tensile strength of the threads used, the chemical analysis of the dyes used, or any one of a number of other facets of this piece of cloth. Each of these will have a social value within its frame of reference. Given enough samples of each of these separate elements, socially meaningful (but not meaningful insofar as this one piece of cloth is concerned) generalizations could be made concerning such thread strengths, stability of such patterns, permanency of such dyes, and so on. But none of these studies of single aspects of this piece of cloth can be taken to represent the cloth; clothwise, such single evaluations or descriptions are meaningless.

The analogy with the examination of the individual—particularly if he is exceptional—need not be labored. The layman or novice tends to make gross evaluations, all of them psychologically valuable and some of them valid regarding the person so evaluated. But the psychologist, aspiring to the objectivity of the scientist, is faced with the two problems of science. He must analyze the whole individual into parts or functions in order that he can get clearer and more objective pictures of those functions. Then, if society is to benefit from his intensive studies of these elements, he must try to reassemble those functions into the whole individual, emphasizing certain of those functions for some purposes, and emphasizing others for other purposes, but at all times concerning himself with the whole individual. This synthesizing process gives psychological meaning to the studies of the artificially isolated functions, enhancing some, limiting others. The psychological tester tends to stop with, or to describe the individual primarily in terms of, his work at the analysis stage. If the psychologist would *assess* the individual, he goes through the analysis stage making as many controlled observations as he deems necessary in order to synthesize his findings into a psychologically meaningful picture of the total functioning dynamic individual. This is not simply an additive process. A person's health may be somewhat below average and his intelligence may seem less than average, yet the strength and nature of his motivation may well be such that he performs on a job considerably better than either of the first two characteristics would lead one to expect.

This need for synthesis holds where any sound psychological evaluation of an individual is undertaken. It is often difficult to achieve when working with the nonexceptional. It is doubly necessary and much more difficult in connection with the exceptional, since misleading or obscuring conditions so often enter their behavioral pictures. This difficulty often is compounded by the fact that, because of a dearth of appropriately well-trained persons, less well qualified individuals endeavor to make assumptions and use procedures that may have more validity in a nonexceptional frame of reference.

The interrelating of the varieties of information obtained in the assessment process must be accomplished with as full a comprehension and understanding as possible of the *total* social picture in which the exceptional child and youth has been, is, and probably will be functioning.

Although it was necessary for convenience of discussion and description to concern ourselves with aspects or functions of the exceptional as though they were pure, isolated identities, the interrelatedness of these five areas of measurement repeatedly became apparent. The paradox of the psychological absurdity of dealing with functions one at a time and the scientific impossibility of meaningfully concerning ourselves with an undifferentiated total called an individual constitutes a continuum within which the psychologist must always operate.

The point was made, in the discussion of intelligence measurement of the severely physically handicapped, that the psychologist had to use an almost intuitive approach but that in doing so he had a fairly meaningful set of reference points as a result of having been well grounded in his training and experience with less handicapped children. As a result of the important part played by such basic training, we encounter the point of view that effective measurement in markedly atypical cases is much more a matter of the person making the examination than it is

of the particular device used. Even though reasonably adequate psychological pictures thus can be obtained of the handicapped, the kind of data so obtained is often recognizably inadequate for rigid statistical analysis. In other words the determination of the mental level or rate of mental development in such cases tends more to be an art than a science. This being the case within a given area of measurement, the synthesizing of these areas of measurement tends even more to be a matter of art. Calling either of these processes something less than scientific need not cause us to reject them as useless and completely meaningless. The need for rigorous research on the validity of these important and necessary processes is unmistakably apparent.

SUMMARY

The concepts and assumptions fundamental to all measurement underlie the examination and assessment of the exceptional. We sample behavior and assume, with varying degrees of confidence, that our samples give us adequate cues as to the totality of learning-proneness, emotionality, achievement, or aptitudes. For a number of reasons, but especially since the organism we are observing under controlled conditions is a growing and adapting one, and since we have to resort to samples of its behavior, we are bound to have errors in our measurements. At times the behavior we observe has to serve as a basis for inferring a capacity for further similar behavior, as in the case of the measurement of mental capacity. Both the performance under observation and the inferred basic capacity to perform are of psychological importance. In the case of the exceptional the gap between the two tends to be greatest. At other times there is less, if any, need for such inference since it is the degree of skill in evidence at the time of observation (testing) that is of primary social value, as in the case of educational achievement or certain vocational aptitudes.

Certain of our assumptions and problems are common to all the areas of the psychological evaluation of the exceptional. Even though measurement error is known or knowable, it is at times not recognized. But it can be reduced. Pervading the processes of psychologically evaluating the exceptional are problems pertaining to the nature and status of their conceptualization processes and problems involved in communication. The first of these necessitates the careful consideration both of the verbalized content employed in the behavior sampling process and of the evaluations made of the responses given in the examination situations. This latter bears also upon the means of communicating, by the exceptional child or youth, with the examiner, and also makes special demands regarding the sensory avenues employed in getting through to him. The communication problem appears to have received more attention than the conceptualization problem.

The examination of exceptional children and youth is, by the very nature of their being exceptional, an exacting and difficult task requiring the services of highly skilled and qualified persons. The presence of motor and sensory handicaps and of major emotional involvements, singly or in combination, materially complicates the process. The psychological assessment of these children and youth, the necessary synthesizing of the results of physical, intellectual, socioemotional, achievement, and aptitude measurements, is even more difficult. Although sound research is badly

needed to show us how to make these processes more scientific and less a matter of art, their results can still play a significant part in educational and social planning for, and in our understanding of, the exceptional.

References

Abt, L. E., & Bellak, L. *Projective psychology: Clinical approaches to the total personality.* New York: Grove Press, Inc., 1959.

Allen, R. M., & Collins, M. G. Suggestions for the adaptive administration of intelligence tests for those with cerebral palsy. *Cerebral Palsy Review*, 1955, *16*, 11–14, 25; and 1958, *19*, 6–7.

Ames, L. B. *et al. Adolescent Rorschach responses.* New York: Harper & Row, Publishers, 1959.

———, Learned, L., Metraux, R. W., & Walker, R. N. *Child Rorschach responses.* New York: Paul B. Hoeber, Inc., 1952. The exceptional children reported on include emotionally maladjusted delinquents, mentally superior, endogenous and exogenous defectives, enuretic children, children with extremes in reading skills, and those with tics.

Ammons, R. B., & Ammons, H. S. *Full Range Picture Vocabulary Test.* Missoula, Mont.: Psychological Test Specialists, 1948.

Anastasi, A. Psychology, psychologists, and psychological testing. *American Psychologist*, 1967, *22*, 297–306.

Arthur, G. *The Arthur Adaptation of the Leiter International Performance Scale* (Manual). Beverly Hills, Calif: Western Psychological Services; or Chicago: C. H. Stoelting Co., 1952.

Baldwin, B. T., & Wood, T. D. *Weight-height-age tables for boys and girls.* New York: American Child Health Association, 1932.

Bayley, N. *The Bayley Scales of Infant Development.* New York: The Psychological Corporation, Inc., 1968.

———. On the growth of intelligence. *American Psychologist*, 1955, *10*, 805–818.

———, and Oden, M. H. The maintenance of

intellectual ability in gifted adults. *Journal of Gerontology,* 1955, *10,* 91–107.

Benton, A. L. *The Revised Visual Retention Test: Clinical and experimental applications.* New York: The Psychological Corporation, Inc., 1955.

Berko, M. J. Some factors in the mental evaluation of cerebral palsied children. *Cerebral Palsy Review,* 1953, *14,* 6, 11, 15.

Bice, H. V. Psychological examination of the cerebral palsied. *Journal of Exceptional Children,* 1948, *14,* 163–168.

Birch, J. R., & Birch, J. W. The Leiter International Performance Scale as an aid in the psychological study of the deaf. *American Annals of the Deaf,* 1951, *96,* 502–511.

———. Predicting school achievement in young deaf children. *American Annals of the Deaf,* 1956, *101,* 348–352.

Blum, L. H., Burgemeister, B. B., & Lorge, I. The Mental Maturity Scale for the Motor Handicapped. *School and Society,* 1951, *73,* 232–233.

———. *Columbia Mental Maturity Scale.* New York: Harcourt, Brace & World, 1954. The only information supplied in the manual for the 1959 revision is a normative data sheet that provides norms for a mental age range from three years five months to thirteen years eleven months, but the norms about ten years suggest the use of extrapolative procedures. The sigmas of the IQs for the separate age levels have been reported as distractingly large.

Blum, L. H., & Fieldsteel, N.D. *Blum-Fieldsteel Development Charts.* New York: Harcourt, Brace & World, Inc., 1953.

Bond, N. B. Cerebral palsy profile in Mississippi. *Exceptional Children,* 1953, *20,* 98–99.

Brown, M. E. Daily activity inventories of cerebral palsied children in experimental classes. *Physical Therapy Review,* 1950, *50,* 415–421. (*a*)

———. Daily activity inventory and progress record for those with atypical movement. *American Journal of Occupational Therapy,* 1950, *4,* 195–204, 261–272; and 1951, *5,* 23–29, 38. (*b*)

———. Pre-Vocational Motor Skill Inventory. *American Journal of Occupational Therapy,* 1953, *7,* 153–163, 188.

Cattell, R. B. Theory of fluid and crystallized

intelligence: A critical experiment. *Journal of Educational Psychology,* 1963, *54,* 1–22.

———. Are I.Q. tests intelligent? *Psychology Today,* 1968, *1,* 56–62.

———, & Butcher, H. J. *The prediction of achievement and creativity.* Indianapolis: The Bobbs-Merrill Co., Inc. 1968.

Cruickshank, W. M. *The teacher of brain-damaged children.* Englewood Cliffs, N. J.: Prentice-Hall, Inc., 1966. See especially Part III, Cognitive, perceptual, and motor competencies, pp. 137–221.

Distefano, M. K., Jr., Ellis, N. R., & Sloan, W. Motor proficiency in mental defectives. *Perceptual and Motor Skills,* 1958, *8,* 231–234.

Doll, E. A. Psychometric pitfalls in clinical practice. *Journal of Consulting Psychology,* 1947, *11,* 12–20.

———. *Measurement of social competence.* Minneapolis: Educational Test Bureau, 1953.

Dunn, L. M. *Peabody Picture Vocabulary Test.* Nashville: American Guidance Service, 1965.

Eichenwald, H. F., & Frey, P. C. Nutrition and learning. *Science,* 1969, *163,* 644–48.

Force, D. A comparison of physically handicapped children and normal children in the same elementary school classes with reference to social status and self-perceived status. Doctoral dissertation, University of Michigan, 1954.

Frandsen, A. N., McCullough, B. R., & Stone, D. R. Serial versus consecutive order administration of the Stanford-Binet Intelligence Scales. *Journal of Consulting Psychology,* 1950, *14,* 316–320.

Frank, L. K. *Projective methods.* Springfield: Charles C. Thomas, Publisher, 1948.

Frostig, M., & Horne, D. *The Frostig Program for the Development of Visual Perception.* Los Angeles: Follett Publishing Company, 1964.

Geist, H. *The Geist Picture Interest Inventory.* Missoula, Mont.: Psychological Test Specialists, 1959.

Gesell, A., & Amatruda, C. S. *Developmental diagnosis* (2nd ed.). New York: Paul B. Heeber, Inc., 1947.

Goodenough, F. L. The appraisal of child personality. *Psychological Review,* 1949, *56,* 123–131.

Graham, F. K., & Kendall, B. S. Memory-for-

Designs Test: Revised general manual. *Perceptual and Motor Skills,* Monograph Supplement No. 2, 1960, *11,* 147–148.

Guertin, W. H., Rabin, A. I., Frank, G. H., & Ladd, C. E. Research with the Wechsler Intelligence Scale for adults. *Psychological Bulletin,* 1962, *59,* 1–26.

Guilford, J. P. *The nature of human intelligence.* New York: McGraw-Hill Book Co., 1967.

———. *Intelligence, creativity, and their educational implications.* San Diego: Robert K. Knapp, 1968.

Hartshorne, H., & May, M. A. *Studies in service and self-control.* New York: Macmillan, 1929.

Haussermann, E. Evaluating the developmental level of cerebral palsied pre-school children. *Journal of Genetic Psychology,* 1952 (first half), *80,* 3–23.

Hecht, P. J., & Newland, T. E. Learning potential and learning achievement of educationally blind third-graders in a residential school. *The International Journal for the Education of the Blind,* 1965, *15,* 1–6.

Herbert, M. The concept and testing of brain-damaged children. *Journal of Child Psychology and Psychiatry,* 1964, *5,* 197–216.

Hiskey, M. S. *Hiskey-Nebraska Test of Learning Aptitude.* Lincoln: Union College Press, 1966.

Hunt, B. M. Differential responses of mentally retarded children on the Leiter Scale. *Exceptional Children,* 1961, *28,* 99–102.

Jay, E. S. *A book about me.* Chicago: Science Research Associates, Inc., 1952.

Johnson, M. K., Zuck, F. N., & Wingate, K. The Motor-Age Test: Measurement of motor handicaps in children with neuromuscular disorders such as cerebral palsy. *Journal of Bone and Joint Surgery,* 1951, *33*A, 698–707.

Katz, E. A method of selecting Stanford-Binet Intelligence Scale test items for evaluating the mental abilities of children severely handicapped by cerebral palsy. *Cerebral Palsy Review,* 1956, *1,* 13–17.

———. The "Pointing Modification" of the revised Stanford-Binet Intelligence Scales, Forms L and M, Years II through VI: A report of research in progress. *American Journal of Mental Deficiency,* 1958, *62,* 698–707.

Klaus, R., & Gray, S. Early Training Project for disadvantaged children. *Monographs of the Society for Research in Child Development,* 1968, *33,* 1–66.

Ledwith, N. H. *Rorschach responses of elementary school children.* Pittsburgh: University of Pittsburgh Press, 1959.

Lessing, E. E. A note on the significance of discrepancies between the Goodenough and Binet I.Q. scores. *Journal of Consulting Psychology,* 1961, *25,* 456–457.

Martin, W. E. *Children's body measurements.* U. S. Office of Education, Special Publication 4. Washington, D. C.: Government Printing Office, 1955.

Minnesota Vocational Interest Inventory. New York: The Psychological Corporation, Inc., 1965.

Mursten, B. I. *Handbook of projective techniques.* New York: Basic Books, Inc., Publishers, 1965. A very good summary of research on the major projective approaches.

Newland, T. E. Language development of the mentally retarded child. In Nancy E. Wood (ed.), Language development and language disorders: A compendium of lectures. *Monographs of the Society for Research in Child Development,* serial No. 77, 1960, *25,* 71–87.

———. Prediction and evaluation of academic learning by blind children: 1—Problems and procedures in prediction and 2—Problems and procedures in evaluation. *The International Journal for the Education of the Blind,* 1964, *14,* 1–7; and *14,* 42–51.

———. *The Blind Learning Aptitude Test.* Report, USOE Grant No. OEG-3-6-061928-1558. Urbana: University of Illinois, 1969.

Nudd, E. M. *Perceptions of pictured social interaction by brain-injured and non-brain-injured children of normal intelligence.* Unpublished doctoral dissertation. University of Illinois, 1957.

Olson, W. C., & Hughes, B. O. *Manual for the description of growth in age units,* Ann Arbor, Michigan: The Edwards Letter Co., 1950.

Parnicky, J. J., Kahn, H., & Burnett, A. D. *Standardization of the Vocational and Sophistication Assessment (VISA): A Reading-Free Test for Retardates.* Bordentown, N. J.: E. R. Johnstone Training and Research Center, 1968.

Pintner, R., Eisenson, J., & Stanton, M. *The psychology of the physically handicapped.* New York: Appleton-Century-Crofts, 1941.

Piotrowski, Z. Positive and negative Rorschach organic reactions. *Rorschach Research Exchange,* 1940, *4,* 147–151.

Pond, D. Is there a syndrome of "brain damage" in children? *Cerebral Palsy Review,* 1960, *4,* 296–297.

Rabin, A. I., & Haworth, M. H. (Eds.) *Projective techniques with children.* New York: Grune and Stratton, Inc., 1960.

Raven, J. C. *Raven Progressive Matrices.* Cambridge, England: H. K. Lewis & Co., Ltd., 1938, 1947, 1956, 1962. Distributed in this country by The Psychological Corporation, Inc., New York, and by Western Psychological Services, Beverly Hills, California.

Reitan, R. M. Qualitative versus quantitative mental changes following brain-damage. *Journal of Psychology,* 1958, *46,* 339–346.

Rowley, V. N. Analysis of the WISC performances of brain damaged and emotionally disturbed children. *Journal of Consulting Psychology,* 1961, *25,* 553.

San Francisco Vocational Competency Scale. New York: The Psychological Corporation, Inc., 1968.

Scherer, I. W. The prediction of academic achievement in brain injured children. *Exceptional Children,* 1961, *28,* 103–106.

Sievers, D. J., & Norman, R. D. Some suggestive results in psychometric testing of the cerebral palsied with Gesell, Binet, and Wechsler Scales. *Journal of Genetic Psychology,* 1953, *82,* 69–90.

Snijders, J. T., & Snijders-Doman, N. *Non-verbal intelligence tests for deaf and hearing subjects.* Groningen, Holland: J. B. Wolters, 1959.

Soldwedel, B., & Terril, I. Sociometric aspects of physically handicapped and non-handicapped children in the same elementary school. *Exceptional Children,* 1957, *23,* 371–372.

Solomon, I. L., & Starr, B. D. *School apperception method.* New York: Springer Publishing Co., Inc., 1968.

Street, R. F. I. Q. changes of exceptional children. *Journal of Consulting Psychology,* 1942, *6,* 243–246.

Taibl, R. M. *An investigation of Raven's Progressive Matrices as a test for the psychological evaluation of cerebral palsied children.* Doctoral dissertation, University of Nebraska, 1951.

Taylor, E. M. *Psychological appraisal of children with cerebral defects.* Cambridge, Mass.: Harvard University Press, 1959.

Tisdall, W. J. *The efficacy of a special class program in the productive thinking abilities of educable mentally handicapped children.* Doctoral dissertation, University of Illinois, 1962.

Tracht, V. S. Preliminary findings on testing the cerebral palsied with Raven's Progressive Matrices. *Journal of Exceptional Children,* 1948, *15,* 77–79, 89.

Van Alstyne, D. *Van Alstyne Picture Vocabulary Test.* New York: Harcourt, Brace & World, Inc., 1960.

Weingarten, K. P. *Picture Interest Inventory.* Los Angeles: California Test Bureau, 1958.

Wepman, J. M., & Weiner, P. S. *Standardization and validation of a diagnostic test battery for language impaired children.* Chicago: University of Chicago Press, 1967.

Werner, H., & Strauss, A. Types of visuomotor activity in their relation to low and high performance ages. *Proceedings of the Association on Mental Deficiency,* 1939, *44,* 163–168.

Wetzel, N. C. *The treatment of growth failure in children.* Cleveland: National Education Association Service, 1948.

Wittenborn, J. R., & Sarason, S. B. Exceptions to certain Rorschach criteria of pathology. *Journal of Consulting Psychology,* 1949, *13,* 21–27.

PART II

Psychological Components of Disability

FOUR

Speech Defects: Nature, Causes, and Psychological Concomitants

JON EISENSON

Jon Eisenson is Professor of Speech and Hearing Sciences and Director of the Institute of Childhood Aphasia, School of Medicine, Stanford University. He is a consultant in clinical psychology and in speech pathology for the United States Veterans Administration and has served as a consultant for agencies of the Department of Health, Education, and Welfare.

DISORDERS OF SPEECH: DEFINITION AND CLASSIFICATION

Speech may be defined as a method of communication that employs oral symbols according to the rules and conventions of a linguistic code. Speech disorders, therefore, may be considered as defects or imperfections in oral (verbal) production when the encoded verbal formulation is presumably intact. Language disturbances refer to defects or impairments of formulation (encoding). The implication of this division between speech and language disorders may be expressed in the generalized statement that speech defects comprise "noise" that, according to nature and degree of severity, interferes with the reception and interpretation (decoding) of the message. We may, however, take the position that speech necessarily involves language, that speech is not solely a manner of producing a code, but requires a symbol (linguistic) code. Language defects, therefore, are subsumed under speech defects.

We shall, in this chapter, limit our discussions to "legal children"—those who are ordinarily considered to be members, or at least eligible for membership, in our school-age population.

Speech Defects: Listener and Speaker

From the point of view of the listener, any child who speaks so that he distracts attention from what he is trying to say (the message) to how he is saying it (manner of production) may be considered to have defective speech.*

The amount of distraction and, therefore, the degree and significance of the defect may vary. Objectively, a child's

---

*We assume, of course, that the age of the child is properly considered.

speech is significantly defective when the amount of distraction is sufficient to make it difficult for him to communicate readily with a normal listener. A normal listener is one whose hearing, visual perceptive abilities, intelligence, expectations, and motivations make it possible for him to wish to and be able to understand what the speaker is attempting to communicate.

Defective speech has another aspect—a subjective one. From this viewpoint speech may be considered defective if the speaker is unduly self-conscious or apprehensive about objectively small deviations. Any speech deviation is a defect when it looms large enough in the speaker's mind so that it becomes a factor that contributes to difficulties in social, educational, and vocational adjustments.

Specifically, speech may be considered defective if it is characterized by any one or more of the following:

1. It is not readily audible.
2. It is not readily intelligible.
3. It is vocally unpleasant.
4. It is visibly unpleasant.
5. It is labored in production or lacking in conventional rhythm and stress.
6. It is linguistically deficient.
7. It is inappropriate to the individual (content or manner of production) in terms of age, sex, and physical development.
8. The speaker responds to his own speech as if one or more of the above were present.

Types of Speech Defects

Speech defects are frequently divided into four major types:

1. Defects of articulation (sound production)
2. Defects of phonation (voice production)
3. Defects of fluency (stuttering and cluttering)
4. Language dysfunctions (delayed speech and aphasia)

For practical purposes a second type of classification may be considered. This classification is based on categories of speech-defective individuals rather than on speech defects. For example, a cerebral-palsied child may show defects of language delay, voice, and articulation. Most children with cleft palates have defects of articulation as well as of voice. With this in mind, the following classification should be found useful:

1. Defects of articulation, including omissions, distortions, or substitutions of speech sounds
2. Defects of voice, including those of quality, loudness, pitch, variety, or adequate duration
3. Stuttering (stammering)
4. Cluttering
5. Delayed language development
6. Cleft-palate speech
7. Cerebral-palsied speech
8. Impairments of previously developed language functions (aphasic involvements)
9. Speech defects associated with defective hearing

INCIDENCE OF SPEECH DEFECTS

Based on the 1966 (March) *Current Population Reports,* and on a rather conservative figure of 4 percent, Johnson (1967, p. 1.) estimated a total of 2,225,000 for speech defective children (ages five to nineteen years).

JON EISENSON

Estimates as to the incidence of type of speech defects vary considerably. In terms of our definition and its implication of either message distortion or subjective maladaptive potential, conservative estimates approximate the following.

TABLE 4-1

PERCENTAGE OF SPEECH
DEFECTIVE SCHOOL-AGE POPULATION

Defects of articulation	2.0-3.0
Stuttering	.7-1.0
Voice	.1
Cleft-palate speech	.1
Cerebral-palsied speech	.1
Retarded language development	.2
Speech defects related to impaired hearing	.5
Cluttering	No reliable figures
Aphasia	No reliable figures
Total:	4–5%

SOURCES: These figures are based on estimates in W. Johnson and D. Moeller (eds.), *Speech Handicapped School Children* (New York: Harper & Row, Publishers, 1967).

We may note that the largest category, exceeding all others combined, is functional articulatory defects. It is likely that among the children with less severe speech defects an even greater proportionate number fall into this category.

SEX DISTRIBUTION

Milisen (1957, p. 249), on the basis of several survey studies on the incidence and sex distribution of speech defects among grade-school children, concluded that "All workers report more males than females for all age levels amd more speech defectives, both male and female, in the first three grades." Both parts of Milisen's observations suggest the likelihood that maturational factors account for the incidence and sex distribution of speech defects among young children. Among typical studies that bear out the general findings are those of Mills and Streit (1942) and, specifically in relationship to the production of articulatory errors, Roe and Milisen (1942). As we have indicated, however, it is by no means certain that the errors in articulation of children in the first three grades should be considered defects of speech which will require remediation. Powers (1957, p. 729), after surveying the literature on the incidence of articulatory defects, concludes "the weight of evidence supports a sex difference in favor of girls, both in the normal development of articulatory skills during the early years and in the smaller percentages of functional articulatory defects among girls throughout the entire educational range from preschool through college."

The somewhat higher proportion of males to females for organic involvements such as cleft palate and cerebral palsy related to speech defects (Berry and Eisenson, 1956, pp. 309 and 354) is another factor increasing the ratio of males to females. The largest factor, however, is the significantly greater proportion of males to females, approximately three to four males to one female, among stutterers (Andrews and Harris, 1964, p. 161; Johnson, 1967, pp. 267–268). In general, therefore, we may conclude that there is a higher incidence of speech defects among boys than among girls in the school-age population as a whole.

SPEECH AS A DEVELOPMENTAL PROCESS

We appreciate, of course, that children are not miniature adults in their acquisition of speech. The vast majority of children develop the proficiencies needed for speech over a period of time beginning in some instances as early as nine months of age and extending, in most instances, through ages seven and eight. In regard to vocabulary, there is no ceiling age either for the comprehension or production of lexical items. If we view speech as consisting of a processing of the sound system (articulate-phonemic component), the lexical system (vocabulary), and the grammatical system (syntax), we can make several statements related to these components. Articulatory proficiency is normally reached between ages seven and eight. That is, most children indicate by the way they speak that they have mastered the sound system, the identifiable phonemes and phonemic combinations, of their language (Johnson, Darley, and Spriestersbach, 1963, pp. 101–103; and Templin, 1957, p. 58). Vocabulary growth, as we have indicated, has no ceiling age. Productive vocabulary, the vocabulary of use, appears to show a faster rate of growth between ages three to five than between six to eight (Templin, 1957, pp. 114–116). Grammar (syntax), at least in regard to the most frequent and conventional forms, is usually well established by age five. However, the use of complex forms, for example, combinations of passive, negative, and interrogative and subordinate structures, are achievements that continue beyond age eight, possibly up to age fifteen (Lenneberg, 1967, p. 130 and Templin, 1957, pp. 103–104).

The following "developmental" schedule for normal language acquisition is based on Lenneberg's observations for the first three years (1967, pp. 128–130). Lenneberg is not, however, responsible for any of the interpretations.

I. *Prelingual Developmental Stages*
Birth Cry
Undifferentiated—birth to three weeks.
Differentiated—beyond three weeks.
Cooing—beginning with eight weeks —"squealing, gurgling sounds, vowellike in character, sustained for fifteen to twenty seconds." *Responds* to human sounds by smiling and possibly by cooing. By twenty weeks vowellike production is modified by consonantlike sounds with labial fricatives. *The infant is a universalist in his sound making.*

Babbling
By or before six months, cooing changes to babbling, which resembles one-syllable utterances. Neither the vowel nor the consonants have fixed recurrences; most frequent utterances resemble *ma, mu, da, di.*

Lalling
By eight months, reduplication (sound repetition) becomes frequent; intonation patterns discernible in utterances; "utterances can signal emphasis and emotion."

Echolalia
By nine to ten months, sound play and apparent imitation of sound patterns of the environment. *Responses—* differential adjustments to utterances of speakers in environment may show clear indication of comprehension of several single words or utterances.

II. *Word Identification and Identification Language*
By twelve months, increase in sound and identification imitation (replication); definite indications of understanding; may say "mama," "dada," may be able to play (obey simple commands) such as "Show me your eyes, . . . nose." May utter words such as "mama," "dada," "doll," to identify events.

III. *True Speech*

By fifteen to eighteen months, uses words to bring about events (anticipatory language); vocabulary may range from three to fifty words. By twenty-four months, vocabulary of more than fifty words.

IV. *Syntactic Speech—twenty-four months*

Words are combined into two-word phrases; many are combinations *not* directly taught.

V. *Communicative Intent*

By thirty months, communicative intent is clear because the child will show frustration if not understood; most rapid increase in vocabulary to date, and proportionately for rest of life.

VI. *Syntactic Competence*

By three years, has mastered most of the grammar (syntax) of the language of his environment.

VII. *Individuolect*

By four years, child shows virtually complete mastery of the grammar used by members of his environment. The child also begins to express himself in his own "rhetorical" style.

CAUSES OF DEFECTIVE SPEECH

We must never lose sight of the truism that a speech defect is the defect of a *person*. Thus, what may constitute a primary cause of a defect for one individual may have little or no etiological significance for another. Some children with minor organic anomalies of the articulatory mechanism, such as malocclusions, may have unmistakable articulatory defects. Others, with measurably greater anomalies, may have entirely adequate articulation. Some children regress in speech proficiency when new siblings are brought into the family. Other children take the arrival of new brothers and sisters in apparently easy stride. Even stutterers, who as a group are fairly predictable as to what factors will increase or decrease the severity of their stuttering, vary extensively when considered as individuals. The causes of speech defects that we shall consider refer to the various groups of speech defectives when they are studied as groups. In the final analysis the only certain way of knowing why a given child has a speech defect, and what this defect may mean to him, is to study him, his dynamics, and his own reactions to his speech. The implications of diagnoses and a philosophy for the management of the child with defective speech related to diagnosis is considered in detail by Johnson, Darley, and Spriestersbach (1963, Chap. I).

Organic Causes

Some speech defects are clearly organic in origin. The articulatory and vocal difficulties of the child with a cleft palate can, at least initially, be attributed directly to the type and severity of the cleft. Hearing impairment, if it begins early and is relatively severe, may directly account for defects in articulation and voice. Malocclusions and dental irregularities, if severe, may be responsible for some degree and some types of defective articulation, though such physical deviations, as indicated earlier, do not make it inevitable that a given child will have faulty articulation. Cerebral palsy conditions that involve the speech mechanism are directly responsible for defective speech. Implications for language acquisition in the cerebral-palsied are related to brain damage associated with aphasic involvements, and problems that may be associated with hearing and listening impairment. Beyond this, there are more general implications related to mental retardation for some cerebral-palsied children. Congenital (developmental) aphasia is, by definition, language delay associated with central nervous system dysfunction and related underlying perceptual impairments (Eisenson, 1968). Cluttering, according to Weiss (1964, p. 1) is "the verbal manifestation of central language imbalance" and is based on hereditary predisposition.

Functional Causes

Many children with apparently normal speech mechanism nevertheless have defects of articulation and/or of voice. In some instances imitation of an older sibling, a playmate, or an adult may account for the defect. Children learn to articulate, vocalize, and use language "by ear." If what they hear is faulty, and if they have no cause to be negatively inclined to what they hear, they will learn to speak in a faulty manner. In an important sense, speech faults that are based on imitative patterns may indicate normal adaptive behavior. If the influential and respected members of a child's environment speak in a given way, the child, having no basis to determine that such speech is not appropriate, should be expected to imitate what he hears, *unless he is negatively inclined either to the individuals or to the general environment.*

Psychogenic Causes

Numerous studies have supplied data which support the clinical impression that many defects of speech are basically psychogenic. When the defects are found in children, their origin, when not organic or imitative, may often be associated with the children's reactions to their environment, particularly to their parents. It is not at all surprising that some investigators have interpreted their findings to indicate that the primary maladjustments exist in the parents of the speech-defective children. Wood (1946), for example, found that on the whole a group of fifty speech-defective children showed better adjustment than the parents. Despite this, about half of the children to whom the Thematic Apperception Test was administered revealed dynamisms that suggested frustration, withdrawing tendencies, and a sense of lack of affection. Only three of the twenty-five children to whom the TAT was administered manifested no preponderance of unfavorable dynamisms. Maladjustments of the parents were determined on the basis of the findings of the Bernreuter Personality Inventory and the California Test of Personality. Both mothers and fathers tended to have poor adjustment scores. 86 percent of the children had one or both parents who were below the 35th percentile in self-adjustment; 64 percent had one or both parents who were below the 35th percentile in social adjustments. The mothers, as a group, were significantly totally less well adjusted than the fathers. A specific significant finding was that the social standards of the mothers were very high in comparison with other adjustment scores.

When this is viewed in relation to the emotional instability of the maternal group, it appears probable that the speech-defective children had imposed upon them a set of very high standards in an atmosphere of habitual emotional outbursts on the part of the parents.

In general, Wood concludes:

... on the basis of this study that functional articulatory defects of children are definitely and significantly associated with maladjustment and undesirable traits on the part of the parents, and that such factors are usually maternally centered.

The findings on stutterers are varied and not altogether consistent. Parents often are considered to be "different" and to have traits with serious implications for their children. Johnson (1967, p. 17) observes that "As a rule, in the beginning it is the mother who is a key member of the problem." However, in regard to stutterers themselves, after surveying the literature on maladjustments of stutterers, Johnson (1967, p. 261) concludes:

It does seem incontrovertible that in some cases the experience of stuttering produces a certain amount of personality maladjustment and, in addition to this, there appears to be no ground for assuming that among people who stutter there would not be the same proportion as of the general population who have the customary kinds and grades of personality maladjustments. By and large, stutterers are people who stutter.

We may question the apparent indictment of the parents of stutterers and the assertion that, despite the influence of their parents, the children who become stutterers are essentially normal persons except that they stutter. In any event we will review several studies that shed light on how the parents of stutterers are different from other parents.

Moncur (1952) compared the responses of the mothers of stutterers and nonstutterers on questionnaires designed to reveal tendencies toward parental dominance and the holding of children to excessively high standards. Moncur found the mothers to be much like those studied by Wood. As a group the mothers of stutterers tended by their responses to reveal a variety of dominating actions which included "domination by disciplinary action, domination by oversupervising and overprotecting the child, domination by holding the child to excessively high standards, and domination by adverse parental criticism."

Andrews and Harris found two trends among the mothers of stutterers based on findings of a school survey in Newcastle on Tyne. One group, coming from the lower socioeconomic class, included a significant portion who

... showed an inability to manage themselves, their homes or their husbands, not so much on account of neuroticism as through some degree of inadequacy of intellect and personality. In the upper social groups, however, there were able neurotic mothers who, fitting Johnson's description, appeared to have made excessive demands on their children (Andrews and Harris, 1964, p. 161).

We shall return to the subject of stuttering and possible causes later in this chapter.

The observations of Wood *et al.* in regard to their special populations may be generalized to include other types of speech-defective children. Pekarsky (1952) studied a population of twenty-six mothers of children with psychogenic delayed speech and a control group of mothers whose children were normal in speech development. Pekarsky found that as a group the mothers of the delayed-speech children were found to be "overprotective, rigid individuals, who are restrictive in their demands upon the children." The home environment is reported to be characterized by "confusion, tension, and a lack of organization in the performing of routine tasks." In fairness to the mothers of the delayed-speech children, it should be noted of the control group mothers that their attitudes were not necessarily different but were more moderate.

Brown (1967) describes several cases of delayed and arrested speech development that he attributes to faulty motivation and excessive expectations on the part of parents.

INTELLIGENCE, EDUCATIONAL ACHIEVEMENT, AND SPEECH DEFECTS

The studies we shall consider will be divided into three categories:

1. The relationship of speech defects to intelligence in children of school age as a whole
2. Intelligence of speech-defective children with physical handicaps
3. The incidence of speech defects among children known to be of below-average intelligence

Intelligence

Carrell (1936) analyzed a school population of 1,174 children. He found that the speech-defective children, taken as a group, were lower in average intelligence than the general population. Curtis (1967, p. 132) makes the general observation that "Speech imperfections are more frequent among children of low intelligence than among those who are average or above in mental capacity." Van Riper (1963, p. 112) stresses the interrelationship between speech and intellectual development with the observation, "It is true that mental deficiency can cause delayed speech; it is also true that delayed speech can contribute to mental retardation." Lenneberg (1967, p. 169), however, stresses the point that only severe mental retardation is to be considered a cause for marked delay of the *onset of speech*. However, we believe that though speech onset may come within or close to the normal age range of expectancy, even moderate mental retar-

dation is associated with the prevalence of defective speech. More generally, mental retardation is related to slower and poorer language development despite instances of normal or near normal date of onset for speech.

Stutterers have been a subject of considerable study relative to their intelligence. Schindler (1955) reported a mean IQ of 94.9 compared with a mean of 100.1 for a control group in an Iowa survey. She concluded that the difference between the groups was not statistically significant. Andrews and Harris (1964, p. 161), after surveying the literature and on the basis of their own study, conclude that "stuttering is more common among those with low intelligence." Surveys among college stutterers (Schindler, 1955, p. 353) tend to show higher IQs for stutterers than in the earlier school grades. We accept Schindler's observation that "It is possible that there is a selective factor operating in that the less intelligent stuttering children drop out of school earlier than the more intelligent ones, which would affect the mean IQ for the high school and college groups."

Among physically handicapped children with speech defects, the cerebral-palsied and the deaf show a higher proportion of those mentally below average than does the total population. Most objective findings, even when allowances are made for the nature of the motor disabilities, indicate that a disproportionately large number of cerebral-palsied children are also mentally retarded. Wolfe (1950), for example, found that 26 percent of the subjects of his study were so limited in intelligence that they had to be considered uneducable. Survey studies by Bice and Cruickshank (1955) support this finding.

Deaf children as a group tend to fall below the mean intelligence level of hearing children, especially where verbal tests are involved. Levine (1948) reported an IQ of 89.6 on the verbal portion of the Wechsler-Bellevue for a population of thirty-one "normal" deaf adolescent girls. Elsewhere the intelligence of the deaf is considered in some detail (see e.g., Pintner & Lev, 1939). Although the findings are not consistent, the consensus suggests a somewhat lower intelligence for the deaf than for the hearing for both verbal and performance tests, with a greater difference for the former.

Hard-of-hearing children were found to fall slightly but significantly below the normal level on tests of verbal intelligence. A slight but not significant difference was also found in a nonlanguage test (Pintner and Lev, 1939). Oleron (1950), using the Raven's Matrices Test, concluded that the deaf were equal to the hearing in concrete mental functioning but inferior to them in abstract intelligence.

The Mentally Deficient

The consistent finding of studies of speech defects among mentally deficient children is that the incidence of defects is considerably higher than it is among the population as a whole. In a pioneer study Kennedy (1930) found that 42.57 percent of children in the moron group (IQs ranging from 50 to 69) had speech defects; 31 of 32 imbeciles (IQs from 21 to 47) had speech defects; and all of the children in the idiot range (IQs from 20 to below test level) had defects of speech. Lewald (1932) found that 56 percent of speaking feeble-minded children had speech defects.

More recent studies present data that support the earliest findings. Sachs (1951), for example, studied the incidence and nature of speech defects in a group of 210 mentally deficient children between the ages of ten and twenty. He found that speech defects were present in 57 percent of the children. Gens (1950) reports an even higher percentage. According to Gens, 70 to 75 percent of institutionalized mentally deficient children have disorders of speech.

Matthews (1957, p. 536), after a survey of the literature on speech defects among the mentally retarded, observes "the data permit us to conclude that the incidence of speech defects in populations of mentally retarded is high—considerably higher than in the general population." Matthews found incidence figures ranging from 5 to 79 percent. The variations are attributed to differences in definition of speech defects, as well as to differences in the population involved in the specific studies.

Smith (1962) after surveying the recent literature on the relationship between mental retardation and defective speech, concluded "The incidence of speech problems was found to range from 8 per cent up to 79 per cent, depending on the intellectual range being studied. With the retarded, specifically, language development was delayed, articulation problems were more prevalent, and voice problems occurred commonly."

An overview of the problems of speech and language development of mental retardates will be found in Lillywhite and Bradley (1969). The treatment in this monograph emphasizes language development and the psychological and educational correlates for mentally retarded children.

Educational Achievement

The consensus of evidence shows that children with defective speech (including students on a college level) are somewhat retarded in school progress as compared with children with normal speech. The amount of retardation would, of course, be much greater if we were to include those speech-defective children who are also mentally deficient and who must therefore either attend special schools or be institutionalized as uneducable. Surveys, such as those of Carrell (1936), upon which the general conclusion of slight educational retardation is drawn, are concerned with children in regular schools and so exclude the severely mentally deficient and other special groups who are more greatly retarded.

The ASHA Committee on the Midcentury White House Conference (1952) includes the following among the well-established effects of speech disorders: "Speech defectives appear to be retarded scholastically and to fail to take advantage of opportunities for college training, out of proportion to expectations based on intelligence test data."

Van Riper (1963, p. 201) notes that "failures in school subjects, especially in reading, may be a direct consequence of defective articulation, and remedial reading can frequently be combined with remedial speech." The relationship of reading disability (dyslexia) to delayed language development is discussed by Eisenson (1963).

Reading Ability and Speech

Although research findings are not unamimous, most of the evidence indicates that difficulties in speech and in reading are somehow related. A recent study suggests that these lack of proficiencies are correlated even at the stage of reading readiness. Weaver, Furbee, and Everhart (1960) found that in a population of 638 first-grade children there was a steady decrease in reading readiness as the number of articulatory faults increased. The relationship, as might be expected, is greater when oral reading disability is correlated with speech disability, especially for articulation and for stuttering. Hildreth (1946), for example, considers a number of language and speech defects that retard reading. These include indistinct, inaccurate articulation; poor auditory discrimination of speech sounds; stuttering; bilingual background; and emotional conflicts due to speech defects that interfere with articulation in oral reading, as well as with the comprehension and interpretation of the written page. Jackson (1944) found that, in comparison with 10 percent of the accelerated readers, 23 percent of the retarded readers had speech defects. Artley (1948) after reviewing the literature, concluded that a majority of studies "lead one to the generalization that speech and reading defects are to a substantial degree associated. Particularly is this true when oral reading is involved."

The possibilities to explain the relationship between speech and reading disabilities may be put into three categories: (1) the two disabilities have a common cause; (2) speech disability may cause reading disability, especially when children are taught reading by the oral method; and (3) reading disability may cause speech deficiency.

Eames (1950) believes that both reading and speech disabilities are likely to have a common cause on the basis of a neurological lesion of the language centers. Emotional reactions may increase the degree of difficulty in either reading or speech or both. Although it is difficult to demonstrate this relationship in young children who do not show obvious neurological involvement, the relationship is frequently demonstrated in cases of acquired aphasia in children and in adults. Limited intelligence, probably more than specific neurological deficit, is likely to be a common cause for speech disability and general linguistic deficiency.

The possibility that speech defects may be the cause of reading disability can be explained along the following lines. Defects of articulation may cause errors of pronunciation and so cause errors in the interpretation of the written word. It is also possible, especially in insecure children, that the child's awareness and concern over his defective speech may reduce his ability to concentrate on and so to comprehend what he is reading. A third factor is that faulty speech, especially faulty articulation and stuttering, may disturb the rate and rhythm of reading, interfere with proper phrasing, and therefore with the comprehension of the written symbol. A fourth possibility is that a child, aware of his speech deficiency, may become negatively inclined to all forms of oral expression. The attitude may be generalized to silent reading and so may indirectly influence an area of achievement that the child might otherwise enjoy and in which normal proficiency might otherwise be expected.

The likelihood that reading disability might be the cause of defective speech, except possibly for stuttering, is remote and small. For most children articulatory proficiency is attained for a large majority of speech sounds before formal training in reading ordinarily begins. This is especially true in schools that have a flexible program in the teaching of reading and do not begin formal teaching until reading readiness is clearly demonstrated. In regard to stuttering, the possibility exists that small children who have difficulty with oral reading may generalize this difficulty to include oral recitations and possibly to conversational speech. Several stutterers who have been treated by the author date the onset of their stuttering to unhappy incidents associated with oral reading. Artley (1948), after noting the absence of research to support the possibility that reading defects may cause speech defects, concludes that "where reading defects exist as a cause of speech defects, an explanation may lie in the fact that reading defects may result in fears, tensions, and various types of nervous behavior that may impair normal speech."

PHYSICAL DEFECTS

Most speech-defective children are physically normal. At least their defects of speech cannot be directly attributed to the existence of a specific physical disability. Among children with serious defects of speech, approximately 320,000, or 16 percent, have physical disabilities etiologically associated with their defects of speech. Chief among these are cleft palate, cerebral palsy, and hearing impairments. Deformities and growths of the larynx or pharynx, and neurological impairments affecting the control of the vocal bands, soft palate, or muscles of the throat may be the cause of vocal defects. These conditions, however, occur relatively infrequently in children. Enlarged adenoids is a much more common cause of voice disturbance. In addition, there are minor organic anomalies such as dental malocclusions and high palatal arch, which are found to occur more frequently among speech-defective children than in the population at large.

Of late, considerable interest has been shown by orthodontists and speech pathologists in oral irregularities and articulatory defects associated with "tongue-thrust" swallow. Many children who habitually protrude their tongues between their teeth in the act of swallowing also demonstrate extreme tension in the mouth-enclosing musculature. The forward thrust of the tongue tends to produce oral malocclusion characterized by anteriorly displaced incisors. In a study of a population of children between six to eighteen years of age, which included 668 with tongue-thrust swallow, 230 of the group were found to have sibilant distortion (Fletcher, Casteel, and Bradley, 1961). This incidence is considerably larger than would be expected by chance and significantly larger than the incidence of sibilant distortion among the children in the study whose normal swallowing habits were free of tongue-thrust.

It is likely that residuals of infant neuropathologies have continued influence in the form of retarded speech development or in defective articulation. Although it is not always possible to demonstrate this relationship, the impression of many speech pathologists, including the present writer, is that it exists among many young children with retarded or distorted speech.

A supporting study along this line was made by Eustis (1947). He reports that 48 percent of individuals over six years of age of a family tree covering four generations, in addition to specific speech and reading disabilities, showed one or more of the following conditions: left-handedness, ambidexterity, body clumsiness. Eustis believes that these conditions suggest a syndrome, hereditary in origin, which is characterized by a slow rate of neuromuscular maturation and probably implies retarded myelination of the motor and association nerve tracts. "It is suggested that this inherited tendency to delayed neuromuscular maturation is the single factor

from which all the various aspects of the syndrome may develop."

Basically the same point of view is expressed by Eames (1950), who holds that many defects of speech and reading are etiologically associated, both essentially being "neurophysiological with psychological overtones."

An excellent survey of organic anomalies associated with articulatory defects may be found in Curtis (1967, Chap. 3).

Motor Development and Motor Abilities

Although it is frequently not possible to find evidence of specific neurological deficit,* or of motor involvement, as an etiological associate for most children with defective speech, there is a fair amount of evidence to indicate that the general picture of the development of motor abilities is less favorable for the defective in speech than for the population at large (Berry and Eisenson, 1956, p. 12).

Bilto (1941) administered a series of tests measuring large-muscle abilities to a group of ninety speech-defective children (stutterers and articulatory defectives) who ranged in age from nine to eighteen years and who had no observable organic defects basic to their speech disturbances. The tests were also administered to a control group of children with normal speech. The test performances called for the use of appropriate rhythm, coordination, and the application of strength. Bilto found that approximately two-thirds of the speech-defective children were inferior to the nor-

*Children who are clearly cerebral-palsied, or dysarthric, and children with so-called minimal brain dysfunction (Clements, 1966) are, of course, by definition and by implication neurologically impaired. However, the vast majority of children with speech defects do not show clear evidence by present standards and measures of assessment of neurological involvement.

Jon Eisenson

mally speaking children in the tested abilities. It is important to note, however, that no single specific type of physical disability characterized the speech-defective children.

Patton (1942) found that articulatory defectives tended to show less kinesthetic sensibility than a matched control group of normal elementary school children. Albright (1948) compared thirty-one college students with good articulation and thirty-six with poor articulation in tests of motor and articulatory skills. The students with poor articulation were inferior to the control group in motor skill and in three of four tests specifically related to articulatory skills.

The results of some studies are not as conclusive as those just considered. Fairbanks and Bebout (1950) compared a group of thirty young adults with functional articulatory defects with thirty free from articulatory defects. Their study was confined to four measurements of the tongue: (1) maximum length of protrusion, (2) length of the tip, (3) maximum amount of tongue force, (4) percentage of error in duplicating a tongue position. They reported small, inconsistent, and not significant differences between the groups. In another aspect of the study with the same group, Fairbanks and Spriestersbach (1950) compared the rate of repetitive movements of the organs of articulation. They found a significant difference for the males only in regard to lip movement.

Reid made a study (1947) of functional articulatory defects in elementary school children. She concluded that degree of neuromuscular control and degree of kinesthetic sensitivity are not related to articulatory ability. She observed, however, that "there are minimum levels of maturity . . . that are requisite for articulatory ability." Reid did find a significant

correlation between articulation ability and the ability to discriminate between speech sounds.

Contrary to the findings reported in most of the studies we have considered are those of Mase (1946). He studied matched groups of 53 fifth- and sixth-grade boys with respect to six factors commonly believed to be associated etiologically with functional articulatory defects. These factors included rate of movement of the articulators and general muscular coordination. Mase found no significant differences between his experimental and control groups on any of the factors studied.

Studies on stutterers as to motor competency and implications for neurological (neuromotor) control have been inconclusive. Rotter (1955) reviewed some of the literature and conducted his own investigations. In his study Rotter compared a group of twenty adult male stutterers and a control group of twenty nonstutterers on card sorting and tapping tests. He found that the nonstutterers scored consistently higher than the stutterers on all tests, but few of the differences were statistically significant. Rotter concluded (p. 376) that "These results do not support the hypothesis that stutterers, at least those selected as right-handed, are less able than non-stutterers to coordinate left and right sides rhythmically or that they are better able to carry on motor activities of the left and right sides which are independent of each other."

It may be that the differences in findings cited may be based on differences in populations studied, instruments and measurements employed, or sizes of groups studied. The present author, in reviewing the literature, noted that, as a general finding, the higher the incidence of males in the experimental population, the greater the likelihood that significant differences were found. Males, as noted earlier, exceed the number of females in the speech-defective population. There is apparently also a greater incidence of both delayed maturation and retarded motor development among males than among females. In any event, it is reasonably safe to conclude that the evidence suggests that some degree of motor involvement is etiologically associated with defective speech development.

SENSORY IMPAIRMENTS

If we approach this matter from the point of view of handicapped children with specific sensory impairments, such as the hard-of-hearing, the deaf, and the blind, we will find a larger incidence of speech defects than we would in the population at large. If we exclude these special populations with significant hearing and visual losses, we will find a lack of unanimity in the results of studies related to sensory impairments among speech-handicapped children. Most of the studies concern children with articulatory defects. Most, also, are concerned with some aspect of auditory functioning.

Reid (1947) found no significant relationship between auditory memory span and articulatory ability. She did, however, find that the ability to discriminate between speech sounds stand out as being positively related to the severity of the speech disorder and also to the response made to special speech training.

Van Riper (1963, pp. 209–212) considers hearing loss (acuity of hearing), poor auditory memory span, and difficulties in phonetic discrimination to be causes of defective articulation. He prescribes specific exercises to improve auditory memory span and phonetic discrimination.

Curtis (1967, pp. 124–126) reviews auditory factors related to defective articulation. Curtis questions the assumption that poor speech sound discrimination is causally related to defective articulation, arguing that "it is not evident that low scores on speech sound discrimination tests are related to some fundamental differences of the auditory mechanism." Curtis holds that "The ability to discriminate among complex auditory patterns, such as speech sounds, is doubtless a cultivated or learned trait." We prefer an alternate explanation and believe that speech sound discrimination is a function that improves with maturation and, of course, with opportunity for practice. Fundamentally, however, we consider the maturation of the auditory system, especially on higher central nervous system (CNS) levels, to be the fundamental factor. This is how we interpret the findings of Cohen and Diehl (1963), who studied elementary grade school children with articulatory defects and a control group of normal-speaking children (thirty in each group) for their ability in speech sound discrimination using the Templin Speech Sound Discrimination Test. Cohen and Diehl found that "children with functional articulation-type speech defects made significantly more speech sound discrimination errors than a matched group of normal speaking children." They also observed that speech sound discrimination ability tends to improve with age but that the speech defective group continued to perform below the level of the normal-speaking group at equivalent grade levels.

Van Riper and Irwin (1958, pp. 22–26) emphasize that the techniques for testing sound discrimination may explain the inconsistent results in the literature pertaining to persons with articulatory defects. They suggest "(1) that our existing tests of speech sound discrimination are not testing speech sound discrimination ability except in a crude and oblique fashion, and/or (2) that poor discrimination may be only one of many factors important in the case's ability to recognize error-signals in his own speech." Van Riper and Irwin look upon speech sound (phonetic) discrimination as a complex of several factors that includes auditory memory span and phonetic analysis as well as the ability to monitor one's own sound production. A test of the ability to discriminate speech sounds should seek to single out the factors involved in the total complex.

Some of the apparent inconsistencies in findings, especially where discrimination for nonspeech events are concerned (for example, musical pitch, pure tones, and so forth) may be appreciated by the position that the speech code (speech mode) is perceived and processed differently and in different parts of the cerebral cortex than nonspeech sounds. Liberman *et al.* (1967) state: "The conclusion that there is a speech mode, and that it is characterized by processes different from those underlying the perception of other sounds, is strengthened by recent indications that speech and nonspeech sounds are processed primarily in different hemispheres of the brain." Thus, an individual may have difficulty in phonemic (speech events) discrimination and processing and yet have no difficulty in the appreciation of musical events or of mechanical or animal noises. The possibility to us that there may really be no such impairment as "functional articulatory defects" is a real one.

Menyuk (1964), from another point of view, argues against the notion of *infantile speech* as constituting a category of delayed or defective articulation. Menyuk studied the grammatical production of children with so-called infantile speech and age peer children (age range three years to five years ten months; mean IQ of the infantile speech group 125.7 compared with 126.4 for the normal speakers as measured by the Ammons, 1958, Full Range Picture Vocabulary Test). The relatively high IQ of the infantile speech group is of special importance in the light of the conclusion that:

The term infantile seemed to be a misnomer since at no age level did the grammatical production of a child with deviant speech match or closely match that of a child with normal speech. The children with deviant speech, in the terms of the model of grammar used for analysis, formulated their sentences with the more general rules whereas children with normal speech used increasingly differentiating structures as they matured.

Hearing Acuity

It is not surprising, of course, to find defects of voice and articulation among children who have significant degrees of hearing loss. The American Speech and Hearing Association's Committee on Legislation lists impaired hearing as the third largest category of causes of defective speech. Estimates of the incidence of impaired hearing in the school population vary from about 3 to as much as 10 percent. Glorig (1959) reported that 3 percent of a male population between the ages of ten through nineteen were found to have a hearing loss of 15 decibels or more. This figure is based on a sample of approximately 400,000. Davis and Silverman (1960, p. 416) are aware that there is considerable variability in estimates of hearing loss. They say "Our best estimate is that 5 percent of school-age children have hearing levels outside the range of normal . . . and that from one to two of every ten in this group require special educational attention." These estimates refer to hearing impairments of such degree that the individual is likely to be aware and think of himself as an acoustically handicapped person. In the speech-defective population as a whole, smaller amounts of hearing loss may have an influence on the quality of speech, even though the speaker may have no awareness of his reduced hearing acuity.

Fiedler (1949) found that among public school children in grades 1 to 3, the incidence of speech defects was higher among children with hearing loss (19.28 percent) than among their normally hearing classmates (6.73 percent). A diagnosis of hearing loss was made on the basis of a 20-decibel loss on two or more frequencies in either ear as measured by individual pure-tone testing on the ADC audiometer. Few of the children found to have hearing loss were identified as such by their teachers.

The specific form of defective speech varies considerably with the type, degree, and age of onset of hearing loss. Children with congenital hearing loss severe in degree are almost always delayed in beginning to speak and continue to be slow in language development. Beyond this, the oral speech they are able to develop is likely to be characterized by articulatory distortion, faulty rhythm, and general vocal inadequacy. Even if the hearing loss is acquired after the normal onset of speech, speech defects are likely to become part of the overall habilitation problem. We may accept the observation of Davis and Silverman (1960, p. 389) as a truism that:

If the ear can no longer serve as a monitor when one talks, slow degeneration of speech results. The sharpness and precision of enunciation disintegrate. The melodies of speech become monotonous. Intonations lose their life. The quality of the voice becomes rigid. Finally, control over the loudness of the voice suffers.

For a more detailed consideration of the relationship between hearing loss and speech, the reader may consult Berry and Eisenson (1956, Chap. 19), Johnson *et al.* (1967, Chap. 8), and West and Ansberry (1968, Chap. 6). A brief overview of problems related to hearing impairment may be found in Newby (1964, Chap. 10).

Auditory Memory and Sequencing

Auditory memory span has been a subject of psychological study for many years, going back to the initial investigations of Ebbinghaus (1913). Most recent studies of auditory memory span have used series of digits or of nonsense syllables as basic measures. The assumption that auditory memory is a factor in intelligence is expressed in the frequent inclusion of memory-span tests employing digits forward, digit series to be recalled in reverse order of presentation (digits backward), and recall of meaningful material as in reproduction of sentences and of units of meaning after the oral presentation of contextual material. There is ample evidence that memory span as measured by recall is positively related to intelligence and to mental development. Many speech pathologists believe that poor auditory memory is related to defective speech, though the results of research are by no means consistent. An excellent brief review of the subject may be found in Van Riper and Irwin (1958, pp. 26–29). The implication that auditory memory for digits (auditory sequential memory) is related to language development is inherent in the inclusion of a digit span test in the Illinois Test of Psycholinguistic Abilities (McCarthy and Kirk, 1968).

JON EISENSON

Despite the inconsistent results of controlled investigations, many language clinicians maintain their clinical impression that speech-defective children with retarded language development and articulatory defects are indeed defective in auditory memory. Perhaps the reason for the difference lies in the nature of the experimental design. Immediate recall when a child is not concerned with meaning calls for a different processing than recall with meaning. Even more crucial, we believe, is the need to distinguish between recall of material to be imitated (immediately reproduced) and a more complex ability to process and sequence a series of sounds into a phonemic-morphemic meaningful unit. Young children who are just beginning to develop verbal habits often transpose sounds and syllables and may say "pests" for "pets," or "ephelant" for "elephant." Such transpositions also feature the paraphasic output of adults who have cerebral damage and become aphasic. Van Riper and Irwin indicate that children with defective articulation are frequently lacking in their ability to combine and analyze speech sound sequences. Because of this lack,

The articulation case can understand the word spoken by another, can recognize it as correct, yet cannot say it correctly himself.... When we find cases with marked deficiencies in phonetic ability of either the analytic or synthesizing type, we can expect difficulty in articulation therapy (1958, p. 29).

Children who are retarded in language development may, we suspect, be lacking in a fundamental ability to analyze any but the shortest auditory sequence, to identify and recall the first item of an aurally received event, or to hold this and succeeding items in mind until a series is recognized as having been completed. Beyond

this, the child must be able to synthesize the series of auditory items into an event appropriate to the demands of a speaking situation.

Eisenson (1966) discusses the underlying auditory perceptual functions for language (speech) processing and the nature of some of the impairments in children with severely delayed language development. Auditory events, unlike visual ones, do not "stay put." Impressions received aurally can be reproduced only by adequate feedback. Such feedback is a function not only of the total number of items that can be recalled but of the sequence or order in which they need to be recalled for acceptable verbal behavior. When recalled, the items must be organized into recognizable verbal events (linguistic units) and be reproduced so that they are intelligible to another listener. For this, the ability for auditory discrimination and production, as we have already noted, must also be adequate. For many young children, and especially those with brain damage, the demands for this complex ability seem to be excessive. As a result they are slow to talk and often defective and retarded after they begin to talk. The need to help brain-injured children to *hear and distinguish* sounds was an integral part of an experimental program conducted by Cruickshank and his associates (1961, pp. 182–183).

The Profoundly Deaf

The problems of the profoundly deaf that are of concern to us relate to language and language as a mediator of thought. An important statement as to the degree of competence the profoundly deaf have for language comes from Furth.

The vast majority of deaf people; i.e., persons profoundly deaf from earliest childhood, do not know the native language of their country with any substantial degree of competence. Even a nonverbal system of manual signs is not readily available to most of the deaf during their formative years. Consequently the deaf child is in the unique position of having to grow up and develop intellectually without the benefit of the conventional system of language which is present to all hearing children. (Furth, 1966, p. *x*).

In his monograph on the deaf Furth (1966) develops a theoretic basis for the following conclusions (pp. 226–227).

1. Because of their linguistic incompetence, the deaf are impaired on all tasks that are specifically verbal as well as on those nonverbal tasks for which linguistic habits (verbal mediation) afford a direct advantage.
2. Indirectly, because of their linguistic limitation (incompetence) the deaf (1) lack information and "do not know facts," (2) manifest minimal intellectual curiosity, (3) "have less opportunity and training to think," and (4) "they are insecure, passive, or rigid in unstructured situations."

Happily, however, Furth concludes that:

Apart from these listed effects, the basic development and structure of the intelligence of the deaf in comparison with the hearing is remarkably unaffected by the absence of verbal language. One can reasonably assume that the major area in which the deaf appear to be different from the hearing is in variables related to personality, motivation and values. If substantial differences are found, they will be likely due to experimental and social factors of home, school, and the deaf community (1966, p. 227).

Some of the implications of Furth's conclusions in relationship to personality and intelligence are considered elsewhere in this text. We consider Furth's conclu-

sions a challenging position statement not yet adequately supported by "hard" data. Nevertheless, we endorse his recommendation that the deficiencies that arise because of the language incompetencies of the deaf may be avoided if nonverbal methods of instruction and communication were encouraged both at home in the earliest years and in formal school education (1966, p. 227). Lenneberg (1967, pp. 320–324) provides related observations that emphasize the desirability of early and increased experience with written materials for the congenitally deaf.

PERSONALITY ASPECTS AND ADJUSTMENT PROBLEMS

Are speech-defective persons, and particularly speech-defective children, likely to be more maladjusted than children who are free of speech defects? Do some speech-defective persons have aspects of personality that our culture tends to consider undesirable? These are questions we raise and anticipate that we will not and probably cannot answer adequately.

In this section we shall first consider studies and points of view on the speech-defective population as a whole and then consider the specialized studies of particular types of speech defectives. Some of the studies and points of view have already been considered in our discussion of the psychogenic basis of defective speech.

Speech Defectives as a Group

Van Riper (1963, Chap. 3) is especially impressed with the speech defective's tendency to employ either aggressive or withdrawal behavior reactions to the penalty behavior of his associates. Hostility and anxiety seem to be the key behavioral traits of speech defectives. These arise as a result of the penalties our culture places on disordered speech.

In summarizing his observations on the emotional problems of the speech-handicapped, Van Riper (1963, p. 68) says:

We have shown that anxiety, guilt, and hostility may arise as a result of this penalty and frustration and that these feelings may, themselves, provoke further reactions which can contribute to the total problem and interfere with its solution. Finally ... the extent of the emotional fraction of the speech handicap may depend upon the severity and frequency of the speech deviations, their type, the person's age, the presence of compensatory assets, and the attitudes of his associates.

Observations such as Van Riper's are made on the basis of clinical experience. The behavioral traits are certainly not unique for speech-defective persons but are found among many persons with minor as well as major adjustment problems. Yet the relationship between speech deficiency and maladjustment is likely to be causal rather than merely coincidental.

Glauber (1944), approaching the problem from a Freudian, psychoanalytic point of view, observed that speech disturbances are common in psychoneurotic patients. In relationship to psychoneurotic personalities, Glauber says:

Speech may be overvalued in all categories. It is most voluminous and indistinct in the oral-clinging, is rapid and distinct in the compulsive, most highly developed in the exhibitionistic and competitive types, and most disturbed in the orally-aggressive and the masochistic which creates the greatest amount of conflict, with resultant tendencies towards repression and other defenses ... The speech disorder or idiosyncrasy is a reflection of a disturbance or idiosyncrasy of the total personality. ...

From a very different orientation, Johnson (1967, pp. 74–75) summarizes the effects of speech disorders on personality to highlight their circular influence.

The psychology of the handicapped is basically the psychology of frustration. The handicap of impaired speech is no exception to this general rule. In fact, there is hardly anything more frustrating, in ways that matter deeply, than something that constantly interferes with our relationship to other people. ...

... The relationship between speech and personality is ... a two-way affair. They affect each other. And the effect is not only circular, but also cumulative. ... speech characteristics, once created, tend to affect the personality in ways that insure their further development.

Up to this point we have presented the opinions of writers in the field of speech correction and psychiatry and their observations, based largely on personal experience, of the relationship between defective speech and personality maladjustments. No attempt has been made to indicate causal relationships. It is fairly apparent, however, that Glauber has in mind that speech defects of the kinds he describes are manifestations of maladjusted personalities. Van Riper, and the authors of the Midcentury White House Conference report (1952), on the other hand, are thinking primarily in terms of the effect on the personality of a speech defect, whatever the origin of the defect may be. Berry and Eisenson (1956, p. 17), after reviewing some of the research literature on the relationship between personality traits and defective speech, conclude:

There seems to be a tendency for speech-defective individuals to present a personality picture which includes traits considered to be socially undesirable. Tendencies towards maladjustments seem to increase as the speech defectives grow older. ... The tendency for speech defectives to have other limitations such as poor motor control, lesser intellectual capacity, and somewhat lower educational achievement, makes it difficult to determine the direct relationship between the personality maladjustment and the defective speech. It may be that together, the speech defect *and* the other limitations constitute a constellation which is conducive to maladjustment. . . .

The circularity of speech defects to personality and adjustment problems is emphasized in the clinical observations cited above. We will now turn our attention to specific studies that derive conclusions from investigations and presumably from objective findings. The implications of the findings may serve to clarify the relationships between speech disorders, personality, and adjustment problems.

Retarded Language Development

Definition: The child with delayed or retarded language is one whose competence (comprehension) and/or performance (production) is significantly below what we expect on the basis of age, sex, and intelligence. Ordinarily, it is performance or production rather than competence that is used as a measure of achievement.* Conventionally, aspects of performance include articulatory proficiency, vocabulary size and sentence production (length and syntactical or grammatical "correctness").†

The discussion that immediately follows

---

*For a discussion of the relationship between competence (comprehension or understanding) and performance, see Lenneberg (1967, pp. 284–292).

†Since the publication of Templin's monograph *Certain Language Skills in Children*, emphasis has changed from the use of length of utterance and type of word used as basic measures of achievement to grammatical (syntactic) development. Templin, however, indicated awareness of the need for a change in one of her concluding observations. "In future studies of language skills, the modification or refinement of the techniques of measurement is probably the most important consideration (1957, p. 149)."

excludes those children who have any recognized organic or intellectual impairment which may directly account for the language delay, both in onset and development. We will reemphasize the point, however, that severe mental deficiency is the most frequent cause of delayed language development.

Parental Influences

In our earlier discussion of the pyschogenic causes of defective speech, reference was made to several studies concerned with the parents of speech-defective children. These studies tended to indicate that parents, and especially the mothers, of young speech-defective children were more maladjusted than control-group parents. Among the undesirable traits and attitudes found to exist to a greater degree among the test-group parents were increased neurotic tendency, lower self- and social-adjustment, greater overall emotional instability, rigidity, perfectionism, overprotectiveness, and restrictiveness. In addition many of the mothers were found to have unrealistically high expectations of what constitutes appropriate language performance for their children. Peckarsky (1952), for example, found that mothers of children with delayed speech were overprotective, rigid, highly critical, and restrictive in their demands upon their children. It is possible, therefore, that when a child who is physically and intellectually normal fails to develop speech, the basis of the retardation may be found in the child's reaction to his parents' maladjustments. The speech delay may often be both a reaction to the psychological environment and a manifestation of the child's own maladjustment.

Rejection. Much of the attitude of the parents considered in the studies previously cited probably constitutes an unconscious rejection of the children. A child who senses such rejection and who cannot identify himself with his parent, and especially with his mother, is likely to be delayed in speech development. Mowrer (1952 and 1960) points out that a child must first identify himself with his parent with respect to speaking behavior before he can begin to wish to speak. He must, of course, be physically and intellectually mature and ready before the identification will motivate true speech. The rejected child either makes no such initial identification or may lose the identification once rejection is sensed.

Parental rejection, which takes the form of continuous disapproval and criticism, of speech as well as of other forms of behavior, may cause the child to stop talking or to reduce his amount of talking. When the rejection takes the form of indifference, the ordinary rewards that strengthen speech behavior and that stimulate renewed efforts at speaking are absent. Speech, then, may continue on an infantile level.

Goldfarb (1961, p. 200), discussing the schizophrenic child, observes:

... the speech model presented by a pathologically perplexed parent may be diminished in phonatory and rhythmic range. Further, in the face of unstructured emotional communication by this kind of parent, the child responds with confusion and unawareness of what is expected of him, so that he never achieves the complicated techniques required for connotative expression.

Ruesch (1957, p. 133), in his discussion of autistic, withdrawn, or outright schizophrenic children and their disturbances in communication or their failure to develop conventional communicative skills, also considers the parents' own behavior to be the fundamental cause. "The parents' unresponsiveness in non-verbal terms prevents the child in the early years of life from learning how to relate through *movement and action*. The absence of early appropriate and gratifying communication through action, gesture, and object leaves traces." Some of the traces are in inadequate speech both for the expression of affect and for developing normal relationships through conventional communicative behavior.

Negativism. When the rejection takes the form of excessive criticism, the child may demonstrate that rejection is a mechanism he too can use. He may begin by rejecting his own parents. If he does so, he may also negate speech, through which he became aware of the parental criticism and disapproval. Such a child may occasionally become overtly unresponsive to humaan sounds and manifest a conscious awareness only of mechanical or animal noises. He may either fail to develop speech or, if he had begun to use speech, regress to preverbal stage of speech development.

The intelligent child who is severely retarded in speech has a deficient tool for making adjustments to his environment. As he grows older, without adequate means for expression and communication, he must frequently deny his own developing needs and so entertains frustration. If he does not engage in self-denial, he invites frustration by having no proficient means to communicate his wishes or to elicit responses for their satisfaction.

We believe that negative familial influences and, more generally a negative environment, are more likely to influence the development of speech than speech onset. The nature and content of what the child may say and the circumstances for talking are likely to be influenced by negative features in the child's speech environment, and so by negativism toward speaking.

Behavioral Traits Accompanying Delayed Speech

It is, of course, not possible to make any direct inquiry or study through adjustment inventories of what is disturbing the child with delayed speech. Conclusions must be drawn from observations of the child's environment, from personality studies of the child's parents, and from direct observation of the child's behavior. Conclusions and implications have been drawn relative to the influence of parental maladjustment on the child. Observations will now be made of the behavior of the child—of what he does in the company of other children. For the most part, these will be limited to direct observations of the child with delayed speech in a play situation in a speech clinic. The author has been in charge of such clinics since 1946 and has had delayed-speech groups under the immediate supervision of a psychologist and one or more speech clinicians since that time. The groups have varied in size from four to nine children.

Most idiopathic delayed-speech children resort to direct means to make their wants known or to impress their feelings upon others. These direct means may include literally forcing another child, or an adult, to enter into a situation and striking out at an undirected object or person. Frequently, the object or person struck at may be one very recently brought into the situation created by the child. The striking out may probably be considered the child's way of responding to something or somebody that does not readily understand why it was wanted and what role it was expected to assume.

Some children with delayed speech iso-late themselves, as far as the physical situation permits, from others in the room. They will spend periods of up to an hour or more "playing" with a single toy object or just sitting off to one side apparently doing nothing. One boy of five spent his first four months in the clinic sitting high up, silent and alone, on the top of a four-foot jungle gym.

Some delayed-speech children appear to enjoy close physical contact with older persons and with inanimate objects. They may be seen to rub their bodies along the walls as they move from place to place. They rub their faces against their toys. Occasionally and very impulsively, they will grab hold of another child, or a clinician, and cling with great force for a moment before releasing the person. Apparently, there is a need for sensuous contact, which the child obtains from accepting unsuspecting individuals or objects.

Emotional lability characterizes the behavior of many delayed-speech children. They act with impulsiveness and excessiveness, at least when compared with most normally speaking children. They yell and cry quickly and more loudly, break toys, knock down block houses, fling objects around, tear papers, throw pencils, chalk, and crayons, and in general keep things flying about them.

All the characteristics just considered do not set the child with delayed speech off from other children. As a group, delayed-speech children differ in degree from normally speaking children. Their mechanisms of adjustment or maladjustment are like those of other children, except that they are less expertly used. Some delayed-speech children are even well behaved and appear to have made an adjustment to not speaking. Some reveal no factors in their case histories that can explain why they do not speak. Most, fortunately, learn to speak after a while and improve in their adjustment patterns as speech is developed.

General considerations of delayed speech and language development may be found in Wood (1964), Renfrew and Murphy (1964), Brown (1967), and Van Riper (1963, Chaps. 5 and 6). Pronovost, Wakstein, and Wakstein (1966) have an excellent research report on the speech behavior and language comprehension of autistic children.

Congenital aphasia and language retardation. Despite opposition to the use of the terms "congenital" and "developmental aphasia", they have become part of the professional literature on severe language retardation in children and so will be used in this discussion.* We take the position that congenital or developmental aphasia (dyslogia) is an identifiable syndrome that must be separately considered among the organic causes of severe language retardation. Perhaps what sets it off most from other kinds of language retardation is that onset as well as development are seriously delayed.

When we make the diagnosis of congenital aphasia, we are obligated first to make certain that the child so designated is not severely mentally retarded, is not suffering from severe hearing impairment, and is not one who is primarily autistic or schizophrenic. On the positive side a diagnosis of congenital aphasia implies a need to establish, directly or on the basis of perceptual dysfunctions, that the child has a central nervous system pathology before language could be normally established or else to demonstrate that the child has atypical CNS functioning on a matura-

*Objections and reservations to the use of these terms may be found in Bender (1958) and Critchley (1967).

tional (congenital) basis. We believe that congenital aphasia is a relatively infrequent cause of language retardation, but it is, nevertheless, a cause that cannot be argued away semantically. Congenital aphasia is not a diagnosis arrived at by default. The term is *not*, from our point of view, synonymous with idiopathic language delay. In the broadest sense the developmentally aphasic child is one with central nervous system impairment (dysfunction) and severe language delay.

Differential diagnostic features of developmental aphasia (dyslogia). Eisenson (1968) amplifies the concept of developmental aphasia and suggests the use of "dyslogia" as a synonymous term. Differential features include the following:

1. Perceptual dysfunction in one or more sensory modalities, but not in all modalities.
2. Auditory dysfunction over and above what would ordinarily be implied on the basis of conventionally determined hearing loss. Such dysfunctions include difficulty in speech sound (phonemic) discrimination and phonemic sequencing.
3. Sequencing difficulties that are especially pronounced for auditory speech events but that may also be present for visual events.
4. Intellectual inefficiency over and above any objectively determined intellectual limitation. The aphasic child needs optimal conditions, an absence of "noise" to determine his intellectual potential.
5. In regard to verbal ability, impairment may be "complete" or virtually so for both the comprehension and production of language. Often children who begin to acquire language continue to use single words or two-

word utterances when their age peers are able to employ conventional grammatical sentences. In general, we may characterize the productive language of the less severely developmentally aphasic child as lacking in conventional syntax and by a marked negative deviation from the language norms of their age peers in regard to size of vocabulary (competence and production), length of utterance, and syntactic formulations.

The underlying perceptual disturbance we believe is primarily for auditory-speech events. This dysfunction we consider to be related initially to defective storage capacity for speech sounds and to a defective capacity for the discrimination and sequencing of sounds in contextual utterance, especially when the child is required to process speech signals at a rate at which such signals are normally produced by most speakers. (See Eisenson [1966 and 1968] for a detailed explanation of perceptual functions and dysfunctions related to developmental aphasia.)

Developmental background: aphasic development and the aphasic child. Children who fail to develop language or are significantly retarded in some aspect of language development because of congenital cerebral pathology or pathology with onset before true speech is normally achieved (by the end of the second year) are frequently found to be *out-of-phase* in their general sensory, motor, and perceptual development. In regard to these functions they are literally dys-phasic or a-phasic in that they do not follow anticipated patterns in the development of their sensory-motor skills and the behavior that is associated with such skills. Their sequential development is more highly individualized than our norms lead us to expect. Developmental manifestations that normally go together—that correlate and are in phase for normal children—show a lack of such correlation or phasing in children with known brain damage.

Clinicians are often confronted with assessing nonverbal children for whom brain damage or atypical cerebral maturation cannot be clearly demonstrated by either clinical history or neurological diagnosis. We consider the diagnosis of congenital aphasia to be in order if the developmental history and psychological evaluation show the predominant features of the child with established brain damage. In a very important sense the psychological findings, especially in regard to perceptual functioning —those that may well be regarded as the "extended neurological"—are the essential determinants.

As a final note on differential diagnosis, we wish to reemphasize that the clinician needs to be certain that severe mental retardation and/or hearing deficiency is not singly, or in combination, basic to the language delay. He needs to be mindful that some clinicians consider such children to be schizophrenic. It might be of some comfort to appreciate that the term "childhood schizophrenia" is really an omnibus designation that in some important respects overlaps our criteria for congenital aphasia. Goldfarb acknowledges this in describing the setting of his research on childhood schizophrenia. Says Goldfarb (1961, p. 7), "The Staff was impressed with the great variation among the children in the single diagnostic category 'childhood schizophrenia.' The children differed markedly with respect to symptoms, defenses, and general level of ego development. They also differed in responsiveness to treatment." We should like to consider the possibility that some children were not responsive to treatment because they were misdiagnosed as schizophrenic rather than congenitally aphasic (dyslogic) children.

CLUTTERING

We shall discuss *cluttering* at this point in our treatment of speech and language disorders because of its apparent resemblance to stuttering and because we accept the position of Weiss that cluttering is a disorder with an "organic flavor," which "might be only one aspect of a generalized disorder of all channels of communication." (1964, p. 5).* Weiss (1964, p. 7) points out that by an "organic flavor" he means that though there are no clear neurologic symptoms, "they run parallel to symptoms caused by an organic disease but have no concomitant signs of organicity."

Symptoms of cluttering include repetition of monosyllabic words or of the first syllable of polysyllabic words, poor formulation of utterance associated with excessive speed of articulation, slurring (telescoping) as rate of utterance increases, and what appears to be a compulsion for rapid utterance, or at least a rate of utterance too rapid for the clutterers' ability as speakers. Weiss also notes (p. 23) that the "clutterer's inability to find the words he needs in sufficient time to maintain a smooth flow of speech causes him to prolong vowels, most often at the ends of words. . . . This is in effect a stalling device during which he searches for the next word." Weiss (p. 24) believes as follows: "Because the clutterer is inept at finding

* The monograph by Deso Weiss on cluttering includes a historical review of the problem and theories as to etiology and treatment.

the necessary words to express his ideas, his speech is studded with clichés and repetition of words and phrases."

Articulation is generally imprecise. Vocal monotony becomes pronounced when speech becomes rapid. Often the total utterances become unintelligible.

Weiss argues (1964, p. 36) that the clutterer has a poorly integrated thought process and generalizes that "the clutterer's haphazard and tentative thinking in preparation for speech reflects his general approach to all undertakings. This is the basic characteristic of cluttering and hence one of the prime targets of therapy."

Background History of Clutterers

The case histories of many clutterers suggest that retarded language development is both an individual and familial trait. Weiss (1964, p. 51) reports a higher than expected incidence of speech disorders, including cluttering on the paternal side, in the family. Although some psychiatrists view cluttering as a neurotic manifestation, the prevailing point of view is that it is probably organic in origin. Luchsinger and Landolt (1951), cited by Weiss, report an incidence of almost 100 percent of positive electroencephalographic findings. DeHirsch (1961) regards cluttering as a manifestation of a lack of maturation of the central nervous system. Arnold (1960) considers cluttering to be an expression of poor auditory perception, which he designates as *perceptual dysgnosia.*

Related Symptoms

Cluttering is viewed by Arnold (1960) and by Weiss (1964, p. 7) as a disorder of *central language imbalance.* According to Weiss, this imbalance includes such features as delayed language onset, delayed language development, dyslalias, reading and writing difficulties, disorders of rhythm and musicality, and, as general characteristics, disorderliness and restlessness.

Clinical Impression and Prognosis

The clinical impression of the cluttering child is that he is "rather loosely put together." He is awkward in his movements and is often ambinondextrous and generally imprecise, if not patently "sloppy" in his productions. Weiss reports (1964, p. 10) that the clutterer is

> ... deficient in his sense of harmony in language functions and must exert extra effort if he wishes to speak, read, and write acceptably. ... Cluttering (Central Language Imbalance), then, we consider to be a basic constitutional characteristic of an individual's general disposition.

A differential diagnostic and therapeutic observation is made by Weiss (1964, p. 69) in distinguishing cluttering from stammering (stuttering). Whereas the stammerer tends to do worse as he attends to his speaking, the clutterer tends to improve. The clutterer speaks more poorly when relaxed; the stammerer tends to speak better. Other differential characteristics are summarized by Weiss (1964, Chap. 4), which, if we accept his notions, clearly differentiate stammering from cluttering and suggest, as well, the differential nature for therapy.

THE RIDDLE OF STUTTERING*

The Problem(s) and a Definition

The literature on stuttering, both professional and lay, is long, vast, and inconclusive as to theories of origin and therapy of choice. Any person with a bias can, by selective reading, find support for a position as to cause, concomitants, or treatment. Perhaps the greatest weaknesses in our study of stuttering, or of stutterers, is the premise or assumption that what we regard as stuttering is indeed a single symptom or symptom complex that therefore should have a single cause. Logically, of course, there should also be one therapeutic approach more efficacious than all others. Experience, however, suggests that this is not so. Stutterers have or have not improved by exposure to varieties of treatment including oral surgery, cauterization, castigation, psychoanalysis, various forms of psychotherapy including behavior modification, conditioning, and desensitization. Some stutterers have improved by direct attention to their symptoms and others by obeying suggestions if not direction to ignore their symptoms. Some insist that they literally "gave up" stuttering by their own determination. The catalog of positions is long, and sometimes "through every passion raging." Each position has claimants and can cite cases for success. Probably because each may be selectively right, we have found no widely accepted theory as to the origin of stuttering; neither have we wide acceptance that perhaps the word ought to take the plural form "stutterings" so that causes for what may be related disorders, and treatments relative to the disorders, may be found.

In their introduction to the Andrews and Harris monograph (1964), Court and Roth state that, based on techniques of covarying clusters of features, the analysis conducted in this study

> ... showed in effect that there were three relatively separate forms of stutter. They dif-

*We shall use the term "stuttering" as essentially synonymous with "stammering".

fered in respect of such features as social class origin, intelligence, personality of the mother, quality of family life, early or late onset of stutter and the presence of other intellectual and emotional disabilities. . . . The utilization of tentative groupings of this kind can also help to ensure that patients submitted to further investigation will be subdivided into relatively homogeneous groups. In this manner, enquiry, whether concerned with the definition of causes or the evaluation of treatment, might be enabled to lead to more clear and fruitful results.

This is a position that we heartily endorse.

Before proceeding further in our discussion, we shall pause for a practical or operational definition, acknowledging that even a definition reveals bias. We shall accept Van Riper's (1963, p. 311) definition to the effect that "*Stuttering occurs when the flow of speech is interrupted abnormally by repetitions or prolongations of a sound or a syllable or posture, or by avoidance and struggle reactions.*" Van Riper, in emphasizing abnormal interruptions, distinguishes stuttering from normal hesitation phenomena and normal disfluencies. We should also note both the similarities and differences between stuttering and cluttering (see page 200) of our discussion on cluttering. Several other definitions may be found in Eisenson (1958).

In this work six authorities present their viewpoints as to the essential cause or causes and therapeutic approaches for stutterers. The present author, who is also the editor of and a contributor to the work, believes that the viewpoints on stuttering in this monograph and in general can be classified into three major but not altogether discrete groups along the following lines:

1. The stutterer has difficulty in speaking—he blocks, hesitates, repeats, grimaces, and so forth—because of an unconscious (repressed) need to do so. The stutterer is essentially a neurotic individual who expresses his neuroticism in part through his deviant speech.

2. Stuttering constitutes a breakdown or failure in functioning of the complex of neuromuscular and intellectual activity required for communicative speaking. This breakdown may occur temporarily for any speaker, but it is likely to be relatively chronic for those who are either emotionally or constitutionally predisposed to such impairment.

3. Stuttering is a learned form of speech behavior characterized by "anticipatory struggle." It thus becomes an avoidance reaction that is associated with a fear of hesitation in speech or otherwise of speaking in a manner the individual has learned to regard as stuttering.

We shall not, in our discussion, seek to support or to refute any of these theoretic positions. Instead we shall evaluate some of the recent literature as it touches upon the psychological implications of being a stutterer. We shall be especially concerned with studies that seek to discover: (1) how the psychological environment of stutterers is different from that of normally speaking children and (2) how the adolescent and young adult stutterers differ psychologically from adolescents and young adults who do not stutter.

Environmental Influences of Young Stutterers

Johnson, an eminent student of stuttering and stutterers, argued emphatically that stutterers are essentially normal children. He held (1967, p. 239) that stuttering arises as a result of an interaction between a listener and a speaker—"that is, of the speaking child, and those others, chiefly the child's authority figures, his parents primarily, who listened and reacted evaluatively to his speech." Presumably, the authority figure or figures misevaluated the child's normal disfluencies as stuttering so that

In due course, evidently by virtue of the disruptive perceptual and evaluative reactions to his own speech behavior, the problem came to involve disturbances of speech, in an overt expressive sense. It seems necessary to conclude, therefore, that the listener does more than the speaker to set in motion the interactions to the creation of the stuttering problem (1959, pp. 261–262).

Johnson therefore directs our attention to an environment that includes authority figures who misevaluate the speech of the child and, by virtue of this misevaluation, create a problem in the child. However, we may ask what is there about this child that influences him to accept misevaluations and so leads him to become a stutterer? The underlying implication is that the parents have excessively and unrealistically high expectations which the child attempts but fails to meet.

Unreasonable expectation of speech performance was also found by Bloodstein, Jaeger, and Tureen (1952). They asked twenty-four parents of young stutterers and twenty-four parents of young nonstutterers to diagnose as "stuttering" or "normal" the recorded spontaneous speech of six stuttering and six nonstuttering children. They found that the parents of the stuttering children significantly exceeded parents of the nonstutterers in the extent to which they diagnosed both the stuttering and the nonstuttering children as stutterers.

Moncur (1952) designed an interview form comprised of 330 items by which he distinguished the attitudes of mothers of stuttering and nonstuttering children in regard to domination. Domination was revealed by the types of disciplinary actions and the standards of performance the mothers had in regard to their children. Moncur concludes that there is a syndrome of environmental factors which seems to precipitate or aggravate stuttering with significant regularity. The syndrome includes a variety of parental actions such as "domination by disciplinary action, domination by oversupervising and overprotecting the child, domination by holding the child to excessively high standards, and domination by adverse parental criticism."

Glasner (1949) made a study of seventy stuttering children under the age of five. Although he believes that young children who stutter are frequently and initially different in personality type from children who do not stutter, he found that on the whole the stuttering children had a background significant for overprotection and pampering, and overanxious, excessively perfectionist parents.

Andrews and Harris (1964, p. 102) in their report on a long-term survey study of stutterers and control children of school age in Newcastle on Tyne (England), found that "Mothers of stutterers gave very similar personal histories to control mothers. They have, however, had significantly poorer school records and significantly poorer work histories. Consistent with this is the finding that more mothers of stutterers appear to be of below average intelligence than do the control mothers." Other findings (pp. 102–103) indicate that (1) psychiatric assessment revealed no significant differences between the stutterers and the control children; (2) psychological testing on the Wechsler Intelligence Scale for Children showed that the stutterers as a group scored lower than the controls, "Thus it appears that there is a higher incidence of stuttering among children of below average intelligence"; and (3) the stutterers were significantly late in onset of talking (four months) and had a higher incidence of developmental disorders compared with the control children. In addition a positive family history of stuttering was common among the stuttering children and virtually absent for the control group.

Adolescent and Young Adult Stutterers

Home influences. Glauber (1951, p. 90) reported on a clinical study of mothers of stutterers. According to his report, the stutterer is an inadequate male who identifies himself almost completely, but defectively, with the mother. The basic fault, and the cause of the stuttering, is to be found in the personality of the mother, in her ambivalent attitudes to the stuttering child in particular as well as to other members of her family, including her own mother. Glauber holds that the nuclear etiological factors in the stuttering syndrome lie in specific elements in the personality structure of the mother. In a later writing Glauber (1958) characterized the mother as suffering from maternal anxieties.

> ... birth, nursing, weaning, and onset of speech were felt by the mother as anxious experiences, with a special quality compounded of both separation and clutching. Also the child's taking control of his own locomotion, elimination, the development of his will in its negative and positive aspects, and of his intellect—all these landmarks of his ego development—were felt by the mother as the child's provocative acts of moving away.

Glauber came to his conclusions in regard to stutterers and their mothers on the basis of "an extensive study of the family constellation of stutterers and material from psychoanalyses of stutterers and of their mothers." Some of the observations differ in at least a few important respects from those previously considered.

Douglass and Quarrington (1952) differentiate between stutterers according to their motivation and degree of success in controlling the outward, secondary manifestation of stuttering. The interiorized stutterers—those who generally succeed in controlling visible and audible aspects of stuttering but who feel and think of themselves as stutterers—are characterized by their sensitivity to their social world. This sensitivity, apparently, originates with their families. On the basis of their case histories and clinical studies, Douglass and Quarrington observe:

> The interiorized stutterer appears to come from a family that is upwardly oriented and employs child-rearing practices and methods of discipline particularly suited to the development of a child who will strive to maintain and enhance the social status of the family. Moral training in such a family is by means of anxiety-producing threats to withhold affection or actual withholding of affection until the child conforms with the expectations of the parent.... Parental expectations in such upwardly-oriented families are characteristically high in respect to most aspects of the child's life.

Another approach to the probable influence of the parents on the personality and speech of the stutterer was undertaken by Moore, Soderberg, and Powell (1952). They employed questions from the Sacks Sentence Completion Test to evoke spontaneous speech from a group of sixteen adolescent male stutterers ranging in age from thirteen to twenty-one. The questions were on the topics of parents, future hopes, misdeeds, fears, associates, and good times. Moore and his associates found that the severity (duration) of stuttering was significantly greater when the stutterers talked about *parents* than on any of the other topics.

Duncan (1949) investigated and compared the home adjustment of sixty-two stutterers and a control group of sixty-two nonstuttering college students. On the basis of answers to questions on the Bell Adjustment Inventory, Duncan found significant differences in regard to five items. As a group the stutterers more often than the nonstutterers felt that they were not understood by their parents, that there was a lack of real affection in their homes, that their maturity was underestimated, that they entertained strong desires to run away from their homes, and that their parents were disappointed in them.

Sheehan (1958) reviewed studies on personality aspects of stutterers which employed projective techniques as the instruments of investigation. Sheehan evaluated the results and concluded: (1) findings based upon projective studies are inconsistent; (2) stutterers as a population do not show a definite personality pattern; and (3) there is very meager evidence "to show that stutterers are different from anyone else." Sheehan did find, in keeping with some of his own studies, that lower levels of aspiration existed among stutterers.

Social adjustments. Except for the subjective opinions in the psychoanalytic literature, in which stutterers tend to be characterized as severely neurotic individuals, there is considerably less unanimity on the overall social adjustment of stutterers. It may very well be that psychoanalysts are correct in their judgments in regard to the limited number of stutterers they treat who may be severely neurotic. Objective studies, for the most part,

do not support the generalized judgments of the psychoanalysts. On the other hand, it should be appreciated that most studies of adolescent and young adult stutterers are made with college students as subjects. These students may be a selected group of comparatively well adjusted stutterers who attend college and accept therapy because they have succeeded in adjusting socially despite their speech impediment. With these reservations in mind, some of the objective studies will now be reviewed.

Fiedler and Wepman (1951) investigated the self-concept of stutterers by comparing a group of ten adult male stutterers and a control group of six nonstutterers in their responses to seventy-six statements descriptive of personality traits taken from Murray. They concluded that the stutterer's self-concept showed no characteristic difference from that of the nonstutterer.

Duncan (1949) found significant differences for stutterers as compared with nonstutterers in only five of thirty-five items related to "home adjustment" on the Bell Adjustment Inventory.

Schultz (1947) compared adult stutterers (twenty college students) with psychoneurotics in a nondirective counseling situation and investigated the responses of the stutterers on the Adult Form A, California Test of Personality. Schultz concluded: "These stutterers had many symptoms common to psychoneurotics. The stutterers . . . had many serious social and self-adjustment problems."

Spriestersbach (1951) compared the evaluation reaction of a group of fifty male stutterers enrolled at the State University of Iowa, 183 normally speaking male students, and twenty male psychotic patients at an Iowa State hospital. The evaluations were of a series of pictures that were to be rated upon the degree to which they fitted such words as "fun," "undesirable," and "worthwhile." Spriestersbach concluded that the stutterers displayed evaluated reactions differing somewhat from the nonstutterers in a way which suggested relatively mild degrees of social maladjustment. The stutterers differed markedly from the psychotic patients in their evaluated reactions.

Murphy and Fitzsimons (1960), based on their own studies and a broad review of the literature, consider that the stutterer's self-concept is dominated by feelings of inadequacy and insecurity, both born of parent-related anxiety. The stutterer's speech as well as his overall adjustment problems are characterized by underlying lower self-concept—lower in comparison with that of ideal-self—than we are likely to find among peer nonstutterers.

Although not particularly concerned with personality aspects of stutterers, clinical theorists such as Brutten and Shoemaker (1967) and Wolpe (1958) take the position that, however learned, stuttering is basically maladaptive behavior that needs to be unlearned. Wolpe tends to emphasize anxiety features in the stutterer, and his therapy is directed, by techniques of reciprocal inhibition, to reduce the anxieties associated with speaking and so to reduce or eliminate stuttering. Essentially the same approaches are recommended by Brutten and Shoemaker.

We have by no means undertaken to do any more than sample the literature on stuttering. The catalogue, as we indicated, is long. Books, monographs, articles— some popular and others presumably scientific—are published in great numbers. Excellent surveys of the literature may be found in a number of publications including Johnson (1967), Van Riper (1963), Andrews and Harris (1964), and Beech and Fransella (1968). A critical reader

may suspect that some of the surveys are somehow more selective than others and tend, somehow, to be supportive of the position of the writer. However, a diligent reader will compare interpretations as well as findings and come, only tentatively, we hope, to his own conclusions—or come to reserve his conclusions for greater weight of evidence for any one position.

Monographs that emphasize therapy are almost too numerous to mention. The Brutten and Shoemaker (1967) book does better than most in reconciling theory to therapy. Gregory (1968) presents several positions in which both the onset and modification of stuttering are explained within a framework of learning theory. The text by Luper and Mudler (1964) emphasizes approaches for the school-age child and the management of the stuttering child in a classroom setting. As a historical note that is still quite contemporary, we recommend Bluemel's study (1957).

CLEFT PALATE

The problems of the cleft-palate child are related to the cosmetic aspects, problems directly involved with speech, and problems related to temporary or chronic hearing loss. Speech difficulties per se are, of course, directly related to the nature and extent of the palatal cleft and/or the lip and dental anomalies. Excessive nasality is a common voice characteristic where palatal cleft or palatal insufficiency is involved. Velar control may also be affected because of neuromuscular impairment (Koepp-Baker, 1957, pp. 577–581).

Varying degrees of hearing loss are relatively common. Pannbacker (1961), in a survey study of 103 subjects ranging in age from three to forty-one years found that subjects with cleft lip only and congenital palatal insufficiency were not found to have "socially significant audiological defects." Cleft-palate cases, with or without cleft lip, were found to have the same frequency of hearing loss. Approximately two-thirds of the cases had hearing loss of 15 decibels or more in either ear.

Smith and McWilliams (1968) reviewed and reported the results of several studies on the general linguistic proficiency of cleft-palate children. They also investigated the linguistic abilities of a group of cleft-palate children (eighty-six males and fifty females) ranging in age from three to eleven years. The Illinois Test of Psycholinguistic Abilities was used to assess language competence and performance. Their data reveal that "cleft-palate subjects manifest a general language depression with particular weakness in vocal expression, gestural output, and visual memory. Moreover, in the samples studied, there was a tendency for language weaknesses to become more marked as age increased."

Van Riper (1963, p. 441) sums up his impression of the adjustment problems of cleft-palate children with the observation that "Many cleft-palate cases have as poor eye contact as do stutterers, a behavior which makes the speech and the condition more noticeable."

For detailed consideration of cleft palate, see Van Riper (1963, Chap. 13), Berry and Eisenson (1958, Chap. 14), and Westlake and Rutherford (1966).

OTHER GROUPS

The personality aspects and, more generally, the psychology of the hard-of-hearing, the deaf, and the cerebral-palsied will not be considered in this chapter. Some aspects of the problems of these groups of speech-defective children with sensory and motor disabilities were taken up in our overview of types of speech defective persons. These groups are considered in detail by recognized authorities elsewhere in this text.

We have paid no special and separate attention to the vocally defective child, except as vocal defects are associated with organic disorders. The reason for this is that, except for clinical case studies, there is a paucity of available literature of objective psychological studies of the vocally defective child. However, the subject is treated in such texts as Johnson (1967, Chap. 4), Van Riper (1963, Chap. 7), and Berry and Eisenson (1958, Chaps. 9 and 10).

SUMMARY

The defective in speech differ in degree but not in kind from the normally speaking population. Taken as a group, the differences are not great. On an individual basis the difference may be great, small, not discernible, or nonexistent. Taken as a group, speech-defectives are somewhat retarded intellectually and educationally. They all have somewhat more difficulty in their adjustment efforts than do the normally speaking. In individual instances it is not clear whether these adjustment problems are caused by the defect in speech or whether the speech defect is but one additional manifestation of the somewhat maladjusted personality.

Objective studies relating to the personality pictures and adjustment problems have, for the most part, been undertaken with adolescents and adults. Some attempts to do as much for children have been reported. On the whole the differences appear to be greater as the children grow older. The adolescent and adult speech-defectives appear to have considerably more problems in adjustment than do the children. This observation, however, may really mean that our measuring devices for adjustment differences are better when applied to older speech-defectives than they are when applied to children. It may also suggest that older children who maintain their defective speech develop experience frustration and develop other reaction patterns which our culture considers to be maladaptive.

References

Albright, R. W. The motor abilities of speakers with good and poor articulation. *Speech Monographs*, 1948, *15*, 164–172.

Andrews, G., & Harris, H. *The syndrome of stuttering.* London: The Spastics Society and William Heinemann, Ltd., 1964.

Arnold, G. E. Studies in tachyphemia: 111 signs and symptoms. *Logos*, 1960, *3,* 25–45. (*a*)

―――. Studies in tachyphemia: *Logos*, 1960, *3*, 82–95. (*b*)

Artley, A. S. Astudy of certain factors presumed to be associated with reading and speech difficulties. *Journal of Speech and Hearing Disorders*, 1948, *13*, 351–360.

ASHA Committee on the Midcentury White House Conference, Speech Disorders and Speech Correction. *Journal of Speech and Hearing Disorders*, 1952, *17*, 129–137.

Beech, H. R., & Fransella, F. *Research and experiment in stuttering.* London: Pergamon Press, 1968.

Bender, L. Psychiatric aspects, the concept of congenital aphasia from the standpoint of dynamic differential diagnosis. S. P. Brown (Ed.), American Speech and Hearing Association Symposium, 1958.

Berry, M. F., & Eisenson, J. *Speech disorders.* New York: Appleton-Century-Crofts, 1956.

Bice, H., & Cruickshank, W.M. Evaluation of intelligence. In W. M. Cruickshank and C. M. Raus (Eds.), *Cerebral palsy.* Syracuse, N.Y.: Syracuse University Press, 1955, Chap. 3.

Bilto, E. W. A comparative study of certain physical abilities of children with speech defects and children with normal speech. *Journal of Speech Disorders*, 1941, *6*, 187–203.

Bloodstein, O., Jaeger, W., & Tureen, J. A study of the diagnosis of stuttering by parents of stutterers and non-stutterers. *Journal of Speech and Hearing Disorders*, 1952, *17*, 308–315.

Bluemel, C. S. *The riddle of stuttering.* Danville, Ill: Interstate Publishing Co., 1957.

Brown, S. In W. Johnson & D. Moeller (Eds.), *Speech handicapped school children.* New York: Harper and Row, Publishers, 1967, Chap. 6.

Brutten, E. J., & Shoemaker, P. J. *The modification of stuttering.* Englewood Cliffs, N. J.: Prentice-Hall, Inc., 1967.

Carrell, J. A. A comparative study of speech-defective children. *Archives of Speech*, 1936, *1*, 179–203.

Clements, S. D. *Minimal brain dysfunction in children.* NINDB Monograph No. 3. U. S. Department of Health, Education, and Welfare, Washington, D. C. : Government Printing Office, 1966.

Critchley, M. Aphasiological nomenclature and definitions. *Cortex*, 1967, *1*, (3), 3–25.

Cruickshank, W. M. *et al. A teaching method for brain injured and hyperactive children.* Syracuse, N. Y.: Syracuse University Press, 1961.

Curtis, J. In W. Johnson & D. Moeller (Eds.), *Speech handicapped school children.* New York: Harper and Row, Publishers, 1967.

Davis, H., & Silverman, S. R. *Hearing and deafness* (rev. ed.). New York: Holt, Rinehart & Winston, Inc., 1960.

DeHirsch, K. Studies in tachyphemia, IV: Diagnosis of developmental language disorders, *Logos*, 1961, 3–9.

Douglass, E., & Quarrington, B. The differentiation of interiorized and exteriorized secondary stuttering. *Journal of Speech and Hearing Disorders*, 1952, *17*, 377–385.

Duncan, M. H. Home adjustments of stutterers and nonstutterers. *Journal of Speech and Hearing Disorders*, 1949, *14*, 255–259.

Eames, T. H. The relationship of reading and

speech difficulties. *Journal of Educational Psychology*, 1950, *41*, 51–55.

Ebbinghaus, H. *Memory: A contribution to experimental psychology.* New York: Columbia University Press, 1913.

Eisenson, J. Aphasia and dyslexia in children. *Bulletin of the Orton Society*, 1963, *13*, 101–109.

———. Developmental aphasia (dyslogia). A postulation of a unitary concept of the disorder. *Cortex*, 1968, *14*, 184–200.

———. Perceptual disturbances in children with central nervous system dysfunctions and implications for language development. *British Journal of Disorders of Communication*, 1966, 21–32.

———. (Ed.), *Stuttering: A symposium.* New York: Harper and Row, Publishers, 1958.

Eustis, R. S. The primary origin of the specific language disabilities. *Journal of Pediatrics*, 1947, *31*, 448–455.

Fairbanks, G., & Bebout, B. A study of minor organic deviations in functional disorders of articulation: 3. The tongue. *Journal of Speech and Hearing Disorders*, 1950, *15*, 348–352.

Fairbanks, G., & Spriestersbach, D. C. A study of minor organic deviations in functional disorders of articulation: 1. Rate of movement of oral structures. *Journal of Speech and Hearing Disorders*, 1950, *15*, 60–69.

Fiedler, M. F. Teacher's problems with hard of hearing children. *Journal of Educational Research*, 1949, *42*, 618–622.

Fiedler, F. E., & Wepman, J. An exploratory investigation of the self-concept of stutterers. *Journal of Speech and Hearing Disorders*, 1951, *16*, 110–114.

Fletcher, S. G., Casteel, R. L., & Bradley, D. P. Tongue-thrust swallow, speech articulation and age. *Journal of Speech and Hearing Disorders*, 1961, *26*, 201–208.

Furth, H. G. *Thinking without language.* New York: The Free Press, 1966.

Gens, G. W. Speech retardation in the normal and subnormal child. *The Training School Bulletin*, 1950, *48*, 32–36.

Glasner, P. J. Personality characteristics and emotional problems in stutterers under the age of five. *Journal of Speech and Hearing Disorders*, 1949, *14*, 135–138.

Glauber, I. P. The mother in the etiology of stuttering. Abstract of an address in *The Psychoanalytic Quarterly*, 1951, *20*, 160–161.

———. The psychoanalysis of stuttering. In J. Eisenson (Ed.), *Stuttering: A symposium.* New York: Harper and Row, Publishers, 1958.

———. Speech characteristics of psychoneurotic patients. *Journal of Speech Disorders*, 1944, *9*, 18–30.

Glorig, A. Hearing conservation past and future. *Proceedings of the Working Conference on Health Aspects of Hearing Conservation, Supplement to the Transactions of the American Academy of Ophthalmology and Otolaryngology*, November–December 1959, 24–33.

Goldfarb, W. *Childhood schizophrenia.* Cambridge: Harvard University Press, 1961.

Gregory, H. H. *Learning theory and stuttering therapy.* Evanston, Ill.: Northwestern University Press, 1968.

Hildreth, G. Speech defects and reading disability. *Elementary School Journal*, 1946, *46*, 326–332.

Jackson, J. A survey of psychological, social and environmental differences between advanced and retarded readers. *Journal of Genetic Psychology*, 1944, *45*, 113–131.

Johnson, W. In W. Johnson and D. Moeller (Eds.), *Speech handicapped school children* (3rd ed.). New York: Harper and Row, Publishers, 1967.

Johnson, W., Darley, F. L., & Spriestersbach, D. C. *Diagnostic methods in speech pathology.* New York: Harper and Row, Publishers, 1963.

Johnson, W. *et al. The onset of stuttering.* Minneapolis: University of Minnesota Press, 1959.

Kennedy, L. Studies in the speech of the feeble-minded. Unpublished doctoral dissertation, University of Wisconsin, 1930.

Kirk, S. A., McCarthy, J. J., & Kirk, W. D. *The Illinois Test of psycholinguistic abilities* (rev. ed). Urbana: University of Illinois Press, 1968.

Koepp-Baker, H. In L. E. Travis (Ed.), *Handbook of speech pathology.* New York: Appleton-Century-Crofts, 1957, Chap. 19.

Lenneberg, E. H. *Biological foundations of language.* New York: John Wiley & Sons, Inc., 1967.

Levine, E. S. An investigation into the person-

JON EISENSON

ality of normal deaf adolescent girls. Unpublished doctoral dissertation, New York University, 1948, University Microfilms No. 1156.

Lewald, J. Speech defects as found in a group of 500 mental defectives. *Proceedings and addresses of the American Association for the Study of the Feeble-minded*, 1932, *37*, 291–301.

Liberman, A. M. *et al.* Perception of the speech mode. *Psychological Review*, 1967, *74* (6), 431–461.

Lillywhite, H., & Bradley, D. *Communication problems in mental retardation*. New York: Harper and Row, Publishers, 1969.

Luchsinger, R., & Landolt, H. EEG investigations in stammering and cluttering. *Folia Phoniatricia*, 1951, *3*, (cited by Weiss, 1964, 48–49).

Luper, H. L., & Mudler, R. L. *Stuttering therapy for children*. Englewood Cliffs, N. J.: Prentice-Hall, Inc., 1964.

Mase, D. J. *Etiology of articulatory speech defects*. Teachers College Contributions to Education, No. 921. New York: Columbia University Press, 1946.

Matthews, J. Speech problems of the mentally retarded, In L. E. Travis (Ed.), *Handbook of speech pathology*. New York: Appleton-Century-Crofts, 1957.

Menyuk, P. Comparison of grammar of children with functionally deviant speech. *Journal of Speech and Hearing Research*, 1964, *7* (2), 109–121.

Milisen, R. In. L. E. Travis (Ed.), *Handbook of speech pathology*. New York: Appleton-Century-Crofts, 1957.

Mills, A. W., & Streit, H. Report of a speech survey, Holyoke, Massachusetts. *Journal of speech disorders*, 1942, *7*, 161–167.

Moncur, J. P. Parental domination in stuttering. *Journal of Speech and Hearing Disorders*, 1952, *17*, 155–164.

Moore, W. E., Soderberg, G., & Powell, D. Relations of stuttering in spontaneous speech to speech content and verbal output. *Journal of Speech and Hearing Disorders*, 1952, *17*, 371–376.

Mowrer, O. H. *Learning theory and the symbolic process*. New York: John Wiley & Sons, Inc., 1960, 79–86.

———. Speech development of the young child: The autism theory of speech development and some clinical applications. *Journal of Speech and Hearing Disorders*, 1952, *17*, 263–268.

Murphy, A. T., & Fitzsimons, R. M. *Stuttering and personality dynamics*. New York: The Ronald Press Company, 1960, Chap. 6.

Newby, H. *Audiology* (2nd ed.). New York: Appleton-Century-Crofts, 1964.

Oleron, P. A study of the intelligence of the deaf. *American Annals of the Deaf*, 1950, 179–195.

Pannbacker, M. Hearing loss and cleft palate. *Cleft Palate Journal*, 1969, *6*, 50–56.

Patton, F. E. A comparison of the kinesthetic sensibility of speech defective and normal speaking children. *Journal of Speech Disorders*, 1942, *7*, 305–310.

Peckarsky, A. Maternal attitudes towards children with psychogenically delayed speech. Unpublished doctoral dissertation, New York University, School of Education, 1952.

Pintner, R., & Lev, J. The intelligence of the hard of hearing school child. *Journal of Genetic Psychology*, 1939, *55*, 31–48.

Powers, M. H. In L. E. Travis (Ed.), *Handbook of speech pathology*. New York: Appleton-Century-Crofts, 1957.

Pronovost, W., Wakstein, M. P., & Wakstein, D. J. The speech behavior and language comprehension of autistic children. A report of Research to the National Institute of Mental Health, Public Health Service, 1966.

Reid, G. The etiology and nature of functional articulatory defects in elementary school children. *Journal of Speech Disorders*, 1947, *12*, 143–150.

Renfrew, C., & Murphy, K. *The child who does not talk*. London: William Heinemann, Ltd., 1964.

Roe, V., & Milisen, R. Effects of maturation upon defective articulation in elementary grades. *Journal of Speech Disorders*, 1942, *8*, 37–50.

Rotter, J. B. In W. Johnson (Ed.), *Stuttering in children and adults*. Minneapolis: University of Minnesota Press, 1955.

Ruesch, J. *Disturbed communication*. New York: W. W. Norton & Company, Inc., 1957.

Sachs, M. H. A survey and evaluation of the existing interrelationships between speech and mental deficiencies. Master's thesis, University of Virginia, 1951.

Schindler, M. D. A study of educational adjustments of stuttering and non-stuttering children. In W. Johnson (Ed.), *Stuttering in children and adults.* Minneapolis: University of Minnesota Press, 1955.

Schultz, D. A. A study of non-directive counseling as applied to adult stutterers. *Journal of Speech and Hearing Disorders,* 1947, *12,* 421–427.

Sheehan, J. Projective studies of stutterers. *Journal of Speech and Hearing Disorders,* 1958, *23,* 18–25.

Smith, J. O. Speech and language of the retarded. *The Training School Bulletin,* 1962, *58* (4), 111–124.

Smith, R. M., & McWilliams, B. J. Psycholinguistic abilities of children with clefts. *Cleft Palate Journal,* 1968, *5,* 238–249.

Spriestersbach, D. C. An objective approach to the investigation of social adjustments of male stutterers. *Journal of Speech and Hearing Disorders,* 1951, *16,* 250–257.

Templin, M. *Certain language skills in children: Institute of child welfare monograph series.* Minneapolis: University of Minnesota Press, 1957.

Van Riper, C. *Speech correction* (4th ed.). Englewood Cliffs, N. J.: Prentice-Hall, Inc., 1963.

Van Riper, C., & Irwin, J. V. *Voice and articulation.* Englewood Cliffs, N. J.: Prentice-Hall, Inc., 1958.

Weaver, C. H., Furbee, C., & Everhart, R. W. Articulatory competency and reading readiness. *Journal of Speech and Hearing Research,* 1960, *3,* 174–180.

Weiss, D. A. *Cluttering.* Englewood Cliffs, N. J.: Prentice-Hall, Inc., 1964.

West, R. W., & Ansberry, M. *The rehabilitation of speech* (4th ed.). New York: Harper and Row, Publishers, 1968.

Westlake, H., & Rutherford, D. R. *Cleft palate.* Englewood Cliffs, N. J.: Prentice-Hall, Inc., 1966.

Wolfe, W. G. A comprehensive evaluation of fifty cases of cerebral palsy. *Journal of Speech and Hearing Disorders,* 1950, *15,* 234–251.

Wolpe, J. *Psychotherapy by reciprocal inhibition.* Stanford, Calif.: Stanford University Press, 1958.

Wood, K. S. Parental maladjustment and functional articulatory defects in children. *Journal of Speech Disorders,* 1946, *11,* 255–275.

Wood, N. *Delayed speech and language development.* Englewood Cliffs, N. J.: Prentice-Hall, Inc., 1964.

FIVE

Psychological Problems of Children with Impaired Vision

BERTHOLD LOWENFELD

Berthold Lowenfeld is Superintendent Emeritus of the California School for the Blind in Berkeley. He is a Fellow of the American Psychological Association, and, among other professional assignments, he was a member of the National Advisory Council on Vocational Rehabilitation.

INTRODUCTION

Impairment of vision causes many practical as well as theoretical problems. The psychological aspects of these problems will be treated here under three headings: Cognitive Functions, Mobility, and Personality and Social Factors. In general it can be said that blindness creates problems *sui generis* only in the area of cognitive functions and mobility. The congenitally and totally blind child experiences the world around him by sensory functions that the seeing child does not employ for this purpose, and he builds up his knowledge of the object world in ways that are essentially different from those of seeing children. As a result, it appears to be as impossible for the seeing to imagine the world of the blind as it is for the blind to really understand the experience of seeing. In achieving mobility the blind also make use of sensory means rarely if ever employed by the seeing. The personality and social effects of blindness, however, are similar to those caused by other conditions that either handicap the individual or set him apart in one way or another from the normal, the majority, the customary, or the better-organized. A blind child may develop feelings of insecurity because of negative parental attitudes due to his blindness just as other children may develop them for the same or for different reasons. Thus social and emotional effects of blindness are nonspecific, although they may be characteristic as reactions to blindness or environmental influences caused by it.

For reasons of presentation the three factors are treated separately. In reality such separation does not exist. Cognitive functions and mobility have their strong emotional and social implications, whereas emotional and social factors may intensely influence cognitive functions and mobility.

Some problems caused by blindness have received much attention and investigation, but others have fared less well. The comparatively small number of blind children with the resulting wide scatter in age, intelligence, socioeconomic background, and geographic location has retarded research. It makes research based on large groups or on matched groups rather difficult and often impractical. Although the past decade has, largely as a result of governmental support, produced more research than ever before, the literature on the psychological effects of blindness in children is still quite limited, and in many areas experiences, observations, and theoretical presentations continue to be the only contributions available. A basic tenet for those concerned with psychological practices has been stated by Raskin (1962, p. 341):

All essential psychological practices can be carried out with persons with visual defects. This includes psychological appraisal from infancy to adulthood, the evaluation of intelligence, aptitude, achievement, adjustment and personality organization, and the procedures of counseling and psychotherapy

Psychological problems of blindness received early attention in the eighteenth century with the question of how a successfully operated congenitally blind person would react to his first optical impressions. The philosophers Locke, Berkeley, and, later, Diderot theorized considerably about sensory problems of the blind. During the early period of scientific psy-chology, William James, as well as Wilhelm Wundt and others, discussed in their standard works problems of the blind, particularly their spatial perception. The first systematic study dealing with psychological problems of blindness as such also dates back to the experimental laboratory of Wundt, where Theodor Heller conducted investigations that he reported in his *Studien zur Blinden-Psychologie* (1895). Psychological research in the field of the blind has dealt mainly with problems of sensory experiences of the blind as compared with those of the seeing, with the ability to perceive obstacles, and with the measurement of intelligence, a field in which Samuel P. Hayes made the outstanding contribution. In 1933 Thomas D. Cutsforth's *The Blind in School and Society* was published as the first major work dealing with personality problems of the blind. Since then the emotional and social implications of blindness have received increasing attention.

A unique contribution was made by Helga Lende when in 1940 the American Foundation for the Blind published her *Books about the Blind: A Bibliographical Guide to Literature Relating to the Blind,* of which a new revised edition appeared in 1953. More recently, in 1960, Graham published a survey, *Social Research on Blindness,* which reports the literature as well as the then on-going research. The American Association of Workers for the Blind, under a grant from the Social and Rehabilitation Service, Department of Health, Education, and Welfare, published a card catalog of references in the field of blindness, edited by Isabella S. Diamond, which is being kept up-to-date by supplements. The American Foundation for the Blind made available a dictionary catalogue of its comprehensive collection of literature dealing with blindness.

DEFINITION, DEGREES, AND CAUSES OF VISUAL IMPAIRMENT

There are mainly three ways in which pathological conditions in the eye may result in impaired vision. The visual acuity may be reduced, the field of vision may be limited or defective, and color vision may be imperfect.

Visual acuity is measured by the use of the Snellen Chart and expressed in the form of a fraction. A visual acuity of 20/200 means that the eye can see at the distance of 20 feet what a normal eye can see at 200 feet, or in other words, an object that a normal eye can see 200 feet away must be brought to within 20 feet in order to be discerned by the eye with a visual acuity of 20/200. In this pseudo-fraction the "numerator" and the "denominator" may be changed. In visual acuities better than 20/200, the denominator is usually changed, as for instance in 20/70; in visual acuities below 20/200, the numerator is usually changed, as for instance in 5/200. This is proper enough since such low acuities are actually measured at distances less than 20 feet.

The *field of vision* may be affected in two ways: an eye may have central vision with the peripheral field restricted to a certain angle, or the eye may have a scotoma, a spot without vision, which, if in the center of the field of vision, may cause loss of central vision. Restrictions in the field of vision are mapped out with the perimeter, an instrument that indicates the field limitations in the various directions on a chart.

Color vision is determined by the discrimination of the three qualities of color: hue, saturation, and brightness. In the rare case of total color blindness, all colors are seen as shades of black, gray, and white.

Most color blindness is partial, the person having difficulty in distinguishing between certain colors, usually reds and greens. Color blindness by itself, though a visual impairment, is generally not regarded as coming within the scope of visual handicaps. However, some eye conditions that reduce vision result also either in total or partial color blindness.

According to the most widely accepted definition of blindness, a person is considered as blind if he has "central visual acuity of 20/200 or less in the better eye, with correcting glasses, or central visual acuity of more than 20/200 if there is a field defect in which the peripheral field has contracted to such an extent that the widest diameter of visual field subtends an angular distance no greater than 20 degrees (Hurlin, 1962, p. 8)". Under this definition, individuals who are totally blind, who have light perception (ability to distinguish darkness and light), or light projection (ability to indicate the source of light), who can distinguish hand movements in front of their eyes, who have form or object perception, who have "traveling vision," and whose vision can be measured with the Snellen Chart up to and including 20/200, are all considered as "blind." This definition does not take into consideration the important factor of near or reading vision, or any defects within the peripheral field that do not result in a contraction of the field itself but block out certain areas.

During an era in which ophthamologists were cautious about the use of the eyes, particularly for reading, the definition of blindness given above was a fairly adequate tool in determining educational placement of children. Although a few decades ago the use of the eyes was considered as harmful for many types of visual handicaps, ophthalmologists recommend now that visually handicapped children use their sight without any special restrictions. The eyes are visual receptors, and just as a camera does not suffer from use, neither do the eyes. This change of approach made the previously defined demarcations of visual acuity far less meaningful. Many children with visual acuities considerably below 20/200 are able to read print, large type or even regular size, if they can bring it close to their eyes or use magnifying glasses, as they are now encouraged to do. A "functional" definition of blindness is sought which will realistically determine for educational purposes which children should be considered as blind or as partially seeing.

Jones (1961) reported statistics on the degree of vision of 14,125 legally blind students enrolled in residential schools and local public schools, as registered with the American Printing House for the Blind in January 1960.

Nolan (1965) reported a replication of this study as of January 1963 and a reappraisal (Nolan, 1967) as of January 1966. In 1966 the total registration of legally blind students with the American Printing House for the Blind was 19,007. This registration does not include any children attending residential or local schools whose vision is better than 20/200, though there are many enrolled in some of these schools. School attendance as well as visual acuity data are given for 18,652 children. Of this total, 10,835 were enrolled in local day school programs, 6,886 in residential schools for the blind, 663 in educational programs coordinated by State Commissions for the Blind, and 268 in residential programs for multihandicapped blind children, mainly mentally retarded and deaf-blind. Their degree of vision was distributed as follows: 22 percent were totally blind, 14 percent had

light perception or projection only, 30 percent had vision ranging from perception of hand movements to 17/200, and 36 percent had 18/200 to 20/200 visual acuity. Of the children enrolled in residential schools, 50 percent were totally blind or had light perception or projection only, whereas the corresponding figure in local day schools was only 25 percent. It is interesting to note that the group of multihandicapped blind children had 83 percent in this severely visually handicapped category. On the other end of the visual acuity range, 17 percent of the children in residential schools had 18/200 to 20/200 visual acuity, whereas in local day schools, 48 percent had that much vision. Of the multihandicapped blind children, only 8 percent fell into this better vision bracket. A full description of educational facilities for blind children is given by Scholl (1967).

The cause of blindness often has psychological implications for the individual. Whether blindness is inherited or acquired through accident or disease may, for instance, be an important factor in explaining an individual's reaction toward his parents. The most recent national data on causes of blindness among school-age children are those published by Hatfield (1963) pertaining to the school year 1958–1959. They included 7,757 of the nearly 13,500 legally blind school children enrolled in that school year. The following percentage distribution of causes of blindness was reported (p. 6). Table 5–1 shows that by far the largest known cause of blindness in children of school age was retrolental fibroplasia (33.0 percent). Retrolental fibroplasia (referred to as RLF) is an eye disease that since 1942, but mainly between 1949 and 1954, caused blindness almost exclusively in prematurely born babies. After intensive and painstaking

BERTHOLD LOWENFELD

TABLE 5-1

Infectious diseases	4.0
Toxoplasmosis	0.8
Rubella	0.6
Syphilis	0.4
Tuberculosis	0.3
Gonorrhea	0.2
Measles	0.1
Other	1.6
Injuries	2.4
Poisonings (excessive oxygen–RLF)	33.0
Tumors	3.5
General diseases	1.6
Prenatal influence	47.8
Unknown to science	1.4
Not reported	6.3

medical research, it was found in 1954 that the major cause of this condition was the administration of high concentrations of oxygen over prolonged periods of time to prematurely born infants. Since 1954 the application of oxygen in incubators has been carefully controlled, and RLF is practically eliminated. In the peak years of this disease, some states reported that almost 80 percent of their blind preschool children were blind as a result of it. It has been estimated that RLF caused blindness in more than 10,000 babies who have now reached adolescence and adulthood.

The large percentage of blindness shown in the table as prenatal influence and unknown to science (49.2 percent) proves that our medical knowledge of causes of blindness is still far from satisfactory.

AGE AT ONSET OF BLINDNESS

Visually handicapped individuals may have been born with a visual impairment or may have lost their sight completely or partially at any time during their lives. The extreme case of blindness is one in which the person is totally blind from birth. According to observations made by Zoltan Toth (1930) and others, individuals who have lost their sight before about five years of age do not retain any useful visual imagery. In a more recent study Schlaegel (1953) confirmed this, stating that visual imagery tends to disappear if vision was lost before the age between five and seven years. He also found that subjects with the poorest vision had the least number of visual responses. Various studies on dreams of the blind, reported by Blank (1958, p. 160), confirm that the critical period for retaining visual imagery in dreams is if sight was lost at the age between five and seven years. This "is also the period of cerebral structural maturation, the completion of early childhood ego development, and the beginning of latency." Therefore, children who lost their sight completely during the early years of their lives must also be regarded as extreme cases. If children have some sight, they observe visually and also visualize in their memory. Those who lose their sight completely or partially after five years of age may retain a more or less active visual frame of reference. They may, for instance, observe an object by touch and form a visual idea of it based on their past visual experiences. Of course their visual observation is limited according to the degree of sight retained.

On the basis of this discussion, we must distinguish the following gradations of visual impairment so far as influence on sensory and memory activities is concerned:

1. Total blindness, congenital or acquired before the age of five years
2. Total blindness, acquired after five years of age
3. Partial blindness, congenital
4. Partial blindness, acquired

5. Partial sight, congenital
6. Partial sight, acquired

Of these six categories, the first four come within the definition of blindness, and children who belong to these four groups are considered as blind for educational purposes. Those who belong to the fifth and sixth groups are partially seeing children, who will be discussed elsewhere.

Hatfield's report (1963, p. 3) shows that 47.1 percent of the students in her study were born blind, that 36.8 percent became blind in the first year of life, and 4.8 percent before five years of age. This gives a total of 88.7 percent who were born blind or became blind before five years of age.

It is estimated (NSPB Fact Book, 1966, p. 33) that in 1962 about 39,000 blind individuals (by legal definition) below twenty years of age lived in the United States. This is less than 10 percent of the estimated total of about 400,000 blind individuals. The rate of blind individuals under twenty years of age per 100,000 of the general population is 54.1, or about one blind individual to 2,000 seeing individuals in this age group.

The effects of the more recent epidemics of maternal rubella have not been statistically determined but may be as severe as those of RLF.

It has been pointed out that a visual-acuity test is in most cases used as the indication of a person's degree of sight. Such a test, however, does not always give a true indication of the individual person's "visual efficiency." Many experienced observers have noted that some children with very low vision make much better use of it than others who have a higher visual acuity. Such factors as general intelligence and environmental influences are assumed to be influential. Lowenfeld (1957, p. 462) considers inclination to-ward the visual type or the haptic type as the most important factor determining whether the remaining sight is an asset or an irritation for the individual. Barker *et al.* (1953) also call attention to this fact and state (p. 271): "It is the adequacy of each individual's vision for the particular tasks of his life that is crucial for a somatopsychological definition of blindness rather than the optically measured visual acuity."

In the following discussions it must be kept in mind that the effects of blindness are fully operative only in those children who have no sight and no workable visual imagery. For all others, adaptations and modifications in kind as well as in degree will have to be made according to the extent of their visual handicap.

COGNITIVE FUNCTIONS

Experiencing the Object World

Children who are blind or have lost their sight early in life must rely upon their remaining senses for gaining knowledge of the world around them. In attempting to determine the importance of the remaining senses for the blind child's development, it is necessary to understand the basic functions of hearing and touch as cognitive means. Hearing gives certain clues in regard to distance and direction of the object, provided the object makes any sound. It does not convey any concrete ideas of objects as such. A blind person may, for instance, walk under a tree and hear the wind blow through the leaves. His past associations and experiences may enable him to interpret what he hears so that he can say whether the tree has leaves, needles, or is barren, whether the leaves are dry or fresh, how far away from the ground they are, and how thick the foliage is. His olfactory impressions may permit him to say whether the tree is in bloom or even what kind of tree it is. But all these clues will not give the blind person any idea of the shape and size of the leaves, the formation of the branches and of the trunk of the tree, and of its general appearance. Knowledge of the spatial qualities of objects can only be gained by touch observations in which kinesthetic sensations take part. The importance of hearing is in the area of verbal communication, in locomotion, and in general as an indicator of audible clues.

Lacking sight, actual knowledge of the object world can be gained only by touch experiences. Lowenfeld (1950 b, p. 91) points out that tactual space perception of the blind is different from the visual space perception of the seeing. The main reason for the difference is to be found in the fact that tactual perception requires direct contact with the object to be observed. As a consequence, blind people can observe only those things that are accessible to them. The sun, the moon, the clouds, the horizon, and the sky are inaccessible and can be explained to blind people only by the use of analogies from other sensory fields. This method must also be used in explaining to blind people such visual phenomena as shadows, perspective, and reflection of light. Many objects are too large to be observed by touch, for instance, a mountain or a large building. Other objects are too small and cannot be observed by touch with any degree of accuracy, for instance, flies or ants. Of course, microscopic observations can only be made visually and are entirely impossible for the sense of touch. Fragile or delicate objects like butterflies, certain flowers or parts of flowers, snowflakes, or a spider's web also cannot be observed tactually. Objects in motion, live objects, and

objects in certain conditions such as burning, boiling, or cooking cannot be observed by touch because they either change their shapes or positions or because direct contact with them would be dangerous. Liquids do not have shapes of their own and are often difficult to observe by touch when kept in containers. This is also the case with mercury in narrow glass tubes as used in thermometers and various gages.

Many of these restrictions in observation hold true not only for the blind person who has never seen but also for the person who becomes blind later in life. Although he may have a very clear idea of the visual appearance of these objects, he cannot actually observe the object itself. He may, for instance, know what a thermometer looks like but cannot read the temperature it indicates. If it is understood that visual observation permits perception of a situation as a whole and of the objects within the situation according to size, shape, distance, position, and color, it must also be recognized that tactual observations have their own characteristics and advantages. Touch perceptions relate, with the restrictions already discussed, the size, shape, and position of objects. In addition, they also give such experiences as surface quality (roughness, smoothness, evenness), temperature, and weight. These qualities cannot be gained by visual observations, although seeing people may secure them if they bring their touch organs into play. The average person is inclined to neglect tactual observations almost completely because of the dominance of sight over all other senses. For instance, most seeing people are completely satisfied by looking at a sculpture without giving themselves the stimulating experience of observing it by touch. Another most important advantage of touch, as compared with vision, is that it does not depend upon light. Also, it is often easier to explore with the fingers rather than to get into a position where sight could be applied. Often tactual observation is the only observation that can be made, as in some medical examinations.

There is a further important difference between sight and touch so far as activity of these senses is concerned. When a person is awake, his eyes are almost continuously open to stimulation coming from the outside world. This is different for touch activities. The hands as touch organs must be actively applied for the purpose of observation. Also, when they are applied, the horizon of touch extends only to the limited area of the outstretched hands. Observations beyond that limit can only be made if the person moves toward or follows the object to be observed. It is true that the exposed areas of the skin are open to stimulation by air currents and temperature, but this in no way compares with the perceptual activity of sight.

Hearing enables a blind person to gain information through verbal communication and to keep in contact with his social and physical environment. However, in respect to the latter, his efficiency is curtailed. People may stop talking or may not talk at all so that he is unaware of their presence; persons may move away or enter a room without being heard; it may not always be obvious to the blind person to whom the comment of somebody else is directed; many things do not give any sound, whereas others that do sound may not always do it, or they may sound only under certain conditions, such as leaves when the wind is blowing; continuous sound such as that of rain may drown out all other audible clues; and snow deadens sounds that may indicate changes in the environment. All these factors contribute

to more chances for being less adequate in meeting the demands of the situation. Therefore, it can be assumed that they increase a blind person's nervous tension and insecurity.

With the exception of taste, which permits touch observations because the tongue and the mouth envelop or at least touch the object, the other senses relate only sensory clues indicating the presence, location, or nature of certain objects. In passing by a garden one can, for instance, smell if there are certain trees or plants around, provided the wind does not blow in the opposite direction. As one walks on the street, such places as a drugstore, a shoestore, or a food market can be ascertained by their specific odors. Also, the exposed skin surface reacts to changes in air current and in temperature, which may give a blind person clues concerning the spatial characteristics of his surroundings. Walking along the walls of buildings feels entirely different from walking along a garden fence, along shrubs, or in open space.

Space and Form Perception

The process by which space perception by touch is attained has been the subject of considerable research. Heller (1895) and Steinberg (1920) agree that the touch sense is the only original spatial sense of those who were born blind. Heller distinguishes two types of tactual perception by the hands: enveloping touch in which small objects are enfolded by letting either one or both hands observe the object. This type of tactual perception he called "synthetic touch" because the form of the object is perceived as a whole, more or less simultaneously. In observing an apple, for instance, children will gain an idea of the shape of the fruit by enfolding it in their hands. This enveloping touch is applied not only to smaller objects but also to larger ones when only parts of them are subjected to closer observation. The other type of tactual perception is applied to large objects which extend beyond the limited scope of one or both hands, as in the observation of a chair. Here the moving hands follow the shape of the object and, if it is a very large one, the whole body may actively participate in the process. This method has been called "analytic touch" because it consists of successive impressions gained by observing parts of the object. These successive impressions, however, cannot remain isolated, but must result in a unified "touch idea" of the object. Without such unification, blind people would not have any workable concept of larger objects nor of their environment.

German psychologists considered this phenomenon of unification the central problem of blindness, and various explanations have been given for it. Steinberg (1920, p. 139) assumes, as a result of experimentation in which Gestalt psychological principles were applied, that there is a mental process of "expansion of tactual space." Heller (1895, p. 68) believes that there is a contraction of tactual space in which large objects are reduced by a special mental act until a simultaneous idea of the total object is achieved. Another theory postulates the perseveration of the earlier perceptions until they combine with the later ones into a spatial and temporary continuum, a spatial Gestalt. Senden (1960, pp. 289–90), published in German, 1932 and translated into English, 1960, reviews the reports and studies of others concerned with the problem of the perception of space and shape in congenitally blind persons who recovered their sight after eye surgery. He comes to the conclusion that tactual perceptions do not result in awareness of space. The congenitally blind person creates temporal schemata and verbal concepts that are "a surrogate for the spatial awareness he lacks." Others disagree with this point of view, and so do even those who discuss in an appendix to the book the significance of Senden's work for related disciplines.

Whatever the explanation may be, the fact that blind individuals are able to reproduce all kinds of objects, small and large ones, in modeling and handwork, and that they can recognize objects on the basis of previous observations, is evidence that they must be able to unify separate perceptions into one total concept of the object. This central problem of space perception, however, needs further investigation.

All tactual observations of the fingers, hands, arms, or other parts of the body have a kinesthetic component because muscle sensations are involved in these movements. For example, in observing a chair with both hands, the touch movements of the two hands and arms may proceed in different directions and with changing distances between them. Therefore, the actual spatial experience is made up not only by the touch contacts with the object but also by the variety of muscular sensations accompanying the touch movements.

Tactual perception results not only in spatial experiences but in a number of other touch sensations. The surface of the skin has specialized nerve endings, which are the receptors for pressure, pain, warmth, and cold. Sensitive spots for these sensations are dispersed over various areas of the body in varying density. Experiments reported by Hayes (1941, pp. 16–48) have shown that blind individuals have no better discrimination in regard to cutaneous sensitivities than the seeing.

Color Ideas

Space and form can be perceived through sight as well as touch. Color perception, however, is a function of the retina, and no other organ can take it over. When the retina is destroyed, when it cannot be affected by light stimulation, when the stimuli received by the retina are not carried back to the interbrain and the cortex, or when the visual areas of the brain are destroyed, total blindness occurs and color vision is absent.

Therefore, persons who have been born blind or lost their sight so early that they do not have any visual memory do not have any real ideas of color. Because they live in a world that makes constant use of color observations and color references, they build up substitutive ideas for color on the basis of verbal, sensory, and emotional associations. They hear people talk, for example, about the blue sky and, as a result, all or some of the different sensations and emotions caused by fine weather may build up as a substitutive idea for the color blue, in this case a pleasant one. On the other hand, the commonly unpleasant connotation that this color carries in the proverbial "blue Monday" may give the word *blue* a different emotional character. Because such color associations vary from individual to individual, and also from time to time, the substitutive color ideas are not constant. Blind children learn the common color associations such as blue sky, red blood, white snow, and green grass because they are a part of their socially needed vocabulary. However, because they cannot experience color, their attention should be directed toward aspects of situations and objects that can be experienced by them in order to avoid purely verbal preoccupation. Excessive and unrealistic use of color words by blind individuals is not rare and can, in many cases, be regarded as a compensatory mechanism.

Colored audition, which is a form of synesthesia, plays an important role in the ideational life of many persons who have lost their sight either during childhood or later on. In this phenomenon color sensations are closely attached to auditory sensations and may appear regularly in response to certain auditory stimulations. These secondary sensations of color are called photisms. Photisms may be attached to a variety of experiences and ideas. Wheeler and Cutsforth have published research on this problem and examined the function of synesthesia in learning (1921), in the development of meaning (1922) and of concepts (1925), and in other thought processes. Voss (1930), in his extensive study of color-hearing of the blind, enumerates photisms attached to timbre of tones and sounds, especially of various musical instruments; varying pitch of tones of an instrument; single tones within a scale; major and minor scales; voices of persons; vowels and consonants; various emotions; numbers; days; months; geographical names, particularly those of cities and countries; names of the notes of the scale, and so on. These photisms, once present in an individual, are quite inflexible, although they vary from person to person. Of course only persons who have seen colors can experience colored audition, because imagination cannot create anything that was not experienced previously by the senses.

Sensory Acuteness

The assumption that the loss of one sense is compensated for by a more or less automatic improvement in the acuity of the other senses is one of long standing

BERTHOLD LOWENFELD

and perseverance. Three explanations might be considered for this fact. The wish to have nature act according to justice and thereby relieve one of feelings of guilt or the responsibility to help, ascribes to other minorities similar facilities. The fact that blind individuals may learn to use their senses better than those who can rely upon sight gives some actual support to this assumption. Finally, there is a widespread tendency to consider anything the blind can do as admirable and superior, which only disguises a tendency to consider them inferior.

It is not surprising that experiments to determine the differences in sensory acuteness of the blind and the seeing were performed to a considerable extent around the turn of the century, when experimental psychology began to be practiced in many laboratories, particularly under Wilhelm Wundt in Germany and William James in the United States. Hayes (1941, pp. 16–48) reviewed in detail the various studies that tested the comparative abilities of the blind and the seeing to distinguish the direction of sound, to determine the distance of sounds, and to discriminate the intensity of sounds; also studies of acuteness of smell, taste, and touch, discrimination of lifted weights, of passive and active pressure, and of tactual space, sensitiveness to changes in temperature, and acuteness of the vibratory sense, particularly in the deaf-blind. Fisher (1964) investigated the capability of spatial localization in blind and sighted subjects. His experiments gave no support to the two hypotheses: (1) that the acuity of hearing is improved in the blind and (2) that they develop an extra sense of some kind. All these studies gave evidence that the blind are not superior to the seeing in their sensory acuteness; some of the studies even indicated that they are somewhat inferior.

There is no experimental research available on pain sensitivity, on the sense of balance, and on the organic sense. Hayes (1941, pp. 63–80) investigated the memory of blind children—rote memory, recall, and logical memory—and found no superiority in this field either. He concludes: "In memory, as in sensation, compensation is not a gift but the reward of persistent effort" (p. 79). Therefore, any higher efficiency of the blind in interpreting the sensory data perceived must be the result of attention, practice, adaptation, and increased use of the remaining faculties.

Almost twenty years later Axelrod (1959) examined the effects of blindness on two levels of sensory functioning: a basic tactile level where light-touch sensitivity and two-point acuity of three finger tips were tested, and a "higher level" where sense data received through the haptic and auditory modalities were utilized. He did not find any generalized rise of sensory acuity in the early-blind group; on the contrary, they did significantly less well than sighted subjects on the "higher level" complex-task performance. These results stress the importance of early visual learning for later problem solving. Axelrod adds that "brain damage associated with, or consequent to, blindness of early onset cannot be ruled out as a factor" but continues: "The difference between early-blind and sighted groups on the complex tasks were, though statistically significant, nonetheless small; they should not be regarded as evidence of gross impairment of intellective processes" (p. 73). A great deal of hypothesizing was required to bring some coherence to the interpretation of the data of this study. This indicates that the last word on the problem of "sensory compensation" may not yet have been spoken.

There may be processes in operation that so far have eluded experimentation.

There are only a few studies on the widely assumed superior abilities of the blind in music. In an early study, Seashore and Ling (1918) compared fifteen blind and fifteen sighted subjects in certain aspects of their musical ability. Their results indicated that the blind and the sighted demonstrated equal sensitivity to the direction, intensity, and pitch of sound. Merry (1931) used the Seashore Musical Talent Tests with a selected group of forty-four blind children. The majority of them ranked superior in the six tests, but because they represented a selected group, their superiority does not permit any general conclusions. Even in this group, Merry points out, there was a significant percentage of inferior performances. Pitman (1965) reviewed a few other publications in which blind persons' musical capacities were examined. He concluded (p. 64): "The studies mentioned, although by no means conclusive, would seem to suggest that in music the blind are of generally average ability by reference to norms available for the sighted." In his own investigation, the musical ability of 90 blind children was assessed by the Wing Test of Musical Intelligence and compared with a control sample of 130 sighted children. The blind children tested higher than the sighted ones, but their superiority showed up in those subtests where perception was of particular importance. This superiority he ascribed to the blind children's concentration on aural communication and concluded (p. 77) "that fundamentally the blind are no better at music than the sighted."

The belief that blind people have a superior ability to interpret human voices also belongs in this category. It is unquestionably true—and we know it from various autobiographical and other reports—that some blind persons can remember and recognize many voices even after a long lapse of time. They also develop through continuous practice the ability to discern in voices moods, emotions, attitudes, and such traits as sincerity, tact, friendliness, and their opposites. On the other hand, it often happens that blind individuals rely too much upon the voice as an indicator of a person's character and either accept or reject the person on that ground alone. In this respect they are not different from seeing persons who form impressions on the basis of pleasant or unpleasant appearances. Cantril and Allport (1935) conducted some experiments in which blind and seeing subjects were asked to judge from voices the vocation, age, interests, and such features of personality as introversion and extroversion. They found, contrary to the popular belief, that the blind are less accurate in their judgments than the seeing. They explained this by the fact that the blind have fewer opportunities to observe and to study personality and also have no visual assistance in correcting their errors in judgment. These experiments have been made with a small number of persons and can only be considered as preliminary. The problem of interpretation of voices and its influence on the blind is one that should receive further attention. Regardless of the objective validity of the judgment which blind people form in listening to voices, it is a fact that they are strongly influenced by them and find in the variety of timbres and modulations a source of enriching social experiences.

Intelligence

Samuel P. Hayes has, since 1918, reported on his studies in connection with

BERTHOLD LOWENFELD

the standardization of intelligence tests for blind children. In his *Contributions to a Psychology of Blindness* (1941), Hayes followed the distribution of IQs of pupils entering two residential schools for the blind from 1915 to 1940 and found in practically all years a mean intelligence of slightly above 93 (pp. 90–98). There were considerable variations in the percentages falling into the various intelligence groups with no trend apparent in the changes over the years. The percentage in the inferior group was consistently higher than that in the superior group.

The question whether congenitally and adventitiously blind children show any difference in their intelligence was also examined by Hayes (1941, pp. 133–45). He found no correlation of general intelligence with the age at which sight is lost, and achievement in different school subjects also did not show any differentiation. He concluded (p. 144): "The *mental constitution* of those born blind may well be essentially different from that of the other group, but the *functioning* of their minds as measured by our tests shows no such difference."

To compile a distribution of IQs of pupils in schools for the blind and draw from this general conclusions upon the intelligence of blind children as compared with seeing children is a somewhat uncertain procedure. Schools for the blind must admit and retain for shorter or longer periods of diagnostic observation children who are of questionable educability. In the case of the seeing school population, such children would not be included in regular classes. Thus the borderline and dull brackets of the intelligence distribution may be overweighted according to the tolerance of a school for low-intelligence children. Hayes (1942) ascribes the retardation frequently found in pupils entering

school to "the inferior environment in which many blind children grow up, and the restrictions placed upon them in their homes" (p. 225) and notes that under the favorable conditions of a good residential school, many of these children "blossom out" although this may not occur for several years. Komisar and MacDonnel (1955) confirmed this in a study of retests of eighty-nine children in a residential school. They found significant gains in IQ (mean gains of 6.3 IQ points), which increased with the years spent at the school. Children with lower IQs gained more than those of average or above average levels.

Another factor to be considered in this connection is Hayes' own recognition that the Hayes-Binet Scale is not entirely satisfactory if used with younger and older children.

Although we have fairly convincing evidence of the general validity and reliability of the Hayes-Binet Scale, the author has long realized that both ends of the scale were far from satisfactory—the tests for very young children have never been properly standardized because so few cases come to the attention of schools and their testers, and the tests above the fourteen year level are too few and too restricted in range to give an adequate measurement of bright adolescents (1942, pp. 225–26).

Since Hayes made this statement, the verbal parts of the Wechsler scales that avoid some of these shortcomings have become widely used in testing the visually handicapped. Hayes (1950) recommended their use and reported consistent high correlations between the Interim Hayes-Binet Intelligence Tests for the Blind 1942 and the Wechsler Bellevue Scale. In an item analysis of the latter, he showed its value in use with blind students.

A thorough investigation of the performance of blind and sighted children on the WISC was undertaken by Tillman (1967), who used 110 educationally blind and an equal number of sighted children, matched for age and sex, in his studies. In order to determine how appropriate the items of the WISC are for blind children, he evaluated their performance in terms of item difficulty curves, t-tests, and subtest reliabilities. He found (p. 73) "that blind children score about the same as normal children on Arithmetic, Information and Vocabulary but did less well on Comprehension and Similarities." The application of factor analyses led him to a number of educationally important conclusions regarding the ability structure of blind as compared with sighted groups: (1) blind children retain experiences as facts equally well as normal children, but these experiences are less integrated and tend to stand alone; (2) blind children tend to approach abstract conceptualization problems from a concrete and functional level and consequently lag behind the sighted children; (3) for blind children Vocabulary appears to be only word-definition whereas it has much more than a word-naming function for sighted children; and (4) the blind are quite comparable to the sighted in numerical ability.

Zweibelson and Barg (1967) investigated one aspect of language development in the blind child, that of concept formation. Eight practically totally blind children, aged eleven to thirteen, were matched in sex, age, intelligence, socio-economic level, and lack of emotional and organic involvement with a group of eight sighted children. WISC test protocols were obtained, and the children's responses in the similarities and vocabulary subtests were rated according to whether they were concrete (a specific characteristic of the object is considered to be the content), functional, or abstract (summing up all essential characteristics of the object) definitions. The blind children functioned primarily on a concrete and functional-conceptual level, using abstract concepts to a far lesser degree than their sighted peers. The authors recommend, therefore, that blind children be supplied with concrete experiences, both with objects and situations, and that a multisensory approach as well as training in reasoning tasks be used according to the child's needs and level development.

These results are in line with Rubin's valuable study (1964) on abstract functioning in the adult blind. Rubin found that adult congenitally blind subjects did less well on abstraction tests than sighted or adventitiously blind groups. He also stressed the importance of the age at onset of blindness for abstract functioning and for tests involving this ability. Studies to be reported on later under the heading Orientation and Locomotion also point out the importance of vision for the ability to visualize in performing spatial tasks.

Juurmaa (1967) raises many interesting and important questions—some similar to those investigated by Tillman and others —which deserve to be topics of research. However, his study has a number of faults, which can be summed up by stating that he applied refined statistical analyses to inexact data, which were collected from inadequate samples under adverse and insufficiently controlled testing conditions. He used tests, many of which were only cursorily described, appear difficult to quantify, and are not replicable.

There were others who recommended the Hayes-Binet and the WISC as alternative testing instruments for the blind. Gilbert and Rubin (1965) found high correlations between the two tests but indicated a preference for the WISC because of its easier application. They also suggested modifications of the Comprehension and Similarities parts of the test to make them more suitable for blind children and recommended the inclusion of verbal reasoning and meaningful verbal memory subtests. The correlations just mentioned have been confirmed by Lewis (1957), who also showed that there is a positive relationship between measured mental ability and academic achievement and survival of blind students in a residential school. On the other hand, Hopkins and McGuire (1966, 1967) questioned the comparability and interchangeability of the two tests and recommended a cautious interpretation of Hayes-Binet scores because of marked variations between test and retest performance.

Newland (1961, 1964) recognized the need for a test of learning aptitude developed specifically for and standardized upon the blind. He suggested an approach by which those psychological processes are assessed which make achievement possible. His Blind Learning Aptitude Test (1961), BLAT, uses a variety of embossed figures of increasing complexity in order to determine the ability of children to distinguish tactually some of the figures that do not belong in a given group. As yet, the standardization of the BLAT has not been fully reported, though a study by Hecht and Newland (1965), conducted on a limited scale, indicated a high positive correlation between scores obtained on the BLAT and those on educational achievement tests.

Wattron (1956) reported a successful attempt to use adapted Kohs-type blocks that have smooth and rough sides instead of the white and red colors. The Ohwaki-Kohs test is a modified version of the Kohs Block-Design Test, which substitutes different types of fabric for the colors used by Kohs. Ohwaki *et al.* (1960) re-

ported significant correlations between its scores and school achievement for Japanese blind children. Suinn, Dauterman, and Shapiro (1966) have used the Ohwaki-Kohs test at Stanford University and found it useful with blind adults, though their experience indicated the need for a modification of the test materials. The use of a number of other performance tests has been reported (Dauterman, Shapiro, and Suinn, 1967), but none of them have been satisfactorily explored or standardized to make them practically applicable, particularly so far as their use with blind children is concerned.

Most of the questions arising from the use of the Hayes-Binet Intelligence Tests may soon become superseded, since a new, much better conceived and standardized adaptation of the Binet-Simon Tests will become available. Davis (1962) reported that he and his associates at the Perkins School for the Blind are nearing completion of an adaptation of the 1960 Standford Revision of the Binet-Simon Scales

in which a definite effort has been made to substitute items calling for the use of tactual perception and organization as substitutes for those items in the original test calling for visual perception and organization. . . . so that a single meaningful test will result (pp. 50–51).

According to recent studies, there are two causes of blindness that appear to have definite effects on the intelligence of children affected by them: retinoblastoma and bilateral congenital anophthalmos. Williams (1968), a British psychologist who also devised the Williams Intelligence Test for Children with Defective Vision widely used abroad, reports on a study of fifty children whose blindness was caused by retinoblastoma, a malignant tumor of the eye, originating from immature retina cells. Retinoblastoma may be present at birth or the tumors are discovered before the child is six years of age. There is a hereditary factor involved in the disease, and there is no sex linkage. Retinoblastoma is a rare disease, and experienced observers have noted that practically all children whose blindness is caused by it show superior intelligence. Williams compared the IQ scores of fifty retinoblastoma cases with seventy-four nonretinoblastoma subjects who were blind but had no additional handicaps. The retinoblastoma group had a mean IQ (on the Williams Intelligence Test Scale) of 119.72 as compared with the control group's mean IQ of 102.81. The difference was highly significant. The IQ range of the retinoblastoma group was from 101 to 146, with 78 percent of the children scoring above 110. No definite explanation for this phenomenon can be given.

Congenital anophthalmos, lack of eye-structure formation in which part of the embryonic structure of the brain fails to develop, is also a rare cause of blindess. In most but not all cases, it results in developmental retardation and is associated with additional handicaps, according to a study by Bachelis (1967). A majority of the cases in the study had subnormal IQs, many of them requiring custodial care, though there were some who showed superior intelligence and good adjustment. There was a high incidence of associated handicaps, most of them neuromuscular and convulsive disorders, maldevelopment of the brain case, and a fairly high incidence of other congenital anomalies, such as polydactyly, missing toes, cleft palate, and congenital heart defects. These results were to be expected because congenital anophthalmos is due to a generalized genetic disturbance. The author recommends early comprehensive diagnostic evaluations in order to identify and treat any possible additional handicaps.

In the past years many things have happened that suggest a reevaluation of the whole problem of intelligence testing of blind children: the increases in blindness in children due first to RLF and lately to maternal rubella, which did not follow any socioeconomic stratification; the increase in the number of blind children attending local public school facilities; the better understanding of parents in bringing up their blind child because of growing emphasis on parent education; and the recognition that tests devised for seeing children may not adequately measure the intelligence of visually handicapped children, particularly if they rely only on verbal items. These are some of the factors that advocate a revision of our testing procedures and of the conclusions drawn from them in the past.

Achievement Test Results

The first report on the use of an achievement test with the blind was published in 1918 by Hayes, who used a reading test with blind pupils. In 1927, Maxfield published her *Adaptation of Educational Tests for Use with Blind Pupils*, in which she gave directions for the administration of parts of the Standford Achievement Tests and the Gray Oral Reading Check Tests. Since then many achievement tests have been used and adapted for use with the blind, such as the Metropolitan Achievement Tests, the Sones-Harry High School Achievement Test, and the Myers-Ruch High School Progress Test. The Stanford Achievement Tests in their various forms have been used most widely in schools for the blind. The College Entrance Examination Board also offers its tests in braille for those blind students who plan to enter college. Hayes (1941, p. 155) found two basic changes necessary in adapting achievement tests for use with blind pupils: (1) greater detail in preliminary instructions and (2) an increase of three times the time allowance given for seeing pupils. This ratio was indicated as desirable in a study by Caldwell (1932).

Nolan (1962) questioned this "somewhat arbitrary ratio" as established by Hayes in 1937. He mentioned particularly (p. 494) the facts that braille Grade 1½ has been replaced by braille Grade 2 and that the ratio between braille and print reading may not be "the same at all grade levels and for all forms of material commonly presented in achievement tests." Lowenfeld, Abel, and Hatlen (1969) investigated the braille reading rate and found that on the fourth-grade level, blind children need about twice as much time and on the eighth-grade level, about one and one-half to twice as much reading time as seeing children. They concluded (p. 92): "As a result of the present study, revision of the time allowance to about twice the time as compared with seeing children seems to be indicated." It should be recognized that these recommendations are based on tests given to 200 blind children (visual acuity of 5/200 or less, of whom 78 percent were totally blind or had light perception only) within the normal range of intelligence and free of "marked" additional handicaps.

Although blind pupils show, grade by grade, about the same achievement as seeing pupils, Hayes pointed out (1941, p. 216) that "blind children average at least two years older than seeing children in the same grades, so comparisons by age, either chronological or mental, demonstrate their retardation." Lowenfeld (1945) reported on the age-grade relationship for 481 pupils in four grades of twelve schools for the blind. In the third and fourth grades, the blind showed an overage of 2.5 years, in the sixth grade of 2.9, and in the seventh grade of 2.8 years (p. 11). He considered various factors responsible for this age-grade retardation, such as environmental influences resulting in lack of opportunities for observations, slower acquisition of knowledge as a result of blindness, and slower braille reading. Lowenfeld (1955, p. 231) indicated that more recent data might "show a change due to the increased use of aural sources of information, such as the Talking Book and the radio, and to the greater integration of blind children with seeing children." Lowenfeld, Abel, and Hatlen (1969) found indeed a considerable narrowing of the age-grade differences between blind and seeing students:

The chronological age of fourth graders showed that blind children in local schools were 0.8 years and in residential schools 1.2 years older than their seeing peers. On the eighth grade level, there were only very small differences between blind and seeing students (p. 111).

It must, of course, be understood that whatever is said about blind pupils as a group does not permit any conclusion concerning the achievement of individual blind students. Many of them are younger than their seeing fellow students and excel in any subject for which they show a particular aptitude.

There are only a very few reports available that deal with the use of achievement tests with visually impaired children. Trismen (1967) undertook an equating study of parts of the Sequential Tests of Educational Progress (STEP) to relate scores on the braille forms to existing norms. The social studies, science, and mathematics tests were give to about 270 visually handicapped students registered as braille readers in twenty-nine residential schools. He established equivalent scores for the braille version, which had certain inappropriate items omitted, and came to the conclusion (p. 423) "that, in general, the blind equating samples used in this study are roughly comparable in achievement level to the national norms samples, when tested under untimed conditions with instruments which have been specially adapted for their use." He noticed, however, that the removal of certain items from the print version, such as those based on political cartoons or complex graphs, may have resulted in an advantage to the blind since (pp. 423–424) "many of these items are concerned with the very concepts and processes which prove most difficult for the blind student."

The Verbal Scale of the Wechsler Adult Intelligence Scale and the Haptic Intelligencs Scale for Adult Blind (Shurrager and Shurrager, 1964) were used by Streitfeld and Avery (1968) with thirty-one residential school students, age sixteen to nineteen years. They found that both tests were equally good in predicting academic achievement for totally blind students, but for the partially sighted the WAIS was better in predicting academic success. They recommended further research using the Haptic Intelligence Scale for a variety of purposes.

The most valuable source of information on tests and testing techniques for use with blind pupils and adults is *A Manual for the Psychological Examination of the Adult Blind* (Bauman and Hayes, 1951), which also includes information concerning special considerations of a blind client's history and sources for securing testing material.

The Use of Touch in Cognition

If blind children are to gain experiences comparable in reality value to those of seeing children, they must acquire them through touch observations. Such experiences are particularly essential during the elementary grades when children form the basic concepts of their environment. Objects or situations can either be observed in reality or as models. If an object is too large, the model will represent it in a contracted form; if an object is too small, the model will show it enlarged and most likely also reinforced. A model is only a substitute for the real experience and is always in some way incomplete or distorted. For example, if animals are represented in stuffed form, they may be true to size, shape, and surface quality, but do not give the feeling of warmth, life, and motion that one gets when observing the animal alive. If only a model of the animal is used, size and texture are given up, the motion is "frozen," and the only quality preserved for observation is shape. These shortcomings are, in one or the other combination, true for all teaching models. It is, therefore, necessary for teachers to take great care that their pupils will not form misconceptions about certain qualities of the object presented, particularly in regard to its actual size.

Mandola (1968) calls attention to the fact that the use of models involves perceptual problems which have not been explored and that the wide use of models by teachers of the blind rests on the assumption that tactual aids make the abstract concrete, which has neither been proven nor systematically investigated. There is certainly need for research in this area. However, with the precautions already voiced and those subsequently given, the use of models appears to be pragmatically

BERTHOLD LOWENFELD

justified until proof to the contrary is provided. It has been found successful with countlesss blind children by generations of experienced teachers in this country and abroad.

Although almost no research is available concerning the psychological and educational problems of touch observation, a few comments based on experience are offered here. The ability to observe by touch and to manipulate develops with the child. The cutaneous senses, prehensory and grasping abilities, kinesthetic sensations, time experiences, and, last but not least, coordination and intelligent interpretation, are brought into action according to the child's developmental level. The younger the child is, the simpler must be the experiences from which he can gain. At first he will be limited in observing as well as in verbalizing his experiences, but by practice he will acquire the ability to observe better, to differentiate objects according to size, weight, shape, material, surface, temperature, and to give verbal reports of his observations. Simultaneousness is characteristic of visual observation, whereas successiveness is characteristic of touch observation. Every part of the object must be covered by or brought under the touching hand, often not only once but frequently, so that the large forms as well as the finer details can be observed. In addition to this individual need for more time, there is a group factor that must be considered. Many children can, at the same time, look at an object, whereas only one child can observe it by touch. If touch observation is limited to the hours of instruction only, it will either consume too much time or the individual child will be confined to only a cursory inspection of the object. For this reason, material for observation should be left in the classroom so that the pupils can continue their observation during their free time. The teacher may call the attention of the pupils to certain characteristic features and let them proceed on their own with the actual observation—either in preparation or in a follow-up of the instruction period. In this directed but unsupervised observation, totally blind children and those with partial sight gain mutually from their experiences.

The fact that blind children must rely in their acquisition of actual object knowledge on the touch senses puts them at a serious disadvantage in experiencing objects and situations in their totality. In seeing children, sight is the unifying agent that enables the individual in a short time to observe situations in toto and to combine part experiences into wholes. Sight also serves as an organizer of discrete experiences and facilitates the reduction of form varieties to simpler patterns or schemata. The blind child gains many impressions by the use of his senses: he may hear or smell something, he may feel air currents or temperature changes, and he may have actual touch contact with the object or situation or with parts of them. But all these experiences are discrete and unorganized and remain so unless guided observation or teaching lends organization and structure to them. Teaching by the unit method has, therefore, a special purpose in the blind child's education. It gives him those unifying experiences that he often cannot gain because of his lack of sight.

The young blind child forms his own concepts of his environment as he grows into it. These concepts, incomplete and distorted as they may be, suffice for his purposes and satisfy the child's restricted curiosity. A desire to know more about things and to know them in reality and fully must often be awakened and encouraged in blind children. The preschool years should encourage such inquisitiveness in the young blind child, but often it is suppressed by an ill-conceived "touch taboo." Then the more difficult task of reestablishing this desire for exploration is left to the teacher.

In the process of his observations, the child does not react with one sense but with his total sensory equipment; he hears, smells, and, if given opportunity, tastes. Hearing and smelling have, in common with sight, the characteristic that they need not be applied but are continuously open to stimulation; the sense of taste, like touch, functions only when its organ comes into direct contact with the object to be tasted. Thus, children will hear and smell while they are awake, although their observations need to become conscious ones in order to be of real value. Children, and also adults, may listen to the twitter of birds again and again without noticing the great variety of bird sounds—it is just twitter to them. Once their attention is called to the specific song of, say, the robin, and this recognition is sufficiently implanted, they will not fail to recognize it and to know when one of these singers is around. Or, in walking through a wood, one may smell a peculiar odor that can be traced to rotting wood. Once this connection between the odor and its source is firmly established, the child will know how to make use of it as a clue to the presence of rotting wood or other material in the same condition. Thus, besides recognition, "implanting" and "establishing" are necessary processes before an experience can become of value for future use. The concept of "passive" and "active" knowledge as elaborated in the field of creative growth by Lowenfeld (1957, p.110) is a most useful one in this connection. The methods by which education succeeds in transforming passive into active knowledge are the same for seeing and blind children and include motivation, insight, exercise, activity, repetition, and various forms of reinforcement. Which of these will be used in a given situation with the individual child or with a group of children is a decision that must be left to the teacher.

Confirmation of the need of congenitally totally blind children for concrete experiences with objects and situations, and for unifying structuring experiences elaborated on above and more closely explained by Lowenfeld (1950b) comes from a variety of recent studies, such as those by Harley (1963), Nagera and Colonna (1965), Omwake and Solnit (1961), Rubin (1964), Zweibelson and Barg (1967), and others. Bauman (1946) states that studies of test results

... point very strongly to the desirability of including in the education of blind children far more contact with practical materials of possible vocational value, such as tools. The inability of some blind individuals to deal with this type of material suggests lack of previous contact with it rather than lack of fundamental ability to comprehend it (p. 153).

Normally a child acquires his knowledge of tools by observing when anyone in the family does some work in which tools are used or when he can watch a workman performing his job. Where the seeing child can watch from a distance, the blind child must have direct contact with the object to be observed, and this is his greatest obstacle to the casual acquisition of knowledge and experience. It implies that blind children must be given special opportunities for observation in order to make their environment real to them. This will help them avoid falling into a pattern of unreality that so often interferes with their later adjustment to the requirements of life.

Deutsch (1940) investigated the effect of lack of sight on the sense of reality in the person born blind. He gave twenty-eight blind pupils a box containing seven wooden blocks of various shapes, which the subjects were asked to name and arrange in the order of preference. They were asked to enumerate the forms of the blocks from memory, and it was also observed how they reacted to removal of one or more of the blocks while they were playing with them. Deutsch noticed that the curiosity of the person born blind was more quickly satisfied than that of the seeing, that some subjects were inhibited about feeling the figures, and that observation of loss of some blocks resulted in a striking readiness to give up reality and to escape into fantasy.

The ability of blind children to recognize by touch simple embossed pictures has been studied and reported on by Merry and Merry (1933). On the basis of a series of experiments, they reached the following conclusions:

It seems unwise to expend any considerable amount of time teaching blind children how to recognize tactually pictures of three-dimensional objects. If, however, the needs of the child demand instruction upon the identification of simple figures in two dimensions, time for such work seems justified. . . . It may be of value to make use of embossed designs of a bi-dimensional type in the education of blind children, but it is very doubtful if embossed pictures of tri-dimensional objects, wherein perspective is involved, possess any real meaning for children without sight even after systematic instruction (p. 163).

The idea of using embossed pictures in the education of blind children is an old and often tried one. In addition to the experiments just discussed, the accumulated experiences of teachers of the blind also prove that embossed pictures of three-dimensional objects are of no practical value. Usually they are made by using three-dimensional dots or lines or raised surfaces for the purpose of making tangible two-dimensional outlines of objects as perceived by vision. Thus, perceptual qualities of vision, such as perspective, base line, light and shadow, and distinctness are presented to the sense of touch, which does not function according to them. To be concrete, the embossed outline of a dog gives the shape of this animal as it is seen. The hands, observing a real dog, or a part of it, by touch, move in three dimensions and embrace the object or parts of it in an act of three-dimensional perception. They do not follow the visually perceived outline of the object. In an embossed drawing the dog's four legs are represented in one plane, whereas to the sense of touch they are actually at the "four corners" of the dog's body, as a blind child expressed it. The embossed outline, therefore, constitutes not a representation but a symbol of the object, which becomes meaningful only by added verbal interpretation and explanation. Of course, the situation becomes far more involved if different objects of varying size and positions requiring perspective drawings are presented.

The Merrys' conclusions indicate that the use of embossed material in the teaching of geometry, geography, and other subjects should be successful and, also, that embossed pictures of essentially two-dimensional objects, such as a wheel, a hand, or a pair of scissors, can be recognized.

Two problems in presenting tactile materials for the use of blind students have been dealt with in separate studies. Schiff and Isikow (1966) examined how tactual information—in the form of histograms varying in bar length, regularity, tactile quality (height, textures), and combinations of these (redundancy)—is accurately interpreted by legally blind high school students. All variables, except for tactile quality and redundancy, had significant effects on response time and error scores, with some qualifications for the latter noted. Time and error measures were found to be relatively independent from each other. The authors discuss theoretical and practical implications of their findings.

Morris and Nolan (1963) used sixty braille-reading students in order to determine (1) minimum outer dimensions for seven discrete areal symbols, such as squares consisting of lines of dots, of straight lines, of slanted lines; and (2) whether differences exist according to the grade placement of the students. Their experiments established minimum outer dimensions for the tactual symbols and also revealed grade-level inequities in the ability to identify correctly areal symbols as they diminished in size.

The whole field of tactual representation of spatial and visual symbols that play such an important role in nonvisual communication is in urgent need of expanded research.

Considerable research is going on in the field of electrical stimulation of the skin. This means of communication is being explored in connection with reading devices to make print accessible to the blind and in connection with guidance devices to improve mobility of the blind (Foulke, 1963).

Creative Activities

Lowenfeld (1939, 1957) has studied extensively the creative activities of blind and partially seeing children and the psychological factors involved. He distinguishes two different modes of perception, the haptic and the visual perception. The haptic mode is based on immediate bodily experiences and is primarily concerned with the tactual space around the individual. The visual mode is concerned with his environment and with the visual integration of it. Lowenfeld found that the amount of sight is not a determining factor in the person's inclination toward one or the other type. A haptically minded individual might be disturbed by his remaining sight, while a visually minded individual will be greatly aided by it. Creative activity, which permits the individual child to express himself according to his mode of functioning, is an important means of adjustment. By releasing emotional tension and rigidity, it can help to overcome feelings of inferiority and isolation from the environment. The author exemplifies his findings with numerous illustrations that show the importance of his distinction as derived from visually handicapped children for the general field of art education. His observations, concerning the tactual-kinesthetic perception of space, show that the blind are capable of achieving simultaneous spatial images through an act of integration of successively perceived tactual impressions. He also concludes that, in the modeling of the blind, objects receive their proportion by the value they have for the individual in a given situation. Thus the perspective of the blind in modeling is a perspective of value. So far as creative activities of blind children are concerned, he warns of the danger of imposition of visual characteristics by the teacher, and stresses (1957, p. 446) "that the most primitive creative work born in the mind of a blind person and produced with his own hands is of greater value than the most effective imitation."

Verbalism and Speech

The congenitally and totally blind child cannot be aided in his learning of speech by imitation, which plays a great role in the development of seeing children. He can only learn from what he hears and from occasional touch observation. Therefore, his progress in speech development may be slower than that of seeing children. But it is not only the speech development but also the acquisition of word concepts that is affected by blindness. Cutsforth (1932) refers to this as "verbal unreality," because the blind child may learn to name many things without having any real experience or idea of them. He investigated this tendency toward verbal mindedness in two groups. He used thirty-nine totally blind pupils of whom thirteen, at one time, possessed good sight and were visually minded, and twenty-six were congenitally blind. The subjects had to respond to the names of forty selected objects with some quality of the object. Fifty-four percent of all responses were visual qualities, the congenitally blind giving 48.2 percent and the adventitious group giving 65 percent. Tactual responses followed next, with the congenital group giving 35.7 percent and the adventitious group giving 24.2 percent. This showed a strong tendency of the blind children participating in this study to employ visual concepts, when other sensory concepts were just as available and would have been much more meaningful and familiar in experience. Naturally, a large number of wrong visual responses was found. Cutsforth believes this indicates that the pupils preferred risking a doubtful visual response rather than giving their own experiences.

Nolan (1960) repeated Cutsforth's experiment and found that significantly fewer visual responses were made by his group of blind children. He concluded "that 'verbal unreality' is not a significant problem for the group studied." He also reported that responses to four of the stimulus words were available for 1,000 sighted children. In a comparison of these with the ones obtained in his study, the responses of the blind children closely resembled those of normally seeing children. Though Nolan's data do not give any reasons for this change, one can assume that modern methods used in the education of present-day blind children may have something to do with it and that Cutsforth's findings by themselves, reinforced by the observations of others, are in part responsible for the change.

The relationship of verbalism among blind children to age, intelligence, experience, and personal adjustment was explored by Harley (1963). Forty children, from seven to fourteen years of age, who were blind or had only light perception were chosen from two residential schools. The children were given three tasks: a pretested list of words from the Gates Reading Vocabulary for the Primary Grades to obtain definition of the words, identification of the items representing these words to obtain verbalism scores, and the Tuddenham Reputation Test to obtain adjustment scores. Verbalism was assumed to exist when a child gave an acceptable definition of a word but could not accurately identify the object by some sensory means. Visually oriented verbalism was assumed to exist when a child employed words referring to color or brightness in defining the name of a given object. The results showed that there is a relationship between verbalism and the three personal variables of chronological age, intelligence, and experience, as predicted. No such correlations were found between personal adjustment (the fourth personal variable) and verbalism, and between visually oriented verbalism and the four personal variables. Verbalisms were higher in the areas of food, farm, and nature than in the areas of home, clothing, and community. The results of this study (p. 53) emphasize "that blind children need a unique program in order to help them learn simple concepts that sighted children have developed through incidental learning."

The concept of verbalism has come under theoretical scrutiny in an article by Dokecki (1966). He argues from the psycholinguistic point of view that word-produced meaning (verbalism) is no less meaningful to the blind individual than word-thing relationships are. Although educators have followed the notion that "verbalism is meaningless and must lead to loose thinking" (p. 527) he contends that there is no proof that this is actually the case. Also, it has not been shown that verbalism results in poor academic performance or poor adjustment. Dokecki differentiates between verbalism as determined by Cutsforth—he considers this a "controlled association method"—and the way in which Harley used it in his study where he asked for identification of the object by sensory means. Only Harley's "visually oriented verbalism" corresponds to the Cutsforth and Nolan definition. Dokecki concentrates his disapproval on Cutsforth's evaluation of the effects of nonsensory-based language in the blind. However, he is implicitly critical of educators of blind children who practice concreteness in teaching as a counter measure against verbalism and its effects, even though this has been practiced since educational methods for blind children were developed.

Maxfield (1936) published a preliminary study of the spoken language of eight preschool blind children based on the verbatim report of observations. Although she regarded her work more as a methodological study, it contains some interesting results. Among the older children, 40 to 50 percent of the responses (about twice the percentage then found in seeing children) were concerned with things. Blind children asked more questions and gave fewer commands than seeing children. Their responses also were more frequently incomplete and emotionally toned. Blind children used proper names of persons more frequently than seeing children, and they also asked more questions than seeing children. Maxfield considers some of these differences as indications of the blind child's need for gaining security.

Stinchfield (1933) discussed speech disorders among blind children and found, in a survey, that about half of the children showed some speech defects, ranging from mild oral inaccuracies and letter substitution to lateral lisping, sigmatism (a form of stammering with imperfect pronunciation of the "s" sounds), and severe oral inaccuracies. She recognized that in blind children such speech defects are usually remedial and that the prognosis is much better than in the case of deaf children. The development of speech disorders in blind children is due to the fact that the congenitally blind child must learn speech without being able to learn the formation of speech sounds and the accompanying bodily movements and gestures by visual imitation. He depends solely on the acoustic imitation and production of speech. Stinchfield found more dyslalia (speech defects of organic or functional origin, dependent upon malformation or imperfect innervation of the tongue, soft palate, or other organs of articulation) than any other type of speech defect. In a speech survey of 220 children in a residential school, she found letter substitution, lisping, and stuttering the most frequently occurring speech defects besides unspecified mild oral inaccuracies.

Various authors have suggested psychological causes for speech defects among the blind such as infantilism, egocentricity, emotional gratification, feelings of inferiority, and overcompensation, but no study has actually demonstrated for blind children the connection between speech defects and any particular psychological reaction pattern.

Brieland (1950a) summarized observations of various authors on differences of speech in blind and seeing children as follows:

(1) The blind show less vocal variety. (2) Lack of modulation is more critical among the blind. (3) The blind tend to talk louder than the sighted. (4) The blind speak at a slower rate. (5) Less effective use of gesture and bodily action is typical of the blind. (6) The blind use less lip movement in articulation of sounds (p. 99).

Berry and Eisenson (1942) considered monotony and lack of appropriate modulation to be characteristic voice defects of the blind. Cutsforth (1951, pp. 103–120) discussed voice and speech and their relationship with personality development. He mentions particularly lack of stimulation, faulty sound analysis, synesthetic imagery, and faulty projection as causes of speech defects. The last-mentioned he considers the most common one and calls the use of a loud voice without specific directional projection the "broadcasting voice of the blind."

Brieland (1950a), in his own study, compared the ratings on speech performances of eighty-four matched pairs of blind and sighted pupils twelve to eighteen years old. The ratings indicate that there were no significant differences in general vocal effectiveness or in vocal variety; the blind were judged significantly superior in pitch modulation, whereas the sighted were favored in ratings of bodily action and in degree of lip movement. He concluded (pp. 102–103) that his findings "failed to show the inferiority in the use of the voice which the literature on speech of the blind would lead one to expect." The superiority in pitch modulation may result from a greater reliance of the blind upon verbal means of expression, whereas the superiority in bodily action of the seeing is due to the influence of the visible components of social communication. He suspects that observers become unduly sensitive to small defects in the blind and thus tend to judge them more unfavorably than they would seeing persons.

A survey by Rowe (1958) arrived at conclusions that even favor the blind. She screened 148 school-age blind children for speech defects and took tape recordings that were independently judged by two speech therapists. Her findings indicate that the percentage of speech defects found was low when compared with general estimates and percentages for the normal school population. She ascribes these favorable results to good preschool counseling services, to the fact that in the surveyed group no cases with major secondary handicaps were included, and to the good schooling which these children received. The methodology of this study, however, is open to serious questioning.

Two studies attempted to clarify the different incidence findings of past studies. Both used as their population only children in residential schools for the blind. Miner (1963) investigated the incidence of speech deviations among 293 children and found 33.8 percent to have some sort of speech deviation. He points out that this is four to five times higher than the incidence in public schools. Articulation problems were found to be the largest category and were present in 25 percent. No differences were found between boys and girls and between braille and sight-saving students. There was only one stutterer among all the children, and he was a partially seeing child. Weinberg (1964), however, found that stuttering in blind children is within the range of incidence for the general population.

LeZak and Starbuck (1964) made a speech survey of 173 children in a residential school. They found that 49.8 percent showed some speech disorders, with 36.9 percent falling into the articulation category. The authors of both studies recommend that residential schools provide speech therapy programs adapted to the needs of the students.

Finally, a study by Tillman and Williams (1968) should be mentioned. They compared thirty-five blind residential school children with thirty-five sighted children in two tasks—word association and word usage. They found (p. 40) that word association results show "that both groups are at the same developmental level, that the sequence of acquisition is similar, that is, first nouns and adjectives, later verbs and adverbs, and that rate of acquisition is about the same. However, with reference to word usage, interpretation of results is less clear."

Practically all incidence data on speech deviations of blind children are derived from surveys of residential school populations and cannot be considered as representative of blind children in general. A comprehensive study of speech problems among blind children is long overdue.

Touch Reading

The psychological processes involved in reading are complex and not less so if the reading organs are the fingers rather than the eyes. Blind children learn to read and write braille, which is a system of embossed dots to be read by the fingers. The full braille sign consists of six embossed dots, two vertical rows of three, of a size that can be covered simultaneously by the pulp of a finger. Braille Grade One is written in full spelling, and Braille Grade Two makes use of contractions representing letter combinations, syllables, or words.

Early research on touch reading has largely centered on the mechanics of the reading process. Bürklen (1932) published his important experimental study on touch reading in German in 1917 (translated into English in 1932). He agrees with Heller (1895) that the vertical arrangement of six dots is the best possible one for touch reading. The readability of the various letters of the alphabet is not determined by the number of dots, but by their characteristic formation. He found that all fingers could be used in touch reading but that the first and second fingers of both hands are the preferred ones. The index fingers of both hands are predominantly used as reading fingers. There are different touch motions employed in reading: the up-and-down motion and the horizontal motion. Good readers move their fingers horizontally with a minimum of up-and-down motions, whereas less skilled readers interrupt their horizontal movement by frequent up-and-down motions, which may also form loops. Bürklen also recognizes that the touch motions are connected with different pressure of the fingers. Good readers exert slight and uniform pressure, whereas poor readers employ strong and variable pressure. There is

BERTHOLD LOWENFELD

little decrease of touch sensitivity even after hours of touch reading, which is also not particularly fatiguing. Touch reading is three to four times as slow as visual reading. Reading of words and sentences is done by a unifying perception of word pictures similar to visual reading. Only with difficult or unknown words is a dissection of the word picture necessary. Reading with both hands is fastest, but the left hand alone reads somewhat better than the right hand.

Maxfield (1928) wrote the first book dealing with methods of teaching braille reading and agrees largely with Bürklen, except that American experiences have demonstrated that one-handed readers who use the right hand are more efficient than those who use the left. She underlines the importance of relaxation and correct posture in reading and recommends that children should be trained to read silently without lip movement or inner speech. She observed that many of the best readers read ahead on a lower line with the left hand before the right hand has finished the preceding line and recommends that this be encouraged if children show any inclination toward it. She also recommended the word method of teaching braille reading and the early teaching of contracted braille.

Holland and Eatman (1933) made moving-picture records of the finger movements, which revealed, among other facts, the importance of the amount of time spent in making return sweeps—between 6 and 7 percent of the total reading time —with good readers spending less time than poor readers. Also good readers make fewer regressive movements than poor readers, whose performance is in general less uniform. Holland (1934) also studied the speed and pressure factors in reading braille and confirmed Bürklen's

findings (1932). He observed that pressure varies within a given line, with less variation in the case of fast readers. Poor readers tend to increase pressure toward the end of a paragraph. Fertsch (1947) also used a moving picture camera in studying hand dominance. She explains the discrepancies in past findings by the differences in performance of good and poor readers. Readers whose hands are equally effective in perceiving braille read faster, and among them are fewer poor readers than among those who use either the right hand or the left hand dominantly. Those with the right hand dominant perform better than those with the left hand dominant. Good readers read a substantial amount of material with the hands functioning independently, of which the right hand reads about twice as much as the left hand. Poor readers read very little material with the hands independently, since they keep right and left fingers close together.

In another study, Fertsch (1946) found silent braille reading considerably faster than oral braille reading. Independence in the functioning of the hands is characteristic of good readers in making return sweeps as well as in regressive movements. She also found that reading habits become established by about the time a pupil has reached the third grade and do not change noticeably with increase in reading experience.

Horbach (1951) published a study in which he reports observations and experiments on touch reading. He concludes that these experiments give full confirmation to his initial assumption that the processes of tactile and visual reading are the same not only in their final results but also in the progress of the reading act. Differences found, particularly in the rate of reading, are only of a gradual nature. Thus he confirmed many of the assumptions of Bürklen's early study.

Lowenfeld, Abel, and Hatlen (1969) presented the results of a braille reading study that was undertaken with the support of the U.S. Office of Education. It describes the status of braille reading instruction in 1965 in local and residential schools in the United States and reports the results of tests and observations that were derived from a sample of two hundred students, fifty each on the fourth- and eighth-grade levels in local and residential school classes for the blind. The book also includes a review of research on braille reading, a chapter dealing with special problems in braille reading, and other information concerning the history of braille and such topics as readiness for learning to read and the teacher's role in the reading program.

The survey of the status of braille reading instruction, representing replies of 520 teachers, revealed a considerable uniformity of methods with only two areas of substantial differences: two-thirds of the teachers used the word or sentence method, and one-third began braille reading instruction with the braille alphabet and shifted to the word method when the children had learned enough letters to permit this; no uniformity was revealed in the use of fingers encouraged by teachers in braille reading instruction. There were no significant differences between methods of teaching braille reading in local schools and in residential schools.

In connection with the application of the reading part of the Sequential Test of Educational Progress and the Paragraph Meaning part of the Stanford Achievement Test, data on personal characteristics of the students and of their reading behavior were secured. Only 11.5 percent of the 200 students in the study had any

measureable visual acuity, with a maximum of 5/200 (Snellen measurement), the optimum vision allowed for participants in the study. Of the fourth-graders, 54 percent, and of the eighth-graders, 70 percent were blind as a result of RLF. The study required that participating students have no marked additional handicaps. In contrast to past studies, it was found that the differences in age between blind students and their seeing peers were not more than 1.2 years on the fourth-grade level and only two to three months on the eighth-grade level. IQs of fourth-graders were about normal and those of eighth-graders above normal as compared with seeing students. Reading comprehension was at least equal to seeing norms. Reading rate was about twice that of seeing readers for fourth-grade students and less than that for those in the eighth grade. On the basis of these results, it was recommended that reading time allowance for blind students should be reduced from the presently practiced two and one-half to three times to only twice that allowed for seeing students. Among the other findings of this study are the following: blind children in local schools were at least equal in reading rate and comprehension to those in residential schools; students with high reading comprehension belong to the group of fast readers and those with low reading comprehension to that of slow readers; specific hand-use or finger-use did not correlate significantly with reading rate scores or with reading comprehension scores. There were trends to have a slightly better chance to be efficient braille readers for those who read with both hands as compared with those who use only one hand and, particularly for reading rate, for those who use more fingers than the index fingers. The study confirmed results of previous studies con-

BERTHOLD LOWENFELD

cerning other aspects of braille reading such as regressive movements, rubbing letters, losing the place in reading, silent speech movements, which are all characteristic of less efficient braille readers. So far as hand-use and finger-use is concerned, the study indicated that there is no justification for considering any specific ones as a prerequisite for being an efficient braille reader. Therefore, teachers should not insist on a specific hand- or finger-use to the exclusion of what an individual student prefers.

Nolan and Morris (1965) developed and validated a Roughness Discrimination Test as a reading readiness test for young blind children. The test consists of a set of sixty-nine cards upon each of which four pieces of sandpaper are mounted. Three of these pieces are alike, whereas one is rougher than the others. The child must find the piece of sandpaper that feels different from the others. The test shows good predictive validity for success in braille reading and also correlates significantly with reading time and reading error scores of second-grade braille reading students.

The problem of how blind children— and adults for that matter—who cover with their reading fingers only one or a few letters at a time, combine these letters into whole words and sentences has been widely discussed but little studied. It is assumed that the word or short sentence when read in braille becomes, similar to visual reading, a whole, a gestalt, and only as such meaningful to the reader. Felden (1955) distinguished four different gestalt formations in the reading process: the acoustical gestalt—the sound of the word; the acoustic-motoric gestalt—the word as it is spoken; the optic gestalt—the meaningful whole word; and the vibratory gestalt—which becomes of great importance

with deaf and deaf-blind children. Whereas the acoustic and the acoustic-motoric gestalt formations are the same for seeing and blind children, the optic gestalt becomes a tactile for the blind. Felden stresses that this is not a simple equation but that tactile gestalt formation in the touch reading process of the blind is in need of scientific research and clarification.

Nolan (1966) and Henderson (1966) discussed some of their research which, they contend, provides some indication that in braille reading it is not the whole-word shape but the individual braille character that is the perceptual unit in word recognition. Nolan found (p. 12): "When we compare the time necessary to recognize a word with the sum of the times required to recognize the characters it contains, we generally find that the word recognition time is longer. This is, of course, opposite to findings for regular print reading." Henderson concluded (p. 10) that "increasing the rate of identification of isolated braille characters was accompanied by a significant increase in the rate and accuracy of the total reading process."

Among the studies that notice and confirm a similarity between braille reading and visual reading is that of Pick, Thomas, and Pick (1966). They presented to twenty-six braille readers two types of pseudowords, one type pronounceable and the other type unpronounceable, and measured the speed with which the two types were read. Most subjects spent more time reading the unpronounceable than the pronounceable pseudowords. The authors concluded that this indicates that braille print readers, just as sighted print readers, use grapheme-phoneme correspondences as grouping principles in the perception of braille.

Although there is no definite research evidence available, the many similarities noted between braille reading and print reading, the success of the whole-word and sentence method with blind children, and the fact that many efficient braille readers read ahead in the next line with the left hand before finishing the preceding line with the right hand, must be regarded as at least tentative proof that tactile reading, similar to visual reading, is a process of recognition of meaningful wholes.

Some studies that investigated problems of touch reading used children who are "legally blind," which means that they have vision of 20/200 or less Snellen measurement. Because many of these "legally blind" children can read braille by the use of their sight, the results of these studies cannot be regarded as valid, even if the children were blindfolded.

An interesting study dealing with a problem, which in the past has received scant, if any, attention, was undertaken by Barraga (1964). It was the purpose of this study to test the hypotheses that low-vision children could achieve an increase in visual discrimination by a short period of experimental teaching in visual discrimination and that their near-vision acuity would be significantly increased by such training. Ten pairs of blind children with low vision (6/200 or less), who also met other specific criteria, were matched on the ability to make visual discriminations of reading readiness items of the Visual Discrimination Test. This test was specifically designed for the study and showed good validity and reliability. Over a two-month period, the experimental group received approximately thirty hours of intensive and individualized teaching geared to improve the functional use of their low vision. All members of the experimental group showed significant enhancement of their Visual Discrimination Test scores. There was also a significant difference between the experimental and control groups.

The hypothesis that recorded near-vision acuity of experimental subjects would increase was not supported by the results and neither was there any difference in visual acuity between the experimental and control group. However, visual word recognition and reading ability were considerably increased for some experimental subjects.

The author states:

The data of this experiment strongly suggest that blind children with remaining vision could improve their visual efficiency to the degree that they would be able to use their low vision more effectively for educational purposes if a planned sequence of visual stimulation were available to them in their early school years (p. 71).

The Visual Discrimination Test as used in the experiment, a lesson-plan sequence, and forty-four daily lesson plans for a visual stimulation program are given in detail.

The results of this study have, indeed, far-reaching implications for low-vision children, and further experiments should be conducted with legally blind children who have better vision than 6/200 and with partially seeing children in order to determine whether their visual discrimination can also be improved by planned visual stimulation lessons.

The whole area of touch reading poses many problems as yet unsolved and even uninvestigated. Readability of letters and contractions, the mental processes involved in touch reading, methods of teaching touch reading to adults, and reading readiness and its indications are all problems that need investigation.

Touch reading is slow, and this slowness

has been made responsible for either retarding blind children in their educational progress or demanding of them a much greater expenditure of time for their studies. The fact that only a limited amount of reading matter is available in braille or in recorded form also exerts its influence, because much material must still be read aloud to blind students. In an early study, Lowenfeld (1945) compared rates and comprehension of braille and Talking Book reading, the latter with and without sound illustrations. He found that story-telling material was equally well comprehended by braille and by Talking Book reading, but comprehension of textbook material was better by braille than by Talking Book reading. He recommended, therefore, the use of Talking Books for supplementary reading on all grade levels and particularly with slow learners, whereas textbooks should preferably be studied in braille. Because Talking Books are normally read with a rate of 180 to 200 words per minute, many blind readers whose braille reading rate is low can cover more reading matter by using Talking Books or other recorded or taped material.

A further speeding up of recorded reading was suggested by Enc and Stolurow (1960), who conducted experiments to determine whether "time compression" as developed by Fairbanks, Gutman, and Miron (1957) would result in more efficient reading. It was found that over the range of 160 to 233 words per minute, faster rates were more efficient than slower ones. Foulke (1967), Kederis, Nolan, and Morris (1967), and others have further studied the use and effect of time-compressed recorded speech.

Foulke *et al.* (1962) also studied the influence of word rate on comprehension and pointed out (p. 141) that "those losses in comprehension that were statistically significant were not all educationally im-

portant, especially when the time saved in presenting the material was considered."

Hartlage (1963) compared listening comprehension of the blind and the sighted and concluded (p. 5): "With the variables of age, intelligence, and sex controlled, sightedness vs. blindness was not found to be a significant variable in listening comprehension." Thus, studies on listening comprehension conducted with the blind and those conducted with the seeing apply equally to both groups, although it must be recognized that reading by listening is far more important for blind students than it is for the seeing.

MOBILITY

For those who are totally blind or who have only light perception, the task of getting about is one of the most difficult to perform. No comprehensive research on the psychological factors involved in mobility is available. Work on the perception of obstacles, which occupied European scientists around the turn of the century, received particular attention in Cornell University studies published from 1944 on. Obstacle perception, however, is only one factor of importance in the ability to get about. It received more intensive scientific attention only because the blind seemed to possess an ability that the seeing appeared not to have, namely, the ability to avoid obstacles without having bodily contact with them. This fact was recognized already by Diderot in 1749 when his "Letter on the Blind for the Use of Those Who See" was published.

Obstacle Perception

Bürklen (1924) and Hayes (1935) reported extensively on the anecdotal and autobiographical material as well as on the first scientific attempts to investigate the hypothetical obstacle sense. Hayes provided a summary of theories to explain the obstacle sense covering the research up to 1935. He distinguished four different types of theories explaining the obstacle sense: (1) a heightened response of some sense organ, known or unknown; in this category belong the pressure theories, the auditory theories, and the temperature theories; (2) perceptual interpretation of cues from one or more sense organs, such as a combination of pressure, sound, and temperature changes; (3) an indirect and complicated response to sensory cues; Dolanski (1931) assumed, for instance, that cues from any sense organ may suggest danger, arouse fear, and produce contraction of muscles under the skin, causing sensation of obstacles; (4) occult explanations that assume magnetic or electrical phenomena, vibrations of the ether or of some other hypothetical substance, or vestigial organs in the skin (paroptic vision), and give other subconscious or miraculous explanations.

Around the turn of the century, German scientists engaged in a heated and often acrimonious controversy in which each of them defended a theory stipulating a heightened response in one or the other sense organ. Truschel (1906, 1907) claimed that his experiments proved that stimulation of the organs of hearing by reflected sound waves is responsible for obstacle perception. Kunz (1907) opposed him and claimed that the blind have a "distance sense" (*Ferngefühl*) based on abnormal sensibility of the skin for pressure and perhaps temperature differences. Krogius (1917) opposed both and considered temperature sensations as the factor responsible for distance perception of obstacles. The experiments of Truschel were perhaps more scientifically conducted

than those of his two opponents, but experimental psychology at that time was not ready to attack the problem with any hope of general agreement. James (1918) discussed "How the Blind Perceive Space" and considered "tympanic pressure" sensations as the responsible factor. Villey (1930) was critical of Kunz and Krogius and thought that audition is mainly responsible for obstacle sensations. He stated that they may not be recognized as auditive impressions, although they belong to the auditive order, and that the pressure sensations reported by many blind persons may be auditory illusions for which there is at present no physiological explanation.

Dolanski (1930) conducted extensive experiments with forty-two subjects in which he moved, without noise and without production of air currents, small disks toward the subject seated in a chair. The disks were moved either in "frontal approach" or in "lateral approach" toward the subject's face or one of his ears. The distance at which disks of a given size were detected was always greater with the lateral approach than with the frontal approach. He used a variety of materials for the disks, but the material of the disks did not affect the results. Dolanski experimented with his subjects in four conditions: with the face uncovered; with thick paper flaps affixed to the sides of the head in perpendicular direction and in front of the ears; with a cardboard mask covering the face; and with ears plugged with cotton. His results indicated that audition is responsible for obstacle perception. In the second series no obstacles were detected on the frontal approach, which made audition impossible, whereas the lateral approach permitting audition showed the same positive results as in the first series, where the face was left uncovered. No obstacles were detected in the fourth series in which audition was eliminated. In the third series, when a cardboard mask covered the face, the disks were discovered as well with as without the mask, which indicated that pressure and temperature cannot be responsible factors. Jerome and Proshansky (1950, p. 466) regret that Dolanski did not present any data on the frequency of mistakes when subjects claimed to detect an object that was not present and also criticize that he did not include any catch tests in his test procedures.

The most extensive research on the perception of obstacles by the blind was undertaken by a team of psychologists at Cornell University and continued elsewhere. In the first of these studies, Supa, Cotzin, and Dallenbach (1944) used blind and blindfolded subjects who were placed at various distances in front of either a wall or a portable masonite board approximately four feet square with its lower edge two feet above the floor. In walking toward the obstacle, they were asked to indicate their "first perception" of it and then to approach it as closely as possible without touching it—the "final appraisal." Experiments in which hearing was not eliminated were conducted, once with the subjects walking on hardwood floor with shoes on and once walking in stockinged feet on a soft carpet runner. The "first perceptions" of the two blind subjects were better than those of the two sighted subjects, whereas in the "final appraisals" the sighted subjects did approximately as well as the blind. In the four main experiments, various controls, similar in effect to those used by Dolanski (1930), were introduced in order to reduce or eliminate certain sensory cues. Two different receptors of sensation were considered: (1) the exposed areas of the skin and (2) the ears.

The stimuli acting on each of those receptors could be either (a) air currents and air waves that are outside the auditory range, arousing only cutaneous sensation, or (b) sound waves that could be heard and that also might arouse cutaneous sensation in the ear or on the exposed areas of the skin. In the first main experiment the exposed areas of the skin were covered, and in the second the ears were plugged and shielded from all stimulation. In the third experiment the exposed areas of the skin were left open to air and sound waves as in the second, but all stimuli that might have reached the ears were drowned by means of a sound screen—a constant, continuously sounding tone of moderate intensity, conducted by wires to a set of headphones worn over the ears of the subject. In the fourth experiment the stimuli were reduced to sound waves, and their action was limited to the ears. This was achieved by placing the subject in a sound-proof room with high-fidelity headphones over his ears through which he could listen to the sounds of the experimenter who, carrying a microphone, walked in another room toward the obstacle. The latter arrangement was criticized by Jerome and Proshansky (1950) because "electrical transmission systems usually respond to sounds in a manner that differs from the ear's response in a number of important ways. Those differences that are probably most relevant to the present problem are amplitude and directional response" (p. 467). The results of the experiments of this study led to the following conclusions:

1. Stimulation of the face and other exposed areas of the skin by "air-" and sound waves is neither a *necessary* nor a *sufficient* condition of the perception of obstacles by our Subjects.
2. Stimulation of the skin by reflected

breath is neither a *necessary* condition nor, as far as "facial pressure" is concerned, a *sufficient* condition for the "final appraisals" by our Subjects.

3. The pressure theory of the "obstacle sense," insofar as it applies to the face and other exposed areas of the skin, is untenable.

4. Aural stimulation is both a *necessary* and a *sufficient* condition for the perception of obstacles by our Subjects (p. 182–183).

Worchel and Dallenbach (1947) followed up the first study with an investigation on the perception of obstacles by the deaf-blind. In it they wanted to determine whether the aural mechanisms found to be responsible for obstacle perception are auditory or cutaneous, or whether both were involved. They found that their deaf-blind subjects did not possess the obstacle sense and were incapable of learning it and that stimulation of the cutaneous surfaces of the external ears (meatuses and tympanums) is not sufficient to the perception of obstacles. They concluded that the pressure theory is untenable and that audition was confirmed as the aural mechanism responsible for the perception of obstacles by the blind. This study still left open the question of whether intensity (loudness) or frequency (pitch) is the auditory dimension involved. This question was the subject of experiments reported by Cotzin and Dallenbach (1950). In preliminary experiments it was established that continuous sounds are as adequate as intermittent sounds to the perception of obstacles under like conditions. The main experiments indicated conclusively that changes in loudness are neither a necessary nor a sufficient condition for the perception of obstacles. Changes in pitch were established both as a necessary and a sufficient condition for the perception of obstacles and considered a result of the

Doppler effect (the phenomenon in which the pitch of a sound rises when the source of the sound approaches the listener). It was also established that at normal walking speed high frequencies of approximately 10,000 cycles and above are necessary, whereas frequencies of about 8,000 cycles and below are insufficient for obstacle perception. The authors recognize that there still remains an unsolved problem: the relation of wave length and velocity of movement to distance at which obstacles are perceived.

McCarthy and Worchel (1954) experimented with an unusually capable blind boy who rode his bicycle over a course on which two movable obstacles had been placed. When riding as swiftly as he could, he was able to avoid obstacles almost as well as in the slow trial runs. This demonstrates that higher speeds do not impair object perception, a finding which lends support to the Doppler shift theory.

The Cornell experiments were repeated outdoors by Ammons, Worchel and Dallenbach (1953) under conditions more nearly approximating everyday situations where cues other than auditory ones could be utilized. Though no single condition was found necessary for obstacle perception, the results confirmed auditory cues as the most reliable, accurate, and universal ones. Other sensory cues such as cutaneous, olfactory, and temperature were utilized when auditory cues were not available.

Worchel, Mauney, and Andrew (1950) examined the distribution of the ability to perceive an obstacle under usual outdoor conditions among thirty-four blind students. The study indicated large individual differences in the "first perceptions" and consistency in the "final appraisals" in those who had the obstacle sense. It was found that seven of the thirty-four subjects did not possess the obstacle sense. Worchel and Mauney (1951) used these seven failures in another study to determine the effect of practice on the perception of obstacles. These seven subjects were given 210 training trials under conditions favorable for learning. The tests after the practice showed that these subjects had developed the ability to perceive obstacles to an extent equal to that possessed by experienced subjects. The authors conclude (p. 176) that "a systematic course in perceptual recognition and detection of objects for the blind may be of considerable aid and shorten the period of trial-and-error procedure usually adopted by the blind."

There is one further study dealing with a problem in this area. The tendency to veer in one direction, when attempting to walk straight, has been ascertained for blindfolded seeing subjects. Rouse and Worchel (1955) confirmed this also for the blind. This tendency is consistent in direction for the same subject, with most subjects veering to the right. Removal of auditory cues and elimination of facial tactile cues does not increase veering tendency.

Cratty (1968) and staff members of the Perceptual-Motor Learning Laboratory at the University of California, Los Angeles, have conducted basic investigations on perceptual-motor behavior, some of them with reference to blind children. An analysis of their data revealed the following details: in the absence of auditory clues, it is predictable that a blind individual will veer about 36 degrees of angular rotation per 100 feet of forward progress; the blind are more sensitive to decline than to incline, or to left-right tilt in their walking surfaces; congenitally blind adolescents are more sensitive to gradients and veer less than the older adventitiously blinded;

the longer an individual has been blind the less he will tend to veer and the more accurately he can detect gradients; tactually inspecting bent wires, indicating the amount and direction of an individual's veering, can significantly reduce his veering tendency; a blind individual using the presently advocated cane techniques can successfully detect the curvature of a curb if it has a radius of at least five feet. These and other of their findings have important implications for mobility training. Cratty et al. (1968), as well as Harris (1967), found that blind individuals with high anxiety walked slower and veered about twice as much as relaxed blind subjects do.

Training normal hearing to greater usefulness was the aim of experiments carried out by Norton (1960) at the Cleveland Society for the Blind. Binaural tape-recordings were made with two microphones located at the normal two-ear distance, picking up the sounds that were played back through earphones, one to each ear. In one part of the training situation, recordings of various sounds were offered for the purpose of locating and identifying these sounds. In another part, "passive listening" was employed in which the trainee responded verbally to situations recorded under active travel conditions. This arrangement permitted him to concentrate fully on various aspects of his changing environment. A manual has been published describing the project and the training procedures.

In search for a guidance device the Haskins' Laboratories examined the problem of the obstacle sense. Jerome and Proshansky (1950) found certain deficiencies in the experiments conducted in the past. They used four blind subjects in their own experiments. In a "differentiation test" the blind person's ability to differentiate between the presence and absence of objects in his immediate environment was examined. It showed that they all possessed an obstacle sense operating with various degrees of accuracy at different distances. With the increase of distance between the subject and the test object, a regular decrease in obstacle perception occurred, but marked individual differences were noted. The subsequent "avoidance test" was designed to test the more complicated task of avoiding obstacles while attempting to circulate among them either with or without aural obstruction. Real obstacles and symbolic obstacles were used and rotated on an obstacle course through which the subject had to make his way without contacting any of the objects. Contacting a real object and passing so close to a symbolic object that it would have been touched were the criteria used. If a subject had no obstacle sense, he should have made as many errors on real obstacles as on symbolic ones; if aural cues were not necessary, he should have made as many errors on real obstacles with ears unobstructed as with ears obstructed. There was a reliable difference between scores on real and symbolic obstacles when no sensory obstruction was used. Also, on real objects, the difference between aural obstruction and no obstruction was reliable. However, the differences between errors on real and symbolic objects were negligible with aural obstruction. These data indicate that the avoidance of obstacles depends upon aural sensations, and the authors conclude:

> . . . because these studies were carried out in a sheltered area from which air currents and abrupt temperature changes were almost completely eliminated, the results must be interpreted as indicating that, when other sources of information have been excluded, the blind person is capable of avoiding obstacles on the basis of aural cues alone (p. 473).

The study reported further on testing procedures for the evaluation of obstacle avoidance devices.

Griffin (1958) reviewed the literature on orientation and made challenging suggestions for future research in this field. He asks the question whether we can learn from the bats and recommends that we first study "the language of audible echoes" and also explore "what kinds of sound field will produce the most information and the most readily recognized echoes." He recommends research to determine the type of sounds that are most effective in echolocation, as for instance, the frequency-modulated pulses used by certain types of bats. "Any human adaptation of echolocation would necessarily require that the blind man generate clearly audible sounds, probably a series of clicks" (p. 320). Blind people, he believes, will not want to make themselves conspicuous unless they can secure real independence in mobility by it. He warns of continuing hasty attempts to construct portable guidance devices and recommends instead a more patient program of basic research.

Although it is recognized that obstacle perception as such is only one factor influencing a person's mobility, the other factors have received little attention and almost no scientific investigation. There is, for instance, no study available that would show the effects of the restriction in mobility on the personality formation of the blind or on his relations to others on whom he must frequently depend in order to get about. It is obvious that blind individuals are from infancy restricted in their ability to expose themselves to experiences as compared with nonhandicapped individuals. Because blindness imposes limitations in the perceptual area, this added restriction due to limited mobility calls for special instructional methods if it is to be compensated for at least partially. Lowenfeld (1950*b,* pp. 94–96) discussed the effects of this restriction and noted that differences in mobility show themselves already among young blind children. Some hardly dare to step out into unfamiliar grounds and hesitate even in familiar surroundings, whereas others show a surprising facility in getting about. While the blind child is very young, he leaves his environment only when accompanied by others. When he gets older and must adjust to living in the world at large, his restriction in mobility becomes a factor of major importance. If he has not been encouraged to develop his ability to move about and has not achieved a reasonably degree of independence in it, his whole success may be jeopardized. He may, in the extreme case, not only take help for granted but may develop a generalized expectancy of help characteristic of regression. He may also develop a resentment against his dependency and project this resentment toward the seeing society as a whole. Educators of the blind are familiar with these reactions although they have not been the subject of systematic studies.

Many have recognized that the task of getting about results in increased nervous strain for the blind person. Cutsforth (1951) also stressed the unavoidable injury to the ego of the blind person as result of his position of dependency in locomotion:

Since the blind live in a world of the seeing, it is necessary to procure visual aid and information. Whether this be volunteered or solicited, it represents a curtailment of self-expression and is registered emotionally as such. Thus, the act of asking a stranger the name of an approaching street car is an admission of inferiority for which there must be compensation. And the though - ful, kind-hearted guide through a traffic jam must be pleasantly thanked for his assistance— society demands it—while the emotions demand that he be cursed or struck down with the cane (p. 73).

Orientation and Locomotion

Lowenfeld (1950*b* pp. 94–96) has pointed out that mobility has two components: mental orientation and physical locomotion. Mental orientation has been defined as the "ability of an individual to recognize his surroundings and their temporal or spatial relations to himself" (*Dictionary of Psychology,* 1934, p. 189), and locomotion as "the movement of an organism from place to place by means of its organic mechanism" (p. 154). Both functions are necessary for mobility but are of a different nature. In the task of orientation, the blind person must keep in his mind a "mental map" and relate himself to it while he is moving toward his intended destination. If he is experienced, he will rely upon various clues coming to him from his environment, as for instance, the audible traffic signal at a certain corner, the change in ground level at a certain point, the air current indicating open space, and of course all kinds of odor sensations. He also will make use of his "muscular memory," which Villey (1930) discussed and described as follows:

It is by it that, without counting the steps and without looking at them, we know that we have reached the top of our staircase. Our legs have registered, in a way, the number of contractions they had to make. Not only can this muscular memory retain very well the height of a staircase, but also the dimensions of a room and the distance between two walls. It instigates the blind man to repeat, with perfect regularity, the movements that have become habitual to him (p. 126).

He also employs his time sense in tracing

his position on the mental map. The more familiar he becomes with his route, the more mechanically he recognizes his surroundings and his own relation to them. But in order to move about safely and in a goal-directed way, the blind person must also be able to follow a safe path and to avoid harmful obstacles. In doing this he makes use of all his senses. His sense of hearing is constantly active in observing all kinds of sounds, including echoes; he interprets odors in relation to their various sources; he notices changes of temperature and air currents and what they indicate; his feet follow the surface of the ground and notice changes in it; he observes distances, not by counting steps but in terms of time, movement, and sound. Thus any observation he can make and any clue he can obtain is interpreted for the purpose of locomotion as well as orientation. Obstacle perception as such also has its important place, although it cannot be employed effectively in many situations; for example, in moving in crowded or noisy places, or under unfavorable weather conditions, when rain and winds drown out and snow deadens the necessary perceptions.

In the task of getting about, blind persons have always relied upon human assistance. They also have made use of the cane and, lately, of dog guides. Human assistance can take over both factors of mobility, locomotion as well as orientation. The cane, which functions as a lengthening touch organ or feeler indicates to the blind person, if skillfully used, an obstacle-free spot where he may put his foot. The dog guide indicates an obstacle-free space into which the blind person may safely move. Both cane and dog guide leave the task of orientation to their user.

Educators and rehabilitation personnel are giving increased attention to mobility training as an essential part of a blind individual's adjustment. Training in mobility under all kinds of conditions and in the use of the cane are included in many school and rehabilitation programs. Although no experimental evidence of the superiority of any method of cane travel is available, practical usage has confirmed the superiority of the Hoover technique of cane travel, which was developed in the rehabilitation program for war-blinded servicemen. According to this technique, the cane is used in a pendulumlike scanning motion to make certain that the place where the foot will be moving is free of obstacles. A white cane, which is longer than the usual cane—it should reach to the breastbone of the user—is required. Techniques to meet various situational demands have been worked out, and training in the use of the cane proceeds according to a set course of study.

Mobility training specialists stress the importance of early childhood experiences in this area. Hapeman (1967) discussed a framework of needed basic concepts, which, though closely dependent upon each other, can be divided into three main classes: (1) concepts needed for understanding the true nature of the environment (body-image, nature of objects, nature of fixed, moveable, and moving objects, nature of terrain, nature of sounds and odors); (2) concepts needed for achieving and maintaining orientation (path of moving objects, positions of objects in space, directions, sound localization); (3) concepts needed for efficient mobility (distance and time, following a sequence of fixed objects, turning, detouring, moving with and against moving objects). He stressed the importance of concrete learning and that, though exactness of many of the concepts is not necessary, awareness of them is important.

A number of articles have appeared that

BERTHOLD LOWENFELD

describe and discuss mobility training from the preschool level through school age (Ball, 1964; Curriculum Guide, 1966; Eichorn and Vigaroso, 1967; Hartong, 1968; Johnson and Gilson, 1967; and Wilson, 1967).

The importance of posture for mobility, as a cause for as well as an effect of its success, was extensively discussed by Siegel (1966).

Finestone, Lukoff, and Whiteman (1960) completed a study dealing with the demand for dog guides and included in it a chapter "Aspects of the Travel Adjustment of Blind Persons." Their findings indicate that "human guide users represent minimal travel performance, cane travelers achieve a midway position well above human guide users, while dog guide users are in turn markedly above both groups."

Worchel (1951) investigated space perception and orientation in the blind by three experiments for which he used thirty-three totally blind students and a matched group of sighted students. In the first experiment, he wanted to determine the role of visualization in tactual form perception. He used simple geometrical blocks and found that in reproductions by drawing and in verbal descriptions, sighted subjects were significantly better than the blind, and accidentally blinded subjects were significantly better than the congenitally blind. He interprets this as indicating that touch alone is not as efficient in the perception of tactual forms as touch aided by visual images. However, in the test on form recognition, in which the subjects had to select among four blocks one that was similar in shape to the stimulus block, the blind and sighted did equally well. In this test, visualization was not required. The author indicates that the tests were done with simple forms and that more complicated ones may show differ-

ent results. Similar, more recent experiments by Ewart and Carp (1963) confirm Worchel's findings that visual imagery is not a critical factor in the form recognition of various shapes of blocks. The second experiment of Worchel's study required the imaginal construction of a total form after parts of the form had been perceived by touch. The results indicated again that "the use of visual imagery is of definite aid to the sighted and to the accidentally blinded in imaginally manipulating tactual perceptions" (p. 20). It is interesting to note that the ellipse and circle were easiest recognized after tactual perception of parts of them, whereas the semicircle was most difficult. The third experiment is the one dealing directly with the problem of spatial orientation and with the role of visualization in it. The subjects were led along two sides of eight different-sized, right isosceles triangles and asked to return without guidance via the hypotenuse to the starting point, or they were led along the hypotenuse path and asked to return without guidance along the two legs of the triangle. The experiments were made in an open area, where auditory cues gave no undue advantage to the blind. The sighted subjects were significantly superior to the blind, and there was no difference between the accidentally and the congenitally blinded. The results indicated that the blind missed the initial position because of angular deviations rather than by errors in estimating the distance. Introspective reports given by some of the subjects indicated that the blind and the sighted used time in estimating distances. The sighted used visual imagery in determining direction. The study demonstrates the importance of visual imagery in orientation and confirms that besides auditory cues time assists the blind in distance orientation.

Worchel's findings that, in the performances which he tested, the sighted were superior to the accidentally blind and to the congenitally blind, were confirmed by Drever (1955) in experiments using spatial tests. His findings also suggest the existence of certain basic skills built up through the early years, and that later learning has little effect.

Congenitally blind children and a group of seeing children, matched in age, sex, and IQ, were compared in their ability to manipulate themselves and objects in space in a study by Hunter (1964). The blind group as compared with the seeing group showed, in general, lower accomplishments in their ability to utilize various types of stimuli involved in spatial orientation. The author concludes that congenital blindness appears to be associated with subtle but significant impairment.

Gratty and Sams (1968, p. 2) started their study on the body-image of blind children with the assumption "that to help a blind child grasp some of the simpler concepts of his spatial world, one must first help him find out about the space nearest him and, indeed, to find out about himself." A body-image survey form was administered to ninety-one children at the Frances Blend School for the Blind in Los Angeles. The children were asked to identify planes of the body (such as front, back, and so forth) and body parts. They were also scored for making accurate movements of the body, discrimination between left-right dimensions of the body, and between the left and right of the tester and of objects. Based on mean scores of responses, the order of difficulties from easiest to most difficult was: body parts, body movements, body planes, laterality, and directionality. Intercorrelations, comparisons of scores of subgroups, of scores

by age, and other statistical details were supplied. The authors discussed the educational implications of their findings and developed a training sequence for the spatial education of blind children, which they consider essential, particularly for mobility instruction.

Geographic orientation in the blind was the topic of another study in which Worchel cooperated with McReynolds (1951). In their geographic orientation tests the congenitally blind did as well as the accidentally blind, and degree of blindness, etiology, age at blindness, age, IQ, and sex were not significant factors in geographic orientation. They conclude that "visual imagery does not seem necessary to geographic orientation."

Garry and Ascarelli (1960) conducted training experiments in orientation and spatial organization with a group of congenitally blind "good" and "poor" performers. They reported positive effects of training in these skills, though the trained "poor" performers did not achieve the level of the untrained "good" performers.

Maze tests have been used to determine learning ability and evaluate intelligence. Studies by Koch and Ufkess (1926), Knotts and Miles (1929), and Merry and Merry (1934) showed that the stylus maze is more difficult for the blind than for the seeing, whereas the high-relief finger maze is less difficult for both groups, that the ability to learn the maze correlated higher with mental age than with chronological age, and that the finger maze is a valuable supplement in testing the intelligence of blind children. There is no agreement concerning the superior or inferior maze-learning ability of the blind as compared with the seeing. Duncan (1934) found that past visual experience influenced success in maze learning more than the actual degree of sight present and also that those who had perfect vision for at least a year seemed to be the most successful ones in learning the maze. She also observed that fifteen of the blind group of fifty-nine failed to draw square corners in reproducing the maze and that the greatest degree of vision among these fifteen was "finger perception." Only two of the thirty sighted subjects failed to draw square corners. This observation tends to support the Worchel findings concerning the difficulty of directional orientation without visualization. MacFarland (1952) was interested in observing in a maze-learning situation the methods used by blind subjects who were visually oriented. He found that tactual methods had more lasting effect than visual orientation, that motivation affected the degree of learning, and that blind persons seemed more motivated than the others. The method of solution used by blind persons was different from that of the other groups.

They worked slowly and carefully in the first trials, exploring every part of the maze; then they began to eliminate errors systematically. It was apparent that this group employed an attack based at least in part on "visualization" (ultimate construction of a mental image of the entire board) plus kinesthetic memory (p. 262).

This ability to construct a mental image of an object or situation as a result of successive observations of parts of it seems to be a decisive factor. Its importance is also stressed by Lowenfeld (1939, pp. 115–124) in his research on the drawings of partially blind children and on the modeling of the blind and the deaf-blind.

Two important distinctions were added by a study on maze learning by Berg and Worchel (1956). They added to the visual and tactual-kinesthetic factors, verbalization as an aid in maze learning and also

concluded that different mazes call for the use of different sensory processes. They used a multiple U maze, which was held to be a motor and visual maze, and a unidirectional X maze, which was held to require verbalization for its mastery. The subjects were twenty-eight totally blind, twenty-eight deaf, and twenty-eight normal children, matched on the basis of age, sex, IQ, and age at the onset of the sensory loss. On the U maze they found the normals and blind equal, and each surpassing the deaf, suggesting that verbalization plays a significant role in the mastery of this kind of maze. On the X maze, normals performed better than the blind and they in turn better than the deaf. This is interpreted as indicating that although verbalization is important, visualization is also an aid in the learning of this kind of maze.

PERSONALITY AND SOCIAL FACTORS

Personality is the psychophysical organization of the individual as modified by his life experiences and this includes hereditary as well as environmental factors. The child who is congenitally blind experiences the world in his own way, which is different from that of most other children, and must also cope with special difficulties in getting about. His personality is affected by these differences, and it can be assumed that, by reason of his handicap, he is more likely to be under nervous strain and to harbor feelings of insecurity and frustration. But before discussing the findings concerning the effects of blindness on the individual, another source of possible conflicts must be considered, that is, the attitudes toward blindness and the blind.

The Influence of Environmental Attitudes

The attitudes of the public toward the blind have been discussed in many articles, and practically all authors of books dealing with the blind felt called upon to make some statements about this topic. Barker *et al.* (1953) have reviewed publications on attitudes toward the blind and found (p. 276) that "there is almost universal agreement among the blind and those who work with them that blind persons are commonly perceived to be helpless and dependent and are frequently placed in underprivileged social situations."

Rusalem (1950) supplied one of the first experimental studies on this problem. One hundred and thirty graduate students in a social psychology class were given a questionnaire listing twenty physical, fourteen sociological, and twenty-six psychological traits allegedly characteristic of the blind. The answers indicate the following primary clusters of identifying characteristics: physical—carry canes, use guide dogs, wear dark glasses, have lack of facial expression; sociological—attend separate schools, rarely work in industry, are economically dependent; psychological—have very great sense of touch, have keen hearing, have better than average memory. These on the whole favorable responses do not support the negative attitudes generally assumed to be operative toward the blind. The fifty-nine subjects who had had contact with visually handicapped individuals did not significantly differ in their responses from those without previous contact with the blind. Rusalem recognizes a number of factors which limit his findings, such as a biased and exceptional group of subjects, the possibility that a list of items does not give opportunity for free expression of attitudes, and

that the consciously selected items may not be significant for the unconscious tendencies. He calls attention (p. 287) to "the urgent need for highly organized social psychological research into the dynamics of attitudes towards the blind" and suggests that "these attitudes are highly complex and may never be explained in terms of a single simple hypothesis."

Chevigny and Braverman (1950) discuss at length the attitudes of the public toward the blind and of those in work with the blind. They call attention to the fact that the blind are a minority group, and that while the content of the set of ideas about the blind may be different from that entertained about other minorities, the manner of operation is the same. They examine the underlying reasons for the particular attitudes toward blindness and the blind in psychoanalytic terms and attempt to give an explanation of the adjustment and reorganization process required in meeting those ideas about blindness that form the constant in the social environment.

Attitudes Toward Blindness (1951) contains three papers representing various fields of learning. The first deals with the problem from the point of view of the psychiatrist (Schauer), the second considers the cultural-sociological aspects (Himes), and the third presents the approach of the clinical psychologist (Braverman).

The minority status of the blind and other attitudinal problems toward blindness were explored in two important studies. Gowman (1957) examined the sociological position of the war blind in American social structure, and Lukoff and Whiteman (1961) published a preliminary report of their experimental research on attitudes toward blindness. The latter research, as many others, was supported by a grant from the Federal Office of Vocational Rehabilitation. Because both studies, though dealing with problems of the adult blind, have in some parts implications for the status of blind youth, their pertinent results will be reviewed here.

Gowman (1957, pp. 64–96) reports on a questionnaire study exploring attitudes of high school seniors toward blindness. When asked to rank five potential injuries as to their impact upon themselves and their prospective mate, four-fifths of them placed blindness for themselves in the first position. There is greater variability concerning the mate, but blindness is still considered the most difficult disability to accept. Middle-class males were the only ones who assigned blindness to the second position as far as its impact on their mate is concerned. The questionnaire also included thirteen interpersonal situations to which alternative responses had to be selected and a series of agree-disagree questions concerning the blind. Lower class subjects showed a tendency to react to blindness by focusing on assumed limitations and by stereotypical conceptions. Middle-class subjects related more to the visually disabled because of an apparent sophistication and their middle-class humanitarian values.

Lukoff and Whiteman (1961) investigated the attitudes of sighted persons toward blindness by questioning three major groups: graduate social work students, undergraduate college students, and a group of middle- and low-income housing inhabitants. Their findings confirm the importance of environmental attitudes for the kind of adaptation the blind person makes to his handicap. Family members and sighted friends of the blind person are most likely to influence his attitudes of independence. Their findings suggest four relatively independent components of sighted people's perception of the blind: (1) the degree to which sighted persons perceive blindness as personally frustrating; (2) the conception of blindness as distinct from attitudes toward blind people; (3) readiness to interact with blind people; and (4) differences in the degree of feelings among the sighted in thinking about or interacting with blind people. The question of how blind people perceive the sighted was examined by an analysis of data derived from a sample of 500 blind individuals in New York State. A majority of them believe that sighted people have little understanding of the blind, that they are surprised if a blind person can do something, that they consider blind people braver than the average sighted, and that most sighted people pity the blind. Members of the blind sample also tended to agree that they expect favored treatment in regard to pensions and job opportunities. Their interaction with sighted people is characterized by a pattern of submissiveness.

The authors summarize the reciprocal perceptions of the blind and sighted groups as follows: blind people's perception of the sighted is realistic in considering them as naïve, lacking understanding of blind people, and as overly pitying—all of which they are; it is unrealistic in ascribing to the sighted both negative and positive stereotyping attitudes which they do not have, since almost half of them contended that blind people are capable of doing just about everything without help.

Parents are the most important persons in the social environment of the child and their attitudes profoundly affect his life. They also reflect in some way those of the general public of which the parents are a part. Sommers (1944) has made a thorough study of "some of the factors conditioning the behavior and the personality of the adolescent blind" and has attempted "to find out whether there exists a relationship between parental attitudes and actions and the blind child's behavior pattern and attitude toward his handicap" (p. 1). She obtained her results by three different methods: (1) the California Test of Personality was administered to 143 adolescent blind; (2) a questionnaire especially designed for blind children was answered by 120 of the adolescent blind subjects and another questionnaire by 72 of the parents of these subjects; (3) controlled interviews were conducted with 50 blind subjects and their parents.

So far as the California Test of Personality is concerned, Sommers concluded that this test, like other personality tests designed for the seeing, does not adequately measure the personal and social adjustment of this group. A test should be designed, especially for use with the blind, which would evaluate the effects of blindness in relation to the total growth pattern and total social environment of the blind individual. Barker *et al.* (1953, p. 282) agreed with Sommers in questioning the general validity of personality inventories in research with the blind. The life situations of the blind differ greatly from those of the groups used in standardizing the inventories, and also many items in such inventories are of "different interpretive significance" for persons with normal sight and for those who are blind. They suggested detailed item analysis of personality inventories that may lead to hypotheses for further investigation.

The questionnaires revealed a wide variety of attitudes and feelings among the visually handicapped. They indicated that emotional disturbances and maladjustments result more frequently from the conditions and social attitudes of the blind person's environment than from the sensory handicap itself. The lack of unifor-

mity in the reactions also disproves any assumption that blindness by itself can be the dominant cause of behavior deviations. The blind children were most aware of their handicap in such social situations as when people refer to their handicap or feel sorry for them or try to help too much; at sports and games requiring sight; when going to or eating at a strange place; when crossing streets, traveling, or window-shopping. The question "What do you feel one misses most by being unable to see?" brought replies clustering around the following activities: sports, games, car driving, traveling; enjoyment of sights of nature; facial expressions; movies, exhibitions, reading material; independence; normal home life, social life in general. More blind than seeing children indicated that they worried. Three times as many blind as seeing children worried about their own future and the future of the world (finding a job, financial insecurity, and the like). But schoolwork, tests, and teachers were the main worries of both blind and seeing children.

The interviews with the parents disclosed that:

> Persistent feelings of frustration on the part of the parent seemed to arise from a sense of unfulfillment resulting from the fact that the birth of a child with a handicap as apparent as blindness failed to meet the concept of the kind of child which the mother had expected; while the contradiction between maternal devotion and an irrepressible sense of repulsion caused by the blindness seemed to create feelings of irreconcilable conflict (p. 102).

The case studies indicated four different reasons why parents manifest conflicts in their relationship with their handicapped child: (1) blindness is considered as a symbol of punishment, and parents look upon their blind child as a visitation of divine disapproval; (2) fear of being suspected of having a social disease; (3) feelings of guilt due to transgression of the moral or social code or to negligence; resentment of the state of pregnancy, attempted abortion, marital discord, and the like may be the reasons for these feelings; (4) blindness in a child is considered a personal disgrace to the parents.

The ways in which the parents reacted to the handicap of their children fell into five fairly distinct categories: acceptance of the child and his handicap, denial reaction, overprotectiveness, disguised rejection, and overt rejection.

Sommers stressed that sharp lines of demarcation cannot be drawn and that some overlapping of attitudes is to be expected. Acceptance of the child and denial reaction are considered positive attitudes because they permit the child to grow, to develop, and to participate. Overprotection and disguised and overt rejection are negative attitudes that interfere with or stunt the child's growth. Although the number of parents reported in Sommers' study is too small to permit any generalization in regard to the distribution of parental attitudes, it is of some interest to know that out of the fifty parents, nine showed acceptance, four denial reactions, thirteen overprotectiveness, sixteen disguised rejection, and eight overt rejection.

Important for the general formation of attitudes toward a blind child is the following statement that Sommers made in connection with parents:

The meaning the child's handicap held for his parents, especially his mother, the intensity of her emotional reactions, and the kind of adjustment she was able to make seemed to depend largely on the psychological makeup of the individual parent, her marital relationships, and

her own personal and social adjustment to life (p. 105).

It is interesting to note that Sommers' five types of parental attitudes resemble very closely those that Kanner (1957, pp. 117–132) distinguishes as operative for children in general: acceptance, perfectionism, non-rejecting overprotection, rejection, overt hostility, and neglect. The category of perfectionism closely resembles Sommers' denial reaction.

The adjustive behavior of the blind adolescents studied by Sommers was closely related to the parental reactions and showed the following six patterns: wholesome compensatory reactions, hypercompensatory reactions, denial reactions, defensive reactions, withdrawal reactions, and nonadjustive behavior reactions.

Sommers considers only the last-mentioned behavior as strictly nonadjustive. So far as the individual is concerned, the other reactions reduce emotional tension and assist him to adjust to his environment although they may not always be approved socially. Even withdrawal assists the individual in making some kind of adjustment to his disability. Although in general one particular adjustment mechanism is predominant, in some instances, several modes of adjustment were used.

Sommers also studies the relationship between the child's adjustment and parental attitudes as rated by a series of twelve evaluation scales covering the physical, cultural, and emotional environment of the home, the parental attitudes toward the child, and the child's attitude and reactions. The statistical data presented by Sommers only complement her qualitative findings and insightful analysis.

Sommers warns against directly attacking a specific personality maladjustment in a handicapped child, because this means merely to battle against the symptoms and not to attack the underlying trouble. According to the findings of her study,

The answer to the problem of how to effect a more satisfactory development in the personality of handicapped children would seem to lie in building up in the parents of these children wholesome attitudes toward the handicap, as well as in the education and guidance of the child himself (p. 105).

In this she finds herself in agreement with others who have studied the emotional problems of physically handicapped children.

Meyerson (1953) pointed out that the Sommers study, though most valuable, has certain weaknesses, particularly in its lack of statistical support. He points to the urgent need for additional research along similar lines. Cowen *et al.* (1961) carries forward our research efforts in this area. This volume will be discussed later because its main emphasis is on personality adjustment, though it deals in some parts with parental attitudes.

The motor performance of visually handicapped children was studied by Buell (1950), who compared scores of the blind, of the visually handicapped, and of the seeing in such activities as track and field, the Iowa Brace Test, in running, jumping, throwing, and so on. Of the 865 pupils in this study, 309 had no useful vision and 556 were partially seeing; their ages ranged from ten to twenty years. Buell asked teachers and staff members of the schools to indicate those children whose parents appeared to overprotect them and found that 27 percent of the blind boys and 30 percent of the blind girls were considered overprotected, whereas only 13 percent of the partially seeing boys and 9

percent of the partially seeing girls were thus classified. Buell found that overprotective attitudes of parents influence performance in track and field events and in a stunt-type test in a significant way. Neglected children were found to perform normally in motor acts. He concluded (p. 59) that "as far as motor performance is concerned, parental neglect is to be preferred to overprotection." Therefore, "one cannot overemphasize the harm done to visually handicapped children by overprotective parents."

Although considerable research has been done on the attitudes of parents toward their visually handicapped children, the important problem of attitudes of professional workers toward the blind has until recently received only scant attention. Blank (1954) discussed from a psychoanalytic point of view the unconscious conflicts about blindness that may interfere with the professional worker's efforts in helping blind individuals. Among these conflicts are overidentification, subjective "blind spots" about blindness, unconscious sadistic trends, and erotic countertransference reactions. He recommends making psychoanalytic consultation available to case workers, teachers, and supervisory personnel but warns against considering psychoanalysis a panacea.

There are a few more recent studies available that deal with attitudes toward visually handicapped children as expressed in, for instance, prestige of and preference for teaching them, acceptance, and social distance. Jones and Gottfried (1966) studied the prestige attributed to teachers of exceptional children. Their findings indicate that teachers of the blind receive top ranking by practicing teachers and teachers of the mentally retarded, and high ranking by college students. In general, special education teaching carries higher prestige than regular class teaching.

In another study (Murphy, 1960) rating scales were administered to 309 teachers, special educators, principals, and other teaching personnel. They were asked to rank eight groups of exceptional children according to their preference for teaching them and according to how much they knew about them. In this study the visually handicapped were ranked least preferred for teaching (except for the delinquents) and also as those about whom the participants considered themselves least informed. However, special educators tended to rank the visually handicapped in a more favorable position. This result is interpreted as a moderate indication that favorable attitudes toward teaching a group are associated with knowledge about the group. Rusalem (1962) pointed out that the results of this study need to be considered with caution, because its participants were confronted with a forced-choice situation in which ranking distance was constant. Also, attitudes toward a specific group are not necessarily expressed by this ranking in which the teacher may indicate what he presumes to be the difficulties in working with this group. For instance, braille may be regarded as extremely difficult, and this may induce the teacher to assign a low-preference rank to the visually handicapped.

The question whether contact with blind persons plays a role in the formation of attitudes held toward them by sighted individuals has been inconclusively answered by past studies, according to Bateman (1964 a). In her own experiments conducted by giving a questionnaire to students in an introductory college course in special education, she found that personal contact with blind individuals does not appear to affect the attitudes of sighted adults, that information-giving

techniques improve expressed adult attitudes toward blind persons, and that one hour "identification with the familiar" (using cartoons in which blind children's abilities are positively related to the subject matter of the cartoon) was as effective in reducing negative attitudes as six traditional lecture-discussion hours plus textbook material. Bateman recognized that expressed opinions may not actually be indicative of attitudes toward blindness and that her study did not examine how durable the changes produced were. Also, college students are not necessarily representative of the general public. Therefore, further studies are needed in this area.

In another study (Wyder, Wilson, and Frumkin, 1967) the hypothesis that the amount of positive knowledge an individual possesses about blindness is directly related to the positiveness of his attitudes toward blindness was tested by administering the Wright-Remmers Handicap Problems Inventory to sixty-four teachers. This inventory is a checklist of 280 items dealing with the impact of disability on personal, family, social, and vocational adjustments. Only in the area of family adjustment did the positively informed group of teachers perceive the blind as significantly less handicapped than did the uninformed group of teachers. There were no significant differences in the perceptions of personal, social, and vocational adjustments by the two groups. The Handicap Problems Inventory used 100 disabled persons as its normative group. These handicapped people viewed blindness significantly more positively than the nondisabled teachers in this study, regardless of the amount of positive information about blindness which they possessed.

Bateman (1962) also investigated sighted children's perception of the abilities of blind children. She used a fifty-item questionnaire listing activities that sighted children can perform with a sample of 232 sighted children, about one-half of whom were acquainted and attended public school with blind children, whereas the other one-half had never known a blind child. She found that subjects who had known blind children appraised blind children's abilities more positively and increasingly so with the number of blind children known; positiveness of appraisal increased with grade levels, particularly in grades three through six; and urban children were more positive in their appraisals than rural children.

The acceptability of twelve groups of exceptional persons and nonexceptional persons by high school students was examined by Jones, Gottfried, and Owens (1966) in terms of scaled social distance in seven interpersonal situations. Their findings indicated that the average and gifted are ranked as the most acceptable groups in most of the situations, whereas the severely mentally retarded are placed at the opposite end of the acceptance continuum of the distance scale. Those with mild incapacitations, among them the partially seeing, are generally higher on the acceptance scale. The blind rank, in general, in the lower or middle section of the acceptance continuum, depending upon the interpersonal situation.

Steinzor published three articles dealing with attitudes toward visually handicapped children and toward blindness that report parts of a demonstration project conducted at the Jewish Guild for the Blind in New York with a grant from the National Institute of Mental Health. In the study "School Peers of Visually Handicapped Children" (1966a), she reported the results of interviews with 108 boys and girls after they completed four

sets of stories dealing with various interpersonal relations in which either sighted or blind individuals were involved. On the elementary school level, lowest attitudes of cooperation and highest attitudes of rejection were found with those classmates who were for the first time in classes with blind children. Attitudes improved as children had more classroom experiences with blind children. Most positive attitudes were found in those sighted children who had been with blind children before and who were presently in other classes. The author interprets this as a reaction of "shock at first encounter" and favorable attitudes *post factum*. In junior high school, attitudes of cooperation toward blind students were positive and highest for those who attended classes with the blind. Attitudes of independence (respect for another person's needs without entering into cooperative activities) diminished under influence of contact and turned into attitudes of cooperation. The author concludes (1966a, p. 314): "According to these results, therefore, one can recommend, without reservation the full participation of visually handicapped adolescents in schools for the sighted."

In the article on attitudes of visually handicapped children toward their blindness, Steinzor (1966b) reported results of interviews with eight "normal" blind children in elementary school and with six in junior high school. The elementary pupils put strong emphasis on visual residues in terms of functions they can perform, with complete blindness having the connotation of a most negative stereotype; they wanted to find a common ground between themselves and the sighted, particularly in learning and in doing things; and their wishes and aspirations for the future were normal, though they did not always show an awareness of positions that could not

BERTHOLD LOWENFELD

be held by visually handicapped people. The junior high school students showed this awareness and also a "feeling of living in two separate worlds divided by a gap that could not be closed no matter how much good will one might have" (p. 310). They also felt that the sighted held attitudes of superiority and expressed the wish for respect and equality, though they recognized the need for interpretation of the sighted world to them. Most of these students, in contrast to those on the elementary level, mentioned the wish to have sight. The author concludes:

The ability to recognize their handicaps and to accept them, their aspirations to find a place in a world based on sight, their ability to identify themselves as persons rather than as blind, and the strength not to gloss over differences between sightedness and blindness seemed to be the main theme expressed by this group of young handicapped people. Their awareness of being blind was paralleled by their recognition of the necessity of adjusting to the sighted, their standards and their ways (p. 311).

Steinzor (1967) also published an article dealing with siblings of visually handicapped children. The exploratory study reported in this article deals with siblings of visually handicapped children, the latter having conditions complicated by intellectual and emotional disturbances. Therefore, it cannot be considered indicative of sibling reactions to "normal" blind children. Such a study is badly needed and should have high priority on any research program involving attitudes toward blind children.

One final point should be made concerning attitudes toward the blind—they are not something static but they are changing. Himes (1958) pointed this out and discussed some indications of this change, such as the growth of a new social consciousness, the change in agency programs, the emphasis on rehabilitation, and the impact of the actively oriented war blind. He states, (p. 334): "Viewed in broad perspective, change appears as a tendency to melt down and remould the traditional stereotypes of the blind." The effects of continued and improved research also help in promoting this change.

Effects on Personality

A contribution unique in its kind and in its influence was made by Cutsforth (1951) with his book *The Blind in School and Society*, which was originally published in 1933. Cutsforth's own insight into the problems of blindness, his training as a clinical psychologist, his knowledge of the literature concerning the blind, his interviews with blind children, and his case studies make the book a most valuable source of information about the psychological effects of blindness. Many research studies were written later which only confirmed what Cutsforth stated, although he was often unable to provide adequate scientific proof of his assumptions. Some of them did not or will not stand up under scientific scrutiny, due, to a certain degree, to the fact that under the influence of his own writings, conditions have changed so that they no longer support his suppositions. Cutsforth discusses the importance of the home environment for the preschool blind child, the problems that blindness creates in his acquisition of language, his confinement to stimulation through touch and sound, his egocentric trends, his verbal unreality, and the developmental retardation that may be a result of all these factors. He considers the reasons for verbalism in blind and deaf-blind children and holds teachers who imposed visual experiences upon children without sight responsible for it. He wants to have the blind child educated "into his own world of experience so that he may live in harmony with himself and his world, whether it be among the blind or the seeing" (p. 70). Cutsforth classified fantasies of the blind into three categories;

(1) Phantasies in which the individual eradicates the source of social annoyance; (2) phantasies in which the individual attains marked superiority or security; (3) phantasies in which the individual withdraws from the active situation in a surrender to a simple, regressive preoccupation, largely emotional in nature (p. 75).

In considering voice and speech and its value for the blind, he emphasizes the psychogenic character of many of their speech defects. In a chapter on emotional problems, he discusses false attitudes toward the blind and false attitudes adopted by the blind and denies that there is anything like a "world of darkness" for the blind. "The dark experiential world of the totally blind from birth consists of visual nothingness so far as its nature can be discovered" (p. 130). He also denies that the blind suffer because they cannot see or have a yearning for sight unless they adopt these attitudes under social pressure. He considers the fear of being watched an important factor in creating an emotional strain, particularly for pupils in schools for the blind, and believes that this phobia of being watched may persist long after the pupil has left the institution.

Cutsforth's book includes the only extensive treatment of sex behavior of the blind, on which information was and is quite meager and but partially understood. His basic assumption is that the blind child does not have as normal a sexual development as the seeing child. Because sexual growth takes place to the very limit

that the environment provides, the environmental conditions and attitudes determine to a large extent the blind child's sexual growth. He does not have the same expanding social or the same stimulating objective environment and is confined in a much greater degree to stimulations which the self provides. The problems of masturbation and of homosexuality are discussed, and the need for a larger heterosexual environment is stressed. Cutsforth is very critical of the practice of segregation of boys and girls in schools for the blind and wants it replaced by a social environment in which the opposite sex is included so that pupils of residential schools can achieve normal growth under normal conditions. In a separate chapter, personality problems in institutions for the blind are considered, and some of Cutsforth's observations in this area are still valid. In general it is Cutsforth's conviction (p. 2) that "blindness changes and utterly reorganizes the entire mental life of the individual," and that this reorganization, and its support or frustration, determines the influence blindness has on the development of the individual.

There are a few studies that deal with the influence of blindness on certain personality traits. Brown (1938, 1939) reported two studies in which he used 359 seeing high school seniors and 218 blind adolescents between the ages of sixteen and twenty-two. The Neymann-Kohlstedt Diagnostic Test for Introversion-Extroversion showed a higher incidence of introversion among blind girls than among blind boys—which did not seem to be true among the seeing. A comparison between blind and seeing boys gave the blind boys "a somewhat more 'extroverted' appearance." This was not indicated when the girls of both groups were compared. Brown believes that the differences re-

BERTHOLD LOWENFELD

vealed in the study are predominantly due to the effects of blindness, sex, and institutionalization. In the other study, Brown (1939) used the Clark Revision of the Thurstone Personality Schedule in which he changed item 15, "Do you cross the street to avoid meeting someone?" to "Do you try to avoid meeting certain people?" and eliminated for the blind group item 23, "If you see an accident does something keep you from giving help?" He found a higher incidence of "neurotic tendency" among the blind than among the seeing, and it was also higher among the girls than among the boys. There was a greater difference between the sexes in the blind group than in the seeing group. According to the results, the groups seemed to arrange themselves in order of decreasingly desirable adjustment as follows: seeing boys, blind boys, seeing girls, blind girls.

McAndrew (1948a,b) investigated the problem of rigidity in the deaf and the blind. She explained that she is using "a broad Lewinian-type concept of rigidity" and defined it as a lack of variability and adaptability which results in persistent repetition or continuation of an activity and interferes with the ability to adjust to small changes in a situation. Her groups of twenty-five deaf, twenty-five blind, and twenty-five normal individuals were equated for both chronological and mental age but not for institutionalization. She arranged three experiments in which the blind participated. The Satiation experiment revealed that the deaf and the blind are more rigid than the normal but that there were such large individual variations that the results may not represent real group differences. In the Level of Aspiration experiments, the records of the blind and normal were similar with reference to success, but the blind appeared slightly more sensitive to failure than the normal. The deaf appeared to be more rigid than the blind and normal groups. In the Restructuring by Classification experiment, in which she sought to determine the degree of social force needed to encourage a child to change his method of classification, all blind and normal subjects succeeded, but the blind required more trials than the normal. Of the deaf, only four of the twenty-five subjects solved the problem. She concludes:

All of the data suggest that the deaf and the blind have smaller life spaces than the normal, being partially isolated from the objective environments in which they live by the barrier qualities of their handicaps; and that they, therefore, develop less-differentiated and more rigid personalities (1948b, p. 77).

According to the results, the blind are more rigid than the normal; the deaf, more rigid than the blind and the normal. McAndrew used in her experiments children from two southern states. It would be interesting to find out whether repetition of these experiments with a more representative sample of blind and deaf children would show different results. The reasoning behind these experiments and their execution makes them very interesting and valuable contributions to the study of personality.

Jervis and Haslerud (1950) placed twenty blind adolescents, twenty blindfolded sighted adolescents, and twenty sighted adolescents in a masked experimental situation that induced frustration. The three groups met the same age, sex, mental, and emotional criteria. Because blindness frustrates the individual directly as well as indirectly, they wanted to determine whether there are different patterns of response to frustrations in any of the three groups and to find out if the reactions of the blind are due to inability to solve the problem or to the cumulative effects of blindness. In the frustrating situation of the experiment, the blind group reacted in a significantly different manner from the sighted group. The physiological reactions and verbal responses were recorded; quantitatively the blind exceeded the sighted in both significantly. In particular, they showed significantly more sighing and rapid and uneven respiration and significantly less flushing and biting tongue and lips than the sighted. In these reaction patterns, auditory and visual cues are of importance. The verbal responses of the blind were characterized by high intropunitiveness, whereas the sighted groups were highest in impunitive response. The blindfold did not change the reaction pattern of the sighted persons. The authors conclude:

The apparent volubility and large amount of overt emotional expression in the blind do not reduce tension because in an unhealthy and immature way they generally have intropunitive reference. The desirability of promoting more direct outlets for tensions would seem indicated in the education of the blind (p. 75).

Brieland (1950a, p. 102) gave the Bell Adjustment Inventory to eighty-four matched pairs of blind and seeing pupils, twelve to eighteen years old. The test items were recorded and played back. The blind students were significantly inferior in health, social and emotional adjustment, whereas the home adjustment did not show any significant difference.

A scale specifically designed to evaluate adjustment to blindness was developed by Fitting (1954). He interprets adjustment to blindness as including six areas: (1) morale, dealing with the individual's confidence in himself, his hopes, and his aspirations; (2) outlook toward sighted people, dealing with the individual's concept of others; (3) outlook on blindness, dealing with the individual and his concept of himself as a blind person; (4) family relationships, dealing with the attitudes toward members of the family in the home situation; (5) attitudes toward training, including the anticipated degree of success in adjustment training and outlook toward education in general; (6) occupational outlook, dealing with the individual's concept of himself as an employee, his expectations in an employment situation, and his feelings about expected concessions because of his disability. The scale includes 42 items that were standardized on a sample of 144 trainees in nine adjustment centers. Among other results, "the study indicated that there was a direct relationship between the amount of education, such as at a school for the blind, and the level of adjustment" (p. 73).

Land and Vineberg (1965) used the concept of locus of control as employed in the Bialer-Cromwell Children's Locus of Control Scale, which they applied to eighteen residential school blind children, eighteen public school blind children, and eighteen sighted children, matched according to certain criteria. Internal locus of control exists if an individual perceives himself as instrumental in the successful outcome of a situation; external locus of control means that an individual feels dependent upon external factors and perceives himself as ineffective. Differences based on mental age as well as differences between the blind and the sighted were found to be significant, with the blind scoring lower for internal control. The difference between the residential and public school group was found to be not significant. Also no significant correlation was found between the degree of blindness and the locus of control. The scale was found to be a valid instrument for the purposes of this study.

Many authors have considered increased anxiety as a personality characteristic of the blind, but no research has been undertaken on this problem. Hardy (1967) recognized (p. 51) that "a general anxiety scale could be less useful with the blind than an instrument constructed specifically for the blind." He constructed the Anxiety Scale for the Blind (1968a), consisting of seventy-eight items, and used it (1968b) with a sample of 122 "normal" blind children, thirteen to twenty-two years of age, in two residential schools. Taylor's Manifest Anxiety Scale was also administered to these students. The data showed that both anxiety scales measure about the same characteristics and are equally useful, at least with the group of students tested. The anxiety level of totally blind students and of those with relatively useful vision did not vary with age, whereas students with light perception and projection showed significantly higher anxiety test scores as their ages increased. There was a significant inverse relationship between verbal intelligence and anxiety scores but no significant relationship between sex and anxiety scores. This study reveals some facts concerning the correlation of anxiety and certain characteristics of blind students in residential schools. A comparative study between anxiety levels of blind and sighted students, in which blind students in residential as well as public schools are represented, is still a project for further research.

As noted before, tests for the personality assessment of the seeing are of questionable value when used with the blind. Recognizing this, Bauman, Platt, and Strauss (1963) developed the Adolescent Emotional Factors Inventory. Its final form is made up of ten subscales (sensitivity, somatic symptoms, social competency, attitudes of distrust, family adjustment, boy-girl adjustment, school adjustment, morale, attitudes toward blindness, validation), each consisting of roughly fifteen items. This scale has proven itself effective in clinical use. A comparison between adolescent students in residential schools and those in integrated classes in public schools shows significant differences between the mean scores of girls in these two types of school settings for seven of the subscales, whereas there were practically no differences of significance for the boys.

Bauman (1964) administered the Adolescent Emotional Factors Inventory to a group of 150 boys and girls attending residential schools and to an equal number attending integrated classes. Various differences were determined between boys and girls, between partially seeing and totally blind students, and between students from residential schools and integrated schools. For instance, the partially seeing students showed significantly higher anxiety and insecurity than the blind, and the residential school group indicated more anxiety and insecurity, more difficulties in relating to the home and parents, and more problems of social and emotional adjustment than the integrated school group. Bauman noted that further research is needed to determine whether the differences between the students attending the two different types of school setting are due to direct effects of the residential school environment, to the separation from the family, or to other socioeconomic differences.

Projective tests for use with the blind obviously cannot offer visual stimuli such as inkblots or drawings but must make use of stimulus situations that are either auditory, tactile-kinesthetic, or ideational-verbal. Lebo and Bruce (1960) published a then-current evaluative review of projective tests. For example, Wilmer and Husni (1953) have used an auditory projective test with blind children which presented a recorded variety of sound sequences. The Twitchell-Allen Three-Dimensional Apperception Test is a tactile-kinesthtic projection test that makes use of twenty-eight plastic pieces with ambiguous shapes. McAndrew (1950) used this test with blind, deaf, and normal children and concluded that it is "applicable to the blind but must be interpreted cautiously." The Rotter Incomplete Sentences Blank is an example of an ideational-verbal projective test. In this test parts of sentences are presented, and the person is asked to complete them in a way that expresses his own feelings. Dean (1957) used this test among others with blind persons and found that its value with the blind is more likely in the qualitative rather than in the quantitative evaluations.

The use of projective tests with the blind is still in an experimental stage. Frequently, new ones are devised rather than established ones applied and investigated. Lebo and Bruce (1960, p. 35) consider this a "dangerous manner."

Cholden (1958) mentioned three special preoccupations of the adolescent that make acceptance of blindness particularly difficult: (1) The importance of bodily attractiveness in the female, and masculine strength and independence in the male. These preoccupations are of course related to sexual fears which are accentuated in the blind adolescent; (2) The problems of developing independence in an adolescent who must accept certain dependencies which are characteristic for blindness; (3)

The exhibitionism accompanied with the desire for anonymity of the adolescent (p. 56).

Cole and Taboroff (1955) reported the successful therapy of a disturbed congenitally blind adolescent girl. They distinguish three categories of special problems of congenitally blind children: the cultural pressures that create a charged atmosphere in which the blind person must make his adjustment; the effects that blindness may have on personality and emotional development; and the problem of semantics of those blind from birth, since "their means of conceptualizing, their orientation, their perception of reality, may be different but also is poorly transmitted in a language manufactured by the seeing" (p. 630).

Special needs of the blind adolescent were discussed by Abel (1961). He needs to be understood and respected as an adolescent who is blind; because he cannot observe visually, he needs to have his questions answered honestly and specifically by people around him and by professional persons; he needs to be a participating member of his family and of his peer group; he needs to acquire an optimistic outlook toward his future; he needs expert instruction in independent modes of travel; and he needs educational facilities and special equipment based on good practice and sound research.

Lowenfeld (1959) examined some difficulties that blindness creates for the adolescent in the areas of sex curiosity, dating, mobility, and concern for the future. These difficulties may influence the blind adolescent's self-concept and his attitudes toward interpersonal relations but "may be simply different but no more severe or serious manifestations of the process of maturation which goes on in all adolescents" (p. 315).

Hooft and Heslinga (1968) discussed the sex education of congenitally blind children, which, though essentially not different from that of the seeing, poses some special problems. They point out the likelihood that blind children learn later about sex differences and are, therefore, more prone to harbor erroneous ideas about them and also about the sex act. Stressing the fact that literature which deals frankly with sex and the sexual organs is far less accessible to blind than to seeing children, they recommend realistic teaching models of male and female nudes and opportunities for frank discussion with educators in whom the blind child has confidence. The living arrangements in residential schools should be as similar as possible to those of the family, with coeducation, free opportunities for boys and girls to get together socially, and with a mixed staff.

Teen-age discussion groups were suggested and arranged (Bucknam, 1967), as a prophylactic measure to avoid some of the difficulties blind adolescents must face in a residential school setting. Group therapy techniques were used with junior high school age groups, separated according to sex. Sex problems arose for discussion only after many months, but when they did, they became a predominant topic during the year in which each group met. The group setting provided opportunities for reality testing of some of the concepts students had about their sexual role.

A growing interest in dynamically oriented research in the field of adjustment to blindness on the adult level is evidenced by such studies as those by Bauman (1954), Gowman (1957), Lukoff and Whiteman (1961), and Cowen, Underberg, and Verrillo (1958). Bauman and Yoder (1966) reviewed the literature on adjustment to blindness and included a follow-up of Bauman's study (1954), which deals with problems of adjustment of the adult blind population. They also discussed and reviewed some literature dealing with various adjustment problems of the growing child and adolescent and covered such topics as Blindness, Frustration and Conflict; Blindness and Anxiety; Blindness as an Assault on the Ego; Blindness as Physical Stress; and Learning, Motivation and Blindness. Pringle (1964) reviewed the literature published on the emotional and social adjustment of blind children during the past thirty-four years. The main contribution in the general field of physical disability is Wright's thought-provoking work (1960), which integrates findings from all areas of disability, including blindness.

A major publication on the adjustment to blindness in adolescence reports on the three-year research program that has been carried on under Emory L. Cowen at the University of Rochester, New York (Cowen *et al.,* 1961). Because the available research studies on attitudes toward the blind and adjustment to blindness have resulted in ambiguous and contradictory findings, the University of Rochester research group set out to examine afresh the essentially unresolved question of the comparative adjustment of visually disabled and sighted adolescents. They also wanted to test the proposition that characteristics of parent behavior (attitudes and understanding) are related to the adjustment of the visually disabled adolescent. They hoped that, in addition, their studies would clarify some other problems, such as the difference in adjustment between adolescents attending a residential school for the blind and those attending public school programs for the blind while living at home.

In their efforts to develop suitable measuring instruments for their research, the research team considered three factors as essential besides those that are required for all studies (reliability and validity): direct applicability to the visually disabled, objectivity of the indices of adjustment, and representation of a variety of situations. They developed, adapted, and adopted instruments to be used for the measurement of child adjustment, parental attitudes, and parental understanding. The child adjustment indices, which yielded seven global measures of adjustment were: A Self-Concept and Ideal-Concept Sort, a Teachers' Behavior Rating Scale, and a newly developed, objectively scorable projective type device, the Situations Projective Test B (SPT-B). Measures of Parental Attitude consisted of the Master Scale of 150 items, testing generalized attitudes toward child-rearing, sociopsychological attitudes toward minority groups and toward authority, and specific attitudes to blindness; and the Situation Projective Test A (SPT-A). Measures of Parental Understanding were in part the same as those used in measuring the adjustment of the children—the Predicted Self-Concept Sort and the Predicted SPT-B—so that the child's responses and the responses his parents predicted for him could be compared; and a "Dummy" Sort control in which the parent was asked to rank certain statements as he thought an "average teen-ager" would rank them.

The population of the study consisted of 167 adolescents aged thirteen to eighteen years, in the seventh through twelfth grades. Of these, 71 were visually disabled adolescents attending public day-school facilities, and 56 were visually disabled adolescents from residential schools for the blind. The control group consisted of 40 sighted adolescents matched as closely as possible to the experimental group in age, grade placement, intelligence, and socioeconomic status. The mothers of all 167 adolescents and the fathers of 66 were tested independently. The experimental groups were also broken down according to their degree of visual disability, and the sex distribution of all three groups was equated. The children were tested in their schools in two sessions of at least 45 minutes duration; parental tests were administered during individual home visits, in one session of about two hours.

So far as the problem of adjustment is concerned, the outstanding result of this study is that no systematic or consistent differences in personality attributes or adjustment were found among the three major groups tested. Elsewhere the authors (Underberg *et al.,* 1961, p. 257) state that their findings "cast an important shadow of doubt on beliefs about inherent associations between visual disability and maladjustment." Although there were no significant differences, partially sighted adolescents ranked slightly lower in adjustment than the legally or totally blind. There were no sex differences found, except that within the residential school sample, male adolescents were significantly better adjusted than their female fellow students. The study revealed no differences in adjustment between those living in residential schools for the blind and those living at home and attending public schools.

In their study of the relationship between attitudes of parents and child adjustment, the authors compared the mothers of the three major groups. They found mothers of adolescents in the residential school group to have more favorable attitudes toward their children than did the other mothers. This they interpret as "a powerful contraindicant" for the belief that children are placed in residential schools because of unfavorable parental attitudes. To their concern the authors found that their data failed to show any relationship between maternal attitudes and child adjustment, a finding contrary to past research as well as to clinical observation and psychological theory. They call attention to the fact that their research used the questionnaire method, which depends heavily on what a parent is willing to verbalize publicly and conclude that continued exploration of this problem is needed.

The third problem area, that of the relationship between parental understanding and adjustment of the visually handicapped child, has not previously been explored. The mothers of the three experimental groups showed no significant intergroup differences in the indices of understanding. However, a high degree of parental understanding, that is, accuracy in predicting the child's test behavior, correlated significantly and consistently with good adjustment of the child for all three experimental groups. This ability to predict apparently indicates an empathy and reality perception that is an essential condition for good child adjustment. The same pattern of relationship, though less clear-cut, was found for fathers.

The study also includes a preliminary attempt toward the construction of a prediction formula for adjustment. The adolescent who perceives a high degree of parental acceptance, who is seen by his mother as well adjusted and similar to other adolescents, and who has a relatively high socioeconomic status, is likely to be a well-adjusted individual.

The authors display a high degree of self-criticism in the appraisal of their research methods and results. This makes the reading of their study a stimulating intellectual exercise and the study itself a good one from which to learn scientific objectivity.

Jervis (1959) used the self-concept for a comparison of blind and sighted adolescents. His subjects were twenty students, seventeen to nineteen years of age, from two residential schools. All were totally blind since their third birthday or before, of normal intelligence, and free from additional physical or severe emotional problems. As a control group he selected twenty sighted students, matched in all essential characteristics except blindness. Each subject had two open-ended interviews to yield a qualitative measure and was given a modification of the Chicago Card-sort to yield a quantitative measure. The interviews were used to explain the purpose of the study, to establish a good relationship, and to encourage the subject to talk freely about himself and his feelings in response to a set of twelve stimulus questions, such as "How would you describe yourself to a stranger? What do you consider some of your strengths? What do you see yourself doing in five or ten years?" In the Q-sorts the subjects were asked to sort twice statements concerning their feelings or attitudes toward themselves—once as they would best describe themselves and once as they would describe their ideal selves. The interviews were independently judged by two psychologists, and no significant differences were found between the self-concepts of the two groups. A breakdown of the data revealed that blind subjects tended to be more apprehensive about their future, more aware of the need to get along with others, and felt less able to control outbursts of temper or aggression. Also, more of them felt that people in general did not expect enough of them. The Q-sort data also showed no significant differences between the two groups in their actual self-concept or in their idealized concept. However, more blind subjects had either high positive or high negative attitudes toward themselves, and the blind as a group exhibited a greater amount of variation. Jervis observes (p. 23) that "blindness may be considered more than sight-deprivation but not a completely crippling factor. The fact that the blind subjects pushed either to an extreme negative or an extreme positive attitude toward themselves would indicate that they have difficulty in normal adjustment."

In general, the studies of the University of Rochester group and of Jervis agree that there are no essential and consistent differences between blind and sighted adolescents as a group, but there appear to be individual differences—and these should be further explored.

Davis (1964) and Jervis (1964) discussed the development of the self-concept and the process of obtaining and maintaining self-esteem in blind children and adolescents, which must be considered as issues of central importance in the personality development of blind individuals.

Zunich and Ledwith (1965) compared the self-concept of visually handicapped children with those of sighted children. They used the self-concept scale designed by Lipsitt with twenty-nine sighted subjects. They found that the visually handicapped tended to use extremes, such as *not at all* and *all of the time* more than sighted subjects as Jervis (1959, p. 23) has also stated. Of the twenty-two trait-descriptive terms, significant differences, with the visually handicapped rating higher, were found in only four, namely: trusted, jealous, loyal, obedient. Only in popularity did nonsighted boys rate themselves significantly lower than the sighted.

Blank (1957) observed that "Psychoanalytic literature abounds in references to the symbolism of the eye, scoptophilia and exhibitionism, hysterical visual disturbances, and Oedipus and his blindness. . . . Yet contributions on the psychic problems of the blind are scant" (p. 1).

Burlingham (1941) reported two case histories of blind children and concluded that the lack of sight disturbs and diminishes the testing of reality, one of the most important functions of the ego. Instead of compensating for this, the blind child turns to fantasy—which leads to denial of reality and to wishful thinking. She stated that there was little new material concerning the early sexual development of the two children and concludes that "the instinctual processes and the attempts to repress them which cause anxiety, act independently of sight" (p. 81). Her observations agree with those of Deutsch (1940), who also noticed a striking readiness to give up reality and escape into fantasy.

Blank (1957) believes that congenital blindness does not always cause ego defect, but blindness which occurs when ego functions are already developed is inevitably traumatic. He distinguishes three factors that underlie personality disturbances of the visually handicapped:

(1) The unconscious significance of the eye as a sexual organ, including the equation of eye with mouth and with genital. (2) The unconscious significance of the eye as a hostile, destructive organ, including the equation of eye with piercing phallus and with devouring mouth. (3) The unconscious significance of blindness as castration, as punishment for sin (p. 1).

In two case presentations he demonstrated the problems of congenitally blind disturbed children and stressed (p. 6) that their ego development "depends primarily upon the physical contacts, consistent communication, and other components of mother love." Therefore, psychotherapy with the mother and assistance to the whole family are important prerequisites for helping the child.

In his discussion of acquired blindness, Blank comes to the same conclusions as Cholden (1958), who distinguished two stages in the reaction of healthy personalities to the loss of sight. The shock stage is a state of "psychological immobility," which can be thought of "as a period of protective emotional anesthesia which is available to the human organism under such stress" (p. 74). The degree of ego strength and maturity will determine the individual's capacity to recover from this initial shock and to enter the next stage of depression. This stage is interpreted as a mourning for the loss of a loved object, and "the patient must die as a sighted person in order to be reborn as a blind man" (p. 76). This stage must be lived through before blindness can be accepted, and attempts to prevent or prematurely shorten this depression may impede the rehabilitation process. Also, the raising of false hopes for the return of sight or, on the other hand, the premature offer of braille can prevent the acceptance of blindness as a reality. The problem of reactions to misfortune, such as mourning, was more thoroughly examined by Dembo, Leviton, and Wright (1956).

Facial Expressions

The problem of facial expression and of its development in the blind is of practical as well as theoretical importance. The questions of the innateness of certain expressions and of the cultural determination of expressive mimicry have received considerable attention. The social value of "normal" facial expression for blind chil-dren and adults has been stressed by many educators. Thompson (1941) studied this problem in twenty-six blind children, from six weeks to thirteen years of age, who had been blind from birth or shortly thereafter. She compared them with a matched group of twenty-nine seeing children. The children were observed and photographed in naturally occurring situations of an emotional nature. The purpose of the study was to determine the effects of maturation and of social mimicry upon the innate neuromuscular mechanisms of emotional expression. Expressions of laughing, smiling, and crying were observed in blind, deaf-blind, and seeing children, although there were certain differences between them. The effect of maturation showed itself in a decrease of facial activity in smiling in older blind children, whereas in crying blind and sighted children showed an increase in facial activity. The emotional responses in blind and deaf-blind children were, in general, appropriate to the situation but did not occur as uniformly among the blind as among the seeing children. These changes were considered to be maturational, because they could not have been brought about in blind children in any other way. The development of facial expressions in seeing children seems largely to be determined by mimicry. Thompson concluded (p. 41): "Since it is believed that the facial musculature is under a dual neural control, it seems that maturation effects the 'emotional' expressions whereas mimicry effects 'voluntary' expression."

Fulcher (1942) asked 118 seeing subjects from four to sixteen years of age and 50 blind subjects from six to twenty-one years of age to form facial expressions of emotions. These were photographed by a motion picture camera. The analysis of the requested expressions revealed: (1) the blind show less facial activity than the seeing in expressing every emotion; (2) the relative amount of facial activity in expressing emotions is about the same for the blind as for the seeing; (3) facial activity increases with age in the seeing but decreases with age in the blind; (4) the blind show slighter, though similar, differences of facial movement in expressing different emotions; (5) the expressions of the seeing are more adequate than those of the blind. He concluded, therefore, that vision is an important means of acquiring the ability to form appropriate facial expressions but that there are other ways of acquiring them besides visual imitation.

After reviewing the literature on innate versus acquired facial expressions, Freedman (1964) reported observations on four congenitally blind infants. He observed that all four babies reacted to touch and voice stimuli with smiles which were extremely fleeting. In two cases who were observed through six months of age, these fleeting smiles gradually changed to normal prolonged smiling. These observations led him to two interim hypotheses: "(1) the initial elicited smiles were reflexive in nature, since there was the typical sharp onset and almost immediate waning; (2) in these early months prolonged social smiling seems to require visual regard as a maintaining stimulus." (1967, p. 162).

Dreams

How blind individuals dream is a topic of frequent discussions and numerous observations, but there are few studies available that investigate the dreams of blind children. Deutsch (1928) presented descriptions of dreams of various children and also her own dreams without discussing the symbolism contained in any of the dreams. She found that children often said that they "saw" an object when they actually meant that they only heard or felt it or just knew that it was present. Therefore, she based her conclusions only on her own dreams and found that the imagery in them is "entirely auditory, kinesthetic, static, and tactile. The sense of hearing usually plays the most important part, while the other three sense modalities seem to be of about equal moment." (p. 293). Taste and smell imagery did not play any part in her dreams. She often carried on long conversations and actually heard what was being said to her by voices, which had all their usual inflections. An Italian study by Costa (1937), in which he analyzed eighty dreams of fifteen blind children, also showed that the dreams of totally blind children are predominantly of a tactual and auditory nature. A French study by Bolli (1932) agrees with this observation and also stresses that the dreams of those born blind are not lacking in variety or richness. In persons blinded later in life, visual imagery deteriorates in proportion to the age of the subject and the duration of his blindness. Schumann (1959), in a German treatise, made prodigious comments on the dreams of those born blind, blind at an early age (two to fourteen years), and at a later age. He agreed essentially with other writers, but his thorough review of the blind in mythology and in various arts is of special value (pp. 61–109).

That the congenitally blind and those who became blind before the age of about five do not have visual dreams was confirmed by the reports of Blank (1958). He also concurred with Deutsch and others that hearing ranks first in importance, tactile and kinesthetic perceptions next— but also found that sometimes blind people's dreams include taste, smell, and temperature perceptions. He described five

BERTHOLD LOWENFELD

cases (three of whom were congenitally blind) and their dreams and concluded that the "typical dream of the blind is a dream 'from above,' one that is determined primarily by serious reality problems and it usually contains some prominent spoken statement, or other superego elements more closely related to the day's residue than to deeply repressed conflicts." He stated (p. 173): "The phenomenological differences between the dreams of the blind and the seeing are not fundamental. They require no revision of the psychoanalytical theory of dreams."

Imaginativeness in dreams and in fantasy plays of blind and sighted children was studied by Singer and Streiner (1966). Twenty matched pairs of blind and sighted children, eight to twelve years of age, were studied and their imaginativeness in self-reports of day and night dreams and plays was judged. Blind children showed themselves less imaginative or flexible than their sighted peers of comparable intelligence and socioeconomic status, except for their greater use of imaginary companions. These results confirmed Blank's (1958) findings on the poverty of content and concreteness in the dream reports of blind children.

Developmental Aspects

There is a large and growing literature that deals with descriptions, observations, and generalizations concerning the development of blind children. In most cases it also includes advice to parents on their functions in rearing a blind child. The number of scientific studies in this area, however, is rather small, although many of the research studies that were reported here have direct or indirect implications of a developmental nature.

Gesell, Ilg, and Bullis (1950) followed

the development of a child, born with clinically complete bilateral anophthalmia (congenital absence of both eyes), up to the age of four years. They took periodic moving-picture records of this child in order to answer such questions as: Is retardation of behavior caused by blindness or by complicating factors? Can blindness by itself produce retardation? How are patterns of behavior affected by blindness? Their observational data demonstrated that in general the sequences of development in this blind child were comparable to those of seeing children. The blind child progressed in the basic patterns of posture, manipulation, locomotion, exploration, language, and social behavior, thus confirming the basic role of maturation in the blind infant's growth. Due to the lack of visual control, the child showed atypical orientational behavior, established no eye-hand coordination, and his head remained in a consistently maintained midposition. The authors concluded (p. 273) that blindness "profoundly alters the structure of the mental life but not the integrity of a total growth complex."

Although Gesell and his associates found that blindness by itself does not produce a serious degree of retardation (at least up to four years of age), another study by Wilson and Halverson (1947) reached a different conclusion. In this study, a totally blind child was observed and tested with a battery of tests including the Gesell Schedules, the Cattell Infant Scale, and the Vineland Social Maturity Scale. Examinations were conducted at fifteen, eighteen, and twenty-four months, and the age at which the child passed various test items was recorded during regular weekly observations. The data indicated a general developmental retardation that was greatest in his motor and adaptive behavior—particularly in all activities involving prehension and locomotion—and least in language. In contrast to the aggressive attitude of seeing children, the child also showed a lack of initiative and spontaneity in his movements. The authors believe that much of the value of touch as an informative sense in early childhood is due to its association with vision and conclude that the blind child's retardation was for the most part caused by inadequate perception of space.

The difference in the findings of these two studies concerning the retarding influence of blindness may be due to a difference in innate potentialities of the two children, although the authors of the latter study do not consider this as a possible cause. It must, however, be recognized that even a single case of a blind child with essentially normal development is sufficient proof that blindness does not necessarily retard a child. As a matter of fact, there are innumerable blind children who have demonstrated normal growth in spite of total blindness.

Maxfield and Fjeld (1942) used the Vineland Social Maturity Scale with 101 visually handicapped children ranging in age from nine months to six years and ten months. The Social Quotient for this group was 83.54 with a standard deviation of 29.28. The wide variability of this group is due to the fact that it included children whose mental ability varied from an extremely low level to very superior and also to the inclusion of partially seeing as well as of blind children. Of great importance in this study are the qualitative results that led to a tentative revision of the Vineland Social Maturity Scale for use with visually handicapped preschool children. Maxfield and Fjeld used the first seventy-seven items of the whole scale and found that fourteen items were relatively more difficult for visually handicapped children than for the seeing. Among them were eating with spoon and fork, buttoning coat or dress, marking with pencil, fetching or carrying familiar objects, cutting with scissors, reaching for familiar person, and playing simple table games. Of the fourteen items, at least four, such as marking with pencil and cutting with scissors, were obviously more difficult for visually handicapped children. Among fifteen items found to be relatively easier for visually handicapped children were sitting unsupported, discriminating foods, washing hands unaided, initiating own play activities, using names of familiar objects, and playing with other children. Thus the blind children revealed a tendency to succeed better on items requiring less initiative, less activity, and less aggressiveness. Maxfield and Fjeld, in their adaptation of the scale, adhered to the categories and age levels of the original scale but included new items and revised some others. They concluded that visually handicapped children as a group appeared to be more docile, less active, and to have less initiative than seeing children of corresponding ages. This trend was more striking in the blind than in the partially seeing. Hayes (1952) used the Maxfield-Fjeld Adaptation of the Vineland Social Maturity Scale with 300 blind babies and reported results closely corresponding to the findings of Maxfield and Fjeld.

Maxfield and Kenyon (1953) prepared a guide for the use of the Maxfield-Fjeld scale. Finally, Maxfield and Buchholz (1957) presented their Social Maturity Scale for Blind Preschool Children. The use of the previous adaptation revealed that some items needed relocation or reformulation, others should be eliminated, and new ones should be added. The new scale consists of 95 items and is based on data and observations of 484 children. The authors aim at providing "as objective a means as possible for comparing the present status, or the progress, of a given blind child, in his acquisition of personal and social independence and competence, with that of other blind children of corresponding chronological age" (p. 8).

Sands (1952) stressed the importance of qualitative observation in connection with any use of preschool tests with blind children; these observations should include:

> . . . the child's spontaneous play activities, his awareness and alertness; his methods of discrimination, exploration, and localization; his means of communication and use of language; his attention span and learning ability; his reactions to routine, and to people he knows as well as to new people (p. 26).

Sound and practical discussions on the psychological evaluation of blind children are offered in articles by Hepfinger (1962) and Kenyon (1959).

Lowenfeld (1950*b*) distinguished three objective effects of blindness: (1) the limitation in the range and variety of experiences; (2) the limitation in the ability to get about; and (3) the limitation in the control of the environment and the self in relation to it. From these limitations he derives the following basic principles in methods of teaching blind children: individualization, concreteness, unified instruction, additional stimulation, and self-activity. The first two limitations have already been discussed here, but the third one, in the control of the environment and the self in relation to it, needs further elaboration.

Sight is the human sense that overcomes distance and, at the same time, gives details and relationships of form, size, and position. This "object quality" of vision permits more effective contact with and control of the environment than are achieved by the other senses. Therefore, lack of sight causes a detachment from the physical and, to a lesser degree, from the social world. As a result, the blind individual is affected in different ways during his development. It has been noted, for instance, that the blind infant does not reach out for objects or crawl toward them because he is not attracted by them unless they emit sounds. Some blind children omit the crawling stage although they follow in general the same sequence of development as seeing children do. Also, the blind child cannot acquire certain behavior patterns on the basis of visual imitation. This factor plays an important role in his learning to walk, to talk, to play, to acquire expressive movements, and to perform the many other actions in which learning by imitation is important. Dressing, eating, and many daily activities are considerably more complicated when they must be learned and performed without sight. For this reason it is generally agreed that some retardation in the blind child's rate of development as compared with that of seeing children can be expected.

The blind child's inability to control his environment by sight also is responsible for his fear of being observed, which has been reported by many observers. He cannot determine whether he is being observed or when the observation begins or ends unless the observer makes himself known by some nonvisual means. This fear by itself is liable to produce tension and self-consciousness. The question of how blind children learn to understand what it means to be watched has not yet received scientific attention. Reported observations have shown that the blind child realizes at an early age that people can tell what he is doing without having bodily contact with him. Thus he learns that others can do something to him which he cannot do to them. Also, he finds out at an early age that he must grope around for something he has lost, whereas his seeing brother or sister or friend can locate it immediately. Thus he learns by experience that he is in some way different from the others, although he may not know or may not be able to verbalize until much later that this is due to his blindness.

A research volume by Norris, Spaulding, and Brodie (1957) reports a five-year longitudinal study conducted under the University of Chicago clinics by an ophthalmologist-psychologist-social worker team that cooperated with available community resources. Sixty-six of the 259 blind children in the study were studied intensively. Fifty-six of the former and 209 of the latter were blind as a result of retrolental fibroplasia. The first part of the study describes its research methods and findings; the second part presents case histories of six RLF children illustrating adjustment "ranging from very favorable to very unfavorable." The Cattell Infant Intelligence Scale, supplemented by certain items from the Kuhlmann Scale of Intelligence, and the Maxfield-Fjeld Tentative adaptation of the Vineland Social Maturity Scale were used with children up to three years. The Interim Hayes-Binet Intelligence Tests for the Blind were used with children above the three-year level. Detailed item analyses are reported for the Cattell and for the Maxfield-Fjeld scales. In interpreting the test results, it is stated (p. 15) that "In the experience of the project staff, any expectation that a psychological test result in itself could be regarded as a valid measure either of a child's capacity or of his functioning level proved unfounded." The importance of readiness is recognized, and the results of

the study suggest "that the more time that elapses between the time of optimum readiness and the time when the opportunity for learning is provided, the greater the difficulties in learning become" (p. 23). Therefore, favorable opportunities for learning "are more important in determining the child's functioning level than such factors as his degree of blindness, his intelligence as measured by psychological tests, or the social, economic, or educational background of his parents" (p. 65).

The general conclusions of the study can be summed up by stating that under favorable conditions "the blind child can develop into an independent, responsible, freely functioning child whose use of his potential compares favorably with that of most sighted children of his age" (p. 65). This result confirms what Gesell and his associates (1950) have found in their study of a child with congenital absence of both eyes. But whereas Gesell states (p. 273) that blindness "profoundly alters the structure of the mental life, but not the integrity of a total growth complex," the University of Chicago study asserts (p. 65): "There are no special problems or 'handicaps' which can be attributed directly to the blindness"—a statement with which many would take issue.

Imamura (1965) compared the behavior of preschool blind children and sighted children and sought to determine what relationship, if any, exists between the children's behavior and that of their mothers. Her results are based on systematic observations of the behavior of children and their mothers in their natural home environment. The study parallels cross-cultural investigations, conducted jointly by Harvard, Yale, and Cornell universities, by using the same observational methods and by matching its blind subjects on certain variables with a group of sighted children in the larger study. Imamura found that, compared with sighted children of the same ages, blind children are more dependent (the author uses the term "succorant") on the nurturance of their mothers, are less aggressive toward their mothers, are more succorant and less aggressive toward other children, have excessive social interaction with their mothers and proportionately less with other children, and are more verbal. So far as the behavior of mothers toward their children is concerned, mothers of blind children performed approximately five times as many responses as the mothers of sighted children. They reacted, in response to the children's request for help, significantly more frequently by compliance, by refusal, and by ignoring. The difference in the category of ignoring was the largest. The correlational data indicated that:

(a) more succorant mothers tend to have more nurturant children; (b) less sociable mothers tend to have more sociably aggressive children; and (c) extremely complaint and extremely noncompliant mothers tend to have children who are more self-reliant, while moderately compliant (equal amount of compliance and noncompliance) mothers tend to have children who are less self-reliant (p. 50).

Thus, in general, the study asserts that blind children are much more dependent than sighted children; that mothers of blind children treat their children's succorant behavior differently than mothers of sighted children by ignoring rather than refusing their children's succorant behavior; and, finally, that there is a relationship between the children's behavior and the way their mothers react to it. Succorance is the behavior characteristic that most clearly distinguishes blind from sighted children. The author concluded (p. 57): "Although we cannot ignore the signifi-cant effect lack of sight has on the blind child's development and behavior, the dependency of the blind child bears a strong relationship to the differential treatment he receives from his mother."

Cutsforth (1951) discussed "blindisms," which are acts of automatic self-stimulation such as rolling or tilting the head, thrusting the fingers into the eyes, and swaying the body. He explains that, in contrast to the seeing child, the blind child must find his stimulation within bodily reach and turns to his own body as the source and the object of stimulation. Thus, lack of stimulation from the external world furthers the blind child's concentration on the self and encourages the exercise of self-stimulation. Totman (1947) believes, on the basis of experience, that like any undesirable activity, blindisms must be replaced by more socially acceptable activities that give pleasure and satisfaction to the child.

Morse (1965) argues that the term "blindism" implies that the behavior described is exhibited only by those who are blind, whereas seeing children actually show the same behavior. Therefore, he suggests the term "mannerisms." He also believes that anxiety and frustration are causal factors in these mannerisms. These and similar behavior patterns such as thumb-sucking, nail-biting, leg-swinging, increase in sighted people as expressions of anxiety or frustration. He recommends finding substitutes for these expressions through the establishment of rewarding relationships with people in the child's environment.

An interesting distinction concerning blindisms was made by Stone (1964) on the basis of observations of forty blind retarded children, most of them institutionalized for a long time. He distinguished "withdrawal" and "alerting" blindisms.

Withdrawal blindisms constitute intense rhythmic behavior that is completely involving and repetitive, thus resulting in a blocking out of environmental stimuli. Alerting blindisms employ small muscle masses and involve often ritualized behavior such as hand-clapping. Children engaged in these blindisms are aware of and responsive to the environment. He found that alerting blindisms resulted always in an increase of rate of a previously slow electroencephalogram. The results of his study suggest that blindisms of retarded blind children are accompanied by changes in the level of consciousness and "must represent an important method for the child in the alteration or regulation of his contact with a stressful reality" (p. 18).

Blindisms in their children are often quite disturbing to the parents because of the unfavorable reactions of other people to them. In most cases blindisms disappear as the child grows up, although observers agree that emotionally disturbed children or those of low mentality may continue to practice them for a long time. This, however, is characteristic not only of blind but also of seeing children who are thus affected.

Some of the most valuable contributions to our knowledge of the influence of blindness on the development of children are coming from the staff of the Educational Unit of the Hampstead Child-Therapy Course and Clinic in London, of which Anna Freud is the head. The research group on blind children is directed by Mrs. Dorothy Burlingham. Burlingham (1961), in reporting her observations on the development of these children, stated (p. 123) that "retardation and restriction of muscular achievement are the order of the day.... The blind baby although not intentionally restricted yet behaves in many respects like a restricted sighted child."

Burlingham considers blindness responsible for this because it prevents stimulation to reach out and causes lack of some incentive, such as the observed approval of the mother, to repeat achievements. The dependency stage of the blind child is enlarged and prolonged; frequent persistence of mouth pleasure is characteristic. Blind children are observed as showing much less aggressive expression and more fear of external aggression. They feel the need for controlling their aggression because they realize how dependent they are on the seeing. Burlingham also observed that blind children often ask strangers immediately for their names, where they live, and so forth. She believes that people are far more attractive to them than objects and imputes frequently occurring faulty methods of verbalization to such factors as speech, which is less firmly connected with sensory experiences, and lack in ego achievement. She raises the question whether this will affect later superego formation and produce "certain ego characteristics such as superficiality, hypocrisy, overcompliance, which are often considered to be connected with blindness" (p. 137). Many of Burlingham's other observations are similar to those made in the United States on disturbed RLF children, but the research on blind adolescents fails to confirm the presence of any of the expected ego characteristics.

Burlingham (1964) also discussed the role of hearing and sound in the development of blind infants. Her observations are limited to a few blind children only, as she herself recognized. She stressed that the lack of visual contact between mother and child cannot be made up for by voice and listening. Thus, mother and infant cannot develop the close relationship that is established otherwise by the reciprocal effects of visual response. Mothers frequently do not understand the importance of silence and sounds for their blind infants. What may appear in the child as passivity may actually mean that he is listening to whatever goes on in his environment. The fact that the blind child later imitates something that he can only have heard during such periods of "passivity" is cited by her as evidence. However, stillness can also be frightening to the child, as for instance, if somebody leaves the room and the child feels that he is left alone. Burlingham believes that any continual auditory stimulation, such as the playing of the radio, has detrimental effects, not only because it blocks out environmental noises which might interest the child but also because it invites passivity and self-stimulation.

In another contribution, Burlingham (1965) dealt with problems of the ego development in blind children. She calls attention to the immobility of the blind child, except where conditions of absolute safety are provided, and contrasts this with the spontaneous active behavior of seeing children. She claims that this "immobilization is displaced from the motor area to other ego functions." She considers verbalization as a problem of the blind and states: "There is, thus, a comparative void left in the minds of those who have to build up their world image without visual impressions" and "from our observations of the blind it appears that this void is filled in part by the child's attentiveness to the sensations arising from his own body" (pp. 203–204). She also observed that blind children possess to an extraordinary degree an excellent memory. This memory plays a role in the impasse that results from the increase in his vocabulary of essentially meaningless words and his frustration in not understanding words which are spoken by people important to him. She gives some examples of speech

observed in the Hampstead Nursery School and classifies them as follows: words acquired normally on the basis of sense experience; verbalizing by sense association; using words of the sighted world; associating from memory to unknown words; confusion between word and thing; undigested parroting (pp. 207–208).

In her discussions of childhood occupations, Burlingham (1967) used the following significant headings: The Mother's Body as the First Toy; Playing with the Feet and Other Body Games; Playing with Sound; A Common Toy for the Blind: The Door; Mastery of Tasks Through Play and Occupations. She gives copious examples of plays and games and professes that she cannot understand why, in view of the great variety of toys and activities which blind children can use, so many of them spend hours of inactivity and boredom and why mothers find it so difficult to keep them happily and satisfactorily occupied. She presents (p. 188) the following important comment: "There is, of course, the possibility that we are wrong in judging the development of the blind child on the basis of comparisons with the sighted. What in this light appears as backwardness or a slowing up may turn out to be a matter of much greater basic difference in kind. To deal with visual representations of things, as the seeing do, is probably a much easier process than to deal with the verbal abstractions to which the blind are confined and for which they depend wholly on the progressive development of verbalization and its ramifications—inevitably later occurrences."

The most elaborate narrative of the psychoanalytic treatment and the recovery of a severely disturbed blind girl was presented by Omwake and Solnit (1961). Their contact with this child began when she was three and a half years old. Treatment continued through her seventh year. They selected for discussion in this presentation four of the child's difficulties: an arrest of libidinal and ego development; the development of an inhibition of touching; the disorganizing effect of memories of painful experiences from the first three years of life; and the gradually developing comprehension of her sensory defect.

Klein (1962) further discussed the case presented by Omwake and Solnit and stressed that blindness must be understood "not in terms of the loss of visual function, but in the manner of organization of the information provided by the residual modalities" (p. 90). In modification of Omwake and Solnit's conclusions, he assures that the cognitive style that a blind child can develop may correspond essentially to that of a seeing child. In other words, vision does not appear to be indispensable for ego functioning. Maladjustments as a result of blindness are seen as consequences of a vacuum created by inadequate ego surrogates.

Passivity and ego development in blind infants was discussed by Sandler (1963). She proposes to provide a tentative theoretical model since psychoanalytic theory gives a basic frame of reference but no specific theory accounting for the peculiarities of the blind child's development.

Briefly, the thesis to be advanced is that the development of blind and sighted children follows roughly parallel courses for about twelve to sixteen weeks after birth, but that at the time of transition from the first (predominantly passive) oral phase to the second (predominantly active) phase, the ego development of the blind child pursues a course which results in his passive self-centeredness and lack of striving toward mastery at later ages (p. 346).

While in the first phase the mouth is the most important organ of exploration for blind as well as seeing children, in the second phase, the hand takes over and sight plays an all-important role in directing the hand's exploratory functions. This leads during the second and third quarters of the first year to a differentiation between the child's own body and the outside world. The blind child is hindered and retarded in this process of turning from the self to the outer world. Although sounds can play some role in this process, the blind child by necessity lacks the sensory continuity of visual impressions. Thus, the blind infant is to a large extent deprived of the satisfactions of external stimulation and turns to repetitive self-stimulating behavior. Sandler notes (p. 356) that even the mother's best handling of her child cannot avoid the basic retardation in ego development. "It is inevitable that this must have a profound effect on later stages of development, ... "

Sandler and Wills (1965, p. 18) reported many observations on totally blind children at the Hampstead Unit in an effort "to trace the baby's early difficulties in moving away from passive instinctual aims to exploration of the world around." They stress the importance of the mother and her body in this process and the significant role that hearing and sound assume. Evidence of this they find in the children's recall of conversations and in their frequent and repetitive imitation of sounds. In role-playing situations, copying adult activities is mostly on the verbal level while the child has difficulties in acting the adult role. The authors suggest that the poor cathexis of adult activities raises the whole question of later sublimation.

Observations on six blind children, illustrating Burlingham's (1961) comments on blind children's conceptualization of the

BERTHOLD LOWENFELD

world around them, were presented by Wills (1965). She concluded that it takes blind children much longer to gain a knowledge of the world around them, that they have difficulties in distinguishing reality from fantasy, that they frequently gain only partial and insufficient knowledge of objects, that they have a tendency toward animistic thinking long after seeing children have overcome it, and that they need help in establishing their own way of thinking and their own methods of understanding and adaptation in order to integrate with the sighted world around them.

There are other psychoanalytically oriented studies that deal with the development of blind children. Fraiberg and Freedman (1964) reported the illuminating case of a nine-year-old blind child with arrested ego development, which they consider typical of deviant blind children. They call attention to the importance of the functions of the mouth as a leading organ of discrimination and perception throughout the blind person's life. The blind child's development proceeds by the hand gradually taking over perceptual functions that were centered in the mouth. Deviant blind children may fail to develop this "hand autonomy."

The importance of the search for the source of sound for the ego development of blind infants was stressed by Fraiberg, Siegel, and Gibson (1966). By observing a totally blind infant, they found that the coordination of prehension and hearing, which begins in seeing children between five and six months of age, occurred in the blind child only in the last quarter of the first year. There was no equivalent for the early visual search for the source of sound in the infant without vision. Only at eleven months of age did the child search or reach out on sound cue alone, which led the authors to the conclusion that

sound does not confer substantiality upon an object at earlier ages. They interpret the searching on sound cue alone as an experience that an object is "out there," the beginning of the discovery of the object world. The blind child must cover a much more complicated route to achieve this discovery than the seeing child and may remain arrested on earlier levels of development, which is characteristic of the deviant blind child.

Nagera and Colonna (1965) examined the ego and drive development of six blind children, age four to eight and one-half years. The authors distinguished two types among the blind children, some who are not far behind sighted children of similar ages in their ego processes, drive development, and object relationships, and others whose developmental processes are atypical, lagging behind in different degrees in the different areas and giving in some extreme cases the impression of marked mental retardation. They dealt mainly with the latter group and reported many observations in line with those made by others analytically oriented.

A broadly conceived research study by Gomulicki (1962), sponsored by the Royal National Institute for the Blind, London, the Cambridge Institute of Education, and the Mental Health Research Fund, has been reported only in a preliminary way with some of its conclusions. The experimental tasks used in this research were designed to throw light on the developmental patterns of perceptual learning in blind children. According to the report:

... Details differed, but in experiment after experiment, regardless of the perceptual modality concerned, much the same picture emerged. At the age of five, the blind child was at a distinct disadvantage as compared with the sighted one, taking decidedly longer to produce results that were markedly inferior. By that age, the sighted child had already achieved the major part of his perceptual development; the blind child still had far to go. But the further progress of sighted children from five onward is, in general, slower than that of the blind, who, over a period varying from about four years to ten or more, manage to draw approximately level. ... by their mid-teens or thereabouts, the blind children become, to all intents and purposes, as good as the sighted children of the same age (p. 120).

The author asks at what cost this is achieved and states (p. 120) that the data of his experiments suggest "that a prolonged effort of the intellect is part of the cost to the blind of a degree of perceptual skill that for the sighted is a relatively effortless product of maturation." Gomulicki believes that parent education is essential in fostering attitudes which would enable them to deliberately encourage their blind child to be active and self-reliant and to provide them with ample opportunities to develop the effective use of their senses. Also, methods of training the children in the various perceptual skills should be cultivated during their school years because for the blind it cannot be taken for granted—as it can safely be done for the sighted—that their "normal" senses will achieve the required efficiency without aid.

If the results of Gomulicki's research can be satisfactorily documented, they would provide an explanation for the contradictory findings of frequent problems in young blind children and generally good adjustment and success among blind adolescents and adults.

MULTIHANDICAPPED BLIND CHILDREN

Since the second edition of this book appeared, retrolental fibroplasia as a cause of blindness has become an issue of historical importance so far as psychological problems of blind children are concerned. The second edition of this book dealt with it extensively (pp. 289–294). This chapter has incorporated some of the research of general importance in its preceeding treatment of developmental aspects.

For many years to come, it is certain that comparatively large numbers of multihandicapped blind children will need educational facilities and psychological services geared to their special needs. An indication of the extent to which blind children have additional handicapping conditions can be found in two studies. Wolf (1967) secured in 1965 data from forty-eight residential schools for the visually impaired who had a total enrollment of 6,696 visually impaired children. Thirty-five of these schools with a pupil population of 4,711 reported 1,170 mentally retarded children, which is a prevalence rate of 250 mentally retarded per 1,000 visually impaired children. His investigation indicated that there was a combined average of 3.18 disabilities for children enrolled in special classes for the mentally retarded blind in residential schools.

Lowenfeld (1968) surveyed educational and other facilities throughout the state of California to determine the prevalence of multihandicapped blind and deaf-blind children in that state. According to his conservative estimate, 80 to 90 percent of the multihandicapped blind children's population is included in his data. He found 1,180 multihandicapped blind children of whom 940 are blind children with multiple handicaps (excluding deafness) and 240 are deaf-blind children. Of the total, 261 children are of preschool age, leaving 919 multihandicapped blind children of school age in the state. To this number 1,217 multihandicapped blind children in state hospitals must be added, of whom about 200 are of preschool age. He concludes:

It can, therefore, be stated that for the school age population, normal blind children (1,111) outnumber the multihandicapped blind children by 11 to 9. If we include the State Hospital population of multihandicapped blind children, multihandicapped blind children of school age (1,919) outnumber 'normal' blind children (1,111) by 19 to 11 (p. 32).

In Lowenfeld's study, children enrolled in residential or public school facilities for the visually handicapped (the deaf-blind not included), had a combined average of 3.0 handicaps per child. The additional handicaps in order of their frequency were: mental retardation, emotional, speech, cerebral palsy, communication, orthopedic, epilepsy, and so forth.

In 1966 Graham (1968) collected descriptive data on 8,887 multiply impaired blind children and estimates that there are about 15,000 such children in the United States.

The number of multihandicapped blind children shows a dramatic increase, largely because of the following factors: (1) there are still older retrolental fibroplasia children of school age; (2) maternal rubella epidemics (Wagner, 1967) have caused comparatively large numbers of multihandicapped blind and deaf-blind children; (3) prenatal causes of blindness, many of which affect not only the eye but also cause additional abnormalities, have increased while other causes such as infectious diseases and accidents, many of which affect only the eye and leave the child's other sensory, intellectual, and physical capabilities intact, have decreased.

Anderson (1965) provided a bibliography on the visually impaired mentally retarded up to 1965 and Lowenfeld (1968) on the multihandicapped up to 1968.

The rubella epidemics, just as the retrolental fibroplasia era, have released a veritable flood of articles, pamphlets, and reports dealing with psychoeducational problems of blind children with additional handicaps. They all stress the importance of emotional acceptance of the child by his parents, of providing early and suitable opportunities for learning at the right time, and of environmental influences— principles that are accepted for children in general but that need to be specially stressed with blind children who have additional handicaps.

Two books, widely acclaimed by parents and professional workers, have been found helpful. Lowenfeld's *Our Blind Children—Growing and Learning With Them* (1964) is a psychologically oriented book dealing with the education of blind children. Spencer's *Blind Children in Family and Community* (1960) is a more sociologically oriented picture story of preschool blind children.

One of the pivotal elements in the placement and provision of education for multihandicapped blind children is that of evaluation or assessment. Intelligence tests, which are only reasonably satisfactory in use with normal blind children, are practically useless with many of the multihandicapped blind children, particularly those who are retarded or emotionally disturbed. These tests are largely verbal, and this is precisely the area in which many multihandicapped blind children are most deficient. For this reason, assessment based on long-term observations is regarded by most teachers and psychologists working with these children as the only way to determine whether an individual child is likely to make progress. It is not the present status of performance of a child that must be considered, but his ability to improve and to progress.

Weiner (1967) identified five characteristics as the most relevant dimensions of educability: level, rate, range, efficiency, and autonomy. *Level* is to be understood as the amount of development or achievement in terms of degree of difficulty or complexity; *rate* refers to the time required for different tasks; *range* means the curriculum and in which parts of it the child is able to function; *efficiency* refers to economy and speed of performance in a wide range of socially and educationally meaningful tasks; *autonomy* is described as evidence of independence, self-actualizing behavior, and how the child chooses, initiates, and executes tasks he has selected for himself and whether he experiences satisfaction from his activity. Weiner comments: "These characteristics reflect the response of the child to the demands made of him in out-of-school as well as in-school activities. They are observable in all stages of development, across the conventional categories of handicaps, and in all social and cultural groups" (p. 74).

Because assessment can be carried out only over prolonged periods of time, various programs serving multihandicapped blind children include assessment as one of their functions. There are many descriptions of such facilities available, as for instance those of Brodey (1962) of the Pilot School for Blind Children in Washington, D.C., who also gives a perceptive account of their developmental learning program and its underlying principles; Cicenia *et al.* (1965) of the Edward R. Johnstone Training and Research Center at Bordentown, New Jersey; Donlon (1964) of the Center for the Development

of Blind Children at Syracuse University; Tretakoff (1966) of the Hope School for the Blind in Springfield, Illinois; and Williams (1964) of Sunland's Program for the Blind.

The Children's Division of the Syracuse Psychiatric Hospital in Fairmount, New York, carries on a program for twenty severely disturbed blind children, six to twelve years of age, in a residential setting (Ross, Braen, and Chaput, 1967). These children were in the beginning without any interest in the external world and in learning, and they had a short attention span and extremely low frustration tolerance. None of them had had any successful school experience.

The heart of the program lay in an expectation that each staff member would show the same respect to each child regardless of his individual developmental level; would provide the child with interpersonal and other kinds of experiences to help guide him to the next step in development; and would patiently allow him to achieve that step at a speed consistent with his specific needs (p. 218).

The difficult and complex progress of some of these children from regression as a reaction to admission, to slowly developing interest in others, use of language, lessening of anxiety and consequent decrease in aggression, and finally to participation in an educational curriculum is described.

Mattis (1967) reported the program of the Mental Health Center for Visually Impaired Multi-Handicapped Children of the Jewish Guild for the Blind in New York. The center conducts two out-patient programs: the Concept Formation Program and the Day Treatment Program. Referral to one or the other depends upon the clinic's diagnostic evaluation, in which a psychological examination over a period of one to two weeks for a total of five to ten hours plays a dominant role. The Concept Formation Program is based on the observation that deficiencies in perceptual-cognitive functioning are a major factor in the children's developmental difficulties. The Day Treatment Program serves children who are often considered autistic, schizophrenic, and profoundly retarded with little or no language and few self-care skills. Group treatment in a large sound-deadened area was planned for these children at the time of the report. Casework with parents is a part of both programs.

Goodman (1967) provided a detailed description of another facet of the guild's activities—the treatment program for multihandicapped blind young adults. This is a two-day-a-week experimental program in which group sessions as well as other training features, such as physical fitness, development of tactile and muscle sense, mobility and orientation, and recreation are employed. The major therapeutic goals of the group sessions are: (1) the development of a sense of self and the emergence of ego identity; (2) improved capacity for reality testing; and (3) increased awareness of feelings. The parents receive counseling, some in the form of a group-counseling experience. It is felt that the program has accomplished much and offers even greater promise for the future.

Pacific State Hospital in Pomona, California, instituted a program to determine the value of having one interested adult devote several hours a day to the training of one retarded blind child (Blanchard, Bowling, and Roberts, 1968). A number of college students participated in this program during the summer of 1966. The children were all severely multihandicapped. At the end of the training period, every child had made some progress in at least one area of acitvity. The authors suggest further investigation to provide evidence of whether such a short-time concentrated one-to-one relationship can be helpful to such children.

Para-analytic group therapy in which the therapist, whose basic role is analytical, also functions as a counselor and supplies accurate factual information (on sex matters and reproduction), was described by Avery (1968). She carried out such a program at the Connecticut Institute for the Blind with two groups of seven and six adolescent girls and gives a detailed account of its progress and effect on the participants.

In another report, three cases of multihandicapped blind children received mobility training in order to prove that this kind of training, with some modifications in technique according to the individual student's needs, was possible and beneficial (Seelye and Thomas, 1966). Though the students were not able to participate in every phase of mobility, the value of the program was demonstrated.

Various reports by Elonen and her co-workers described the arrangements, experiences, and results of programs carried out by the Michigan School for the Blind. Elonen and Polzien (1965) described summer session programs for multihandicapped blind children during the summers of 1961 through 1964 and the very favorable results that were obtained with extremely deviant blind children by individual, intensive therapy. A surprisingly large percentage of these children were sufficiently rehabilitated to be referred to either day-school classes or residential schools.

As a result of this success, the Michigan School for the Blind established a full program to which some children, formerly committed to institutions for the retarded, were admitted (Elonen, Polzien, and Zwarensteyn, 1967). These children reacted to their frustrations with such aggressive violence that their families had removed them from their homes. They were considered as emotionally disturbed and non-stimulated blind children. Some others in the group remained on a very infantile level because of their parents' overprotective attitude. Frequently long periods of institutionalization had prevented any developmental progress. The provisions at the school include psychological therapy, speech and language training or speech therapy, physical and occupational therapy, music therapy, remedial reading, and special living conditions with hand-picked, understanding housemothers. The cases of six children were reported in some detail.

Elonen and Cain (1964) and Elonen and Zwarensteyn (1964) discussed in greater detail the methods applied in the Michigan programs. In the first paper, they stress that the therapist needs to have a deep personal commitment toward these children and must work with them in the same way in which he works with psychotic children. They warn that in this process the therapist may overidentify with a blind child to the extent that he negatively interprets actions of other people in the child's environment. The relationship is usually on a one-to-one basis and demands a high degree of skill and dedication on the part of the therapist.

In the second paper, the authors discuss in detail the deviations that may occur in the development of the young blind child in the areas of independence; of mobility, sensory, and motor skills; of speech and language; and of mental activities such as conceptualization, memory, humor, and socialization. They believe that in many of the deviant children retarded development, autistic behavior, and apparent brain damage may be only pseudocondi-

tions. For the prevention of such pseudo-conditions, they recommend intensive counseling for parents, information and demonstration of techniques in managing the child, information about developmental expectations for each individual child, and support for the parents on the basis of long-term observation of the child through his various developmental stages. Preconceived attitudes of parents and also of many professional people to whom the parents turn may affect the development of these children so severely that pseudoconditions become irreversible. More research is needed to ascertain this point of irreversibility and the indications for it. "Certainly, the earlier the parents can be encouraged to provide maximal nurture, motivation, and opportunity for growth, the more hopeful are the children's chances for attaining normal development" (pp. 609–610).

The cases of three blind children and their psychiatric therapy were presented by Green and Schecter (1957). Two were RLF cases showing severe disorders; the third, blind from early infancy, was not as autistic or retarded as the other two. Four phases of the therapeutic program are described:

(1) The individual work of the psychiatrist with the child. (2) Consultations with parents by the psychiatrist and the psychiatric social worker. (3) Placement of the child in daytime school programs, with regular consultations with the teachers. (4) Placement in institutions for disturbed blind children for those who could not be treated on a once-a-week clinic basis.

Attention is called to the need for early detection of such emotional disturbances, and the authors warn (pp. 645–646) of "the danger of explaining, all too easily, the psychological deviations on the basis of a child's handicap, rather than exploring the severe child-parent disturbances which have become organized around the handicap."

To the many case studies that have already been mentioned, Cohen's (1966) report on a blind spastic child must be added. He presented this case as an example of how a child can overcome the severe disadvantages of gross multiple handicaps (blindness, spastic quadriplegia, and hearing disorder) and early emotional deprivation. A stimulating school environment, a good program of physical therapy, special attention and help for specific problems, an accepting foster home, and above all, the child's own inner courage and drive toward growth were instrumental in achieving a healthy psychological and physical development despite a gloomy early picture.

Play therapy has also been found to be successful in restoring a measure of mental health to many blind children (Avery, 1968; Axline, 1947; Raskin, 1954; Rothschild, 1960).

There are two reports that deal with electroencephalographic findings of multihandicapped blind children. Akiyama, Parmelee, and Flescher (1964) studied the electroencephalograms of children who had varying degrees of visual handicaps. The frequency of abnormal EEGs was higher when the visual handicap was more severe, but there was no relationship between abnormal EEGs and the occurrence of seizures or the intellectual development. The authors conclude (p. 241): "These EEGs should not be interpreted as indication for a poor prognosis in terms of behavioral development." Similar observations are available in a study dealing with school-age children with retrolental fibroplasia (Boshes *et al.,* 1967).

Although there is very useful material available on the education of deaf-blind children (Robbins, 1960, 1963; Robbins and Stenquist, 1967; Contemporary Papers, 1967) that has psychological implications, and a valuable chapter on deaf-blindness in the adult population by Rothschild (1962), practically no psychological research studies dealing with this highly challenging group of multihandicapped children can be reported. This may be due to the fact that in the past their numbers were only very small, though during the more recent years they have greatly increased due to the unfortunate results of rubella epidemics.

Jordan (1964) draws attention to differences within the group of the deaf-blind, distinguishing those who are deafened-blind, blinded-deaf, and those who lack both senses from birth or early childhood on. These groups should be clearly distinguished in any future research.

H. and R. Rusalem (1964) examined the reactions of high school students and H. Rusalem (1965) those of college students (freshmen) to deaf-blindness. Both groups reported that they had practically no contact with any deaf-blind person—not surprising because of their small numbers. They tended to maintain a social distance from deaf-blind individuals, which prevented correction of their negative percept of deaf-blindness. The high school students were exposed to an unusually gifted deaf-blind speaker at a school assembly, which produced more accepting verbalized feelings that could, if reinforced, lead to attitude changes.

In summing up the discussion of multihandicapped blind children, some facts stand out as a result of experiences with them reflected in the literature. Any effective program to assist these children therapeutically must be based on a clinical approach. Ashcroft (1966, p. 93) stressed this by saying: "The therapeutic intervention must be rather drastic as compared to conventional educational programs. The program should be 'clinical' in nature—that is, it should be conducted virtually on a one-to-one basis." Cruickshank (1964) warned that in order to understand multihandicapped children, one cannot think of them in a generic sense. Each one is an individual and his special condition must be considered in clinical terms in order to find a workable solution, only after careful and frequently long exhaustive periods of study.

The effects of multiple handicaps cannot be understood by simply adding those of every handicap found in an individual child. They lead to something more and different than would be the result of a mere addition of the handicapping conditions. This idea has been expressed by Curtis (1966) as follows:

It is necessary for the examiner to recall throughout the interview and examination process that the list of characteristics which we associate with a certain degree of hearing loss, type of brain injury, or particular physical disability, when viewed in isolation, does not have the same significance when that particular disability occurs simultaneously with one or more other severe disabilities (p. 374).

So far as the causes of the problems in many of these children are concerned, Guess (1967) summed them up well in reviewing Sandler's (1963) study:

The blind child turns inward because he receives less stimulation in quantity and variety from his environment. Moreover, the blind child does not receive emotional feedback from his mother to reward and stimulate him. He lacks the continuity with environment afforded by vision and consequently directs his attention to his own bodily experiences. This drive for bodily gratification impairs his relationships to things and people around him (p. 473).

Finally, there is an obviously noticeable difference between the writings of psychoanalysts and of others concerning the outlook for successful improvement in the condition of retarded or disturbed blind children. The psychoanalytically oriented group is far less optimistic about it than the clinical-educationally oriented group. Most of the psychoanalytically oriented studies consider the ego damage resulting from congenital blindness either as irreversible or at best as only partially compensable. The clinical-educational group believes more optimistically that therapy and a wholesome environment can successfully restore the child's mental health, though they recognize that at a certain not-yet-determined point conditions caused by environmental deprivation may become irreversible.

Effects of Physical Factors

A number of physical factors related to the eyes doubtlessly affect the individual, although no research has clarified the extent and kind of this influence. Facial disfigurement is a frequent result of eye defects. The eyeball may be enlarged (as in congenital glaucoma) or abnormally small (microphthalmia), or there may be no eyeball at all (anophthalmia); the muscles controlling the movements of the eyeball or of the eyelids may not function normally and thus cause strabismus, nystagmus, or ptosis (dropping of the upper lid); X-ray treatment of the eyes to control malignant growths may have resulted in disfiguring X-ray burns; pathological changes in the eyeball or parts of it may be quite apparent. All these and other disfigurements are liable to make the individual quite self-conscious and ill at ease. The eye condition responsible for the visual defect may not be static but

BERTHOLD LOWENFELD

progressive, and this may cause anxiety and feelings of insecurity. There may be actual pain as a result of the eye defect (as, for instance, in glaucoma), or discomfort and irritation may sometimes serve to make the child acutely conscious of his eye trouble. Also, frequent and prolonged hospitalization because of eye pathology exerts its influence on the child, particularly if it necessitates separation from the mother during the earlier years of life. It may result in developmental retardation as well as in emotional reactions characteristic of deprivation of maternal care (Kanner, 1957, pp. 722–725; Spitz, 1946). Prolonged treatment of eye diseases by medication also has emotional effects on the child and his environment. Finally, any blindness that occurs late in life results in an emotional trauma which may manifest itself in various reaction forms.

CONCLUSION

Blindness is a defect of one sense, but it affects the individual in various ways. Though studies on the psychological implications of blindness have increased, research to connect behavior with specific effects of blindness is still needed. Personality inventories, scales, and interviews record only reported behavior, judgements (often about oneself), and opinions. Therefore, any analyses of these must be accepted with caution, no matter how refined and objective the statistical treatment may be. The problem of a blindness-adequate intelligence test still awaits solution.

The distinction between those who are totally and congenitally blind and those who are only partially blind or partially seeing or those who became blind later in life has not received due attention. The

lack of this distinction is responsible for ambiguity in the results of many studies and for contradictions between the results of some of them.

Behavioral studies (research as well as observations) provide increasing evidence that blindness, uncomplicated by other disorders of either organic or environmental nature, does not cause developmental disturbances. However, the chances that these may occur are heightened by the effects that the child's blindness may have, from early infancy on, on his social environment, particularly in the mother-child relationship. The effects of blindness modify some cognitive functions, and this may have a retarding influence, more noticeable during the preadolescent period. All this, however, does not prevent normal achievement according to the individual's capacity.

THE PARTIALLY SEEING CHILD

When Pintner in 1941 reviewed the literature on the partially seeing, he concluded his chapter by saying:

This chapter shows our ignorance rather than our knowledge. The special education of the partially seeing child is so recent that practically all of the effort and interest in this work has been concentrated on the organization, administration, and equipment of these classes. About the children themselves from a psychological point of view we know practically nothing (pp. 259–260).

Since then, conditions have not changed to any considerable extent, as indicated by Massie (1965) who concluded a review of a random sample of fifteen studies, published before 1963, dealing with partially seeing children by stating: "Research in the area investigated is scanty, and the results provide more questions than answers" (p. 58). Since 1963 some increase in the research activities dealing with this group of children can be noted, but it cannot compare, at least in quantity, with that in research in the area of the blind or with that of many other groups of impaired children.

We may be able to explain, at least in part, the reasons for the lack of research concerning partially seeing children. Most of them are, for all practical purposes, seeing children, and their handicap, if it is one, does not affect them in any different way from other children who slightly deviate from "the normal." It would, however, be quite valuable to know more about the ways in which children react to visual handicaps that put them into the category of partially seeing children.

According to Hathaway's (1959) revised book, the following children should be considered possible candidates for special education as partially seeing children:

(1) Children having a visual acuity of 20/70 or less in the better eye after all necessary medical or surgical treatment has been given and compensating lenses provided when the need for them is indicated. Such children must, however, have a residue of sight that makes it possible to use this as the chief avenue of approach to the brain. (2) Children with a visual deviation from the normal who, in the opinion of the eye specialist, can benefit from the special educational facilities provided for the partially seeing (p. 16).

Special educational opportunities should also be provided for children after eye operations, if readaptation in eye use and psychological readjustment is required, and for those with muscle anomalies, such as strabismus, which demand reeducation of an eye and psychological readjustment.

Kerby reported in 1952 (there are no more recent national data available) on causes and degrees of defective vision in 4,179 boys and 3,131 girls in 600 classes for partially seeing children. Of them, 20.8 percent had vision of 20/200 or less, 29.5 percent had vision from 20/70 to 20/200, 16 percent from 20/50 to 20/70, 24 percent better than 20/50, and for 9.7 percent, vision was not reported. These figures show that less than one-third of these children really come within the visual acuity range of partially seeing pupils. One-fifth of the pupils receiving education as partially seeing children fall under the definition of blindness. They are apparently able to take part in the instruction offered, and this may be taken as another proof of the already noted fact that visual acuity by itself is not a true indication of "visual efficiency." Forty percent of all pupils classified as partially seeing have vision better than 20/70, which, so far as visual acuity is concerned, would place them beyond the category of the partially seeing. They were most likely placed in these classes for other than visual reasons. As mentioned in the discussion of Definition of Visual Impairments, the last few decades have seen a change in the medical approach to the use of sight in defective eyes. Ophthalmologists now encourage unlimited use of sight, no matter how closely the eye must be brought to the object or to printed matter to be read. This change must undoubtedly permit many children, who in the past attended educational provisions for partially seeing children, to take part as regular pupils in normal classroom work. More up-to-date statistics would most likely show considerable changes in the above-given statistics of Kerby.

Table 5-2 shows the percentage distribution of causes of visual defects in the group of partially seeing children reported on by Kerby (1952, p. 138).

TABLE 5-2

Developmental Anolamies of structure		21.5%
Cataract and/or dislocated lens	11.3	
Albinism	3.7	
Other	4.3	
Multiple anomalies	2.2	
Diseases or defects of eyes		10.2%
Infectious diseases	3.4	
Injury	1.5	
Other	.4	
Cause unknown	4.9	
Refractive errors		48.7%
Myopia (incl. myopic and mixed astigmatism)	35.5	
Hyperopia (incl. hyperopic astigmatism)	12.8	
Type not known	.4	
Defects of muscle function		18.2%
Squint (incl. strabismus and amblyopia exanopsia)	8.8	
Nystagmus	9.4	
Cause undetermined		1.4%

A national study, in which hundreds of teachers reported details about over 1,000 fifth- and sixth-grade partially seeing children in more than a dozen states, was undertaken and reported on by Peabody and Birch (1967). They presented a composite portrait of a typical partially seeing child from which the following facts stand out. He lives with his parents who cooperate with the school; he is in a special class for the visually handicapped, and his next most likely placement would be in a resource-type program; he is most likely visually handicapped as a result of congenital myopia, and, though the teacher may not be informed about it, his near-point visual acuity is somewhat superior to his far-point visual acuity; he has no further educationally significant handicap though emotional problems may be pres-

ent; although he can read any type size from 12- to 24-point, he is more at ease with one type size, and there is no relation between type size and his far-point visual acuity; his reading distance is 6.5 inches, and he will use only his glasses with regular correction, but no visual aid; if given extra time, he does better in schoolwork involving reading, but his overall achievement is rated poorest in reading and spelling and best in music and physical education; his most serious academic weaknesses are in science, social studies, and language, and his highest achievement is in arithmetic computation; his IQ can be assumed to be at least 100. The most significant educational effect of his visual impairment is fatigue and underachievement. The author's summary portrait, which is even more abbreviated here, can only become meaningful for practical purposes if the study itself is consulted.

In their article the authors present some salient observations resulting from the study. Preschool identification and assessment should become common practice and should be considered in determining special educational placement. Materials need not be limited to a particular type size for the majority of partially seeing children unless this is medically contraindicated. Though most partially seeing children need more time for study than their seeing peers, planned instruction may reduce this need. The authors conclude their article by a call for reexamination of traditional educational practices and for development of new knowledge and procedures.

Bateman (1963) investigated the effect of limited vision on the reading and psycholinguistic processes of partially seeing children. In the course of this investigation, she gave details on her sample of 131 children who attended Grades 1 to 4 in classes (either of the resource or special class type) for partially seeing children in Illinois outside of the city of Chicago. This can well be considered a representative sample, and therefore, her more recent report on certain personal characteristics of these students is of special value because no national data are availabe. There were 59.5 percent boys, indicating a majority of boys as compared with girls. The mean IQ was 100, with the boys scoring 100.7 and the girls 97.5. Of the children, 23.5 percent had less than 20/200 vision, 34 percent had visual acuity from 20/70 through 20/200, 21 percent visual acuity from 20/40 to 20/70, and 17 percent visual acuity better than 20/40. This distribution is very similar to that reported by Kerby in 1952. It appeared that the girls were more severely handicapped than the boys. The distribution of causes of blindness showed some differences from that reported by Kerby. Myopia, the largest percentage, was reported for 24 percent (35.5 percent in the Kerby study); cataracts for 15 percent (11.3); hyperopia, 8 percent (12.8); albinism, 5 percent (3.7); nystagmus, 8 percent (9.4). Some of the other classifications were not directly comparable. In summary, refractive errors were found in 37 percent (48.7); muscle defects in 17 percent (18.2); developmental anomalies (cataract and albinism only) in 20 percent (15.0); and retrolental fibroplasia, 13 percent (none).

When cause of blindness was compared with intelligence and age, myopes and hyperopes were less severely handicapped, older, and showed lower IQ scores than the other groups. A comparison of visual acuity and intelligence showed that those with severe visual handicaps had the highest mean IQs (106.1); those with moderate defects came next (101.1); and those with mild defects had the lowest mean IQ

(95.0). This trend was statistically significant.

In a study limited to an unselected group of sixty partially seeing children in a large city school system, Livingston (1958, p. 37) collected data in order "to discover clues to the intelligence strengths and weaknesses of partially seeing children and whether enlarging the revised Stanford-Binet Intelligence Test would increase their score". Photographic enlargements of the tests did not produce any significant IQ gains as compared with the standard forms. In comparing the partially seeing with 407 normally seeing children, the normally seeing did better in visual-motor coordination, and the partially seeing were superior in two abstract word tests. The author concludes that there was little evidence that the partially seeing child performs less adequately than the normally seeing in broad areas of mental functioning. Nevertheless, he refers repeatedly to the weaknesses of partially seeing children in certain areas such as social judgment involving interaction, conceiving and executing a planning operation, and emotional security. There are no data given on any of these and other observations, which, as presented in this abridged version of a doctor's thesis, must be considered unconfirmed.

Relationships among certain educational and psychological variables as they pertain to partially seeing children were investigated in an exploratory study by Bateman and Wetherell (1967). Questionnaire responses were obtained from thirty-one teachers of partially seeing children in Illinois, exclusive of Chicago, giving individual information on 297 children in Grades 1 through 12. In their article Bateman and Wetherell quote some findings of a previous study dealing with the same population (Bateman, 1964 *b*) which have psychological significance. The mean IQ, reported for 167 children, was 99.2, with 15 and 16 percent, respectively, having IQs below 84 and above 115; 69 percent had IQs between 84 and 115. There were significant differences between resource room teachers and special class teachers, with the former being more positive in their perception of the ability of children to compete with normal children and in being more dependent on large-type books and less inclined to use optical aids. The resource room teachers did not differ in their responses to items concerning perceived attitudes of regular classroom teachers toward having a partially seeing child, concerning academic achievement, intelligence, behavior or discipline problems, social acceptance, emotional adjustment, and concerning parental attitudes toward program and child (p. 34).

Bateman and Wetherell divided the partially seeing children into three groups: severely, moderately, and mildly visually impaired. They found that the severely impaired group scored higher in individual intelligence tests than the mildly impaired group. So far as social-emotional adjustment is concerned, the midly impaired showed better adjustment than the severely impaired, though both were better than the moderately impaired group. There was no difference in the attitudes of parents of the two groups toward the special program, and about three-fourths of the parents in both groups were judged as having normal attitudes toward their children. There was a strong relationship between poor adjustment and low intelligence, but social adjustment was not significantly related to either vision, age, or type of program.

In her already mentioned study, Bateman (1963) determined reading achievement and grade level by administration of four of the most widely used reading tests. Fourth-graders read 3.5 school months below, whereas the average reading grade of third-graders corresponded with their average grade placement. However, when reading grades were converted to reading ages, reading age of third graders was 5.2 months and of fourth graders 6.5 months below their mental age. There was a significant trend for brighter children to read less well in relation to their mental age than did slower children. These and other findings led Bateman to the conclusion (p. 18) that "mental age alone is not an adequate predictor of the reading performance of these children." There was no difference in reading achievement between boys and girls although the boys' IQs and mental ages were found to be slightly higher than those of the girls.

So far as errors in reading are concerned, partially seeing children made excessive errors only in vowel discrimination. This is explained as a result of the fact that in print all five vowels are of the same height and, with the exception of the "i," quite similar in shape, thus almost inviting errors for those who have visual defects. So far as visual acuity and reading achievement are concerned (p. 24), a "clustering of mild visual defect, refractive errors, lower intelligence, and lower reading achievement strongly suggests again that these children were placed in classes for the partially seeing for reasons beyond visual defect per se." This confirms a conclusion stated before in connection with Kerby's report.

In the course of the study, the Illinois Test of Psycholinguistic Abilities (ITPA) was administered to ninety-three partially seeing children, Grades 1 to 3, in order to determine whether and how their performances differed from those of normally seeing children. As a group, the partially seeing children were significantly inferior to normals in visual-decoding, motor-encoding, visual-motor sequential, and visual-motor association subtests but did equally well on the auditory-vocal channel subtests. As to be expected, children with severe visual defects showed more marked visual channel deficits than children with mild and moderate visual defects. Performance on the ITPA was found to be related to eye condition only through the indirect effect of visual acuity.

From the results it was concluded that, in general, methods of teaching reading to partially seeing children are beyond serious criticism, though the author suggests that visual discrimination of vowels, reading of all visual symbols, and elimination of faulty eye movements should receive emphasis. Also, partially seeing children should be given special assistance in expressing ideas and emotions motorically. Experimentation in the area of helping children to interpret or obtain meaning from visual symbols is also recommended. The study has supplied evidence (p. 43) that "minimal sensory intake may be sufficient for near maximal central efficiency" because partially seeing children "did not necessarily show a visual channel psycholinguistic deficit." This moved the author to conclude her study (p. 44) by saying: "Speculative, theoretical justification has thus been presented for continuing with increased zeal an already established precept of special education—helping each child use *centrally* what he has *peripherally*."

Karnes and Wollersheim (1963) investigated the specific strengths and weaknesses of sixteen partially seeing children. They formulated many pertinent hypotheses, but the results of their study are scientifically untenable because they were based on a sample of only sixteen children, ranging in age from seven years to fourteen years and eleven months, with a wide visual acuity range from 20/70 to 20/200. Their use of percentages (two children—12.5 percent!) and of averages with such small numbers are examples of their approach. The studies of Bateman (1963) and Peabody and Birch (1967) raised practically the same questions and answered them by sound research based on statistically reliable data.

Because reading plays such an important role in our culture, particularly in acquiring an education, much attention has been given to the kind of print and the size of type that would be most adequate for partially seeing children. Past studies have not demonstrated how 24-point compares with 18-point type, the two types most widely used in books especially printed for partially seeing children. Nolan (1959) studied this problem in a carefully designed experiment and found that both types were read with equal reading speed, the readability criterion selected for his study. Also, a common textbook letter type was read more rapidly than an experimental type thought to be more legible. These findings are an experimentally founded sanction for the enlarged presentation of regularly printed textbooks.

A study of Mueller (1962) sheds more light on the use of enlarged material. He investigated the effects of illustration size on test performance of visually limited children and administered the Peabody Picture Vocabulary Test, plates of which are availabe in two forms and in two sizes, 5 by 7 inches (used in the regular published edition) and 8½ by 11 inches. The thirty-nine subjects of the study were divided into two visual acuity groups (p. 126), one with vision of 20/70 to 20/200 and the other of 20/200 to 10/200, 10/200 being regarded "as the least de-

BERTHOLD LOWENFELD

gree of vision which is generally useable in reading ink print." The results show that children with mild visual impairments (20/70 to 20/200) did not show any difference in their performance by using the two different sizes of the test. Children in the lower vision group (20/200 to 10/200) showed significant gains when the larger plates were used. The test results as a whole were lower than those of a population with no visual handicap. Mueller concluded that the Peabody Picture Vocabulary Test was appropriate for use with visually limited children. The author suggested that the results of his study may be applicable to type size and indicated that children with vision better than 20/200 derive little benefit from large type, which may be useful to children with lower visual acuity.

In an evaluation of large-type usage, Fonda (1966), an opthalmologist, stated (p. 297) that such type is indicated in the following situations:

1. When distant vision ranges from 2/200 to 10/200 (decisions are often difficult for upper and lower limits);
2. When the patient cannot read 12-point type (pica typewriter) at 2 inches from the eye;
3. When a greater reading distance is mandatory, for example, for mathematics and accounting;
4. When a patient insists that large type is more comfortable and easier on his eyes. (This statement may be valid, but the advantage is offset by the need for a larger book).

Eames (1959) studied a population of 3,500 school children, half of them reading failures and half unselected. He found a much greater incidence of hypermetropia and exophoria at the reading distance (a type of strabismus) in the reading fail-

ure group, whereas myopia occurred with similar frequency in both groups. Also (p. 27), "Pathological eye conditions as distinguished from eye defects and deficiencies have appeared to the extent of nearly five percent among reading failures which is slightly less than twice the frequency found among the non-failures." Eames offers a valuable discussion of the physiology of seeing to read and of the educational indications and implications of various eye conditions. It must be concluded that learning to read is affected by vision problems and that partially seeing children need special attention in order to avoid reading difficulties, or remedial services if such have developed.

Bixel (1966) pointed out that, according to present practices, children who pass the Snellen test are expected to do the culturally demanded vision task of absorbing meaning from print. He believes that reading as a skill is a comparatively new activity for mankind for which man is visually not adapted. This causes visual problems in reading for which Snellen tests are of little help.

Nolan (1959) determined that partially seeing children have a reading rate of 106 words per minute (p. 43). This slow rate, considerably less than half than that of their seeing peers, makes the use of recorded material, such as Talking Books with about 180 to 200 words read per minute, advantageous to partially seeing students.

Bischoff (1967) adapted the Listening Test of the Sequential Tests of Educational Progress and administered it to sixty-three partially seeing students divided in two experimental groups and one control group. The two experimental groups received listening comprehension lessons consisting of different material for ten weeks, whereas the control group did not receive any. The results of the experiment showed that both instructional groups increased their listening efficiency significantly, whereas the noninstructional group actually showed a decrease. Bischoff concluded that teachers should become aware that listening efficiency is a skill that can be improved by listening instruction lessons and that with increased skills, recorded material could effectively supplement reading media presently used.

There are two papers available dealing with the relationship between visual defects and juvenile delinquency. Wallace (1940) found that refractive errors are more frequent in juvenile delinquents than in the normal population. He concluded that the visual defect may cause discomfort which can lead to maladjustment in school, followed by truancy and ultimately by delinquency. Blumenthal (1941) described a case in which, after an eye was lost as a result of injury, such symptoms as disobedience, quarrelsomeness, cruelty, temper tantrums, and truancy were observed. He believes that this adolescent wanted to regain status by being "tough" and thus compensated for the feelings of insecurity by developing aggressive behavior patterns.

Pintner and Forlano (1943) administered in large-type print the Aspects of Personality Test and the Pupil Portraits Test to more than 400 children in classes for the partially seeing. The scores did not reveal any consistent difference from the norms established for seeing children.

Benton (1951) underlined the importance of parental responsibility and of the child's feelings of security. He emphasized that in the case of handicapped children (p. 25), "their emotional difficulties bear a closer relationship to their early home experiences and to their general background than to their visual defect." He also called attention to the possibility that emotional conflicts may be channeled through conversion to the visual apparatus, thus causing complaints of visual disturbance ranging from blinking to actual complete blindness.

Young (1952) discussed the results that some of the more common eye defects may have in causing fears and anxieties, self-centeredness or extroverted behavior, and worry about the cause and final outcome of the eye disorder. She called attention to the effect of disfigurements due to certain visual handicaps, which may cause feelings of embarrassment or inferiority and make the individual avoid social experiences. Strabismus may lead to shyness and introverted behavior unless the eyes are straightened before school age when the social effects of the condition may become active. Myopia, in which distance vision is poor, may cause self-centeredness and a desire to confine oneself to solitary activities; but hyperopia, in which near vision is poor, may lead to neglect of school activities requiring close eye work and encourage interest in athletics.

The psychological effects of strabismus were discussed by Lipton (1967). He used observations of a number of psychoanalysts about themselves, about their own strabismic children, and about patients. He differentiated effects for those who have the condition from birth and those who acquired it, usually at two-and-one-half to three years of age. For the former, the effects are mainly in the reactions of the environment to the cosmetic defect, since only one eye is usually functionally blind (amblyopia ex anopsia) and the child can see with the other. For those who became strabismic later in childhood, the effects may be

BERTHOLD LOWENFELD

similar to a surgical trauma. Learning difficulties, fears, and fantasies may be the result (p. 782), although the strabismus is not a severe eye condition but "a cross to bear."

McLaughlin (1964) discussed strabismus and amblyopia ex anopsia (deterioration of vision though disuse), the latter usually being considered a result of the former. He presented evidence that the strabismus-amblyopia syndrome's underlying disorder is a previously unrecognized anomaly of visual perception, leading to a "suppression" of images perceived by the affected eye.

Froistad (1966) calls attention to the emotionally disturbing effects of being called "blind" on those who have some useful vision on the one hand and of not recognizing the effects of a visual handicap on the other hand. He gives the tragic case history of a boy exemplifying both conditions.

Hackbusch (1950) recommended the use of various tests with the partially seeing, such as the Stanford-Binet, the Wechsler-Bellevue Intelligence Scale, the Jastak Wide Range Achievement Test, and the Vineland Social Maturity Scale. Some of these can be copied on yellow paper in as large size print as is necessary and comfortable for the child. She found the Human Figure Drawings Test and the Rorschach Test the most useful personality tests for this group but does not give any results of their application. She called attention to "problem parents" whose anxiety, sadness, or ambitiousness affects the child. Some parents have "paranoid attitudes" and refuse to accept or face the child's handicap. Various instances of social and educational maladjustment are given in which visual defects were the causative factors but were not recognized until discovered in specific situations.

Lowenfeld (1950 a) called attention to the need for medical and psychological research in this area and discussed some basic needs of visually handicapped preschool children. He found them to be identical with those of all children but stressed that they must be satisfied according to the child's sensory capacities.

Even if research on the effects of eye difficulties on the personality of children is practically nonexistent, there are enough observations available to prove that they may cause more or less severe forms of maladjustment. There are largely three ways in which an eye defect may show its psychological effects:

1. It may limit the child in his visual activities and in those others which are governed by vision. The kind and severity of the defect determines the nature of the limitations; its degree depends on personality and environmental factors.

2. The eye condition may be a changing one or cause actual discomfort or pain, thus creating feelings of insecurity and anxiety about imminent attacks as well as about the future progress of the pathological process.

3. There are various forms of mild or more severe facial disfigurements, for instance in strabismus or nystagmus, which may create a particular social reaction in the child's environment. The wearing of glasses, particularly heavy ones, is a cause of physical discomfort and also frequently evokes among children social reactions that are quite negative in their effects. Also the one-eyed child, even with good visual acuity in the remaining eye, may feel self-conscious, particularly if he must wear an artificial eye.

How an individual child reacts to any of these three basic factors will depend on his personality, his past experiences (which of course have become a part of his personality), and on his environment, which includes his family, his school, and his friends. We have no evidence of particular reaction patterns, but it is safe to assume that children react to eye difficulties essentially in the same way in which they react to other similar conditions affecting them.

Stolz and Stolz (1950) confirmed this in discussing the emotional effects of wearing glasses (p. 95):

> ... for every example we may give of a girl disturbed because she has to wear glasses or a boy disturbed by his large, prominent nose, the reader can probably match a case with similar characteristics who gave no evidence of any disturbance. Of four girls in the California study who wore glasses, three were concerned about their appearance, while one showed no evidence of disturbance, nor did the fact seem in any way to interfere with her satisfactory social relations.

If a child is unable to succeed in his school work because of a visual defect, it may make him feel inadequate and inferior to his peers. Therefore, an effective screening program for eye difficulties is of great importance because it is instrumental in finding those children who need special educational assistance in order to cope with their eye problems.

The need for the best possible improvement of any individual's vision is unquestioned; it is the more necessary if he is a visually impaired child with some useful vision. Hoover and Kupfer (1959) reported on the work of seven low-vision clinics and concluded (p. 187): "The most valuable aid to vision is the proper correction of the refractive error. This accounted for the largest improvement in visual acuity. Further improvement in reading and close work was obtained with the use of special low-vision aids."

Lowrey (1965) stressed that the patient should be psychologically prepared to accept a low-vision aid and observed that children and young people usually adjust rapidly to their use.

Freudenberger and Robbins (1959) also called attention to the need for assistance in accepting optical aids, rendered either by a social worker or a psychologist according to the patient's need. They distinguished three types of attitudes toward the use of optical aids. The "acceptor" is one who can perceive situations rationally and without undue neurotic involvement. He tends to be a friendly, optimistic, active, and self-accepting person, neither submissive nor dominant. He wants to be helped and is ready to try adjustment. "Rejectors" tend to be negativistic, hostile, maybe pessimistic and rejecting of themselves and their eye conditions, inactive, and submissive or dominant. The "mixed type" is not clearly accepting or rejecting and needs a cautious approach. Rejectors and those of the mixed type will only slowly adjust to a low-vision aid and frequently need assistance over a long period of time.

A few studies dealing with the blind have furnished some indication that the partially seeing tend to be less well adjusted than either the blind or the seeing (Brieland, 1950 b; Cowen and Bobgrove, 1966; Cowen et al., 1961; Greenberg and Jordan, 1957). Apparently the marginal, or better overlapping position (as explained by Meyerson in Chapter 1) of the partially seeing child often intensifies his personality and adjustment problems. For example, teachers in schools for the blind have frequently voiced complaints that children with considerable sight in these schools are "problem cases." This may be explained as a reaction of children who are placed in an environment that does not permit them to make full use of their vision, which they consider their greatest sensory asset. Being frustrated in their visual functioning, they may develop resentment and asocial or even hostile behavior. For this and other reasons it is recognized that partially seeing children should preferably attend regular classes in public schools and receive any needed assistance in a special room with a resource teacher or from a special itinerant teacher, as described by Scholl (1967, pp. 307–311).

This survey shows that, though remarkable progress has been made in the last decade, our knowledge of the psychological implications of partial sight is still fragmentary. The assumption that partially seeing children are, in general, basically functioning like seeing children has received support in many of the studies. It appears that a functional differentation within the heterogeneous group of children with visual impairments, already evidenced in some studies, is a prerequisite for future successful research efforts.

References

Abel, G. L. The blind adolescent and his needs. *Exceptional Children,* 1961, *27,* 309–310, 331–334.

Akiyama, Y., Parmelee, A., & Flescher, J. The electroencephalogram in visually handicapped children. *The Journal of Pediatrics,* 1964, *65,* 233–242.

American Association of Workers for the Blind. *Contemporary papers.* Vol. 2. Washington, D.C., 1967.

Ammons, C. H., Worchel, P., & Dallenbach, K. M. "Facial vision": The perception of obstacles out of doors by blindfolded deafened subjects. *American Journal of Psychology,* 1953, *66,* 519–553.

Anderson, R. M. The visually impaired mentally retarded: A selected bibliography. *New Outlook for the Blind,* 1965, *59,* 357–360.

Ashcroft, S. C. Delineating the possible for the multi-handicapped child with visual impairment. *Sight-Saving Review,* 1966, *36,* 90–94.

Avery, C. Para-analytic group therapy with adolescent multi-handicapped blind. *New Outlook for the Blind,* 1968, *62,* 65–72.

———. Play therapy with the blind. *International Journal for the Education of the Blind,* 1968, *18,* 41–46.

Axelrod, S. *Effects of early blindness: Performance of blind and sighted children on tactile and auditory tasks.* New York: American Foundation for the Blind, 1959.

Axline, V. M. *Play therapy.* Boston: Houghton-Mifflin Company, 1947, Chap. XXI.

Bachelis, L. A. Developmental patterns of individuals with bilateral congenital anophthalmos. *New Outlook for the Blind,* 1967, *61,* 113–119.

Ball, M. J. Mobility in perspective. *Blindness 1964.* Washington, D.C.: American Association of Workers for the Blind, pp. 107–141.

Barker, R. G. *et al. Adjustment to physical handicap and illness: A survey of the social psychology of physique and disability* (rev. ed.) New York: Social Science Research Council, 1953.

Barraga, N. *Increased visual behavior in low vision children.* New York: American Foundation for the Blind, 1964.

Bateman, B. The modifiability of sighted adults' perceptions of blind children's abilities. *New Outlook for the Blind,* 1964, *58,* 133–135. (*a*)

———. *Reading and psycholinguistic processes of partially seeing children.* Research Monograph. Washington, D. C.: Council for Exceptional Children, 1963.

———. Sighted children's perception of blind children's abilities. *Exceptional Children,* 1962, *29,* 42–46.

———. Some educational characteristics of partially seeing children. In *Selected Convention Papers.* Washington, D.C.: Council for Exceptional Children, 1964, pp. 74–82. (*b*)

———, & Wetherell, J. L. Some educational characteristics of partially seeing children. *International Journal for the Education of the Blind,* 1967, *17,* 33–40.

Bauman, M. K. *Adjustment to Blindness.* Pennsylvania: State Council for the Blind, 1954.

———. Group differences disclosed by inventory items. *International Journal for the Education of the Blind,* 1964, *13,* 101–106.

———. Studies in the application of motor skills techniques to the vocational adjustment of the blind. *Journal of Applied Psychology,* 1946, *30,* 144–154.

——— & Hayes, S. P. *A manual for the psychological examination of the adult blind.* New York: The Psychological Corporation, 1951.

Bauman, Platt, H., & Strauss, S. A measure of personality for blind adolescents. *International Journal for the Education of the Blind,* 1963, *13,* 7–12.

Bauman & Yoder, N. M. *Adjustment to blindness—reviewed.* Springfield, Ill.: Charles C. Thomas, 1966.

Benton, P. C. The emotional aspects of visual handicaps. *Sight-Saving Review,* 1951, *21,* 25.

Berg, J., & Worchel, P. Sensory contributions to human maze learning: A comparison of matched blind, deaf, and normals. *Journal of General Psychology,* 1956, *54,* 81–93.

Berry, M. F., & Eisenson, J. *The defective in speech.* New York: Appleton-Century-Crofts, 1942, Pp. 340–353.

Bischoff, R. W. Improvement of listening comprehension in partially sighted students. *Sight-Saving Review,* 1967, *37,* 161–165.

Bixel, G. Vision: Key to learning or not learning. *Education,* 1966, *87,* 180–184.

Blanchard, I., Bowling, D., & Roberts, R. L. Evaluation of an educational testing program for retarded blind children. *New Outlook for the Blind,* 1968, *62,* 131–133.

Blank. H. R. Countertransference problems in the professional worker. *New Outlook for the Blind,* 1954, *48,* 185–188.

———. Dreams of the blind. *The Psychoanalytic Quarterly,* 1958, *27,* 158–174.

———. Psychoanalysis and blindness. *The Psychoanalytic Quarterly,* 1957, *26,* 1–24.

Blumenthal, F. Physical defects in the genesis of juvenile delinquency. *New York State Journal of Medicine,* 1941, *41,* 154–159.

Bolli, L. Le rêve et les aveugles. *Journal de Psychologie,* 1932, *29,* 2–73, 258–309.

Boshes, L. D. *et al.* Longitudinal appraisal of school-age children with retrolental fibroplasia. *Diseases of the Nervous System,* 1967, *28,* 221–230.

Braverman, S. The psychological roots of attitudes toward the blind. In *Attitudes Toward Blindness.* New York: American Foundation for the Blind, 1951, pp. 22–32.

Brieland, D. M. A comparative study of the speech of blind and sighted children. *Speech Monographs,* 1950, *17*(1), 99–103. *(a)*

———. Personality problems of the blind and visually handicapped as revealed by a projective technique. *The American Psychologist,* 1950, *5,* 340. *(b)*

Brodey, W. M. Normal developmental learning and the education of the child born blind. *Gifted Child Quarterly,* 1962, *6,* 141–149.

Brown, P. A. Responses of blind and seeing adolescents to an introversion-extroversion questionnaire. *Journal of Psychology,* 1938, *6,* 137–147.

———. Responses of blind and seeing adolescents to a neurotic inventory. *Journal of Psychology,* 1939, *7,* 211–221.

Bucknam, F. G. Preventive child psychiatry at a residential school. *New Outlook for the Blind,* 1967, *61,* 232–237.

Buell, C. E. *Motor performance of visually handicapped children.* Berkeley: Charles Edwin Buell, 1950.

Bürklen, K. *Blinden-psychologie.* Leipzig: Johann Ambrosius Barth, 1924.

———. *Touch reading of the blind.* Trans. by F. K. Merry. New York: American Foundation for the Blind, 1932.

Burlingham, D. Developmental considerations in the occupations of the blind. In *The Psychoanalytic Study of the Child.* New York: International Universities Press, Inc., 1967, *22,* 187–198.

———. Hearing and its role in the development of the blind. In *The Psychoanalytic Study of the Child.* New York: International Universities Press, Inc., 1964, *19,* 95–112.

———. Psychic problems of the blind. *American Imago,* 1941, *2,* 43–85.

———. Some notes on the development of the blind. In *The Psychoanalytic Study of the Child.* New York: International Universities Press, Inc., 1961, *16,* 121–145.

———. Some problems of ego development in blind children. In *The Psychoanalytic Study of the Child.* New York: International Universities Press, Inc., 1965, *20,* 194–208.

Caldwell, F. F. *A comparison of blind and seeing children in certain educational abilities.* New

York: American Foundation for the Blind, 1932.

Cantril, H., & Allport, G. W. *The psychology of radio*. New York: Harper & Row, Publishers, 1935.

Chevigny, H., & Braverman, S. *The adjustment of the blind*. New Haven: Yale University Press, 1950.

Cholden, L. S. *A psychiatrist works with blindness*. New York: American Foundation for the Blind, 1958.

Cicenia, E. F., *et al.* The blind child with multiple handicaps: A challenge. *International Journal for the Education of the Blind*, 1965, *14*, 65–71, 105–112.

Cohen, J. Development of a blind spastic child: A case study. *Exceptional Children*, 1966, *32*, 291–294.

Cole, N. J., & Taboraff, L. H. The psychiatric problems of the congenitally blind child. *The American Journal of Orthopsychiatry*, 1955, *25*, 627–639.

Costa, A. Sogni di fanciulli ciechi e semiveggenti. *Rivista de Psicologia*, 1937, *33*, 44–52.

Cotzin, M., & Dallenbach, K. M. "Facial vision": The role of pitch and loudness in the perception of obstacles by the blind. *American Journal of Psychology*, 1950, *63*, 485–515.

Cowen, E. L., & Bobgrove, P. H. Marginality of disability and adjustment. *Perceptual and Motor Skills*, 1966, *23*, 869–870.

Cowen, E. L., Underberg, R. P., & Verillo, R. T. The development of an attitude to blindness scale. *Journal of Social Psychology*, 1958, *48*, 297–304.

Cowen, E. L., *et al. Adjustment to visual disability in adolescence*. New York: American Foundation for the Blind, 1961.

Cratty, B. J. *et al.* The development of perceptual-motor abilities in blind children and adolescents. *New Outlook for the Blind*, 1968, *62*, 111–117.

Cratty, B. J., & Sams, T. A. *The body-image of blind children*. New York: American Foundation for the Blind, 1968.

Cruickshank, W. M. The multiple-handicapped child and courageous action. *International Journal for the Education of the Blind*, 1964, *13*, 65–76.

Curriculum guide: Pre-cane mobility and orientation skills for the blind. Lansing: Michigan School for the Blind, 1966.

Curtis, W. S. The evaluation of verbal performance in multiply handicapped blind children. *Exceptional Children*, 1966, *32*, 367–374.

Cutsforth, T. D. *The blind in school and society* (rev. ed.). New York: American Foundation for the Blind, 1951.

———. The unreality of words to the blind. *The Teachers Forum*, 1932, *4*, 86–9.

Dauterman, W. L., Shapiro, B., & Suinn, R. M. Performance tests of intelligence for the blind reviewed. *International Journal for the Education of the Blind*, 1967, *17*, 8–16.

Davis, C. J. The assessment of intelligence of visually handicapped children. *International Journal for the Education of the Blind*, 1962, *12*, 48–51.

———. Development of the self-concept. *New Outlook for the Blind*, 1964, *58*, 49–51.

Dean, S. I. Adjustment testing and personality factors of the blind. *Journal of Consulting Psychology*, 1957, *21*, 171–177.

Dembo, T., Leviton, G. L., & Wright, B. A. Adjustment to misfortune—A problem of social-psychological rehabilitation. *Artificial Limbs*, 1956, *3*, 4–62.

Deutsch, E. The dream imagery of the blind. *Psychoanalytic Review*, 1928, *5*, 288–293.

Duetsch, F. The sense of reality in persons born blind. *Journal of Psychology*, 1940, *10*, 121–140.

Diderot, D. *Letter on the blind for the use of those who see*. Chicago: Open Court Publishing Co., 1916, pp. 88–104. Reprinted: *Blindness 1966*. Washington, D.C.: American Association of Workers for the Blind, pp. 210–230.

Dokecki, P. R. Verbalism and the blind. A critical review of the concept and the literature. *Exceptional Children*, 1966, *32*, 525–530.

Dolanski, V. Les aveugles possèdent-ils le "sense des obstacles"? *L'Année Psychologique*, 1930, *31*, 1–50.

———. Do the blind "see" obstacles? ... *And There Was Light*, 1931, *1*, 8–12.

Donlon, E. T. An evaluation center for the blind child with multiple handicaps. *International Journal for the Education of the Blind*, 1964, *13*, 75–78.

Drever, J. Early learning and the perception of space. *American Journal of Psychology*, 1955, *68*, 605–614.

Duncan, B. K. A comparative study of finger-maze learning by blind and sighted subjects. *Journal of Genetic Psychology,* 1934, *44,* 69–94.

Eames, T. H. Visual handicaps to reading. *Journal of Education,* 1959, *141,* 1–34.

Eichorn, J. R., & Vigaroso, H. R. Orientation and mobility for pre-school blind children. *International Journal for the Education of the Blind,* 1967, *17,* 48–50.

Elonen, A. S., & Cain, A. C. Diagnostic evaluation and treatment of deviant blind children. *The American Journal of Orthopsychiatry,* 1964, *34,* 625–633.

Elonen, A. S., & Polzien, M. Experimental program for deviant blind children. *New Outlook for the Blind,* 1965, *59,* 122–126.

Elonen, A. S., Polzien, M., & Zwarensteyn, S. B. The "uncommitted" blind child: Results of intensive training of children formerly committed to institutions for the retarded. *Exceptional Children,* 1967, *33,* 301–7.

Elonen, A. S., & Zwarensteyn, S. B. Appraisal of developmental lag in certain blind children. *The Journal of Pediatrics,* 1964, *65,* 599–610.

Enc, M. E., & Stolurow, L. M. A comparison of the effects of two recording speeds on learning and retention. *New Outlook for the Blind,* 1960, *54,* 39–48.

Ewart, A. G., & Carp, F. M. Recognition of tactual form by sighted and blind subjects. *American Journal of Psychology,* 1963, *76,* 488–491.

Fairbanks, G., Gutman, N., & Miron, M. Effects of time compression on auditory comprehension of spoken messages. *Journal of Speech and Hearing Disorders,* 1957, *22,* 10–19.

Felden, H. W. *Die ganzwortmethode im erstleseunterricht der blindenschule (The whole-word method in the beginning reading instruction in the school for the blind).* Hannover-Kirchrode: Verein zur Förderung der Blindenbildung, 1955.

Fertsch, P. An analysis of braille reading. *New Outlook for the Blind,* 1946, *40,* 128–131.

———. Hand dominance in reading braille. *American Journal of Psychology,* 1947, *60,* 335–349.

Finestone, S., Lukoff, I. F., & Whiteman, M. *Aspects of the travel adjustment of blind persons.* New York: American Foundation for the Blind, 1960.

Fisher, G. H. Spatial localization by the blind. *American Journal of Psychology,* 1964, *77,* 2–14.

Fitting, E. A. *Evaluation of adjustment to blindness.* New York: American Foundation for the Blind, 1954.

Fonda, G. An evaluation of large type. *New Outlook for the Blind,* 1966, *60,* 296–298.

Foulke, E. A language of the skin. *New Outlook for the Blind,* 1963, *57,* 1–3.

———. Time compressed recorded speech and faster aural reading. *Blindness 1967.* Washington, D.C.: American Association of Workers for the Blind, pp. 11–20.

Foulke, E., *et al.* The comprehension of rapid speech by the blind. *Exceptional Children,* 1962, *29,* 134–141.

Fraiberg, S., & Freedman, D. A. Studies in the ego development of the congenitally blind child. In *The Psychoanalytic Study of the Child.* New York: International Universities Press, Inc., 1964, *19,* 113–169.

Fraiberg, S., Siegel, B. L., & Gibson, R. The role of sound in the search behavior of a blind infant. In *The Psychoanalytic Study of the Child.* New York: International Universities Press, Inc., 1966, *21,* 327–357.

Freedman, D. B. Smiling in blind infants and the issue of innate vs. acquired. *Journal of Child Psychology and Psychiatry,* 1964, *5,* 171–184. Reprinted in *New Outlook for the Blind,* 1967, *61,* 156–163, 194–201.

Freudenberger, H. J., & Robbins, I. Characteristics of acceptance and rejection. *American Journal of Ophthalmology,* 1959, *47,* 582–584.

Froistad, W. M. The partially seeing are not blind. *New Outlook for the Blind,* 1966, *60,* 239–242.

Fulcher, J. S. *"Voluntary" facial expression in blind and seeing children.* New York: Archives of Psychology, no. 272, 1952.

Garry, R. J., & Ascarelli, A. Teaching topographical orientation and spatial organization to congenitally blind children. *Journal of Education,* 1960, *143,* 1–48.

Gesell, A., Ilg, F. L., & Bullis, G. E. *Vision: Its development in infant and child.* New York: P. B. Hoeber, Inc., 1950.

Gilbert, J. G., & Rubin, E. J. Evaluating the intellect of blind children. *New Outlook for the Blind,* 1965, *59,* 238–240.

Gomulicki, B. R. The development of perception and learning in blind children. *The New Beacon,* 1962, *46,* 118–121.

Goodman, L. A treatment program for multiply-handicapped blind young adults. *Blindness 1967.* Washington, D. C.: American Association of Workers for the Blind, pp. 89–103.

Gowman, A. G. *The war blind in American social structure.* New York: American Foundation for the Blind, 1957.

Graham, M. D. *Multiply impaired blind children: A national problem.* New York: American Foundation for the Blind, 1968.

————. *Social research on blindness: Present status and future potentials.* New York: American Foundation for the Blind, 1960.

Green, M. R., & Schecter, D. E. Autistic and symbiotic disorders in three blind children. *The Psychiatric Quarterly,* 1957, *31,* 628–646.

Greenberg, H., & Jordan, S. Differential effects of total blindness and partial sight. *Exceptional Children,* 1957, *24,* 123–124.

Griffin, D. R. Echolocation by the blind. In *Listening in the dark.* New Haven, Conn.: Yale University Press, 1958, pp. 297–322.

Guess, D. Mental retardation and blindness: A complex and relatively unexplored dyad. *Exceptional Children,* 1967, *33,* 471–479.

Hackbusch, F. Psychological study of partially seeing and children with other visual problems. *Sight-Saving Review,* 1950, *20,* 157–162.

Hapeman, L. B. Developmental concepts of blind children between the ages of three and six as they relate to orientation and mobility. *International Journal for the Education of the Blind,* 1967, *17,* 41–48

Hardy, R. E. *The anxiety scale for the blind.* New York: American Foundation for the Blind, 1968. *(a)*

————. Prediction of manifest anxiety levels of blind persons through the use of a multiple regression technique. *International Journal for the Education of the Blind,* 1967, *17,* 51–55.

————. A study of manifest anxiety among blind residential school students. *New Outlook for the Blind,* 1968, *62,* 173–180. *(b)*

Harley, R. K., Jr. *Verbalism among blind children.* New York: American Foundation for the Blind, 1963.

Harris, J. C. Veering tendency as a function of anxiety in the blind. *Research Bulletin No. 14.* New York: American Foundation for the Blind, 1967, pp. 53–63.

Hartlage, L. C. Differences in listening comprehension of the blind and the sighted. *International Journal for the Education of the Blind,* 1963, *13,* 1–6.

Hartong, J. R. A special orientation and mobility project at a residential school. *New Outlook for the Blind,* 1968, *62,* 118–121.

Hatfield, E. M. Causes of blindness in school children. *Sight-Saving Review,* 1963, *33,* reprint.

Hathaway, W. *Education and health of the partially seeing child* (rev. ed. by F. M. Foote, D. Bryan, & H. Gibbons). New York: Columbia University Press, 1959.

Hayes, S. P. Alternative scales for the mental measurement of the visually handicapped. *Outlook for the Blind and the Teachers Forum,* 1942, *36,* 225–230.

————. *Contributions to a psychology of blindness.* New York: American Foundation for the Blind, 1941.

————. *Facial vision, or the sense of obstacles.* Watertown, Mass.: Perkins Institution for the Blind, 1935.

————. *First regional conference on mental measurements of the blind.* Watertown, Mass.: Perkins Institution for the Blind, 1952, pp. 26–30.

————. Measuring the intelligence of the blind. In P. A. Zahl (Ed.), *Blindness.* Princeton, N. J.: Princeton University Press, 1950, pp. 141–173.

Hecht, P. J., & Newland, T. E. Learning potential and learning achievement of educationally blind third-eighth graders in a residential school. *International Journal for the Education of the Blind,* 1965, *15,* 33–38.

Heller, T. *Studien zur blinden-psychologie.* Leipzig: Wilhelm Engelmann, 1895.

Henderson, F. The rate of braille character recognition as a function of the reading process. *48th Bienniel Conference of the American Association of Instructors for the Blind,* 1966, Pp. 7–10.

Hepfinger, L. M. Psychological evaluation of young blind children. *New Outlook for the Blind,* 1962, *56,* 309–315.

Himes, J. S. Changing attitudes of the public

toward the blind. *New Outlook for the Blind,* 1958, *52,* 330–335.

———. Some concepts of blindness in American culture. In *Attitudes toward blindness.* New York: American Foundation for the Blind, 1951, pp. 10–22.

Holland, B. F. Speed and pressure factors in braille reading. *The Teachers Forum,* 1934, *7,* 13–17.

———, & Eatman, P. F. The silent reading habits of blind children. *The Teachers Forum,* 1933, *6,* 4–19.

't Hooft, F., & Heslinga, K. Sex education of blind-born children. *New Outlook for the Blind,* 1968, *62,* 15–21.

Hoover, R. E. The cane as a travel aid. In P. A. Zahl (Ed.) *Blindness.* Princeton, N. J.: Princeton University Press, 1950, pp. 353–365.

———, & Kupfer, C. Low-vision clinics: A report. *American Journal of Ophthalmology,* 1959, *48,* 177–187.

Hopkins, K. D., & McGuire, L. IQ constancy in the blind child. *International Journal for the Education of the Blind,* 1967, *16,* 113–114.

———. Mental measurement of the blind: The validity of the Wechsler Intelligence Scale for Children. *International Journal for the Education of the Blind,* 1966, *15,* 65–73.

Horbach, H. *Taktiles lesen.* Hannover: Verein zur Förderung der Blindenbildung, 1951.

Hunter, W. F. An analysis of space perception in congenitally blind and in sighted individuals. *Journal of General Psychology,* 1964, *70,* 325–329.

Hurlin, R. G. Estimated prevalence of blindness in the U.S., 1960. *Sight-Saving Review,* 1962, *32,* 4–12.

Imamura, S. Mother and blind child. New York: American Foundation for the Blind, 1965.

James, W. *The principles of psychology.* New York: Holt, Rinehart & Winston, Inc., 1918, *2,* pp. 202–211.

Jerome, E. A., & Proshansky, H. Factors in the assay and use of guidance devices. In P. A. Zahl (Ed.), *Blindness.* Princeton, N. J.: Princeton University Press, 1950, pp. 462–494.

Jervis, F. M. A comparison of self concepts of blind and sighted children. In C. J. Davis (Ed.), *Guidance programs for blind chil-*

dren. A report of a conference. Watertown, Mass.: Perkins Institution for the Blind, 1959, pp. 19–25.

———. The self in process of obtaining and maintaining self-esteem. *New Outlook for the Blind,* 1964, *58,* 51–54.

———. & Haslerud, G. M. Quantitative and qualitative difference in frustration between blind and sighted adolescents. *Journal of Psychology,* 1950, *29,* 67–76.

Johnson, D. E., & Gilson, C. Teenagers evaluate mobility training. *New Outlook for the Blind,* 1967, *61,* 227–231, 237.

Jones, J. W. *Blind children: Degree of vision, mode of reading.* Washington, D.C.: U. S. Department of Health, Education, and Welfare, 1961.

Jones, R. L., & Gottfried, N. W. The prestige of special education teaching. *Exceptional Children* 1966, *32,* 465–468.

———, & Owens, A. The social distance of the exceptional: A study at the high school level. *Exceptional Children,* 1966, *32,* 551–556.

Jordan, S. The deaf-blind: A clarification. *Perceptual and Motor Skills,* 1964, *18,* 503–504.

Juurmaa. *Ability structure and loss of vision.* New York: American Foundation for the Blind, 1967.

Kanner, L. *Child psychiatry* (3rd ed.). Springfield, Ill.: Charles C. Thomas, 1957.

Karnes, M. B., & Wollersheim, J. P. An intensive differential diagnosis of partially seeing children to determine the implications for education. *Exceptional Children,* 1963, *30,* 17–25.

Kederis, C. J., Nolan, C. Y., & Morris, J. E. The use of controlled exposure devices to increase braille reading rates. *International Journal for the Education of the Blind,* 1967, *16,* 97–105.

Kenyon, E. L. Diagnostic techniques to be applied with blind children. In C. J. Davis (Ed.), *Guidance programs for blind children.* Report of a conference. Watertown, Mass.: Perkins Institution for the Blind, 1959, pp. 31–40.

Kerby, C. E. A report on visual handicaps of partially seeing children. *Exceptional Children,* 1952, *18,* 137–142.

Klein, G. S. Blindness and isolation. In *The Psychoanalytic Study of the Child.* New

York: International Universities Press, Inc., 1962, *17*, pp. 82–93.

Knotts, J. R., & Miles, W. R. The maze-learning ability of blind compared with sighted children. *Journal of Genetic Psychology,* 1929, *36,* 21–50.

Koch, H. L., & Ufkess, J. A comparative study of stylus maze learning by blind and seeing subjects. *Journal of Experimental Psychology,* 1926, *9,* 118–131.

Komisar, D., & MacDonnel, M. Gains in I.Q. for students attending a school for the blind. *Exceptional Children,* 1955, *21,* 127–129.

Krogius, A. Zur frage vom sechsten sinn der blinden. *Zeitschrift für Experimentelle Pädagogik,* 1917, *5,* 77–89.

Kunz, M. Das orientierungsvermögen und das sog. ferngefühl der blinden und taubblinden. *Internationales Archiv für Schulhygiene,* 1907, *4,* 80–179, 282–286.

Land, S. L., & Vineberg, S. E. Locus of control in blind children. *Exceptional Children,* 1965, *31,* 257–260.

Lebo, D., & Bruce, R. S. Projective methods recommended for use with the blind. *Journal of Psychology,* 1960, *50,* 15–38.

Lende, H. *Books about the blind* (new ed.). New York: American Foundation for the Blind, 1953.

Lewis, L. L. The relation of measured mental ability to school marks and academic survival in the Texas School for the Blind. *International Journal for the Education of the Blind,* 1957, *6,* 56–60.

LeZak, R. J., & Starbuck H. B. Identification of children with speech disorders in a residential school for the blind. *International Journal for the Education of the Blind,* 1964, *14,* 8–12.

Lipton, E. L. The cross eyed bear—the cross I bear: Selections from a study of the psychological effects of strabismus. *American Journal of Orthopsychiatry,* 1967, *37,* 281–282.

Livingston, J. S. Evaluation of enlarged test form used with the partially seeing. *Sight-Saving Review,* 1958, *32,* 37–39.

Lowenfeld, B. The blind adolescent in a seeing world. *Exceptional Children,* 1959, *25,* 310–315.

———. *Our blind children—growing and learning with them* (2nd ed.). Springfield, Ill.: Charles C. Thomas, 1964.

———. Braille and talking book reading: A comparative study. New York: American Foundation for the Blind, 1945.

———. Meeting the needs of visually handicapped preschool children. *Sight-Saving Review,* 1950, *20,* 145–150. (*a*)

———. *Multihandicapped blind and deaf-blind children in California.* Sacramento: State Department of Education, 1968.

———. Psychological foundation of special methods in teaching blind children. In P. A. Zahl (Ed.), *Blindness.* Princeton, N. J.: Princeton University Press, 1950, pp. 89–108. (*b*)

———. Psychological Problems of children with impaired vision. In W. M. Cruickshank (Ed.), *Psychology of exceptional children and youth* (1st ed.). Englewood Cliffs, N. J.: Prentice-Hall, Inc. 1955, pp. 214–283.

———, Abel, G. L., & Hatlen, P. N. *Blind children learn to read.* Springfield, Ill.: Charles C. Thomas, 1969.

Lowenfeld, V. *Creative and mental growth* (3rd ed.). New York: The Macmillan Company, 1957.

———. *The nature of creative activity.* New York: Harcourt, Brace & World, Inc., 1939.

Lowrey, A. Plan for a low vision clinic. *New Outlook for the Blind,* 1965, *59,* 275–277.

Lukoff, I. F., & Whiteman, M. Attitudes toward blindness—some preliminary findings. *New Outlook for the Blind,* 1961, *55,* 39–44.

MacFarland, D. C. An exploratory study comparing the maze learning ability of blind and sighted subjects. *New Outlook for the Blind,* 1952, *46,* 259–263.

Mandola, J. A theoretical approach to graphic aids for the blind. *International Journal for the Education of the Blind,* 1968, *18,* 22–24.

Massie, D. Guidelines for research in the education of partially seeing children. *New Outlook for the Blind,* 1965, *59,* 57–58.

Mattis, S. An experimental approach to treatment of visually impaired multi-handicapped children. *New Outlook for the Blind,* 1967, *61,* 1–5.

Maxfield, K. E. *Adaptation of educational tests for use with blind pupils.* New York: American Foundation for the Blind, 1927.

———. *The blind child and his reading.*

New York: American Foundation for the Blind, 1928.

———. *The spoken language of the blind preschool child.* New York: Archives of Psychology, 1936, No. 201.

———, & Buchholz, S. *A social maturity scale for blind preschool children: A guide to its use.* New York: American Foundation for the Blind, 1957.

Maxfield, & Fjeld, H. A. The social maturity of the visually handicapped preschool child. *Child Development,* 1942, *13,* 1–27.

Maxfield, & Kenyon, E. L. *A guide to the use of the Maxfield-Fjeld tentative adaptation of the Vineland Social Maturity Scale for use with visually handicapped preschool children.* New York: American Foundation for the Blind, 1953.

McAndrew, H. Rigidity and isolation: A study of the deaf and the blind. *Journal of Abnormal and Social Psychology,* 1948, *43,* 476–494. (*a*)

———. Rigidity in the deaf and the blind. *Journal of Social Issues,* 1948, *4,* 72–77. (*b*)

———. The use of projective techniques in the personality evaluation of the blind. *American Psychologist,* 1950, *5,* 340.

McCarty, B. M., & Worchel, P. Rate of motion and object perception in the blind. *New Outlook for the Blind,* 1954, *48,* 316–322.

McLaughlin, S. C. Visual perception in strabismus and amblyopia. *Psychological Monographs: General and Applied,* 1964, *78.*

McReynolds, J., & Worchel, P. Geographic orientation in the blind. *Journal of General Psychology,* 1951, *51,* 221–236.

Merry, R. V. Adapting the Seashore Musical Talent Tests for use with blind pupils. *The Teachers Forum,* 1931, *30,* 15–19.

———, & Merry, F. K. The finger maze as a supplementary test of intelligence for blind children. *Journal of Genetic Psychology,* 1934, *44,* 227–230.

———. The tactual recognition of embossed pictures by blind children. *Journal of Applied Psychology,* 1933, *17,* 148–163.

Meyerson, L. The visually handicapped. *Review of Educational Research,* 1953, *23,* 476–491.

Miner, L. E. A study of the incidence of speech deviations among visually handicapped children. *New Outlook for the Blind,* 1963, *57,* 10–14.

Morris, J. E., & Nolan, C. Y. Minimum sizes for areal type tactual symbols. *International Journal for the Education of the Blind,* 1963, *13,* 48–51.

Morse, J. L. Mannerisms, not blindisms: Causation and treatment. *International Journal for the Education of the Blind,* 1965, *15,* 12–16.

Mueller, M. W. Effects of illustration size on test performance of visually limited children. *Exceptional Children,* 1962, *29,* 124–128.

Murphy, A. T. Attitudes of educators toward the visually handicapped. *Sight-Saving Review,* 1960, *30,* 157–161.

Nagera, H., & Colonna, A. E. Aspects of the contribution of sight to ego and drive development: A comparison of the development of some blind and sighted children. In *The Psychoanalytic Study of the Child.* New York: International Universities Press, Inc., 1965, *20,* pp. 267–287.

Newland, T. E. The blind learning aptitude test. *Report Proceedings of Conference on Research Needs in Braille.* New York: American Foundation for the Blind, 1961, pp. 40–51.

———. Prediction and evaluation of academic learning by blind children, II: Problems and procedures in evaluation. *International Journal for the Education of the Blind,* 1964, *14,* 42–51.

Nolan, C. Y. Blind children: Degree of vision, mode of reading, a 1963 replication. *New Outlook for the Blind,* 1965, *59,* 233–238.

———. Evaluating the scholastic achievements of visually handicapped children. *Exceptional Children,* 1962, *28,* 493–496.

———. A 1966 reappraisal of the relationship between visual acuity and mode of reading for blind children. *New Outlook for the Blind,* 1967, *61,* 255–261.

———. On the unreality of words to the blind. *New Outlook for the Blind,* 1960, *54,* 100–102.

———. Perceptual factors in braille word recognition. *48th Biennial Conference of the American Association of Instructors for the Blind,* 1966, 10–14.

———. Readability of large types: A study of type sizes and type styles. *International Journal for the Education of the Blind,* 1959, *9,* 41–44.

————, & Morris, M. E. Development and validation of the Roughness Discrimination Test. *International Journal for the Education of the Blind*, 1965, *15*, 1–6.

Norris, M., Spaulding, P. J., & Brodie, F. H. *Blindness in children.* Chicago: University of Chicago Press, 1957.

Norton, F. M. *Training hearing to greater usefulness, a manual.* Cleveland: Cleveland Society for the Blind, 1960.

NSPB fact book: Estimated statistics on blindness and vision problems. New York: National Society for the Prevention of Blindness, Inc., 1966.

Ohwaki, Y., *et al.* Construction of an intelligence test for the blind. *Tohoku Psychological Folia*, 1960, *18*, 45–65.

Omwake, E. G., & Solnit, A. J. It isn't fair: The treatment of a blind child. In *The Psychoanalytic Study of the Child.* New York: International Universities Press, Inc., 1961, *16*, 352–404.

Peabody, R. L., & Birch, J. W. Educational implications of partial vision: New findings from a national study. *Sight-Saving Review*, 1967, *37*, 92–96.

Pick, A. D., Thomas, M. L., & Pick, H. L., Jr. The role of grapheme-phoneme correspondences in the perception of braille. *Journal of Verbal Learning and Verbal Behavior*, 1966, *5*, 298–300.

Pintner, R., Eisenson, J., & Stanton, M. The psychology of the physically handicapped. New York: Appleton-Century-Crofts, 1941, pp. 252–261.

Pintner, R., & Forlano, G. Personality tests of partially sighted children. *Journal of Applied Psychology*, 1943, *27*, 283–287.

Pitman, D. J. The musical ability of blind children. *Review of Psychology in Music*, 1965, *2*, 19–28. Also in *Research Bulletin No. 11.* New York: American Foundation for the Blind, 1965, pp. 63–79.

Pringle, M. L. K. The emotional and social adjustment of blind children. *Education Research*, 1964, *6*, 129–138.

Raskin, N. J. Play therapy with blind children. *New Outlook for the Blind*, 1954, *48*, 290–292.

————. Visual disability. In J. F. Garrett and B. S. Levine (Eds.), *Psychological practices with the physically disabled.* New York: Columbia University Press, 1962, pp. 341–375.

Robbins, N. *Educational beginnings with deaf-blind children.* Watertown, Mass.: Perkins Institution for the Blind, 1960.

————. *Speech beginnings for the deaf-blind child: A guide for parents.* Watertown, Mass.: Perkins Institution for the Blind, 1963.

————, & Steinquist, G. *The deaf-blind rubella child.* Watertown, Mass.: Perkins Institution for the Blind, 1967.

Ross, J. R., Braen, B. B., & Chaput, R. Patterns of change in disturbed blind children in residential treatment. *Children*, 1967, *14*, 217–222.

Rothschild, J. Deaf-blindness. In J. F. Garrett and B. S. Levine (Eds.), *Psychological practices with the physically disabled.* New York: Columbia University Press, 1962, pp. 376–409.

————. Play therapy with blind children. *New Outlook for the Blind*, 1960, *54*, 329–333.

Rouse, D. L., & Worchel, P. Veering tendency in the blind. *New Outlook for the Blind*, 1955, *49*, 115–119.

Rowe, E. D. *Speech problems of blind children: A survey of the North California area.* New York: American Foundation for the Blind, 1958.

Rubin, E. J. *Abstract functioning in the blind.* New York: American Foundation for the Blind, 1964.

Rusalem, H. The environmental supports of public attitudes toward the blind. *New Outlook for the Blind*, 1950, *44*, 277–288.

————. Research in review. *New Outlook for the Blind*, 1962, *56*, 66–68.

————. A study of college students' beliefs about deaf-blindness. *New Outlook for the Blind*, 1965, *59*, 90–93.

————, & Rusalem, R. Students' reactions to deaf-blindness. *New Outlook for the Blind*, 1964, *58*, 260–263.

Sandler, A. M. Aspects of passivity and ego development in the blind infant. In *The Psychoanalytic Study of the Child.* New York: International Universities Press, Inc., 1963, *18*, 343–360.

————, & Wills, D. M. Preliminary notes on play and mastery in the blind child. *Journal of Child Psychotherapy*, 1965, *1*, 7–19.

Sands, H. H. The psychological appraisal of young blind children. In S. P. Hayes (Ed.), *First regional conference on mental mea-*

surements of the blind. Watertown, Mass.: Perkins Institution for the Blind, 1952, pp. 25–26.

Schauer, G. Motivation of attitudes toward blindness. In *Attitudes toward blindness*. New York: American Foundation for the Blind, 1951, pp. 5–10.

Schiff, W., & Isikow, H. Stimulus redundancy in the tactile perception of histograms. *International Journal for the Education of the Blind*, 1966, *16*, 1–11.

Schlaegel, T. F., Jr. The dominant method of imagery in blind as compared to sighted adolescents. *Journal of Genetic Psychology*, 1953, *83*, 265–277.

Scholl, G. T. The education of blind children. In W. M. Cruickshank and G. O. Johnson (Eds.), *Education of exceptional children and youth* (2nd ed.). Englewood Cliffs, N. J.: Prentice-Hall, Inc., 1967, pp. 287–342.

Schumann, H. J., von. *Träume der blinden, vom standpunkt der phänomenologie, tiefenpsychologie, mythologie und kunst*. Basel and New York: S. Karger, 1959.

Seashore, T. E., & Ling, T. L. The comparative sensitiveness of blind and seeing persons. *Psychological Monograph*, 1918, *25*, 148–158.

Seelye, W. S., & Thomas, J. E. Is mobility feasible with multiply handicapped blind children? *Exceptional Children*, 1966, *32*, 613–617.

Senden, M., von. *Space and sight*. Glencoe, Ill.: The Free Press, 1960.

Shurrager, H. C., & Shurrager, P. S. Haptic Intelligence Scale for adult blind. Chicago: Psychology Research, 1964.

Siegel, I. M. *Posture in the blind*. New York: American Foundation for the Blind, 1966.

Singer, J. L., & Streiner, B. F. Imaginative content in the dreams and fantasy play of blind and sighted children. *Perceptual and Motor Skills*, 1966, *22*, 475–482.

Sommers, V. S. *The influence of parental attitudes and social environment on the personality development of the adolescent blind*. New York: American Foundation for the Blind, 1944.

Spencer, M. B. *Blind children in family and community*. Minneapolis: University of Minnesota Press, 1960.

Spitz, R. A. Anaclitic depression. In *The Psychoanalytic Study of the Child*. New York:

International Universities Press, Inc., 1946, *2*, 313–342.

Steinberg, W. *Die raumwahrnemug der blinden*. Munich: Reinhardt, 1920.

Steinzor, L. V. School peers of visually handicapped children. *New Outlook for the Blind*, 1966, *60*, 312–314. *(a)*

———. Siblings of visually handicapped children. *New Outlook for the Blind*, 1967, *61*, 48–52.

———. Visually handicapped children: Their attitudes toward blindness. *New Outlook for the Blind*, 1966, *60*, 307–311. *(b)*

Stinchfield, S. M. *Speech disorders*. New York: Harcourt, Brace & World, Inc., 1933, pp. 62–76.

Stolz, H. R., & Stolz, L. M. Adolescent problems related to somatic variations. In *Adolescence, National Society for the Study of Education, Yearbook XLIII*. Vol. 1. Chicago: University of Chicago Press, 1950, 95.

Stone, A. A. Consciousness: Altered levels in blind, retarded children. *Psychosomatic Medicine*, 1964, *26*, 14–19.

Streitfeld, J. W., & Avery, C. D. The WAIS and HIS as predictors of academic achievement in a residential school for the blind. *International Journal for the Education of the Blind*, 1968, *18*, 73–77.

Suinn, R. M., Dauterman, W., & Shapiro, B. The Stanford Ohwaki-Kohs Tactile Block Design Intelligence Test for the Blind. *New Outlook for the Blind*, 1966, *60*, 77–79.

Supa, M., Cotzin, M., & Dallenbach, K. M. "Facial vision": The perception of obstacles by the blind. *American Journal of Psychology*, 1944, *57*, 133–183.

Thompson, J. *Development of facial expression of emotion in blind and seeing children*. New York: Archives of Psychology, no. 264, 1941.

Tillman, M. H. The performance of blind and sighted children on the Wechsler Intelligence Scale for Children. *International Journal for the Education of the Blind*, 1967, *16*, Study 1, 65–74, Study 2, 106–112.

———, & Williams, C. Associative characteristics of blind and sighted children to selected form classes. *International Journal for the Education of the Blind*, 1968, *18*, 33–40.

Toth, Z. *Die vorstellungswelt der blinden*. Leipzig: Johann Ambrosius Barth, 1930.

Totman, H. E. Training problems and techniques. In B. Lowenfeld (Ed.), *The blind preschool child*. New York: American Foundation for the Blind, 1947, pp. 57–72.

Tretakoff, M. What they are all doing. *American Association of Instructors for the Blind Convention Report*. Washington, D. C.: 1966, 42–44.

Trismen, D. A. Equating braille forms of the sequential tests of educational progress. *Exceptional Children*, 1967, *33*, 419–424.

Truschel, L. Der sechste sinn der blinden. *Zeitschrift für Experimentelle Pädagogik*, 1906, *3*, 109–142; 1907, *4*, 129–155; 1907, *5*, 66–77.

Underberg, R. P. *et al.* Factors relating to adjustment to visual disability in adolescence. *New Outlook for the Blind*, 1961, *55*, 252–259.

Villey, P. *The world of the blind*. Trans. by A. Hallard. New York: The Macmillan Company, 1930, pp. 101–117.

Voss, W. *Das farbenhören bei erblindeten*. Hamburg: Psychologisch-Aesthetische Forschungsgeselleschaft, 1930.

Wagner, E. M. Maternal rubella: A general orientation to the disease. *New Outlook for the Blind*, 1967, *61*, 97–105.

Wallace, E. Physical defects and juvenile delinquency. *New York State Journal of Medicine*, 1940, *40*, 39–56.

Warren, H. C. (Ed.). *Dictionary of psychology*. Boston: Houghton Mifflin Company, 1934.

Wattron, J. B. A suggested performance test of intelligence. *New Outlook for the Blind*, 1956, *50*, 115–121.

Weinberg, B. Stuttering among blind and partially sighted children. *Journal of Speech and Hearing Disorders*, 1964, *29*, 322–326.

Weiner, B. B. A new outlook on assessment. *New Outlook for the Blind*, 1967, *61*, 73–78.

Wheeler, R. H., & Cutsforth, T. D. The role of synaesthesia in learning. *Journal of Experimental Psychology*, 1921, *4*, 448–468.

———. Synaesthesia and meaning. *American Journal of Psychology*, 1922, *33*, 361–384.

———. Synaesthesia in the development of the concept. *Journal of Experimental Psychology*, 1925, *8*, 149–159.

Williams, D. Sunland's Program for the blind. *Mental Retardation*, 1964, *2*, 244–245.

Williams, M. Superior intelligence of children blinded from retinoblastoma. *Archives of Disease in Childhood*, 1968, *43*, 210–214.

Wills, D. M. Some observations on blind nursery school children's understanding of their world. In *The Psychoanalytic Study of the Child*. International Universities Press, Inc., 1965, *20*, 344–364.

Wilmer, H. A., & Husni, M. A. The use of sounds in a projective test. *Journal of Consulting Psychology*, 1953, *17*, 377–383.

Wilson, E. L. A developmental approach to psychological factors which may inhibit mobility in the visually handicapped person. *New Outlook for the Blind*, 1967, *61*, 283–289.

Wilson, J. W., & Halverson, H. M. Development of a young blind child. *Journal of Genetic Psychology*, 1947, *71*, 155–175.

Wolf, J. M. *The blind child with concomitant disabilities*. New York: American Foundation for the Blind, 1967.

Worchel, P. Space perception and orientation in the blind. *Psychological Monographs*. Washington, D. C.: American Psychological Association, 1951, *65*, (332).

———, & Dallenbach, K. M. "Facial vision": Perception of obstacles by the deaf-blind. *American Journal of Psychology*, 1947, *60*, 502–533.

Worchel, & Mauney, J. The effect of practice on the perception of obstacles by the blind. *Journal of Experimental Psychology*, 1951, *41*, 170–176.

———, & Andrew, J. G. The perception of obstacles by the blind. *Journal of Experimental Psychology*, 1950, *40*, 746–751.

Wright, B. A. *Physical disability—a psychological approach*. New York: Harper & Row, Publishers, 1960.

Wyder, F. T., Wilson, M. E., & Frumkin, R. M. Information as a factor in perception of the blind by teachers. *Perceptual and Motor Skills*, 1967, *25*, 188.

Young, M. A. C. The partially seeing. In J. F. Garret (Ed.), *Psychological aspects of physical disability*. Service series No. 210. Washington, D. C.: Office of Vocational Rehabilitation, 1952, pp. 162–178.

Zunich, M., & Ledwith, B. E. Self-concepts of visually handicapped and sighted children. *Perceptual and Motor Skills*, 1965, *21*, 771–774.

Zweibelson, I., & Barg, C. F. Concept development of blind children. *New Outlook for the Blind*, 1967, *61*, 218–222.

SIX

Psychological Considerations with Crippled Children

FRANCES P. CONNOR
HERBERT RUSALEM with
WILLIAM M. CRUICKSHANK

*Frances P. Connor is Professor of Special Education
and head of the Department of Special Education,
Teachers College, Columbia University. Herbert Rusalem is Associate Professor of Education and Assistant
Director of the Research and Demonstrations Center
for the Education of Handicapped Children, also at
Teachers College, Columbia University.*

Children and youths who are disabled by an orthopedic impairment will be considered in this chapter. Thus a child who has a deformity that causes interference with the normal use of bones, muscles, or joints would come within the province of this discussion. Included are children with poliomyelitis, osteomyelitis, tuberculosis of the bones or joints, and those with congenital deformities such as clubfoot or spina bifida; also included are children and youths who are handicapped by cerebral palsy, with the recognition that although this condition is neurological rather than orthopedic, the cerebral-palsied child usually has limitations in mobility and dexterity and, to the extent that this is true, may be grouped with crippled children in educational and theraputic centers. Some of the psychological considerations relating to crippled children, in general, apply equally to the child with cerebral palsy. However, because there are special considerations that should be taken into account when working with the cerebral-palsied, a separate section of this chapter will focus directly on this group. Except for certain comparative purposes, cardiac children, who sometimes are included in legal classifications of crippled children, will be excluded from the discussion, but are considered elsewhere in this book.*

THEORIES OF THE IMPACT OF DISABILITY ON ADJUSTMENT

Numerous theoretical positions have been taken regarding the impact of physical disability upon social and emotional adjustment. Although considerable thought has been given to this problem, little research in support of these positions has provided consistent verification of any

*See Chapter 9.

308

of them. Thus, relatively little is known about the effects of the degree and duration of disability, the age of onset, the family and home situation, and the socioeconomic status on the development of crippled children.

Although the basic adjustment problems of the crippled child are the same as those of physically normal children of comparable chronological and mental development, disability does introduce psychologically significant variables. This viewpoint was expressed by Cruickshank (1948) in a phenomenological frame of reference.

It is seen that the physically handicapped child in his social relationships is, as are all children, attempting to insure not his physical organic self, but his phenomenal self, the concept of himself of which he is cognizant. Two types of problems are to be observed in the handicapped child from this point of view: (1) adjustment problems which might occur in the normal developmental progress of any individual who is simultaneously striving for expansion of self and for the maintenance of the self-concept already developed, and (2) adjustment problems which are solely resultant from the fact that a physical handicap is inserted between the goal and the self-desire to achieve such a goal.

Although such a dichotomy is useful for the sake of discourse, no such clean-cut separation ever exists in reality. However, "the failure to recognize the duality of the problem accounts for much current misunderstanding with reference to the handicapped (Cruickshank, 1948)." It also helps to explain why some lay and professional persons continue to conceive of the personality problems of crippled children as an inherent part of being crippled rather than adjustive mechanisms of crippled children adopted in the course of development in an effort to integrate the crippling condition into his life space.

Field Theory

The difference in adjustment potentials of crippled and noncrippled individuals has been interpreted in terms of Lewinian field theory (Cruickshank, 1948). Figure 1–1, as depicted earlier by Meyerson, illustrates the problem under consideration. It illustrates the life space of a person (P) in his attempt to effect an adequate adjustment in a new social situation (N.S.) different from an old situation (O.S.) that no longer holds value for him. In the course of his attempts to adjust, numerous avenues are open to him—direct movement into the new situation as the result of no barrier (B) or as the result of his ability to surmount the barrier or the development of substitute satisfaction (see Figure 1-1) if the barrier is temporarily or permanently insurmountable. Within the limits of his culture and his self-concept, great freedom of adjustment is permitted the individual. In rare instances, when both the new and the substitute are unattainable, the individual may escape from his life space entirely into one of unreality or psychosis.

The avenues are not equally open to the handicapped person. In the first place the barrier to achievement for the non-handicapped child rarely remains the same in the attempts of the personality to adjust to different situations. For the non-disabled person the barrier may change as the situation and the self-concept are subject to or have experienced modification (Cruickshank, 1948).

The barrier for the handicapped child may remain the same. If the child conceives his physical disability as an organic or psychological barrier to satisfactory adjustment, the barrier remains the same regardless of the type of adjustment being attempted. Note that not all handicapped children conceive of their handicaps as being restrictive in nature. The theory thus holds only in those instances wherein the handicapped child conceives of himself as being handicapped. As will be shown, however, this comprises a relatively large proportion of disabled children.

The situation is basically different for a physically handicapped child attempting

> . . . to move from an old situation (O.S.) which at the moment holds no value to the self (—) into a new life space (N.S.) which does hold value (+). The barrier (B) to successful adjustment is the physical handicap . . . which is irremediable in actuality or which the child feels is irremediable. When the normal personality was confronted by the barrier . . . one of his avenues for successful adjustment was that of developing substitute satisfactions which contained nearly the same positive value as the originally desired new situation. Substitute satisfactions comparable to the original goal region are rarely possible to the handicapped child, because the same barrier to the original goal region is also a barrier to the development of substitute satisfactions of a value (+) equal in any respect to that contained in the originally desired new situation. Thus the handicapped individual's personality, in addition to the possibilities of escaping the life space into unreality to protect the self, has added the negative possibility of developing substitute satisfactions within the old situation life space. All of these avenues have little value (—) to the personality as the behaver conceives his needs. Thus a condition of continued frustration frequently is to be observed in the handicapped person (Cruickshank, 1948).

This situation is well illustrated in a protocol of a counseling situation with a sixteen year-old boy, a quadriplegic handicapped by athetoid cerebral palsy.

> SUBJECT: I just don't know why the doctors let me live when I was born. I'm no use to anyone the way I am.
> COUNSELOR: You feel that you are of no value to society and that discourages you.

> SUBJECT: Yes, I know what I want to do and I can talk O.K., but every time I try to do anything I'm stymied. I can't walk or even eat without some help.
> COUNSELOR: You feel, because of your physical condition, that you can't do many of the things you want to do and you feel frustrated when this happens.
> SUBJECT: It's worse than that. When I can't succeed in something and when I know I could succeed if I weren't a C. P. [cerebral palsy], I get more than discouraged because I'm so helpless. You're stuck and you hate yourself ·for being stuck (Cruickshank, 1948).

This young man represents the situation demonstrated by numerous handicapped persons in their attempt to obtain satisfactions when the handicap represents a barrier organically or psychologically. The handicap sets into operation a circular situation: "The handicap is the barrier to success; frustration results; attempts are made to substitute satisfactions for the original activity; the handicap is again a barrier; greater frustration results; more activity; more blocking ad infinitum (Cruickshank, 1948)." Although no experimentation has been undertaken to test the adequacy of this hypothesis, Lewinian field theory may explain the problem of adjustment that is faced by some disabled children and young people. Wright (1960) goes far to establish definitively the somatopsychological relationship (suggested in the preceding discussion) of physical disability to general adjustment and personality development.

Organic Inferiority

The theory of organic inferiority as developed by Adler has close relationship to the problem under consideration. However, as one evaluates the research and later theoretical considerations in comparison to Adler's earlier writings, the implications for understanding the handicapped become somewhat vague. Adler (1917) originally hypothesized and assumed an undetermined, but specific, neurological basis between organ inferiority and behavior mechanisms of a compensatory nature. In later writings, the psychic need for control of inferiority of whatever kind was added, although Adler (1926) continued to refer to the organic basis of feelings of inferiority as the central theme around which his concepts were developed. The hypotheses thus become more indefinite and less subject to careful experiment or control, so that today his concepts, although important in stimulating further thought, have largely been supplanted by other ideas. To discount completely Adler's contribution, however, would be an injustice to him, for without question his contribution was an important one, and the impact of his writings has weighed heavily on the later thinking of his students and his associates. Crookshank (1936) and Dreikurs (1948), among others, have individually contributed detailed reviews of Adlerian concepts. Crookshank suggests that an individual may recognize his inferiority on a "Somatic level," a "sympathetic level," or on a "psychic level." He feels, thus, that in a child with a clubfoot, for example, the "other leg may . . . try to grow longer to compensate." From the point of view of either a functional or sympathetic level, he feels that the body may "assume" an attitude or posture as a compensatory mechanism. On the psychic level, the individual is more conscious of the disability or physical inferiority, and he will attempt to deal with it with whatever techniques he can. Dreikurs, following the careful evaluation of three cases in which he applies Adlerian theory, states: " . . . the life style of each individual is not only influenced by the disability, but in turn determines the final effect of any physical disability."

He further states:

Each handicapped individual formulates his own response to his disability in accordance with his life style, which can only be determined through dynamic psychological investigation. Alfred Adler developed a specific technique to determine the life style of each individual. This life style is developed in early childhood through the interpretation which the child makes of all the experiences and difficulties with which he is confronted. The disability is only one, although often an important factor. Not what he has—in heredity endowment and environment—but what he does with it, is important. Courage and social interest, or the lack of them, determine whether a disability permits a good social adjustment or leads to permanent failure (Dreikurs, 1948).

Dreikurs' last statement, while leaning heavily on and in defense of Adler's views, is in effect more closely related to concepts of mental hygiene and compares to the thinking of Allen and Pearson (1938), who feel that behavior problems of crippled children are directly related to inadequate parental attitudes rather than to the child's inability to encompass psychologically the physical disability per se.

Freudian Theories and Body-Image

Numerous writers have looked to the work of Freud as a basis for their concepts regarding physically handicapped persons. Chief among these are Meng and Schilder. Schilder sees a direct relationship between the perception of the body-image and action. He states:

Our study is primarily a study of the body-image which lies on the impressive side of our psychic life. But there are no impressions which are not directional and do not find at the same time an expression. There are no perceptions without actions. Every impression carries with it efferent impulses. Even this formulation does not emphasize sufficiently that impression and expression form a definite unit which we can separate in its parts only by artificial analysis (Schilder, 1950).

From this he concludes:

Experiences in pathology show clearly that when our orientation concerning left and right is lost in regard to our own body, there is also a loss of orientation in regard to the bodies of other persons. The postural model of our own body is connected with the postural models of the bodies of others. There are connections between the postural models of fellow human beings. We experience the body-images of others. Experience of our body-image and experience of the bodies of others are closely interwoven with each other. Just as our emotions and actions are inseparable from the body-image, the emotions and actions of others are inseparable from their body-images. The postural image of the body must be studied, if we desire to gain a deeper insight into social psychology (Schilder, 1950).

Bender (1934), and Bender and Silver (1948) have further contributed to Schilder's concept of the body-image. The latter, in particular, have related the theory to an understanding of the brain-damaged child. They point out that a disturbance in the body-image may occur at any period in the development of the individual or at any level in the perceptual or integrative growth of the person. "In its early development, emphasis upon one particular part of the body by disease or by the attention of others, creates an increased psychological value to that part which disturbs the body-image."

Although not wholly related to the physically disabled child or youth, the important work of Machover (1949) is in large measure based upon the projection in drawings of unconscious determinants related to the body-image. Although little research has been done with drawings of crippled children or youth, Machover reports on the drawings of twenty orthopedically handicapped persons. She states that the preliminary findings were notable and that the individual's projections of the disability into the drawings varied "according to the basic personality of the individual afflicted, the degree of disability, and the duration of the disease, but important features of the subject's reaction to the disease were made graphically explicit in most of the cases." Studies utilizing large groups of physically disabled persons are needed to supplement Machover's findings, but the clinical evidence drawn from single cases wherein body-image manifestations are apparent in drawings of the human figure are common experiences of clinical psychologists.

Examples of the relationship between unconscious motivation for body-image projections are to be observed in Figures 6-1 and 6-2.*

Fig. 6–1. Drawing of a man by an eighteen-year old boy with congenital amputation of left arm and mild paraplegic ataxic cerebral palsy.

*See also drawings included in Z. S. Klapper and H. Werner, Developmental deviations in brain-injured (cerebral-palsied) members of pairs of identi-

Fig. 6–2. Drawing of a man by an adolescent male with congenital deformities involving both hands.

The drawing in Figure 6-1 was made by an eighteen-year-old boy with a congenital amputation of the left arm coupled with a mild paraplegic ataxic cerebral palsy. Without fully elaborating the personality dynamics depicted in the drawings, it is interesting to observe the treatment that is given the legs and the right arm in the drawing. The legs in the drawing are indefinite and generally appear useless. So too in reality, the subject's lower extremities were a source of worry to him insofar as gait and steadiness of locomotion were concerned. In a counseling session this boy commented, "If my pins would only go where I really want them to go, I'd be a lot more satisfied." Although the boy's left hand is actually completely impaired, the drawing shows an incomplete right hand. Evidence of concern is depicted in interchange. It may be that in drawing the incomplete right hand, the

tical twins. *The Quarterly Journal of Child Behavior*, 1950, *2*, 288–313.

boy is even more than in real life punishing himself for being handicapped, because the right hand symbolically relates to power and force. In the second drawing, Figure 6-2, the hands are again hidden from view. This drawing was made by an adolescent boy who also has a congenital deformity—one involving both hands. The usable fingers on the right hand include only the index finger and the thumb; on the left, the thumb alone.

It is hypothesized that, until the child has a coordinated and coherent understanding of the body-image, learning in the form of reading and number concepts, for example, will either not take place or will be severely retarded. In working with a small group of hyperactive children, some with and some without the diagnosis of central nervous system impairment, Cruickshank (1963) observed a close relationship in several children between the developing body-image concept as depicted in the children's drawings of a person and their initial development of reading and number concepts. In a group of forty such children, those who achieved most academically had well-developed body-image concepts and were able to depict these with accuracy. Those who did not achieve in reading and related learning areas, on the contrary, were those whose body-image concepts were immature or almost nonexistent. The author suggests that a very close relationship exists between the two types of learnings. Until the child realizes that his total body functions in a coordinated way, that there is meaning and reason to the relationship of the several parts, and that each part has its separate and appropriate functions in relation to the total, learning of a socially acceptable nature cannot take place. As these concepts enter the conscious understanding of the child, achievement may be observed to take place in the abstract areas of reading and arithmetic. Careful study of this situation should be undertaken, for if such is found to be generally true, there are major implications for preschool and early elementary and home activities, the goal of which would be the earlier development of positive and accurate notions of the body-image and self-concept. The unique relationship between self-concept and adjustment of many types has been emphasized also by Wright (1960).

Any summarization of the Freudian formulations of Meng do him injustice, for without question much further consideration needs to be given to his understanding of the problem. Both qualitative and quantitative research is needed for verification of his theory. Meng (1938) stresses the importance of the frequently impossible transition of physically handicapped children from the pleasure principle to the reality principle because of the child's inability to participate in normal play activities. Little contact with reality through play brings the crippled child to an adult state of maturity too soon and without basic reality testing and understanding. Meng also stresses the commonness of narcissistic pleasures among the handicapped group. As a result of his disability the individual lays claim to importance and distinction. He is different by reason of his disability, and as such, through such experiences as the necessity for undue physical exertion, pain, misfortune, fears, and other factors associated with the disability itself, the handicapped person considers himself in a position of uniqueness and narcissism.

Of considerable importance also in Meng's formulation is the factor of overcompensation, which, he points out, frequently occurs in handicapped individuals. Meng, however, draws a sharp distinction between overcompensation as he is considering it and overcompensation as a result of organic inferiority described by Adler. Meng is considering unfavorable parent-child relationships and unfavorable cultural-child relationships basic to compensatory behavior. As a result of too much parental attention or as a result of condescending attitudes on the part of society, for example, the handicapped child comes to feel inferior and unconsciously overcompensates so as to achieve psychic stability.

Closely related to this point is a second which Meng stresses. In keeping with Freudian concepts, stress is placed upon the close and intimate relationships between the child and his parents. The child comes to look upon the parent as the source of all his satisfactions and as the person who must supply all of the basic needs that he as a child feels. At the same time the child sees the parent (1) as the source of his handicap, which causes hate, and (2) also as the source of the solution to this handicapping situation, which results in ambivalence, because the emotions related to both roles in the same situation are distinctly different. Conflict and maladjustment ensue when the child is unable to rationalize the two opposing points of view confronting him. Often, when a satisfactory solution is not reached, the handicapped person is noted to resort to hypochondriacal solutions as a compensatory mechanism. The close relationship between the defect and the body structure increases the ego libido. As the individual feels rejected by the parent, by his peers, and by the culture, the importance of this relationship becomes greater. As the need to protect the defect, the body, and, in fact, the ego itself becomes more apparent, hypochondriacal solutions are often used.

Experience Deprivation

Evidence is accumulating that suggests that exposure during the formative years to reduced sensory input, both in number and variety of stimuli, exercises an effect upon human development. A review of the literature by Brownfield suggests that sensory (and probably experiential) deprivation plays a part in infant growth and has pervasive ramifications for a child in the intellectual, social, and affective domains. Although this approach to understanding crippled children is gathering momentum, deprivation theory formulation is in its early stages insofar as psychology and education of the handicapped is concerned. Yet, important clues to the effects of deprivation are beginning to appear in the literature. Lemkau (1961) holds that prolonged stimulus deprivation is a relevant variable in the development of the handicapped child and that restoration of stimulus input is required to prevent disordered personality formation. Attempts have been made to coordinate data concerning the lack of mothering with experience deprivation among exceptional children. Although the issue is far from settled, Richmond (1962), following the work of Bowby (1951), holds that sensory deprivation is more important to such children than a lack of mothering, especially during critical learning periods. If learning fails to take place during these critical periods, the effects of the "bypass" may not be fully compensated for in subsequent learning experiences. Gibbs (1959), in discussing the implications of Piaget's work on developmental patterns of children with cerebral palsy and other handicaps, suggests that some of the spastic child's educational difficulties may be due as much to sensory deprivation imposed by brain damage as to the brain damage itself. He suggests further the possibility that some of the effects of brain damage are reversible if we had but the know-how.

Although dim outlines of theory are taking shape, the experience deprivation approach is just beginning to be tested in relation to exceptional children. In an early study, Larson (1958) noted that the experiential background of a sample of 135 physically handicapped children aged three to six years was less rich than that of a comparable group of physically normal children. In this instance the exceptional children were at a disadvantage in almost every aspect of socialization, recognition, outside experiences, and knowledge. A study currently in progress at the Research and Demonstration Center for the Education of Handicapped Children, Teachers College, Columbia University and United Cerebral Palsy of Queens suggests that some experience deprivation among cerebral-palsied children can be traced to the disengagement of fathers of such children from involvement at home and in school programs. This deprivation appears to be a factor in determining the degree of overall deprivation suffered by such children and the consequent intellectual and social losses that appear to flow therefrom.

As in the case of other theories of exceptionality, experience deprivation contributes to an understanding of only selected child behaviors. It seems particularly relevant in generating explanations for socially induced retardation among children with intact learning mechanisms. However, even in this area, relatively little is known about the impact of various types of deprivation at different stages of growth, the effects of varying durations of deprivation, and the reversibility of deprivation under different conditions. At least one attempt is now being made to present a systematic conceptual framework concerning experience deprivation in the hope that it will stimulate further theory-building and research.

Other Theoretical Positions

The importance that Allen and Pearson place upon the parental attitudes as being basic in the development of healthy adjustment among handicapped children has been mentioned. Similarly, numerous other authors have made contributions to psychological theory relating to crippled individuals. Among these should be recorded the writings of Phelps (1948), Dembo (1948), Winkler (1931), Landis and Bolles (1942), Menninger (1949), Meyerson (1948), and Barker (1948). Clark (1934), also in psychoanalytic terms, has pointed out that the ego loss due to a somatic defect resolves itself in emotional compensatory behavior, whereas Kubie (1945), in the same frame of reference, points out that the impact of the handicap will be the result of the interaction of three factors—reality, conscious fantasy, and unconscious fantasy and feeling. Several studies based upon small samples of twins have in large measure supported the conclusion of Allen and Pearson, namely, that the impact of the disability is closely related to the adequacy or inadequacy of the parental attitudes that surround the child (Jenkins, 1934; Klapper and Werner, 1950; Bradway, 1937; Newell, 1930). Barker and his associates have summarized the theoretical assumptions that are proposed as etiological problems in individuals with physical disability:

1. Compensation for inferiorities (Adler).
2. Easy narcissistic satisfactions from pain and uniqueness (Meng, Clark).
3. Lack of normal plan and expressive actions (Meng, Wurtz [1932]).
4. Easy cathexis to disabled part (Meng).
5. Unrelated anxieties transferred to bodily handicap (Meng, Stafford [1939]).
6. Blame of parents (Meng, Allen, and Pearson).
7. Feeling of guilt for hostility toward parents (Meng, Winkler).
8. Body-image at variance with reality (Schilder, Bender).
9. Efforts to achieve social acceptance (Meng, Lowman [1942], Allen and Pearson).
10. Dependent, demanding apathetic behavior deriving from over-solicitous protective situation (Meng, Allen and Pearson).
11. Variable, conflicting behavior in response to variable, inconsistent attitudes of others (Allen and Pearson).
12. Goals beyond achievement possibilities due to pressure from parents, and to physical, social, and economic restrictions (Lord, Landis, and Bolles).
13. Conflict between withdrawal and compensatory tendencies (von Baeyer [1928]).
14. Acceptance of disability as a punishment for sin (Winkler).
15. Retaliatory behavior for "unjust" treatment by nature (Meng).
16. Self-concept (Fishman [1949]).
17. Degree of acceptance of disability by disabled person (Fielding [1950]).
18. Value systems of disabled person and his associates (Dembo).
19. Cultural role of disabled person (Schneider [1947], Fitzgerald [1951]).
20. Intergroup dynamics (Schneider) (Barker *et al.*, 1953).

EMOTIONAL AND SOCIAL ADJUSTMENT

Studies of Adjustment

Information regarding the adjustment of crippled children in comparison to that of nondisabled children is, in general, unsatisfactory. Numerous studies in the literature point up differences in the adjustments of the two groups of children (Strauss, 1936; Brockway, 1936; Rosenbaum, 1937). In most instances, however, such studies can be offset by others which generally show the converse of the situation—that the adjustments of crippled and noncrippled children can be favorably compared (Gates, 1946). The situation is worthy of some detailed consideration. Cruickshank and Dolphin (1949 *a, b*) report the results of a study of the emotional needs of crippled and noncrippled children. These authors administered the Raths Self-Portrait N Test to two groups of children: one, a group of 87 crippled children, the other, a group of 193 noncrippled children. The group of crippled children consisted of 42 boys and 45 girls; the group of noncrippled children, 97 boys and 96 girls. The former included children handicapped by cardiac conditions, cerebral palsy, poliomyelitis, Perthe's disease, progressive muscular dystrophy, spina bifida, and other orthopedic or neurological impairments. Table 6-1 shows the mean scores achieved by both groups of children in eight areas of emotional need as included in the test. As seen in the table, no statistically significant differences were observed between the two groups of children.

The authors had earlier felt that the need to be free from feelings of fear and guilt would be predominantly characteristic of the crippled children, but when the adjustment of the crippled children was compared with normal children's emotional needs in these two areas, similar results were obtained. In view of the findings of certain studies to be noted below, objective tests such as Raths Self-Portrait N Test and others used in earlier studies of the adjustment of crippled and noncrippled children are not sensitive enough to point up differences if they do exist. The objective tests certainly do not depict the possible differences in dynamics inherent in the quantitative results, and these quite possibly differ between the groups. The objective test may contain too great a threat to the child to permit honest responses; it may not anticipate a wide enough scope of situations to produce answers that are typical of the child at the time he is completing the test; it may simply not be an adequate measure of emotional adjustment.

Illness can be used as a defense against anxiety or escape from intolerable social situations. In a survey of 12,000 children in a New York State school district, Keeve (1967) found that 7 percent were given prolonged medical excuses from physical education. Although this study did not generate definitive evidence, it was presumed that about half of these conditions were "phantom" disabilities with strong illusory or imagined components. The author suggests that educators and physicians are influential in initiating and supporting the use of disability as a defense. Although the appearance of physical symptoms in apparently nondisabled children raises important social-psychological concerns, the central problem continues to be the emotional response of children to physical limitations.

TABLE 6-1

SIGNIFICANCE OF THE DIFFERENCES IN MEANS
OBTAINED BY CRIPPLED AND NONCRIPPLED CHILDREN

Need	Means			
	Crippled Group n 87	Noncrippled Group n 193	t-scores	Percent level of significance of t
Part A: Presence of Needs				
Belonging	3.46	2.88	1.4367	10-20
Achievement	4.45	3.81	1.4286	10-20
Economic security	3.90	3.97	.0147	90
Freedom from fear	6.37	6.07	.4517	60-70
Love and affection	2.56	2.28	.8505	30-40
Freedom from guilt	5.63	7.12	1.9487	5-10
Decision making	4.57	3.77	1.7010	5-10
Understanding world	4.99	5.99	1.5242	10-20
Part B: Fulfillment of Needs				
Belonging	5.92	5.82	.1558	80-90
Achievement	5.05	5.02	.0532	90
Economic security	4.24	3.83	.8888	30-40
Freedom from fear	4.09	4.43	.6730	50-60
Love and affection	5.34	6.19	1.2513	20-30
Freedom from guilt	3.49	3.47	.0488	90
Decision making	4.24	4.35	.2171	80-90
Understanding world	3.41	3.02	.9934	30-40

SOURCE: By permission from W.M. Cruickshank and J.E. Dolphin. The emotional needs of crippled and noncrippled children. *Journal of Exceptional Children*, 1949, *16*, 33-40.

In psychosocial terms, Ladieu, Adler, and Dembo (1948) attribute the problem primarily to the belief of the disabled individual that others overestimate the disability. Closely associated with this phenomenon is the nondisabled person's tendency to resist making concessions to the disability and to regard his association with the disabled person negatively. Consequently, exclusion from activities that can be performed despite the disability extends and enlarges the scope of the real limitation. A central source of frustration for the exceptional child is that such discrepant perceptions of his capacity reduce his participation in socially satisfying activities. This position was confirmed by Block (1951) in his review of historical, theoretical, and experimental approaches to the understanding of disabled persons. A common thread in the various formulations is the suggestion that disabling effects were due not so much to the physical condition as to the disabled individual's interaction with others in the social milieu. For example, Freedman (1967), among others, in a comprehensive review of the subject, observed that environmental factors are at least as important in the genesis of emotional disturbances as is the handicap. Parent-child relationships are often viewed as the central consideration in the adjustment of the physically limited child. An example of work in this area appears in Miller's study (1958) of clients in a child guidance clinic. Although cautious in generalizing her findings to all children with cerebral palsy, the author notes that disturbed parent-child relationships tend to play a more significant role in personality development among such children than the severity of the disability. Although the disability may "trigger" the emotional response, the troubled child with a physical disability functions in a manner similar to that of his nondisabled counterpart. However Cruickshank and Dolphin noted that some differences may be characteristic of the crippled child. In their study, although the exceptional children compared favorably with the normal group in needs for belonging, achievement, economic security, freedom from guilt, and understanding of the world, they lacked independence in their thoughts and actions. In general, although these needs were being met by parents in varying ways to varying degrees, the authors suggest that desires for sharing in decision making and affection were being overmet by the parents concerned.

Explorations of child adjustment using paper-and-pencil tests have not produced uniform results. Depending upon the instrument used, the variable presumably being measured, and the interests of the investigator, comparable studies of this kind contradict almost as frequently as they confirm each other. An early study by Rosenbaum (1937), using the Thurstone Personality Schedule with crippled girl campers, found the test group to be emotionally maladjusted. Using the Neyman Kohlsted Test in the same era, Nagge and Sayler (1933) found no differences between crippled and nondisabled high school students on introversion-extroversion. Using the Minnesota Multiphasic Inventory with handicapped college students in a later study, Linde and Patterson (1958) noted, on the other hand, that their cerebral-palsied subjects tended to score in the direction of emotional maladjustment. However, no specific patterns or personality types appeared to differentiate the disabled from the nondisabled group. Some of the differences were attributed to the anxiety generated by the disability and the concomitant tendency of the disabled to withdraw from social contacts.

In a more recent consideration of differences in adjustment between physically limited and other persons, Michal-Smith (1962) observed that the status a physically handicapped individual has in society contributes to feelings of inadequacy, rejection, frustration, hostility, and guilt. Social perceptions of the disability accentuate feelings of social devaluation and deter the individual from making an adequate social adjustment. At times, however, the disabled person may turn this social devaluation to his own advantage, using his perceived helplessness to avoid responsibilities and to project blame for failure upon others. The critical role of interaction with others in an unstructured social field in creating problems for disabled individuals was underscored in Meyerson's study (1948) in which an artificial injury was imposed upon a group of children and adults for a period of twenty-four hours. The subjects in this experiment reported that the difficulties they experienced were due not so much to the limitations associated with the physical conditon as to the quality of their life experiences.

There has been considerable interest in ascertaining the incidence of adjustment problems among physically exceptional children. Using data obtained from semistructured clinical interviews, supplemented in some cases by test findings,

Siller (1960) investigated the psychological concomitants of amputation in a group of children aged two and one-half to seventeen years. Sixty percent of these subjects had an adequate or better adjustment. Prominent in the dynamics underlying the adjustment of the Siller group was concern with restitution or avoidance of the loss. Gates' (1946) analysis of data obtained from autobiographies written by crippled and noncrippled children, coupled with some test results, revealed no statistically significant difference in social or emotional adjustment between groups. Although it may be argued that disability imposes extra burdens upon children and thus renders them more vulnerable to adjustment problems, conclusive evidence supporting this position has not yet emerged from studies comparing groups of physically exceptional children with normal children. Conversely, the position that disability constitutes an adequate defense against frustration and, thus, shields the individual from marked adjustment problems also lacks unequivocal research support. Consequently, at this point in psychological research, it must be conceded that physically disabled children as a group do not appear to differ qualitatively in adjustment from other children. Also lacking is conclusive evidence to support the belief that mental health problems occur with greater frequency among the disabled.

Notwithstanding their equivocal character in certain instances, the data on social and emotional adjustment of crippled children suggest that the disability experience renders the goal of sound mental health difficult but not impossible to attain. The barriers created by the physical limitations themselves are not inconsiderable, but the core of the matter seems to be treatment accorded to crippled children by the non-disabled. In effect, if real and consistent differences in adjustment do exist between the crippled and the nondisabled, they probably are a product of the negative and inconsistent attitudes of the latter group. To the degree that this is so, social maladjustment is preventable and, in all probability, remediable if only the perceptions of disability in the social milieu could be modified in a favorable direction.

A variety of projective techniques have been administered to groups of crippled children in an effort to avoid the defects of paper-and-pencil tests and to explore more profound aspects of the individual. Using the Rosenzweig Picture Frustration Test, Smock and Cruickshank (1952) found the level of frustration tolerance of handicapped children to be lower than that of normal children. Whereas the normal population concentrated upon a solution to the problem that was causing frustration, the handicapped subjects were likely to ignore the barrier and/or project blame and hostility upon it. The authors noted that social relations constituted an area of frustration which was a greater problem for handicapped children than for other children. A similar finding was derived by Fitzgerald (1951) through the use of the thematic apperception test. In this study family reactions appeared to be a source of more frustration in orthopedically handicapped adolescents than the disability per se. Using the Rosenzweig Picture Frustration Test, Lange (1959) found frustration reactions of handicapped children with cogenital disabilities did not differ from children with acquired ones. The generalization emerging from this study was that when he reaches the age when denial of freedom and independence becomes important to him, the congenitally disabled child suffers as much frustration as his adventitiously disabled peer.

Reports in the literature suggest that when exposed to stimuli which relate to a physical disability, physically limited children tend to maintain a higher threshold for threat stimuli. Lipp and his associates (1968) found physically exceptional children to be less perceptive than nondisabled peers of handicap-related details of disabled figures. The authors of this study believe that their finding lends support for a denial theory of defense. Such a theory holds that the perception of the disabled child that he is "different" usually is managed by denying the difference.

Projective techniques have been used to assess discrepancies between the goals that crippled children set for themselves and their measured capacities. A study by Harway (1952) revealed that exceptional youngsters tend to overestimate and to be inconsistent in their self-evaluations in some, but not all, situations. One of the areas of the crippled child's self-evaluation that has relevance for professional workers is that of body-image. Through the use of a draw-a-person test developed by Machover, Wysocki (1965) found that crippled children can be differentiated from noncrippled children in terms of their higher levels of feelings of inferiority, anxiety, and aggression. Physical insults appearing in the figure drawings tended to correspond with the child's own disability. Also using figure drawings in an earlier study, Centers and Centers (1963) reported that the figures produced by amputee children provided clues to their own disabilities in drawing a deformed limb or omitting a limb entirely. In drawing nondisabled persons, crippled children tend to be realistic about the differences that exist between themselves and others. This sense of reality is not accompanied by extreme anxiety or conflict. In contrast to figure-drawing studies that differentiate disabled and nondisabled children, Lambright (1967) found that an administration of such an instrument to adolescents in special education and in regular programs yielded no consistent differences in self-concept or personal adjustment.

Projective techniques have been useful in exploring the social needs of crippled children. Broida, Izard, and Cruickshank (1950) used the Symonds Picture Story Test to differentiate three groups of crippled children who varied in the presence of feelings of fear. A subgroup that had unmet needs to be free of fear revealed a great need for social acceptance and participation. Such children experience conflict in that their needs for increased social integration are counterbalanced by fear of entering social situations. Using a sentence completion test with crippled junior and senior high school children, Cruickshank (1952) found that social relationships do constitute a problem area for many crippled youngsters. In their desire to be treated as individuals, not as handicapped persons, these subjects wanted peers and adults to forget their disabilities, but they lacked some of the social attributes necessary to bring this about. As a group they were less able than the nondisabled control subjects to evaluate interpersonal relationships. They tended to withdraw from social contacts, and they had fewer "normal" adolescent interests. Indicative of their reduced social competency, moderately handicapped children responding to the World Test were reported by Wenar (1956) to be more vulnerable than nondisabled children to feelings of fear from a world perceived to be dangerous and from their own impulses. Simultaneously, the exceptional group had fewer defenses that could be used in coping with such threats.

In general, projective techniques appear

to constitute a promising avenue of investigation into the personality dynamics of crippled children. Currently, methodology is still being tested, but data derived from this source suggest some special problems in frustration, self-image, and social interaction. Projective instruments seem to generate less equivocal data regarding personality comparisons between disabled and nondisabled groups. This may be because the projective instruments attempt to tap the inner feelings and perceptions of young people through the use of loosely structured stimuli rather than verbal stimuli, which call forth socially desirable responses.

The complex and pervasive character of the disabilities imposed by cerebral palsy are so psychologically significant that Haring (1959) recommends avoidance of comparisons with nondisabled children. However, some of the special adjustment problems that confront children with this disability merit investigation. Operating out of a longitudinal frame of reference, Gesell and Zimmerman (1937) reported on a fourteen-year development study of a cerebral-palsied child. Their observations indicated that a functional personality organization is possible even when severe limitations exist in the sensory and motor mechanism. Intact auditory and visual functions contributed substantially to the positive adjustment made by this subject throughout the period of observation. Phelps (1948) also viewed sound emotional adjustment as possible for severely disabled cerebral-palsied persons despite apparent neurological impairment. He concluded that parental attitudes and home and school training were crucial in promoting social competency in such children.

Adopting a multicausal approach to the development of personality in cerebral-palsied children, Denhoff (1960) notes the importance of such variables as inherited intellectual, perceptual, and emotional traits, the effects of brain damage during the early years of life, the dynamics of the mother-child relationship, and the impact of sensory deprivation. Similarly, Hopkins, Bice, and Colton (1954) relate emotional conditions to restriction of movement, pain, failure experiences, parent reactions, and perceived social inadequacy.

Several studies of specific characteristics of cerebral-palsied children shed light on adjustment problems. On the basis of data derived from personality measures and a task that measures self-reliance in a social situation, Gunn (1965) concluded that cerebral-palsied children tend to be emotionally and socially immature and hypothesized that this immaturity was a result of parental handling. Realistic fear of movement among these children was associated with an intensified fear of emotional expression and assertiveness. Reiterating a common theme in the literature, Holden (1957) reported that the condition of cerebral palsy does not necessarily impoverish the adjustment of those who have this disability. On the contrary, 74 percent of his sample of cerebral-palsied nursery school children were rated as having average or high motivation. In this study, satisfactory motivation correlated very well with good progress in the nursery school program.

Nussbaum's work (1962) suggests that the personality development of cerebral-palsied children is related to the attitudes of significant adults in their lives. Generally, however, these children revealed less of a reality orientation to themselves than did the adults around them. Working with older individuals who had cerebral palsy, Muthard (1965) noted that groups of severely, moderately, and mildly disabled college students were comparable in personality. However, when compared to other college students, Muthard's subjects required more counseling and assistance with their problems.

Although the data are not conclusive, the trend thus far suggests that cerebral-palsied children and adolescents are subject to a multiplicity of negative developmental influences in the personality area and run greater risks of having adjustment problems. However, such problems seem more closely related to the social response to cerebral palsy than to the disability itself. This position is supported in the finding that cerebral palsy does not necessarily engender adjustment problems and that favorable social conditions tend to neutralize aspects of the disability which accentuate problems and heighten the probability of a positive social adjustment occurring.

Attitudes of the Handicapped Child Toward the Culture

Building upon the earlier work of McKibben (1943), Franke (1932), Kammerer (1940), and Sohn (1914), Cruickshank (1952) administered a sentence completion test to 264 handicapped children and 400 nondisabled children in the junior and senior high schools of six cities. The normal children responded to virtually all the items. On the other hand, the disabled subjects produced a statistically significant greater number of neutral, ambivalent, or nonsensical responses or failed to respond altogether. The investigator suggested that this may be attributed to the higher level of experience deprivation among the exceptional youngsters in his study. Some of the characteristic attitudes of physically limited children uncovered

by this study were: a feeling that adults are impressing an awareness of the disability upon the child, an acceptance of the status quo in relation to adults even though relations with such adults are imperfect, a wish for less adult interference in the life of the child, especially in the direction of forgetting or ignoring the handicap, and a need to be treated like others. In contrast the nondisabled subjects in this study expressed a desire to be treated as special people. Thus, having achieved equality, they were reaching for a relationship with adults that goes beyond mere acceptance.

Relatively little additional systematic information is available concerning the attitudes of physically exceptional children toward their society. However, a number of retrospective follow-up investigations have encouraged physically limited individuals to look back at their educational experiences and report their attitudes toward them. Thus, graduates of a hospital school studied by Brieland (1967) reported generally favorable perceptions of their experiences at the school but suggested that students should be given opportunities for the attainment of greater independence and self-sufficiency. Furno and Costello (1963) reported on a follow-up study of graduates of a school for physically handicapped children. Their sample expressed positive attitues toward independence, self-confidence, acceptance of the handicap, and interest in other people, aspects of personality that were thought by these graduates to be related to postschool success. In another follow-up study, Carlsen (1957) found that among graduates of a special school for crippled children fewer than the expected number of these individuals reported negative attitudes toward their postschool social situations. However, confinement at home was associated with increased dissatisfaction in this group. On the college level, Muthard (1964) found that cerebral-palsied students differed only slightly from matched nondisabled college students in their attitudes toward their educational experiences. In the main, therefore, it may be concluded that the available studies support the values of current special education practices because they reflect positive retrospective attitudes on the part of the consumers of these services. It is not known how much these positive results are biased by selection factors, the response sample, or by the possibility that the "old oaken bucket" delusion may be operating to transform the memories into sweeter ones than the original experience would merit.

In view of the fact that the social and personal attitudes of physically disabled children fail to reflect the reality of their situation or exercise a destructive influence on their social interactions, professional workers have made a variety of attempts to reshape such attitudes in a more favorable direction. An important guideline for attitude change suggested by Patterson (1963) is that of minimizing threat to the individual concerned. Through a genuine interest in the student and a sincere attempt to understand and accept him, educators and others may have the greatest success in changing perceptions of self and others among exceptional children. Although occasional mention is made of the use of behavior modification techniques in the reorganization of the attitudes of the disabled, most of the work in this area has been accomplished through the use of group approaches (Whelan and Haring, 1966).

In an early experiment in the therapeutic use of groups in an orthopedic hospital school, Rubenstein (1945) found that the group experience eased superego and enabled them to use the group as a family situation in which reality could be tested and new perceptions could be formed. Similar results were reported by Zeichner (1957) in his work with cerebral-palsied group participants and by Wilson (1962) in a study of homebound physically handicapped students. In the latter, as a result of the group experience, five of eight severely limited homebound children acquired more realistic perceptions of themselves and the world around them and made an adequate adjustment to their disabilities and their families. These studies barely scratch the surface of attitude modification for orthopedically disabled children. However, they do suggest that attitude change is possible and that group interventions constitute a promising procedure. Other interventions that need to be explored include milieu therapy, behavior modification, and individual psychotherapy.

Attitudes Toward the Handicapped Child

Not all societies view the disabled in a similar manner. In reviewing the situation in some non-Occidental areas, Hanks and Hanks (1948) concluded that attitudes toward them are more favorable in those societies that maintain higher levels of industrial productivity, have a more equitable diet, minimize competitive factors in individual and group achievement, and maintain a concern for individual capacity rather than setting formal standards of attainment. Reiterating the role of social attitudes in fashioning the behavior of exceptional children, Trippe (1959) observed that America's cultural dedication to success coupled with the opening of relatively few channels for the disabled to achieve that success creates anxiety and insecurity with possible personality disorganization. In attempting to cope with this situation, disabled children adopt different means, one of which is to abandon the goal of social success while retaining the accepted means of achieving success. The consequence of this adjustive mechanism often is rigidity, compulsivity, and personality constriction. Pressed into this life style by their lack of access to opportunities to become successful, disabled children are forced into deviant behavior associated with poor reality testing and unrealistic goals. The problem for the disabled child starts quite early in his life. Silberberg (1967) found that nondisabled children evidence consistent and negative perceptions of orthopedic disability by age four years.

Avoiding euphemisms about social attitudes, Gellman (1959) observed that prejudice toward the disabled exists at all socioeconomic levels in all regions of the United States. Stereotypical behavior toward the exceptional in our society has its roots in child-rearing practices that stress normalcy, social customs and norms that institutionalize pity, the arousal of neurotic childhood fears among nondisabled persons under stress, and the impact of behaviors exhibited by the disabled which invite discrimination. Through emphasizing the concept that difference among people is acceptable and normal, schools and other social institutions can improve the social climate in which the disabled child lives. In studying attitudes toward disabled students on a college campus, Yuker (1965) noted nondisabled individuals with negative attitudes toward disability tended to avoid interactions with members of this group and that even if such nondisabled individuals were helped to accept their disabled peers, the quality of the acceptance was superficial. Consis-

tent with the finding that those who held negative attitudes toward the exceptional have similar feelings toward certain ethnic groups, Yuker observed a tendency for such persons to assign the disabled to a class and to attribute to them presumed class characteristics.

In exploring attitudes of first, third, and sixth grade nondisabled children toward the crippled, Billings (1963) used two projective techniques, one requiring a written story in response to a picture stimulus and the other a picture completion test. The attitudes of these fifty-four children toward the crippled were significantly less favorable than their attitudes toward the noncrippled with an increase by grade (age) in their "unfavorableness." The children rated high in adjustment by their teachers evidenced the more unfavorable attitudes toward the disabled. Negative attitudes, even among educators, are often engendered merely by identifying an individual as exceptional. In this regard, Combs and Harper (1967) found that teachers in their sample reacted more negatively to descriptions of cerebral-palsied children than they did to the same descriptions presented without the disability label. Reporting a comparable finding in a sample of disabled high school seniors, Jaffe (1967) concluded that when the disability as a stimulus appears in the context of a disabled person's other traits, it is accorded more favorable attitudes. However, Mader (1967) found that teachers of different disability groups had comparable attitudes toward physically exceptional individuals.

Few investigators have reported studies dealing with the impact of the handicap on cultural attitudes toward disabled children. Coughlin (1941) selected a group of fifty-one children from the files of the Detroit Orthopaedic Clinic. In all cases the parents of the children were living and the attitudes of the parents were known to the worker. Coughlin defines four broad categories of parental attitudes. "The attitude considered most constructive was that of the relatively small number of parents who had sufficient intellectual insight and were so well adjusted personally that they were able, while fully realizing the implications of the orthopedic problem, to accept it and turn their attention and energies toward finding means of compensating for it." A second generally positive attitude was expressed by some parents who apparently had a "complete acceptance of a handicapped child on an emotional level with very little or no intellectual insight." A number of parents had an adequate intellectual understanding of the child's problem but emotionally were unable to provide him with complete acceptance. Thus these parents demonstrated such feelings as overanxiety, overprotection, and "overstimulation of the patient to accomplish more than he was capable." Finally, a group of parents were observed who neither intellectually nor emotionally were able to accept the child. These parents possessed both a lack of understanding of the physical condition of the child and "destructive attitudes" toward the child. Included among these latter were such factors as fear of surgery, fear that the child might get worse, fear of what society would think, and fear of inability to be economically independent.

Mussen and Barker (1944) also reported a study on attitudes toward the crippled. Although the study does not relate specifically to children or youth, the attitudes expressed toward crippled people in general undoubtedly apply to cripples regardless of age. The authors report on the responses of 117 college students to a rating scale developed for the purpose of determining beliefs held toward the behavior characteristics of cripples. On twenty-four characteristics the ratings varied from favorable to unfavorable. In general, the ratings concerning cripples were less favorable than "ideal ratings," although there were a few exceptions to this statement. Greatest variation was to be seen on such characteristics as vitality, self-confidence, submissiveness, realism, aggressiveness, social adaptability, and sensitiveness. On each of these characteristics the ratings of attitudes toward cripples was in the unfavorable range.

In an unpublished study, Cruickshank, Wiberley, and Summers investigated the social acceptance of crippled children by their physically normal peers. Twenty-eight classrooms were located within a series of public school systems wherein no special programs differing from those planned for all of the children of a particular class were prepared for the crippled child. Included on the total class registers were 29 crippled children and 807 physically normal children. Two crippled children were registered in one of the classes and the remaining 27 classes each contained one crippled child. To all of the children in the seventh-grade groups the investigators administered a sociometric test to determine the degree of social acceptance or rejection of each child. The crippled children included those with poliomyelitis, cerebral palsy, congenital amputations, Perthe's disease, and other categories of disability. One finding of the study is pertinent at this point. Three classifications were made for the positions achieved by the children on the sociometric test through the responses given, that is, stars, neutral groups, and isolates. Among the physically handicapped children there were 7 stars, 7 neutrals, and 15 isolates; among the physically normal children, 205 stars, 227 neutrals, and 375 isolates. When these two sets of figures are compared statistically, there appears to be no significant difference in the rate of acceptance or rejection between the crippled and noncrippled children of these classrooms as demonstrated by the children's own choices. The factor of visible physical disability alone, in other words, is apparently not the basis on which acceptance or rejection of a crippled child is made.

Tithy (1966) found that a greater degree of alienation and introversion was attributed by a sample of nondisabled subjects to disabled as compared to nondisabled persons. The greater the perceived ability of the disabled to compensate for the limitations, the lower the level of alienation and introversion that these nondisabled subjects attributed to them. Persons with cosmetic disabilities generally were perceived to have less compensation potential than those with motor handicaps. Reporting equivalent findings, Jones, Gottfried, and Owens (1966) noted that their nondisabled subjects expressed greater acceptance of exceptionalities that reflect mild handicaps, that is, promise greater compensation potential.

Investigations of attitudes toward the physically exceptional do not agree in all details concerning the incidence of avoidance and rejection in society. Undoubtedly, these differences stem, in part, from variations in the reference groups and the instrumentation used in these studies. It may be hypothesized that young elementary school age children find themselves subject to fewer negative attitudes from peers than do physically disabled teenagers. Furthermore, college students probably encounter fewer negative attitudes on campus than they do in seeking employment. The most valid conclusion regarding attitudes seems to be that physically dis-

abled children will experience such attitudes from time to time but because the attitudes vary from situation to situation and are applied inconsistently to the same disabled individual, uncertainty in new situations is engendered whenever a disabled child enters unfamiliar sectors of life. Somatopsychologists have studied this problem in depth and Barker and his associates suggest that the phenomenon accounts for some of the tensions felt by disabled individuals in social situations.

The most hopeful note about attitudes is that educators and other professional persons can influence the disabled under selected conditions. The most promising approach seems to be planned interaction between disabled and nondisabled children under conditions favorable for both groups. Such arrangements require both social psychological sophistication and educational engineering. Yet the stakes are sufficiently high for the adjustment of the exceptional child to warrant carefully planned interventions. Thus far, group encounters under adult leadership seem to offer the most productive approach to attitude modification in this context. Other approaches merit further study.

Family Adjustment

Relationships within the family constitute one of the critical problem areas for the disabled child. Although the establishment of unequivocal links between parental response to, and emotional disorders within, the physically exceptional child are difficult to document, Allen and Pearson (1938), Lord (1930), Kammerer (1940), Oettinger (1938), and Rosenbaum (1943), among others, have suggested such a relationship. Indeed, general acceptance in education and psychology of the role of the family in fashioning child behavior seems to make the issue self-evident. Some verification does exist in the literature. For example, Schecter (1962) found that certain reactions in the parents, such as guilt, are reflected in the fantasy life and, by implication, in the behavior of the physically limited child.

Observations of parent groups conducted in Los Angeles County, California, by Carr (1968) revealed recurrent patterns of concern that suggest the difficulties encountered by parents of cerebral-palsied children. These parents expressed concerns revolving around uncertain information about the cause and diagnosis of the child's disability, the hope that a cure could be effected, awareness that the child at school accomplished much while away from them, lack of clarity concerning how to explain the cerebral palsy condition to the child, his siblings, and others, confusion about the relationship between cerebral palsy and mental retardation, the issues related to the handicapped child's play with nonhandicapped children, possible placement of the child away from home, the desire to assist the child to avoid certain forms of undesirable behavior, the hope that speech therapy would be effective in promoting improved oral communication, the amount of love and attention required by the handicapped child, and the matter of handling the disability situation with nondisabled siblings. In view of the complexity of these problems, it may be expected that many parents of physically exceptional children are troubled and, in turn, convey some sense of their perplexity to their children. In working with the parents in his sample, Carr was impressed repeatedly by the closeness of the emotional tie that developed between a disabled child and his parents. Unfortunately, this tie appears to have been used to inhibit independence for the child and to limit other interests and relationships for the parents.

A number of general studies have underscored the depriving effects of separation from the mother for whatever reason during the early stages of life. In a follow-up study of one hundred children with poliomyelitis, Copellman (1944) confirmed for exceptional individuals findings that had been reported for nondisabled infants. Separation from parents during hospitalization is difficult both for disabled children and their parents. Typically, the younger group tends to be withdrawn and bewildered, whereas the older children become aggressive and resist adult demands. Yet, necessary separation can, in time, be managed to some degree by the physically limited. In a study of crippled children in an orthopedic hospital school, Donofrio (1949) discovered that his sample had an above average adjustment to home and family, a finding that he explained on the basis of "absence makes the heart grow fonder."

The entry into the family of a severely physically disabled child can be exceedingly stressful for the parents. In a review of the literature on this matter, Collins (1965) concludes that mothers of severely defective children are under a strain and that the family suffers adverse effects as a consequence. However, when mothers were given adequate supportive services in conjunction with education and treatment of their children, feelings of inferiority and difference tended to dissipate, reducing parental tension. In an observational study Mowatt (1965) characterized her sample of mothers of physically exceptional individuals as evidencing low levels of spontaneity and as conflicted by feelings in the areas of guilt, separation, and independence. Here again, participation in a group process resulted in alleviation of most of these problems.

Much of the literature concerning the family relationships of physically limited children is confined to the mother-child constellation. By and large, fathers have either been inaccessible to investigators or have avoided entry into study samples. In the earlier mentioned study being completed at the Teachers College, Columbia University Research and Demonstration Center for the Education of Handicapped Children, Rusalem is finding a "cop-out" syndrome among fathers. Deeply concerned about their relationships with their physically disabled children and denied many of the opportunities that mothers have to act out such concerns, fathers tended, in this sample, to disengage themselves from their exceptional children and to focus their interests upon work, out-of-home social contacts, or other activities that denied their children an intimate association with a male figure. Thus, Rusalem recommends a restructuring of child-care arrangements that provide fathers not only with a role in rearing the exceptional child but that endows this role with the attributes of reinforcing his sense of "maleness."

The data on family relationships are unequivocal regarding the role of the mother in the development of the physically limited child. Bender's (1949) recommendation that early mothering and continued emotional support for both the mother and the child are essential cannot be questioned. Yet mothers may be so distressed by the demands of the mother role vis-à-vis the severely disabled child that they may be lacking in emotional readiness to provide the child with the warmth and acceptance he needs. As in other areas of exceptionality, educators and psychologists working with the physically handicapped recognize the values of early professional intervention in working with mothers. To an increasing degree, schools and agencies are entering the developmental process at the earliest possible moment, sometimes within the first year of the child's life.

Social Status with Peers

As increasing proportions of physically disabled children participate in classes with the nondisabled peers, the quality of their relationships with such children is being studied. As a result of using incomplete sentences with physically limited and nondisabled children, Cruickshank (1952) reported that handicapped children reveal insecurity relative to the negative feelings expressed about them by their nondisabled peers. Despite this, however, the relationships between the two groups are, in most instances, favorable. Comparing cardiac and orthopedic with nonhandicapped adolescents, Giovannoni (1967) found that the two groups were not differentiated on the basis of membership in informal social groups or social relations with the opposite sex. However, the disabled indicated less participation in formal social groups. Giovannoni concluded that the disabled do not constitute a deviant group in society and that the disability is not useful in determining social role behavior or level of social participation.

On the other hand, at least one investigation resulted in sociometric data suggesting that disability constitutes an important variable in determining children's social status. Nondisabled subjects aged ten to twelve were asked by Richardson and Royce (1968) to rank preference for drawings in which skin color and physical handicap were systematically varied. The authors concluded that physical handicap is such a powerful determiner of attitudes that it masks skin color in children's social preferences. At least one group of physically limited children, the homebound, expressed their own needs in relation to nondisabled students. Responding to questions, put to them by Rusalem and Jenkins (1961), relating to their home instruction experience, these homebound teen-agers noted that special deprivation and isolation from peers constituted the most important limitation imposed upon them by their inability to attend classes in a regular school building. In considering a possible return to classroom instruction, they expressed their greatest degree of anxiety relative to the manner in which other students would accept and integrate them into their social fields.

Studies related to the perceptions held by physically exceptional students concerning the nondisabled are few in number and, in at least one instance, so contradictory that few generalizations can be made about this area other than to indicate that exceptional students see it as an important one for them. Much additional work has to be done relative to the interaction between disabled and nondisabled students before the dynamics of the situation are clarified. Experience suggests that in regard to some disability areas, exceptional children do not differ materially from other children in having their social status determined by factors other than the disability. On the other hand, study has not been made of severe disabilities, especially those which impair communication, to determine the extent to which the disability, per se, interferes with the achievement of a satisfactory social status with one's peers.

Guilt, frustration, and fear were found by Cruickshank (1952) to be more common among physically disabled than nondisabled children and to play a part in determining their social adjustment. One means through which these feelings are controlled is through conformity behavior. To the extent that this is so, disabled children would be expected to scale down some of their goals to what society believes they should be. However, this hypothesis has not been adequately tested by research. At present, as exemplified by Allen's study (1967) of the aspirations of disabled and nondisabled high school students, the tendency is to regard level of aspiration as an individual matter. This is supported by the finding that within each of the two groups, a broad range of aspiration and reality levels could be found. As Linde and Patterson (1958) indicated in their work on the influence of orthopedic disability on conformity behavior, even the underlying assumption that greater conformity exists among the disabled is open to question.

Although there is a paucity of data in many areas of the study of psychosocial impact of disability upon personal and social functioning, that of self-concept is relatively well developed. Body-image as a reflection of total self-concept has interested a number of investigators. Because crippling produces differences in body structure and/or function that set the child aside from the physically normal, authors have sought to understand the psychosocial implications of such variations for the manner in which one sees his own body. In exploring the stable cognitive structure of body self-concepts (body schema) of child amputees, Simmel (1966) found that sensations apparently emanating from the amputated limb (phantom limb) are found among children who have lost a limb during development rather than in children with congenital amputations. Because body schema is plastic, new postures and movements are incorporated into it over time. Eventually, these sensations are brought into relationship with each other and incorporated into the schema until a new organization of perceptions is formed. When the reorganization process is completed, an altered body schema emerges which more nearly reflects the objective body structure.

In an experimental study of the relationship between the severity of the disability and self-concept, Smitts (1964) found that severely disabled adolescents have lower self-concept scores than mildly disabled ones. Within the disabled adolescent group, as a whole, physical disability had its most significant and negative effect on severely disabled females. Richardson, Hastorf, and Dornbuser (1964) discovered that a group of physically disabled campers aged nine to eleven years had introjected the prevailing peer value emphasizing physical activities and, consequently, offered a higher proportion of negative statements about themselves than did nondisabled children. Realistic in their self-descriptions, the handicapped children were aware of their shortcomings in the physical area, a condition reflected in comparative lack of social experience and greater concern for the past.

The available evidence suggests that physically disabled children and adolescents perceive themselves in unfavorable terms when making comparisons with nondisabled peers. However, as Rusalem (1963) concluded after studying one-hundred homebound teen-agers, this does not obtain in comparisons between self and other disability groups. In this context almost all of Rusalem's disabled subjects preferred their own disability to others mentioned. It may be assumed that fantasy wishes and envy extend to those without a disability, but are less significant in relation to other limitations. Apparently, with few exceptions, if a teen-ager has to be disabled, his own disability has

no more negative valence to him than any other condition. As indicated earlier, body-image is a fluid aspect of self-concept and is influenced by life experiences. In a study of the effects of a two-week camp experience, Holdren (1961) confidently suggested that even such a brief experience can change a child's body-image. Although such differences do not ordinarily manifest themselves in figure drawings, they are reflected in counselor's judgments on behavior rating scales.

In the more general area of self-concept, Fairchild (1967) reported that the self-concept of handicapped elementary school children did not differ from that of their nondisabled peers to a significant degree. However, the handicapped group was found to have more unrealistic components in their concepts of self. In another investigation, Pomp (1963) found that the self-concepts of seventh- and eighth-graders in special classes had a greater degree of distortion than those of comparable nondisabled children. Beyond this general finding, Pomp reported that self-concept as a student was more distorted among the disabled subjects than the nondisabled ones. The atypical school experience of the former is suggested as a partial explanation for this finding. Lambright's study (1967) of adolescents sheds some light on Pomp's conclusion. She compared the self-concepts of eighteen physically disabled adolescents enrolled in public school classes with a comparable group attending public and private school special education classes. Because no significant differences were found between the two groups, she concluded that school placement does not affect self-concept and personal adjustment.

Self-concept has been studied in older disabled individuals as well. Dunn (1968) compared a sample of disabled students enrolled at the University of Illinois with nondisabled peers and found that self-esteem among the handicapped was at least equivalent to that of the nondisabled. In this specialized sample, satisfaction with social relationships (and, consequently, self-esteem) was higher for the severely disabled than for the nondisabled. Dunn also reported that the self-esteem level was not related to the degree of disability. Among physically disabled adults, Shelsky (1957) found that an overt visible injury does not necessarily have a more negative effect upon self-concept than a nonvisible injury or illness.

Cutter (1962) suggests that because learning is an ego function, disorder in a physically handicapped child's self-concept will manifest itself in educational problems. Consequently, the evidence concerning self-deprecation should be taken into account in planning educational programs for physically disabled children. Within the limits of the studies conducted in the self-concept area, self-deprecation is more evident in adolescents than in children. However, regardless of age, self-concept of physically disabled children seems vulnerable, particularly when intact and smoothly functioning bodies are highly valued. Implications strongly support structuring preschool experience to maximize realistic feelings of self-regard and, when self-concept distortions do occur, exploring means of modifying such perceptions in a positive direction within the framework of the school experience.

Parent Reactions to the Physically Limited Child

In recognition of the critical role of family response to the exceptional child in personality formation, many writers have addressed themselves to interactional problems in this area. Zuk (1962) contends that some of the difficulties confronting parents of physically exceptional children are traceable to their functioning in a society that has contradictory values regarding disability. When a family becomes aware of the exceptional child, disappointment, anger, and guilt soon follow. Guilt has value in controlling the anger that is turned toward the child, a control that is sometimes manifested through denial of anger of any type. Despite such generalizations, most observers agree that a physical handicap in a child is not inevitably associated with inability of parents to respond warmly and sensitively to a child. Denhoff holds that all parents, whether of disabled children or not, have essentially comparable feelings toward their children. Yet, a severe disability in a child can traumatize the family. When this occurs, family and other environmental reactions to the disability can affect the child's development. Citing cases illustrating the influence of adverse family reactions on physically handicapped children, Gasson (1966) concluded that the resultant emotional defect of such reactions may be more handicapping to the child's functioning than the disability per se.

Hall (1963), studying a sample of cerebral-palsied children in Minnesota, concluded that the family into which a cerebral-palsied child is born is high risk in terms of potential family breakdown. Faced with a multiplicity of problems and harsh realities, such families ordinarily experience feelings of uncertainty, hopelessness, desperation, guilt, and frustration. The preponderance of potential family difficulties is supported by Boles' study (1959) in which he found mothers of cerebral-palsied children to be more anxious, guilty, overprotective, unrealistic, maritally conflicted, and socially withdrawn than were mothers of nonhandicapped children. The age of the child and the mother's religious affiliation were significantly correlated with personality characteristics. Yanagi (1962) suggests that the greater the severity of the neurological involvement, the greater the risk that the family faces in coping with its responsibilities to the child. Professional intervention seems indicated early in the child's development, when the family in crisis may be susceptible to assistance and before the family problems become chronic and resistant to solution.

In studying fifty-eight families having an orthopedically disabled child, Coughlin (1941) noted that the attitudes of the parents did not differ significantly in quality from those of parents of nondisabled children. However, the feelings expressed by Coughlin's parent sample were more intense, although most of them tended to have constructive attitudes toward their exceptional children. The handicap seemed to have less influence on the attitudes of parents on lower social-economic levels than of more affluent and intellectually able parents. In any case there is a reality in rearing a physically disabled child, a reality that has some unpleasant social, economic, and psychological connotations. As Freedman (1967) noted, concern for the child and confusion about what is best for him accounts for some parental behavior of a destructive nature.

Numerous suggestions have been made about the types of help that are effective in improving parent performance in the rearing of an exceptional child. Among these are Carr's suggestion (1968) that parents share responsibility with community agencies and avail themselves freely of community resources, Ware's recommendation that parents mobilize their inner resources and obtain help to accept what

cannot be changed, Cardwell's (1956) emphasis upon family participation in community action to improve conditions for the handicapped child, and the feelings of Mosher and Stewart (1958) and Thurston (1969) that parents enter into a program of family counseling and rehabilitation.

Family members can take steps to evaluate the child's capacities realistically and establish reasonable goals for him. In comparing mothers' and staff ratings of the intellectual ability of cerebral-palsied children, Barclay and Vaught (1965) noted that mothers of younger and more severely disabled cerebral-palsied children tended more often to overrate intellectual potential. Regardless of age or degree of handicap, a cerebral-palsied child in the Barclay and Vaught sample who scored in the mental retardation range was likely to have his ability overestimated by his mother. Jensen and Kogan (1962) reported comparable findings for cerebral-palsied children, indicating that most parental overrating of intellectual ability occurred when the subject was younger, less handicapped, or suffering from both a physical and an intellectual disability.

The critical role of family interactions with the child in fashioning the child is well documented. Although the nature of family reactions to the physically exceptional child vary with socioeconomic status, the family structure, personality characteristics, and cultural factors, it can be generalized that many families are not fully prepared to cope with the child-rearing process unaided. The data support the contention that families containing an exceptional child are vulnerable to breakdown, and that mothers and siblings seem to be in an especially precarious position. Early professional intervention is recommended almost universally by writers in the field whose clinical judgement dictates that assistance of various types will result in more realistic expectations of the child and healthier responses to him.

Studies of Intelligence of Crippled Children

As stated earlier, few recent investigations have been conducted regarding the intelligence of crippled children as a group. Lee (1931) reports the results of a study of intelligence of 148 crippled children in the Children's Orthopedic Hospital in Seattle, Washington. She utilized the Binet Test. The age range of her group was between three and sixteen years; the intelligence quotient range, 35 to 138, with a mean of 86.8. Lee found that the children with poliomyelitis had the highest mean intelligence quotient score, 92. Children with "spastic paralysis" had a mean intelligence quotient of 69; tuberculosis of bone and joint, 88; congenital deformities, 61; and central nervous system involvements, 74. Of particular interest is a recent comprehensive study of hemophiliac boys in Los Angeles (Dietrich, 1968). Their mean IQ on the WISC was 121. Yet, as a group, they suffer academic and vocational frustration.

Witty and Smith (1932) have reported a study that included 1,480 crippled children. They obtained a mean intelligence quotient of 84.5 with a range of from 50 to 130. Pintner, Eisenson, and Stanton (1941) and Gordon, Roberts, and Griffiths (1939) present differing results with two populations of crippled children. The former, utilizing a group of 300 crippled children (which excluded cerebral-palsied children), obtained a mean intelligence quotient of 88; the latter, a mean quotient of 103.9 from a group of 98 children with poliomyelitis. Fernald and Arlitt (1925), in one of the earliest studies reported, found a mean intelligence quotient of 82.35 and a range of 30 to 138 in a group of 194 crippled children, representing many different types of physical conditions, including cerebral palsy. Donofrio (1949) reported that the distribution of Stanford-Binet scores obtained with 157 crippled children were skewed toward the lower end of the curve.

Practically all of the studies mentioned appeared prior to the publication of even the 1937 revision by Terman and Merrill of the Stanford-Binet Intelligence Scale. The 1960 revision of the scale has a much more adequate standardization and, in general, is a great improvement in terms of items and administrative procedures over earlier forms of the same test. New studies need to be completed to provide information regarding the intelligence of crippled children on this scale. It has previously been pointed out that the intelligence range of children with cerebral palsy is apparently considerably different from that of the normal population and may, as well, be different from that of other types of crippled children. Hence, those studies that included cerebral-palsied children within their populations need to be tentatively considered and need to be reevaluated with populations that exclude this group of children. More and more information is being received from clinical observation and group study to the effect that crippled children cannot be considered as a homogeneous group insofar as psychological characteristics are concerned. Cardiac children, often included in group studies of crippled children, for example, appear to be characterized in many instances differently from other crippled children. Cerebral-palsied children have already been discussed in this respect. It is likely that other groups of crippled children will likewise have characteristics which distinguish one from the other. The impact of congenital defects on intelligence and personality versus adventitious disabilities needs to be seriously investigated. It can undoubtedly be expected that the intelligence level of some groups of crippled children will be below national norms or will have a different curve from that of the general population. Although Briggs (1960) reported that scores achieved on the WAIS Performance Scale when only the dominant hand is available do not suffer significant decrements, the same probably does not hold true if the dominant hand is affected. Consequently, limitations in manipulation should be taken into account in assessing intelligence test performance when the stimulus tasks require dexterity or rapid movement. In considering the multitudinous factors that may depress the intelligence test scores of physically exceptional children, Braen and Masling (1959) question the indiscriminate application of general population norms to handicapped children and advocate modifications devised for each case. Children who have been markedly restricted in their experiences and activities will, with the present instruments of evaluation, achieve lower-than-average scores. Children who have been restricted in their experiences through long periods of hospitalization and convalescence may be expected to show differences in intelligence scores and personality factors. Children who have suffered a cerebrospinal involvement may be expected to achieve lower scores on tests due to the interaction in function of the cerebral cortex. However, studies that continue to group all types of handicapped children together, regardless of etiological factors or type of involvement, will add little to the present meager fund of knowledge of this problem.

The Binet-type tests and the revisions of them have limitations in their application to disabled children. The preponderance of verbal material serves as a disadvantage to children with speech disorders or auditory impairments, whereas the heavy emphasis on motor activities in the remaining items often makes the test inappropriate for children with severe motor involvements. Such factors as these are basic to the criticism heard of the studies of the intelligence of cerebral-palsied children noted earlier. Several authors have made serious attempts to circumscribe the criticisms of the Binet materials. Chief among these are Ammons and Ammons (1949), and Blum, Burgemeister, and Lorge (1951 a,b). Both of these groups of investigators have attempted to develop scales that require little or no verbalization and that can be completed through the utilization of gross motor activities rather than through the fine muscle movements required on previously mentioned intelligence scales. The attempt in each instance is to produce a scale that permits a more accurate evaluation of the innate ability of the crippled child and that reduces to a minimum the impact of the disability on test performance. Other tests in current use include Haeussermann's test of the educability of young handicapped children, the Illinois Test of Psycholinguistic Abilities, and the Peabody Picture Vocabulary Test. These instruments have not received sufficient use as yet to be able to ascertain accurately whether or not the goals of the authors have been achieved. The Leiter International Intelligence Scale was developed with the assessment of intelligence of physically handicapped children as one of its major goals. The test is ingenious in several of its parts; however, the scale consists of dozens of items, many of which are composed of many tiny pieces to be placed together in a variety of ways. These pieces are so small that subjects with almost any degree of motor incoordination involving the hands are seriously restricted in their ability to participate in the test. As a test of motor performance the Leiter not only has all of the restrictions of performance tests generally but has intensified some of them to a point that renders almost useless an interesting and potentially useful instrument. These tests, however, together with careful modifications required on Raven's Progressive Matrices may provide resources for clinical psychologists which in the future will permit more accurate research and greater understanding of the intellectual potential of individual crippled children.

SPECIAL CONSIDERATIONS IN CEREBRAL PALSY

Most crippling conditions do not alter directly the learning mechanism of the disabled individual. With few exceptions, the damage is localized in the limbs, the spine, the joints, or the trunk. Learning deficits, if they occur at all, result from environmental influences. On the other hand, the tissue damage that causes cerebral palsy lies in the brain of a child and, not infrequently, involves neurological structures and processes that determine perception and intellectual capacity. Although direct neurological involvement of this type is not inevitable, it happens often enough to justify separate consideration of the special psychological problems of cerebral-palsied children who do suffer an insult to the learning mechanism. Obviously, their adjustment problems are even more complex than those of other crippled children because the whole gamut of human response—communication, perception, and controlled movement—may be impaired. Consequently, as indicated earlier in this chapter, a special section will be devoted to a review of the intellectual and perceptual problems of this disability group.

Intelligence

In 1946 McIntire reported the results of a study to which Phelps and others have referred. Phelps (1948) suggests that approximately 30 percent of the cerebral-palsied group is mentally retarded as a result of brain damage; the remaining 70 percent is normal "in the sense that these individuals show the normal spread of the population seen at large." This statement had been widely accepted until about 1950 when, simultaneously and independently, several studies appeared—each of which is markedly similar to the others in methodology, treatment of data, and results (Asher and Schonnel, 1950; Holoran, 1952; Miller and Rosenfeld, 1952; Heilman, 1952; Hopkins et al., 1954; Bice and Cruickshank, 1955). Heilman has compared the results of these studies in Table 6–2. It is interesting to observe the close similarity of the results of the five investigations and to note the results of the combined data. Among the 1,002 children included in the studies, 25 percent have average or above average intelligence; 30 percent, borderline-dull intelligence; and 45 percent are in the mentally defective range. Fouracre (1953) reports similar findings in still another study, although his population was considerably smaller than those previously mentioned. Likewise, Hopkins et al. (1954), in a study involving 992 cerebral-palsied children, report 487 children or 49.0 percent with intelligence quotients between 0 and 69; 224 children

TABLE 6-2

COMPARISON OF INTELLIGENCE TEST RATINGS OF CEREBRAL-PALSIED CHILDREN FOR WHOM RATINGS WERE DETERMINED IN FIVE RECENT STUDIES

Estimated intellectual level	Miller and Rosenfeld	Strong Memorial Hospital Staff	Asher and Schonell	Holoran	Heilman	Combined Data
	% of 261	% of 90	% of 340	% of 133	% of 178	% of 1,002
Mentally defective	49	43	47	36	47	45
Borderline dull	25	30	28	38	30	30
Average and above	26	26	25	26	23	25

SOURCE: From A. Heilman, Intelligence in cerebral palsy. *The crippled child*, 1952, *30*, 12. By permission.

or 22.5 percent, between 70 and 89; 212 children or 21.9 percent, between 90 and 109; and 69 children or 6.6 percent, with IQs above 109. All these studies have employed the 1937 Stanford revision of the Binet Intelligence Scale as a basis of their evaluations. It is recognized that the Binet-type tests are not the most satisfactory measures of intellectual evaluation for severely disabled children. However, the independent nature of the studies which have been cited, the knowledge that the psychologists involved in the studies were exceedingly well prepared for their responsibilities, and the increased understanding which clinical psychologists now have regarding the problems of mental measurement with handicapped children lend stature to these studies and credence to their collective findings.

The large population of cerebral-palsied children reported by Bice, Hopkins, and Colton, and later analyzed in greater statistical detail by Bice and Cruickshank, supports the other studies with respect to the percentages of cerebral-palsied children in the several classifications of intelligence. Some minor differences were noted particu-

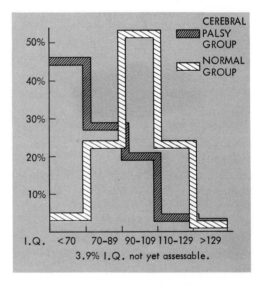

Fig. 6–3. Distribution of intelligence quotients of normal and cerebral-palsied populations, British study [from Asher and Schonnel, *Archives of Diseases of Children*, XXV (1950). Reproduced with permission.]

larly relating to the triplegia spastic group, but the meaning of these differences is not clear and is certainly not basic to psychological or educational planning.*

*It is recommended that the reader refer himself to an excellent discussion of intelligence and cerebral

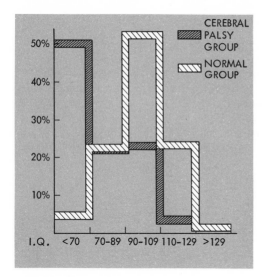

Fig. 6–4. Distribution of intelligence quotients of normal and cerebral-palsied populations, Buffalo (N.Y.). Children's Hospital study [from Miller and Rosenfeld, *Journal of Pediatrics*, XLI (November 1952). Reproduced with permission.]

Taibl (1951), utilizing Raven's Progressive Matrices Test, examined 115 cerebral-palsied children who ranged in age from six years to adulthood. The school grade placement of the subjects was from Grade 1 through Grade 8 with the exception of Grade 5. No high school students were represented in his study, although two university students were included. The group consisted of sixty-nine spastics, six ataxics, one rigidity, and four mixed types. Seventy-two of the children were educationally classified as either "special class" or "ungraded group." The findings indicated that the cerebral-palsied children of Taibl's population ranged from intellectually superior to mentally defective, the distribution not being a "normal" one. The performance of the spastic group was

palsy, by Viola E. Cardwell, which appears in Chapter 14 of *Cerebral palsy: Advances in understanding and care* (New York: Association for the Aid of Crippled Children, 1956).

in keeping with the distribution of intelligence scores in earlier studies cited. The athetoid group, however, showed a close relationship to normal comparative groups. In general the author concludes that the cerebral-palsied children perform on Raven's Progressive Matrices in a manner closely similar to that of other North American children. This points to the need for further examination of the problem because his findings are in contrast to those of Bice, Holoran, Heilman, Asher, Miller, and others. Taibl also states that he is encouraged in the use of Raven's Progressive Matrices as a test for cerebral-palsied children. A later statement by Banks and Sinha (1951), however, indicates that the average reliability (0.88) of the matrices is considerably smaller than that given by Raven and "appreciably below the minimum needed for a satisfactory test of intelligence."

With respect to validity, the findings showed that some of Raven's items have undoubtedly been badly selected and poorly constructed. Banks and Sinha point out that several items have little discriminative value and others are comparatively worthless. "The average validity, whether judged by internal or external criteria, was decidedly poor (0.54)." Other statements from this study require that opinions regarding Taibl's data be held in abeyance until further basic work has been done on the test itself, and then corroborative studies must be completed. Further, Taibl's study can hardly have been considered conclusive, nor was it intended as such by the author, because it deals with a relatively small heterogeneous population. The small number of children per type of cerebral palsy, the wide chronological age span, the limited number of children at any one chronological age level, and the complete omission of children at certain age and grade levels necessitate that this study be considered as one pointing to new directions for investigation but one which is not definitive.

Because cerebral palsy is not a homogeneous system of symptoms and because persons with this diagnosis vary one from another in numerous ways, attempts have been made to differentiate the intellectual functioning of various subgroups. Comparing intelligence test scores after a fourteen-year lapse, Klapper, Zelda, and Birch (1967) found that, in general, retest scores indicated a significant increase in IQ for the sample. However, the greatest variability occurred in the paraplegic and monoplegic subgroups and the least variability in those having hemiplegia and athetosis. Prediction of retest scores was most difficult in those who had originally tested in the 75 to 89 IQ range. Wedell's (1961) retesting perceptual ability of spastic hemiplegic children after six years indicated considerable rise in performance levels. All improved on at least one test and more than half improved on four or more tests. He noted that superiority of right hemiplegics over the left group persisted. Additional support for age differences in performance was provided by Delaney (1962), who reported that younger subjects (aged four to ten years) taking four perceptually oriented tests scored higher than an older group (aged ten to eighteen years) on all subtests, total score, and mental age. However, when the scores were translated into IQs, the younger group was found to be superior. Spastic and extrapyramidal children could not be differentiated on three of the four subtests. However, the extrapyramidal group did perform better on the Goldstein-Scheerer Test. In this instance, visual and visual-motor perception were found to be positively related to mental age. The role of

chronological age is suggested by Hirschenfang and Benton (1965), indicating that the intelligence test scores of cerebral-palsied children tend to rise with age. They concluded that it takes a longer time for such children to reach mental maturity.

In performance comparisons of spastic and athetoid children, Katz noted no differentiation on Stanford Binet scores in either mental age or IQ terms. In an investigation of reading skills, Jones (1966) found that athetoids tend to suffer more severely from disordered eye movements, but that the frequency of such defects was greater among spastics. Consequently, measures of intellectual ability that rely upon some degree of reading speed may be influenced by the visual factors described in this study.

Psychologists have been troubled by the sources of invalidity that may lie even within the best-designed measures of intellectual ability when such measures are used with cerebral-palsied children. In addition to exercising great caution in using the standardized instructions, time limits, and test materials, examiners have been comparing the disabled child with the normal groups assembled by the test-makers. As a consequence, great reliance has been placed on the judgment of the well-trained and experienced examiner whose observations during the testing session are considered more appropriate than indiscriminate use of numerical scores. Simultaneously, the search for valid and functional instruments goes on. This search often takes the form of comparisons among respected standardized instruments in the hope that one or another, in original or adapted form, will provide a ready yardstick of intellectual functioning, especially for individuals with cerebral palsy. Dunn and Harley (1969) in a comparison of the results yielded by the Peabody Picture Test, the Ammons, the Van Alstyne, and the Columbia Mental Maturity Tests, concluded that all four tests had utility as predictors of the school success of children with cerebral palsy, correlating as they did in the .80s with teacher ratings. The Peabody and the Ammons were useful with a wider range of age groups than the other two tests examined. In fact the Van Alstyne seemed applicable to children whose mental age was below 8.0, whereas the Columbia had its greatest value in use with children with MAs above 4.0. Similarly, Ando (1968), comparing the values for the cerebral-palsied of the Peabody Picture Vocabulary Test with the Verbal Scale of the Wechsler Intelligence Scale for Children, found the two instruments to be highly correlated. If anything the Peabody scores were less affected by the degree of physical and speech limitations in cerebral-palsied children. In another study with a sample of cerebral-palsied children, Hammill and Orvis (1966) noted that the Peabody Picture Vocabulary Test does not overlap, but is supplementary to scores obtained on tests of sound discrimination and abstraction.

In assessing the values of the Gessell Developmental Scale for young cerebral-palsied children, Sievers and Norman (1961) concluded that physical, visual, and speech handicaps and limited life experiences tended to depress children's scores and to give evidence of retardation. Older cerebral-palsied children who were given the Stanford-Binet seemed to do less well than expected in verbally describing objects, forming blocks into a bridge, and working with picture stimuli owing to problems of perception, life experience, and limited environments. Finally, with cerebral-palsied children aged fourteen years and older, these authors found the

Wechsler-Bellevue Verbal to be relatively accurate in assessing intellectual ability. As a caution to examiners and teachers, they advise intraindividual rather than interindividual comparisons and selective alteration of the standardized testing conditions in accordance with the needs of the child. In still another comparison study concerning three well-known tests, Richardson and Kobler (1955) concluded that the Binet, the Ammons Full-Range Picture Vocabulary Test, and the Ravens Progressive Matrices correlated quite well with each other when used with a sample of thirty-two cerebral-palsied children aged 61 to 138 months. The Ravens and the Ammons were recommended for use with severely handicapped children because they both elicit nodding and pointing responses. However, it was noted that the Binet produced an acceptable score in the cases in this sample, including a basal age.

Discussion about the most favorable techniques of assessing the intellectual functioning of cerebral-palsied children continues. Allen (1960) focused upon biological fact of neurological impairment, considering it an important but not the only factor to be taken into consideration in evaluating the individual. Thus, perceptual processes are significant as reflected in test behaviors. Because these test behaviors in the cerebral-palsied constitute an atypical situation, the psychological evaluation is useful when regarded as an approximation of individual potentialities and current efficiency. In line with the thinking of some specialists in the field, Cotton (1941) departed from standardized batteries and worked with a custom series in testing spastic children in his sample. This series consisted of a sorting technique, a string pattern test, completion tests, and pattern memory tests. As the author views it, this series constitutes an effective mental test that is especially adapted for spastic children.

Other investigators have attempted to adapt standardized instruments for use with cerebral-palsied children. In working with the Stanford-Binet, using a "pointing modification method," Katz (1955) prepared tables indicating the physical capacities required for various test items, enabling an examiner to select those items that are within the physical range of the subject. Allen and Collins reported on the selection of tests that were found suitable for psychological evaluation purposes by a cerebral palsy clinic team. Among the tests they selected were: the Ammons Full-Range Picture Vocabulary Test, the Columbia Mental Maturity Test, Raven's Progressive Matrices, the Leiter International Performance Scale, the Cattell Infant Intelligence Scale, the Gesell Preliminary Behavior Inventory Scale, and the Stanford-Binet. In the light of the nature of the limitations found in any sample of cerebral-palsied children, adaptations may be required in these instruments from time to time.

In accordance with the feeling of some examiners that special tests are needed for severely disabled children, Haeussermann (1952) developed test items that require minimal response from the child—usually affirmation or negation. Although the level of abstractness of these test items increases progressively, the response modality remains the same. Presenting items to the child that are either life-size concrete objects or large clear pictures, the examiner offers him at least two alternatives to be indicated in any manner possible. This individualized approach, relying heavily upon observations of the examiner rather than upon standardized procedures is based upon the tester's knowledge of the child (familiarity with the case record is recommended) and awareness of such problems as immaturity and infantilization, negation, experience deprivation, concretization, mental retardation, visual difficulties, inaccessibility to human speech, delayed responses, and behavior deviations. In another attempt to develop a custom-made battery, Peters (1964) combined nine subtests into an instrument that presents stimulus tasks on graduated levels of concreteness until relative abstractness of objects, agents, and actions are reached. This battery is thought to measure developmental aspects of the conceptual components of presymbolic behavior.

Although the references noted above do not designate solutions to all testing problems in cerebral palsy, they do suggest that standardized measurement may be less informative about the cerebral-palsied child than other children. The pervasive physical, social, and neurological effects of this disability usually generate such great differences from the usual in the testing situation that comparisons with nondisabled norms and the imposition of ordinary testing procedures become exceedingly risky. In place of definite quantitative mental ages, IQs, and other test score variants, the psychologist and educator are well advised to think in terms of ranges. Generally, the most useful product of a testing experience is a workable estimate both of current intellectual functioning and estimated potential. In time, as experience with the child accumulates in the service situation and as repeated contacts are made with the examiner, these estimates can be revised. However, for the present they serve as functional hypotheses concerning the child and allow tentative program decisions to be made for him. Although reports in the literature generally indicate a higher incidence of low intelligence test scores among other children, it is probable that some part of this finding can be traced to the concepts and procedures used in assessing the handicapped group and to a changing population seeking community service. Classification is difficult because performance is influenced by all factors that enter into any testing situation coupled with the physical, neurological, and environmental factors that make cerebral palsy such a complex condition. It must be concluded that the present crucial variable in evaluating the cerebral-palsied child is the competence and experience of the tester.

Effects on Educationally Related Processes

Prior to reviewing the perceptual consequences of cerebral palsy, an overview of the related educational processes that are affected by this disability will be presented. In a study of the language development of children ranging in age from 7.9 to 10.6 years, Dillon (1966) found that the severely involved cerebral palsy group scored unfavorably when compared to the nondisabled on most of the variables measured by the Illinois Test of Psycholinguistic Abilities and, to an even greater extent, on reading tests. He concluded that a lag may be expected among the cerebral-palsied in all language aspects, but especially in reading. In a study of cerebral-palsied children aged six to seventeen years, Irwin and Hammill (1965) reported deficiencies in abstraction and vocabulary. Problems in the language area were confirmed by Trombly (1968), who noted that the language development of cerebral-palsied children lags behind that of normal children and suggested, as a remedy, enrich-

ment of the disabled child's environment. In a study assessing listening comprehension, however, de Hoop (1965) found no statistically significant differences between cerebral-palsied and nondisabled subjects.

The educational implications of cerebral palsy were described globally by Fouracre (1952), who based his formulations on the concept that the cerebral-palsied child lacks normal learning experiences and, consequently, requires educational compensation. Among the areas of developmental deficiency considered important for educational planning are communication and language development, emotional and social adjustment, and mental development, including consideration of perceptual disturbances. Among other basic treatment tools suggested by Fouracre is a psychological evaluation by a skilled examiner. In recognition of deficits that a cerebral-palsied child may bring into the classroom with him, a number of educational interventions have been tried with varying success. Among the more promising of these are preschool treatment programs similar to those reported by Diedrich, Allender, and Byrne (1960) and Zimmerman and Jones (1965), and suggested by Robinault and Connor (1968), for cerebral-palsied children who are so limited that they are homebound and must participate in teleteaching programs as described by Carr (1964). It is widely recognized by educators, psychologists, social workers, and counselors that the implications of cerebral palsy extend far beyond the classroom. For example, Carlsen (1957) has discussed in detail vocational and social consequences of severe motor limitations. These consequences become even more compelling when perceptual and related problems impose their effects upon limited mobility and experience deprivation.

Perception in Children with Cerebral Palsy

For many years psychologists have been interested in the effect of brain lesion upon learning, intelligence level, personality, and perception. Doll and his associates (1932) early pointed to the relationship between birth injury, brain lesion, and mental retardation. The universal effect of brain lesion is seen in Doll's statement that such may produce "(1) motor impairment, (2) retardation of intelligence, (3) disturbance of personality and conduct, and (4) consequent handicaps in learning." Although Doll was not the first psychologist to be concerned with this problem, his organization of the problem stimulated many others to further consideration of it. Neurologists and psychiatrists likewise have contributed much to psychological understanding of this type of impairment (Penfield and Rasmusses, 1952). Goldstein (1942) and Halstead (1940), who have worked primarily with adults, have also contributed much to the understanding of similar conditions in adulthood. Piotrowski (1937) and Harrower-Erickson (1940) also focusing on adults, have stimulated numerous later psychological investigations of central nervous system disorders through the use of the Rorschach Test.

With children, Meyer (1947), Cotton (1941), Lord (1930), and Sarason (1949), among other research workers, have contributed important studies to the further understanding of the implications of brain injury for psychology. Werner and Strauss* have made a remarkable contribution to an understanding of the impact of brain injury on the perception of exogenous mentally retarded children. Because

*The reports of their research may be found in A. A. Strauss and L. Lehtinen, *Psychopathology and education of the brain-injured child* (New York: Grune and Stratton, 1947).

their work has received a penetrating critique from Sarason (1952), no further elaboration will be made here. Suffice it to say that although some limitations are inherent in the studies of Werner and Strauss, as Sarason points out so well, the importance of their contribution to psychology and education is exceedingly great. Further, it has a pertinent relationship to the cerebral-palsied child.

Many of the contributions of the previously mentioned writers have directly or indirectly related to perception, and specifically to perception in individuals with brain pathology. Because cerebral palsy, in its numerous forms, is a cerebrospinal condition, it has been the opinion of many that much of what has been written by these authors would normally also hold in a study of the psychopathology of children with cerebral palsy. It is recognized at the outset that the problem of individual differences is perhaps seen at its greatest among cerebral-palsied children. Thus, there may be those who show marked degrees of impairment, psychologically, from brain injury, whereas others may show little or no effects of the lesion insofar as psychological growth, learning, and adjustment are concerned. This discussion will be amplified when the multiple-handicapped cerebral-palsied child is discussed. Bender (1949) has stated, for example, that "cerebellar disorders often exist in relatively pure form and are not complicated with other perceptual or impulse disorders." Later she states that "in some organic brain disorders, the ability to draw a man is not impaired due undoubtedly to different localizations of pathology." The extreme variability of performance of brain-injured children and adults in psychological tests presents interesting and sometimes baffling situations to psychologists and illuminates the paucity of accurate knowledge about these problems. Location of the lesion, extent of the lesion, innate intellectual capacity, and many other variables add to the complexity of the problem and make controlled research with large groups still to be desired.

Stimulated by the publications of Werner and Strauss relating to exogenous mentally retarded children, Cruickshank and Dolphin have been concerned with their findings as they may relate to cerebral-palsied children. In 1950 Dolphin undertook a study of the psychopathology of cerebral-palsied children that became the basis for later investigation. As a preliminary study to ascertain the worth of further investigation, Dolphin obtained two carefully matched groups of thirty children each: one a group of cerebral-palsied children, the other, physically normal children. The former group included children with a chronological age range of between eight and thirteen years, a mental age range from six to fifteen years, and an intelligence quotient range from 78 to 129. The mean CA was 10.02 years, the mean MA, 9.57 years, and the mean IQ, 93.66. Children were paired on the above bases and were matched by sex as well.

An experimental test battery consisting of six parts was administered to the two groups of children. In general, the results of these tests showed that the cerebral-palsied children as a group differ significantly from physically normal children in several phases of perception. These results will be discussed subsequently under various topics. Before that is done, a few general findings relating to the perceptual problems of cerebral-palsied children will be discussed.

Cruickshank, Bice, and Wallen (1957) have presented one of the definitive discussions of perceptual problems in cerebral palsy, concluding that such children do, indeed, differ in certain essential perceptual characteristics from other children and that these differences influence educational progress. In an earlier consideration of the evidence on this subject, the California State Department of Education (1954) stressed individual differences among cerebral-palsied children but noted as well perceptual problems in the group manifested in limited attention span and high levels of distractibility, poor size, shape, and color discrimination, inadequate motor-visual coordination (especially in the eye-hand area), and emotional problems.

Using a custom-made test battery, Peters (1964) made the following observations of perception among the cerebral-palsied: (1) the lack of speech or hearing did not necessarily impede the formation of concepts, (2) the degree of involvement had little, if any, relationship to concept formation, and (3) the ability to identify objects was not necessarily indicative in these children of the ability to form concepts. Basing his opinions on test results derived from 300 children, Berko (1954) concluded that cerebral-palsied children suffered significant perceptual deficits and, therefore, suggested that tests based on abstract perceptual tasks are of questionable validity in assessing the capacities of these children. After analyzing test results obtained from thirty spastic and thirty athetoid children, Simpson noted that the perceptual function of cerebral-palsied children could be divided into at least two components rather than being regarded as a homogeneous entity. The two components are: (1) discrimination from memory and from model and (2) perceptual motor integration from memory and from model. Simpson found that his sample of cerebral-palsied children performed more favorably on discrimination than on integration tasks and that perceptual functioning and IQ had little relationship to each other.

In summarizing the findings, it is possible to state that the evidence supports the existence of important perceptual and visuomotor problems among cerebral-palsied children. These problems appear in many areas of functioning and have educational significance that cannot be ignored in planning and executing classroom programs for these children. Most special educators agree that differentiated teaching materials and techniques are required to enable the cerebral-palsied child to cope with his perceptual limitations. A full discussion of these teaching approaches appears in the educational literature and does not warrant review here except, owing to its controversial neurological and psychological evidence, the patterning approach should be mentioned. With Doman and Delacato (1966) as strong advocates of this position, patterning has attracted both avid believers and avid critics. Regardless of the results of an ultimate and impartial assessment of its merits, this formulation has influenced psychologists and educators who are adapting certain elements of the approach. In at least one instance, this occurred through providing the child with practice experiences at his stage of development and gradually moving him into the next stage as he achieved readiness for it. In this case, Lills and Shofer (1965) assisted the cerebral-palsied child through each stage that a normal child experiences naturally in the course of neurological development. Programming for the child under these circumstances closely follows a neurological model and is consistent with the presumed status of the central nervous system. Up to the present, the controversy has been more productive of heat than light. At this writing, without the benefit of more definitive and impartial data, it is difficult, if not impossible, to determine the degree to which the patterning concept is applicable to the now well-documented perceptual problems of cerebral-palsied children.

The figure-background relationship. The pathology of the figure-background relationship in individuals of all ages is an important differential diagnostic sign pertinent to cerebrospinal conditions, and it has been recognized as such by clinical psychologists for some time. Rorschach himself commented upon the reversal-of-field phenomenon in individuals with organic pathology (Rorschach, 1942). Since his first investigations with the cards later to bear his name, numerous others have commented upon this now common finding. Werner (1945), in a study utilizing the Rorschach cards, noted the increased number of white-space responses perceived by brain-injured mentally retarded children and notes that this category of responses "was more than twice as high with the brain-injured in comparison to the non-brain-injured group." The Werner and Strauss study of the figure-background relationship stimulated a reevaluation of their test with the cerebral-palsied children in the present experiment (Werner and Strauss, 1941; Strauss and Lehtinen, 1947). Table 6–3 shows the results of the tachistoscopic presentation of nine stimulus pictures to the cerebral-palsied and normal children of the Dolphin study (1951). It will be noted that the preponderance of responses of the normal children are those of the figure (either the correct figure or the incorrect figure, but nevertheless response to figure); those of the cerebral-palsied children, the background (background with incorrect figure and background only). A second test involved the children's matching an initial stimulus

TABLE 6-3

COMPARISON OF FREQUENCY SCORES OF CEREBRAL-PALSIED
AND NORMAL GROUPS FOR THE PICTURE TEST

Type of Response	Cerebral Palsy Group Frequency Scores	Normal Group Frequency Scores	Chi Squares	Level of Significance
Correct figure	16	74	44.86	.001
Incorrect figure	8	56	40.84	.001
Background with correct figure	55	53	.0378	.90
Background with incorrect figure	97	60	12.36	.001
Background	94	27	47.8126	.001

SOURCE: From J. E. Dolphin and W. M. Cruickshank. The figure-background relationship in children with cerebral palsy. *Journal of Clinical Psychology*, VII, 1951, 228-231. By permission.

card with one of three other cards: (1) a card containing the background only, similar to that appearing on the stimulus card; (2) a card containing the original background with a different figure; and (3) a card with a different background and the original figure. Although the difference was not statistically significant, a trend was observed in this test for the cerebral-palsied children to select the card with the background only, whereas the normal children were differentiated statistically in their selection of the card that had the original figure but a different background. The results of this portion of the study are in agreement with earlier studies of other types of brain-injured individuals to the effect that many of the cerebral-palsied children have difficulty in distinguishing figure from background in a field which simultaneously contains both. The degree to which cerebral-palsied individuals differ among themselves in this respect is not known from the reported data. However, the results indicated that not all of the responses of these children were psychopa-

thological in nature and that individual differences were present. Numerous cerebral-palsied children responded in a manner similar to the normal children. For many cerebral-palsied children, the figure-background differentiation is difficult or impossible and must be considered an important psychological characteristic of the group. Bender (1949), in this connection, has stated that "perceptual or intellectual problems are due to difficulties in organizing or interpreting and appreciating the totality of perception, which leads to frustration due to poor relationship with reality." Findings, almost identical to those described by Dolphin, are also reported by Klapper and Werner (1950) in the clinical reports of behavior of three cerebral-palsied members of pairs of identical twins. Also similar to the Dolphin study is the report of these latter authors with respect to the fact that the three physically normal members of the sets of twins responded to figure-background tests with predominantly figure responses.

An extensive study of figure-background relationships in the child with cerebral palsy was reported by Cruickshank, Bice, and Wallen (1957). This study, sequential to the initial exploratory work of Dolphin, utilized large and relatively homogeneous groups of athetoid and spastic types of cerebral palsy children. One hundred fourteen athetoid and two hundred eleven spastic cerebral palsy children were examined and compared to one hundred ten physically normal children. Chronological age, mental age, degree of stability, intelligence quotient, basis of physical diagnosis, and other variables were controlled.

In contradistinction to the earlier studies of Werner, Strauss, Dolphin, and others, Cruickshank and his associates utilized a three-dimensional tachistoscopic method of presentation, the Syracuse Visual Figure-Background Test. The following findings, as reported by the authors, are significant in relationship to the present discussion:

a. No sex differential was indicated in terms of the number of errors made by either sex within each age level within each diagnostic group.

b. Analysis of the number of slides correctly identified . . . revealed significant differences between the group means based on "number correct" scores for the three diagnostic groups; a mean of 7.04 for the spastic group, of 8.22 for the athetoid group, of 10.05 for the non-handicapped group.

c. Examination of the mean "number correct" scores at the various age levels for the three diagnostic groups revealed a fairly constant superiority of the non-handicapped group over the spastic group. The relative performance of the athetoid group, however, varied with age level approximating that of the spastic group at the younger ages and then approaching the performance of the non-handicapped at the older ages.

d. The spastic group made a significantly greater mean number of responses including reference to background (the number background score) than did either the athetoid or non-handicapped group. The difference between these latter two groups was not significant (Cruickshank *et al.*, 1957).

The evidence seems to point in the direction of a higher incidence of figure-background perceptual difficulties at all ages in the spastic group with such disturbances apparently having greater significance with athetoid children at the lower age levels.

Reed and Pollock (1963) also evidenced interest in visual perceptual function. They devised a display of black dots forming bars of different densities with patterns projected in a darkened room, which was considered to be a method of quantifying the parameters of a hidden figure test. Using ninety-nine palsy subjects and seventy nonhandicapped matched for age and sex, they found that the bar detection was significantly more difficult for the cerebral-palsied than for the normals and that there was no difference between the function of the spastic and athetoid groups. Children with clinical oculomotor problems erred significantly more even on comparatively simple tests than did the cerebral-palsied children without such difficulties. The authors suggest the possibility that oculomotor control may be a limiting factor of cerebral palsy children, including those in whom the defect is not grossly apparent.

Concern over underestimation of the importance of disordered eye movements in cerebral palsy has also been expressed by Abercrombie (1964). She suggests further study of the relationship of various kinds of squint to pattern (including figure-ground) and depth perception, noting that, in some cases, squint is successfully corrected with full stereoscopic vision resulting and that, in others, vision becomes uniocular by suppressing acuity in one eye. However, in many cerebral palsy children, the squint is of an intermittent kind with good visual acuity in both eyes and varying degrees of ability to attain fusion of two images. It is in this group that she believes that the greatest difficulties in perception occur.

Visual-motor perception. A disturbance in the visual-motor relationship of brain-injured children has also been reported by Werner (1944). Marble boards similar to those used by Werner and described elsewhere (Dolphin and Cruickshank, 1951) were administered to cerebral-palsied and normal children by Dolphin. In this test one is able to ascertain to a large degree through the child's performance his method of visual perception. Although both groups of children utilized similar methods of visuomotor performance, the trend established by the cerebral-palsied children was toward a constructive and incoherent approach; the normal children tended to use a constructive and global approach in their responses. It is hypothesized that, as in the test of figure-background relationship, the cerebral-palsied children were disturbed in their perception of the marble pattern (the figure) by reason of the large number of holes in the marble board and the marbles themselves, all of which constitute extraneous stimuli to which the cerebral-palsied children find it difficult to refrain from reacting. Compulsivity to react, as described in numerous cited works, undoubtedly plays

a role in the performance of some of the cerebral-palsied children of this study. Also suggestive of the insecurity felt by the cerebral-palsied children on the marble board test was their observed moving of marbles from place to place on the boards almost twice as many times as the normal children did. Further, some of the cerebral-palsied children, as in an attempt to gain security in space on the marble board, compressed their figures close to the edge of the board itself and in numerous instances actually utilized the holes along the edge of the board as the point of departure for the remaining portion of the design on which they were working. As long as these children had the security and stability of an edge or fixed point, they could operate satisfactorily; when they attempted to operate in space in the center of the boards they were confused and were ineffectual in their efforts. It must be pointed out that these findings again pertained to an undetermined number of cerebral-palsied children. Nevertheless, this clinical observation involved a considerable proportion of the children. Similar behavior is also to be observed in the drawings of Bender-Gestalt designs by two of the cerebral-palsied members of pairs of identical twins reported by Klapper and Werner (1950).

The Cruickshank, Bice, Wallen study (1957), to which earlier reference has been made, revealed a statistically significant difference between spastic, athetoid, and nonhandicapped groups of children on the marble board test. The median total error score for the spastic group was 23; for the athetoid group, 12.5; and for the nonhandicapped group, 3. No consistent sex superiority was evidenced in this study. Examination of combined sex-age groups in terms of medians and proportions of perfect scores for "total error" and "total changes" scores, respectively, supported previous findings of improved performance with increasing chronological age. These data further indicated that performance stabilized at an earlier age for the nonhandicapped children than for the spastic or athetoid groups of children.

Distinction between perceptual and perceptual-motor dissociation in cerebral-palsied children has been highlighted by several researchers. Bortner and Birch (1962), using the WISC Block Design, studied twenty-eight cerebral-palsied (nineteen spastic and nine athetoid) individuals eight to eighteen years of age with no significant difference in age or IQ of spastics and athetoids. They noted that athetoids made significantly more correct designs than spastics and that accurate discrimination was a factor of severity of motor impairment in that mild cases were accurate 94 percent of the time, moderate 81 percent, and severely handicapped 6 percent. The ability to discriminate was intact even though the ability to reproduce the designs was impaired. They concluded that the apparent inability to translate a perceptual organization into an appropriate action pattern might be a reflection of different stages of ontogenetic development. Thus, they suggest that functionally autonomous systems may exist with a recognition and discrimination system developing earlier and a perceptual-motor, or more complex integrative system, maturing later and that these levels are differentially affected by brain damage.

In a review of the literature on perceptual and visuomotor disorders of educable cerebral-palsied children, Abercrombie (1964) notes little evidence that these children see things in a distorted way, although they may see them in a primitive or immature manner, that is, they fail to make differentiations at the level of complexity suggested by their MA. Therefore, she refers to a developmental lag in perceptual skills. On the other hand, she sees the bizarre constructions as unlike what other children produce at any age and as a possible mixture of immature and mature performance. She too notes that visuomotor disturbances do not occur so frequently or so severely in children with athetosis as in spastics and that there is less evidence of perceptual, as distinct from visuomotor, disorders in the different types of cerebral palsy.

It is felt from the work described above, and from similar observations which have been made with many adults having cerebral involvements, that the disturbance of visual perception and the inability of many patients to interpret visual stimuli into motor activity is another important psychological characteristic.

Tactual-motor perception. One set of form boards, consisting of raised wooden geometrical figures on wooden blocks, was presented to cerebral-palsied and physically normal children (Dolphin and Cruickshank, 1952). A second set of forms consisted of the same geometrical figures —this time made up of large rubber-headed tacks surrounded by smooth metal thumbtacks pushed flat against the surface of the wooden blocks. The children, blindfolded, felt the surface of the blocks with their hands and fingers and then drew what they felt. In the first test situation there was marked similarity in the performance of the two groups of children. Even in this situation, however, where the background was purposely minimized, trends were observed for the cerebral-palsied children toward background responses; for physically normal children, toward figure responses. However, in the second presentation, the results from the tactual-motor experiment were comparable to those obtained from the figure-background experiment noted before, that is, cerebral-palsied children produce a significantly larger number of background drawings but physically normal children produce a significantly larger number of figure drawings. These findings from Dolphin's study are compatible with the trends noted by Werner and Strauss (1941) in a comparable experiment with exogenous mentally retarded children. In the Cruickshank, Bice, Wallen study (1957) of figure-background relationships, the nonhandicapped children again performed significantly better than either the spastic or athetoid groups on a tactual-motor performance test. This test involved a modification of the Bender-Gestalt test wherein Bender abstracts were converted into a tactual-motor test and administered to blindfolded subjects. This study, which utilized large numbers of children, corroborated the findings of the earlier Dolphin pilot investigation.

Concept formation. In their studies of concept formation with exogenous mentally retarded children, Strauss and Werner (1942) relied extensively on earlier work in grouping behavior reported by Cotton (1941) and Halstead (1947). Likewise, Dolphin (1951) modeled an experiment with cerebral-palsied children, following these earlier investigators. The Cruickshank, Bice, and Wallen study did not extend itself to the problem of concept formation. Hence, no corroborative data to the Dolphin investigation is available from this source. The close relationship between the findings of Strauss, Werner, Halstead, Cotton, and Dolphin should be noted. Dolphin requested children to place before one or two pictures objects that they felt were appropriate to the picture. A miscellaneous collection of 102 objects was available for the children's se-

lection. All of the objects were either to be placed before one of the pictures or discarded. The cerebral-palsied children placed a mean of 8.26 objects before the first of the two pictures; the normal children, a mean of 4.03 objects. To the second picture the cerebral-palsied children attributed a mean of 27.63 objects; the normal children, a mean of 17.36 objects. Statistically significant differences were obtained in each instance. The much larger number of objects and the more frequent usage of uncommon objects by the cerebral-palsied children corroborates the similar findings of Strauss and Werner with exogenous mentally retarded children. It is also in keeping with the observation of Cotton that cerebral-palsied children differed from normal children in three ways; namely, through a wider range of individual differences of the type of response within a given test situation, a greater tendency toward concrete types of responses with less ability to shift to more abstract forms of behavior and a greater tendency toward stereotyped responses. The second characteristic is one that Goldstein and Scheerer (1941) feel is typical of individuals with organic brain pathology and that clinical psychologists have come to feel is an almost classic sign in psychological evaluations.

Dolphin, as did others in similar experiments, observed the cerebral-palsied children reacting to the objects on the basis of secondary characteristics—soap was placed before one of the pictures because soapsuds could be waves. A burned match "is a toothpick because it has a sharp end on it." The selection of objects because of their secondary characteristics was also noted by Strauss and Werner with their group of brain-injured mentally retarded children; in the Dolphin study this tendency was rarely demonstrated by the physically normal children. The selection of larger numbers of objects, the utilization of uncommon objects, and the projection of the static situations into three-dimensional realities are all in large measure due to the forced responsiveness of the cerebral-palsied children to stimuli and to compulsivity characteristic of so many brain-injured individuals. The latter caused the child to feel forced to utilize all of the objects in his grouping activities. Strauss and Werner had observed a marked degree of meticulosity among their brain-injured subjects. To a lesser degree this was also observed by Dolphin in the performance of the cerebral-palsied children during the grouping test. It was, however, a reported clinical observation made of the cerebral-palsied children when drawings were done in connection with the previously discussed tactual-motor test.

More recently, Irwin and Hammill (1965) investigated levels of abstraction in 142 cerebral-palsied children. No significant differences in this variable were found among quadriplegics, hemiplegics, and paraplegics, among mildly, moderately, and severely involved subgroups, and among spastics and athetoids. Although the correlation between abstraction test scores and mental age was relatively high, it was modest in relation to abstraction scores vis-à-vis both chronological age and speech and language ability ratings. In a study of the relationship of sensory motor experience with concept formation, Melcer (1967) found that his handicapped subgroup had a deficit of action concepts which seemed related to their restricted sensory-motor experiences. In the belief that sensory-motor experiences in early childhood are a necessary precursor to concept formation, Melcer concluded that sensory-motor de-

privation along with neurological factors influence the intellectual development of cerebral-palsied children.

Also to be considered are Piaget's theories (1952, 1953, 1956) about the origins of intelligence in childhood, which highlight the fundamental role that the understanding of spatial relationships play in the development of number concept and all that depends upon it. It is also possible that the ability to cope with visuo-spatial relationships may well take precedence over verbal skills in the service of the needs of biological survival, with important consequences for lateralization of brain function.

Summary. Differences have been reported between the two groups of children, cerebral-palsied and normal, in discrimination of figure from background, in visual-motor and tactual-motor perception, and in generalized concept formation. It was not known to what extent all of these aspects of pyschopathology were present simultaneously in a single child or whether or not certain characteristics appeared in some children whereas others were absent. However, the Cruickshank, Bice, and Wallen study (1957) minimizes the notion of a general perceptional impairment. In general this study reported low relationships between the four tests that were employed within the three diagnostic groups studied. "Though the diagnostic groups differ considerably with respect to level of performance, there is not much evidence of individuals with overall perceptual 'problems.'" In fact, recent studies direct much more attention to visual-motor dysfunction than to perceptual disorders per se and note that spastics are much more susceptible to such problems than are athetoids. These results certainly emphasize the importance of careful assessment and evaluation by competent clinicians of each cerebral-palsied child and the necessity of adequate assessment information before educators can adequately prepare optimal learning situations for these children.

In addition to the differences already noted and discussed, certain other psychopathological characteristics were observed in the behavior of some of the cerebral-palsied children. Perseveration was common among the cerebral-palsied children. The impact of certain perceptions was observed to influence subsequent performance and activities on numerous occasions. Dissociation, the inability to relate objects in a unified Gestalt, has been observed by many investigators in the drawings by cerebral-palsied children and during their performance on the marble boards. This does not appear to be a function of motor dysfunction due to gross motor impairment per se. Klapper and Werner (1950) likewise have reported this as a characteristic of varying degrees of severity in the cerebral-palsied members of the pairs of identical twins whom they studied.

The studies of Werner and Strauss, of Dolphin, and of Cruickshank, Bice, and Wallen, and others tend to corroborate one another extensively. Further psychological studies reported in an educational demonstration project lend further credence to the data reported herein (Cruickshank *et al.*, 1961). Statistically significant differences do obtain between groups of children with some type of central nervous system disorder and comparable groups of children without such disabilities. Differences between and within groups of cerebral-palsied children are described in 95 detailed clinical case portraits of children with cerebral defects obtained from the administration of almost 300 psychological tests to them. The im-

plication of these findings, however, for learning and learning situations is still subject to much more needed research. The early reports of Strauss and Lehtinen, based on studies by Strauss and Werner, point out the necessity of significant modifications in the learning situation itself and in the educational methodology employed. The studies of Cruickshank and his associates referred to previously and the study of Gallagher (1960) corroborate statistically much of what was suggested as important by Strauss, Werner, and Lehtinen. Certain other studies, however, demonstrate no difference or exceedingly minimal differences between populations of children with central nervous system disorders and those of normal physique. Studies by Capobianco and Funk (1958) and Capobianco and Miller (1958) are examples in this instance. These two studies, like the early studies of Strauss and Werner, were concerned essentially with the learning characteristics of exogenous and endogenous groups of mentally retarded children. In general no statistically significant differences were noted between the groups of children studied.

On the surface it would appear that the studies of Capobianco, Funk, and Miller were in opposition to the previous studies which have been discussed in this section of the chapter. From the point of view of critique, as presented by Cruickshank (1963), two factors that stand out in the studies by Capobianco and his associates must be considered. The studies of Dolphin utilized children up to a maximum chronological age of sixteen years. The studies of Strauss and Werner were essentially limited to children between the chronological ages of twelve and eighteen years. The Cruickshank, Bice, and Wallen population were children between six years and fifteen years eleven months.

The later work of Cruickshank *et al.* (1961) utilized children between the chronological ages of seven and eleven years. The studies by Capobianco and his associates were, in effect, made on older populations, utilizing groups of subjects with chronological ages of eleven years seven months to twenty-two years of age (means in the range of fourteen to fifteen years). The heavy reliance on older subjects puts the findings of these authors in a position where comparisons cannot easily be made. The studies of Cruickshank, Bice, and Wallen, utilizing the Syracuse Visual Figure Background Test, indicate that at least two groups of cerebral palsy children show a marked loss in amount of psychopathology as age increases. It would not be expected, on the basis of the latter data, that statistically significant differences would obtain beyond the chronological age of fourteen (Capobianco's mean) if comparisons were made with endogenous type children. Thus the findings of Capobianco, Funk, and Miller are to be expected and are in line with previous research.

Cruickshank's more significant criticism of the Capobianco studies, however, pertains to the methods employed in grouping. Two items were used. The Riggs and Rain classification system was employed in considering institutional records to differentiate the subjects into the two groups, that is, exogenous or endogenous. No neurological appraisal was employed. When considering the generally unsatisfactory state of clinical records, the variability that may exist between medical and psychological diagnosticians, and the lack of reliability in a pencil-and-paper classification instrument, one has to reserve judgment as to the degree to which the two groups of subjects represented clear-cut differences and were indeed exogenous or endogenous. Furthermore, a second basis of grouping subjects involved the Syrause Visual Figure-Background Test. A decision was made to define children as exogenous if they demonstrated four or more background responses on this test. Although it might be assumed that all exogenous subjects produced four or more background responses, one has to raise the fact that numerous endogenous subjects may also produce four or more background responses. This fact, coupled with the crude appraisal through the Riggs and Rain system of the presence or absence of central nervous system disorder, raises doubt that two completely different groups of subjects were obtained; the results, therefore, must be questioned. One of the great needs in both psychology and education is for a carefully controlled study, longitudinal in nature, that seeks to study differences in psychopathology and achievement at various age levels from early childhood well into early adulthood. One of the values of the educational studies of Cruickshank and his associates was the availability of a unique medical-psychological-educational diagnostic team. The results obtained in this study can be compared to known quantified data and its population can be described with a unique degree of accuracy. Until similar careful diagnostic studies are made to precede psychological and educational investigations, the results of such studies will of necessity have to be considered tentative. The data that are presented by Capobianco are interesting and of value in the degree to which they corroborate the findings of earlier investigations regarding age changes.

It is possible that such findings are related to Wedell's (1961) conclusion, after studying visual perceptions of seventy-three cerebral-palsied and forty controls matched by age and IQ, that perceptual impairment is not a general concomitant of cerebral palsy but that it is mainly associated with bilateral and left-sided spasticity. He attributed the athetoids' superiority over the controls to the possibility of underestimation of the formers' IQs. Of particular interest here is his evidence that the spastics' inferiority tends to decrease with higher CA and MA levels and his suggestion that improvement may be due to accumulation of limited sensory-motor experience and to the unravelling of confused kinesthetic and other sensations. Thus, as proposed by Bortner and Birch (1962) and others, the factor of age might well be operating. As Teuber and Rudel (1962) showed clearly, whether the brain-injured differ from normals of the same age depends to a considerable extent on the kind of test used and the age at which it is administered.

THE MULTIPLY HANDICAPPED CEREBRAL-PALSIED CHILD

Reference has been made previously in this chapter and elsewhere to the problem of the multiply handicapped cerebral-palsied child (Cruickshank, 1953). It is, however, such an important consideration for psychologists and educators that, at the expense of being redundant, further mention of the problem will be made here. Only three variables have been isolated for consideration in this connection, with full realization that many others may be present in a given child and thus will have to be considered by the psychologist. The three that have been chosen for discussion are (1) the presence in the cerebral-palsied child of other physical or sensory defects, for example, impaired hearing, impaired vision, epilepsy; (2) the presence in the cerebral-palsied child of retarded mental development; and (3) the presence in the cerebral-palsied child of psychopathological characteristics of perception that are independent of mental retardation. Both of these last factors have been independently discussed earlier in this chapter. Table 6-4 illustrates the complexity of this problem and demonstrates the combinations of disabilities that may be observed in a consideration of the three variables which we have mentioned.

Type 1. This type simply involves the basic form of the disability, i.e., cerebral palsy of whatever variety and with no other physical or psychological deviations.

Type 2. This group of children includes those with cerebral palsy who also show defects of perception, but in whom there is no evidence of mental retardation or other type of physical disability. Type 2 in our classification of multiply handicapped cerebral-palsied children constitutes a group about which we admittedly know relatively little at the present time. The validity of this clinical type is assured, however, in the opinion of this writer. Strauss and Werner (1942) briefly report findings which are subjective, but which were nevertheless gathered from the responses of a small group of children of normal intelligence and who demonstrated perceptive defects. In the group of children studied by Dolphin and Cruickshank there were 14 children whose intelligence quotients were above 95. Within this group numerous children showed defects of perception which significantly differentiated them from their control subjects who were physically normal. . . . The prognosis for this type of multiply handicapped child is good educationally and psychologically provided the child receives his educational experiences in an environment which recognizes his basic learning problems, (Cruickshank and Dolphin, 1951), and in the degree to which he can profit from a total program of physical reconstruction.

Type 3. This group includes those cerebral-

TABLE 6-4

MAJOR VARIETIES OF MULTIPLY HANDICAPPED
CEREBRAL-PALSIED CHILDREN

Type	Presence of Cerebral Palsy	Presence of Other Physical Defect	Presence of Retarded Mental Development	Presence of Perceptive Pathology
1	yes	no	no	no
2	yes	no	no	yes
3	yes	no	yes	no
4	yes	yes	no	no
5	yes	no	yes	yes
6	yes	yes	yes	no
7	yes	yes	no	yes
8	yes	yes	yes	yes

SOURCE: From W.M. Cruickshank, The multiply handicapped cerebral-palsied child. *Exceptional Children*, XX, 1953, 16-22. By permission.

palsied children who show no physical handicap other than the basic one and who are free of perceptive disabilities but whose intelligence is retarded significantly. Psychologically these children appear like the endogenous mentally retarded children as defined by Strauss (1939). Many of these children show the classical symptoms of primary mental retardation, indicating that mental retardation might have existed even had cerebral palsy not been present. Such children, in addition to the physical characteristics of cerebral palsy (which are assumed throughout the remaining discussion of each type), exhibit lack of ability to form insight, poor comprehension, restricted memory functions, poor judgment, faulty reasoning, and limited problem-solving ability. These factors are those, among others, which characterize all primary forms of mental retardation. In general, each of the above factors will, of course, be accentuated in direct proportion to the degree of mental impairment. Both the rate of mental growth and the ultimate level of achievement, physical as well as mental, will be governed primarily by the innate mental ability of the child. While no adjustments are required

in the learning environment, such as are suggested in connection with Type 2, the same sort of adjustments in curriculum and teaching materials are necessary as for endogenous mentally retarded children. Prognosis—educationally, psychologically, and to a somewhat lesser degree, physically—depends directly upon the intelligence level and the adequacy of the educational program. At best, the level of achievement is significantly limited.

Type 4. This group of cerebral-palsied children included numerous problems of great seriousness. These are children who possess secondary physical disabilities other than cerebral palsy but whose intelligence is determined to be within normal limits and who do not show characteristics of perceptive difficulties. The frequency with which visual and auditory impairments accompany cerebral palsy is well known. Epilepsy ... is common among children with cerebral palsy. As a matter of fact, there is no physical disability which might not also occur in conjunction with cerebral palsy. The degree of visual or auditory defect may, of course, vary from mild impairments to those of a profound nature. Epilepsy may take the form of petit mal or grand mal seizures.

Children who present this variety of multiple disorder constitute one of the most difficult educational and psychological problems of any to be mentioned. Teachers, psychologists, and medical personnel may well be confused with respect to the appropriate methods of education and physical training for these children. Secondary physical defects of mild degree may not constitute a serious block to the learning or to the adjustment of cerebral-palsied patients. More involved physical defects, however, may seriously retard learning. Prognosis with Type 4 children is undetermined. Outcome is based primarily on the degree of severity of the secondary handicap and on the adequacy of the educational and therapeutic programs to cope with both primary and secondary disabilities. Educational methodology and therapy requisite to the secondary defect must, of course, be available to the child in order to insure even the most moderate psychological growth and educational achievement.

Type 5. With Types 5, 6, 7, and 8 the problem of multiple handicaps becomes more complicated. Cerebral-palsied children in Type 5 category are those who have no secondary physical defects, but who demonstrate both retarded mental development and psychopathological perceptive functions. This group insofar as psychological development is concerned corresponds to the mixed category in the classification of mental deficiency as described by Strauss (1939). These children will demonstrate the psychological characteristics of both the exogenous and endogenous types of retarded children. Insofar as educational and therapeutic programs are concerned, this writer feels that the perceptive problems of exogeny will demand major consideration in program planning, in learning or therapy situations, and in teaching materials. On the other hand, the professional worker will also have to keep in mind those psychological characteristics briefly mentioned in connection with Type 3 which are typical of endogeny. Prognosis—educationally and psychologically—will depend directly on the level of innate intellectual ability and the extent of the cranial damage which has caused both the manifestations of cerebral palsy and those of exogeny.

Type 6. These cerebral-palsied children are those who are characterized by secondary physical defects of a nature described in Type 4 who also show retarded mental development, but who do not have perceptive malfunction. It must be pointed out that to measure the intelligence of such children with accuracy is a most difficult operation since satisfactory instruments for the assessment of multiply handicapped children, and in particular, those with cerebral palsy, are not yet available.... When cerebral palsy, secondary physical disturbances, and mental retardation are found in combination, extreme caution must be exercised and careful periodic reassessments be made before a final decision is made regarding the mental level of the child. Even then accuracy in establishing a mental age may be impossible. If mental retardation is a bona fide diagnosis, then the prognosis for the child will depend upon the level of mental ability. At best, the outcomes, educationally and psychologically, may be significantly restricted.

Type 7. Type 7 includes those cerebral-palsied children who have secondary physical disabilities and who also demonstrate the peculiarities of perception which have been commented upon above, but who are of normal intelligence. Prognosis here is better than in Type 6 because of the better intellectual ability of the child, although it, of course, depends upon the severity of the secondary physical disabilities. Experience has shown that some cerebral palsied children will superficially demonstrate auditory and visual impairments, but that in reality these may be manifestations of the perceptive difficulties and not actual sensory disorders. Such findings and observations would warrant careful and cautious psychological, audiological, and/or ophthalmological evaluations of cerebral-palsied children to ascertain the exact etiology of the secondary physical manifestations.

Type 8. This final group of cerebral-palsied children is one in whom are observed secondary physical disabilities, accurately diagnosed mental retardation, and the psychopathological perceptive characteristics. This group will constitute the most serious educational, social, and therapeutic problem. Prognosis will be exceedingly poor, and the possibility of any independent adult experiences will be significantly limited. Comments which have been made in connection with other appropriate groups of children will, in combination, all apply in this instance.

A classification of eight distinct types of multiply handicapped cerebral-palsied children has been made. This classification is based upon the type of physical and psychological problem which the child demonstrates. It is a functional classification. Research of an educational and psychological nature is necessary with each type to determine the most adequate procedures which can be used to facilitate learning, social adjustment, and physical growth and development (Cruickshank, 1953).

Multiple disabilities in cerebral palsy complicate the process of family adjustment. Adams (1968) noted the incidence of parental overconcern and overreaction with such children, particularly among those who because of mental retardation cannot take initiative in learning self-care activities. Where additional handicaps accentuate the child's dependence, there is a greater danger of a symbiotic bond developing, which can impede the child's later autonomy. Similar learning and parent-relationship problems were described for cerebral-palsied children with hearing handicaps by Sister Rose Gertrude (1961), who noted the special vulnerability of these children to impairments in the language area. Communication problems in this instance can be made even more difficult by such symptoms of neurological impairment as improperly patterned behavior, anxiety reactions, and perceptual distortions.

As Burks (1960) indicated, cerebral-palsied children may show symptoms of hyperkinesis in conjunction with other symptoms of the disorder. In these instances, a short attention span, restlessness and overactivity, impulsive behavior, irritability and low frustration tolerance, impaired perceptual abilities, undefinitive concept formation mechanisms, poor memory, and limited muscular coordination make the educational task infinitely more challenging for the special educator. Owing to the family and community response to hyperkinetic children, such youngsters run greater than average risks in the emotional adjustment area.

The evidence concerning cerebral palsy suggests that multiple disability is common to children with this diagnosis. The involvement of more than one body system or function in the child's total problem usually is not additive in the sense that now there are two disabilities with which the child and his family must cope. On the contrary, the combination of disabilities comprises a new gestalt—one that usually is more complex and difficult than the addition of the individual disabilities would suggest. Each area of disability in the multihandicapped child interacts with the others so that it becomes disabling beyond its original boundaries. Thus, in educating and treating such children, interventions must be selected not only in terms of the discrete areas of limitation but also in regard to the totality of disability that emerges from their interrelationships.

References

Abercrombie, M. L. J. *Perceptual and visuomotor disorders in cerebral palsy.* London: Spastic Society/William Heinemann, 1964.

Adams, M. E. Problems of management of mentally retarded children with cerebral palsy. *Cerebral Palsy Journal,* 1968, *29,* 3–7.

Adler, A. *The neurotic constitution.* New York: Dodd, Mead & Co., 1926.

————. *Study of organ inferiority and its psychical compensation: A contribution to clinical medicine.* New York: Nervous and Mental Disease Publishing Co., 1917.

Allen, F. H., & Pearson, G. H. J. The emotional problems of the physically handicapped child. *British Journal of Medical Psychology,* 1938, *8,* 212–235.

Allen, G. Aspirations and expectations of physically impaired high school seniors. *Personnel and Guidance,* 1967, *46,* 59–62.

Allen, R. M. One point of view: Intellectual evaluation in cerebral palsy. *Exceptional Children,* 1960, 202–204.

————, & Collins, M. G. Suggestions for the adaptive administration of intelligence tests for those with cerebral palsy. *Cerebral Palsy Review, 16* (3), 27–33.

Ammons, R. B., & Ammons, H. S. The full-range picture vocabulary test: 1, preliminary scale. *Journal of Psychology,* 1949, *28,* 51–64.

Ando, K. A comparative study of Peabody Picture Vocabulary Test and Wechsler Intelligence Scale for Children with a group of cerebral palsied children. *Cerebral Palsy Journal,* 1968, *29,* 7–9.

Asher, P., & Schonnel, F. E. A survey of 400 cases of cerebral palsy in childhood. *Archives of Disease in Childhood,* 1950, *25,* 360–379.

Baeyer, W., von. Zur psychologie verkrüppelter kinder und jugendlicher. *Zeitschrift für Kinderforschung,* 1928, *34,* 229–292.

Banks, C., & Sinha, U. An item analysis of the Progressive Matrices Test. *British Journal of Psychology, Statistical Section,* 1951, *4,* 91–94.

Barclay, A., & Vaught, G. Maternal estimates of future achievement in cerebral palsied children. *American Journal of Mental Deficiency,* 1965, *69,* 62–65.

Barker, R. G. The social psychology of physical disability. *Journal of Social Issues,* 1948, *4,* 28–38.

————, et al. *Adjustment to physical handicap and illness: A survey of the social psychology of physique and disability.* Bulletin 55. New York: Social Science Research Council, 1953.

Bender, L. Psychological problems in children with organic brain disease. *American Journal of Orthopsychiatry,* 1949, *29,* 404–415.

————. Psychoses associated with somatic diseases that distort the body structure. *Archives of Neurology and Psychiatry,* 1934, *32,* 1000–1024.

————, & Silver, A. Body image problems of the brain injured child. *Journal of Social Issues,* 1948, *4,* 84–89.

Berko, M. J. Some factors in the perceptual deviations of cerebral palsied children. *Cerebral Palsy Review, 15* (2), 34.

Bice, H., & Cruickshank, W. M. Evaluation of intelligence. In W. M. Cruickshank and G. M. Raus (Eds.), *Cerebral palsy, its individual and community problems.* Syracuse, N.Y.: Syracuse University Press, 1955.

Billings, H. K. An exploratory study of the attitude of non-crippled children toward crippled children in three selected elementary schools. *Journal of Experimental Education,* 1963, *31,* 381–387.

Block, W. E. Personality of the brain-injured child. *Exceptional Children,* 1951, *21,* 91–100.

Blum, L. H., Burgmeister, B., & Lorge, I. The Mental Maturity Scale for the motor handicapped. *School and Society,* 1951, *73,* 232. *(a)*

————. Trends in estimating the mental maturity of the cerebral palsied child. *Journal of Exceptional Children,* 1951, *17,* 174–177. (*b*)

Boles, G. Personality factors in mothers of cerebral palsied children. *Genetic Psychology Monograph,* 1959, *59,* 159–218.

Bowlby, J. *Maternal care and mental health.* Monograph 2. Geneva: World Health Organization, 1951.

Bortner, M., & Birch, H. G. Perceptual and perceptual motor dissociation in cerebral palsied children. *Journal of Nervous and Mental Disorders,* 1962, *134,* 103–108.

Bradway, K. Birth lesions in identical twins. *American Journal of Orthopsychiatry,* 1937, *7,* 194–203.

Braen, B., & Masling, J. M. Intelligence tests used with special groups of children. *Exceptional Children,* 1959, *21,* 42–45.

Brieland, D. A follow-up study of orthopedically handicapped high school graduates. *Exceptional Children,* 1967, *33,* 555–562.

Briggs, P. F. The validity of WAIS Performance Subtests completed with one hand. *Journal of Clinical Psychology,* 1960, *16,* 318–320.

Brockway, A. The problems of the spastic child. *Journal of the American Medical Association,* 1936, *106,* 1635–1638.

Broida, D. C., Izard, C. E., & Cruickshank, W. M. Thematic apperception reactions of crippled children. *Journal of Clincial Psychology,* 1950, *6,* 243–248.

Burks, H. The hyperkinetic child. *Exceptional Children,* 1960, *27,* 18–26.

California State Department of Education. The special education needs of the cerebral palsied child. *Bulletin of the California State Department of Education.* November 1954, 1–12.

Capobianco, R. J., & Funk, R. A. *A comparative study of intellectual, neurological, and perceptual processes as related to reading achievement of exogenous and endogenous retarded children.* Syracuse, N. Y.: Syracuse University Research Institute, 1958.

Capobianco, R. J., & Miller, D. Y. *Quantitative and qualitative analysis of exogenous and endogenous children in some reading processes.* Syracuse, N. Y.: Syracuse University Research Institute, 1958.

Cardwell, V. *Advances in understanding and care.* New York: Association for the Aid of Crippled Children, 1956.

Carlsen, A. Vocational and social adjustment of physically handicapped students. *Exceptional Children,* 1957, *23,* 364–376.

Carr, D. B. Teleteaching—A new approach to teaching elementary and secondary homebound pupils. *Exceptional Children,* 1964, *31,* 118–126.

Carr, J. Psychological problems of the cerebral palsied child, his parents, and siblings as revealed by dynamically oriented group discussions with parents. *Cerebral Palsy Review,* *19* (5), 3–5; 11–15.

Carr, L. B. Problems confronting parents of children with handicaps. *Exceptional Children,* 1968, 251–255.

Centers, L., & Centers, R. A comparison of the body images of amputee and non-amputee children as revealed in figure drawings. *Journal of Projective Personality Assessment,* 1963, *27,* 158–165.

Clark, L. P. What is the psychology of Little's Disease? *Psychoanalytic Review,* 1934, *21,* 131–145.

Collins, H. A. Introversion and depression in mothers of cerebral palsied children. *Missouri Medicine,* 1965, *62,* 847–850.

Combs, R., & Harper, J. Effects of labels on attitudes of educators toward handicapped children. *Exceptional Children,* February 1967, 399–403.

Copellman, F. A follow-up of one hundred children with poliomyelitis. *The Family,* 1944, *25,* 289–297.

Cotton, C. B. A study of the reaction of spastic children to certain test situations. *Journal of Genetic Psychology,* 1941, *58,* 27–44.

Coughlin, E. W. Some parental attitudes toward handicapped children. *The Child,* 1941, *6,* 41–45.

Crookshank, F. G. *Organ inferiorities.* London: The C. W. Daniel Company, Ltd., 1936.

Cruickshank, W. M. The impact of physical disability on social adjustment. *Journal of Social Issues,* 1948, *4,* 78–83.

———. The multiply handicapped cerebral palsied child. *Exceptional Children,* 1953, *20,* 16–22.

———. *Psychology of exceptional children and youth.* Englewood Cliffs, N. J.: Prentice-Hall, Inc., 1963.

———. A study of the relation of physical disability to social adjustment. *American Journal of Occupational Therapy,* 1952, *6,* 100–109.

———, Bice, H. V., & Wallen, N. E. *Perception and cerebral palsy: A study in figure background relationship.* Syracuse, N. Y.: Syracuse University Press, 1957.

Cruickshank, W. M., & Dolphin, J. E. The educational implications of psychological studies of cerebral palsied children. *Exceptional Children,* 1951, *17,* 1–18.

———. The emotional needs of crippled and non-crippled children. *Journal of Exceptional Children,* 1949, *16,* 33–40. (*a*)

———. A study of the emotional needs of crippled children. *Journal of Educational Psychology,* 1949, *40,* 295–305. (*b*)

Cruickshank, W. M., *et al. A teaching method for brain injured and hyperactive children.* Syracuse, N. Y.: Syracuse University Press, 1961.

Cutter, A. V. The place of self-concept in the education of the physically different child. *Exceptional Children,* 1962, *28,* 343–349.

Delacoto, C. H. *Neurological organization and reading.* Springfield, Ill.: Charles C. Thomas, 1966.

Delany, F. I. Cerebral palsy—An investigation into certain aspects of visual and visiomotor perception in children with cerebral palsy. *Dissertation Abstracts,* 1962, *28* (4-A).

Dembo, T., Ladieu, G., & Wright, B. A. *Adjustment to misfortune: A study in social-emotional relationships between injured and non-injured people.* Washington, D. C.: War Department, Office of the Surgeon General, 1948.

Denhoff, E., & Robinault, I. P. *Cerebral palsy and related disorders.* New York: McGraw-Hill Book Company, 1960.

Diedrich, W., Allender, B., & Byrne, M. The value of a preschool treatment program. *Exceptional Children,* 1960, *27,* 187–190.

Dietrich, S. *Hemophilia: A total approach to treatment and rehabilitation.* Los Angeles: Orthopedic Hospital, 1968.

Dillon, E. An investigation of basic psycholinguistic and reading abilities among the cerebral palsied. *Dissertation Abstracts,* 1966, *27* (4-A).

Doll, E. A. Psychological significance of cerebral birth lesions. *American Jouranal of Psychology,* 1933, *45,* 444–452.

———, Phelps, W. M., & Melcher, R. T. *Mental deficiency due to birth injury.* New York: The Macmillan Company, 1932.

Dolphin, J. E. A study of certain aspects of the psychopathology of cerebral palsy children. Unpublished doctoral dissertation, Syracuse University, 1950.

———, & Cruickshank, W. M. The figure-background relationship in children with cerebral palsy. *Journal of Clinical Psychology,* 1951, *7,* 228–231. (*a*)

———. Pathology of concept formation in children with cerebral palsy. *American Jour-*

nal of Mental Deficiency, 1951, *41,* 392–336. (*b*)

———. Tactual motor perception of children with cerebral palsy. *Journal of Personality,* 1952, *20,* 466–471.

———. Visuo-motor perception in children with cerebral palsy. *Quarterly Journal of Child Behavior,* 1951, *3,* 198–209. (*c*)

Donofrio, A. F. A study of crippled children in an orthopedic hospital school. *Exceptional Children,*1952, *18,* 33–38.

———. A study of the intelligence, achievement, and emotional adjustment of crippled children in an orthopedic hospital school. Unpublished doctoral dissertation, New York University, 1949.

Dreikurs, R. The social psychological dynamics of physical disability. *Journal of Social Issues,* 1948, *4,* 39–54.

Dunn, L. M., & Harley, R. K. Comparability of Peabody, Ammons, Van Aldstyne, and Columbia Test Scores with cerebral palsied children. *Exceptional Children,* 1969, *35,* 5–21.

Dunn, M. Satisfaction with social relationships of college students who are physically disabled. *Dissertation Abstracts,* 1968, *28* (8-A).

Fairchild, S. Achievement motivation, self-concept, and independence of physically handicapped children. *Dissertation Abstracts,* 1967, *28* (6-B).

Fernald, M. R., & Arlitt, A. H. Psychological findings regarding crippled children. *School and Society,* 1925, *21,* 449–452.

Fielding, B. B. Attitudes and aspects of adjustment of the orthopedically handicapped woman. Unpublished doctoral dissertation, Columbia University, 1950.

Fishman, S. Self-concept and adjustment to leg prothesis. Unpublished doctoral dissertation, Columbia University, 1949.

Fitzgerald, D. C. Success-failure and TAT reactions of orthopedically handicapped and physically normal adolescents. *Personality,* 1951, *1,* 67–83.

Fouracre, M. H. *Realistic educational planning for children with cerebral palsy.* New York: United Cerebral Palsy Association, Inc., 1952.

———, & Theill, E. A. Education of children with mental retardation accompanying cerebral palsy. *American Journal of Mental Deficiency,* 1953, *57,* 401–414.

Franke, K. Erforschung der Krüppelpsyche

durch Selbstdarstellungen gebrechlicher jungendlichen. *Zeitschrift für Krüppelfürsorge,* 1932, *25,* 251–271.

Freedman, R. D. Emotional reactions of handicapped children. *Rehabilitation Literature,* 1967, *19,* 274–282.

Furno, O. F., & Costello, M. Activities and attitudes of physically handicapped special education graduates. *Exceptional Children,* 1963, *30,* 85–92.

Gallagher, J. J. *The tutoring of brain injured mentally retarded children: An experimental study.* Springfield, Ill.: Charles C. Thomas, 1960.

Gasson, W. Psychopathological environmental reaction to congenital defect. *Journal of Mental and Nervous Disease,* 1966, *142,* 453–459.

Gates, M. F. A comparative study of some problems of social emotional adjustment of crippled and non-crippled girls and boys. *Journal of Genetic Psychology,* 1946, *68,* 219–244.

Gellman, W. Roots of prejudice against the handicapped. *Journal of Rehabilitation, 25,* 4–6.

Gertrude, Sister Rose. Psychological and intellectual problems of the multiple handicapped. *National Catholic Education Association Bulletin,* 1961, *58,* 399.

Gesell, A., & Zimmerman, H. M. Correlations of behavior and neuropathology in a case of cerebral palsy from birth injury. *American Journal of Psychiatry,* 1937, *94,* 505–535.

Gibbs, N. Deprivation of experience—Does it matter? *Spastics Quarterly,* 1959, *8,* 22–31.

Giovannoni, J. Social role behavior and extent of social participation in disabled and nondisabled adolescents. *Dissertation Abstracts,* 27 (11-A).

Goldstein, K. *Brain injuries due to war.* New York: Grune & Stratton, Inc., 1942.

———, & Scheerer, M. Abstract and concrete behavior: An experimental study with special tests. *Psychological Monographs,* 1941, *53,* 1–151.

Gordon, R. G., Roberts, J. A. F., & Griffiths, R. Does poliomyelitis affect intellectual capacity? *British Medical Journal,* 1939, *2,* 803–805.

Gunn, R. Some personality characteristics of cerebral palsied children. *Dissertation Abstracts,* 1965, *25* (12) 73–79.

Haeussermann, E. *Evaluating the developmental level of preschool children handicapped by cerebral palsy.* New York: United Cerebral Palsy Association, Inc., 1952.

Hall, W. T. Physical handicap to family stress. *Cerebral Palsy Review,* 1963, *24* (4), 8–11.

Halstead, W. C. Preliminary analysis of grouping behavior in patients with cerebral injury by the method of equivalent and nonequivalent stimuli. *American Journal of Psychiatry,* 1940, *96,* 1263–1294.

———. *Brain and intelligence.* Chicago: University of Chicago Press, 1947.

Hammill, I., & Orvis, C. Relations among measures of language of cerebral palsy and mentally retarded children. *Cerebral Palsy Journal,* 1966, *27* (1), 8–9.

Hanks, J. R., & Hanks, L. M. Jr. The physically handicapped in certain nonoccidental societies. *Journal of Social Issues,* 1948, *4,* 11–20.

Haring, N. A review of research on cerebral palsy and emotional adjustment. *Exceptional Children,* 1959, *26,* 191–194.

Harrower-Erickson, M. R. Personality changes accompanying cerebral lesions. *Archives of Neurology and Psychiatry,* 1940, *43,* 859–890.

Harway, V. T. Self-evaluation and reactions to success and failure experiences in orthopedically handicapped children. Unpublished doctoral dissertation, University of Rochester, 1952.

Heilman, A. Intelligence in cerebral palsy. *The Crippled Child,* 1952, *30,* 11–13.

Hirschenfang, S., & Benton, J. Delayed intellectual development in cerebral palsy children. *Journal of Psychology,* 1965, *60,* 235–238.

Holden, R. H. Motivation, adjustment, and anxiety of cerebral palsied children. *Exceptional Children,* 1957, *24,* 313–316.

Holden, R. Changes in body imagery of physically handicapped children due to summer camp experience. *Dissertation Abstracts,* 1961, *21* (10), 3165.

Holoran, I. M. The incidence and prognosis of cerebral palsy. *British Medical Journal,* 1952, *4751,* 214–217.

De Hoop, W. Listening comprehension of cerebral palsied children as a function of two speaking rates. *Exceptional Children,* 1965, *31,* 233–240.

Hopkins, T. W., Bice, H. V., & Colton, K. C. *Evaluation and education of the cerebral palsied child.* Council for Exceptional Children, Washington, D. C.: 1954.

Irwin, O., & Hammill, D. Effect of type, extent and degree of cerebral palsy on 3 measures of language. *Cerebral Palsy Journal,* 1965, *26,* 7–9.

Jaffe, J. What's in a name: Attitudes toward disabled persons. *Personnel and Guidance Journal,* 1967, *45,* 57–60.

Jenkins, R. L. Dissimilar identical twins: Result of brain injury at birth. *American Journal of Orthopsychiatry,* 1934, *5,* 39–42.

Jensen, C. D., & Kogan, K. L. Parental estimates of the future achievements of children with cerebral palsy. *Journal of Mental Deficiency,* 1962, *6* (1), 56–64.

Jones, M. H. Pilot study of reading problems of cerebral palsied adults. *Developmental Medicine and Child Neurology,* 1966, *8,* 417–427.

Jones, R., Gottfried, N. W., & Owens, A. The social distance of the exceptional: A study at the high school level. *Exceptional Children,* 1966, *32,* 551–556.

Kammerer, R. C. An exploratory psychological study of crippled children. *Psychological Record,* 1940, *4,* 47–100.

Katz, E. Intelligence test performance of athetoid and spastic children with cerebral palsy. *Cerebral Palsy Review, 16,* 17–19.

———. Method of selecting Stanford-Binet Intelligence Scale Tasks for evaluating the mental abilities of children severely handicapped by cerebral palsy. *Cerebral Palsy Review, 16,* 14–17.

Keeve, P. J. Perpetuating phantom handicaps in school age children. *Exceptional Children,* 1967, *33,* 539–544.

Klapper, R., Zelda, A., & Birch, H. G. A fourteen-year follow-up study of cerebral palsy: Intellectual change and stability. *American Journal of Orthopsychiatry,* 1967, *37,* 540–547.

Klapper, Z. S., & Werner, H. Developmental deviations in brain-injured (cerebral palsied) members of pairs of identical twins. *Quarterly Journal of Child Behavior,* 1950, *2,* 288–313.

Kubie, L. S. Motivation and rehabilitation. *Psychiatry,* 1945, *8,* 69–78.

Ladieu, G., Adler, D. L., & Dembo, T. Studies in adjustment to visible injuries: Social acceptance of the injured. *Journal of Social Issues,* 1948, *4,* 55–61.

Lambright, C. A comparative analysis of self-concept of physically disabled adolescents in two types of school organizations. *Dissertation Abstracts,* 1967, *28* (3-A).

Landis, C., & Bolles, M. M. *Personality and sexuality in the physically handicapped woman.* New York: Paul B. Hoeber, Inc., 1942.

Lange, P. Frustration reactions of physically handicapped children. *Exceptional Children,* 1959, *25,* 355–357.

Larson, L. Preschool experiences of physically handicapped children. *Exceptional Children,* 1958, *24,* 310–312.

Lee, M. V. The children's hospital: A survey of the intelligence of crippled children. *Journal of Educational Research,* 1931, *23,* 164–167.

Lemkau, P. V. Influence of handicapping conditions on child development. *Children,* 1961, *8,* 43–47.

Lilly, E. C. & Shafer, S. A. Developmental training for the cerebral palsied. *Cerebral Palsy Review,* 1965, *26,* 7–8.

Linde, T., & Patterson, C. H. The MMPI in cerebral palsy. *Journal of Consulting Psychology,* 1958, *22,* 210–212.

Lipp, L., *et al.* Denial of disability and internal control of reinforcement: A study using a perceptual defense paradigm. *Journal of Consulting and Clinical Psychology,* 1968, *32,* 72–75.

Lord, E. E. *Children handicapped by cerebral palsy.* New York: New York Commonwealth Fund, 1930.

Lowman, C. L. *Survey of the vocational, educational and social status of poliomyelitis patients.* New York: National Foundation for Infantile Paralysis, 1942.

Machover, K. *Personality projection in the drawing of the human figure.* Springfield, Ill.: Charles C. Thomas, 1949.

Mader, J. Attitudes of special educators toward the physically handicapped and toward education. *Dissertation Abstracts,* 1967, *28* (5-A).

McIntire, J. T. The incidence of feeble-mindedness in the cerebral palsied. *American Journal of Mental Deficiency,* 1946, *50,* 491–494.

McKibben, S. The spastic situation. *Journal of Speech Disorders,* 1943, *8,* 147–153.

Melcer, J. D. Sensory motor experience and concept formation in early childhood. *Dissertation Abstracts,* 1967, *27* (10-B).

Meng, H. Zur socialpsychologie der körperbeschädigten: Ein beitrag zum problem der praktischen psychohygiene. *Schweizer Archiv für Neurologie und Psychiatrie,* 1938, *40,* 328–344.

Menninger, W. C. Emotional adjustments for the handicapped. *Crippled Child,* 1949, *27,* 4.

Meyer, E., & Simmel, M. The psychological appraisal of children with neurological defects. *Journal of Abnormal and Social Psychology,* 1947, *42,* 193–205.

Meyerson, L. Experimental injury: An approach to the dynamics of disability. *Journal of Social Issues,* 1948, *4,* 68–72. (*b*)

———. Physical disability as a social psychological problem. *Journal of Social Issues,* 1948, *4,* 2–10. (*a*)

Michal-Smith, H. Psychological factors in the therapist-patient relationship in the rehabilitation process. *Rehabilitation Literature,* 1962, *23,* 66–69.

Miller, E. A. Cerebral palsied children. *Exceptional Children,* 1958, *24,* 298–302.

———. & Rosenfield, G. The psychological evaluation of children with cerebral palsy and its implications in treatment. *Journal of Pediatrics,* 1952, *41,* 613–621.

Mosher, F., & Stewart, M. Parents' expectations in planning for their child's rehabilitation. *Exceptional Children,* 1958, *25,* 119–122.

Mowatt, M. Emotional conflicts of handicapped young adults and their mothers. *Cerebral Palsy Journal,* 1965, *26,* 6–8.

Mussen, P. H., & Barker, R. G. Attitudes towards cripples. *Journal of Abnormal and Social Psychology,* 1944, *34,* 351–355.

Muthard, J. E. Attitudes of cerebral palsied college students toward college and their education. *Journal of College Student Personnel,* 1964, *5,* 202–209;216.

———. MMPI findings for cerebral palsied college students. *Journal of Consulting Psychology,* 1965, *29* (6), 599.

Nagge, J. W., & Sayler, R. H. Physical deficiency and extroversion-introversion. *Journal of Social Psychology,* 1933, *4,* 239–244.

Newell, H. W. Differences in personalities in the surviving pair of identical triplets. *American Journal of Orthopsychiatry,* 1930, *1,* 61–80.

Nussbaum, J. An investigation of the relationship between the self-concept and reality orientation of adolescents with cerebral palsy. *Dissertation Abstract,* 1962, *22,* 4410–4411.

Oettinger, K. B. An experiment in teaching physically handicapped children at home. *Mental Hygiene,* 1938, *22,* 245–264.

Patterson, C. H. Influencing work and social attitudes of cerebral palsied children. *Cerebral Palsy Review,* 1963, *24,* 9–11.

Penfield, W., & Rasmusses, T. *The cerebral cortex of man.* New York: The Macmillan Company, 1952.

Peters, D. M. Developmental conceptual components of the normal child. A comparative study with the C. P. child. *Cerebral Palsy Reveiw,* 1964, *25,* 3–7.

Phelps, W. M. Characteristic psychological variations in cerebral palsy. *Nervous Child,* 1948, *7,* 10–13. (*a*)

———. Description and differentiation of types of cerebral plasy *Nervous Child,* 1948, *8,* 107–127. (*b*)

Piaget, J. *The child's conception of number.* London: Routledge & Kegan Paul, Ltd., 1952.

———. *The origin of intelligence in the child.* London: Routledge & Kegan Paul, Ltd., 1953.

———, & Inhelder, B. *The child's conception of space.* London: Routledge & Kegan Paul, Ltd., 1956.

Pintner, R., Eisenson, J., & Stanton, M. *The psychology of the physically handicapped.* New York: Appleton-Century-Crofts, 1941.

Piotrowski, Z. The Rorschach Inkblot Method in organic disturbances of the central nervous system. *Journal of Nervous and Mental Diseases,* 1937, *86,* 525–537.

Pomp, H. A study of self-concept distortion in physically disabled and non-disabled eighth grade students. *Dissertation Abstracts,* 1963, *24* (2), 824.

Reed, C. F., & Pollock, A. Statistically defined displays and pattern detection of cerebral palsied children. *Science,* 1963, *140,* 1331–1333.

Richardson, E., & Kobler, F. Testing the cerebral palsied—A study comparing the Binet, Raven, and Ammons. *Exceptional Children,* 1955, *21,* 101–103; 108–109.

Richardson, S. Race and Physical handicap in children's preference for other children. *Child Development,* 1968, *32* (2). 467–480.

———, Hastorf, A., & Dornbuser, S. Effects of physical disability on a child's description of himself. *Child Development,* 1964, *35,* 893–897.

Richmond, J. B. Modern understandings of child development implications for exceptional children. *Exceptional Children,* 1962, *28,* 233–236.

Robinault, I., & Connor, F. P. *Realistic educational planning for children with cerebral palsy, pre-school level.* New York: United Cerebral Palsy Association, Inc., 1968.

Rorschach, H. *Psychodiagnostics.* Berne, Switzerland: Verlag Hans Huber, 1942.

Rosenbaum, B. B. Neurotic tendencies in crippled girls. *Journal of Abnormal and Social Psychology,* 1937, *31,* 423–429.

Rosenbaum, S. Z. Infantile paralysis as the source of emotional problems in children. *Welfare Bulletin,* 1943, *34,* 11–13.

Rubenstein, B. Therapeutic use of groups in an orthopedic hospital school. *American Journal of Orthopsychiaty,* 1945, *15,* 662–674.

Rusalem H. Comparative values in a population of homebound individuals. *Exceptional Children,* 1963, *29,* 460–465.

———, & Jenkins, S. Attitudes of homebound students toward return to regular classroom attendance. *Exceptional Children,* 1961, *28,* 71–74.

Sarason, S. B. *Psychological problems in mental deficiency* (2nd ed.). New York: Harper & Row, Publishers, 1952.

———, & Sarason, E. K. The discriminatory value of test pattern with cerebral palsied, defective children. *Journal of Clinical Psychology,* 1949, *2,* 141–147.

Schecter, M. D. Psychiatric views and recommendations on orthopedic problems in children. *American Journal of Physical Medicine,* 1962, *41,* 6–8.

Shelsky, I. The effect of disability on self-concepts. Unpublished doctoral dissertation, Teachers College, Columbia University, 1957.

Schilder, P. *The image and appearance of the human body.* New York: International Universities Press, Inc., 1950.

Schneider, D. M. The social dynamics of physical disability in army basic training. *Psychiatry,* 1947, *10,* 323–333.

Sievers, D. J., & Norman, R. D. Some suggestive results in psychometric testing of the cerebral palsied with Gesell, Binet, and Wechsler Scales. *Genetic Psychology,* 82, 69–90.

Silberberg, N. and Silberberg, M. Hyperplexia-Specific word Recognition Skills in Young Children. *Exceptional Children,* 1967, *34,* 41–42.

Siller, J. Psychological concomitants of amputation in children. *Child Development,* 1960, *31,* 109–120.

Simmel, M. Developmental aspects of the body schema. *Child Development,* 1966, *37,* 83–95.

Smitts, S. Reactions of self and others to the obviousness and seriousness of physical disability. *Dissertation Abstracts,* 1964, *25,* 1324–1325.

Smock, C., & Cruickshank, W. M. Responses of handicapped and normal children to the Rosenzweig P-F Study. *Quarterly Journal of Child Behavior,* 1952, *4,* 156–164.

Sohn, D. L. The psychic complex in congenital deformity. *New York Medical Journal,* 1914, *100,* 959–961.

Stafford, G. T. *Sports for the handicapped.* Englewood Cliffs, N. J. : Prentice-Hall, Inc., 1939.

Strauss, A. A. Typology in mental deficiency. *Proceedings of American Association on Mental Deficiency,* 1939, *46,* 85–90.

———, & Lehtinen, L. *Psychopathology and education of the brain injured child.* New York: Grune & Stratton, Inc., 1947.

——— & Werner, H. Disorders of conceptual thinking in the brain injured child. *Journal of Nervous and Mental Diseases,* 1942, *96,* 157–172.

Strauss, F. The initiative of the crippled child. *The Crippled Child,* 1936, *13,* 164–165.

Taibl, R. M. An investigation of Raven's "Progressive Matrices" as a tool for the psychological evaluation of cerebral palsied children. Unpublished doctoral dissertation, University of Nebraska, 1951.

Teuber, H., & Rudel, R. G. Behavior after cerebral lesions in children and adults. *De-*

velopmental *Medicine and Child Neurology,* 1962, *4,* 3–20.

Thurston, J. Counseling the parents of the severely handicapped. *Exceptional Children,* 1969, *26,* 139–147.

Titley, R. Perception of the physically atypical: The attribution of alienation, introversion and compensatory potential to the injured and disfigured. *Dissertation Abstracts,* 1966, *26* (11), 6860.

Trippe, M. J. The social psychology of exceptional children, part II, in terms of factors of society. *Exceptional Children,* 1959, *26,* 71–75.

Trombly, T. Linguistic concepts and the cerebral palsied child. *Cerebral Palsy Journal,* 1968, *29,* 7–8.

Ware, L. E. Parents of the orthopedically handicapped child. In M. E. Frampton and E. D. Gall (Eds.), *Special education for the exceptional.* Vol. 2. Boston: Porter Sargent, 1955.

Wedell, K. Follow-up study of perceptual ability in children with hemiplegia. In *Hemiplegic cerebral palsy in children and adults.* London: Spastic Society/William Heinemann, Ltd., 1961.

Wenar, C. The effects of a motor handicap on personality: III The effects on certain fantasies and adjustment techniques. *Child Development,* 1956, *27,* 9–15.

Werner, H. Development of visuo-motor performance on the marble board test in mentally retarded children. *Journal of Genetic Psychology,* 1944, *64,* 269–279.

———. Perceptual behavior of brain-injured, mentally defective children: An experimental study by means of the Rorschach technique. *Genetic Psychology Monographs,* 1945, *31,* 51–110.

———, & Strauss, A. A. Pathology of figure-background relation in the child. *Journal of Abnormal and Social Psychology,* 1941, *36,* 236–248.

Whelan, R. J., & Haring, N. Modification and maintenance of behavior through systematic application of consequences. *Exceptional Children,* 1966, *32,* 281–288.

Wilson, E. L. Group therapy experience with eight physically disabled homebound students in a prevocational project. *Exceptional Children,* 1962, *29,* 164–169.

Winkler, H. *Psychische entwecklung and krüppeltum.* Leipzig: Leopold Voss, 1931.

Witty, P. A., & Smith, M. B. The mental status of 1,480 crippled children. *Educational Trends,* 1932, *1,* 22–24.

Wright, B. A. *Physical disability—a psychological approach.* New York: Harper and Row, Publishers, 1960.

Wurtz, H. *Zerbrecht die krucken.* Leipzig: Leopold Voss, 1932.

Wysocki, B. Body image of crippled children as seen in draw a person test behavior. *Perceptual and motor skills,* 1965, *21,* 499–504.

Yanagi, G. An appraisal of psychological deficit in children with CP. *Dissertation Abstracts,* 1962, *22,* 4088–4089.

Yuker, H. Attitudes as determinants of behavior. *Journal of Rehabilitation,* 1965, *31,* 15–16.

Zeichner, A. Observations on individual and group counseling. *Exceptional Children,* 1957, *23,* 350–352.

Zimmerman, I., & Jones, M. Changes in intellectual ratings of cerebral palsied children with and without prenursery school training. *Exceptional Children,* 1965, *31,* 486.

Zuk, G. H. The cultural dilemma and spiritual crisis of the family with a handicapped child. *Exceptional Children,* 1962, *28,* 405–408.

SEVEN

The Psychological Characteristics of Brain-Injured Children

WILLIAM M. CRUICKSHANK
and JAMES L. PAUL

William M. Cruickshank is Professor of Psychology and Education and Director of the Institute for the Study of Mental Retardation at The University of Michigan. James L. Paul is senior education consultant with the North Carolina State Department of Mental Health and Associate Professor of Special Education, College of Education, at the University of North Carolina, Chapel Hill.

The authors of this chapter wish to express their appreciation to Mrs. Rebecca Dixon, Social Research Assistant, State Department of Mental Health, Raleigh, North Carolina, and Mr. Daniel P. Hallahan, Research Assistant, Institute for the Study of Mental Retardation, The University of Michigan, for significant contributions which they made to its preparation.

TERMINOLOGY AND LABELS

No presentation of the psychological characteristics of brain-injured children would be complete without specific acknowledgment of controversy surrounding the use of the term "brain-injured." This chapter might have been titled "Psychological Characteristics of Brain-Damaged Children," or "The Psychological Characteristics of Perceptually Handicapped Children," or "The Psychological Characteristics of Children with Learning Disabilities," or any one of more than forty labels that have been used interchangeably to designate *these* children. The words "brain," "damage," "neurological," "injury," "organic," "minimal," "disorder," "learning," "disability," "handicap," and others have been used in a variety of combinations.

In 1964 a task force, cosponsored by the National Society for Crippled Children and Adults, Inc., and the National Institute of Neurological Diseases and Blindness of the National Institutes of Health, was appointed to study the issues of terminology and identification. A report (Clements, 1966, p. 9) of the work of this task force, which adopted the term "minimal brain dysfunction," included the following statement:

A review of selected literature revealed a total of 38 terms used to describe or distinguish the conditions grouped as minimal brain dysfunction in the absence of findings severe enough to warrant inclusion in an established category, e.g., cerebral palsies, mental subnormalities, sensory defects. Several methods of grouping these terms are possible, such as:

Group I—Organic Aspects
Association Deficit Pathology
Organic Brain Disease
Organic Brain Damage

Organic Brain Dysfunction
Minimal Brain Damage
Diffuse Brain Damage
Neurophrenia
Organic Drivenness
Cerebral Dysfunction
Organic Behavior Disorder
Choreiform Syndrome
Minor Brain Damage
Minimal Brain Injury
Minimal Chronic Brain Syndromes
Minimal Cerebral Damage
Minimal Cerebral Palsy
Cerebral Dys-synchronization Syndrome
Group II—Segment or Consequence
Hyperkinetic Behavior Syndrome
Character Impulse Disorder
Hyperkinetic Impulse Disorder
Aggressive Behavior Disorder
Psychoneurological Learning Disorders
Hyperkinetic Syndrome
Dyslexia
Hyperexcitability Syndrome
Perceptual Cripple
Primary Reading Retardation
Specific Reading Disability
Clumsy Child Syndrome
Hypokinetic Syndrome
Perceptually Handicapped
Aphasoid Syndrome
Learning Disabilities
Conceptually Handicapped
Attention Disorders
Interjacent Child

Cruickshank (1966, pp. 10–18) convened a distinguished panel of professional leaders who had had specific interest in these children and suggested that they address themselves to the question, among others, of labels. There was, predictably, reasonable professional defense for several of the labels already listed. In addition, a new term, "developmental imbalances," was suggested by Gallagher at this meeting.

It was recognized by this group as by previous groups that no single term would serve all purposes. Cruickshank suggested that in the absence of a completely adequate label, the term "brain-injured" be used. This label did not satisfy all the logical criteria required for a label, but it was hoped that it might be used to obtain a professional meeting of the minds until a more generally acceptable label could be adopted. For those who for good reasons preferred other labels, at least the general characteristics of the children being discussed would be understood and planning discussions could proceed. This has not occurred.

Other labels have been suggested since that time, again failing to unify professional opinion. Nellhaus (1968, p. 536), for example, suggests the term "dyssynchronous child" as being more generic and providing a better basis for communication between parents and professionals.

The problem of terminology should not be considered simply a semantic lag, an annoying hang-up in the interest of a better name, which will placate the idiosyncrasies of different disciplines and interest groups. The issue is grossly oversimplified if one assumes that the existing conceptualizations of etiology and the complex learning and behavior problems presented by this group of children are waiting for a uniting banner or a magical solution to the difficult problems by the genius of a better name. The hard-core problems are conceptual and empirical. The energy dissipated in disagreement over a name for the child may serve to keep the child in the corridors waiting for a more adequate treatment or educational program. This is not to suggest that terminology is unimportant; it certainly is. We often act, however, as though the resolution of problems lies primarily in the clarification of language. If we could find the *correct* label, then it follows that we could in some important sense advance in treating these children. This may be a mythical search. The problem lies rather in the clarification of concepts, their accurate description, and their social consequences. A more acceptable label may well communicate our solutions; it will never be the solution.

The ultimate resolution of the terminology issue, like that of definition, must satisfy certain criteria. The task force (Clements, 1966, p. 8) on terminology and definition states that certain professional and interest groups with their own built-in criteria must be satisfied: clinicians, researchers, other professionals, and parents. Cruickshank (1966, pp. 17–18) indicated that definition should include the concepts of etiology, developmental imbalances, ego problems, and interdisciplinary interest. Obviously, a satisfactory label would be judged by its adequacy to reflect these issues and, at a minimum, to not exclude by implication one of these aspects. An example of exclusion by implication would be a strictly medical label, such as brain damage, which might not suggest an interdisciplinary point of view and consequently could exclude the nonmedical interest, such as that of teachers.

One aspect of the terminology question is essentially phenomenological. It is useful to distinguish between the act of naming what is seen and naming what is thought to be seen or what is decided upon as the salient view. Elementary concerns in a philosophy of science ought to force a rejection of the assumption that a one-to-one correspondence exists between what is there and what we see as being there. This is at the center of the interdisciplinary question and the implications for terminology. Whether a reductionistic psychological point of view or an existential psychological perspective is utilized makes an important difference in the kind of reality under consideration. The assumptions, the priorities of interest, the view of man, the rules for discovery, and so forth are different. Similarly, the language for describing and explaining is different.

Professional groups only partially represent the different philosophic orientations. There is much overlap. Rhodes (1966), Hewett (1968, pp. 8–41), and Bateman (1967) have described these orientations. They may be grouped in terms of the psychoanalytic, behavioral, neurosensory or communicative, and ecological.

The way in which a disability is named, described, explained, and treated usually betrays the set of assumptions we employ and the general view we accept as most valid or useful. The reader should recognize that these are not pure or mutually exclusive positions but rather represent general philosophic stances. The brain-injured child has been named, described, and treated as such primarily within the neurosensory or communication frame of reference. This point of view is essentially the basis of discussion in this chapter. It provides a specific view of the child as a receiver and processor of stimuli with consequent behavioral acts or responses. The adequacy of these perceptual and perceptual-motor acts are the specific clinical concerns. Treatment is specified in terms of work with the specific dysfunction. There is not complete agreement in the field as to whether the clinician or teacher identifies and exploits the appropriately engaged processes or whether he focuses specifically on the disabled or disengaged processes. Similarly there is some difference in professional opinion as to whether the child is viewed and worked with as a whole or a unity or whether he is viewed as a complex interaction of parts, some of which are working appropriately and some

WILLIAM M. CRUICKSHANK AND JAMES L. PAUL

of which are not. The senior author of this chapter has taken the latter position in both instances.

The neuro-sensory position has two aspects: descriptive and explanatory. The descriptive aspect focuses upon the process of describing, in objective behavioral terms as much as possible, the abilities and disabilities of the child. The explanatory aspect is more difficult. Explanations are postulated in terms of the integrity of the central nervous system. The distinction between description and explanation is essentially the same as the distinction between what and why.

The phenomenological question is no less relevant in the more apparent aspect of describing the behavior. It is, however, the explanatory aspect that is more difficult in terms of empirical defense. It is this aspect that provides the basis for many of the labels applied to these children, for example, brain damage, brain injury, and so forth. Explanations or attempts to formulate answers to the questions of cause have always been difficult in the behavioral sciences. With human behavior we do not have the kind of freedom in experimental design to deal effectively with the question of causality. Behavioral data is based, for the most part, on correlational analyses. It should be noted, however, that even with freedom in design to control and manipulate experimental variables, the philosophic issues of causality would still be extremely difficult to manage.

For the most part, our understanding of brain-behavior relationships is based on experimental laboratory research with animals and studies of adults, much of which is based on studies of casualties in wars. Neither of these translates directly to children. The study of brain-injured children, their characteristics, and their treatment is very new compared to the other disability groups described in this volume. Much of the original work was with captive institutionalized retarded groups.

The importance of labels should not be underestimated. The *academic* concern is only one aspect, perhaps even the least important in terms of the child. Different labels have different public meanings and associations. They *do* communicate something to the parent, the teacher, the neighbor, the minister, and the child, who will hear the label eventually assigned. The label affects what is expected of the child, elicits feelings in the adult about the child, often even before the child and the adult have interacted, and can subvert the child's chance to interact as a child with an adult who chooses to interact with the child as being *brain-injured*, in which case the child is the victim of whatever myths, fantasies, or associations that adult may have about brain injury. The whole issue of expectancy is extremely important. The influence value of the researcher on the outcomes of his work is one way of thinking about the determinate influence of the teacher on the outcomes of her teaching. The outcomes of the former are expressed in data terms. The latter are expressed in human-life terms, that is, educational gains of students.

The expectancy phenomenon is not new to literature on experimental design. The Hawthorne effect, for example, was described by Roethlisberger and Dickson in 1939. More recently, the work of Rosenthal and Jacobson (1968) has dealt specifically with the question of teacher expectancy on pupil gain. They concluded (p. 98) that "teachers' favorable expectations can be responsible for gains in their pupils' IQs and, for the lower grades, that these gains can be quite dramatic."

Their work has been seriously questioned (Barber and Silver, 1968*a;* Barber and Silver, 1968*b;* Snow, 1969; Thorndike, 1968). The criticisms have been leveled primarily in terms of measurement and data analysis questions. Thorndike (1968) who considered the Rosenthal and Jacobson study "so defective technically that one can only regret that it ever got beyond the eyes of the original investigators!" went on to point out in his review that "the general reasonableness of the 'self-fulfilling prophecy effect' is not at issue." He concluded, "the indications are that the basic data upon which this structure has been raised are so untrustworthy that any conclusions based upon them must be suspect. The conclusions may be correct, but if so it must be considered a fortunate coincidence."

Snow (1969), who also raised serious measurement and data analysis questions and suggested that Rosenthal and Jacobson may be guilty of the bias they describe, further indicated that "teacher expectancy may be a powerful phenomenon which, if understood, could be used to gain much of positive value in education."

The salient point for the present writing is that, in the opinion of the authors, teacher expectancy is a real phenomenon and possibly never more dramatically evident than in the teacher-handicapped child relationship. The extent to which the labels we assign communicates what is to be expected of a child indicates the seriousness of the issue. This is not easily rationalized by supposedly positive statements such as, "we reduce our expectations to what is more reasonable in terms of the child's abilities." The child's abilities and disabilities are appropriately communicated by a careful and thorough diagnosis, not a label. The label communicates a total picture of all the retarded, the emotionally disturbed, the brain-injured, and so forth. This *total picture* is never a portrait of the individual child.

The hazards of expectancy and labels are not limited to the public without relevant professional training. Gallagher (1966. p. 27) has suggested that professionals, who sit around the conference table representing different disciplinary points of view, often relax when the results of their different evaluations of the child are brought together and a label is selected and agreed upon. In such an instance, the label might be expected to do what only the diagnosis can do. It might be expected to communicate what only the complete diagnostic study could communicate.

Trippe (1966), writing about the emotionally disturbed child, has suggested that the purpose of the label is often to get the child somewhere. This is not less true of the retarded, the brain-injured, or any other *special* child. Clinical evaluations of children generally are initiated following the child's exhibition of his incompetence or his noncompliance with certain performance standards or regulations. This is always in a context or a system that has a purpose and a set of expectations and values. When there are resistances or experienced frustration in meeting the system's perceived objectives, there are alternative courses of action available to alleviate the frustration, to circumvent or otherwise reduce the resistance. These alternatives most often require action in terms of the resistance or frustration—that is, the incompetent, the incompatible, the incongruous, the noncompliant, and so forth. The alternatives in terms of modifying the system in which the stress or the concern is experienced are almost never as well developed.

This is most clearly evident in the public school system. Hence, the question What is to be done with the child? is answered by a pursuit of an answer to the question What is wrong with the child? or

WILLIAM M. CRUICKSHANK AND JAMES L. PAUL

Why does he act that way? or Why can he not learn? An alternative set of questions might involve the appropriateness of the teaching methods and materials, what is wrong with the teaching space, the teacher, and so forth. Whereas the most honest appraisals involve answers that reflect an interaction of these two sets, the relevant point here has to do with the purpose of labeling which goes beyond academic questions of accuracy.

The implications of labels are profound for parents. Some labels subtly communicate parental responsibility—not because of the label but the parents' associations with it. The term "emotionally disturbed" is a good example. Many parents have read popular journal articles and books written for lay consumption on the psychosexual development of children. Their translations of these concepts are within the guilt and concern and disturbed relationships that already exist.

Another communication is that of futility. Brain injury or damage communicates irreversibility which may be construed that little or nothing can be done. Rappaport (1966) has attacked the irreversibility notion from an ego psychological (not neurological) point of view. The label, however, is neurological in its reference and, consequently, in the associations it generates.

The concept of degree has been reflected in labels by the use of the word "minimal." Cruickshank (1966, p. 13; 1967, pp. 5–6) has criticized this concept because the psychological problems are anything but minimal and also because of the fact that injury either exists or it does not, and the concept of *minimal* distorts the picture. Birch (1964, p. 5) similarly pointed out that minimal, as a descriptive adjective, does not increase the descriptive accuracy or add to the validity or utility of terms such as "brain injury" or "brain damage."

The concept of the brain-damaged child has been used to indicate a pattern or set of patterns of behavioral aberrance. Birch (1964, pp. 3–11) and others have criticized this concept because of the problem of evidence with reference to the question of causality. There are children who manifest the patterns of behavior associated with brain injury or brain damage who cannot be diagnosed with the procedures and instruments available as in fact having an injury to the brain. Also, there are children who have diagnosable injury who do not display the behavioral pattern. The position is argued both ways, and solid empirical support is yet to be obtained for either. The relevant immediate point is that brain damage is applied to some children in which there is no demonstrable damage to the brain. Using the label in this way rests on the assumption that aberrations in the normal functions of the central nervous system become manifest in certain patterns of behavior and learning. Hence, the existence of such patterns which, some (for example, Cruickshank, 1966, pp. 13–14; Cruickshank, 1967*a*, pp. 3–4; Strauss and Kephart, 1955, pp. 41–42) have argued, are symptomatic of injury or damage to the brain. When such injury is not verified in clinical assessment, it is assumed to be due to the lack of sophistication and precision in our methods and procedures.

It may be argued, and many have done so (Bateman, 1964; Hanvik, 1966; Hewett, 1968, p. 77), that the question is academic. In settings where the pragmatic concern dominates, such as in a classroom where the teacher is faced with the decision as to what will be done in teaching the child how to read, the behavioral characteristics are obviously the most crucial.

That is, the fact that a child is reversing figure and background and that he perseverates is much more important to the teacher in teaching the child to read than the most basic cause of these behaviors. The child *may* in fact have suffered insult to the brain, but it is not this fact that answers the practical methodologic question. This kind of rationale has precipitated the use of such labels as learning disabled. Some (Hanvik, 1966) have suggested that the child should be described behaviorally and not labeled. This is not to say that the question of cause is in any sense unimportant. It is to suggest that the setting in which the child is identified and eventually labeled has something to do with the label, has some implications for the relevant action to be taken and who is most responsible for taking that action.

CHARACTERISTICS

Numerous investigations have found brain-injured children to possess psychological aberrations, which Rappaport (1964) has included under the rubric of "Inadequate Impulse Control or Regulation." These are: hyperactivity, hyperdistractibility, disinhibition, impulsivity, perseveration, lability of affect, and motor dysfunction. As the reader will soon see, many of these characteristics can be thought of as interrelated in some way. The following are taken from Hirt, a former associate of Rappaport's, and are descriptions of the above characteristics. As Hirt presents no empirical data, the characteristics are based on observation.

Hyperactivity

Hirt (1964) describes the hyperactive child as one "who is always in motion, and whose motion is always in double

time." In and out of his seat all of the time, this is a child who is particularly disturbing to the classroom teacher.

Hyperdistractibility

"This is often viewed as the result of an inadequate attention span. Actually, it is the inability to focus attention selectively on one major aspect of a situation" (Hirt, 1964). Hyperdistractibility is of two general types: (1) overresponse to external stimuli and (2) overresponse to internal stimuli. The former is evident in the child who is unable to filter out extraneous stimuli in his environment. The hair ribbon on the girl across the row from him, the crack in the plaster on the ceiling, the barking dog outside the window—all unnoticeable to the normal child—serve as distractors for the brain-injured child. "The second type . . . is exemplified by the child who repeatedly interrupts his seatwork to ask irrelevant questions, such as 'Is this Monday, Miss Doan?' " (Hirt, 1964).

Disinhibition

This manifests itself in the lack of normal propriety. "It is exemplified by the child who asks a visitor, 'How come you are so fat?' " (Hirt, 1964).

Impulsivity

This is described by Hirt (1964) as the inability to control an overvalent impulse regardless of the situation or the consequences. This is the child who is intrusive, unable to delay gratifications, and makes a general nuisance of himself by constantly pushing and hitting others around him.

Perserveration

This refers to the lack of impulse control of a motor act of some kind. For example, the child may repeat the same words over and over again or start drawing a line on a page and be unable to stop this motor act until he has drawn the line off the page and onto the desk.

Lability of Affect

Hirt (1964) refers to this as "an emotional instability in which the child overreacts to minimal stimulation either by an inordinately intense or mobile response. For example, upon accomplishing a task at which she had been working for several days, a ten-year-old girl burst into tears accompanied by loud sobs. Another example is an eleven-year-old boy who begins to giggle and speak rapidly as soon as he feels unsure of himself."

Motor Dysfunction

This refers to difficulties in both gross and fine motor movement. These problems are considered by Rappaport and his associates from the point of view of segmentation and inadequate laterality and directionality. The former is "the inability to move one's body or its parts in a synchronized and intergrated fashion" (Hirt, 1964). The latter refers to problems in crossing the body midline, reversals of figures, and lack of discrimination of left from right.

The present writers consider distractibility to be the more central of the above characteristics. Rappaport's characteristics of hyperactivity, disinhibition, impulsivity, and perseveration may all be explained, to some extent, by the brain-injured child's distractibility, that is, his inability to filter out extraneous stimuli and focus selectively on a task. Cruickshank (1967b, pp. 252–253) gives the following example:

It can be argued, however, that hyperactivity as Rappaport describes it, is a function of hyperdistractibility and that disinhibition and impulsivity are also manifestations of the same factors, namely, the *inability of the child to refrain from reaction to extraneous external or internal stimuli*. The inability to refrain from reacting to stimuli is a characteristic of the brain-injured which has been commented upon frequently by many writers. Werner and Strauss [1962] often refer to this phenomenon. It is called being "stimulus-bound" (tied to stimuli) by Homberger [1926]. Others have mentioned a "drive" to respond to unessential stimuli. Goldstein [1939] speaks of the behavior as hyperactivity in the face of being unable to do other than to react to stimuli on an unselective basis. Dolphin and Cruickshank [1951] speak of distractibility in their group of cerebral palsy children, and similarly Cruickshank, Bice, Wallen, and Lynch [1965] report this factor an essential one in the inability of their large groups of spastic and athetoid cerebral palsy children to function in a variety of experimental test situations (Cruickshank, 1967b, pp. 252–253).

Although the statement of the problem by Cruickshank and his associates is perhaps the more parsimonious, there is no real fundamental difference between the two writers. It is largely a matter of semantics. Both view the same behavioral characteristics from slightly different perspectives.

Studies of Inadequate Impulse Control in Brain-Injured Children

Williams, Geiseking, and Lubin (1961) compared groups of normal, dull normal, and brain-injured subjects using the Block Design Rotation Test (Shapiro, 1951). It was found that, under conditions of reduced peripheral cues, the normals and dull normals rotate the figures more but the brain-injured group rotate less. It is hypothesized, by the authors, that with the reduction of peripheral cues there is also a reduction of distracting stimuli.

Thus, when the range of possible distracting stimuli is reduced, the brain-injured subject is better able to focus his attention on the more essential stimuli. It is important to note that what prove to be extraneous stimuli for the brain-injured are actually an aid to the non-brain-injured groups. They are able to integrate the additional information from the peripheral cues and this lessens their tendency to rotate; whereas this extra information is a burden for the brain-injured subjects and leads them to errors in rotation.

Other authors (Garfield, Benton, and MacQueen, 1966) compared a group of brain-injured children with a group of familial retarded children, matched for age and IQ, on eight tasks of "motor impersistence." The eight tasks were: keeping the eyes closed; protruding the tongue, both blindfolded and with eyes open; fixation of gaze in lateral visual fields; keeping the mouth open; fixation on the examiner's nose during confrontation testing; head turning during sensory testing; and holding a prolonged "ahh" sound. It was found that the brain-injured children performed significantly poorer than the familials on all but the last two of the eight tasks. In both groups, there was a greater tendency for the younger subjects (*Ss*) to be impersistent. No relationship between motor impersistency and IQ was found. Because the investigators included only those brain-injured *Ss* with no apparent damage to the muscles involved in the tasks, it may be concluded that the brain-injured *Ss* were displaying disturbances of a central nature.

Rosvold *et al.* (1956) compared three groups on a continuous performance test (CPT): Defective Group, brain-damaged and familials; Child Group, brain-damaged and normals; Adult Group, brain-damaged and normals. Analysis of covariance was

performed in order to control for significant age difference between the child subgroups and significant IQ difference between the adult subgroups. The CPT allowed *S* to choose his own time to respond and required a high level of continuous concentration. There were two tasks: X Task—letters were presented approximately every 0.92 second. Every time an X was presented, the *S* was to press a response key. AX Task—*S* was to respond to an X every time it was presented after an A. The results indicated that the brain-injured *Ss* perform poorer than the non-brain-injured *Ss*. This difference is greater on the more complex AX Task and between the two children subgroups.

Rosvold notes that it has been shown that brain-injured *Ss* generally show either random bursts of hypersynchronous activity or a general hypersynchrony on their EEGs. The authors suggest that if hypersynchrony is associated with reduced attention, as suggested by its presence in sleep, then hypersynchrony might be an indication of inattention when an individual is awake. The authors admit that this is only a hypothesis and that this study does not really measure this directly. What would be needed is a measure of the *S*'s EEG while he is responding to such a vigilance task.

Schulman *et al.* (1965) found in a study of brain-injured children that the level of total day activity did not correlate significantly with any of the diagnostic or behavioral clusters of brain damage. These authors are convinced that the majority of brain-injured children have total activity levels, as measured by an actometer, that are similar to normal children. However, in a highly social situation which requires the child to prescribe to rigid rules of behavior, the brain-injured child becomes either hypoactive (he overcompensates for his not being able to control his behavior) or hyperactive. The *Ss* in this study became hypoactive, but the authors suggest that this was probably due to selection by the school from which they were drawn. To summarize, no evidence was found that hyperactivity is a correlate of brain injury except in highly socially structured situations (for example, a testing situation). Distractibility, however, did correlate significantly with measures of brain injury.

Activity was measured by means of an instrument called an actometer. This instrument consists of an automatically winding calendar wrist watch modified so that there is direct drive from pendulum to hands. The amount of "time" recorded on the watch indicates the amount of activity the child undergoes. Each child wore two actometers, one on the wrist and one on the ankle, both on the dominant side. The validity and reliability of this instrument have been demonstrated.

There were four different tests of distractibility:

1. The clock test. Briefly, this test consists of a toy mouse, a piece of cheese, and a mousetrap attached to a clock. *S*'s task was to allow the mouse to reach the cheese, which was placed at position twenty-two, but to push a lever to return the mouse to the start before it reached the mousetrap affixed to a position between positions twenty-three and thirty-two.

2. The box test. Three boxes each with a figure of a different color and shape painted on the front (red circle, yellow triangle, and blue square) were placed before *S*. At varying intervals, *E* exposed a hand puppet to view above one of the boxes. The child was to name, by shape, color, or position, which box the puppet came from after each time it was shown.

3. The card test. Two hundred cards were shown to each *S* at one-second intervals. On 180 of the cards, there was a picture of a rabbit. Interspersed randomly were 20 cards with a picture of a baby. *S* was to indicate whenever he saw a "baby" card.

4. The tone test. Twenty-five tones of 2,000 cycles per second were randomly distributed among 50 tones of 750 cycles per second. The interval between tones was varied throughout the tape. *S*'s task was to raise his hand whenever he heard a 2,000 cps tone.

Each of the above tests was administered to each *S* twice. On one administration there was an external distractor and on the other administration there was not. The external distractor for the Clock and Box tests was a tape recording of *Winnie the Pooh*. On the card and tone tests, a sound track of a Yogi Bear cartoon and another reading from *Winnie the Pooh* served as the distractors.

Thus, the measure of hyperactivity used by Schulman *et al.* is primarily a measure of gross motor activity, whereas the measures of distractibility are concerned with the *S*'s ability to concentrate and attend to a task. The finding that distractibility correlated with brain-injury whereas hyperactivity did not lends support to the contention of the present authors, mentioned earlier, that distractibility is the more central of the two characteristics.

Cruse (1961) compared brain-injured and familial children matched for MA and CA on a reaction-time task under low stimuli and distractible conditions. The highly distracting condition consisted of a room filled with balloons, toys, and a mirror. No differences in reaction time performances were found between the two groups. However, he further subdivided the brain-injured group. Brain-injured children with "determinate" and known etiologies were compared with children whose brain injury was considered definitely prenatal but with no differentiating clinical characteristics. The brain-injured *Ss* with known etiologies were more distractible (that is, had slower reaction times) than the group with unknown etiologies or the familial group. Both groups, the determinate brain-injured and familial, benefited the same amount from the reduction of the external distractions.

In terms of the possible neurological mechanisms involved in inadequate impulse control, many authors have suggested *cerebral inhibition* (Birch, Belmont, and Karp, 1965; Eisenberg, 1964; Paine, 1966). For example, Eisenberg (1964), although he presents no data on the subject, states the following:

Pathways from cortex to reticular system provide for cortico-reticulo-inhibition. In this way, signals arriving at a primary receptive zone can initiate a depression of response in other cortical zones. Interference with these precisely interdigitated inhibitory systems might very well be the basis for the attention deficits observed in so-called minimal brain damage, in which no gross lesion with motor or sensory consequences can be identified.

Birch, Belmont, and Karp (1965) conducted a study of brain-injured adults that has significance for children, particularly in terms of a hypothesis that distractibility is due to defects in cortical inhibition. It was shown that brain-injured *Ss*, when presented with two tones of equal intensity three seconds apart, underestimated the loudness of the second tone in contrast to the non-brain-injured *Ss* who tended to overestimate the second tone or say the two tones were equal. As the interval between the two tones was increased, the brain-injured *Ss* gradually approached normal levels of responsiveness until at

nine seconds they were responding as the non-brain-injured did at the three-second interval. Thus, the first tone seems to be interfering with the judgment of the second tone. The neural impulses to be fired by the second tone seem to be inhibited by the neural impulses fired by the first tone. The authors suggest that this prolonged inhibition in the subject with the brain-injury is due to a defect in the recovery mechanisms of the reticulocortical system or changes in the rate of decay or spread of inhibition of a local excitation.

The above findings are quite interesting in that, at first glance, they go counter to what might be expected of the brain-injured group. It would seem, as the interval between the two tones is increased, that there would be more chance for the brain-injured *S* to become distracted from the task. Instead, an increase in interval leads to a level of responsiveness indistinguishable from that of the normal *S*.

It would be interesting to conduct a developmental study of this task on normal and brain-injured children in order, first of all, to see if the results above found with brain-injured adults could be replicated with brain-injured children. Secondly, a developmental study would allow one to determine whether the effects of the increased interval were peculiar only to brain-injured *Ss* or whether younger normal *Ss* would also respond in the same way.

Numerous investigators have noted that the brain-injured individual's impulsive, hyperactive behavior tends to diminish with time (Menkes, Rowe, and Menkes, 1967; Pincus and Glaser, 1966; Rappaport, 1965). They all agree that by adolescence there is considerable likelihood that the brain-injured child will no longer manifest extremely hyperactive behavior.

Menkes, Rowe, and Menkes (1967) conducted a follow-up study on individuals fourteen years to twenty-seven years (X = 24 years) after they had originally been seen in a clinic and had been described as displaying hyperkinetic behavior and neurological abnormalities. The follow-up study revealed that only three of the original fourteen *Ss* were still hyperactive. The disappearance of hyperactivity had occurred between the ages of eight and twenty-one in the others.

Rappaport (1965) asserts that psychological and educational concern for these children should not decrease as the hyperactive behavior decreases. He notes that hyperkinesis may decline with age but also warns that, if proper educational measures are not provided early in this child's life, he may become antisocial.

Perseveration is another frequently observed psychological characteristic of the brain-injured child. Hunt and Patterson (1958), for example, in comparing brain injured and familial children matched for IQ, MA, CA, and sex, found that the brain-injured *Ss* perseverated more on an auditory-sequence task where the child was required to repeat a story told to him by the experimenter. Perseveration is included under "inadequate impulse control" by Rappaport. Perseveration, however, seems to be more of an independent psychological factor than the others already discussed under inadequate impulse control. As Cruickshank *et al.* (1961, pp. 7–8) state:

Perseveration is the inability to shift with ease from one psychological activity to another. More precisely, it is the apparent inertia of the organism which retards a shift from one stimulus situation to another, and it results in a prolonged after-effect of a given stimulus to which the individual has made an adjustment. There is an overlap in time between a shift from an old situation to a new situation. As is the case with many other characteristics which have been mentioned, perseveration is not restricted solely to children with central nervous system disorders. While it may be observed frequently in such patients, it is also a characteristic of psychopathology in many other clinical groups. It is difficult to understand how perseveration could be related to hyperactivity and distractibility, although Werner and Strauss on one occasion intimated that this might be possible.

Perseveration appears to be an independent psychological variable whose presence may impede learning in as significant a way as can distractibility in all of its various forms.

One might, however, think of perseveration as another manifestation of defective cortical inhibition, which was discussed above. For example, two different stimuli, A and B, impinge on the organism at Time 1 and Time 2, respectively. It might be hypothesized, following a prolongation of inhibition model, that Stimulus A fires a neural impulse which inhibits for an abnormal amount of time the firing of an impulse to Stimulus B. Thus, the response to the first stimulus remains salient for a longer period of time than normal. In other words, the child perseverates.

Figure-Ground Disturbances

Figure-ground disturbances may be characterized by any one or a combination of the following: (1) confusion of figure and background, (2) reversal of figure and background, (3) inability to see any difference between figure and background. This disturbance can be considered as closely related to those under inadequate impulse control. The brain-injured child is unable to attend to the figure. The background becomes highly distractible to the child and he is forced to respond to it. He is unable to selectively respond to the essential stimuli while filtering out the inessential stimuli.

This disturbance has been demonstrated with cerebral palsy children in the visual modality (Dolphin and Cruickshank, 1951a) and in the tactual sense (Dolphin and Cruickshank, 1952; Cruickshank, Bice, and Wallen, 1957).

This disturbance is also well documented in non-cerebral-palsied brain-injured children in both the tactual (Werner and Strauss, 1941) and the visual modalities (Vegas and Frye, 1963; Werner and Strauss, 1941). Vegas and Frye (1963) compared groups of brain-injured and familial retardates matched for MA on their abilities to name as many objects as possible in pictures containing nonhidden and hidden objects. Although the total response rate was much greater for the familials, there was a greater percentage of responses for hidden objects for the brain-injured children as compared to the familial children. Thus, the brain-injured child manifested a forced responsiveness to the hidden objects, that is, the background stimuli.

Birch and Lefford (1967) have obtained results which indicate that the ability to separate figure from background is of a developmental nature. They presented different age groups of children of above average intelligence with tasks that required them to copy geometric figures. In one condition, the geometric forms were presented on blank sheets of paper and the S was asked to draw the form on a separate blank sheet of paper. In another condition, the forms were presented on sheets of paper with a grid-line background and the child was also given a response sheet with these grid lines. It was found that the youngest group of children (five years old) performed more poorly when the grid lines were presented than when the forms were presented on blank sheets of paper. The seven year and older groups of children, however, performed better when the grid lines were presented than when they were not. Apparently, the older children were able to use the extra structure provided by the guidelines whereas, perhaps because of figure-ground disturbance, the grid lines distracted the younger children.

Visual-Motor Disturbances

Studies have shown that the brain-injured child, compared to the familial retardate and the normal child, has an impaired ability to coordinate the visual system and the motor system. This child, for example, is unable to draw what the eyes see. Thus, when asked to copy a figure, his representation is a distortion of the true figure. One can also hypothesize that he draws what he sees all right, but what he sees is so distorted by cerebral disorganization that his drawing results in what to us is a distorted figure.

Frostig, Lefever, and Whittlesey (1961) compared a group of children with learning disabilities, many of whom were diagnosed as neurologically handicapped, with a group of normal children on five areas of visual perception—eye-motor coordination, constancy of form, figure-ground relationships, position in space, and spatial relations. They found that the overall perceptual quotient (PQ) obtained from these tests was lower for the group with probable brain damage. Frostig (1962) also found that the average PQ was significantly lower than the average IQ for those children with probable brain injury.

Bensberg (1950) found familials superior to brain-injured Ss on reproducing designs on a marble board task. The brain-injured children were characterized by their inability to construct the design as a totality. They had a tendency to jump from one part of the design to another. This mode of construction was first observed by Werner and Strauss (1939) and has been named "dissociation" by Cruickshank (1961). As noted previously (Cruickshank, 1961), this characteristic is thought to be closely related to distractibility. Placing two boards, each containing one hundred holes, and a few dozen marbles in front of the child creates a highly stimulating and potentially distracting testing situation.

Bensberg (1952), among many others, has also found that brain-injured children are deficient in performance on the Bender Gestalt Test. This visual-motor test requires the child to copy various designs. He found that a group of familial retardates were more accurate in their reproductions than a group of brain-injured children. The brain-injured children were characterized, in particular, by their tendency to reverse figures, repeat parts of the designs, and to use lines when dots were required.

Performance on visual-memory tests may also be included as indicators of visual-motor disturbances. When an individual is required to reproduce a design that was previously presented to him, he must be able to both remember what the design looked like and then be able to reproduce it using his visual-motor skills.

Cassel (1949) compared brain-injured and familial children, matched for MA and CA, on their abilities to reproduce geometric designs. The experimenter then asked these two groups of children to identify these same designs when seen in a different context. The familials and the brain-injured children did not differ in their ability to do this. It was therefore concluded by Cassel that lower scores of brain-injured subjects on reproduction from memory tasks must be interpreted with caution. The poorer performance may be due to an inability to express what has been apprehended. In other words, poor performance of brain-injured children in reproducing designs from memory may be due, in large part, to a visual-motor deficit rather than a memory deficit.

It is possible that, just as with the Marble Board Task discussed by Cruickshank (1961), brain-injured children perform poorly on copying and reproducing designs because they are distracted by extraneous stimuli and are unable to attend to the task. Although there are no doubt more extraneous stimuli presented to S in the Marble Board Task, some general concentration deficit may still be hindering the performance of the brain-injured individual on tests like the Bender Gestalt Test.

Rowley and Baer (1963) attempted to determine the influence of lack of attention and concentration on performance on the Benton Visual Retention Test. Assuming that emotionally disturbed youngsters exhibit the same lack of concentration as brain-injured children, they compared a group of each of these kinds of children matched for age and IQ. Grossly defective performances were displayed by 28 percent of the brain-injured group but by only 4 percent of the emotionally disturbed group. Rowley and Baer thus concluded that poor performance on the Benton Visual Retention Test is not caused by attention or concentration difficulties but by more specific disabilities, for example, visual-motor coordination, visual memory, and spatial relations.

That emotionally disturbed and brain-injured children display the same kind and degree of inattention, however, is an assumption that the present writers feel should be viewed with some caution.

More research is needed into the relative affects of distractibility and visual-motor defects in the poor performance of brain-injured children on visual-motor tasks. Until such research is done, distractibility should not be discounted as at least a partial determiner of such defective performance.

It has been noted by many that there are large individual differences in the scores of brain-injured children on the various visual-motor tests (Colman and Com, 1966; Hunt, 1959; Koppitz, 1962).

Colman and Com (1966) compared the performances of brain-injured, emotionally disturbed, and normal groups of children matched for age and IQ on the Marble Board Test and Ellis Visual Designs Test. They found that 10 of the 28 brain-injured *Ss* received 3 or more ratings of both incoherent procedure and linear organization on the Marble Board Test and scores of less than 4.5 on the Ellis Visual Designs Test. This was in sharp contrast to the other 2 groups where none of the *Ss* in either of these 2 groups scored this poorly. However, as Colman and Com point out, 18 of the 28 brain-injured children did not receive such poor scores, indicating that one should not attribute the same behavioral characteristics to all brain-injured children.

Hunt (1959) compared groups of familial and brain-injured children on their abilities to construct three-dimensional designs from pictures. In addition, the brain-injured group was further broken down into two subgroups depending, on the basis of observable behavior displayed in the classroom, on whether they had visual-motor problems or auditory problems. The brain-injured group with visual-motor deficits performed the poorest on the task. The brain-injured group that displayed severe auditory disturbances, how-ever, obtained the highest scores on these visual-motor tasks. Such results should caution one from attempting to describe "a typical brain-injured child," particularly with respect to his visual-motor abilities.

Koppitz (1962) also concludes that, when attempting to diagnose brain injury, it is unwise to rely upon the performance score of only one test. She has observed, for instance, that some brain-injured children may score well on the Bender Gestalt Test by compensating for their difficulties. This is often done by taking an unusually long time to complete the test. Also, some may anchor the design with their hands while copying it; some trace the design with a finger first before attempting to copy it; some may even turn both the stimulus card and paper upside down and then draw the design in this way.

Such methods of attacking the task differ from those of normal children. In light of the evidence cited above that a score on a visual-motor test may not always discriminate the brain-injured from the non-brain-injured child, more attention should be given to the way in which the child goes about accomplishing the task. In other words, instead of considering only the quality of the finished product, research also needs to be focused on how the brain-injured child accomplishes this final product, whether it be equal in quality to that of the non-brain-injured child or not.

Visual-Perceptual Disturbances

Size-distance judgment. Jenkin and Morse (1960) compared the abilities of brain-injured, mentally retarded adolescents; familial adolescents; normal adolescents and normal adults to make size-distance judgments. It was found that, whereas the latter three groups tended to overestimate, the brain-injured retardates tended to underestimate the size of a distant object in comparison to a proximal object. In this respect, Jenkin and Morse point out that the brain-injured adolescents in this study perform similarly to the youngest children (seven to eight years) in Piaget and Lambercier's study (1951) of normal children. Piaget and Lambercier found that the youngest group made judgments that fell short of size constancy and that their older groups, starting from eight to ten years, progressively overestimated the size of the object. It may thus be concluded that the brain-injured adolescents, in contrast to familial adolescents, have not proceeded beyond the developmental level of seven or eight years with respect to their ability to make size-distance judgments.

The authors conclude that the brain-injured Ss fail to combine several sources of information in making their judgments. It is pointed out that in making size-distance judgments, various depth cues and the integration of these with other sources of information (for example, size of the proximal stimulus) must be taken into account by the individual. The brain-injured S is unable to integrate this information and thus tends to be "stimulus bound."

Apparent movement. When a person placed in a dark room is presented with a stationary point of light, he will perceive this light as moving. This is referred to as the "autokinetic phenomenon." It is generally accepted that this phenomenon has a cerebral rather than a retinal basis (Haggard and Rose, 1944; Werner and Thuma, 1942).

Bennet and Poit (1963) compared brain-injured and familial children matched for age and IQ on their abilities to detect au-

tokinetic movement. There was little differentiation between the two groups with regard to the total amount of movement seen. The brain-injured Ss, however, reported that the light moved for much shorter periods of time and that they saw the light start and stop more frequently than the familial control group. The authors explain these results as being due to disturbances in the neural pathways of brain-injured Ss resulting in more frequent interruptions in cerebral streaming. This finding is yet another explanation of the distractibility of the brain-injured child.

Mark and Pasamanick (1958) found higher asynchronism thresholds for two points of light in a group of brain-injured children compaired to a control group matched for age, sex, and IQ. Such a finding indicates a loss of visual efficiency in brain-injured children in the detection of a pause between the onset time of two lights. Because the brain-injured children had no primary diagnosis of opthalmologic disturbance, it may be concluded that the loss in visual efficiency is due to cerebral dysfunctioning of some kind.

Aftereffects. Levine and Spivack (1962) compared the reports of brain-injured, emotionally disturbed, and normal Ss on the Spiral Visual Aftereffects Test (SVA). The normal and emotionally disturbed Ss showed a decrease in SVA sooner than did those with brain injury. In addition, the normal and emotionally disturbed groups were characterized by an increase of failure to report SVA in later trials, whereas the brain-injured group did not. It is thus concluded by Levine and Spivack that the brain-injured Ss are characterized by a different adaptation pattern to the SVA. This finding may have explanatory value with regard to perseveration. The brain-injured individual may have a tendency to perseverate because of the prolonged aftereffect of a stimulus.

Day (1960) notes, however, that studies on SVA have obtained conflicting results. Some studies have shown that brain-injured *S*s see little or no aftereffect. He points out that, in order for an individual to experience an aftereffect of seen movement for a rotating spiral pattern, it is necessary for him to fixate steadily on a stationary point in or near the moving stimulus pattern. Damage to a location in the brain that controls voluntary eye movement (for example, the frontal region) might render the individual unable to fixate on a stationary point and thus hinder his seeing an aftereffect. Day concludes that inconsistencies in results may be due to differences in the brain-injured *S*s studied with regard to locus, extent, and nature of the injury.

Efstathiou and Morant (1966) lend some empirical support to Day's conclusions. They conclude from a study comparing brain-injured adults with normal adults that when proper measures are taken to assure fixation on the SVA test, brain-injured patients function at about normal level. Efstathiou and Morant also tested the two groups on the Waterfall Illusion Aftereffect (WIAE), a test that does not depend as critically on fixation as the SVA test. If one fixates on a stationary terrain after having looked at a waterfall, the terrain is then experienced as moving upwards. This phenomenon can be replicated in a laboratory situation with a moving set of parallel lines. On this WIAE test, where much less fixation is required, there were no significant differences between brain-injured and normal *S*s.

Schein (1960) has also called into serious question cortical inhibition explanations of failure to report afterimages. He found in a study comparing brain-injured, psychotic and normal individuals on their abilities to report an Archimedes Spiral afterimage that, whereas the brain-injured *S*s failed to report any afterimage significantly more frequently than the control groups, when the afterimage was seen, none of the variables of age, intelligence, drugs, or *diagnosis* differentiated the groups with regard to the *duration* of the afterimage. He suggests, apparently as a result of the effect of instructions on the frequency of responses, that these findings indicate that the brain-injured *S*s *perceive* the afterimage as frequently as the control groups but that the brain-injured individuals are more easily confused by the task and thus fail to *report* their perceptions more frequently.

Garner, Neuringer, and Goldstein (1966) found no differences between brain-injured and normal adults on duration of the spiral aftereffect. They suggest that some brain-injured individuals, particulary those with language disturbances, may be impaired in their ability to report subjective experiences.

From the above studies it would appear safe to conclude that the inconsistent findings may be resolved by considering the locus, extent, and nature of the lesion to the brain. It would also appear that in explaining the reason for no report of a visual afterimage in some brain-injured *S*s there are at least three explanations more parsimonious than a cortical-inhibition explanation:

1. Failure of some brain-injured *S*s to fixate on a steady point due to damage to brain centers controlling voluntary eye movements
2. Failure of some brain-injured *S*s to *report* subjective experiences
3. Failure of some brain-injured *S*s to understand the task

It should be pointed out, however, that, because the above studies were dealing with adults, these conclusions may not necessarily apply to brain-injured children. Furthermore, they do not explain the findings of Levine and Spivack (1962), discussed above, that the brain-injured *S*s showed a longer SVA than normal and emotionally disturbed *S*s. Research is now needed on brain-injured children, taking account of the pitfalls encountered in the adult studies.

Auditory Disturbances

Brain-injured children also frequently have problems of an auditory nature. Sabatino (1969), in fact, points out that one can often miss neurologically handicapped children if only the visual modality is tested. Sabatino found that all of the subtests of his Test of Auditory Perception (TAP) correlated negatively with scores of the Bender Visual Motor Gestalt Test. The TAP's subtests are: recognition of sounds, recognitions of words, immediate memory for digits, immediate memory for speech, auditory integration, and auditory comprehension. He found that under conditions of background noise, a group of brain-injured children was significantly poorer on all six subtests than a non-brain-injured control group matched for age, sex, and verbal IQ. With normal background noise, the two groups were significantly differentiated on all but two subtests—immediate memory for digits and auditory integration. (The *S* was required to duplicate prerecorded patterns of tapping.) With regard to this finding, Sabatino concludes that meaningful language is necessary to differentiate normal and brain-injured children on auditory perception. It is also important to note that this finding is additional empirical evidence for the hyperdistractibility of the brain-injured child.

Schlanger (1958) found that varying the background noise made no difference in the performance of brain-injured children in discriminating pairs of words that were close in sound (for example, pin—pen). This task is highly similar to Sabatino's subtests of recognition of sounds and recognition of words. The findings of the two studies indicate that background stimuli may be distracting for brain-injured children only on certain kinds of auditory perceptual tasks. Schlanger concludes that the low performance of brain-injured children in discriminating sounds is of a psychological nature due to limited attention span, lack of concentration, and distractibility to *internal* factors rather than due to a general or specific auditory factor.

Other studies have shown brain-injured children to be deficient on tone-discrimination tasks (Birch, Belmont, and Karp, 1965; Stevens *et al.,* 1967). Closely related to this deficiency is the brain-injured child's problem in determining initial, final, and medial sounds of even short words (Kaliski, 1959). The separate sounds that go into making up these words tend to run into one another for the brain-injured child. If such a child is unable to discriminate the sounds of single words, it is evident that his problem is multiplied to an even greater extent when he is presented with a string of words in a sentence.

From the Birch, Belmont, and Karp study (1965) previously cited, in which it was found that a longer period of time between two tones was required for brain-injured as contrasted to normal *S*s before the second tone was not interfered with by the first tone, we might posit that a disturbance in cerebral inhibition is a factor in the inability to discriminate sounds. Belmont, Birch, and Karp (1965), furthermore, have concluded from a study of intersensory and intrasensory relations that brain-injured individuals are often characterized by a lack of spread of inhibition.

Either because of a prolongation of inhibition, as demonstrated in the Birch, Belmont, and Karp study, or because of a lack of inhibition, sounds run together and are not integrated into a meaningful sequence or pattern. Considering two sequential sounds—A and B—in the first case, sound A would interfere with sound B; in the latter case, B would interfere with A. To determine which of these two processes was working, one could set up an experimental situation in which brain-injured children with auditory disturbances and normal controls were presented verbally with a list of about seven random words and then asked to repeat the words they could remember. Looking at words 3, 4, and 5 in order to eliminate primacy and recency effects (assuming that the serial position curves are the same in the two groups), if prolongation of inhibition is occurring, the third word would tend to be remembered better than either the fourth or fifth word. If, however, there is a defect that was keeping inhibition from occurring at all, the fifth word would be remembered better than either the third or fourth word.

Intersensory Disturbances

Many investigators have concluded that organized behavior is the result of an integration of the different sensory systems (Birch, 1954; Maier and Schneirla, 1935; Sherrington, 1951). The ability to integrate information from more than one sensory system comes at a more advanced stage of development than the ability to integrate information from a single sensory system.

Referring to the classic writings of Goldstein (1939) in which he posits a "hierarchy of disintegration" whereby the higher, more complex behaviors of an organism are the first to be impaired by cortical injury, one can readily see why investigators have concluded that intersensory organization is more impaired than intrasensory organization in brain-injured individuals. Birch (1964), for example, has noted that, at the very least, the emergence of intersensory relations is delayed in the brain-injured child. As Birch points out, inadequate intersensory organization may not only result in the inability to organize input from two different sensory modalities, but may also predispose the child to develop bizarre types of integrations.

Hunt and Patterson (1958) found that brain-injured children, in contrast to familial controls, were characterized by an inability to coordinate information from two sensory modalities—auditory and visual. When given a task which required that they listen to a story read by the examiner and then rearrange a group of pictures to coincide with the story, they, instead of benefiting from the two different sources of cues, tended to select one or the other sensory modality as their sole base of operation.

The inability on the part of brain-injured children to integrate and organize inputs from more than one sensory modality may be viewed as another manifestation of distractibility. The neurologically impaired individual is limited in the amounts and sources of information he can deal with. It is difficult for him to attend to one stimulus at a time because so much of his attention is taken up with the impingement of other stimuli. But when he attends to these others, he is unable to integrate them in a meaningful way.

Conceptual and Abstract Thinking Disturbances

Another characteristic of the brain-injured child that is often referred to in the literature is his inability to deal with objects and ideas on an abstract level. This inability requires that he operate on a concrete level (Paine, 1966). Goldstein (1939) in his investigation of brain-injured war patients noted that these patients could perform concrete tasks but were unable to function on tasks that required abstract thinking.

Hand in hand with this deficiency in abstract thinking goes the brain-injured child's inability to form concepts (Kaliski, 1959). He is often deficient in seeing the relationships and similarities in things, that is, he has conceptual difficulty (Burks, 1960; Rappaport, 1964). As Burks notes, poor conceptual ability usually leads to serious academic deficiencies.

Strauss and Werner (1942) compared a group of familials and a group of brain-injured children matched for MA and CA (MA =nine years) on a Sorting Test and a Picture-Object Test. On the Sorting Test the S was required to sort fifty-six common objects into groups on the basis of their belonging together. On the Picture-Object Test, S was instructed to place objects in front of one of two pictures on the basis of the most appropriate matching. One picture was of a boy drowning and the other was of fireman attempting to rescue a burning building.

On both tests the brain-injured S s, compared to the familial controls, formed more groups and made far more uncommon responses. The principle by which the brain-injured children made their selections seemed to be based particularly upon unusual or accidental or apparently insignificant details. Furthermore, on the Picture-Object Test the brain-injured S s more often than the familials arranged the objects in circumscribed units, manifested formalistic behavior (for example, meticulosity, organic pedantry, arbitrary patterning), and dramatized the pictures in their selection of objects.

Dolphin and Cruickshank (1951b), comparing cerebral palsy children and non-brain-injured children matched for MA and CA, replicated the above results found by Strauss and Werner on the Picture-Object Test. The cerebral palsy children chose significantly more objects than the controls, made more selections based on secondary qualities of the objects, chose a larger number of uncommon objects, and more often dramatized the pictures in their selection of objects.

Gallagher (1957) compared a group of familials and a group of brain-injured children matched for MA and CA on tasks requiring quantitative conceptual ability. He found no differences between the two groups on these measures of quantitative concepts. He did find, however, that the brain-injured group was inferior on a task that required the integration of verbal concepts. This task required that the S supply the missing word in a sentence.

Ernhart et al. (1963) compared a group of brain-injured preschool children with a group of normal preschool children. Scores on the measures were adjusted for age, sex, and socioeconomic status. Covarying for vocabulary subtest score on the Stanford-Binet, it was found that the brain-injured preschoolers performed poorer on a conceptual task requiring S s to group blocks differing on the dimensions of color, size, and form.

However, Reed and Reed, Jr. (1967) found in a study of brain-injured and normal children (ten years to fifteen years) that, when level of intellectual functioning is controlled, the two groups are indistinguishable with regard to abstract reasoning tasks and concept-formation tasks as measured by the Wechsler-Bellevue Block Design Test and Halstead Category Test, respectively. They have concluded that one accompanying characteristic of brain injury in older children is a general lowering of intellectual ability rather than specific deficiencies in nonverbal abstract reasoning or concept formation. They do not imply, however, that specific impairment does not occur. They point out that such variables as type of lesion, age of onset, lateralization, location, and rate of progression or severity need to be further investigated in order to determine their effects on selective impairment.

Language Disturbances

The authors mean to deal here briefly with the more common language disturbances of the child with neurological impairment. We shall exclude, in this study, those brain-injured children whose primary problem lies in the language area—the aphasics. Although, as Thelander, Phelps, and Kirk (1958) state, the most easily recognized disturbances of the learning-disabled child with brain injury are in the area of language, these children do not display the profound language aberrations that are characteristic of the child with aphasia. For a good account of the child with aphasia, see McGinnis (1963) and Wepman (1951).

As Luria (1966) states, speech is the result "of highly complex integration of nervous processes. All complex forms of human mental activity involve direct or indirect participation of speech." Because it is the higher mental processes in the hierarchy of complexity that are the most easily deranged by local or general brain lesions (Luria, 1966; Goldstein, 1939), it follows that language processes should be among those behaviors that are most significantly affected.

Fisichelli et al. (1966) have made extensive phonetic analyses of infants with brain injury. They found from the tape recordings of normal and brain-injured infants at three age levels—first week of life, approximately six months of age, and approximately one year of age—that the normal infants produce significantly more total sounds, significantly more vowel sounds, and significantly less nasal sounds than the brain-injured infants. Other studies cited by Fisichelli et al. have found significant differences between these two groups in regard to threshold (Karelitz and Fisichelli, 1962) and latency (Fisichelli and Karelitz, 1963). Another study (Karelitz, Karelitz, and Rosenfeld, 1960) has found that the cries of normal infants are more rhythmic and are characterized by earlier appearance of inflectional changes than those of brain-injured infants.

These infant studies have thus shown that the consequences of brain injury appear early in the area of language development. These findings reflect early disturbances in the motor area of speech production, however, and might best be considered as disturbances that might later be concomitant with language disturbances of a conceptual nature.

Sievers (1959) compared the performances of normal, brain-injured retardates, and familial retardates matched for MA on the Differential Language Facility Test. The MAs ranged from 2-0 years to 5-11 years. The normals were superior to the brain-injured and non-brain-injured groups in areas of language ability that require verbal production without semantic reasoning. However, a surprising finding

WILLIAM M. CRUICKSHANK AND JAMES L. PAUL

was that the familial retardates were superior to normals on the subtest requiring semantic meaning but not verbal production. It was also found that the familials tended to perform better than the brain-injured group on subtests that required the subject to make semantic connections between visual objects as in the Object Association and Picture Series Description subtests.

Reed, Jr., Reitan, and Klove (1965) compared a group of brain-injured children ranging in age from ten to fourteen years with another group of children controlled for age but not for education or general intelligence. It was found that the brain-injured group was more frequently inferior in performance on tests directly dependent upon language functions. The authors note that this finding is in contrast to a previous study on adults (Reitan, 1959). The authors thus conclude that children and adults may differ quite significantly with respect to behavioral consequences of brain injury. The adult brain-injured *Ss* differ far more from their control group on tasks involving adaptive and problem-solving ability than on stored experience and memory abilities.

Socioemotional Disturbances

It is well established that the brain-injured child frequently presents a behavior problem to his peers, family, and teachers (Bender, 1956; McCartney, 1956; Farnham-Diggory, 1966; Gallagher, 1957; Jacobs and Pierce, 1968; Rappaport, 1964). Keeping in mind that how the child views himself is to a large extent dependent upon how others perceive and react to him, it becomes apparent that the behavior characteristics we have been describing above, impulsivity and hyperkinesis in particular, predispose the brain-

injured child to personality problems. This impulsive behavior he displays causes others to reject and exclude him from their groups. Especially during the stage of preadolescence, when peer groups are so important, we can see the devastating effects that this rejection can have on the child's personality development. It is no wonder that Bender (1956) has stated that all brain-injured children suffer from profound anxiety. Not only is the brain-injured child rejected by his peers, but often his own mother and father have rejected him in some way. Right from the first time the mother attempts to feed the child and he is unable to suck or sucks too briefly (Decker, 1964), there is a conflict that may continue for years.

Farnham-Diggory (1966) found that brain-injured children, in contrast to normals, have an immature view of life ahead and a lack of awareness of personal development and change. They also show a high degree of death imagery in their responses. She has concluded that their overall picture suggests that of the "catastrophic" reaction observed by Goldstein (1939) in his war patients. This was particularly true of the younger children. Briefly, for Goldstein, a catastrophic reaction arises in a brain-injured patient when the whole organism is unable to function adequately. There is some degree of realization that time has slowed down and that death has, in a sense, already begun.

Farnham-Diggory did not find on a self-evaluation questionnaire (SE) that the brain-injured group made lower evaluations of themselves than the normal control group. (The subject indicated his evaluation on each item by moving a red wooden arrow along on a scale.) Also, a highly significant negative correlation ($r = -.54$) was found between the mean SE and IQ of the brain-injured group. Thus, the more intelligent the child, the less he thought of himself.

As with all findings based on questionnaires, there is the problem of how honest the reporter is when giving his answers. The fact that in this particular case the experimenter was present with the subject while he was responding to questions prefaced with "show me how good you are at ... " makes the results even more questionable. Furthermore, the negative correlation found between IQ and SE may indicate that the more intelligent the child, the more honest he is in evaluating himself. Perhaps because of his higher level of functioning, he does not feel as threatened when it comes to evaluating himself.

Gallagher (1957) in his comparison of brain-injured and familial children found the brain-injured poorer on all personality variables measured. On rating scales, the brain-injured *Ss* were judged to be more hyperactive, inattentive, fearful, unpopular, and uninhibited. Gallagher has proposed two possible explanations for the brain-injured child's poor personality ratings: (1) he does not perceive social situations correctly and consequently acts inappropriately; (2) his general lack of inhibition presents behavior that is unacceptable to peers.

Jacobs and Pierce (1968) analyzed responses to sociometric questions ("Which of the boys and girls in the class would you like most [least] to work with on some special project? Which of the boys and girls in the class would you like most [least] to play with outside of school?") distributed to children in twelve public school classes for the educable mentally retarded. When the students were divided into those diagnosed as brain-injured and those diagnosed as familial, it was found that the brain-injured children were more often rejected by their peers than the

familials were. The correlation of brain-damage characteristics with number of times rejected was .426 (significant at .001 level). Short attention span was the most commonly mentioned characteristic of those subjects who were most often rejected. Hyperkinesis, emotional lability, and impulsivity were also quite frequently associated with those students most often rejected. An insignificant correlation ($r = .14$) was found between IQ and number of brain injury associated characteristics, and thus IQ was not considered a significant variable.

Variability of Performance and Orderliness

Investigators (Cruickshank *et al.*, 1961; Francis-Williams, 1965) have noted that the behavior of the brain-injured child is extremely variable. One day he is attentive to the task, the next day he cannot sit still. It is quite likely that the hyperdistractibility of brain-injured children is a major cause of this variability. Francis-Williams (1965) attributes variable performance of these children to their hypersensitivity to slight changes in their environment. Thus, one moment they may be attentive, but with a slight movement by another child in the classroom or the roar of an automobile outside the window, they may lose their level of concentration and remain in this condition for some time. It may also be that there are neurological changes constantly occurring within the brain-injured child's brain that cause this variation in performance ability.

Investigators (Cruickshank *et al.*, 1961; Goldstein, 1939; Mackie and Beck, 1966) have also noted that individuals suffering from brain injury often display a tendency toward orderliness in their behavior. Goldstein (1939) suggests that this behavior is a reaction to avoid catastrophic

WILLIAM M. CRUICKSHANK AND JAMES L. PAUL

situations that we have mentioned above.

One might also consider the possibility that this ordered behavior is a reaction to the disordered perception and behavior of the child. The world can be a frightening place for a child who is constantly bombarded by stimuli that he is unable to organize and integrate into meaningful patterns. From the review of the studies above, it is evident that the brain-injured child is indeed unable to deal in an organized manner with the input of information. Considered from this point of view, then, the brain-injured child may frequently order his behavior to the point of becoming compulsive and rigid in defense against what is for this child an extremely disorganized environment.

This may be achieved in numerous ways. The child may insist, for example, that everything on his desk be in its proper place, and if he finds an item out of place, he may go into a tantrum. It can be seen from this example that although this orderliness to a certain extent defends the child from overreacting to stimuli, it also takes up an inordinate amount of energy.

Self-Concept

The research literature on the self-concept of brain-injured children is very weak. At least three monumental issues account for this situation. First, clarity and consistency in the definition of brain injury, discussed elsewhere in this chapter, have not been adequate to aid in the systematic inquiry into characteristics such as negative self-concept of these children. Secondly, constructs of self "have been stretched to cover so many inferred cognitive and motivational processes that their utility for analytic

and predictive purposes has been greatly diminished (Wylie, 1961, p. 318). Lack of empirical evidence supporting theories of self-concept

... seems to be due in part to each of the following four factors: (1) the lack of proper scientific characteristics of the theories themselves; (2) the inevitable difficulties encountered in formulating relevant, well-controlled research in a new area; (3) the understandable fact that individual researches in a new area are not part of a planned research program and therefore cannot be easily synthesized; (4) avoidable methodological flaws (Wylie, 1961, p. 323).

The third has to do with the conceptual and empirical issues posed by bringing the two together. That is, a vague construct, self-concept, utilized in the description of a group of children who are not clearly specified in terms of their uniqueness and homogeneity can but compound the conceptual problem and add to the empirical questions. This observation, of course, applies generally to the behavioral and social sciences. The point is made here not in defense but as challenge to the serious-minded student who would pursue the difficult questions of a field where the development of thinking and practice is very young yet well beyond its formulation of operational definitions and constructs.

The discussion of self-concept here will not be restricted to the neurosensory view of the child, as is implied in the title of the chapter. Rather, this view will be integrated in part with other viable psychological points of view necessary to a more adequate discussion of the complex issues involved. The social competence and ego psychological views of child development and behavior, for example, provide fundamental concepts in our attempts at explanation. The assumption of injury to the brain is neither adequate nor essential for full understanding of stress to the child who is different.

Self-concept occupies a central position in several personality theories, for example, Rogers (1951). Self-concept is often considered the fundamental focus for behavioral change and for learning. Fennimore (1968, p. 448) has suggested that it is inconceivable that anyone could learn something inconsistent with his self-concept. Literature on early education is filled with the assumption that experiences to enhance the child's positive feelings about himself and to encourage the child's rejection of negative self-views are crucial (for example, Goodlad, 1964; Sears and Sherman, 1964).

That man, early in life, must accept a positive view and reject a negative view of himself—worthy, good, and valued rather than unworthy, mean, or unimportant—is not singularly a moral concept. It is a profound psychological concept in child development.

Hawk (1967, p. 196) has stated, "To understand the behavior of a person, one must understand how that person sees himself." He summarizes (pp. 196–197) the self as a dynamic unity of

... sensing, remembering, imagining, perceiving, wanting, feeling and thinking ... The individual's idea of what he looks like and his ideas of how he affects other persons ... the meaning of one's distinctive characteristics, abilities, and unique resources ... attitudes, feelings, and values one holds about oneself, one's self-esteem or one's self-reproach or both.

Davidson and Lang (1960, p.107) state: "The child's self concept arises and develops in an interpersonal setting." Researchers (for example, Ausubel et al., 1954, p. 182; Coppersmith, 1968; Davidson and Lang, 1960) have accumulated support for the notion that significant adults affect the child's feelings about himself. These include his parents and, later, his teachers.

The self is something which has development; it is not initially there, at birth, but arises in the process of social experience and activity, that is, develops in the given individual as a result of his relations to that process as a whole and to other individuals within that process (Mead, 1934, p. 135).

Mead (1934, p. 164) also states that "Selves can only exist in definite relationship to other selves."

Starting at a very early age, perhaps as early as the first feeding experiences, the matter of competence and mastery becomes a significant aspect of this very crucial relationship. The experience of being a mother, a good and competent mother, is almost as new to the mother as being a baby is to the infant. Both have important needs to be met and, even at this very elementary stage, certain abilities are required. The mother, if she is to nurse the child, must be physically able to provide the infant with adequate nourishment. The infant, on the other hand, must be able to receive and use that nourishment. If the infant cannot suck, then he is not able to satisfy the mother's need to feed him. There are physical as well as psychological hurts in the breach of this two-directional, need-satisfying experience. The infant has negative internal stimulation from pains of hunger while the mother has the discomfort of breasts unreleased from their fullness. These mutual discomforts become a part of the psychological experience of closeness in the process of feeding. The physical and emotional stimulation, so crucial in the infant's initial experiences with his world, bears the consequences of the dissatisfaction of mother and infant. The frustration of those biological and emotional needs in one creates frustration for the other. The mother's feeling of adequacy is measured in the response of the infant. Similarly, the infant's sense of well-being in a world that is pleased with his presence is dependent on the quality of the mother's presence. The first psychological task for the infant is the development of a basic sense of trust in himself and his environment (Erikson, 1960, p. 45).

Part of the social-psychological structure provided by the mother and later the family is elicited by the child. That is, normal maternal responses exist and are elicited by the child's behavior. The gross motor activity and the variety of sounds produced, for example, by the healthy, happy baby bring the mother's relaxed attention. Her response is of equal delight—including her own gestures, verbal and physical —which is an important, total, affective communication. As empty of precise associations and meanings of words that comprise the English language as the sounds of the Lovedu tribe, the messages do exist and they are communicated. "I am very happy and my happiness has much to do with you. Right now you have my undivided attention. I will take care of you and not abandon you." All are interwoven in the gestures. The infant's narcissism and omnipotence are then unchallenged. The lack of differentiation between the infant and mother for approximately the first six months makes the quality of this exchange particularly crucial. He learns to trust that his needs are cared for and that he can find pleasure in sensory and motor responses. The child's sense of trust is a reflection of his mother's sensitivity to his needs and her sturdy and realistic attitude (Rosenblith and Allinsmith, 1962, p. 206).

Mead (1934, p. 208) has stated that "we have to distinguish ourselves from other people and this is accomplished by doing something which other people cannot do, or cannot do as well." The psychological saliency of the experience of competency, as already indicated in the most basic relationship, is a crucial concept. Importantly, as Mead pointed out, this experience is obtained in a social context. It is in relation to the perceived competency of others.

Parents and teachers know the requirements of children to have the adult recognize skills they have acquired. With siblings, for example, an older child may have learned to skip, to count to ten, to recognize certain letters of the alphabet, to print his name, or to perform any one of literally thousands of skills that are part of the natural growth and development of children. The younger child will often require equal time to display his skill for the adult's approval. The skill the younger child displays may not be a skill at all but an impromptu performance designed specifically to elicit reassurance from the adult. Equal stage time and equal credit will not be based on equal performances. Importantly, the younger child fares well in skill comparison with age peers. He will not always be better than age peers, but he is competing on an equal footing and he knows it.

Some children do not compete so well. They consistently lose. Losing becomes even more devastating when the consistent winners are younger than he. The child knows when his relative performance is inferior. Caring and sensitive adults want so much for this child to also feel satisfied by his acts and may constantly reassure him of their love and his value to them. If, however, their reassurance is based on dishonest appraisal of his performance, both the child and the adult are locked into a futile engagement.

How the child thinks about himself has a major influence on his behavior. The child's image of himself has two main souces: the way he sees others viewing him and what he sees himself as able to do—and hence to be. Others' views are first his parents' views. If they cannot provide the warm acceptance that underlies the sense of personal worth for the normal child, the inner core of his self-concept will be one of worthlessness. His extrafamilial experiences with peers and teachers often further self-depreciation as others display impatience with his limitations and shun his company. Even with the good fortune of having sympathetic parents and companions, he must daily face the painful realization of his incompetence at play and at work. No "reassurance" will satisfy him that he is capable as a person when he sees that he is not (Eisenberg, 1964, p. 70).

The child will have to continue to create pseudoskills, which often become either clownlike or defeatist in nature. The child may try to elicit humor and sympathy responses in the absence of real competence to elicit genuine pride. Neither he nor his parents nor his teacher can feel good about his development as a "good" student, a responsible host to friends, a competent negotiator of the mealtime activities, and so on.

There are various ways in which we can realize that self. Since it is a social self, it is a self that is realized in its relationship to others. It must be recognized by others to have the very values which we want to have belong to it. It realizes itself in some sense through its superiority to others, as it recognizes its inferiorities in comparison with others. The inferiority complexes are the reverse situations to those feelings of superiority which we entertain with reference to ourselves as over against people about us.... We do belong to the community and our self-respect depends on our recognition of ourselves as such self-respecting individuals. But that is not enough for us, since we want to recognize ourselves in our differences from other persons.

. . . It would seem childish to intimate that we take satisfaction in showing that we can do something better than others. We take a great deal of pains to cover up such a situation; but actually we are vastly gratified. Among children and among primitive communities these superiorities are vaunted and a person glories in them; but even among our more advanced groups they are there as essential ways of realizing one's self, and they are not to be identified with what we term the expression of the egoistic or self-centered person.... But there is a demand, a constant demand, to realize one's self in some sort of superiority over those about us (Mead, 1934, pp. 204–205).

The development of the central nervous system is inextricably related to the psychological and social development of the child. The nature-nurture issue, although inviting in discussions of the psychological development of brain-injured children, has served, for the most part, to disguise or distort the real matter of complex interaction of the two. Discussion of either one proceeds, at a minimum, with assumptions about the other.

Ego functions such as impulse control, frustration tolerance, ability to mediate between biological drives and environmental demands, and awareness of others are not present at birth. They are developed, rather, as an outgrowth of more primary ego functions, such as attention span, communication, perception, and motor control. These more primary functions emerge in the *normal* course of development according to a generally predictable pattern. This occurs if certain conditions are met, part of which are internal to the human organism. An intact central nervous system is one fundamental condition that provides the neonate an opportunity to develop those functions (Rappaport, 1966, p. 47). Although not a sufficient condition, this genetic endowment is

WILLIAM M. CRUICKSHANK AND JAMES L. PAUL

necessary to normal growth and development and the acquisition of phase-specific competencies.

Rappaport (1964, pp. 40–41) has described the extrauterine epigenesis of the ego.

Because ego development is first of all contingent upon the fetal development of the central nervous system and its extrauterine maturation, any neurological insult which the child experiences must interfere to some extent with his ego development. Only when born with his central nervous system intact does the child have the inborn capacities that develop, through growth, experience, and learning, to become the *primary apparatuses* of the ego. These include such important basic skills as motility, perception, concept formation, and language. Unlike the average child, the brain-damaged child is not born with these intact ego apparatuses which serve as the primary guarantees of the organism's adaptation to its environment.

The control of gross motor discharges in the early phases of cephalocaudal neural maturation is an important source of gratification. This gratification is of primary value in the child's accomplishment of subsequent developmental tasks. The issue here is one of self-mastery, an aspect of his ego development.

With further neural maturation, cortical inhibition takes place, allowing him the opportunity for volitional practice. That, in turn, provides him with greater opportunity for mastery and the resultant gratification of self-esteem. The first few years of life—in which a child learns such sensori-motor skills as to walk, talk, perceive, feed himself, and be toilet trained—provide literally hundreds of daily opportunities for being pleased with himself, for the budding of a positive identity which later will bloom into the conviction of "I am one who can!" (Rappaport, 1966, p. 48).

Rappaport (1964, pp. 49–51) has discussed reaction patterns associated with defective self-concept and narcissistic hypersensitivity in brain-injured children. His outline of these patterns will be used here. The patterns are not mutually exclusive in that discrete behaviors can always be identified as characterizing one pattern and not another. The outline is, however, very useful in providing a basis for discussion of the basic issues involved.

The first reaction pattern is *low frustration tolerance*. This is very much related to the gratification schedule required by the child who must succeed in his acts and whose success must be sufficiently gratifying to him. Delays in response, inadequate response, or negative response regarding his acts are often intolerable. It is his self-value that, to him, is at stake. The distinction between "I like you, but I do not approve of your behavior" frequently used by adults in managing abberrant behavior is very difficult for these children. No child is so devoid of a basic feeling of well-being and personal worth as the child whose books kept on success are almost always unbalanced and whose account is always in the red. The reasonable tolerance for failure or the positive use of the failure experience, so important in the realities of child growth and development, is predicated on assumptions of success histories and reasonable self-confidence. These children often do not fit the assumptions. The good they would, they do not. The essential equipment required for mastery—for example, of gravity, of behavioral expectations, of language, of one's own acts or patterns of movements—has not worked properly for them. This, coupled with our child-rearing practices, which are almost never aligned with the environmental and managerial needs of these children (to be discussed later), make them particularly vulnerable to failure.

These children become hyperaggressive in defense of self. This serves both to obtain some response, albeit usually negative, and also to protect their weaker self from the aggression—such as the negative judgment of their acts—of stronger selves. This aggression is usually physical and becomes increasingly verbal as they acquire nonphysical aggressive capability.

Flight from challenge is the second reaction pattern. The last thing the child with a conviction of negative personal worth wants is social confirmation of unworthiness. He is convinced of low self-value and is equally certain that others will level their demeaning guns at him. He will find ways of avoiding the reality that he experiences as a challenge or threat. What he protects is an ego, short-changed in its primary gratification, and wounds to esteem too deep to risk another loss. The child who has always failed does not expect to succeed and probably cannot be expected to try.

Defending himself against the threat of failure, he may take other roles that remove him from the present demands of performance in his real role. A barrage of verbiage is not uncommon if it keeps him from the task. He may attack others if this will head off expected attack from others and further reduction of personal esteem.

The third reaction pattern listed by Rappaport is *overcompensation*. The child utilizing this defense will invest an inordinate amount of energy to excel in one area. This is often a skill or body of knowledge that has little payoff to the child except to provide him with a sense of pseudocompetence. It is usually something that other children his age typically do not know or cannot do and with which they are not likely to involve themselves sufficiently to become serious competitors. Rappaport describes two children to illus-

trate this pattern. One memorized all the Gilbert and Sullivan operettas and sang them when he was in a situation where he could compete successfully. Another memorized the names and complete records of every major league baseball player.

The fourth aspect is *control and manipulation of others*. These children who do not have sufficient mastery over themselves and are most frequently not able to obtain positive regard for age appropriate performance will often resort to the control of others. A child does battle with guts bared and both hands down when he *must* control those much larger and those much wiser than he. It is frightening for him to win, whereas the prospect of losing feels like devastation. This may be, after all, his sole engagement with the world from his point of view. If he does not withdraw from the world in which he has failed, he must control that world which will declare him unfit.

The fifth aspect listed by Rappaport (1964, p. 51) is *power struggle* or *negativism*. "In this reaction pattern the brain-damaged child attempts to stave off a sensed impending loss of identity by total noncompliance. This pattern is characterized by the child's absence of regard for the wishes, requests, and feelings of others. His own sense of weakness and inadequacy is protected by his contumelious behavior aimed at the vulnerabilities of others. A child who is *against* everything has found too little he can be *for* safely. The reward of success he wants so much is precluded by his inability to risk failure.

To this point the discussion has centered on the child and his immediate and intimate relationships. The cultural issues are not separable from the view of the child already expressed. This is particularly true in terms of Mead's formulation

WILLIAM M. CRUICKSHANK AND JAMES L. PAUL

(1934, pp. 173–78) of the concept of "me," the internalized attitude of the community, in the development of self. It would be a gross omission, however, to discuss these children and their appropriated self-feelings without more specific reference to the broader community. The error in reductionistic formulations is one well practiced in this area, many of the preceding statements in this chapter not withstanding. Only a brief statement will be included here, though much more elaborate treatment is needed.

The community and its institutions have an essentially normative orientation. At certain ages certain things are expected, and the community reacts in terms of the congruence of the behavior and the expected behavior. An individual's need to test his worth or reestablish the trustworthiness of his world (the first task facing an infant during his first year of life) will be responded to as immaturity if he is, for example, sixteen years old. Depending on the extent of the demand on the community, for example, violation of legal codes, the sixteen-year-old will be ignored, rejected or punished, none of which are appropriate to the child's implied need statement. The community tolerance threshold is more or less age specific.

If the child feels too much mistrust, shame, uncertainty, or inferiority too long after he qualified by age to engage with adults to satisfactorily resolve these feelings, he has to deal with them in a special setting—special classes, special schools, clinics, hospitals, or correctional institutions. This is obviously not a conscious rational phenomenon with either the child or the culture that prescribes time bands and places.

The importance of this conceptualization here is that the development of brain-injured children is very uneven. Every child has a biologically and genetically determined ceiling rate of development. Rosenblith and Allinsmith (1962, p. 202) state that "Proper rate and normal sequence is necessary if functional harmony is to be secured." The interaction between his rate potential and his culture determines his actual development.

The brain-injured child has been referred to by Gallagher (1966) as the child with developmental imbalances. He is *not* necessarily retarded in his measured intelligence but may be grossly retarded in one or more certain basic skills, such as perceptual-motor, or in his development of a positive self-concept.

The interaction between the community's expectations, or those of any one of the community's child-socializing agents or agencies, and the child's response to those expectations constitutes the proving ground of mutual accord. The quality of the action of either has proportional consequences in the interaction. It is here that mutuality of regard is established. It is here that the self and personal values are presented and matched for fit with the perceptions, values, and expectations of the community. It is here that leaders are recognized and also where extrusion of certain members is accomplished. Rhodes (1967, p. 451) has described emotional disturbance in children as a crisis in the exchange between culture bearer and culture violator.

Brain-injured children are often alien in a competence-oriented culture and tried and found wanting in their abilities. The nine-year-old child may not, in fact, understand the parent's verbal request to hang up his coat because of other demanding and competing auditory stimulations, such as television, the dishwasher, and baby sister crying—all at once. He does, however, get the affective quality of the exchange that follows—"Are you absolutely stupid? Can't you do anything? You don't do anything you are told!"

This is a small sample of his failure in interactions in which his feelings and self were never really represented. This failure is augmented in the school and the community, where innaccurate or inappropriate responses interacting with his own feelings from a history of failure characterize his role in the engagement with the bearers of culture. The conviction that "I cannot" will over time be confirmed by significant others.

Body-Image

Body-schema, the precursor to body-image, derives from very early sensory experiences (Dubnoff and Chambers, 1966, p. 9). "From the point of view of sensory motor development, the child brings more or less isolated and uncorrelated experiences into a complete form by continual effort" (Schilder, 1950, p. 106).

Body-image development proceeds in terms of certain biologic laws of growth and the "integration of new experiences, physical and psychological, arising from one's self and from relationships and attitudes of others, into a gestalt" (Bender and Silver, 1948, p. 89). Continual modification is required as new adaptive capacities are obtained by the organism as a result of its physical and psychological maturation. As abilities to perceive and integrate stimuli increase, so must prior judgments be modified on the nature of the body, how it works, and how its parts are interrelated in relation to its surrounding space and objects in that space.

Kessler (1966, p. 21), in a discussion of the discovery of physical self, noted that the distinction between self and nonself is first made on the basis of physical differences. The infant usually first notices his hands and experiences touching, being touched, and then seeing these simultaneously. Initially he views his hands as playthings and then moves quickly to viewing them as tools. After a sense of permanence and predictability about them is established, the eyes will lead and direct the hands, for example, in grasping and touching. During the first six months every object is given an oral trial, and later tactile and visual exploration is used. With this growing ability he learns what is self and what is nonself.

The baby does not become equally familiar with all physical boundaries of his body at the same time. He first becomes acquainted with the physical limits, capabilities, and sensations of his upper extremities; he must similarly discover his legs when he crawls and walks.

In the development of a sense of reality, the conception of one's own body plays a very special role. It takes the better part of a year for the baby to form a complete image of his body (Kessler, 1966, pp. 21–22).

A differentiation in the body parts and their comparative relationship is required. This is a complex process which characterizes the neurosensory development of children. An adequate body-image provides the child with a dependable point of reference for his motor responses and the development of perception. It is the essence of a concept of volitional movement, of a basis for purposeful body action in space and of complex goal-directed behavior. An adequate body-image includes the almost infinite set of perceptual-motor linkages in the neurophysiological system of the organism which provides the preconditions for patterns of movement and associations on command.

The reader should here be alerted to the

nature of the statements being utilized to describe a concept of body-image. The empirical basis of the concept is not given. Rather, like the concept of self, the concept of body-image has resisted the operational clarity needed to significantly advance our knowledge in this area. Wylie (1961, p. 272) indicated that "Body image is a term with no clear literary or operational definition." Traub and Orbach (1964, p. 53) have more recently stated:

> Though broadly applied within the context of psychological, psychiatric, and neurological theory, the concept of body-image (body schema, postural model of the body, perceived body, body ego, body boundaries, etc.) has neither been satisfactorily defined nor rigorously measured in the clinic or laboratory. In its most literal sense, body-image refers to "the picture of our own body which we form in our mind, that is to say, the way in which the body appears to ourselves."

The initial thrusts in formulating the concept of body-image were made by neurologists in their attempts to explain certain phenomena associated with cerebral lesions. Poetzl, Critchley, Gerstmann, Bartlett, Head, and others did much of the beginning conceptual and experimental work on the organization and development of body attitudes. Head, a British neurologist, was the first to develop a rather elaborate theory in this regard. Since then considerable work has been done on the concept of body-image, and numerous definitions have been postulated.

Schilder (1950, p. 11) has defined body-image as "the picture of our own body which we form in our mind, that is to say the way in which the body appears to ourselves." Kephart (1960, p. 51) has defined it as "a learned concept resulting from the observation of movements of parts of the body and the relationship of the different parts of the body to each other and to external objects." McAninch (1966, p. 140) conceptualized body-image as a referential point, "a conceptual and operative image which includes an awareness of the body in relation to the physical world or in other words, an image of the body and its boundaries, and an inner view of the self." Horowitz (1966, p. 456) views body-image as:

> ... a specialized, internal analogue data-center for information about the body and its environment. It is in constant transactional relationship with internal and external perceptions, memories, affects, cognition, and actions. It provides economical and specific information concerning the morphology, position, and relationships of the body as well as the structure of the space, objects, and persons that are in some relation to it. This information has been compiled from all sources and is available to all mental mechanisms. Thus, while residues of prior sensations build the body-image, the momentary and immediate nature of the body-image affects the interpretations of current sense data and may even result in the apperceptive distortion of such sense data.

Part of the definitional confusion has to do with the lack of clear delineation of the concept of body-image from the concept of self-concept. Freud (1960, p. 38) states, "The ego is first and foremost a bodily ego; it is not merely a surface entity, but is itself the projection of a surface."

Since then, the clarification of either concept has, for the most part, increased the clarity of the relationship of the two. Wylie (1961, p. 159) observed, "It seems safe to say ... that self-concept theorists agree on the general idea that body characteristics which are lowly valued by S may be expected to undermine his general self-regard, while highly valued body characteristics should enhance self-regard." Prosen (1965, p. 1262) defines body-image as a visual image with attached emotions —emotions concerned with self-esteem, feelings of adequacy, influence on or relations with others. "The body image is determined to a large extent by a person's sense of his own worth."

Zion (1965) investigated certain relationships between self-concept and body-image, using a sample of 200 college freshman women. A significant linear relationship was found between self-description and body description, ideal self and ideal body, and self-description-ideal discrepancy and body description-ideal discrepancy. The self-acceptance and body-acceptance relationship was ambiguous. It was concluded that the security one has in one's body appears related to the security with which one faces one's self and the world (Zion, 1965, p. 494). Although extreme caution should be exercised in generalizing the results of this study to brain-injured children, the conclusion of the study is generally consistent with the view of the very close relationship between concepts of the self and the body.

Fisher and Cleveland (1958, p. 111) considered the body-image a "summary in body terms of a great many experiences the individual has had in the course of defining his identity in the word. . . . The body image is a sensitive indicator which registers many of the individual's basic social relationships, especially those early involved in his development of a sense of identity."

Although much conceptual work remains for researchers who will pursue new knowledge in this area, existing constructs have provided the practitioner with a useful frame of reference for the sequence and pace of developmental tasks of children. A basis has been established for analysis and understanding of behavior. An adequate body-image, for example, is essential to the development of laterality and directionality, which is so important in the development of integrity in body movement and increasingly complex competencies.

Laterality, which Radler and Kephart (1960, p. 33) describe as "the inner sense of one's own symmetry" is usually learned by the child's continual experimentation with movement—comparison of movements on the right side with movements on the left side with undifferentiated movements. Multiple proprioceptive, kinesthetic, tactile, visual, and other stimuli serve to inform the child of the consequences of his acts. Over time the child succeeds in movements of his own determination. This is vastly gratifying. Through this learning process the child begins "to build up an image of his own body, a visual and kinesthetic awareness of how he fills the space within his own skin. This awareness is basic to motor control; . . . fundamental to our perception of the world outside our skins, the left and right or up and down of things" (Radler and Kephart, 1960, p. 9).

The distinction between left and right and the simultaneous and separate control of the two sides is a crucial aspect of development dependent upon an adequately developed body-image. The human body is bilaterally symmetrical, anatomically and neurologically designed to develop right-left orientations (Kephart, 1960, p. 43). If it were not so, it would be very difficult, if not impossible, to sort and keep physical relationships in the world about us straight.

After developing body awareness and learning to control and integrate its parts, the child perceives the world around him —at first by relating all ideas of form to

WILLIAM M. CRUICKSHANK AND JAMES L. PAUL

himself and his own body. "The first 'space world' develops within an arm's reach" (Radler and Kephart, 1960, p. 25).

After laterality is developed, it is then possible to develop concepts of space outside the body. Directionality is the projection of laterality into space (Radler and Kephart, 1960, p. 34). The relationship of an object to the self precedes the development of relationships betwen objects (Radler and Kephart, 1960, p. 39).

Spatial relations and directions in the environment, such as up, down, right, left, and behind, are established with reference to the body. They are not *given* in the physical construction of the environment. The human body must become oriented to the characteristics—space, gravity, form, motion, and so forth—of the world in which that body is to meaningfully and volitionally act. The functional relationship between the two, that is the body and its action space, must be developed and meaningfully conceptualized.

From the development of laterality and the concert of volitional movements, the child can develop balance. He begins to negotiate the innervation of one side against the other, the complex sensorimotor process that eventually involves countless linkages and message transmissions between sensory receptors and the motor neurons. The whole pattern of movement with reference to a specific task is developed through successive approximations of the goal in which self-corrective movements are required. Errors in posture, appendage position, speed, and so forth must be integrated into the movement pattern being executed in walking, for example. As Barsch (1966, p. 184) has pointed out, this is occurring with reference to three ordinates: vertical, horizontal, and depth. A dynamic match between the demands endemic to the task and the capabilities of the organism is required for successful sensorimotor development.

The image of the body that is developed is, then, psychologically salient to the functional integrity of the organism. It has important implications, as has been indicated, for the feelings about self that are developed.

To suggest that the development of body-image and the feelings that derive from a satisfying, normative development of the sensorimotor system are adequately understood by events essentially internal to the organism would be in error. The social aspects of self-concept development already discussed are very much relevant here because, as has been suggested, self-concept and body-image development are not mutually exclusive or discrete entities.

Interesting work has been done on some of the social-psychological implications, for example, of relative body-size perception. Beller and Turner (1964), investigating certain personality correlates of children's perception of human size, found that autonomous achievement striving was significantly correlated with accuracy of the child's estimation of his own and other people's sizes. Their sample included fourteen preschool normal children.

Although not typically discussed in the context of writing on body-image and brain-injured children, work on the social meaning or social stimulus value of the body provides an even broader sociological view. As an image of one's own body is developed, the adopted view gains social definition with reference, for example, to value.

Staffieri (1967), in a study of social stereotype of body-image in normal male children (ages six to ten), found a significant relationship between the adjectives of various behavior/personality traits assigned by children to body types (endomorph, mesomorph, and ectomorph). The adjectives assigned the mesomorph image were favorable, whereas those assigned endomorph and ectomorph images were not. The *S*s in the study clearly preferred to look like the mesomorph image. The older the children, the more accurate the perception of their own body type.

Staffieri (1968) obtained similar findings on the favorable social connotations of mesomorphs based on the adjectives assigned by thirty-three mentally retarded male *S*s (ages fifteen to twenty-five).

Discussion of body-image to this point has centered primarily on the sensorimotor development of all children. A child is born into a world with physical, psychological, social, and cultural demands already established. He brings with him a genetic endowment, a constitutional readiness and potential, and his own growth demands. The interaction between his demands and the demands of the world in which he happens to be born is the story of child growth and development. The characters in the story are in every instance different and the plot is infinitely varied. That variation is accounted for by the nature and extent of the demands in either and the capacity of coping in the other. The biological laws that govern child development and the principles of socialization are so carefully interwoven into the fabric of this interaction that aberrance in either is experienced as such by the other.

The brain-injured child's neural maturation is aberrant, and hence his sensorimotor task negotiation is not always consonant with the normative expectations. The predominance of harmony over disharmony in the interaction for most children may be reversed for these children. Such reversal constitutes failure both in the child and in the socializing system. The absorption of and recovery from experienced failure takes much less toll on the system than on the child.

These children may not establish adequate cerebral dominance or mature at the expected rate (Gubbay *et al.,* 1965). They may not be able to use kinesthetic feedback properly, such as in discriminating between similar and different sensations in various parts of the body, or to accurately classify motor responses to provide feedback necessary for the repetition of an act (McAninch, 1966, p. 153). Because of overall gross or fine motor skill disabilities, these children are often described as clumsy. (See, for example, Haring and Schiefelbusch, 1967, p. 366; Illingworth, 1968; Walton, Ellis, and Court, 1962.) Gerstmann (1924, 1940), Strauss and Werner (1938, 1939), and others have described the phenomena of finger agnosia and deficiencies in finger schema in these children.

Whether the activity is walking, jumping, or negotiating a pencil or a glass of milk, a body that does not work as a unity in response to a demand or goal will often fail. The very complex sensorimotor task involved in catching a ball when age peers are enjoying the game may keep this child on the bench. The concert of movement of eyes, hands, fingers, feet, head, and all other parts of the sensorimotor system in the interest of the organism's goal, the acquiescence of some body parts while other parts do their job—these are essential.

These children become convinced they *cannot* because they have learned their bodies *will not*. When rewards of adult approval, so important in the self-esteem of children, are forthcoming for those who are good at the act, these children often miss out and accept the fact that they *are not* because they *have not.* To be angry and seriously hurt is no uncertain human consequence of such human failure.

TREATMENT

The treatment of brain-injured children has been formulated on several bases. The neurosensory view, which provides the primary frame of reference for child development as discussed in this chapter, has been one important basis for formulating treatment. The psychopathology described here is taken seriously in the formulation of the problems, the goals, and the methods of treatment. The child who has not developed an adequate image of his body, how its various parts work both singly and in concert as a unity, is treated in terms of this deficiency because of its central importance to other learnings. The child who has not developed a basis of self-confidence and esteem sufficient to secure his personal conviction of self-value is treated accordingly. The absence of a success history states the condition of treatment, which must be predicated on the child's succeeding.

For children whose failures have inordinately exceeded their successes, whose normal development of complex sensory-motor integrity has not occurred, whose bodies are "programmed" for error and work in opposition to the child's intent, including the intention to elicit warm parental response, survival becomes the primary and defense the predominant strategy. Trust of and autonomy from others have not been accomplished because the trustability of self has not been established. The adult, be he parent, teacher, therapist, or friend who would enter into the important living or learning space of this child, must know that a positive relationship will not come easily. Most adults, in this child's view, cannot be trusted and depended upon, not necessarily because of adult behavior error but because of constant failure in this child's use of self in social and physical space and in most of his transactions with adults.

The conditions of treatment are established by the primary negative life assumptions already adopted by the child. The ego resources of the adult must be more than adequate for him. His resources will be needed and must be available for use by the child. Rappaport (1966, pp. 50–51) has referred to these children as ego bankrupt and in need of adults to act as ego banks. That the child appreciates or otherwise gratifies the adult cannot be a precondition for the interaction. The child brings only need to the relationship and promises to resist all good intentions of adults.

The adult who would "help" this child or successfully treat him must be psychologically prepared for the job. The child will not lose an ego struggle with the adult —it is too important. The adult must also be carefully prepared technically for the task.

The technical aspects of treatment from the neurosensory point of view have had considerable development in the last decade. The increased understanding and development of these procedures has been accompanied by recognition of the essential alliance with other points of view. The utility of ego psychological constructs, for example, is well established. The application of principles of learning and conditioning paradigms in treatment has also gained substantial acceptance. A senior researcher with responsibilities for dispensing monies for behavioral research in one of the federal offices recently commented that no more money could be obtained to determine if behavior-modification principles work.

A broader social view of discordant child behavior currently being developed particularly with reference to emotionally disturbed children—the ecological view—also has specific implications in understanding these children. This view suggests that behavior disorders in children must be viewed as problems in interaction with reference to cultural rules. The cultural rites and rules are protected, the cultural standard must be kept. It is the breach of these rites and rules or standards that constitutes the basis of discord and generates concern. Professionals are utilized in the reduction of tension between the standard bearer—parents, teachers, neighbors, peers, and so forth— and discordancy represented by the child. As indicated earlier, the problem of emotional disturbance as conceptualized by Rhodes (1967) is a crisis in the interaction between culture bearer and culture violator.

The utility of this view is to avoid the dilemma of assigning responsibility entirely inside the organism such as is suggested by a vigorous application of the medical disease or sickness model. Szasz (1961), Trippe (1963, 1966), Albee (1969), Lewis (1965), Hobbs (1966), and others have clearly described the hazards of exclusive applications of medical constructs, including total assignment of responsibility for behavior to the brain as is implied in the label used in the title of this chapter. To view the child, rather, as a dynamic organism within dynamic systems with socializing responsibility is to suggest that abberrance in the child can also be accounted for by failures in the socializing systems. To take this stance is to become involved in a broader definition and analysis of problems and intervention on a broader basis. The questions now must include the nature of influences external to the child and responsibility for including the modification of those influences when indicated as goals in a total treatment or intervention plan.

These points of view are not mutually exclusive but provide important bases for understanding the multiple aspects of the problem any treatment would attack. There are real differences in these views, and a smorgasbord approach justified by a banner of eclecticism based on a clear understanding of neither point of view will not work. The professional must have a solid technical base from which to work and must know what deviations from his orientation mean. Equally important is the rejection of a religious commitment to his professional technical beliefs to the exclusion of other points of view. The therapy or treatment that *must* work and is viewed as adequate to all tasks for all children is simply unreasonable. A type of treatment that would be adequate for all children does not exist, and if a single method should be forced on all children, it would be unfortunate for many of them.

Obviously the many treatment procedures and implications of these multiple points of view cannot be described here. Some of the specific work related to the treatment of body-image and self-concept as described in this chapter will be included.

Kephart (1960, pp. 53, 129–139) has suggested specific sensory-motor training activities to guide the child toward an awareness of his body in space and what it can do. He suggests five techniques for helping the child gain knowledge and control of his body parts which have implications for laterality, directionality, control, and rhythm, as well as body-image. These are: (1) the identification of body parts on the basis of verbal cues, (2) the imitation of movement based on visual cues accompanied by knowledge of these parts and their position, (3) the display of knowledge of body parts in reference to outside objects and amount of space occupied by the body or its parts by the use of an obstacle course, (4) the development of

WILLIAM M. CRUICKSHANK AND JAMES L. PAUL

knowledge of parts and position in various combinations of movements and ability to control upper and lower extremities in all combinations by use of the angels-in-the-snow exercise, and (5) the use of stepping stones to demonstrate control of parts on the basis of interpretation of outside stimuli.

Kephart (1960, pp. 222–230) also suggests use of the balance board in combination with movements and identification of body parts to help create a more adequate body-image. Postural flexibility is required. Laterality, involved in maintaining balance, is approached specifically when the child is required to walk on the board sideways. Kephart points out that the correction of balance, not the simple maintenance of it, is the important activity. The trampoline is particularly useful in developing coordination and muscular control. It requires balance and right-left and fore-aft directions. Kephart (1960, pp. 233–235) goes on to describe games and stunts such as the duck walk, rabbit hop, crab walk, measuring worm, and elephant walk, which involve movement in space with patterns different from the usual walking and running. As different relative positions and functions of body parts are assumed, the altered body position helps the child with location and function of various limbs, and the body-image is strengthened.

All motor training exercises must be purposeful and have specific goals. Once a skill is accomplished, it must then be generalized. The specific task performance is secondary to the generalization. As McAninch (1966, p. 165) has pointed out, the learning experiences are selected and organized so that transfer is insured. The child must ultimately develop "a generalized response rather than a limited skill for a specific task."

The child must be moved quickly beyond easily negotiable tasks to avoid boredom. Again, this movement must be purposeful and sequential.

Chalkboard training (Kephart, 1960, pp. 161–215) is also important in helping the child learn on the chalkboard certain patterns of movement and then gradually transfer the learning to smaller and smaller paper which requires finer and more precise patterns of movement. Gross patterns of movement and the existence of up, down, right, and left directions on a large vertical scale are involved. The child changes gradually to large sheets of newsprint, to regular tablet paper, and then to regular 8½ by 11 inch sheets lying flat on a desk. Movement patterns must then be transferred to the smaller sheets and his orientation to a vertical direction transferred to conventional directions. Directionality and ability in crossing the midline, as Kephart points out, are aided by this training.

Finger painting, with the freedom of movement, is also useful. Technique, not product, is important.

Kephart (1960) also describes ocular-motor training and training in form perception.

Barsch (1965, p. 5) developed a curriculum based on movigenics, "the study of the origin and development of movement patterns leading to learning efficiency." The goal of the curriculum was to "achieve a state of physiologic readiness in the learner to bring the children to a level of total organization which would enable them to profit from the existing curriculum." Barsch's movigenic curriculum was therefore developed as a supplement to existing public school curriculum. It is still undergoing revision and modification, but the reader is referred to the curriculum itself and Barsch's state-

The Psychological Characteristics of Brain-Injured Children   **403**

ment (1965, pp. 5–6) of the rationale and movigenic constructs.

The Doman-Delacato treatment of neurologically handicapped children has received wide publicity. The program of the Institute for the Achievement of Human Potential was described in *The Journal of the American Medical Association,* September 17, 1960. Based on neurological organization, the program emphasizes the injured brain levels rather than the resulting peripheral symptoms, operating on

> ... the premise that certain brain levels ... have separate, consecutive responsibilities in terms of mobility. The goal ... is to create a climate in which a brain-injured child may develop and utilize those brain levels which are uninjured as they are developed in the normal child (Doman *et al.,* 1960, p. 261).

The procedures which, the authors state, must be carried out wholistically include (1) providing opportunities for the brain-injured child to spend prolonged periods of time on the floor to promote unaided development, (2) externally imposing patterns of activity on the child, reproducing mobility functions for which the injured brain levels are responsible, (3) sensory stimulation to make the child body conscious in terms of position and proprioception, (4) establishment of laterality and hemispheric dominance, and (5) a breathing program to improve vital capacity. Progress is measured by a developmental mobility scale (designed by the authors) of thirteens levels involving various stages of crawling, creeping, and walking.

There has been some research done which failed to confirm the validity and practicality of this theory of neurological organization (Robbins, 1966). The seriousness of the questions, however, was more directly underlined by a statement made by the Joint Executive Board of the American Academy of Pediatrics and the American Academy of Neurology (1967). The following is an excerpt from that statement.

Studies Not Available

To our knowledge, no controlled studies are available to support the greater value claimed for the program as compared with conventional treatment of the neurologically handicapped child. Without such studies, a medically acceptable evaluation is not thought possible.

However, because of the demanding nature of the program and its seemingly unreserved promise of benefit, it is important that some preliminary opinion be passed which may be of assistance to our members pending a more definitive and accurate appraisal, now long overdue. In our judgment, there are several factors to be noted:

First, varying degrees of progress are made in the handicapped from maturation. In addition, individual attention and care, and physiotherapy techniques offer some benefits (though quite limited in many cases). Some of the improvements noted in Doman-Delacato treated cases may accrue from these factors.

Second, physicians should be aware of the sacrifices which a family must make in order to participate in this program. Success or failure largely devolves on parents to follow a regimen which, if taken literally, is extremely demanding. Failure, therefore, may implicate parents in the ultimate outcome. The demands on the family to sacrifice untold time and energy and to create obligations on volunteer assistants, not to mention cost and transportation burdens, are factors to be weighed particularly when the point is made that "nothing to date has helped and if it can do no harm, let's give it a try."

Evaluation Needed

Third, more than five years have passed since the publication of the preliminary results of the studies of the program. Granted, the necessary controlled studies are fraught with great diffi-

WILLIAM M. CRUICKSHANK AND JAMES L. PAUL

culty. Matching cases at the outset of treatment is open to considerable error. Controlling variables likely to affect the outcome in some way is extremely difficult. Recording data uniformly and judging outcome as it pertains to the host of phenomena involved, presents a challenge to the serious investigator. But whatever the reason, the absence of an acceptable evaluation of the program after such a period of time is a disservice to the program if, in fact, it is responsible for the successes claimed for it.

Fourth, individual members report they have been informed of cases in which the Doman-Delacato program appears not to have helped the patient.

The Executive Boards of the American Academy of Pediatrics and the American Academy of Neurology, acting jointly, feel, therefore, that physicians should make their decisions and recommendations for management of the neurologically handicapped child on the basis that there is as yet no firm evidence substantiating the claims made for the Doman-Delacato methods and program. What is needed are well controlled studies by recognized experts.

Getman (1966, pp. 165–167) has developed specific visuomotor training procedures. These involve training in eye-movement patterns, eye-teaming skills, eye-hand coordination, and visual-form perception. Procedures may include pursuit eye-movements for localization and identification of moving targets or developing awareness of distance, size, and color through side-to-side or near-far-near eye movements; use of eyes to steer and monitor movements while executing various tasks of balance (for example, jump rope, hopscotch, balance board); practice in eye-hand coordination where the eyes guide the hands, such as chalkboard routines of drawing geometric forms; and gross movement activities, such as walking on geometric forms painted on the floor, and reproduction of forms through tracing and use of templates.

Frostig and Horne (1964) and others have developed diagnostic and remedial materials and procedures for use with children who have visual perceptual problems. The program is intended to be both corrective and preventive but places primary emphasis on early diagnosis and remediation of difficulties in visual perception. The Marianne Frostig Development Test of Visual Perception and work sheets designed for the program focus on diagnosis of the five visual perceptual abilities most relevant to academic development: perception of position in space, perception of spatial relationships, perceptual constancy, visual-motor coordination, and figure-ground perception. The work sheets include exercises in printing, writing, and drawing skills; working with letters, numbers, and other symbols in proper sequence; recognition of geometric forms regardless of color, size, brightness, or position; directionality; and pattern matching with beads, marbles, pegs, or geometric blocks. The pencil and paper exercises must be supplemented with specified training in eye movement, gross motor coordination, fine motor coordination, and development of balance and accurate perception of body-image, body-concept, and body-schema. Exercises in these areas, such as cutting, sorting, playground activities, and drawing of human figures, are outlined. "Such a program provides training for every muscle group, and involves the coordination of vision with musculature" (Frostig and Horne, 1964, p. 17).

Video tapes and motion pictures have been used in the development of more appropriate self-image and self-concept. Geertsma (1965) reported a case study of an emotionally disturbed girl and the effects of video tapes used in seven weekly sessions. The video tapes provided a strong stimulus and reportedly aided in the more realistic rating of herself.

Cornelison (1966) has described preliminary experiments with the Self-Image Experience (SIE) technique. This involves making color motion pictures with sound of a patient and showing them to him. Considerable behavior changes have been reported following the use of this technique with alcoholics and mentally ill patients.

Boyd and Sisney (1967) observed changes in self-concept and concepts of interpersonal behavior of inpatients on a psychiatric ward as measured by Leary's Interpersonal Check List following self-image confrontation via video tape. The authors used a control group that was not given the self-image confrontation for comparison. Interpersonal concepts of the self, the ideal self, and the public self reportedly became less pathological and less discrepant with one another following the self-image confrontation. Differences between experimental and control groups remained significant two weeks later, with one exception.

Various tactile-kinesthetic procedures such as the Fernald method (1943) have been developed to aid in teaching academic subject areas. The sensorimotor and perceptual training methods suggested by the Montessori method (1965) have also been used rather extensively and have been found to be of considerable value.

The specific work with the self-esteem problems of these children cannot be separated from the work on body-image problems. This idea follows logically from the rationale statements on the development of body-image and self-concept in children.

The child who has failed so much in his primary developmental tasks and has accepted so completely the negative self-constructs must be guided in a carefully designed program oriented toward success. The self-assumption must be changed by his acceptance of positive self-experience data. That he *can* is a view available only as he feels and sees that he *has*. The experience of competence must be real and must be attached directly to areas of previously experienced incompetence.

The child has literally thousands of experiences each day in which he succeeds or fails. The physical activities in which he engages, such as eating, running, walking, climbing, throwing, catching, kicking, riding, and countless others, are purposeful for him and provide satisfaction if done well. Listening, observing, feeling, tasting, smelling, and understanding also have important psychological value. Social relationships with other children and adults and the very basic familial relationships are sources of important gain or profound loss.

The day is a constant imposition of challenge, a moment by moment impingement of physical and social stimulation that must be responded to and managed only to find the threat or opportunity of the next moment. The child described in this chapter who has low self-esteem is failing in his real-life experiences. The moment by moment process for him has been more characterized by the unmanageable, the overwhelming, the vague, and, ultimately, the damaging than the understandable, the negotiable, and the rewarding. A well-developed ego with the resources for meaningful engagement in social, intellectual, and physical activities does not derive from continual failure and negative reinforcement of worth.

Treatment for these children, then, must accommodate the scope of their failure. A single professional service will usually not be adequate. Rappaport (1964, p. 43) stated:

WILLIAM M. CRUICKSHANK AND JAMES L. PAUL

As a child learns to face his handicaps, by means of the special educational program, parental counselling, and individual psychotherapy, the catastrophic anxiety and the non-adaptive behavioral reactions begin to diminish. It is only then that the child can begin to assess his assets and to instrument them for realistic accomplishment and gratification. This, of course, is the best antidote for his defective self-concept, and it paves the way for belatedly achieving his rightful ego autonomy.

It is not suggested here that all of these services are always essential for all of these children. It should be clear, however, that the therapeutic interventions must go well beyond a singular focus on "adjusting" the child. The life forces and the stimulus impingements must be modified so that he has a realistic opportunity for succeeding. A one-hour-per-week therapy session, for example, that is not part of a broader effort to do something with the successes and failures of the child during the other 167 hours of the week, will rarely be adequate.

Cruickshank (1967, pp. 235–238) and others have pointed out that psychotherapy can help the child restructure his life relationships and help him reach a level of personality integration and learning acceptable to society. Cruickshank also indicated the desirability of a more structured therapeutic intervention, such as is provided by a structured milieu, over a nondirective therapy. The suggestion for structured therapeutic intervention is based on the stimulus-adjustment characteristics of these children, their inability to make decisions, and the relationship as well as physical structure required for their treatment.

Someone has commented that winning may not be everything but losing is nothing. Winning, in the sense of succeeding, feels like everything to these children because so much is at stake. To engage in a treatment and management program for one of these children, one must take this concept seriously. This child will not be gratified by *your* efforts. The goal is that he eventually be gratified by *his*.

References

Albee, G. W. Emerging concepts of mental illness and models of treatment: The psychological point of view. *American Journal of Psychiatry,* 1969, *125,* 42–48.

American Academy of Pediatrics and American Academy of Neurology. Doman-Delacato treatment of neurologically handicapped children. *Neurology,* 1967, *17,* 637.

Ausubel, D. P. *et al.* Perceived parent attitudes as determinants of children's ego structure. *Child Development,* 1954, *25,* 173–183.

Barber, T. X., & Silver, M. J. Fact, fiction, and the experimenter bias effect. *Psychological Bulletin,* 1968, *70* (6), 1–29. (*a*)

————. Pitfalls in data analysis and interpretation: A reply to Rosenthal. *Psychological Bulletin,* 1968, *70* (6), 48–62. (*b*)

Barsch, R. H. *A movigenic curriculum.* Bulletin No. 25. Madison: State Department of Public Instruction, 1965.

————. Teacher needs—motor training. In W. M. Cruickshank (Ed.), *The teacher of brain-injured children: A discussion of the bases for competency.* Syracuse, N. Y.: Syracuse University Press, 1966, pp. 181–195.

Bateman, B. Learning disabilities—yesterday, today and tomorrow. *Exceptional Children,* 1964, *31,* 167–178.

————. Three approaches to diagnosis and educational planning for children with learning disabilities. *Proceedings: 1967 International Convocation on Children and Young Adults with Learning Disabilities.* Pittsburgh: Home for Crippled Children, 1967, 120–130.

Beller, E. K., & Turner, J. L. Personality correlates of children's perception of human size. *Child Development,* 1964, *35,* 441–449.

Belmont, I., Birch, H. G., & Karp, E. The disordering of intersensory and intrasensory integration by brain damage. *The Journal of Nervous and Mental Disease,* 1965, *141,* 410–418.

Bender, L. *Psychopathology of children with organic brain disorders.* Springfield, Ill.: Charles C. Thomas, Publisher, 1956.

———, & Silver, A. Body image problems of the brain-damaged child. *Journal of Social Issues,* 1948, *4,* 84–89.

Bennett, S. W., & Poit, C. H. The perception of autokinetic movement by brain-injured and familial retardates. *American Journal of Mental Deficiency,* 1963, *68,* 413–416.

Bensberg, G. J. A test for differentiation of endogenous and exogenous mental defectives. *American Journal of Mental Deficiency,* 1950, *54,* 502–506.

———. Performance of brain-injured and familial mental defectives on the Bender Gestalt Test. *Journal of Consulting Psychology,* 1952, *16,* 61–64.

Birch, H. G. Comparative psychology. In F. L. Marcuse (Ed.), *Areas of psychology.* Harper & Row, Publishers, New York: 1954.

——— (Ed.). *Brain damage in children: The biological and social aspects.* Baltimore: The Williams & Wilkins Co. Association for the Aid of Crippled Children, 1964.

———, Belmont, I., & Karp, E. The prolongation of inhibition in brain-damaged patients. *Cortex,* 1965, *1,* 397–409.

Birch, H. G., & Lefford, A. Visual differentiation, intersensory integration, and voluntary motor control. *Monographs of the Society for Research in Child Development,* 1967, 32.

Boyd, H. S., & Sisney, V. V. Immediate self-image confrontation and changes in self concept. *Journal of Consulting Psychology,* 1967, *31,* 291–294.

Burks, H. F. The hyperkinetic child. *Exceptional Children,* 1960, *27,* 18–26.

Cassel, R. H. Relation of design reproduction to the etiology of mental deficiency. *Journal of Consulting Psychology,* 1949, *13,* 421–428.

Clements, S. D. *Minimal brain dysfunction in children: Terminology and identification, phase one of a three-phase project.* U. S. Department of Health, Education, and Welfare. NINDB monograph No. 3. Washington, D. C.: Government Printing Office, 1966.

Colman, P. G., & Com, B. A comparative study of the test performances of brain-injured, emotionally disturbed and normal children. *South African Medical Journal,* 1966, *40,* 945–950.

Coopersmith, S. Studies in self-esteem. *Scientific American,* 1968, *218,* 96–106.

Cornelison, F. S., Jr. Learning about behavior. A new technique: Self-image experience. *Mental Hygiene,* 1966, *50,* 584–587.

Cruickshank, W. M. *The brain-injured child in home, school, and community.* Syracuse, N.Y.: Syracuse University Press, 1967. (*a*)

———. The education of the child with brain injury. In W. M. Cruickshank and G. O. Johnson (Eds.), *Education of exceptional children and youth.* (2nd ed.). Englewood Cliffs, N.J.: Prentice-Hall, Inc., 1967, pp. 238–283.

——— (Ed.). *The teacher of brain-injured children: A discussion of the bases for competency.* Syracuse, N.Y.: Syracuse University Press, 1966.

Cruickshank, W. M., Bice, H. V., & Wallen, N. E. *Perception and cerebral palsy.* Syracuse, N.Y.: Syracuse University Press, 1957.

——— et al. *Perception and cerebral palsy* (2nd ed.). Syracuse, N.Y.: Syracuse University Press, 1965, pp. 1–172.

———et al. *A teaching method for brain-injured and hyperactive children.* Syracuse, N.Y.: Syracuse University Press, 1966.

Cruse, D. B. Effects of distraction upon the performance of brain-injured and familial retarded children. *American Journal of Mental Deficiency,* 1961, *66,* 86–92.

Davidson, H. H., & Lang, G. Children's perceptions of their teacher's feelings toward them related to self-perception, school achievement and behavior. *Journal of Experimental Education,* 1960, *29,* 107–118.

Day, R. H. The aftereffect of seen movement and brain damage. *Journal of Consulting Psychology,* 1960, *24,* 311–315.

Decker, R. J. Manifestations of the brain damage syndrome in historical and psychological data. In S. R. Rappaport (Ed.), *Childhood aphasia and brain damage: A definition.* Narbreth, Pa.: Livingston Publishing Company, 1964.

Dolphin, J. E., & Cruickshank, W. M. The figure-background relationships in children with cerebral palsy. *Journal of Clinical Psychology,* 1951 *7,* 228–231. (*a*)

WILLIAM M. CRUICKSHANK AND JAMES L. PAUL

————. Pathology of concept formation in children with cerebral palsy. *American Journal of Mental Deficiency,* 1951, *56,* 386–392. (*b*)

————. Tactual motor perception of children with cerebral palsy. *Journal of Personality,* 1952, *20,* 466–471.

Doman, R. J. *et al.* Children with severe brain injuries: Neurological organization in terms of mobility. *The Journal of the American Medical Association,* 1960, *174,* 257–262.

Dubnoff, B., & Chambers, I. A multifocal approach to the development of the concept of body image. In Council for Children with Behavioral Disorders (Ed.), *Yearbook 1966.* Washington, D. C.: Council for Children with Behavioral Disorders, 1966.

Efstathiou, A., & Morant, R. B. Persistence of the waterfall illusion aftereffect as a test of brain damage. *Journal of Abnormal Psychology,* 1966, *71,* 300–303.

Eisenberg, L. Behavioral manifestations of cerebral damage in childhood. In H. G. Birch (Ed.), *Brain damage in children.* Baltimore: The Williams & Wilkins Co., 1964, pp. 61–73.

Erikson, E. H. Youth and the life cycle. *Children,* 1960, *7,* 43–49.

Ernhart, C. B. *et al.* Brain injury in the preschool child: Some developmental considerations, II: Comparison of brain-injured and normal children. *Psychological Monographs,* 1963, *77,* 17–33.

Farnham-Diggory, S. Self, future, and time. *Monographs of the Society for Research in Child Development,* 1966, *31.*

Fennimore, F. Reading and the self-concept. *Journal of Reading,* 1968, *11,* 447–451.

Fernald, G. M. *Remedial techniques in basic school subjects.* New York: McGraw-Hill Book Company, 1943.

Fisher, S., & Cleveland, S. E. *Body image and personality.* Princeton, N. J.: D. Van Nostrand Company, Inc., 1958.

Fisichelli, V. R., & Karelitz, S. The cry latencies of normal infants and those with brain damage. *Journal of Pediatrics,* 1963, *62,* 724–734.

———— *et al.* The phonetic content of the cries of normal infants and those with brain damage. *The Journal of Psychology,* 1966, *64,* 119–126.

Francis-Williams, J. Special educational problems of children with minimal cerebral dysfunction. *Spastics Quarterly,* 1965, *14,* 71.

Freud. S. *The ego and the id.* trans. by J. Strachley (Ed.), New York: W. W. Norton & Company, Inc., 1960.

Frostig, M. Visual perception in the brain-damaged child. *American Journal of Orthopsychiatry,* 1962, *32,* 279–280.

————, & Horne, D. *The Frostig Program for the Development of Visual Perception, Teacher's Guide.* Chicago: Follett Publishing Company, 1964.

Frostig, M., Lefever, D. W., & Whittlesey, J. R. B. A developmental test of visual perception for evaluating normal and neurologically handicapped children. *Perceptual and Motor Skills,* 1961, *12,* 383–394.

Gallagher, J. J. Children with developmental imbalances: A psychoeducational definition. In W. M. Cruickshank (Ed.), *The teacher of brain-injured children.* Syracuse, N. Y.: Syracuse University Press, 1966, pp. 21–43.

————. A comparison of brain-injured and non brain-injured mentally retarded children on several psychological variables. *Monographs of the Society for Research in Child Development,* 1957, *22,* 51.

Garfield, J. C., Benton, A. L., & MacQueen, J. C. Motor impersistence in brain-damaged and cultural-familial defectives. *The Journal of Nervous and Mental Disease,* 1966, *142,* 434–440.

Garner, F. E., Neuringer, C., & Goldstein, G. The spiral aftereffect, extraneous stimulation and brain damage. *Cortex,* 1966, *2,* 385–397.

Geertsma, R. H., & Reivich, R. S. Repetitive self-observation by videotape playback. *Journal of Nervous and Mental Disease,* 1965, *141,* 29–41.

Gerstmann, J. Fingeragnosie: eine umschriebene stoerung der orientierung am eigenen koerper. *Wiener Klinische Wochenschrift,* 1924, *37,* 1010–1012.

————. Syndrome of finger agnosia, disorientation for right and left, agraphia and acalculia: Local diagnostic value. *American Medical Association Archives of Neurology and Psychiatry,* 1940, *44,* 398–408.

Getman, G. N., & Hendrickson, H. H. The needs of teachers for specialized information on the development of visuo-motor skills in relation to academic performance. In W. M. Cruickshank (Ed.), *The teacher of brain-injured children.* Syracuse, N. Y.:

Syracuse University Press, 1966, pp. 153–168.

Goldstein, K. *The Organism.* New York: American Book Company, 1939.

Goodlad, J. I. Understanding the self in the school setting. *Childhood Education,* 1964, *41,* 9–14.

Gubbay *et al.* Clumsy children: A study of apraxic and agnosic defects in 21 children. *Brain,* 1965, *88,* 295–312.

Haggard, E. A., & Rose, G. J. Some effects of mental set and active participation in the conditioning of the autokinetic phenomenon. *Journal of Experimental Psychology,* 1944, *34,* 45–59.

Hanvik, L. J. And the beanstalk grows. *Exceptional Children,* 1966, *32,* 577–578.

Haring, N. G., & Schiefelbusch, R. L. (Eds.). *Methods in special education.* New York: McGraw-Hill Book Company, 1967.

Hawk, T. L. Self concepts of the socially disadvantaged. *The Elementary School Journal,* 1967, *67,* 196–206. Permission to quote granted by the University of Chicago Press.

Hewett, F. M. *The emotionally disturbed child in the classroom.* Boston: Allyn & Bacon, Inc., 1968.

Hirt, J. B. Manifestations of the brain damage syndrome in school. In S. Rappaport (Ed.), *Childhood aphasia and brain damage: A definition.* Nabreth, Pa.: Livingston Publishing Company, 1964.

Hobbs, N. Helping disturbed children: Psychological and ecological strategies. *American Psychologist,* 1966, *21,* 1105–1115.

Homberger, A. *Vorlesungen über psychopathologie des kindersaleters.* Berlin: Julius Springer, 1926, pp. 1–318.

Horowitz, M. J. Body image. *Archives of General Psychiatry,* 1966, *14,* 456–460.

Hunt, B. J. Performance of mentally deficient brain-injured children and mentally deficient familial children on construction from pattern. *American Journal of Mental Deficiency,* 1959, *63,* 679–687.

Hunt, B. J., & Patterson, R. M. Performance of brain-injured and familial mentally deficient children on visual and auditory sequences. *American Journal of Mental Deficiency.* 1958, *63,* 72–80.

Illingworth, R. S. The clumsy child. *Clinical Pediatrics,* 1968, *7,* 539–543.

Jacobs, J. F., & Pierce, M. L. The social position of retardates with brain damage associated characteristics. *Exceptional Children,* 1968, *34,* 677–681.

Jenkin, N., & Morse, S. A. Size-distance judgment in organic mental defectives. *Journal of Consulting Psychology,* 1960, *24,* 139–143.

Kaliski, L. The brain-injured child—learning by living in a structured setting. *American Journal of Mental Deficiency,* 1959, *63,* 688–695.

Karelitz, S., & Fisichelli, V. R. The cry thresholds of normal infants and those with brain damage. *Journal of Pediatrics,* 1962, *61,* 679–685.

Karelitz, S., Karelitz, R., & Rosenfeld, L. S. Infants' vocalizations and their significance. In P. W. Bowman and H. V. Mautner (Eds.), *Mental retardation: Proceedings of the first international medical conference.* New York: Grune and Stratton, Inc., 1960, pp. 439–446.

Kephart, N. C. *The slow learner in the classroom.* Columbus: Charles E. Merrill Books, Inc., 1960.

Kessler, J. W. *Psychopathology of childhood.* Englewood Cliffs, N. J.: Prentice-Hall, Inc., 1966.

Koppitz, E. M. Diagnosing brain damage in young children with the Bender Gestalt Test. *Journal of Consulting Psychology,* 1962, *26,* 541–546.

Levine, M., & Spivack, G. Adaptation to repeated exposure to the Spiral Visual Aftereffect in brain-damaged, emotionally disturbed, and normal individuals. *Perceptual and Motor Skills,* 1962, *14,* 425–426.

Lewis, W. W. Continuity and intervention in emotional disturbance: A review. *Exceptional Children,* 1965, *31,* 465–475.

Luria, A. R. *Higher cortical functions in man.* New York: Basic Books, Inc., Publishers, 1966.

Mackie, J. B., & Beck, E. C. Relations among rigidity, intelligence, and perception in brain-damaged and normal individuals. *The Journal of Nervous and Mental Disease,* 1966, *142,* 310–317.

Maier, N. R. F., & Schneirla, T. C. *Principles of animal psychology.* New York: McGraw-Hill Book Company, 1935.

Mark, H. J., & Pasamanick, B. Asynchronism and apparent movement thresholds in brain-injured children. *Journal of Consulting Psychology,* 1958, *22,* 173–177.

McAninch, M. Body image as related to perceptual-cognitive-motor disabilities. In J. Hellmuth (Ed.), *Learning disorders.* Vol. 2. Seattle: Special Child Publications of the Seattle Seguin School, Inc., 1966, pp. 137–170. Quotations by permission of Special Child Publications, Inc., Seattle, Washington.

McCartney, L. D. Helping mentally deficient children of the exogenous type showing central nervous system impairment to make better social adjustments. *American Journal of Mental Deficiency,* 1956, *61,* 121–126.

McGinnis, M. A. *Aphasic children: Identification and education by the association method.* Washington, D. C.: Volta Bureau, 1963.

Mead, G. H. *Mind, self and society: From the standpoint of a social behaviorist.* C. W. Morris (Ed.), Chicago: University of Chicago Press, 1934.

Menkes, M. N., Rowe, J. S., & Menkes, J. H. A twenty-five year follow-up study on the hyperkinetic child with minimal brain dysfunction. *Pediatrics,* 1967, *39,* 393–399.

Montessori, M. *Dr. Montessori's own handbook.* New York: Schocken Books, 1965.

Nellhaus, G. What name for "these" children? *Developmental Medicine and Child Neurology,* 1968, *10,* 536–537.

Paine, R. S. Neurological grand rounds: Minimal chronic brain syndromes. *Clinical Proceedings of the Children's Hospital.* Washington, D. C.: 1966, *22,* 21–40.

Piaget, J., & Lambercier, M. La comparison des grandeurs projectives chez l'enfant et chez l'adulte. *Archives of Psychology,* 1951, *33,* 81–130.

Pincus, J. H., & Glaser, G. H. The syndrome of "minimal brain damage" in childhood. *The New England Journal of Medicine,* 1966, *275,* 27–35.

Prosen, H. Physical disability and motivation. *Canadian Medical Association Journal,* 1965, *92,* 1261–1265.

Radler, D. H., & Kephart, N. C. *Success through play.* New York: Harper & Row, Publishers, 1960.

Rappaport, S. R. (Ed.). *Childhood aphasia and brain damage: A definition.* Narbreth, Pa.: Livingston Publishing Company, 1964.

———. Diagnosis, treatment, and prognosis. In S. R. Rappaport (Ed.), *Childhood aphasia and brain damage: Volume II, Differential diagnosis.* Narbreth, Pa.: Livingston Publishing Company, 1965.

———. Personality factors teachers need for relationship structure. In W. M. Cruickshank (Ed.), *The teacher of brain-injured children.* Syracuse, N. Y.: Syracuse University Press, 1966, pp. 45–55.

Reed, H. B. C., Jr., Reitan, R. M., & Klove, H. Influence of cerebral lesions on psychological test performances of older children. *Journal of Consulting Psychology,* 1965, *29,* 247–251.

Reed, J. C. & Reed, H. C., Jr. Concept formation ability and non-verbal abstract thinking among older children with chronic cerebral dysfunction. *The Journal of Special Education,* 1967, *1,* 157–161.

Reitan, R. M. The comparative effects of brain damage of the Halstead impairment index and the Wechsler Bellevue scale. *Journal of Clinical Psychology,* 1959, *15,* 281–285.

Rhodes, W. C. Preface. In J. Hellmuth (Ed.), *Educational therapy.* Vol. 1. Seattle: Special Child Publications of the Seattle Seguin School, Inc., 1966, pp. 16–26.

———. The disturbing child: A problem of ecological management. *Exceptional Children,* 1967, *33,* 449–455.

Robbins, M. P. A study of the validity of Delacato's theory of neurological organization. *Exceptional Children,* 1966, *32,* 517–523.

Roethlisberger, F. J., & Dickson, W. J. *Management and the worker.* Cambridge, Mass.: Harvard University Press, 1939.

Rogers, C. R. *Client-centered therapy.* Boston: Houghton Mifflin Company, 1951.

Rosenblith, J. F., & Allinsmith, W. (Eds.). *The causes of behavior: Readings in child development and educational psychology.* Boston: Allyn & Bacon, Inc., 1962.

Rosenthal, R., & Jaconson, L. *Pygmalion in the classroom, teacher expectation and pupils' intellectual development.* New York: Holt, Rinehart & Winston, Inc., 1968.

Rosvold, H. E. *et al.* A continuous performance test of brain damage. *Journal of Consulting Psychology,* 1956, 20.

Rowley, V., & Baer, P. Visual retention test performance in emotionally disturbed and brain-damaged children. *American Journal of Orthopsychiatry,* 1963, *31,* 579–583.

Sabatino, D. A. The construction and assessment of an experimental test of auditory perception. *Exceptional Children,* 1969, *35,* 729–737.

Schein, J. D. The duration of the Archimedes Spiral Afterimage in the diagnosis of brain damage. *Journal of Consulting Psychology,* 1960, *24,* 299–300.

Schilder, P. *The image and appearance of the human body.* New York: John Wiley & Sons, Inc., 1950.

Schlanger, B. B. Results of varying presentations to brain-damaged children of an auditory word discrimination test. *American Journal of Mental Deficiency,* 1958, *63,* 464–468.

Schulman, J. L., Kaspar, J. C., & Throne, F. M. *Brain damage and behavior—A clinical experimental study.* Springfield, Ill.: Charles C. Thomas, Publisher, 1965.

Sears, P. S., & Sherman, V. *In pursuit of self esteem: Case studies of eight elementary school children.* Belmont, Cal.: Wadsworth Publishing Company, Inc., 1964.

Shapiro, M. B. Experimental studies of a perceptual anomaly: I. Initial experiments. *Journal of Mental Science,* 1951, *97,* 90–110.

Sherrington, D. S. *Man on his nature.* Cambridge, England: Cambridge University Press, 1951.

Sievers, D. J. A study to compare the performance of brain-injured and non-brain-injured mentally retarded children on the Differential Language Facility Test. *American Journal of Mental Deficiency,* 1959, *63,* 839–847.

Snow, R. E. Unfinished Pygmalion. *Contemporary Psychology,* 1969, *14,* 197–199.

Staffieri, J. R. Body image stereotypes of mentally retarded. *American Journal of Mental Deficiency,* 1968, *72,* 841–843.

———. A study of social stereotype of body image in children. *Journal of Personality and Social Psychology,* 1967, *7,* 101–104.

Stevens, D. A. *et al.* Presumed minimal brain dysfunction in children: Relationship to performance on selected behavioral tests. *Archives of General Psychiatry,* 1967, *16,* 281–285.

Strauss, A. A., & Kephart, N. C. *Psychopathology and education of the brain-injured child.* Vol. 2. *Progress in theory and clinic.* New York: Grune & Stratton, Inc., 1955.

Strauss, A. A., & Werner, H. Deficiency in the finger schema in relation to arithmetic disability. *American Journal of Orthopsychiatry,* 1938, *8,* 719–725.

———. Disorders of conceptual thinking in the brain-injured child. *The Journal of Nervous and Mental Disease,* 1942, *96,* 153–172.

———. Finger agnosia in children. *American Journal of Psychiatry,* 1939, *95,* 1215–1225.

Szasz, T. S. *The myth of mental illness.* New York: Hoeber-Harper, 1961.

Thelander, H. E., Phelps, J. K., & Kirk, E. W. Learning disabilities associated with lesser brain damage. *The Journal of Pediatrics,* 1958, 53.

Thorndike, R. L. Review. *American Educational Research Journal,* 1968, *5,* 708–711.

Traub, A. C., & Orbach, J. Psychophysical studies of body-image: I. The adjustable body-distorting mirror. *Archives of General Psychiatry,* 1964, *11,* 53–66.

Trippe, M. J. Conceptual problems in research on educational provisions for disturbed children. *Exceptional Children,* 1963, *29,* 400–406.

———. Educational therapy. In J. Hellmuth (Ed.), *Educational therapy.* Vol. 1. Seattle: Special Child Publications of the Seattle Seguin School, Inc., 1966, pp. 45–48.

Vegas, O. V., & Frye, R. L. Effect of brain damage on perceptual performance. *Perceptual and Motor Skills,* 1963, *17,* 662.

Walton, J. N., Ellis, E., & Court, S. D. M. Clumsy children: A study of developmental apraxia and agnosia. *Brain,* 1962, *85,* 603–612.

Wepman, J. M. *Recovery from aphasia.* New York: The Ronald Press Company, 1951.

Werner, H., & Strauss, A. A. Disorders of conceptual thinking in the brain-injured child. *Journal of Nervous and Mental Diseases,* 1952, *96,* 153–172.

———. Types of visuo-motor activity in their relation to low and high performance ages. *Proceedings of the American Association on Mental Deficiency.* Mansfield Depot, Conn.: American Association on Mental Deficiency, 1939, pp. 163–169.

———. Pathology of figure-background relation

in the child. *Journal of Abnormal and Social Psychology,* 1941, *36,* 236–248.

Werner, H., & Thuma, B. A deficiency in perception of apparent motion in children with brain damage. *American Journal of Psychology,* 1942, *55,* 58–67.

Williams, H. L., Gieseking, C. F., & Lubin, A. Interaction of brain injury with peripheral vision and set. *Journal of Consulting Psychology,* 1961, *25,* 543–548.

Wylie, R. C. *The self concept: A critical survey of pertinent research literature.* Lincoln: University of Nebraska Press, 1961.

Zion, L. C. Body concept as it relates to self-concept. *The Research Quarterly,* 1965, *36,* 490–495.

EIGHT

A Psychology of Auditory Impairment

JOHN WILEY

John Wiley is Professor in the Departments of Physical Medicine and Rehabilitation and Speech at The University of Michigan. He was formerly Associate Professor, Department of Neurology and Psychiatry, College of Medicine, University of Nebraska, and has also served as Chief of the Division of Communicative Disorders, Nebraska Psychiatric Institute.

Loss of hearing is a common health problem affecting millions of people in the United States. Most of us know someone who has difficulty in hearing. Under noisy conditions at a party or at work, all of us may have some difficulty hearing another person's voice. We may associate hearing loss with the effect of aging, someone wearing a hearing aid, or the temporary effect of a severe cold and accompanying ear infection. Defining the extent of loss of hearing and its possible effects on human behavior involves many factors. Two people with apparently normal hearing may listen to the same physical stimulus and perceive something quite different. Two parents serve as chaperons at a junior high school dance. After hearing the music at a distance, they venture into the room with the band and are overwhelmed with the sound from the huge speakers and amplifiers. Their reactions are not the same as those of the young people listening to the music. What they perceive reflects not only the physical state of their hearing mechanism but their previous learning and their attitudes at the moment. A discussion of auditory disabilities must include not only the characteristics of hearing as defined by careful hearing tests but the attitudes and experiences of the listener.

"It's a noisy world." As the number of people and machines increase, the types of noises in our environment multiply. No longer do we need to listen to the twig crackling underfoot to warn us that someone else approaches, friend or foe. Indeed, we could not hear the twig crackling because of the noise of automobiles, airplanes, televisions and other sounds of the modern world. Although we ignore many environmental sounds because they are not important to us, the total level of sound is so high in some places that investigators are evaluating noisy environments

414

to see how much our ears can tolerate without damage. At the busy airport, men on the flight line wear big earmuffs to protect their ears from the sound of the jet engines. Investigators are able to tell us what constitutes a safe level of sound and how long we can be exposed safely to a given level of sound before damage to our ears may occur. Industries have programs of noise abatement to protect the ears of their workers and people living nearby. Cities have noise ordinances specifying the maximum allowable level of noise for motorbikes and other noisy machines.

The care and treatment of hearing loss and the prevention of damage to hearing has become the concern of many specialists. Impaired hearing concerns not only the physician (particularly the otologist and otolaryngologist) but the psychologist, physiologist, audiologist, special educator, speech pathologist, psychophysicist, and many others. Efforts have been made to arrive at common terms to define the extent and nature of hearing loss so that specialists can speak the same language about hearing impairments.

MEASUREMENT OF HEARING LEVEL

Although new developments are occurring in the measurement of hearing impairments in children, the most common measurement of auditory sensitivity is still the pure-tone audiogram. Measurement of hearing by common sounds, such as the watch tick and the casual human voice, has become rare in professional settings. The pure-tone audiometer produces a variety of controlled tones that vary in pitch and loudness. Under the best clinical conditions, pure-tone testing yields valuable information about the child's auditory abilities. Detailed procedures for testing

hearing have been described in a number of books (Bunch, 1943; Davis and Silverman, 1960; Hirsch, 1952; Jerger, 1963; McConnell and Ward, 1967; and Newby, 1964).

In the traditional pure-tone hearing test, the subject is asked to make a voluntary response, such as raising his finger or pushing a button, to sounds he hears through earphones placed over his ears. With most children four years of age or older, pure-tone testing is relatively fast and accurate. Adaptations of pure-tone testing may be successful at even younger ages (Lowell *et al.,* 1956). As the child responds to a series of sounds, ranging from about middle C to five octaves above, in each ear, his responses are recorded by the examiner on a form called the audiogram. In addition, bone-conduction testing may be done, in which the sound source, a vibrator, is placed on the mastoid area back of the ear, and the child responds in the same fashion as described above. Figure 8–1 shows a sample audiogram. Line A represents normal hearing, Line B a slight hearing loss, Line C a moderate hearing loss, Line D a severe hearing loss, and Line E a profound hearing loss. These levels are general indicators, and the effects of this amount of loss for pure tones in a given child may vary widely. The term used to describe the loudness of the sound presented is the decibel (dB), and the pitch is described in terms of the frequency of the vibration of the sound source. The unit of frequency used until recently was cycles per second (cps), but the current term is hertz (Hz.). On the sample audiogram the important frequency range for speech is from 500 Hz. (about an octave above middle C) to 2,000 Hz. (about three octaves above middle C). In screening audiometry, tones may be presented at 500, 1,000, and 2,000 Hz.,

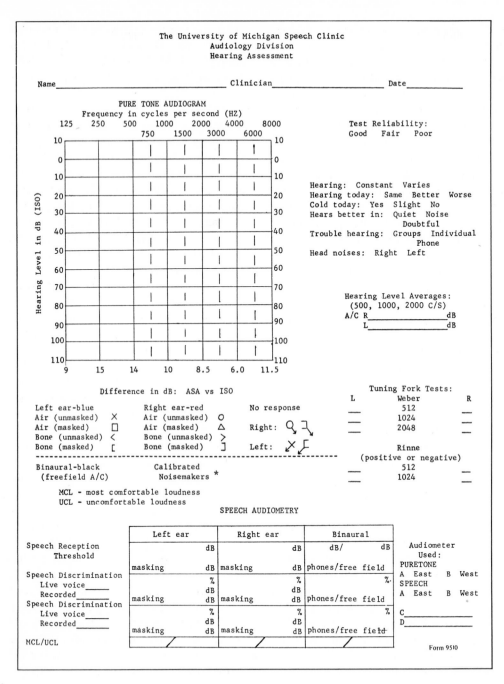

Fig. 8–1.

JOHN WILEY

whereas more detailed testing usually includes 250, 4,000, and 8,000 Hz. as well.

The important sounds for most human beings are not pure tones but the speech of other humans. For some children, it is possible to predict, within certain limits, the hearing for speech from the pure-tone audiogram. For many children, valuable additional information about hearing can be obtained from speech audiometry. Most of the speech tests used in measuring hearing have been developed from investigations at the Bell Telephone Laboratories during the 1920s and 1930s and from extensive studies done during World War II at Harvard Psycho-Acoustic Laboratories and several field stations. Unfortunately, most of these measures were developed for adults with normal language abilities. These tests are not accurate for young children or for many language handicapped children. Of the tests developed, the most widely used are the spondee words (two-syllable words with equal stress on both syllables), used to get a speech reception threshold (SRT), and the phonetically balanced (PB) words used to test auditory discrimination (or the ability to hear differences between sounds). Adaptations and extensions of these tests to use with children have been developed (Siegenthaler and Haspiel, 1966; Siegenthaler, Pearson and Lezak, 1954).

Normal levels for hearing for pure tones and speech stimuli have been derived from tests of large populations. Consequently, they represent averages, not the absolute limits of human hearing. Under careful laboratory conditions, some human beings can hear sounds considerably fainter than those represented by the zero line on the audiogram. The frequency range of sounds usually included in pure-tone hearing tests and recorded on the audiogram is not the total range of human hearing. The range of human hearing may extend as low as 20 Hz. to an upper limit of 20,000 Hz., or perhaps higher. Thus, the dog whistle, at about 20,000 Hz., may be audible to some humans and inaudible to some dogs. A child may hear little or nothing above 4,000 Hz. and yet not be handicapped in everyday language situations. A hearing loss above 4,000 Hz. may be of medical interest but not of educational significance to the teacher or parent. Some people may have normal hearing for speech, but their hearing may be too "low fidelity" to appreciate their high-fidelity stereophonic record player, which requires a response from 100 Hz. to 15,000 Hz.

Because most of the hearing testing procedures mentioned thus far involve a voluntary response from the child, they may not be suitable for many very young children or for retarded, physically handicapped, or multiply handicapped children. Consequently, a number of investigators have developed procedures that do not involve a voluntary response on the part of the child.

One widely used procedure has been called psychogalvanic skin-resistance audiometry and now is more appropriately described as electrodermal audiometry. Electrodes are attached to the hand, or the sole of the foot, and measurements of changes in skin resistance or potential are made when a tone is presented to the child. In some cases, conditioning has been used, with a tone and electrical shock sequence. The child anticipates the shock and responds to the tone by a change in skin resistance. Although the basic principles of this response have been investigated for about eighty years, applications to the testing of hearing are more recent. Doerfler (1948); Bordley and Hardy (1949); Hardy and Pauls (1952); Stewart (1954); and Grings, Lowell, and

Honnard (1960) have described this approach to the testing of hearing. Currently, audiologists are using electrodermal audiometry less frequently than they did ten years ago. Results with retarded and brain-damaged children have been equivocal. Investigators have explored the use of electrodermal audiometry with speech stimuli as well (Ruhm and Carhart, 1958). Among the investigators of electrodermal audiometry, Hardy has remained one of the most consistent proponents. Recently, he has stated (1967, p. 6):

I believe that most of my colleagues will agree that the EDR (electrodermal audiometry) is more economical of time and effort, but is fraught with a host of possibilities of misinterpretation. In careful and experienced hands, and with due regard for the many behavioral pitfalls involved, the measurement by EDR can offer much useful clinical information.... The EER (electroencephalographic audiometry) measurement, on the other hand, is more accurate, although it, too, is not without some difficulties. In general, there is ample evidence from various basic and clinical studies that electroencephalographic audiometry with the help of an electronic averaging computer is the most advanced electro-physiological measurement of auditory function.

Although earlier attempts to identify EEG responses to sound stimuli were largely unsuccessful, the advent of the average response computer and later more sophisticated computers have enabled investigators to average many responses and more easily identify changes time-locked to sound stimuli. Davis, formerly Director of Research at the Central Institute for the Deaf, one of the major investigators in EEG audiometry, has stated (1967, pp. 13–14):

It appears to be superior, as a method of so-called "objective audiometry" to both classical EEG audiometry and electrodermal or GSR audiometry.... With children 4 years of age and older it compares favorably in reliability and in sensitivity with behavioral audiometry either finger-response audiometry or so-called "play audiometry."

On the other hand, the equipment required is more expensive and complicated than for any of the above mentioned methods and some experience is required to recognize correctly the electroencephalographic patterns that are evoked by signals near the threshold of hearing. Davis feels this technique will not be used for screening but as a diagnostic test in major centers. While the technique is promising, there are many aspects of the clinical applications to be worked out. A number of other investigators have reported on studies in this area (Derbyshire *et al.*, 1962; Goldstein, Kendall, and Arick, 1963; Lowell *et al.*, 1960; Lowell *et al* 1961; McCandless, 1967). Evoked-response audiometry has been used to explore hearing in neonates (Goodman *et al.*, 1964).

A variety of other approaches that eliminate voluntary responses on the part of the child include measures of respiration and electronystagmography (Rosenberg and Toglia, 1967; Tell *et al.*, 1967).

Some investigators have used operant-conditioning procedures to train the child to respond to test stimuli. Operant conditioning has been used extensively with the retarded child. Meyerson and Michael (1960) described an approach and apparatus that was reported to be quite successful. The apparatus is now available commercially. Investigators at the Parsons Language Project (Lloyd, Spradlin, and Reid, 1968) have used operant conditioning with the difficult to test (sometimes called untestable) retarded patients.

Perhaps the most important new developments in the detection of hearing loss have come in the extension of testing to infants. As stated earlier, conventional pure-tone techniques are successful most of the time with children four years of age and above. Even younger children may respond reliably with various play techniques. EDR audiometry has been used on children as young as six months of age, and EEG audiometry has been used experimentally in the first few days of life.

Simple techniques of testing infants have been developed by some investigators. Whereas pediatricians and others have been using sudden loud sounds such as a handclap for many years, somewhat more detailed testing with noisemakers was developed by the Ewings at the University of Manchester. Their techniques have been modified by Sheridan (1958) in England and by investigators at Johns Hopkins (Hardy and Bordley, 1952; Hardy, Daugherty, and Hardy, 1959) in the United States. A program of infant testing in Colorado has lead to the development of a portable sound generator, which can be taken into the nursery (Downs, 1962; Downs, 1967; Downs and Sterritt, 1967).

Although improved techniques of testing young children have become available, frequently children are not referred for these evaluations unless parents are aware of a possible hearing loss. Peters (1967) describes a study of the parents of 396 deaf and 249 hard-of-hearing children from three to seventeen years who were questioned about the detection of hearing impairment in their children. Deaf children were detected in nine out of ten cases by the mother, and in 90 percent of the cases during thier first three years. Only 29 percent of the hard-of-hearing children had been recognized by the age of three. Again, the mother first suspected the impairment in nine out of ten cases.

OTHER FACTORS IN AUDITORY IMPAIRMENT

The extent of hearing loss is not the only factor determining the degree of impairment of language and other behavior in the child. If hearing loss is present at birth, or occurs before language develops, the child's normal pattern of acquiring language is altered and behavior is profoundly affected. Cawthorne, in the keynote speech at the National Symposium on Deafness in Childhood, 1966, said: "Severe or total deafness which does not develop until after language has been learned, though tragic, is not such a handicap as deafness at birth which prevents the normal development of language." Severe hearing loss after the acquisition of language may produce severe emotional disturbances in the child struggling to adjust to a drastically altered world of silent lip movements. Serious acquired hearing loss will produce deterioration in speech sounds because the child can no longer monitor his sound production by listening. Prompt treatment by a skilled speech pathologist will minimize this loss by teaching the child to attend to tactile and kinesthetic cues. During World War II, rehabilitation facilities for servicemen with recently acquired hearing losses developed programs of speech insurance to prevent deterioration of speech. Variations of these techniques can be used with the child who acquires a severe hearing loss.

Other factors that influence the amount of impairment related to hearing loss include environment, intelligence, and other physical handicaps. The interaction between intelligence and hearing loss and learning impairment has not been adequately defined, but it is generally agreed that the slow learning or retarded child may be more impaired by a given degree of hearing loss. On the other hand, the bright, responsive child, in a supportive environment, may be able to compensate for part of his hearing loss. Helen Keller, both blind and deaf, acquired language skills of a high order and developed intelligible speech in spite of double sensory handicaps. Some graduates of the Perkins Institute program for the deaf-blind have intelligible speech, even though the visual and auditory cues are diminished or absent. Physical handicaps may make movements for speech more difficult or may diminish tactile or kinesthetic feedback needed to compensate for the lack of hearing. The child living in a secure environment, with adequate home training, may have many more language experiences than the child in an institution or less well-stabilized home. I observed a three-year-old boy with a severe hearing loss who would hop up into his father's lap and put his ear close to his father's mouth to hear what was being said to him.

This arrangement was worked out at home without any previous professional advice. A six-year-old girl with good speech and language development in spite of a severe hearing loss had had excellent stimulation from her mother. As a smaller child, she sat on the drainboard while her mother washed dishes and talked to her. Each household activity had been planned so the child could take part, and, whenever possible, be close to her mother so she could hear as much as possible.

DEFINITION OF TERMS:

Because all of the factors described above, and many others, enter into the extent of impairment, terms are hard to define briefly and clearly. The White House Conference on Child Health and Welfare (1931) proposed the following definitions:

The deaf are those who were born either totally deaf or sufficiently deaf to prevent the establishment of speech and natural language; those who became deaf in childhood before language and speech were established; or those who became deaf in childhood so soon after the natural establishment of speech and language that the ability to speak and understand speech and language has been practically lost to them.

The hard of hearing are those who established speech ability to understand speech and language, and subsequently developed impairment of hearing. These children are sound-conscious and have a normal, or almost normal, attitude towards the world of sound in which they live.

This definition includes time of onset as differentiating whereas the 1937 recommendation of the Committee on Nomenclature of the Conference of Executives of American Schools for the Deaf proposed the following classification and definitions:

1. The deaf: Those in whom the sense of hearing is non-functional for the ordinary purposes of life. This general group is made up of two distinct classes based entirely on the time of the loss of hearing:

(A) The congenitally deaf: Those who were born deaf.
(B) The adventitiously deaf: Those who were born with normal hearing but in whom the sense of hearing became non-functional later through illness or accident.

2. The hard of hearing: Those in whom the sense of hearing, although defective, is functional with or without a hearing aid.

Estimates of the number of children with hearing losses have varied widely. A 1939 survey involving nearly 1 million children in New York City revealed that 4 percent had an impairment of hearing. S. R. Silverman (1947) estimated that 5 percent of the children in the nation had a hearing loss. This figure includes those with monaural hearing loss and does not mean that all require hearing aids or special educational training. Of this number, only a small percentage would be classified as deaf. Even in the residential schools for the deaf, the majority of the children have some response to a hearing test and have some usable hearing.

Although many of the hard-of-hearing children are in regular schools, there are a number in special schools or classrooms. Each year, the *American Annals of the Deaf* publishes a survey of these programs. Approximately 75 percent of the 21,545 pupils enrolled in schools and classes for the deaf in the United States in 1953 were enrolled in residential schools. By 1961 the percentage enrolled in residential schools had dropped to 58 percent. In 1966 there were approximately 36,000 children enrolled in special schools and classes, with 56 percent enrolled in residential schools. Day school and day classes for the deaf have increased steadily in number and enrollment. Obviously, the pattern is not the same across the country. Day schools and classes are found primarily in large cities. The alternatives for education for the deaf child in rural areas or smaller cities are residential schools, regular public schools, or an institution for the retarded or mentally ill.

PROBLEMS IN INVESTIGATING AUDITORY IMPAIRMENT

Studies of the characteristics of the deaf child have been difficult to evaluate in part because of the difficulty in comparing results. Labels such as deaf, acoustically handicapped, children with auditory handicaps, moderate, severe, and profound hearing loss, and so forth, have been used without adequately defining the

terms. As we have seen before, the pure tone or speech audiometric evaluation is not enough to define the actual impairment of the child. Some of the investigators did not have sufficient information about deaf children to know how to evaluate their results. Most of the investigators have used special schools and special rooms for the deaf in their studies, so we have relatively little information about the hearing-handicapped child who is in the regular classroom and manages to get along in that setting.

Several years ago (1963, p. 125) Meyerson said:

In addition to subjects who have mild, moderate, or even questionable losses of hearing, the author examined children in schools for the deaf who were feeble-minded or mentally retarded; mongoloid children, children who had congenital.... thyroid and pituitary disorders, brain damage, aphasia, epilepsy, various kinds of cerebral palsy, impaired vision verging on blindness, and emotional disorders ranging from psychic deafness to pre-psychosis. Some of these children had physiological impairments of hearing so mild that they probably would not be handicapping if it were not for their other disabilities. Other children had severe losses of hearing, but the hearing impairment was not their greatest problem nor the major contributing source of their behavior.

In the same chapter, Meyerson pointed out that there had been many psychological investigations of the deaf and hard-of-hearing, but the meaning of the findings was uncertain. There are several reasons why this is true. As we have seen earlier in this chapter, the terms "deaf," "hard-of-hearing," "acoustically impaired," "auditory handicaps," and so forth, have different operational definitions for various investigators. In many cases the operational definition used in the study is not clear.

Although valid auditory sensitivity data can be collected on most impairments of hearing, many of the older studies do not have these data. Even when well-defined terms and adequate audiological data are used at a given time in the child's life, there is not always adequate evidence about his hearing at an earlier period in his life. Some investigators regard as deaf all children in school programs for the deaf, whereas others may regard as deaf only those children who do not respond to speech, even with amplification. Many years ago, Bezold (quoted by Bunch, 1943, p. 133) said

> ... up to 1898, I tested 276 organs of hearing of deaf-mutes. Of these only 79 were totally deaf. The others had remnants of hearing of various extents. Both ears were totally deaf in only 27 pupils or 19.7 percent of those 138 pupils. The other 53 or 38.4 percent showed such extensive remnants of hearing distributed over a large part of the sound scale that they were not different from a large number of adult hard-of-hearing people with whom one can converse easily.

Hughson and his co-workers in an audiometric study (1939, p. 403) of the hearing of the children in the Pennsylvania School for the Deaf found that "95% of the children examined could perceive at least one frequency by air conduction in one or the other ear, and 85% perceived at least one in both ears."

In an unpublished study by Hiskey and Wiley at the Nebraska School for the Deaf, 21 out of 36 students had pure-tone averages (speech range) of 90 dB or better in at least one ear, whereas 15 had pure-tone averages greater than 90 dB. All of these students were sixteen years old or older. Of the 15 with the greatest hearing losses, only 4 did not respond to pure-tone testing at any frequency in the speech range in either ear.

Because schools for the deaf were among the first special schools to be established, children who did not talk, or had other learning disabilities, were sent there in the absence of other facilities. With the development of other special schools and classes, it should not be necessary for schools for the deaf to care for so many other problems. Obviously, no adequate statistics on the changes in the population of the schools exist because classification procedures and methods of diagnosis have been changing.

We do not know if the children enrolled in the residential schools are typical of the deaf population. There are a number of apparently deaf children in regular public or private schools who are not reported in statistics on the deaf. Some years ago I interviewed a high school student who had no usable hearing. She was enrolled in a regular public high school and had had all of her educational experiences in regular schools. With the help of her sister, this girl was doing acceptable work. Very likely, some of the brightest deaf children, with the most home support, are students in regular public schools.

BEHAVIORAL CHARACTERISTICS OF THE AUDITORILY IMPAIRED

Evaluation Procedures

Progress in clarifying the issues of deafness and other handicaps has been made in recent years. Myklebust (1945 and 1967) has described detailed clinical procedures for distinguishing among auditory disorders due to peripheral deafness, aphasia, mental retardation, and other disorders. Differences between an aphasic and deaf population have been explored at the Central Institute for the Deaf by Goldstein, Landau, and Kleffner (1960).

Many of the measures used to evaluate intelligence, personality, and language were not designed for the deaf and may not reflect their abilities accurately. The group intelligence tests and many of the individual intelligence tests have verbal instructions that may not be meaningful to the deaf child and that may require verbal responses which the deaf child cannot produce. The Nebraska Test of Learning Aptitude, developed by Marshall Hiskey, is one of the few psychological tests specifically designed for the deaf. This test has been standardized for both deaf and hearing populations. The revised version has norms for children from three to sixteen years of age. The Leiter International Performance Scale (Birch and Birch, 1951) and the Arthur revision of the Leiter, with no verbal instructions or responses required, has been widely used with the hearing impaired. The Ontario Scale, developed at the Ontario School for the Deaf, is designed for use by the deaf. Performance items from the Wechsler Individual Scale for Children and the Stanford-Binet have been widely used. Some of the performance scales (which have verbal directions) have been adapted for use with the deaf. The Randall's Island Test, for example, has been used at the Central Institute for the Deaf. Raven's Progressive Matrices, the Chicago Non-Verbal, and the Terman Non-Language Test have been used with some success in a recent study (Goetzinger, Wills, and Dekker, 1967). The cautions in administering these tests have been well expressed by Vernon and Brown (1964, p. 415):

Tests given to deaf children by psychologists not experienced with the deaf or hard of hearing are subject to appreciably greater error than is the case when the service is rendered by one familiar with deaf youngsters. The atypical attentive set of the hearing impaired child to testing which has been frequently cited in the literature is felt to be one of the reasons for this.

Intelligence

Vernon and Brown (1964) have rated the psychological tests frequently used with the deaf, indicating that relatively good tests include the Wechsler Performance Scale for Children, the Leiter, Raven's Progressive Matrices, the Ontario School Ability Examination, the Nebraska Test of Learning Aptitude, and, for preschool children, the Randall's Island Performance Scale. Other tests, which they rate as poor to fair, include the Chicago Non-Verbal Examination, the Grace Arthur Performance Scale, the Merrill-Palmer Scale of Mental Tests, and the Goodenough Draw-a-Man Tests. They suggest that the Goodenough has some value as a projective test for the deaf. They feel that hard-of-hearing children may appear to understand verbal tests, when actually they do not. Test results on preschool and early school age deaf and hard-of-hearing children tend to be less reliable than on hearing subjects. In addition, Vernon and Brown (1964, p. 415) say: "There is far more danger that a low I.Q. score is wrong than that a high one is inaccurate." Problems in testing deaf children include difficulties in communication and lack of language experiences on the part of the child as well as the failure of the deaf child to understand that he must hurry on timed tests.

In evaluating the intelligence of the deaf, we are faced with a variety of confusing evidence, largely due to the factors mentioned above. Some studies, such as MacKane (1933), Peterson (1936), Zeckel and Van der Kolk (1939), and Oleron (1953) have shown the deaf to have lower intelligence. Other studies, such as Bishop (1936), Kirk (1938), Streng and Kirk (1938), Lane and Schneider (1941), and Burchard and Myklebust (1942) have shown intelligence levels that were normal. A few studies, such as MacPherson and Lane (1948) have indicated above average intelligence for the deaf.

For a long time professional people working with the deaf have been influenced by the findings of Pintner, who conducted investigations of the deaf until his death in 1942. He stated (1941, pp. 177–179):

The results of these tests seem to indicate slightly lower general intelligence for the deaf as a group when compared with the hearing. . . . The motor and mechanical ability and the concrete intelligence of the deaf are their great assets. Their abstract verbal intelligence, their academic achievement (which was found to be about four years behind that of the hearing) are their great liabilities.

On the basis of these findings, he recommended education be oriented to motor skills and mechanical and concrete materials. He felt the learning of language should be subsidiary and ancillary to making and building and doing. Pintner's point of view represented a step forward at the time, but more recent investigations have indicated that the deaf are indeed academically disadvantaged but may not be handicapped in dealing with abstractions.

On group nonverbal and nonlanguage tests, some investigators have found lower IQs (Peterson and Williams, 1930; Shirley and Goodenough, 1932; and Springer, 1938), whereas other investigators have found normal intelligence. Lane and Silverman (1947) point out that the results of tests to 242 nursery school age children who applied for admission to the Central Institute for the Deaf indicated an average

IQ of 102.7, with a range from 62 to 151. They say (1947, p. 374): "The mental abilities of deaf children as a group are equal, except for language, to those of children who can hear." Whether or not the children who apply to the Central Institute for the Deaf are typical of all deaf children, we do not know.

Generally, it appears that the deaf are not inferior in intelligence if appropriate tests are administered by psychologists accustomed to working with the deaf. If items involving language are used, the results may be different.

Language

The obsolete term "deaf-mute" implied that the deaf person was unable to speak. This term has fallen into disuse because teachers and investigators discovered that there were no organic conditions usually accompanying deafness which prevented the development of speech. In fact, many deaf children develop speech and other language skills. Nevertheless, children who are deaf or severely hard-of-hearing do not learn language in the same way or at the same rate. For many years, teachers of the deaf have tried to develop more satisfactory ways to teach speech to deaf children. Since World War II, speech and language pathologists and audiologists have been concerned more and more with these problems. More recently, linguists, psycholinguists, and psychologists have applied new approaches to the study of the language of the deaf.

The term "language" is being used here in a general sense, which includes comprehension and use of oral and written symbols and the use and comprehension of finger spelling and signs. "Speech" refers to oral language, including the motor acts involved in speech sound and voice production.

In the normal hearing child, comprehension of oral language is learned first and oral language expression second, with recognizable words being produced about the age of one year. The deaf and severely hard-of-hearing child will produce similar crying and babbling sounds, but before the age of one year, it is apparent that he is not imitating the sounds he makes or the sounds others make. If the hearing loss is severe, he will not learn to speak without a great deal of special help. With a less severe loss, speech development will be delayed, comprehension and expression vocabulary may be reduced, and speech may be hard to understand. The deaf child misses many experiences in his preschool years because he does not hear human voices and many environmental sounds. Later, language learning, such as reading and writing, may be delayed because the deaf child does not develop adequate language concepts in his preschool years. Thus, the teaching of reading becomes much more than a task of relating visual patterns to language concepts already formed.

The speech patterns of the deaf child are usually easy to recognize for the experienced clinician. There are omissions or slighting of less-visible consonants, distortion of vowels, lack of inflection, alterations of nasality and other voice quality characteristics, and, frequently, abnormal pitch levels. The intelligibility of speech is related to the amount of hearing loss, but the correlation is far from perfect. Other factors, including intelligence, education, and motivation, are involved. Thus, a moderately hard-of-hearing child may have very defective speech, whereas some deaf children have intelligible and close to normal speech.

Because speech and speech reading are hard to learn, using visual communication, such as finger spelling or signs, has been recommended by many educators of the deaf. The debate between the supporters of the manual method and the oral method has raged on for many years. Although most schools for the deaf are primarily oral in formal instruction, at least for the most rapid learners, many children learn manual communication informally from other children. Most schools offer manual instruction for the child who does not learn speech and speech reading in the usual amount of time. Supporters of manual teaching feel it is most important for the deaf child to have some communication. They particularly recommend manual communication for the child who has unusual difficulties in learning speech and speech reading. Proponents of the oral method feel that once the child learns manual methods he will be less motivated to try to learn the more difficult tasks of speech and speech reading. These issues are discussed in detail in several recent books (Di Carlo, 1964; Ewing and Ewing, 1967; Groht, 1958; O'Neill and Oyer, 1961; Oyer, 1966; Proceedings of International Conference on Oral Education of the Deaf, 1967). Myklebust (1967) warns of the dangers of learning manual methods first, because he feels it becomes the "native" tongue and will be used for thought processes, even if speech and speech reading are taught later. Others have pointed out that dependence on sign language and finger spelling restricts the deaf child to a small group of people, even cutting him off from his own family. The essential question becomes one of determining if all or most deaf children can learn oral language well enough to use it effectively with our present educational system or even an ideal one. Is it better to work through an intact sensory input than through a poorly functioning one? The questions have not been answered as yet. Rosenstein (1967,

p. 1383) says: "At the present time, however, we do not have a sufficient body of information that allows for a comprehensive description of language acquisition and development in deaf children." After four years of research utilizing psycholinguistic approaches at the Lexington School for the Deaf, he states (1967, p. 1391): "We concluded that deaf children do not have a language system of their own, but certainly have difficulties in learning fully the grammatical sequences and constraints of English." Templin (1967, pp. 1428–1429) in discussing the difficulties in studying language in the deaf, states:

The title of this paper ["Methodological Variations in Language Research with Deaf Subjects"] implies the systematic study of the effect of variations in methodology. Unfortunately, this is still a goal, and not an accomplished fact. This paper merely identifies some methodological considerations that are important in planning and carrying out research with the deaf.

Brannon and Murry (1966) have reported on a spoken language sample of fifty sentences obtained from thirty normal and thirty hearing impaired children. A total score of structural accuracy (syntax) was obtained by combining the errors of addition, omission, substitution, and word order. The hard-of-hearing subgroup resembled the control group in its total output of words, but the deaf subgroup was significantly lower in this measure. There was moderate correlation between average hearing loss and total words uttered and a higher correlation when hearing loss was related to measures of syntax. In a later study, Brannon (1968) studied the spoken language of thirty normal junior high students, fifteen hard-of-hearing children, and fifteen children from special classes for the deaf. Fourteen colored pictures were used as stimuli to elicit fifty spoken sentences. These responses were classified into fourteen word classes, as proposed by Jones, Goodman, and Wepman. Brannon concluded that a significant hearing impairment reduces productivity of both tokens and types of words. A moderate impairment lowers the use of adverbs, pronouns, and auxiliaries; a profound impairment reduces nearly all classes. Some of the difficulties in learning language for the deaf were illustrated in the study by Odom and Blanton (1967). Two groups of twenty-four deaf subjects each were compared with twenty-four fifth-graders and twenty-four twelfth-graders with normal hearing on the learning of segments of written English. Eight subjects in each group learned meaningful phrases, eight more learned the same words in acceptable English word order but nonmeaningful, whereas the remaining eight in each group learned the same words scrambled. Both groups of hearing subjects showed facilitation on the meaningful phrases, and interference on the scrambled segments, whereas the deaf group showed no such difference. Thus, memory processes in relation to meaning were not operating in the same way for the deaf.

Two studies by Blank and Bridger (1966) indicated that deaf subjects, although deficient in general language, possessed number symbols and used them as efficiently as hearing subjects. In both experiments, one using subjects in the three- to five-year range and the other, five- and six-year-olds, deaf subjects were more proficient in using tactual cues. Kates et al. (1961) reported on a study of categorization and verbalization processes of twenty-four adolescents, eight of whom were profoundly deaf. The sixteen hearing subjects were divided into two groups, one matched with the deaf subjects for age and IQ and the other matched on Stanford Achievement Test scores and IQ. The Goldstein-Scheerer Object Sorting Test was administered and the deaf subjects categorized as adequately as the hearing subjects on this task, even though they had more inadequate verbalization than the hearing subjects. They did not differ from the hearing subjects on the type of verbalization, in the developmental level of verbalizations used, or in spontaneous changes of categorization.

Some deaf adolescents are able to understand single words and short phrases but cannot get the total meaning of a paragraph. Some years ago I worked with a young man who had been classified as deaf. He had had training in a school for the deaf, some regular high school experiences, and was a sophomore in a university. We were trying to improve his speech, which was quite intelligible. As we worked on connected speech, I had him read aloud anecdotes from the *Reader's Digest.* These anecdotes were never funny to him. As I investigated, I found he was unable to get the point of the jokes because he could not put the whole anecdote together. Visual jokes were funny to him, but auditory ones were not. Even at this high educational level, language problems occur.

Other questions arise in considering language learning in the deaf. Earlier investigators have felt that the deaf may be adequate in "concrete" intelligence but lacking in "abstract" abilities. They cite the higher scores made on performance items as compared to verbal items. Careful examination of two of the widely used tests with the deaf, the Hiskey and the Leiter, does not indicate that these scales are limited to testing concrete behavior.

As the title of the Hiskey test indicates, it was designed to measure aptitude for learning, and it is used with hearing as well as deaf children. Dr. Ralph Gibson, chief psychologist in the Pediatrics Department at the University of Michigan, has collected a great deal of data on the Leiter test, with both hearing and deaf children. He has found it to be a good measure of conceptual ability and useful as a predictor of future academic progress in preschool children. Furth (1963) cites a series of experiments indicating that language is not necessary to thinking. Furth noted that the deaf were retarded in some areas of cognitive development but felt this was due to experiential deficits. In a recent book (1967), he reviews the literature and the results from twelve experiments, comparing the thinking of deaf, mentally retarded, and normal hearing children. He feels words and language are not synonymous, words and cognition are not synonymous, and cognition and language are not synonymous. Therefore, he does not believe the deaf are as handicapped in cognitive development as earlier investigators have thought.

Lenneberg (1967) has discussed the role of biological development in the development of language. If the child's brain functions are not yet ready to do language synthesis, he cannot be taught to talk. Lenneberg feels language development shows the characteristics of maturationally dependent behavior. Thus, all the teacher of the deaf can do is feed language into the child, hoping he is ready to synthesize it. Another implication of this point of view is that if language learning experiences are delayed too long, the child may be past the period when he is most ready to learn language. Lenneberg feels it is more important to teach the child language concepts than individual language skills, such as lip reading, articulation, signing, and so forth. He discusses another aspect of the disabilities imposed by deafness when he states (1967, p. 1347):

Deafness imposes a formidable handicap upon the child as far as the learning of facts is concerned. He cannot ask the millions of questions that hearing children ask and he does not receive the millions of incidental explanations that older children and adults give us in early childhood. In this sense, the deaf are greatly deprived.

Moores (1967) has discussed some of the other applications of psycholinguistic investigations to the development of linguistic skills in deaf children. The implications of the psycholinguistic investigations are not fully apparent yet, but they offer some fresh and important approaches to the study of language learning in the hearing-handicapped child.

Educational Achievement

Earlier studies of educational achievement by means of standard tests revealed that children in schools for the deaf were retarded three years or more. (Day, Fusfeld, and Pintner, 1928; Hall, 1929; Reamer, 1921). In many deaf children educational retardation begins with problems in learning to read and becomes progressively worse as the child grows older. Arithmetic is usually less affected, whereas the greatest difficulty occurs in understanding words and paragraphs. Kates, Kates, and Michael (1962) feel that the primary effect of deafness is a retardation in the development of connections between verbal symbols and their nonverbal referent categories, with this retardation falling along normal developmental lines.

Superintendents of residential schools for the deaf say that a good graduate of their program (at age nineteen or twenty) is about two years behind an average hearing high school graduate in overall educational achievement. Obviously, some students do much better than that, but even the students who enter Gallaudet (the only college for the deaf in the United States), who represent some of the best graduates of schools for the deaf, are behind the typical high school graduate academically.

In a recent study of deaf students in colleges and universities, Quigley, Jenne, and Phillips (1968) attempted to locate deaf students who had succeeded in pursuing their education in regular colleges and universities and to determine the factors relating to success, the problems encountered, and how the problems might be eliminated or decreased. They found that there was no easy way to determine who these deaf students were or even how many there were.

After a lengthy investigation, they located 992 persons, and were able to collect and analyze 653 usable questionnaires. Students were divided into five groups: Group A, with 224 students, was composed of those who had been awarded at least a bachelor's degree; Group B had 131 students who had terminated college before the bachelor's degree; Group C had 161 students who were still in college; Group D had 39 students who began in regular colleges and then transferred to Gallaudet; and Group E had 98 students who had graduated from Gallaudet and had attended graduate schools in regular universities. About half of Group E had acquired one graduate degree. Grades for A and E were good. Group B had lower grades than A, and Group D had lower grades than B. Groups A and E were quite successful vocationally, earning salaries comparable to those of hearing people of equal training. Group A were largely graduates of day school programs or oral residential schools and were from socioeconomic groups comparable to other college students. Group E had largely attended residential schools and were from lower socioeconomic groups than Group A. The married graduates in Group E were primarily married to deaf partners. This was less true in Group A, but the majority were still married to deaf partners. Group C was, of course, the youngest group and will be followed carefully in the next several years. There is no way of knowing if this group is typical of the deaf population who attend college or what proportion they represent. Nevertheless, the study indicates that some deaf students can graduate from college and compete in a hearing world successfully. It seems to indicate that even these educationally elite deaf tend to socialize with other deaf people and perhaps are isolated from the rest of the community. The interactions of type of early education and socioeconomic level are well worth further investigation.

Under present conditions, both language and general educational level are significantly retarded in the child with severe auditory impairment, even though intelligence in the deaf seems to be normal.

Personality

Investigations employing paper and pencil tests of personality have revealed generally that deaf children are less well adjusted than normal hearing children, especially in school and social adjustment. Only a few attempts have been made to develop personality scales for the deaf. One attempt was the Brunschwig Person-

ality Inventory for Deaf Children. Brunschwig (1936) reported that the general adjustment score of deaf children was lower than that for normal hearing children. Using the Vineland Social Maturity Scale, Bradway (1937) found the deaf to be 20 percent inferior to hearing subjects throughout all age levels examined. Burchard and Myklebust (1942) found much the same thing, whereas Streng and Kirk (1938), looking at preschool and day school deaf, classified their subjects as average in social maturity. Kirk (1938), using the Haggerty-Olson-Wickman Behavior Rating Schedules with teachers of the deaf, found a significantly greater number of problem tendencies among the deaf than among normal hearing children. Myklebust and Burchard (1945) studied 187 children in a residential school and found the deaf presented a higher incidence of behavior problems. There were no differences between the groups with congenital and acquired deafness, or between those who had been in residence less than four years or more than four years. Bindon (1957) compared rubella deaf children, nonrubella deaf children, and hearing children on the Rorschach, the Wechsler-Bellevue Performance Scale, and Schneideman's adaptation of the MAPS tests and found the deaf group to be functioning at a less mature level, although the performance of the rubella and nonrubella group were similar. Gregory (1938) reported that deaf children formed less adequate social relationships than hearing children. Lyon (1934) studied 87 male and female adolescent students in a residential school, using the Thurstone Personality Schedule, and found the incidence of poor adjustment twice as high as the norms. Levine (1956) used the Rorschach with 31 deaf children and found them inferior in conceptual thinking, with more limited interest and greater emotional immaturity than the hearing. Myklebust (1964) used a Human Figure Drawing Test, a modified form of the Goodenough, with 830 deaf children and found the deaf children's drawings more immature in use of space and placement of the figure on the page, and in drawing the boy, parts were disproportionately large. He found perceptual distortions.

Rigidity, or a tendency to persist in an action that is no longer appropriate and to be unable to see new ways of responding, has been mentioned frequently as a characteristic of the deaf. McAndrew (1948), using the Rorschach with twenty-five children in a residential school, concluded that deaf children were more rigid than the normal hearing children he studied. On the other hand, Myklebust (1964) cites a study by Neyhus (1962) indicating that language facility is related to Rorschach performance, and the better the language, the more normal the personality pattern.

Rutledge (1954) compared a deaf group of fifty-two adolescent deaf boys and girls with a matched group of normal adolescents. He studied aspiration behavior and found the aspiration levels of the deaf on the Heath Rail-Walking Task to be significantly lower than normals but similar in level on the Rotter Aspiration Board. If aspiration level was compared to previous performance on repeated administrations of the items, the deaf set lower aspiration levels than the hearing subjects, except for similar scores for boys on the Rotter test. Observation of overt behavior indicated the deaf students seemed to be more unsure.

Meyer (1953) has said that the attitude that handicapped children do not differ from normal ones except for one specific disability is ill-chosen and unrealistic. The child's impairment modifies his adjustment and makes him need more emotional support. Myklebust (1963) has discussed the role of hearing as a scanning, alerting sense and the effects of deprivation of hearing.

Vernon and Brown (1964) have evaluated personality testing with hearing-impaired children. They discuss Machover's Draw-a-Person Test, the Thematic Apperception Test, the Children's Apperception Test, the Rorschach Ink Blot Test, and the H-T-P technique. The Rorschach, TAT, and CAT require considerable verbal skill, and all require skillful interpretation by a psychologist well versed in the test. They point out several cautions in relation to these tests. Personality evaluation is a far more complex task than intelligence testing, and test findings need to be related to case history data and personal experience with the child. In addition to the unusual verbal skills required of the children in some of these tests, excellent rapport is necessary. It is questionable if the norms derived from hearing populations can be used for the deaf, because deafness alters the perceived environment.

Furfey and Harte (1964), in a sociological study of relationships between deaf and hearing, point out that the deaf are not a homogeneous group and successful adjustment of the deaf requires planning by both the community and the deaf person.

Morkovin has discussed some of the problems of the deaf in his book, aptly titled *Through the Barriers of Deafness and Isolation* (1960).

In an earlier comprehensive review of intelligence and personality testing, Berlinsky (1952, p. 45) said: "The tests which have been used to date are largely those which have been designed specifically for hearing groups and possess corresponding language and situation complexities which are outside the range of experience and abilities of the average deaf individual." He points out that when the investigator modifies the language of the personality test to fit it into the comprehension of the deaf child the differences between deaf and hearing children become small. The differences that remain indicate the deaf find it more difficult to adjust and are somewhat more introverted, a little more emotionally unstable, and have more feelings of depression and suspicion.

One large, long-term study has been completed recently on some aspects of family and mental health problems in the deaf in New York State (Rainer *et al.*, 1963). In this study, nearly 12,000 names and addresses of literate deaf adolescents and adults were amassed, and sampling techniques were employed to gather genetic data, family characteristics, and so forth. In regard to the socialization of the sample studied, Rainer *et al.* (p. 115) state:

> The data indicate that persons with early total deafness can establish adequate socialization patterns and are able to participate in and utilize general community services. However, qualitative and quantitative differences between the deaf and the hearing in the nature of their social and community integration exist.

This group found the serious psychiatric problems to be similar in type and characteristics in the deaf and normal hearing populations, estimating the incidence of schizophrenia to be 2.5 percent of the deaf population. One interesting bit of data, in reporting from 536 respondents, was that of those entering school before age four, 16.7 percent went on to higher education, whereas of those entering at age six or over, 7.6 percent went on to higher education.

MULTIPLY HANDICAPPED DEAF CHILDREN

Children who are hearing impaired may have other handicaps that interfere with learning. Clinical reports indicate that the number of multiply handicapped deaf children is on the increase, although accurate statistics are not available. The presumption is that improvements in medicine have enabled more of these multiply handicapped children to survive. Schools for the deaf must deal not only with the "normal" deaf child, but with the aphasic deaf, the retarded deaf, the emotionally disturbed deaf, the motor-handicapped deaf, the visually handicapped deaf, and the deaf with other learning disorders. There is special cause for concern now because of the rubella epidemic of 1963–1964, which produced an increased number of multiply handicapped deaf. Hardy (1967, pp. 7–8) has described the seriousness of the problem in these terms:

> At the risk of overspecialization I would like to call your attention to a particular problem which faces us in this country pertaining to the multiple facets of behavior and function relatable to hearing impairment. . . . From Maine to Florida, it is estimated, there are probably 25,000 of the most multiply involved children our nation has ever known.

Provisions for these multiply handicapped deaf have been slow to develop. At the Perkins Institute, there has been a program for the deaf-blind for many years, and there are a few other such programs. As far as this author knows, only two state schools for the deaf have developed special programs for the emotionally disturbed deaf, the California School at Riverside and the Michigan School at Flint. Anderson and Stevens (1969) reported that in 1966, four states, California,

Michigan, Tennessee, and Minnesota, reported having a program for the retarded deaf. Since that time, the program at Lapeer State Home in Michigan has been closed.

In recent years, particular attention has been paid to the relationship between deafness and mental retardation. Because the deaf are usually educationally retarded and have speech and other language problems, they have been regarded as retarded in some cases. Individual cases of near normal or normal intelligence, coupled with deafness, have been found in a number of institutions for the retarded. For example, the author found a man in his early forties who had been institutionalized for more than twenty years in a state institution for the retarded. He played such a responsible role on the ward that we reevaluated his apparent retardation. This man had a very severe hearing loss and had been in a school for the deaf for a short time as a child. When he was not learning at the expected rate, he was taken out of school and sent home. Later, because he did not fit into the community and there were no other facilities available, he was sent to the institution for the retarded. His intelligence, on a nonverbal test, was in the normal range. These individual clinical experiences have been reinforced by the results of a number of studies showing a high incidence of hearing loss in institutions for the retarded (Foale and Paterson, 1954; Johnston and Farrell, 1954). These results have led to a belief that hearing loss might play a critical role in the problems of the institutionalized retarded person. A study by Gaines (1961), supervised by the author, used two entirely separate hearing-testing procedures to evaluate a group of institutionalized youngsters. Examination of the results indicated an apparent incidence of hearing loss above 20 percent on each procedure, but when the results of the two procedures were combined, the incidence of hearing loss dropped to 12 percent. Because this study suggested that the apparent high incidence of hearing loss in the retarded population might be related to testing procedures, a follow-up study (Wiley and Jacobs, 1965) was conducted. All of the mildly retarded patients between ten and twenty years of age in a state institution were tested, and the results indicated that the incidence of hearing loss was not significantly different from that found in a population of normal intelligence. La Crosse and Bidlake (1964), in a study conducted in a state institution, found a much lower incidence of hearing loss than reported in previous studies. Whether or not these conclusions can be extended to other levels of retardation, or to noninstitutionalized retarded children, we do not know. Lloyd and Reid (1967) have found an incidence of hearing loss over 20 percent in a population at the Parsons State Home and Training School, where many of the children are moderately or severely retarded. Webb *et al.* (1966) have discussed the problem of the validity of hearing-test procedures on retardates. A number of investigators (Fulton and Graham, 1966; Fulton, 1967; Hogan and Graham, 1967; Reneau and Mast, 1968; Rose and Rittmanic, 1968) have been exploring more satisfactory approaches to evaluating hearing levels in retarded children and adults.

NEW DEVELOPMENTS

One of the most promising developments in the treatment of the deaf has been the extension of training into earlier preschool years. In 1942 the John Tracy

Clinic in Los Angeles started a program on the University of Southern California campus that emphasized training the mothers of deaf children. This program, started by Mrs. Spencer Tracy, with suggestions from Dr. Boris Morkovin and many others, required mothers to attend the preschool program at least once a week. Thus, the mothers were trained to work more effectively with their children at home. A correspondence course for parents, developed by Mrs. Harriet Montague, has been sent all over the world. All services to parents are free, as the clinic has been largely supported by contributions. The success of this program has led to the establishment of many preschool programs, on much the same model, in many American cities. In the beginning, these programs started at age three, to give the deaf child language-learning experiences, experiences with amplification, and social experiences to prepare him for other school experiences at ages five or six. Harris (1963) has discussed some of these learning experiences, which she developed at the Tracy Clinic and in other programs. More recently, some of these programs have accepted children at one year of age, or even younger, for beginning sensory training. Many of these children whom the author has observed have quite good oral communication by age five.

One controversial program has been described by Griffiths (1957). She reported on the experiences of forty-two infants who were equipped with hearing aids at ages from thirty days to eight months and one week of age. All of these infants were diagnosed as having a hearing loss by pediatricians and/or otologists, and the diagnosis was confirmed at the HEAR Foundation, which is directed by Dr. Griffiths. Dr. Griffiths feels that myeliniza-

tion of the neural pathways in some children will not occur because of a maturational lag unless amplified sound is supplied before birth. Of the group of forty-two, thirty-one advanced to normal hearing, whereas seven were still employing aids at the end of therapy, ranging up to one year in duration. Four children discarded aids with normal responsiveness, and then regressed and returned to using hearing aids. Dr. Griffiths states that this normalization of hearing does not occur when the child is over eight or nine months of age when the hearing aids are fitted. Other investigators have criticized these apparently miraculous results by pointing out the uncertainties of diagnosis of hearing loss at these very young ages. Other studies with babies have not been achieving similar results. Nevertheless, Dr. Griffiths has dramatized the importance of infant testing and the possibility of instruction for deaf infants.

Other stimulating changes in the education of the deaf are occurring. Fusfeld's (1967) book of readings on the education of the deaf reviews some of the developments prior to 1967. The application of new educational approaches to the education of the deaf is producing important changes. This author served on the advisory committee of a project to develop a learning laboratory for hard-of-hearing children (Stepp, 1965). In this project, directed by Dr. Robert Stepp, of the University of Nebraska, single-language concept films were developed for use by young deaf children. The films were placed on closed-loop cartridges, which could be handled by the children and were made available for their use at any time. The purpose of this project was to provide for additional language learning experiences in a situation controlled by the child, who could see the film as many times and as often as he wished, with no teacher intervention. Films of this type are continuing to be produced and are widely used in programs for the deaf and hard-of-hearing.

Many new educational developments for the deaf have been sponsored by the Captioned Films for the Deaf agency of the U. S. Office of Education. This agency, directed by Dr. John Gough, has sponsored many individual projects and has set up four Media Centers for the Deaf, each with a special area of development. Films, filmstrips, transparencies, and new applications of educational technology are being developed. One center is developing new ways to use television in training the deaf. These materials are being distributed to schools for the deaf. Meantime, the original purpose of the Captioned Films program—to provide printed captions on films, so the deaf can use them more effectively—continues. In addition, these centers provide special conferences for teachers of the deaf and other professional workers to teach them how to make use of these new developments. One center, the Midwest Regional Media Center for the Deaf, has sponsored a series of yearly meetings on new developments in teaching the deaf, with published reports (Symposium on Research and Utilization of Educational Media for Teaching the Deaf, 1965, 1966, 1967, 1968). In 1969 the functions of the regional media centers were being enlarged to provide materials for teachers and clinicians working with other handicapped children. Stepp (1968) has reviewed many of the contributions of educational media to deaf education.

These new educational developments of extending education to the deaf babies and providing for the extension of new educational technology, should provide investigators with an increased opportunity to see if the educational deficiencies of the deaf can be remedied with changes in educational approaches.

Another development of great interest has been the extension of amplification to deaf children who have been unable to use hearing aids. Ling, (1968a); Ling and Druz (1967); and LaFon (1967) in France have reported on transposition hearing aids. In these aids, the frequency range of speech is transposed down to lower frequencies to take advantage of the remaining hearing for low pitch sounds, which some children have, even with very severe hearing losses. Thus far, the results have been somewhat equivocal.

SOURCES OF INFORMATION ON THE PSYCHOLOGY OF THE DEAF

As cited in the bibliography, articles on the psychology of the deaf appear in *The American Annals of the Deaf, Volta Review, Journal of Speech and Hearing Disorders, Journal of Speech and Hearing Research, Child Development,* and a number of other journals in psychology, medicine, and education. Abstract sources that are particularly useful include *Psychological Abstracts, DSH Abstracts,* and *Communication Disorders. DSH Abstracts* is a quarterly devoted to the areas of deafness, speech, and hearing, sponsored by the American Speech and Hearing Association and Gallaudet College. *Communication Disorders* is prepared by the Information Center for Hearing, Speech, and Disorders of Human Communication at the Johns Hopkins Medical Institutions. Additional information on the psychology of the deaf is available in the books by Levine (1960) and Myklebust (1964) as well as the chapters concerning the deaf in previous editions of this book.

CONCLUSIONS

This is a time of rapid change in the evaluation and education of the deaf child. Since most of the recent evidence indicates that the deaf are not inferior in intelligence and yet are usually handicapped educationally, particularly in language, some of the new educational procedures described here may produce significant changes. Although the deaf are isolated socially and tend, as adults, to move into groups with other deaf adults, the best available evidence suggests that serious mental illness is not significantly more common in the deaf than in other groups.

References

Anderson, R., & Stevens, G. Deafness and mental retardation in children: The problem. *American Annals of the Deaf,* 1969, *114,* 15–22.

Berlinsky, S. Measurement of the intelligence and personality of the deaf: A review of the literature. *Journal of Speech and Hearing Disorders,* 1952, *17,* 39–54.

Bindon, M. Personality characteristics of rubella deaf children: Implications for teaching of the deaf in general. *American Annals of the Deaf,* 1957, *102,* 264–270.

Birch, J. R., & Birch, J. W. The Leiter International Performance Scale as an aid in the psychological study of deaf children. *American Annals of the Deaf,* 1951, *96,* 502–511.

Birch, J. W. The hearing of mental defectives, its measurement and characteristics. *American Journal of Mental Deficiency,* 1951, *55,* 384–393.

Bishop, H. Performance scale tests applied to deaf and hard of hearing children. *Volta Review,* 1936, *38,* 484–485.

Blank, M., & Bridger, W. Conceptual cross-modal transfer in deaf and hearing children. *Child Development,* 1966, *37,* 29–38.

Bordley, J., and Hardy, W. A study of objective audiometry with use of a psychogalvanometric response. *Annals of Otology, Rhinology and Laryngology,* 1949, *48,* 3.

Bradway, K. The social competence of deaf children. *American Annals of the Deaf,* 1937, *82,* 122–140.

Brannon, J. B., Jr. Linguistic word classes in the spoken language of normal, hard-of-hearing and deaf children. *Journal of Speech and Hearing Research,* 1968, *11,* 279–287.

———, & Murry, T. The spoken syntax of normal, hard-of-hearing, and deaf children. *Journal of Speech and Hearing Research,* 1966, *9,* 604–610.

Brunschwig, L. *A study of some personality aspects of deaf children.* New York: Teachers College, Columbia University, 1936.

Bunch, C. C. *Clinical audiometry.* St. Louis: The C. V. Mosby Company, 1943.

Burchard, E., & Myklebust, H. A. Comparison of congenital and adventitious deafness with respect to its effect on intelligence, personality, and social maturity, part I: Intelligence. *American Annals of the Deaf,* 1942, *87,* 140–154.

Cawthorne, T. Children with defective hearing. In F. McConnell & P. Ward (Eds.), *Deafness in Childhood.* Nashville: Vanderbilt University Press, 1967.

Conference of Executives for the Deaf. Report of the conference committee on nomenclature. *American Annals of the Deaf,* 1938, *83,* 1–3.

Davis, H. The present status of evoked response audiometry. *Proceedings of the International Conference on Oral Education of the Deaf,* Vol. I. Washington, D. C., The Alexander Graham Bell Association for the Deaf, Inc., 1967.

———, & Silverman, R. (Eds.). *Hearing and deafness* (rev. ed.). New York: Holt, Rinehart, & Winston Inc., 1960.

Day, H., Fusfeld, I., & Pintner, R. *A Survey of American schools for the deaf.* Washington, D.C.: National Research Council, 1928.

Derbyshire, A. *et al.* Components of hearing measured by EEG and its responses to sounds. *International Audiology,* 1962, *1,* 254–256.

Di Carlo, L. *The deaf.* Englewood Cliffs, N. J.: Prentice-Hall, Inc., 1964.

Doerfler, L. Neurophysiological clues to auditory acuity. *Journal of Speech and Hearing Disorders,* 1948, *13,* 227–232.

Downs, M. Audiometry in children (infants). *International Audiology,* 1962, *1,* 268–270.

———. Organization and procedures of a newborn infant screening program. *Hearing Speech News,* 1967, *35,* 26–36.

———, & Sterritt, G. A guide to newborn and infant hearing screening programs. *Archives of Oto-laryngology,* 1967, *85,* 15–22.

Ewing, A., & Ewing, E. *Hearing aids, lipreading and clear speech.* Washington, D.C.: Volta Bureau, 1967, p. 118.

Foale, M., & Paterson, J. The hearing of mental defectives. *American Journal of Mental Deficiency,* 1954, *59,* 254–258.

Fulton, R. Standard puretone and Bekesy audiometric measures with the mentally retarded. *American Journal of Mental Deficiency,* 1967, *72,* 60–73.

———, & Graham, J. Conditioned orientation reflex audiometry with the mentally retarded. *American Journal of Mental Deficiency,* 1966, *70,* 703–708.

Furfey, P., & Harte, T. *Interaction of deaf and hearing in Frederick County, Maryland.* Washington, D.C.: Catholic University Press, 1964, p. 100.

Furth, H. *Report of the proceedings of the International Congress on Education of the Deaf and of the 41st meeting of the Convention of American Instructors of the Deaf.* Washington, D.C: Gallaudet College, 1963.

———. *Thinking without language.* New York: The Free Press, 1966.

Fusfeld, I. (Ed.). *A handbook of readings in education of the deaf and postschool implications.* Springfield, Ill.: Charles C. Thomas, 1967.

Gaines, J. *A comparison of two audiometric tests administered to a group of mentally retarded children.* Master's thesis, University of Nebraska, 1961.

Goetzinger, C., Wills, R., & Dekker, L. Nonlanguage IQ tests used with deaf pupils. *Volta Review,* 1967, *69,* 500–506.

Goldstein, R., Kendall, D., & Arick, B. Electroencephalic audiometry in young children. *Journal of Speech and Hearing Disorders,* 1963, *28,* 331–354.

Goldstein, R., Landau, W., & Kleffner, F. Neurologic observation on a population of deaf and aphasic children. *Annals of Otology,* 1960, *69,* 756.

Goodman, W. *et al.* Audiometry in newborn children by electroencephalography. *Laryngoscope,* 1964, *74,* 1316–1328.

Gregory, T. A comparison of certain personality traits and interests in deaf and hearing children. *Child Development,* 1938, *9,* 277.

Griffiths, C. *Conquering childhood deafness* (1st ed.). New York: Exposition Press, 1957.

Grings, W., Lowell, E., & Honnard, R. Electrodermal responses of deaf children. *Journal of Speech and Hearing Research,* 1960, *3,* 120–129.

Groht, M. *Natural language for deaf children.* Washington, D.C: The Alexander Graham Bell Association for the Deaf, Inc., 1958.

Hall, P. Results of recent tests at Gallaudet College. *American Annals of the Deaf,* 1929, *74,* 389–395.

Hardy, J., Daugherty, A., & Hardy, W. Hearing responses and audiologic screening in infants. *Journal of Pediatrics,* 1959, *55,* 382–390.

Hardy W. Early detection and assessment. *Proceedings of the International Conference on Oral Education of the Deaf.* Vol. I, Washington,, D.C.: The Alexander Graham Bell Association for the Deaf, Inc., 1967.

———, & Bordley, J. Evaluation of hearing in young children. *Acta Otolaryngolica,* 1952, *40,* 346–360.

———, & Pauls, M. The test situation in PGSR audiometry. *Journal of Speech and Hearing Disorders,* 1952, *17,* 13–24.

Harris, G. *Language for the preschool deaf child* (2nd ed.). New York: Grune & Stratton, Inc., 1963.

Hirsch, I. *The Measurement of hearing.* New York: McGraw-Hill Book Company, 1952.

Hiskey, M., & Wiley, J. Intelligence achievement and hearing levels of older deaf children in a state school for the deaf. Unpublished study, 1963.

Hogan, D., & Graham, J. The use of summing computer for analyzing auditory evoked responses of mentally retarded adults. *Journal of Auditory Research,* 1967, *7,* 1–13.

Hughson, W., Ciocco, A., & Palmer, C. Studies of the pupils of the Pennsylvania School for the Deaf. *Archives of Otolaryngology,* 1939, *29,* 403.

Jerger, J. (Ed.). *Modern developments in audiology.* New York: Academic Press, Inc., 1963.

Johnson, D., & Myklebust, H. *Learning disabilities.* New York: Grune & Stratton, Inc., 1967.

Johnston, P., & Farrell, M. Auditory impairment among residential school children at the Walter E. Fernald State School. *American Journal of Mental Deficiency,* 1954, *58,* 640–643.

Kates, S., Kates, W., & Michael, J. Cognitive processes in deaf and hearing adolescents and adults. *Psychological Monographs,* 1962, *76,* 34.

Kates, S. *et al.* Categorization and related verbalizations in deaf and hearing adolescents. *Journal of Educational Psychology,* 1961, *52* (4), 188–194.

Kirk, S. Behavior problem tendencies in deaf and hard of hearing children. *American Annals of the Deaf,* 1938, *83,* 131–137.

La Crosse, E., & Bidlake, H. A method to test the hearing of mentally retarded children. *Volta Review,* 1964, *66,* 27–30.

La Fon, J. Hearing aids for the extreme deaf. *International Audiology,* 1967, *6,* 343–345.

Lane, H., & Schneider, J. A performance test for school age deaf children. *American Annals of the Deaf,* 1941, *86,* 441–447.

Lane, H., & Silverman, S. Deaf children. In H. Davis (Ed.), *Hearing and deafness.* New York: Murray Hill Books, Inc., 1947.

Lenneberg, E. *Biological foundations of language.* New York: John Wiley & Sons, Inc., 1967.

————. Prerequisites for language acquisition. *Proceedings of the International Conference on the Oral Education of the Deaf.* Washington, D.C.: The Alexander Graham Bell Association for the Deaf, Inc., 1967.

Levine, E. *Youth in a silent world.* New York: New York University Press, 1956.

————. *The psychology of deafness.* New York: Columbia University Press, 1960.

Ling, D. Frequency transposition and programmed instruction. *Ami Sourds,* 1968, *2,* 1–4. (*a*)

————. Frequency transposition and programmed instruction. *Ami Sourds,* 1968, *3,* 8–11. (*b*)

————, & Druz, W. Transposition of high frequency sounds by partial vocoding of the speech spectrum: Its use by deaf children. *Journal of Auditory Research,* 1967, *7,* 133–144.

Lloyd, L., & Reid, M. The incidence of hearing impairment in an institutionalized mentally retarded population. *American Journal of Mental Deficiency,* 1967, *71,* 746–763.

————, & Spradlin, J. An operant audiometric procedure for difficult-to-test patients, *Journal of Speech and Hearing Disorders,* 1968, *33,* 236–245.

Lowell, E. *et al.* Evaluation of pure tone audiometry with preschool age children. *Journal of Speech and Hearing Disorders,* 1956, *21,* 292–302.

————. Measurement of auditory threshold with a special purpose analog computer. *Journal of Speech and Hearing Research,* 1961, *4,* 105–112.

————. Temporal evannation: A new approach in diagnostic audiology. *Journal of Speech and Hearing Disorders,* 1960, *25,* 340–345.

Lyon, U. The use of vocational and personality tests with the deaf. *Journal of Applied Psychology,* 1934, *18,* 224.

MacKane, K. A comparison of the intelligence of deaf and hearing children. *Teachers College Contributions to Education,* No. 585. New York: Columbia University Press, 1933.

MacPherson, J., & Lane, H. A comparison of deaf and hearing on the Hiskey test and performance scales. *American Annals of the Deaf,* 1948, *93,* 178–184.

McAndrew, H. Rigidity and isolation: A study of the deaf and the blind. *Journal of Abnormal and Social Psychology,* 1948, *43,* 476.

McCandless, G. Clinical application of evoked response audiometry. *Journal of Speech and Hearing Research,* 1967, *10,* 468–478.

McConnell, F., & Ward, P. *Deafness in childhood.* Nashville: Vanderbilt University Press, 1967.

McCroskey, R. Progress report on a home training program for deaf infants. *International Audiology,* 1967, *6,* 171–177.

Meyer, E. Psychological and emotional problems of deaf children *American Annals of the Deaf,* 1953, *98,* 472–477.

Meyerson, L. A psychology of impaired hearing. In W. Cruickshank (Ed.), *Psychology of exceptional children and youth* (2nd ed.). Englewood Cliffs, N.J.: Prentice-Hall, Inc., 1963.

———, & Michael, J. The measurement of sensory thresholds in exceptional children. *Monographs in Somatopsychology*. No. 4. Houston: University of Houston, 1960.

Midwest Regional Media Center for the Deaf. *Designing instructional facilities for teaching the deaf: The learning module.* Symposium on Research and Utilization of Educational Media for Teaching the Deaf. Lincoln: University of Nebraska, 1968.

———. *The educational media complex.* Symposium on Research and Utilization of Educational Media for Teaching the Deaf. Lincoln: University of Nebraska, 1967.

———. *Systems approach in deaf education.* Symposium on Research and Utilization of Educational Media for Teaching the Deaf. Lincoln: University of Nebraska, 1966.

———. Symposium on Research and Utilization of Educational Media for Teaching the Hearing Impaired. Lincoln: University of Nebraska, 1965.

Moores, D. Projected trends in language development for the deaf. *Deaf american,* 1967, *20,* 5–7.

Morkovin, B. *Through the barriers of deafness and isolation.* New York: The Macmillan Company, 1960.

Myklebust, H. The measurement of language. *Proceedings of the International Conference on the Oral Education of the Deaf.* Vol. 2. Washington, D.C.: The Alexander Graham Bell Association for the Deaf, Inc., 1967.

———. Psychological and psychiatric implications of deafness. *Archives of Otolaryngology,* 1963, *78,* 790–793.

———. *Psychology of deafness* (2nd ed.). New York: Grune & Stratton, Inc., 1964.

———, & Burchard, E. A study of the effects of congenital and adventitious deafness on intelligence, personality, and social maturity of school children. *Journal of Educational Psychology,* 1945, *34,* 321.

Newby, H. *Audiology* (2nd ed.). New York: Appleton-Century-Crofts, 1964.

Neyhus, A. The personality of socially well-adjusted adult as revealed by projective tests. Unpublished doctoral dissertation, Northwestern University, 1962.

Odom, P., & Blanton, R. Phrase learning in deaf and hearing subjects. *Journal of Speech and Hearing Research,* 1967, *10,* 600–605.

Oleron, P. Conceptual thinking of the deaf. *American Annals of the Deaf,* 1953, *98,* 304–310.

O'Neill, J., & Oyer, H. *Visual Communication for the hard of hearing.* Englewood Cliffs, N.J.: Prentice-Hall, Inc., 1961.

Oyer, H. *Auditory Communication for the hard of hearing.* Englewood Cliffs, N.J.: Prentice-Hall, Inc., 1966.

Peters, C. Early detection of impaired hearing in young children. *Practica Oto-Rhino-Laryngologica,* 1967, *29,* 295–300.

Peterson, E. Testing deaf children with Kohs Block Designs. *American Annals on the Deaf,* 1936, *81,* 242–254.

———, & Williams, J. Intelligence of deaf children as measured by drawings. *American Annals of the Deaf,* 1930, *75,* 242–254.

Pintner, R. *The psychology of the physically handicapped.* New York: Appleton-Century-Crofts, 1944.

Proceedings of the International Conference on the Oral Education of the Deaf. Vol. 1 and 2. Washington, D.C.: The Alexander Graham Bell Association for the Deaf, Inc., 1967.

Quigley, S., Jenne, W., Phillips, S. *Deaf students in colleges and universities.* Washington D. C.: The Alexander Graham Bell Association for the Deaf, Inc., 1968.

Rainer, J. *et al.* (Eds.). *Family and mental health problems in a deaf population.* New York: Department of Medical Genetics, N.Y. State Psychiatric Institute, Columbia University, 1963.

Reamer, J. Mental and educational measurements of the deaf. *Psychological Monographs,* 1921, *29* (132).

Reneau, J., & Mast, R. Telemetric EEG audiometry instrumentation for use with the profoundly retarded. *American Journal of Mental Deficiency,* 1968, *72,* 506–511.

Rose, D., & Rittmanic, P. Evoked response tests with mentally retarded. *Archives of Otolaryngology,* 1968, *88,* 495–498.

Rosenberg, P., & Toglia, U. Electronystagmography in clinical audiology. *Journal of Speech and Hearing Disorders,* 1967, *32,* 170–176.

Rosenstein, J. Research in the linguistic behavior of deaf children. *Proceedings of the In-*

ternational Conference on the Oral Education of the Deaf. Washington, D.C.: The Alexander Graham Bell Association for the Deaf, Inc., 1967.

Ruhm, H., & Carhart, R. Objective speech audiometry: A new method based on electrodermal response. *Journal of Speech and Hearing Research,* 1958, *1,* 168–179.

Rutledge, L. Aspiration levels of deaf children as compared with those of hearing children. *Journal of Speech and Hearing Disorders,* 1954, *19,* 375–380.

Sheridan, M. Simple clinical hearing tests for very young or mentally retarded children. *British Medical Journal,* 1958, *2,* 999–1009.

Shirley, M., & Goodenough, F. A survey of intelligence of deaf children in Minnesota schools. *American Annals of the Deaf,* 1932, *77,* 238–247.

Siegenthaler, B., & Haspiel, G. *Development of two standardized measures of hearing for speech by children.* University Park: Pennsylvania State University, 1966.

Siegenthaler, B., Pearson, J., & Lezak, R. A speech reception threshold test for children. *Journal of Speech and Hearing Disorders,* 1954, *19,* 360–366.

Silverman, S. Hard-of-hearing children. In H. Davis (Ed.), *Hearing and deafness.* New York: Murray Hill Books, Inc., 1947.

Springer, N. A comparative study of the intelligence of a group of deaf and hearing children. *American Annals of the Deaf,* 1938, *83,* 138–152.

Stepp, R. *A feasibility study to investigate the instrumentation, establishment, and operation of a learning laboratory for hard-of-hearing children.* Final report. Lincoln: University Extension Division, University of Nebraska, 1965.

———. Educational media and deaf education: The emerging literature. *Volta Review,* 1968, *70,* 465–474.

Stewart, C. Some basic considerations in ap-plying the GSR technique to the measurement of auditory sensitivity. *Journal of Speech and Hearing Disorders,* 1954, *19,* 174–183.

Streng, A., & Kirk, S. The social competence of deaf and hard of hearing children in a public day school. *American Annals of the Deaf,* 1938, *83,* 244–254.

Tell, J. *et al.* Thresholds of hearing by respiration using a polygraph. *Archives of Otolaryngology,* 1967, *86,* 172–174.

Templin, M. Methodological variations in language research with deaf subjects. *Proceedings of the International Conference on the Oral Education of the Deaf.* Washington, D.C.: The Alexander Graham Bell Association for the Deaf, Inc., 1967.

Vernon, M., & Brown, D. A guide to psychological tests and testing procedures in the evaluation of deaf and hard-of-hearing children. *Journal of Speech and Hearing Disorders,* 1964, *29,* 414–423.

Webb, C. *et al.* Incidence of hearing loss in institutionalized mental retardates. *American Journal of Mental Deficiency,* 1966, *70,* 563–568.

White House Conference on Child Health and Protection. *Special Education, the Handicapped and the Gifted: Report on The Committee on Special Classes. Section III, Education and Training.* Vol. III-F. New York: Appleton-Century-Crofts, 1931.

Wiley, J., & Jacobs, G. The incidence and characteristics of hearing loss in an institutionalized, mildly retarded population. In L. Lloyd, & R. Frisina (Eds.), *The audiologic assessment of the mentally retarded: Proceedings of a national conference.* Parsons, Kans.: Parsons State Hospital and Training Center, 1965.

Zeckel, A., & Van der Kolk, J. A comparative intelligence test of groups of children born deaf and of good hearing by means of the Parteus Test. *American Annals of the Deaf,* 1939, *84,* 114–123.

NINE

Psychological Problems of Children and Youth with Chronic Medical Disorders

JOSEPH NEWMAN

Joseph Newman is Professor of Education and Psychology at the University of Pittsburgh. He has served as Chief of Psychology Service, Veterans Administration Hospital, Pittsburgh, and as Director of Rehabilitation, Municipal Sanatorium, Otisville, New York.

THEORETICAL MODELS IN THE PSYCHOLOGY OF ILLNESS

Since the first edition of this book in 1955, there has been a prodigious growth in interest and in programs for exceptional children and youth. The increased number of published works in the psychological literature on chronic disorders among children and youth reflects this state of affairs. With this growth, theoretical concepts guiding research have become diversified so that where once the psychoanalytic approach was dominant, today other orientations appear, particularly those stemming from general psychological theory.

Moreover, the literature on chronic medical disorders among children and youth has changed its emphasis from focus on specific disease entities to focus on more general elements present in all disorders. There is perhaps one exception, asthmatic conditions, in which a large literature has developed, as will be seen. Nevertheless, here too, the trend in published studies is to point up similarities to other disorders. Thus, the literature on chronic disease among children continues to affirm a fundamental postulate of Chapter 1, that there are more similarities in the psychological aspects of different chronic disorders than dissimilarities. In addition, the search for unifying concepts to attack the psychological problems of children with chronic disorders is receiving its most vigorous stimulation from the broad field of psychology, especially developmental psychology.

In the early period of psychological study of chronic disorders the influence of Freud and psychoanalytic theory was strong. The frequent focus of research efforts was on parent-child relationships, but the variables developed proved to be complicated. Consequently, the studies were both time consuming and expensive, with the result that the research was limited in both output and impact, and the generalizations derived from a psychoanalytic frame of reference had less than adequate empirical foundations. Nevertheless, psychoanalytic orientation still remains a major influence in research among chronically ill children. The explanation for this continued theoretical dominance would seem to be the medical context in which much of the research takes place. Another factor to be kept in mind is the significant amount of research being carried out by investigators with medical backgrounds, principally psychiatrists and pediatricians. A frequent occurrence is collaborative research between medical men and nonmedical professionals, usually psychologists and social workers.

The next period of influence was derived from the general field of psychology, especially from learning theory. The attractiveness of this approach was in the ready availability of testable hypotheses and developed techniques, particularly for studies in developmental psychology. There was interest in the effects of stress or strong stimulation during infancy and early years, which served as a reminder that the environment is a source of interaction with the individual. This interest continues, but in broadened fashion, from preoccupation with conditioning and motor development to concern with such problems as perception, attention, and curiosity. All varieties of psychological phenomena are taken to be understood best within sociocultural settings. This, of course, is not a new notion but one that dates back to antiquity.

The involvement of psychological phenomena in illness is generally referred to as psychosomatic disorders. These psychosomatic or psychophysiologic disorders represent one end of the continuum of physiological reactions that occur in response to a variety of life experiences or in association with emotional status. These reactions may range from minor physiological changes to those resulting in severe tissue damage. Everyone has had symptoms, such as heartburn, palpitations, or dry mouth, as consequences of emotional experiences without pathology in the gastrointestinal, cardiovascular, or secretory systems. Psychosomatic considerations are generally recognized in contemporary pediatrics. Prugh (1963, p. 246) states:

... the concept of comprehensive pediatric care rests upon two basic assumptions: (1) both somatic and psychologic factors may act as predisposing, contributory, precipitating, and perpetuating forces in illness; (2) the prevention of disease and the promotion of healthy growth and adaptation must include attention to all aspects of the developing child's psychobiological equipment as well as the psychological setting in which he exists.

Within this context, there is no dichotomization of wholly somatic or completely psychological disease.

In the past most of the literature in psychosomatic disorders was based upon studies of adults. This is less true now with a growing literature dealing specifically with children and youth. It is possible that psychosomatic disorders are more prevalent among adults and that they are more readily identified. On the other hand, there is little question that psychosocial stresses in children may be associated with significant physiological changes.

Theoretically, the questions confronting workers in the field may be stated as follows: (1) How are life experiences translated into physiological changes? (2) What factors determine which persons are most likely to develop psychosomatic disorders?

and (3) What factors determine the "choice" of the organ system? (Lipton, Steinschneider, and Richmond, 1966).

Several theoretical models have been developed to explicate these problems. Already mentioned are the approaches derived from concepts elaborated by Freud. One approach postulated that psychosomatic disorders are basically conversion reactions and represent symbolic expressions of repressed feelings. For any individual the process whereby this takes place may be understood only after knowledge is gained of repressed thoughts and feelings with elaboration of the symbolic meanings associated with them. There is little support for this formulation.

Departing from the orthodox Freudian approach, Dunbar (1948) attempted to develop personality profiles in which specific personality constellations were associated with specific disorders. Again, specificity theories have not been supported in research studies.

Alexander (1950) presented a model in which he hypothesized that each conflict situation and emotional state is accompanied by a specific pattern of physiological alteration. Persisting strong unresolved conflicts may lead to psychophysiological disorders. The nature of the conflict situation determines to some extent the selection of the disorder organ. Predisposition also plays a role. Alexander's model is also a specificity theory that has not been substantiated.

More prevalent currently are the nonspecific theories that attribute psychosomatic disease to general psychological stress reactions. Some writers emphasize the common origins of many diverse psychosomatic symptoms (Kubie, 1954). Thus, psychosomatic disturbances are multiplexly expressed in various systems of the body and not in just one organ system. They are the end result of a series of events. This series of events may appear to have been initiated by some easily visible life stress such as school failure, injury, or death. However, the way in which a person reacts to stress is a highly individual matter, which can be understood only by appreciation of the many factors operating in that person's situation (Ehrentheil, 1959; Stevenson and Matthews, 1953).

Hence, the psychological component in any illness is variable; it may range from incidental to central importance. Starr (1955) has conceptualized a schema, a psychosomatic spectrum, in which he describes a continuum of psychological complications as they may occur in all types of clinical illness. The range is from illnesses in which the psychological factor is regarded as causative to those illnesses in which it is incidental.

These considerations are applicable to the conditions surrounding exceptionality among children and youth as well as to every variety of medical disorder affecting them. Parenthetically, it should be noted again, such considerations are applicable to the nonexceptional as well.

In the explication of the complexly related somatic and psychological states, it is not necessary to analyze an example of each variety of disorder along the continuum of psychosomatic reactions. From among the chronic disorders, we have chosen four severe and common disorders: asthma, diabetes mellitus, heart ailments, and tuberculosis. These disorders illustrate two psychosomatic relationships—psychophysiological and somatopsychological. However, before discussing these specific diseases, it is fundamental to present some general observations and findings about significant psychological factors in illness in general among children. Basic to our approach is Thompson's observation (1959, p. 1) that "the living organism is a dynamic and developing system, variable in its functioning according to inherent genetic characteristics which interact with selected environmental antecedents. We now know that alteration in one part of this system can have widespread and enduring consequences."

INFLUENCE OF EARLY EXPERIENCE IN CHRONIC DISORDERS

Noted previously was the interest in seeking answers to questions about the effects of early experience on individuals and the consequent growth of a large theoretical and research literature. Practically no one today denies the importance of early experience. Much of this interest, to be sure, stems from Freud's writings and has led to investigations of the effects of trauma and the effects of mothering, but with the research sophistication and theoretical refinements derived from experimental psychology. Both of these investigation areas are significant to a psychology of illness.

A crucial component of Freud's notions about early experience has been the effects of trauma. The first investigations generally proceeded on the hypothesis that emotional development was most importantly, if not exclusively, involved in traumatic events. More recently, stemming from Hebb's writings (1949), perceptual and cognitive development are believed to be even more significantly affected.

One avenue of investigation has been to relate psychosomatic disorders to psychological traumas having their origin in the very early life of the individual. Mohr and others (1955) studied a group of psychosomatically ill children. They found that these children were consistently exposed to inadequate mothering care during the first year of life.

In a later report, Garner and Wenar (1959) more systematically explored the hypothesis that susceptibility to psychosomatic illness in children develops in the first year of life when somatic response patterns are laid down in an atmosphere of close but mutually frustrating mother-child interaction. Mothers of physically ill children had positive attitudes toward pregnancy and early child care; mothers of neurotic children had negative attitudes toward both; and mothers of psychosomatically ill children had positive attitudes toward pregnancy but not toward child care. Mothers in this last group were seen as ambitious, controlling, driving women, who victimized their children. They expected conformity but lacked tenderness and the spontaneous enjoyment of children. They were mothers who "loved" their children and did all the "right" things. Although this study did not have a control group and the number of subjects was relatively small, it is regarded as a contribution to the growing literature about psychosomatically ill children.

In a study (Carter and Chess, 1951) of factors influencing the adjustment of organically handicapped children, the most prominent single factor in determining whether anxiety would become an important element seemed to be parental attitude. It was found that the amount of anxiety and the manner in which it found expression bore no predictable relationship to the handicap per se. There was no predictable relationship between the severity of the handicap and parental attitudes, such as overprotection or underprotection. The amount of parental anxiety and the manner in which it found expression seemed more related to the parents' own particular emotional needs and basic attitudes toward the child than to realistic elements of the handicap.

Again, Tuttman (1955), in an investigation of the influence of the severity of disability and parental authoritarianism in the child's acceptance of disability, found that children of authoritarian parents have more difficulty in accepting disability than do children of less authoritarian parents.

Parsons (1952) has emphasized that the concept of illness as applied to the sick adult cannot be applied to the sick child. The immature child cannot be expected to assume the same roles and levels of responsibility as the adult. For example, the child cannot be held responsible for getting out of his condition by an act of will. He is not held responsible in usual dealings with others and, therefore, is not to be held responsible for recognition of his own condition, its disabilities, and his need for help. Therefore, third parties—parents—must play an especially important role in the child's illness.

The most severe trauma faced by the chronically ill child is separation from parents, especially the mother, when hospitalization becomes necessary. This trauma is indeed a common experience. The earlier research on maternal separation led to broad generalizations, many of which are now regarded as oversimplified interpretations. Yarrow (1964, p. 91) has reviewed the literature in this area and does not regard separation from the mother as a simple, delimited event with simple predictable consequences.

The meaning to the child of the event of separation and the experiences subsequent to separation will also vary with individual and experiential factors, such as the child's unique vulnerabilities and sensitivities, his developmental stage, and his experiences prior to separation.

Separation that occurs after a long period of indifferent parental care or overt rejection and hostility is likely to have a different meaning to the child from that representing a break in an intimate, protective, gratifying relationship. It is also likely that the meaning of separation to the child will vary with such characteristics of the experience as: the degree of concomitant trauma; whether it is permanent or temporary; and if temporary, whether it is of long or short duration; whether any contact is maintained with the parents; and whether it is the first or one in a series of similar experiences.

In summary, the effects of separation from the mother have been the subject for much reassessment. It may be said that a more balanced orientation exists in that the effects of maternal deprivation do not inevitably and inexorably lead to psychologically disastrous consequences, nor is there a negation of the importance of early maternal care. It seems clear that all separation experiences cannot be equated as to their consequences. Such experiences vary widely from minor events with which most children are able to cope to very traumatic disruptions of relationships. Important here are the situational circumstances.

HOSPITALIZATION

Studies of hospitalization for children emphasize that separation from parents and from familiar surroundings is but one element in the total experience. The other elements identified are feelings of helplessness and the increased dependency associated with illness, threats to bodily integrity through medical and surgical procedures, and, finally, effects of a strange environment filled with strange people (Shore, 1967).

Interest in the effects of hospitalization was stimulated by the studies on the effects of institutionalization by Spitz (1946) and Goldfarb (1945, 1947). Their studies showed that favorable conditions of shelter, food, medical care, schooling, and supervised social life are not in themselves sufficient to assure adequate physical growth and emotional development. Developmental retardation, emotional disturbances, and language dysfunctions have been reported. Influential also were reports of World War II experiences in England with children separated from their families. Evacuated children displayed evidences of severe personality damages (Freud and Burlingham, 1944).

Critical in the institutional situation is not separation from the mother, but the lack of intellectual and social stimulation. It was this observation that has led to efforts to modify institutional circumstances to prevent harmful effects to whatever extent possible. Both the age of the child and the duration of institutional care are significant; the earlier the age of placement and the longer the duration, the greater the deleterious effects.

These findings have face validity in application to hospitalized children and spurred investigations of the effects of hospitalization (Bowlby, 1951). The hospitalized child has a different psychological situation; he has a family, an illness, and continued contact with parents. It was the work of Bowlby (1952, 1956) in England and particularly that of his associate, Robertson (1959, 1962), that advanced the hypothesis that maternal separation experiences during hospitalization were pathogenic. Robertson states that when hospital admission deprives a child of a warm, intimate, and continuing relationship with his mother, particularly before the age of four, he reacts emotionally in a characteristic manner. This reaction has three phases. The first phase is protest, in which the child strongly and consciously demonstrates his grief. Next is despair in which the child is less active in showing a conscious need of his mother but experiences an increasing hopelessness. He may become withdrawn, apathetic, and may make no demands. Sometimes this stage is presumed to indicate that distress has lessened. A common remark is "He was quite settled until his mother came." With short hospitalization, some children just reach this stage or may go home in the stage of protest. In the third phase, denial, the child shows more interest in his surroundings. He may appear stable and sociable. However, this is believed to be a superficial impression and actually is a manifestation of a defensive or adaptive maneuver. When the previously lamented mother comes, the child hardly knows her and no longer cries when she leaves. He is reluctant to leave the hospital. Robertson believes that the aftermath of long hospitalization in the early years is an extended period of serious emotional maladaptation. The two main dangers of hospitalization are the traumatic (shock of losing the mother and the pain and fright of treatment) and the deprivational—a function of lengthy separation.

In this country, studies were also stimulated, and the most notable were those by Prugh and his associates (1953, 1954, 1955). The purpose of the studies was to investigate the nature of the effects of brief hospitalization upon both children and parents. Two groups of 100 children, matched for age, sex and diagnosis and hospitalized for relatively acute illnesses and for relatively short periods of time, formed the basis of one investigation. The results supported the impression of other investigators that children under three years of age are the most susceptible to the negative aspects surrounding hospital care. Separation from the mother is often interpreted as a punishment or desertion. This reaction, separation anxiety, was most frequent among the younger children. It was also common in older age groups but in less severe form and not as frequently. Among the older children, anxiety was the most common persisting posthospital reaction. Depression and various disturbances, such as in feeding, sleeping, and toilet behavior, were noted. Regressive phenomena constituted the most common defense. Among older children, withdrawing behavior became common. Frequent among all children was the reaction to treatment and diagnostic procedures as punishment. In the main, children who showed the most successful adjustment to hospitalization were those who seemed to have the most satisfying relationship with their parents, especially the mother. The highest positive correlation was reported between apparent adaptive capacity and adjustment to hospitalization. Children with limited adaptive capacity showed the most severe reaction to the total experience of hospitalization. The reactions of the parents to hospitalization were found to be dependent upon the adjustment of the parents and the nature of their relationships with the child.

Other studies revealed essentially similar findings. Gofman, Buckman, and Schade (1957) undertook to assess the preparation for hospitalization among 100 children, ages three to fifteen years, as well as their understanding of illness and their reaction to hospital care. They found that 75 percent of their group were not prepared for hospitalization. It was felt by these investigators that children as young as three or four years of age could understand something of their illness and the necessary treatment if explanations were made in terms suited to their levels. Marlens (1960) compared emotional attitudes toward self and the environment for a group of children hospitalized and a group with similar complaints but not hospitalized. The hospitalized children were significantly higher in feelings of rejection and punishment, in somatic preoccupation, and in anxiety and depression. There was no difference between the groups in feelings of hostility.

At the University of Maryland Hospital, Glaser (1960), by means of group discussions with mothers, elicited descriptions of the reactions of their children to hospitalization. These reactions included: increased dependency needs and physiological regression in behavior, withdrawal from others, and need for continued contact with the outside world. This last reaction made mothers fearful that mention of friends, pets, and other familiar aspects of home life would make the child homesick. Actually, it was found that talking about these matters was helpful. The technique of group discussions for mothers was found to be useful in dealing with the mother's anxieties, fears, and misconceptions about the illness and the hospitalization.

In another study, Vaughan (1957) undertook to investigate the attitudes toward hospitalization and an impending operation for correction of strabismus in a group of twenty children and a group of twenty controls. He found that all children had varied, bizarre, and sometimes frightening ideas about the hospital. The children reflected the parents' anxieties. However, he gave (to his experimental group) simple and brief explanations and reassurances of what to expect. He found that this was enough to result in a significant benefit.

Schaffer and Callendar (1959) studied

twenty-five infants hospitalized less than two weeks. They found distinct differences between infants under seven months of age and infants between seven and twelve months of age. The younger infants adapted to the entire hospital experience with little evidence of disturbance. The older infants showed a variety of disturbances associated with maternal separation—marked anxiety with strangers, desperate clinging to mothers, and vigorous crying when the mother left.

These and similar experiences led to actions to minimize, if not eliminate, the hazards of hospitalization for children. This subject was the concern of a study group of the World Health Organization (WHO) in meetings held in Stockholm in September 1954. It was pointed out that the best place to care for the ill child is at home. The child under five is unable to understand the meaning of illness. Even for an adult, going to a hospital is a major event. For the small child, the break in relationships occasioned by hospitalization seems final and irrevocable.

The remedial efforts suggested by the WHO meetings (Capes, 1956) proceeded along three lines: elimination of force or actual pain in contact between staff and child, preparation for hospitalization, and continuing close contact between the mother and child. This last is most controversial and has met with the most resistance. Nevertheless, there have been efforts to modify the separation of mother and hospitalized child that is customary in this country.

In England these recommendations were incorporated in the Platt Report of 1959 (Robertson, 1962). This report encouraged hospitals to provide unlimited visiting to all children in hospitals and to develop living-in arrangements for mothers of preschool patients. The British hospitals, as well as those in the United States, have been slow in acting upon the recommendations of the Platt Report.

On the other hand, some students of the problems, recognizing the potential deleterious effects of hospitalization, insisted that these effects were not inevitable. They were agreed that, with prophylactic measures, hospitalization could be a constructive experience (Sonit, 1960).

Illingworth (1958) believes that the case has been overstated, particularly the danger that children who experience institutionalization and similar forms of deprivation, especially in early life, commonly develop psychopathic or affectionless characters. The exaggeration of the risk can cause much unnecessary anxiety in parents and might possibly delay necessary hospital treatment. Exaggeration can also lead to the minimizing of this risk or denial of its existence. On the basis of his experience in the follow-up of all children discharged from a medical ward in an English hospital, Illingworth found that it was exceptional for the child to show behavior problems which could be ascribed directly to hospital stay and experiences. Certainly, the majority of children cry in hospitals, especially young children, when parents leave at the end of visiting time. Some may show other types of emotional behavior. But the existence of this sort of behavior does not mean that the hospital experience leads to behavior problems which persist for weeks or months after discharge. Indeed, it would be surprising if young children below four years of age were not upset by hospital admission. Nevertheless, Illingworth believes that the problem of psychological trauma is great, and the fact that "only a small majority" show any lasting ill effects must not be a basis for minimizing it.

At this point in discussing remedial and preventive measures for the harmful consequences of hospitalization, it would be instructive to scan briefly similar actions with regard to the broader problems of institutionalization. Certainly, the findings on the destructive effects of institutional care on young children led to an avoidance, if not rejection, of all forms of group care for young children. However, since alternatives were not easy to find, exploration of changes in institutional child care was begun. This development was reinforced by reevaluations and reinterpretations of the early studies. The new findings provided a more precise understanding of the parameters of institutional environments that are associated with deleterious effects of institutional life. Thus, bases were established for changes in institutional care.

A recent report of one such institutional effort concerned eighty-five children between the ages of three months and three years (Flint, 1966). Despite numerous difficulties and resistances, many and varied changes were introduced. Marked alterations were made in the physical environment to increase the quality and variety of sensory stimulation. Especially significant were the attempts to create an environment conducive to the development of feelings of individuality in the children. Each child was given special possessions—clothes, bedcovers, toys— with some unique characteristics. The management of routines was altered to provide greater flexibility and recognition of individual differences. Equally important was the redefinition of the role of the caretakers to emphasize individualized relationships with the children. The number of caretakers was increased to enhance the possibility of closer relationships. A central element in those relationships was the effort to elicit initiative and to encourage persistence in mastering simple defined tasks.

Systematic study identifies the several factors that are causative in behavior problems associated with hospital stay. First is the disturbance in parent-child relationship before admission or after; the better this relationship, the less likely the development of disturbance. Lack of or inadequate preparation for admission is another factor. A third is unwise or excessive preparation as a result of anxiety about hospitals on the part of the parents. Frequently encountered are threats to the child—to do as they are told or lose love. Also implicated is a lack of daily visiting. Parental anxiety during visits, along with unkept promises, are potent in creating problems. Parental attitudes on discharge, overindulgence, and the like, especially after serious illness, are important. Age at hospitalization is a critical factor; children are likely to be susceptible to psychological damage from about seven months to seven years, with the most vulnerable period from seven months to three years. Hospital procedures also stimulate anxieties regarding bodily injury.

Unquestionably, there is broad recognition of the problem of psychological trauma for hospitalized children and the realization that many areas of hospital procedure can be modified for the welfare of the child. The measures recommended are implicit in the discussion of factors believed to be causative of disturbance. It is felt that many illnesses can be treated at home and, hence, unnecessary admissions should be avoided. When admission to a hospital becomes necessary, then there should be appropriate preparation for such admission. Where possible, admission should be to a children's hospital rather than to a general hospital and certainly never to an adult ward. Upon admission, the child should not be separated from the mother; the mother should go up to the ward with him. Daily visiting should occur. Routines should be explained to the child. Unpleasant sights and sounds should be avoided, and painful procedures should be carried out in treatment rooms away from the observations of children. Ward rounds should be conducted with some consideration of the child as an understanding individual with feelings. Educational and recreational facilities should be available. Staff contacts with the family, especially the mother, should be maintained either through individual or group meetings.

These measures, pediatric authorities are convinced, would contribute to positive experiences as a result of the hospital stay—in that solution of mother-child problems would be furthered and healthy maturational forces encouraged. There are many constructive forces within the hospital, and with the aid of these forces (for example, parent substitutes and family substitutes) the child may grow emotionally (Blom, 1958).

A study incorporating such preventive measures was conducted by Faust and his associates (1952), involving 140 children hospitalized for tonsillectomies. The preventive procedures included preparation for the hospital experience through discussion with parents, helping the parents prepare the children for the hospitalization, careful timing and elective hospitalization in terms of the child's developmental stage and emotional state in relation to other experiences in the home, such as the arrival of a sibling or a move to a new home or school. In the hospital itself, changes permitted the mother to remain with the child. Potentially traumatic procedures such as

enemas and venipunctures were kept to a minimum. Most of the children in the immediate postoperative period, and again three months later, showed no adverse effects. Only a small number, thirteen, displayed changes indicative of emotional trauma. Generally, younger children showed more adverse behavior changes, but these were considered essentially mild in nature. The children more seriously affected were those who had been sensitized to separation through previous traumatic experiences and those who had essentially poor relationships with their parents prior to hospitalization.

OTHER PSYCHOLOGICAL CONSIDERATIONS IN CHRONIC ILLNESS

In addition to the study of the relationships of early experience, hospitalization, and separation to illness, there has been some attention to other psychological aspects of illness among children. Illness, like any stress, may accentuate a preexisting problem or awaken a previously dormant problem. Prugh *et al.* (1953), for example, found that a child's reaction to illness was appropriate for age level rather than stemming from illness itself in a specific sense. Thus, anxiety was exaggerated by fantasies and fear of an overwhelming attack on the part of the preschool child but not on the part of the older child.

Many authors have observed that physical illness in a child, no matter how trivial, has its own unique meaning to the child and to his parents. When a child becomes ill, many things happen to him that are strange, new, and poorly understood. He does not feel well, understands little of why he has become sick, is irritable, and perhaps wants to be left alone. His own anxiety is often intensified by that of his parents, who may become guilty and anxious about their own part in the production of the illness or their failure to have prevented it. Indeed, many observers feel that parents form the most significant source of anxiety in children (Sontag, 1946, 1953; Szurek, 1951).

Although the meaning of a specific illness to a particular child depends upon a large number of factors in his past experience and on the attitudes of his parents, there are certain common reactions in most children who become sick. Prominent among these are guilt and fear and the belief that illness is a punishment. In one study, 90 percent of a group of hospitalized children stated that they became sick because they were "bad." Eighteen out of a group of twenty-one diabetic children said they "ate too much sugar." In a group of cardiac children, 90 percent believed they were ill because they "ran too much." In another group of children with rheumatic heart disease, almost all thought that their illness was in some way caused by disobedience of parental commands. When these same children were placed for treatment outside their homes, some felt that they were being sent away because they were bad (Langford, 1948).

To be sure, parental admonitions will intensify any latent fear that the child may have that his illness comes as a punishment. Thus, colds come because the child disobeys and does not wear his rubbers. A leg is broken because the child disobeys and does not heed his mother's caution not to roller skate in the street. Upset stomachs could be avoided if the child would eat properly, and so on. When something does happen to the child, warnings are supplemented with "I told you so." These practices are very common and contribute to the child's belief that when he is sick,

he is being punished. The use of the doctor as a "bogey" man will also reinforce the belief that illness is punishment. If the medical treatment is painful, it is looked upon as deserved punishment. Anna Freud (1952) has discussed this aspect of illness in an enlightening way. She points out that the child is unable to distinguish between feelings of suffering caused by the disease and suffering imposed in order to cure the disease. The child is forced to submit uncomprehendingly. She identifies several factors as being more significant in illness. First is a change in the emotional climate of the home—increased attention and indulgence along with overconcern where formerly coercion may have been the rule. Then, the experience of being nursed may have negative psychological implications. In this, there is infringement on developing processes of self-determination, independence, and privacy, which may be difficult for the child to tolerate because they are relatively recent acquisitions and hence more difficult to relinquish. A third factor is the restriction of bodily movement, which inhibits the child's usual motoric activity and leads to irritability and restlessness. Lastly, the threat of operations stimulates fears of bodily integrity and fantasies of mutilation.

The second group of common reactions are regressive phenomena (Josselyn, 1950; Korsch, 1958). It has been observed frequently that with almost any illness there occurs some degree of regression to an earlier level of emotional and social functioning. In the child, regression takes place as an adaptive device to mobilize defenses against anxiety. The degree of regression is dependent upon the severity of emotional disturbance and length of illness. With more prolonged and traumatic illnesses, there are more severe regressions to infantile preoccupations with need for affection and purely physical functions such as food intake and excretion. The younger the child at the time of illness, the more quickly the regression occurs. In general, the most recently acquired behavior habits and social techniques are first to go.

Persistent dependency reactions form the third group. Some children try to perpetuate infantile relationships to their environment which have given them an enjoyable security and satisfaction during illness. These secondary gains of illness are reluctantly given up, even though there were no particular symptoms of maladjustment prior to illness. The most persistent of these dependency states are those in which there is intense anxiety on the part of parents because of illness in the child.

Fourth of the common reactions is rebelliousness. Some children react by developing resentment and rebellion. They blame others for their illness and incapacitation. This reaction is probably related to anxiety over illness as a punishment and, as a compensatory mechanism, serves to deny the presence of fears.

Chronic invalid reactions form the fifth group. These are the result of parental overconcern, and they continue long after there is any need for realistic concern about the effects of illness. There is continued preoccupation with bodily functioning on the part of the child.

Finally, there are the constructive reactions to illness. Some children respond to difficult situations in a constructive manner, and illness may cause a minimum of emotional disturbance. If illness is well handled and the child stable and healthy emotionally, then illness may be a constructive growth experience.

Psychological reactions to illness also extend to the sequelae of illness, that is, to the reduced or limited function and disability. In addition to the awareness concerning his limitations gained in the family constellation, the child may become aware of his physical inadequacies as a result of limitations in his ability to compete and (consequently) because of the attitudes of his peers. This situation has a profound effect on his social adjustment, sense of personal adequacy, and very probably on the development of drives and motivation. Sontag (1946) has described such environmental settings into which the child may be thrust as being unyielding and disregarding of any differences and limitations. Children may be unconsciously cruel in their uninhibited and unthinking treatment of physical defects and deficiencies of their fellows. Fatty, Skinny, Shorty, nicknames implying physical differences, are indicative of the readiness with which children call attention to the physical differences and deformities of their fellows. This emphasis on physical deformity or lack of physical attractiveness comes at a time when it can be most important for personality delineation and emotional adjustment.

The child's physical state helps to shape his environment, which in turn affects his emotional life. His energy level is an important determining factor in the nature of his responses to environmental pressures, whether of an active or passive sort. The adaptive process of a child to his handicap is quite different from that of an adult. The adult makes use of many past experiences in which problems were solved; the child's experience is limited. He must learn through experimentation.

These psychological phenomena continue to exert their influences when disease becomes long-term and/or chronic. The continued stress necessitates adaptive actions on the part of the family and the individual. In general, these adaptive maneuvers are not new but derive from the existing patterns established previously in the earlier phases of the illness.

One particularly useful and unifying frame of reference in understanding the effects of chronic illness is in terms of the body-image, body-concept, and self-concept (Wright, 1960). Body-image and body-concept refer to the subjective impressions of one's own body and to the way it is perceived in relation to the outside world during growth and development. The self-concept is a broader construct (Lowe, 1961). It is also formed over time out of the rewarding and punishing experiences with the world and reflects how the individual sees himself. It is an organizing factor in behavior, a mediator between the individual and experience.

Wylie, in her review of the self-concept (1961), remarks on the theoretical importance of a person's body characteristics as he perceives them to the development of his self-concept. Self-concept theorists agree on the general idea that body characteristics that have low value may be expected to undermine self-regard, whereas highly valued body characteristics should enhance self-regard. However, no controlled study has explored this proposition directly. The total pattern of findings from different investigations is congruent with the assumption that deviations of body characteristics from the individual's ideal may lead to lowered self-regard. However, no firm cause-effect inferences can be drawn.

It seems reasonable and significant to relate the self-concept to physical health and specifically to illness. Some have theorized that low self-regard leads to or involves anxiety and tension and that anxiety may lead to various psychophysiological expressions. Wylie is of the opinion that there seems to be no strong support for the rationale that low self-regard is connected with poor physical health.

On the other hand, there is a persistent opinion that ill health may undermine self-esteem and distort the self-concept, that is, produce effects of a somatopsychological kind. Wright (1960) feels that, although group data do not show consistent relationships between the self-concept and physical disability and although there is wide variability in these data, there is a relationship in the attitudes of the disabled to personality characteristics existing prior to disability. She feels that physical disability has a profound effect upon the individual. From this frame of reference, some recent studies may be considered.

Barker and Wright report that the attitudes of a disabled person toward self are frequently devaluating (1954). In a similar way, Shelsky (1957) found that disabled and chronically ill patients are more self-rejecting and less self-accepting. This process is affected by the nature of the disability; persons with tuberculosis are more negatively affected than amputees. In a study by Kimmel (1959), the kind of personality problems created by orthopedic disability was related to the period in life in which the handicap occurred. Children with acquired orthopedic handicaps have greater confidence in and more esteem for their bodies, and they can cope more adequately with anxiety than children with congenital handicaps. Kimmel felt that the results supported theories of personality development which emphasized the importance of motor maturation in the development of body confidence and ability to cope with anxiety.

JOSEPH NEWMAN

TUBERCULOSIS

Nature of the Disease

Tuberculosis is an infection to which apparently all humans are susceptible. It is caused by *Bacillus mycobacterium tuberculosis,* which can and does infect almost any tissue or organ in the body. In addition to the pulmonary form, which accounts for the vast majority of cases of tuberculosis, the two most serious complications are hematogenous spread (miliary tuberculosis) and spread to the central nervous system (tuberculous meningitis).

The initial infection is called *primary* tuberculosis. This usually occurs in childhood but now appears increasingly in adulthood. A new infection after the primary lesion has been brought under control is referred to as *reinfection* tuberculosis. Reinfection usually happens in adulthood but may strike in childhood. Primary tuberculosis has a great tendency to heal and consequently is regarded as benign. In contrast, reinfection tuberculosis has a tendency to progress. However, primary infection is not always benign and reinfection not always devastating. Some authorities are of the opinion that arrested primary infection exerts an immunizing effect against reinfection. It remains a controversial issue (Rich, 1951; Smith, 1967).

In this country, the tuberculosis situation has undergone a remarkable change during the past four decades. In the early 1930s large numbers of children had primary tuberculosis. Many died in infancy and early childhood from acute reinfection forms of tuberculosis such as meningitis, pneumonia, and miliary disease. Large numbers were suffering from tuberculosis of the bones and joints. Since 1930, a marked decline was observed in primary tuberculosis among children in nearly every region of this country. In the age groups under twenty-one years, 5 percent have been infected with tuberculosis bacilli as determined by skin tests, compared with a rate of 90 percent infected prior to 1930 (Myers, 1951).

There has been a continued and marked decline in the mortality rate of tuberculosis since 1900 and a precipitous drop since 1947, corresponding with the introduction of antibiotic and chemical therapy. In 1900 the tuberculosis death rate in the United States was about 200 per 100,000; in 1945, the death rate was less than 50 per 100,000; and in 1965, 4.2 per 100,000 (U. S. Department of Health, Education, and Welfare, 1965). Tuberculosis workers felt this heralded the beginning of the complete eradication of tuberculosis; indeed, the Arden House Conference in November 1959 agreed that the elimination of tuberculosis as a public health problem was a realizable goal by 1970 (Lincoln, 1961). That goal is now recognized as a premature aspiration. Eradication of tuberculosis is still a major public health problem and much work still must be done if that prospect is ever to become a reality (Holquin, 1966; U. S. Department of Health, Education, and Welfare, 1965).

Although some observers felt that this decline in mortality rate did not reflect a corresponding decline in the incidence of the disease, the prevailing opinion is that there is a corresponding reduction in the active case rate; the active case rate in 1950 was estimated at 80 per 100,000; in 1965 the active case rate was 25.3 per 100,000 (U. S. Department of Health, Education, and Welfare, 1965). The goal of 10 per 100,000 by 1970 had been set by tuberculosis workers (Lincoln, 1961), but again that achievement was beyond reach. Newer therapeutic and surgical techniques have provided many years of survival to persons who would have rapidly died of tuberculosis in the past. It is believed that more success was achieved in retarding death from tuberculosis than in protecting from infection or in curing the disease (Lincoln, 1966; Lincoln and Vera Cruz, 1960; Smith, 1953). The exact incidence of tuberculosis is not known.

In general, there is a direct relation between the amount of active tuberculosis in any geographic area and the socio-economic level of the inhabitants. Wherever living conditions are poor and diet is inadequate, it is usual to find more tuberculosis than in areas where the standard of living is higher. Thus, tuberculosis is more common in the slum areas. This fact is illustrated by the higher tuberculosis rate for the nonwhite population, which is more than three times the rate for whites. Among children and youth under twenty-one years of age, the nonwhite rates are almost five times the white rates (Lincoln, 1966; U. S. Department of Health, Education, and Welfare, 1965).

During recent years, there has also been a noticeable shift in the age period at which the height of tuberculosis mortality is reached. The active case rates rise until the highest rates are reached for those sixty-five years of age and older. Tuberculosis is now beginning to be spoken of as a disease of older people, particularly men. These older groups remain the largest source of infection (Dubos, 1953).

Smith (1967) has analyzed the special vulnerability of adolescents to tuberculosis for reasons not yet understood. This authority and others (Lincoln, 1966) regard no segment of the population more important for the control and eradication of tuberculosis than adolescents.

The implications of this situation are important for a work such as this text, which covers the age groups up to about twenty-one years. The shifting of the greater incidence of tuberculosis to older age groups within the last twenty odd years has coincided with the rise in greater interest in the psychological factors in tuberculosis. Consequently, the groups to which psychological study has been applied have mainly been adults. Hence, the number of psychological studies specifically dealing with tuberculous children have been very few and have been even fewer in recent years.

Psychological Vulnerability Among the Tuberculous

Before we consider specific studies, it will be of value to review some of the aspects of tuberculosis that have implications for psychological reverberations. First is the chronic nature of tuberculosis. The disease process, once brought under control, lies dormant. This dormancy is termed "inactive" or "arrested" but not "cured." Thus there is always the potential for reactivation, although with passage of time the probability of reactivation is reduced. Nevertheless, the danger is ever present.

This fact leads to the second aspect of tuberculosis, which is important psychologically. Reactivation of dormant lesions can be caused by a variety of factors as apparently unrelated as puberty, fatigue, malnutrition, uncontrolled diabetes, and emotional disturbances.

Third is the contagious nature of the disease. This leads to isolation, usually carried out in a hospital, although much less frequently than in the era before the early 1950s. Isolation, entailing separation from family and friends, is continued until noncontagiousness is established and maintained and the disease process is rendered inactive. With antibiotics and chemotherapy the period of treatment,

JOSEPH NEWMAN

formerly extending over months and years, has been shortened. During this time the threat of possible lung surgery is present. Paradoxically, the patient usually feels fine from the outset of treatment.

Fourth, tuberculosis as a leading cause of death carries with it the threat of death. To this statistical fact must be added the folklore about consumption as a wasting disease leading to certain fatality.

Fifth, in considering the folklore of tuberculosis, the sense of ostracism must be recorded. Further, tuberculosis is a disease, in the main, of the least-favored social classes. As one writer put it, "Tuberculosis is not a disease which spells retirement with honor." It is often felt by patients, and to a certain degree by society, to be evidence of failure.

Sixth, the susceptibility to tuberculosis becomes high shortly after puberty and during early adulthood, following the previous age period, which is called the "golden age" of resistance to tuberculosis. Thus, for many young people, tuberculosis comes at a period of life in which important adjustments are being made, and the long illness serves to complicate these processes. This is not to say that tuberculosis contracted in childhood is of little consequence.

Finally, for those with reinfection tuberculosis, changes in the mode of life are necessary, the extent and length of time for these adjustments being dependent upon the extent of the disease.

The literature on the psychological aspects of tuberculosis is extensive and has been reviewed by several authors (Barker et al., 1953; Berle, 1948; Derner, 1953; Harris, 1952; Korkes and Lewis, 1955; Merrill, 1953; Wittkower, 1952). It has been concerned almost exclusively with adult groups. As a matter of fact, although there are references to add since our

previous review, we have not been able to find any new studies involving age groups below adults and only one or two additional general discussions (Marker, 1956; Rosenbluth and Bowlby, 1955).

Up to about 1940, the literature was mainly the result of subjective observation and clinical experience. Observations were usually made on small numbers of cases; contradictory conclusions were frequent; and systematic work with adequate experimental designs was virtually nonexistent. In sum, this work served as a source of hypotheses for study, but it did not provide useful knowledge.

Within recent years, studies of a systematic and experimental nature have appeared, and a more consistent body of knowledge has evolved. Despite its hoary tradition, the notion of a "tuberculosis personality" has been discarded. Differences in scores on psychological tests of tuberculosis patients and non-ill people do occur, but these are seen in the context of the patients' experience of hospitalization; in other words, the effects seen in the tuberculosis patient may be reactive to the illness and its treatment. A number of studies report specific emotional characteristics such as depression and anxiety and enable us to conclude that these are frequently found in tuberculosis patients. Some relationship between psychological factors and response to treatment has been suggested (Vernier et al., 1961).

Attempts have been made to relate the onset of tuberculosis or its relapses to emotional stress (Hartz, 1944). This association has been noted by nonpsychiatric observers such as Dubos (1953). The exact relationship of emotional factors to the onset of active disease has not been established. The various efforts to formulate tuberculosis as a psychosomatic disease have served to offer some explanation as to why a person falls ill and why he falls ill when he does, but have failed to explain why he falls ill with pulmonary tuberculosis (Wittkower, 1959).

A thoroughgoing psychological study has been reported by Vernier and her associates (1961). For some 814 adult patients in 18 hospitals, several psychological variables were related to hospital adjustment, response to medical treatment, and posthospital adjustment. One psychological variable, anxiety, was found to be related to all three criteria.

Anxiety appears to play an important role in poor adjustment as seen both in the hospital and in the posthospital situations. Further, among those hospitalized patients with far advanced disease, the presence of anxiety was significantly related to less satisfactory response to the medical treatment of the disease process itself. These results lend some confirmation to the concept that anxiety is a central psychological variable in determining a wide variety of behaviors.

These investigators feel that in this disease, "the need to maintain anxiety at a minimal state makes sense both logically and psychologically."

This last study deals essentially with the somatopsychological effects of tuberculosis. From a practical point of view, these are especially significant. In addition, there is much agreement among the various studies on such psychological effects of the disease.

Somatopsychological Aspects

The effect of the diagnosis of tuberculosis is a traumatic one—a reaction of shock. This is followed by anxiety and depression. The specific reaction for each individual, Derner (1953) found, was related to the individual's perception of the meaning of the disease. The defenses against anxiety and depression are frequently seen in defiance, cheerfulness, resentment, and apathy. The feelings of anxiety and depression are normal and adequate so long as they are in keeping with the nature and degree of the tuberculosis process and with the repercussions that the illness has for the individual's life situation. However, the situation may be complicated by existing conflicts and disturbances. In this fashion, neurotic anxiety may be superimposed on justifiable fear.

Tuberculous patients have to subject themselves to complete inactivity or enforced idleness for a prolonged period. Some may surrender to this, finding in the disease a welcome refuge from the vicissitudes of life; others, prematurely and unwisely, try to escape this period of inactivity. Derner has emphasized that the basic psychological problem in tuberculosis is the sharp conflict between dependence needs and independence needs.

Hospital and sanatorium life is highly artificial (Ludwig, 1948). Tuberculosis is the center of all interest and the chief preoccupation of all patients. Surgery is an ever-present threat and a source of anxiety about mutilation. Hospitalization also keeps to the fore the fact that the patients are social menaces. The most frequent thought of one group of patients studied was to go home. Often this thought is implemented by action, so that premature interruptions of treatment in hospitals and sanatoria have become a major problem in the treatment of tuberculosis. Interestingly enough, most patients feel anxious or insecure upon discharge.

Psychological Effects in Children

The psychological effects of tuberculosis upon children have been the concern of several investigators. Kramer (1948) has not found any specific personality type among children suffering from tuberculosis, a finding consistent with other tuberculosis workers among both children and adults (Demuth, 1951; Derner, 1953). Kramer also is of the opinion that the psychopathology of tuberculous children does not differ essentially from the psychopathology of those who are nontuberculous. In addition, infection with tuberculosis does not necessarily lead to psychopathology; it is dependent on the reactions to the disease, not on the disease itself. Kramer found no specific reaction pattern among the tuberculous children. The last finding is at variance with the results of Dubo's study (1950).

Because Dubo's study is an extensive investigation of tuberculous children, it might be well to present Dubo's findings in some detail. Twenty-five children, ages six to thirteen years, were studied in Bellevue Hospital, New York City. These children came from deprived homes of low economic status in congested neighborhoods where the tuberculosis incidence is high. Data were gathered through individual interviews and group sessions. The Rorschach technique was also utilized.

It was found, despite wide diversity of premorbid personalities, that there was a remarkable similarity of specific reactions. These reactions appeared to be closely linked with the difficulties in medical management encountered with these children. Ward behavior was characterized by diffuse motor activity, aggressive outbursts, and inability to cooperate in bed rest. The necessary limitation of activity was intolerable. These reactions were believed to stem from the intense anxiety that characterized the children's reaction to tuberculosis. Their thinking was preoccupied with death and other morbid content. Tuberculosis was equated with death.

Dreams, fantasies, and drawings were filled with morbid and threatening symbols.

To these children, tuberculosis was a highly abstract phenomenon. It was symptomless and yet terrible, because they had seen relatives and other patients die of it. In the face of this terrifying threat, the children were not allowed to react with the usual psychological response—fight or flight. They were forced to remain inactive and passive. It is not surprising, therefore, that Dubo found that the fantasies of these children were filled with constant motion —running, dancing, roller-skating.

Regressive phenomena were observed but were expected in a prolonged, confining, and anxiety-producing illness. Yet strong resistance was found to these regressive trends. Another source of disturbance was the necessity for isolation. The children could not comprehend the abstract concept of contagion, much less the measures utilized to reduce contagion. They felt different and stigmatized; the most forceful term of opprobrium was to be called "TB patient." They believed that tuberculosis was contracted through lack of cleanliness and, therefore, was shameful. In addition, the children tended to assume personal responsibility for being ill and looked upon the illness as punishment. The reactions to these feelings of guilt and shame were resentment and a feeling of being wronged. Aggression and defiance of authority were frequent problems.

The results of Dubo's study fit in with some of the findings of research with the adult tuberculous, particularly the reaction of anxiety. To be sure, this appears to be the basic generalized reaction to great threat. Important to note is the failure of the children to comprehend the meanings of tuberculosis and contagion, which remained abstract concepts. We may wonder, indeed, if adults do not have the same difficulty (Hartz, 1950). Dubo's study appears to have wide usefulness despite the fact that it is probably of limited general applicability because of the nature of the group studied. It is quite likely that many of the attitudes and reactions expressed by these children reflect their sociocultural backgrounds.

Bowlby *et al.* (1956) conducted an investigation of sixty children who were under treatment for tuberculosis. The children were between six and fourteen years of age and had been hospitalized at various times before their fourth birthday for treatment of tuberculosis. They received the standard tuberculosis treatment while visits from parents were maintained. No special attention was given to the problems of separation.

The findings indicate that these children suffered no significant damage to intellectual functions. There were, however, some indications of personality damage. On the basis of teachers' reports and interviews with the parents, the sanatorium children were judged to be showing tendencies toward withdrawal and apathy, as well as agressiveness. Contrary to expectations, however, disturbance in the capacity to establish relationships with peers was not found in any significant number of these cases. On the basis of judgments of overall adjustment, a fairly high proportion of the children who had been hospitalized during their preschool years were considered maladjusted (63 percent of the sanatorium children as compared with 40 percent of a control group of eight-year-olds). In the interpretations of findings, the authors felt that factors in addition to separation may have influenced these outcomes, for example, concomitant deprivation of maternal care. These children were not only ill and

hospitalized, but in many there were also histories of disruption and stress in their families—factors which were undoubtedly important for their subsequent adjustment.

In summing up the findings of this study, the investigators emphasized the great variations in personality patterns among the hospitalized children and pointed out that only a small minority developed very serious personality disabilities. On the other hand, they stressed that the potentially damaging effects of this kind of experience should not be minimized and felt that there were similarities in persisting personality deviations in some of these children reminiscent of those found in studies of severely deprived institutionalized children.

Bellak (1950), in a study of forty-six patients, emphasizes the problems of the tuberculous adolescent. These patients face many problems upon their return home after long absence. In the hospital sanatorium, they had lived under altogether different conditions in a sexually mixed group of all ages and had been exposed to many ideas. Thus, with the usual problems of adolescent growth, they encounter special difficulties at home and in their social relationships. Instead of growing up with their problems, absorbing changes in small doses, there are sudden changes and clashes. Bellak calls attention to these difficulties as one of the most clear-cut results of his study.

There may be some question of the continued relevance of the concerns expressed in studies of the effects of separation through hospitalization for children with tuberculosis. Until very recently, the tuberculosis hospital was the foundation upon which the treatment regimen was built. The effectiveness of chemotherapy brought to a climax the many dissatisfactions with hospital treatment in tuberculosis. Ambulatory treatment while at home through clinics and private physicians became increasingly practiced and recommended. The tuberculosis hospital has come in for critical appraisal as a necessary element in the treatment program (Isbister, 1967).

A Field-Theory Contribution

A particularly clarifying approach to the understanding of the tuberculous individual has been formulated by Barker *et al.* (1953). These authors have undertaken to state, in terms of Kurt Lewin's topological psychology, the nature of the problems encountered in the adjustment to tuberculosis. This approach considers the psychological position of the tuberculous as influenced by overlapping "healthy" and tuberculous situations, which give rise to a great amount of interfering and antagonistic behavior. There are, to be sure, other elements developed in this analysis, and the interested reader would do well to consult the work of Barker and his associates.

Tuberculous Children in School

A practical issue in the care of tuberculous children, of particular interest to school authorities, is the provision of special facilities for education. In the past thirty years, attitudes have undergone considerable change. At one time there was much enthusiasm about the treatment of children with primary tuberculous infections by removal from the home to preventoriums and camps. For those at home, attendance in special buildings, special schools, and "fresh-air" classes were recommended. In addition, as measures to prevent tuberculosis, malnourished and anemic children were sent to institutions set up for the purpose.

Experience, however, has shown that these facilities make no difference in treatment, and the results are the same whether the children are treated at home or in any of these special facilities. Consequently, most of these facilities have been closed. The prognosis in primary tuberculosis is excellent. For those with active reinfection tuberculosis, the proper place is to be decided by medical authority. When hospitalization is necessary, hospitals with patients of school age usually provide bedside instruction. Once the tuberculosis has been rendered inactive and the child discharged to his home, the physician may institute a period of progressive increases in activity during which the child may attend regular classes, beginning at first on a part-time basis. Segregation in special classes is not warranted medically or psychologically (Cruickshank and Peacher, 1950). This is not to say that there will not be problems arising from the integration of children with inactive tuberculosis in class activities. However, to the interested teacher, these problems are no greater than for any child who requires some adjustment in classroom routine. The problem of tuberculosis among children, which at one time appeared to be a vanishing one, persists, but is, in the main, a public health and medical issue.

HEART DISORDERS

Nature of Heart Disorders Among Children

Fifty years ago, the focus of attention in heart disorders among children and youth was rheumatic heart disease. Today, in the light of a broadened interest in heart disease, with more detailed examination of the available facts about heart disorders and with the changing epidemiological picture of infectious diseases, especially streptococcal disease, it has become clear that there are many more children suffering from congenital heart defects than from rheumatic heart disease. However, until the advent of cardiac surgery, interest in congenital heart defects was largely academic. With remarkable advances in diagnostic and surgical techniques achieved in recent decades, the prognosis in most forms of congenital heart defect was converted from hopeless to surgically curable (Morse, 1963).

There are many types of congenital heart defects; each may occur alone or in combination with other defects. The various anatomical subdivisions of the heart or of the great vessels leaving the heart may be affected. Some are more lethal or disabling than others; some produce little obvious handicap in childhood but may cause difficulty at a later age. The symptom that is most usually associated with congenital heart defects is cyanosis, hence, for children, the term "blue baby." However, not all heart defects present this symptom, and it may be associated with conditions other than congenital heart defect.

The causes of congenital heart defects are not known. Some implicate occurrence of German measles (rubella) during the first three months of pregnancy. Other virus diseases are also believed to be involved. One author states that approximately 6 babies in 1,000 live births are born with congenital heart disease; another author estimates this to amount to 30,000 to 45,000 children each year. Many die in the first few weeks of life, and a further number succumb before the end of the first year (Gluck, 1961). A New York study reported that congenital heart defects at present account for approximately half of the organic heart conditions found in school-age children (Wrightstone et al., 1961).

It is believed that 75 to 80 percent of the children with congenital heart disease can be helped by surgery. Not all congenital heart defects can be successfully corrected. With some, children may be restored to a normal life; other defects may still require that the child be restricted in activity.

The costs of diagnosis and surgical treatment of congenital heart defects are high. These procedures require large teams of many kinds of specialists and comparatively long periods of medical and hospital care. Hence, cardiac surgery is out of the reach of many families who can ordinarily meet medical expenses. Fortunately, there are two major sources of help —the state crippled children's programs and the state vocational rehabilitation programs.

Rheumatic fever is a clinical syndrome whose chief manifestations are heart disease, arthritis, chorea, skin rashes, and subcutaneous nodules. The importance of the disease centers around the fact that it produces heart damage. Until the 1930s it was one of the chief causes of illness and death in childhood and early adult life. It is now less common and has dropped from second to the third cause of death among school children. One authority states that there is the clinical impression that rheumatic fever is milder in its virulence (Keith, Rowe, and Vlad, 1958).

The most important causative factor is accepted to be Group A hemolytic streptococcus. The disease rarely begins in the first four years of life. As adolescence is approached, the incidence rises from 40 cases per 100,000 at age six to 340 cases per 100,000 at age fourteen. The prevalence of rheumatic fever among school populations has been estimated from one to six per thousand. There has been, in the last few decades, a trend toward lowered incidence. The death rate is less than 1 per 100,000 (Gasul, Arcilla, and Lev, 1966).

Rheumatic heart disease is found in only 1 or 2 school children per 1,000. Approximately an equal number have rheumatic fever but no residual heart involvement. Of children who have recovered from an attack of rheumatic fever 95 percent are able to lead an average existence. Perhaps 5 percent are semi-invalids and lead restricted lives. The vast majority are able to go to school and take part in ordinary activities that do not involve strenuous effort. In a study of 699 surviving patients out of 1,000 rheumatic fever patients who twenty years before had acute attacks, it was found that 3 out of 4 had little or no limitation in their activities (Keith, Rowe, and Vlad, 1958).

Climate appears to be an important factor in incidence. The colder, wetter parts of the temperate zone as well as the colder, wetter seasons of the year favor rheumatic disease. It is far more common, also, among the poor than among the well-to-do in almost every community; as a matter of fact, the decline in incidence is not as great among the nonwhite populations as it is among the white. In general, the nonwhite populations occupy lower socioeconomic positions than do the white. Rheumatic fever is infrequently seen in private schools but is relatively frequent in large public schools. Crowded living conditions seem to be the most important epidemiological factor as well as exposure to cold and wet without sufficient protection, and malnutrition and fatigue (Gasul, Arcilla, and Lev, 1966).

The periods of illness in rheumatic fever are often prolonged despite the fact that the earliest infection is often mild. In addition, the child with rheumatic fever is subject to repeated attacks of acute infection, and if the heart escapes damage during earlier attacks, it rarely escapes as the result of the repeated attacks. The greater the number of recurrences, the greater the heart damage. In the past, once the acute infection phase was over, convalescent care was recommended for long periods of time, sometimes for years. At present, bed rest is a controversial therapeutic measure. No one strongly advocates the prolonged and rigid regimen once employed. Authorities question the value of bed rest in preventing or minimizing heart damage. Thus bed rest, although still widely used, is not prescribed routinely, and adaptation to individual needs, both clinically and psychologically, is recommended. There has been no specific therapy for rheumatic fever. Antibiotics and salicylates are the most frequently used therapeutic agents. Prevention of streptococcal infection is widely practiced by the prophylactic use of penicillin and sulfonamides.

Many children with rheumatic fever may be regarded as being cardiac, even though they do not have heart disease, because of the necessity for close health supervision and prophylactic medication. The prognosis in rheumatic fever has improved, mortality is falling, recurrences are less common, initial attacks are less severe, streptococcal disease is more readily treated, and increasingly successful surgical techniques for valvular damage are available. The prospects for good health and longevity are excellent.

Psychological Sensitivity of the Cardiovascular System

Psychological factors have been associated with the functioning of the heart since time immemorial. There are numerous allusions in literature to the particular vulnerability of the heart to emotional influence, if not to its being the actual seat of emotion. In view of the critical importance of the heart for life or death, it is not at all surprising that the heart has been probably the most heavily emotionally invested organ of the body. Any threat to the heart is a threat to life itself. Thus, the accumulated folklore concerning the heart would be expected to cause immediate psychological repercussions whenever there is the slightest implication of heart disease.

However, before discussing these somatopsychological aspects of heart disease, the psychosomatic elements of heart disease should be considered. Interest in psychosomatic aspects of heart disease has been expressed along with the general development of psychosomatic medicine (Garner, 1952). Dunbar (1948), in particular, has formulated psychosomatic hypotheses in many forms of heart disease, including one for a psychosomatic predisposition to rheumatic heart disease. Except for rheumatic heart disease, the diseases implicated are those of adulthood and so do not directly concern the age groups under study. Moreover, the evidence presented is based almost entirely on adult groups. Nevertheless, her hypotheses have not been supported—no distinct personality has been found for children with heart disease (Crowell, 1953; Neuhaus, 1958; Wrightstone et al., 1961).

In patients with structural heart defects, there is a basic physiological problem that can be stated in terms of supply and demand. As long as it is possible for the heart to maintain circulation at an adequate level, the patient is compensated, that is, an adequate blood supply is maintained to tissues in response to varying functional demands. Whenever the balance between circulatory demands and the capacity of the heart to meet these demands cannot be maintained, heart failure develops. This balance may be disrupted by factors which increase the demand to a level greater than can be met or by factors that lead to reduction of the capacity of the heart to meet demands. In both these situations, psychological stress may operate to increase demand and/or decrease available supply (Reiser, Ferris, and Levine, 1954).

Many studies have been conducted that demonstrate this. Wolff and Wolff (1946) and the various studies of the Cornell group have shown that variations in pulse rate, cardiac output, and blood pressure, as well as other cardiovascular changes, may be induced under conditions of psychological stress having specific meaning for the individual. These stress conditions include the persistent low-grade strains of everyday living. Insofar as the patient with heart disease is concerned, there is little doubt as to the influence of psychological stress on the course of his disease (Boshes, 1958). However, the etiological role of psychological stress is not firmly established.

Anxiety is an inevitable consequence of heart disease, as of disease in general. Koenig (1959) studied this phenomenon in children with rheumatic fever. She investigated the relationship between recurrences of rheumatic fever and Rorschach indices of anxiety. She found that children with recurrences of rheumatic fever exceeded normal children in degree of anxiety. Children who had experienced several attacks exhibited more marked anxiety than those who had suffered a single attack. She also found that the younger the child during the first and ensuing attacks, the greater the anxiety in extent of indicators and intensity.

Green and Levitt (1962), using drawings of human figures by a group of children with congenital heart disease, found that those children tended to depict themselves as graphically smaller than did a group of normal children. Reed (1959) compared a group of children with congenital heart disease with nondisabled controls and found no significant differences in intelligence test scores, social maturity scores, and judgments about personal adjustment.

Josselyn, Simon, and Eells (1955) describe rheumatic children who came to a convalescent home after hospitalization as having "unwarranted anxiety in regard to their heart." They point out that anxiety may persist where damage to the heart is severe. Among their children, anxiety was also provoked by other factors than the actual cardiac condition—factors they classify under neurotic anxiety. Neurotic anxiety includes such sources of disturbances as the nature of the parent-child relationships and utilization of the illness for secondary gain—for attention, avoiding responsibility, controlling and tyrannizing the family, and the like.

In a group of 262 cardiac adolescents who responded to a questionnaire, about half reported worries about their heart condition. About two-thirds of the rheumatic heart cases reported a higher incidence of worries. In every group of this study, the adolescent felt that his parents were much more concerned about the cardiac limitation than he was (Wrightstone *et al.,* 1961).

Whitehouse (1964) has explicated the problems of the cardiac adolescent. These are emotional immaturity, cultural isolation, academic deficiency, and vocational ineptitude. Together, these problems constitute a social handicap. These problems, of course, refer to children with long-standing heart disorders.

Neuhaus (1958) compared the personalities of asthmatic, cardiac, and normal children. The cardiac children exceeded the normals in degree of neuroticism and in dependency feelings but were not significantly different from asthmatic children. The younger sick children in the study groups showed more intense maladjustment.

It seems clear that anxiety among cardiac children is invariably aroused. Once aroused, it cannot fail to reverberate to the cardiovascular system as a stress factor. Inevitably, the physiological reserve and heart function will be taxed—and possibly contribute to further disability. Finally, symptoms that are psychogenic in origin, the results of anxiety, may be misinterpreted as being based on heart disease (Bellak and Haselkorn, 1956).

Psychological factors have been found to be influential in determining the continuation of recommended prophylactic treatment to prevent recurrent rheumatic fever attacks. A group of 284 college students with histories of rheumatic fever were interviewed, and it was found that their conscientiousness in maintaining prophylaxis depended upon beliefs and attitudes rather than objective experiences (Heinzelmann, 1962).

Psychological Factors in the Home

The outcome of these psychological forces is to place the heart in a central position in the phenomenological scheme of patients. With children, the intensity and content of anxiety about the heart seem to be derived from parental influences rather than from self-awareness except, of course, as children grow older. Brazelton, Holder, and Talbot (1953) found that parent-child relationships, particularly before illness, greatly influenced the way in which the child subsequently handled his disease. This fact is emphasized by most investigators. It must be remembered, too, that anxiety in cardiac disease is realistic to a certain extent. The potential dangers of heart damage and death are constantly in the awareness of the parents, who in turn impress them upon the child. As a result, these authors believe that rheumatic fever is a real trauma which, because of these threats, lowers the capacity of the child to withstand daily stresses.

Intensifying these effects is confusion about the nature of heart disease (Bauer, 1952). Children found it especially difficult to comprehend the concept of heart disease; their concepts were as vague as those of their mothers.

Psychologically, another complication is that treatment programs in heart disorders usually have been guided by the demands of the pathologic process. Generally this meant adherence to strict bed rest with gradual resumption of activity. Emphasis was placed on lessened participation. Furthermore, most children with rheumatic heart disease were hospitalized because of the need for nursing care and close medical supervision. This experience of hospitalization is a very significant one, as we have seen.

In contrast, for his group of children, Bauer (1952) found that the anxiety coming out of separation was usually of short duration. The adjustment to hospitalization seemed to have been dependent upon the nature of developmental relationships with parents. Those who adjusted best had experiences of emotional security and growth with their parents. Other factors in hospital adjustment were found in the nature of the specific practices of the hospital to provide for emotional needs of the children, such as frequency of visits, and opportunities and encouragement to form attachments to parental substitutes. As we have noted, the aseptic and impersonal atmospheres in hospitals have served to enhance anxiety feelings.

The recognition among cardiologists of the importance of psychological factors in the care of children with long-term illness has led to increased attention to the extramedical aspects of treatment. One study, for example, undertook to investigate the suitability of home care for children with active rheumatic fever (Young and Rodstein, 1953). It was found that children could be cared for as well as in the hospital, provided certain initial criteria were met. The most important criterion was the willingness and ability of the parents to undertake a long, exacting regimen of unpredictable duration and outcome. Both the children and parents preferred the home treatment to that in a hospital. There seems little doubt that the homes in this study were in many ways superior to those ordinarily found among cardiac children. As such, this study is limited in its usefulness. Nevertheless, as noted above, there have been changes in the rigid activity restrictions formerly practiced. Indeed, Gasul, Arcilla, and Lev (1966) state that "no proof (exists) . . . that (rest) prevents or minimizes heart damage."

Restriction of Physical Activity

Regardless of the extent of the activity restriction, the single element running through every phase of the care of children with heart disorders is the necessity for some degree of restriction of physical activity. This necessity dictates the need for extended convalescence and continued efforts to teach the child to live within his limitations. It dictated the policy of many school systems to make arrangements for the education of children with heart disease in other than regular classes. It is important, therefore, that the psychological implications be considered.

Holder (1953) found that the restrictions placed upon children because of heart disease impressed upon them that they were sick and were constant reminders of their illness. The child finds it difficult to understand the necessity for limited activity beyond the acute phases of illness when he readily accepts restrictions. As he begins to feel better, the restrictions become onerous. Hence, it is necessary to use pressure to maintain restricted activity, and this is a persistent source of conflict. The parents' anxiety may lead them to overcontrol. Bauer (1952) felt that much overemphasis on restrictions was an unconscious expression of the parents' hostility engendered by the hardships the illness caused the family.

It is not surprising to find that cardiac children dislike the restrictions placed on their activity (Wrightstone, Justman, and Moskowitz, 1953). They resent the segregation at school; they feel singled out and "different." They regard themselves as adequate and not different from other children. They miss the identifications with their peers and the competitive outlets afforded in their relationships both at school and in their neighborhoods. The net effect of these restrictions is to engender hostility, anxiety, and feelings of low self-esteem and insecurity. Passive children accept the restrictions, and the others become resigned despite initial resistiveness.

On the other hand, a group of adolescent cardiac students on a self-report questionnaire tended to underestimate the restrictions imposed by the physicians. In distinction to the findings reported among elementary-school cardiacs, very few of the adolescents felt that their limitation had affected their ability to make friends. Virtually none of the students reported having no friends. Two factors should be kept in mind in interpreting these findings. One is that the data are based on self-reports, and two, adolescents would be loath to admit they have few or no friends. This is a reflection of the cultural stereotype of popularity (Wrightstone *et al.,* 1961).

The advisability for a regimen of limited activity and graded steps in increasing activity at one time meant that the cardiac child went to a convalescent home where he stayed perhaps up to a year after discharge from the hospital; the procedure is not as commonly practiced today. Here again, lack of understanding on the part of the child of the need for a convalescent period was found. The reactions noted among the children were accentuated guilt feelings and anxiety. During the period of convalescent care, the concepts of controlling and limiting his activity are emphasized as are the precautions necessary to avoid infection. Summer camps for cardiac children were also utilized to help these children adapt to the regimen imposed by their illness (Lammers, 1956).

The Return Home

Eventually the child returns home and all observers agree that this situation is fraught with difficulties. After so long an absence, the child may have developed feelings of rejection and, hence, hostility toward his parents and siblings (Taran and Hodsdon, 1949). In a sense the child has grown away from the family. Bauer found that whereas the home could do much to help the child in this difficult period, more often than not the child's problems are enhanced. The parents' anxieties tend to maintain the child's separation from his age group; overprotectiveness and over-control are common. Without the experience in relationships with healthy peers, the child hesitates in or withdraws from competition with his playmates. Holder saw the uncertainties of outlook and the possibility of recurrence of rheumatic fever as leading parents to curb and cripple the expression of positive social interactions.

Another contributing element to negative psychological development in the cardiac child is the ambivalent attitude of parents, as shown in a New York City Board of Education study. There was a limited acceptance of the child. The attitude of the parents was related to the degree of marital harmony existing between them. When the marriage was harmonious, the attitudes toward the child were positive, and when disharmony prevailed, negative attitudes were the rule (Wrightstone, Justman, and Moskowitz, 1953).

The Personality of the Cardiac Child

The net result of these forces seems to be to encourage passive, dependent reactions. One study found that cardiacs exceed normal children in degree of neuroticism and dependency (Neuhaus, 1958).

The picture of the cardiac child, as drawn by the study of the New York City Board of Education, portrays him as one who has come to accept his disability with persistent withdrawal behavior. The data, based in part on the use of projective techniques, show definite personality trends. As a group, the cardiac children tend to be unresponsive. They are unable to cope with many situations in which they find themselves. They are passive and lacking in initiative and drive for achievement.

They do not make adequate use of their intellectual capacity and tend to be apathetic mentally. They require stimulation in order to be productive. Emotionally, the children are immature, constricted, and regressed. They are given to daydreaming and brooding. As in other studies, a high percentage of children are judged to be maladjusted. They have few friends and do not engage in organized play activities outside the home. Withdrawal behavior is characteristic.

On the other hand, a later study of adolescents reported that the cardiac group was representative of the general adolescent population. There was no distinct personality pattern for the adolescent cardiac. Dependency was not a significant factor. The greatest amount of deviation from average was in sex anxiety. This finding was adjudged to be not unusual because one of the outstanding changes in adolescence is sexual maturity. The investigators in this study of adolescents felt that the evidence did not indicate that cardiac illness per se was related to any of the personality traits investigated. Where disturbances were found, it was not believed they were the results of cardiac illness. It is difficult to evaluate these results, whether they are the outcomes of the techniques and criteria of investigation or whether they represent developmental change. They stand in contrast to the findings of other investigations (Wrightstone *et al.,* 1961).

In the New York City study, teachers of children in special cardiac classes evaluated their adjustment by means of a rating scale. It was observed that the teachers were biased in favor of the children, tending to assign more favorable ratings in practically all categories of the scale. In contrast to the ratings by specialists, the children showed the best adjustment in (1)

JOSEPH NEWMAN

relationship to parents, (2) relationship to other children, (3) attitude to group control, and (4) adjustment to leadership. Their poorest adjustment was reported in (1) leadership, (2) work habits, (3) nervous habits, (4) self-confidence, and (5) responsibility. Furthermore, according to the teachers, the children tended to adopt aggressive, rather than withdrawing, mechanisms of adjustment.

In the study of adolescents, the teachers reported the majority of students as socially adjusted. With this group, psychologists were in agreement.

It is not easy to reconcile these contradictory findings within the same study and between studies. The reports do not attempt to do so. In addition to the probably different frames of reference for the teachers and specialists in rating the cardiac children, it seems that the biases of the teachers in favor of the children were potent factors in contributing to much of the difference.

In the high school grades, the situation is altered. The student is less well known to any single teacher. The teacher usually feels competent to provide information on academic achievement but less able to provide information on other aspects of the student. The majority of students were reported as socially adjusted. Academic adjustment was rated as wholly positive for 48 percent of the students and wholly negative for 20 percent in the tenth grade. The majority of teachers felt that the cardiac students showed interest in the classroom and possessed other positive attributes about school.

On both group and individual tests of intelligence, the cardiac children in elementary schools were found to fall into the low-average category. The distribution of scores showed a wide range of variability. There were no data available to evaluate this finding, but it seemed to be due mainly to sociocultural phenomena. Most of the children came from below-average socioeconomic homes, and the deficit may be a function of cultural deprivation. It may be speculated, also, that the restriction of activities due to illness, with limited opportunities for social, cultural, and intellectual stimulation, were contributory. Certainly, the data presented previously on personality evaluation, indicating mental apathy and lack of drive, tend to support these speculations.

Eighth-grade cardiacs attained an average IQ of 95.3 on a group intelligence test; the city-wide average for eighth-graders was 101.8. Here again, the cardiacs as a group fell into the low-average category.

As part of the New York City study, a group of 108 cardiac students in the eleventh grade were given individual intelligence examinations. The average IQ for this group was 105.7. This places them in the slightly above-average group and compares favorably to the level achieved by the noncardiac New York City eleventh-grade population. The latter had achieved an average IQ of 103.7 on a group intelligence test when they were in the eighth grade.

The discrepancy between the mean IQs of the eleventh-graders and eighth-graders is believed to be due to selective factors. Most of the school drop-outs occur in the tenth and eleventh grades and generally are for poor scholarship. Hence, the eleventh-graders are superior students. The proportion of dropouts by school year is much the same in the cardiac and in the total school population.

The Cardiac Child in School

The New York City study found that in other areas as well cardiac children showed retardation. On tests of achievement, wide variability was seen. The children performed below the level of nonhandicapped children in the same grade level. Analysis indicated that the cardiac children, as compared to the total school population of New York City in the grades studied, were in far larger proportion overage for their grade. This high percentage of overageness was believed to be due, mainly, to irregular attendance and consequent nonpromotion.

In the eighth grade, cardiac adolescents obtained a mean grade reading score six months lower than that of the city-wide population (7.1 versus 7.7). In arithmetic the corresponding grade scores were 7.3 for the cardiac group and 8.1 for the city-wide population.

In the eleventh grade, about 2 percent of the cardiac students were failing, that is, showed a high school average below 65. For the entire group the average was 78.2. Again, the better achievement of the eleventh-graders was undoubtedly due to selective factors.

It is significant to note that those students who had received some type of special instruction—special classes at home or in the hospital—achieved scores below the intellectual and achievement scores of those who had attended regular classes for their entire school career.

It is appropriate at this point to discuss the advisability of special educational arrangements for cardiopathic children. In the past there have been three types of school provisions for these children: (1) day schools—special provisions in regular classes, special classes in regular schools, special centers for the handicapped in schools for normal children, and special schools; (2) residential provisions in institutions, sanatoria, convalescent homes, and hospitals; (3) homebound provisions for those children who are too handicapped to go to school, who cannot be transported, or who are excluded for whatever reasons.

In the past these educational provisions were dictated by purely medical considerations so as to provide for limited activity. Usually the anxieties of the school administrator and the teacher caused the child to be set apart. Furthermore, it had been customary to stress cardiac damage and resulting cardiac disability as the starting points in the education of the cardiopathic child. In other words, once the child was sick, he was to be trained for a life of cardiac disability. From this frame of reference, segregation in special classes and training in the realization of limitations were logical developments.

However, current medical thinking does not accept this point of view. The child is either completely handicapped because of rheumatic activity and cannot attend classes, or, as in the vast majority of cases, he can participate in all childhood activities when his illness is quiescent (Levitt and Taran, 1948). White (1951) shares this view and believes that most children with heart disease at any age, once the disease is not active, can safely attend school and need not or should not be separated in special categories or classes. The exceptions would be those children with such congenital or organic defects as to make them actual cardiac cripples. Thus, with the medical necessity for special facilities for the education of cardiac children placed in doubt, it is not surprising that many educational authorities are taking another look at their special educational facilities. This, of course, does not take into consideration the many compelling psychological arguments and findings against such segregation. These have been indicated throughout the present discussion.

In New York City, the Board of Education undertook to determine whether its program was meeting adequately the needs of children with physical limitations. This study was extremely broad and comprehensive and delved into every aspect of education of cardiopathic children. One part of the study was an evaluation of a sampling of special classes for physically handicapped children, not only for cardiac children. The physical and recreational facilities of these classes seemed to be adequate. The classroom climates in less than one-third of the rooms observed were regarded as attractive; the others were "neat, staid, static." The large majority of the classes were friendly in atmosphere. About one-third of the classes were conducive to the development of pupil initiative. Few were stimulating for the children; in most, interest was either forced or passive and indifferent. Formal control by the teacher was the role assumed in the great majority of classes. However, in most classes, the pupil-teacher attitudes were friendly and sharing. From these data, it does not seem that these classes reflect the best practices for providing the stimulation and opportunities for emotional growth. They tend to reinforce the trends toward passivity and lack of initiative.

Studies such as these are difficult to evaluate because their results provide no frame of reference against which they may be evaluated. For example, for the special classes, it is necessary to know something of the regular classroom facilities and practices to learn whether the results are typical of the schools themselves or are specific for the special classes. This situation serves to point out again the need for controlled study.

Our discussion of heart disorders among children and youth seems to have been concerned mainly with rheumatic heart disease. This is a reflection of the psychological literature that deals almost exclusively with children suffering from rheumatic heart disease. Until the advent of heart surgery, these were the children with heart disorders who survived and came to the attention of other professional groups than the medical. Although it is likely that the picture will change as the experiences with heart surgery among children are accumulated, the current literature has not yet indicated this. Nevertheless, the discussion presented should still be appropriate to all children with heart disorders.

DIABETES

The Nature of Diabetes

The history of diabetes has been described as illustrative of the progressive refinement of medical concern and care in a disease from a focus on physical aspects, reduction of mortality, and lessening of morbidity to an awareness and acceptance of the psychological aspects. In the preinsulin era, the central objective of the physician was quite simply that of the patient's survival. The early 1920s ushered in the insulin era, and there ensued an increasingly successful effort to reduce the physical aspects of diabetic morbidity. The 1940s heralded a third era in which increased attention was devoted to the psychological management of the diabetic, an interest epitomized by the ironic paraphrase: "the diabetes was successfully regulated, but the patient decompensated emotionally." (Starr, 1955)

The progressive mastery of the disease permitted attention to case finding and prevention. Contributing to the growing number of known diabetics is the rising number of aging individuals, among whom the incidence of diabetes is the highest in our population.

Diabetes mellitus is a disorder of metabolism; the basic defect is an inefficient metabolism of carbohydrates. The disease is characterized by abnormal concentrations of sugar in the blood (hyperglycemia) and in the urine (glycosuria) and by abnormal metabolism of fat and protein. In untreated cases, there is marked loss of weight and the development of acidosis. The inadequately treated child under five years of age may be retarded in height and weight (Danowski, 1957). Eventually, if the diabetes remains uncontrolled, serious complications such as sepsis, nerve-tissue damage, or vascular disease may develop.

There is no agreement on statistics regarding the prevalence of diabetes; no single figure would be acceptable to all authorities. However, there are increasing numbers of cases with diabetes. In the 1950s, there were about 2 million diabetics; currently about 3 million persons are estimated to have the disease, and it is predicted that 4 million will have the disease by 1970. In these estimates, only slightly more than half are recognized cases. Thus, it is believed that diabetes should be suspected in a large number of the population, especially among older age groups. About 5 percent of diabetics are under fifteen years of age (Eli Lilly, 1967). It is estimated that about 150,000 children under the age of fifteen have diabetes. There is an almost equal group of patients in whom the diagnosis of diabetes is first made after fifteen years of age but who had juvenile diabetes (Danowski, 1957).

The life expectancy of the diabetic is below that of the general population; seventeen fewer years for the ten-year-old diabetic to almost four years less for the seventy-year-old. However, the life expectancy is increasing. Nevertheless, diabetes is the eighth leading cause of death and the third leading cause of blindness. The mortality for diabetics under the age of fifteen has been falling (Forsham, 1959).

A differentiation is made between diabetes in the younger age group (juvenile diabetes) and the disease in the older group (adult diabetes); there is some opinion that the disease mechanism is different in each. Among the differences between the two types is the fact that diabetes tends to be more severe in the child. The disease runs a notoriously stormy course; it stabilizes as the child gets older but frequently becomes stormy again during adolescence. There is a great frequency of symptoms among juvenile diabetics (Forbes, 1956), and greater fluctuations prevail in day-to-day control. Psychologically there are important differences. As a growing, maturing, and developing organism, the child is affected in a much more comprehensive and complex fashion. In addition, the child has the problem of rationalizing a regimen of living—an infinitely more difficult task for the younger age groups than for the older age groups (Peters, 1954).

There is not complete evidence to establish any specific cause for the disease. Many elements seem to be associated: hereditary factors, infection, overeating, dysfunction of the endocrine glands, and psychological factors.

The Treatment of Diabetes

Treatment of the diabetic child aims at enabling the child to compete with his peers physically, mentally, and socially. Insofar as he is not able to do so, to that degree he is considered inadequately treated (White, 1952); the total welfare of the patient is the only acceptable medical goal (Starr, 1955). In the treatment program, diet has to be regulated and insulin taken. Exercise has to be watched in relation to the need for insulin, because exercise tends to lower blood sugar. Diabetic shock and coma are ever-present dangers, and the child has to learn to recognize the first symptoms of shock and to carry sugar to take for its avoidance. Infection is also a danger.

There is not complete agreement among physicians as to the degree of control necessary in the management of diabetic patients—whether there should be chemical control or clinical control (White, 1952). Those who favor chemical control have rigid rules and procedures to be followed very strictly and carefully, such as frequent urine examinations, keeping of daily records, and others. Those physicians who favor clinical control usually recommend liberal handling of diabetic patients. Their patients have only a few rules to follow, one of which is never to omit insulin. These physicians emphasize psychological elements in the treatment of diabetes (Forsyth and Payne, 1956; Tolstoi, 1948). In general, there is increased recognition of the difficulty in expecting a program of rigid control, especially among juvenile diabetics, and more attention to the interpersonal elements of the doctor-patient relationships to achieve effective management of the diabetes.

Psychological Ramifications

The importance of psychological factors in diabetes has been recognized for a long time. However, in the preinsulin era, it was quite impractical to be concerned with the emotional health of diabetics when the physician was struggling to stem the death-dealing effects of unregulated diabetes. With the discovery of the physiological mechanism, particularly insulin, systematic attention to psychological variables slowly evolved.

The work of Menninger (1935), pointing out striking temporal correlations between changes in diabetes and changes in the mental states of a number of psychotic patients, helped to stimulate interest in the importance of psychological experiences. Other investigators noted that the severity of the metabolic disturbances in diabetes can be aggravated by emotional disturbances. Hinkle, Evans, and Wolf (1951) have demonstrated that emotional stress factors can produce undesirable changes in diabetic regulation, which clear up upon the removal of stress. These authors look upon diabetes as a disorder of adaptation. Others have also demonstrated these phenomena (Rosen and Lidz, 1949).

To move to the position that diabetes can be caused by emotional factors is another matter. To be sure, the work pointing to emotional effects on regulation of diabetes is highly suggestive, but Danowski (1957, p. 417) states: "there is no extensive support for the suggestion that diabetes actually originates as a result of such stress." As with tuberculosis, the data tell why an individual becomes ill at the time he develops symptoms, but they do not tell why he becomes ill with diabetes. Hinkle and Wolf (1952) attempt to do so, but the stresses they describe are no different from the types of stresses that many individuals encounter without developing diabetes. On the other hand, Danowski believes it is wise to keep in mind that emotional conflicts have very specific meaning for individuals, implying the possibility of a causative relationship under certain circumstances.

Dunbar (1948) has been especially positive in asserting that the diabetic has a distinctive behavioral pattern. However, her hypothesis has not been supported in subsequent research (Falstein and Judas, 1955). It seems well accepted that diabetics, adult or juvenile, do not have distinctive personality patterns that are different from those in other disease entities, rheumatic fever, for example (Crowell, 1953).

Starr places diabetes among the psychopathophysiological reactions in his psychosomatic spectrum. The somatic component is in the dominant relationship and psychological factors would be exacerbating and/or perpetuating of the somatic manifestations. This point of view is one to which most writers in the field would subscribe. As a matter of fact, Hinkle's extensive investigation precisely demonstrates the influence of emotional stress on the diabetic's course. It should be noted that the subjects involved in these studies were almost exclusively adults.

In some early studies, a marked incidence of mental retardation among diabetic children was reported. However, the recent work of Kubany, Danowski, and Moses (1956) found that the intelligence of diabetic children is like that of the nondiabetic population. They are of the opinion that the differences found in the past were mainly due to sampling biases.

Developmentally, the diabetic is not different from nondiabetic children except in height and weight. Hormonal secretions also are not strikingly variant from normals (Danowski, 1957).

Psychological Elements in Treatment

In addition to the effects of illness in general, diabetes has its specific implications. First of all, diabetes in childhood is a severe, lifelong, life-threatening disease (Bruch, 1949). Diabetic children, as a rule, are healthy until they are struck by the disease. Within a short time, they become desperately ill, even comatose. With insulin, their outlook has changed in terms of life expectancy and normal functioning. Despite this more favorable outlook, diabetes in a child means constant awareness of danger. Ever present is the fear of hypoglycemic shock and possible coma. Avoidance of infections because they affect the physiology of the body calls for special vigilance. Blood-vessel complications are always a danger. Consequently, a feeling of apprehension surrounds the life of the diabetic child. Complicating these fears are the usual bewilderment and lack of understanding of the illness on the part of both the family and the child.

The responses of the family to chronic illness, previously discussed, have special pertinence here because of the critical responsibility of the mother in the daily management of the diabetes. The mother has the realization that the health and the life of her child depend upon her ability to get the child to follow the prescribed regimen. To be sure, the entire constellation of psychological elements in the family is involved, and, as Bruch and Hewlett (1947) have shown, the extent of success or failure in the daily management of the diabetic child is dependent upon these psychological elements in the home.

Crain, Sussman, and Weil (1966) pursuing an interest in effects of the illness of one family member upon other members, studied fifty-four diabetic children and seventy-six controls. The investigation found that parents of diabetic children have lower marital integration, less agreement on how to handle the child, and greater marital conflict. The authors believed that the diabetes produced an intrafamilial crisis.

In the prescribed regimen for the diabetic are fertile sources of psychological disturbance (Podolsky, 1955). Fischer (1948) studied these various factors among a group of diabetic children followed for ten years. The necessity for dietary restriction, although made more liberal with the advent of insulin, is still an important part of the daily routine. Parents develop many anxieties about food, fearing carbohydrates in particular. They hesitate to give sugar; they tend to repeat the same foods day after day, and lack of variety often provokes resistance. The children commonly become hungry after meals, and extra between-meal snacks are permitted. Not infrequently, diabetic children do their own supplementing, and this provokes violent reaction from the parents because of "cheating" or "stealing." The parents become overzealous in enforcing the diet and begin to use detective methods. The work of Hinkle and his associates suggests that the attempt to regulate the diets of many diabetic children is fruitless because such attempts are opposed by strong psychological drives. Food becomes an area of struggle. The accusations of the parents bring guilt feelings and induce more concealment. Thus, another vicious circle is set up—more guilt, more anxiety, and more conflict. Food comes to be regarded as a poison, which not only intensifies the child's anxieties but also may be used as a weapon in his relationship to the environment.

Probably the most important aspect of daily routine is the necessity of insulin injections. This necessity most pervasively affects the emotions of the diabetic child. The use of the hypodermic syringe cannot be avoided even though the frequency of its use is reduced with slower-acting insulin preparations. The emotional effects of the injections are often traumatic. Some children regard them as punishment. Physiological reactions from insulin are very disturbing, and after a child has experienced several, he becomes very fearful and may seek to avoid or in some way weaken the insulin injection. The latter may occur when the child administers his own injection. Dread of insulin reactions may upset parents even more, particularly if the reactions come at night. Insulin reactions are indicated by pallor, sweating, and faintness. The effects of hypoglycemia are irritability, sleepiness, crying, temper tantrums, and mischievousness. The child may fall asleep in the classroom or become unconscious after heavy exercise. Not infrequently, these symptoms of diabetic children are misunderstood and the children are punished for "bad" behavior (Fischer, 1948).

A third aspect of the regimen of the diabetic child is the necessity to test the urine. Although testing of every voided specimen is unnecessary, urination takes on much emotional color. Aside from any diabetic disorder, this eliminative function seems to have an especially high potential for involvement in emotional disturbances. Added to this sensitivity is the anxiety of the diabetic surrounding the urine specimen and analysis. There is, not infrequently, bed-wetting among diabetic children because of a greater necessity for frequent voidings (polyuria) as a result of increased thirst and water intake (polydipsia). This bed-wetting is an aspect of the diabetes, but, of course, it may become involved with bed-wetting that is symptomatic of emotional disturbance. In any event, the parents and the child are upset and embarrassed by bed-wetting when it occurs. Here again, the relationships and the attitudes that exist in the family are important.

Anna Freud (1952) illuminates an inherent conflict in the management of the diabetic. The goal, as seen, is to teach the child the various requirements of self-care, among which is self-administration of insulin. The young child who is slowly and uncertainly moving away from dependence on the mother suffers a blow to this developmental progress when he falls ill with diabetes. The regimen of treatment requires that he begin to learn how to take care of himself. Anna Freud believes this burdens the child with excessively grave responsibilities and takes away the feeling that his parents will see to it that he is well and safe.

Limitation of activity occupies a prominent place in the daily routine of the diabetic child. The first limitation is in physical activity because of the fear of shock due to rapid depletion of blood sugar as the result of heavy exercise. Although restriction is observed, especially when the child is young and not fully capable of self-regulation, it seems all too frequently carried over into later years. The social life of the child is also limited. For example, a child is not permitted to attend parties because it is feared he may indulge in the excessive eating of sweets. In addition, parents may be fearful of letting the child out of sight for any length of time for fear of insulin reactions. Excursions and visits away from home are difficult because of insulin and meals. These difficulties serve to impress on the child the fact that he is different (Johannsen and Bennett, 1955).

The many and complex problems of the diabetic's life led Bennett and Johannsen (1954) to conclude that the disease makes a real and tangible impact on the personality of the child. They are of the opinion that the child never gets used to diabetes and its restrictions. They feel that the older child just gets more capable of controlling negative reactions. They go on to state that the results of the restricted life of the diabetic cannot but help to have effects on personality which, in their group, produced a constricted passive-dependency.

Starr (1955), in a comprehensive discussion of the psychosomatics of juvenile diabetes, points out that the child's adjustment to the sudden illness depends upon the premorbid emotional state of affairs for the child and his family. Given the same degree of life stress, that is, the appearance of diabetes, afflicted children and their families will react varyingly to such an emotional trauma. Where the intrafamilial adjustment has been adequately successful, the diabetic illness, after a short period of reactive disturbance, will be taken in stride. On the other hand, where faulty interpersonal relationships and extensive conflicts were quite prevalent, diabetes will result in emotional upheavals.

The most interesting and crucially significant phenomenon observed in such poorly adjusted family situations is the fact that the diabetic management per se becomes the arena and battleground for the expression of irrational preexisting attitudes in the mother-child relationship. The different problems of that situation contaminate the various details of diabetic regulation. The family's individualized reactions toward the child and his diabetes are of central importance in determining the type and specific nature of the adverse adjustment the child will make in connection with his illness. That adjustment may range from an excessively anxious and endangered personality to a compulsive, overly-regulated, and regimented personality, a depressive and self-destructive personality, a delinquent and rebellious personality, and a submissive, passive, and excessively dependent personality (Starr, 1955).

The Adolescent Diabetic

The social stigma of being diabetic becomes more apparent as the child moves into adolescence. In the earlier years, management is a problem mainly of the interplay between child and parents, particularly the mother, in order to achieve adherence to the diabetic regimen. Awareness that the diabetic routine does not make for social success begins to make its appearance as adolescence approaches. There seems to be general agreement among the workers in the field that adherence to the prescribed regimen becomes a real problem during adolescence (White, 1952). It is interesting that this rebellion seems to coincide with the need in those years to achieve independence and emancipation from the home.

This rebellion is short-lived because there is no escape from diabetes. We do not have information as to the consequences of the defeat. There are suggestive data, as reported by Fischer, that many diabetic children begin to fail in studies after elementary school. Whether this is due to physical or psychological factors is not known. Still fewer go on to college and fewer of these complete college and go on to professional life. In general, there seems to be better adjustment after adolescence and college years have passed.

There is evidence that diabetic control in young children, say under the age of nine, is less reactive to group participation than among older children. Weil, Sussman, and Crain (1967) found that participation in group activities, especially the conditions of that activity, has an important effect on diabetic control. The less competitive and more crisis-free groups tend to have more stabilizing effects.

During adolescence, problems involving future aspirations arise—problems of mar-

riage, parenthood, and career (Kennedy, 1955). As for marriage and parenthood, there are many risks to be faced by the future mother with diabetes. There is a high rate of abortions, stillbirths, and neonatal deaths as well as hazards for the diabetic who is pregnant (Forsham, 1959). This is a matter for skilled and wise counseling, one that has to be faced candidly and honestly.

The employment of diabetics is a problem that is beginning to be given systematic attention. Surveys of the employment practices of industry pertaining to diabetics have been carried out (Forsham, 1959). In a sense, employability depends upon the diabetic. If control is achieved by diet alone, then the problem is relatively simple. If insulin is required, then questions arise. The problem of insulin is mitigated by the development and growing use of oral preparations.

Forsham (1959) gives five most frequent reasons for rejecting diabetics for employment: (1) insulin shock (sudden unconsciousness); (2) prolonged absenteeism; (3) increased compensation costs (prolonged disability following industrial accident); (4) complications of diabetes (prolonged or permanent disability, which may be expensive to management); (5) increased insurance costs (reported to be unfounded although frequently given as a reason for rejection).

The American Diabetes Association takes the position that although the poorly controlled, uncooperative diabetic should be refused employment, the well controlled, cooperative diabetic is a good employment risk. The results of studies in industry show that the diabetic may be compared to the nondiabetic in his ability to work, caliber of work and absentee record (Analysis of a Survey

Concerning Employment of Diabetics in Some Major Industries, 1957).

The Diabetic Children in School

In contrast to children with tuberculosis and heart disease, there is no mention in the literature of special educational facilities for the diabetic child. Certainly there do not seem to be compelling medical or psychological reasons for such. His educational needs apparently can be met most adequately in regular classes.

As with tuberculosis and heart disease, but more obviously so, diabetes seems to require a life style that serves to set the diabetic apart, at least in his own eyes. Because of the necessity to train the child in this style of life and yet to make him feel part of a group, summer camps for diabetics have been developed in many parts of the country. The stated values of these camps are to train the diabetic child in the prescribed diabetic regimen, but to do so in an atmosphere of recreation, companionship, and emotional support. Such camps seem to be established as a part of the educational program in the disease for diabetic children. The therapeutic evaluation of the camps are mainly impressionistic and generally favorable. Camp sessions have been utilized as occasions for studies of diabetic children. As elements in the treatment scheme, the camps seem to be pleasant interludes but are not of critical significance (Geist, 1964; Hurd, 1957; Jacobi, 1954; Marble, 1957; Smelo and Eichold, 1955; Weil and Sussman, 1961).

Finally, psychological attention is recommended consistently for the diabetic child. Throughout the literature, there is the theme that preventive measures should be observed and, when needed, psychotherapeutic programs should be set up for both child and parents. Group programs are also reported (Luzzati and Dittman, 1954).

ASTHMA

The Nature of Asthma

Asthma is a common disorder of respiration affecting persons of all ages with repeated episodes of difficulty in breathing, characterized by wheezing, labored. breathing, cough, and sputum. These symptoms may range from the mildest cough and wheeze to respiratory distress of such severity as to obstruct breathing with fatal consequences. The usual cause of asthma derives from an allergic disorder.

Allergic disorders constitute a variety of reactions which may affect practically every organ and tissue of the body. These reactions result from antigen-antibody union, antigen being the substance (food, dust, drugs, bacteria) which, when introduced into the body, creates antibodies. Tissue sensitivity is created so that when there is antigen exposure in the future, the antigen-antibody union causes the allergic reaction. Histamine, or some similarly acting substance, is produced which, in turn, reacts on the neuromuscular apparatus of the affected organ. It is not known what determines for an individual the tissue or area to be involved, called the shock organ. This may be the skin, the lungs, or another part of the body. The allergic reactions are well known and may include wheals, coughing, gasping, sneezing, among others. These reactions do not take place unless there is tissue sensitivity. Sensitivities may disappear spontaneously, or spread to new allergens or antigens, or manifest themselves in new forms or in new shock organs (Prigal, 1960).

Allergies are long lasting and may extend throughout life. Most children do not outgrow their allergies; rather, they tend to develop complications. Thus eczema, the most common allergic reaction in infants, is not outgrown, as is a prevalent misconception. Usually, the child goes through a sequence, referred to as the eczema-hay fever-asthma complex, and emerges with a respiratory allergy— asthma (Nelson and Stoesser, 1953).

In allergy, the inciting factors, once an antigen-antibody reaction is established, are extremely varied, as are the manifestations elicited by them. There is no common agent, such as in tuberculosis, through which many quite different manifestations may be related; there are instead, a number of nonspecific factors in addition to allergens. The nonspecific factors include infection and psychological stress. Actually, the approach favored is the seeking of interactions among three forces—allergy, infection, and psychological stress—which ultimately produce the symptoms. Each of the forces may affect the other; each may be able to initiate vicious cycles or chain-type reactions. For any individual, the symptoms may be due to allergy, infection, or psychological stress (Prigal, 1960). This theoretical formulation follows Selye and Wolff in looking upon allergy as a maladaptive response to stress in which the protective mechanism an individual employs in his constant need for adaptation may produce disease, either because it is called into play when not needed or because in "its magnitude and direction the adaptive protective reaction may be more damaging to the individual than the effects of the noxious agent per se" (Prigal, 1960). Prigal raises the intriguing possibility of the establishment of Pavlovian conditioned response in this situation. Since the

publication of a Soviet monograph describing the relationship of conditioned reflex and asthma, there have been a number of studies which have attempted to explore this psychological mechanism (Nodine and Moyer, 1962). The importance of classical conditioning phenomena in the understanding of asthma is apparent.

There seems to be general acceptance of the role of psychological forces in allergic disorder but not as a specific mechanism of causation. Although psychological factors play a role in the modification of symptoms, and perhaps trigger symptoms, there is little or no evidence to demonstrate their ability to modify the actual antigen-antibody reaction.

Some Statistics

There is no agreement about statistics on the incidence of allergic disorders. Part of the difficulty lies in the matter of definition. If a liberal definition is followed, the incidence would be about 50 percent of the population. This figure is indicative of the wide prevalence of allergic reactions. However, if only recognized allergic disorders are included, the general opinion is that the rate would be 10 percent (Rappaport, Appel, and Szanton, 1960). One authority states that allergic disorders account for one-third of all chronic conditions occurring annually among children under seventeen years of age. The rate given is 74.3 per 1,000, and the rate for asthma 25.8 (Dees, 1967). Asthma is taken to occur in about 5 percent of the general population (Prigal, 1960). Figures for the incidence of asthma in groups of individuals in the United States are not readily available. In a study of 2,169 children under the age of fifteen years, it was found that 20 percent had major allergic disorders, but only one-third of this group was receiving treatment. The investigators felt that this situation pointed to a public health problem. If two-thirds of the allergic children are untreated, how many learning problems and how much school difficulty and absenteeism may have roots in allergy? (Rappaport, Appel, and Szanton, 1960). The National Health Survey, 1959–1961, reported that asthma was the chronic condition that caused the greatest percentage of days lost from school, 22.9 percent of all days lost (Dees, 1967).

Psychological Determinants in Asthma

In the past decade, investigations of psychological factors in asthma have grown at an accelerated rate and involve the largest and most active literature of the four disorders considered in this chapter. Although that literature still has a psychoanalytic frame of reference, there is an increasing number of reports which reflect psychodynamic points of view that are not necessarily psychoanalytic. Maurer (1965) has published a comprehensive assessment of the relative importance of emotional factors in asthma which contains discussions of the various psychological views about asthma.

Impetus to the psychoanalytic approach came from the work of French and Alexander (1941), who pointed out the particular significance of the interrelationships between the mother and the asthmatic child. They found that the child is more or less rejected by the mother or both parents and that the mother is much too preoccupied with her own problems to give adequate love to the child, although she often overcompensates for this unconscious rejection by an overprotective attitude. They also noted the overambition of the mother for the child and the over-dependence of the child upon the mother, with the result that the child is immature and lacking self-confidence in most situations. Thus, French and Alexander formulated their hypothesis that the psychological conflict in asthma is a repressed longing, basically for the mother. When this desire is frustrated or threatened with frustration, an asthmatic attack is precipitated. The asthmatic attack becomes, symbolically, the protest of a crying spell.

This hypothesis formed the basis for further investigations, which followed psychoanalytic formulations and supported French and Alexander's observations. Miller and Baruch (1957) have carried out an extensive series of studies. They have observed and treated some 201 clinically allergic children since 1946. Psychological tests were used, and the parents were interviewed. Similarly treated was a group of 110 children with no allergic disorder but with behavior problems. Miller and Baruch found that 97 percent of the allergic children had mothers who verbally expressed rejecting attitudes, whereas 37 percent of the mothers of nonallergic children did so—the difference being highly significant. This theme of maternal rejection has become the dominant one in the literature on asthma.

Miller and Baruch believe that maternal rejection preceded the development of symptoms. They studied hostility in allergic children as a reaction to the experience of rejection. As compared to non-allergic children, the allergic child did not dare to express his hostile feelings to the same extent or as freely as did the non-allergic child. The allergic child apparently developed guilt and anxiety in relation to his hostility and was more frequently in conflict about bringing out his hostile feelings. He is like a cornered animal. He feels and hates the impact of his mother's rejection, as all children do. But he is not able to express this hostility in either direct or indirect fashion. Consequently, he cannot get release from the tension of his hostile feeling. He turns his resentment on himself and uses his allergic condition as satisfaction for his conflicting needs.

An elaboration of Miller and Baruch's thesis is the concept of mutual engulfment, advanced by Abrahamson (1954). The rejecting mother is found to be ambitious, willful, and oversolicitous of her child. She wants to mold the child along the lines she wishes. When the child rebels, as frequently happens, she rejects him. This raises anxiety for the child. Thus the basic conflict is dependence-independence, and the anxiety emerging from this conflict is expressed through a somatic response—asthma.

A more broadly conceived factor is advanced by Rees (1963) who found faulty parental attitudes to be significantly higher among parents of asthmatic children than among parents of a control group. Rees did not find parental rejection to be the significant factor reported by Miller and Baruch. Similarly, Jacobs (1963), in a study of fantasies among children with hay fever, found significant differences for stories of maternal domination than for stories of maternal rejection.

Maternal rejection concepts have found support in a number of studies which sought to verify the frequent observation that asthmatic children invariably showed an abatement of their symptoms when they were away from homes and families —for example, in a hospital or a camp. Equally invariably, the symptoms recurred when the children returned home (Jessner et al., 1955).

Long and his co-workers (1958) undertook to investigate this phenomenon in a study of eighteen children hospitalized for asthma. After their symptoms had been relieved while in the hospital, the children were exposed to heavy concentrations of house dust from their homes but showed no demonstrable reaction. This finding was interpreted to indicate that allergen is not the only necessary factor to produce asthma and points to a complex etiology of asthmatic episodes.

An extension of these approaches is found in the development of therapeutic methods for the severely asthmatic child. One such method is the so-called parentectomy school of thought, which recommends the separation of the asthmatic child from his family for effective treatment. The reported results of a residential treatment center in Denver, which follows this method, indicate that of 500 children admitted over a period of years, only 10 percent did not achieve any improvement or amelioration of symptoms (Peshkin, 1960; Tuft, 1957).

The results of the various studies that support the fact of maternal rejection are generally accepted. However, what is challenged is the concept itself—that the psychological conflict and trauma lead to the asthmatic reaction. Harris and Shure (1956), Leigh (1953), Lipton, Steinschneider, and Richmond (1966), and others insist that the psychological reactions observed are the results of the asthma, not the causes. For example, Fitzelle (1959), in a controlled study involving 100 mothers of asthmatic children and 100 mothers of children with other ailments, found no differences in personality tests and child-rearing attitude surveys between the two groups. Both groups deviated from the normal. Dubo and her co-workers (1961) report similar negative results as to severity, cause and response to treatment, and family situations.

Margolis (1962) failed to find support for the psychosomatic interpretation of asthma, using the PARI scales. However, the use of the Blacky test indicated that mothers of asthmatic children are more psychologically disturbed.

Coolidge (1956) observed that the conflictual mother-child relationship is not specific for asthma but that ambivalence conflict is a basic characteristic of development.

Implicit in the challenge of the concept of maternal rejection as a causative factor is the questioning of the existence of a unique or specific personality pattern in the child as a significant etiological element. Harris and Shure (1956), in a survey of the incidence of asthma among school children ages six to twelve, found twenty-five cases of asthma. Among these twenty-five asthmatic children, Harris and Shure did not find any specific personality pattern. Similarly, Knapp and Nemetz (1957, 1960) found no single personality type in their adult group, nor did Herbert (1964) in his group of children. Rees (1956, 1959), reporting on his studies in England, did not find a specific personality type among his patients. Moreover, he did not find a significant psychological factor in 64 percent of a group of 50 patients. In general, the opinion of various investigators is that there is no common personality type in asthmatic children (Herbert, 1964; Purcell, Turnbull, and Bernstein, 1962).

The studies of asthma as a learned response, stemming from classical conditioning theory, have been suggestive but not conclusive (Dekker and Groen, 1956; Dekker, Pelser, and Groen, 1957; Stubblefield, 1966). Purcell advanced the hypothesis that children with rapidly remitting disease may have learned asthma as a defensive-adaptive response. Turnbull (1962) developed a theoretical model to explicate asthma within a classical conditioning frame of reference. Thus, asthma-like behavior could be learned and would persist as a means of resolving conflicts and problems.

Friend and Pollock (1954) criticized the predominant focus on intrapsychic elements in the study of the asthmatic child. They believe there has been a neglect of situational and social factors. Certainly, the existing literature supports this criticism. The probable explanation is that the almost exclusive source of the hypotheses pursued in the study of asthma has been in psychoanalytic theory. Rees (1964) attributes the controversial nature of published material on asthma to poorly designed research and failure to view asthma as the consequence of multiple causation. Other criticisms emphasize the accumulating evidence that the asthmatic population is heterogeneous (Baraff and Cunningham, 1965).

Psychological Effects of Asthma

The alternate approach to the psychological variables discussed above is to assume that they are somatopsychological and result from the disorder. According to this view many of the psychological effects have already been considered. There is, as we have seen, virtually complete acceptance of the fact that psychological variables influence the frequency and severity of asthmatic episodes in children. The earlier discussion of the characteristics of chronically ill children will be pertinent here.

Bakwin (1954) is of the opinion that when attacks occur frequently and are difficult to control, emotional factors should be suspected. In general, he believes that any circumstance that makes the child anxious and unhappy may intensify the allergic symptoms. The asthmatic child, becoming aware of the agitation produced by his attacks and the concern displayed by his parents, finds in his illness a ready means of getting his own way and of evading responsibilities. Guilt feelings are common in both the child and parents. The child fears that he may have caused his illness or attacks by not carrying out his mother's directions, as by not wearing his rubbers or by eating something forbidden. When he becomes ill, he hurts himself and his guilt is relieved. He is conflicted over the restrictions that surround him—he wants greater freedom but also wants to obey his mother. On the other hand, the parents may also feel guilty that they are the cause of illness through heredity or poor care. The asthmatic attacks are in themselves very frightening, and the dread of future attacks may haunt the child and the parents. Weiss (1966) found that asthmatics show more negative moods during asthma attacks than during nonattack periods.

With backgrounds of experiences such as these, the personality characteristics ascribed to asthmatics should not be surprising. One writer has remarked on the exclusiveness in the relationship between the mother and asthmatic child. Another refers to the mother's need to be close to the child and to the fact that, in this, their needs are complementary. Despite overt complaints, the mother actually rewards the dependence of the child. "She can give love and care only to the sick child. . . . The illness provides the mother with the setting for acting-out more deeply repressed unconscious impulses. . . . Consequently the mother unconsciously fosters the illness." Little has been written of the father. He is described by Kripke (1957) as "a passive individual who plays a subordinate role in the family."

The closeness of the identification between mother and asthmatic child has led to observation that the mothers are overcontrolling and overambitious for the child and that the child is overly dependent and overconforming (Knapp and Nemetz, 1957). Little and Cohen (1951) and Morris (1959) undertook studies in the area of achievement, utilizing goal-setting tasks. In these studies, hypotheses were confirmed as to higher goals set by both asthmatic children and their mothers and to the effect that the asthmatic child's level of aspiration rises when the mother is present and participating in goal setting. Also, Morris found that asthmatic child-mother pairs were more alike in goal-setting than nonasthmatic child-mother pairs. Both studies used control groups. Owen (1963) reports that asthmatic children show significant differences in aspiration patterns when compared to controls in responses to the mother's voice.

Another personality characteristic noted in the asthmatic child was the presence of a significantly greater degree of neurotic behavior than normal; this behavior contained such traits as anxiety, insecurity, and dependency. However, the asthmatic children did not differ from cardiac children. Interestingly, Neuhaus (1958) did not find any significant differences between asthmatic children and their nonasthmatic siblings on these variables. On the other hand, Fine (1948) found such differences in his study.

The asthmatic child has also been described as being very sensitive emotionally and as being typically negativistic and emotionally inhibited (Creak and Stephens, 1958). Furthermore, he lacks self-confidence and has feelings of inferiority (Kripke, 1960).

There are few data on the school adjustment of asthmatic children. One report states that they are often retarded in their school achievement, mainly because of frequent absences (Bakwin and Bakwin, 1948). Their school adjustment is described as poor; they tend to be fidgety, demanding, and immature. The experience of the Jewish National Home for Asthmatic Children in Denver, a residential treatment center, is very much the same. Many of the children admitted to the center have had difficulties in school because of frequent and extended school absences. In addition, the center found many of the children to have negative attitudes toward school. The children admitted to the center are the more severely asthmatic (Bukantz and Peshkin, 1949).

Psychotherapeutic Procedures

Psychotherapeutic procedures are more recognized as an integral part of the care of asthmatic children than of children with the other disorders we have considered, with the possible exception of diabetes.

Miller and Baruch (1960) have reported most extensively on psychotherapeutic efforts with asthmatics. They see treatment as long and involved. The focus of therapy is the parents, and Miller and Baruch generalize that parents of severely allergic children are severely ill emotionally.

The asthmatic children who attend the residential home in Denver are severely ill, and in this home and similar facilities, psychological help is provided for the children. In addition, the parents of the children attend regular group-therapy sessions on a continuing basis in their home communities. Here, too, the reported experience is that the parents need help (Abrahamson and Peshkin, 1960; Hallowitz, 1954).

CONCLUSIONS AND IMPLICATIONS

The study of these four chronic disorders serves to emphasize that the psychology of the ill and the disabled is to be understood in terms of the psychology of other groups, the normal and the deviant. The reactions of any child or youth to the stress of illness and disability depend upon a complex interplay of many forces, both internal and external. There is no simple predictable relationship between any single factor and the reaction displayed by the individual, whether this relationship is between a psychological variable and a physical response or between a physical event and a psychological response. Rather, the evidence is in the direction of interactional effects which, in turn, are influenced by situational, developmental, and psychosocial factors.

There are, to be sure, psychological reactions that occur with sufficient frequency to be regarded as being common, but those are by no means inevitable or invariant. Prominent among the common reactions to illness are anxiety and guilt feelings. Children often feel that their illness is a punishment. For them, illness is a poorly understood phenomenon and is clouded by subjective and irrational forces.

Inextricably implicated and strongly influential in these reactions are family forces that have their origin in parent-child relationships. There is a continuing interplay between these familial and subsequent experiences. Consequently, even though we are concerned with children and youth, it is appropriate to consider the reactions of adults to illness because the content of those reactions are communicated and provide the core of the children's reactions.

In our discussion, we began to discern developmental trends in reactions to illness and disability. There are suggestions that adolescence does not play an invariant role in chronic illness; the cardiac adolescent seems to be different from the diabetic adolescent.

Hospitalization is not inevitably a negative experience; certainly not with the changes in hospital practices being initiated to insure positive reactions.

Finally, in educational settings, chronically ill children are likely to appear in any classroom. As adults, teachers show the lack of knowledge, limited understanding, and distorted attitudes about chronic illness that adults as parents demonstrate (Connor, 1958).

Although there is much we still have to learn about the psychological aspects of chronic medical disorders among children, there is much we do know and can make available. Considerable research interest and activity are apparent; we also need a corresponding attack on the lag between knowledge about chronic disorders among children and the application of that knowledge.

References

Abrahamson, H. A. Evaluation of maternal rejection theory in allergy. *Annals of Allergy,* 1954, *12,* 129–140.

————. Intractable asthma: Conflict of period of toilet training. *Journal of Psychology,* 1961, *52,* 223–229.

————, & Peshkin, M. M. Psychosomatic group therapy with parents of children with intract-able asthma. *Annals of Allergy,* 1960, *18,* 87–91.

Adams, M. L., & Berman, D. C. Hospital through a child's eyes. *Children,* 1965, *12,* 102–104.

Ainsworth, M. D. *et al. Deprivation of maternal care: A reassessment of its effects.* Geneva: World Health Organization, 1962.

Alcock, T. Some personality characteristics of asthmatic children. *British Journal of Medical Psychology,* 1960, *33,* 133–141.

Alexander, F. *Psychosomatic medicine: Its principles and applications.* New York: W. W. Norton & Company, Inc., 1950.

American Heart Association. *If your child has a congenital heart defect.* New York: American Heart Association, 1960.

Analysis of a survey concerning employment of diabetics in some major industries. *Diabetes,* 1957, *6,* 550–553.

Bakwin, R. M. Essentials of psychosomatics in allergic children. *Pediatric Clinics of North America,* 1954, *1,* 921–928.

————, & Bakwin, H. The child with asthma. *Journal of Pediatrics,* 1948, *32,* 320–323.

Baraff, A. S., & Cunningham, A. P. Asthmatic and normal children. *Journal of the American Medical Association,* 1965, *192,* 99–101.

Barker, R. G., & Wright, B. A. Disablement: The somatopsychological problem. In E. D. Wittkower and R. A. Cleghorn (Eds.), *Recent developments in psychosomatic medicine.* Philadelphia: J. B. Lippincott Co., 1954, pp. 419–435.

Barker, R. G. *et al. Adjustment to physical handicap and illness: A survey of the social psychology of physique and disability.* Bulletin 55 (rev. ed.). New York: Social Science Research Council, 1953.

Bauer, I. L. Attitudes of children with rheumatic fever. *Journal of Pediatrics,* 1952, *40,* 796–806.

Beech, H. R., & Nace, E. D. Asthma and aggression: The investigation of a hypothetical relationship employing a new procedure. *British Journal of Social and Clinical Psychology,* 1965, *4,* 124–130.

Bellak, L. Psychiatric aspects of tuberculosis. *Social Casework,* 1950, *31,* 183–189.

————, & Haselkorn, F. Psychological aspects of cardiac illness and rehabilitation. *Social Casework,* 1956, *37,* 483–489.

Bennett, E. M., & Johannsen, D. E. Psychodynamics of the diabetic child. *Psychological Monographs,* 1954, *68,* 1–23.

Berle, B. B. Emotional factors and tuberculosis. *Psychosomatic Medicine,* 1948, *10,* 366–373.

Block, J. *et al.* Clinician's conceptions of the asthmatogenic mother. *Archives of General Psychiatry,* 1966, *15,* 610–618.

——, *et al.* Interaction between allergic potential and psychopathology in childhood asthma. *Psychosomatic Medicine,* 1964, *26,* 307–320.

Blom, G. E. The reactions of hospitalized children to illness. *Pediatrics,* 1958, *22,* 590–600.

Borenz, H. F. Children's personality reaction to chronic illness. *Wisconsin Medical Journal,* 1962, *61,* 551–554.

Boshes, B. Emotions, hypothalamus, and the cardiovascular system. *American Journal of Cardiology,* 1958, *1,* 212–223.

Bostock, J. Asthma; A synthesis involving primitive speech, organism, and insecurity. *Journal of Mental Science,* 1956, *102,* 559–575.

Bowlby, J. *Maternal care and mental health.* Geneva: World Health Organization, 1951.

——, Robertson, J., & Rosenbluth, D. A two year old goes to the hospital. *The psychoanalytic study of the child.* Vol. 7. New York: International Universities Press, 1952, pp. 82–94.

——, *et al.* The effects of mother-child separation: A follow-up study. *British Journal of Medical Psychology,* 1956, *29,* 211–247.

Brazelton, T. B., Holder, R., & Talbot, B. Emotional aspects of rheumatic fever in children. *Journal of Pediatrics,* 1953, *43,* 339–358.

Bruch, H. Physiologic and psychologic interrelationships in diabetes in children. *Psychosomatic Medicine,* 1949, *11,* 200–210.

——, & Hewlett, I. Psychological aspects of the medical management of diabetes in children. *Psychosomatic Medicine,* 1947, *9,* 205–209.

Buck, C., & Hobbs, G. E. The problem of specificity in psychosomatic illness. *Journal of Psychosomatic Research,* 1959, *3,* 277–233.

Bukantz, S. C., & Peshkin, M. M. Institutional treatment of asthmatic children. *Pediatric Clinics of North America,* 1949, *6,* 755.

Capes, M. The child in the hospital. *Mental Hygiene,* 1956, *40,* 107–159.

Carter, V. E., & Chess, S. Factors influencing the adaptations of organically handicapped children. *American Journal of Orthopsychiatry,* 1951, *21,* 827–837.

Clayton, L. B. Respiratory disease—how much of a problem. *Bulletin of the National Tuberculosis Association,* 1967, *53* (4), 5–6.

Clifford, E. Connotative meaning of self- and asthma-related concepts for two subgroups of asthmatic children. *Journal of Psychosomatic Research,* 1964, *8,* 467–475.

Connor, F. P. The education of children with chronic medical problems. In W. M. Cruickshank and G. O. Johnson (Eds.), *Education of exceptional children and youth,* 2d rev. ed. Englewood Cliffs, N. J.: Prentice-Hall, Inc., 1967, 498–554.

Coolidge, J. C. Asthma in mother and child as a special type of intercommunication. *American Journal of Orthopsychiatry,* 1956, *26,* 165–178.

Crain, A. J., Sussman, M. B., & Weil, W. B., Jr. Effects of a diabetic child on marital integration and related measures of family functioning. *Journal of Health and Human Behavior,* 1966, *7* (2), 122–127.

Creak, M., & Stephens, J. M. The psychological aspects of asthma in children. *Pediatric Clinics of North America,* 1958, *5,* 731–747.

Crowell, D. H. Personality and physical disease: A test of the Dunbar hypothesis applied to diabetes mellitus and rheumatic fever. *Genetic Psychology Monographs,* 1953, *48,* 117–153.

Cruickshank, W. M., & Peacher, W. G. Special education for the epileptic, the tubercular, and children with glandular disorders. In N. B. Henry (Ed.), *49th yearbook of the N.S.S.E.* Chicago: University of Chicago Press, 1950, 218–235.

Danowski, T. D. *Diabetes mellitus.* Baltimore: The Williams and Wilkens Co., 1957.

Davis, E. L. Play interviews used to evaluate child's reactions to hospitalization. *Hospital Topics,* 1961, *39,* 63–67.

Debuskey, M. Hospital vs. home care in childhood illness. *Maryland State Medical Journal,* 1961, *10,* 59–65.

Dees, S. C. Asthma. In E. L. Kendig (Ed.), *Disorders of the respiratory tract in children.* Philadelphia: W. B. Saunders Co., 1967, pp. 449–487.

Dekker, E., Barendregt, J. T., & DeVries, K. Allergy and neurosis in asthma. *Journal of Psychosomatic Research,* 1961, *5,* 83–89.

———, & Groen, J. Reproducible psychogenic attacks of asthma. *Journal of Psychosomatic Research,* 1956, *1,* 58–67.

———, Pelser, H. E., & Groen, J. Conditioning as a cause of asthma. *Journal of Psychosomatic Research,* 1957, *2,* 97–108.

Demuth, E. L. Is there a specific personality in tuberculous patients? *Archives of Neurology and Psychiatry,* 1951, *66,* 30–37.

Derner, G. F. *Aspects of the psychology of the tuberculous.* New York: Paul B. Hoeber, 1953.

Dimock, H. G. *The child in hospital.* Philadelphia: F. A. Davis Co., 1960.

Dow, T. E. Optimism, physique, and social class in reaction to disability. *Journal of Health and Human Behavior,* 1966, *7,* 14–20.

Dubo, S. Psychiatric study of children with pulmonary tuberculosis. *American Journal of Orthopsychiatry,* 1950, *20,* 520–528.

———, *et al.* A study of relationships between family situations, bronchial asthma and personality adjustment in children. *Journal of Pediatrics,* 1961, *59,* 402–414.

Dubos, R. J. Biologic and epidemiologic aspects of tuberculosis. *American Review of Tuberculosis,* 1953, *67,* 1–8.

Dunbar, F. *Psychosomatic diagnosis.* New York: Paul B. Hoeber, 1948.

Ehrentheil, O. F. Some remarks about somatopsychic compared to psychosomatic relationships. *Psychosomatic Medicine,* 1959, *21,* 1–7.

Endler, N. S., Boulter, L. R., & Osser, H. (Eds.). *Contemporary issues in developmental psychology.* New York: Holt, Rinehart & Winston, Inc., 1968.

Falstein, E. I., & Judas, I. Juvenile diabetes and its psychiatric implications. *American Journal of Orthopsychiatry,* 1955, *25,* 330–342.

Faust, O. A. *et al.* Reducing emotional trauma in hospitalized children. Albany, N. Y.: Albany Research Project, Albany Medical College, 1952.

Finch, S. M. The treatment of children with ulcerative colitis. *American Journal of Orthopsychiatry,* 1964, *34,* 142–145.

Fine, R. The personality of the asthmatic child. *Abstracts of Dissertations.* New York: University Publishers, 1948, p. 165.

Fischer, A. E. Factors responsible for emotional disturbance in diabetic children. *The Nervous Child,* 1948, *7,* 78–83.

Fishbein, G. M. Perceptual modes and asthmatic symptoms: An application of Witkin's hypothesis. *Journal of Consulting Psychology,* 1963, *27,* 54–58.

Fitzelle, G. T. Personality factors and certain attitudes toward child rearing among parents of asthmatic children. *Psychosomatic Medicine,* 1959, *21,* 208–217.

Flint, B. M. The child and the institution: *A study of deprivation and recovery.* Ontario: University of Toronto Press, 1966.

Forbes, G. B. The juvenile diabetic. *G. P.,* 1956, *13,* 99–110.

Ford, R. M. The causes of childhood asthma: An assessment of the relative importance of the allergic, infective and emotional factors in childhood asthma. *Medical Journal of Australia,* 1963, *50,* 128–130.

Forsham, P. H. (Ed.), Current trends in research and clinical management of diabetes. *Annals of the New York Academy of Sciences,* 1959, *82,* 229–235.

Forsyth, C. C., & Payne, W. W. Free diets in treatment of diabetic children. *Archives of Diseases of Childhood,* 1956, *41,* 245–253.

French, T. M., & Alexander, F. Psychogenic factors in bronchial asthma. *Psychosomatic Medicine Monographs.* Washington, D. C.: National Research Council, 1941. Parts 1 and 2.

Freud, A. The role of bodily illness in the mental life of children. *The psychoanalytic study of the child.* Vol. 7. New York: International Universities Press, 1952, pp. 69–81.

———, & Burlingham, D. I. *Infants without families.* New York: International Universities Press, 1944.

Friend, M. R., & Pollock, O. Psychosocial aspects in the preparation for treatment of an allergic child. *American Journal of Orthopsychiatry,* 1954, *24,* 63–72.

Gambrill, E. Post-hospitalized disabled children. *Journal of Health and Human Behavior,* 1963, *4,* 206–210.

Garner, A. M., & Wenar, C. *The mother-child*

interaction in psychosomatic disorders. Urbana: University of Illinois Press, 1959.

Garner, H. H. A psychosomatic view of cardiovascular disease. *Chicago Medical School Quarterly,* 1952, *14,* 8.

Gasul, B. M., Arcilla, R. A., & Lev, M. *Heart disease in children.* Philadelphia: J. B. Lippincott Co., 1966.

Geist, H. *The psychological aspects of diabetes.* Springfield, Ill.: Charles C. Thomas, Publisher, 1964.

Gibbs, G. E. Management of juvenile diabetes. *Journal-Lancet,* 1966, *86,* 319–325.

Glaser, H. H., Harrison, G. S., & Lynn, D. B. Comprehensive medical care for handicapped children: I. Patterns of anxiety in mothers of children with rheumatic fever. *American Journal of Diseases of Children,* 1961, *102,* 344–354.

————. Emotional implications of congenital heart disease in children. *Pediatrics,* 1964, *33,* 367–379.

Glaser, K. Group discussion with mothers of hospitalized children. *Pediatrics,* 1960, *26,* 132–140.

Gluck, R. *Diagnosis of congenital cardiac defects in general practice.* New York: American Heart Association, 1961.

Gofman, H., Buckman, W., & Schade, G. H. The child's emotional response to hospitalization. *A.M.A. Journal of Diseases of Children,* 1957, *93,* 157–164.

Goldfarb, W. Psychological privation in infancy and subsequent adjustment. *American Journal of Orthopsychiatry,* 1945, *15,* 247–255.

————. Variations in adolescent adjustment of institutionally reared children. *American Journal of Orthopsychiatry,* 1947, *17,* 449–457.

Green, M., & Levitt, E. E. Constriction of body image in children with congenital heart disease. *Pediatrics,* 1962, *29,* 438–441.

Grinker, R. R. Psychosomatic approach to anxiety. *American Journal of Psychiatry,* 1956, *113,* 443–447.

Hallowitz, D. Residential treatment of chronic asthmatic children. *American Journal of Orthopsychiatry,* 1954, *24,* 576–587.

Ham, G. D. The cardiovascular system. *Psychosomatic Medicine,* 1962, *24* (1), 31–36.

Harris, D. H. Psychological aspects of tuberculosis. In J. F. Garrett (Ed.), *Psychological aspects of physical disability.* Washington, D. C.: Government Printing Office, 1952, pp. 97–111.

Harris, M. C. Is there a specific emotional pattern in allergic disease? *Annals of Allergy,* 1955, *13,* 654–661.

————, & Shure, N. A study of behavior patterns in asthmatic children. *Journal of Allergy,* 1956, *27,* 312–323.

Hartz, J. Human relationship in tuberculosis. *Public Health Reports,* 1950, *65,* 1293.

————. Tuberculosis and personality conflicts. *Psychosomatic Medicine,* 1944, *6,* 17–22.

Hebb, D. O. *Organization of behavior.* New York: John Wiley & Sons, Inc., 1949.

Heinzelmann, F. Factors in prophylaxis behavior in treating rheumatic fever: An exploratory study. *Journal of Health and Human Behavior,* 1962, *3* (2), 73–81.

Herbert, M. Personality factors and bronchial asthma: A study of South African Indian children. *Journal of Psychosomatic Research,* 1964, *8,* 353–364.

Herold, A. A., Jr. Juvenile diabetes. *Journal of Louisiana Medical Society,* 1966, *118,* 429–432.

Hinkle, L. E., Evans, F. M., & Wolf, J. Studies in diabetes mellitus. *Psychosomatic Medicine,* 1951, *13,* 184–202.

————, & Wolf, S. A summary of experimental evidence relating life stress to diabetes mellitus. *Journal of the Mount Sinai Hospital,* 1952, *19,* 537–570.

Holder, R. *Rheumatic fever project* (typescript). Boston: Massachusetts General Hospital, 1953.

Holquin, A. H. The child-centered program to prevent tuberculosis. *Bulletin of the National Tuberculosis Association,* 1966, *52* (7), 4–7.

Howell, M. C. Some effects of chronic illness on children and their mothers. *Dissertation Abstracts,* 1963, *23* (8), 2976–2977.

Hurd, J. B. Report of the committee on camps. *Diabetes,* 1957, *6,* 97.

Illingworth, R. S. Children in hospital. *Lancet,* 1958, *2* (7039), 165–171.

Isbister, J. L. A health officer speaks his mind. *Bulletin of the National Tuberculosis Association,* 1967, *53* (7), 2–5.

Jacobi, H. G. Nutritional studies of juvenile diabetics attending summer camp. *Journal of Clinical Nutrition,* 1954, *2,* 22.

Jacobs, M. A. Fantasies of mother-child interaction in hay fever sufferers. *Dissertation Abstracts,* 1963, *24* (4), 1698–1699.

Jensen, R. A. The hospitalized child: Round Table, 1954. *American Journal of Orthopsychiatry,* 1955, *25,* 293–318.

Jessner, L. *et al.* Emotional impact of nearness and separation for the asthmatic child and his mother. *The psychoanalytic study of the child.* Vol. 10. New York: International Universities Press, 1955, 353–375.

Johannsen, D. E., & Bennett, E. M. The personality of diabetic children. *Journal of Genetic Psychology,* 1955, *87,* 175–185.

Josselyn, I. M. Treatment of the emotionally immature child in an institution framework. *American Journal of Orthopsychiatry,* 1950, *20,* 397–409.

———, Simon, A. J., & Eells, E. Anxiety in children convalescing from rheumatic fever. *American Journal of Orthopsychiatry,* 1955, *25,* 109–119.

Kangery, H. Children's answers. *American Journal of Nursing,* 1960, *60,* 1748–1751.

Kaplan, H. I., & Kaplan, H. S. Current theoretical concepts in psychosomatic medicine. *American Journal of Psychiatry,* 1959, *115,* 1091–1096.

Kazan, A. T., Browning, T. R., & Cohen, A. D. Emotional implications of child care practices on pediatric units of general hospitals in Westchester County: Survey and recommendations. *New York State Journal of Medicine, 65,* 2568–2572.

Keith, J. D. Modern trends in acute rheumatic fever. *Canadian Medical Association Journal,* 1960, *83,* 789–796.

———, Rowe, R. D., & Vlad, P. *Heart disease in infancy and children.* New York: The Macmillan Company, 1958.

Kendig, E. L. (Ed.). *Disorders of the respiratory tract in children.* Philadelphia: W. B. Saunders Co., 1967. (*a*)

———. Tuberculosis. In E. L. Kendig (Ed.), *Disorders of the respiratory tract in children.* Philadelphia: W. B. Saunders Co., 1967, 656–701. (*b*)

Kennedy, W. B. Psychologic problems of the young diabetic. *Diabetes,* 1955, *4,* 207–209.

Kennell, J. H., & Bergen, M. E. Early childhood separations. *Pediatrics,* 1966, *37,* 291–298.

Kimmel, J. A comparison of children with congenital and acquired orthopedic handicaps on certain personality characteristics. *Dissertation Abstracts,* 1959, *19,* 3023–3024.

Kirk, S. A., & Weiner, B. B. (Eds.). *Behavioral research on exceptional children.* Washington, D. C.: Council for Exceptional Children, 1963.

Knapp, P. H., & Nemetz, S. J. Acute bronchial asthma. *Journal of Psychosomatic Medicine,* 1960, *22,* 42–56.

———, & Nemetz, S. J. Personality variations in bronchial asthma. *Psychosomatic Medicine,* 1957, *19,* 443–465. (*a*)

———. Sources of tension in bronchial asthma. *Psychosomatic Medicine,* 1957, *19,* 466–485. (*b*)

Koenig, F. G. A study of anxiety in children with rheumatic fever. *Dissertation Abstracts,* 1959, *20,* 1438–1439.

Korkes, L., & Lewis, N. D. C. An analysis of the relationship between psychological patterns and outcome in pulmonary tuberculosis. *Journal of Nervous and Mental Disease,* 1955, *122,* 524–563.

Korsch, B. M. Psychological principles in pediatric practice: The pediatrician and the sick child. In S. L. Levine (Ed.), *Advances in pediatrics.* Chicago: The Year Book Medical Publishers, 1958, 11–73.

———. Psychological reactions to physical illness in children. *Journal of the Medical Association of Georgia,* 1961, *50,* 519–523.

Kramer, H. D. Psychopathology of childhood tuberculosis. *The Nervous Child,* 1948, *7,* 102–114.

Kripke, S. S. Psychologic aspects of bronchial asthma. *American Journal of Diseases of Children,* 1960, *100,* 935–941.

Kubany, A. J., Danowski, T. S., & Moses, C. The personality and intelligence of diabetics. *Diabetes,* 1956, *5,* 462–467.

Kubie, L. S. The problem of specificity in the psychosomatic process. In E. D. Wittkower and R. A. Cleghorn (Eds.), *Recent developments in psychosomatic medicine.* Philadelphia: J. B. Lippincott, 1954, pp. 29–40.

Lammers, M. A. Where children take heart. *American Journal of Nursing,* 1956, *56,* 854.

Langford, W. S. Child in the pediatric hospital: Adaptations to illness and hospitalization. *American Journal of Orthopsychiatry,* 1961, *31,* 667–684.

———. Physical illness and convalescence: Their meaning to the child. *Journal of Pediatrics,* 1948, *33,* 242–250.

Laybourne, R. C., & Miller, J. M. Pediatric hospitalization of psychiatric patients: Diagnosis and therapeutic implications. *American Journal of Orthopsychiatry,* 1962, *32,* 596–603.

Leigh, D. Asthma and the psychiatrist: A critical review. *International Archives of Allergy,* 1953, *4,* 227–246.

Lemkau, P. V. The influence of handicapping conditions on child development. *Children,* 1961, *8* (2), 43–47.

Levitt, J., & Taran, L. M. Some of the problems in the education of rheumatic children. *Journal of Pediatrics,* 1948, *32,* 553–557.

Lewis, M. Management of parents of acutely ill children in the hospital. *American Journal of Orthopsychiatry,* 1962, *32,* 60–66.

Lilly, Eli, Co. *Diabetes mellitus.* Indianapolis: Eli Lilly Co., 1967.

Lincoln, E. M. Eradication of tuberculosis in children. *Archives of Environmental Health,* 1961, *3,* 444–455.

———. The continuing menace of tuberculosis for children. *Journal-Lancet,* 1966, *86,* 49–54.

———, & Vera Cruz, P. G. Progress in treatment of tuberculosis. *Pediatrics,* 1960, *25,* 1035–1042.

Linde, L. M. Cardiovascular problems in adolescence. *Arizona Medicine,* 1966, *23,* 843–846.

Lipton, E. L., Steinschneider, A., & Richmond, J. B. Psychophysiologic disorders in children. In L. W. Hoffman and M. L. Hoffman (Eds.), *Review of Child Development Research.* New York: Russell Sage Foundation, 1966, 169–220.

Little, S. W., & Cohen, L. D. Goal setting behavior of asthmatic children and of their mothers for them. *Journal of Personality,* 1951, *19,* 376–389.

Long, R. T. *et al.* A psychosomatic study of allergic and emotional factors in children with asthma. *American Journal of Psychiatry,* 1958, *114,* 890–899.

Lowe, C. M. The self-concept: Fact or artifact. *Psychological Bulletin,* 1961, *58,* 325–336.

Ludwig, A. O. Emotional factors in tuberculosis. *Public Health Reports,* 1948, *63,* 883–890.

Luzzati, L., & Dittman, B. Group discussion with parents of ill children. *Pediatrics,* 1954, *13,* 269–272.

Lynn, D. L., Glaser, H. H., & Harrison, G. S. Comprehensive medical care for handicapped children: III. Concepts of illness in children with rheumatic fever. *American Journal of Diseases of Children,* 1962, *103,* 120–128.

Mahaffy, P. R., Jr. Effects of hospitalization on children admitted for tonsillectomy and adenoidectomy. *Nursing Research,* 1965, *14,* 12–19.

Marble, A. The future of the child with diabetes. *Journal of the American Dietetic Association,* 1957, *33,* 565–574.

Margolis, M. Mother-child relationships in bronchial asthma. *Journal of Abnormal and Social Psychology,* 1961, *63,* 360–367.

———. A psychological study of mothers of asthmatic children. *Dissertation Abstracts,* 1962, *23* (1), 311–312.

Marker, C. B. Psychological care of tuberculosis in children. *Journal of the Maine Medical Association,* 1956, *47,* 60.

Marlens, H. S. A study of the effect of hospitalization on children in a metropolitan municipal institution. *Dissertation Abstracts,* 1960, *20,* 3385–3386.

Mason, E. A. The hospitalized child, his emotional needs. *New England Journal of Medicine,* 1964, *272,* 406–414.

Maurer, E. The child with asthma: An assessment of the relative importance of emotional factors in asthma. *Journal of Asthma Research,* 1965, *3* (1), 25–79.

McCord, W., McCord, J., & Verden, P. Family correlates of "psychosomatic" symptoms in male children. *Journal of Health and Human Behavior,* 1960, *1,* 192–199.

McGovern, J. P., & Fernandez, A. A. On the role of emotional factors in allergy. *Journal of Asthma Research,* 1964, *1,* 213–217.

Mechanic, D. Perception of parental responses to illness: A research note. *Journal of Health and Human Behavior,* 1966, *6,* 253–257.

Meek, H. W., Sr. An investigation of certain psychological variables in diabetes mellitus. *Dissertation Abstracts,* 1960, *20,* 4176.

Menninger, W. C. Psychological factors in the etiology of diabetes mellitus. *Journal of Nervous and Mental Disease,* 1935, *81,* 1–13.

Merrill, B. R. Some psychosomatic aspects of

pulmonary tuberculosis. *Journal of Nervous and Mental Disease,* 1953, *117,* 9–28.

Miller, F. J. W., Seal, R. M. E., & Taylor, M. D. *Tuberculosis in Children.* London: J. & A. Churchill, Ltd., 1963.

Miller, H. Evaluation of the emotional factors in eczema and urticaria. *Annals of Allergy,* 1960, *18,* 161–166.

———, & Baruch, D. W. The emotional problems of childhood and their relation to asthma. *A.M.A. Journal of Diseases of Children,* 1957, *93,* 242–245.

———. Psychotherapy of parents of allergic children. *Annals of Allergy,* 1960, *18,* 990–997.

Mohr, G. J. *et al.* A program for the study of children with psychosomatic disorders. In G. Caplan (Ed.), *Emotional problems of early childhood.* New York: Basic Books, 1955, pp. 251–268.

Morris, R. P. Effect of mother on goal setting behavior of the asthmatic child. *Dissertation Abstracts,* 1959, *20,* 1440.

Morse, D. P. *Open heart surgery.* Springfield, Ill.: Charles C. Thomas, Publisher, 1963.

Moskowitz, J. A. Caring for the young diabetic patient. *New York Journal of Medicine,* 1966, *66,* 2519–2522.

Mussen, P. Developmental psychology. In P. R. Farnsworth (Ed.), *Annual review of psychology.* Palo Alto, Calif.: Annual Reviews, 1960, pp. 439–478.

Mutter, A. Z., & Schleifer, M. J. The role of psychological and social factors in the onset of somatic illnesses in children. *Psychosomatic Medicine,* 1966, *28,* 333–343.

Myers, J. A. *Tuberculosis among children and adults.* Springfield, Ill.: Charles C. Thomas, Publisher, 1951.

Nelson, L. S., & Stoesser, A. V. Allergic diseases of infancy and childhood. *International Record of Medicine and General Practice Clinics,* 1953, *166,* 95.

Neuhaus, E. C. A personality study of asthmatic and cardiac children. *Psychosomatic Medicine,* 1958, *20,* 181–186.

Nodine, J. H., & Moyer, J. H. (Eds.). *Psychosomatic Medicine.* Philadelphia: Lea & Febiger, 1962.

Ongley, P. A., & DuShane, J. W. Rehabilitation of the child with congenital heart disease. *American Journal of Cardiology,* 1961, *7,* 335–339.

Owen, F. W. Asthma and maternal stimuli. *Dissertation Abstracts,* 1961, *22,* 644.

———. Patterns of respiratory disturbance in asthmatic children evoked by the stimulus of the mother's voice. *Acta Psychotherapeutica et Psychosomatica,* 1963, *11,* 228–241.

Parsons, T. Illness and the role of the physician: A sociological perspective. *American Journal of Orthopsychiatry,* 1952, *21,* 452–460.

Pasamanick, B., & Knobloch, H. Brain damage and reproductive casualty. *American Journal of Orthopsychiatry,* 1960, *30,* 298–305.

Peay, R. Emotional problems of children facing heart surgery. *Children,* 1960, *7,* 223–228.

Peshkin, M. M. The emotional aspects of asthma in children. *Journal of Asthmatic Research,* 1966, *3,* 265–275.

———. Management of the institutionalized child with intractable asthma. *Annals of Allergy,* 1960, *18,* 75–79.

———. The role of emotions in children with intractable bronchial asthma. *Journal of Asthma Research,* 1964, *2,* 143–146.

Peters, J. P. Management of diabetes. *Yale Journal of Biology and Medicine,* 1954, *27,* 75–79.

Pinneau, S. A. The infantile disorders of hospitalism and anaclitic depression. *Psychological Bulletin,* 1955, *52,* 429–452.

Podolsky, E. Physical ailments and the frightened child. *Mental Hygiene,* 1955, *39,* 489–497.

Pomp, H. C. A study of self-concept distortion in physically disabled and nondisabled seventh and eighth grade students. *Dissertation Abstracts,* 1963, *24,* 824.

Potts, W. J. The hospitalized child. *Illinois Medical Journal,* 1963, *123,* 235–239.

Prick, J. J. G. A psychosomatic approach to asthma. *Acta Psychotherapeutica et Psychosomatica,* 1963, *11,* 81–112.

Prigal, S. J. (Ed.). *Fundamentals of allergy.* New York: McGraw-Hill Book Company, 1960.

Provence, S. A., & Lipton, R. C. *Infants in institutions.* New York: International Universities Press, 1962.

Prugh, D. G. Investigations dealing with reactions of children and families to hospitalization and illness: Problems and potentialities. In G. Caplan (Ed.), *Emotional problems of early childhood.* New York: Basic Books, Inc., Publishers, 1955, pp. 307–321.

——, & Cath, S. Psychosocial stress: Children's reactions to hospitalization and the use of the respirator. *Journal of Nervous and Mental Disease,* 1954, *120,* 399–400.

Prugh, D. G. *et al.* A study of the emotional reactions of children and families to hospitalization and illness. *American Journal of Orthopsychiatry,* 1953, *23,* 70–106.

Purcell, K. Distinction between subgroups of asthmatic children: Children's perceptions of events associated with asthma. *Pediatrics,* 1963, *31,* 486–494.

——, Bernstein, L., & Bukantz, S. C. A preliminary comparison of rapidly remitting and persistently "steroid-dependent" asthmatic children. *Psychosomatic Medicine,* 1961, *23,* 305–310.

Purcell, K., & Metz, J. R. Distinctions between subgroups of asthmatic children: Some parent attitude variables related to age of onset of asthma. *Journal of Psychosomatic Research,* 1962, *6,* 251–258.

Purcell, K., Turnbull, J. W., & Bernstein, L. Distinctions between subgroups of asthmatic children: Psychological tests and behavior rating comparisons. *Journal of Psychosomatic Research,* 1962, *6,* 283–291.

Rappaport, H. G., Appel, S. J., & Szanton, V. L. Incidence of allergy in a pediatric population. *Annals of Allergy,* 1960, *18,* 45–49.

Read, C. H. Management of diabetes in children. *Journal-Lancet,* 1965, *85,* 35–41.

Reed, M. K. The intelligence, social maturity, personal adjustment, physical development, and parent-child relationships of children with congenital heart disease. *Dissertation Abstracts,* 1959, *20,* 385.

Rees, L. The importance of psychological, allergic, and infective factors in childhood asthma. *Journal of Psychosomatic Research,* 1964, *7,* 253–262.

——. Physical and emotional factors in bronchial asthma. *Journal of Psychosomatic Research,* 1956, *1,* 98–114.

——. The role of emotional and allergic factors in hay fever. *Journal of Psychosomatic Research,* 1959, *3,* 234–241.

——. The significance of parental attitudes in childhood asthma. *Journal of Psychosomatic Research,* 1963, *7,* 181–190.

Reiser, W. F., Ferris, E. B. Jr., & Levine, M. Cardiovascular disorders, heart disease and hypertension. In E. D. Wittkower and R. A. Cleghorn (Eds.), *Recent developments in psychosomatic medicine.* Philadelphia: J. B. Lippincott Co., 1954, pp. 300–325.

Rich, A. R. *The pathogenesis of tuberculosis.* Springfield, Ill.: Charles C. Thomas, Publisher, 1951.

Robertson, J. *Young children in hospitals.* New York: Basic Books, Inc., Publishers, 1959.

—— (Ed.). *Hospitals and children.* London: Victor Gollancz, Ltd., 1962.

Rogerson, C. H., Hardcastle, D. H., & Duguid, K. A psychological approach to the problem of asthma and the asthma-eczema-prurigo syndrome. *Guy's Hospital Reports,* 1935, *85,* 289–308.

Rosen, H., & Lidz, T. Emotional factors in precipitation of recurrent diabetic acidosis. *Psychosomatic Medicine,* 1949, *11,* 211–215.

Rosenbluth, D., & Bowlby, J. The social and psychological backgrounds of tuberculous children. *British Medical Journal,* 1955, *1,* 946–949.

Ruesch, J. Psychosomatic medicine and the behavioral sciences. *Psychosomatic Medicine,* 1961, *23,* 277–286.

Sandler, L. Child-rearing practices of mothers of asthmatic children. Part I. *Journal of Asthma Research,* 1964, *2,* 109–142.

——. Child-rearing practices of mothers of asthmatic children. Part II. *Journal of Asthma Research,* 1965, *2,* 215–256.

Schaffer, H. A., & Callender, W. M. Psychologic effects of hospitalization in infancy. *Pediatrics,* 1959, *24,* 528–539.

Schneer, H. I. (Ed.). *The asthmatic child.* New York: Harper & Row, Publishers, 1963.

Schneider, E. Psychodynamics of chronic allergic eczema and chronic urticaria. *Journal of Nervous and Mental Disease,* 1954, *120,* 17–21.

Schwartz, B. Emotional problems of children attending a heart clinic. *Ohio State Medical Journal,* 1966, *62,* 125–128.

Seiden, R. The psychoanalytic significance of onset age in bronchial asthma. *Journal of Asthmatic Research,* 1966, *3,* 285–289.

Selye, H. Recent progress in stress research, with reference to tuberculosis. In P. J. Sparer (Ed.), *Personality, stress and tuberculosis.* New York: International Universities Press, 1956, 45–64.

Shelsky, I. The effect of disability on self concept. *Dissertation Abstracts,* 1957, *17,* 1598–1599.

Shore, M. F. (Ed.). Red is the color of hurting. *Public Health Service Bulletin, No. 1583,* Washington, D. C.: Government Printing Office, 1967.

———, Geiser, R. L., & Wolman, H. Constructive uses of a hospital experience. *Children,* 1965, *12* (1), 3–9.

Simon, A. J. Illness and the psychosomatics of stressful life situations as seen in a children's clinic. *Journal of Health and Human Behavior,* 1960, *1,* 13–17.

Sipowicz, R. R., & Vernon, D. T. A. Psychological responses of children to hospitalization. *American Journal of Diseases of Children,* 1965, *109,* 228–231.

Smelo, L. S., & Eichold, S. Conduct of camp for diabetic children. *Diabetes,* 1955, *4,* 219–222.

Smith, D. T. Tuberculosis today and tomorrow. *American Review of Tuberculosis,* 1953, *67,* 719.

Smith, M. H. D. Tuberculosis in adolescents: characteristics, recognition, management. *Clinical Pediatrics,* 1967, *6,* 9–15.

Solnit, A. J. Hospitalization: An aid to physical and psychological health in childhood. *A.M.A. Journal of Diseases of Children,* 1960, *99,* 155–163.

———, & Provence, S. A. (Eds.). *Modern perspectives in child development.* New York: International Universities Press, 1963.

Sontag, L. W. The genetics of differences in psychosomatic patterns in childhood. *American Journal of Orthopsychiatry,* 1950, *20,* 479–489.

———. Some psychosomatic aspects of childhood. *The Nervous Child,* 1946, *5,* 296–304.

Sperling, M. Psychosomatic medicine and pediatrics. In E. D. Wittkower and R. A. Cleghorn (Eds.), *Recent developments in psychosomatic medicine.* Philadelphia: J. B. Lippincott, Co., 1954, 381–396.

Spitz, R. A. Reply to Dr. Pinneau. *Psychological Bulletin,* 1955, *62,* 453.

———, & Wolf, K. Anaclitic depression. *Psychoanalytic Study of the Child,* 1946, *2,* 313–342.

Starr, P. H. Psychosomatic considerations of diabetes in childhood. *Journal of Nervous and Mental Disease,* 1955, *121,* 493–504.

Stevenson, I., & Matthews, R. A. Fact and theory in psychosomatic medicine. *Journal of Nervous and Mental Disease,* 1953, *118,* 289–306.

Stubblefield, R. L. Psychiatric observations of asthma in children. *Southern Medical Journal,* 1966, *59,* 306–310.

Sussman, M. B., & Weil, W. B. An experimental study of the effects of group interaction upon the behavior of diabetic children. *International Journal of Social Psychiatry,* 1960, *6,* 120–125.

Symposium on rehabilitation in cardiovascular disease. *American Journal of Cardiology,* 1961, *7,* 315–319.

Szurek, S. A. Comments on the psychopathology of children with somatic illness. *American Journal of Psychiatry,* 1951, *107,* 844–849.

Taran, L. M., & Hodsdon, A. F. Social and psychologic problems associated with prolonged institutional care for rheumatic children. *Journal of Pediatrics,* 1949, *35,* 648–661.

Thompson, G. G. Developmental psychology. In P. R. Farnsworth (Ed.), *Annual Review of psychology.* Palo Alto, Calif.: Annual Reviews, Inc., 1959, 1–41.

Thompson, W. R. Early environment—its importance for later development. In P. A. Hoch and J. Zubin (Eds.), *Psychopathology of childhood.* New York: Grune & Stratton, Inc., 1955, pp. 120–139.

Tisza, V. B. Management of the parents of the chronically ill child. *American Journal of Orthopsychiatry,* 1962, *32,* 53–59.

Tolstoi, E. The objectives of modern diabetic care. *Psychosomatic Medicine,* 1948, *10,* 291–294.

Tuft, H. S. The development and management of intractable asthma of childhood. *A.M.A. Journal of Diseases of Children,* 1957, *93,* 251–254.

Turnbull, J. W. Asthma conceived as a learned response. *Journal of Psychosomatic Research,* 1962, *6,* 59–69.

Tuttman, S. Children's reactions to their physical disabilities in relation to parents' personalities. *Dissertation Abstracts,* 1955, *15,* 1909–1910.

United States Department of Health, Education and Welfare, Public Health Service. *Reported tuberculosis data, 1965.* Publication

No. 638. Washington, D. C.: Government Printing Office, 1967.

Vaughan, G. F. Children in hospital. *Lancet,* 1957, *272,* 1117–1120.

Vernier, C. M. *et al.* Psychosocial study of the patient with pulmonary tuberculosis. *Psychological Monographs,* 1961, *75,* 1–32.

Vernon, D. T. A., & Schulman, J. L. Hospitalization as a source of psychological benefit to children. *Pediatrics,* 1964, *34,* 694–699.

Weil, W. B., Jr. Social patterns and diabetic glucosuria: A study of group behavior and diabetic management in summer camp. *American Journal of Diseases of Children,* 1967, *113,* 454–460.

———, & Sussman, M. B. Behavior and diet and glycosuria of diabetic children in a summer camp. *Pediatrics,* 1961, *27,* 118–123.

Weiss, J. H. Mood states associated with asthma in children. *Journal of Psychosomatic Research,* 1966, *10,* 267–273.

Welfare of children in hospital. *British Medical Journal,* 1959, *1,* 166.

White, P. Diabetes in childhood. In G. G. Duncan (Ed.), *Diseases of metabolism.* Philadelphia: W. B. Saunders Company, 1952.

White, P. D. *Heart disease.* New York: The Macmillan Company, 1951.

Whitehouse, F. A. Problems of the cardiac adolescent. *New York State Journal of Medicine,* 1964, *64,* 1108–1111.

Wittkower, E. *A psychiatrist looks at tuberculosis.* London: National Association for the Prevention of Tuberculosis, 1959.

———. Psychology of the tuberculosis patient. In T. H. Sellors and J. L. Livingstone (Eds.), *Modern practice in tuberculosis.*

London: Butterworth & Co. (Publishers), Ltd., 1952.

Wolf, G. A., & Wolff, H. G. Studies on the nature of certain symptoms associated with cardiovascular disorders. *Psychosomatic Medicine,* 1946, *7,* 293–319.

Work, H. H. Making hospitalization easier for children. *Children,* 1956, *3,* 83–86.

Worth, J. M. Juvenile diabetics: the educational experience for diabetics using programmed instruction. *Southern Medical Journal,* 1966, *59,* 585–588.

Wright, B. *Physical disability—a psychological approach.* New York: Harper & Row, Publishers, 1960.

Wrightstone, J. W., Justman, J., & Moskowitz, S. *Studies of children with physical handicaps, No. 1, the child with cardiac limitations.* New York: Board of Education, 1953.

Wrightstone, J. W. *et al.* (Eds.), *Studies of children with physical handicaps, No. 6, adolescents with cardiac limitations.* New York: Board of Education, 1961.

Wu, R. Explaining treatments to young children. *American Journal of Nursing,* 1965, *65,* 71–73.

Wylie, R. C. *The self concept.* Lincoln: University of Nebraska Press, 1961.

Yarrow, L. J. Separation from parents during early childhood. In M. L. Hoffman and L. W. Hoffman (Eds.), *Review of Child Development Research.* New York: Russel Sage Foundation, 1964, pp. 89–136.

Young, D., & Rodstein, M. Home care of rheumatic fever patients. *Journal of the American Medical Association,* 1953, *152,* 987–990.

PART III

Psychological Factors in Intellectual
and Emotional Disabilities

TEN

Psychological Characteristics of the Mentally Retarded

G. ORVILLE JOHNSON

G. Orville Johnson is Professor of Education and Chairman of the Faculty for the Education of Exceptional Children, College of Education, Ohio State University. He is also an associate editor of Exceptional Children.

No field of human behavior has been studied as extensively by persons in such a number of varied disciplines as mental retardation and the problems associated with it. No other field has been of as great concern to the state legislatures and national governing bodies. Each of these groups has selected terms to define the specific groups of children or aspects of the total problems in which they have an interest. As a result, there has been built up a large group of terms by physicians, social workers, rehabilitation counselors, psychologists, educators, and others. In some instances common terms have been employed by two or more disciplines—but not always to denote the same problem. In other instances, specific vocabularies have been developed to refer to narrow, clinical groups. The latter is true particularly of the medical profession.

One additional factor has entered the picture during the past two or three decades to further becloud or confuse clear communication. This has been the advent and expansion of organized groups of parents of retarded children. They have tended to use broad, descriptive terms when referring to their children, apparently feeling these terms make the children appear more nearly normal or less deviate in the eyes of the general public. The more specific and technical terms sound harsh and leave little room for doubt. Newspapers and popular periodicals have tended to adopt these all-inclusive, nonspecific terms. To add to the general confusion, they have also used the technical terms, such as "moron," incorrectly and inappropriately.

The entire issue of terminology has been so acute that the *American Association on Mental Deficiency* has considered it a problem of major importance. Five manuals have been published in an attempt to propose solutions that will receive popular acceptance. The last (Heber, 1959) appeared following two years of extensive work. The stated purpose of this manual is to increase uniformity in classification. If this is accomplished, the manual will prove to be a very real boon to research and communication.

Classifications can generally be divided into two major categories—medical and behavioral. The medical classifications are fairly well defined and accepted, although disagreement sometimes exists concerning etiology or cause. When this occurs there may also be a consequent lack of agreement in regard to the category in which an individual should be placed. The degree of agreement has been much less in the acceptance and use of behavioral classifications. This has been due to a number of factors. Two of the primary ones are scientists' inability to definitively describe categories and characteristics and the numbers of disciplines (sociology, education, and psychology—to name only a few) involved, each observing the behavior from its frame of reference and for its own purposes. It is also in the descriptive, behavioral area that lay and legislative usage have been an added confusing factor.

It is essential that any serious discussion concerned with a description of the mentally retarded, particularly in the behavioral area, must first be directed to the clarification of the terminology to be subsequently used. Only then can it become involved in the more fundamental aspects of the problem. This is true whether the discussion is centered around characteristics (physical, motor, psychological, social, educational, and so forth) or programs (day school, residential, workshops, and so forth). Without a clear definition of terms, effective communication between the discussant and the reader and/or listener is impossible.

The two basic classifications, medical and behavioral, are not mutually exclusive. A mentally retarded individual, in order to be adequately described and classified, must be included under each one. The medical classification is primarily concerned with etiology, physical characteristics, and consequent treatment and prevention. The behavioral classification is primarily concerned with the degree of mental retardation, the resulting performance level of the individuals in various situations, and programs. Persons interested in the behavioral aspects of the problems of and related to mental retardation have little need to know the medical classification. The exception to this statement is where unique patterns of behavior are existent in individuals belonging to a specific medical or etiological category.

The following discussion will, therefore, be largely descriptive in nature, directed to the behavioral characteristics and problems of the mentally retarded. The various medical categories will only be referred to as they are important within this context. Thus, the broad, generic terms "mentally retarded" and "mental retardation" will be used as all-encompassing referring to all degrees of mental deficit. Where available information indicates psychological characteristics are restricted to an etiological group or to a group performing at a certain adaptive behavioral level, more specific terms with appropriate definitions will be introduced at that time.

CONCEPTS OF MENTAL RETARDATION

When one discusses the field of mental retardation with persons from the various disciplines, he is often faced with more than the requirement of coping with a

G. ORVILLE JOHNSON

number of terminologies. He is likely to be faced with the problem of these persons having different conceptualizations of mental retardation. Mental retardation is literally many things to many people. To some it is a symptom. Some physicians may consider it a symptom indicating a chemical imbalance or the inability of the body to assimilate and digest certain foods. This would be in the case of such entities as phenolketonuria, galactosemia, and cretinism. Some psychiatrists and clinical psychologists consider mental retardation a symptom of a severe emotional disturbance. The individual is retarded intellectually only because of his inability to relate adequately with other persons and to his environment. In other instances these same persons may consider that mental retardation is a symptom of a sensory handicap or that the sensory disability has been the indirect cause of the emotional disturbance. This attitude is also held by some educators and many parents. Thus, a deaf, blind, or cerebral-palsied child cannot be mentally retarded. The apparent retardation in these children is merely a reflection or symptom of their inability to benefit from the normal environmental stimuli that encourages intellectual development in most children. The literature is replete with articles and statements purporting to prove or attempting to justify the assumption of normal intellectual development for the children and youth who comprise these handicapped groups.

The sociologists and developmental psychologists often apparently feel that mental retardation is a reflection of a lack of psychosocial stimulation. It is a symptom of inadequate social concern and an inadequacy of social structure. The fact that most mentally retarded persons (particularly where there is no apparent etiological factor such as disease, trauma, or chemical imbalance present) tend to be born to parents residing in subcultural, low socioeconomic environments indicates to them the validity of their contention. Numerous educators feel mental retardation is a symptom of poor or inadequate instruction. It may also be a symptom of disinterest and inattention on the part of the child or youth. Consequently, the individual does not derive adequate or sufficient benefit from the instruction provided him.

Where mental retardation is considered as purely a sympton, the solution is either a simple one or hopeless as far as present knowledge is concerned. Cure by attacking the cause is the only correction possible. If the cause cannot be corrected with presently known methods, techniques, or treatment, there is nothing that can be done at least at the immediate time. Selective feeding, changing bodily chemical balance, and providing psychotherapy are all purported cures. When the cure does not produce results it is because it is not specific for the disease under treatment or because there is inadequacy of available information and treatment. Similarly, children having severe sensory disabilities cannot be helped unless substitute stimuli can be provided to compensate for the lack of experiences in certain areas. The latter solution, of course, is far more acceptable to many parents, sociologists and others, and provides the basis for a number of treatments. Following this train of reasoning, there can be no truly retarded blind, deaf, or cerebral-palsied children.

The sociologist would feel that mental retardation along with many social ills are strictly the product of slum-area living. It can all be eliminated by the razing of substandard dwellings and the erection of community housing projects; addition of parks, playgrounds, and recreational facilities; and the provision of various cultural experiences for the residents. More homework, higher academic standards, different methods, and insistence on attention and satisfactory performances in the schools will solve the problem of the mentally retarded child in the school, according to some educators.

These theories sound fine and attract many disciples. The theories make it possible to conceive of a society where nothing so unpleasant as mental retardation exists. They are not proven by pointing at a case where apparently dramatic changes occurred following a prescribed treatment. No one has ever held that some of these factors do not cause mental retardation or that some persons having problems in the previously mentioned areas may not also have a number of behavioral characteristics usually attributed to mental retardation. Mental retardation, however, must be accepted as an entity in itself. It may also be associated with one or more of these symptoms, but it exists as a valid, unique characteristic. In the case of phenolketonuria, if treatment is initiated at an early enough date, the individual *may* never become mentally retarded. In other words, the inability of the body to assimilate certain foods may be a cause of mental retardation, but mental retardation is not necessarily a symptom. Severe emotional disturbance many cause an individual to be inadequate insofar as his abilities to relate to other persons and his environment are concerned. Mentally retarded persons, like the normal and superior, may become emotionally disturbed. But because a mentally retarded person is emotionally disturbed does not mean that the retardation is a symptom.

The mentally retarded, particularly those who are capable of independently maintaining themselves, tend to reside in the subcultural, low socioeconomic areas of the community. They hold jobs that are rated toward the bottom of the vocational ladder. In childhood and youth they do poorly in school. Does this mean that the environment is the sole cause of their retardation, or does this environment reflect their behavioral level? Where else in the community could they maintain themselves without outside help? What kinds of better jobs could they hold? What else could they do in school? Studies (Cassel, 1949 *b;* Cassidy and Stanton, 1959; Johnson, 1961; Pertsch, 1936) have not indicated that the educable mentally retarded perform any higher in special classes, theoretically designed in consideration of their characteristics and needs, than they do in the regular grades. Others beside the mentally retarded also live in these areas, are employed on similar low-level positions in industry, and do poorly in school—but for numerous other reasons. Again, mental retardation cannot be considered a symptom.

Mental retardation, by definition, is exactly what the term itself describes. The mentally retarded are individuals who are retarded and inadequate in their intellectual development and ability. The term states unequivocally that this is their characteristic now. It indicates nothing in regard to either the past, the future, or the cause. The definition thus used is one concerned with the intellectual operational level of individuals. Measures of the more finite variety (pound, ounce, gram, inch, centimeter, and so forth) used in the physical sciences have not been developed. Yet intelligence can be measured by comparing the behavior of one individual to that of the population. These comparisons have been made in many ways. Gross or severe retardation has been recognized

G. Orville Johnson

down through the centuries much as it is today, by merely observing the behavior of an individual and making a gross comparison to the way persons of his age behave. This kind of evaluation fails at the higher levels where the deviation from the norm is relatively small. It was not until the advent of the standard intelligence test that an instrument that could make these finer differentiations was available. Binet's original instrument was designed for the purpose of measuring those aspects of intelligence that are important to school success. This is still its primary application, although the Terman and Merrill Revision (1937) has been found to be one of the best predictors of vocational success for the retarded as well (Loomis, 1959). Since Binet completed his original work, numerous revisions of his scale, as well as additional intelligence tests, have been developed. A number of these have attempted to measure other, or additional, facets of intelligence. Thurstone, for example, attempted to determine all of the factors that contribute to a concept of total intelligence. After defining and describing these factors, he selected and devised items designed to measure them. These items were combined into the Tests of Primary Mental Abilities.

Intelligence is measurable on a comparative basis. The intelligence tests have been designed and standardized to perform this function. Because mental retardation involves some degree of deficit in intelligence, the intelligence tests are the instruments that have been developed to determine the intellectual level at which an individual is functioning. Through use of the intelligence tests, it can be determined whether or not a person is mentally retarded. Clinical judgment, use of projective material, and psychiatric and psychological interviews can help only in deter-

mining if the individual performed at or near his ability level on the intelligence test and/or other kinds of psychological problems he may have in addition to mental retardation.

Once an instrument had been developed that was capable of making finer measurements of intellectual development than had been possible using observation alone, placement of persons (particularly children) in categories began. It was, of course, recognized immediately that those categorized as mentally retarded were incapable of learning the same things as normal children of the same age. They could, however, often learn these things at a later date. Thus the concept of their being slow to learn or slow learners developed.

Diagnostic instruments have also provided the means whereby fairly accurate estimates of the incidence of mental retardation can be made. Unfortunately, no extensive and reliable epidemiological or demographic studies have been made to either verify or refute estimates, based upon school surveys and the assumed distribution of intelligence, that are available. School surveys are poor because numbers of the lowest pupils have been excluded. In addition, the surveys are subject to errors engendered by the nature of the population being served. As a result, other methods must be relied upon. If intellectual abilities follow the same normal distribution as other physical characteristics (and there is no reason to think they do not), the incidence of mental retardation should be between 3 and 4 percent. About one half of 1 percent will be of such a low level that they will require custodial care, supervision, and direction for their entire lives. The majority of the remainder are educable as children and able to care for themselves socially and economically as adults. Of the low-grade retarded, more than half of them can be considered trainable. They can learn to take care of their personal needs. There are approximately 2.7 trainable mentally retarded children per 1,000 school children. Of these, 1 has been institutionalized and 1.7 are still residing in the community (Kirk, 1957; State Superintendent of Public Instruction, 1954).

As psychology gradually came of age and more and more information concerning human behavior and individual differences became available, theories or hypotheses began to be developed regarding the psychological characteristics of persons included in the several intellectual categories. Psychologists began to look for ways in which the mentally retarded differed from the normal and a whole psychology of the retarded began to develop. Work has been done in the areas of learning, adjustment, social maturity, psychomotor skills, and even differentiation of characteristics for special etiological groups. The basic assumption seems to have been that here was a unique organism (Baker, 1953; Duncan, 1943; Wallin, 1924), or possibly a number of unique organisms (Strauss and Lehtinen, 1947), that needed to be described psychologically in order that educators, social workers, and other persons who might be responsible for them would, in having this information, become more knowledgeable and able to plan more effective programs.

INFLUENCE OF PSYCHOSOCIAL STIMULATION

There are several ways in which cultural factors may be related to and have an influence on mental retardation. One is in the impact that cultural factors have upon the individual who is, for any reason, retarded. Another is in the effect the retarded person has on his society. The third concerns the part which cultural factors play in the etiology of mental retardation.

There is little question that cultural factors play some part in the development of an intelligence that is appropriate to the society in which an individual exists. It has been shown that different attitudes and values in different cultures are associated with different child-rearing practices. Further, sociologists contend that more than one culture exists in the United States. The predominant one is the middle class; thus poor performance of lower class children on mental tests can be explained, at least partially, in terms of their lack of environmental stimulation. The fact that there is a markedly higher percentage of mentally retarded persons among the lower socioeconomic groups is commonly accepted. In fact, the statement is circular because any test item that did not indirectly measure socioeconomic status would probably be discarded as not assessing intelligence. Depending upon one's philosophical persuasion, it may be argued that people belong to the lower classes because they are unintelligent or that they may be unintelligent because they get insufficient stimulation from their lower class environment.

There have been many different approaches used to study the extent to which cultural factors are responsible for the incidence of mental retardation. Or, to put it in another context, many studies have attempted to determine how the rate of intellectual growth can be controlled by changes in environment. One of these methods is to study children who have been reared in an environment other than the home of their natural parents. They may then be compared to their earlier development or with siblings who remained in the original home. Freeman, Holzinger, and Mitchell (1928) studied 130 pairs of siblings who had been separated for at least four years in various foster homes. They found that the correlation between siblings was only .25, whereas the correlation between the intelligence of these children and the socioeconomic conditions of the foster homes was .48. In order of ascending economic levels of their foster homes, mean IQs of the children were 91, 103, and 111. The twin studies reported by Newman, Freeman, and Holzinger (1937) showed that IQs of fraternal twins correlated .63; those of identical twins reared together correlated .88; and those of identical twins reared apart correlated .77. In a few cases where identical twins were reared in very different environments, IQs showed differences as great as 24 points. A number of additional studies have been conducted using siblings raised in different environments. In most of these studies, although correlations continued to remain positive, they dropped significantly lower as the environments changed. This was especially true for children originally placed under five or six years of age.

In studying children with parents of subnormal intelligence and/or coming from lower socioeconomic group homes, which provided them with little stimulation, a number of interesting results were reported. Skeels and Fillmore (1937) found that, although the intelligence of young children showed fluctuation by age, it remained higher than the intelligence of the older children. A successive drop in intelligence was noted for each successive age group of children who remained in these homes over seven years. In another study, Skeels (1936) followed a group of children who had been taken out of the poor environment into which they were born and placed in foster homes at an early age. He found that their average intelligence was higher than one would expect in terms of their parentage. Whereas a correlation of .50 is consistently found between the intelligence of parents and children, the correlation between the intelligence of these children and their true mothers was zero. The average IQ of the mothers was at the borderline level, while the average for the children was 115.5. When comparing the intelligence of the children with the occupational level of the foster father, no correlation was found for children under two years of age. After this age, the correlations tended to become positive.

Skeels and Dye (1939) report what is probably the most dramatic study in the literature relating to the effects of environmental change on IQ. Thirteen children under three years of age having an average IQ of 64 were taken from an orphanage, where they had received a minimum of attention, and were placed in an institution for the feeble-minded. They were assigned to various wards where they received a great deal of attention from older patients and attendants. After a year and a half, their IQs showed an average increase of 27.5 points. A contrast group of twelve infants remained in the orphanage. The initial average IQ of this group was 87.6. After thirty months, with adequate physical care but a minimum of stimulation, they had dropped an average of 26.2 points in IQ. Twenty-seven years later Skeels (1966) reported on the adult status of the two groups. The changes noted in early childhood continued to hold. The institutional group had made good social and vocational adjustment, whereas the adjustment of the orphanage group was marginal.

In relation to the findings concerning increases in IQ or tested mental ability, a number of persons have discussed the age at which a child must be taken from a poor environment and placed in a stimulating one if the change is to prove of value. The general consensus among investigators holding that environment is an extremely important factor in mental development is that the change must be made very early in life. Wells (1939) felt that if children were taken from poor homes and placed in good foster homes before five years of age, sufficient change upward in intellectual development would occur to render invalid earlier predictions concerning intellectual attainment at adulthood. If, however, the change in environment were made after the age of five, neither significant gains nor losses would occur. Reymert (1939) felt that the change must be made before the age of six. He found, by examining children at the time they entered school and annually throughout the ensuing five years, that no changes in IQ occurred for those whose home environments were changed during this period of time.

One of the more recent and extensive studies in this area was conducted by Kirk (1958). He identified eighty-one mentally retarded children from three to six years of age. They were divided into four groups: Community Experimental, Community Contrast, Institutional Experimental, and Institutional Contrast. The experimental groups attended preschool programs, the contrast groups did not. It was found that the rate of mental growth of 70 percent of the children who received the preschool education was accelerated during the preschool period; the rate was maintained after they entered a regular school program. When the social and intellectual growth increases of the experimental groups were compared to similar evaluations of the contrast groups, the differences were significant. Additional analyses were made on such factors as

organicity and home environment. The study strongly indicates that a stimulating preschool program can do much to materially increase the rate of intellectual growth of many mentally retarded children, but if optimum results are expected, the program must extend beyond the school and into the community where the children reside in undesirable homes that provide little in the way of psychosocial stimulation.

All preschool intervention programs have not consistently demonstrated the same kinds of results (Blatt and Garfunkel, 1967; Hodges, McCandles, and Spicker, 1967; Weikart, 1967). In a number of instances early gains in intelligence either have not held or after a year follow-up differences found with contrast or control groups have been canceled out. When changes in language development and academic achievement are also considered, however, it must be concluded that preschool programs for high grade (mildly) mentally retarded children with no organic brain impairments but who reflect lower social class backgrounds are of very real value. There is little or no evidence to indicate that similar findings will be obtained for lower grade trainable and custodial groups.

LEARNING CHARACTERISTICS

Studies concerned with the learning characteristics of mentally retarded persons are by far the most numerous among all the reported research projects conducted for the purpose of obtaining information related to their psychological behavior. The investigator who begins to examine the literature is faced by one problem that at first glance appears to be almost insurmountable. How is it possible to bring the many results together into

G. ORVILLE JOHNSON

some kind of a meaningful relationship when they have been obtained by study of quite diverse groups or populations? At times, it is difficult, because of differences in terminology, to even determine the exact nature of the group from which the subjects were selected. When the types of groups are clearly defined, one finds that some comparative studies have used institutional mentally retarded and noninstitutional normal subjects. Other studies have included subjects selected in a variety of ways—from public school, special class, and so forth. The various studies have also used mentally retarded subjects of differing degrees or levels of retardation. One soon begins to speculate upon the influences the matter of selection of subjects may have on the reported results. Yet, with all these apparently contaminating influences there is remarkable agreement in the results, regardless of the environment or degree of intellectual deficit.

A number of kinds of learning and use of a variety of appropriate tasks have engaged the attention of many investigators. The verbal learning ability of two groups of retarded subjects and one group of normal subjects, all of equivalent mental ages, was reported by Cassell (1957). He was primarily interested in the problem of retroactive inhibition although he studied serial learning as well. The subjects were first required to learn an experimental list of six words. Next, an interpolated list of words was presented to half of each group. Although the results indicated that retroactive inhibition did obtain, there was no evidence of any significant difference between the groups (the two retarded and one normal) either on this factor or on the serial learning. Johnson (1958) also studied serial learning and proactive and retroactive inhibition. Both the subjects and tasks selected were different from Cas-

sell's. The normal and retarded subjects were selected from the public schools. The serial learning task consisted of memorizing a list of nonsense syllables by using the anticipation method. A cancellation task was used in the other study. He found no significant differences in serial learning between the normal and retarded groups. Like Cassell, he also found that the learning of normal children and mentally retarded children was affected by a previously learned task of the same nature. However, on the particular tasks used, which were somewhat psychomotor in nature, the mentally retarded were affected to a significantly smaller degree than the normal children. Berkson and Cantor (1960) concerned themselves with a problem of verbal mediation. Following an A-B, B-C, A-C paradigm with the experimental subjects and an X-B, B-C, A-C paradigm with the controls, they compared the performances of a normal group and a mentally retarded group. The results indicated that the facilitation effects were of a comparable magnitude for the two groups. There was no significant difference between their performances.

Cruickshank and Blake (1957) and Johnson and Blake (1960) reported the results of comparative studies with normal and retarded institutionalized boys on tasks requiring associative learning, transfer, sensory-motor learning, and discovery and application of a principle. The only differences they found caused them to conclude that the normal subjects were "probably superior" on the paired associates task. McCullock, Reswick, and Roy (1955) studied the abilities of institutionalized mentally retarded subjects on tasks involving repetitive learning. Their results indicated that there was a positive relationship between mental age and initial scores, final scores, and the amount learned. Sloan and Berg (1957), using a similar task—also with institution inmates —reported the same results. Jensen (1965) also found normal children superior to institutional, retarded adults in rote learning.

The facts that appear to be clear in regard to rote learning is that the mentally retarded are not superior to their normal mental-age peers as was once thought by some persons. And, when the factor of institutional environment for the mentally retarded is added, they appear to perform more poorly than comparative normal groups.

The problem of transfer has also been investigated, and is the subject of a number of published reports. Among the earliest is a study by Woodrow (1917), in which he compared the abilities of normal and mentally retarded children of the same mental age. He concluded that there was no significant difference between the performances of the two groups. Johnson (1958, 1960), using a psychomotor task, found that his retarded group showed significantly superior performance on a task requiring the transfer of a principle than did his normal group. Tizard and Loos (1954) reported that considerable transfer of training took place and that, among a group of residential retarded subjects, practice brought improvement in performance of a complex laboratory task.

Kingsley (1968), in studying associative learning of public school mentally retarded and normal children (with equal mental ages), found no differences. When equal CA groups were compared on associative learning ability (Prehm, 1966; Ring, 1965), the mentally retarded were found to be inferior.

Several studies on set have been conducted with the mentally retarded. Unlike the majority of the previously cited investigations, these are not comparative in nature. Rather, the investigators were interested in determining whether the same theories that had been postulated for learning in general held true for the mentally retarded. Barnett and Cantor (1957) took a group of adult mentally retarded subjects and provided them with stimuli and instructions that were designed to facilitate learning. Their performance was then compared to that of another group which had not had the training. It was reported that discrimination set facilitated performance. When the experimental group was divided into groups of high and low mental-age subjects, it was further found that the degree to which performance was facilitated was comparable for these two groups. Bensberg (1958) concluded from his work that by developing in the mentally retarded sets to attend to appropriate or inappropriate aspects of presented stimuli, the rate of learning can be controlled.

The search for qualitative learning differences between normal and mentally retarded children has resulted in very little data to support the thesis that the differences exist when mental age is held constant. Miller, Hale, and Stevenson (1968) found significant differences in learning and problem solving of equal CA groups of normal and mentally retarded subjects. For equal MA groups, learning was similar, but the retarded were somewhat poorer in the concepts of conservation and probability. Schusterman (1964) found that problem solving strategies of normal and retarded children was related to mental age. In studying temporal orientation of retarded and normal children of equal CA, Roos and Albers (1965) found the retarded have shorter future extensions, longer past extensions, and look at the past more negatively.

The concept that the mentally retarded require more time to learn a task they are capable of learning than do normal children certainly has not been verified by most of the reported research. The same is true for the often expressed necessity for the inclusion of more repetition or practice in their learning activities. Most of the evidence, instead, indicates that the mentally retarded learn in the same way as normal children, youth, and adults. The laws of learning that hold true for the normal also hold true for the mentally retarded. They are not slow learners in the sense that they comprehend slowly or grasp new concepts slowly or learn a skill slowly. The slowness is related to their rate of intellectual development. That is one of the prime determiners of when they will be able to comprehend, grasp a concept, or learn a skill.

Studies using mentally retarded persons as subjects have carefully employed tasks that are within their ability to master. When they can learn to perform the required task, they follow the same laws of learning and show little or no difference from normal persons of the same intellectual developmental level—mental age. If more difficult tasks were posed, the normal subjects of the same *chronological* age would be able to learn them; the mentally retarded would not. Then a difference would be demonstrated between the two groups. The difference, however, would not be one of learning but rather one of development.

Many statements concerning the learning rate of retarded children are undoubtedly made by persons who (a) are unfamiliar with the basic concepts involved in an understanding of the learning process, (b) have failed to differentiate immediate and sequential learning, or (c) lack an understanding of child development. Often they have not differentiated in their own thinking between learning and development, using the terms interchangeably. As a result, articles concerned with development rate have appeared where the author has used the term "learning," and in other writing, the author has used a reverse of the terms and concepts involved. This has resulted in a great deal of confusion on the part of readers. The confusion on the part of authors has thus been compounded to the extent that numerous dogmatic statements appear in print concerning the learning abilities (or disabilities) and characteristics of retarded children that are erroneous in light of interpretations that can be made concerning the findings reported in the learning studies.

When concerned with child development and rate of development in general, one may be referring to the growth rate of an individual or group in one or more of a number of somewhat discrete and only distantly related areas —physical, mental, academic, social, and so forth. The mentally handicapped group for education purposes is defined (as the name implies) upon the basis of retarded or slow intellectual development. This is reflected in the theoretical meaning of the I.Q. which, on most standardized intelligence tests, is a ratio showing the relationship between intellectual growth and number of years lived. The individual's present intellectual behavior upon a selected sample of tasks is compared to the average responses of a large sample of the population of the same life age.

Thus, a child with an I.Q. of 75 has an intellectual developmental rate three fourths that of the average or normal. A child with an I.Q. of 66 or 67 is developing intellectually at two thirds the rate of the average or general population. It will, consequently, take this individual from one-fourth to one-third times longer to "pass through" a specified developmental growth period than is required for the "average" or normal child. Assuming each of three children has an intellectual developmental level (mental age) of 6–0 years, the normal child will achieve one year of intellectual growth in one chronological year, and after a one-year interval will have an intellectual developmental level of 7–0 years. During this same period of time, the child with an I.Q. of 75 will have grown intellectually 9 months, and the child with an I.Q. of 66 or 67 only 8 months. The child with an I.Q. of 75 will require one year and 4 months and the child with an I.Q. of 66 or 67 will require one year and 6 months to develop intellectually the one year that the normal child accomplished in a one-year period of time.

The I.Q., therefore, does not provide the observer with an evaluation of the present intellectual power or ability of the individual but is rather derived from this knowledge plus a knowledge of the individual's life age. On such standardized instruments as the *Stanford Binet,* the intellectual developmental level (mental age) may be derived from a knowledge of the developmental age (intelligence quotient) and life age (chronological age.)

Learning is dependent upon a number of variables of which intellectual developmental level is an important one. This factor will largely determine the maximum complexity and level of learning that can possibly take place at any specified time. Thus, in comparing the learning ability (level, rate, and so forth) of two groups of children at the same intellectual developmental level, and assuming the same degree of readiness to learn in terms of background experiences, attitudes, desires, quality of instruction, and so forth, one would expect that they would learn the skill or concept in the same period of time. Although the two groups (normal and mentally handicapped) may differ significantly on such developmental factors as life age, physical and motor development, or social development, as long as they are equated for intellectual developmental levels, experiences, and previous learnings to ensure equal readiness, they should have similar patterns of learning, require the same amounts of practice, and retain equal amounts of the material learned.

The preceding statement should hold true in terms of immediate learnings within the intellectual abilities of the subjects included within the respective group. In the case of learning studies, it should hold true for the younger,

normal subjects and older, retarded subjects of the same mental age. This statement would not apply, however, to a sequence of learning activities (such as learning to read, which actually consists of many discrete learnings). Where sequential learning is properly placed in terms of an intellectual developmental scale and each successive learning activity requires: (1) greater intellectual maturity as well as, (2) previous learning, then the concept of intellectual rate of development as well as the concepts involved in learning must be incorporated into planning for the learning of the entire, total sequence.

The subject with normal or "average" intelligence will learn the sequence in a specified period of time. The subject developing more slowly requires that successive learning be spaced farther apart, thus extending the sequence of learnings over a longer period of time, but no more practice time in learning a specified skill or concept and consequently no more total instructional time to learn the entire sequence should be necessary. The only additional time devoted to skill instruction for the slower group should be in terms of additional review to overcome the factor of forgetting (Johnson, 1959).

The basic learning characteristics of the mentally retarded, summarized briefly, are in all probability the same as for normal children of approximately the same mental age. Differences that have been noted by teachers using rather subjective observational methods and by some research workers probably are due to controllable factors. Cruickshank (1946) found that mentally retarded boys were retarded in their arithmetic vocabulary, had less understanding of the correct process to use in solving problems, and tended to guess or give some unsuitable response more often than did normal boys. In the area of reading, Dunn (1954) found, when comparing two groups of boys (retarded and normal equivalent mental ages), that the mentally retarded did not do as well in silent and oral reading. In addition, the two groups differed markedly in regard to the patterns of reading errors. Numerous other studies of somewhat less extensive nature have amply supported these findings.

Because the learning of arithmetic and reading are important skills, usually emphasized by the schools, it would appear that the results discussed above would be contradictory to the earlier statement concerning no learning differences. The results reported by Cruickshank, Dunn, and others may have been influenced by many factors unrelated to "ability" to learn. An important factor may be one of instruction. Klausmeir, Feldhusen, and Check (1959) in studying the learning efficiency in arithmetic of mentally retarded, normal, and high intelligence children found no differences in acquisition, retention, and transfer. Kirk (1934), in surveying the reading progress of an institutional population, reported good reading ability. The average reading achievement of 100 children (averaging fourteen years ten months of age, 69 IQ, and mental age slightly over ten years) was grade 4.3. MacIntyre (1937) also states that mentally retarded children can perform at a level at least equal to their mental age. Numerous comparative studies, such as those reported by Bennett (1932), Pertsch (1936), and Johnson (1961), further indicate the probable influence of instruction. These studies compared the achievement of mentally retarded children in special classes with the achievement of like children in regular classes. They showed that those mentally retarded children who remained in the regular grades were achieving higher than those who had been placed in special classes. Because in Johnson's study the factor of selection for placement in the special class was controlled, the differences had to be caused by instruction or emphasis of academic instruction in the respective curricula.

Anyone desirous of knowing more about the mentally retarded and/or working with them should also be aware of some of the other variables that may affect learning. The various groups within the total society place varying amounts of value upon different kinds of learning. The middle and upper class groups as well as the upwardly mobile in American culture tend to stress academic accomplishment as a means of maintaining or improving their status. The lower class groups tend to emphasize traditional academic learnings and the need for formal education to a much lesser degree. Because the majority of the higher grade retarded who can benefit from education and eventually maintain themselves independently come from lower class homes, their felt needs for high academic achievement are often much less than for children in general. This statement should not be construed to mean that mentally retarded children do not want to learn. It means that anyone working with them must have an awareness of individual backgrounds and values. Only in this way can learning experiences be placed in contexts whereby each child will understand the value of learning and have the necessary desire to achieve.

The above statements are well documented with a number of studies reported by Zigler and his colleagues (Berkowitz, Butterfield, and Zigler, 1965; Stevenson and Zigler, 1957; Zigler, 1961, 1963; Zigler and deLabry, 1962; Zigler and Yvell, 1962). Their general conclusion was that the differences that have been noted between the mentally retarded and normal can be attributed to emotional and motivational factors rather than to the existence of mental retardation per se. They replicated and/or redesigned a number of studies concerned with rigidity, satiation, learning, and so forth that had indicated differences. By controlling variables that had not been considered originally, they were able to show that the differences in performance and behavior that had originally been noted could be explained upon the bases of differences in motivational systems. The initial studies had not taken into consideration the past experiences the mentally retarded and normal subjects brought with them to the experimental situation.

Among the factors that Zigler and others identified as being important and accounting for the observed differences between the two groups were (1) the relative deprivation of adult contact among the institutionalized mentally retarded, (2) their lack of experience of being correct or having success, and (3) their lack of experience of placing importance upon being right or correct. These deprivations and differences in background experiences then resulted in the development of differences in the values placed upon the reinforcers used. For example, intangible reinforcers were found to be of relatively low value and tangible reinforcers of higher value. Also, their problem-solving approach was different in that they sought to avoid failure rather than achieve success.

Thus, in studying the behavior of the mentally retarded, one must look beyond the mental retardation and develop an understanding of the reinforcer hierarchy operating. Thus, one must continually be asking oneself, "Is the individual deriving satisfactions from the activity and reinforcers based upon his previous experiences?" When the mentally retarded child or youth is constantly compared with nor-

mal or bright siblings and/or classmates, he may soon become so sufficiently frustrated that he will refuse to apply himself to school-centered activities. If the variables mentioned, as well as many more, are not understood, it is very easy to come to the conclusion that mentally retarded children learn differently from normal children.

It should be remembered that these same factors also operate with the normal. Teachers, psychologists, and social workers who work with the retarded are usually most familiar personally with middle-class values and objectives. It is difficult to understand that other value systems exist. Because most of society is designed to meet the needs of this large, middle group, these variables that affect learning adversely have much less chance of achieving the same degree of importance with normal children than they do with most of the mentally retarded.

The continuity of the learning process across all IQ levels was commented on by Ellis *et al.* (1960) in a discussion of their findings on serial verbal and finger-maze learnings with subjects at various intelligence levels. This concept, along with a recognition of variables effecting learning, has been accepted by numbers of psychologists and educators. Future research is undoubtedly going to include larger numbers of studies directed toward factors (psychological, physiological, and sociological) that influence learning. As information of this kind becomes available, more realistic and influential programs (educational and community) will be able to be planned for the mentally retarded. As a result, the mentally retarded will learn to operate more effectively in society and to improve their positions and conditions within the community.

G. ORVILLE JOHNSON

PSYCHOMOTOR ABILITIES

The relationship of general physical growth and maturation of the mentally retarded was investigated fairly thoroughly during the first third of the twentieth century. From these studies it is generally accepted today that the high-grade mental retardate who is potentially capable of maintaining himself independently follows the same sequence of growth at approximately the same rate as the normal individual. Some evidence indicates that the mentally retarded may be, on an average, slightly smaller and somewhat more prone to illness than the general population. This is supported in a series of recent reports by Klausmeier (1958), Klausmeier, Lehman, and Beeman (1959), and Klausmeier and Check (1959). They studied relationship between chronological age, height, weight, grip, number of permanent teeth, carpal age, intelligence, reading, arithmetic, and language for three groups of children eight years five months of age. The group classified as low in IQ was not significantly different from the average or high groups in any of the physical measurement areas. They were, however, fairly consistently lower on most of the measures.

As one considers the physical development of the low-grade retardate who requires perpetual supervision and direction, the similarity in physical growth no longer holds true. These persons develop significantly more slowly than the normal in all areas of physical growth. Many never achieve complete physiological maturity no matter how long they may live. A strong contributing factor here, of course, is that much of the severe retardation is either caused by or associated with gross physical deviations or malfunctionings.

The area of motor and psychomotor abilities is a much newer field of study. As a result, less information is available. Historically, Europe seems to have been more interested in the entire subject of physical and motor development at an earlier date than the Western Hemisphere. It is only in recent years that this, too, has changed. Three tests are European in origin, but not all have found equal favor in this country. A test of motor proficiency developed by a Russian named Oseretsky has proved to be the most popular of the three. Many investigators have made use of it or adapted it to their use. The Vineland (Cassel, 1949b) adaptation was one of the first to be used. Later, Sloan (1954) developed and standardized the Lincoln-Oseretsky Motor Development Scale.

Francis and Rarick (1960) reported a study concerned with the motor characteristics of the mentally retarded. Their subjects included 284 children (boys and girls) from special classes in Milwaukee and Madison, Wisconsin. They found that the mentally retarded children were from two to four years retarded as compared to published norms. They also found that the discrepancy tended to increase with age. They felt that their evidence indicated that the motor abilities of the mentally retarded were organized in much the same way as in children with normal intelligence but that the ability level is lower than has often been suspected.

Beaber (1960) compared mentally retarded and normal children in four tests of simple motor performance. The subjects were divided into three groups—two normal and one retarded. One normal group and the retarded group were matched on mental age. The other normal group and the retarded group were matched on chronological age. The results showed that the performance of the mentally retarded was below that of normal children of the same chronological age but was very similar to the performance of intellectually normal children of the same mental age.

Howe (1959) also compared the motor skills used on eleven tests of mentally retarded and normal children. He used eighty-six subjects ranging from six and a-half to twelve years of age. The groups were matched with respect to chronological age, socioeconomic background, and sex. He found that the normal children were consistently superior to the mentally retarded.

A number of studies concerned with motor skills have been conducted using institutional populations. Sloan (1951), using the Oseretsky, determined that normal children were significantly better than the mentally retarded on all subtests. Malpass (1960), using institutionalized and noninstitutionalized mentally retarded subjects, reported that when he compared the motor performance of the combined group to the performance of a group of normal children of the same chronological age, the normals were significantly better. Rubin (1957), using the Lincoln-Oseretsky, studied the relationship of age, intelligence, and sex to motor proficiency in a group of institutionalized retarded children. He found motor proficiency to have a significant positive relationship to age, to be insignificantly related to intelligence, and to bear no relationship to sex at these ages (ten to fourteen years). He comments, however, that the lack of significant relationship to intelligence may well have been due to the method of statistical analysis used.

The preceding studies, while few in number, are consistent in the information provided. The psychomotor (defined as pertaining to activities requiring coordination or direction from the brain) develop-

ment of the mentally retarded is significantly below that found in the normal population. All the evidence strongly indicates a high, positive relationship between level of intelligence and level of psychomotor development. This condition apparently can be mitigated, at least to some extent with training programs. Lillie (1966) found that although motor development lessons for preschool mentally retarded children had little effect over no training in gross motor gains, for fine motor abilities significant changes occurred.

PERSONAL AND SOCIAL ADJUSTMENT

Attitudes concerning personal adjustment, mental illness, social behavior (including delinquency and crime), and their causes have undergone long and interesting development. Notwithstanding the information that has been provided through research, many of the ancient attitudes continue to persist. When efforts were first made to understand deviate and asocial behavior, the assumption was that abnormality was basically physical and that deviates could be typed. Further, it was felt that criminals, for example, were born. Measurements of hundreds of prison inmates were eventually required to help dispel this idea. The next assumption was that criminals and delinquents were mentally retarded.

Today it is generally argued that there is no direct cause-and-effect relationship between discernible mental defect and delinquency. Mental retardation is usually considered to be associated with from 15 to 20 percent of the cases of delinquent behavior, although studies such as that reported by Levy (1954) indicate that the relationship may be as low as 1 percent. Sociologists feel that delinquent behavior

G. ORVILLE JOHNSON

is actually produced by a multiplicity of causes. The focus on unitary causes, such as physical type, race, nationality, or mental retardation, is gradually being replaced by theories of frustration and multiple factors and their effects upon one another. Haggerty (1925) suggests that low intelligence may be of importance but indicates that the cause is basically extreme deviation from the normal. Thus, the same factor may, on occasion, also operate for the very bright as well.

Kvaraceus (1944) emphasizes that the nature of the curriculum in school is an important element to consider. The delinquent is typically a nonbookish, nonintellectual, nonacademic, nonverbal student who does poorly in the traditional school subjects. For instance, in a group of 761 delinquents, 44 percent had repeated at least one term of school, as compared with only 17 percent of all other children in the same school. He also found that 60 percent of these delinquent children expressed a definite dislike for school, and 34 percent had been truants as compared with 7 percent among the nondelinquents. It is obvious that the majority, if not all, of these young delinquents had experienced a considerable degree of frustration in connection with their school life.

Following the thinking connected with the multifactor theory, a delinquency-producing environment consists of several of the listed items or elements: a home in which parents are unsuccessful economically, are of average or below-average intellectual ability, are of undesirable personal habits, are of questionable morality, are ineffective in discipline, are unable to furnish the children with a feeling of emotional security, and are inclined to reject their delinquent child both before and after his misdeeds; a neighborhood that is devised for adults, without safeguards for children, largely without safe outlets for emotional and social life, and full of unsatisfactory models and conflicting standards; and a school that attempts to make academic scholars out of nonacademic children and sometimes furnishes them with teachers who are too rejecting in their attitudes. When many of these elements are affecting the same unstable child, retarded or normal, a delinquent is likely to be produced.

That this is the environment of many of the mentally retarded is well recognized. The majority of the mentally retarded children and youth are raised (or allowed to grow up) in the delinquency-producing areas of the community. It is little wonder that most studies show a higher delinquency rate for them than is true for the total population. The question that has not been answered is "How does their delinquency rate compare with others raised in the same environment, in the same culture?" Understanding the contributory factors that result in delinquent behavior, it is now possible to understand such behavior when it is observed in the mentally retarded. It is also possible to establish school and community programs designed to eliminate these conditions.

The past quarter of a century has seen many of the earlier attitudes and feelings regarding the relationship of mental retardation and behavior vanish among professional workers as greater understanding has developed. Unfortunately, this is not as true of the public in general. In the late 1930s another movement relating behavior, adjustment, and intelligence came to the forefront. During the decade between 1940 and 1950 there was a flurry of activity related to the testing of personality and the use of projective tests with the mentally retarded. Some of the reports (Jolles, 1947; Sloan, 1947) went so far as to intimate that certain types of mental retardation may be a symptom of personality disorder. In these cases the apparent limited mental ability is due to the problems related to personality and adjustment. These persons can, consequently, be better diagnosed or differentiated with standard intelligence tests. Both Sarason (1959) and Wallin (1949) were extremely critical of these studies.

The general feeling among psychologists is that projective tests and psychological interviews have primary value in determining the existence and nature of problems related to personal adjustment that may be facing the mentally retarded person. From studies, such as those reported by Sarason (1944), Abel (1945), and Gothberg (1947), it is apparent that the mentally retarded have much the same psychological needs and face much the same kinds of personality stresses as normal persons. They have fears and feelings of inadequacy, anxiety, aggression, and guilt like anyone else. These stresses may or may not interfere with their intellectual functioning. The one point that was brought out in a number of studies was that the feelings usually thought of as being unhealthy in nature were exaggerated in the mentally retarded. Guthrie *et al.* (1964) in studying the self-attitudes of mentally retarded females found that although they considered themselves as popular, friendly, and conforming among their peers, they felt that they were ignored and isolated by others. They suggest these attitudes are the result of their past experiences. Because most of these studies were performed with institutional populations, one cannot generalize from the findings of the studies to the total population. The high-grade mentally retarded persons who are ordinarily committed are either dependent or delinquent in their

behavior. Furthermore, they represent a very small fraction of the total retarded population. Johnson (1961), using the California Test of Personality, found that the mentally retarded children who remained in regular grades, as well as those who had been placed in special classes, scored significantly lower than normal children on both the personal adjustment and social adjustment parts of the test. These results can be explained on the basis of the added frustrations faced by mentally retarded children both in school as well as in community situations.

During the years of high activity with personality assessment and recommendations advocating greater use of projective instruments, their use with the mentally retarded was frequently discussed in professional literature. The general thesis contained in the writing of Cassel (1949 *a*), Guertin (1950), Kanner (1952), and others was essentially that often unrecognized personality disorders may be misinterpreted as mental retardation, because their learning and responses to items on standard intelligence tests were in many ways similar. At a slightly later date this movement also provided another explanation than that used earlier for apparent retardation in children with physical or sensory disabilities. Not only could the reduced level of intellectual operation now be blamed upon lack of learning due to deprivation of sensory stimulation, it could also be explained by the presence of an assumed severe personality disorder. For a time it almost appeared as if it were impossible for blind, deaf, or cerebral-palsied children to be mentally retarded, although it was known that a number of the causes of these disabilities were also causes of mental retardation.

The hypothesis upon which these assumptions are founded is that a person will be unable to perform adequately in either a learning or testing situation if a severe personality disorder is present. Knowing that this is true in mental hospitals, where one is dealing with cases of schizophrenia and autism, it seems reasonable that it would still hold for somewhat less acute problems in children who are still capable of relating to a certain extent with persons about them and of having an awareness of their environment. The hypothesis can also be very easily tested. Reduction or alleviation of the problem should increase learning and test performance. Although counseling and psychotherapy have been used with the mentally retarded (as well as with children who have physical or sensory disabilities and behave like retarded persons), no research reports using numbers of subjects and control groups have been published that show significant IQ changes. Undoubtedly success has been achieved in individual cases. But that the problem of pseudoretardation is an extensive one or can be ordinarily solved in this manner has not been demonstrated.

There is no reason to suspect that the mentally retarded, because they are retarded, are consequently immune to personality disorders. They are, instead, probably somewhat more prone to having emotional problems because of their limited intellectual abilities. As a result they understand their problems less clearly, perceive the demands of their environment less accurately, and are more restricted in the number of available possible solutions to their problems. The discussions and reviews concerning psychotherapy with the mentally retarded by Abel (1953), Burton (1954), Neham (1951), and Sarason (1959) indicate that the use of this treatment approach with the retarded has not been generally received with enthusiasm by the majority of the therapists. The various reasons for this are as follows:

1. A feeling that, due to an unawareness of his problems, the retarded do not seek help.
2. A feeling that the mentally retarded lack sufficient intelligence essential to developing understanding and insights required in modifying behavior.
3. A feeling that the mentally retarded are unable to delay or control expression of impulses or, due to lack of ego strength, to develop self-dependence.
4. A feeling that any small results obtained are not worth the necessary involvement of time, effort, facilities, and money.
5. A feeling that many therapists who attempt treatment of this type have insufficient understanding of mental retardation.
6. A conflict of values between those of the therapists and those that are appropriate for the mentally retarded.

Despite these initial rather negatively biased attitudes, a goodly amount of work has been done, particularly in institutions, with some apparent success. Only a few of the studies, in which groups of subjects were used, will be briefly cited. Heiser (1954), using individual psychotherapy with fourteen subjects over about a one-year period, reported little increase in IQ. The majority, however, showed an improvement in behavior and adjustment. Thorne (1948), working with thirty males and thirty-eight females over a two-year period, reported that 66 percent improved. Cotzin (1948), using group therapy with nine boys, reported initial improvement of behavior for each one. After an interval of time a reevaluation indicated continued behavioral changes—some positive and others negative. Fine and Dawson (1964) report feeling an improvement of behavior and better placement results as well as adjustment on the wards as the result of psychotherapy. A methodological study using fifty-four chronically delinquent males is reported by Snyder and Sechrest (1959). Their results indicated a significantly greater increase in positive behavior on the part of those subjects with whom directive therapy was used as compared to those with whom other methods were employed. General success in psychotherapy with twelve female subjects was also reported by Fisher and Wolfson (1953).

These articles, as well as most other studies, indicate more successes than failures, which is also true for normals. Such factors as the generally subjective tone of the majority of the evaluations, the unreliability of many of the more objective attempts at rating therapy, the lack of control groups in many instances, the general lack of control for such variables as mental age, chronological age, length of stay in the institution, positive or negative influences of the institutional environment, types of behavior manifested, and personality and theoretical orientation of the therapists leave most of the results open to question. Considered as a group, however, the studies repeatedly indicate that the mentally retarded individual is capable of deriving some benefit from psychotherapy. There is no doubt that the processes and outcome are difficult to measure in a reliable and objective manner. One is eventually impressed by the quantity if not the individual quality of the evidence.

The greatest success appears to be achieved when the therapist is accepting, relatively permissive, but by no means passive. He allows and encourages expressions of feeling but, when necessary, places definite limits on overt behavior. In many of the studies reported the therapist continually found it necessary to take an active role in defining the purpose of therapy, in giving the patients direction and structure in recognizing and delineating their problems, and in some cases developing topics of discussion or activities to be developed. Practically no studies reported the use of a classical psychoanalytical approach. Where a completely nondirective approach was utilized in a group therapy situation (Mehlman, 1953; Ringelheim and Polatsek, 1955), complete failure was reported. There seems to be a feeling developing among therapists generally that a reality-oriented approach (which may also apply to the mentally retarded) is most effective. The flexibility and sensitivity of the therapist himself to the needs of his patients, however, may be more crucial than any specific technique.

The fundamental problem then appears to eventually center around the effectiveness of the social adjustment of the mentally retarded—the effectiveness with which they can relate to others. Although this problem has been investigated sporadically over an extended period of time, little in the way of direct, definitive information is available for a number of reasons. First, most comparisons have been made against a norm or average for the total population. Although the mentally retarded show up at a disadvantage on these comparisons, there is good reason to believe they are neither valid nor meaningful. These comparisons do not take into consideration the society with whom the retarded ordinarily associate and maintain themselves. The social maturity of those who are able to operate independently in society over an extended period of time must be satisfactory, at least in terms of the demands made on them. Second, instruments available for evaluating social maturity are poorly standardized and seldom based upon any theory of social behavior or adjustment. In this area, as in a number of others, instrumentation is badly needed.

According to Clarke (1957), all mentally retarded above the very lowest levels have some degree of social adaptation, although this level will vary widely. He lists the reasons for social maladjustment as lack of educational achievement, poor home and background conditions, prolonged stays in residential situations, poor emotional control, lack of experience, resentful attitudes toward authority, poor work habits, and lack of initiative. In order to effect proper social adjustment a program based upon the learning of good work habits should be emphasized. This idea is comparable to those expressed in curricula used for the mentally retarded in numbers of school systems.

One of the major reasons for the placement of mentally retarded children in special classes is that many educators feel that adequate social adjustment does not and cannot take place in the regular class. Johnson (1950) and Johnson and Kirk (1950) report that the mentally retarded are less accepted than normal children. They are also more actively rejected. The reasons given for the rejection are in relation to the retarded children's unacceptable behavior rather than low academic ability. Lapp (1957) and a number of other investigators have supported these findings with respect to lack of acceptance. Blatt (1958) compared mentally retarded children in special classes with those in regular classes. He found the special class children to be socially more mature and emotionally stable. Kern (1962)

also found that special school children are superior to similar children in regular grades in some areas of social adjustment, whereas the two groups are equal in others. Snyder's study (1966) indicated a relationship between achievement and personal adjustment with the high achievers scoring high on the California Test of Personality as compared to low achievers.

Pero (1955) conducted a study in which he used a social orientation method of social training with a group of mentally retarded persons within an institutional setting. His sample consisted of twenty students selected on the basis of the possibility that they might eventually be released. The objectives of the project were to prepare the students for a better-adjusted life while in and after leaving the school. The program was set up to be a guidance medium through which the personnel might delve deeper into the true nature of each student as an individual and as a member of a group.

Tests were used to measure the amount of responsibility that could be handled, how well each student undertook and completed tasks, leadership potential, awareness of daily needs and responsibilities, the ability to make and keep friends, self-confidence, dependability, and social adjustment in school. The results were discussed with the group. In addition, individual conferences were provided for those who desired them. Each student was thus given an opportunity to seek advice on anything that might be troubling him. The orientation lessons were so prepared as to give a complete social training related to occupational and social adjustment, human relations, improved daily living, personal growth and development, and total school adjustment. It was observed that the students formed a code of ethical values helpful to everyday living and that conduct and behavior improved within the institution. There was a general increase of competencies necessary for adequate social adjustment. Chaires (1967), by pairing low status and high status special class children in school activities, was able to change the peer acceptance of the low group significantly.

With young children, Capobianco and Cole (1960) showed that play activities produce more acceptable behavior among mentally retarded children. It has long been recognized that the level of social behavior has a positive, although not perfect, relationship to the mental age of the individual. This was verified in this study. That is, the lower the mental age, the lower one can generally expect the social level of the individual to be. His rate of social growth will also follow the rate of intellectual growth more closely than his rate of chronological growth. This is of utmost importance when one plans programs taking into consideration the kinds of occupations and social relations the mentally retarded adult will be capable of maintaining for himself. Thus, there appears to be simple and effective means of changing existing situations where it is appropriate and necessary.

The final criterion of effective personal and social adjustment is the effectiveness with which the mentally retarded adjust to society. Two primary sources have commonly been used for purposes of obtaining populations of retarded adults for studies in these areas. One source is the institution; the other, special classes within the public schools. In interpreting results obtained using these populations, some cautions must be observed. It is estimated that only about 5 percent of the mentally retarded population can be found in institutions and that only 20 to 40 percent can be found in special classes, depending upon the state and community. Any conclusions are consequently based upon samples taken from approximately 30 percent of the mentally retarded population. It is obvious that a certain amount of care needs to be applied in generalizing from these studies, because one is not completely aware of the factors that determine the composition of the population.

Once information has been collected, there still remains the task of determining a causal relationship for the behavior. If one group performs in a superior manner to another, is this the result of special training? A study by Porter and Milazzo (1958) would seem to indicate that special class training does result in better social and economic efficiency. This view receives some support from Bobroff (1956). Closer examination of the study indicates that one cannot make too broad generalizations based upon these results alone. First, the populations were small, consisting of only twenty-four subjects. Second, the amount of time spent in a special class was fairly short, ranging from 1.1 to 5.5 years with a mean attendance of only 3.2 years. Fortunately, a number of additional studies concerned with the social and vocational adjustment of the mentally retarded are available.

One of the earliest extensive studies is reported by Channing (1932). She studied the work success of 949 mentally retarded adults who had been enrolled while still children in special classes in a number of cities. Ninety-four percent were found to have been employed, although first jobs tended to be of short duration. Baller (1936) compared the status of a group of former special class pupils with a group of normal adults. He found that the mentally retarded were socially, economically, and vocationally inferior. Less than 50 percent were maintaining themselves independently continuously. The rate of permanent employment was very low. On the more positive side, the mentally retarded had had only a few more contacts with law enforcement agencies, and these were of a minor nature. Charles (1953) followed the same group of mentally retarded individuals about fifteen years later, when their mean age was in the early forties. He found the majority of them were now maintaining themselves and that their whole social and economic adjustment had improved considerably. Kennedy (1948) studied 256 mentally retarded adults who were matched with 129 normal adults. She concluded that the mentally retarded had come from families that were less well adjusted, more disturbed, and economically less well off. Despite this and the mental retardation, the families were very similar in their economic, marital, and social adjustment. Again the mentally retarded had had a few more contacts with the police—but of a minor nature, such as traffic violations and disturbing the peace.

Peterson and Smith (1960) also compared groups of mentally retarded and normal adults. The groups were matched on the basis of age. The retarded had attended special classes for an average of four years. It was observed that the mentally retarded worked at low-level jobs and maintained their first jobs for varying periods of time. Ninety-three percent of the retarded group lived in substandard housing. More than 50 percent were unmarried. Among those who had married, the divorce rate was high. As in other studies, they showed a higher incidence of minor civil offenses. The area in which the two groups were most similar was in their avocational interests—reading and television.

The relationship between personal adjustment, social skills, and vocational success with the mentally retarded has received some attention. Although the answers to these problems are still problematical, some indications are available from work done with vocational rehabilitation. Generally speaking, the results of these programs have been good. It should be remembered, however, that the state vocational rehabilitation agencies accept only those clients who show not only eligibility for service but also show high feasibility. The local office determines eligibility, often through the use of achievement and aptitude tests. Many of the most difficult cases are never accepted.

Cowan and Goldman (1959) concluded that level of education and past work experience were not significant factors in vocational adjustment. The effort exerted to find employment, however, is significant. Peckham (1959) studied eighty closed rehabilitation cases. The following job adjustment problems were noted: (1) a lack of acceptance by co-workers was felt, (2) a lack of social and vocational sophistication existed, (3) the retarded employees indicated a dissatisfaction with level of salary, (4) they quit their jobs for capricious reasons, (5) parents were unrealistic regarding the capacity of their children, (6) the family tended to overprotect the retarded person. Personnel from Departments of Vocational Rehabilitation attempted to solve these problems by counseling with employers, parents, and clients and providing an on-the-job training program. As a result of the study, recommendations concerning job practice supplemented by classroom instruction, guidance on the job, and an active follow-up program were made.

Engel (1952) made an extensive survey of studies related to the employment of the mentally retarded adult. The following points and recommendations seemed to be important in their achieving success.

1. Social and vocational adjustment should be given specific attention.
2. School programs should be centered around personal adjustment, social skills, and good work habits.
3. The mental level is not as important as personal traits and characteristics of the worker. The most important traits in workers according to employers are dependability, ability to get along with co-workers, ability to accept criticism, and a desire to do one's best.
4. Handwork in school has no apparent relationship to success on the job.
5. Students should be encouraged to remain in school until they are ready for employment.
6. There is a need for good guidance of the mentally retarded.
7. Counseling, personal and vocational, should be provided before the termination of schooling.
8. A follow-up program is necessary to provide support for the initial job experience.

Follow-up studies with low grade or severely retarded persons presents quite a different picture. Contribution to the general welfare of the home and community, or even demonstrated ability for self-direction, is the exception rather than the rule for these persons. Delp and Lorenz (1953) did a follow-up study of eighty-four severely retarded persons who had been in special classes. By the age of twenty-two (average), nine were deceased, twenty-five had been institutionalized, nine had moved out of the state, and forty-one were still at home in that community. A more extensive study of somewhat higher grade retardates was reported by Saenger (1957). His findings are based upon a sample of 520 cases taken from a population of 2,640 persons who between the years 1929 and 1955 had attended special classes for children with low IQs. Of these retardates 66 percent were still residing in the community, 26 percent had been committed to an institution, and 8 percent were deceased. Of those still living in the community, only 33 percent were able to leave the home and neighborhood unattended. Thirty-six percent were employed or had worked at some time. Less than half of them had found positions themselves, outside of jobs directly or indirectly controlled by parents, relatives, or family friends.

PARENTAL AND FAMILY ADJUSTMENT

Among psychologists it is widely recognized that many of the problems presented by children are reflections of and/or caused at least in part by problems in their parents and family. It is almost axiomatic that the parents must be included in the treatment when therapy or counseling with children is done. It is, therefore, appropriate to take a brief look at the problems facing parents of mentally retarded children. As a better understanding of their problems and attitudes is developed, greater insights into the behavior and problems of retarded children and youth should result.

Most of the research that has been conducted to date in this area consists of studies involving parents of severely retarded children who come predominantly from the middle class. A much smaller amount of work has been concerned with the attitudes and problems of parents (again from the middle class) of higher grade, educable retarded children. The problems faced by these parents are in many ways identical.

Therefore, it should come as no surprise that the findings of the studies are very similar. Middle-class parents are faced with a problem that essentially has no satisfactory solution. The mentally retarded child, whether severely or mildly retarded, is a deviate of such a nature that it is impossible for him to achieve at or even near the hopes and aspirations his parents have for him. He poses a problem of perpetual care and supervision for them. They usually cannot accept institutional care because it represents rejection of the child.

In some ways the problems are less acute and better defined (consequently, easier to deal with) when the child is severely retarded. Then the deviation is so great from early childhood or even infancy that it is obvious that some kind of custodial plans must be made. Even so, many parents never face this fact and die leaving the problems still unsolved. The higher grade retardate has the potential of self-support and self-direction when the environmental demands are not too great. Too often the level at which he can maintain himself is unacceptable to the middle-class parent. As a result he is seldom given the opportunity. If he does find employment, he continues to reside in his parents' home where many of his middle-class needs are still provided. Once the father has retired, or the parents have died and can no longer supplement his income, make many of his purchases, and so forth, his problem becomes acute. He has not learned how to provide for many of his needs nor has he been prepared for the lower standard of living he must assume. Relatives and agencies must take over the role of the parents at this point.

The presence of a severely retarded child within the middle-class home, as previously indicated, is a very traumatic occurrence. Farber (1959, 1960) and Farber, Jenne, and Toigo (1960) studied the problem of marital integration. Farber found that the degree of marital integration among middle-class, Caucasian families having a severely retarded child was dependent upon a combination of the severity of the problem and the methods used by the parents. That is, the type of family orientation was very important to marital integration. If institutionalization of the retardate were to be recommended, it should be recommended upon this basis. As far as the effect of the retardate upon the siblings was concerned, mothers saw their daughters as being affected to a greater degree than their sons. Farber also found the marital integration of families with severely retarded boys lower than those with retarded girls. The boys, in addition, became a more disruptive influence as they became older. This sex difference vanished in cases in which the children had been placed in an institution. Among the supportive factors reported were religion and close interaction between the mother and the child.

Parental aspiration and ability to evaluate their children in regard to their growth and potential has also been studied to some degree for the severely retarded. Goldstein (1956) found that the aspirations of parents were quite unrealistic but tended to improve (become more realistic) following the enrollment and attendance of their children in a school program. Johnson and Capobianco (1957) provided a parent educaton program in conjunction with a school program for the children. Only a few of the parents attended the sessions with any regularity. It appeared that parents who did participate could evaluate the present behavioral level of their children quite accurately. However, they had relatively little understanding of either what other children of the same chronological ages are usually capable of doing or what this level of behavior in their own children meant in terms of ultimate abilities in the future. About half of the parents felt that their children would become fairly normal, be able to learn academic skills, and eventually earn their living. It would only take them longer than the normal.

Fliegler and Hebeler (1960) reported a study of middle-class parents who had an educable retarded child. In regard to parental attitudes they stated:

Adjustment for the entire group . . . showed that greater relief was evident in a reconciliation to the handicap and parental satisfaction with educational and organized activities-goals. Somewhat less familial adjustment was noted in the reaction of the local community members toward the retardate, intrafamilial relationships which concern disciplinary measures, special considerations and the relationship between the retardate and his siblings, and the impact upon the parents' social life as a consequence of the retardation. Although the patterns for mothers and fathers was similar to the combined group, mothers indicated a greater dissatisfaction with the neighborhood contacts. Since mothers are more directly related to the neighborhood, this difference is plausible.

It seems that acceptance of retardation and the ways of coping with it through education are viewed with comparatively less concern than the more personalized areas. Significantly, in each of the cities from which the population emanated, special classes and clinical medical facilities are available. However, neglect of the more personally involved areas of behavior leads to greater discomfort. The interpretation of retardation for personal adjustment to the familial and community relationships is obviously needed to enhance over-all adjustment (Fliegler and Hebeler, 1960).

The studies mentioned are related to the parental problems of approximately 25 percent of retarded children. The remainder of the children and their parents are of the lower class. Because no studies are available, one can only hypothesize concerning parental attitudes, family adjustment, and the impact of these factors upon the children. With this group the total problem of mental retardation is probably considerably different and in many ways simplified for both the retardate and his parents. For one thing, among parents of severely retarded children evidence indicates that lower class families institutionalize their children much more readily than parents in the middle class. Thus, this problem is fairly readily solved to a large extent. The retardate receives care and supervision in an environment designed in terms of his needs and abilities. The demands placed upon him are realistic. The parents, at the same time, are relieved of the necessity for care, direction, and planning.

As far as the high-grade, educable retardate is concerned, the hopes and aspirations of the parents are in harmony with the ability of the child. He is living at a socioeconomic and cultural level that it is within reason to expect him to at least maintain. The jobs he qualifies for and can obtain as a youth and adult are equal to those held by his parents. Here the primary problem should not be one of family integration due to the presence of a retarded child or unrealistic aspirations on the part of the parents. Often he is not recognized as being mentally retarded. The primary problem is that the retarded child is too often growing up in an environment where the value system is inappropriate for keeping out of trouble with the law and the community in general. Ways must be devised that will provide

G. ORVILLE JOHNSON

him with more appropriate values if he is to be able to use his abilities in maintaining himself.

SUMMARY

Mental retardation is a comparative concept based upon the distribution of intelligence in the total population. The mentally retarded ordinarily include those persons in the lowest 3 or 4 percent of this distribution. If this concept is kept clearly in mind, a clearer and more accurate understanding of the mentally retarded and their psychological characteristics can be developed. The entire field has been plagued too long with misconceptions and misunderstandings unfortunately still fostered by groups because they are thus enabled to keep the truth from coming into the foreground of their own thinking. Too much time has been devoted to studying the characteristics of the mentally retarded from biases based upon an assumption of uniqueness or that they comprise a population apart from the rest of the human race.

Recent studies indicate quite conclusively that the mentally retarded learn in the same way as the normal. Their motor development follows the same sequence and pattern as the normal. Their level of achievement or performance, however, can be best estimated upon the basis of mental rather than chronological age. The modes or methods of adjustment are also like those of the normal. This is, they have desires, fears, hopes, frustrations, and so forth as does anyone else. The dynamics of their approach to solutions to problems is also the same, although the methods may vary somewhat due to the nature of the problem, their background of experience, and the depth of understanding they can bring to bear in seeking to reduce tension.

The majority of the mentally retarded come from lower social class homes that provide a minimum of psychosocial and cultural stimulation. Thus, it has been found that, for many, a dramatic change in their environment may cause significant changes to occur in their intellectual developmental rate. When and if a solution is found for this broad sociological problem it does not mean that mental retardation will vanish from the scene, although it may well be materially reduced at least insofar as it is recognized at the present time. There is no reason to suspect that intelligence does not follow the same characteristics in regard to its distribution that has been found to be true for other physical growth.

The mentally retarded who reside in the low socioeconomic areas of the community face many problems—problems that the retardation tends to make more acute. These areas of the community are also the high delinquency areas. Placing a child with limited intelligence in continuous contact with antisocial values and behavior over an extended period is providing him with learning experiences that will make his total community adjustment even more difficult. Often he may be unable to foresee all the implications and consequences of his behavior. As a result, much of the crime and delinquency attributed to the retarded is due not to the retardation directly but rather to the lack of appropriate learning experiences. Society is at fault.

The mentally retarded child, youth, or adult in a better home is, in many ways, no better off. Although parents may intellectually understand his problems, it is seldom that they can truly accept them emotionally. The program of training or the most appropriate disposition of his problems may not be acceptable to them. They may understand intellectually that he can only earn his living as an adult in an unskilled position but be unable to accept his employment in a position of this type. In some instances he, his siblings, and the parents might be better off if he were placed in an institituion, but they feel they are rejecting him by placing him there—"Nice" people do not reject their children and, furthermore, what would their neighbors and friends think?

Programs cannot be planned for the total population of mentally retarded. The mentally retarded represent a broad cross section of the human race in terms of their social, physical, motor, and cultural abilities and backgrounds. Experiences that may be correct for one child may be all wrong for another. By understanding the laws of learning in the individual's intellectual development, the level of learning experiences can be recommended. By understanding human behavior and adjustment, the individual's behavior can be understood and controlled. Each retardate is an individual with his characteristics, problems, abilities, and experiences. Individual rather than group or category understanding and appropriate planning must be provided.

References

Abel, T. M. Resistances and difficulties in psychotherapy of mental retardates. *Journal of Clinical Psychology,* 1953, *9,* 107–109.

———. Responses of negro and white morons to the Thematic Apperception Test. *American Journal of Mental Deficiency,* 1945, *49,* 463–468.

Baker, H. J. *Introduction to exceptional chil-dren* (rev. ed.). New York: The Macmillan Company, 1953.

Baller, W. R. A study of the present social status of a group of adults, who, when they were in elementary schools, were classified as mentally deficient. *Genetic Psychology Monographs,* 1936, *18* (3), 165–244.

Barnett, C. D., & Cantor, G. N. Discrimination set in defectives. *American Journal of Mental Deficiency,* 1957, *62,* 334–337.

Beaber, J. D. The performance of educable mentally handicapped and intellectually normal children on selected tasks involving simple motor performance. Unpublished doctoral dissertation, Syracuse University, 1960.

Bennett, A. *A comparative study of the subnormal children in the elementary grades.* New York: Teachers College, Columbia University Press, 1932.

Bensberg, G. J. Concept learning in mental defectives as a function of appropriate and inappropriate "attention sets." *Journal of Educational Psychology,* 1958, *49,* 137–143.

Berkowitz, H., Butterfield, E. C., & Zigler, E. The effectiveness of social reinforcers on persistence and learning tasks following positive and negative social interactions. *Journal of Personality and Social Psychology,* 1965, *2,* 706–714.

Berkson, G., & Cantor, G. N. A study of mediation in mentally retarded and normal school children. *Journal of Educational Psychology,* 1960, *51,* 82–86.

Blatt, B. The physical, personality, and academic status of children who are mentally retarded attending special classes as compared with children who are mentally retarded attending regular classes. *American Journal of Mental Deficiency,* 1958, *62,* 810–818.

———, & Garfunkel, F. Educating intelligence determinants of school behavior of disadvantaged children. *Exceptional Children,* 1967, *33,* 601–608.

Bobroff, A. Economic adjustment of 121 adults, formerly students in classes for mental retardates. *American Journal of Mental Deficiency,* 1956, *60,* 525–535.

Burton, A. Psychotherapy with the mentally retarded. *American Journal of Mental Deficiency,* 1954, *58,* 486–489.

Capobianco, R. J., & Cole, D. A. Social behavior of mentally retarded children. *American Journal of Mental Deficiency,* 1960, *64,* 638–651.

Cassel, J. T. Serian verbal learning and retroactive inhibition in aments. *Journal of Clinical Psychology,* 1957, *13,* 369–372.

Cassel, R. H. Notes on pseudo-feeblemindedness. *Training School Bulletin,* 1949, *46,* 119–127. (*a*)

———. The Vineland Adaption of the Oseretsky Tests. *Training School Bulletin,* 1949, *46,* 1–32. (*b*)

Cassidy, V. M., & Stanton, J. E. *An investigation of factors involved in the education placement of mentally retarded children.* Columbus: Ohio State University Press, 1959.

Chaires, M. C. Improving the social acceptance of unpopular mentally retarded pupils in special classes. *American Journal of Mental Deficiency,* 1967, *72,* 455–458.

Channing, A. *Employment of mentally deficient boys and girls.* Washington, D. C.: Government Printing Office, 1932.

Charles, D. C. Ability and accomplishment of persons earlier judged mentally deficient. *Genetic Psychology Monographs,* 1953, *47,* 9–71.

Clarke, A. D. B. The social adjustment of the mentally deficient: A symposium. *American Journal of Mental Deficiency,* 1957, *62,* 295–299.

Cotzin, M. Group psychotherapy with mentally defective problem boys. *American Journal of Mental Deficiency,* 1948, *53,* 268–283.

Cowan, L., & Goldman, M. The selection of the mentally deficient for vocational training and the effect of this training in vocational success. *Journal of Consulting Psychology,* 1959, *23,* 78–84.

Cruickshank, W. M. *A comparative study of psychological factors involved in the responses of mentally retarded and normal boys to problems in arithmetic.* Unpublished doctoral dissertation, University of Michigan, 1946.

——— & Blake, K. A. *A comparative study of the performance of mentally handicapped and intellectually normal boys and transfer.* Syracuse, N. Y.: Syracuse University Research Institute, 1957.

Delp, H. A., & Lorenz, M. Follow-up of 84 public school special class pupils with I.Q.'s below 50. *American Journal of Mental Deficiency,* 1953, *58,* 175–182.

Duncan, J. *The education of the ordinary child.* New York: The Ronald Press Company, 1943.

Dunn, L. M. Studies of reading and arithmetic in mentally retarded boys. A comparison of the reading processes of mentally retarded and normal boys of the same mental age. *Monographs of the Society for Research in Child Development,* 1954, *19* (1), 7–99.

Ellis, N. R., *et al.* Learning in mentally defective, normal and superior subjects. *American Journal of Mental Deficiency,* 1960, *64,* 725–734.

Engel, A. M. Employment of the mentally retarded. *American Journal of Mental Deficiency,* 1952, *57,* 243–267.

Farber, B. Effects of a severely mentally retarded child on family integration. *Monographs of the Society for Research in Child Development,* 1959, *24* (2), 73.

———. Family organization and crisis: Maintenance of integration in families with a severely mentally retarded child. *Monographs of the Society for Research in Child Development,* 1960, *25* (1), 1–95.

———, Jenne, W. C., & Toigo R. Family crisis and the retarded child. *Council for Exceptional Children Research Monograph,* 1960, *25,* (1), 463–476.

Fine, R. H., & Dawson, J. C. A therapy program for the mildly retarded adolescent. *American Journal of Mental Deficiency,* 1964, *69,* 23–30.

Fisher, L. A., & Wolfson, I. N. Group therapy of mental defectives. *American Journal of Mental Deficiency,* 1953, *57,* 463–476.

Fliegler, L. A., & Hebeler, J. *A study of the structure of attitudes of parents of educable mentally retarded children and a study of a change in attitude structure.* Syracuse, N.Y.: Syracuse University Research Institute, 1960.

Francis, R. J., & Rarick, G. L. *Motor characteristics of the mentally retarded.* Cooperative Research Monograph No. 1. Washington, D.C.: U. S. Office of Education, 1960.

Freeman, F. N., Holzinger, K. J., & Mitchell, B. C. The influence of environment on the intelligence, school achievement and conduct of foster children. *Twenty-seventh year-*

book *National Society Study of Education.* Vol. I. Chicago: University of Chicago Press, pp. 103–217.

Goldstein, H. *Report number two on study projects for trainable mentally handicapped children.* Springfield, Ill.: State Superintendent of Public Instruction, 1956.

Gothberg, L. C. A comparison of the personality of runaway girls with a control group as expressed in the themas of Murray's Thematic Apperception Test. *American Journal of Mental Deficiency,* 1947, *51,* 627–631.

Guertin, W. H. Differential characteristics of the pseudo-feeble-minded. *American Journal of Mental Deficency,* 1950, *54,* 394–398.

Guthrie, G. M., *et al.* Non-verbal expression of self-attitudes of retardates. *American Journal of Mental Deficiency,* 1964, *69,* 42–49.

Haggerty, M. E. The incidence of undesirable behavior in public school children. *Journal of Educational Research,* 1925, *12,* 113–114.

Heber, R. *A manual on terminology and classification in mental retardation.* Washington, D.C.: American Association on Mental Deficiency, 1959.

Heiser, K. Psychotherapy in a residential school for mentally retarded children. *Training School Bulletin,* 1954, *50,* 211–218.

Hodges, W. L., McCandles, B. R., & Spicker, H. H. *The effectiveness of a diagnostic curriculum for pre-school psycho-socially deprived retarded children.* U. S. Office of Education, project No. 5–0350. Bloomington: Indiana University, 1967.

Howe, C. E. A comparison of motor skills of the mentally retarded and normal children. *Exceptional Children,* 1959, *25,* 352–354.

Jensen, A. R. Rote learning in retarded adults and normal children. *American Journal of Mental Deficiency,* 1965, *69,* 828–838.

Johnson, G. O. *Comparative studies of some learning characteristics in mentally retarded and normal children of the same mental age.* Syracuse, N. Y.: Syracuse University Research Institute, 1958.

———. *A comparative study of the personal and social adjustment of mentally handicapped children placed in special classes with mentally handicapped children who remain in regular classes.* Syracuse, N.Y.: Syracuse University Research Institute, 1961.

———. The relationship of learning rate and developmental rate. *Exceptional Children,* 1959, *26,* 68–69.

———. A study of the social position of mentally handicapped children in regular grades. *American Journal of Mental Deficiency,* 1950, *55,* 60–89.

———, & Blake, K. A. Learning performance of retarded and normal children. *Syracuse University Special Education and Rehabilitation Monograph Series 5.* Syracuse, N.Y.: Syracuse University Press, 1960.

———, & Capobianco, R. J. *Research project on severely retarded children.* Special Report to New York State Interdepartmental Health Resources Board. Albany, N. Y.: State Dept. of Mental Hygiene, 1957.

———, & Kirk, S. A. Are mentally retarded children segregated in the regular grades? *Exceptional Children,* 1950, *17,* 65–67, 87–88.

Jolles, I. The diagnostic implications of Rorschach's test in case studies of mental defectives. *Genetic Psychology Monographs,* 1947, *36,* 89–197.

Kanner, L. Emotional interference with intellectual functioning. *American Journal of Mental Deficiency,* 1952, *56,* 701–707.

Kennedy, R. J. R. *The social adjustment of morons in a Connecticut city.* Hartford: Social Service Department, State Office Building, 1948.

Kern, W. H., & Pfaeffle, H. A comparison of social adjustment of mentally retarded children in various educational settings. *American Journal of Mental Deficiency,* 1962, *67,* 407–413.

Kingsley, R. F. Associative learning ability in educable mentally retarded children. *American Journal of Mental Deficiency,* 1968, *73,* 5–8.

Kirk, S. A. The effects of remedial reading on the educational progress and personality adjustment of high grade mentally deficient problem children. *Journal of Juvenile Research,* 1934, *18,* 140–162.

———. *Early education of the mentally retarded.* Urbana: University of Illinois Press, 1958.

———. *Public school provisions for severely retarded children.* Special Report to New York State Interdepartmental Health Resources Board. Albany, N. Y.: New York State Dept. of Mental Hygiene, 1957.

Klausmeier, H. Physical growth of mentally retarded children. *School and Society,* 1958, *86,*
140.

————, & Check, J. Relationships among
physical, mental, achievement, and personality measures in children of low, average,
and high intelligence at 113 months of age.
American Journal of Mental Deficiency,
1959, 63, 1059–1068.

————, & Feldhusen, J. *An analysis of learning*
efficiency in arithmetic of mentally retarded
children in comparison with children of aver-
age and high intelligence. Madison: University of Wisconsin Press, 1959.

Klausmeier, Lehman, I.J., & Beeman, A. Relationships among physical, mental, and
achievement measures in children of low,
average, and high intelligence. *American*
Journal of Mental Deficiency, 1959, *63,*
647–656.

Kvaraceus, W. C. Delinquency—a by-product
of the school? *School and Society,* 1944,
59, 330–341.

Lapp, E. R. A study of the social adjustment of
slow-learning children who were assigned
part-time to regular classes. *American Jour-*
nal of Mental Deficiency, 1957, *62,* 254–
266.

Levy, S. The role of mental deficiency, the causation of criminal behavior. *American Jour-*
nal of Mental Deficiency, 1954, *58,*
455–464.

Lillie, D. L. *The effects of motor development*
lessons on the motor proficiency of preschool
culturally deprived children. Unpublished
doctoral dissertation, Indiana University,
1966.

Loomis, C. M. (Coordinator). *A study of social*
adequacy and of social failure of mentally
retarded youth in Wayne County, Michigan.
Detroit: Wayne State University Press,
1959.

MacIntyre, G. M. Teaching of reading to mentally defective children. *Proceedings Ameri-*
can Association on Mental Deficiency, 1937,
41, 59–67.

Malpass, L. F. Motor proficiency in institutionalized and non-institutionalized retarded
children and normal children. *American*
Journal of Mental Deficiency, 1960, *64,*
1012–1015.

McCulloch, T. L., Reswick, J., & Roy, I. Studies of word learning in mental defectives.

I. Effects of mental level and age. *American*
Journal of Mental Deficiency, 1955, *60,*
133–139.

Mehlman, B. Group play therapy with mentally retarded children. *Journal of Abnor-*
mal and Social Psychology, 1953, *47,*
53–60.

Miller, L. K., Hale, G. A., & Stevenson, H. W.
Learning and problem solving by retarded
and normal Ss, *American Journal of Mental*
Deficiency, 1968, *72,* 681–690.

Neham, S. Psychotherapy in relation to mental
deficiency. *American Journal of Mental*
Deficiency, 1951, *55,* 557–572.

Newman, H. H., Freeman, F. H., & Holzinger,
K. J. *Twins: A study of heredity and environ-*
ment. Chicago: University of Chicago Press,
1937.

Peckham, R. A. Problems in job adjustment of
the mentally retarded. *American Journal of*
Mental Deficiency, 1959, *56,* 448–453.

Pero, J. F. Social orientation method of social
training in an institution. *American Journal*
of Mental Deficiency, 1955, *60,* 390–396.

Pertsch, C. F. *A comparative study of the pro-*
gress of subnormal pupils in the grades and
in special classes. Unpublished doctoral dissertation, Teachers College, Columbia University, 1936.

Peterson, L., & Smith, L. L. A comparison of
the post-school adjustment of educable
mentally retarded adults with that of adults
of normal intelligence. *Exceptional Chil-*
dren, 1960, *26,* 404–408.

Porter, R. B., & Milazzo, T. C. A comparison
of mentally retarded adults who attended a
special class with those who attended regular school classes. *Exceptional Children,*
1958, *30,* 410–412.

Reymert, M. L. The effect of a change to a
relatively superior environment upon the
I.Q.'s of one hundred children. *Thirty-ninth*
yearbook National Society of Education, II,
1939, *40,* 189.

Ring, E. M. The effect of anticipation internal
on paired-associate learning in retarded and
normal children. *American Journal of Men-*
tal Deficiency, 1965, *70,* 466–470.

Ringelheim, D., & Polatsek, I. Group therapy
with a male defective group. *American Jour-*
nal of Mental Deficiency, 1955, 60, 157–
162.

Roos, P., & Albers, R. Performance of retardates and normals on a measure of temporal orientation. *American Journal of Mental Deficiency,* 1965, *69,* 835–838.

Rubin, H. M. The relationship of age, intelligence, and sex to motor proficiency in mental defectives. *American Journal of Mental Deficiency,* 1957, *62,* 507–516.

Saenger, G. *The adjustment of severely retarded adults in the community.* A Report to New York State Interdepartmental Health Resources Board. Albany, N.Y.: New York State Dept. of Mental Hygiene, 1957.

Sarason, S. B. Dreams and thematic apperception test stories. *Journal of Abnormal and Social Psychology,* 1944, *39,* 486–492.

———. *Psychological problems in mental deficiency* (3rd ed.). New York: Harper& Row, Publishers, 1959.

Schusterman, R. J. Strategies of normal and mentally retarded children under conditions of uncertain outcome. *American Journal of Mental Deficiency,* 1964, *69,* 66–75.

Shallenberger, P., & Zigler, E. Rigidity, negative reaction tendencies, and cosatiation effects in normal and feebleminded children. *Journal of Abnormal Psychology,* 1961, *63,* 20–26.

Skeels, H. M. Mental development of children in foster homes. *Journal of Genetic Psychology,* 1936, *21,* 91–106.

———. Adult status of children with contrasting early life experiences. *Monographs of the Society for Research in Child Development,* 1966, *3,* 1–65.

———, & Dye, H. B. A study of the effects of differential stimulation on mentally retarded children. *Proceedings and Addresses of the Sixty-Third Annual Session of the American Association on Mental Deficiency,* 193, *44* (I), 114–136.

———, & Fillmore, E. A. Mental development of children from underprivileged homes. *Journal of Genetic Psychology,* 1937, *50,* 427–439.

Sloan, W. Mental deficiency as a symptom of personality disturbance. *American Journal of Mental Deficiency,* 1947, *52,* 31–36.

———. The Lincoln-Oseretsky Motor Development Scale. *Genetic Psychology Monographs, 55,* 183–252.

———. Motor proficiency and intelligence. *American Journal of Mental Deficiency,* 1951, *55,* 394–406.

———, & Berg, I. A. A comparison of two types of learning in mental defectives. *American Journal of Mental Deficiency,* 1957, *61,* 556–566.

Snyder, R. Personality adjustment, self attitudes and anxiety differences in retarded adolescents. *American Journal of Mental Deficiency,* 1966, *71,* 33–41.

———, & Sechrest, L. An experimental study of directive group therapy with defective delinquents. *American Journal of Mental Deficiency,* 1959, *64,* 117–123.

State Superintendent of Public Instruction. *Report on study projects for trainable mentally handicapped children.* Springfield, Ill.: State Superintendent of Public Instruction, 1954.

Stevenson, H. W., & Zigler, E. Discrimination learning and rigidity in normal and feebleminded individuals. *Journal of Personality,* 1957, *25,* 699–711.

Strauss, A. A., & Lehtinen, L. E. *Psychopathology and education of the brain-injured child.* New York: Grune & Stratton, Inc., 1947.

Terman, L. M., & Merrill, M. A. *Measuring intelligence.* Boston: Houghton Mifflin Co., 1937.

Thorne, F. C. Counseling and psychotherapy with mental defectives. *American Journal of Mental Deficiency,* 1948, *52,* 263–271.

Tizard, J., & Loos, F. M. The learning of a spatial relations test by adult imbeciles. *American Journal of Mental Deficiency,* 1954, *59,* 85–90.

Wallin, J. E. W. *Children with mental and physical handicaps.* Englewood Cliffs, N. J.: Prentice-Hall, Inc., 1949.

———. *The education of handicapped children.* Boston: Houghton Mifflin Company, 1924.

Weikart, D. P. Preliminary results from a longitudinal study of disadvantaged children. *CEC selected convention papers.* Council for Exceptional Children, Washington, D.C., 1967, pp. 161–170.

Wells, J., & Arthur, G. Effect of foster-home placement on the intelligence ratings of children of feebleminded parents. *Mental Hygiene,* 1939, *23,* 277–285.

Woodrow, H. Practice and transference in normal and feebleminded children. *Journal of Educational Psychology,* 1917, *8,* 85–96, 151–165.

Zigler, E. Rigidity and social reinforcement

G. ORVILLE JOHNSON

effects in the performance of institutionalized and noninstitutionalized normal and retarded children. *Journal of Personality,* 1963, *31,* 258–269.

———. Social deprivation and rigidity in the performance of feebleminded children. *Journal of Abnormal and Social Psychology,* 1961, *62,* 413–421.

———, & deLabry, J. Concept-switching in middle-class, lower-class, and retarded children. *Journal of Abnormal and Social Psychology,* 1962, *65,* 267–273.

Zigler, E., & Yvell, E. Concept-switching in normal and feebleminded children as a function of reinforcement. *American Journal of Mental Deficiency,* 1962, *66,* 651–657.

...hology of Gifted
Cm..dren And Youth

E. PAUL TORRANCE

E. Paul Torrance is Professor of Psychology and Educational Psychology and Chairman of the Division of Educational Foundations at the University of Georgia. His wide range of experience as a teacher has included work with preprimary children, all elementary and high school students, college and university graduates and undergraduates, and other groups.

Psychology during recent years has witnessed the emergence of new and broadened concepts of gifted children and youth. Witty (1953) paved the way for broader concepts by defining as gifted children and youth those whose performance is consistently remarkable in music, art, social leadership, and other forms of expression. However, it took the national and international needs and research productivity of the 1960s to bring about a widespread acceptance of a broadened concept of giftedness and to make it possible to implement it. Along with the development and refinement of new conceptualizations of giftedness, there have arisen new interests in finding "hidden giftedness," especially among children born and reared in poverty and deprivation. These interests in turn have given rise to issues of early identification and educational stimulation and of identifying and cultivating those talents that are highly valued by disadvantaged cultures. Interest in the problem of giftedness among disadvantaged groups has stimulated renewed interest in issues concerning the roles of heredity and environment. Protesting and dissident high school and college students are now bringing about a new interest in sociocultural concepts of divergent behavior as they relate to gifted children and youth.

HISTORICAL OVERVIEW OF THE CONCEPT OF GIFTEDNESS

Interest in giftedness and in gifted children and youth has virtually replaced interest in genius, distinction, eminence, and fame. Albert (1969) has called attention to the fact that the concept of genius was prevalent at least among the early Greek philosophers and was tremendously popular among early eighteenth century writers. The first significant study of genius was Francis Galton's *Hereditary Genius,* first published in 1869. There has always been a great deal of mysticism about the concept of genius. Along with the idea that geniuses represent the ultimate in intelligence and creativity, there has also been the idea that such people are unexplainable by modern concepts of human behavior and personality development. This is perhaps one of the most important reasons why psychologists have turned to concepts of giftedness, gifted children, and creativity.

Shifts in the interests of psychologists in this area have been documented by Albert (1969) through an analysis of the *Cumulated Subject Index to Psychological Abstracts* from 1927 to 1960 and *The Psychological Abstracts* from 1960 to 1965. Albert's data show that 67 percent of the references of genius, distinction, and eminence occurred prior to 1944. In the period 1937 through 1944, only 23 percent of the literature on giftedness, gifted children, and creativity was published. The terms "giftedness" and "gifted children" had their greatest popularity between 1958 and 1961. A steady upsurge in studies of creativity began in 1958. In 1965, the last year of Albert's survey, 139 publications on creativity were cited in *The Psychological Abstracts* compared with a grand total of 135 for genius from 1927 to 1965. This picture is extended by Frierson (1969) in his review covering the period from 1965 to 1969, which concluded that research related to giftedness has shifted dramatically from concern for gifted children and youth to concern for the creative process. Noffsinger (1968) in his survey of research on giftedness published between 1961 and 1966 has also confirmed this shift. In 1961, 61 percent of the studies in this area dealt with the gifted child, and in 1966, 66 percent of them were concerned with creativity.

Concern about creativeness has also been voiced by historians such as Arnold Toynbee (1962) and national leaders such as John F. Kennedy (1963), Lyndon B. Johnson (1965), and Hubert H. Humphrey (1965). Toynbee (1962, p. 10) declared that "to give a fair chance to potential creativity is a matter of life and death for any society." He warned that potential creative ability can be stifled, stunted, and stultified by adverse social attitudes.

About the time Toynbee made the above declaration, leaders in almost every area of life in the United States became alarmed by increasing societal pressures in the direction of conformity and the stifling of the creative spirit and mind.

The late John F. Kennedy, during the time he was President, was especially articulate on this topic (Gardner, 1964). As an advocate of the "new frontier," he was ever aware of the difficulties. On one occasion, he pleaded, "I call upon all of you to join in a journey to the new frontier. The voyage is a long and hazardous one, but we are all partners in a great and historic journey." He felt strongly that creative artistic, literary, scientific, dramatic, and other achievements should be valued. He warned, "If you scoff at intellectuals, harass scientists, and reward only athletic achievements, then the future is dark indeed."

The late Adlai E. Stevenson, in characterizing the late President, described what might well be considered the embodiment of the creative spirit and mind. He wrote on November 27, 1963, "President Kennedy was so contemporary a man—so involved in our world—so immersed in our times—so responsive to its challenges—so intense a participant in the great events and decisions of our day, that he seemed the very symbol of the vitality and exuberance that is the essence of life itself" (Gardner, 1964). The creative mind and spirit is characterized by just this involvement, absorption, responsiveness, and intensity; and anything that makes a person less alive reduces his creativity.

Lyndon B. Johnson, in his fight for a Great Society, likewise championed the need for a more creative society and a greater respect for creative potentialities. In his Special Message to Congress on Education, January 12, 1965, he announced the goal that "Every child must be encouraged to get as much education as he has the ability to take." In this same message, he showed a recognition of the importance of the creative spirit and mind among all of the people of our country. For example, he asserted, "But we will not accept the peace of stifled rights, the order imposed by fear, the unity that stifles protest. For peace cannot be purchased at the cost of liberty."

Vice-President Hubert H. Humphrey was perhaps even more forthright in his concern about creative people. In his address before the White House Conference on Education, July 21, 1965, he expressed the hope that "Our monument can be a society of free and creative people, living at peace and with the knowledge that each new day can be a better day." He urged, "We must ... continue eliminating obsolete and outmoded teaching methods and curricula—methods and curricula which stunt the development of creative thinking and understanding.... We must have the courage and foresight to use new mechanisms and devices to help the learning process." In this address he also expressed his faith in the creative potentialities of children who live in poverty and cultural deprivation. He declared, "Here is the chance to prove that children —regardless of their immediate environment—do respond to determined and creative efforts to illuminate their lives."

Perhaps the fundamental reason for the shift of scholarly interest from genius to giftedness and then to creativity was the growing recognition that the distinguishing characteristic of the truly gifted person is creativity or originality. It had become obvious by 1950 that not even the combination of high intelligence and special talent are enough to produce outstanding achievement (Guilford, 1950; Educational Policies Commission, 1950).

CONTEMPORARY CONCEPTS OF GIFTEDNESS

For many years, psychologists and educators have tried to destroy the predominant concepts of a single type of giftedness. Many of them have sensed that such concepts lead to errors and inhumane treatment of many children. A major problem has been in finding ways of conceptualizing the various kinds of giftedness and developing measures of the different kinds of mental abilities and personality qualities involved. Some brave attempts have been made, and some of them have had powerful influence on action. For example, on the basis of the Norwood Committee in England (Burt, 1958), the Education Act of 1944 in that country implemented the idea that there are different kinds of intellectual giftedness. Burt, an eminent British psychologist, maintains that the Education Act of 1944 assumes that children differ more in quality of ability than in amount. This act resulted in a tripartite classification of secondary schools, based on the idea that there are three major types of giftedness: a literary or abstract type to be educated at gram-

E. PAUL TORRANCE

mar schools, a mechanical or technical type to be educated at technical schools, and a concrete or practical type to be educated at modern schools. Burt reports that this scheme has not worked out as well as had been hoped. Many observers believe, nevertheless, that this tripartite system in England is much superior to earlier systems based on the theory of a single type of giftedness.

STRUCTURE OF INTELLECT MODEL

There are current today a number of models that may give a more psychologically sound and adequate basis for devising the education of gifted children and youth. Most of these models have been inspired by Guilford's Structure of Intellect Model (1956, 1959, 1967). As late as 1958 leaders in the study of giftedness such as Strang (1958, p. 64) were struggling with such categories as scientific, artistic, musical, and leadership giftedness and saying that "giftedness may take many forms, depending upon the circumstances."

Guilford's work marks a turning point because it directed both psychologists and educators away from dependence upon a single measure of giftedness. In his Structure of Intellect Model depicted in Figure 11–1 in the shape of a cube, Guilford has given us what virtually amounts to a periodic table of different kinds of intelligence. As shown in Figure 11–1, the model has three dimensions: operations, contents, and products.

In the model the operations are the major kinds of intellectual activities or processes that a person does with the raw materials or information. The first, *cognition,* includes discovery, awareness, recognition, comprehension, or understanding. The second, *memory,* refers to retention

or storage, with some degree of availability of information. Then there are two types of *productive thinking* in which something is produced from what has been cognized and memorized: *divergent production,* or the generation of new information from given information where emphasis is upon variety and quantity or output from the same source, and *convergent production,* or the generation of information where emphasis is upon achieving unique or conventionally accepted best outcomes (the given information fully determines the response). The fifth operation is *evaluation,* making decisions or judgments concerning the correctness, suitability, adequacy, desirability, and so forth of information in terms of criteria of identity, consistency, and goal satisfaction.

These five operations act upon each of the kinds of content (figural, symbolic, semantic, and behavioral) and products (units, classes, systems, transformations, and implications). Theoretically, this yields 120 different kinds of mental ability. Ever since the formulation of this model, Guilford and his associates (Guilford, 1967; Guilford, Hendricks, and Hoepfner, 1968) have been engaged in the measurement and validation of these abilities.

TWO-MODE MODELS

This monumental work of Guilford and his associates remained almost totally neglected by both educators and psychologists until Getzels and Jackson (1962) showed that highly divergent or creative adolescents achieved as well as their highly intelligent peers, in spite of the fact that their average IQ was 23 points lower. This study attracted widespread national and international attention and was vigor-

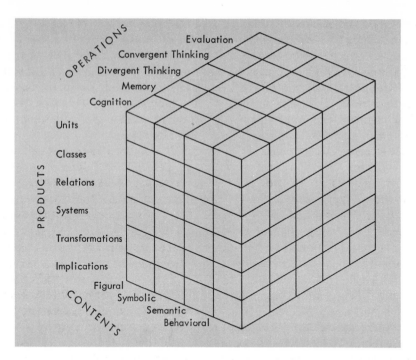

Fig. 11–1. Guilford's structure of intellect model

ously and widely criticized. The study had many acknowledged limitations, but it and the other investigations that it inspired showed quite clearly that creatively gifted children and youth could not be equated with highly intelligent ones. In eight partial replications of the Getzels and Jackson study, Torrance (1962) found that if one identified as gifted the upper 20 percent of a given population on an intelligence test alone, he would miss 70 percent of those who would be identified as gifted by a test of creative thinking. In his eight partial replications of the Getzels-Jackson study, Torrance (1962) obtained results similar to the original study, and in the other two cases the results were dissimilar. These studies gave clues about the conditions that generate the Getzels-Jackson effect and those that do not. Torrance then conducted seven additional partial replications of the Getzels-Jackson study

to pursue these clues further. In these partial replications, all subjects in the upper 20 percent on the measure of intelligence and all in the upper 20 percent on the creativity measure were included, whereas Getzels and Jackson included only those not in the upper 20 percent on some other ability. In ten of the total of fifteen studies the Getzels-Jackson effect was found; in the other five this effect did not occur. In all of the schools where this effect did not occur, two conditions seemed to be common: (1) the children were taught primarily by methods of authority and had little chance to use their creative thinking abilities to acquire information and educational skills and (2) the average IQ of the children was considerably lower than in the other ten situations and in the Getzels-Jackson study.

It was observed that the highly creative pupils in two of the five divergent schools

E. PAUL TORRANCE

achieved educational quotients higher than their intelligence quotients. Thus, Torrance and his associates thought that an ability gradient might be operating. According to the concept of the ability gradient suggested by J. E. Anderson (1960), ability level can be thought of in terms of thresholds, and questions can be asked about the amount of ability necessary to accomplish a task. Then consideration can be given to the factors that determine function beyond this threshold. There are cutoff points or levels about which the demonstration of ability in relation to minimum demands is determined by other factors. In other words the creative thinking abilities might show their differential effects only beyond certain minimal levels of intelligence.

To test this possibility, Yamamoto (1964) reanalyzed data from six of the Torrance partial replications of the Getzels-Jackson study. In each case, students were divided into three groups according to IQ (above 130, 120 to 129, and below 120). In general, the achievements of the first two groups did not differ from each other but were significantly higher than that of the third group (IQ below 120). In a correlation study involving ninth-grade students, Bowers (1966) found that relationships between creativity test scores and achievement were higher than between intelligence test scores and achievement among those at the lower end of the intelligence continuum.

Still almost unnoticed is that part of the Getzels-Jackson study (1962) dealing with two kinds of psychosocial excellence—that is, high social adjustment and high moral courage. It was found that just as the highly intelligent student is not always highly creative, the highly adjusted student is not always high in moral courage. Further, it was found that although the

students high in moral courage achieved at a higher level than highly adjusted students, the teachers perceived the highly adjusted students as the leaders rather than those high in moral courage. This is especially significant in a peer-oriented culture such as predominates in the United States.

Rather than going beyond the intelligence-creativity distinctions in searching for giftedness among children and youth, however, researchers have had a kind of fixed interest in this distinction, and hundreds of studies have dealt with it (Torrance, 1967a). Perhaps the most notable work concerning this distinction is that of Wallach and Kogan (1965) and Wallach and Wing (1969). Wallach and Kogan's criterion tests for creativity were five tasks each requiring the generation of different kinds of associates. The tests were administered individually in a gamelike atmosphere without time limits. The associates generated were scored for uniqueness and number. Five measures of general intelligence were also used. These included verbal and performance subtests from the Wechsler Intelligence Scale for Children, the School and College Ability Tests (verbal and quantitative), and the Sequential Tests of Educational Progress. A single index of creativity and a single index of intelligence were derived for each child on the basis of these ten measures. Wallach and Kogan then composed four groups within each sex: those in the top half of the distribution on intelligence and also in the top half on creativity; those in the top half on intelligence and in the lower half on creativity; those in the lower half on intelligence and in the top half on creativity and those in the lower half on both intelligence and creativity.

In summarizing their results, Wallach and Kogan concluded that whatever their measure of creativity assesses is different from what intelligence as now measured assesses and makes a big difference in the behavior of children. In their study involving fifth-grade children, they found that those high on both creativity and intelligence can exercise both control and freedom and engage in both adultlike and childlike behavior. Those high on creativity and low in intelligence appear to be in angry protest with their school environment and are bothered by feelings of unworthiness and inadequacy. In a stress-free context, as in the gamelike tests of creativity, they can blossom forth cognitively. Wallach and Kogan described those high in intelligence but low in creativity as addicted to school achievement. They continually strive for academic excellence. Those low in both are basically bewildered and engage in various defensive strategies, ranging from intensive social activity to regressive behavior such as passivity and psychosomatic symptoms.

To further validate the creativity-intelligence distinction, Wallach and Wing (1969) followed up the study described above with college students as subjects and academic and extracurricular achievement as the criteria. Their criteria of extracurricular achievement included attainments in the exercise of leadership, in various creative arts, in scientific endeavors, and in social services. Their criteria were especially concerned with excellence in self-initiated activities. They found that level of intelligence was strongly related to academic grades, but only to grades. Intelligence was not at all related to the level or quality of achievement in any of the forms of extracurricular activities studied. Performance on the measures of creativity or ideational resourcefulness, however, were unrelated to grades but strongly related to nonacademic achievements, especially those in which innovation plays a major role.

Hudson (1966), in England, has been trying to validate a different but somewhat similar set of distinctions, the abilities that differentiate successful students in the arts from those successful in science. Hudson characterizes the successful arts students as divergers and the successful science students as convergers. He defined the converger as the boy who is substantially better at the intelligence test than he is at the open-ended tests; the diverger is the reverse. Then there are those who are equally good or poor on both types of tests. On the basis of his research, Hudson concluded that the academically successful boy is not distinguished by his intellectual apparatus but by the use he sees fit to make of it. He found that most arts specialists, weak on the intelligence tests, were much better at the open-ended ones. Most scientists were the reverse. Arts specialists are on the whole divergers; physical scientists are convergers. From his samples, Hudson concluded that students in the classics resemble those in physical science and that biology, geography, economics, and general arts attract convergers and divergers in about the same proportions.

MULTIPLE-TALENT MODELS

Whereas Guilford's Structure of Intellect Model (1967) with its 120 abilities and even Thurstone's 20 primary mental abilities (1938) may be too complex for practical use, and the two-way distinctions of Getzels and Jackson (1962), Wallach and Kogan (1965), Wallach and Wing (1969), and Hudson (1966) may be too simplified, some of the moderately complex models now being suggested may push us closer to a practical, working con-

E. PAUL TORRANCE

ceptualization to guide identification and development of the many different types of gifted children and youth. Some of the more promising of these will now be considered.

One of the more promising multiple-talent models has been suggested by Calvin W. Taylor and is represented graphically in Figure 11–2. Taylor's (1968) groupings of talents are based on world-of-work needs and specify at present academic talent and 5 other important types: creative (and productive) talent, evaluative or decision-making talent, planning talent, forecasting talent, and communication talent. Taylor argues that if we consider only the upper 10 percent on each talent group as gifted, the percentage of gifted will increase from 10 percent for 1 talent area to 30 percent across the 6 talent areas. He argues further that if we limit ourselves to cultivating 1 of these talent groups, only 50 percent of our students will have a chance to be above average (the median) in classes. If all six talent groups are considered, about 90 percent will be above average in at least 1 group and almost all others will be nearly average in at least 1 of them.

Taylor (1968) believes that we now know enough about measuring and fostering multiple talents to find ways of cultivating most of them in school rather than letting them lie largely dormant. He also believes that in classrooms where multiple talents are cultivated all students will learn more. In other words, by having many pathways through their complex nervous systems, students can use several different abilities at one time or another to process information during the school week. He believes that this will happen if teachers sharpen their abilties to cultivate these talents and deliberately work across a greater number of these talents.

Taylor recommends that teachers give greater emphasis to their talent developer role and less emphasis to their role as information dispenser. He suggests further that each teacher might specialize to become experts in developing particular talents and that students could study under each of these separate talent development specialists. He proposes that educational programs be evaluated by determining how much students have developed each of these talents as well as how much they have gained in subject mastery. He suggests that the best place to begin is by cultivating the creative and productive type of talent, because creative teaching approaches do most to expand the narrow band of talents with which schools now concern themselves.

Taylor's Multiple-Talent Model (1968) represents one of the cleanest departures yet offered from traditional conceptualizations of talents in terms of subject-matter content such as science, art, music, dramatics, creative writing, mechanics, social leadership, and the like. The latter model is perhaps best represented by the Quincy, Illinois, and Portland, Oregon, gifted-child projects of the 1950s (De Haan and Wilson, 1958). Although Taylor's Multiple-Talent Model is based on world-of-work needs, it also seems to be a departure from the vocational-guidance-oriented models born largely in the 1940s and thrust into prominence in the 1950s. These models are represented by test batteries such as the Differential Aptitude Tests (Bennett et al., 1959), the General Aptitude Test Battery (Bureau of Employment Security, 1958), the Multiple Aptitude Tests (Segel and Raskin, 1959), and the Flanagan Aptitude Classification Tests (Flanagan, 1959). Although the models upon which these test batteries were designed guide job selection and personnel selection, Taylor's model seems to be

These multiple-talent
totem poles designed
by Darrel Allington
and Vern Bullough
illustrate that most
individuals possess
above average talents
in at least one of
the six basic fields.

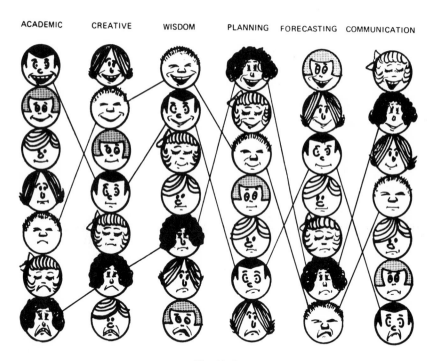

ACADEMIC   CREATIVE   WISDOM   PLANNING   FORECASTING   COMMUNICATION

Fig. 11–2.

designed for talent development in education.

A number of models similar to Taylor's have been offered, but none of them has been developed and instrumented to the extent that Taylor's has been. Douglass (1968), for example, has suggested the following basic types of gifted children and youth and other types that are hybrids of these:

E. PAUL TORRANCE

1. *The blotter mind.* This type of learner can learn quickly materials from the printed page and from lectures and retain them fairly well.
2. *The understanding mind.* This type of learner is able to generalize and grasp meanings and is not dependent upon rote memory. He tends to generalize his experiences, including his readings.
3. *Problem-solving mind.* This type of learner is able, with a little guidance, to apply his knowledge or what knowledge he can find in various sources to contribute to the solving of problems.
4. *The creative mind.* This type of learner possesses imagination and an urge to create in some form such as art, crafts, music, and the theater.
5. *The skilled mind.* This type of learner has great capacity for developing a variety of skills including typewriting, skating, and dancing.
6. *The social and leadership mind.* Some youngsters, who may or may not be superior in respect to the foregoing areas, seem to possess unusual skills for getting along with people, being well regarded, and exerting leadership.

FOUR TYPES OF GIFTED ADOLESCENTS

A somewhat different model of gifted adolescents has been developed by Drews (1961, 1963) and is illustrated in Figure 11–3. This conceptualization grew out of Drews' disconcerting experience in which she had found that gifted adolescents appear very much alike when viewed in terms of group intelligence and achievement tests. She sensed that adolescents showing gifted performances not only have more talents than others, but they often have unusual combinations of talents and styles with limitless contraditions and inconsistencies. She points out that the boy scientist may also be a poet and the May Queen may take computer programming on the side. Out of the discomfort of her disconcerting findings, Drews developed the following four-way classification of gifted adolescents:

1. The high-achieving studious. These adolescents think hard work is a good thing and are highly attuned to what parents and school expect. They usually conform to what teachers demand or suggest. They generally put their school work ahead of pleasure. They are rarely school leaders and may not be highly creative and original. They are productive, however, in terms of number of problems completed or number of words in a theme. They like highly structured activities and often reject learning approaches that lack apparent structure. They are highly favored by teachers. Their ambition is to be hard working and conscientious, to help others, and to live by the rules.

2. The social leaders. These adolescents are popular and well liked by their peers. They tend to conform more to teenage mores than to teachers' expectations. They are generally quite successful academically. Drews reports that while the studious are preparing for examinations and the creative intellectuals are reading about existentialism, the social leaders are out electing someone to office or getting themselves elected. Although they receive good grades, they do not achieve very well on difficult scholarship examinations.

3. The creative intellectuals. In general, this group of adolescents receives lower grades than the studious or social leaders. However, their achievement test

Fig. 11–3. Drews' four faces of gifted adolescents. Saturday Review, Inc.] [used by permission of Doug Anderson; copyright 1963

scores are higher than their grades. On creativity tests they tend to be both fluent and original. They also tend to ask provocative, below-the-surface or, for some teachers, below-the-belt questions. This group contains future scientists (but not engineers), artists, writers, musicians, and scholars-at-large. As adolescents they delve into such matters as extrasensory perception. They buy books and read them. Unlike the high-achieving studious group, they do not want explicit assignments and thrive on free choice. Often they do not want or expect rewards.

4. The rebel. Drews describes rebels as individualistic, creative nonintellectuals. Their noncomformity serves no social or intellectual purpose and shows only their dislike for regimentation. Though some of them are brilliant, they are extremely low achievers. Although they are not leaders in school, they may be masterminds in a

E. PAUL TORRANCE

subculture that borders on delinquency. Rejection between rebels and teachers is mutual. Rebels measure low on social responsibility and test higher on nonverbal than on verbal sections of intelligence tests. On creativity measures they are not highly fluent, yet they are highly original. They are sometimes responsive to unusual ideas. They are alienated from school, but sometimes they can be reclaimed if approached in ways that make sense to them.

PROFILE OF EMINENT CREATIVE ADULTS

From studies of eminent creative adults and other highly productive, creatively gifted adults, there has emerged a fairly consistent profile. One of the most intense and comprehensive investigations of the productively creative personality is being carried out by MacKinnon (1961) and his associates at the Institute for Personality Assessment and Research (IPAR) at the University of California at Berkeley. Most of their studies have been based on investigations of highly productive persons, in various occupations, who have achieved eminence because of their creativity. These groups include: scientists, architects, writers, artists, students, and others. In summarizing this work, MacKinnon identifies the following characteristics of the productively creative person:

1. Intelligent—but the most intelligent persons are not always the most creative (Concept Mastery Test and creativity correlate .08 among architects and .07 among scientists).
2. Original.
3. Seeks deeper meanings, implications, possibilities.
4. Independent in judgment and in thought and action.

5. Often chafes and rebels; a high level of energy is channeled toward activities and goals the individual has set for himself.
6. Perceptive, open to experience both of the inner and outer world.
7. Intuitive, both in perceptions and in thought processes.
8. Has an image of himself as a responsible person and a sense of destiny about himself as a human being; has a belief in the worth and validity of one's creative efforts.
9. Entertains both theoretical and aesthetic values; has the capacity to tolerate the tension created in him by conflicts and effects some reconciliation.
10. Similarly, concerning masculinity-femininity, there is a resolution of the conflict with creative male subjects appearing to give more expression to the feminine side of their nature than do less creative persons.
11. Is not stimulus and object bound in perceptions but is ever alert to the as-yet-not-realized.

Barron (1963), one of the members of MacKinnon's research team at IPAR, has called attention to certain other aspects of the personality of the productively creative individual. One of these is the creative person's preference for complexity and his tolerance for disorder, imbalance, ambiguity, and incompleteness. Barron (1963) has also emphasized the idea that the creative individual not only respects the irrational in himself but courts it as the most promising source of originality in his thought. According to Barron, the creative person rejects the demands of society that he should shun in himself the primitive, the uncultured, the naïve, and the nonsensical. He rejects this demand because he wants to own himself totally and because he perceives a short sightedness in the claim of society that all its members should adapt themselves to a norm for a given time and place. Barron maintains that this type of imbalance is more likely to be healthy than unhealthy. The truly creative person is ready to abandon old classifications and to acknowledge that life, particularly his own unique life, is rich with new possibilities; disorder offers the potentiality of order.

IDENTIFYING GIFTED CHILDREN AND YOUTH

The New Problem

The emergence of new and broader concepts of giftedness has been quite confusing to teachers, administrators, and parents who insist upon strict adherence to rules and demand precision. Man's enormously strong need for simplicity of structure has perhaps, more than any other factor, impeded the emergence and implementation of appropriate complexity in educating gifted children and youth. Illustrative of this concern is the following quotation from a letter to the editor of *The Instructor* magazine (Troutman, 1969):

> Our school has been working on a project of identifying and setting up a program for gifted children. A major concern is to find an operational definition of the gifted to apply to our study. When we went to books and articles, we found little agreement as to what exactly giftedness is.

Acceptance of any of the complex models of giftedness sketched in the preceding section commits one inalterably to complexities in identifying gifted children and youth. The procedures, means, and goals for identifying gifted children and youth under these complex models become fairly clear when the task is perceived as one of searching for unusual potentialities which, if given intelligent guidance and encouragement, can result in outstanding achievements of value to society.

In approaching problems of identifying gifted children and youth, it is of great importance that there be compatibility between the criteria of identification and the goals of the program to be established. The author has known of excellent programs for gifted children with considerable emphasis on creative activities for children identified as gifted on the basis of intelligence test scores and teacher grades. It was obvious that many of these children were miserable and felt extremely out of place. It would be just as cruel to identify as gifted a group of children on the basis of creativity tests and then give them a program that emphasized only knowledge acquisition by highly structured and authoritarian procedures.

The author has worked with one highly successful program for upper elementary gifted children that uses high achievement as measured by standardized tests as the criterion of selection (Gilbertson, 1960). The children in this program are rather well adjusted socially and have good backgrounds of achievement. On the average they read at about the tenth-grade level. With the strong motivation of these children and the almost total absence of behavior problems and time-consuming problems of classroom discipline, it is possible to achieve impressive results. One might be concerned about the absence of maladjusted children with brilliant minds or of highly creative children who do only moderately well on objective tests of achievement. However, the school made the choice to establish a particular kind of

E. PAUL TORRANCE

program for gifted children and used appropriate criteria in selecting children for it.

In the light of the complexity that exists, how can decisions be made concerning the identification of gifted children and youth? Newland (1963) has proposed that giftedness be defined in terms of social need. In suggesting this approach Newland recognized that it would appear to be an oversimplification. He believes, however, that a definition of giftedness in terms of social need is necessary as a socially promising first step and that a kind of evidence of social reality can be communicated in simple yet sound psychometric terms. Accordingly, he collected opinion data from professional educators and students in a course on the gifted child in school and society to make estimates concerning the percentage of school children who should be accorded special educational stimulation to meet society's needs for gifted adults. He estimates that from 5 to 8 percent of children should be defined as gifted and that this decision should be made on the basis of the Binet and Wechsler intelligence scales. He acknowledges that these measures are susceptible to error and reflect only one facet of total intelligence, but he believes that these instruments provide the best single piece of objective evidence in terms of which gross educational planning can start.

One senses the wisdom of Newland's suggestion when he confronts the elaborate psychometric procedures necessary to implement some of the models of giftedness presented in the first part of this chapter. To administer properly the psychometric procedures necessary to implement Guilford's Structure of Intellect Model would require several days of testing. To date, instrumentation for about 80 of the 120 hypothesized abilities have been completed and validated, and there are several tests for each ability. Furthermore, most of the tests were designed for superior adults, and the task of adapting them for use with school children and youth has barely been touched (Gardner and Cox, 1964; Guilford, Merrifield, and Cox, 1961; Hoepfner and Guilford, 1965; Merrifield, Guilford, and Gershon, 1963).

Reinterpretation of Old Measures

The hope is that out of the complexity of the Structure of Intellect Model and the great mass of test devices that have been invented to implement it will come simpler, practical procedures that will distill most of the essence of the more complex model. One approach to this goal has been the reinterpretation of data from existing psychometric procedures such as the Binet and Wechsler in terms of Structure of Intellect concepts, and the other has been efforts to invent complex tasks that can be scored in a variety of ways and in terms of Structure of Intellect concepts. The efforts of Meeker (1969) and Bruch (1969) are perhaps the best exemplars of the former, and the work of Torrance and his associates (Torrance, 1962, 1965, 1966, 1968), the latter.

Meeker (1969) has made a systematic attempt to develop practical ways to translate the Stanford-Binet, the Wechsler Intelligence Scales for Children, and the Wechsler Pre-Primary Scales of Intelligence into Guilford's Structure of Intellect Model so that a graphic profile of a child's intellectual abilities becomes evident. In her book Meeker provides specific profiles of gifted children and discusses how the information from these profiles can be used as guides for tailoring programs.

Bruch (1969) is engaged in the process

of validating a special scoring of the Stanford-Binet to yield a creativity score. Many of her case studies indicate that the procedure holds special promise for identifying gifted children and youth among disadvantaged groups who would be identified as only average or slightly below average on the routine scoring of a Stanford-Binet test record.

Complex Tasks with Multiple Scoring

Over a period of ten years, Torrance and his associates (1962, 1965, 1966, 1968) have developed and published alternate batteries of tests of creative thinking that have been used successfully in a variety of cultures and subcultures and at all educational levels from kindergarten through graduate school. Deliberate efforts were made to construct test tasks that are models of the creative thinking process, each involving different kinds of thinking and each contributing something unique to the batteries, both verbal and figural. These batteries, or test tasks from them, have been used in over 400 investigations and have been translated into more than 15 different languages. A great variety and bulk of validity and reliability data are presented in the norms-technical manual (Torrance, 1966), but thus far the number of longitudinal validity studies is small. In one of these predictive validity studies, a class of high school seniors were tested in 1959 and followed up in 1966. Validity indexes at the .05 level of significance or better were obtained for the following creative achievements (Erickson, 1966):

1. Wrote a poem, story, song, or play
2. Wrote a book
3. Suggested innovations in policies that were adopted by superiors or co-workers

4. Received a research grant for original research
5. Had a scientific or scholarly paper published in a scientific or professional journal
6. Developed an original experimental design

In another predictive validity study (Torrance, Tan, and Allman, 1967), 325 elementary education majors at the University of Minnesota were tested in 1958 and followed up in 1966. The major criterion instrument was a checklist of creative achievements and teaching behaviors. Many of the subjects could not be located and many had dropped out of teaching or had never gone into teaching and data were obtained from only 114 subjects. Satisfactory validity indices were obtained for 69 creative achievements and/or teaching activities. The following are examples of these:

1. Wrote a story
2. Wrote a play
3. Wrote a professional article
4. Wrote a book
5. Published a research paper
6. Won a contest for some creative work
7. Improved a teaching device
8. Improved an instructional method
9. Developed a new method of teaching
10. Used research as a method of teaching

Torrance and Khatena (1969) reported a study to validate the originality score of *Sounds and Images* (Cunnington and Torrance, 1965) for identifying creative talent in music. A total of 137 students enrolled at Westminister Choir College were administered both Forms A and B of the test, and information was obtained concerning their creative achievements in music. Both forms of the test successfully discriminated between the music students as a group and a sample of education students. Scores also satisfactorily differentiated those who had had experience in original composition of music, those who had composed in different performance media, and number of awards for outstanding music achievement.

Other Promising Approaches

Among other published tests of creativity are: (1) a test of creativity in machine design by Owens (1968), (2) the Remote Associates Test by Mednick (1968), and Flanagan's (1968) Ingenuity Test. Owens' test has been used primarily with engineering students; Mednick's, with college students; and Flanagan's, with high school students.

Taylor and his associates (Taylor, 1960, 1961, 1963; Taylor *et al.* 1961) have been engaged for over fifteen years in the development of measures to implement the Multiple-Talent Model presented in the first section of this chapter. These ability measures, however, have not been published and made generally available to schools.

A wide variety of nontest and observational measures have also been suggested by various investigators. These suggestions are so numerous and so varied, however, that no attempt will be made here to summarize them. Nevertheless, such indicators of giftedness should not be neglected. Perhaps as psychologists and educators achieve greater consensus concerning a model of giftedness, it will be possible to identify a set of powerful but plainly observable critical behaviors indicative of giftedness. For example, it has been shown

already by Durkin (1966) and others that children who read early tend to be gifted. In one study, Durkin found that the median IQ of a sample of 49 early readers was 121; in a second sample of 156 early readers, the median IQ was 132. It is likely that many of these children were also gifted in other abilities.

Some educational leaders also advocate the use of self-identification procedures. One very successful program based on self-identification in high school science has been described by Brandwein (1955).

Issues in Identifying Gifted Disadvantaged Children and Youth

Increased concern about the education of disadvantaged children in the late 1960s brought about increased interest in the identification of giftedness among disadvantaged groups and the search for hidden talents. The theme of this increase is rather well summarized in the following quotation from Wolfle's introduction (1969, p. *xx*) to the Walter Van Dyke Bingham Lectures on the Development of Exceptional Abilities and Capacities:

. . . there has come to be widespread recognition of the huge social loss we suffer in all ranges of the ability distribution. Far too many children are born into homes that give them no intellectual stimulation, in which their potentialities cannot mature, in which attitudes and customs are so rigid that originality and creativeness cannot flourish, in which the traits and abilities required for effective participation in a complex technological society have little chance to develop.

Before this, numerous scholars (Anderson, 1960; Riessman, 1962; Taba and Elkins, 1966) had written of the hidden talents among disadvantaged children. There has long been a general recognition that existing methods of psychological assessment fail to discover these talents (Terman, 1925, 1954; Davis, 1948). Attempts to develop culture free (Cattell, 1949) and culture fair (Davis and Eels, 1953) tests of intellectual talent have not been very successful.

At the First Minnesota Conference on Gifted Children in 1958, Anderson (1960) urged that we set up a searching procedure for identifying and utilizing talent throughout all socioeconomic levels. Somewhat later, Riessman (1962) proposed the category of slow-gifted students among disadvantaged populations. In the late 1960s, as colleges and universities initiated programs of high-risk admissions for disadvantaged young people, they ran squarely into the major issues of identifying and encouraging giftedness among disadvantaged groups. As the author perceives the situation, there are three major issues:

1. Should we seek to identify and cultivate those kinds of talents that the dominant society values or look for talents of the type that are highly valued in the particular disadvantaged subcultures?
2. Are there important kinds of talents found in abundance among disadvantaged subcultures?
3. How early should attempts be made to identify and give special encouragement to outstandingly gifted children among disadvantaged sub-cultures? Is the time of college admission too late?

Talents Valued by the Subculture

It is safe to say that most recent programs for disadvantaged groups have been unconcerned about the identification and encouragement of the gifted members of these groups. Occasionally it has hap-pened, but it has not been planned deliberately. It is also safe to say that where there has been some degree of concern about talent identification and encouragement, the search has been for those kinds of talent that are highly valued by the dominant society. The instruments usually employed in these searches have been traditional tests of scholastic achievement and aptitude.

A few years ago the concern of the dominant culture was the discovery and encouragement of scientific talent, particularly creative scientific talent. At that time Roe (1963) made some very important observations about this problem and about the first issue. She pointed out that we can start in the early elementary grades and see what sorts of problems inhibit development in the direction of creative scientific talent. According to her, the earliest and most important of these is the conflict between the value structure of the home and the value structures that underlie education. If children are selected from homes in which book learning is not valued—even distinctly devalued—and if these children are encouraged into scientific fields, they will find themselves in the midst of severe and continuing conflict with home values. Many dropouts of intellectually able scholarship are the result of such conflicts. These individuals are unable to become members of any group in college and do not stay.

There are numerous things that may be done to reduce the stress that results from the conflict between the values of the disadvantaged subculture and the values of the educational establishment. One thing that may happen is that the values of the family may change and the support that comes from this may be crucial where it occurs. This happened in the case of Jesse Stuart (Tucker, 1964), the writer

E. PAUL TORRANCE

who came from the poverty of Appalachia. It is reported that when he came home from school the first day he said, "Pa, I can do somethin' you cain't." When his father asked, "What's that, Jesse?" he responded, "Write my name." He reports further, "Pa was embarrassed. He was so embarrassed he turned red. That night he sat down and made Ma teach him how to write his name in a certain way. Ma could teach him, too. She had gone to the second grade in school."

Jesse Stuart's father was first a coal miner and then tried farming, and Jesse was reared in poverty. He began teaching school for a living even before he himself had completed high school. He waited until the last minute to inform his mother that he was going to college. At first, she forbade his going. Jesse expressed strong determination and she gave in, saying "Son, go on. Go out in the world. Go to college. Then come back and tell me what the world is like." Regarding his father, Jesse reported, "I went off down the road and out the holler. Pa was walking along the ridge, so I missed him. It is a good thing I missed Pa, too. I would never have gotten past him."

One may think that the support given Jesse Stuart was very small. Actually, it was very large compared to the support received by many disadvantaged youngsters wanting to "make a go of it." Not all fathers have wanted to learn how to sign their names. Not all mothers have wanted their children to come back and tell them what the world is like. When they have returned and tried to tell about the world, there has been no interest.

The gifted disadvantaged youngster can rarely solve his problems of conflict and isolation by staying in his family and community because of his superior talent or achievement. Frequently, however, the latter occurs because the young person believes that the stress from the conflict and isolation in his family and community is less than the stress he will encounter in the outside world of college and profession.

Roe (1959, 1963) has suggested that the careful selection of a college may help and that it might be possible in colleges to establish some kind of ingroup with which the disadvantaged student can become closely enough identified to receive some support. She has warned, however, that there are still other hazards encountered by the gifted disadvantaged student in science. The potential scientist must be above average in intelligence and creativity, but many of them have relatively lower verbal than nonverbal ability. In both high school and college, they will experience severe restrictions on their curiosity, and teachers rather characteristically make sweeping devaluations and ridicule "wild ideas."

We need to draw as much information as we can from the experiences of disadvantaged individuals who have broken through their unfavorable environments and achieved outstanding success. Thus far, we have had little serious study in this area. Goldman (1968) reports autobiographical accounts of eleven men and women in England who have broken through from poor social beginnings and deprived backgrounds into high levels of professional achievement. They include notables in the academic world, Parliament, the theater, and art. In most of these autobiographies, it becomes clear that the talents that resulted in outstanding achievements were valued in the particular disadvantaged subcultures. Most of them would not have had a chance to have worked for success in the ordinary flow of events. Their chances came through some unorthodox channel, such as attending evening classes sponsored by the Worker's Educational Association, military service schools, young people's societies in churches, and the like. When they entered college, almost all of them felt keenly the great gulf betwen themselves and other college and university students. By this time most of them had learned how to tolerate loneliness and conflict rather well. In most cases, they were able to reduce their loneliness by going back and forth to some supporting group back home. In some cases a compatible and supporting marriage turned the tide.

Talents Common in Disadvantaged Groups

Most of the lists of intellectual characteristics of disadvantaged children that have been compiled from research are lists of deficits. Such lists include: impaired auditory and visual perception, decelerating intellectual growth, limited interests, inability to classify data, inability to give verbal explanations and to observe and state sequences of events, lack of responsiveness to verbal stimuli, short attention span in listening to verbal material, and the like. Riessman (1962) was the first to call to our attention in any very effective way the positives of culturally disadvantaged children. He emphasized the need for recognizing and building upon these positives, which he identified as the following:

1. Slow learning but not necessarily dull —careful, cautious, one-tracked, physical learners.
2. Hidden verbal ability—very verbal out of school, articulate with peers, and articulate in role playing.
3. Positive attitude toward education, though unfavorable attitude toward school.

On the basis of three years of exploratory work with disadvantaged groups, primarily blacks, the author has suggested a set of creative positives that exist to a high degree among disadvantaged children and upon which he believes we can build successful educational programs and, ultimately, successful lives:

1. High nonverbal fluency and originality. On the figural forms of the Torrance Tests of Creative Thinking (1966), disadvantaged groups almost always hold their own or even excel similar advantaged groups. This seems to hold true in a variety of localities throughout the United States and for Negroes, American Indians, Mexican-Americans, and Caucasians. Frequently, however, their figural flexibility and elaboration are less outstanding. High fluency and originality, and sometimes flexibility and elaboration as well, are evident in creative movement or dance. These also come out in games, problem-solving activities, and the like.

2. High creative productivity in small groups. The author has found disadvantaged children to be more highly productive in small groups than in individual or large-group situations. They even become quite verbal in small group creative problem-solving situations and seem less inhibited than more advantaged children. Leaders emerge and are given support by the rest of the group.

3. Adept in visual art activities. In every disadvantaged group with which the author has worked there have been surprisingly large numbers of gifted artists. In some cases, they have persisted in being copyists rather than trusting their originality. This seems to be more characteristic of the Negro than of the American Indian and Mexican-American groups on which we have data. Even the gifted black artists become more imaginative and inventive as

E. PAUL TORRANCE

they become involved in group activities such as puppetry, making giant murals, and the like.

4. Highly creative in movement, dance, and other physical activities. Disadvantaged children seem to take naturally to work in creative movement, dance, and other physical activities. Many of them will work hard at these activities and develop considerable discipline. In our workshop last summer we gave some emphasis to hula hoop activities. Two of the girls in the workshop won city district championships and one of them later won the city championship and was second-place winner in the state contest.

5. Highly motivated by games, music, sports, humor, and concrete objects. The warm-up effects of games, music, sports, humor, and the like seem to enable disadvantaged children to achieve a higher level of mental functioning than otherwise attained.

6. Language rich in imagery. In telling stories, making up songs, and producing solutions to problems, their language is rich in imagery.

Rather than attempt to document these creative positives and elaborate upon them, the author will simply state in gross terms what he regards as their implications. First, if one is searching for gifted individuals among disadvantaged populations, he is likely to have better success if he seeks them in the areas identified here than in traditional ways. Second, we need to give more serious consideration to careers in the creative arts and sciences for disadvantaged youth than we have in the past. When asked about their aspirations, almost no disadvantaged children express choices in the creative fields (Torrance, 1967 *b*). Yet many of those who achieve outstanding success do so in creative

fields, especially where talent has known no boundaries.

Early Identification and Encouragement

Most talent searches have been leveled at high school seniors. In recent years the Upward Bound and similar programs for disadvantaged youths have been designed to appeal to younger groups. Now there are some talent searches aimed at the junior high school level group. The younger the person, the better the chance he has of overcoming the deficits he has developed along the way and the better the chance he has of developing his positives more fully. Even junior high school, however, is rather late.

Studies in recent years by Bloom (1964) and others have shown that it is extremely difficult to overcome deficits acquired after age five or so. Insights arising from these findings have done much to inspire Headstart and other preprimary programs. The author knows of no instances, however, where deliberate efforts have been made to identify outstanding talent among disadvantaged preprimary age children and give special encouragement to the development of this outstanding talent. In fact, the only attempt at the elementary level of which he is aware is that of Witt in New Haven, Connecticut. Witt's project has demonstrated that it is possible to identify disadvantaged children who possess the creative positives to an outstanding degree at an early age and that it is possible to work with such children and their families in productive ways.

Witt (1968) initiated a program over four years ago for a group of sixteen highly creative, lower class Negro children in a ghetto setting. He believed that highly creative children are injured more in such settings than are their creative peers. Witt selected his sixteen highly creative children from the second through fourth grades of a ghetto school solely on the basis of tests of creative thinking (the Torrance Tests of Creative Thinking and one test task that Witt himself devised).

Twelve of the original sixteen children have continued in the program for over four years, and all of them have manifested high level creative skills in such fields as music, art, science, and writing. Much work has been done with the families. In many instances, the high creative talents of siblings have been recognized and opportunities have been provided for them to have music, art, ballet, and other kinds of lessons from outstanding teachers. In a few instances it has been possible to help parents of the children upgrade their job skills and acquire better jobs.

In fashioning a program for highly creative, inner-city children, Witt (1968) attempted to incorporate the following major characteristics:

1. Be clearly structured but flexible.
2. Provide for opportunities to be rewarded for solving problems.
3. Be viewed by one and all in a positive light.
4. Be tangible, and have many activities conducted in the homes.
5. Have enough competent adults in charge to minimize the need for the ubiquitous instant jeering and quarreling.
6. Continue controls indefinitely.
7. Involve exciting people from the inner and noninner city.
8. Design all learning experiences so that exciting perceptual-motor experiences precede, accompany, and follow cognitive growth.
9. Be intimately coordinated by a di-

rector expert in individual, group, and community dynamics.
10. Provide for the support, control, and involvement of the children's families, parents, and siblings.

Each year, Witt reports, new structural elements have been added to the program as the children, their families, and the program have grown.

During the first part of the program the specialists who worked with the program began to doubt that the children who had been selected had any kind of creative potentialities. Witt encouraged them to keep working, however, and he continued working with the children and involving their families. Before the end of the first summer, all of the children had exhibited outstanding promise in at least one creative field and many of them had shown unusual promise in two or more areas.

It would be hazardous to predict the adult futures of the twelve children who have continued in the program devised by Witt and called LEAP (Life Enrichment Activity Program). The present indications, however, are that these children are developing talents which are highly valued both in their own subcultures and in the dominant culture and that their families are supporting their development and in most cases developing along with them. There are indications that such talents can be identified at least as early as age eight and that there is a bountiful supply of such talent in almost all disadvantaged groups.

NEW CONCERN ABOUT ROLES OF HEREDITY AND ENVIRONMENT

New interest in improving the education of disadvantaged and minority subculture children has brought renewed

E. PAUL TORRANCE

concern about the roles of heredity and environment in giftedness. The problem is indeed a complex one, and as evidence concerning the issue has been presented and discussed, teachers and parents with low tolerance for complexity have been disturbed and professed confusion. This state of affairs is reflected in the following quotation from a letter by an Alabama teacher (Carswell, 1969) to the editor of *The Instructor* magazine:

One article I read recently said that "the maximum contribution of the best environment to intelligence is about 20 IQ points." The next book I took from the shelf said, "It is possible to envision a 40- to 60-point difference produced by a minimum negative environment and a maximum positive environment."

The IQ boys don't seem to be able to get together. Some insist that the IQ is fixed by the time a child is four, others by the time he is seven, and still others that it can change throughout childhood. I think it's time we should throw out the IQ scores.

Actually there is not as much discrepancy between this teacher's two sources as she implies. If a maximum positive environment can serve to raise the IQ 20 points and an extreme negative environment can lower the IQ 20 points, it could be argued that environment might possibly make a 40-point difference. This, in fact, was rather close to the facts in the well-known study of Skeels (1936, 1940, 1966) conducted in the 1930s and followed up in the 1960s. In this study, the children placed in the stimulating care of mentally retarded adolescents gained an average of 27.5 IQ points, whereas the comparison group placed in an institution lost an average of 26.2 IQ points. This experiment yields a difference of 53.7 IQ points between what was far from the

maximum positive environment and the negative environment of a state institution for mentally defective children in the 1930s.

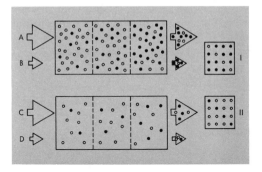

Fig. 11–4. Jensen's model of the growth of intelligence.

One center of the 1969–1970 controversy has been the work of Jensen (1969). Jensen presented his model for examining the roles of heredity and environment in a paper first published in 1966. This model is depicted in Figure 11–4. In his synthesis of research, Jensen concluded that genes and prenatal development account for 80 percent of the variance in intelligence, leaving 20 percent of the variance to the environment. In Figure 11–4 the arrows represent individuals with different amounts of innate intelligence. A and C were born with more intelligence than B and D. The large rectangles are the environments these four individuals must pass through. The broken lines signify the various stages of environment influence. The dots symbolize the various elements of the environment. The greater the number of dots, the richer the stimulation for intellectual growth. The black dots represent learning that has broad application to all future learning, and the white dots represent perceptual learning. When these four individuals are placed in Test Situation I (highly loaded with items testing learning with broad application) and Test Situation II (highly loaded with items testing perceptual learning), we obtain the results symbolized by the second set of arrows. Although A and C began with the same intellectual capacity, A will achieve higher scores. B and C will have about the same scores, but B will be ahead in black dots. Jensen (1968) points out that even this difference of 20 or 30 IQ points that can be effected through the environment is clearly enough to have significant consequences.

The most controversial of Jensen's papers is his lengthy article in the *Harvard Educational Review* (1969). In this paper he argued that the failure of recent compensatory education efforts to produce lasting effects on children's IQ and achievement called for a reexamination of the premises on which these efforts have been based. He especially questioned the idea that IQ differences are almost entirely a result of environmental differences and the cultural bias of intelligence tests. As in his earlier papers, he argued that environmental factors are less important in determining IQ than genetic factors. After examining the recent research concerning compensatory educational programs for young children, Jensen concluded that extreme environmental deprivation can keep a child from performing up to his genetic potential, but an enriched educational program cannot push the child above that potential. Jensen argues, however, that there are other mental abilities not included in intelligence tests that might be capitalized upon in educational programs. He believes that current educational attempts to boost IQ have been misdirected, and he advocates the development of educational methods that are based on other mental abilities besides IQ.

Another controversial document of the late 1960s was Rosenthal and Jacobson's report of their "Pygmalion experiment" (1968). This experiment was conducted in a public elementary school in a lower class community where one-sixth of the pupils were Mexican-Americans. In September 1964, the school's teachers were told that on the basis of intelligence tests conducted the previous spring about 20 percent of the students would be expected to show significant increases in intelligence during the year, and each teacher was given the names of the potential "spurters" in his class. Four months later and again the following May, the children were given the same intelligence test they had been given the preceding spring. Children in both the experimental and control groups scored higher, but the first- and second-grade children in the experimental group—the ones the teachers had been told were the potential spurters—scored significantly higher than the children in the control group. About 21 percent of the children in the experimental group gained 30 or more IQ points, but only 5 percent of those in the control group attained gains this great. Almost half of the experimental group gained 20 or more IQ points compared with 19 percent in the control group. Changes for children in the upper grades were not as dramatic as for the children in the first and second grades but still tended to confirm the basic theory that children will respond in terms of teachers' expectations of them. Rosenthal and Jacobson believe that by many verbal and nonverbal cues the teachers communicated to the children in the experimental group that they expected improved intellectual performance. They believe that by such communications and changes in teaching techniques the teachers helped the children in the experimental group to learn by changing their self-con-

E. PAUL TORRANCE

cepts, their expectations of their own behavior, their motivations, and their cognitive styles and skills.

Some psychologists and educators have criticized the Rosenthal and Jacobson study quite vigorously (Thorndike, 1968). Even discounting for these criticisms, however, it seems clear to the present author that the expectations that teachers have of children have a great deal to do with which ones perform at a gifted level. He has seen it happen in too many cases to be able to deny its reality.

Hunt (1961, 1968) has been especially effective in summarizing and synthesizing research concerning environmental influences on intellectual growth. He believes that this body of research has changed or is changing the following six beliefs (Hunt, 1968, p. 294):

1. A belief in fixed intelligence
2. A belief in predetermined development
3. A belief in the fixed and static, telephone-switchboard nature of brain function
4. A belief that experience during the early years, and particularly before the development of speech, is unimportant
5. A belief that whatever experience does affect later development is a matter of emotional reactions based on instinctual needs
6. A belief that learning must be motivated by homeostatic need, by painful stimulation, or by acquired drives based on these

The implications of these changes or possible changes in beliefs are obviously far-reaching insofar as the identification and treatment of gifted children and youth are concerned.

CHARACTERISTICS OF GIFTED CHILDREN AND YOUTH

In the past, teachers and other educators have not found studies of the psychological characteristics of gifted children and youth to be very helpful. Perhaps a major reason is that these studies had not differentiated the various types of giftedness and had not specified the type of gifted children or youth being studied. Certainly the acceptance of a more complex concept of giftedness requires a reorientation of studies in this area. Thus far, few such studies have been reported and these have been primarily concerned with differentiations between highly creative children and youth and highly intelligent ones and between different types of creatively gifted children and youth. A few of the results of these studies will illustrate some of the promise of such studies.

Westinghouse Science Talent Search Winners

One of the more productive studies of creatively gifted youths in the sciences is Parloff and Datta's (1965) study of Westinghouse Science Talent Search winners. From the more than 2,500 male applicants who completed successfully all entry requirements, Parloff and Datta selected the 573 who scored above the 80th percentile on a science aptitude examination. Judges scored the projects submitted by these subjects for creativity and potential creativity. Basically, the criteria used by the judges included evidence that the applicant recognizes and formulates novel relationships and that his formulations are plausible and/or effective. The sample was subdivided into three groups to reflect different levels of creative potential. Group I, High Potential Creativity, included 112 young men; Group II, Moderate Potential

Creativity, included 140; and Group III, Low Potential Creativity, included 285. The groups were then compared on the basis of a variety of life experience and personality test variables.

The investigators found statistically significant differences on five scales of the California Psychological Inventory when the members of Groups I and III were compared. The young men in Group I were more ambitious and driving; more independent, autonomous, and self-reliant; more efficient and perceptive; more rebellious toward rules and constraints; and more imaginative.

Parloff and Datta found no meaningful differences among the three groups on age, intelligence, measured scientific aptitude, vocations of fathers, socioeconomic status, and intactness of family.

The investigators (Parloff and Datta, 1965) asked Gough, the author and developer of the California Personality Inventory, to provide clinical interpretations of five mean profiles without identification. The profile of Group I (High Potential Creativity) was described by Gough as follows: (1) a high level of intellectual ability, that is, a level consistent with the group's being excellent students with a zest for independent effort and constructive endeavor; (2) a high level of resourcefulness, that is, adeptness at coping with new and different situations and in evolving effective techniques for dealing with new problems; (3) the capacity for independent work, that is, the ability to generate internal motivation without need for external props and reinforcements; and (4) a capacity for original and innovative work.

Group II was characterized by its complexity. This group was described by Gough on the basis of their profile as strong, resolute, and forceful and yet at the same time unsure of themselves,

doubting, and pessimistic. They were characterized as valuing themselves and their work and seeking recognition and yet were dubious and even annoyed when recognition was forthcoming. They welcome change, uncertainty, and emotional expressiveness, and yet become anxious.

In contrast, the members of Group III were characterized as less concerned with individuality and freedom from external coercion and showed less of the spontaneity that leads to creativity. They showed less zest for counteracting complacency and inertia and less zest for innovation. They were described as insightful, intelligent, autonomous, constructively motivated, resourceful, and able to pursue meaningful goals.

In the field of art, Hammer (1961) has reported a provocative in-depth study of a small group of creative artists at the high school level attending the High School Scholarship Painting Workshop at New York University. The workshop faculty, distinguished painters themselves, classified the eighteen students into three categories on the basis of their productions: (1) a group that is merely facile and lacks creativity and originality, (2) an intermediate group, and (3) a truly creative group, with a high degree of promise for serious painting. Five were placed in the merely facile group and five in the truly creative group. All subjects were administered the Rorschach ink blots, the Thematic Apperception Test, House-Tree Person Drawings, and the Unpleasant Concept Test.

In this exploratory investigation, Hammer concluded that the "truly creatives" differed from the "merely faciles" in the following ways (pp. 92–93):

1. Greater depth of feeling and closeness to basic emotional tones

E. Paul Torrance

2. Personal, original responsiveness from within
3. A retreat from people into an observer rather than into a particular role
4. Confidence and determination
5. Ambition and striving for power to influence
6. Feminine components combined with masculine strength
7. Personal uniqueness and independence
8. Rebelliousness
9. A psychological habit of self-observation and a capacity to become aware of conflict
10. Exhibitionistic needs, more active than passive in form
11. A tolerance for suffering
12. Full range of emotional feeling, breadth of emotional horizons
13. A sense of inner emotional disequilibrium converted into a striving for outer balance on canvas

The Creativity and Intelligence Modes

Getzels and Jackson (1962) succeeded in differentiating by means of test criteria two distinct types of gifted secondary school students and their characteristics. These researchers used the following battery of tests in determining their index of creative ability: Word Association, Unusual Uses, Hidden Shapes, Fables, and Make-Up Problems. Their high creatives were defined as those whose creativity indexes placed them in the upper 20 percent of students of their age and sex but were not in the upper 20 percent of intelligence or any other indicator of giftedness available to the researchers. Their high intelligence group was similarly defined as those who were in the top 20 percent on IQ when compared with others in the sample

of the same sex and age and who were not in the upper 20 percent on the index of creativity or other measures of giftedness. This meant that students high on both creativity and intelligence were excluded, as were those high on measures of psychological adjustment and morality. The total pool of subjects was 543 students in a private high school ranging from the sixth through the twelfth grades. Twenty-six qualified for the high creative group and twenty-eight for the high intelligence group. The mean IQ for the high IQ group was 150 and for the high creativity group, 127. Thus, both groups were rather highly intelligent, even though there was a difference of 23 IQ points between them.

In this study it was found that the measured school achievement of the highly creative and highly intelligent groups was equally superior to that of the total population from which they were drawn. The high IQ students were rated by their teachers as more desirable than the average student but the highly creative students were not. On their fantasy productions, the creatives made significantly greater use of stimulus-free themes, unexpected endings, and playfulness. On the basis of these findings, Getzels and Jackson have suggested that an essential difference between the two groups is the creative adolescent's ability to produce new forms and to risk joining together elements usually seen as independent and dissimilar. They also suggested that the creative adolescent seems to enjoy the risk and uncertainty of the unknown. The high IQ adolescent prefers the anxieties of safety to those of growth. These differences are reflected in the occupational choices of the two groups. Of the creatives 62 percent chose unconventional occupations such as adventurer, inventor, writer, and the like. Only 16 percent of the high-intelligence subjects chose such occupations; 84 percent of them chose conventional occupations, such as doctor, lawyer, engineer, and the like.

Getzels and Jackson (1962) interviewed the parents of their two groups of subjects. The parents of the high IQ students tended to recall greater financial difficulties during their childhoods and at the interviews expressed greater real or imagined personal insecurity than those of the high creatives. The parents of the high IQ adolescents also seemed to be more vigilant with respect to their children's behavior and academic success. These parents were more critical of both their children and the school than were the parents of the highly creative students. The parents of the high IQ youths focused their attention on immediately visible virtues such as cleanliness, good manners, and studiousness. The parents of the creatives focused theirs on less visible qualities such as the child's openness to experience, his values, and his interests and enthusiasms.

Originality and Elaboration Modes

A study of Dauw (1965) attempts to differentiate between two types of creative ability among secondary students. His subjects were 712 seniors in a metropolitan public high school who had been administered a battery of four of the creative thinking ability tests developed by Torrance and his associates (two figural tasks, Incomplete Figures and Circles, and two verbal tasks, Product Improvement and Unusual Uses). All four tasks were scored for originality (statistical infrequency and relevance) and elaboration (number of details or additional ideas produced beyond the minimum required to communicate the basic ideas). On the basis of these measures, six groups were identified

within each sex: high (upper 20 percent in all cases) on both originality and elaboration, high on originality but not on elaboration, high on elaboration but not on originality, low on both, low on originality but not elaboration, and low on elaboration but not originality. The 311 members of these criterion groups were then administered a life-experience inventory, a creative personality self-description checklist, and the Minnesota Importance Questionnaire (a measure of vocational needs).

The high-original boys described themselves characteristically as adventurous, curious, independent in thinking, willing to take risks, and having a sense of humor. They characteristically rejected as descriptive of themselves such characteristics as timidity, boredom, conformity, and quietness. Their career aspirations tended to be creative and unconventional, such as archeologist, anthropologist, actor, and the like. They expressed stronger vocational needs than any of the other groups of boys in creativity, recognition, and social service. Their second-order needs were for authority, social status, moral values, responsibility, and achievement.

The high-elaborating boys characteristically regarded themselves as healthy, desiring to excel, considerate of others, willing to take risks, adventurous, and having a sense of humor. They rejected as descriptive of themselves such qualities as timidity, fearfulness, and boredom. They disliked working alone and did not regard themselves as emotionally sensitive. Their school grades were higher than those of the high-original boys but their scholastic aptitude scores (Minnesota Scholastic Aptitude Test) were slightly, though not significantly, lower. Their career aspirations were more conventional than those of the high originals, although a few of them selected such unusual occupations as marine biologist, entertainer, and philosopher. The strength of their expressed vocational needs was quite low. Of the six groups of boys, the high-elaborating boys were lowest on good working conditions, compensation, security, ability utilization, company practices and policies, supervision, activity, moral values, achievement, advancement, and good co-workers.

Boys high in both originality and elaboration saw themselves as willing to take risks, unwilling to accept things on others' say-so, always asking questions about puzzling things, and having a sense of humor. They most emphatically rejected as self-descriptive such qualities as timidity, good guessing ability, fearfulness, quietness, and having the tendency to disrupt the procedures and organization of the group. Their grades and scholastic ability scores were higher than for any of the other groups of boys. Their career aspirations were about as unconventional as those of the high-original boys. They expressed stronger vocational needs than the high originals and high elaborators for variety, activity, and responsibility. They also tended to be high on good working conditions, ability utilization, achievement, advancement, and independence. They were lower than the other highly creative boys on social status, compensation, security, and recognition.

The high-original girls characteristically described themselves as adventurous, desirous of excelling, curious, emotionally sensitive, often bored, and having a sense of humor. They rejected most strongly such qualities as being timid, fearful, negativistic, haughty, and self-satisfied. Their grades and scholastic aptitude scores were lower than those of the high elaborators. Their career choices tended to be creative and unconventional, including artist, actress, advertiser, author, entertainer, and interior decorator. Their vocational need

for good working conditions was stronger than for the high elaborating girls.

The high-elaborating girls saw themselves as adventurous, affectionate, emotionally sensitive, strongly emotional, and having a sense of humor. They did not see themselves as quiet, timid, haughty, self-satisfied, and often bored. Their career aspirations tended to focus on such occupations as teaching, direct services to others, psychology, and social work.

Girls highest in both originality and elaboration characteristically described themselves as desiring to excel, competitive, strongly emotional, emotionally sensitive, nonconforming, and as having a sense of beauty. They rejected most strongly such characteristics as negativism, fearfulness, faultfinding, haughtiness, and self-satisfaction. Their school grades and scholastic aptitude scores were higher than those of any of the other groups. Their career aspirations tended to be along such lines as biochemist, interior decorator, poetess, and the like. Their creativity needs and needs for authority were higher than those of any of the other groups of girls. They also had strong needs for variety, ability utilization, moral values, responsibility, achievement, and social service. They expressed weaker needs than other creative groups for security, recognition, supervision, and independence.

A number of life experience variables also differentiated the groups under study. The high originals seemed to feel that their home disciplinary atmosphere was "probably less strict than average" to a greater extent than do the high elaborators. Fathers seemed to encourage independence more in their highly original daughters and in daughters who were high in both categories than in the high-elaborating girls.

Psychology of Gifted Children And Youth

The high elaborators tended to be more perfectionistic than the high originals and repeated tasks until satisfied with the results. The high originals—especially the girls—tended to set higher standards and goals for themselves more often than the high elaborators.

Highly original boys appeared to have more close friends older than they were in comparison with the high-elaborating boys. The highly original boys appeared to prefer a more competitive work relationship, whereas the high elaborators seemed to prefer a more cooperative one.

The highly elaborating girls liked to attend lectures as often as possible but not the highly original girls. The highly original boys and girls were more likely than the others to make up games, build models, compose music, and write prose and poetry. The elaborators were more likely to play musical instruments, to improvise, to paint and draw, and to participate in dramatics.

In the sphere of athletics, golf attracted the high originals of both sexes more frequently than the high elaborators. Tennis and track appealed more to the original boys. Highly elaborating girls tended to like gymnastics, wrestling, and track.

In classes the highly elaborating more frequently than the highly original girls seemed to volunteer answers every time they knew or thought they knew the answers. Among the boys, however, the high originals were more likely to volunteer answers. The best teachers, according to the high elaborators, were very strict, whereas the high originals preferred their teachers to be more permissive.

Highly original boys tended more frequently to have cars at an early age and to learn to drive them than the high elaborators. Having bank accounts at earlier ages —under ten years—seemed to be more characteristic of high originals than high elaborators.

Studies of Dissident Youth

Of increasing interest in the psychology of giftedness is the phenomenon of dissident youth. Of course, there have always been dissident, protesting youth among the gifted. During the 1968–1969 academic year and the summer of 1969, leaders working with gifted high school and college youth sensed a stronger and more active dissidence among them. At this point there are few studies to guide workers in coping constructively with this dissidence. A voluminous literature of observational studies of rebellious college students is accumulating, however, and these provide many provocative clues. One of the few empirical studies of the characteristics of dissident gifted youth is one by Whittaker (1967), which illustrates the promise of such studies.

Whittaker's (1967) subjects were 151 members of Berkeley's underground subculture and a comparison group of 56 University of California students. Both groups were equally gifted according to measures of verbal intelligence. The nonstudents expressed disdain of formal educational experiences and had been attracted to the University of California at Berkeley environment as a source of cultural stimulation and asylum. Compared with the students, the nonstudents were more unconventional in appearance and described themselves as more untidy, free, eccentric, and imaginative. Their vocational choices tended to be in the creative arts. On the Allport-Vernon-Lindzey Study of Values, their preferences were for esthetic, theoretical, social, political, religious, and economic values in that order. On the Omnibus Personality Inventory, the non-students were high on impulse expression, estheticism, complexity, autonomy, and religious liberalism and low on personal integration, anxiety level, practical outlook, and masculinity. Compared with the students, they were more intellectually oriented, less authoritarian, more psychologically maladjusted, lower on self-control, and higher on lability. The nonstudents' high needs were for autonomy, change, exhibitionism, and succorance, and they were low on needs for order, endurance, deference, achievement, and dominance. They also seemed to have a greater propensity for the use of drugs and to have engaged in a prolonged and stressful search for identity.

SPECIAL PROBLEMS OF ADJUSTMENT OF GIFTED CHILDREN AND YOUTH

Those who have been interested in special provisions for gifted children and the improvement of the skills of all teachers for working with gifted children have usually met with opposition and discouragement. Critics of proposals for improving the education of gifted children and youth have said that the plight of the mentally retarded, the blind, the deaf, and the crippled arouses sympathy but that the gifted are well endowed and can take care of themselves. They generally believe that gifted children who do not succeed are morally delinquent and should be punished.

These critics may express shock when the town's "model" honor student commits murder, arson, or rape and express

delight when the town's brilliant but non-conforming young artist, scientist, musician, or writer is imprisoned for a minor misdemeanor. They may express surprise when some young prisoner is acclaimed for a great novel, work of art, or important invention executed while in prison. They will still say, "If a child has any spark of creativity or anything good in him, it will come out regardless of what happens to him." They fail to recognize the compelling fact that the gifted young child is frequently completely unable to help himself and to cope with hate, aggression, coercion, poverty, and other negative forces. Yet this helpless, gifted young child is potentially an awesomely powerful force. He can advance civilization or destroy it. The creative energies of gifted children need to be activated and guided early, or else they can be lost—or prove dangerous.

Self-Concepts of Gifted Children and Youth

The search of gifted children and youth for their identity and for a realistic and favorable self-concept is frequently painful and prolonged. The feedback that the gifted child receives is conflicting and confusing. He is puzzled. He performs outstandingly and is punished rather than rewarded. He is taught that the good child is a modest child. He is also taught that he should at all times "do his best." In doing his best, however, he breaks norms, and this brings punishment, hostility, and rejection. He is made to feel ashamed and unworthy. Thus, the gifted child frequently derogates himself and is severely handicapped by his low estimate of himself.

Torrance (1960) studied a group of underevaluating gifted college freshman (students actually ranking in the upper 10 percent in scholastic ability but estimating their ability as below average). The portrait developed through this study of the underevaluating gifted college freshmen is that of an intellectually sublimating, overrational, self-punishing individual who sees himself basically as a little boy. In spite of the great energy invested in intellectual control, he occasionally gives way to emotional outbursts and tries to hide his inner disturbance by isolation and intellectual achievement. He thus avoids group participation and association with the opposite sex. He sees himself as stubborn, reserved, bashful, impetuous, tactful, conscientious, nervous, anxious, and depressed. As a function of his immaturity, he is unable to picture himself in any mature vocational role. He is socially conforming, represses his aggression and hostility, and is generally inhibited in the sphere of emotion and will. Basically, he is dependent but, because of previous disappointments, he cannot accept his need for dependence.

Purkey (1967), reviewing research concerning the self-concepts of gifted children and youth, found that the evidence refutes the popular idea that gifted individuals see themselves as superior, are filled with self-satisfaction, or have contempt for their less able peers. Purkey (1966) himself conducted a study of intellectually gifted high school students and compared their test-estimated and self-estimated personality characteristics. The results of this study showed that gifted high school students are markedly above average in personal adjustment. They saw themselves as simply average on these qualities, however.

Werblo and Torrance (1966) conducted a study of gifted upper elementary children to test the hypothesis that the gifted who engage in research, using the process of historiography to investigate their own development, will achieve more realistic self-evaluations in such areas as size of vocabulary, reading speed, and curiosity. The study involved 69 sixth-graders in three classes for high achievers in a public school system. As a part of a unit taught by Torrance on how to do research, these gifted children were asked to estimate on a set of graphs their own growth, including height, curiosity, reading speed, imagination, spelling, independence in thinking, and arithmetic computation. Next, they were asked to indicate the point on their graph where they thought average boys and girls their age would be. Then they were encouraged to collect as much data from witnesses and records as possible to test their hypotheses and to modify them, if necessary.

Results of the study showed that self-evaluations of vocabulary, curiosity, and reading speed showed significant changes at the end of the research training, all in the direction of higher self-evaluations. For example, in curiosity, of fifty-three students rating themselves as average or below average at the start of the unit, only twenty-eight remained the same at the end, with fifteen changing to above average.

It was clear from this study that even gifted, high-achieving, and socially well-adjusted children tend to underevaluate themselves on such variables as size of vocabulary, reading speed, and curiosity, even after thorough testing and segregation from regular classes. Werblo and Torrance suggest that gifted students can apply the concepts and methods of research to attain more realistic self-evaluations in the areas discussed and perhaps in others. One can only imagine the plight of emotionally disturbed and low achieving gifted children and youth.

E. Paul Torrance

Bright Underachievers and Dropouts

Although there have been hundreds of studies of the incidence of underachievement among gifted students and of their characteristics, there have been few reported all-out efforts to aid such students. In 1962 Lichter *et al.* reported an unusually provocative and illuminating study of such an attempt by counseling and guidance personnel to concentrate their full resources on highly able dropouts at the high school level. There were evidences that many of the students in this study changed their behavior markedly and achieved improved emotional adjustment. Their teachers and the rest of the school program were not changed, however, and seemed to be unwilling to accept the changes that these students achieved. Because their teachers expected these students to fail and to misbehave, they found it extremely difficult to continue their changed behavior and retain their improved emotional adjustment.

Raph, Goldberg, and Passow (1966) reported a set of studies of bright underachievers in which the school did make some changes designed to help such students succeed. In the first two studies conducted at the DeWitt Clinton High School, the Bronx, New York, the outcomes strongly pointed to the importance of the teacher who works with bright underachieving students. Such students seemed to be at their best when the teacher was able to accept their limitations and was sufficiently flexible to allow the students the freedom they seemed to need. The students also responded to high standards or expectations on the part of the teacher. In these first two studies the teacher taught a subject, and most of his contact was in the teaching-learning situation. The third study placed these students in a guidance situation with a selected teacher but did not achieve positive effects equal to those in the first two studies. The investigators recognized the difficulties of evaluating the ultimate effect of the interventions used in these studies but were generally pessimistic. They are especially pessimistic about such efforts initiated as late as the high school level.

Creatively Gifted Children and Youth

Many creatively gifted children and youth are so severely handicapped in adjusting and learning in the typical school that this author has suggested that such children and youth be recognized as a new category in the field of special education. There are many children in this category whose behavior problems stem from the differences their abilities create between them and other children and between them and their teachers. Their learning difficulties arise from the incompatibility between their abilities and learning preferences on one hand and the teaching methods and system of rewards of the school on the other. If brought together with other creatively gifted youngsters, they would no longer be misfits. If taught in ways compatible with their abilities and interests, their achievement might soar.

Out of a series of studies dealing with mental health problems, the author (Torrance, 1963) has offered the following conceptualization for investigating and ameliorating the problems of highly creative children and youth. Because almost all definitions of creativity involve the production of something new, original, or divergent, it is inescapable that the creatively gifted person repeatedly will find himself a minority of one. Even when matters of fact are involved, as in Asch's (1955) famous experiments in social psychology, there are few people who can endure being a minority of one. Being a minority of one leaves a person with too few anchors in reality or guides to behavior. Because creative behavior requires independence of mind, divergence from group norms, or unusualness, it is inevitable that highly creative persons will experience many problems of adjustment. The highly creative child must either repress or sacrifice his creativity or learn to cope with or reduce the tensions that arise from being so frequently a minority of one. Repression, if prolonged or severe, leads to uncertain or inadequate self-concepts, learning difficulties, behavior problems, neurotic distortions, or even psychotic breakdowns. The continued expression of creative needs in spite of tensions and pressures may lead to loneliness, conflicts, or other types of alienation.

From existing evidence it does not seem possible to say to what extent a breakdown occurs because a person sacrifices his creativity. It has been shown, however, that the fourth-grade slump in creativity (Torrance, 1967b) is accompanied by an increase in mental health referrals and classroom behavior problems. The roots of the difficulty seem to stem from the inevitable pressures that are exerted against the expression of creative needs and abilities and the child's difficulty in learning adequate controls without becoming overcontrolled. The stronger the needs and the higher the abilities, the more severe the pressures are likely to be. As a consequence, at each critical stage of development, many children sacrifice their creativity. For some, this begins at age five or six, when the child first enters school. For others, it comes at age nine, or twelve, or at some later time. As a child learns to cope with the new demands of a stage, he may recover or he may apparently abandon creativity, distort it, or hold tight rein on it.

It now seems that different types of creatively gifted children and youth experience different kinds of mental health problems. In a population of 712 high school seniors, Torrance and Dauw (1965) studied the mental health problems of youths characterized by high originality, high elaboration, and high originality and elaboration. Their findings confirmed the findings of other studies that highly creative youths frequently experience rather intense and prolonged stresses that reduce creativity and that the stresses of the highly original youth differ in important ways from those characteristically experienced by those who excel in elaboration. Those high on both originality and elaboration share many of the vicissitudes of the high originals but apparently escape some of the discomforts and strains that result from nonconformity.

The high originals and those high on both originality and elaboration tend to be characterized by concern about ridicule, restriction of freedoms, and pressures of time, whereas the high elaborators are more frequently concerned about possible failure and inability to meet the expectations their parents and teachers have of them. The high originals and those high on both seem to cope with stresses by changes in strategies and the initiation of new projects whereas the high elaborators more frequently report using withdrawal strategies and resort to eating, sleeping, and drinking. All three groups rely rather frequently on absorption in work and creative activities and discussion of their problems with others.

The high originals reported more frequently than the other groups special problems involving parental disagreements and estrangement, whereas the other

E. PAUL TORRANCE

groups reported concerns about meeting the high expectations of their environment. In general, the environment of the high originals does not seem to hold very high expectations of them, tending instead to disparage them and to frustrate their craving for independence and achievement. At least, this is the way that the highly original high school seniors in the Torrance and Dauw study perceived the situation.

CONCLUSION

It is obvious from the analysis that has been presented in this chapter on gifted children and youth that the acceptance of a more complex concept of giftedness creates many new problems and calls for a reexamination of much of the research and development of the past. The new concept provides exciting ways of examining the problems of gifted children and youth, however, and offers hope for a more humane and liberating approach to their problems and their education.

References

Albert, R. S. Genius: Present-day status of the concept and its implications for the study of creativity and giftedness. *American Psychologist,* 1969, *24,* 743–753.

Anderson, J. E. The nature of abilities. In E. P. Torrance (Ed.), *Talent and education.* Minneapolis: University of Minnesota Press, 1960, Pp. 9–13.

Asch, S. E. *Studies of independence and submission to group pressure. I. A minority of one against a unanimous majority.* Swarthmore, Pa.: Swarthmore College, 1955.

Barron, F. *Creativity and psychological health.* Princeton, N.J.: D. Van Nostrand Co., Inc., 1963.

Bennett, G. K. The DAT—a seven year follow-up. *Test Service Bulletin No. 49.* New York: The Psychological Corporation, 1959.

———, *et al. Differential Aptitude Tests: Manual.* New York: The Psychological Corporation, 1959.

Bloom, B. S. *Stability and change in human characteristics.* New York: John Wiley & Sons, Inc., 1964.

Bowers, J. E. A study of the relationships among measures of productive thinking, intelligence, and ninth grade achievement. Unpublished doctoral dissertation, University of Minnesota, 1966.

Brandwein, P. F. *The gifted student as future scientist.* New York: Harcourt, Brace & World, Inc., 1955.

Bruch, C. B. A creativity score from the Stanford-Binet and its applications. Paper presented at the meetings of the Council on Exceptional Children International, Denver, Colorado, April 10, 1969.

Bureau of Employment Security. *General aptitude test battery: Section III, development: Guide.* Washington, D.C.: U.S. Department of Labor, 1958.

Burt, C. The inheritance of mental ability. *American Psychologist,* 1958, *13,* 1–15.

Carswell, F. D. IQ scores. *The Instructor,* 1969, *79* (1), 12.

Cattell, R. B. *The culture-free intelligence test.* Champaign, Ill.: Institute for Personality Assessment and Testing, 1949.

Cunnington, B. F., & Torrance, E. P. *Sounds and images.* Boston: Ginn and Company, 1965.

Davis, A. *Social class influence on learning.* Cambridge, Mass.: Harvard University Press, 1948.

———, & Eels, K. *Davis-Eels games.* New York: Harcourt, Brace & World, Inc., 1953.

Dauw, D. C. Life experiences, vocational needs and choices of original thinkers and good elaborators. Unpublished doctoral dissertation, University of Minnesota, 1965.

De Haan, R. F., & Wilson, R. C. Identification of the gifted. In N. B. Henry (Ed.), *Education for the gifted.* Chicago: University of Chicago Press, 1958, pp. 166–192.

Douglass, H. Types of abler students. Personal communication to the author, April 28, 1968.

Drews, E. M. A critical evaluation of approaches to the identification of gifted students. In A. Traxler (Ed.), *Measurement and research in today's schools.* Washington, D. C.: American Council on Education, 1961, 109–121.

―――. The four faces of able adolescents. *Saturday Review,* 1963, *46,* 68–71.

Durkin, D. *Children who read early.* New York: Teachers College Press, Columbia University, 1966.

Educational Policies Commission. *Education of the gifted.* Washington, D. C.: National Education Association, 1950.

Erickson, G. The predictive validity of a battery of creative thinking tests and peer nominations among University of Minnesota High School seniors seven years later. Master's research paper, University of Minnesota, 1966.

Flanagan, J. C. *Flanagan aptitude classification tests: Technical report.* Chicago: Science Research Associates, 1959.

―――. Ingenuity test. *Journal of Creative Behavior,* 1968, *2,* 215–216.

Frierson, E. C. The gifted. *Review of Educational Research,* 1969, *39,* 25–37.

Gallagher, J. J., Aschner, M. J., & Jenné, W. *Productive thinking of gifted children in classroom interaction.* Washington, D. C.: Council on Exceptional Children, National Education Association, 1967.

Galton, F. *Hereditary genius: An inquiry into its causes and consequences* (first published, 1869). London: Macmillan & Co., Ltd., 1892.

Gardner, G. (Ed.). *The shining moments: The words and moods of John F. Kennedy.* New York: Pocket Books, 1964.

Getzels, J. W., & Jackson, P. W. *Creativity and intelligence.* New York: John Wiley & Sons, Inc., 1962.

Gilbertson, S. *The second report on the high achievers room.* Bloomington, Minn.: Bloomington Public Schools, 1960.

Goldman, R. J. (Ed.). *Breakthrough.* London: Routledge & Kegan Paul, Ltd., 1968.

Guilford, J. P. Creativity. *American Psychologist,* 1950, *5,* 444–454.

―――. *The nature of human intelligence.* New York: McGraw-Hill Book Company, 1967.

―――. Structure of intellect. *Psychological Bulletin,* 1956, *53,* 267–293.

―――. Three faces of intellect. *American Psychologist,* 1959, *14,* 469–479.

―――, Hendricks, M., & Hoepfner, R., Solving social problems creatively. *Journal of Creative Behavior,* 1968, *2,* 155–164.

Guilford, J. P., Merrifield, P. R., & Cox, A. B. *Creative thinking in children at the junior high school level.* Los Angeles: Psychological Laboratory, University of Southern California, 1961.

Hammer, E. F. *Creativity: An exploratory investigation of the personalities of gifted adolescent artists.* New York: Random House, Inc., 1961.

Hoepfner, R., & Guilford, J. P. *Figural, symbolic, and semantic factors of creative potential in ninth-grade students.* Los Angeles: Psychological Laboratory, University of Southern California, 1965.

Hudson, L. *Contrary imaginations.* New York: Schocken Books, 1966.

Humphrey, H. H. Remarks before White House Conference on Education, Washington, D. C., July 21, 1965.

Hunt, J. M. Environment, development, and scholastic achievement. In M. Deutsch, I. Katz, & A. R. Jensen (Eds.), *Social class, race, and psychological development.* New York: Holt, Rinehart & Winston, Inc., 1968, pp. 292–336.

―――. *Intelligence and experience.* New York: The Ronald Press Company, 1961.

Jensen, A. R. How much can we boost IQ and scholastic achievement? *Harvard Educational Review.* 1969, *39,* 1–119.

―――. Social class and verbal learning. In M. Deutsch, I. Katz, & A. R. Jensen (Eds.), *Social class, race, and psychological development.* New York: Holt, Rinehart & Winston, Inc., 1968, pp. 115–174.

―――. Verbal mediation and educational potential. *Psychology in the Schools,* 1966, *3,* 99–109.

Johnson, L. B. Special message to Congress on education, Washington, D. C., January 12, 1965.

Kennedy, J. F. Address to the National Academy of Sciences. Washington, D. C., October 22, 1963.

Lichter, S. O. *et al. The drop-outs.* New York: The Free Press, 1962.

MacKinnon, D. W. *The creative person.* Berkeley: University of California General Extension, 1961.

Mednick, S. A. The remote associates test.

E. PAUL TORRANCE

Journal of Creative Behavior, 1968, *2,* 213–214.

Meeker, M. N. *The structure of intellect: Its interpretation and uses.* Columbus: Charles E. Merrill Books, Inc., 1969.

Merrifield, P. R., Gardner, S. F., & Cox, A. B. *Aptitudes and personality measures related to creativity in seventh-grade children.* Los Angeles: Psychological Laboratory, University of Southern California, 1964.

Merrifield, P. R., Guilford, J. P., & Gershon, A. *The differentiation of divergent production abilities at the sixth-grade level.* Los Angeles: Psychological Laboratory, University of Southern California, 1963.

Newland, T. E. On defining the mentally superior in terms of social need. *Exceptional Children,* 1963, *29,* 237–240.

Noffsinger, T. Creativity: A critique. *Science Education.* In press.

Owens, W. A. The predictive validity of certain measures of creativity in machine design. *Journal of Creative Behavior,* 1968, *2,* 211–212.

Parloff, M. B., & Datta, L. E. Personality characteristics of the potentially creative scientist. *Science and Psychoanalysis,* 1965, *8,* 91–106.

Purkey, W. W. Measured and professed personality characteristics of gifted high school students and an analysis of their congruence. *Journal of Educational Research,* 1966, *60,* 99–104.

———. *The self and academic achievement.* Gainesville: Florida Educational Research and Development Council, College of Education, University of Florida, 1967.

Raph, J. B., Goldberg, M. L., & Passow, A. H. *Bright underachievers.* New York: Teachers College Press, Columbia University, 1966.

Riessman, F. *The culturally deprived child.* New York: Harper & Row, Publishers, 1968.

Roe, A. Personal problems and science. In C. W. Taylor and F. Barron (Eds.), *Scientific creativity: Its recognition and development.* New York: John Wiley & Sons, Inc., 1963, pp. 132–138.

Rosenthal, R. & Jacobson, L. *Pygmalion in the classroom.* New York: Holt, Rinehart & Winston, Inc., 1968.

Segel, D. & Rashkin, E. *Multiple aptitude tests.* Monterey, Calif.: California Test Bureau, 1959.

Skeels, H. M. Adult status of children with contrasting early life experiences. *Monographs of the Society for Research in Child Development,* 1966, *31* (3), 1–65.

———. The mental development of children in foster homes. *Journal of Genetic Psychology,* 1936, *49,* 91–106.

———. Some Iowa studies of the mental growth of children in relation to differentials of the environment: A summary. In *Intelligence: Its nature and nurture.* 39th yearbook, Part II. Chicago National Society for the Study of Education, University of Chicago Press, 1940, pp. 281–308.

Strang, R. The nature of giftedness. In N. B. Henry (Ed.), *Education for the gifted.* Chicago: University of Chicago Press, 1958, pp. 64–86.

Taba, H., & Elkins, D. *Teaching strategies for the culturally disadvantaged.* Chicago: Rand McNally & Co., 1966.

Taylor, C. W. Be talent developers as well as knowledge dispensers. *Today's Education,* 1968, *57* (9), 67–69.

———. The creative individual: A new portrait in giftedness. *Educational Leadership,* 1960, *18,* 7–12.

———. Finding the creative. *Science Teacher,* 1961, *28,* 593–606.

———. Some possible relations between communication abilities and creative abilities. In C. W. Taylor & F. Barron (Eds.), *Scientific creativity: Its recognition and development.* New York: John Wiley & Sons, Inc., 1963, pp. 365–371.

——— et al. *Explorations in the measurement and prediction of contributions of one sample of scientists.* USAF Personnel Research Laboratory Report No. ASD-TR-61-96. Lackland Air Force Base, Texas: USAF Personnel Research Laboratory, 1961.

Terman, L. M. The discovery and encouragement of exceptional talent. *American Psychologist,* 1954, *9,* 221–230.

———. *Mental and physical traits of a thousand gifted children.* Stanford, Calif.: Stanford University Press, 1925.

Thorndike, R. L. Review of Rosenthal, R. and Jacobson, L. "Pygmalion in the Classroom." *American Educational Research Journal,* 1968, *5,* 708–711.

Thurstone, L. L. Primary mental abilities. *Psychometric Monographs,* 1938, (1), 1–121.

Torrance, E. P. Personality dynamics of under-self-evaluation among intellectually gifted college freshmen. In E. P. Torrance (Ed.), *Talent and education.* Minneapolis: University of Minnesota Press, 1960, pp. 165–172.

———. *Education and the creative potential.* Minneapolis: University of Minnesota Press, 1963.

———. Examples and rationales of test tasks for assessing creative behavior, *Journal of Creative Behavior,* 1968, *2,* 165–178.

———. *Guiding creative talent.* Englewood Cliffs, N. J.: Prentice-Hall, Inc., 1962.

———. The Minnesota studies of creative behavior: National and international extensions. *Journal of Creative Behavior,* 1967, *1,* 137–154. (*a*)

———. *Rewarding creative behavior.* Englewood Cliffs, N. J.: Prentice-Hall, Inc., 1965.

———. *The Torrance tests of creative thinking: Norms-technical manual* (research ed.) Princeton, N.J.: Personnel Press, 1966.

———. *Understanding the fourth grade slump in creative thinking.* Final Report on CRP No. 994. Washington, D. C.: Bureau of Research, U. S. Office of Education, 1967. (*b*)

——— & Dauw, D. C. Mental health problems of three groups of highly creative high school seniors. *Gifted Child Quarterly,* 1965, *9,* 123–127, 130.

Torrance, E. P., & Khatena, J. Originality of imagery in identifying creative talent in music. *Gifted Child Quarterly,* 1969, *8,* 3–8.

Torrance, E. P., Tan, C. A., & Aliman, T. *Verbal originality and teacher behavior: A predictive validity study* (mimeographed). Athens: Georgia Studies of Creative Behavior, University of Georgia, 1967.

Toynbee, A. Has America neglected her crea-tive minority? *Utah Alumnus,* February 1962, *10,* 29–37.

Troutman, M. R. Who are the gifted? *The Instructor,* 1969, *79* (1), 10.

Tucker, R. L. Jessie Stuart, here's to you! In M. B. Smiley, F. B. Freedman, & J. J. Marcatante (Eds.), *A family is a way of feeling.* New York: The Macmillan Company, 1964, pp. 18–19.

Wallach, M. A., & Kogan, N. *Modes of thinking in young children: A study of the creativity-intelligence distinction.* New York: Holt, Rinehart & Winston, Inc., 1965.

———, & Wing, C. W, Jr. *The talented student: A validation of the creativity-intelligence distinction.* New York: Holt, Rinehart & Winston, Inc., 1969.

Werblo, D., & Torrance, E. P. Experiences in historical research and changes in self evaluations of gifted children. *Exceptional Children,* 1966, *33,* 137–141.

Whittaker, D. N. E. Psychological characteristics of alienated, nonconformist, college-age youth as indicated by AVL, OPI, ACL, and SVIB-M/W group profiles. Unpublished doctoral dissertation, University of California, Berkeley, 1967.

Witt, G. *The life enrichment activity program: A brief history* (mimeographed), New Haven Conn.: LEAP, Inc., 1968.

Witty, P. How to identify the gifted. *Childhood Education,* 1953, *29,* 313.

Wolfle, D. The discovery of talent. Cambridge, Mass.: Harvard University Press, 1969.

Yamamoto, K. Threshold of intelligence in academic achievement of highly creative students. *Journal of Experimental Education,* 1964, *32,* 401–405.

TWELVE

Psychological Considerations of Emotionally Disturbed Children

PETER KNOBLOCK

Peter Knoblock is Associate Professor of Special Education and Administrator of the Children's Psychological Services, Division of Special Education and Rehabilitation, Syracuse University. He is a past president of the Council for Children with Behavioral Disorders.

This chapter is a new addition to this text. Its inclusion can be viewed as a recognition of the many factors we need to consider when interacting with children labeled "emotionally disturbed." Professional workers, parents, and the lay public all view the problem of disturbance in children from different perspectives. This chapter will not attempt to reconcile these variant perspectives, nor will it approach inclusiveness in terms of the available philosophies, interventions, and research.

In many ways the battle lines have been hastily and firmly drawn. Some professional workers place their diagnostic and intervention emphases on the behavior of the child. Others look for the psychodynamic explanations behind such symptomatic behaviors or to the parents, who could be accountable for the genesis of disturbance in the child. Still others do not view emotional disturbance as a condition at all. To this group emotional disturbance resides in the eyes of the beholder and is a reality only insofar as we are willing to label it as such. Closely related are those who feel that the environmental pressures under which children operate are overly burdensome to their psychosocial development.

Any or all of these perspectives may be useful as explanatory concepts or as points of view that allow for greater accessabilty of assistance to the child. This chapter takes the point of view that any effort to understand emotional disturbance in its many manifest forms will need to view the child in the context of his many environments. That the child labeled emotionally disturbed by adults, be they professionals or nonprofessionals, is capable of making an impact on those around him is well recognized but not necessarily accepted or acceptable to those with whom he interacts. The reciprocal impact of the situational determinants on a child's emotional status and responsiveness is not nearly as well recognized or recognizable. Yet we seem to operate on the basis that accurate understanding of environments can effectively assist a child in difficulty.

The interaction of the child we are referring to as emotionally disturbed and the many environments and people who inhabit those environments will be the central focus in this chapter. Explicit in such an approach is the fact that we need extensive understanding of both children and environments. As a matter of fact, there is much we do know of children's emotional development. To keep things in perspective, we should remind ourselves that we are still speaking of children and not necessarily referring to some irrational being who is helpless and totally removed from society. Those serious students of child development and behavior are also encouraged to pursue studies in normal child development so as to gain some perspective on the prevalence of what we call childhood problem behavior (Macfarlane, Allen, and Honzik, 1962). For the purposes of this chapter, only those interpersonal and intrapersonal behaviors and reactions that seem pivotal to our better understanding of "these children" will be discussed in any detail.

ENVIRONMENTAL DEFINITIONS OF EMOTIONAL DISTURBANCE IN CHILDREN

In defining environment, we advocate an adherence to a life-space formulation in its broadest sense. The dynamic considerations we are willing to put into the equation B = f (PE), where behavior is a function of the person interacting with his environment, will largely determine our definition.

As professional workers interact with

problem children, it becomes more apparent that many children do not exhibit maladaptive behaviors in every situation and environment. There are great numbers of children, normal and otherwise, who exhibit interpersonal and environment-specific problems. If this is the case, and our clinical experience indicates that it is, then environmental expectations and psychological climates would need to be considered in any attempt to conceptualize the type of children with whom we are concerned.

School Definitions

For many decades a rather awkward discussion raged in public schools as to whether teachers should be as concerned with the shy, withdrawn child as they are with the aggressive, acting-out child. This argument was awkward because a great many of the critics had insufficient information as to the shades and nuances of behavior in operation in a typical classroom. It is only within the past few years that direct observation and recording of child behaviors and teacher-child interactions has assumed a degree of respectability (Smith and Geoffrey, 1968; Jackson, 1968). As Beilin (1959) points out, there may be very appropriate reasons for teachers focusing on more overt, acting-out behaviors. These are the behaviors that directly subvert the instructional and management approaches of teachers. Of more subtle significance is Beilin's finding that over the years since the publication of the Wickman study (1928), the correlation between clinicians' and teachers' judgments as to what constitutes problem behavior is increasing. One possible interpretation might be that teachers have become more like clinicians in their perceptions. Those of us involved in schools, however, do not see this. What is seen are teachers focusing very directly on those children manifesting deviant behavior, usually taking the form of physical or verbal aggression.

According to Gnagey (1965) "deviancy" is used synonomously with "misbehavior." "A deviancy occurs when a student takes actions which are prohibited by the teacher" (p. 4). It would seem, then, that a great number of school environments, while paying lip service to the quiet and shy, are labeling and focusing on aggressive children. It is this labeling of aggressive behavior as emotional disturbance and placing it in the realm of deviance that accounts for a large group of children being presented to special education for assistance.

The intrapsychic model for looking at emotional problems of children undoubtedly contributed to the placing of responsibility on the child for the control or mismanagement of his behavior. The locus of the problem, that of transgressing against the norms of the school, is viewed in this context as stemming from internal problems of the child. He is admonished to try harder, to respond to the interventions by adults, to re-set his behavioral goals, and, failing to do one or all of these, to suffer the consequences of his behavior.

A dramatically different approach to the defining of emotional disturbance in children is an ecological one in which environmental variables are viewed as possible determinants of children's emotional reactions and adjustments. Such a point of view would not rule out the psychodynamic forces operating within the child but, rather, place such forces within the context of the environment in which the child operates (Barker and Gump, 1964). Carried to a logical conclusion, such an emphasis upon the environmental pressures of schools should make us ask why some behaviors are considered deviant and disturbed? Have we redefined emotional disturbance in terms of what the school can and cannot tolerate without looking inward to examine the abrasive characteristics of our schools?

Out of an ecological orientation have come references to the disturbing child— one who may act out due to psychonoxious qualities in the environment. The matter becomes complex because it quickly leads to the observation that only some children are defined this way. The process of defining is rarely as clear as the above implies. School agents frequently believe that the child is doing things *to* the environment rather than acknowledging the reciprocal impact of school practices on the child (Trippe, 1963).

Rhodes (1966) pleads eloquently for a merger of education and ecological sciences, which would include behavioral, social, and mental-health approaches. He paints the picture of many ancillary workers flitting about in the school.

> ... whirling giddily around the outside periphery of the central instructional arena. All of these are patched onto the school as extraneous foreign bodies which are easily cast out, like the unassimilable appendages they are, every time it suits the administrators, the funding sources or reactionary power groups. In the center we see the regular teacher and the instructional program ploughing its way through the core of the curriculum, no matter what the balanced growth and learning needs of the children happen to be (p. 5).

One of the more dramatic examples of an ecological approach gone somewhat awry has been the rise and subsequent disillusionment of many with the formation of special classes for disturbed children. To this day many administrators would like to utilize the most effective forms of professional intervention by surrounding the special class with a form of milieu therapy in which many individuals such as psychologists, school social workers, and remedial specialists could assist in effecting child change (Redl, 1957). Experience has been showing, however, that to mobilize anything resembling a team effort in the schools often meets with resistance by teachers and administrators, usually due to a lack of any clear set of goals or procedures to be implemented by out-of-the-classroom workers.

The designing of a special class as a specific environmental intervention has been based on a number of assumptions:

1. Emotional disturbance, as manifested in the public schools is observable in a general form. In other words, "Everyone knows who the disturbed children are."
2. The children under consideration are too disturbed to be educated and handled in the regular classroom.
3. Placement into a special-class program will modify behavior in a positive direction.

These assumptions, particularly the last, carry explicit beliefs as to what contributes to child improvement and change. Similarly, then, assumptions about principles of change are adhered to by proponents of special-class environments. They are:

1. Children who are changed and who exert influence for change feel a sense of groupness or belongingness to the special class.
2. The attractiveness of the group contributes to individual and group child change.
3. Communication of goals and procedures between all children in the

group and the adults involved contributes to improvement.
4. The prevalence of the design of special classes for disturbed children is evidence of the efficacy of this intervention.

Serious professional workers contemplating the reworking of the "regular" school environment and turning it into something "special" need to examine the assumptions underlying the development of special classes (or any rearrangement for that matter) and the principles upon which they are basing change and improvement. Before committing ourselves to one environmental and interpersonal intervention—such as the special class—to the exclusion of other approaches, we need to look at the accumulating body of evidence that is raising some question as to the efficacy of special-class programs, or we should at least question our global approach and subsequent unwillingness to specify what type of program and interventions are being used (Johnson, 1962; Knoblock, 1964; Morse, Cutler, and Fink, 1964).

Much of what we say about the definition of emotional disturbance in the schools has been imported from other settings and mental-health workers. Considering the developmental tasks of childhood, the importance schools place on learning, and what constitutes deviant school behavior, we are in need of a school-based definition of emotional disturbance. One such definition has been drawn up by Thompson and Trippe (1965) and is as follows:

In its most broad sense, an emotionally disturbed child, from the point of view of the schools, is a child whose needs cannot be met through the ordinary provisions of elementary and secondary education because of disorders of behavior or disorders of learning even though the ordinary provisions are maximally flexible and oriented toward individualized instruction.

These two large areas of childhood disorder result in departure from school expectations and represent failures on the part of the children to meet the standards or norms of the schools even though these norms may be quite adaptable to a wide range of individual differences. Many of these difficulties spring from conditions rooted in the central nervous system or other physiological conditions; many can be traced to grossly unfavorable environments; a majority represents some imponderable combination of constitutional misadventure and societal mismanagement. The resulting impact on learning and/or behavior causes the child to be deviant from school expectations and, consequently, require special educational efforts aimed at behavior construction and the reduction of learning disabilities.

Most are born to well-meaning, able parents. All of them exhibit persistent problems. Many of their abilities may be thought of as falling within the usual range of mental potential, but they often have difficulty in school. They may appear mentally retarded, socially inept, incorrigible, physically clumsy, or emotionally unresponsive. In some areas of development they are retarded; in others they are competent or even precocious. Many of them may be resistant and unmanageable both at home and at school. Often they are hyperactive, inattentive, distractible, and unable to concentrate. They may not conform to classroom behavior standards, and they may pose constant harrassment to the teacher and to the school. They may be withdrawn or isolated and continually on the fringes of the group. Frequently, they cannot get along with others because they are abusive and antagonistic or socially immature. Some have ungovernable temper outbursts, episodes of destructiveness or violence. Usually there are several symptoms appearing together in varying severity: disordered visual-perceptual development, motor limitations, poor impulse control, and learning and memory deficits (particularly in reading and spelling). Emotion, em-

pathy, and judgment are quite often seriously affected, and quite often, there are deficiencies in abstract thinking.

These children find very little success. The disjunctions in their perceptions, their thinking, their emotional life, their conduct, cannot be corrected by teaching procedures and classroom direction adapted to either normal or defective children.

As time goes by, the effects of failure, retardation, ostracism, criticism, and punishment invade the child's self-concept. He senses his inadequacies, and internalizes them. Some of his rebellion and clamor represents, then, the conflict between his poor self-esteem and his struggle for stature. With little positive initiative and incentive, he is reduced to continual discouragement. Such children have been greatly misunderstood. They have been thought to be stubborn, lazy, stupid, perverse, incorrigible, and wayward.

Classroom teachers can readily nominate disturbed children by their behavior. They are to be found in almost every schoolroom. Learning and behavior problems exhibit themselves in many ways: inattention, hyperactivity, disobedience, defiance, poor grades, refusal to complete work, daydreaming, annoyance to other children, and agitation or exclusion on the playground. The teacher can refer to the school psychiatrists or psychologists those children who are not adapting to or profiting from regular classroom procedures. In turn, these personnel can investigate the condition in detail: background, educational history, academic achievement, medical evidence, family circumstances; and mental, emotional, and motor functioning. Such evaluation can appraise the potential strengths within his makeup that might properly be exploited toward rendering him an adequately functioning child.

If the child appears to be potentially within the average mental ability range but manifests persistent irregularities in learning and behavior, he may be considered emotionally disturbed. Sometimes the estimate of mental ability must be presumptive because the child may not be able to mobilize or exhibit his abilities. Careful appraisal procedures do not always clearly identify children with potential learning ability. Therefore, the major criteria for selection are likely to be observational and descriptive: learning and behavior problems. Competent quality appraisal should be made at the time of referral for purposes of assignment to a program or sequence of services judged to be most appropriate in relation to the needs of the child and availability of resources.

In addition to failing to meet the standards or expectations of the schools, some children violate the norms of other professionalized social systems. Some children violate the law and are provided for in detention facilities, foster homes or training schools. The families of some children are unable to provide adequately for them or the families may not be suitable for child rearing. These children may be placed in day care centers, foster homes, group homes or residential homes. Finally, some children with innate ability may fail to develop along expected lines or may develop such extremes of behavior that health, social welfare and/or legal correctional agencies desire and secure services of private mental health specialists, mental health clinics, day treatment centers, residential treatment centers or mental hospitals. Many of the children in these groups that violate the norms of other social systems also have disorders of learning and behavior as viewed by the school. Many more develop disorders of learning and behavior associated with the disruptions in their lives and the cumulative effects of negative experiences and social stigma. These children also are considered emotionally disturbed as viewed by the school and require special educational efforts.

Peer-Group Definitions of Emotional Disturbance

Some professional workers look to the peer group as a yardstick of who in the group represents deviant behavior and requires labeling as an emotionally disturbed child. Undoubtedly, this definitional stance has come about through the study of children who are scapegoated by groups. Not all of these observations are dramatically available to the observer, however. As children's groups develop greater cohesiveness, there is a greater tolerance for deviations from group norms, thus allowing for a greater range of behavior from individual members and less chance for clear labeling by adults. Studies of child group-behavior seem to point out that the environment in which behavior occurs defines certain limits as to the behavior of group members (Barker, 1963).

In an interesting study of social distance generated by the exceptional at the high school level (Jones, Gottfried, and Owens, 1966), it was found that acceptance was related to both interpersonal situations and the type of exceptionality. Using high school students in grades 9 through 12, the acceptability of emotional disturbance varied according to the specific situation under consideration. Along with the importance of the interpersonal situation were the variables of sex and grades of the respondents. Thus, in response to the statement: "I would accept this person as a coworker in my occupation," the emotionally disturbed were rated very low. In contrast, this exceptionality fared much better when considered in the interpersonal situation, "I would accept this type of child as a playmate for my children."

Although it is of interest to know how normal children view deviant behavior, it is of even greater value for us to examine more direct forms of peer-group involvement to determine just how far children can go in their own groups before they are labeled deviant. Lesser (1959) reports on a study which supports the notion that groups of children are capable of making determinations as to which responses are acceptable and to be differentially rewarded or punished by peers. His study explored the relationships between different forms of aggression and peer-group approval or disapproval. In this sociometric approach he used five categories of aggression: provoked physical aggression; outburst aggression; unprovoked physical aggression; verbal aggression; and indirect aggression. His sample consisted of upper lower class boys, ten to thirteen years old. He found provoked physical aggression a relatively approved form of aggression, with indirect aggression ("to attack or injure indirectly through another person or object") strongly disapproved.

Not all children, however, will communicate their definitions to us quite so clearly. Redl (1949) has pointed out that individual members in a group will be drawn into acting-out behaviors, a phenomenon he refers to as contagion, depending on group psychological factors such as the status of the initiator. This would be an example, then, of deviant behavior displayed by a high-status group member, which would be followed by others and not singled out negatively by others in the group. This type of child, often referred to as the "master manipulator" has the power to pull deviant behavior from others while remaining almost unobtrusive to the untrained eye. It is the wise group-leader who focuses on the influence such a child may have on others.

All of us know of many good examples of disturbed children's keen ability to diagnose their differences from other children. A teacher of disturbed children reported to us that he asked a boy in his class who was having a particularly bad day to write out what was bothering him about being in a special class. His questions reflect a sensitivity to and concern about his status with peers:

1. Why do we get out at 2:30 (instead of the regular dismissal time)?
2. Why don't we use a pen?
3. Why don't we use our textbooks more?
4. Why don't we have lockers?
5. Why don't we get homework for sixth to get ready for seventh?
6. Why don't we ride a bike to school?
7. Why do we use these workbooks so often?

This writer can recall many instances of youngsters labeled as schizophrenic coming to him and insisting that other children in their group be removed because *they* were too crazy! The child as diagnostician is well accepted by other children who frequently feel the slings and arrows of peer disapproval.

There is also rather convincing evidence from follow-up and follow-back or retroactive studies of children either identified as disturbed or traced back from a state of adult mental illness to childhood status to show that effective peer-functioning was a problem for many in the childhood years (Gronlund and Anderson, 1957; *Onondaga County School Studies,* 1963; Zax, Cowen, and Rappaport, 1968). These studies and others tend to show that there is often a pulling back from group and peer participation on the part of troubled youngsters. The reciprocal response on the part of other children is difficult to sort out. In other words, which comes first, the strange behavior that alienates peers or peer rejection, based on a host of factors, which then exacerbates a troubled child's self-esteem and prevents greater group-interaction skills from developing?

One word of caution in the interpretation of the above studies in general is raised by Lewis (1965) in his discussion of the continuity hypothesis, which maintains that emotional disturbance in childhood is the precursor of adult mental illness. Only moderate support for this hypothesis has been accumulated according to his review and interpretation of available studies. Also Robins (1966) found that shy and withdrawn personality characteristics in childhood were not necessarily predictive of later adult maladjustment. The finding of estrangement from peers appears in a sufficient number of studies of childhood interactions of disturbed children to alert us to potential social interaction problems faced by children without such findings necessarily pointing to later problems.

Many investigators find that the social-interactional systems operative in children's groups are not often recognized and channeled for constructive purposes. This inattentiveness to group process and dynamics would be as true for classroom groups as it is for institutional programs (Getzels and Thelen, 1960; Polsky, 1962). Polsky's participant observation study in a residential treatment center for disturbed boys clearly demonstrates that the peer culture of the center functioned in a powerful manner in terms of influencing children and, of course, the adults. The professional staff, concerned at the roadblocks thrown up by the children to the treatment program, sought an analysis of the peer social and emotional climate. Some of us joke with each other from time to time about the strong possibility that children plot and scheme against the kinds of notions we have for helping them. Ironically enough, Polsky's study shows how well organized some delinquent subgroups can be in order to accomplish their own survival goals.

A common observation in classrooms of the disturbed is the pattern of teacher behavior often described as sequential tutoring. Youngsters are assisted on an individual basis, with the rest of the group learning to wait their turn. Although there is nothing wrong with this particular style of interaction, it tends to cast some doubt on adequate recognition of group interactions. To go even one step beyond this is the concern expressed by many regular classroom teachers who have disturbed children placed with normal children. As teachers they feel they cannot "sacrifice" their entire class for the benefit of a few. There is some strong evidence which does not completely support this teacher concern, and puts the question of how destructive is it to have disturbed children in a regular class more within the domain of understanding group dynamics. It is no longer sufficient to believe that how we manage a disturbed child's behavior in a regular classroom goes unnoticed by the other children. It is more realistic to assume that individual children are carefully watching the teacher as he interacts around other children (Kounin and Gump, 1958). Further, in a study of emotionally disturbed children in regular classrooms (Kounin, Friesen and Norton, 1966), it was found that teachers who were able to effectively cope with the management problems of a classroom were also relatively successful in handling the disturbed children in their classrooms. In keeping with our emphasis on the differential importance of different environments on behavior is Kounin, Friesen, and Norton's finding that the most appropriate school behavior occurs in subgroup recitation periods and the most deviant behavior in seatwork situations.

Parent Definitions of Emotional Disturbance

The prevalent notion that it is the professionals who seek out and define disturbance does not give credit to parent detection. Those responsible for clinic and child-welfare services will attest to the numerous requests for assistance made by parents.

Others would be willing to go a step further, such as Vogel and Bell (1960), who maintained that not only can some parents define emotional disturbance but that they may, in fact, create it. In such instances the child's role is that of family scapegoat, and his problem is either created or exacerbated due to the marital conflicts and needs of the parents. In a study of disturbed children's parents, who were themselves disturbed, several definitional approaches were utilized by the parents. Such approaches revolved primarily around dynamic family-need patterns. Vogel and Bell indicate that the selection of a particular child as the scapegoat could be related to one or more of the following: value orientation conflicts of parents and the degree to which the child represents that conflict in the parents' minds; sibling order and sex of child; physical, emotional, and intellectual resemblances or dissimilarities of child to parent.

Lest one come away with the notion that great numbers of parents deliberately set about to harm their children, the current attention being paid to the "direction of effects" research strategy (Bell, 1968) places this notion in proper perspective. As Bell points out, most research on parent-child relations has typically looked at the influence of the parent being directed at the child. He argues for a bidirectional model, which would then allow for the investigation of the impact the child's behavior may have on the parent and the relationship between parent and child.

Along with some of the research supporting the powerful influence of child behavior on adult behavior is the observation by many engaged in working with emotionally disturbed children that different children seem to "pull" rather dramatic behaviors from their parents. This is as true for professional workers as it is for parents. Professionals find themselves gravitating toward work with certain groups of disturbed children and often expressing, at the same time, the feeling that they couldn't really work with disturbed children manifesting certain behaviors.

Definitions Based on Perceptions of Others

The summary publication of the Joint Commission for Mental Health, *Action for Mental Health* (1961), spells out the many fears and concerns held by the general public toward the mentally ill and the resultant lack of progress. The commission makes reference to society's pursuit of punishment for those who are markedly deviant from sets of norms; ineffectual functioning of voluntary mental-health organizations such as the National Association for Mental Health; lack of strong, visible leadership in mental health; an emphasis on prevention despite lack of promising evidence to support such an orientation; and, most basically, the public's attitude of rejection toward children and adults who are labeled disturbed.

In a well-designed study of attitudes toward mental health, Nunnally (1961) reports that, in terms of the information possessed by the public, the problem seems to be lack of information rather than misinformation. Mental illness, then, remains an abstract term, and Nunnally found very negative attitudes toward the mentally ill. Although this study used adult respondents as the sample, the findings would seem to apply to adult attitudes toward children as well as toward other adults. There are many who feel that the acting out and apparently deviant behavior of children is willful in nature. Efforts are often made toward exhorting the child to conform so that he makes his life easier and avoids conflict with adults.

Many of the attitude studies indicate that those considered mentally ill are thought of as exhibiting unpredictable behavior. Such a belief would seem to apply to perceptions of deviant children. Those professional workers directly involved with children, regardless of the setting, repeatedly receive the message that they are unique in their interest in working with such a child. How can they do it, they are asked, considering the types of problems being presented? There is a subtle amount of pressure being exerted on such workers and reflected in results of attitude studies of special-education teachers and prospective teachers. Public attitudes, then, may really have a rather dramatic influence on those employed in child-care work and may even serve to discourage and limit others who might consider such a professional endeavor.

Societal influence in the choice of special education has been reported by Gottfried and Jones (1964), Meyers (1968), and Lord and Wallace (1949). The experience that many have had in talking with young people considering a career in special education confirms the observation reported in the above studies that direct experience and contact with exceptional children is a powerful determiner of career choice.

Less obvious societal influence is revealed in those studies of preferences for teaching various *types* of exceptional chil-

dren. In many of these (Badt, 1957; Jones and Gottfried, 1962), teaching and working with emotionally disturbed children had high valence for many responding in these studies. Badt's study (1957), however, points out the discrepancy between the possible glamour and visibility a preference area such as emotional disturbance has and the actual commitment to working in that area. Badt found that although this area was considered highly attractive, many rating it as such would not actually want to teach disturbed children.

Certainly, the demand for personnel in the education of disturbed children remains high and continues to increase. The kinds of attitudes cited above and held by both the public, professionals, and prospective teachers all highlight the dilemma. For the public, the disturbed individual is seen in an essentially negative light. For professionals and prospective teachers, there is a relatively high prestige factor associated with teaching disturbed children, but this does not necessarily mean they would engage in such professional activity themselves.

The ways emotionally disturbed children feel about themselves are influenced heavily by many of the factors outlined in the previous sections. Although there is interesting work currently being done on temperament factors within children, which may account for certain manifestations of behavior, many researchers adhere to an interactionist orientation when explaining the child's acquisition of perceptions of himself (Knoblock and Garcea, 1969). Many are intrigued with the realization that we can so effectively convince a child that he is deviant. The matter then becomes as much the adult's business as the child's concern. This is a dilemma that many professional workers with children are facing—and doing so

PETER KNOBLOCK

with some alarm. There are those who feel they have compensated for this problem by communicating to children that what they as adults disapprove of is the behavior and not the child. Although adults may be able to make this distinction, there is question as to whether children can. Practitioners such as Redl (1959) and Dreikurs (1968) prefer to deal less moralistically with behavior and approach the situation in terms of the natural consequences of what the child has done.

Schwartz, Fearn and Stryker (1966) studied self-perceptions of disturbed children in two inpatient institutions. They found that those children classified as having a poor prognosis by therapists came to see themselves as settling into the role of "disturbed." In essence they came to identify rather heavily with the perceptions they thought their therapist had. Negative perceptions they had of themselves were matched by their therapists' negative perceptions. In short, the authors felt the poor-prognosis group had come to accept their role as disturbed and were, in fact, committed to it. The poor-prognosis group tended to assign higher self-meanings to themselves. Positive self-meanings with this group were interpreted as a settling into the role and as a result the children had diminished feelings of anxiety about themselves. Of interest was the finding that those children least committed to the deviant role could be more heavily influenced by others and were not as dependent upon the therapist for a definition of their problem. We can see, then, that adults can hold powerful sway over a child, not only in relation to what they can and cannot do with him but also because of what they can make the child feel and come to believe about himself. Nowhere is this seen more dramatically than in a surge of interest, although still not

reaching enough attention, in the alarming suicide rate in children. A study documenting suicides in New Jersey (Jan-Tausch, 1964) highlights many provocative implications for all of those in contact with children. Suicide in children, as the ultimate example of acting-out behavior, is at the same time an illustration of a child's turning inward against himself, with the specific reasons and causes remaining elusive. This study identified forty-one children, thirty-two boys and nine girls, ages seven to nineteen, who committed suicide between 1960 and 1963. Although the report draws no definitive conclusions based on its descriptive data, these children as a group were found to be of normal intelligence, but their academic achievement was poor in relation to intellectual potential. The majority had no interest in extracurricular activities, and perhaps of greatest significance was the lack of a close friend in all forty-one cases of suicide.

HOW DO THE EMOTIONALLY DISTURBED FEEL?

It can be seen from all that has been written so far that considerations of how emotional disturbance is defined are tied closely to the environment and the people within that environment. In this section an attempt will be made to describe how such children have come to see themselves or, in other words, define themselves. In the process of relating research and clinical information, some discussion of implications for changing negative self-perceptions will be presented.

Disturbed children are often seen as unpredictable, "bad," and presenting serious problems. But the disturbed are not necessarily the type of youngsters people would want to interact with professionally or socially. Certainly such attitudes are results of complex factors and are held by adults to different degrees and in different combinations. Such attitudes are communicated to disturbed children, and many professionals feel the children's responses reflect prevalent attitudes toward them. Just as society sees and prefers to place disturbed children apart from whatever it defines as the mainstream, there is evidence that disturbed children also see *themselves* as apart from the mainstream. In an interesting methodological approach, Weinstein (1965) utilized concepts of social distance and had children organize social stimuli in a free-placement situation. This was accomplished by using flannelboards and felt figures representing humans and rectangles. Weinstein asked the question, "First, like normal adults, do emotionally disturbed children group humans closer than nonhuman objects?" The disturbed children, in contrast to a normal group, placed the human figures farther apart than they did rectangles. The interpretation of such findings is based upon conceptualizations of the importance of social schemata and their possible reflection of cultural norms (Keuthe, 1962). For example, we typically think of the closeness of certain relationships, such as the mother-child relationship, or perhaps, we even think of humans as belonging together in close proximity both emotionally and physically. Weinstein raises the question of whether physical distance can be equated with emotional distance. Findings similar to Weinstein's have been reported by Fischer (1967), and, with our concerns about changing negative self-concepts in children, perhaps we would do well to investigate social schemata as perceived by children. Some evidence for the impact of meaningful treatment environments on the restructuring of interpersonal space

has been reported by Hobbs (1966). Comparisons of different studies reporting how disturbed children view psychological relationships must be made with some caution, and researchers need to consider methodology and impact of the particular stimuli used to measure social distance (Tolor, 1968).

Failure in school is often thought to reflect inadequate self-perceptions. After an investigation of high school students who were failing (Jan-Tausch and Granstrom, 1967, p. 14) stated: "School failure in these cases is symptomatic of neurotic behavior." Regardless of whether or not we agree with this, of importance for our purposes is their presentation of findings from interviews with the children. The children saw themselves at fault for not working hard enough; there was nothing the teacher could have done differently; and they felt guilty and ashamed when they came to class unprepared. And just as revealing was their inability to organize themselves to study and their very unclear perceptions of what teachers expected of them. These children seemed to be caught up in a cycle that rapidly spiraled them downward. They turned the burden of responsibility inward but at the same time expressed having inadequate skills and no clear guidelines as to expectations from school or home. Interviews with teachers showed essentially an undynamic view of these children. They were perceived as less intelligent than their IQ test results showed, and, in effect, the teachers saw the children failing in much the same terms expressed by the children—lack of effort. One could hypothesize, based on surveys such as this, that as the external realities provided by negative teacher feedback and internalized failure feelings of the children move closer, there is less chance for a child to break out of such a failure cycle. Some ways to possibly avoid such a spiraling effect would be to view the school failure problems of children in more dynamic terms by attempting to obtain the perceptions of the children and by looking to the expectations of the school environment and the teachers within it.

In line with the above discussion of school failure, one could conceptualize and explore the self of the disturbed child in terms of the child's self-image, which is being influenced by his observing his own behavior (Ganter, Yeakel and Polansky, 1967). This is just a short step from our discussion of how important other people's perceptions, such as the therapist's, are to the child, as seen in the Schwartz, Fearn, and Stryker study (1966). Farnham-Diggary (1966) makes the distinction between self-as-being and self-as-doing. She states (p.13): "The best way to avoid such confusions may be to limit self-image analysis to clear instances of imaged action, to behavior that the child can observe in himself, just as he observes it in others." Using a sample of twenty-four psychotic children, twenty-four brain-injured, and forty-eight normal children, each normal was matched on sex, age, race, IQ, and socioeconomic status with a nonnormal. Her study explored concepts these groups held of self, future, and time.

Farnham-Diggary developed a self-evaluation scale using a wooden rating scale on which a child could show the answer to such questions as "When you're doing something you love to do, show me how good you are at it." By using a three-dimensional motor-activity stimulus, she hoped to prove that disordered children need to observe themselves doing and that their self-images would be defective. The scale measured their perception of skill, influence, independence, likability, dependability, judgment, decisiveness, and

success. With the exception of "likability," the psychotic children were not distinguished from the other two groups. In other words, they saw themselves as less able to arouse affection in others. The profile similarities of the three groups lends support to the observation that those who designate and place children into categories such as psychotic, brain-damaged, and normal do so because they feel there are distinct differences among children, but the children in all the groups saw themselves in similar terms. Apparently our classification scheme does not always get through to the child! This is said only partly in jest. All too often children in difficulty come to believe what is communicated to them by others. Perhaps more activities that would involve them in acquiring perceptions of themselves as they do things would provide them with more accurate and useful self-concepts. Although the implications for prognosis remain obscure, one could argue that as long as a child, or adult for that matter, continues to live under someone else's label and set of expectations, the less opportunity he has to be himself and to find out about himself.

Changing and Modifying Self-Concepts

What to change and how to do it remain perplexing questions, made even more difficult by the reluctance to change evidenced by some groups of children whose behavior, while maladaptive by some standards, serves useful purposes for the child. Groups of delinquent children might comprise such a resistant group. Further, it may be rather presumptuous of us to continue thinking of the problem as residing in the child. Those practitioners who are exploring the impact of the school environment on the child prefer to think of some children as disturbing, that is, acting out in direct retaliation against a hostile and threatening environment.

Regardless of what we do, we had better do it rapidly. There is a sense of urgency to findings such as those of Morse (1964), who reports that children's concepts about themselves and about school become more negative with more time in school. A first line of attack used by many professional workers centers around the use of praise as a social reinforcer. In light of what we already know of the negative and alienated feelings many disturbed children have of themselves, the use of praise may have more limited effectiveness than we realize. In a conditioning study of fifteen emotionally disturbed boys, Levin and Simmons (1962) found that praise was not particularly effective as a reinforcer. In their study, patterns of operant response were unrelated to age, IQ, and psychiatric diagnoses. McDavid and Schroeder (1957) point up the dramatically different interpretations delinquent adolescents may have of approval and disapproval. Although approval and disapproval may be clear messages from the standpoint of the sender, McDavid and Schroeder found their delinquent sample to experience difficulty in adequately discriminating between positive and negative interpersonal events. Such interpretational difficulties may account for the lack of impact reinforcers such as approval and disapproval may have with this type of youngster.

Several lines of evidence regarding the difficulty disturbed children experience in understanding themselves in relation to their environment lend support to change efforts that focus on assisting the child to gain self-esteem in clearly definable environments. Basically, such evidence comes from the leads supplied by Weinstein

(1965), who reports on how disturbed children organize their social relationships; increasingly negative self-concepts children have of their performance in school environments as reported by Morse (1965); and McDavid and Schroeder's findings (1957) concerning the difficulty delinquent adolescents have in discriminating between approval and disapproval in interpersonal environments. A case could be made, in line with Farnham-Diggary's thesis (1966), that children need to function in environments which allow them to see changes in their performance and receive help in evaluating it.

Again, we are faced with the harsh reality that concepts of change are as elusive as definitions of emotional disturbance. From whose vantage point do we assess change? Issues revolving around improvement have major implications for the designing of school and community programs for disturbed children. Program designs such as the special class in public schools have failed to capture the imagination of children and parents (and an increasing number of professionals) mainly because these programs have not been able to establish their specialness. The same could be said for traditional child-guidance clinic programs, which have similarly failed to make significant enough differences with large enough numbers. But again, by whose standards have these approaches failed? For the teacher in the special class may feel that he is able to establish the kind of interpersonal relationship with individual children and design curriculum approaches that just would not be possible in larger regular classrooms. The staff in a particular school, however, may feel just as strongly about the preciousness of such a small intervention when their regular classrooms are filled with other youngsters equally in need of assistance.

But what about children's perceptions of change? Perhaps this dimension should be our guidepost. Redl (1965) cautions us that perceptions of improvement may, in fact, place a child, as well as adults, under great pressure. He mentions a child's concern for raised expectation levels of others toward him and whether he can match them; his concern in moving away psychologically from the peer group, based on improvement; and his difficulty in handling praise, a topic touched on earlier.

The only large-scale study of disturbed children's perceptions of change is incorporated in Morse, Cutler and Fink's (1964) research analysis of special-class programs. In line with this chapter's theme of the interdependence of environment and behavior, the authors were able to relate child change to the type of program the child was in. Those pupils involved in a program type referred to as psychoeducational generally reported the greatest number of gains. By "psychoeducational" we mean a design in which efforts are made to coordinate clinical and educational data by involving various disciplines, in which teachers' relationships with children are viewed as central to the learning process, and in which curriculum is placed in the context of a therapeutic classroom environment.

Pupils perceived themselves as improving more in general feelings, as experiencing reduced school anxiety, and as experiencing more positive perceptions of improved relationships with teachers. Also, as we might expect, changes in teachers' perceptions of pupil control were greater within psychoeducational classroom environments. The authors conjecture that the progress of the children within this program aided the teachers' performances by making them more comfortable, and, in turn the teachers' changes in the direction of seeing children under greater control is a reflection of this reciprocal pattern. Such a pattern would involve the designing of an environment in which behavior is channeled in a firm and consistent manner so that children can feel safe to interact and learn. It is then hypothesized that when such child-behavioral changes occur, the teacher responds positively and is similarly able to cope with the situation more effectively and view the children more positively. The authors feel that pupil problems, teacher reactions, and program environments are intimately related. The authors (p. 129) go on to make a rather interesting statement: "the teachers' personal style and comfort in the setting is probably the major determiner of both operating program type and pupil responses." Their statement is interesting because if we are really serious about facilitating change in children's self-concepts and responses, then we may need to focus on changing perceptions and behaviors of significant others in the disturbed child's life.

Further evidence for such a focus is found in a study of a nonclinical child and parent population by Medinnus and Curtis (1963). They and others found a correlation between parental self-acceptance and the parents' acceptance of their children. Many case-study descriptions of disturbed children allude to the rejection of the child by one or both parents. Certainly, the same could be said of some teachers with disturbed children and certain therapists with some patients (Schutz, 1966). In another study using normal elementary age boys, Weinstein (1967) found that the boys' positive views of human relationships reflected acceptance by parents. One of her points is that perceptions of human relationships are learned through social experience and that such experiences influence social behavior.

Farnham-Diggary's (1966) emphasis on self-observation is also seen in a study of emotionally disturbed boys placed in a residential treatment hospital (Rosengren, 1961). In findings that Rosengren refers to as suggestive, it was found that those boys whose perceptions of self changed most positively also manifested improved overt behavior, and the converse was true for those whose perceptions of self changed the least. It could be inferred from this study that, in this therapeutic environment, disturbed boys were provided with the opportunity to test their concepts about themselves, and, in the process of looking at their behavior, they gathered more realistic feedback about themselves from their behavior. The interactional quality of self-evaluation and behavior seems apparent, and one could get into an endless discussion of which came first, the change in self-perception or the changes in behavior.

EMOTIONALLY DISTURBED CHILDREN AS LEARNERS

It is generally assumed that emotional disturbance is primarily a concept revolving around behaviors and feelings. As White and Charry (1966) point out, however, it would be a mistake not to realize that disorders in children, at least those in schools, are detected and defined often on the basis of learning behaviors. In their study of the relationship between school disorders, intelligence, and social class, the greatest number of children referred to school psychologists were singled out on the basis of learning difficulties. A second large group was singled out on the basis of behavior characterized by psychological

disturbances. Further findings linked the educationally disturbed group with lower IQ, social class, and achievement in contrast to the emotionally disturbed group. Such findings as these need to be looked at in the light of the referring persons (in this study they were all school personnel) and age at referral, which was mostly ages six to ten. Also, several reasons could be given for each referral, thus making the dichotomy between the educationally and the emotionally disturbed less dichotomous.

Of interest in the White and Charry study was the differential intervention service-patterns different groups were assigned to based on school performance. In brief, those children designated as educationally disturbed had lower IQ, achievement, and social-class designations, with the emotionally disturbed being higher. Selective intervention practices tended to assist the former group with educational interventions and the latter with psychotherapy approaches. The authors (p. 80) state: "It appears that we are treating the potentially healthier pupils with psychotherapy, while the potentially sicker ones are treated with educational methods."

The above study attempted to look at school disorder in broad definitional terms, and found, as we discussed earlier, that in essence the particular environment, in this case the school, defines its concerns in its own terms and with concepts most relevant for its welfare.

Several studies have demonstrated that school age children labeled as emotional problems (although various labels are assigned them) have low IQs, experience failure in one or more content areas such as reading and mathematics, and perform below expectancy for their age and ability (Kvaraceus, 1961; Powell and Bergen, 1962; Scarpitti, 1964).

Issues Related to the Learning Characteristics of Emotionally Disturbed Children

Before proceeding to a discussion of some of the specific learning problems experienced by disturbed children, three issues are deserving of mention. First, most analyses, clinical and experimental, make reference to the discrepancy between the potential of the disturbed child and his actual performance. The majority of studies reported in the literature indicate that, as a group, disturbed children possess at least average intelligence. In clinical investigations of individual children, however, we find many for whom the assumption of normal intelligence is less clear. What is typically done by clinical psychologists and clinical teachers is to speculate that many of these children possess greater potential than they show and frequently base this on an inconsistent functioning pattern. For example, results on the Wechsler Intelligence Scale for Children might reveal areas of strength as well as weakness, thus lending support to definite skills in certain areas. Similarly, a child may excel in certain subject-matter areas and fail in others. Diagnosing a child's potential can be even more subtle, particularly when a child presents a flat learning-profile. In such instances cues may need to be taken from the child's language pattern, nonverbal behaviors, motor skills, or other unobtrusive behaviors.

One assumption many of us continue to make, then, is that the personality and behavior traits of disturbed children contribute to discrepant achievment. In a review of the literature relating personality to discrepant achievement, Taylor (1964), investigating studies using many different populations, found seven factors contributing to achievement behavior. They were (1) ability to handle anxiety, (2) feelings of self-worth, (3) conformity to authority demands, (4) peer acceptance, (5) less conflict over independence and dependence, (6) engagement in activities of an academic nature, and (7) setting of realistic goals. Again, although these seven considerations represent a compilation of findings from many diverse populations, experience has shown that disturbed children lack many of the above attributes.

Second, a new category of exceptionality is being advocated, that of learning disabilities. This category immediately raises questions as to which youngsters can be grouped under this rubric. Is it conceivable to separate out children with degrees of emotional disturbance from those we are calling learning-disabled? Of course it would be conceivable, depending on the definition we give to either term. What is of interest is the observation that many school and learning clinics identify large numbers of children referred to them for learning problems as manifesting emotional problems (Coleman and Sandher, 1967). The Coleman and Sandher study also highlighted the interaction of emotional status, intelligence, age, and sex in the learning condition of children. This study and others may give us cause to be cautious in our willingness to continue to carve youngsters up into mutually exclusive categories that in reality overlap considerably.

The third issue concerns our tendency to overlook very bright and creative disturbed children. These children remain an enigma to many professional workers largely because of the dramatic discrepancy between ability and achievement. One useful way of developing a frame of reference for understanding the psychological and educational needs of bright underachievers is in a case-study approach.

Kimball (1953) used a case-history approach to generate hypotheses and then tested her hypotheses by using results of psychological testing. Her results included a picture of bright underachievers as those who experience difficulty with relationships with fathers, demonstrated extreme passivity, demonstrated physical aggression toward inanimate objects, and showed feelings of inferiority. Those who have taught emotionally disturbed gifted children will attest to the challenge they present. For many of them, intellectualizing as a way of life can become so pronounced that enormous barriers are erected to prevent communication on an interpersonal basis. Often forgotten is the need on the part of the adult, be it therapist, teacher, or parent, to remain comfortable when confronted with flashes of brilliance and, in fact, to be intellectually able to respond so that the threat level of the adult does not interfere with the relationship.

Studies of the Learning Behavior of Emotionally Disturbed Children

As is the case with many problems attributed to emotionally disturbed children, there are many assumptions made about their reading status and really only descriptive evidence to carry us further. Those who have worked with disturbed children in educational settings are well aware of how discouraged many children become at not being able to read and of not being able to devote sufficient psychological energy to the learning of this skill. Their problems are exacerbated by increasing feelings of inadequacy as they grow older and feelings of remorse over not being able to meet peer and adult expectations in the area of learning to read. Often we see disturbed adolescents who refuse to even acknowledge that they have a reading problem.

Rabinovitch *et al.* (1956) have identified a group of nonreaders who have proved to be almost completely resistant to remediation efforts. This writer recalls working in a remedial situation with an adolescent boy who absolutely denied that he could not read. Once having erected such a strong defense, he would not even go near the learning situation that had been developed for him. The erecting of self-preservation defenses tends to mask the potential for learning a youngster may have as well as keep us from validating or even developing remedial interventions that are soundly based on deficit functioning of the child.

The literature on learning problems of the disturbed, scarce as it is, tends to focus on anecdotal statements such as the above with little research available pointing to differences in learning behaviors of disturbed versus normal children. Despite the lack of available research, we have noted that large numbers of school children are labeled school disordered on the basis of learning problems.

One of the consistent findings that has turned up in descriptive and survey studies of normal and disturbed children has been the progressive decline in reading and arithmetic achievement as children identified as emotionally disturbed progress through the grades. Perhaps such findings gain importance and should attract our concern when we view them in light of Morse's (1964) finding, reported earlier, of diminished feelings of self-regard as children progressed in school.

The early California studies on an early identification process for emotionally handicapped children approached the problem at some points by comparing achievement of the normal and the dis-

PETER KNOBLOCK

turbed. One such survey by Bower, Tashnovian, and Larson (1958) demonstrated that the differences in grade-level achievement in reading and arithmetic for the emotionally handicapped in contrast to normal children increased between grades 4 and 6.

A more recent study attempts to link classroom behavior, intelligence, and achievement (Feldhusen, Thurston, and Beaning, 1967) indicated that by the third grade those children nominated by teachers as manifesting socially disapproved behavior (aggressive and disruptive) had already fallen far behind in both reading and arithmetic achievement. These researchers raise the need for exploring early interventions into the academic problems presented by such children, that is before grade 3.

Only a few studies have investigated the interrelationship of behavior and reading. As stated above, there are many clinical discussions but few attempts to clearly delineate the type or grouping of disturbed children under investigation.

One such attempt to find patterns between psychopathological labels and reading skills is found in a study by Wilderson (1967), which he labeled as exploratory. His study provided some valuable clues worthy of follow-up and showed that traditional psychiatric labels based on symptom expression still do not get us close enough to the reading behavior of disturbed children. Wilderson points out that the same problem plaguing our understanding of the emotionally disturbed is faced in understanding the reading process —namely looking at reading as a unitary concept. In a factor analytic approach to reducing large numbers of symptomatic behaviors to fewer clusters or factors, he identified four factors: schizoid withdrawal, character disorder, borderline psychosis, and somatic complaints. Similarly, seven reading-skill deficiency factors were obtained: word recognition, perceptual efficiency, intellectual maturity, visual efficiency, auditory inflectional awareness, memory, and hyperactive style. Correlations among the two sets of factors—the psychiatric factors and reading skill factors—yielded a number of low, but significant, correlations. The reader is encouraged to refer to Wilderson's study, for it is rich with clinical hunches. Perhaps if we could develop a system for more accurately describing and labeling children's behavior, an approach such as the one used in this study would yield even greater translation value for us in developing remedial programs. For example, Wilderson found that the factor *character disorder* correlated at or close to significance with *intellectual maturity* and *hyperactive style*. He considers these variables as representing inadequate impulse control. We can see, then, that the more specific we can become in dissecting the learning deficit and learning *style* of children, the closer we can come to responding appropriately to the deficit.

In line with this plea for more clearly defining the population of disturbed delinquent children, Graubard (1967) studied a group of disturbed delinquent children, using a variety of diagnostic instruments including the Illinois Test of Psycholinguistic Abilities (ITPA) and measures of auditory closure, right-left discrimination, and eye-hand coordination. In many ways Graubard's subjects would fall close to the group labeled as character disorders in Wilderson's study above. Graubard's group manifested, among other factors, a diffuseness in language structure and difficulty in right-left orientation and perceiving wholes from parts. Graubard (p. 366) states: "Much of the pathology of this sample lies in the fact that these subjects cannot delay gratification and have poor impulse control and a disturbed time sense."

Only a narrow band of findings has been pulled from these two studies, but they have served our purpose, namely to demonstrate that the behavior of the child may have implications for the learning environment we create for him. The tragedy for many difficult and troubled youngsters has been that their behavior has had such an impact on their environments that we remain focused on the behavior to the exclusion of effecting remedial programs based on their learning deficits. These learning deficits are often considered secondary to the dramatic behavior, but in reality they serve as a constant reminder to the youngster that his world remains unmanageable. The assumption that many apparently operate under is that, first, we must cure the sickness, and then learning can take place. It may be just as valid to use a more reciprocal notion, which would maintain that accurate remediation of a child's learning deficits would go a long way toward modifying his behavior. After all, feeling of failure, diminished self-esteem, and lack of communication with adults arise from school failures and carry over into behavior styles that are manifested in many of the child's environments.

THE SEARCH FOR A FRAMEWORK

The existing research and literature on interventions to assist disturbed children reveal several unsettling findings. The first is the discrepancy between the identified types of syndromes of emotional disturbance and types of programs planned for such children. Empirical evidence for this finding has long been available for anyone who has made the effort to examine the chaotic manner in which groups of disturbed children are placed into classroom units. A survey of the literature reveals only one serious attempt to realistically group disturbed children on the basis of psychoeducational dimensions (Cohen *et al.,* 1965). More recently, the extensive special-class study conducted by Morse, Cutler, and Fink (1964) demonstrated the incongruity between the characteristics of children served in special-class programs and the aims of the programs. The second finding of concern revolves about the issue of curriculum utilization. Defining curriculum in the broad context of the total daily plan for a child, which would include the presentation of learning materials, the important question is one of uniqueness or overlapping of curriculum approaches with those present with normal children. Whereas there are basic philosophical differences presently coming to the fore, the issue is to determine how such differences are being translated into classroom practice. Again, it is necessary to turn to the Morse, Cutler, and Fink study mentioned above for a reasonably systematic look at curriculum utilization and adaptation by special-class teachers of disturbed children. After surveying curriculum practices, the authors concluded that they were unable to uncover practices which were essentially different from those of regular classroom teaching.

The implications of the above two findings are enormous in terms of what we should do and avoid doing with disturbed children. Without belaboring the point, it is entirely possible that the qualitative differences between disturbed and normal children are such that one model, that of extending and stretching the normative approach commonly employed for the majority, is acceptable. The point is, however, that we are not really in possession of sufficient data to substantiate such a far-reaching conclusion. *The major problem is that children are being placed into special groupings without adequate conceptualization on the part of educators of the type of program needed, and, therefore, the program which is designed appears quite similar to regular classroom procedures.*

Basically, the research and clinical problems confronting investigators in the education of emotionally disturbed children center around two related concerns: (1) Can one develop a framework that is comprehensive enough to include major features of an emotionally disturbed child's school life which are considered important by practitioners? and (2) Is there some way to design diagnostic teaching and grouping procedures that are measurable and effective?

In some ways it is almost paradoxical, at this date, to discuss the importance of diagnostic teaching approaches. Certainly, the entire special education movement is built on diagnostic teaching, individualizing such approaches. Before and after World War II, efforts to ameliorate learning problems in adults focused attention on the diagnostic approach and the ulilization of specific techniques. Fernald (1943, p. *v*) had commented:

The contrast between the status of the men who were given the opportunity to do remedial work as children and that of the men of equal intelligence who reached adult life with the handicap of extreme disabilities in these essential skills seems to typify the whole program of specific disabilities.

Again, in Harold Benjamin's introduction to Fernald's book (p. *xv*), specific reference is made to the scientific movement, which he said "tended to substitute precise observation for passionate exhortation, accurate description for stern prescription, and tested generalization for general prayer."

Although many have clung tenaciously to this interest in the scientific movement in education, we can look back to many movements and swings of the pendulum as they affect the mental health of all children, including emotionally disturbed children. Allinsmith and Goethals (1962) have presented a very clear discussion of the shifting curriculum and programming interests of educators and the mental-health implications of such interests. A careful study of the various curriculum and/or programming approaches quickly reveals that if a practitioner (or therapist, for that matter) should decide to apply and practice life-adjustment education or content-matter approaches, for example, he would be forced by the very nature of his choice to delimit and constrict not only his view of emotionally disturbed children but his practices as well.

It would seem clear that we are still grappling with the scientific movement in developing educational programs for disturbed children. Our concern is, as Benjamin stated it, a need for precise observation, accurate description, and tested generalizations. The implication is that any approach which takes a fragmented point of view thus runs the risk of omitting important considerations necessary for achieving our goals for emotionally disturbed children.

Unfortunately, there is overwhelming evidence to indicate that we are still asking questions reflecting a fragmented approach, such as, "Should we deal with a child's mental health or academic progress?" or "Which is a more parsimonious approach to data collection, the case-history or life-space approaches?"

We should not be so deluded as to believe that merely because we have the evidence to support a more encompassing framework or point of view that teachers will translate such theory into practice. In a study of normal children, Morse, Bloom, and Dunn (1961) investigated the utilization of diverse evaluative frameworks, which included developmental, mental-health, substantive-learning, and group-process approaches. One significant finding was the negative relationship between a teacher's philosophy and actual practice. Other disturbing findings included the observation that teachers tended to view one particular classroom approach as mutually exclusive from another. The authors cite the example that if there was an emphasis on mental health, then group process or learning was excluded—at least in the teacher's perception. Interestingly enough, the perceptions of the pupils were quite the opposite. Morse and his colleagues found that pupils felt that one positive factor tended to operate in conjunction with others, specifically, that the presence of an emphasis on learning was accompanied by mental-health and group-process approaches. Perhaps the most significant finding of this study is the conclusion that effective teachers operate in many areas and on many levels, often without conscious recognition of such flexible performance.

Of current significance is the choice by the Association for Supervision and Curriculum Development to devote their 1966 yearbook to the topic of learning and mental health in the school (Waetjen and Leeper, 1966). Mental health in the words of Waetjen (p. 2):

. . . is not something out of which one makes a curriculum unit but rather it is something that occurs in the context of the moment-to-moment discourse and interaction between pupils and teachers in classrooms. We have taken the position that there are potentialities for influencing mental health in teaching the skills and understanding necessary to cope with the environment, the skills of communication, the ways of identifying and solving problems rationally, and the basic requirements needed for pursuing a vocation.

Waetjen supports the findings of the Morse *et al.* project (1961) in his observation that teachers, either on a preservice or inservice basis, do not see a mental-health orientation as a reality. He goes on to make the point that whereas positive valence may be attributed to mental-health principles, the actual practices are seen as nonoverlapping with the teaching function. One might argue, as did Morse *et al.,* that investigation of the teachers' styles might not support the prevalent contention that teachers believe "Our job is to teach and that's all." Many more complex classroom operations undoubtedly exist, and by necessity it behooves us to specify and chart the correlation between sound mental-health approaches and curriculum orientations as mutually interrelated rather than as antagonistic components of the teaching-learning process.

The essential ingredients of a framework should include characteristics of emotionally disturbed children, curriculum or programming implications of the identified characteristics, and measures of the academic and interpersonal interactions in order to evaluate the effectiveness and progress of curriculum and/or programming approaches.

PETER KNOBLOCK

How the Child Processes Information: An Ego-Process Approach

Recently a group of college students viewed the film, *The Quiet One,* depicting an emotionally and economically impoverished boy's life in a large city and his subsequent placement and partial rehabilitation in a residential setting. In the discussion that followed, questions were raised as to the nature of the discipline and the punishments for certain behaviors. The contrast was made between what was seen as a benign orientation to children placed in the residential center and what some of the college students knew of what happens in other institutional programs, namely repressive and harsh measures against children rather than for them.

The question of how and when to respond to children's behavior is at the heart of much of what this chapter has been addressing itself to. We began by looking at various definitional postures taken by schools, parents, the child himself, and the public. Another large focus has been how the child feels about himself and how he learns or rejects learning. None of these sections can stand alone, particularly when we ask the question of from where and when do controls come. The question needs to be raised, if only to allow us to look at the interrelationship of all of the factors referred to in this chapter.

We might begin by looking at the question of responsibility. Our search for the scapegoat, be it the child, the parent, or the school, has led us nowhere and was probably somewhat destructive. Often our anger at what has been done to disturbed children and our frustrations at not seeing more direct results of our work serves to continue the hunt for a scapegoat.

The position taken here is that we need to cease looking for the external cause and investigate more intensively what the child does to the environmental and interpersonal messages, in other words how he processes them. What is needed is some way of conceptualizing how the child organizes the incoming stimuli of ego processes as a framework for understanding what the disturbed child does with a world that seems confusing and confused to him. By utilizing an ego-process model to understand the behavior and the organization of a child's inner life in relation to the external world, we have more of an opportunity to view the disturbed child as an active, seeking organism who is in a constant state of flux and at the same time striving for growth. Bower (1967, p. 51) states:

> There is one characteristic of the organization of ego-processes which puts it in the forefront in relationship to the external world. The ego is an active seeker of inputs, a constructor of patterns, mosaics, and meanings. Objects and events do not enter ego-processes; they are selected, assigned properties and meaning, and actively ingested.

Perhaps the most direct application of an understanding of ego processes and its relationship to the behavior of disturbed children is in looking at the impulsive behavior of many children and the controls such children need to handle themselves and their environments. Redl and Wineman (1957, p. 59) make the following observation:

> In spite of the known complexity and multiplicity of causes in human motivation, the question as to why a particular piece of behavior occurs in a particular individual can be viewed in terms of two larger sets of "variables." One may be summarized under the term "impulsive system." By this is meant the sum total of all urges, impulses, strivings, desires, needs which

seem to push in the direction of gratification, goal attainment, or expression at any one time. It is somehow held in check by what might crudely be referred to as the "control system"—by which is meant those parts of the personality which have the function and the power to decide just which of a given number of desires or strivings will or will not be permitted to reach the level of behavioral action, and in which form.

Redl and Wineman (1957) have provided us with the most extensive descriptions of ego processes that relate to the acting out of impulses in groups of children they refer to as "children who hate." They specify four ego functions.:

1. *Cognitive function, externalized.* This resembles most closely what has come to be referred to as a child's reality testing, that is, his making contact with and responding appropriately to environmental and interpersonal stimuli which impinge on him. Implied is a degree of accuracy of perception and an active orientation toward validating or discarding of perceptions and feelings.
2. *Cognitive function, internalized.* The ego skills associated with this function allow the child to become aware of internal drive status in the form of impulses and recognition of internalized standards.
3. *Power function of the ego.* This is the function that would allow the child to get up and go, that is, to assist him in carrying out the kinds of activities and behaviors which are in keeping with his reality awareness of both external and internal forces.
4. *Selective function of the ego.* Given a wide or even limited repertoire of responses to choose from, the child is constantly placed in situations that require the selection of appropriate responses and relationship techniques.
5. *Synthetic function of the ego.* The several functions already outlined are thought to be in need of some coordination and integration. Given the complexity of environmental circumstances in which a child finds himself, and the range of behaviors that could be used, some kind of balance is needed to sort out reality, impulses, and appropriate response.

Cognitive Styles of Disturbed Children

It may prove very productive to combine our focus and explore the learning or cognitive styles of disturbed children rather than dichotomize affect and learning. Such a focus might allow us to move from psychiatric labels, which do not appear to be educationally relevant, to examining groups of children sorted out on the basis of direct observation of behaviors, such as socially acting-out children, or perhaps even to examining socioeconomic status and learning styles.

Auerswald's orientation (1969) represents a step in the direction of unifying some of our notions of psychopathology in an urban environment. Looking at acting-out children's cognitive development, he argues that such children manifest behaviors reflecting a cognitive structure which is relatively undifferentiated. Disorientation in time and space and lack of useful categories in which to place and process incoming stimuli may make such a youngster more vulnerable to his environment. It could be argued that such children would need excessive stimuli and environmental messages because they lose so much in the translation process. Auerswald uses a communications theme that seems appropriate to the problem of the school environment's need to hook up with such children. He states (p. 193):

And since he cannot learn or put words to use in many contexts, the richness and depth of meaning which words acquire through varied usage in many different life transactions will not develop for him. As a result, he is not likely to see words as useable and valuable tools. Furthermore, he is not likely to develop a clear concept of himself as a user of words. On the contrary, he will be deficient in communications skills and without motivation to acquire them. Thus, efforts to teach him these skills are likely to fail.

He will not be able to differentiate a wide variety of inner feeling responses. On the contrary, he is likely to be clearly aware only of feelings that create widespread physiological responses in him, which he perceives as high level stimuli in themselves. Such feelings, of course, are primarily the emotions of individual survival, fear and rage, species survival, or sexual sensation.

The above statements by Auerswald point up how futile it may be to continue to separate the child's self-concept, his behavior in his environment, and his learning or lack of it in school.

Spending time with various kinds of children labeled emotionally disturbed, one is struck with the diffuseness Auerswald refers to above. It takes various forms and is often perceived as a type of inflexible approach to meeting internal and external demands. Some workers refer to this diffuseness in connection with some children's self-defeating behaviors. Some children seem to place themselves "on the chopping block" even when it is obvious they will be caught. Self-defeating acts can take the form of repetitive misbehavior, which serves only to drag disturbed children deeper into difficulty. Although there may be as many explanations as there are forms of this behavior, it would seem to represent, at least on one

level, the lack of alternative forms of behaving available to such children.

This narrowing of the cognitive field of disturbed children has been discussed in considerable detail by Gardner (1966), who presents many implications for the classroom teacher who is concerned with the impact of disturbance on cognitive functioning. Insofar as the narrowing or constriction of awareness is concerned, anxiety is thought to play a major role in bringing about such a phenomenon. It has been well established that an excessive degree of anxiety impairs the learning of complex tasks, and certainly reality testing must be high on the list of complex maneuvers all children must go through.

Attentional processes, as closely related to anxiety, have received much clinical attention. The hyperactivity and impulsiveness characterizing many disturbed children remains a very big source of concern for those dealing with disturbed children. Some researchers have attempted to design environmental interventions (Cruickshank et al., 1961) that would superimpose an external source of support to bolster chaotic inner controls. Other points of view might approach the problem by assisting the youngsters in more direct ways of examining their behavior, as in psychotherapy.

Regardless of the theory of psychopathology under which one may operate, central to most theories is that of anxiety (Levitt, 1967). Our discussion so far has alluded to the fact that anxiety may contribute both to disorganization in a child and to a blurring of his consciousness or reality testing. Still, one other possibility exists, and that is that a high degree of selectivity can take place which might be attributed to anxiety and could represent a degree of regression. A compartmentalized view of self is characteristic of many disturbed children, and approaches to tasks often reveal an inability to conceptualize and look at the big picture, so to speak.

Despite the indefiniteness many attach to the term "cognitive style" there have been several attempts to both conceptualize and articulate what can be encompassed under the term. Basically, it seems that we are in need of some measurement approach or approaches which would aid us in translating the seemingly discrepant messages and behaviors of disturbed children. Further, there must be some way to clearly articulate the "point" at which we find children so that we may appropriately program for them and hopefully move them further along.

One potentially useful approach to the measurement of cognitive behaviors is the work on impulsive and reflective attitudes in children (Kagen, *et al.,* 1964). Kagan and his colleagues (p. 1) specify three sequential processes that occur in problem solving: "the initial categorization of information, storage of the encoded information and the imposing of transformations or mediational elaborations upon the encoded material."

They go on to point out that we have come to expect, and justifiably so, that with increasing age children show more competent problem-solving behavior. Kagan and his co-workers (p. 1) argue that such well-established findings may cause us to ignore the potential importance of other factors, such as children's reflective or impulsive attitudes:

It is not surprising, therefore, that psychologists have not seriously entertained the possibility that other factors may contribute to age and individual differences in cognitive products. Specifically, there has been a tendency to ne-

glect the relevance of individual differences in the processing of information—differences in the aspects of stimuli that are initially selected for labeling and the degree of reflection attendant upon classification of events or the selection of solution hypotheses. For children and adults have a clear preference hierarchy with respect to the stimulus characteristics to which they initially attend and the speed with which classification decisions are made.

Fisher (1966) in an attempt to utilize Kagan's Conceptual Styles Test (CST) to discriminate normal and impulsive children did not find differences between the groups. Her study was an attempt to test Kagan's contention that impulsivity and the inferential style of thinking are related. Fisher is of the opinion that, based on her findings, the CST could not discriminate a highly impulsive group of disturbed from normal children. Kagan's own findings are at variance, and undoubtedly further research is in order before this avenue is closed.

Conceptual-Systems Approach and Environmental Planning

All that has been said to this point argues loudly for a conceptual and operational scheme that would allow us to look at characteristics of emotionally disturbed children in ways that would move us closer to designing curriculum and management approaches which are more nearly relevant to these characteristics. It is at this point of tying characteristics and management of emotionally disturbed children together that we need to look toward the designing of relevant environments which would accommodate the behaviors and provide for a progression to other behaviors and environments.

The conceptual-systems approach

PETER KNOBLOCK

(Hunt, 1956 *b*) may offer a bridge for those interested in both ego processes, breakdowns and programming for change on the basis of more clearly differentiated self-other orientations.

From the Conceptual Systems view, development is seen as a continuous process which, under optimal conditions, proceeds in a given order to a higher conceptual level. Higher conceptual level is associated with greater conceptual complexity and interpersonal maturity and thus, is considered a desirable state. Under optimal conditions, progression on the conceptual level dimension is viewed in terms of a series of successive stages, each characterized by a specific interpersonal orientation and conceptual structure. These developmental stages characterize the person's interpersonal orientation, and the major stage characteristics deal with the "Conceptual work" occurring at a given stage. This developmental theory emphasizes interpersonal aspects pertaining to learning about oneself, about others, and about the relations between self and others, as well as structural organization (p. 2).

Figure 12–1 is a diagram of the stages, ranging from the more concrete Sub I stage to the more abstract Stage IV, the self-other orientations of children located at each stage, and the behavioral characteristics found at each stage.

Knoblock and Farrell (1969), using the above approach of characterizing children by conceptual levels, identified groups of slow learners and emotionally disturbed children who were in the sixth grade and would be moving to seventh the following fall. This project had several purposes. Perhaps the most important one was an attempt to find a more educationally relevant method of grouping children without creating the stigma characterized by the labels emotionally disturbed and slow learners. Meaningful ways to group difficult children have particular relevance at the junior and senior high school levels, when peer pressure is so great and the tolerance for deviant group-member behavior is so low.

Knoblock and Farrell were strongly impressed by how important the role of expectation may be in how teachers view their children (Rosenthal and Jacobson, 1968). Shortly after the school year began, the children were divided into two groups: slow learners and the emotionally disturbed. Several teachers commented that a job must have been done on these children over the summer in light of how well they were doing. But no child was seen during the summer months for purposes of this study. And further, several boys who had been designated by their sixth-grade teachers as emotionally disturbed were never so clearly identified as such by their junior high teachers. Many were referred to as Sub I and Stage I children. One important purpose of the study was to see if relevant instructional practices were designed based on the conceptual level of the child and the teacher's understanding of that level.

In a further attempt to validate empirically the efficacy of using such a stage-specific model to relate to observable behaviors, Hunt and Hardt (1964) studied the occurrence of delinquent offenses by boys classified at one of three stages—Sub 1, Stage 1, Stage 2. Hunt and Hardt's assumption was that more delinquent offenses could be expected from Sub 1 group members, based on less internalization of cultural norms at that stage. This assumption was supported along with a higher incidence of boys classified as delinquent in that stage. In this paper the authors also discuss the environmental prescriptions most meaningful for each stage.

STAGE	SELF-OTHER ORIENTATION	STAGE CHARACTERISTIC
SUB I	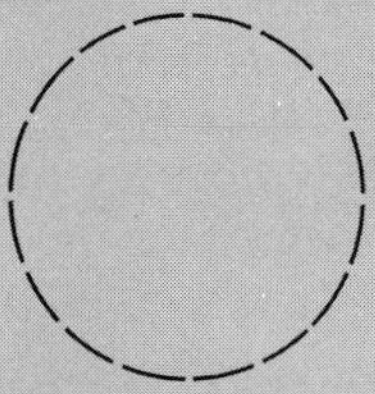	Unorganized — before assimilation of cultural standards
I	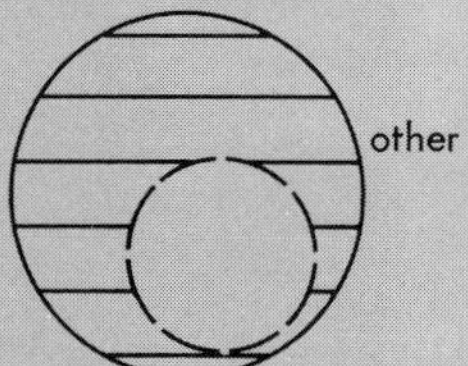 other	Learning cultural standards
II	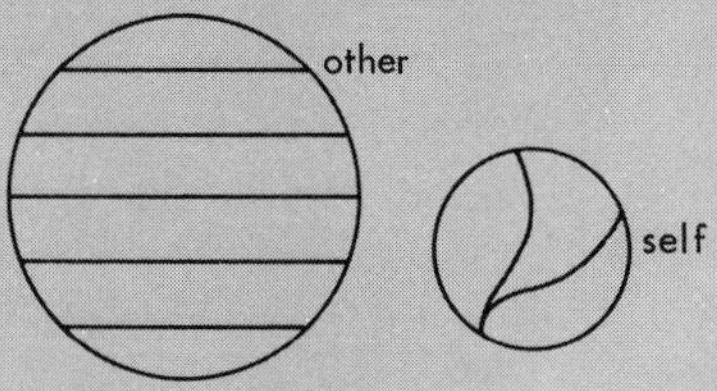 other, self	Learning how self is distinct from standards
III	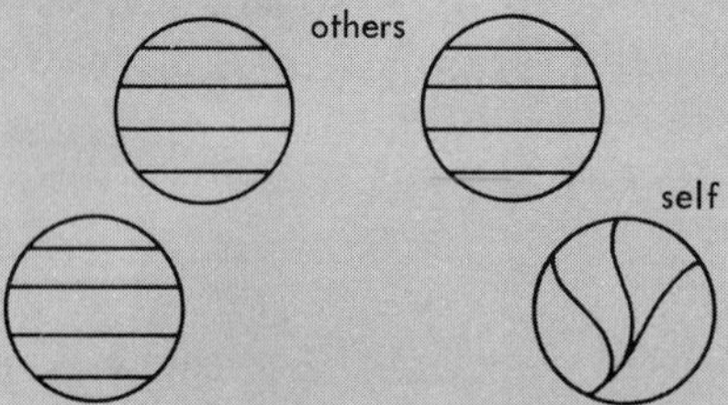 others, self	Learning about others through empathic matching
IV	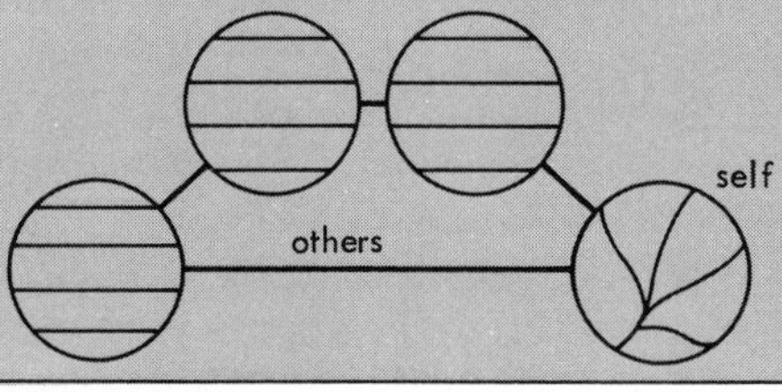 others, self	Placing self and others into integrated relation

Fig. 12–1 Conceptual work at each stage (Hunt, 1965 *b*).

Changing the Self-Other Orientations of Disturbed Children

In this section reference will be made to the goal of aiding disturbed children to maximize their potential by presenting them with environments that allow them to solve the tasks required at one stage and to move upward to another stage which requires even greater integration of self and differentiation of self and others. This movement upward from one stage to another is referred to by Hunt (1965 *a,* p. 10) as "a change model":

By a change model we mean a set of logically derived statements of the "if . . . then" variety which are conditional upon the developmental stage of the person with whom one is working. Thus, if we know the present stage or conceptual level, then we can derive the specific environment most likely to produce progression for that person. The issue is not "which environment is best?" but rather "which environment is most likely to produce the desired effect for a specified person or persons?" That educational environments such as highly organized or completely free classrooms are differentially effective with students of varying personalities or abilities, is widely recognized. Our attempt here is to coordinate or "match" the environment and person most effectively by use of a theoretical model.

The environmental prescriptions for each stage are derived from the "conceptual work" in Figure 12–1 by simply reasoning that the optimal environment for a person at a given stage will be that one which will foster the specific conceptual work at that stage. These stage-specific optimal environments which summarize the change model are shown in Table 12–1.

In attempts to test the relevance of these developmental stages for prescribing specific environments, Hunt combined theoretical deductions and some empirical observation in the form of teacher responses to what procedures were most effective with children at different stages. Many of these empirical observations were obtained by Hunt (1965*a*) when he formed three stage-similar classrooms in three grades in a junior high school which remained together for the school year. It was from this pilot study that empirical observations were taken from teacher feedback.

Environmental prescriptions or the programming of environmental experiences designed to enhance the functioning of disturbed children who manifest certain behaviors or clusters of behaviors may move us closer to effectively meeting such children's needs.

Mann and Phillips (1967) criticize the tendency to fractionate a child's problems and approaches to assisting him. Environmental programming that assumes a broader stance in terms of intervention may help us avoid this tendency. The current interest in learning problems of children, including disturbed children, may represent Mann's concern in that the child is viewed as composed of an almost infinitesimal number of functions, many of which may be in need of remediation. In itself, this view may not be unfavorable, but the translation to programs remains elusive. A review of

TABLE 12-1
STAGE CHARACTERISTICS AND OPTIMAL ENVIRONMENTS

Stage	Characteristics	Optimal Environment
Sub I	Impulsive, poorly socialized, egocentric, inattentive	Accepting but firm; clearly consistent with minimum of alternatives.
Stage I	Complaint, dependent on authority, concerned with rules	Encouraging independence within normative structure
Stage II	Independent, questioning, self-assertive.	Highly autonomous with numerous alternatives and low normative pressure

the literature points out some beginning trend toward more unified frameworks (Hewett, 1968; Warren, 1966; Quay, 1968).

Taking Bower's (1967) notion of "programming specific ego-processes into educational experiences," the procedures specified by Goodrich and Boomer (1958, p. 286) appear to be aimed at Stage II children who are resistant to change.

Preventive: (avoid threatening existing ego controls)
1. Therapist recognizes that he is not obligated to interpret or limit symptomatic behavior that is not disruptive or currently operating as resistance.
2. Therapist deliberately avoids mobilizing currently uncontrollable core conflict.
3. Therapist refrains from confronting child with his psychopathology when the intervention seems likely to generate a disruptive degree of anxiety.

Supportive: (help child maintain ego controls under stress)
1. Therapist is alert to situations that are likely to overload children's ego controls and he provides clear supportive structuring.
2. Therapist helps child to maintain his ego control in a variety of situations by constantly evaluating the child's current frustration tolerance.
3. Therapist helps child to maintain or regain control by deliberate expression of positive interest.
4. Therapist firmly and clearly limits socially intolerable behavior.

Restitutive: (help child regain control after temporary failure)
1. Therapist, when setting limits to disapproved behavior, relates the intervention to an established policy.
2. In dealing with a child who is temporaily flooded by anxiety, therapist promotes recovery by:

a. Permitting the child to regain control in his own way.
b. Giving the child the undivided attention of a trusted adult.
c. Permitting the child as much interpersonal distance as he needs.

The pioneering work by Redl, growing out of a number of group-care projects such as the Detroit Group Project, Pioneer House, and the National Institute for Mental Health project for severely aggressive boys; Bettelheim (1950) in his organizing every aspect of a residential treatment program to meet the emotional growth needs of disturbed children; and the University of Michigan Fresh Air Camp (McNeil, 1957) are all dramatic testimony to the efficacy of designing environment-specific interventions based on the ego dimensions children present themselves with.

The resistance to change evidenced by many disturbed children may reflect the type of ego structure that is closed or resistant as opposed to an open structure. Education should take on, as do other mental health fields, the goal of aiding the child to progress from closed to open conceptual structures. Harvey, Hunt, and Schroeder, (1961, p. 340) state the following:

The goal of education in a democratic society such as ours is (or should be) to provide the conditions to produce more abstract conceptual structure. Educational procedures therefore aim not only to induce progression to the next abstract stage, when such progressive leaps are appropriate, but also to maintain sufficient openness to progression continuously so that closedness and arrestation do not occur. If the child can be kept either in progression or in preparation for progression, the necessity for use of time-consuming, difficult procedures for decreasing closedness described in the last section is unnecessary. Thus, one goal of education is also the prevention of excessive arrestation or closedness.

For those disturbed children who are most resistant to change because of a lack of ego skills or the closedness of their conceptual stage, there is a need for direct and extensive intervention. One example of such an intervention would be play therapy which offers the advantage of placing the child into an environment that is interpersonal in nature and allows him to look at himself as well as his interactions with the therapist.

In discussing the essential aspects of play therapy, Cowen and Trippe (1963, p. 536) state: "Probably the area of greatest agreement among child therapists representing different schools, would be in the fundamental importance of the therapist-child relationship." Cowen and Trippe's discussion is a rather complete one and places the broad range of play-therapy techniques and concepts into perspective for those interested in such interventions.

Perhaps it is significant that this chapter ends on a theme that emphasizes the value of positive relationships with children. All too often we tend to think of doing things to children and not with them. The programs and techniques we have discussed are only as effective as the adults involved and the relationships they have with the children. There may not be any magic in our skills and procedures, but there may be potential healing power in adult-child relationships.

THE BEGINNING

More appropriate than a summary statement may be a statement of where we go from here. It is too early to write a summary and conclusion. It is hoped that this chapter has captured some of the exciting developments currently taking place in our efforts to assist children who experience difficulties in learning and adjusting. A survey of the references used points out how diverse are the interests and concerns of an equally diverse sample of professional practitioners.

It would seem a healthy thing if many types of professionals and disciplines continue to express research and clinical interests in assisting disturbed children. In the process of capitalizing on the varied interests of many groups, it would be equally healthy if we allowed many points of view to mature to the point where more definitive results and information could be obtained. It is alarming to see professionals prematurely closing off areas of investigation.

Similarly, we need to stretch our sights to encompass even more creative sources of mental-health manpower. The use of children to tutor other children is exciting and is often referred to as cross-age relationships. There are tutoring projects being conducted in neighborhood fire stations using firemen as tutors! The range of possibilities is only now becoming apparent.

Whatever our theoretical and practical orientations may be, we are still talking about human relationships—the children and our interactions with them. In the development of programs, environments, and interventions, we need to display the kinds of creative planning and openness we hope they will achieve some day. When all is said and done, the outcome needs to be that of providing disturbed children with opportunities for communicating with others and with themselves. Their learning experiences need to take place in environments that provide alternatives for them and with individuals who believe in children's capacities to grow and profit from concerted efforts to assist their "becoming."

And, finally, as we come to identify rather heavily with these children, many of whom have been exposed to gross distortions in their encounters with life, we must heed Maslow's (1968) reminder "to transcend our foolish tendency to let our compassion for the weak generate hatred for the strong." We need to keep in mind that as we focus on child change, we need to place ourselves in the equation and be equally willing to change and look at our behavior in order that we may be of value to children.

References

Allinsmith, W., & Goethals, G. W. *The role of schools in mental health.* New York: Basic Books Inc., Publishers, 1962.

Auerswald, E. H. Cognitive development and psychopathology in the urban environment. In P. S. Graubard (Ed.), *Children against schools.* Chicago: Follett Publishing Company, 1969, pp. 181–201

Badt, M. I. Attitudes of university studies toward exceptional children and special education. *Exceptional Children,* 1957, *23,* 286–290.

Barker, R. G. (Ed.). *The stream of behavior.* New York: Appleton-Century-Crofts, 1963.

———, & Gump, P. V. *Big school, small school: High school size and student behavior.* Stanford, Calif.: Stanford University Press, 1964.

Beilin, H. Teachers' and clinicians' attitudes toward the behavioral problems of children: A reappraisal. *Child Development,* 1959, *30,* 9–25.

Bell, R. Q. The problem of direction of effects in studies of parents and children. Paper presented at the Conference on Research

Methodology in Parent-Child Interaction, Upstate Medical Center, Syracuse, N. Y., October 1968.

Bettelheim, B. *Love is not enough.* Glencoe, Ill.: Free Press, 1950.

Bower, E. M. The confluence of the three rivers—ego-processes. In E. M. Bower and W. G. Hollister (Eds.), *Behavioral science frontiers in education.* New York: John Wiley & Sons, Inc., 1967, pp. 48–71

———, Shellhammer, T. A., & Daily, J. M. School characteristics of male adolescents who later became schizophrenic. *American Journal of Orthopsychiatry,* 1960, *30,* 712–719.

Bower, E. M., Tashnovian, P. J., & Larson, C. A. *A process for early identification of emotionally disturbed children.* Sacramento: California State Department of Education, 1958.

Cohen, *et al.* An inquiry into variations of teacher-child communications: Implications for treatment of emotionally ill children. In P. Knoblock (Ed.), *Educational programming for emotionally disturbed children: The decade ahead.* Syracuse, N.Y.: Syracuse University Press, 1965, pp. 71–101.

Coleman, J. C., & Sandher, M. S. A descriptive-relational study of 364 children referred to a university clinic for learning disorders. *Psychological Reports,* 1967, *20,* 1091–1105.

Cowen, E. L., & Trippe, M. J. Psychotherapy and play techniques with the exceptional child. In W. M. Cruickshank (Ed.), *Psychology of exceptional children and youth.* New York: Prentice-Hall, Inc., 1963, pp. 526–591.

Cruickshank, *et al.* *A teaching method for brain-injured and hyperactive children.* Syracuse: N. Y.: Syracuse University Press, 1961.

Dreikurs, R. *Psychology in the classroom* (2nd ed.). New York: Harper & Row, Publishers, 1968.

Farnham-Diggary, S. Self, future, and time: A developmental study of the concepts of psychotic, brain-damaged, and normal children. *Child Development Monographs,* 1966, *31* (1), 1–63.

Feldhusen, J., Thurston, J., & Benning, J. Classroom behavior, intelligence and

PETER KNOBLOCK

achievement. *Journal of Experimental Education,* 1967, *36,* 82–87.

Fernald, G. M. *Remedial techniques in basic school subjects.* New York: McGraw-Hill Book Company, 1943.

Fisher, R. Failure of the conceptual styles test to discriminate normal and highly impulsive children. *Journal of Abnormal Psychology,* 1966, *71,* 429–431.

———. Social schema of normal and disturbed school children. *Journal of Educational Psychology,* 1967, *58,* 88–92.

Ganter, G., Yeakel, M. & Polansky, N. A. *Retrieval from limbo: The intermediary group treatment of inaccessible children.* New York: Child Welfare League, 1967.

Gardner, R. W. The effects of emotional disturbance on cognitive behavior. Paper presented at the Meeting of the California Department of Education, San Francisco, October 1966.

Getzels, J. W., & Thelen, H. A. The classroom group as a unique social system. In N. B. Henry (Ed.), *The dynamics of instructional groups.* 59th yearbook. Chicago: University of Chicago Press, National Society for Study of Education, 1960.

Gnagey, W. J. *Controlling classroom misbehavior.* Washington, D. C.: NEA, 1965.

Goodrich, D. W., & Boomer, D. S. Some concepts about therapeutic intervention with hyperaggressive children. Parts I and II. *Social Casework,* 1958, *39,* 207–213, 286–292.

Gottfried, N. W., & Jones, R. L. Career choice factors in special education. *Exceptional Children,* 1964, *30,* 218–223.

Graubard, P. Psycholinguistic correlates of reading disability in disturbed, delinquent children. *Journal of Special Education.* 1967, *1,* 363–368.

Gronlund, N. E., & Anderson, L. Personality characteristics of socially accepted, socially neglected, and socially rejected junior high school pupils. *Educational Administration and Supervision,* 1957, *43,* 329–338.

Harvey, O. J., Hunt, D. E., & Schroeder, H. M. *Conceptual systems and personality organization.* New York: John Wiley & Sons, Inc, 1961.

Hewett, F. M. *The emotionally disturbed child in the classroom.* Boston: Allyn & Bacon, Inc., 1968.

Hobbs, N. Helping disturbed children: Psycho-

logical and ecological strategies. *American Psychologist,* 1966, *21,* 1105–1115.

Hunt, D. E. Conceptual systems assessment in planning differential educational treatment and in measuring developmental change. Paper presented at the meeting of the American Psychological Association, Chicago, September 1965. (*b*)

———. Developmental change in culturally disadvantaged children and its implication for differential treatment. Paper presented at the 43rd International Convention of the Council for Exceptional Children, Portland, Oregon, April 1965. (*a*)

———, & Hardt, R. H. Developmental stage, delinquency, and differential treatment. *Journal of Research in Crime and Delinquency,* 1964, in press.

Jackson, P. W. *Life in classrooms.* New York: Holt, Rinehart & Winston, Inc., 1968.

Jan-Tausch, J. *Suicide of children: 1960–1963.* Trenton, N. J.: Special Education Services, Department of Education, 1964.

———, & Granstrom, R. *Who failed? A study of subject failure at the secondary school level.* Trenton, N. J.: New Jersey State Department of Education, 1967.

Johnson, G. O. Special education for the mentally handicapped—a paradox. *Exceptional Children,* 1962, *29,* 61–69.

Joint Commission on Mental Illness and Health. *Action for Mental Health.* New York: Science Editions, 1961.

Jones, R. L. & Gottfried, N. W. Preferences and configurations of interest in special class teaching. *Exceptional Children,* 1962, *28,* 371–377.

———, & Owens, A. The social distance of the exceptional: A study at the high school level. *Exceptional Children,* 1966, *32,* 551–556.

Kagan, J., *et al.* Information processing in the child: Significance of analytic and reflective attitudes. *Psychological Monographs,* 1964, *78,* (1), 1–37.

Ketcham, W. A., & Morse, W. C. Dimensions of children's social and psychological development related to school achievement. Cooperative Research Project No. 1286. Washington, D. C.: U. S. Office of Education, 1965.

Keuthe, J. L. Social schemas. *Journal of Abnormal and Social Psychology,* 1962, *64,* 31–38.

Kimball, B. Case studies in educational failure

during adolescence. *American Journal of Orthopsychiatry,* 1953, *23,* 406–415.

Knoblock, P. The concept of the special class in the education of emotionally disturbed children: Implications for placement of children and training of personnel. In Vivian Harway (Ed.), *The social and emotional problems of the school child.* Rochester, N. Y.: University of Rochester, 1964

————, & Farrell, R. A conceptual systems approach to grouping emotionally disturbed and slow learning children. Unpublished manuscript. Syracuse, N. Y.: Division of Special Education and Rehabilitation, 1969.

Knoblock, P., & Garcea, R. A. Teacher-child relationships in psychoeducational programming for emotionally disturbed children. In J. Hellmuth (Ed.), *Educational therapy.* Seattle: Special Child Publications, Inc., 1969, pp. 391–411.

Kounin, J. S., Friesen, W. V. & Norton, A. E. Managing emotionally disturbed children in regular classrooms. *Journal of Educational Psychology,* 1966, *57,* 1–13.

Kounin, J. S., & Gump, P. V. The ripple effect in discipline. *Elementary School Journal,* 1958, *59,* 158–162.

Kvaraceus, W. C. Forecasting delinquency: A three-year experiment. *Exceptional Children,* 1961, *27,* 429–435.

Lesser, G. S. The relationships between various forms of aggression and popularity among lower-class children. *Journal of Educational Psychology,* 1959, *50,* 20–25.

Levin, G. R., & Simmons, J. B. Response to praise by emotionally disturbed boys. *Psychological Reports,* 1962, *11,* 10.

Levitt, E. E. *The psychology of anxiety.* New York: The Bobbs-Merrill Company, 1967.

Lewis, W. W. Continuity and intervention in emotional disturbance: A review. *Exceptional Children,* 1965, *31,* 465–475.

Lord, F. E., & Wallace, H. M. Recruitment of special education teachers. *Exceptional Children,* 1949, *15,* 171–173.

Macfarlane, J. W., Allen, L., & Honzik, M. P. *A developmental study of the behavior problems of normal children between 21 months and 14 years.* Berkeley and Los Angeles: University of California Press, 1962.

Mann, L., & Phillips, W. A. Fractional practices in special education: A critique. *Exceptional Children,* 1967, *33,* 311–317.

Maslow, A. H. *Toward a psychology of being* (2nd ed.). New York: Van Nostrand, 1968, iv (Preface).

McDavid, J., & Schroeder, H. M. The interpretation of approval and disapproval by delinquents and non delinquent adolescents. *Journal of Personality,* 1957, *25,* 196–207.

McNeil, E. B. (Ed.). Therapeutic camping for disturbed youth. *Journal of Social Issues,* 1957, *13,* 3–63.

Medinnus, G. R., & Curtis, F. J. The relation between maternal self-acceptance and child acceptance. *Journal of Consulting .and Clinical Psychology,* 1963, *27,* 542–594.

Mental Health Research Unit. Persistence of emotional disturbances reported among second and fourth grade children. *Onondaga County School Studies.* Interim report No. 1. Syracuse, N. Y.: Mental Health Research Unit, 1963.

Meyers, C. E. Realities in teacher recruitment. *Mental Retardation,* 1968, *2,* 42–46.

Morse, W. C. Self concept in the school setting. *Childhood Education,* 1964, *41,* 195–201.

————, Bloom, R., & Dunn, J. *A study of school classroom behavior from diverse evaluative frameworks: Developmental mental health, substantive learning, group process.* United States Office of Education, 1961.

Morse, W. C., Cutler, R. L. & Fink, A. H. *Public school classes for the emotionally handicapped: A research analysis.* Washington, D. C.: Council for Exceptional Children, 1964.

Nunnally, J. C. *Popular conceptions of mental health: Their development and change.* New York: Holt, Rinehart & Winston, Inc., 1961.

Polsky, H. W. *Cottage six: The social system of delinquent boys in residential treatment.* New York: Russell Sage, 1962.

Powell, M., & Bergen, J. An investigation of the differences between tenth-, eleventh-, and twelfth-grade conforming and nonconforming boys. *Journal of Educational Research,* 1962, *56,* 184–190.

Quay, H. The facets of educational exceptionality: A conceptual framework for assessment, grouping, and instruction. *Exceptional Children,* 1968, *34,* 25–32.

Rabinovitch, R. D. *et al.* A research approach to reading retardation. *Neurology and Psychiatry in Childhood,* 1956, *34,* 363–396.

Redl, F. Clinical speculations on the concept of improvement. In N. J. Long, W. C. Morse, & Ruth G. Newman, *Conflict in the classroom*. Belmont, Calif.: Wadsworth Publishing Co. Inc., 1965, pp. 453–465.

———, The concept of the life space interview. *American Journal of Orthopsychiatry,* 1959, *29,* 1–18.

———, The concept of a therapeutic milieu. *American Journal of Orthopsychiatry,* 1959, *29,* 721–734.

———, The phenomenon of contagion and "shock effect" in group therapy. In K. R. Eissler (Ed.), *Searchlights on delinquency*. New York: International Universities Press, 1949, pp. 315–328.

———, & Wineman, D. *The aggressive child*. Glencoe, Ill.: Free Press, 1957.

Rhodes, W. C. Presidential Address, Council for Children with Behavioral Disorders. *Newsletter,* 1966, *4,* (1)

Robins, L. N. *Deviant children grow up*. Baltimore: The William & Wilkins Co., 1966.

Rosengren, R. The self in the emotionally disturbed. *American Journal of Sociology,* 1961, *66,* 454–462.

Rosenthal, R., & Jacobson, L. *Pygmalion in the classroom*. New York: Holt, Rinehart & Winston, Inc., 1968.

Scarpitti, F. R. Can teachers predict delinquency? *Elementary School Journal,* 1964, *65,* 130–136.

Schutz, W. C. *The interpersonal underworld*. Palo Alto, Calif.: Science & Behavior Books, Inc., 1966.

Schwartz, M., Fearn, G., & Stryker, S. A note on self conception and the emotionally disturbed role. *Sociometry,* 1966, *29,* 300.

Smith, L. M., & Geoffrey, W. *The complexities of an urban classroom: An analysis toward a general theory of teaching*. New York: Holt, Rinehart & Winston, Inc,, 1968.

Taylor, R. G. Personality traits and discrepant achievement: A review. *Journal of Counseling Psychology,* 1964, *11,* 76–82.

Thompson, A. C., & Trippe, J. J. A school based definition of emotionally disturbed children. Paper presented at meeting of university personnel training teachers of emotionally disturbed children, United States Office of Education, Washington, D. C., June 1965.

Tolor, A. Psychological distance in disturbed and normal children. *Psychological Reports,* 1968, *23,* 695–701.

Trippe, M. J. Conceptual problems in research on provisions for disturbed children. *Exceptional Children,* 1963, *29,* 400–406.

Vogel, E. F., & Bell, N. W. The emotionally disturbed child as the family scapegoat. In N. W. Bell and E. F. Vogel (Eds.), *The family*. Glencoe, Ill.: Free Press, 1960.

Waetjen, W. B., & Leeper, R. R. *Learning and mental health in the school*. Washington, D. C.: Association for Supervision and Curriculum Development, 1966.

Warren, M. Q. Classification of offenders as an aid to efficient management and effective treatment. Paper prepared for President's Commission on Law Enforcement and Administration of Justice, Task Force on Corrections, 1966.

Weinstein, L. Social Experience and Social Schemata. *Journal of Personality and Social Psychology,* 1967, *6,* 429–434.

———. Social Schemata of Emotionally Disturbed Boys. *Journal of Abnormal Psychology,* 1965, *70,* 457–461.

White, M. A. & Charry, J. (Eds.). *School disorder, intelligence, and social class*. New York: Teachers College Press, 1966.

Wickman, E. K. *Children's behavior and teachers' attitudes*. New York: Commonwealth Fund, 1928.

Wilderson, F. B. An exploratory study of reading skill deficiencies and psychiatric symptoms in emotionally disturbed children. *Reading Research Quarterly,* 1967, *2,* 47–73.

Zax, M., Cowen E. L., & Rappaport, J. Follow-up study of children identified early as emotionally disturbed. *Journal of Consulting and Clinical Psychology,* 1968, *32,* 369–374.

Delacato, C. H., 345
Delaney, F. I., 339
Delp, H. A., 518
Dembo, T., 50–52, 63, 269, 316, 318
Demuth, E. L., 457
Denhoff, E., 322, 332
Dentler, R. A., 79, 101, 110
Derbyshire, A., 418
Derner, G. F., 455–57
Detroit, Group Project, 594
Deutsch, E., 231, 270
Deutsch, F., 268
DeWitt Clinton High School (Bronx, New York), 559
Dexter, L. A., 78–79
Diamond, Isabella S., 212
Di Carlo, L., 425
Dickson, W. J., 369
Dictionary of Psychology, 247
Diderot, Denis, 212
Diedrich, W., 342
Diehl, C. F., 188
Dillon, E., 342
Distefano, M. K., Jr., 134
Dixon, Rebecca, 366
Doerfler, L., 417
Dokecki, P. R., 234
Dolanski, V., 242–43
Doll, E. A., 134, 154, 343
Dolphin, J. E., 317–19, 344–53, 378, 385; on distractibility, 373
Doman, R. J., 345, 404
Donlon, E. T., 282
Donofrio, A. F., 328, 334
Dornbuser, S., 331
Douglass, E., 203
Douglass, H., 536–37
Downs, M., 419
Dreikurs, R., 311, 575
Drever, J., 250
Drews, E. M., 537–38
Druz, W., 434
Dubnoff, B., 396
Dubo, S., 457, 479–80
Dubos, R. J., 454, 455
Dunbar, F., 442, 462, 471–72
Duncan, B. K., 250–51
Duncan, J., 500
Duncan, M. H., 204
Dunn, J., 586
Dunn, L. M., 100, 339–40, 506–7
Dunn, M., 33–34
Durkin, D., 543
Dye, H. B., 501

Eames, T. H., 184, 186, 293
Eatman, P. F., 237
Ebbinghaus, H., 190
Eddy, E. M., 101–2
Edgerton, R. B., 81–82, 101
Educational Policies Commission, 530
Eells, E., 463
Eells, K., 544
Efstathiou, A., 382
Ehrentheil, O. F., 442
Eichenwald, H. F., 145*n*
Eichold, S., 476
Eichorn, J. R., 249

Eisenberg, L., 376, 392
Eisenson, J., 147, 175, 177, 186, 190, 201, 206, 334; on aphasia, 180, 197–98; on auditory perceptual functions, 191, 197; on personality, 193–94; on voice defects in the blind, 235
Elkins, D., 543
Ellis, E., 400
Ellis, N. R., 134, 508
Elonen, A. S., 283–84
Enc, M. E., 241
Engle, A. M., 517–18
Erickson, G., 542
Erikson, K. T., 79, 110, 391
Ernhart, C. B., 385
Eustis, R. S., 186
Evans, F. M., 471
Everhart, R. W., 184
Etzel, B. C., 69
Ewart, A. G., 249
Ewing, A., 419, 425
Ewing, E., 419, 425
Exceptional Children, 147
Eysenck, H. J., 3

Fairbanks, G., 187, 241
Fairchild, S., 331
Falstein, E. I., 472
Farber, B., 96, 97, 100, 104, 108, 109, 519
Farber, D. J., 49
Farina, A., 96
Farnham-Diggory, S., 387, 577, 578, 580
Farrell, M., 432
Farrell, R., 591
Faust, O. A., 449
Fearn, G., 575, 577
Federal Office of Vocational Rehabilitation, 252
Felden, H. W., 239
Feldhusen, J., 507, 583
Fennimore, F., 390
Fernald, G. M., 406, 585
Fernald, M. R., 334
Ferris, E. B., Jr., 462
Ferster, C. B., 64, 71
Fertsch, P., 237
Festinger, L., 79
Fiedler, F. E., 204
Fiedler, M. F., 190
Fieldsteel, N. D., 133
Fillmore, E. A., 501
Fine, R., 481
Fine, R. H., 514
Finestone, S., 249
Fink, A. H., 568, 579, 584
Fischer, A. E., 473, 475
Fisher, G. H., 221
Fisher, L. A., 514
Fisher, R., 576, 590
Fisher, S., 398
Fisichelli, V. R., 386
Fiske, D. W., 3
Fitting, E. A., 262
Fitzelle, G. T., 479
Fitzgerald, D. C., 320
Fitzsimmons, R. M., 205
Fjeld, H. A., 272
Flanagan, J. C., 535, 543
Flescher, J., 285
Fletcher, S. G., 186

Groen, J., 480
Groht, M., 425
Gronlund, N. E., 571
Gruenberg, E. M., 104
Guertin, W. H., 122, 512
Guess, D., 286
Guilford, J. P., 122*n*, 146, 530, 541; intellect model of, 136, 531, 532, 541
Gullion, M. E., 64
Gump, P. V., 567, 572
Gunn, R., 322
Guskin, S. L., 75, 76, 80, 83–86, 97, 103, 104
Guthrie, G. M., 512
Gutman, N., 241

Hackbusch, F., 295
Haeussermann, E., 335, 341
Haggard, E. A., 381
Haggerty, M. E., 511
Hale, G. A., 504
Hall, J., 62
Hall, P., 428
Hall, W. T., 332
Hallahan, D. P., 366
Halstead, W. C., 343, 350
Halverson, H. M., 271
Hamilton, K. W., 7
Hammer, E. F., 552–53
Hammill, D., 342, 351
Hammill, I., 340
Hanks, J. R., 12, 324
Hanks, L. M., Jr., 12, 324
Hanvik, L. J., 371, 372
Hapeman, L. B., 248
Hardt, R. H., 591
Hardy, J., 419
Hardy, R. E., 263
Hardy, W., 417–19, 431
Haring, N., 322, 324
Haring, N. G., 400
Harley, R. K., 339–40
Harley, R. K., Jr., 230, 233–34
Harper, J., 325
Harris, D. H., 455
Harris, G., 433
Harris, H., 177, 181, 182, 200, 202–3, 205
Harris, J. C., 245
Harris, M. C., 479, 480
Harrower-Erickson, M. R., 343
Harte, T., 430
Hartl, E. M., 3
Hartlage, L. C., 241
Hartong, J. R., 249
Hartshorne, H., 155
Hartz, J., 455, 458
Harvard Educational Review, 550
Harvard Psycho-Acoustic Laboratories, 417
Harvey, O. J., 594
Harway, V. T., 321
Haselkorn, F., 463
Haskins, R. G., 4
Haskins' Laboratories, 245
Haslerud, G. M., 261–62
Haspiel, G., 417
Hastorf, A., 331
Hatfield, E. M., 214, 216
Hathaway, W., 288

Hatlen, P. N., 227, 238
Haussermann, E., 141
Hawk, T. L., 390
Haworth, M. H., 157
Hayes, S. P., 150, 272; on achievement tests, 226–28; on intelligence, 212, 222–23; on obstacle perception, 241–42; on sensory acuteness, 219, 221
HEAR Foundation, 433
Hebb, D. O., 443
Hebeler, J., 520
Heber, R., 496
Hecht, P. J., 150, 225
Heilman, A., 336–38
Heinzelmann, F., 463
Heiser, K., 513
Heller, Theodor, 212, 218, 236
Henderson, F., 239
Hendricks, M., 531
Hepfinger, L. M., 273
Herbert, M., 145
Herbert, M., 480
Hersh, J. B., 82
Heslinga, K., 265
Hewett, F. M., 368, 371, 594
Hewlett, I., 472
Hildreth, G., 184
Himes, J. S., 252, 259
Hinkle, L. E., 471–73
Hirsch, I., 415
Hirschenfang, S., 339
Hirt, J. B., 372–73
Hiskey, M., 422, 423
Hobbs, N., 402, 576
Hodges, W. L., 502
Hodsdon, A. F., 465
Hoepfner, R., 531, 541
Hogan, D., 432
Holden, R., 331
Holden, R. H., 322
Holder, R., 463–66
Holland, B. F., 237
Holoran, I. M., 336–38
Holquin, A. H., 453
Holzinger, K. J., 500–1
Homberger, A., 373
Honnard, R., 418
Honzik, M. P., 566
Hooft, F. 't, 265
Hoop, W. de, 342
Hoover, R. E., 296
Hopkins, K. D., 225
Hopkins, T. W., 322, 336–37
Horbach, H., 237–38
Horne, D., 405
Horowitz, M. J., 397
Howe, C. E., 510
Hudson, L., 534
Hughes, B. O., 135
Hughes, E. C., 87
Hughson, W., 422
Humphrey, Hubert H., 529, 530
Hunt, B. J., 377, 380, 384
Hunt, B. M., 145
Hunt, D. E., 590–91, 593, 594
Hunt, J. M., 551
Hunter, W. F., 250
Hurd, J. B., 476

Hurlin, R. G., 213
Husni, M. A., 264
Hutterites, 102–3

Ilg, F. L., 271
Illingworth, R. S., 400, 447
Imamura, S., 274–75
Institute for Personality Assessment and Research (IPAR), 539
Institute for the Achievement of Human Potential, 404
Instructor, The, 540, 549
Irwin, J. V., 188–91
Irwin, O., 342, 351
Isbister, J. L., 459
Isikow, H., 231–32
Izard, C. E., 321

Jackson, J., 184
Jackson, P. W., 531–34, 553–54, 566
Jacobi, H. G., 476
Jacobs, G., 432
Jacobs, J. F., 387, 388
Jacobs, M. A., 479
Jacobson, L., 88, 91, 369, 370, 550–51, 591
Jaeger, W., 202
Jaffe, J., 85, 325
James, William, 212, 221, 242
Jan-Tausch, J., 575, 576
Jay, E. S., 156
Jenkin, N., 380–81
Jenkins, R. L., 316
Jenkins, S., 330
Jenne, W., 428
Jenne, W. C., 428
Jensen, A. R., 101, 504, 549–50
Jensen, C. D., 333
Jerger, J., 415
Jerome, E. A., 243, 245
Jervis, F. M., 261–62, 267–68
Jessner, L., 479
Jewish Guild for the Blind in New York, 258, 282–83
Jewish National Home for Asthmatic Children, 482
Johannsen, D. E., 474
John Tracy Clinic, 432–33
Johnson, D. E., 249
Johnson, G. O., 495, 498, 503, 568; on adjustment, 512, 515; on development, 505–6; on instruction, 507; on parent education, 519–20; on transference, 504
Johnson, Lyndon B., 529, 530
Johnson, M. K., 133
Johnson, W., 176–79, 190, 205, 206; on personality, 181, 193; on stuttering, 201–2
Johnston, P., 432
Joint Commission for Mental Health, 573
Jolles, I., 511
Jones, J. W., 214
Jones, M. H., 339, 342
Jones, R. L., 95–96, 256–58, 327, 570, 574
Jordan L. J., 103–4
Jordan, S., 285, 296
Josselyn, I. M., 450, 463
Journal of Applied Behavior Analysis, 71
Journal of Experimental Child Psychology, 71

Judas, I., 472
Justman, J., 465, 466
Juurmaa, 224

Kagan, J., 590
Kahn, H., 163
Kaliski, L., 383, 385
Kammerer, R. C., 323, 327
Kanner, L., 255, 287, 512
Kaplan, B., 101, 102
Karelitz, R., 386
Karelitz, S., 386
Karnes, M. B., 292
Karp, E., 376, 383–84
Kates, S., 426–28
Kates, W., 428
Katz, E., 130, 339, 341
Kederis, C. J., 241
Keeve, P. J., 317
Keith, J. D., 460, 461
Keller, Helen, 420
Kelley, H. H., 76
Kemph, J. P., 62
Kendall, B. S., 134
Kendall, D., 418
Kennedy, John F., 529
Kennedy, L., 183
Kennedy, R. J. R., 517
Kennedy, W. B., 475
Kenyon, E. L., 272, 273
Kephart, N. C., 371, 397–99; on sensory-motor training, 402–3
Kerby, C. E., 288–91
Kern, W. H., 515
Kerr, C., 65–70
Kerr, N. C., 43
Kessler, J. W., 396
Keuthe, J. L., 576
Khatena, J., 542
Kimball, B., 582
Kimmel, J., 452
Kingsley, R. F., 504
Kirk, E. W., 386
Kirk, S., 424, 429
Kirk, S. A., 103, 145, 500, 502, 507, 515
Klapper, R., 339
Klapper, Z. S., 312*n,* 316, 346, 348, 352
Klaus, R., 152
Klausmeier, H., 507, 509
Klebanoff, L., 97
Kleck, R., 62
Kleck, R. E., 95
Kleffner, F., 422
Klein, G. S., 278
Klein, H. P., 62
Klineberg, O., 3
Klove, H., 387
Knapp, P. H., 480, 481
Knoblock, P., 565, 568, 574, 591
Knotts, J. R., 250
Kobler, F., 340
Koch, H. L., 250
Koenig, F. G., 462
Koepp-Baker, H., 205
Kogan, K. L., 333
Kogan, N., 533–34
Komisar, D., 223
Koppitz, E. M., 380

MacIntyre, G. M., 507
MacKane, K., 423
McKibben, S., 323
Mackie, J. B., 388
MacKinnon, D. W., 539
McLaughlin, S. C., 295
McNeil, E. B., 594
MacPherson, J., 424
MacQueen, J. C., 375
McReynolds, J., 250
McWilliams, B. J., 206
Mader, J., 325
Maier, N. R. F., 384
Malpass, L. F., 510
Mandola, J., 228
Mann, L., 598
Marble, A., 476
Margolis, M., 480
Mark, H. J., 381
Marker, C. B., 455
Marlens, H. S., 446
Martin, W. E., 134
Mase, D. J., 187
Masling, J. M., 335
Maslow, A. H., 596
Massie, D., 287–88
Mast, R., 432
Matthews, J., 183
Matthews, R. A., 442
Mattis, S., 282
Mauney, J., 244–45
Maurer, E., 478
Maxfield, K. E., 226, 234, 237, 272–73
May, M. A., 155
Mayman, M., 78
Mead, G. H., 390–92, 394–95
Medinnus, G. R., 579
Mednick, S. A., 543
Meeker, M. N., 541
Mehlman, B., 514
Melcer, J. D., 351
Meng, H., 311, 314
Menkes, J. H., 376, 377
Menkes, M. N., 376, 377
Menninger, K., 78
Menninger, W. C., 316, 471
Mental Health Research Fund, 279
Menyuk, P., 189
Merrifield, P. R., 541
Merrill, B. R., 455
Merrill, M. A., 499
Merry, F. K., 231, 250
Merry, R. V., 222, 231, 250
Meyer, E., 343, 430
Meyerowitz, J. H., 98, 104
Meyers, C. E., 574
Meyerson, Lee, 1, 13, 296, 309, 316; on auditory
    measurement, 418; on behavior modification,
    64–70; on personality, 256; on rehabilitation,
    62; on role of interaction, 319; on schools for
    the deaf, 421
Michael, J., 64, 66, 418, 428
Michal-Smith, H., 319
Michigan School at Flint, 431
Michigan School for the Blind, 283–84
Midcentury White House Conference, 184, 193
Midwest Regional Media Center for the Deaf,
    434

Milazzo, T. C., 516
Miles, W. R., 250
Milisen, R., 177
Miller, D. Y., 352–53
Miller, E. A., 319, 336–38
Miller, H., 107
Miller, H., 478–79, 482
Miller, L. K., 504
Mills, A. W., 177
Mills, C. W., 107
Miner, L. E., 235–36
Miron, M., 241
Mitchell, B. C., 501–3
Moeller, D., 177
Mohr, G. J., 443
Moncur, J. P., 181, 202
Montague, Harriet, 433
Montessori, M., 406
Moore, W. E., 203–4
Moores, D., 428
Morant, R. B., 382
Morkovin, B., 430, 433
Morris, J. E., 232, 241
Morris, M. E., 239
Morris, R. P., 481
Morse, D. P., 460
Morse, J. L., 275
Morse, S. A., 380–81
Morse, W. C., 568, 582, 584, 586; on self-con-
    cept, 578; on special classes, 579
Moses, C., 472
Mosher, F., 333
Moskowitz, S., 465, 466
Moss, J. W., 103–4
Mowatt, M., 328
Mowrer, D. E., 68, 195
Moyer, J. H., 477
Mudler, R. L., 205
Mueller, M. W., 292–93
Murphy, A. T., 205, 257
Murphy, G. E., 50, 51
Murphy, K., 197
Murry, T., 426
Mursten, B. I., 157
Mussen, P. H., 326
Muthard, J. E., 322–24
Myers, J. A., 453
Myklebust, H., 422, 424, 425, 429, 430, 434

Nagera, H., 230, 279
Nagge, J. W., 319
National Association for Mental Health, 573
National Health Survey, 478
National Institute of Mental Health, 258, 594
National Institute of Neurological Diseases and
    Blindness, 366
National Society for Crippled Children and
    Adults, Inc., 366
Neham, S., 513
Nellhaus, G., 367
Nelson, L. S., 477
Nemetz, S. J., 480, 481
Neuhaus, E. C., 462, 463, 466, 481
Neuringer, C., 382
New York City Board of Education, 466–69
Newby, H., 190, 415
Newell, H. W., 316
Newland, T. E., 115, 129, 225, 541

Newman, H. H., 501
Newman, J., 440
Neyhus, A., 430
Nodine, J. H., 477
Noffsinger, T., 529
Nolan, C. Y., 214, 227, 232–34, 239, 241; on type size, 292, 293
Norman, R. D., 130, 340
Norris, M., 274
Norton, A. E., 572
Norton, F. M., 245
Norwood Committee on England, 530
NSPB fact book, 216
Nudd, E. M., 146
Nunnally, J. C., 573–74
Nussbaum, J., 322

Oden, M. H., 122
Odom, P., 426
Oettinger, K. B., 327
Ohwaki, Y., 225
Oleron, P., 183, 423
Olshansky, S., 98, 104–5
Olson, W. C., 135
Omwake, E. G., 230, 277–78
O'Neill, J., 425
Onondaga County School Studies, 571
Orbach, J., 397
Orvis, C., 340
Oseretsky, 509
Osborne, J. G., 70
Owen, F. W., 481
Owens, A., 258, 327, 570
Owens, W. A., 543
Oyer, H., 425

Pacific State Hospital (Pomona, California), 283
Paine, R. S., 376, 385
Pannbacker, M., 205–6
Parloff, M. B., 551–52
Parmelee, A., 285
Parnicky, J. J., 163
Parson, O. A., 62
Parsons, T., 444
Parsons Language Project, 418
Parsons State Home and Training School, 432
Pasamanick, B., 381
Passow, A. H., 559
Paterson, D. G., 3
Paterson, J., 432
Patterson, C. H., 319, 324, 330
Patterson, G. R., 64
Patterson, R. M., 377, 384
Patton, F. E., 187
Paul, J. L., 366
Pauls, M., 417
Payne, W. W., 471
Peabody, R. L., 289, 292
Peacher, W. G., 459
Pearson, G. H. J., 311, 316, 327
Pearson, J., 417
Peck, J. R., 104
Peckarsky, A., 181, 194
Peckham, R. A., 517
Pelser, H. E., 480
Penfield, W., 343
Perceptual-Motor Learning Laboratory, 245
Perkins Institute, 431

Perkins School for the Blind, 225, 240
Pero, J. F., 515
Perrott, M. C., 64
Pertsch, C. F., 498, 507
Peshkin, M. M., 479, 482
Peters, C., 419
Peters, D. M., 341, 344
Peters, J. P., 470
Peterson, D. R., 78
Peterson, E., 423, 424
Peterson, L., 517
Pfaeffle, H., 515
Phelps, J. K., 386
Phelps, W. M., 142, 316, 322, 336
Phillips, S., 428
Phillips, W. A., 593
Piaget, J., 315, 351, 381
Pick, A. D., 239
Pick, H. L., Jr., 239
Pierce, M. L., 387, 388
Pincus, J. H., 376
Pintner, R., 147, 183, 334, 428; on gifted children, 149–50; on intelligence of the deaf, 424; on the partially seeing, 287, 294
Pioneer House, 594
Piotrowski, Z., 134, 343
Pitman, D. J., 222
Platt, H., 263
Platt Report of 1959, 447
Plant, T. F. A., 101, 102
Podolsky, E., 473
Poit, C., 381
Polansky, N. A., 577
Polatsek, I., 514
Pollock, A., 347
Pollock, O., 480
Polsky, H. W., 572
Polzien, M., 283–84
Pomp, H., 331
Pond, D., 145
Porter, R. B., 516
Powell, D., 203–4
Powell, M., 580
Powers, M. H., 177
Preger, P., 78
Prehm, 504
Prigal, S. J., 476, 477
Pringle, M. L. K., 265
Proceedings of International Conference on Oral Education of the Deaf, 425
Pronovost, W., 197
Prosen, H., 398
Proshansky, H., 243, 245–46
Prugh, D. G., 441, 445–46, 449
Psychological Abstracts, 71
Purcell, K., 480
Purkey, W. W., 558

Quarrington, B., 203
Quay, H., 594
Quiet One, The (film), 587
Quigley, S., 428

Rabin, A. I., 122, 157
Rabinovitch, R. D., 582
Radler, D. H., 398–99
Rainer, J., 431
Raph, J. B., 559

Schutz, R. E., 68
Schutz, W. C., 579
Schwartz, M., 575, 577
Scott, R. A., 87
Sears, P. S., 390
Seashore, T. E., 222
Sechrest, L., 514
Seelye, W. S., 283
Segel, D., 535
Selye, H., 477
Senden, M. von, 219
Shapiro, B., 225
Shapiro, M. B., 373
Sheehan, J., 204
Sheldon, W. H., 3–4
Shelsky, I., 332, 452
Sheridan, M., 419
Sherman, V., 390
Sherrington, D. S., 384
Shirley, M., 424
Shoemaker, P. J., 205
Shofer, 345
Shontz, F. C., 60, 62
Shore, M. F., 444
Short, J. F., 99
Shure, N., 479, 480
Shurrager, H. C., 228
Shurrager, P. S., 228
Siegel, B. L., 279
Siegel, I. M., 249
Siegenthaler, B., 417
Sievers, D. J., 130, 340, 386–87
Silberberg, N., 325
Siller, J., 62, 320
Silver, A., 312, 396
Silver, M. J., 369–70
Silverman, S. R., 189–90, 415, 420–21, 424
Simmel, M., 330-31
Simmons, J. B., 578
Simon, A. J., 463
Simpson, 344–45
Singer, J. L., 271
Sinha, U., 338
Sisney, V. V., 406
Skeels, H. M., 501, 549
Skinner, B. F., 64
Sloan, W., 134, 504, 509–12
Sloane, H. N., Jr., 71
Smelo, L. S., 476
Smith, D. T., 454
Smith, J. O., 183
Smith, L. L., 517
Smith, L. M., 566
Smith, M. B., 334
Smith, M. H. D., 453, 454
Smith, R. M., 206
Smitts, S., 331
Smock, C., 320
Snow, R. E., 370
Snyder, R., 514, 515
Society for the Hard of Hearing, 49
Soderberg, G., 203–4
Sohn, D. L., 323
Soldwedel, B., 154
Solnit, A. J., 230, 277–78, 447
Solomon, I. L., 157
Sommers, V. S., 253–56
Sontag, L. W., 450, 451

Spaulding, P. J., 274
Spencer, M. B., 281
Spicker, H. H., 103, 104, 502
Spiegel, L. A., 11
Spitz, R. A., 287, 445
Spivack, G., 381, 383
Spradlin, J., 418
Spriestersbach, D. C., 178, 179, 187, 204–5
Springer, N., 424
Stachnik, T., 64
Staffieri, J. R., 399–400
Stanton, J. E., 498
Stanton, M., 147, 334
Starbuck, H. B., 236
Starr, B. D., 157
Starr, P. H., 442, 469, 471, 472, 474
State Superintendent of Public Instruction, 500
Steinberg, W., 218, 219
Steinquist, G., 285
Steinschneider, A., 442, 479
Steinzor, L. V., 258–59
Stephens, J. M., 481
Stepp, R., 433, 434
Sternfeld, L., 105
Sterritt, G., 419
Stevens, D. A., 383
Stevens, G., 431–32
Stevens, S. S., 3
Stevenson, Adlai E., 529–30
Stevenson, H. W., 504, 507
Stevenson, I., 442
Stewart, C., 417
Stewart, M., 333
Stinchfield, S. M., 234–35
Stoesser, A. V., 477
Stolurow, L. M., 241
Stolz, H. R., 13, 296
Stolz, L. M., 13, 296
Stone, A. A., 275–76
Stone, D. R., 126
Strang, R., 531
Strauss, A. A., 345, 400, 500; on brain damage, 145, 343, 344, 347, 350, 352, 354, 356, 371, 373, 378, 379, 385; on meticulosity, 351; on perseveration, 377
Strauss, F., 317
Strauss, S., 263
Street, R. F., 153
Streiner, B. F., 271
Streit, H., 177
Streitfeld, J. W., 228
Streng, A., 424, 429
Stryker, S., 575, 577
Stuart, Jesse, 544–45
Stubblefield, R. L., 480
Suinn, R. M., 225
Summers, L., 326
Supa, M., 243
Supreme Court, U.S., 101n
Sussman, M. B., 472, 475, 476
Sutherland, E. H., 83
Syracuse Psychiatric Hospital (Fairmont, New York), 282
Szanton, V. L., 477, 478
Szasz, T. S., 402
Szurek, S. A., 450

Taba, H., 543

Taboroff, L. H., 264
Taibl, R. M., 143, 338–39
Talbot, B., 463–64
Tallman, I., 96
Tan, C. A., 542
Tappan, P. W., 101
Taran, L. M., 465, 468
Tashnovian, P. J., 583
Taylor, C. W., 535–36, 543
Taylor, E. M., 130, 164
Taylor, R. G., 581
Tell, J., 418
Templin, M., 178, 194*n,* 426
Terman, L. M., 499, 544
Teuber, H., 354
Thelander, H. E., 386
Thelen, H. A., 572
Thomas, J. E., 283
Thomas, M. L., 239
Thompson, A. C., 568–70
Thompson, J., 269
Thompson, G. G., 443
Thoresen, C. E., 71
Thorndike, R. L., 88, 370, 551
Thorne, F. C., 513
Thuma, B., 381
Thurston, J., 333, 583
Thurstone, L. L., 499, 534
Tillman, M. H., 224, 236
Time Magazine, 103, 103*n*
Tisdall, W. J., 136
Titley, R., 327
Tizard, J., 504
Toglia, U., 418
Toigo, R., 519
Tolor, A., 576
Tolstoi, E., 471
Torrance, E. P., 528, 541, 542, 547, 554; on
    adolescents with originality, 260–61; on the
    creative, 559–60; on fourth-grade slump in
    creativity, 560; on Getzels-Jackson effect, 532–
    33; on music ability, 542–43; on self-concept,
    557–58
Toth, Z., 215
Totman, H. E., 275
Toynbee, Arnold, 529
Tracht, V. S., 143
Tracy, Mrs. Spencer, 433
Tracy Clinic, 432–33
Traub, A. C., 397
Tretakoff, M., 282
Trippe, M. J., 324–25, 370, 402, 567, 568–70,
    595
Trismen, D. A., 227–28
Trombly, T., 342
Troutman, M. R., 540
Truschel, L., 242
Tucker, R. L., 544–45
Tucker, W. B., 3
Tuft, H. S., 479
Tumin, M. M., 107
Tureen, J. A., 202
Turnbull, J. W., 480
Turner, J. L., 399
Tuttman, S., 444

Ufkess, J., 250
Ullmann, L. P., 64, 71

Ulrich, R., 64
Underberg, R. P., 265, 266
Union League of the Deaf, 47
United Cerebral Palsy of Queens, 315

Van der Kolk, J., 423
Van Riper, C., 197, 205, 206; on aggressive be-
    havior, 192–93; on articulation, 184, 188–89,
    191; on auditory memory, 189, 190; on delayed
    speech, 182; on intellectual development, 182;
    on reading, 184; on stuttering, 201
Vaughan, G. F., 446
Vaught, G., 333
Vegas, O. V., 378
Vera Cruz, P. G., 454
Vernier, C. M., 455, 456
Vernon, M., 423, 430
Verrillo, R. T., 265
Vigaroso, H. R., 249
Villey, P., 242, 247
Vineberg, S. E., 262
Vlad, P., 460, 461
Vogel, E. F., 573
Volta Review, 147
Voss, W., 220

Waetjen, W. B., 586
Wageman, R. M., 70
Wagner, E. M., 281
Wakstein, D. J., 197
Wakstein, M. P., 197
Wallace, E., 294
Wallace, H. M., 574
Wallach, M. A., 533–34
Wallen, N. E., 344, 347, 350–53, 378; on dis-
    tractibility, 373
Wallin, J. E. W., 500, 512
Walton, J. N., 400
Ward, P., 415
Ware, L. E., 333
Warren, M. Q., 599
Watson, L. S., Jr., 70–71
Wattron, J. B., 225
Weaver, C. H., 184
Webb, C., 432
Wedell, K., 339, 353–54
Weikart, D. P., 502
Weil, W. B., Jr., 472, 475, 476
Weinberg, B., 236
Weiner, B. B., 282
Weingarten, K. P., 163
Weinstein, L., 576, 578–80
Weiss, D. A., 180, 199–200
Weiss, J. H., 481
Wells, J., 502
Wenar, C., 321, 443
Wepman, J., 204, 386
Werblo, D., 558
Werner, H., 316, 344, 347, 378, 379, 400; on
    autokinetic phenomenon, 381; on brain-injured,
    145, 312*n,* 343, 346, 350; on conceptualization,
    385; on dissociation, 352; on figure-ground
    perceptions, 345; on meticulosity, 351; on per-
    severation, 377; on stimulus-bound concept,
    373; on visual-motor perception, 348
West, R. W., 190
Westinghouse Science Talent Search, 551–52
Westlake, H., 206

GENERAL INDEX

Adjustment (cont.)
41, 45; counseling on, 45–59; evaluation of, 41; of externally controlled, 92; in illness, 451; patterns of, 43–49; perceptions of disabled in, 55–58; problem of, 42–43; self-perceptions in, 154–55, 309–10; testing of, 153–58; values in, 48, 54–55, 57. *See also* Emotional adjustment; Maladjustment; Vocational adjustment; *and specific disability*

Adolescent Emotional Factors Inventory, 263

Adolescents: brain injury in, 376, 377, 381; with chronic illness, 483; creativity in, 531, 553–56; with diabetes, 470, 475–76; dissident youth as, 556–57; emotionally disturbed, 582; gifted, 531, 537–39, 553–56, 560; with heart disorders, 463, 465–67; impaired vision in, 253–56, 259, 263–68, 276, 283, 285, 294; orthopedically handicapped, 320, 321, 331, 332; speech defects in, 203–5, 207; tuberculosis affecting, 454, 458. *See also* Delinquent behavior and delinquents

Albinism, 289, 290

Alcoholism, 406

Allergic disorders, 476–78

Allport-Vernon-Lindzey Study of Values, 556–57

Ambidexterity, 186

Amblyopia ex anopsia, 294, 295

Ammons Full-Range Picture Vocabulary Test, 142, 189, 340, 341

Amputations, 320, 321, 330, 452

Anophthalmia, 286; congenital, 225, 226, 271

Anxiety, 317, 324; in hospitalization, 446–48, 456; in illness, 449–52, 462, 482; maladjustment and, 41, 319; neurotic, 456, 463; parental attitudes and, 443–44, 446, 450, 463; in self-concept, 452; in speech defects, 192, 205

Anxiety Scale for the Blind, 263

Aphasia and aphasics, 386; with auditory impairments, 421, 422, 431; congenital, 180, 197; learning capacities with, 141; speech defects and, 176, 177, 179, 180, 184–85, 191, 197–99

Aptitude, defined, 162

Aptitude measurement, 160–62

Archimedes Spiral Afterimage, 382

Architectural barriers, 43

Arthur Adaptation of the Leiter International Performance Scale, 148

Articulation, defects of, 176, 177, 179, 180, 183–91, 199

Aspects of Personality Test, 294

Asthma and asthmatics, 440, 442, 476–82; anxiety in, 478–79, 481; education for, 482; hospitalization for, 479; incidence of, 477–78; nature of, 476–77; parents of, 478–82; personality with, 463, 480–82; psychological determinants in, 478–80; psychological effects of, 480–82; psychological stress and, 477; treatment for, 479, 482

Athetoids, 146, 310, 338, 339, 354, 373; concept formation of, 351; perceptualization in, 347–49, 351

Attention span, 62, 392, 441; in brain-injured, 372, 379–80, 388; in cerebral-palsied, 344, 357; in emotionally disturbed children, 379–80, 569, 589

Attitude modification, 324, 327

Audiogram, 415

Auditory (hearing) impairment, 414–35; acceptance of, 40–41, 59; acoustic handicap as, 50,

Auditory (hearing) impairment (cont.)
116; adjustment patterns with, 43–59, 261, 429–31; adventitiously deafened, 49, 59–60, 420, 429; age at onset of, 419, 420; behavioral characteristics with, 6, 20–21, 58–59, 422–31; in brain-injured, 380, 383–84, 395, 418, 421; causes of, 5, 429, 431; in cerebral-palsied, 354, 355, 357, 421; in children, 47–49; conceptual thinking with, 146, 428, 429; congenital, 49, 59, 420, 429; deaf, 421; deaf-mute, 424; defined, 116, 146, 420–22; education with, 41, 42, 48, 51–52, 149, 189–90, 421, 424, 431–35; emotional problems with, 419, 421, 429–31; environment and, 419–20, 425, 430; group membership with, 46–48, 58–59, 429, 435; hard of hearing with, 433–34; hearing acuity in, 9–10, 188–90; hearing aids for, 433, 434; incidence of, 189–90, 420–21; information on, 434; impaired vision and, 214, 221, 244, 259, 280–81, 285, 420, 421, 431; institutionalization of, 41, 48, 51–52; intelligence with, 128, 129n, 182–83, 192, 419, 423–25, 429, 435; labeling of, 83, 421; language handicap with, 191–92, 417, 419, 420, 422–28, 430, 432; life space of, 261; lip reading with, 32–33, 41, 51–53, 55–56, 60; measurement of, 134, 415–19, 432; memory with, 426; mental retardation with, 417–19, 421, 422, 431–32, 497, 512; motivation with, 425; motor development with, 424; multiply handicapped with, 417, 421, 431–32; new psychological situations and, 32–33; noise and, 414–15; obstacle perception with, 244; operant techniques for, 70; parents and, 419, 420, 431, 433; personality with, 192, 429–31; physical handicaps with, 419, 420; psychogenic, 5; sex distribution of, 177, 188–89; speech defects associated with, 117, 176, 177, 179, 182, 185, 188–92, 197, 198, 205–6, 281, 419–20, 424, 425, 432; superiority with, 53; testing with, 126–29, 144–47, 156, 158, 335, 423, 430–31; treatment for, 42, 415, 419, 432–34; values and perceptions with, 55–59; vocational success with, 47, 428–29

Autistic children, 197, 198, 513; multihandicapped, 283, 284

Autokinetic phenomenon, 381

Basic capacity, 136–39, 151, 153

Beauty criteria, 11–12, 36–37

Behavior: avoidance, 81; bidirectional model for, 573; cognitive guidance for, 58, 59; creative, 136; dependent, 87; disability affecting, 6–7; ego process model in, 587–88; environment and, 5–6, 63–65, 69, 566; evaluation of society affecting, 77–78; explanations of, 20–21, 62–63; judging of, 90; in new psychological situations, 26–34, 42; normal, 58–59, 395; in overlapping psychological roles, 34–38, 42; of physically disabled, 4–7, 12, 14–16, 23, 25–26, 28; of physically handicapped, 16–18, 25–26; prediction of, 28, 31; problem behavior defined, 566–67; relation to physique of, 2–6, 12, 14, 19, 26; sampling in psychological testing, 117–22, 126, 128–30, 139, 148–49, 151, 158, 162–63, 168–69; self-defeating, 43; self-evaluation and, 91–92; in socioemotional assessment, 154–56; terminal (molar), 66; terminology for, 63. *See also specific disability*

Behavior modification, 63–71, 200; attitudes of

Behavior modification (cont.)
disabled changed by, 324; with brain-injured, 401
Bell Adjustment Inventory, 204, 262
Bender-Gestalt Test, 348, 350, 379, 380
Bender Visual Motor Gestalt Test, 383
Benton Visual Retention Test, 134, 379
Bernreuter Personality Inventory, 180
Bailer-Cromwell Children's Locus of Control Scale, 262
Binet tests, 147, 150, 156, 157, 334, 335, 337, 340, 499, 541; Terman and Merrill Revision, 499. *See also* Binet-Simon Tests; Hayes-Binet Intelligence Tests; Stanford-Binet Intelligence Scales
Binet-Simon Tests, 225
Black box, 144–46, 165
Blacks, 546–48
Blacky test, 480
Blind Learning Aptitude Test (BLAT), 150, 225
Blindisms, 151, 275–76
Blindness. *See* Impaired vision
Block Design Rotation Test, 373
Bodily integrity, 444, 450
Body clumsiness, 166, 186, 200, 400, 569. *See also* Motor handicapped
Body-image, 311–14, 321, 330, 331, 396–400; in chronic illness, 452; defined, 397–98; directionality in, 398, 399, 402; laterality in, 398–99, 402–4; sensory-motor training for, 402–3, 405. *See also* Self-concept; *and specific disability*
Braille, 227–28, 236–41, 257, 269
Brain-injured (brain-damaged) children, 343, 366–407; aggression in, 394; anxiety in, 387, 407; attention span in, 372, 379–80, 388; attitudes toward, 369; auditory disturbances in perception of, 380, 383–84, 395, 418, 421; body-image in, 312, 396–403, 405–6; cause of, 369; central nervous system in, 369, 371, 377; cerebral inhibition in, 376, 377, 382, 383; in cerebral-palsied, 315, 322, 336, 343, 366–67, 373, 378, 385; characteristics of, 372–407; compulsivity in, 351, 389; conceptual and abstract thinking disturbances, 385–86; control and manipulation of others by, 394; defined, 116, 144–45, 366–67; developmental imbalances in, 395; disinhibition in, 372, 373, 388; education of, 152, 191, 372, 402–7; ego of, 401, 406; figure-ground disturbances in perception of, 345–48, 372, 377–78, 405; flight from challenge by, 394; frustration tolerance in, 393–94; hyperactivity in, 372, 373, 375, 377, 388; hyperdistractibility in, 372, 373, 375–77, 379–81, 383, 384, 388; hyperkinesis in, 367, 377, 387; impaired vision in, 117, 221; inadequate impulse control in, 372, 387; intersensory disturbances in, 384; intelligence in, 385–86, 388, 395; labeling of, 134, 366–72; lability of affect in, 372, 373, 388; language disturbances in, 382, 386–87; memory in, 379, 383, 387; mental retardation with, 144–45, 380–81, 386–88; minimal brain dysfunction, 186, 366–67, 371, 376; motor control in, 400; motor dysfunction in, 372, 373; perseveration in, 372–73, 377, 381–82; studies on, 373–77; negativism in, 394; orderliness in, 388–89; overcompensation in, 394; parents of, 97, 387, 390–92, 401, 404, 407; perceptual handicaps of, 344–45, 366, 368, 389, 403; psychotherapy

Brain-injured (brain-damaged) children (cont.)
for, 407; self-concept of, 389–96, 400–402, 405–7, 577; socioemotional disturbances in, 387–88; speech defects and, 179, 191, 198; testing of, 139, 144–46, 354, 380; treatment for, 401–7; variability of performance in, 388; visual-motor disturbances in, 368, 378–80, 405; visual-perceptual disturbances in, 380–83, 405
Brain lesions, 343–44, 382, 386. *See also* Brain-injured children
Brown-Bogert Pre-Vocational Motor Skill inventory, 133–34
Brunschwig Personality Inventory for Deaf Children, 429

California Personality Inventory, 552
California Psychological Inventory, 552
California Test of Personality, 182, 204, 254, 512, 515
Cardiac disorders. *See* Heart disorders
Cataracts, 289, 290
Cattell Culture-Fair Tests, 120, 121
Cattell Infant Intelligence Scale, 271, 274, 341
Central nervous system, 392–93; in brain injury, 369, 371, 377; in cluttering, 199; in congenital aphasia, 180, 197; disorders of, 343, 352; tuberculosis meningitis in, 453
Cerebral inhibition, 393; in brain-injured, 376, 377, 382, 383
Cerebral palsy and cerebral-palsied, 336–57; acceptance of, 41; acculturation of, 118; adjustment of, 319, 322–23, 336, 357; attention span in, 344, 357; with auditory impairment, 354, 355, 357, 421; brain damage in, 315, 322, 336, 343, 366–67, 373, 378, 385; conceptualization of, 141, 344, 350–51; counseling for, 323, 324; defined, 140n; education of, 34, 324, 342–44, 352, 354–57; emotional problems of, 344, 357; environment affecting, 342, 354; experience deprivation of, 315, 342; family adjustment in, 357; hyperkinesis in, 357; with impaired vision, 281, 339, 347–48, 354, 355; intelligence in, 141, 333, 334, 336–43, 351, 355; language and reading by, 342, 357; mental retardation among, 143, 179–80, 182, 336, 343–44, 354–57, 497, 512; motivation (drive) in, 143–44, 144n, 322; with multiple handicaps, 343, 354–57; neurological impairment in, 144, 308, 322, 333, 336, 340–42; oculomotor control in, 347–48; with orthopedic impairment, 308; parents of, 319, 322, 328, 332–33; perceptualization of, 141–44, 336, 339, 340, 342–54, 356–57; sensory deprivation affecting, 315; speech defects of, 176, 177, 179–80, 182, 185, 186n; testing of, 127–30, 138–44, 146, 159, 334–42, 344; types of, 354–57
Cerebrotonia, 4
Chalkboard training, 403
Change model, 593
Chicago Card-sort, 267
Chicago Non-Verbal Examination, 423
Children's Apperception Test, 430
Chronic medical disorders, 440–83; early experience affecting, 443–44. *See also specific disorder*
Clark Revision of the Thurstone Personality Schedule, 261
Cleft palates, 176, 177, 179, 185, 205–6, 226
Clubfoot, 308, 311

Clumsiness, 166, 186, 200, 400, 569. *See also* Motor handicapped

Cognition, 531

Cognitive development, 588; clarity in, 58; trauma affecting, 443. *See also specific disability*

College Entrance Examination Board, 226–27

Colored audition, 220

Columbia Mental Maturity Scale, 142, 143, 340, 341

Communication, 392; with auditory impairment, 425, 433; with impaired vision, 218, 222, 232, 235; in psychological assessment, 129, 131, 141–44, 146–47, 149–51, 154–56, 158–59, 161, 163, 165, 169, 423; in speech defects, 175–76, 195, 199

Concept Mastery Test (CMT), 122, 539

Conceptual Styles Test (CST), 590

Conceptualization, 130, 131, 155, 158, 161, 164, 169, 393, 594–95; with auditory impairment, 146, 428, 429; in the brain-injured, 385–86; in the cerebral-palsied, 141, 344, 350–51; in the emotionally disturbed, 590–91, 593, 595; with impaired vision, 150, 224–25, 234, 264, 278–79

Contemporaneous explanations, 21–23

Convergers, 534

Correlational explanations, 23

Counseling: on adjustment patterns, 45–59; of adventitiously impaired persons, 59–60; for dropouts, 559; not helpful, 58–59; for parents, 283, 284, 328, 329, 333, 518; for reading disabilities, 24; in rehabilitation, 71; on validity of perceptions of the disabled, 57

Creativity: in adolescents, 531, 553–56; adult profiles with, 539–40; divergent thinking as, 136; in the gifted, 529–30, 531–37, 539–40, 546–48, 551–57, 559–60, 581–82; with impaired vision, 232

Criminal behavior and criminals, 99–100, 102; mental retardation and, 510–11, 517, 520, 521

Crippling. *See* Orthopedic impairment and orthopedically impaired

Daily Activity Record of M. E. Brown, 133–34

Deafness. *See* Auditory impairment

Dearborn and Lincoln Hollow Square tests, 121

Defective speech. *See* Speech defects

Delinquent behavior and delinquents, 102, 257, 577; careers of the exceptional in, 106–7; of the emotionally disturbed, 570, 572, 577, 578, 583–84, 591; evaluation of, 80; of the gifted, 539, 557; labeling and, 83; life chances and, 108; mental retardation and, 510–11, 521; parents of, 511; social class and, 99, 521; visual defects and, 294

Dental irregularities, speech and, 181, 185–86, 205

Detroit Mechanical Aptitude Test, 163n

Developmental imbalances, 367

Deviance, 574; in child group-behavior, 570; detection of, 98–100, 104, 109, 151; extermination of, 100–101; formal and informal management of, 98–99; punishment for, 573; rehabilitation (treatment) of, 98, 100–105; roles of, 106; sequential and simultaneous models of, 105–7; social class and, 99–100

Deviant types, 79–81

Diabetes mellitus and diabetics, 442, 450, 469–76; anxiety with, 473; education of, 475, 476; emotional disturbance with, 473; employment of, 475–76; exercise in, 471, 473, 474; incidence of, 470; insulin in, 471, 473–74; intelligence of, 472; nature of, 469–70; parents of, 472–76; personality of, 473, 474; psychological factors in, 471–72, 474; treatment of, 470–71, 476; tuberculosis and, 454

Differential Aptitude Tests, 535

Differential Language Facility Test, 386

Disabilities and disabled persons: acceptance of, 6, 40–42, 54, 444; cultural relativity of, 6–9, 12; disabled role of, 92–93; interaction with, 95–96, 318, 319; interrelation of handicap with, 6–8; psychological effects of, 17, 18; psychosomatic, 5; reduction of, 42–43, 110; research on, 18–25, 62–63; social consequences of, 76, 318; as a social value judgment, 7, 9. *See also* Handicaps and handicapped persons; Physical disabilities and physically disabled; *and specific disability*

Disadvantaged children, 528; education of, 543–55; gifted as, 151–52; talents in, 546–47; testing of, 151–53, 543–44; values of, 544–45

Discredited and discreditable individuals, 94

Dissident youth, 556–57

Dissociation, 352, 379

Divergers, 534

Doll's Vineland Social Maturity Scale, 154

Doman-Delacato treatment, 404–5

Doppler effect, 244

Drive. *See* Motivation

Dropouts, 559

Dyslexia. *See* Reading disability

Dyslogia, 197–99. *See also* Aphasia and aphasics

Dyssynchronous child, 367

Echolocation, 246, 248

Ectomorph, 4, 400

Eczema, 477

Educability, 282

Education, 584–95; for chronically ill, 483; curriculum utilization in, 584; diagnostic teaching in, 585; for disabled, 34, 41, 42, 81, 97, 125; expectancy phenomenon in, 87–95, 369–70, 550–51, 559, 561, 569, 577, 579, 591; goal of, 594–95; life chances in, 107; of multihandicapped, 280–86; of public, 34, 43, 257; self-evaluation and performance in, 91–92. *See also specific disability*

Educational achievement testing, 127, 128, 160–62. *See also specific disability*

Ego development, 392–93, 397, 406–7

Ego processes, 587–88

Electrodermal audiometry (EDR), 417–19

Electroencephalographic audiometry (EEG), 418–19

Ellis Visual Designs Test, 380

Emotional adjustment: of special-class retardates, 104; testing of, 155–60. *See also* Adjustment; Maladjustment; Vocational adjustment; *and specific disability*

Emotional handicaps, relation to physique variations, 13–15

Emotionally disturbed children, 565–96; acceptability of, 570–71; anxiety in, 581, 589, 594; attention span in, 379–80, 569, 589; attitudes

Emotionally disturbed children (cont.)
toward, 573–76; with auditory impairment, 431; behavior of, 566, 569, 574, 583, 584, 588–90; behavior modification procedures for, 70; cognitive styles of, 588–90; conceptualization by, 590–91, 593, 595; defined, 395, 402, 566, 569–70; delinquent behavior of, 570, 572, 577, 578, 583–84, 591; in diabetes, 473; ecological view of, 401–2, 567–68; education of, 566–86, 589, 591; ego-process model of, 587–88, 590, 594; environment affecting, 565–66, 569, 572, 576–80, 584, 587–93, 595–96; environmental definitions of, 566–75, 577; in illness, 450–51; inadequate impulse control in, 569, 583, 584, 587, 590; institutionalization and, 445, 572, 587; intelligence of, 569–70, 576, 580–83; labeling of, 82, 370, 371, 565, 570, 573, 583, 588, 591; learning behavior of, 569–70, 576, 580–84; memory of, 569; mental retardation and, 497, 498, 507, 513, 569; multihandicapped, 284–85; parents of, 565, 569, 573, 576, 579–80, 582, 587; perceptions of, 381, 569, 583, 588; personality of, 569, 572, 594; play therapy for, 595; psychotherapy for, 580; reality testing by, 588, 589; role-acceptance by, 575; self-concepts of, 405, 558, 569, 571, 574–81, 587, 589; self-other orientations in, 592–95; shyness as, 566–67; testing of, 160. *See also* Mentally ill
Emotionally maladjusted children: basic capacity of, 138; testing of, 124, 139
Empirical explanations, 23
Employment, 97. *See also specific disability*
Endomorph, 4, 399–400
Environment, 399, 441, 451; adjustment and, 55; behavior and, 5–6, 63–65, 69, 566; conceptual work and, 593; environmental prescriptions for, 593–94; formula on, 5–6, 566; in hospitalization, 444, 548; labeling and, 83–84; in socioemotional assessment, 154, 159–60. *See also* Acculturation; *and specific disability*
Epilepsy and epileptics, 8, 356; with auditory impairment, 421; in cerebral-palsied, 354–56; with impaired vision, 281; learning capacities of, 141
Ethnocentrism, 14
Evaluation, in intellect model, 531
Exceptional children, 440, 574; acceptability of, 258, 574; basic capacities of, 137–38, 151; careers of, 105–7; creative production of, 136; defined, 116; disadvantaged children as, 151–52; experience deprivation in, 315–16; interpersonal relationships of, 153–56, 164–65; manifest capacities of, 137–38, 151; psychological assessment of, 115–69; pure types of, 117; right to be different of, 166; teachers of, 256–57, 574. *See also specific disability*
Exophoria, 293
Expectancy phenomenon, 87–95, 369–70, 550–51, 559, 561, 569, 577, 579, 591
Experience deprivation, 315–16
Explanations, 19–25; contemporaneous, 21–23; diagnostic psychological procedures as, 62; empirical (correlational), 23; historical, 21–23; naming, 19–21
Extermination, 100–101
External control, 88–89, 91–92
Eye-hand coordination, 62, 69, 344, 378–80; training for, 405. *See also* Visual-motor disturbances

Fables test, 553
Fernald method, 406
Field theory, 64, 309–10, 459
Finger agnosia, 400
Finger painting, 403
Flanagan Aptitude Classification Tests, 535
Flanagan Ingenuity Test, 543
Fluency, defects of, 176
Frame of reference: individual, 156–59; in psychological assessment, 125, 137, 154–59, 164, 167–68; social, 154–56
Frontal lisp, 66, 68
Frustration: in delinquent behavior, 511; labeling and, 370; in new psychological situations, 28, 33; tolerance for, 33, 53, 393. *See also specific disability*
Functional disabilities, 5

Gates Reading Vocabulary for the Primary Grades, 233
General Aptitude Test Battery, 535
Gesell Developmental Schedules, 133, 148, 271, 340, 341
Gifted children and giftedness, 528–61; academic achievement by, 534, 537–38, 540, 544, 553–56, 558, 559, 581–82; acceptability of, 258; adjustment of, 557–61; adolescents, 531, 537–39, 553–56, 560; anxiety in, 552, 553; blotter mind in, 537; characteristics of, 551–57; concepts of, 530–31, 540; convergers and divergers as, 534; creativity in, 529–30, 531–37, 539–40, 546–48, 551–57, 559–60, 581–82; defined, 528, 540, 541; as disadvantaged children, 151–52; education of, 152, 528, 530–31, 535, 540, 541, 543–48, 550, 557, 561; elaboration by, 554–56, 560; environment and, 528, 548–51, 561; hereditary factors in, 528, 548–51; identification of, 139, 141, 528, 540–48; intellect models of, 531–39; intelligence of, 117, 531–34, 537, 539, 540, 549–51, 553–54; intuition in, 539; moral courage in, 533; motivation in, 552; multiple talents in, 535–37; originality in, 554–56, 560; parents of, 537, 540, 544–45, 548, 549, 554, 555, 560–61, 582; problem-solving mind in, 537; profile of, 539–40; rebelliousness in, 538–39, 552, 553, 556–57; in science, 534, 544, 545, 551–52; self-concept in, 539, 550–51, 554–58, 560; skilled mind in, 537; socially adjusted and leaders as, 533, 537, 540; testing of, 532, 541–44, 550–51; types of, 537–39, 551; as underachievers, 559, 581–82; understanding mind in, 537; vocational choices of, 553–55, 558
Glaucoma, congenital, 286–87
Goals: in acceptance of disability, 40; in adjustment, 309, 321, 325, 330; in adventitiously impaired persons, 59; alternative routes to, 42; cognitive, 67; goal-setting and, 154, 481; inaccessible, 37–38, 43, 44, 52, 53; in motor training exercises, 403; in new psychological situations, 33, 43; occupational, 51; in overlapping excluding roles, 37–39, 43; in rehabilitation slogans, 38; replacement of, 56
Goldstein-Scheerer Test, 339, 427
Goodenough Draw-a-Man Tests, 423
Grace Arthur Performance Scale, 423
Graham-Kendall Memory-for-Designs Test, 134
Gray Oral Reading Check Tests, 226

Group membership, 58; of the deaf, 46–48, 58–59, 429, 435; of the disadvantaged, 546–47

Haggerty-Olson-Wickman Behavior Rating Schedules, 429
Halstead Category Test, 386
Hampstead Child-Therapy Course and Clinic in London, 276
Handicaps and handicapped persons: acculturation of, 118; defined, 75, 76, 110, 116; deviant role of, 106; disabled role of, 92–93; formal management of, 98–99; as incompetence, 81; interrelation of disability with, 6–8; labeling of, 77, 81–86, 96, 98, 99; life chances of, 107–9; psychological, 7; socially imposed, 10–13, 75–81, 109, 110, 324–25; societal reduction of, 110; status relationship of, 75; testing of, 121–22, 124, 125, 138–39; as unattractive, 81; visibility of, 94. *See also* Disabilities and disabled persons; Physical disabilities and physically disabled; *and specific disability*
Haptic Intelligence Scale for Adult Blind, 228
Hard of hearing. *See* Auditory impairment, hard of hearing with
Hawthorne effect, 369
Hayes-Binet Intelligence Tests, 150, 223–25; for the blind, 223, 274
Headstart, 547
Hearing acuity, 9–10, 188–90
Heart disorders, 442, 459–69; adjustment with, 463, 466–67; anxiety and, 462–65; blue baby (cyanosis) in, 460; cardiac children, 308, 329, 334, 450, 463; cardiovascular system in, 461–63; causes of, 460; congenital, 460, 463, 468; education for, 465, 467–69; hospitalization for, 464; incidence of, 460; intelligence with, 334, 466, 467; parents and, 463–67; personality with, 329, 463, 466–67, 481; physical activity with, 464–65; psychological stress affecting, 462, 463; psychosomatic aspects of, 462; somatopsychological aspects of, 461–62
Heath Rail-Walking Test, 430
Height, 2–3; norms, 134–35
Hemiplegia, 339, 351
Hemophilia, 334
Heredity factors, 5
Hertz, 415–17
Hidden Shapes test, 553
Hiskey-Nebraska Test of Learning Aptitude, 147, 148, 427
Historical explanations, 21–23
Hoover technique of cane travel, 248
Hospitalization, 444–49, 483; for asthmatics, 479; for heart disorders, 464; with impaired vision, 287; parents and, 287, 444–49, 458; for tuberculosis, 454–56, 458–59. *See also* Institutionalization
Hothousing. *See* Acculturation
House-Tree-Person Drawings, 552
H-T-P technique, 430
Human Figure Drawings Test, 295, 430
Hyperkinesis, 357, 367, 377, 387
Hypermetropia, 293
Hyperopia, 289, 290, 294
Hypothyroid condition, 5

Illinois Test of Psycholinguistic Abilities (ITPA), 145, 190, 206, 291–92, 335, 342, 583

Illness, 444, 447; psychology of, 440–43, 449–52, 482; as punishment, 450, 451, 457, 482; reactions to, 451
Impaired vision, 211–87; achievement tests results in, 226–28, 238; adjustment in, 16, 230, 232, 234, 247, 248, 254–55, 261–69, 278, 291, 294–96; in adolescents, 253–56, 259, 263–68, 276, 283, 285, 294; adventitiously blind, 217, 224, 245; age at onset of, 215–16, 224, 268–69, 287; anxiety and, 263, 268, 275, 287, 294; attitudes of the, 253, 258–60, 262, 267; attitudes toward the, 252–60, 265; auditory impairment and, 214, 221, 244, 259, 280–81, 285, 420, 421, 431; behavior with, 6, 14, 39, 93, 94, 151, 254; blindisms (motor behavior patterns) in, 151, 275–76; body image of the, 250; braille reading with, 227–28, 236–41, 257, 269; brain damage and 117, 221; causes of, 1, 214–15, 225–26, 288–90; cerebral-palsied with, 281, 339, 347–48, 354, 355; cognitive functions with, 211–13, 216–41, 278, 283, 287; color ideas and vision and, 58, 213, 220; communication with, 218, 222, 232, 235; conceptualization and perceptualization with, 150, 224–25, 228, 231, 234, 242, 247, 264, 278–80, 283; congenital, 215–16, 224, 264, 268; congenital anophthalmos, 225, 226, 271; creative abilities and, 232; curiosity and, 229–31; defined, 116, 117, 213–14, 288; dependence in, 150–51, 246–47, 252, 264, 275, 276; developmental aspects in, 271–80, 282–84; diabetes as cause of, 470; dog guides and, 248, 249; dreams with, 215, 270–71; echolocation and, 246, 248; education with, 213–14, 221, 223, 224, 228–32, 234, 238–39, 245, 248–50, 256–57, 262, 273; ego development and, 277–79; emotional problems with, 151, 254, 255, 259–63, 290–91, 294; environment and, 223, 227–30, 232, 245–48, 252, 259–61, 273–75, 277, 281, 286, 287, 294–96; experiencing object world with, 216–18; facial expression and, 252, 269–70; facilities for education for, 280–81; fantasies of those with, 260, 268, 271, 295; fear of being observed and, 260, 273; field of vision in, 213; frustration and, 251, 253, 254, 260–62, 275, 277, 284; hearing and 216–18, 220, 221, 242–45, 247–49, 252, 270, 276–79; hereditary factors in, 214, 226; institutionalization of, 102, 260, 261, 266–67, 280, 283–284; intelligence and, 23, 129n, 150, 212, 216, 221–27, 238, 274, 290–91; laser beam procedure for, 42; life space of, 261; light perception in, 213, 214, 241; light projection in, 213, 214; listening efficiency and, 293–94; locus of control in, 262–63; maladjustment in, 295; maturation and, 269, 271, 280; maze learning by, 250–51; memory and, 221, 224, 225, 231, 247, 251, 252, 277; mental retardation and, 214, 226, 227, 241, 259, 275–76, 279–84, 286, 287, 497, 512; minority status of, 252–53; mobility and, 42, 211–12, 230, 241–51, 283; motivation with, 230, 251; motor performance with, 256, 271–72, 276; multihandicapped with, 214, 226, 280–87; musical ability and, 220, 222; nervous tension and, 218, 247, 251, 273; new psychological situations and, 29–32; objective effects of, 273; obstacle perception and, 241–48; olfactory sense and, 217, 221, 247, 248, 252, 270; orientation and locomotion and, 247–51, 271–

Marianne Frostig Development Test of Visual Perception, 405
Maturation, 69, 154, 396, 452; auditory impairment and, 427; with impaired vision, 269, 271, 280; of mentally retarded, 509; neural, 393, 400; sexual, 4; speech defects and, 177, 186, 188, 197
Measures of Parental Attitude, 266
Mediational process, 144–46, 165
Memory, 130, 137, 537; with auditory impairment, 426; in brain-injured, 379, 383, 387; defined, 531; in emotionally disturbed, 569; with impaired vision, 221, 224, 225, 231, 247, 251, 252, 277; with speech defects, 188–91
Meningitis, 5, 146
Mental ages, 140
Mental health, 311, 320, 573, 585–86; acceptance and, 40; behavior and, 59; in the gifted, 559–60; values and, 38
Mental retardation and the mentally retarded: acceptability of, 258, 515–17, 521–22; adjustment of, 104, 500, 501, 510–18, 521; auditory impairment with, 417–19, 421, 422, 431–32, 497, 512; in behavior modification example, 66–67; behaviorial classification of, 496; body-image in, 400; brain damage in, 144–45, 380–81, 386–88; in cerebral-palsied, 143, 179–80, 182, 336, 343–44, 354–57, 497, 512; concepts of, 496–500; criminal and delinquent behavior in, 510–11, 517, 520, 521; defined, 496, 498, 521; dependency relationship of, 81; as deviant types, 80; with diabetes, 472; education of, 79, 100, 103–5, 125, 497, 498, 502, 507, 512, 515–16, 518; emotional problems of, 497, 498, 507, 513, 569; employment of, 498, 516–18, 522; environment and, 497, 500–504, 511, 513, 517–18, 520, 521, 549; foster homes for, 103, 501, 502; with impaired vision, 214, 226, 227, 241, 259, 275–76, 279–84, 286, 287, 497, 512; incidence of, 499–500; institutionalization of, 102–3, 500–502, 504, 508, 518–20, 522, 549; intelligence of, 116, 498–503, 505–7, 509, 511–13, 521, 549; labeling of, 81–86, 93; learning characteristics of, 350, 352, 499, 500, 502–8, 521, 522; medical classification of, 496; motor coordination of, 132, 134; motor impersistence in, 374; parents' organizations of, 495; parents of, 97, 104–5, 497, 501, 502, 517, 518–22; perceived subnormality of, 83–85; as a personality disorder, 512–13; play therapy for, 516; psychomotor abilities of, 374, 500, 503, 504, 509–10, 521; psychosocial stimulation affecting, 497, 500–502; psychotherapy for, 497, 513–14; sensory disability causing, 497, 512; social training for, 515–16; socially induced, 315; speech defects and, 182–84, 194, 197, 198; as surplus population, 109; terminology about, 495–96; testing of, 139, 141, 149, 153, 155, 158, 161, 499, 511–13; treatment for, 497–99; vocational testing of, 163–64, 499
Mentally ill, 572–74; attitudes toward, 573–74; behavior of, 83, 92–93; foster homes for, 103; institutionalization of, 93, 103; labeling of, 81–83; treatment for, 406. See also Emotionally disturbed children
Merrill-Palmer Scale of Mental Tests, 423
Mesomorph, 4, 400
Metropolitan Achievement Tests, 226

Microphthalmia, 286
Miller Analogies, 122
Minnesota Importance Questionnaire, 554
Minnesota Multiphasic Inventory, 319
Minnesota Scholastic Aptitude Tests, 554
Minnesota Vocational Interest Inventory, 164
Monoplegia, 339
Montessori method, 406
Motion pictures: for auditory impairments, 433–34; for brain-injured, 405–6
Motivation (drive), 52, 144n, 163, 165, 167; with auditory impairment, 425; in the blind, 230, 251; in cerebral-palsied, 143–44, 144n, 322; in the gifted, 552; illness affecting, 451
Motor behavior, 132–34
Motor control, 392–93, 398, 400
Motor development, 396, 452; with auditory impairment, 424; of mentally retarded, 132, 134, 374, 500, 503, 504, 509–10, 521, 569; in speech defects, 134, 186–88, 194, 200
Motor-handicapped, 396; with auditory impairment, 431; in brain-injured, 372, 373, 400; with brain lesions, 343; in cerebral-palsied, 345, 348–50; testing of, 126, 160, 161, 335–36
Motor training exercises, 403–5
Movigenics, 403–4
Multiple Aptitude Tests, 535
Multiply handicapped: with auditory impairment, 417, 421, 431–32; with cerebral palsy, 343, 354–57; educability of, 282; education of, 280–86; with impaired vision, 214, 226, 280–87; parents of, 281, 283, 357; testing of, 117, 281–82
Music talent, 542–43; with impaired vision, 220, 222
Myers-Ruch High School Progress Test, 226
Myopia, 289, 290, 293, 294

Nebraska Test of Learning Aptitude, 423
Neurologically handicapped, 404–5; in cerebral-palsied, 308, 322, 333, 336, 340–42
Neurotic anxiety, 456, 463
Neuroticism, in speech defects, 199, 201, 204
Neymann-Kohlstedt Diagnostic Test for Introversion-Extroversion, 260, 319
Norms, meanings of, 123–26
Nystagmus, 141, 166, 286, 289, 290, 295

Occupational aptitudes, 117, 127, 128, 132, 137, 162–64, 535
Ohwaki-Kohs test, 225
Omnibus Personality Inventory, 557
Ontario School Ability Examination, 147, 148
Operant conditioning, 68, 70–71
Organic inferiority, 310–11
Orthopedic impairment (crippling) and orthopedically impaired, 308–57; adjustment of, 41, 155, 308–24; anxiety in, 317, 319, 321; attitudes of, 323–24; attitudes toward, 324–27; body-image in, 311–14, 321, 330, 331, 452; education of, 42, 78, 152, 323–24, 332; ego loss in, 316; emotional needs in, 317–18; environment and, 318; experience deprivation and, 315–16, 323, 335; fantasy life of, 328, 331; field theory in, 309–10; Freudian theories in, 311, 314; frustrations in, 310, 318, 320, 330; with impaired vision, 281; intelligence in, 334–36; learning behavior of, 143, 313–14,

Orthopedic impairment (cont.)
332; mental health in, 320; organic inferiority in, 310–11; parents and, 311, 314–16, 318–20, 326–29, 332–34; projective tests in, 320–22, 325; social relationships in, 321, 326–27; social status with peers in, 329–32; testing of, 124, 131, 139, 140, 157. *See also* Cerebral palsy and cerebral-palsied
Oseretsky Tests, 134, 509, 510
Osteomyelitis, 1, 308
Otis Gamma IQ, 121

Para-analytic group therapy, 283
Paraplegia, 339, 351
Parents: bidirectional model in emotional disturbance of, 573; in careers of the exceptional, 106; children affected by attitudes of, 48, 51–52; chronic medical disorders and, 440, 472, 482–83; cop-out fathers as, 329; counseling for, 283, 284, 328, 329, 333, 518; of delinquents, 511; hospitalization and, 287, 444–49, 458; labeling affecting, 369, 371; in life chances, 107–9; of multihandicapped, 281, 283, 357; physical behavior affected by, 135; psychosomatic disorders and, 443–44; psychotherapy for, 482; research on, 97–98; response to disability of, 96–98, 326; responsibility of, 17, 55; self-concept affected by, 91, 390–92; in value development, 51, 55. *See also specific disability*
PARI scales, 480
Peabody Picture Vocabulary Test, 89, 142, 152, 292–93, 335, 340
Perception and perceptualization, 392, 393, 396, 441; in aphasia, 197–98; of cerebral-palsied, 141–44, 336, 339, 340, 342–54, 356–57; of the emotionally disturbed, 381, 569, 583, 588; in the gifted, 539; with impaired vision, 150, 228, 231, 242, 247, 264, 279–80, 283; of physically disabled, 321, 324, 330; training for, 403, 405, 406; trauma affecting, 443. *See also* Brain-injured children, perceptual handicaps of
Perceptual dysgnosia, 199
Perseveration, 352, 372–73, 377, 381–82
Personality: brain lesions affecting, 343; endocrine secretion affecting, 4; physical disability and, 60, 325; physique affecting, 3–4, 12. *See also specific disability*
Personality disorders, 512–13
Pharynx growths, 185
Phenolketonuria, 497, 498
Phonation, defects of, 176, 177, 180, 183
Photisms, 220
Physical area, in testing, 132–35
Physical disabilities and physically disabled, 1–2, 6–7; adjustment to, 308–16, 443–44; attitudes about, 318, 323–27; auditory impairment and, 419, 420; behavior and, 4–7, 12, 14–16, 23, 25–26, 28; body-image in, 311–14, 321, 330, 331, 396–400; defined, 6, 7, 116; as deviant types, 80; experience deprivation of, 315–16, 323; family adjustment of, 327–29, 332–33; hypochrondriacal solutions of, 314–15; internally and externally controlled, 92; labeling of, 85; life space of, 31–32, 42, 309–10; life style of, 311; narcissism in, 314; in new psychological situations, 28–34, 42; overcompensation by, 314, 316; in overlapping excluding

Physical disabilities (cont.)
roles, 38–42; personality adjustment and, 60, 325; phantom disabilities as, 317; pleasure principle in, 314; prejudices against, 34, 37–38, 58, 325, 329–30; psychological problems in children with, 16–17, 23; reality principle in, 314, 324, 325; self-concept of, 62, 91–92, 309–11, 321, 324, 330–32, 452; social acceptance of, 33–34, 319; social status with peers of, 329–32. *See also* Disabilities and disabled persons; handicaps and handicapped persons; *and specific disability*
Physical therapy, 66
Physique, relation to behavior of, 2–6, 12, 14, 19, 26
Physique variations, 7, 451; in emotional handicaps, 13–15; in limitation in ability, 7–10; in socially imposed handicaps, 10–15; value systems on, 16
Pintner Non-Language Mental Tests, 147
Play therapy, 285, 516
Poliomyelitis, 1, 22, 308, 328, 334
Porteus Mazes, 143
Prejudice, 34, 37–38, 58, 325, 329–30
Primary Mental Abilities Test, 121
Product Improvement test, 554
Prosthetic aids, 42
Psychiatric classification schemes, 78
Psychological assessment and testing, 115–69; acculturation affecting, 118, 123, 124, 126, 128, 129*n*, 136, 137, 142, 146, 150, 151, 159–60, 164, 544; aptitude measurement in, 162–64; assessment process in, 164–68; assumptions underlying, 117–19, 168; clinician in, 117, 164–66, 168, 341–42; communication in, 129, 131, 141–44, 146–47, 149–51, 154–56, 158–59, 161, 163, 165, 169, 423; conceptualization affecting, 130, 131, 155, 158, 161, 164, 169; of creativity, 542–44; defined, 116, 117; of the disadvantaged, 151–53, 543–44; of educational achievement, 127, 128, 160–62; error in, 118, 119, 127, 137–39, 160, 161, 163, 168–69; frames of reference in, 125, 137, 154–59, 164, 167–68; future behavior inferred in, 118–19, 168–69; group averages in, 161; mediational process (the black box), 144–46, 165; of motor skills, 117, 162–63; of multihandicapped, 117, 281–82; norms in, 123–26, 129, 155–56, 160; perceptualization affecting, 141–44, 150; physical area of, 132–35; present behavior observed in, 118–19; process-product perception in, 122–23, 131, 143, 149, 150, 152; projective approaches in, 157–58, 321–22, 325, 511–21; quantitative and qualitative, 116, 137, 141; sampling of behavior in, 117–22, 126, 128–30, 139, 148–49, 151, 158, 162–63, 168–69; of socioemotional area, 117, 119, 127, 128, 137, 153–60, 511–12; standardization of tests in, 123–26, 128, 147, 153, 155, 158, 159, 223, 225, 228, 254, 334, 339–41, 423; synthesizing process in, 166–69; test adaptations in, 126–31, 140–41, 147, 160–61, 339–41; variability among tests in, 119–23; vocational aptitude and interests, 117, 127, 128, 132, 137, 162–64, 535. *See also* Intelligence testing; *and specific disability*
Psychological conflict, 58
Psychological predictions, 18, 29, 31

Psychological situations, new, 26–34, 42–43, 53, 309–10, 327

Psychology: in chronic disorders, 440–43, 449–53, 483; of illness, 440–43, 449–52, 482; learning theory in, 441; psychoanalytic approach in, 440–41

Psychophysiological disorders, 442

Psychosomatic disabilities, 5

Psychosomatic disorders, 441–42, 472; self-concept and, 452; trauma affecting, 443–44; tuberculosis as, 455–56

Psychotherapeutic programs, 476, 482; for the brain-injured, 405; for the emotionally disturbed, 580; for the mentally retarded, 497, 513–14

Ptosis, 286

Punishment: in behavioral modification, 64–65, 68; for deviance, 573; gifted receiving, 557; illness as, 450, 451, 457, 482

Pupil Portraits Test, 294

Quadripligia, 351

Randall's Island Performance Scale, 423

Raths Self-Portrait N Test, 317

Raven's Progressive Matrices, 122, 143, 148, 149, 183, 336, 338, 340, 341, 423

Reading: giftedness and, 543; learning in, 506, 507

Reading disability, 367; of emotionally disturbed, 569, 582–83; with impaired vision, 227–28, 236–41, 257, 269; remedial work or counseling for, 24; speech defects and, 184–85, 199–200

Reading vision, 213

Reality testing, 588, 589

Regressive phenomena, 446, 450–51, 457

Rehabilitation, 1, 60–64, 71, 110; behavior of client in, 63–64; client as comanager in, 63; education in, 42–43; in formal management of deviance, 98, 101–3; goals of, 38, 76; slogans in, 38. See also specific disability

Reinforcement, 64–68, 70, 230, 578

Remote Associates Test, 543

Research: on disabled persons, 18–25, 62–63; on families of the exceptional, 97–98. See also specific disability

Retardates. See Mental retardation and the mentally retarded

Retinoblastoma, 225–26

Retrolental fibroplasia (RLF), 214–15, 226, 238, 274, 280, 281, 284, 285, 290

Rheumatic fever, 460–62, 466

Rheumatic heart disease, 450, 459–61, 463, 464, 469; predisposition to, 462

Riggs and Rain classification system, 353

Roles: antagonistic overlapping, 36, 42, 46, 49, 50, 53, 55, 59; in careers of the exceptional, 106, 575; deviant, 106, 575; disabled, 92–93; interfering overlapping, 35–36; overlapping, 26, 34–42, 58; overlapping excluding, 36–39, 41, 42; role-acceptance and, 87, 93, 575; role expectations and, 87–95, 574–75; role performance and, 88–89, 91; social, 87, 329

Roosevelt, Theodore, 5

Rorschach Test, 295, 343, 429–30, 457, 462, 552

Rosenzweig Picture Frustration Test, 320

Rotter Aspiration Board, 430

Rotter Incomplete Sentences Blank, 264

Roughness Discrimination Test, 239

Rubella, 431; auditory impairment from 429, 431; congenital heart defects caused by, 460; impaired vision from, 216, 226, 281, 285

Sacks Sentence Completion Test, 203

San Francisco Vocational Competency Scale, 164

Schizophrenic children, 283, 513, 571; with auditory impairment, 431; parents of, 97; speech defects and, 195, 198–99

School and College Ability Tests, 533

School Apperception Method, 157

Schools, 75, 96; intellectual deviance in, 79, 101, 104; labeling in, 82, 98, 370–71; learning aptitude measured for, 135–36, 148, 149; social categorization in, 78, 82, 98, 100; special classes in, 103–5, 108, 559, 567–68, 574, 578–79, 584–85. See also Education; and specific disability

Scotoma, 213

Seashore Musical Talent Tests, 222

Seguin Form Board, 121

Self-concept, 62, 91–92, 154–55, 309–11, 321, 324, 330–32, 389–97, 399, 452; in chronic illness, 452; parents affecting, 91–92, 390–92. See also Body-image; and specific disability

Self-Concept and Ideal-Concept Sort, 266

Self-fulfilling prophecy, 87–88, 370

Self-Image Experience (SIE), 406

Sensorimotor development, 399–400

Sensory-motor training, 402–6

Sequential Test of Educational Progress (STEP), 227–28, 238, 293–94, 533

Shoe tying, 66, 68–70

Situations Projective Test A (SPT-A), 266

Situations Projective Test B (SPT-B), 266

Snellen Chart, 142, 213, 238, 240, 293

Snjiders-Oomen Non-Verbal Intelligence Scale, 148

Social categorization, 78–79, 109

Social classes, 99; in life chances, 107, 109

Social distance, 570, 576

Social Maturity Scale for Blind Preschool Children, 272–73

Social pressures, 56–57

Social status, 153–55, 329–32

Socioemotional area of testing, 117, 119, 127, 128, 137, 153–60, 511–12

Somatopsychology: adjustment and, 310; concepts for, 25–26; defined, 2; explanations in, 19–25; function of, 2–6; research in, 18–19, 62–63; science and theory in, 16–18, 25; variables in, 60

Somatotonia, 4

Somatotypes, theory of, 4

Sones-Harry High School Achievement Test, 226

Spastics, 285, 354, 373; concept formation in, 351; intelligence in, 334, 337–41; perceptualization in, 347–49, 352

Speech, 177, 424; with auditory impairment, 32–33, 51–53, 55–56; as a developmental process, 177–79, 233; infantile, 189; language development and, 190–91; speech mode in, 189. See also Language; Language disturbances

Speech defects, 175–76; adjustment with, 180–81, 192–97, 204–7; aphasia and, 176, 177, 179, 180, 184–85, 191, 197–99; of articulation, 176,

Speech defects (cont.)
177, 179, 180, 183–91, 199; auditory impairment and, 32–33, 51–53, 55–56, 117, 176, 177,
179, 182, 185, 188–92, 197, 198, 205–6, 281,
419–20, 424, 425, 432; auditory memory span
and, 188–91; in behavior modification, 66, 68,
200; brain injury and, 179, 191, 198; in cerebral-palsied, 176, 177, 179–80, 182, 185, 186n,
344; with cleft palate, 176, 177, 179, 185, 205–
6, 226; cluttering, 176, 177, 180, 199–200;
communication with, 175–76, 195, 199; delayed
speech (retarded language), 176, 180–82, 194–
99; educational achievement and, 183–84, 194,
206; emotional conflicts in, 184, 196, 201;
environmental factors in, 180–81, 194–96,
201–3; of fluency, 176; frustration and, 193,
195, 207; functional causes of, 180; hereditary
factors in, 180, 186; impaired vision and, 117,
188, 234–36, 260; incidence of, 176–77, 190;
infantile speech as, 189; intelligence and, 182–
85, 189, 194, 195, 197, 203, 206; kinesthetic
sensitivity and, 187; labeling of, 85; maturation and, 177, 186, 188, 197; mental retardation and, 182–84, 194, 197, 198; motor development and abilities in, 134, 186–88, 194,
200; organic causes of, 179–80, 199; parents
affecting, 180–82, 194–96, 199, 201–5; personality and, 192–94, 204, 205–7; of phonation
(voice production), 176, 177, 180, 183; physical defects and, 185–88; psychogenic causes of,
180–82; reading disability and, 184–85, 199–
200; remedial work (therapy) on, 24, 71, 188,
205; sensory impairments with, 188–92; sex
distribution of, 177, 187–88; sibilant distortion,
68, 186; sound discrimination and, 187, 188;
speech deviation as, 176; stuttering (stammering), 176, 177, 179, 180, 182, 184, 185, 187,
199–205; testing of children with, 117, 124,
126, 129, 139, 142, 335; types of, 176; vocal
defects as, 176, 185, 189, 206. See also Language disturbances; Language dysfunctions
Spina bifida, 308
Spiral Visual Aftereffects Test (SVA), 381–
83
Spread effect, 83, 92
Stammering. See Stuttering
Stanford Achievement Tests, 226, 238, 427
Stanford-Binet Intelligence Scales, 116–17, 122,
126, 140, 148, 290, 295, 334, 337, 339–41, 385,
423, 506, 541, 542; Revised Binet Form, 138,
225. See also Binet tests
Stereotyping, 83, 90
Sterilization, 101
Stigma management, 94
Strabismus, 286, 288, 289, 293–95, 446
Stuttering, 176, 177, 179, 180, 182, 184, 185,
187, 199–205
Suicide, 575
Surgery: cardiac, 460, 469; in disability reduc-
tion, 42; for stuttering, 200; in tuberculosis,
455, 456
Surplus population, 108
Symbiotic bond, 357
Symbols and symbol acquisition, 121, 122, 136,
137, 142, 177, 424
Symonds Picture Story Test, 321
Syracuse Visual Figure-Background Test, 347,
353

Talking Books, 241, 293
Taylor's Manifest Anxiety Scale, 263
Taylor's Multiple-Talent Model, 535–36
Teachers' Behavior Rating Scale, 266
Templin Speech Sound Discrimination Test, 188
Terman and Merrill Revision of Binet tests, 499
Terman Non-Language Test, 423
Test of Auditory Perception (TAP), 383
Tests of Primary Mental Abilities, 499
Thematic Apperception Test (TAT), 180, 430,
552
Therapy, 60–71, 402; for attitudes in handi-
capped, 324; for brain-injured, 402–7; for mul-
tihandicapped, 482–86; para-analytic group,
283; for parents, 283, 284, 328, 329, 333, 518;
physical, 66; physiotherapy techniques in, 404;
play therapy in, 285, 516, 595; in schools, 568.
See also Psychotherapeutc programs; and spe-
cific disability
Thinking, abstract, 385–86, 531, 569
Thinking, divergent, 136
Thinking, productive, 531
Thurstone Personality Schedule, 319, 429
Tongue-thrust swallow, 185–86
Tonsillectomies, 449
Torrance Tests of Creative Thinking, 545, 548
Touch taboo, 230
Trauma, 443–45, 447–49; in rheumatic fever,
464; in tuberculosis diagnosis, 456
Tuberculosis, 308, 334, 442, 453–59; adjustment
with, 459; education during, 459; hospitaliza-
tion with, 454–56, 458–59; incidence of, 453–
54; nature of the disease of, 453–54; psycho-
logical factors in, 454–59; self-concept with,
452
Tuddenham Reputation Test, 233
Twitchell-Allen Three-Dimensional Apperception
Test, 264

Underachievers, 559, 581–82
Unpleasant Concept Test, 552
Unusual Uses test, 553, 554
Upward Bound, 547

Van Alstyne Picture Vocabulary Test, 142, 340
Verbal unreality, 58, 233–34, 259
Vineland Social Maturity Scale, 271, 272, 274,
295, 429, 509
Viscerotonia, 4
Visual acuity, 213, 214, 216, 240, 288–90, 292,
296
Visual Discrimination Test, 240
Visual-motor disturbances, 345, 348–49, 351, 368,
378–80, 405
Visual-perceptual development, 569; in brain-
injured, 380–83, 405
Visuomotor training, 405
Vocational adjustment, 157; of special-class re-
tardates, 104. See also specific disability
Vocational aptitudes, 117, 127, 128, 132, 137,
162–64, 535
Vocational Interest and Sophistication Assess-
ment, 163–64
Vocational planning, 125; of the gifted, 553–55,
558

Wallin Peg Boards, 121
Waterfall Illusion Aftereffect (WIAE), 382